Poverty, Health and Law

Poverty, Health and Law

Readings and Cases for Medical-Legal Partnership

Edited by

Elizabeth Tobin Tyler

Ellen Lawton

Kathleen Conroy
Megan Sandel
Barry Zuckerman

CAROLINA ACADEMIC PRESS
Durham, North Carolina

Library of Congress Cataloging-in-Publication Data

Poverty, health and law : readings and cases for medical-legal partnership / edited by
Elizabeth Tobin Tyler ... [et al.].
    p. cm.
  Includes bibliographical references and index.
  ISBN 978-1-59460-779-0 (alk. paper)
  1. Medical laws and legislation--United States. 2. Legal assistance to the poor--United
States. 3. Health facilities--Law and legislation--United States. 4. Medical care--Law and
legislation--United States. 5. Social legislation--United States. 6. Old age assistance--
Law and legislation--United States. I. Tyler, Elizabeth Tobin. II. Title.

  KF3825.P68 2011
  344.7304'1--dc23

                                                                        2011014320

Carolina Academic Press
700 Kent Street
Durham, North Carolina 27701
Telephone (919) 489-7486
Fax (919) 493-5668
www.cap-press.com

Contents

Part I
Poverty, Health and Law: Making the Connections

Part V
Using Medical-Legal Partnership to Improve Population Health

Foreword:
Medical-Legal Partnerships
Raise the Bar for Health[1] and Justice

Martha L. Minow, JD, EdM
Dean and Jeremiah Smith, Jr. Professor, Harvard Law School

A good idea deserves attention, especially when the idea offers promise for seriously improving human welfare. Medical-legal partnerships—involving legal advocacy in healthcare to secure access to benefits and protections—can measurably improve health status of individuals and improve institutions affecting health while also advancing justice. Yet, as Admiral Hyman Rickover once noted, "Good ideas are not adopted automatically. They must be driven into practice with courageous patience."[2]

The essays in this book document and exhibit the vigorous practices and courageous patience of those pursuing medical-legal partnerships. The chapters, at the same time, offer serious analysis of the motivation, design and strategy of the initiative. This book is the first to document and analyze the development of now over 240 examples of medical-legal partnerships in the United States that promote health for vulnerable individuals through integrated healthcare and legal advocacy.

The chapters offer crucial insights into how better to deploy the resources spent on healthcare in this country, where we spend more money on healthcare per person than any other nation and yet fall behind comparable nations in life expectancy and infant mortality and in effectiveness of healthcare.[3] Doing more of the same is not improving the health status of Americans. Medical-legal partnerships recognize that people's health can be keenly affected not only by access to medical care but also by access to affordable food, safe housing, heat and electricity, and workplace adjustments for parents and caretakers of individuals with illness and chronic conditions. Individuals with these kinds of needs require advocates and also better practices and systems so that red-tape, indifference and short-sightedness does not get in the way of needed services.

Lawyers have the tools to provide individual advocacy and to reform systems and policies. Participation in medical-legal partnerships benefits the legal community as well by orienting lawyers to attend to prevention and problem-solving, to analyze data and promote best practices, and to redress the deficit in justice in the crucial domains of health and quality of life. Critics urge lawyers to do more to prevent and solve problems rather than simply spot them or grow conflicts around them.[4] The persistent justice gap for low-income Americans requires tough choices about what priorities should guide limited legal resources.[5] The Legal Services Corporation, the national non-profit organization allocating scarce federal funds, supports medical-legal partnerships because they "make meaningful differences in the lives of low-income Americans across the nation."[6] Drawing from the practice of evidence-based service-delivery in medical care, medical-legal partnerships can calculate the value of legal and policy interventions in containing and reducing the costs of healthcare while improving the quality of health outcomes and the public and private systems meant to serve low-income communities.

The joint efforts of medical and legal professionals to advance the health of vulnerable individuals thus offer opportunities to tackle chronic national shortfalls in health and justice. Here is where the partnership element is pivotal. A partnership allows individuals or groups to cooperate to advance each of their interests. When physician Barry Zuckerman and attorney Ellen Lawton developed the medical-legal partnership model at Boston Medical Center, they laid the ground for the initiatives that they and others are developing across the country.

This book is itself proof of the power of medical-legal partnerships in drawing together people with contrasting backgrounds and training to advance real problem-solving. This interdisciplinary book offers a tool for new generations of lawyers and healthcare providers in learning how to collaborate in tackling persistent and complex problems and enhancing the quality of life for vulnerable individuals. May this book bring attention and further assessment of the powerful idea of medical-legal partnerships, now developed and put into action!

Notes

1. This is the phrase used by the National Center for Medical-Legal Partnerships. See *www.medical-legalpartnership.org/*.

2. Admiral Hyman Rickover, "Doing a Job," Speech delivered at Columbia University, 1982, available at: http://govleaders.org/rickover.htm.

3. "World Health Statistics 2009," World Health Organization (May 2009). available at: http://www.who.int/whosis/whostat/2009/en/index.html.

4. William M. Sullivan, et al., "Educating Lawyers: Preparation for the Profession of Law," Carnegie Foundation for the Advancement of Teaching (2007); Lisa A. Kloppenberg, "Engaging Students to Educate Problem-Solving Lawyers for Clients and Communities," available at: www.aals.org/documents/curriculum/documents/Dayton; Todd D. Rakoff and Martha L. Minow, "A Case for Another Case Method," Vanderbilt Law Review 60 (2007): 597.

5. See "Documenting the Justice Gap in America: The Current Unmet Civil Legal Needs of Low-Income Americans," Legal Services Corporation (2007), available at: www.lsc.gov/justicegap.pdf.

6. LSC Updates, LSC Leaders on Panel at Medical-Legal Partnership Summit, April 1, 2010 (quoting President Victor Fortuno), available at: www.lsc.gov/press/updates_2010_detail_T259_R6.php.

Foreword: Making the Case for Health

James S. Marks, MD, MPH
Senior Vice President and Director, Health Group,
Robert Wood Johnson Foundation

"The physician, whether he chooses it or not ... is placed by his job, by his patients, and by society right where the demands of the individual and of society clash."[1]

At every income and education level there is a tremendous gap in health between those individuals at the upper and lower ends of the distribution. Further differences in overall health among communities are more closely correlated with social factors, like education and employment, than with access to quality medical care. It is apparent that many people live and work in places where healthy living is nearly impossible. This means that where and how people live, learn, work and play are central to whether they are likely to become ill or injured. How can medical care providers respond to this reality? They are ill trained to deal with the social factors affecting health, must respond to the acute event that brings the patient to them, and often have little time to connect patients and their families to the solutions that may lie outside the clinical setting. This book is about the societal factors that negatively or positively affect people's health and an effective response being implemented through medical-legal partnerships around the country.

Law and public policy frame how a society indicates what it wishes to become. If our institutions were effectively meeting the standards set by laws or public policies, new laws and advocacy to ensure that existing laws are being adequately enforced would be unnecessary. But laws and public policies are, in a sense, always aspirational. This is as true for laws affecting health as it is for laws governing education or business: whether legal protections will be applied to those most in need or only to those with more means; whether workers and patrons are exposed to the cigarette smoke of others; whether cars have seat belts and air bags, or whether housing has heat or clean running water and functioning toilets. These are all about both the framing of the law and its implementation or enforcement.

The chapters in this book are about moving from aspiration to execution: how to ensure that existing laws and policies are being fully applied to those in great need and determining where legal and policy changes need to occur to better protect the health of vulnerable populations. What is most surprising and inspiring is that the method by which this is taking place is within the medical care system through partnership between lawyers and healthcare providers. Often solutions to health problems come from outside the healthcare system, such as through improving housing, education or income supports. These are areas in which legal expertise and patient advocacy can be important tools for ensuring that necessary services are applied to help an individual patient or family. This book provides discussion of the medical-legal partnership model and multiple illustrations of its implementation. Lawyers and social workers are key allies in helping individuals who are unable to advocate effectively on their own behalf, and medical care providers are crucial to identifying the link between social circumstances and health. Ultimately, the solutions will come from healthcare providers and lawyers partnering to ensure that legal protections are enforced and services are administered to improve the health of vulnerable populations, those who are otherwise left without protection.

This book also explores the role of public policy advocacy when laws and systems are found to be inadequate and solutions need to be multi-faceted. This type of advocacy is explored in the context of a current health crisis: obesity. This discussion further solidifies a central point of the book that the important health problems of our time will not be solved by medical care, public health agencies or by research alone. They will be solved by assessing what our society and its organizations foster or inhibit. Which policies reduce disease or injury and which make their likelihood more common—even if these health outcomes were not the initial or principal purpose of the policies or laws in question? Medical-legal partnership is often where larger policies and laws are connected "on-the-ground" to those whose need is both acute and sustained.

At a time when our country's financial future is critically linked to escalating costs for medical care, when the prevalence of conditions like obesity, smoking, asthma and many others are all integrally linked to social policy decisions, it has become even more crucial that we look outside the medical system for solutions. This book highlights this understanding of what we need as a nation and offers a structure for how law and legal remedies can be used to improve the health of vulnerable populations. It also offers a way forward in addressing our nation's crisis in medical care costs by showing that the changes we consider do not have to be only about how much we pay per visit or procedure or about how many we insure. We can do much more to reduce disease and injury than we do now by ensuring that our communities, schools, worksites and homes are healthier places for all of us to live.

Our health begins, is nurtured, protected and preserved in our homes and communities by our laws, policies and actions. This book is about how to harness those forces and structures on behalf of us all, but especially for our most vulnerable.

Note

1. D. Rennie, R.A. Rettig, and A.J. Wing, "Limited Resources and the Treatment of End-Stage Renal Failure in Britain and the United States," *Quarterly Journal of Medicine* 56 (1985): 334.

Contributors

Megan Bair-Merritt, MD, MSCE
Assistant Professor of Pediatrics
Division of General Pediatrics & Adolescent Medicine
Johns Hopkins University

Meredith A. Benedict, JD, MPH
Independent Consultant

Steven D. Blatt, MD
Associate Professor of Pediatrics
Director of General Pediatrics
Co-Director, Syracuse Medical-Legal Partnership
Upstate Medical University
College of Law, Syracuse University

Lisa R. Bliss, JD
Associate Clinical Professor
Co-Director, HeLP Legal Services Clinic
Georgia State University College of Law

Debra Braun-Courville, MD
Assistant Professor of Pediatrics
Mount Sinai School of Medicine

Alison Brock, BA
2013 MD candidate
The Warren Alpert Medical School at Brown University

Sylvia B. Caley, JD, MBA, RN
Associate Clinical Professor
Co-Director, HeLP Legal Services Clinic
Director, Health Law Partnership
Georgia State University College of Law

Ellen Cohen, MD
Associate Professor of Clinical Medicine
Mount Sinai School of Medicine
Program Director, Internal Medicine Residency
Newark Beth Israel Medical Center

Jeffrey Colvin, MD, JD
Assistant Professor of Pediatrics
Mercy Hospital
The University of Missouri—Kansas City School of Medicine

Kathleen Conroy, MD, MSc
Instructor
Harvard Medical School
Staff Pediatrician
Children's Hospital Boston

Jayson Cooley, BA
2011 JD candidate
Roger Williams University School of Law

Mallory Curran, JD
Manager of Health and Government Benefits
Manhattan Legal Services

Cristina Dacchille, JD
Staff Attorney
Medical-Legal Partnership | Boston

Edward De Vos, EdD
Director
Pediatric Program Evaluation and Development Group
Boston Medical Center

Angela Diaz, MD, MPH
Jean C. and James W. Crystal Professor
Department of Pediatrics and Preventive Medicine
Mount Sinai School of Medicine

Abigail English, JD
Director
Center for Adolescent Health and the Law

Ann Hilton Fisher, JD
Executive Director
AIDS Legal Council of Chicago

Patricia Flanagan, MD
Professor of Pediatrics
Warren Alpert Medical School of Brown University
Chief of Clinical Affairs
Hasbro Children's Hospital

Chong-Min Fu, BA
Research Associate
Division of General Pediatrics
Boston Medical Center

Paula Galowitz, JD, MSW
Clinical Professor of Law
New York University School of Law

MaryKate Geary, BA
2011 JD Candidate
Roger Williams University School of Law

Samantha Graff, JD
Director of Legal Research
National Policy & Legal Analysis Network to Prevent Childhood Obesity
A Project of Public Health Law and Policy

Joshua Greenberg, JD
Vice President
Government Relations
Children's Hospital Boston

Eric J. Hardt, MD
Associate Professor of Medicine,
Boston University School of Medicine
Geriatrics Section, Department of Medicine
Boston Medical Center

Alan W. Houseman, JD
Executive Director
Center for Law and Social Policy

Manel Kappagoda, JD, MPH
Deputy Director
National Policy & Legal Analysis Network to Prevent Childhood Obesity
A Project of Public Health Law and Policy

Kevin Kappel, BA
Manager, Government Relations
ML Strategies

David Keller, MD
Associate Clinical Professor of Pediatrics
University of Massachusetts Medical School
Medical Director
Family Advocates of Central Massachusetts

Chen Kenyon, MD
Instructor in Pediatrics
Children's Hospital Boston

Rebecca Lawrence, MPH, MSW
Research Coordinator
Boston Medical Center

Ellen Lawton, JD
Executive Director
National Center for Medical-Legal Partnership

Jane Liebschutz, MD, MPH
Associate Professor of Medicine and Community Health Sciences
Boston University School of Medicine
Department of Medicine
Boston Medical Center

Betsy McAlister Groves, LICSW
Associate Professor of Pediatrics
Boston University School of Medicine
Director, Child Witness to Violence Project
Boston Medical Center

Kate Mewhinney, JD
Clinical Professor, Managing Attorney of the Elder Law Clinic
Wake Forest University School of Law
Associate, Department of Internal Medicine (Section of Geriatrics and Gerontology)
Wake Forest University School of Medicine

Tenley Mochizuki, BA
Intern, LegalHealth 2010

Samantha Morton, JD
Executive Director
Medical-Legal Partnership | Boston

Robert Needlman, MD
Associate Professor of Pediatrics
Case Western Reserve University School of Medicine
Developmental and Behavioral Pediatrics
MetroHealth Medical Center

Wendy E. Parmet, JD
George J. and Kathleen Waters Matthews Distinguished University Professor of Law
Northeastern University School of Law

Edward G. Paul, MD
Associate Professor
Family & Community Medicine
University of Arizona College of Medicine
Director of Medical Education
Yuma Regional Medical Center

Robert Pettignano, MD, FAAP, FCCM, MBA
Associate Professor of Pediatrics
Emory University School of Medicine
Medical Director — Campus Operations
Medical Champion — HeLP
Children's Healthcare of Atlanta at Hughes Spalding

Lisa Pilnik, JD, MS
Staff Attorney
American Bar Association Center on Children and the Law

Randye Retkin, JD
Director, LegalHealth
New York Legal Assistance Group

Josiah D. Rich, MD, MPH
Professor of Medicine and Community Health
The Warren Alpert Medical School at Brown University
Director, the Center for Prisoner Health and Human Rights

Melissa A. Rodgers, JD, EdM
Founding Legal Director
Peninsula Family Advocacy Program

Kerry Rodibaugh, MD
Associate Professor
Department of Obstetrics and Gynecology
University of Nebraska Medical Center

Sara Rosenbaum, JD
Professor of Health Services Management and Policy
Chair of the Department of Health Policy
School of Public Health and Health Services
George Washington University

Anne M. Ryan, JD
Clinical Assistant Professor
University of Arizona Department of Family & Community Medicine
Director, Tucson Family Advocacy Program

Megan Sandel, MD, MPH
Assistant Professor of Pediatrics
Boston University School of Medicine
Medical Director
National Center for Medical-Legal Partnership

Samuel Senft, JD, MPH
Health Program Manager
Alaska Division of Public Health
Section of Epidemiology, HIV/STD Program

Lynda Shuster, MSW, LICSW
Manager of Mental Health and Medical Management Services
Center for Infectious Diseases
Boston Medical Center

Gerry Singsen, JD
Consultant

Lauren A. Smith, MD, MPH
Medical Director
Massachusetts Department of Health

Megan Sprecher, JD
Staff Attorney
Community Advocacy Program
Legal Aid Society of Cleveland

Leanne Ta, BA
Projects Coordinator
National Center for Medical-Legal Partnership

Pam Tames, JD
Director of Training
National Center for Medical-Legal Partnership
Medical-Legal Partnership | Boston

Joel Teitelbaum, JD, LLM
Associate Professor and Vice Chair for Academic Affairs, Department of Health Policy
School of Public Health and Health Services
George Washington University

Jerome Tichner, JD
Partner, Heath Industry Advisory Practice Group
McDermott Will & Emery LLP

Elizabeth Tobin Tyler, JD, MA
Director of Public Service and Community Partnerships
Lecturer in Public Interest Law
Roger Williams University School of Law

Paul R. Tremblay, JD
Clinical Professor and Law Fund Research Scholar
Director, Community Enterprise Clinic
Boston College Law School

Deborah J. Weimer, JD
Professor of Law
Clinical Law Program
University of Maryland School of Law

Dana L. Weintraub, MD
Clinical Assistant Professor
Division of General Pediatrics
Lucile Packard Children's Hospital at Stanford
Medical Director, Peninsula Family Advocacy Program

Debra J. Wolf
Senior Attorney, LegalHealth
New York Legal Assistance Group

Shale L. Wong, MD, MSPH
Associate Professor of Pediatrics
University of Colorado School of Medicine

Barry Zuckerman, MD
Joel and Barbara Alpert Professor of Pediatrics
Boston University School of Medicine
Professor of Public Health
Boston University School of Public Health
Chief of Pediatrics at Boston Medical Center

Editorial Advisors

Jeffrey Colvin, MD, JD
Assistant Professor of Pediatrics
The University of Missouri — Kansas City School of Medicine

James Corbett MDiv, JD
Vice President of Mission
Steward Health Care System, LLC

Katie Cronin, JD
Adjunct Professor
University of Kansas School of Law

Richard Daynard, JD
Professor of Law
Northeastern University School of Law

Ann Dibble, JD
Senior Staff Attorney
LegalHealth, New York Legal Assistance Group

Eric Fleegler, MD
Instructor in Pediatrics
Harvard Medical School

Daniel Graver, MPP
2013 JD Candidate
The University of Texas School of Law

Robert S. Kahn, MD, MPH
Associate Professor, Division of General and Community Pediatrics
University of Cincinnati College of Medicine

Melissa D. Klein, MD
Adjunct Assistant Professor of Pediatrics
University of Cincinnati College of Medicine

J. Michael Norwood, JD
Professor of Law and Associate Dean for Clinical Affairs
University of New Mexico School of Law

Michael L. Pates, JD
Center for Human Rights
American Bar Association

Chad Priest, RN, MSN, JD
Chief Executive Officer
Managed Emergency Surge for Healthcare, Inc.

Preface

To our knowledge, this book is the first of its kind to comprehensively discuss the ways in which legal remedies may be used to address the social determinants of health. In the past ten years, the number of medical-legal partnerships in the United States has gone from fewer than ten to more than ninety, existing now in over 240 healthcare institutions. In addition, medical-legal partnership (MLP) continues to take hold in law school, medical school and public health curricula through interdisciplinary courses and clinical and internship opportunities. It is out of this burgeoning field of medical-legal teaching and practice that this book developed.

This book is intended as a teaching tool for courses in medicine, law, public health, nursing and social work to explore the connections among poverty, health and law and to prepare future practitioners to effectively address the medical-legal needs of their patients and clients. It will be especially useful in teaching across disciplines. It is also meant to serve as a useful resource for legal and healthcare practitioners already engaged in MLP, or those interested in better understanding the convergence of health and law in their patients' or clients' lives.

If we have learned anything from MLP practice and teaching, it is that members of all professions who touch the lives of vulnerable populations must become better skilled at communicating across disciplines, doing our best to leave our particular narrow professional perspectives and jargon at the door. This book represents our effort to bring disciplines together for a common purpose: to offer a better understanding of our roles in improving the health of our patients and clients. Authors from multiple disciplines collaborated on the chapters in this book. To make the concepts accessible to readers from different disciplines, they strove to present complex medical or legal information in generally accessible language. In addition, to educate readers about concepts from the different disciplines, we have included a *glossary of terms,* divided by topics addressed in the book: poverty and health, public health, medicine, health and the healthcare system, law and the legal system, and medical/healthcare partnership. We hope that this glossary will provide readers with the background knowledge needed to engage with the substantive material in the book.

Because this book is intended as both a teaching tool and a resource for those engaged or interested in MLP, we include several features throughout the book to support those goals:

Discussion Questions: Questions to help guide and expand the discussion of the material in educational settings or in medical-legal trainings for MLP practitioners.

Cases for Medical-Legal Partnership: Cases that help students to identify the connections among poverty, health and law and to apply what they have learned in the preceding sections. The cases include discussion questions that ask readers to think about how healthcare and legal professionals should respond to the complex problems faced by their patients and clients.

Best Practices and Advocacy Strategies for Medical-Legal Partnership: Examples of approaches used by MLPs to address a particular medical-legal issue or problem. These may include highlighted strategies or a specific description of particularly effective practices currently being used by MLPs around the country.

Practice to Policy: Examples of how MLP practitioners may identify areas in which systemic or policy changes can benefit a wider population of vulnerable patients and communities. These may include policy advocacy strategies or specific examples of successful policy change initiatives undertaken by MLPs.

Acknowledgments

This book would not have been possible without the work of several people who devoted many hours of research assistance and editorial support. Chong-Min Fu, Research Associate for the National Center for Medical-Legal Partnership, provided exceptional assistance on every aspect of the book from the day we started the project until the day we completed the editing process. We are grateful for her incredible work ethic, the many long hours she devoted to this project and for her calm and kind manner throughout the process. We also thank Jayson Cooley and MaryKate Geary, Roger Williams University law students, and Claudia Coronel-Moreno, Emily Suther and Johnna Murphy, of Boston Medical Center, for their excellent research and editorial assistance. They, too, committed long hours and helped us to meet our deadlines all along the way. Leanne Ta, Brandy Gonzales, and Kate Marple from the National Center for Medical-Legal Partnership stepped in to help whenever asked and provided much needed support. We also gratefully acknowledge help provided by Melissa Brennan of Boston Medical Center, Lauren Fiechtner of Children's Hospital Boston, and Amy VanHeuverzwyn of MLP|Boston. We also acknowledge the staff at Carolina Academic Press, for their professionalism, flexibility and helpfulness. Many thanks to Laura Poole for her assistance with copyediting and to Noeline Bridge for her work on the index.

Liz Tobin Tyler would like to thank David Logan, David Zlotnick, Andy Horwitz, Laurie Barron, Eliza Vorenberg, Suzanne Harrington-Steppen, Jennifer Lashley and Lauren Macbeth from Roger Williams University School of Law for their generous support of this book. I would also like to acknowledge Professor Mark Hall for his helpful suggestions on the original book proposal and Roger Williams University law students Brandy Hughes, Amy Peltier, Amanda Walsh and Jane Duket for their early research assistance as the book was being conceptualized. Finally, I thank my patient, loving and supportive family — my husband, John, and my children, Graham, Tobin and Clare, who endured many nights and weekends with me on my computer editing chapters, and my parents, Robert and Maurine Tobin, for their encouragement and for modeling a lifelong commitment to social justice.

Ellen Lawton would like to acknowledge current and former National Center and Medical-Legal Partnership | Boston staff — especially Josh Greenberg, Samantha Morton, Lauren Smith and Pamela Tames — as well as the hundreds of MLP Network members past and present who have contributed to the development of the medical-legal partnership model. Several key advisors helped advance the MLP model including Steve Scudder at the American Bar Association and Tom Koutsoumpas and Kevin Kappel of Mintz Levin/ML Strategies. But my key to success was the endless support, love and encouragement of my husband Jon, and my boys Louis and Charlie — who cheered me on and helped me keep my sense of humor and perspective. I owe a debt of gratitude also to my parents — Nancy Lawton, whose wit, wisdom and compassion inspire me every day, and Tom Lawton, whose memory I cherish and honor — and my siblings Thomas, Jamie, Maura and Andrew — each of whom helped me get here.

Introduction

Elizabeth Tobin Tyler, JD, MA

"There is more to health than health care."

In this era of healthcare reform, discussion among policy makers, the press, and the general public has focused primarily on how to expand health insurance coverage, cut costs in the system, and preserve or improve the quality of care. Lawyers continue to play a large role in shaping healthcare reform, particularly in the wake of passage of the Patient Protection and Affordable Care Act—interpreting legislative language, drafting regulations and crafting arguments to bring or respond to legal challenges to reform laws. Healthcare providers are on the front lines of reform efforts, some advocating for change, some bracing for a major transformation of the system in which they care for patients.

As the national debate continues about how to achieve reform of the healthcare system, researchers, foundations, public health officials, healthcare providers and lawyers are beginning to raise a point often left out of the discussion: "There is more to health than healthcare."[1] If the goal is to improve health, not just reform the system, different questions and different answers need to be part of the national conversation.

In recent years, researchers have documented the significant disparities in *health* in the United States (not just in *healthcare access*) that exist across racial, ethnic and socioeconomic lines.[2] They have concluded that the answer to improving health, particularly among vulnerable populations, reaches far beyond expanding and improving access to the healthcare system. They have pointed to a much more complex problem—that "where we live, learn, work and play can have a greater impact on how long and how well we live than medical care."[3] The social determinants of health—social environment and social history—may have a more significant impact on health than does access to quality healthcare.

Since Sir Michael Marmot published his groundbreaking Whitehall studies in the 1960s, which exposed differences in disease prevalence and mortality rates of British civil servants according to their grade levels,[4] social epidemiologists have explored how the social environment (e.g. food availability, housing and neighborhood conditions, access to educational opportunities and the experience of social isolation and racism) contributes to poor health outcomes and health disparities across the population.

More recently, health reform advocates are taking notice of the high healthcare costs associated with vulnerable populations who suffer a disproportionate share of chronic illness, do not receive adequate primary care and experience multiple social conditions that complicate the delivery of high-quality healthcare.[5] Researchers and policy makers are also beginning to recognize that failure to address health disparities may have broad consequences for society. A recent study notes that "the aggregate economic gains from interventions that improve the health of disadvantaged Americans are potentially large."[6] But failure to address the adverse effects of poverty and poor social conditions on health is most stark when viewed in terms of the human costs. The human impact of health is clear: "Good health is essential to well-being and full participation in society, and ill health can mean suffering, disability, and loss of life."[7] Healthcare providers see the human costs of ill health among their most vulnerable patients on a daily basis, yet often do not have the tools to address the complex social needs impacting their health. Lawyers who serve vulnerable clients and communities also witness the cyclical consequences of poverty and poor health. Poor health leads to economic and social instability; economic and social instability in turn leads to or exacerbates poor health.

Researchers and practitioners point to the role of social conditions in health disparities, but identifying solutions has been much more difficult. As one scholar notes, "Reducing social disparities in health (i.e., health differences by racial or ethnic group or by socioeconomic factors like income and education) will require solutions that address their root causes."[8] Hence, there is increasing recognition that the healthcare system as it currently exists cannot alone address the "root causes" underlying health disparities.

What, then, is the role of law and public policy in understanding and addressing the social determinants of health? Public health policy makers have long sought "upstream" policy interventions that seek to prevent health problems before they impact the population. The role of law as a social determinant itself is also being explored. As Wendy Parmet notes, "By establishing the social framework in which populations live, face disease and injury and die, law forms an important social determinant of population health."[9] Thus, lawyers concerned with improving health for vulnerable populations have a role to play in challenging the social framework underlying health disparities.

With this understanding of the role of law in the social determinants of health, healthcare providers and lawyers are joining forces to explore preventive interventions in the healthcare setting. This role for lawyers diverges from their traditional approach to health law. Rather than helping design and regulate the healthcare system, they use the law as a tool to address the social conditions of low-income and vulnerable patients — such as ensuring safer housing, overcoming access barriers to public benefits and income supports, enforcing employment protections and seeking safety for their clients from violence.

Since the early 1990s, lawyers have been partnering with healthcare providers to form medical-legal partnerships (MLPs) designed to use law as a tool to combat systemic and social barriers and conditions that disproportionately impact the health of low-income and vulnerable patients. Started in 1993 at Boston Medical Center, the MLP model has expanded to over ninety programs in more than 240 healthcare settings. Initially focused on preventive advocacy to address legal issues impacting child health (such as poor housing conditions causing asthma or lead poisoning), the MLP model is now used to address the legal needs affecting the health of vulnerable populations, including the elderly and patients with cancer or HIV/AIDS. Partnering healthcare providers and lawyers has not only brought new resources for patients and their families into the healthcare setting, it has also challenged healthcare and legal services providers to transform their practice to focus on preventive approaches to medicine and law and advocate for their patients and clients within and outside the healthcare system.

This book investigates the role of law in the social determinants of health and the potential for legal advocacy, both at the individual and policy levels, to improve the health of vulnerable individuals and populations. It explores how MLP creates the potential for preventive interventions by leveraging the resources of interdisciplinary partners and systems. Because MLPs have the potential to transform practice as well as policy, they also offer a unique training ground for medical, public health, nursing, social work and law students interested in improving care to vulnerable populations. This book, therefore, is intended as both a resource for practitioners and as a learning tool for students—the next generation of health and legal professionals. (See Preface for discussion of the types of settings and ways in which the book may be useful.)

Each chapter is written by an interdisciplinary team drawn from the fields of medicine, nursing, public health, law and social work. The authors draw on their collective wisdom derived from medical, healthcare, public health, and legal research, practice and policy. The book exemplifies the value of bringing together a talented group of health and legal professionals devoted to exploring the connections between poverty, health and law and the potential remedies that are possible when these professions partner to serve vulnerable patients and populations.

Part I lays the groundwork for understanding the social determinants of health and the role of law in contributing to and addressing those determinants (Chapter 1), the traditional approaches of the healthcare and legal systems to the needs of the poor (Chapter 2) and the more preventive approach to the care of vulnerable populations offered by MLP (Chapter 3).

Part II explores MLP in practice and the unique challenges and opportunities brought by partnering the healthcare and legal professions—how students and practitioners understand and respond to the cultural context of their patients and clients (Chapter 4), the benefits and challenges of medical-legal education and training (Chapter 5) and how MLP practitioners can provide ethically responsible care to patients and clients within the bounds of professional ethical rules (Chapter 6).

Part III (Chapters 7–11) describes the substantive role that law and legal advocacy plays in improving health outcomes by exploring five areas in which poverty, health and law converge: income and employment, housing, education, legal status and personal safety.[10]

Part IV (Chapters 12–15) offers ways legal remedies in the healthcare context can benefit the health and well-being of special populations, including cancer patients, survivors, and their families; people living with HIV/AIDS; elders and their caregivers; and adolescents and young adults.

As noted earlier, MLP also offers a unique opportunity to advance population health by leveraging the resources of the healthcare and legal professions to promote system and policy changes. Part V (Chapters 16–19) offers insight into the ways MLP has and may in the future affect policy change to benefit vulnerable populations. Chapter 17 explores the role MLP can play in promoting policy changes to address the obesity epidemic. Chapter 18 outlines how researchers are evaluating the potential benefits of MLP for patients, practitioners and systems. Finally, Chapter 19 concludes the book with a view toward the future by offering perspective on the role MLP may play in the future of healthcare in the era of healthcare reform.

Despite the many challenges ahead, this is an exciting time for those focused on improving the health of vulnerable populations. Healthcare reform efforts are opening the door to innovative service delivery models like MLP that seek more preventive, comprehensive and interdisciplinary approaches to improving health. This book captures the importance of partnering professionals across disciplines to explore, discuss and teach the connections between poverty, health and law to change the way we care for our most vulnerable patients, clients and communities.

Notes

1. Risa Lavizzo-Mourey, David R. Williams, "Strong Medicine for a Healthier America (Introduction)," *American Journal of Preventive Medicine,* 40 (2011): S1.

2. Paula A. Braveman, et al., "Broadening the Focus: The Need to Address the Social Determinants of Health," *American Journal of Preventive Medicine,* 40, no. 1S1 (2011): S4–18.

3. Robert Wood Johnson Foundation, Commission to Build a Healthier America, "Issue Brief 7: Message Translation" (2009).

4. See M. G. Marmot, et al., "Employment Grade and Coronary Heart Disease in British Civil Servants," *Journal of Epidemiology and Community Health,* 32, no. 4 (1978): 244–49. M. G. Marmot, et al., "Health Inequalities among British Civil Servants: The Whitehall II Study," *Lancet,* 337 (1991): 1387–93. The following websites describe Marmot's ongoing work in this area in the United Kingdom and Europe: http://www.marmotreview.org/ and http://www.ucl.ac.uk/silva/epidemiology/people/marmotmg.htm.

5. See Atul Gawande, "Can We Lower Medical Costs by Giving the Neediest Patients Better Care?" *New Yorker* (January 24, 2011), http://www.newyorker.com/reporting/2011/01/24/110124fa_fact_gawande.

6. Robert F. Schoeni, et al., "The Economic Value of Improving the Health of Disadvantaged Americans," *American Journal of Preventive Medicine,* 40 (2011): S67.

7. Braveman, et al., "Broadening the Focus," S1.

8. Ibid., S5.

9. Wendy E. Parmet, *Populations, Public Health, and the Law* (Washington, DC: Georgetown University Press, 2009), 31. Also see Scott Burris, Ichiro Kawachi, Austin Sarat, "Integrating Law and Social Epidemiology," *Journal of Law, Medicine and Ethics,* 30 (2003).

10. These five areas represent those most commonly used by MLPs to screen for unmet legal needs. The mnemonic I-HELP (developed by Megan Sandel, MD) addresses issues that have been shown to directly impact patient health and well-being, including Income supports; Housing and utilities; Education and employment; Legal (immigration) status; and Personal and family stability and safety. For further discussion of healthcare provider screening for these issues, see Chén Kenyon, Megan Sandel, Michael Silverstein, et al., "Revisiting the Social History for Child Health," *Pediatrics,* 120 (2007): e734–38.

Part I

Poverty, Health and Law:
Making the Connections

Chapter 1

Social Determinants, Health Disparities and the Role of Law

Wendy E. Parmet, JD
Lauren A. Smith, MD, MPH
Meredith A. Benedict, JD, MPH

The components of health addressed in the traditional medical model focus on the biomedical status of individuals. In this model, biology, genetics and individual behaviors are the primary forces shaping an individual's health status. Simultaneously, the public health profession's examination of population-based data has long recorded significant differences in the health of populations within and among societies. They understand that there are multiple causal and associative relationships between one's health and environment.

Advances in scientific knowledge in the past several decades have begun to unite these two approaches, uncovering relationships between environmental conditions and individual biology and genetics that have specific, measurable impacts at the individual level and are further reflected as population-based differences.[1] Factors making up the social determinants of health are one's physical and social environments and access to resources.[2] Their impact is not confined to people living in poverty but to all people in every type of society. This impact moves along a gradient as socioeconomic status improves. As the World Health Organization has stated, "The social gradient in health means that health inequities affect everyone."[3]

Leaders in medicine, public health and other arenas are increasingly taking account of the profound connections between social determinants and the health of individuals and populations, and reevaluating how to shape policies to foster healthier living for people in all strata of society. This chapter introduces this body of research and discusses the breadth of social, environmental and legal forces that affect the health of populations and lead to health inequities. The socioecological approach to health that has arisen from this growing evidence demonstrates how medical-legal partnerships (MLPs) can have a powerful impact.

Explaining Health Disparities

"The first wealth is health,"[4] wrote nineteenth-century American essayist Ralph Waldo Emerson, underscoring the foundational role that good health plays in one's ability to pursue a livelihood. A review of U.S. population health data might move one to observe further that "wealth *is* health," for, as shown Figures 1.1 and 1.2, "health disparities across income and education groups are seen in a range of health conditions from the beginning of life to old age."[5] Racial and ethnic health disparities also persist across the life span.[6]

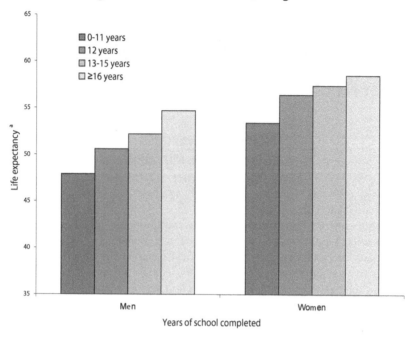

Figure 1.1 More Education, Longer Life

Source: P. A. Braveman, et al., "Broadening the Focus: The Need to Address the Social Determinants of Health," *American Journal of Preventive Medicine*, 40, no. 1S1 (2011): S5.
Data Source: U.S. Census Bureau, National Longitudinal Mortality Study (NMLS), 1988–1998.
Note: [a] Number of additional years of life expected at age 25 years

The Social Determinants of Health

Increasingly, researchers and policy makers have focused attention on the social influences on health as they seek to understand and address population differences in health status or health disparities. The idea that social circumstance impacts health is not novel; it has existed at least since the founding of the scientific discipline of epidemiology in the early nineteenth century, which recognized the "truism that social as well as biological processes inherently shape population health."[7] Called the social determinants of health, these factors are "the conditions in which people are born, grow, live, work and age."[8] Addressing these conditions is "primary prevention" in the medical context and a main objective of public health practitioners: inhibiting or reducing risk factors before disease or conditions develop. Ultimately, social determinants play a greater role in health disparities than access to health insurance and health care, which are important pathways to reducing health disparities but do not address the root causes of illness.[9]

Research Findings on How the Social Environment Impacts Health

A growing body of research in the latter half of the twentieth and early twenty-first century has provided a "more precise definition of both the physical dimensions of the environment that are toxic to health as well as conditions in the social environment, such as social exclusion, racism, educational achievement and opportunities to advance in the

Figure 1.2 Health Status by Income Level

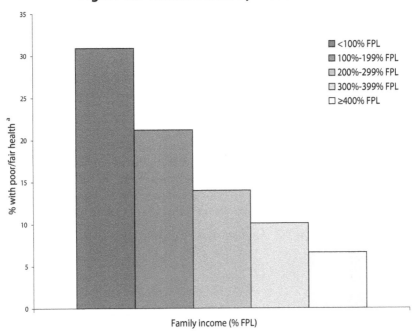

Family income (% FPL)

Source: P. A. Braveman, et al., "Broadening the Focus: The Need to Address the Social Determinants of Health," *American Journal of Preventive Medicine,* 40, no. 1S1 (2011): S6.
Data Source: CDC, National Health Interview Survey (NHIS) 2001–2005.
Note: ª At age ≥25 years; age-adjusted. FPL, Federal Poverty Level

workplace, that shape behavior and access to resources that promote health."[10] Seminal work in the field includes the Whitehall studies, launched in Britain in 1967, which revealed differences in the disease prevalence and mortality rates of British civil servants according to their grade levels.[11] Such studies uncovered "social gradients" in health and revealed that "the overall structure of hierarchy somehow has a significant effect on health, over and above the general issue of whether people are suffering from material deprivation."[12] For example, Whitehall I (1967–77) showed that the coronary heart disease (CHD) mortality of men in the lowest civil service grade was 3.6 times higher than men in the highest grade; adjusting for health and lifestyle factors did not obviate the strong "inverse association between grade of employment and CHD mortality," leading researchers to conclude that established risk factors only partly explain the higher mortality of working-class men in the study and in national statistics.[13]

In recent years, a new area of study called "social epidemiology," in which scholars "explicitly [investigate] social determinants of population distributions of health, disease, and wellbeing, rather than treating such determinants as mere background to biomedical phenomena" has emerged.[14] The Whitehall study is a memorable and often cited example of the social gradient of health; other studies explore the interplay of race, income, wealth and geography on health.

Personal Responsibility and Social Exposure

The influences on health of individuals are multifactorial. " 'Personal responsibility,' motivation, and self-discipline" are key factors enabling informed individuals to make behavioral change to achieve greater health.[15] Yet there is growing recognition and acceptance that personal health is linked not only to personal behavior and medical care but also to living and working conditions in homes and communities and the broader economic and social opportunities and resources that surround an individual.[16]

Researchers are documenting how one's local environment promotes or dissuades individuals from engaging in behaviors that promote health.[17] Environmental conditions, such as extreme poverty, substandard housing, exposure to environmental toxins and lack of access to resources, all affect an individual's ability to control his or her health and make healthy choices. Figure 1.3 illustrates these types of influences on health. Children may be the most vulnerable to poor social conditions and the impact of those conditions on their health because they are least able to control their environment.[18]

Figure 1.3 Factors That Influence Health

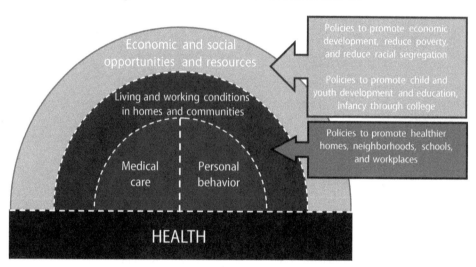

Source: P. A. Braveman, et al., "Broadening the Focus: The Need to Address the Social Determinants of Health," *American Journal of Preventive Medicine*, 40, no. 1S1 (2011): S10.
Note: Prepared for the Robert Wood Johnson Foundation Commission to Build a Healthier America by the Center on Social Disparities in Health, University of California San Francisco

Racial and Ethnic Health Disparities

As discussed earlier, studies confirm a social gradient in health outcomes—people with higher socioeconomic status (SES) have better health outcomes than people with lower SES. The relationships among SES, race or ethnicity and health status are not easy for researchers and policy makers to untangle. Some disparities that were once thought to be race-based today have been shown to be better understood as SES-based. As Paula Braveman and colleagues note:

> Without adequate socioeconomic information, racial or ethnic differences in health may be interpreted, implicitly if not explicitly, as reflecting genetic or entrenched "cultural" differences that are unlikely to be influenced by policy. In fact, modifiable social factors shaped by income, education, wealth, and childhood and neighborhood

socioeconomic conditions, which vary systematically by race or ethnic group, are likely to be more important in explaining health differences by race or ethnicity.[19]

In recent years, careful attention has been paid by the research community to these issues; although certain disparities that once were deemed to be race-based are now more correctly understood as SES-based, racial and ethnic disparities in health persist.[20] Figure 1.4 shows that race and ethnic health disparities exist in each income group. For example, black:white mortality ratios remain > 1 through the largest age categories even after SES adjustments for income and education are made.[21] For black men, race has a residual

Figure 1.4 Health Status, by Income Level and Race/Ethnicity

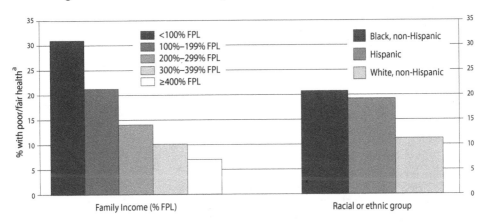

Source: P. A. Braveman, et al., "Broadening the Focus: The Need to Address the Social Determinants of Health," *American Journal of Preventive Medicine*, 40, no. 1S1 (2011): S9.
Data Source: CDC, National Health Interview Survey (NHIS) 2001–2005.
Note: [a] At age ≥25 years; age-adjusted. FPL, Federal Poverty Level

effect in elevated mortality rates for five of six education levels; black women had higher mortality rates than white women for the three higher education levels, but the inverse was true at lower levels of education.[22] There are markedly higher rates of infant mortality for children born to black mothers over the age of 20, regardless of the mother's educational attainment.[23] Racial differences have also been measured even among high SES groups (e.g., black and white physicians).[24]

The reasons for persistent racial and ethnic health disparities are not well understood. Some posit that they may be due to the "adverse health effects of more concentrated disadvantage ... or a range of experiences related to racial bias that are not captured in [routine SES studies]."[25] Some of the social factors that may contribute to racial and ethnic health disparities are discussed shortly.

Diminishing Returns

One explanation is that gains in SES are experienced with "diminishing returns" by minorities.[26] The standard measures of SES (income, education) that have been used in many research studies fail to capture important racial/ethnic differences in economic resources. As Table 1.1 shows, racial differences in wealth are much larger than those for income. Looking at home ownership as a proxy for wealth, one sees that 71 percent of white households own their home, whereas the rate hovers just above and below 50

Table 1.1 Demographic and Socioeconomic Characteristics by Race and Ethnicity: United States, 2000

Indicator	White	Black	Am. Indian/ Alaska Native	Asian	Native Hawaiian and Pacific Islander	Other	Hispanic Race
Hispanic, %	8.0	2.0	16.4	1.2	11.4	97.0	—
Foreign born, %	3.5	6.1	5.4	68.9	19.9	43.4	40.2
Median age, %	37.7	30.2	28.0	32.7	27.5	24.6	25.8
Female-headed, %	9.2	30.8	20.9	9.1	16.1	19.3	17.8
White collar, %	36.6	25.2	24.3	44.6	23.3	14.2	18.1
High school+, %	85.5	72.3	70.9	80.4	78.3	46.8	52.4
College grad+, %	27.0	14.3	11.5	44.1	13.8	7.3	10.4
Poor, %	8.1	24.9	25.7	12.6	17.7	24.4	22.6
Own home, %	71.3	46.3	55.5	53.4	45.0	40.5	48.0

Source: D. R. Williams, "The Health of US Racial and Ethnic Populations," *Journals of Gerontology, Series B,* 60B (special issue 11) (2005): 56.
Data Source: U.S. Census (2000).

percent, respectively, for American Indians and Asians, and for blacks, Native Hawaiians, and Hispanics.[27] For blacks in particular, these data reveal the multigenerational legacy of institutionalized racism that prohibited black ownership of property; the data also illustrate how socioeconomic disadvantage and immigration influence health.[28]

As Figure 1.5 shows, racial and ethnic health disparities persist along with disparities based on SES for children. To illustrate further, consider the results of one study that examined the association of race/ethnicity and family income with the prevalence of childhood asthma among 14,244 U.S. children: data revealed that only among the very poor were non-Hispanic black children at substantially higher risk of asthma than were non-Hispanic white children.[29] The study authors used this analysis to make the point that "patterns of social and environmental exposures must overshadow any hypothetical genetic risk."[30]

Residential Racial Segregation

The concentration of racial groups in specific neighborhoods as a result of residential segregation means that the social conditions in those communities impact racial differences in health.[31] Thus, "race is a marker for differential exposure to multiple disease-producing social factors," with racially unequal patterns in exposure to societal risks and resources forming a critical component of racial disparities in health.[32]

Area-based differences in SES "are likely an important contributor to the residual effects of race after adjustment for individual and household level indicators of SES. These differences in neighborhood quality are driven by residential segregation by race—a neglected but enduring legacy of institutional racism in the United States."[33] Health and development impacts arising from this legacy are irrefutable. One study found that 76 percent of black children and 69 percent of Latino children live under worse conditions than the worst-off white children in one hundred U.S. metropolitan areas.[34] An assessment of the 171 largest U.S. cities "reported that there was not even one city where blacks lived

Figure 1.5 Child Health Status by Family Income, Household Education Level, and Child's Racial or Ethnic Group

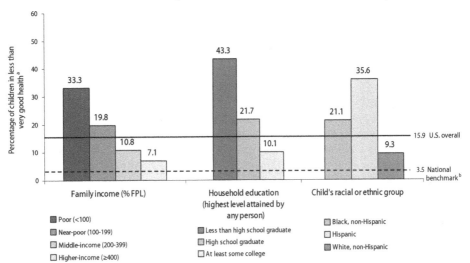

Source: W. D. Miller, et al., "Healthy Starts for All: Policy Prescriptions," *American Journal of Preventive Medicine*, 40, no. 1S1 (2011): S24.

Notes: [a] Aged ≤17 years; based on parental assessment and measured as poor, fair, good, very good, or excellent; health reported as less than very good was considered to be less than optimal; [b] The national benchmark for children's general health status represents the level of health that should be attainable for all children in every state. The benchmark used here—3.5% of children with health that was less than optimal, seen in Colorado—is the lowest statistically reliable rate observed in any state among children whose families were not only higher income but also practiced healthy behaviors (i.e., nonsmokers and at least one person who exercised regularly). Rates with relative SES of ≤30% were considered statistically reliable.

under similar ecological conditions to those of whites in terms of concentrated poverty and female headed households."[35]

Pathways through Which Concentrated Poverty Arising from Segregation Adversely Affect Health

1. Limiting socioeconomic mobility by limiting access to high-quality education and employment

2. Creating conditions in which practicing healthy behaviors is more challenging—limited availability of affordable, healthy foods and opportunities for exercise, greater exposure to tobacco and alcohol advertising

3. Heightening exposure to economic hardship and other stressors, including neighborhood disorder, crime, community violence and incarceration, that affect individuals, communities and neighborhoods

4. Adversely affecting interpersonal relationships and trust among neighbors due to weakened community and neighborhood infrastructure

5. Increasing exposure to environmental toxins, poor-quality housing, and criminal victimization due to institutional neglect and disinvestment

6. Limiting access to medical care and the quality of health services received

Source: D. R. Williams, et al., "Race, Socioeconomic Status, and Health: Complexities, Ongoing Challenges, and Research Opportunities," *Annals of the New York Academy of Sciences*, 1186 (2010): 79.

Hypersegregation is a term that identifies intensely segregated areas; 40 percent of black women of childbearing age live in such areas.[36] Black infants born in these areas are more likely to be preterm, and "black-white differences in pre-term birth were larger in hyper-segregated areas than in less segregated ones."[37] Alternatively, the protective effects of racial concentration have been measured in some communities—such as lower mortality rates among Hispanics in some concentrated communities and lower rates of discrimination in others leading to lower levels of mental health symptoms.[38] Further research is needed to elucidate both the protective effects of racial concentration and the "ways in which specific features of residential areas lead to altered biological processes that have adverse consequences on health and the extent to which such exposures are reflected in the elevated health risks of minority populations."[39]

Generational Exposure and Discrimination

Additionally, the early onset of disease for minorities, measured across SES, and the accumulation of exposures over the life course and across generations affect current health status. As noted earlier, evidence increasingly suggests that "psychological, social and economic adversity in childhood can have long-term consequences for health" for all races.[40] However, given that more blacks and other minorities live in poorer quality environments than do whites, these groups suffer in a greater proportion from these risks. Studies are beginning to document the multigenerational impact of environmental contaminants and stressors. For example, prenatal exposure to pollutants has been linked to neurodevelopmental impacts well into childhood.[41] More research is needed to illuminate how events or conditions at critical periods during the life course and accumulated health risks impact the later health status of racial minority populations.[42]

Additionally, studies have begun to measure the impact of racism and discrimination on health. Nancy Krieger and colleagues have documented associations between self-reported experiences of racial discrimination and poor health outcomes; for example, associations between self-reported experiences of racial discrimination and preterm and low-birth-weight deliveries among black women.[43] It is possible that discrimination (or perceptions thereof) play an influential role in disparities measured among minorities who have achieved middle-class SES.[44] The "costs of caring" for family members with lower SES as well as the health impacts of the "disidentification, distancing, and alienation from one's community of origin" are other suggested areas requiring further study to understand risk factors for middle-class minorities.[45]

The Effects of Migration on Health Status

The immigrant composition of U.S. society calls for special attention to how migration impacts health status. In some cases, immigrant status seems to be protective of health; in other cases, there are associations between immigration status and poor health. For example, in a recent study examining sex and education variations in obesity among U.S.- and foreign-born whites, blacks and Hispanics using data on over 250,000 adults, researchers found that "foreign-born black men had the lowest odds for obesity relative to U.S.-born white men. The largest racial/ethnic disparity in obesity was between U.S.-born black and white women. High educational attainment diminished the U.S.-born black-white and Hispanic-white disparities among women, increased these disparities among men and had minimal effect on foreign-born Hispanic-white disparities among women and men."[46]

As public health scholar, David Williams, has noted:

> Because processes linked to migration make an important contribution to health, the large number of immigrants within both the Asian and Hispanic population importantly affects the health status of these groups. National data reveal that immigrants of all the major racial groups in the United States have lower rates of adult and infant mortality than their native-born counterparts. However, with length of stay in the United States and acculturation to American society, the health advantage of immigrants tends to decline over time.... The relationship between immigrant status and health also varies by the health status indicator under consideration, such that our knowledge of the health of immigrants may be importantly shaped by the availability of data for certain health outcomes.[47]

The health and healthcare concerns of immigrants are discussed in detail in Chapter 10.

The Hispanic Paradox

"The Hispanic paradox" is the phrase coined for the relatively high level of health of Hispanic immigrants despite their low SES. For example, in 2010 the Centers for Disease Control and Prevention (CDC) reported, "The Hispanic population has a life expectancy advantage at birth of 2.5 years over the non-Hispanic white population and 7.7 years over the non-Hispanic black population."[a]

There is not a complete understanding of this epidemiological phenomenon. "Possible under-reporting of Hispanic deaths, 'salmon bias' [aging and unhealthy immigrants return to their homeland when in state of decline and death] and healthy migrant effects, and risk profile may contribute to, but do not explain, the paradox. The reasons for this paradox are likely to be multifactorial and social in origin."[b]

Further scholarly attention is needed to the SES characteristics of immigrant populations, the health trajectories they may be on with multiple generations in the United States, and the collection of data to accurately measure their experience. Varying trajectories for socioeconomic mobility among immigrants will likely lead to divergent patterns of health over time.[c]

Notes: [a] E. Arias, "United States Life Tables by Hispanic Origin," National Center for Health Statistics, *Vital Health Statistics*, 2, no. 152 (2010): 1, http://www.cdc.gov/nchs/data/series/sr_02/sr02_152.pdf; [b] L. Franzini, J. C. Ribble, A. M. Keddie, "Understanding the Hispanic Paradox," *Ethnic Disparities*, 11, no. 3 (autumn 2001): 496–518, http://www.ncbi.nlm.nih.gov/pubmed/11572416; [c] D. R. Williams, "The Health of US Racial and Ethnic Populations," *Journals of Gerontology*, Series B, 60B (special issue 11) (2005): 57.

Research has pointed to the many ways social conditions and experiences can affect health and lead to health disparities. How social experience leads to biological responses causing poor health, however, is not obvious. The next section explores how the "social becomes biologic."

Questions for Discussion

1. What is the relationship between individual choices and social environment in determining an individual's health status?

2. What does research tell us about the role socioeconomic status (SES) plays in racial and ethnic health disparities? What questions remain unanswered?

How the Social Becomes Biologic

Social Environment and Stress

In the past few years researchers have developed a better understanding of the effect of social environment in producing stress and, in turn, the effect of this stress on long-term health outcomes. "Stress responses" are specific physiological expressions that impact brain circuitry and other health factors. The scientific community is increasingly uncovering evidence of specific changes to brain structure—including in areas that help us respond to stress—as a result of chronic stress,[48] and documenting stress effects on child development and subsequent adult health.

The Effects of Toxic Stress on Brain Development in Early Childhood

The ability to manage stress is controlled by brain circuits and hormone systems that are activated early in life. When a child feels threatened, hormones are released and circulate throughout the body. Prolonged exposure to stress hormones can impact the brain and impair functioning in a variety of ways.

- Toxic stress can impair the connection of brain circuits and, in the extreme, result in the development of a smaller brain.

- Brain circuits are especially vulnerable as they are developing during early childhood. Toxic stress can disrupt the development of these circuits. This can cause an individual to develop a low threshold for stress, thereby becoming overly reactive to adverse experiences throughout life.

- High levels of stress hormones, including cortisol, can suppress the body's immune response. This can leave an individual vulnerable to a variety of infections and chronic health problems.

- Sustained high levels of cortisol can damage the hippocampus, an area of the brain responsible for learning and memory. These cognitive deficits can continue into adulthood.

Source: U.S. Centers for Disease Control and Prevention, "The Effects of Childhood Stress on Health Across the Lifespan," 4, http://www.cdc.gov/ncipc/pub-res/pdf/Childhood_Stress.pdf.

The "physiological expression of the stress response system" occurring in the context of stable, protective relationships can be a normal and necessary part of healthy development (positive stress) or have no lasting impact (tolerable stress). But children who have stress response from "frequent or sustained adverse experiences such as extreme poverty, physical or emotional abuse, chronic neglect, maternal depression, parental substance abuse, and exposure to violence, without the buffer of adult support" experience harm (toxic stress).[49]

The Adverse Childhood Experiences (ACE) study by the CDC and Kaiser Permanente found among 17,000 adults that "exposure to ACE showed a strong, graded relationship with conditions and outcomes including ischemic heart disease, cancer, chronic lung disease, depression, alcoholism, illicit drug use, sexually transmitted diseases, suicide attempts, smoking, and premature death."[50] Children of lower SES have greater likelihood of experiencing toxic stress, and research examining underlying physiological responses (salivary cortisol levels, for example) show children of lower SES have higher levels of this stress indicator on a daily basis than children of higher SES.[51]

Stress in adulthood has a negative health effect. Research shows that the experience of environmental conditions, work stressors, discrimination, and chronic poverty can impact adult health. Higher stress reactivity—a predictor of adult mood and anxiety disorders—is associated with lower SES childhood environments with high conflict and adversity.[52] Similarly, researchers point to social experiences such as discrimination and exposure to violence and the ways these experiences affect stress and health. For example, recent research has documented the negative impact of discrimination on the health of working-class lesbian, gay, bisexual and transgender community members.[53]

Social Domains That Impact Health

There is an extensive and growing body of literature on the impact of multiple social domains on health, including (among other issues) nutrition, housing, employment, energy and neighborhood safety.[54] It is beyond the scope of this chapter to review this body of work. However, we highlight two strands to illustrate the kinds of proximal and distal effects social factors have on health:

- Food availability and affordability
- Housing affordability and safety

Access to an Adequate Supply of Affordable, Healthy Food

Good nutrition promotes the healthy development of a child's body and mind and impacts the health status of adults. A family's ability to afford and purchase healthy foods has multiple effects on a child's health, growth and development even before conception. Examination of families' levels of food insecurity, defined as not having access at all times to enough food for an active healthy life,[55] show that poor children are five times more likely to experience food insecurity and hunger and have significantly lower intake of calories, iron, folate and other nutrients, compared with nonpoor children.[56] Among food-insecure families with children, half reported that they were sometimes not able to feed their children balanced meals, and 25 percent reported that their children did not have enough to eat.[57]

There is substantial evidence indicating that food insecurity poses a substantial threat to child health and well-being, which in turn may have lifelong implications for an individual's health and ability to work, play and achieve. A nutritionally inadequate diet makes children susceptible to an "infection-malnutrition cycle" by impairing their immune function.[58] An inadequate food supply prevents children from fully recovering from weight loss or interrupted growth during illness episodes, leading to poor nutritional status that puts them at risk for a subsequent illness, creating a cycle of poor growth and increased risk of illness.

Food insecurity also has a pernicious effect on the health of adults, especially those with chronic disease or advancing age.[59] In families, a "child preference" "at lower levels of food insecurity, [may cause] adult care givers [to sacrifice] their own food consumption to maintain adequate levels for their children."[60] People with chronic illnesses, such as hypertension and diabetes, may struggle to manage their disease; poor self-management increases their risk and rate of complications, in turn increasing morbidity and mortality. Elders who are food insecure have poor overall health status and compromised ability to resist infections, experience deteriorating mental and physical health, show a greater incidence of hospitalizations and extended hospital stays and place increasing caregiving demands on their families.[61] Some studies have found an association between very low food security and lower cognitive performance, although causality requires further study.[62]

Adverse Health Effects of Food Insecurity

Food-insecure children:

- Are two to three times more likely to be in fair or poor health or chronically ill[a]
- Are 30 percent more likely to be hospitalized by age three years[b]
- Are more likely to show poor growth[c]
- Score lower on measures of physical and psychosocial functioning[d]
- Have deficits in cognitive and behavioral development that affect school performance[e]

Food-insecure adults more frequently:

- Report poorer health status[f]
- Score significantly lower on measures of physical and mental health[f]
- Have greater likelihood of hypoglycemia if diabetic[f]
- Have compromised health status if elderly[f]

Notes: [a] L. Weinreb, et al., "Hunger: Its Impact on Children's Health and Mental Health," *Pediatrics*, 110, no. 4 (October 2002): e41; [b] J. T. Cook, et al., "Food Insecurity is Associated with Adverse Health Outcomes among Human Infants and Toddlers." *Journal of Nutrition*, 134, no. 6 (2004): 1432–38; [c] A. H. Fierman, et al., "Growth Delay in Homeless Children," *Pediatrics*, 88, no. 5 (1991): 918–25. Children's Sentinel Nutrition Assessment Program, "The Safety Net in Action: Protecting the Health and Nutrition of Young American Children," 2004; [d] P. H. Casey, et al., "Child Health-Related Quality of Life and Household Food Security," *Archives of Pediatrics and Adolescent Medicine*, 159, no. 1 (2005): 51–56; [e] K. Alaimo, C. M. Olson, E. A. Frongillo, "Food Insufficiency and American School-Aged Children's Cognitive, Academic, and Psychosocial Development," *Pediatrics*, 108 (2001): 44–53; Children's Sentinel Nutrition Assessment Program, "Protecting Children from Hunger and Food Insecurity in 2005–2006," (C-SNAP Brief, 2005); J. M. Murphy "Relationship between Hunger and Psychosocial Functioning in Low-Income American Children," *Journal of the American Academy of Child and Adolescent Psychiatry*, 37 (1998): 163–70; [f] J. E. Stuff, et al., "Household Food Insecurity Is Associated with Adult Health Status," *Journal of Nutrition*, 134, no. 9 (2004), http://jn.nutrition.org/ content/134/9/2330.abstract.

In addition to the relationship between food insecurity and poor health outcomes, there is a relationship between availability of healthy food and poor health outcomes. In recent years, researchers have increasingly focused on disparities in populations' access to healthy foods. Researchers have documented the "food deserts" of many low-income communities, where affordable, healthful food is not available. One influential report, "The Grocery Gap," reports that although 31 percent of whites live in a census tract with a grocery store, only 8 percent of African Americans do.[63] Twenty percent of rural U.S. counties are food desert counties where all residents live more than ten miles from a supermarket or supercenter.[64]

There are well-established relationships between healthy food access and health: "residents who live near supermarkets or in areas where food markets selling fresh produce (supermarkets, grocery stores, farmers' markets, etc.) outnumber food stores that generally do not (such as corner stores) have lower rates of diet-related diseases than their counterparts in neighborhoods lacking food access."[65] There are also substantial data documenting the increased density of fast-food restaurants, which are known to offer food that is higher in fat, sodium and calories, in low-income and minority neighborhoods.[66] See Chapter 17 for further discussion of how social conditions, such as food deserts, impact obesity rates.

Housing Affordability and Safety

Housing costs are usually the largest portion of household budgets and are usually paid first, limiting income available for other expenses such as food, clothing, health care, utilities or transportation. Although housing is considered affordable if a family spends less than 30 percent of their income on it, half of low-income working families with children spend more than half of their income on rent.[67] Families facing high housing costs combined with limited income experience "shelter poverty," which means they cannot adequately meet their other needs after paying for housing.[68]

Confronted with unaffordable housing, families make budget trade-offs between housing and important basic needs. A 2005 national study of housing costs indicated that low-income families who pay more than 50 percent of their income for housing spend: 30 percent less on food, 70 percent less on health care, and 70 percent less on transportation.[69] Trade-offs resulting in food insecurity are particularly important for children's health and well-being. "Rent or eat" is a well-documented dilemma. Children whose families are eligible for but not receiving rent subsidies are up to eight times more likely to demonstrate malnutrition and stunted growth.[70]

Physical housing conditions have been associated with many common chronic diseases in children and adults. The most common of these are asthma, lead poisoning and unintentional injuries. The American Housing Survey conducted by the Department of Housing and Urban Development has found that rodent and cockroach infestation, lack of heat during the winter, leaks and related mold, uncovered radiators, peeling paint and lead paint, exposed wires, holes in walls, and lack of running water in past three months increase the risk of asthma, injuries, lead poisoning and infectious diseases.[71]

The lack of affordable housing is one of multiple factors that can lead to housing instability and homelessness. Homeless families experience overcrowding, often with entire families living in one room; inadequate food preparation and storage facilities; unsanitary conditions; sleep deprivation; lack of transportation to get to school, work and healthcare appointments; and social and geographic isolation.[72] Both homeless families and those in unsanitary conditions have higher exposure to allergens that cause or exacerbate asthma, such as cockroach and rodent infestations, dust mites, inadequate heat, excess moisture, poor ventilation and mold.[73] Medical management of asthma or other health conditions may be more difficult for homeless than housed families due to inability to purchase and/or store medications as well as limited access to electricity and refrigeration. See Chapter 8 for a detailed discussion of housing and health.

Pathways of Impact

The foregoing discussion lays the foundation for understanding how social factors can profoundly influence health and well-being. To further illustrate how "the social becomes biologic," this section describes in greater detail potential pathways of this transformation. The multiple intervening steps between the social domain, where the transformation from social to biologic starts, and the health and medical domains, where the adverse impacts are identified, are often not fully appreciated by those working in the other domain. It is also important to understand that this transformation of the social into the biologic can occur, and usually does, without active intent. Rather, these can be thought of as *unintended* yet *predictable* consequences.

As noted, there are numerous examples of the transformation of the social into the biologic. One could document the multiple intervening steps for each example. However, the topic of energy costs effectively elucidates the pathways connecting a particular social issue to its health consequences. It also highlights how social domains overlap and may affect health at multiple levels. As explored shortly, energy costs relate to housing costs, safety and stability; they may also impact the ability to purchase food, thus affecting food security.

The high cost of home energy places a substantial burden on many families, especially low-income families.[74] There is substantial evidence supporting at least four potential pathways through which high energy costs impact health and well-being. Low-income families facing high energy costs:

- are forced to make household budget trade-offs that jeopardize their health;
- often resort to alternative, unsafe heating sources, such as space heaters, ovens and stoves;
- accumulate substantial unpaid utility bills, leading to disconnections that adversely affect health; and
- are likely to endure substandard housing conditions because they are not able to afford higher quality housing.

Each of these pathways are described in more detail.

Household Budget Trade-Offs

The high cost of home heating and cooling places many low-income individuals and families at risk, with many "caught in the gap between rising energy prices and available energy assistance."[75] There is compelling evidence that when faced with higher energy costs in the winter, low-income families are forced to choose between paying energy bills and purchasing food. "Heat or eat" is a familiar choice for many families in poverty. In 2003, the U.S. Department of Agriculture's Economic Research Service researchers merged data on heating degree-days, reflecting the energy necessary to heat a home based on the outside temperature, with data on household food insecurity, income, employment and other characteristics. They found that "households with incomes below the poverty line were substantially more vulnerable to hunger during the winter and early spring than during the summer."[76]

Strong evidence supports the conclusion that children in low-income families are nutritionally at risk during the winter and early spring because they take in fewer calories and other micronutrients.[77] One report notes that "poor parents are only imperfectly able to protect their children from cold-weather resource shocks."[78] A study of Boston children between six months and two years of age treated at a safety-net hospital found that the children's growth decreased during winter months. Families without heat or threatened with utility disconnections were twice as likely to have children experiencing hunger or be at risk for hunger.[79]

Budget trade-offs that result in food insecurity, medical care forgone or medications skipped have clear health impacts. A 2005 survey performed by state officials charged with providing low-income energy assistance through the federal Low Income Home Energy Assistance Program (LIHEAP) found that a significant proportion of LIHEAP participants in the Northeast reported making precisely these kinds of budget trade-offs due to high energy costs:

- 73 percent reported that they reduced expenditures on household necessities because they did not have enough money to pay their energy bills;
- 20 percent went without food;
- 35 percent went without medical or dental care; and
- 30 percent did not make a full rent or mortgage payment at least once.[80]

Alternative, Unsafe Heating Sources

Faced with high energy costs, low-income families resort to using risky alternative sources of supplemental heat to warm their homes, such as portable space heaters (often in bedrooms), kitchen stoves or fireplaces. A survey of low-income service providers, including state LIHEAP directors, weatherization assistance program directors, community action administrators and public utility commissions, reported that low-income families respond to unaffordable energy bills by relying on alternative heating sources.[81]

The 2005 survey by the National Energy Assistance Directors Association found that 22 percent of LIHEAP households in the Northeast used the kitchen stove or oven to heat their homes due to not having enough money for their energy bill in the past year.[82] This is consistent with national data indicating that 14.5 percent of low-income households used stoves or ovens for heat, compared with 6 percent of higher income households.[83] The use of these alternative sources of heat is risky because they are associated with increased likelihood of house fires, burns and carbon monoxide poisoning. Unintentional, nonfire or automobile-related carbon monoxide poisoning, which can cause seizures, coma and death, sends 15,000 people to emergency departments and results in 500 deaths annually. Not surprisingly, the incidence of both fatal and nonfatal carbon monoxide poisoning increases during the fall and winter months.[84]

Utility Arrearages, Disconnections, Eviction and Homelessness

It is well documented that high energy costs can result in unpaid bills, leading to substantial arrearages and subsequent utility disconnections. These high energy costs can lead to eviction and homelessness in two major ways. First, families may not be able to pay both the energy bills and the entire rent or mortgage. A recent survey documented that 25 percent of LIHEAP recipient households surveyed had made a partial rent or mortgage payment or missed an entire payment altogether because of unaffordable energy bills.[85] This situation is even more dire in regions with cold climates, such as the Northeast: 42 percent reported not paying or paying less than their entire home energy bill because of not having enough money; one in four reported receiving a notice of disconnection of electricity or heating fuel in a 12-month period.[86]

Second, families who have unpaid energy bills develop substantial arrearages that can result in utility service disconnection. Once this occurs, a family whose utility service is disconnected may be evicted for failure to maintain the habitability of their home.[87] Although many states prohibit winter utility disconnection for households experiencing financial hardship, these shut-off protections usually end in the spring, resulting in disconnections in late spring.[88] During the shut-off moratorium period, families continue to accrue debt for their utility bills. In addition to imposing general hardship, disconnected utilities make it difficult to manage chronic conditions such as asthma or diabetes, which require electricity to operate medical equipment or refrigerate medications.

Unaffordable Housing and Unhealthy Housing Conditions

The constraints that high energy costs place on low-income families reduce their ability to afford appropriate housing, increasing the likelihood that they and their children experience unhealthy housing conditions. As discussed earlier, unsafe housing conditions lead to numerous health risks, such as asthma, lead poisoning and injury. See Chapter 8 for discussion of the relationship between substandard housing conditions and health. Figure 1.6 illustrates four pathways leading from high energy costs to adverse health outcomes.

Figure 1.6 The Impact of Energy Costs on Health

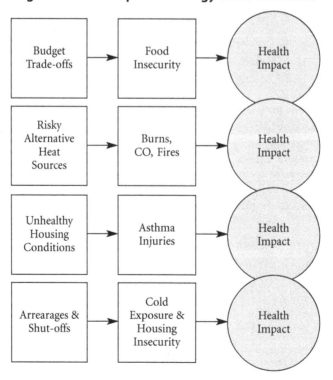

Uncoupling the Social from the Biologic: Looking for the Pump Handle

The primary task of uncoupling social factors from their adverse health outcomes is related to changing the social contexts in which people live, work and play. At the population level, it can be very difficult to make healthy choices when the constraints of the environment tend to promote less healthy choices. For example, a study of cardiovascular health and diet documented racial differences in access to supermarkets — blacks had decreased access to healthy food, with only 8 percent living close to a supermarket.[89] Even more important, the differential access to grocery stores had a dramatic effect on whether study participants met the recommended dietary guidelines, including eating more fruits and vegetables and less saturated and total fat.

Most physicians who counsel their patients on dietary interventions to manage chronic disease, such as hypertension, elevated cholesterol, coronary artery disease or diabetes, would not consider the proximity of their patients to grocery stores. Yet without access to affordable, healthy food, patients who want to follow the sound advice offered by clinicians will not be able to do so. At the same time that low-income and minority populations experience decreased access to healthy nutrition options, they have increased exposure to unhealthy ones. Fast-food restaurant density is related to both race and income with increased density in minority and low-income neighborhoods. In a recent study, predominantly black neighborhoods had up to six times more fast-food restaurants.[90] A recently published Massachusetts report on childhood body mass index by town showed a striking correlation between a biologic condition, obesity and overweight, and a social factor, median household income. Those towns with lower median household income had significantly higher rates of childhood obesity and overweight. This suggests that income associated differences in social context are at play, including easy access to affordable, healthy food and safe opportunities for physical activity.[91]

Influences may be the result of restrictive policies, lack of services or facilities or collective decision making that limits individual choices, but may also arise from contextual cues within an environment, such as fast-food and tobacco advertising or the opinions of peers.[92] Such cues and influences exist in all social strata but with different messages and pressures — differences that may partially explain behavior variations among groups.[93]

Although healthcare has a critical role in avoiding or mitigating adverse health outcomes once individuals have already experienced social health risks, public health advocacy can prevent exposure to those risks in the first place. There is a strong tradition in public health for primary prevention from exposure to or experience of risk.[94] An often cited example is that of John Snow, who during a cholera outbreak in London in 1854 removed a pump handle from a water supply he suspected was the source of the illness. By preventing access to the contaminated water, he averted subsequent deaths.[95] Snow's elegantly simple intervention illustrates the power of changing the social context to promote health. Figure 1.7 illustrates the distinct but mutually enhancing roles that healthcare and public health and advocacy can play in uncoupling social threats from their health effects.

A focus on primary prevention and influencing the social context is also at work in the Health Impact Pyramid (see Figure 1.8) introduced in 2010 by Thomas R. Frieden after he assumed leadership of the CDC.[96] He makes the case for the importance of working on issues that will change the context of individual decision making so that healthier choices become easier, sometimes "default" choices. This approach does not eliminate

Figure 1.7 Uncoupling Social Threats: A Role for Public Health Policy and Legal Advocacy

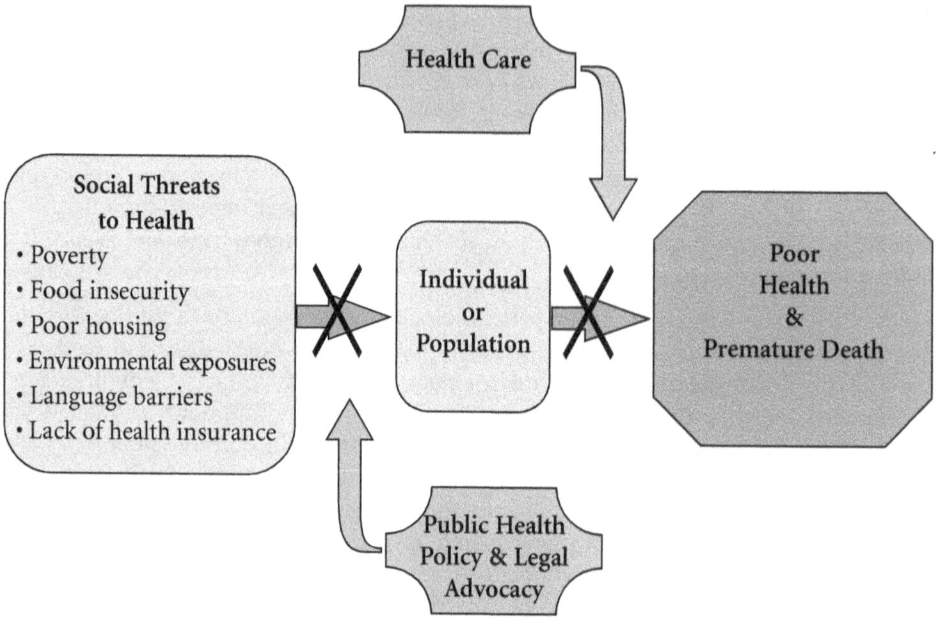

Figure 1.8 Health Impact Pyramid

Source: Adapted from T. R. Frieden, "A Framework for Public Health Action: The Health Impact Pyramid," *American Journal of Public Health*, 100, no. 4 (April 2010): 590–595.

individual responsibility for behavior, but it recognizes that people develop preferences and make choices in contexts that can be more or less supportive of healthier choices. Changing contexts may be more cost-effective and yield more sustainable population-level changes than efforts focusing on individual behavioral change through counseling and education or clinical intervention alone.

As Frieden notes, "Interventions focusing on lower levels of the pyramid tend to be more effective because they reach broader segments of society and require less individual effort. Implementing interventions at each of the levels can achieve the maximum possible sustained public health benefit."[97] For example, sidewalks and safety lighting promote physical activity, and nearby grocery stores support a healthier diet. Alternatively, an abundance of liquor stores, tobacco advertising, corner stores with junk food and vacant lots will discourage healthful habits.[98]

Role of Public Policy

As the understanding of the social determinants of health has deepened, scholars and policy makers have come to realize that "policies in societal domains far removed from traditional health policy can have decisive consequences for individual and population health."[99] Many laws and policies have an unrecognized impact on health. A salient example is the federal welfare reform law, the Personal Responsibility and Work Opportunity Reconciliation Act of 1996,[100] which instituted strict work requirements and time limits for cash assistance. Although two-thirds of welfare recipients at the time were children, the health impact of these provisions on them or their parents, primarily mothers, was essentially ignored by policy makers. However, some health impact studies were conducted that focused particularly on cash assistance recipients with chronically ill children.[101] These studies showed that recipients with chronically ill children face substantial barriers to successful employment, including unmet needs for experienced child care and missed work due to child illness. These barriers were shown to negatively impact the parents' health status due to stress; lack of access to insurance, preventive, and primary care; and other factors.[102]

One effective strategy used by health advocates to evaluate the impact of particular laws and policies on health outcomes is the health impact assessment.[103] These assessments offer an objective, evidence- and experience-based method through which to evaluate the implications of policy, regulations and legislation for health and well-being. These focus on policy arenas outside the traditional realm of health care, public health, and health policy, such as education, housing and landlord/tenant laws, immigration and naturalization, criminal justice and employment and income supports. In this way, health impact assessments can be seen as a structured way to illuminate the transformation of the social to the biologic. See Appendix 1.1 for further information about these assessments.

Just as health advocates explore ways to identify the impact of particular practices and policies on health, lawyers and legal scholars analyze the role of law in the social determinants of health. The following section explores the role law plays in determining the health of individuals and populations as well as potential ways legal advocacy may improve the health of individuals and populations.

Questions for Discussion

1. Explain the concept of "the social becomes biologic" using a different example than those highlighted in the chapter.

2. You are advocating for an increase in LIHEAP in a meeting with your state's congressional leader. How would you describe the potential health benefits of such assistance?

The Role of Law in Addressing the Social Determinants of Health

Law is one of the most important social determinants of health. It helps establish the framework in which individuals and populations live, face disease and injury, and eventually die. By so doing, law influences myriad other social determinants, including education, income, housing, racial and ethnic disparities, nutrition and access to health care. In short, law is one factor that helps determine other social determinants.[104]

The Meaning of Law

To understand law's role as a social determinant, it is useful to consider what we mean by the term *law*. Often in health and public health literature the word *law* is used in its most narrow sense to refer to the constitutions and duly enacted statutes of the federal government, states and localities. Thus, the statement "federal law requires hospital emergency rooms to screen everyone who appears asking for care," refers to a specific federal statute, commonly known as the Emergency Medical Treatment and Active Labor Act (42 U.S.C. § 1395dd). Likewise, when we say "Massachusetts law prohibits driving while texting," we are referring to a Massachusetts state statute (Mass. G.L. ch. 90 § 12A) that makes it a traffic offense to engage in the prohibited act.

The term *law*, however, encompasses far more than constitutions and legislative enactments. It also includes binding regulations and decisions of administrative agencies when they act within the scope of their statutory authority, including the regulations and orders of federal, state or local agencies charged with protecting public health. Hence, the regulations of a city housing department that require landlords to keep their apartments in a sanitary condition are relevant sources of law. In addition, decisions by courts and administrative tribunals not only apply the law to the facts before them but are also part of the law.

Increasingly, scholars recognize that international law belongs within our understanding of the law. International law includes both binding treaties and adjudications between nations, commonly called "hard international law," as well as the declarations and guidance of international agencies and organizations, often known as "soft international law." Both hard and soft international laws can have a profound influence on the health of populations. For example, the International Covenant on Economic, Social and Cultural Rights obligates signatory states to recognize "the right of everyone to the enjoyment of the highest attainable standard of health."[105] Although that right has certainly not been fully realized (and the U.S. is not a signatory to the document), international law's recognition of it has certainly helped move state and nonstate actors to address global health inequities.[106]

The discussion of soft international law suggests a broader point. The term *law* refers to more than simply the authoritative pronouncements or rules of sovereign governments, or so-called positive law. Law also includes deeply held norms and understandings that underlie much of social life. In the United States, as in many other countries, these norms may include the rights to equal opportunity and to control private property. Such norms may be reflected in and enforced by positive law, but they need not be.

One other use of the term *law* warrants consideration. Law can also be understood to refer to the processes and structures that a society uses to organize itself and settle disputes among its members.[107] In other words, the law includes the social system in which norms are applied to particular individuals and groups in specific contexts. The practice of law, whereby lawyers and other advocates represent the interests of individuals or groups within that system, can and should also be viewed as part of the law. By helping determine which norms are recognized as positive laws and how these laws are applied to distinct people in different contexts, law understood as the practice of law can be a powerful social determinant of health.

Law as a Social Determinant

As a social determinant of health, law can have a direct and obvious impact on health or an indirect and subtle effect. For example, laws that establish health departments and authorize them to inspect restaurants or provide vaccinations are "core public health laws." These laws clearly concern public health, and it should not surprise us if they impact the health of populations. Most laws, however, pertain less overtly to public health, yet they may still have a substantial impact on a population's health. Consider the laws that exist in every state requiring children to be schooled. These laws were presumably enacted to educate the next generation of workers and citizens. They are not generally thought of as health laws. Nevertheless, once we recall the well-established connection between education level and health,[108] we may begin to suspect that public education laws may have a profound (albeit perhaps incidental) effect on a population's health. Importantly, because education may be associated with numerous other social determinants, such as income and health literacy, public education laws may influence health through multiple pathways.

Broadening the Scope: Laws That Affect Health

Figure 1.9 illustrates how different types of laws can serve as social determinants of health. In the center of the circle are core public health laws. These laws target health and affect it directly. As we move away from the core, we find other laws, like education laws, that may nevertheless have a robust impact on health. Farther away from the center are laws such as the U.S. Constitution or general common law norms, such as contract law, that help shape other laws and the legal system itself. Surprisingly, these laws may have a more substantial impact on public health than core public health laws do. For example,

Figure 1.9 Laws as Social Determinants*

Constitutional and general common
laws affecting distribution of societal
resources and access to healthcare within a society

Other laws, e.g.,
education and zoning,
affecting health of individuals
and communities

Core public health
laws targeting health
of individuals and
communities

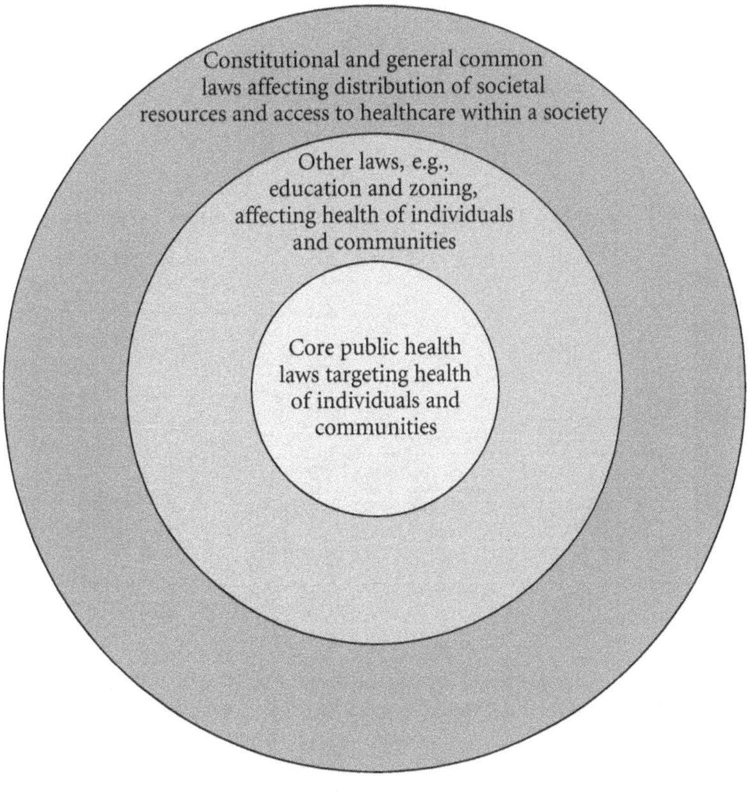

a law authorizing a health department to isolate a tuberculosis patient who fails to take his medication clearly concerns public health; however, this provision may be used rarely and affect the health of relatively few people. In contrast, broad constitutional norms may determine the distribution of resources within a society and whether the government guarantees access to healthcare. These remote but far-reaching laws may have a broad population-wide impact.[109]

Laws as Positive and Negative Determinants of Health

Law's effect on health is not always beneficial. For example, zoning laws that concentrate environmental risks in low-income neighborhoods or make it difficult to challenge such concentrations may exacerbate health disparities.[110] Other zoning laws may promote a sedentary lifestyle and thereby increase a population's risk of obesity, diabetes and coronary artery disease.[111] In contrast, laws that tax cigarettes or prohibit indoor smoking may act as positive determinants of health.[112]

Many of the most important public health gains of the past century have been made using positive law.[113] For example, laws have helped reduce tobacco use, increase childhood vaccination rates and improve motor vehicle safety by requiring cars to have (and individuals to wear) seatbelts.[114] Importantly, such laws often do not always work by prohibiting particular dangerous activities or products. Laws can also affect public health by offering individuals incentives, providing benefits and structuring the environment in a way that makes it easier to stay healthy. Figure 1.10 uses a modified version of the Health Impact Pyramid to demonstrate the different types of laws that can influence a population's health, displaying broadly based measures that alter the social environment and affect broad populations at the bottom of the pyramid and more individually oriented (and often more intrusive) laws, such as individual mandates, closer to the pyramid's peak.

Figure 1.10 Health Impact Pyramid with Legal Intervention

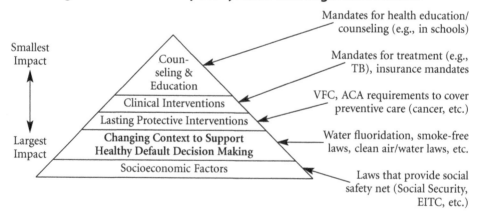

Source: Adapted from T. R. Frieden, "A Framework for Public Health Action: The Health Impact Pyramid," *American Journal of Public Health*, 100, no. 4 (April 2010): 590–595.

Using Law as a Public Health Tool: Individual and Systemic Approaches

Individual Approaches

According to the CDC's Public Health Law Program, "law is a foundational tool for disease prevention and health promotion."[115] In recent decades, many public health practitioners, public health advocates, healthcare workers and lawyers have agreed and have self-consciously sought to use the law and legal tools to promote population health. Legislation, regulation, litigation and nonlitigation-based legal advocacy all offer proponents of health ways to alter the social and physical environment, helping both individuals and communities live healthier lives.

In thinking about the use of law to promote health, it is useful to distinguish between approaches that focus on the interests of particular, identified individuals (patients or clients) and approaches that emphasize systemic, population-wide changes. This section describes individual approaches. The next section looks at the use of law to generate systemic changes.

Lawyers and advocates can use a variety of techniques, including client education, advocacy with government officials, negotiation and even litigation to alter the social conditions faced by specific individual patients and clients, thereby improving their health. These individualized, client-centered approaches may produce faster results for vulnerable clients than would more comprehensive, systemic approaches. After all, a client facing an immediate health crisis can seldom wait for systemic change.

Individual Approaches to Advocacy

Enabling a hearing-impaired child with cerebral palsy maximize her potential: Lack of special supports impeded 11-year-old Grace's ability to thrive in school. Her mother mentioned her concerns to Grace's pediatrician, who then connected the family to the Washington, DC-based Children's Law Center. Advocacy on Grace's behalf resulted in equipment and resources she needed for her special health and education challenges. Grace now keeps up with her schoolwork with an at-home tutor, and she has a desk that enables her to read and write with no limitations.[a]

Ensuring access to safety-net supports for a cancer patient: When Lonnie was treated for cancer at age 62, he found he could no longer earn an income. Lonnie and his wife found that they could not survive on her pension alone. Inexplicably their applications for financial assistance through the federal food stamps and Social Security programs were denied. The Tucson Family Advocacy Program helped them successfully appeal and obtain Social Security disability benefits, assisted them to get health insurance under the state's Medicaid program, and secure food stamps, relieving them of significant economic burdens as they fought the cancer battle. Advocates not only represented them in their appeals but also helped the couple become advocates for themselves. These new skills empowered the couple as they confronted future denials of benefits. Lonnie's wife said, "[my attorney] showed me that it's not that hard to stand there on your own and say: 'Wait a minute, this is not right.'"[b]

Bridging the gap between agencies serving the poor: An ophthalmologist treating a homeless woman in New York City refused to perform glaucoma surgery until the patient's immune system improved. The patient's multiple health ailments, including diabetes, breast cancer, and a weakened immune system due to cancer treatments, and the communal, unsanitary living arrangements provided by her community's homeless authority made it nearly impossible for her to improve her immune system. A LegalHealth advocate worked with the client's healthcare providers to gather the necessary medical records and present the findings to the homeless authority, which granted the client an emergency transfer to new housing with her own bathroom. As a result of the transfer, the client was able to take better care of her immune system and was soon able to undergo the much-needed glaucoma surgery. Without the aid of a legally trained advocate to bridge the gap between the client's medical providers and the city's homeless authority, such a quick transfer would not have been possible.[c]

Notes: [a] See http://www.medical-legalpartnership.org/impact/patient-client-stories/jane-and-grace-washington-dc; [b] See http://www.medical-legalpartnership.org/impact/patient-client-stories/edith-and-lonnie-evans-tucson-az; [c] See R. Retkin, et al., "Medical Legal Partnerships: A Key Strategy for Mitigating the Negative Health Impacts of the Recession," *Health Law*, 22 (2009): 31.

The Benefits of Individual Advocacy

Studies have confirmed that individualized advocacy can improve the health of those who are represented. For example, a 2006 study conducted by St. Luke's-Roosevelt Hospital and LegalHealth researchers found that asthma patients receiving legal interventions experienced "significant improvements in the severity of their condition, and fewer emergency room visits, than patients who did not receive legal assistance."[116] LegalHealth conducted a second study in 2007, surveying fifty-one clients living with cancer. In that study, 83 percent of clients receiving legal assistance reported a significant reduction in stress, and 51 percent reported an improvement in their financial situation.[117] Chapter 18 discusses evaluating the impact of legal interventions for individual patients.

Lawyer-Client Relationship

One often overlooked advantage of an individualized approach is that it permits a close client-attorney relationship. One author examined the importance of individual attorney-client relationships in the context of educational reform litigation, noting that "by making an effort to understand their clients' situations; engaging clients in identifying their own objectives, alternatives, and concerns; and offering empathy ... lawyers assist clients in making their own decisions and thereby protect individual autonomy."[118] Such a client-centered approach to the practice of law is more readily accomplished in an individual context because advocates who seek systemic change and try to address determinants affecting broad populations are usually unable to give the specific individuals who comprise those populations the attention they need to become empowered. Nor can advocates using systemic strategies be confident that they truly understand and are advancing the interests of their clients.

The Broader Impact of Individual Cases

Although individual representation seeks to advance the interests of an individual, it may have a broader impact, thereby affecting the health of many people other than the individual client. For example, when appellate courts decide individual cases, they establish precedent that can reaffirm or alter the law. Thus, the case of *Tarasoff v. Regents of the University of California* (17 Cal. 3d 425 (1976)) was brought to seek compensation for the family of a woman who died after a psychologist failed to warn her that one of his patients intended to kill her. In deciding the case, the Supreme Court of California found that a therapist owes a duty to exercise reasonable care to warn third parties from the dangers posed by their patients. Although the court's opinion was relatively narrow and based on the facts before it, one study found that the case was widely known by mental health professionals, that three out of four respondents thought that the opinion created a duty to warn intended victims, and that the decision — or a least their perception of the decision — appeared to have altered the behavior of many mental health providers.[119] More generally, empirical studies have resulted in conflicting and inclusive results regarding the ability of private litigation to deter dangerous practices.[120]

Individualized approaches may also provide lawyers and advocates with insight as to the types of systemic litigation or reform that may be useful to address growing health problems. For example, advocates who represent individuals with housing problems may notice a pattern of cases suggesting that housing inspectors need tougher enforcement tools. Advocates may then organize around the need for stronger regulations and more vigorous enforcement. ("From Practice to Policy" examples presenting this approach are provided throughout this book.) Or the information uncovered via the discovery process in litigation may reveal that a product is more dangerous than was previously thought. Safety agencies may then take action and remove the product from the market or promulgate stricter regulations.

The Disadvantages of the Individual Approach

Despite the potential benefits to both clients and the broader public, there are significant costs to relying on individualized approaches. Most of the time, a victory for any particular client in either a housing or malpractice case will not inspire the inattentive landlord or the careless hospital to change their ways. (This is especially true if a case is settled with a nondisclosure agreement, barring the parties from informing the broader public about the events leading to the client's injury.) Moreover, even when an individual case results in an appellate decision (which rarely happens), its facts may be so unique that it will be read narrowly, resulting in little or no impact on future behavior. Under such circumstances, the advocate may be better able to promote the health of a broader population by employing a systemic tool, either by seeking a legislative or regulatory change or by bringing an impact lawsuit.

Systemic Approaches

Lawyers and advocates hoping to use the law to address and improve public health on a population level may want to remember a key insight from social epidemiology: prevention strategies that focus on high-risk individuals (including individual clients) may have a less substantial impact on the health of a large population than do strategies that address more broadly based social forces.[121] To put it another way, measures that yield small gains in health among many people may prevent more morbidity and mortality than do interventions that result in substantial benefits for only a few people. By using the law to implement changes affecting many people, systemic approaches may result in greater improvements to public health than approaches that resolve the severe problems of particular clients.

Legislation

Perhaps the most important and influential systemic legal tool is legislation. Under the U.S. Constitution, Congress can only legislate pursuant to a grant of authority enumerated by the Constitution. The most important sources of constitutional authority for federal health legislation are the Commerce Clause (Art. I, Sec. 8, clause 3), which states that Congress shall have the power "to regulate Commerce with foreign Nations, and among the several States," and the Tax and Spending Clause (Article 1, Sec. 8, clause 1), which gives Congress the express power to tax and provide for the "general Welfare." The "necessary and proper clause" under Article I (Sec. 8, clause 18) permits Congress to enact laws that effectuate Congress's commerce or tax and spending powers. The scope of federal authority under these clauses remains highly contested, as the political debates and litigation concerning the 2010 Patient Protection and Affordable Care Act, commonly known as federal health reform, attests.[122]

In contrast to the federal government, states possess what is known as the "police power." This broad and difficult to define power can be thought of as the attributes of sovereignty that the states retained when they joined the federal Constitution.[123] Traditionally, the police power has been closely associated with the protection of health and safety. The idea that states may legislate to protect the health of their residents is well recognized in American constitutional jurisprudence.[124] All state and federal laws, however, are valid only if they do not run afoul of another constitutional provision, such as those found in the Bill of Rights.[125]

Using their constitutional powers, state and federal governments can enact public health laws that have positive effects on public health. For example, finding that the rapid growth of urbanization, industrial development and use of motor vehicles endangered public health, Congress enacted the Clean Air Act (CAA; 42 U.S.C. § 7401 et seq.) to regulate emissions into the air. A study by the Environmental Protection Agency (EPA) conducted in the 1990s found that had the CAA not been enacted, an estimated 205,000 additional Americans would have died prematurely and millions more would have suffered respiratory illnesses including heart disease, chronic bronchitis and asthma. Translated into economic terms, the EPA study estimated the overall benefits of the CAA at a mean of $22 trillion, whereas the costs of enforcement were $523 billion.[126]

Many state laws have helped improve public health. For example, states and their cities have taken the lead in restricting indoor smoking. Studies have found that young people who live in communities with strong indoor smoking laws have less exposure to second-hand smoke.[127] Local indoor smoking laws have also been found to be associated with a decline in hospital admissions for acute myocardial infarction,[128] as well as a decline in respiratory symptoms of workers.[129]

State laws may also interact synergistically with federal laws. For example, in the 1960s federal regulations first required that new cars come equipped with seatbelts and shoulder harnesses.[130] In 1985, New York built on this mandate by requiring seatbelt use.[131] Then in 1998, Congress enacted the Transportation Equity Act for the 21st Century (25 U.S.C. § 405), which provided grants to states that initiated new seatbelt laws. By 2010, forty-nine states had some form of seatbelt law. These laws vary from state to state. Some, known as primary enforcement laws, allow officers to stop cars for violations of the act; others allow only for secondary enforcement, which means that individuals may be cited for violations of the act only if they also commit another motor vehicular offense. Fines range from $10 up to $200 for having a child unbuckled, and $5 up to $124 for an adult's failure to buckle up.[132] In a study examining the impact of seatbelt laws on driving safety and fatalities, researchers concluded that "seat belt legislation unambiguously reduces traffic fatalities."[133] The researchers found that the passage of state seatbelt laws caused a significant increase in seatbelt usage, which in turn resulted in thousands of saved lives each year.[134] The National Highway Traffic Safety Administration reported that increased seat belt use saved an estimated 147,246 lives in the period from 1975 to 2001.[135]

Regulation

Although legislation can impact public health directly, legislatures frequently rely on administrative agencies to promulgate regulations to implement legislation. For example, in 2009, Congress enacted the Family Smoking Prevention and Tobacco Control Act (P.L. 111-31) that gave the Food and Drug Administration (FDA) the power to regulate tobacco marketing. Likewise, the CAA has been implemented through regulations promulgated by the EPA. State and local health regulations are also critically important to health. Many local health agencies have taken the lead in promulgating regulations pertaining to tobacco use, the use of trans fats in restaurants and menu labeling. These regulations in turn may spur further legislative development. For example, the Patient Protection and Affordable Care Act (P.L. 111-148, §4205) builds on local menu labeling initiatives by requiring chain restaurants to provide calorie labeling on their menus.

To realize the enactment of health-benefiting legislation or regulations, and thus systemic change, lawyers and advocates often help mobilize grassroots efforts. For example, during the 1960s a broad movement helped pave the way for the creation of Medicare and Medicaid, which have provided health insurance and thereby healthcare access to millions of Americans.[136] Grassroots law reform efforts can also be addressed to administrative agencies. At the start of the AIDS epidemic in the 1980s, a patient-centered AIDS movement helped convince the FDA to speed up the approval of new medications.[137] Today activists seek to influence a wide array of state and local health, environmental and safety agencies to promote health-protecting laws. Not surprisingly, these movements often face significant resistance from a range of interest groups opposed to enhanced regulation.

Impact Litigation

Sometimes advocates either within or outside of government rely on impact litigation (including class actions) to attempt to improve public health. Impact lawsuits differ from traditional, individually centered advocacy in that they self-consciously seek to utilize the judicial system to make broadly-based changes. For example, both private litigators and the attorneys general of many states brought lawsuits to compel the tobacco industry to change its marketing practices, as well as the price of its products.[138] Despite the fact that the tobacco companies prevailed in most cases, the threat posed by the litigation persuaded the companies to enter into a "master settlement agreement," whereby the companies agreed to cease some of their prior marketing practices.[139] Historian Allan M. Brandt concluded that "tobacco litigation—even when plaintiffs lost—had a major impact on the larger social and political debates about cigarette smoking, the industry and responsibility for harm."[140]

Of course, systemic legal approaches face some significant disadvantages. In particular, large-scale litigation requires a great deal of time and financial resources—things that many people requiring assistance with their health problems lack. In the case of a client seeking immediate legal intervention for a housing or medical issue, an individualized approach may prove superior. Another considerable downside of systemic approaches is the increasing difficulty of bringing class actions.[141] Moreover, the empirical question— whether impact litigation can change the social landscape in a meaningful way—remains highly contested.[142]

In conclusion, law is both a positive and negative social determinant of health. It is also a tool that can be used to improve the health of populations. Although each approach — the individual, client-centered and the broader-based, impact — has much to recommend it, both face unique challenges. More research is needed to understand the impact and efficacy of each approach in relationship to the universe of social determinants of health. There is, however, no doubt that law is a powerful force that advocates can use to improve population health.

Questions for Discussion

1. Explain the role of law in the social determinants of health. How is law itself a social determinant?

2. What are the relative merits of individual and systemic approaches to using law to address health? Thinking of examples of each, which approach do you think has the greatest impact on health?

Conclusion

It is clear that to improve health outcomes and reduce health disparities, interventions that address the social determinants are critical. While expanding access to health insurance and preventive healthcare is an important first step, broader interventions are needed. Healthcare providers, lawyers and other advocates are learning the importance of law and legal interventions to alter the social environment and improve the health of individuals and their communities. Sometimes these efforts focus on the needs of identified patients and clients. Other times, the efforts reach more broadly and seek systemic changes.

The foundation underlying the development of medical-legal partnership is the understanding of the connections between social determinants, health disparities and the law. MLP is premised on the idea that bringing health care professionals and legal professionals together to address the social determinants of health not only addresses the immediate health concerns of patients through legal intervention but also changes systems — both within and outside the healthcare system — to improve the health of populations. The MLP model is discussed in detail in Chapter 3. Examples of medical-legal interventions to address health disparities are explored throughout this book.

Note

Wendy Parmet would like to thank Laura Healy for her assistance with this chapter.

---

1. See, e.g., N. E. Adler, J. Stewart, "Health Disparities across the Lifespan: Meaning, Methods, and Mechanisms," *Annals of the New York Academy of Sciences*, 1186 (February 2010): 5–23, at http://onlinelibrary.wiley.com/doi/10.1111/j.1749-6632.2009.05337.x/abstract;jsessionid=355B9E54DFFC71F9D D9664B407AD17DB.d01t02, 14 (accessed February 11, 2011). For example, "'Allostatic load' provides a useful heuristic model accounting for such changes in response to chronic stress. Allostatic load scores reflect how well or poorly the cardiovascular, metabolic, nervous, hormonal and immune systems are functioning. Higher scores indicate greater dysregulation and greater vulnerability to disease and predict subsequent onset of cardiovascular disease and mortality. Several studies have shown that allostatic load scores increase as SES decreases. Work to determine the best operationalization

for allostatic load continues, but the evidence is growing that it captures biological consequences of stress that may help account for the linkage between socioeconomic disadvantage and a wide array of disease outcomes, and all-cause mortality."

2. U.S. Centers for Disease Control and Prevention, "Social Determinants of Health" (official definition used by the U.S. Centers for Disease Control, the U.S. Department of Health and Human Services, in Healthy People 2020, and the World Health Organization), http://www.cdc.gov/social determinants/Definitions.html (accessed February 11, 2011).

3. World Health Organization, "Backgrounder 3: Key Concepts [Social Determinants]," 1, http://www.who.int/social_determinants/thecommission/finalreport/key_concepts/en/index.html (accessed February 11, 2011).

4. Attributed to Ralph Waldo Emerson, BrainyQuote.com, http://www.brainyquote.com/quotes/ quotes/r/ralphwaldo105704.html (accessed February 7, 2011).

5. P. A. Braveman, et al., "Broadening the Focus: The Need to Address the Social Determinants of Health," *American Journal of Preventive Medicine*, 40, no. 1S1 (2011): S7.

6. See, e.g., Adler and Stewart, "Health Disparities across the Lifespan."

7. N. Krieger, "A Glossary for Social Epidemiology," *Epidemiological Bulletin*, 23, no. 1 (March 2002), http://www.paho.org/english/sha/be_v23n1-glossary.htm (accessed November 8, 2010).

8. World Health Organization, *Closing the Gap in a Generation: Health Equity through Action on the Social Determinants of Health* (2008).

9. See, e.g., T. Pincus, et al., "Social Conditions and Self-Management Are More Powerful Determinants of Health Than Access to Care," *Annals of Internal Medicine*, 129, no. 5 (September 1, 1998): 406–11.

10. Grantmakers in Health, *Knowledge to Action: Social and Environmental Determinants of Health* (2007), 163.

11. See M.G. Marmot, et al., "Employment Grade and Coronary Heart Disease in British Civil Servants," *Journal of Epidemiology and Community Health*, 32, no. 4 (1978): 244–49. M. G. Marmot, et al., "Health Inequalities among British Civil Servants: the Whitehall II Study," *Lancet*, 337 (1991): 1387–93. The following websites describe Marmot's ongoing work in this area in the United Kingdom and Europe: http://www.marmotreview.org/ and http://www.ucl.ac.uk/silva/epidemiology/people/ marmotmg.htm.

12. Grantmakers in Health, *Knowledge to Action*,165.

13. See Marmot, et al., "Employment Grade and Coronary Heart Disease in British Civil Servants," 244.

14. Krieger, "A Glossary for Social Epidemiology." Further publications by these scholars can be accessed at http://www.hsph.harvard.edu/faculty/nancy-krieger/publications/, http://www.hsph.harvard. edu/faculty/ichiro-kawachi/publications/, and http://healthresearchforaction.org/about/leonard-syme-selected-publications.html.

15. Steven H. Woolf, et al., "Citizen-Centered Health Promotion: Building Collaborations to Facilitate Healthy Living," *American Journal of Preventive Medicine*, 40, no. 1S1 (2011): S39.

16. See Braveman, et al., "Broadening the Focus," S10.

17. Ibid.

18. Ibid.

19. Ibid., S7.

20. D. R. Williams, et al., "Race, Socioeconomic Status, and Health: Complexities, Ongoing Challenges, and Research Opportunities," *Annals of the New York Academy of Sciences*, 1186 (2010): 76.

21. Ibid.

22. Ibid., 77.

23. Ibid., 72.

24. See Ibid., 76–77, for further discussion of studies on this aspect of racial disparities.

25. P. A. Braveman, "Socioeconomic Disparities in Health in the United States: What the Patterns Tell Us," *American Journal of Public Health*, 100, no. S1 (2010): S189.

26. Williams, et al., "Race, Socioeconomic Status, and Health," 77.

27. D. R. Williams, "The Health of US Racial and Ethnic Populations," *Journals of Gerontology, Series B,* 60B (special issue 11) (2005): 56.

28. Ibid.

29. L. A. Smith, et al., "Re-Thinking Race, Income and Childhood Asthma: Exploring Racial Disparities Concentrated among the Very Poor," *Public Health Reports*, 120 (2005): 109–16.

30. Ibid.

31. Williams et al., "Race, Socioeconomic Status, and Health," 74.

32. D. R. Williams and P. Braboy Jackson, "Social Sources of Racial Disparities in Health," *Health Affairs*, 24, no. 2 (March/April 2005): 325.

33. Williams, et al., "Race, Socioeconomic Status, And Health," 78.

34. Ibid.

35. Ibid., 79.

36. Ibid.

37. Ibid.

38. Ibid., 80.

39. Ibid.

40. Williams, "The Health of US Racial and Ethnic Populations," 59.

41. Ibid.

42. Ibid., 60.

43. S. Mustillo, et al., "Self-Reported Experiences of Racial Discrimination and Black-White Differences in Preterm and Low-Birthweight Deliveries: The CARDIA Study," *American Journal of Public Health*, 94, no. 12 (December 2004): 2125–31. See, e.g., Nancy Krieger "Discrimination and Health," in L. Berkman and I. Kawachi (eds.), Social Epidemiology (Oxford: Oxford University Press, 2000), 36-75; and N. Krieger, et al., "Occupational, Social, and Relationship Hazards and Psychological Distress among Low-Income Workers: Implications of the 'Inverse Hazard Law,'" Journal of Epidemiological Community Health (2010), doi:10.1136/jech2009.087387.

44. D. Williams, "The Health of US Racial and Ethnic Populations," 59.

45. Ibid.

46. D. S. Barrington, "Racial/Ethnic Disparities in Obesity among US-Born and Foreign-Born Adults by Sex and Education," *Obesity,* 18, no. 2 (February 2010): 422.

47. Williams, "The Health of US Racial and Ethnic Populations," 56.

48. See, e.g., http://www.sciencedaily.com/releases/2010/04/100410141344.htm.

49. W. D. Miller, et al., "Healthy Starts for All: Policy Prescriptions," *American Journal of Preventive Medicine*, 40, no. 1S1 (2011): S20 (citing to Shonkoff).

50. Ibid.

51. Ibid., S21.

52. K. A. McLaughlin, et al., "Childhood Social Environment, Emotional Reactivity to Stress, and Mood and Anxiety Disorders across the Life Course," *Depression and Anxiety*, 27, no. 12 (December 2010): 1087–94.

53. D. H. Chae, et al., "Implications of Discrimination Based on Sexuality, Gender, and Race/Ethnicity for Psychological Distress among Working-Class Sexual Minorities: The United For Health Study, 2003–2004," *International Journal of Health Services*, 40, no. 4 (2010): 589–608.

54. L. F. Berkman, I. Kawachi, Social Epidemiology (New York: Oxford University Press, 2000).

55. Child Health Impact Working Group, "Affordable Housing and Child Health: A Child Health

Impact Assessment of the Massachusetts Rental Voucher Program" (draft report, June 2005), http://www.hiaguide.org/hia/child-health-impact-assessment-massachusetts-rental-voucher-program.

56. A. Meyers, et al., "Subsidized Housing and Children's Nutritional Status: Data from a Multisite Surveillance Study," *Archives of Pediatric and Adolescent Medicine*, 159, no. 6 (2005): 551–56; J. T. Cook, K. S. Martin, *Differences in Nutrient Adequacy among Poor and Non-Poor Children* (Medford, MA: Tufts University School of Nutrition, 1995).

57. M. Nord, "Food Insecurity in Households with Children," Food Assistance Research Brief, U.S. Department of Agriculture Economic Research Service, no. 34-13 (July 2003), http://www.ers.usda.gov/publications/fanrr34/fanrr34-13/fanrr34-13.pdf.

58. J. T. Cook, et al., "Food Insecurity Is Associated with Adverse Health Outcomes among Human Infants and Toddlers," *Journal of Nutrition* 134, no. 1 (June 1, 2004): 1432–38.

59. "Recent research shows that the odds of consuming intakes <50 percent of the recommended dietary allowance (RDA) are higher for adult women and elderly individuals from food-insufficient households." Donald Rose, Symposium Paper: "Economic Determinants and Dietary Consequences of Food Insecurity in the United States," http://jn.nutrition.org/content/129/2/517.full.pdf+html (accessed December 8, 2010).

60. Ibid., 519S.

61. J. S. Lee, J. G. Fischer, M. A. Johnson, "The Causes, Consequences, and Future of Senior Hunger in America," *Journal of Nutrition for the Elderly,* 29, no. 2 (2010): 116–49.

62. http://www.ajcn.org/content/89/4/1197.full (accessed December 8, 2010).

63. Food Trust and Policy Link, "The Grocery Gap," http://www.policylink.org/atf/cf/ %7B97c6d565-bb43-406d-a6d5-eca3bbf35af0 %7D/GROCERYGAP_EXECSUMMARY.PDF, Exec Summary, 7.

64. Ibid.

65. Ibid., 8; See also J. N. Bodor, et al., "Disparities in Food Access: Does Aggregate Availability of Key Foods from Other Stores Offset the Relative Lack of Supermarkets in African-American Neighborhoods?" *Preventive Medicine,* 51, no. 1 (July 2010): 63–67. "Other store types did not offset the relative lack of supermarkets in African-American neighborhoods in the provision of fresh produce, though they did for snack foods. Altering the mix of foods offered in such stores might mitigate these inequities."

66. J. P. Block, et al., "Fast Food, Race/Ethnicity, and Income: A Geographic Analysis," *American Journal of Preventive Medicine,* 27, no. 3 (October 2004): 211–17. Other examples can be found here: http://www.policylink.org/atf/cf/ percent7B97c6d565-bb43-406d-a6d5-eca3bbf35af0 percent7D/DESIGNEDFORDISEASE_FINAL.PDF.

67. B. Sard, Testimony before the Senate Committee on Banking, Housing, and Urban Affairs Hearing on Housing and Community Development Needs: The FY 2003 HUD Budget (November 29, 2001).

68. M. E. Stone, E. Werby, D. H. Friedman, "Situation Critical: Meeting the Housing Needs of Lower-Income Massachusetts Residents," working paper, University of Massachusetts Boston, 2000.

69. Joint Center for Housing Studies of Harvard University, "State of the Nation's Housing," Cambridge, MA: President and Fellows of Harvard College, 2003.

70. A. Meyers, et al., "Housing Subsidies and Pediatric Undernutrition," *Archives of Pediatrics and Adolescent Medicine,* 149, no. 10 (1995): 1079–84. A. Meyers, et al., "Subsidized Housing and Children's Nutritional Status: Data from a Multisite Surveillance Study," *Archives of Pediatric and Adolescent Medicine*, 159, no. 6 (2005): 551–56.

71. Department of Housing and Urban Development, *Healthier Homes, Healthier Children*, http://www.huduser.org/portal/periodicals/ResearchWorks/oct_08/RW_vol5num9t1.html.

72. Child Health Impact Working Group, "Affordable Housing and Child Health," 5.

73. B. Lanphear, et al., "Contribution of Residential Exposures to Asthma in US Children and Adolescents," *Pediatrics*, 107, no. 6 (2001): e98. M. Sandel, G. O'Connor, "Inner-City Asthma," *Immunology and Allergy Clinics of North America,* 22, no. 4 (2002): 737–52.

74. LIHEAP Home Energy Notebook for Fiscal Year 2003, Department of Health and Human Services, 2005. J. Bhattacharya, et al., "Heat or Eat? Cold-Weather Shocks and Nutrition in Poor American Families," *American Journal of Public Health*, 93, no. 7 (2003): 1149–54.

75. Child Health Impact Working Group, "Unhealthy Consequences: Energy Costs and Child

Health Impact Assessment of Energy Costs and the Low Income Home Energy Assistance Program" (April 2007), Exec. Summary, 1.

76. M. Nord, "Keeping Warm, Keeping Cool, Keeping Food on the Table: Seasonal Food Insecurity and Costs of Heating and Cooling," Economic Research Service, July 2003.

77. Food and Research Action Center, "Heat and Eat: Using Federal Nutrition Programs to Cushion the Shock of Skyrocketing Heating Bills," 2005. Child Health Impact Working Group, "Unhealthy Consequences." D. Frank, et al., "Heat or Eat: Low Income Home Energy Assistance Program and Nutritional Risk among Children Under 3 Years Old," *Pediatrics*, 18, no. 5 (2006).

78. J. Bhattacharya, et al., "Heat or Eat?"

79. D. A. Frank, N. Roos, A. Meyers, et al., "Seasonal Variation in Weight-for-Age in a Pediatric Emergency Room," *Public Health Reports*, 111, no. 4 (1996): 366–71.

80. 2005 National Energy Assistance Survey, National Energy Directors Association, 2005.

81. R. Colton, "Measuring LIHEAP's Results: Responding to Home Energy Affordability," Report prepared for the Iowa Department of Human Resources (1999).

82. 2005 National Energy Assistance Survey.

83. Centers for Disease Control and Prevention, "Use of Unvented Residential Heating Appliances — United States, 1988–1994," *Journal of the American Medical Association*, 279, no. 6 (1998): 423–24.

84. "Unintentional Non-Fire-Related Carbon Monoxide Exposures-United States, 2001–2003," *Morbidity and Mortality Weekly Report*, 54, no. 2 (January 25, 2005): 36–39.

85. 2005 National Energy Assistance Survey.

86. Ibid.

87. Code of Massachusetts Regulations, Occupancy Standards and Tenant Participation for State Aided Housing, 760 CMR 6.06 5(a); Code of Federal Regulations, Housing and Urban Development, 24 CFR 982.404(b)(i).

88. Public Service Commission Consumer Protection Rules and Regulations, National Energy Assistance Directors Association, 2006.

89. See K. Morland, et al., "The Contextual Effect of the Local Food Environment on Residents' Diets: The Atherosclerosis Risk in Communities Study," American Journal of Public Health, no. 11 (2002): 1761–67.

90. Block, et al., "Fast Food, Race/Ethnicity, and Income."

91. Massachusetts Department of Public Health, "The Status of Childhood Weight in Massachusetts, 2009: Preliminary Results from Body Mass Index Screening in 80 Essential School Health Districts, 2008–2009" (September 2010).

92. Woolf, et al., "Citizen-Centered Health Promotion," S39.

93. Braveman, et al., "Broadening the Focus."

94. F. D. Scutchfield, C. W. Keck, *Principles of Public Health Practice* (New York: Delmar, 2009).

95. "150th Anniversary of John Snow and the Pump Handle," http://www.cdc.gov/mmwr/preview/mmwrhtml/mm5334a1.htm. For a longer account of this milestone work in public health by the "father of modern epidemiology," see S. Johnson, *The Ghost Map: The Story of London's Most Terrifying Epidemic — and How It Changed Science, Cities, and the Modern World* (New York: Penguin, 2006).

96. T. Frieden, "A Framework for Public Health Action: The Health Impact Pyramid," *American Journal of Public Health*, 100, no. 4 (April 2010): 590–95. For an interesting argument for constructing contexts to promote preferable "default" choices to promote health made by a behavioral economist and legal scholar, see R. H. Thaler and C. R. Sunstein, *Nudge: Improving Decisions about Health, Wealth, and Happiness* (New York: Penguin, 2009).

97. T. Freiden, "A Framework for Public Health Action."

98. Prevention Institute, Foreword, "The Built Environment and Health: 11 Profiles of Neighborhood Transformation," 2004, http://www.preventioninstitute.org/index.php?option=com_jlibrary&view=article&id=114&Itemid=127 (accessed December 9, 2010).

99. D. R. Williams and P. Braboy Jackson, "Social Sources of Racial Disparities in Health," *Health*

Affairs, 24, no. 2 (March/April 2005): 332.

100. P.L. 104–193 (Aug. 22, 1996) 110 Stat. 2105 (for further info: http://frwebgate.access. gpo.gov/cgi-bin/getdoc.cgi?dbname=104_cong_public_laws&docid=f:publ193.104.pdf).

101. L. A. Smith, et al., "Implications of Welfare Reform for Child Health: Emerging Challenges for Clinical Practice and Policy," *Pediatrics*, 106 (2000): 1117–25.

102. L. A. Smith, et al., "Employment Barriers among Welfare Recipients and Applicants with Chronically Ill Children," *American Journal of Public Health*, 92, no. 9 (September 2002): 1453. L. A. Smith, J. L. Hatcher, and R. Wertheimer, "The Association of Childhood Asthma with Parental Employment and Welfare Receipt," *Journal of American Medical Women's Association*, 57 (2002): 11–15.

103. For further information on HIAs, see Centers for Disease Control, "Health Impact Assessments," http://www.cdc.gov/healthyplaces/hia.htm (accessed February 11, 2011).

104. S. Burris, I. Kawachi, and A. Sarat, "Integrating Law and Social Epidemiology," *Journal of Law Medicine and Ethics*, 30 (2002): 510.

105. International Covenant on Economic, Social and Cultural Rights, G.A. Res 2200A (XXI) (1966), Art. 12.

106. S. Gruskin and P. Braveman, "Addressing Social Injustice in a Human Rights Context," in *Social Injustice and Public Health*, ed. Barry S. Levy, Victor W. Sidel (Oxford: Oxford University Press, 2006).

107. W. E. Parmet, "Introduction: The Interdependency of Law and Public Health," in *Law and Public Health Practice*, 2nd ed., ed. Richard Goodman et al., (Oxford: Oxford University Press, 2007).

108. See, for example, Barbara Noah, "The Participation of Underrepresented Minorities in Clinical Research," *American Journal of Law & Medicine*, 29 (2003): 228 ("persons with lower incomes and lower levels of educational attainment generally also have lower rates of health literacy than higher-income, well-education individuals"). See also M. Rebell, "Poverty, 'Meaningful' Educational Opportunity, and the Necessary Role of the Courts," *North Carolina Law Review*, 85 (June 2007): 1475 ("Inadequate education dramatically raises crime rates and health costs").

109. W. E. Parmet, "The Impact of Law on Coronary Heart Disease: Some Preliminary Observations on the Relationship of Law to 'Normalized' Conditions," *Journal of Law, Medicine and Ethics*, 30 (2002): 608.

110. For example, *South Camden Citizens in Action v. New Jersey*, 274 F.3d. 771 (3d. Cir. 2001).

111. W. C. Perdue, L. O. Gostin, L. A. Stone, "Public Health and the Built Environment: Historical Empirical and Theoretical Foundations for an Expanded Role," *Journal of Law, Medicine and Ethics*, 31 (2003): 557–66.

112. Centers for Disease Control and Prevention, "State Cigarette Excise Taxes—United States 2009," 9 *Morbidity and Mortality Weekly Report*, 59 (2010): 385–88; Centers for Disease Control and Prevention, "State-Specific Secondhand Smoke Exposure and Current Cigarette Smoking among Adults—Unites States, 2008," *Morbidity and Mortality Weekly Report*, 58 (2009): 1232–35.

113. Centers for Disease Control and Prevention, "Ten Great Public Health Achievements—United States, 1900–1999," *Morbidity and Mortality Weekly Report*, 48 (1999): 241–43.

114. Ibid.

115. Public Health Law Program, CDC, About the Program, http://www2a.cdc.gov/phlp/about.asp (accessed October 6, 2010).

116. R. Retkin, et al., "Medical Legal Partnerships: A Key Strategy for Mitigating the Negative Health Impacts of the Recession," *Health Law*, 22 (2009): 31.

117. Ibid.

118. A. Reichbach, "Lawyer, Client, Community; To Whom Does the Education Reform Lawsuit Belong?" *Boston College Third World Law Journal*, 27 (2007): 131, 142.

119. D. J. Givelber, W. J. Bowers, C. L. Blitch, "Tarasoff, Myth and Reality: An Empirical Study of Private Law in Action," *Wisconsin Law Review*, 84, no. 2 (1984): 443.

120. W. E. Parmet, *Population, Public Health, and the Law* (Washington, DC: Georgetown University Press, 2009), 236–38.

121. G. Rose, "Sick Individuals and Sick Populations," *International Journal of Epidemiology*, 30 (2001): 427, 430.

122. Pub. L. No. 111-148, 124 Stat. 119 (2010), amended by the Health Care and Education Reconciliation Act of 2010, Pub. L. No. 111-152, 124 Stat. 1029 (2010). Compare *Commonwealth ex rel Cuccinell v. Sebelius*, 2010 U.S. Dist. LEXIS 130814 (E.D. Va. Dec. 13, 2010) (finding that the individual health insurance mandate within the law exceeds Congress's authority) with *Thomas More Law Ctr. v. Obama*, 2010 U.S. Dist. LEXIS 107416 (E.D. Mich. Oct. 7, 2010) (finding that the Affordable Care Act was within Congress's constitutional authority).

123. *Gibbons v. Ogden*, 22 U.S. (9 Wheat.) 1 (1824).

124. L. O. Gostin, *Public Health Law: Power, Duty, Restraint*, 2nd ed. (Berkeley: University of California Press, 2008), 78–114.

125. Ibid.

126. Environmental Protection Agency, *The Benefits and Costs of the Clean Air Act, 1970 to 1990*, http://www.epa.gov/oar/sect812/copy.html.

127. M. S. Dove, et al., "Smoke-Free Air Laws and Secondhand Smoke Exposure among Nonsmoking Youth," *Pediatrics*, 126 (2010): 85.

128. H. R. Juster, et al., "Declines in Admissions for Acute Myocardial Infarction in New York State after Implementation of a Comprehensive Smoking Ban," *American Journal of Public Health*, 97 (2007): 2035.

129. J. Pearson, et al., "The Evaluation of the Immediate Impact of the Washington, D.C., Smoke-Free Indoor Air Policy on Bar Employee Environmental Tobacco Smoke Exposure," *Public Health Reports*, 124 (Supp. 1, 2009): 155.

130. National Committee on Uniform Traffic Laws and Ordinances, Laws Requiring Seat Belts 1 (1972).

131. Governor's Highway Safety Association, Occupant Protection: Seat Belts, http: www.ghsa.org/html/issues/occupantprotection.html (accessed January 10, 2010).

132. Governors Highway Safety Association, *Seat Belt Laws*, September 2010, http://www.ghsa.org/html/stateinfo/laws/seatbelt_laws.html.

133. A. Cohen and L. Einav, "The Effects of Mandatory Seat Belt Laws on Driving Behavior and Traffic Fatalities," *Review of Economics and Statistics*, 85 (2003): 828.

134. Ibid., 829.

135. D. Glassbrenner, *Estimating the Lives Saved by Safety Belts and Airbags*, National Center for Statistics and Analysis, NHTSA, Paper No. 500, http://www-nrd.nhtsa.dot.gov/pdf/nrd-01/esv/esv18/CD/Files/18ESV-000500.pdf.

136. A. Hussain, and P. Rivers, "Policy Challenges in US Health Care System Reform," *Journal of Health Care Finance*, 36, no. 3 (spring 2010): 34.

137. See, for example, B. Rossen, "FDA's Proposed Regulations to Expand Access to Investigational Drugs for Treatment Use: The Status Quo in the Guide of Reform," *Food and Drug Law Journal*, 64 (2009): 183–222.

138. P. Patterson and J. Philpott, "In Search of a Smoking Gun: A Comparison of Public Entity Tobacco and Gun Litigation," *Brooklyn Law Review*, 66 (2000): 549.

139. A. M. Brandt, *The Cigarette Century: The Rise, Fall, and Deadly Persistence of the Product that Defined America* (New York: Basic Books, 2007), 431–42.

140. Ibid., 439.

141. L. S. Mullenix, "Abandoning the Federal Class Action Ship: Is There Smoother Sailing for Class Actions in Gulf Waters?" *Tulane Law Review*, 74 (2000): 1709; E. A. Purcell Jr., "The Class Action Fairness Act in Perspective: The Old and the New in Federal Jurisdiction Reform," *University of Pennsylvania Law Review*, 156 (2008): 1864.

142. W. E. Parmet and R. A. Daynard, "The New Public Health Litigation," *Annual Review of Public Health*, 21 (2000): 437.

Chapter 2

Who Cares for the Poor? Understanding the Healthcare and Civil Legal Systems in the United States

Sara Rosenbaum, JD
Alan Houseman, JD
Gerry Singsen, JD
Jeffrey Colvin, JD, MD

This chapter describes the healthcare and legal assistance systems that have emerged to meet the needs of the most vulnerable individuals and communities in the United States. Each section details the framework for healthcare and legal service delivery for the poor, offers some historical background and reviews funding mechanisms, challenges and opportunities. The healthcare section integrates analysis of recent healthcare reform legislation. We also review how the medical and legal professions regard their responsibilities to meet the health and legal needs of the poor.

A structured background of the healthcare and civil legal landscapes in the United States is critical to understanding the current and unrealized potential of the medical-legal partnership (MLP) model. In particular, the juxtaposition of increased healthcare access for low-income individuals and families under healthcare reform, alongside the persistent dearth of civil legal services, means that newcomers to the health system arrive with significant social and legal challenges that may remain unaddressed without better integration between the two domains.

Healthcare for Vulnerable Populations

This section explores healthcare access for low-income people. Even in the wake of passage of the Patient Protection and Affordable Care Act (the Affordable Care Act, ACA),[1] the United States remains a nation committed to market principles in healthcare. In the context of healthcare access for the poor, these principles play out as a seller's market, in which buyers are either unable to afford the options or rejected as customers outright because their healthcare needs are more likely to be clinically demanding and their insurance more likely to be inadequate.

Defining Low-Income and Vulnerable Populations

Low-income: Frequently defined as individuals and families whose income is less than twice the poverty level (about $44,000 in 2011) and who do not earn enough to cover the everyday costs of living; low-income individuals and families may receive help from government work supports including tax credits, food stamps and heating subsidies.

Vulnerable Populations: Can be defined as groups that are not well integrated into the healthcare system because of ethnic, cultural, economic, geographic or health characteristics. This isolation puts members of these groups at risk for not obtaining necessary medical care, and thus constitutes a potential threat to their health. Commonly cited examples of vulnerable populations include racial and ethnic minorities, the rural and urban poor, undocumented immigrants and people with disabilities or multiple chronic conditions.

Source: Gregory Acs, Pamela J. Loprest, *Who Are Low-Income Working Families?*, Urban Institute (September 20, 2005). Sheila Zedlewski, Ajay Chaudry, Margaret Simms, *A New Safety Net for Low-Income Families*, Urban Institute (July 2008).

The challenge of healthcare access for the poor plays itself out in thousands of lower-income urban and rural communities that experience the absence of available, accessible primary and specialty services. The underlying cause of this problem is essentially the same as that which drives shortages of other essential goods and services in poorer communities: an insufficient supply of attractive customers with substantial purchasing power. Federal and state policy makers have developed interventions, collectively referred to as the "healthcare safety net," that together work to mitigate — but by no means eliminate — the access problems that confront low-income populations. For this reason it is also important to understand the regulatory environment in which the healthcare system operates and the duties imposed by law that may help spur access.

This section begins with a discussion of health insurance, which forms the financial basis of healthcare in the United States. It then turns to healthcare safety-net programs and briefly considers laws that regulate provider conduct.

An Evolving Public and Private Health Insurance Market

Being uninsured in the United States is a phenomenon that is both widespread and concentrated in lower-income individuals and families. Because health insurance is how healthcare services are financed in the United States, the transformation of both the public and private U.S. health insurance system resulting from the ACA has the greatest implications for the low-income population. Of the 50 million Americans who were uninsured in 2009, only 10 percent lived in families with incomes exceeding 400 percent of the federal poverty level (see Figure 2.1).[2] Furthermore, although this figure presents a grim snapshot of the magnitude of the health insurance problem in the United States, rolling estimates paint an even grimmer picture: 70 percent of the uninsured have gone without coverage for a year or longer (see Figure 2.2).[3]

Figure 2.1 Characteristics of the Uninsured, 2009

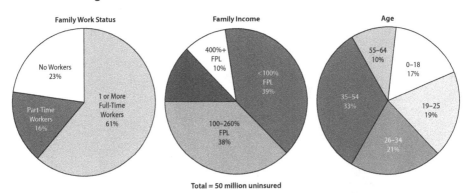

Total = 50 million uninsured

Note: The federal poverty level was $22,050 for a family of four in 2009. Data may not total 100% due to rounding.
Source: "The Uninsured: A Primer," Henry J. Kaiser Family Foundation, December 2010, http://www.kff.org/uninsured/upload/7451-06.pdf (accessed January 1, 2011). *Data Source:* KCMU/Urban Institute analysis of 2010 ASEC Supplement to the CPS.

Medicaid

Passage of the ACA officially places the nation's health insurance system in transition. Effective January 1, 2014, the health insurance picture for the poor changes profoundly, considerably enhancing the ability of poor and low-income people to access coverage. Implementation of the ACA will face multiple challenges, including lawsuits challenging constitutionality of its provisions as well as congressional attempts to repeal the legislation. Prior to that date, Medicaid[4]— the single largest health insurance program in the nation— remains virtually the only form of federally financed public health insurance coverage for nonelderly low-income people.

State participation in the federal Medicaid program is voluntary (all states participate). The federal government contributes toward the cost of the medical assistance furnished under state plans, as well as toward the cost of state program operations. States have considerable leeway in designing and administering their programs because federal law gives them enormous discretion over the structure and shape of Medicaid. As a result, state programs vary greatly; at the same time, minimum eligibility, coverage and operational standards apply under extensive federal requirements. Federal requirements also govern questions of state residency and legal status. Emergency Medicaid coverage only is available to otherwise eligible individuals barred from coverage because they are not legally present in the United States. In addition, Medicaid imposes a five-year waiting period on eligible legal residents, which states may waive at their option in the case of children and pregnant women.[5]

Children and Pregnant Women

As of January 2011, all state Medicaid programs cover low-income children under age 18 and pregnant women regardless of family composition. Financial eligibility rules can vary significantly, subject to a federal income eligibility floor of 133 percent of the federal poverty level for pregnant women and children under age 6 and 100 percent of the federal poverty level in the case of children ages 6–18.[6] States further extend public health insurance

Figure 2.2 Duration of Time without Insurance Coverage among the Uninsured, 2009

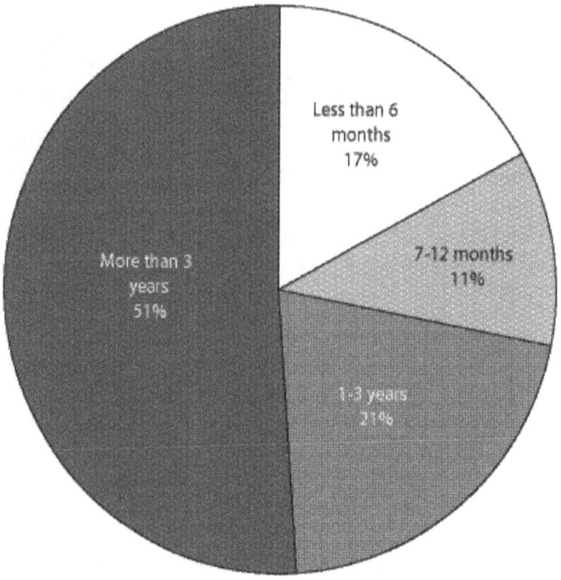

Note: More than three years includes those who said they never had health insurance. Percentages are age adjusted.
Source: "The Uninsured: A Primer," Henry J. Kaiser Family Foundation, December 2010, http://www.kff.org/uninsured/upload/7451-06.pdf (accessed January 1, 2011). *Data Source*: *Summary Health Statistics for the U.S. Population: National Health Interview Survey, 2009* (2010).

coverage for children through the Children's Health Insurance Program (CHIP), a small Medicaid companion that, at the state's option, can be administered either as a separate insurance program, a Medicaid expansion, or a combination of the two (i.e., Medicaid coverage for children with family incomes under 150 percent of the federal poverty level and CHIP for children whose family incomes fall between 150 percent and 300 percent of the federal poverty level).[7]

Medicaid benefits for children are particularly comprehensive as a result of Medicaid's Early and Periodic Screening, Diagnosis and Treatment (EPSDT) benefit, to which all individuals under 21 are entitled.[8] The EPSDT benefit consists of periodic and as-needed health exams to detect physical or mental health conditions, immunizations, vision, dental and hearing care and all medically necessary diagnosis and treatment services recognized under federal Medicaid law, regardless of limits that might apply to adults (42 U.S.C. § 1396d(a) and (r)). Medicaid benefits for pregnant women are similarly comprehensive, reaching not only prenatal, delivery and postpartum care but also treatments for conditions that may affect the pregnancy (42 U.S.C. § 1396a(a)(10)).

Nonelderly, Nonpregnant, Nondisabled Adults

The full impact of Medicaid's limitations under current law is felt in the case of coverage of adults. Federal Medicaid financing is unavailable in the case of coverage of nonelderly adults who are neither disabled within the meaning of the Social Security Act, nor parents of minor children, nor pregnant. Nonelderly adults who lack one of these categorical connections to Medicaid lack recognition as a federal Medicaid-eligible group; as a result, states cannot receive federal funding toward the cost of their coverage. If noncategorical adults qualify for Medicaid (or a similar form of public health insurance coverage) at all, it is because their state of residence either funds some level of public health insurance coverage or operates its Medicaid program as a federal demonstration program that enables the state to receive federal funding toward the cost of their coverage.[9]

Even where an adult falls within a coverage category other than pregnancy (which is governed by minimum federal income standards), states retain considerable discretion over financial eligibility rules, especially in the case of parents with minor children. In many states, financial eligibility standards for parents are so low that employment full time at the minimum wage would disqualify the individual for coverage.[10]

Adults who qualify for coverage receive comprehensive benefits with low cost sharing. At the same time, federal Medicaid requirements related to adult coverage are looser than is the case for children under 21, and states may impose many coverage limitations on adults that would be unlawful under EPSDT.[11] For example, a state may completely exclude vision and dental care for adults, because both services are optional. Similarly, a state, like a private insurer, may place arbitrary limits on covered benefits and services, such as limiting the number of visits or treatments permitted or excluding or limiting prescription drug coverage.[12]

Subsidized Private Health Insurance under the ACA

The ACA fundamentally restructures the health insurance system by forcefully moving the nation toward universality and creating the tools that position the nation for universal coverage.

Historically, the issue of whether to obtain health insurance has been a matter of choice for nonelderly adults. Traditionally however, low-income populations have been far more likely to be uninsured, not because they choose to be but because they are ineligible for public insurance and lack access to affordable coverage because of their jobs, their income, their health status or some combination of these factors, all of which are unrelated to the need for healthcare.

The ACA changes this. Effective January 1, 2014, taxpayers who are citizens or lawfully present in the United States will incur a legal obligation to secure coverage for themselves and their families (known as the "individual mandate") if they are determined to have access to affordable coverage, defined as coverage that costs no more than 9.5 percent of modified adjusted gross income (MAGI) (ACA §§ 1501 and 1401). To make this obligation achievable, the ACA transforms the health insurance system. Part of this transformation is a set of sweeping reforms of the health insurance market, made possible by the establishment of a healthy risk pool. The uninsured poor tend to be disproportionately somewhat younger and healthier than those with coverage as a result of Medicaid's greater availability for adults with disabilities.[13] These reforms, which build on prior federal insurance regulations,[14] collectively bar discrimination in enrollment and coverage based on health status or preexisting conditions.[15] In addition, health reform establishes *health insurance exchanges* (see Health Insurance Exchange: Background).

Health Insurance Exchange: Background

Aim: To (1) create more stable and better quality individual and small group health insurance markets, and (2) create affordable private health insurance options for otherwise ineligible individuals and families through federal subsidies and tax credits.

How it Works: At their option, states may either operate health insurance exchanges or elect to default to the federal government; as of the end of 2010, nearly all states had elected to at least commence a multiyear planning cycle in preparation for operating their own exchanges.[a] Where individual coverage is concerned, the "qualified health plans" sold through health insurance exchanges are to be made available to individuals who are citizens or lawfully present in the United States and are ineligible for Medicaid, Medicare, an affordable employer plan or some other form of "minimum essential coverage."[b] Other key components:

- Exchanges are obligated to screen applicants for Medicaid eligibility and enroll them if eligible to ensure that there is "no wrong door" to health insurance coverage.

- For exchange-eligible applicants and participants whose MAGI falls between 100 percent and 400 percent of the federal poverty level, participating in the exchange market also will entitle them to receive advance refundable tax credits toward payment of their monthly premiums; the value of the credits falls as income rises.[c]

- Exchange participants with family incomes below twice the federal poverty level also will qualify for federal cost-sharing subsidies.[d]

Notes: [a] State-by-state overview of planning activities see http://www.healthcare.gov, the official health reform site of the Obama administration. http://www.healthcare.gov/news/factsheets/grantawardslist.html (accessed January 1, 2011); [b] ACA § 1401; [c] Recently arrived legal residents with family incomes low enough to qualify for Medicaid but who are ineligible because they do not satisfy the program's five-year waiting period will be eligible to secure tax-subsidized policies through exchanges during this waiting period. ACA § 1401; [d] Henry J. Kaiser Family Foundation, *Summary of New Health Reform Law*, Focus on Health Reform (last modified March 26, 2010), http://www.kff.org/healthreform/upload/8061.pdf (accessed January 4, 2011).

The ACA and Medicaid Reforms

In addition to establishing the tax-subsidized exchange market, the ACA expands Medicaid to require participating states to cover all nonelderly persons with MAGI below 133 percent of the federal poverty level (a figure that rises to 138 percent of the federal poverty level as a result of a special 5 percent income disregard).[16] This change in Medicaid eligibility primarily benefits nonelderly adults ages 18–64 who previously were excluded because they were not disabled, pregnant, the parents of minor children or because, even if categorically eligible, their family incomes exceeded their state's Medicaid eligibility standards for adults. Under the ACA, states can add coverage for this population as an option prior to January 1, 2014.[17]

The ACA is thus aimed at closing the enormous gap in health insurance coverage created by a healthcare system that is the world's costliest,[18] lacks universally available public insurance and in which access to coverage among working-age Americans and their families essentially depends on having a job with an employer that elects to offer a tax-subsidized group health plan.[19] Employer-sponsored group health benefit plans are extremely costly; indeed, the average annual family premium in 2010 approached $14,000. As a result, smaller firms that employ predominantly low-wage workers (incomes less than $30,000) are significantly less likely than non-low-wage-dominated firms to offer a group health plan (an offer rate of less than 26 percent in small predominantly low-wage firms, compared to 66 percent in small firms whose low-wage workers comprise 25 percent or less of the total workforce).[20] Even large firms are affected if dominated by low-wage workers, with an offer rate of 71 percent compared to a 100 percent offer rate in large firms dominated by higher income workers.[21]

Figure 2.3 shows the estimated impact of the ACA on the distribution of health insurance coverage in the United States. As Figure 2.3 indicates, the major changes that enable the extension of health insurance coverage to an additional 32 million people are the expansion of Medicaid as well as the establishment of a subsidized individual private health insurance market through health insurance exchanges. By contrast, the Congressional Budget Office (Congress's cost estimation arm) projects that the employer-sponsored market will remain consistent in size.

Figure 2.3 Estimated Health Insurance Coverage in 2019

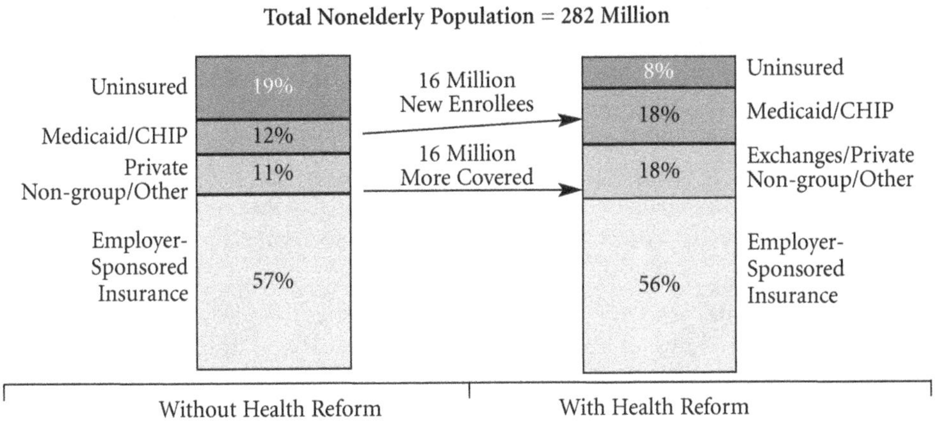

Total Nonelderly Population = 282 Million

Without Health Reform		With Health Reform	
Uninsured	19%	8%	Uninsured
Medicaid/CHIP	12%	18%	Medicaid/CHIP
Private Non-group/Other	11%	18%	Exchanges/Private Non-group/Other
Employer-Sponsored Insurance	57%	56%	Employer-Sponsored Insurance

16 Million New Enrollees

16 Million More Covered

Source: Henry J. Kaiser Family Foundation, "Health Reform—An Overview," 2011, kaiserEDU.org.

Medicaid for Medicare Beneficiaries

Medicare beneficiaries with low incomes are also entitled to Medicaid (either full coverage or coverage for Medicare premiums and cost sharing). Individuals enrolled in both programs are commonly referred to as "dual eligibles." As of 2007 the dual eligible population approached 9 million.[22]

The various pathways to dual Medicaid eligibility are numerous and vary with state Medicaid plans.[23] Supplemental Security Income (SSI) recipients are entitled to full dual coverage as a mandatory coverage group, and states have the option to extend full dual status to other groups who either have very low family income or else "spend down" to Medicaid eligibility by incurring high out-of-pocket healthcare expenses. Other elderly and disabled beneficiaries, including beneficiaries who are permitted to work under special Social Security rules, may qualify for Medicaid assistance with Medicare premiums and cost sharing even if their incomes are too high to permit full Medicaid eligibility.[24] Twenty-five percent of all state Medicaid spending on dually eligible beneficiaries can be attributed to state expenditures related to Medicare premiums and cost sharing.[25]

Full Medicaid coverage is of crucial importance to low-income beneficiaries because of Medicare's coverage limits and cost-sharing responsibilities. In addition to other Medicare noncovered items and services that may be covered for adults under a state's Medicaid plan (e.g., dental care, vision care, hearing aids), Medicaid is the nation's main source of coverage for long-term institutional and home and community care services, such as nursing home care, personal care and home health services. Medicaid spending on dually eligible persons can be attributed disproportionately to the sickest persons; in 2007 approximately 10 percent of all dual eligibles accounted for over 60 percent of all dual eligible spending.[26]

Medicare

Medicare provides health insurance coverage for individuals who are entitled to Social Security benefits on the basis of age or disability. Also see Chapter 14 for discussion of Medicare. Medicare is also available for individuals of any age who are diagnosed with end-stage renal disease. Medicare eligibility based on age commences at 65. Beneficiaries who are entitled to Medicare on the basis of disability must undergo a 24-month waiting period before coverage begins;[27] during this interim period, individuals may be entitled to full Medicaid coverage if they also receive SSI benefits or their incomes are low enough to qualify for Medicaid under their state Medicaid plan. Persons with disabilities in Medicare's 24-month waiting period also may qualify for COBRA continuation coverage through their employer plans, assuming they were previously employed in a job that carried employer-sponsored health benefits, and assuming that they can pay the premiums, which can be set at 102 percent of the employer's payment and with no employer contribution.[28]

Consisting of four parts (A, B, C and D), Medicare offers federally administered public insurance covering a range of institutional and professional healthcare services as well as outpatient prescription drugs.[29]

- *Part A* is compulsory and prefunded through deductions from Social Security-taxed earnings. It consists of hospital, extended care services in both institutional and in-home settings, and hospice care.

- *Part B* is voluntary, and a monthly premium must be paid. It consists of physician and other professional and healthcare diagnostic and medical services. The ACA also expands Medicare coverage of preventive services under Part B, including annual preventive exams.

- *Part C*, known as Medicare Advantage (MA), allows individuals to enroll in MA plans that may be available in their service areas.[30] MA plans offer Part A and B services as well as Part D outpatient prescription drug coverage. Premium and cost-sharing rules vary for MA plans. As of 2010, nearly 12 million beneficiaries were enrolled in MA plans, some 25 percent of all program beneficiaries.[31] Plans range from traditional HMOs offering the lowest monthly premium rates to fee-for-service plans, which offer the loosest provider networks and are the most costly. The ACA increases federal oversight of plan costs and federal regulations issued

Figure 2.4 Standard Medicare Prescription Drug Benefit, 2011

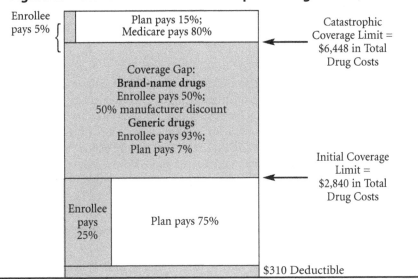

Note: Amounts rounded to nearest dollar.
Source: Kaiser Family Foundation, "The Medicare Prescription Drug Benefit—An Updated Fact Sheet," #7044-11, October 2010.

pursuant to the ACA establish a $6,700 limit on out-of-pocket costs. Medicaid covers out-of-pocket payments in the case of dual enrollees enrolled in MA plans.[32]

- *Part D* is Medicare's voluntary prescription drug program, offering comprehensive coverage through private prescription drug plans. As noted, Part D prescription drug coverage is a basic component of all MA plans, whereas beneficiaries who remain in the "original" fee-for-service Medicare program may purchase a stand-alone part D plan. In 2011 more than 1,100 part D plans will be offered across thirty-four federal regions; each region offers a choice of more than twenty-eight stand-alone plans, as well as MA plans where available.[33] Like Part B, Part D requires payment of both premiums and cost sharing. Low Income Subsidies (LIS) are available to assist in the cost of prescription drug coverage for low-income beneficiaries;[34] beneficiaries who receive LIS assistance are eligible to enroll in a more limited group of "benchmark" plans.[35]

Part D employs a unique coverage design that uses federally regulated drug formularies and offers front-end and back-end coverage; however, currently, the program contains a large coverage gap in the middle (see Figure 2.4). In 2011 Part D will provide an initial $2,840 in outpatient prescription drug coverage after a $310 deductible is met; cost-sharing requirements also apply to initial coverage. When the initial coverage limit is reached, beneficiaries encounter a coverage gap, known as a "donut hole" that excludes all drug coverage until a beneficiary satisfies the program's out-of-pocket payment rules ($6,448 in 2011). At this point, a 95 percent catastrophic coverage component begins.[36] The ACA gradually eliminates this coverage gap between 2010 and 2020 and also requires manufacturers to offer brand-name prescription drugs at discounted prices. Under this gradual improvement, beneficiaries who hit the coverage gap in 2011 will be responsible for 50 percent of the cost of brand-name drugs and 93 percent of the cost of generic drugs until they reach the catastrophic limit. In addition, many states offer gap coverage assistance, and charitable assistance sources also may be available.[37]

Access to Care

Despite the major restructuring of the public and private health insurance market anticipated under the ACA, access to healthcare can be expected to remain a challenge for the low-income population. Several factors account for this. First, the ACA does not take effect until 2014, and although enrollment is expected to proceed rapidly, the inevitable confusion and slowed implementation that accompanies any major shift in public policy can be anticipated to result in slower enrollment and a slower reduction in the number of uninsured. Because of the state of the economy, moreover, the number of uninsured individuals (which surpassed 50 million in 2009) can be expected to continue to rise. As is the case today, the uninsured, as well as those who will face enrollment delays in the wake of full ACA implementation, can be expected to be disproportionately lower income persons.

Second, the ACA is projected to leave some 23 million Americans uninsured because they have no affordable health coverage; included in this group are individuals not lawfully present in the country, as well as those who do not qualify for Medicaid or subsidies and whose MAGI, when compared to available health insurance plans in the exchange, leaves them with a cost exposure that exceeds the law's affordability threshold. In addition, frequent movement among health insurance markets—Medicaid, exchange coverage and employment-based coverage—can be anticipated as a result of changes in income, economic or family circumstances. With this frequent movement can come gaps in coverage.[38]

Third, low-income populations, insured or otherwise, are disproportionately concentrated in poorer urban and rural communities that lack basic resources of all types, including healthcare services. An estimated 96 million persons (nearly twice the total number of uninsured persons) live in communities that can be considered medically underserved as a result of poverty, a lack of primary care resources and elevated health risk indicators.[39] These communities are more likely to be uninsured: approximately 28 percent of residents of medically underserved communities are estimated to lack coverage, a figure nearly twice the national average of 17 percent. Furthermore, Medicaid coverage dominates medically underserved communities because of poverty and the lack of a strong employment base that creates stable, well-paying jobs that come with employee health benefits.

Fourth, even when the poor live in communities that have a reasonable supply of health professionals and healthcare institutions, access to care can be significantly diminished for Medicaid beneficiaries. One study projects that even before an increase in demand is factored in as a result of health insurance reform, the nation can expect to experience a shortage of 200,000 physicians and 1 million nurses by 2020.[40] Medicaid makes a profound difference where healthcare access is concerned, dramatically reducing the likelihood that an individual will report no usual source of primary healthcare or delaying or forgoing necessary care because of cost.[41] At the same time, Medicaid beneficiaries may still experience problems with access to appropriate healthcare. Fewer physicians accept Medicaid patients reportedly as a result of numerous factors, including the program's structure (i.e., depressed payment levels, a potential for more red tape than private insurance or Medicare) as well as provider perceptions of stigma and a greater clinical burden presented by Medicaid patients.[42] One expert in the field reported that in 2009, 53 percent of physicians were accepting all or most new Medicaid patients compared to

87 percent of physicians in the case of privately insured patients and 74 percent in the case of Medicare patients. Acceptance rates varied significantly by specialty, with the lowest rates in three primary care specialties (internal medicine, family practice, and obstetrics and gynecology), as well as in psychiatry.[43] The same research also found that the proportion of private physicians accepting *no* Medicaid patients vastly exceeded the proportion refusing either privately insured or Medicare patients (28 percent for Medicaid versus 4 percent in the case of private insurance and 14 percent in the case of Medicare).[44]

A separate body of research shows that with the exception of dental care, Medicaid patients have a level of preventive primary care access that is comparable to that found among privately insured patients and far better than persons without health insurance.[45] But when these findings are considered in light of those studies that focus on physician acceptance of Medicaid, a clear implication is that equality in primary care access may be principally a result of efforts by federal and state policy makers to intervene formally into matters of healthcare distribution and access. Furthermore, although studies show access comparability for Medicaid beneficiaries in the case of primary healthcare, others suggest serious access constraints in the area of specialty care.[46]

To mitigate access problems and address the unique health needs of medically underserved populations, federal, state and local governments have made certain direct investments in healthcare services and public health measures. In addition, certain laws regulating the conduct of private healthcare institutions become pertinent when considering strategies to ensure healthcare access for low-income persons.

Direct Investments
Community Health Centers and the National Health Service Corps

Community health centers are the primary healthcare delivery system for the poor. The federal community health centers program awards grants to develop and operate health centers in communities and for populations (such as migrant farm workers or homeless persons) designated as medically underserved. In 2009, 1,200 federally funded health centers operating in over 8,000 sites provided comprehensive primary healthcare to nearly 20 million people.[47] An additional one hundred entities meeting all federal requirements but funded with state or local financing reached an additional 1 million persons. Ninety percent of all health center patients have family incomes below twice the federal poverty level, and health center services are available to patients across the full age spectrum.[48]

Organized as nonprofit clinical care providers and operated in accordance with extensive federal requirements, health centers are governed by four key requirements: location in and service to medically underserved populations, provision of a comprehensive range of "primary" healthcare services, the use of prospective adjusted charges based on family income, and governance by a community board, the majority of whose members are health center patients. A significant proportion of the more than 51,000 clinicians (including physicians, dentists, nurses, case managers, social workers and psychologists) who work at health centers are scholarship and loan recipients under the National Health Service Corps (NHSC), which provides scholarship and loan repayment support in exchange for service in urban and rural communities identified as experiencing a shortage of primary healthcare services.[49]

Health centers can be found in all states, the District of Columbia and the territories,[50] and their reach is extensive. In 2009 health centers served one in eight Medicaid beneficiaries, one in seven uninsured persons (including one in five low-income uninsured persons), one in three individuals living in poverty, and one in seven rural Americans. The ACA makes a major investment in health centers and the NHSC with the aim of doubling the program's reach by 2019.[51]

Public Hospitals and Health Systems

Public hospitals and health systems are a feature of many urban and rural communities. An annual survey of hospitals that are members of the National Association of Public Hospitals (NAPH) shows that in 2009, ninety-two hospitals averaged nearly 600,000 ambulatory care patient visits, 21,000 discharges, and accounted for 20 percent of the uncompensated care furnished in the United States.[52] Relying on federal, state and local funding as well as Medicare and Medicaid (including special "disproportionate share" payments under both Medicare and Medicaid), public hospitals are a principal source of not only primary care but highly specialized care and services for the low-income population in their communities. Furthermore, public hospitals frequently are a key source of advanced and specialized care for the entire population, particularly in the case of shock trauma, emergency care, advanced newborn care and critical care units for catastrophic injuries such as burns.[53]

In 2009, member hospitals experienced a 23 percent increase in the number of uninsured patients and a 10 percent increase in uncompensated care. Public hospitals and health systems play a particularly critical role in pregnancy-related care; 70 percent of all births at NAPH-member hospitals were financed by Medicaid in 2009. In many parts of the country, public hospitals are leaders in health professions training, with medical residencies across the major specialties, nurse training programs and programs in other health profession fields.

Family Planning under Title X and Medicaid

Low-income individuals can obtain free and subsidized family planning services. Title X of the Public Health Service Act provides grants to develop and operate family planning clinics offering comprehensive primary family planning and related services to both men and women. In 2008, ninety-one family planning grantees served 5.1 million patients across 4,597 sites.[54] Nearly 2.1 million patients received a Pap test and over 2.3 million received a breast exam. Oral contraceptives (37 percent) and hormonal injections (13 percent) accounted for the majority of family planning services used by Title X female patients.

As of July 2010, twenty-two states had expanded their Medicaid programs on a demonstration basis to offer coverage for family planning and related services to both men and women who meet the eligibility criteria, capped at the highest income level for pregnant women under the state plan. The ACA allows states to add family planning coverage as an option without the use of waivers.[55] Services covered under this option include family planning services and supplies, as well as diagnosis and treatment for conditions (such as infections and STDs) whose treatment during a family planning visit is customary or that arise as a result of family planning services (e.g., treatment of a perforated uterus).[56]

The Ryan White Care Act and AIDS Drug Assistance Program

The Ryan White Care Act (RWCA) provides primary care, care support services and drugs to more than a half million persons living with HIV/AIDS. Grants to states, localities and directly to primary care grantees (many community health centers also receive RWCA funding) comprise a portion of the funding, and services available through grantees can include ambulatory care, AIDS Drug Assistance Program (ADAP), oral health, premium and cost-sharing assistance for low-income persons, medical nutrition therapy, hospice services, home- and community-based health services, mental health and substance abuse outpatient services, home healthcare, and medical case management, including treatment adherence services. ADAP is perhaps the most important component of the RWCA program, providing drug assistance to both uninsured and underinsured persons. Waiting lists for services existed in eleven states as of July 2010.[57]

State and Local Public Health Agencies and Free Clinics

Free or low-cost clinical care for maternal and child health conditions (including conditions experienced by children with special healthcare needs), as well as the prevention and treatment of tuberculosis, immunization services, STDs and other conditions affecting public health may be available through state and local health agencies. Agencies use federal, state and local funding to maintain clinics, award subrecipient grants to clinical providers and otherwise take steps to better ensure the accessibility of care. In addition, the National Association of Free Clinics provides information on local free clinics and other community resources for uninsured persons.[58]

Public Accountability

Beyond direct investments in healthcare for medically underserved and vulnerable populations, federal law (as well as the law in many states) imposes certain healthcare access obligations on private healthcare providers.

The Emergency Medical Treatment and Labor Act (EMTALA)

Federal law requires hospitals to screen and treat individuals with emergent conditions without regard to ability to pay. EMTALA (42 U.S.C. § 1395dd) creates privately enforceable legal obligations on Medicare-participating hospitals with emergency departments. Hospitals governed by EMTALA requirements must provide an "appropriate" (i.e., nondiscriminatory) screening examination to any individual who comes to the emergency department and on whose behalf a request for an examination is made. If the exam identifies an emergency medical condition,[59] the hospital must either stabilize the condition[60] within the meaning of the law or arrange for an appropriate transfer to a medical facility as defined under the law.[61]

Anecdotal evidence suggests that in recent years, hospitals have been increasingly willing to partner with and help support community clinics such as health centers to reduce the frequency with which uninsured or underinsured patients (including Medicaid patients enrolled in managed care plans that lack sufficient network access) seek treatment for nonemergent conditions. At the same time, EMTALA litigation is extensive, and the law remains a powerful tool for gaining access to the specialized services and procedures needed to diagnose and treat emergent medical conditions.

Tax-Exempt Status of Nonprofit Healthcare Entities

Section 501(c)(3) of the Internal Revenue Code establishes the legal standard for determining whether a not-for-profit entity, including nonprofit hospitals, will be exempt from federal income tax.[62] Prior law required the actual provision of uncompensated care; since 1969, the IRS has required not-for-profit hospitals to meet a looser community benefit standard.[63] This standard uses a facts and circumstances test that assesses a hospital's eligibility for tax exemption by measuring whether they promote the health of a broad class of individuals in the community. The community benefit standard has been judged sufficiently vague as to make measurement and enforcement difficult.[64] Certain states have taken an aggressive stance over the years with respect to state property tax exemption and have refused to recognize property tax exemption in the absence of measurable performance standards, but the federal government has not followed suit. States have also been active in imposing community benefit requirements for nonprofit hospitals in state statutes.

Between 2007 and 2009, a series of media reports and government studies found extensive evidence of hospitals' refusal to discount or forgive bills in the case of the poor, as well as imposition of the highest charges on those least able to pay. A 2008 Government Accounting Office report[65] valued the federal tax exemption alone at nearly $13 billion in 2002 (a figure that does not include the total value of the exemption to hospitals when state tax laws also are considered) and concluded that the vagueness of federal requirements precluded effective enforcement. Although a Supreme Court decision held that taxpayers have no standing to enforce the Internal Revenue Code against nonprofit hospitals,[66] in recent years not-for-profit hospitals have been the subject of more than forty-five class-action lawsuits challenging their tax-exempt status on the basis of their billing practices and treatment of low-income or uninsured individuals.[67] In 2009, all not-for-profit hospitals were required to file supplemental information with the IRS to illuminate their community benefit-related spending.[68]

The ACA amends the Internal Revenue Code by adding new section 501(r), titled "Additional requirements for certain hospitals."[69] The new requirements apply to "a facility which is required by a State to be licensed, registered, or similarly recognized as a hospital," and "any other organization which the Secretary determines has the provision of hospital care as its principal function or purpose."[70] Where a hospital organization operates more than one facility, each and every facility is required to meet the requirements set forth in the new provisions.[71] The following ACA provisions relate to charitable hospitals.

- A not-for-profit hospital must conduct a "community health needs assessment" every three years, in addition to adopting an "implementation strategy" to meet the needs established by the assessment.[72] This provision applies beginning with the taxable year two years after the enactment of the law. To qualify as a community health needs assessment the following conditions must be met: the assessment and implementation strategy must be carried out on a recurring basis; the assessment must "take into account" input from persons who represent the "broad interest" of the "community served by the hospital facility"; the assessment must include those with "special knowledge or expertise in public health," suggesting a link to public health not only in terms of the content of information collected through the assessment but also the assessment process itself; the assessment must be made "widely available" to the public; the hospital must have adopted an "implementation strategy."

- A hospital must adopt financial assistance and emergency medical care policies that set forth eligibility criteria for free or discounted care, "the basis for calculating amounts charged to patients"; "the method for applying for financial assistance," the actions the hospital will take in the event of a nonpayment; and measures to widely publicize the policy within the community."[73]

- A hospital must also have a written emergency medical care policy that includes a statement "requiring the organization to provide, without discrimination, care for emergency medical conditions to individuals regardless of their eligibility under the financial assistance policy."[74]

- In addition, to receive the benefits of a 501(c)(3) tax-exempt organization, a hospital must place a limit on "amounts charged for emergency or other medically necessary care provided to individuals eligible for assistance under the financial assistance policy … to not more than the lowest amounts charged to individuals who have insurance covering such care"; and the hospital organization must "prohibit the use of gross charges."[75]

This brief overview has examined financing, service delivery, and regulatory policies that can help promote access to healthcare among the low-income population. The ACA is poised to make changes of enormous consequences to the poor, particularly where coverage is concerned. At the same time, many challenges remain given the fundamentally market nature of the U.S. healthcare system, the added health burdens created by poverty and the economic and social isolation in which the poor so frequently live. Addressing these challenges requires a multipronged strategy, one that combines efforts to ensure access to health coverage, with perhaps even more sophisticated efforts to deliver and improve care, including cost-saving preventive treatment and interventions addressing underlying social determinants of health.

Questions for Discussion

1. How would you describe healthcare access for vulnerable populations in the United States? What are the strengths and weaknesses of the system?

2. How will the ACA change access to care for vulnerable populations? What gaps will remain?

3. Based on your understanding of social determinants of health (see Chapter 1), how effective is our current healthcare system at addressing root causes of illness?

Legal Services for Low-Income Populations

Almost everything an individual does raises legal questions. Driving a car, buying a newspaper, swiping a credit card, enrolling in the fourth grade, getting married, getting paid on the job, paying taxes and eating lunch are all acts done in a context defined by laws that create, implicate or fulfill legal rights, duties and privileges. As naturally as learning a language, a child absorbs society's legal context while growing up. When the car hits a pedestrian, the newspaper is censored, the credit card bill goes unpaid, fourth grade is barred because the child is disabled, divorce looms, the paycheck is withheld, the tax rules are complex, or a foreign substance appears in the sandwich, suddenly the help of a lawyer is important.

Unlike our healthcare system, insurance for legal issues plays only a small role in the United States. Most people are "self-insured," meaning that when they need legal help they find it by hiring a lawyer. If all they need is a little advice, a simple will, review of a lease, or guide to small claims court, gaining access to legal help may cost relatively little. In the past twenty years, a great deal of legal information and advice has become available in books, court self-help centers and free websites. Using these helpful sources of legal insight, a competent adult is often able to work out legal options, prepare legal papers, learn enough to negotiate a resolution to a dispute, or decide that he or she has no legal recourse in a situation.

Frequently, however, individuals would prefer the actual assistance of a legal professional. In some cases, such as a battle over child custody, an eviction from an apartment, permanent expulsion from school, or facing jail time on a felony charge, the potential consequences can change one's life forever. In others, such as liability for personal injuries caused by a car accident, foreclosure on a home, the loss of retirement savings because of fraud, or denial of health insurance benefits for major surgery, the amount of funds at risk threaten a way of life. Sometimes a lawyer is essential because the law is very complicated, a business opportunity requires an advanced understanding of commercial transactions, or access to a benefit is blocked by a bureaucrat.

There are significant obstacles to gaining access to the legal help one needs. The first is failure to recognize that one has legal rights or can look to the law for assistance. Similarly, cultural traditions may deter a battered woman from speaking out or a victim of fraud from seeking redress. In addition, the network of self-representation opportunities doesn't work well for people who are illiterate, who didn't finish high school or for whom English is a foreign language. Mental disabilities, intellectual deficiencies and physical illness can render legal information and advice unusable. Although many people have some means of access to the Internet today, effective navigation of self-help websites is a skill that eludes many, particularly older individuals; without help, the self-representation system is inaccessible.

The greatest obstacle to getting the legal help one needs is the cost of a lawyer's services. Private lawyers may charge by the hour or the job, or work for a percentage of the recovery in some situations. A "simple" divorce may involve just a few hours of a lawyer's work, defending against an eviction a few more, and fighting for child custody can take many hours every year until a child reaches majority. A lawyer may deliver a simple will at a very low cost, a basic estate plan with a revocable trust for $1,000, and a careful plan involving multiple trusts and Medicaid planning for $5,000. Representation by a top criminal defense lawyer at a trial on a manslaughter charge might cost more than $100,000.

The high costs of some legal proceedings are daunting even to wealthy individuals; middle-class families with modest savings will mortgage their house to pay for a lawyer if the cause is important enough. People with fewer resources pay for some services from lawyers who charge lower fees but may have to rely on self-help even when a lawyer is needed. Low-income individuals often cannot find a private lawyer to take their cases, but they may obtain legal help through legal aid programs and organized pro bono systems. Like health, it seems that justice is elusive for many low-income individuals who have legal problems.

The Right to Counsel

"You have a right to remain silent. You have a right to a lawyer. If you cannot afford a lawyer, one will be provided for you, free of charge." These famous Miranda[76] rights capture the letter of the law when an individual is arrested on criminal charges. Although subject to an increasing number of exceptions, the right to free counsel in criminal cases sharply distinguishes such matters from civil cases, where there is no right.

Criminal cases make up a small percentage of the legal problems individuals face. The Sixth Amendment to the Constitution guarantees the accused in all criminal prosecutions "the Assistance of Counsel for his defence," but it was not until 1932, when the Supreme Court in *Powell v. Alabama* declared a right to counsel in cases in which the potential punishment was death that the justice system developed capacity to provide free counsel to defendants.[77] Over the next thirty years, that right was extended to federal felony cases, and a number of states adopted the concept. In 1963, the Supreme Court declared in

Gideon v. Wainwright that states must provide indigent felony defendants with free counsel.[78] Later cases incorporated appeals and misdemeanors where the defendant, if convicted, faces the possibility of jail time.

The fundamental distinction is that defendants in criminal cases have a right to a free lawyer, provided by the government, whereas in the civil domain (with limited exceptions) people have no such right, however critical their need may be. What has been done to remedy this situation? What is still needed?

Civil Legal Assistance

The United States provides some free legal services for low-income people with civil legal problems.

Examples of Civil Legal Problems for Low-Income Individuals

1. Housing evictions and home foreclosures.

2. Consumer problems including predatory lending.

3. Family law problems such as divorce, child support, custody and domestic violence.

4. Access to government benefits such as Social Security, disability unemployment insurance, food stamps, Medicaid and Medicare.

The largest segment of the civil legal aid system (see Table 2.1) is made up of the 136 programs that are funded by the federal Legal Services Corporation (LSC). These are generally staff-based providers.[79] They are joined by numerous other staffed legal aid programs that are not funded by LSC, as well as approximately 900 pro bono programs without LSC funding that exist in every state and virtually every locale.[80] Over 200 law school clinical programs and several hundred self-help programs also supplement the staff delivery system. In addition, thirty-eight state support organizations provide

Table 2.1 Landscape of the Civil Legal Aid System (2010)

Total Number of Programs (Excluding Pro Bono)	
LSC	123
Non-LSC	727
Pro-Bono Programs for the Poor	
Bar or Free-Standing and Law Firm	900
Other Advocacy Organizations	
State	38
National	30

Note: Recent reports from the American Bar Association Standing Committee on Pro Bono and Public Service show that when specialty (domestic violence, AIDS, homelessness, etc.), law firm and law school pro bono programs are considered, there are over 1,500 pro bono programs across the country.
Source: Alan W. Houseman, *Civil Legal Aid in the United States: An Update for 2009*, Center for Law and Social Policy, July 2009.

training and technical support to local legal aid advocates on key substantive issues[81] and advocate before state legislative and administrative bodies on policy issues affecting low-income people.[82] Finally, more than thirty entities advocate on behalf of low-income people at the federal level, fifteen of which were formerly part of the national support network funded by LSC.[83]

The current total funding for civil legal assistance in the United States is approximately $1.4 billion, with LSC as the largest single funder.[84] In addition, considerable funds come from other federal sources, from state sources (primarily appropriations), and from Interest on Lawyer Trust Account (IOLTA) programs.[85] Finally, there are a variety of other funding sources, including local governments, bar associations, law firms, individual members of the private bar, United Way and private charitable foundations (see Figure 2.5).

A Brief History of Civil Legal Assistance Programs

Civil legal assistance for low-income people in the United States began in 1876 with the founding of the Legal Aid Society of New York. Over the next several decades, the legal aid movement caught on in the urban areas of the United States. By 1965, virtually every major city had some kind of locally funded legal aid program; there were 157 organizations employing over 400 full-time lawyers with an aggregate budget of nearly $4.5 million, but there was no national legal aid structure or national funding source.[86]

In part due to grossly inadequate resources and a high number of eligible clients, legal aid programs generally gave relatively perfunctory service to a high volume of clients. Legal aid attorneys rarely went to court with their clients, and appeals were virtually non-

Figure 2.5 Civil Legal Aid Funding Sources (2008 Data)

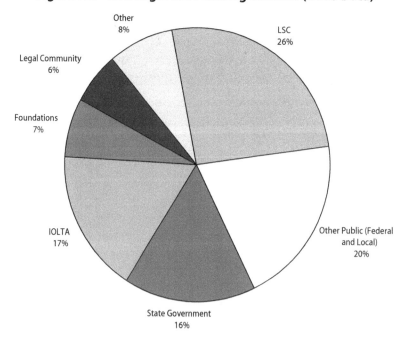

Source: Alan W. Houseman, *Civil Legal Aid in the United States: An Update for 2009,* Center for Law and Social Policy, July 2009.

existent. Administrative representation, legislative advocacy, and community legal education were not practiced. As a result, legal aid provided limited benefits for those it served and little impact on the client population as a whole.

In 1965, the federal Office of Economic Opportunity (OEO) established the first federal legal services program. The OEO funded full-service providers, each serving one geographic area, with the obligation to ensure access for all clients and client groups to the legal system. The local legal services programs made all the key decisions about who would be served, the scope of services to be provided, the substantive areas in which legal assistance would be provided, staffing mix, and so on. The OEO also developed a unique infrastructure that provided national leadership and support on substantive poverty law issues as well as undertook major impact litigation and representation before state and federal legislative and administrative bodies.

On July 25, 1974, President Richard Nixon signed into law the Legal Services Corporation Act.[87] The delivery and support structure put in place by the OEO was carried over fundamentally unchanged by the LSC when it began to function in 1975. The major accomplishment of the LSC in its early years was the expansion of the federal legal services program from a predominantly urban program to one providing legal assistance in virtually every county in the nation and in most U.S. territories. In 1975, the LSC had inherited a program that was funded at $71.5 million annually; by 1981, the LSC budget had grown to $321.3 million. Most of this money went into creating new programs and expanding old ones to cover larger service areas; 325 programs were funded, which operated out of 1,450 neighborhood and rural offices throughout the fifty states, the District of Columbia, Puerto Rico, the Virgin Islands, Micronesia and Guam. Poor people in every county had access to a legal services program.[88]

Since that time, Congress has not provided sufficient funding to maintain the level of access achieved in 1981; indeed, the LSC lost considerable ground due to significant budget reductions in 1982 and 1996 and the inability to keep up with inflation, even when funding was increased. Though local and state funding for legal services has grown considerably — and in 2010 exceeds LSC funding in terms of the overall system — the funding diversity has not been evenly distributed across the country. As a result, large sections of the South, Southwest, and Rocky Mountain states have few nonfederal resources and are almost entirely dependent on federal funds to maintain a minimum of legal services.

Over the past thirty years, the American Bar Association (ABA) has increasingly promoted the idea that lawyers in private practice should fill the gap in legal services for the poor. As part of the complex struggle for the survival of the federally funded LSC after 1980, the LSC required all of its grantees to expend "a substantial amount" of their grants on involving private attorneys in the delivery of legal services to low-income individuals.[89] The ABA, which had called for such a commitment by the LSC, received a modest LSC grant to set up a support project for new bar association programs offering free or reduced-fee services to the poor. Across the country, new pro bono, contract and judicare programs[90] sprung up that featured private attorneys handling cases for low-income clients.

Alongside the dramatic expansion of pro bono activities came a number of service delivery experiments, including legal information hotlines, but the structure of the federal legal services program remained essentially unchanged until 1996.[91] At that point, Congress reduced overall LSC funding by a third, completely defunded the support system, and imposed new and unprecedented restrictions.

1996 Congressional Restrictions on LSC Programs

- Prohibited from representing most undocumented immigrants and other categories of aliens.

- Prohibited from initiating or participating in any class actions.

- Precluded from advocacy and representation before legislative bodies and in administrative rule-making proceedings (with some exceptions).

- Prohibited from claiming attorneys fees.

- Prohibited from representing prisoners and participating in any litigation related to abortion.

Note: For a more detailed discussion of the restrictions, see Alan W. Houseman, "Restrictions by Funders and the Ethical Practice of Law," *Fordham Law Review*, 67 (1999): 218–40. See also Rebekah Diller, Emily Savner, *A Call to End Federal Restrictions on Legal Aid for the Poor*, Brennan Center for Justice, June 2009.

In the wake of the 1996 restrictions, some LSC providers gave up their federal funds and focused on securing unrestricted, non-LSC funds to pursue restricted activities. State and local programs reorganized, more sophisticated pro bono projects were developed, and new, technology-driven systems and strategies were introduced, including self-help websites, hotlines and remote video conferencing in rural areas. States continued to strengthen IOLTA programs to generate funds for staffed legal aid programs.

An Evolving Civil Legal Aid System

To ensure equal justice for all, the United States as a whole and each of the states and jurisdictions must develop a comprehensive and integrated system that delivers high-quality civil legal assistance that meets the legal needs of low-income people. The legal community is at the beginning stages of that process, which will require at a minimum (1) increased funding, (2) leadership to support improved national legal aid infrastructure and (3) increased private attorney commitment to civil legal assistance.

Funding Insufficient to Meet U.S. Legal Needs

Current federal and state funding is simply insufficient to meet the pervasive legal needs of low-income individuals and families. The 2009 LSC Report, "Documenting the Justice Gap in America: The Current Unmet Civil Legal Needs of Low-Income Americans,"[92] details the continued need for civil legal aid among low-income Americans.[93] Study findings include that:

- LSC programs turned away at least half of all eligible applicants for services due to lack of resources.

- Multiple state legal needs studies findings are consistent with the national American Bar Association study that demonstrated that less than 20 percent of the legal needs of low-income Americans were being met.[94]

- The ratio of legal aid attorneys to low-income persons is unsustainable (see Figure 2.6).

In 2011, the LSC continues to be the largest single funder and standard setter for civil legal assistance in the United States, providing core operating funds supplemented by

Figure 2.6 Comparison of Private Lawyers to General Population and Legal Aid Lawyers to Low-Income Population

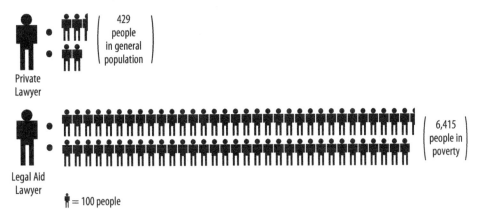

Private Lawyer

429 people in general population

Legal Aid Lawyer

6,415 people in poverty

= 100 people

Source: Legal Services Corporation, *Documenting the Justice Gap in America: The Current Unmet Civil Legal Needs of Low-Income Americans* (September 2005), http://www.lsc.gov/press/documents/ LSC%20Justice%20Gap_FINAL_1001.pdf.

local and state funding. Although legal aid leadership has made significant progress in developing a much stronger bipartisan consensus in favor of LSC funding, Congress remains divided about the necessity of continued federal support for LSC, and, if federal support continues, what the appropriate scope and mission of the program should be.[95]

State and Local Support for Legal Aid

Since 1982, state and local funding for the provision of civil legal services has increased to approximately $500 million in 2010.[96] Until recently, this increase has come primarily from IOLTA programs, which have now been implemented in every state. Over the past decade or so, substantial new state funding has also been generated from general state or local governmental appropriations, as well as resources such as filing fee surcharges, state abandoned property funds and a variety of other state governmental initiatives. With the onset of the 2008 recession, leading to historically low interest rates, state and IOLTA funding declined sharply. Any increases will depend on increases in interest rates and resurgence in the real estate market and general business cycle, the success of IOLTA programs negotiating with banks for comparable interest rates, and the relative health of state fiscal conditions.

IOLTA: Background

Interest on Lawyers Trust Accounts (IOLTA) is a unique and innovative way to increase access to justice for individuals and families living in poverty and to improve our justice system. Without taxing the public, and at no cost to lawyers or their clients, interest from lawyer trust accounts is pooled to provide civil legal aid to the poor and support improvements to the justice system.

A lawyer who receives funds that belong to a client must place those funds in a trust account separate from the lawyer's own money. Client funds are deposited in an IOLTA account when the funds cannot otherwise earn enough income for the client to be more than the cost of securing that income. The client—not the IOLTA program—receives the interest if the funds are large enough or will be held for a long enough period of time to generate net interest that is sufficient to allocate directly to the client.

IOLTA programs were first established in Australia and Canada in the late 1960s and early 1970s to generate funds for legal services to the poor. In the late 1970s, the Florida Bar and other organizations filed a petition to establish the first U.S. IOLTA program. After legislation permitted the establishment of interest-bearing checking accounts in the early 1980s and the Florida advocates obtained important tax rulings from the IRS, the Florida Bar Foundation launched the first IOLTA program in 1981. Shortly thereafter, Oregon, California, Idaho and Maryland followed suit.

In 2011, all fifty states, the District of Columbia and the U.S. Virgin Islands operate IOLTA programs. Forty-two jurisdictions require lawyers to participate in IOLTA. Lawyers can opt out of participation in eight states, and participation is voluntary in two others.

Source: ABA Commission on Interest on Lawyers' Trust Accounts, "Overview," www.americanbar.org/groups/legal_services/interest_lawyers_trust_accounts/overview.html.

Another local component in the legal services delivery system is the law school clinic, which has the dual role of providing legal services to clients and also providing hands-on legal experience to law school students. Directed by law school faculty, student law clinics typically focus in discreet areas of law and provide a low volume of service. Additionally, as will be discussed later in the chapter, law school accreditation standards have been amended to require all ABA-approved schools to offer substantial opportunities for student participation in pro bono activities.

Leadership and Planning for Effective Legal Aid Systems

A second element of an efficient, effective twenty-first-century civil legal aid system is a comprehensive infrastructure at the state and national level. The legal aid community requires improved data systems, monitoring and analysis to help local programs meet the complex needs of a future client cohort that may differ considerably from the client community of past decades.

The national civil legal aid system should also have an ongoing and institutionalized capacity to conduct research on the delivery of civil legal aid and conduct and evaluate demonstration projects, testing new ideas and innovations for possible replication across the system. Many civil legal aid systems in Europe and Canada have entities that conduct research on the civil legal aid system and pilot demonstration programs to improve the delivery of civil legal aid.

Fellowship programs through Equal Justice Works and Skadden Arps Fellowship Program, together with Americorps, have provided a crucial capacity to struggling legal aid offices across the country, while at the same time encouraging innovation and leadership development for the next generation of legal aid leaders.[97] The legal community will need additional investments, analogous to the National Health Service Corps, to meet needs, particularly in underserved and rural parts of the country. A good example is the Public Service Loan Forgiveness Program established by the College Cost Reduction and Access Act offering loan forgiveness after ten years of public service employment.[98]

Additionally, each state should have an effective planning and oversight capacity. As of 2010, twenty-five states and the District of Columbia have functioning access to justice commissions. Another five states have similar planning entities. Among other functions, the access to justice commissions and state planning entities work to integrate all institutional and individual providers and partners, expand pro bono and self-help initiatives, allocate resources among providers to ensure that representation can occur in all forums for low-income persons, and provide access to a range of services for all eligible clients regardless of where they live, the language they speak, or the ethnic or cultural group of which they are a member.[99] Some access to justice or state planning entities have been effective in increasing state funding for civil legal assistance.

Other strategies to realign the civil legal aid system to meet the needs of the vast low-income population include the recent movement toward expansion of a right to counsel for civil cases where "basic human needs" are at stake. Known as "civil *Gideon*," the ABA has passed a resolution in support of the expansion, citing shelter, safety, family integrity and sustenance as examples of basic human needs.[100] Legal aid leaders are also strengthening their traditional collaborations with social service providers to broaden access.

The MLP model contributes substantially to the goal of expanding access to legal resources by cementing local partnerships with healthcare leaders and leveraging scarce resources on behalf of legal aid clients. In bridging the healthcare and legal domains, MLP drives resources and expertise into the legal aid community that will increase effectiveness at the local, regional and national levels, especially as leaders in the legal community look to health and public health for insights about measuring the impact of legal intervention and integrating prevention strategies into legal aid activities.

The Role of Pro Bono Service

Pro bono publico is a Latin phrase meaning "for the public good." The tradition of lawyers in the private sector providing legal service to those who cannot afford it is discussed in greater detail in the next section. Pro bono is more fully integrated into the overall legal services delivery system than it was a quarter century ago. The quality and scope of pro bono programs has improved, private law firms and law schools have become increasingly more organized and committed to public service, innovative pro bono delivery models have been developed, and statewide policies have been adopted that focus more attention on pro bono work. Pro bono expansion has contributed substantially to the fabric of the legal services community, expanding capacity especially in legal domains where funding restrictions have limited access to services, such as immigration and prisoner's rights.

In 1996, to support the development of high-quality pro bono programs, the American Bar Association House of Delegates adopted the ABA Standards for Programs Providing Civil Pro Bono Legal Services to Persons of Limited Means,[101] which recognized that pro bono programs and their volunteer lawyers need to view their clients and cases in a holistic way. Standard 2.10, under the Program Effectiveness section, states: "A pro bono program should strive to develop and maintain active and cooperative relations with community organizations and social service agencies that serve clients."[102] The Commentary to Standard 2.10 discusses the value of these relationships in helping serve the client beyond the immediate legal needs presented. This principle has led to many programs working with social workers and other nonlegal supporter providers and, notably, to the involvement of private attorney volunteers in MLPs.

Pro bono or reduced-fee programs for low-income clients are a critical component of the civil legal assistance system. Such programs are typically part of the bar association, a unit within the staffed legal services office, or independent nonprofit entities with paid staff that refer cases to private attorneys who provide services from their private law offices. Finally, law school programs are collaborating with law firms and community-based service providers to provide pro bono services to help fill the gap.[103]

Increasing pro bono efforts and expanding the activities pro bono lawyers undertake can contribute substantially to the provision of necessary legal services for vulnerable communities. However, there are challenges to effectively increasing and deploying pro bono services in the legal aid context, including the need for training, coordination and oversight. Legal aid agencies can better optimize private bar resources and be creative in how they deploy this valuable resource by investing in better systems to monitor pro bono cases and use pro bono services for systemic impact beyond handling individual cases.

Individual Responsibility and Professional Standards for Attorneys and Physicians

Both the law and medical professions are attentive to their respective commitments to care for the underserved, and each profession maintains different standards — within vastly different systems — for teaching and promoting such commitments. Within the safety-net systems that have been created for the poor in both the healthcare and legal systems, how do the professions understand individual responsibility to serve the poor? Do these professions perceive a unique responsibility? If so, in what capacities are individual professionals equipped to meet this obligation?

Physicians and the Poor

A sense of obligation to society as well as the values of compassion, honesty and beneficence seem inherent in the practice of medicine. These qualities, often prominent in students entering medical school, are further instilled through their medical education, training and the codes of ethics they profess. Reflecting this commitment to altruism, physicians in private practice provide the majority of free medical care for the uninsured in the United States.[104] An estimated 68 percent of physicians (or 397,000 physicians) provide free care to the uninsured as a part of their regular practice.[105] Approximately 80 percent of patients who are either uninsured or have Medicaid will be cared for by a physician in private practice.[106] Physicians provide this care through their private practices, at free clinics, or through volunteer referral networks, in which they agree to treat patients for free or at a nominal charge.[107] The willingness of physicians in private practice to treat patients with Medicaid, however, is often influenced by Medicaid reimbursement rates.[108]

The Hippocratic Oath, written in the fifth century B.C., did not specifically address the care of patients living in poverty.[109] In contrast, the American Medical Association's (AMA) first code of ethics (written in 1847) required physicians to provide free care for indigent patients: "Poverty ... should always be recognized as presenting valid claims for gratuitous services."[110] The AMA's code required that physicians place the interests of their patients above "all pecuniary consideration" and "considerations of personal advancement."[111] The current Code of Medical Ethics of the AMA and its associated opinions continue this mandate by directing physicians to "ensure that the needs of the poor in their community are met," through both medical service and political advocacy.[112]

The education and training of physicians further reinforces the professional tradition of altruism. Medical schools require their students to show a "commitment to provide care to patients who are unable to pay and to advocate for access to health care for members of traditionally underserved populations."[113] Medical students have demonstrated this commitment through the creation of student-run free clinics operated at nearly half of U.S. medical schools.[114] After medical school, students enter residency training programs, where they must demonstrate "accountability to patients, society and the profession."[115] Whether altruism is inherent in the desire to become a physician, or whether it is instilled through medical education and codes of medical ethics, physicians continue to demonstrate a commitment to patients living in poverty.

Like the legal profession, incorporating pro bono work into the private practitioner's schedule is difficult. And because of how the healthcare system's financial incentives are aligned, physicians are even less likely than lawyers to offer individual pro bono services to the poor.[116] As detailed earlier in this chapter, the multiple government programs that comprise the U.S. health system for the poor, elderly and disabled—however disjointed it may be—may serve to diminish the notion of a professional obligation of individual physicians to provide free indigent care.[117] Ultimately, "true charitable care" is less likely in today's healthcare climate, for the myriad reasons detailed earlier, related to the role of health insurance, coupled with the recognition that a healthcare system that relies on inconsistent charitable care for some of its most vulnerable patients may be insufficient.

Attorneys and the Poor

In medieval times, lawyers were forbidden under canonical law to charge a fee for aiding a person in court because it would set a price on the injured party's search for justice. The core English legal declaration of rights, the Magna Carta, declared: "To no one will we sell, to no one will we refuse or delay, right or justice" (Chapter 40). Examples of principled lawyers stepping in without fee to represent unpopular clients have stirred the blood of the noble profession for centuries.

The constitutions of many states emulate the standard set by Massachusetts in 1780:

> Every subject of the Commonwealth ought to find a certain remedy, by having recourse to the laws, for all injuries or wrongs which he may receive in his person, property, or character. He ought to obtain right and justice freely, and without being obliged to purchase it; completely, and without any denial; promptly, and without delay; conformably to the laws. (Part I: Declaration of Rights, Art. XI)

In 1919, Reginald Heber Smith published a groundbreaking analysis of the ways the legal system denied justice to low-income Americans.[118] He was forced to conclude:

> The system of assignment of counsel looms large in the books, but has amounted to very little in practice. Analytically, it would appear that this power of the courts to assign attorneys to assist poor persons in cases where representation was necessary was a complete answer to the difficulty of the expense of attorneys. Practically, it has been no solution at all.[119]

Since the very earliest days of the legal profession in the United States, lawyers have had a tradition of providing volunteer legal services. Beginning in 1906, this tradition was codified into rules of profession responsibility for lawyers. In the modern era, the ABA continues to provide leadership in promoting pro bono contributions by private attorneys through its rulemaking capacity. In 1983, the ABA House of Delegates adopted Rule 6.1

of the Model Rules of Professional Conduct, which stated that a lawyer "should render public interest legal service."[120]

In 1993, the rule was amended to prioritize that lawyers should serve low-income people without charge as well as perform other forms of volunteer legal service.[121] For the first time, an aspirational hourly goal was included in the rule as a way of setting a target for lawyers. The current Rule 6.1 reads: "Every lawyer has a professional responsibility to provide legal services to those unable to pay. A lawyer should aspire to render at least (50) hours of pro bono publico legal services per year."[122] Although some states have adopted the model rule in its entirety, others have modified versions.[123] The LSC has also sought to expand private attorney involvement in addressing the unmet legal needs of the poor. In April 2007, the LSC published an action plan for private attorney involvement for its grantee legal services agencies, which includes strategies for partnering with the private bar, the judiciary and law schools.[124]

Studies suggest, however, that the model rules have not significantly increased pro bono legal service by the private bar. A 2005 survey by the ABA, *Supporting Justice: A Report on the Pro Bono Work of America's Lawyers*, found that only 66 percent of the attorneys surveyed said that they did some pro bono work. But a 2008 update of that report found that 73 percent of respondents reported that they provided pro bono services to people of limited means and organizations serving the poor, and 27 percent of lawyers surveyed reported that they met the ABA's aspirational goal of providing at least fifty hours of pro bono legal assistance annually.[125] Given the enormous unmet need for legal assistance, some analysts have suggested that the aspiration to provide pro bono service should be superceded by a mandate that all lawyers provide pro bono service.[126] There are two primary arguments supporting mandating pro bono service. First, supporters of mandatory pro bono work argue that access to legal services is a fundamental need affecting basic human rights; therefore, all lawyers have a responsibility to provide service to those who cannot afford it.[127] Second, some argue that lawyers have a government-sponsored monopoly on the practice of law and therefore have an obligation to serve those without access to the system.[128]

Opponents of mandatory pro bono work argue that although lawyers may have a moral obligation to serve the poor, mandating that they do so is unrealistic and an inefficient means of solving the problem of unmet legal needs.[129] Thus far, the idea of mandating pro bono service has not found traction.

Legal educators, on the other hand, have been more willing to embrace required pro bono service for law students as a way to inculcate the value and practice of serving those who are unable to pay. The ABA, which accredits law schools, and the American Association of Law Schools (AALS) have both focused efforts in the past two decades on encouraging law schools to incorporate pro bono service into the law school experience. In 1996, the ABA amended its accreditation standards to provide that "a law school should encourage its students to participate in pro bono activities and provide opportunities for them to do so."[130] The accreditation standard for curriculum was amended in 2006 to provide that "a law school shall offer substantial opportunities for ... student participation in pro bono activities."[131] Similarly, in 1999, the AALS Commission on Pro Bono and Public Service Opportunities issued a report that recommended "that law schools make available to all law students at least once during their law school careers a well-supervised law-related pro bono opportunity and either require the students' participation or find ways to attract the great majority of students to volunteer."[132] Partly in response to this guidance from the ABA and the AALS, law school pro bono programs have flourished in the past fifteen years, with some schools adopting mandatory pro bono graduation requirements.[133]

Questions for Discussion

1. Define "access to justice." What are the barriers to access to justice for low-income people?

2. Why is there so much unmet legal need in the United States? What models of legal service are most effective in addressing unmet legal need?

3. What are some of the ways that legal services for the poor can be made more accessible and effective in addressing their needs?

Conclusion

The health and legal systems in the United States may seem to have few commonalities, outside the vulnerable populations they both serve. The health system appears more vast in every way—certainly more substantially resourced and regulated. But the legal system that serves the low-income community is much more than the sum of the parts described here (federal and nonfederal legal aid providers, pro bono, etc.) because it implicates the entire justice system as well—federal, state and municipal courts, administrative agencies, and other domains.

This summary of the health and legal systems, coupled with descriptions of the physician and attorney professional mandates to serve the poor, is designed to give a snapshot of both systems, enabling students and practitioners to grasp the relevance of MLP in the landscape of healthcare and law. Indeed, as each sector is poised for change (especially the health sector under the Affordable Care Act) this foundation can set the stage for understanding the transformative nature of the MLP model, detailed in Chapter 3.

---

1. P. L. 111-148 (111th Cong., 2d sess.).

2. Henry J. Kaiser Family Foundation, "The Uninsured: A Primer," December 2010, http://www. kff.org/uninsured/upload/7451-06.pdf (accessed January 1, 2011).

3. Ibid., fig. 6.

4. Medicaid is one of the nation's most complex social welfare programs. It is not possible to do more than slightly sketch out the program here. Readers who want in-depth information on Medicaid eligibility, benefits and state plan administration should consult other sources, including the Centers for Medicare and Medicaid Services (CMS) (http://www.cms.gov, the agency within the Department of Health and Human Services that administers Medicaid), the National Health Law Program (http://www.healthlaw.org) and the Henry J. Kaiser Family Foundation (http://www.kff.org). Because Medicaid varies tremendously by state, the other starting point is the Medicaid program for the state of residence.

5. For a general discussion of Medicaid citizenship and legal residency requirements and options, see Ruth Ellen Wasem, "Medicaid Citizenship Documentation," Congressional Research Service, February 12, 2009, http://aging.senate.gov/crs/medicaid14.pdf.

6. 42 U.S.C. § 1396a (a)(10). An excellent source of state-by-state information on Medicaid eligibility for all groups is the Henry J. Kaiser Family Foundation, "State Health Facts," http://www.statehealthfacts.org (accessed January 1, 2011).

7. See "State Health Facts" for state-by-state information.

8. Sara Rosenbaum, Paul Wise, "Crossing the Medicaid-Private Insurance Divide: The Case of EPSDT," *Health Affairs,* 26 (2007): 382–93.

9. See "State Health Facts" to determine eligibility standards for adults in each state.

10. Sara Rosenbaum, "Medicaid and National Health Reform," *New England Journal of Medicine* 361 (2009): 2009–12.

11. Rosenbaum and Wise, "Crossing the Medicaid-Private Insurance Divide."

12. State Medicaid plans should be consulted for limitations and exclusions applicable to adults.

13. Benjamin Sommers, Sara Rosenbaum, "Shifting between Medicaid and Exchange Eligibility under the Affordable Care Act: Implications for Implementation," *Health Affairs* (2011).

14. The health insurance market reforms contained in ACA §§ 1201 and amending both the Public Health Service Act and ERISA (ACA § 1563) build on the Health Insurance Portability and Accountability Act of 1996, P.L. 104-191 (104th Cong., 2d sess.), the first federal law to set federal limits on discrimination by health insurers operating in the group market and ERISA-governed self-insured group health plans.

15. ACA § 1001 and 1201 amending Public Health Service Act Title XXVII; ACA § 1563, applying most insurance reforms to the ERISA group health plan market as a matter of federal law, thereby reaching both self-insured and insured plans.

16. ACA as amended by the Health Care and Education Reconciliation Act, P.L. 111-152 (11th Cong., 2d sess.). For a discussion of the exchange subsidy system, see Health Reform GPS, "Update: Health Insurance Exchanges," November 22, 2010, http://healthreformgps.org/resources/health-insurance-exchanges/.

17. ACA § 2001.

18. Gerard F. Anderson and David A. Squires, "Measuring the U.S. Health Care System: A Cross-National Comparison," The Commonwealth Fund (June 2010).

19. David Blumenthal, "Employer-Sponsored Health Insurance in the United States—Origins and Implications," *New England Journal of Medicine,* 355 (2006): 82–88.

20. Henry J. Kaiser Family Foundation, "Health Benefit Offer Rates and Employee Earnings," November 16, 2010, http://www.kff.org/insurance/snapshot/Health-Benefit-Offer-Rates-and-Employee-Earnings.cfm.

21. Ibid.

22. Kaiser Family Foundation, "Dual Eligibles: Medicaid Enrollment and Spending for Medicare Beneficiaries in 2007," http://www.kff.org/medicaid/upload/7846-02.pdf (accessed January 1, 2011).

23. Ibid. See table 1 for a comprehensive chart setting forth all possible dual eligibility pathways.

24. Ibid.

25. Ibid.

26. Ibid.

27. Special rules apply to individuals with Lou Gehrig's disease (amyotrophic lateral sclerosis).

28. For general information about COBRA continuation benefits, see U.S. Department of Labor, "Frequently Asked Questions About COBRA Continuation Coverage," http://www.dol.gov/ebsa/faqs/faq_consumer_cobra.HTML (accessed January 1, 2011).

29. The Centers for Medicare and Medicaid Services publishes a highly useful *Medicare Handbook*, http://www.medicare.gov/Publications/Pubs/pdf/10050.pdf (accessed January 1, 2011).

30. Complete information about Medicare Advantage plans, including a plan locator and more general Medicare information, can be found at http://www.medicare.gov/choices/advantage.asp (accessed January 1, 2011). A Medicare Plan Finder for MA plans and prescription drug plans can be found at https://www.medicare.gov/find-a-plan/questions/home.aspx (accessed January 1, 2011).

31. Kaiser Family Foundation, "Medicare Advantage 2011 Data Spotlight," http://www.kff.org/medicare/upload/8117.pdf (accessed January 1, 2011).

32. Ibid.

33. Henry J. Kaiser Family Foundation, "Medicare: The Medicare Prescription Drug Benefit," October 2010, http://www.kff.org/medicare/upload/7044-11.pdf.

34. Dually eligible beneficiaries are automatically enrolled, whereas less than half of all low-income Medicare beneficiaries not eligible for autoenrollment (because they are not enrolled in Medicaid) actually receive a low-income subsidy. Laura Summers, Jack Hoadley, Elizabeth Hargrave, "The

Medicare Low Income Subsidy Program: Experience to Date and Policy Issues for Consideration," Henry J. Kaiser Family Foundation, http://www.kff.org/medicare/upload/8094.pdf (accessed January 1, 2011).

35. Ibid. Since the Medicare Part D program was originally enacted in 2003 and fully implemented in 2006, the number of benchmark plans available for LIS recipient enrollment has dropped by 26 percent, causing dislocation and premium increases.

36. The Henry J. Kaiser Family Foundation has prepared a particularly helpful fact sheet on prescription drug coverage, http://www.kff.org/medicare/upload/7044-11.pdf (accessed January 1, 2011), as well as numerous other analyses and studies of Part D.

37. These sources are described at https://www.medicare.gov/health-and-drugs/bridging-the-coverage-gap.aspx (accessed January 1, 2011).

38. Indeed, coverage gaps are expected to be sufficiently common that the law does not penalize individuals who experience brief coverage gaps of three months or less. ACA § 1501.

39. Sara Rosenbaum, Emily Jones, Peter Shin, Leighton Ku, "National Health Reform: How Will Medically Underserved Communities Fare?," Geiger Gibson/RCHN Community Health Foundation Research Collaborative, George Washington University, Washington, DC, Department of Health Policy, 2009.

40. Center for American Progress, "Closing the Health Care Workforce Gap," Washington D.C. 2009, http://www.americanprogress.org/issues/2010/01/pdf/health_care_workforce.pdf (accessed December, 31, 2010).

41. Henry J. Kaiser Family Foundation, "The Uninsured and the Difference Health Insurance Makes (Figure 3)," http://www.kff.org/uninsured/upload/1420-12.pdf (accessed December 31, 2010).

42. Testimony of Dr. Peter Cunningham to the Medicaid and CHIP Payment Access Commission, Physician Reimbursement and Participation in Medicaid (September 23, 2010), http://www.hschange.org/CONTENT/1157/1157.pdf (accessed December 31, 2010).

43. Ibid.

44. Ibid.

45. Kaiser Commission on Medicaid and the Uninsured, "Medicaid Beneficiaries and Access to Care," 2010, http://www.kff.org/medicaid/upload/8000-02.pdf (accessed December 31, 2010).

46. Ibid.

47. National Association of Community Health Centers, "What Are Community Health Centers?," http://www.nachc.com/client/US10.pdf (accessed January 1, 2011).

48. Sara Rosenbaum, Peter Shin, Emily Jones, Jen Tolbert, "Community Health Centers: Opportunities and Challenges in Health Reform," Henry J. Kaiser Family Foundation, 2010, http://www.kff.org/uninsured/upload/8098.pdf (accessed January 1, 2011).

49. Ibid.

50. The Health Resources and Services Administration (HRSA) the agency within the Department of Health and Human Services that administers the program, offers a health center locator tool: http://findahealthcenter.hrsa.gov/GoogleSearch_HCC.aspx (accessed January 1, 2011).

51. Ibid.

52. National Association of Public Hospitals and Health Systems, "America's Public Hospitals and Health Systems," 2009, http://www.naph.org/Main-Menu-Category/Our-Work/Safety-Net-Financing/Characteristics-Report/2009-Public-Hospital-Financial-Characteristics-.aspx?FT=.pdf (accessed January 1, 2011).

53. Ibid.

54. The Deputy Assistant Secretary for Population Affairs (DASPA), the agency within the Department of Health and Human Services that administers Title X, offers a family planning locator tool: http://www.hhs.gov/opa/familyplanning/database/index.html (accessed January 1, 2011).

55. ACA § 2303.

56. CMS, State Medicaid Directors Letter, 10-013 (July 2, 2010).

57. Health Resources and Services Administration, "Fact Sheet: The Ryan White HIV/AIDS Program—the AIDS Drug Assistance Program," http://www.hhs.gov/news/press/2010pres/07/adap.html (accessed January 1, 2011).

58. National Association of Free Clinics, http://www.freeclinics.us/ (accessed January 1, 2011). The locator is found at http://www.freeclinics.us/freeclinic.php (accessed January 1, 2011).

59. Under EMTALA, the phrase "emergency medical condition" means: (A) a medical condition manifesting itself by acute symptoms of sufficient severity (including severe pain) such that the absence of immediate medical attention could reasonably be expected to result in (i) placing the health of the individual (or, with respect to a pregnant woman, the health of the woman or her unborn child) in serious jeopardy, (ii) serious impairment to bodily functions, or (iii) serious dysfunction of any bodily organ or part; or (B) with respect to a pregnant woman who is having contractions: (i) that there is inadequate time to effect a safe transfer to another hospital before delivery, or (ii) that transfer may pose a threat to the health or safety of the woman or the unborn child. 42 U.S.C. § 1395dd(e).

60. The phrase "to stabilize" means "with respect to an emergency medical condition described in paragraph (1)(A), to provide such medical treatment of the condition as may be necessary to assure, within reasonable medical probability, that no material deterioration of the condition is likely to result from or occur during the transfer of the individual from a facility, or, with respect to an emergency medical condition described in paragraph (1)(B), to deliver (including the placenta)."

61. An "appropriate transfer" to a medical facility is "a transfer—(A) in which the transferring hospital provides the medical treatment within its capacity which minimizes the risks to the individual's health and, in the case of a woman in labor, the health of the unborn child; (B) in which the receiving facility—(i) has available space and qualified personnel for the treatment of the individual, and (ii) has agreed to accept transfer of the individual and to provide appropriate medical treatment; (C) in which the transferring hospital sends to the receiving facility all medical records (or copies thereof), related to the emergency condition for which the individual has presented, available at the time of the transfer, including records related to the individual's emergency medical condition, observations of signs or symptoms, preliminary diagnosis, treatment provided, results of any tests and the informed written consent or certification (or copy thereof) provided under paragraph (1)(A), and the name and address of any on-call physician ... who has refused or failed to appear within a reasonable time to provide necessary stabilizing treatment; (D) in which the transfer is effected through qualified personnel and transportation equipment, as required including the use of necessary and medically appropriate life support measures during the transfer; and(E) which meets such other requirements as the Secretary may find necessary in the interest of the health and safety of individuals transferred."

62. Sara Rosenbaum, Ross Margulies, "New Requirements for Tax-Exempt Charitable Hospitals," Health Reform GPS, December 20, 2010, http://www.healthreformgps.org/resources/new-requirements-for-tax-exempt-charitable-hospitals.

63. Ibid.

64. Ibid.

65. Ibid.

66. Ibid.

67. Ibid.

68. Ibid.

69. Ibid.

70. Ibid.

71. Ibid.

72. Ibid.

73. Ibid.

74. Ibid.

75. Ibid.

76. *Miranda v. Arizona*, 384 U.S. 436 (1966).

77. *United States v. Powell*, 379 U.S. 48 (1964).

78. *Gideon v. Wainright*, 372 U.S. 335 (1963).

79. Alan W. Houseman, *Civil Legal Aid in the United States: An Update for 2009*, Center for Law and Social Policy, July 2009. In addition to the staff-based programs, the LSC funds one small "judicare program" that delivers services through panels of private attorneys who receive reduced rates to handle civil legal aid cases. This program now also has staff attorneys and paralegals who deliver legal assistance in some cases. In addition, some staff attorney civil legal aid programs have created judicare components or contracted with individual lawyers and law firms, who are paid by the staff program to provide legal assistance to certain groups of clients that the staff attorneys do not represent either because they do not have the expertise or are geographically isolated from program offices. Data obtained from the LSC indicates that of the 93,168 cases closed through LSC-funded programs' private attorney involvement efforts in 2008, 31,052 came from judicare, reduced-fee panels and contracts with private attorneys or law firms. Legal Services Corporation, *Factbook* 2008 (August 2009).

80. See Standing Committee on Pro Bono and Public Service, American Bar Association, Directory of Pro Bono Programs (January 23, 2007), http://www.abanet.org/legalservices/probono/directory.html#.

81. Houseman, *Civil Legal Aid in the United States*, 3; Alan W. Houseman, *The Project for the Future of Equal Justice, The Missing Link of State Justice Communities: The Capacity in Each State for State Level Advocacy, Coordination and Support*, Center for Law and Social Policy, November 2001, http://www.clasp.org/publications/missing_link.pdf.

82. Ibid.

83. Pine Tree Legal Assistance (PTLA) lists 24 national advocacy centers on its website. PineTree Legal Assistance, National Support Centers, http://www.ptla.org/ptlasite/links/support.htm. The Sargent Shriver National Center on Poverty Law lists six additional centers on the inside back cover of the *Clearinghouse Review*.

84. Houseman, *Civil Legal Aid in the United States*, 12.

85. IOLTA programs capture pooled interest on small amounts or short-term deposits of client trust funds used for court fees, settlement payments, or similar client needs that had previously been held in non-interest-bearing accounts.

86. See Alan W. Houseman, Linda E. Perle, *Securing Equal Justice for All: A Brief History of Civil Legal Aid in the United States*, http://www.clasp.org/admin/site/publications/files/0158.pdf.

87. Legal Services Corporation Act of 1974, Pub. L. No. 93-355, 88 Stat. 378, codified at 42 U.S.C. §2996 (1994). The LSC Act does not provide a sunset provision terminating the corporation at a specific date. However, the 1974 Act only authorized appropriations through FY 1977. The Act was reauthorized once in 1977, providing for appropriations through FY 1980. Since 1980, the Act has not been reauthorized; the LSC has continued because Congress has appropriated funds to fund the program.

88. See Legal Services Corporation, *Annual Report 1981*, 8.

89. The story is told in G. Singsen, "PAI—A Time for Reflection," *MIE Journal* (spring 2005): 206.

90. The lawyer is not paid for providing pro bono services. A contract attorney is paid a fee that is lower than the going rate and agrees to take cases of a certain type or from a particular town or county on referral by a legal aid society. A judicare attorney also is paid a reduced fee and is on a list of attorneys from which a client may choose.

91. The first significant effort to dismantle the LSC came in 1981–1984 with the election of President Ronald Reagan and his appointment of Attorney General William Smith, both of whom were explicitly hostile to the program. Reagan proposed to eliminate funding for the LSC in his first budget request and continued in that posture for a number of years, although Congress continued to appropriate funding for the program. The second effort began in 1995 when the leadership of the Republican-controlled Congress sought to eliminate the LSC and replace it with a state block grant program. See Legal Aid Act of 1995, H.R. 2777, 104th Cong. (1995). When that effort failed, the congressional leadership sought to eliminate funding for the LSC over three years. See John McKay, "Federally Funded Legal Services: A New Vision of Equal Justice Under Law," *Tennessee Law Review* 68 (2000): 109–12.

92. Legal Services Corporation, *Documenting the Justice Gap in America: The Current Unmet Civil Legal Needs of Low-Income Americans* (September 2005), http://www.lsc.gov/press/documents/LSC%20Justice%20Gap_FINAL_1001.pdf.

93. Legal Services Corporation, *Documenting the Justice Gap in America: The Current Unmet Civil Legal Needs of Low-Income Americans* (September 2009), http://www.lsc.gov/pdfs/documenting_the_justice_gap_in_america_2009.pdf.

94. American Bar Association, "Legal Needs and Civil Justice: A Survey of Americans," (March 1994), http://www.americanbar.org/content/dam/aba/migrated/legalservices/downloads/sclaid/legal-needstudy.authcheckdam.pdf.

95. McKay, "Federally Funded Legal Services."

96. Houseman, *Civil Legal Aid in the United States*, 12.

97. See http://www.equaljusticeworks.org/post-grad and http://www.skaddenfellowships.org/.

98. College Cost Reduction and Access Act, H.R. 2669 § 301 (2007).

99. See ABA Principles of a State System for the Delivery of Civil Legal Aid, developed to provide guidance to state access to justice commissions and similar entities in assessing their state systems, planning to expand and improve them, and ensuring ongoing oversight of their development. American Bar Association, *Report to the House of Delegates, Principles of a State System for the Delivery of Civil Legal Aid (112B)* (August 2006), http://www.abanet.org/legalservices/sclaid/downloads/06A112B.pdf.

100. Ibid. Clearinghouse Review, *Right to a Lawyer? Momentum Grows* (July 2006).

101. ABA Standards for Programs Providing Civil Pro Bono Legal Services to Persons of Limited Means (1996), http://www.abanet.org/legalservices/probono/standards.html.

102. Ibid.

103. Laurie Barron, et al., "Don't Do it Alone: A Community-Based, Collaborative Approach to Pro Bono," *Georgetown Journal of Legal Ethics*, 23 (spring 2010): 323–51. Elizabeth Tobin Tyler, "Allies Not Adversaries: Teaching Collaboration to the Next Generation of Doctors and Lawyers to Address Social Inequality," *Journal of Health Care Law & Policy*, 11 (2008): 249–94.

104. Stephen L. Isaacs, Paul Jellinek, "Is There a (Volunteer) Doctor in the House? Free Clinics and Volunteer Physician Referral Networks in the United States," *Health Affairs*, 26, no. 3 (2007): 871–76.

105. Peter J. Cunningham, Jessica H. May, "A Growing Hole in the Safety Net: Physician Charity Care Declines Again," Center for Studying Health System Change Health Tracking Rep. no. 13 (2006), http://www.hschange.com/CONTENT/826/826.pdf.

106. Isaacs and Jellinek, "Is There a (Volunteer) Doctor," 871.

107. Ibid., 872.

108. Diane Rowland, James R. Talon Jr., "Medicaid: Lessons from a Decade," *Health Affairs*, 22, no. 1 (2003): 138–44.

109. National Library of Medicine, History of Medicine Division, *The Hippocratic Oath*, http://www.nlm.nih.gov/hmd/greek/greek_oath.html (accessed January 17, 2011). National Library of Medicine, History of Medicine Division, *Hippocrates and the Rise of Rational Medicine*, http://www.nlm.nih.gov/hmd/greek/greek_rationality.html (accessed January 17, 2011).

110. American Medical Association, "Code of Medical Ethics," in *Code of Medical Ethics of the American Medical Association*, ch. 3, art. I, § 3 (Chicago: American Medical Association, 1847), http://www.ama-assn.org/ama1/pub/upload/mm/369/1847code.pdf.

111. Ibid., ch. 1, art. I, § 5; American Medical Association, "Introduction to the Code of Medical Ethics," in Code of Medical Ethics of the American Medical Association, 83 (Chicago: American Medical Association, 1847), http://www.ama-assn.org/ama1/pub/upload/mm/369/1847code.pdf.

112. American Medical Association, Opinion 9.065 ("Caring for the Poor"), in *Code of Medical Ethics* (2001), http://www.ama-assn.org/ama/pub/physician-resources/medical-ethics/code-medical-ethics/opinion9065.shtml.

113. Association of American Medical Colleges, *Learning Objectives for Medical Student Education: Guidelines for Medical Schools*, 9 (1998), https://services.aamc.org/publications/index.cfm?fuseaction=Product.displayForm&prd_id=198&prv_id=239.

114. Scott A. Simpson, Judith A. Long, "Medical Student-Run Health Clinics: Important Contributors to Patient Care and Medical Education," *Journal of General Internal Medicine*, 22, no. 3 (2007): 352–56.

115. American College of Graduate Medical Education, *Common Program Requirement: General Competencies*, http://www.acgme.org/outcome/comp/GeneralCompetenciesStandards21307.pdf (accessed January 17, 2010).

116. Deborah L. Rhode, "Cultures of Commitment: Pro Bono for Lawyers and Law Students," in *Ethics in Practice: Lawyers' Roles, Responsibilities, and Regulation,* Ed. Deborah L. Rhode (New York: Oxford University Press, 2000), 264–82.

117. Ibid.

118. Reginald H. Smith, *Justice and the Poor: A Study of the Present Denial of Justice to the Poor and of the Agencies Making More Equal Their Position Before the Law With Particular Reference to Legal Aid Work in the United States* (New York City: Carnegie Foundation for the Advancement of Teaching, 1919).

119. Ibid., 100.

120. Model Rules of Professional Conduct, Rule 6.1 (1983). Accord American Bar Association Standing Committee on Pro Bono and Public Service, *Supporting Justice: A Report On The Pro Bono Work of America's Lawyers* 6 (2005).

121. Model Rules, Rule 6.1 (1994).

122. Model Rules, Rule 6.1 (2006).

123. American Bar Association Standing Committee on Pro Bono and Public Service. Seventeen states have adopted the rule verbatim or with minor modifications; 26 states have adopted a version of the 1983 rule.

124. Legal Services Corporation, *LSC 2007 Action Plan for Private Attorney Involvement* (2007), http://www.lri.lsc.gov/LRI/LSC_2007_Action_Plan_for_PAI.pdf.

125. American Bar Association Standing Committee on Pro Bono and Public Service, *Supporting Justice II: A Report on the Pro Bono Work of America's Lawyers* (February 2009).

126. Barlow F. Christensen, "The Lawyer's Pro Bono Publico Responsibility," *American Bar Foundation Research Journal,* 6, no. 1 (1981): 1–19. See also Jennifer Murray, "Comment, Lawyers Do It for Free? An Examination of Mandatory Pro Bono," *Texas Tech Law Review,* 29 (1998): 1141–90 (outlining the arguments in favor of mandatory pro bono legal services).

127. Rhode, "Cultures of Commitment," 265.

128. Kellie Isbell, Sarah Sawle, "*Pro Bono Publico*: Voluntary Service and Mandatory Reporting," *Georgetown Journal of Legal Ethics,* 15 (2002): 845–64.

129. Denise R. Johnson, "The Legal Needs of the Poor as a Starting Point for Systemic Reform," *Yale Law and Policy Review,* 17, no. 1 (1998): 479–88; Murray, "Lawyers Do It for Free?," 1162–63 (discussing the administrative difficulties and functional objections to mandatory pro bono service).

130. Office of the Consultant on Legal Education, *Standards for Approval of Law Schools and Interpretations,* 1996 ABA Sec. Legal Educ. & Admissions Bar 31.

131. Office of the Consultant on Legal Education., *Standards and Rules of Procedure for Approval of Law Schools,* 2006 ABA Sec. Legal Educ. & Admissions Bar 18.

132. Association of American Law Schools, *Learning to Serve: The Findings and Proposals of the AALS Commission on Pro Bono and Public Service Opportunities* (1999).

133. Thirty-nine law schools have mandatory pro bono requirements; 116 have formal voluntary pro bono programs. American Bar Association, Chart of Law School Pro Bono Programs (November 3, 2010), http://www.abanet.org/legalservices/probono/lawschools/pb_programs_chart.html.

Chapter 3

Medical-Legal Partnership: A New Standard of Care for Vulnerable Populations

Ellen Lawton, JD
Megan Sandel, MD, MPH
Samantha Morton, JD
Leanne Ta, BA
Chen Kenyon, MD
Barry Zuckerman, MD

As discussed in Chapter 1, a growing body of evidence finds that social and environmental factors fundamentally shape individual and population health. Poor housing conditions, food and energy insecurity, and unequal educational and employment access are a few examples of nonmedical problems that present significant barriers to health for low-income individuals and families across the country. Though a variety of evidence-based public policy programs and public health protections are designed to address such issues, thousands of people continue to lack the basic benefits these programs afford. What is the right set of interventions to address the gap in care for underserved populations? How are these problems related to legal needs? What is medical-legal partnership, and how does it address these issues?

This chapter explores medical-legal partnership (MLP), a healthcare delivery model that incorporates legal services as a vital component of healthcare. It provides an overview of the MLP model: its core components and activities; how MLP transforms medicine and law; and the multilevel impact of MLP on patients, communities, and the broader health and legal systems. Last, this chapter describes MLPs in practice, the national MLP Network and the future of the MLP in light of healthcare reform.

Addressing Unmet Legal Needs as Social Determinants of Health

Recognizing the significant impact of social circumstances on health, Congress and federal and state agencies have created hundreds of safety net programs for low-income individuals and families to reduce the negative impacts of poverty on health and well-being. These programs are designed to address the adverse social conditions that negatively impact health and livelihood and improve quality of life for those in need. Such programs include supplemental nutrition assistance programs, disability benefits, housing subsidies, utility shutoff protections, Medicare and Medicaid, among others.

Although the size, scope and services provided by public health and benefit programs vary, these programs share a common goal: to help individuals and families satisfy their basic needs by invoking the power of laws, regulations and policies. These basic needs can be viewed within the framework of "legal needs," or adverse social conditions with legal remedies. A 2010 article in *Health Affairs* offers an example of how basic needs are often legal in nature:

> A patient might not have enough food, which is frequently seen as a "social" need. But when that patient is wrongly denied Supplemental Nutrition Assistance Program (SNAP) benefits—formerly known as food stamps—what was a social need becomes a legal need, because access to the benefit is prescribed by law.[1]

What Are Legal Needs?

A legal need is an adverse social condition with a legal remedy—that is, an unmet basic need that can be satisfied via laws, regulations, and policies. Unmet legal needs, which can lead to poor health outcomes, are critical social determinants of health.

Material hardships associated with poverty, including hunger, threats to safety, utility access barriers and substandard housing generally constitute unmet basic needs with legal remedies. These unmet legal needs often have important health consequences, particularly for low-income and medically vulnerable individuals and communities. When unmet legal needs lead to poor health outcomes, they become important social determinants of health.

Examples of legal needs that constitute social determinants of health are presented in Figure 3.1.

Given the prevalence of legal needs among disadvantaged populations,[2] targeted interventions to detect and address legal needs have emerged as an important component of local, state, and national safety net programs. Still, thousands of low-income individuals and families continue to confront unmet legal needs.

According to the most recent national assessment of unmet legal needs, low-income households experience on average one unmet legal need per year.[3] Of course, this does not account for the existence of unmet legal needs that are not recognized as such by low-income households—for example, utility shutoffs. A key finding in most legal needs studies is the failure of many respondents to identify problems like poor housing conditions as having legal remedies.[4] In 2003, a statewide legal needs survey in Massachusetts concluded that low-income households confronted an average of 2.4 unmet legal needs per year.[5] These needs remain unmet in part because of the scarcity of low-cost legal intervention,[6] and the fact that civil legal aid organizations are inadequately supported, as discussed in Chapter 2.

The lack of access to low-cost legal services results in underutilization of local, state and federal programs designed to protect well-being and health, leading to acute health problems or, in the case of people with chronic illness, exacerbation of health problems. For example, in some states, up to 50 percent of eligible people are not receiving food stamps due to complex application processes, burdensome documentation requirements, and other administrative and regulatory barriers. This has important public health consequences. Health is undermined at both an individual and population level when people do not receive the benefits or protections that safety net laws and programs afford them,

Figure 3.1 Legal Needs that Affect Health

Legal Need	Examples of Legal Needs That Affect Health
Income/Insurance	Insurance access and benefits Food stamps Disability benefits Social Security benefits
Housing and Utilities	Shelter access Access to housing subsidies (such as Section 8 program) Sanitary housing conditions (such as mold or lead) Foreclosure prevention Americans with Disabilities Act compliance Utilities access
Education/Employment	Americans with Disabilities Act compliance Discrimination Individuals with Disabilities in Education Act compliance
Legal Status	Immigration (asylum, Violence Against Women Act) Criminal record issues
Personal/Family Stability	Guardianship, custody, and divorce Domestic violence Child and elder abuse and neglect Capacity/competency Advance directives Powers of attorney Estate planning

Source: Adapted from C. Kenyon, M. Sandel, M. Silverstein, A. Shakir, B. Zuckerman, "Revisiting the Social History for Child Health," *Pediatrics*, 120 (2007): e734–38. These authors adapted the I-HELP assessment tool.

including a safer environment and better housing, nutrition and healthcare coverage. Although the healthcare system can play a role in mitigating the unwanted health effects of poor social conditions, the traditional medical treatment model will never adequately address or prevent these problems.

For instance, an elderly person continues to be at risk for a fall if he or she is not in a safe housing arrangement. A child living with asthma will continue to experience respiratory problems, no matter how much medicine is administered, if he or she returns to a mold-infested home. Repeated trips to the doctor will not help a cancer patient return to full health if he or she does not have access to adequate nutrition. For these patients and thousands of others, healthcare is necessary but insufficient. The key to better health is improving the social and environmental conditions in which they live, work and play.

A commitment from providers who care for the poor — including healthcare and legal professionals — to ensure that the health-related legal needs of vulnerable populations are met is essential to help make safety net programs more effective and promote better health and well-being.

Questions for Discussion

1. What explains the underutilization of safety net laws and programs designed to protect health of vulnerable populations?

2. What is the relationship between unmet legal needs and health?

Medical-Legal Partnership: A New Standard of Care

As evidence on the significant impact of social determinants of health builds, an increasing number of healthcare, legal and public health professionals have teamed up to address these factors. Across the country, healthcare professionals are turning to lawyers to form MLPs, striving to achieve a new standard of care for low-income, vulnerable populations, joined by legal aid and pro bono attorneys and paralegals.

MLP is a healthcare delivery model that integrates legal assistance as a vital component of healthcare. MLP is built on the understanding of three key factors: (1) the social, economic and political context in which people live has a fundamental impact on health; (2) these social determinants of health often manifest in the form of legal needs; and (3) attorneys have the special tools and skills to address these needs. MLP brings legal and healthcare teams together to provide high-quality, comprehensive care and services to patients who need it most.

MLP: The Core Components

MLP's three core components and activities transform the delivery of health and legal services for vulnerable populations. Although MLP programs vary in many ways, all engage in the following activities: providing legal assistance in the healthcare setting, transforming health and legal institutions and practices and influencing policy change (see Figure 3.2).

Legal Assistance

MLP brings legal professionals into the healthcare setting to address the complex legal needs that confront low-income patients every day. With a focus on early detection of legal problems and prevention of legal and health crises, MLP legal practice is frequently understood as analogous to primary care.

Figure 3.2 MLP Core Components

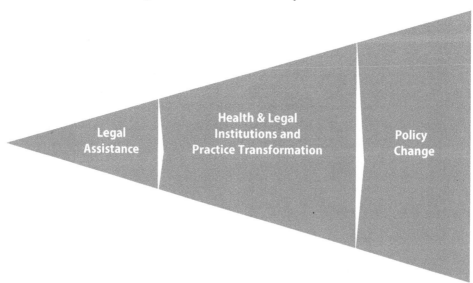

Legal Assistance

Health & Legal Institutions and Practice Transformation

Policy Change

MLP attorneys provide on-site assistance to patients needing legal help in the form of consultations, brief advice and direct legal representation. Cases are referred to attorneys by frontline clinicians, who are trained to screen for and identify patients struggling with unmet legal needs. Attorneys communicate frequently with providers and provide feedback on advocacy outcomes. In this way, MLP is more than a referral service — it is an integrated approach to health and legal services that facilitates critical, efficient, shared problem solving among health and legal teams who care for patients with complex health and legal needs.

The legal issues addressed by MLPs are broad, but all focus on ensuring, through enforcement of legal rights, that a low-income individual's and/or family's basic needs are met. Doctors and other members of the healthcare team often use the assessment tool I-HELP (Income Supports, Housing and Utilities, Education, Legal Status/Immigration, and Personal and Family Stability and Safety) to identify unmet basic needs that may be responsive to legal remedies (see the previous section "Addressing Unmet Legal Needs as Social Determinants of Health").

Transforming Health and Legal Institutions and Practices

MLPs transform health and legal practices in multiple ways, including training frontline providers to screen for, identify and refer patients with potential legal needs; facilitating joint data tracking and the documentation of legal information within patient medical records; and, at the institutional level, providing evidence-based recommendations to conduct quality improvement processes to improve internal systems to better serve patients and families.

MLP staff dedicate a significant amount of resources to the development and delivery of advocacy training curricula to medical faculty, residents, nurses, social workers, attorneys and students. The goals of these efforts are to (1) enhance provider understanding of the social determinants of health and unmet legal needs of patients in their community, (2) increase provider awareness of the resources and interventions available to address these unmet needs and (3) encourage screening for remediable unmet legal needs and appropriate referral of patients who screen positive for potential legal problems. See Chapter 4 for more information on interdisciplinary training.

A critical component of MLP is enhancing a healthcare provider's ability to identify legal needs early and help address them through improved frontline advocacy, since healthcare teams have frequent access to vulnerable populations. Along these lines, MLPs develop and disseminate tools and resources to help providers identify and "treat" legal needs that impact health. For instance, MLP | Boston staff created a form letter for physicians to use when requesting utilities shutoff protection for chronically ill patients. An MLP in Cleveland developed a Special Education Calculator to help physicians stay on top of school timelines when advising families of children with special needs on compliance with the Individuals with Disabilities Education Act (see Chapter 16).

As MLP attorneys become a part of the healthcare team, sharing information with allied professionals in a structured manner is also an important core activity. With patient consent, MLP attorneys share information with frontline providers about patient needs and case outcomes. In fact, a number of MLPs have integrated legal information into patient medical records. Thus, MLPs transform the way that legal needs and the use of available legal resources are tracked and documented.

Finally, through frequent interaction with patients, clinicians and the healthcare system, MLP staff members are in a unique position to identify patterns of unmet need among patient populations, as well as opportunities for institutional and systemic improvement to better address those needs. A core MLP activity is providing evidence-based recommendations to improve the programs and policies within health and legal institutions. Drawing on the combined insight and expertise of health and legal professionals who care for vulnerable populations in their day-to-day roles, MLPs can help make institutional programs and policies more effective and efficient.

Policy Change

Although direct legal assistance and institutional change can improve the health and well-being of hundreds of individuals and families who are cared for in health settings with MLPs, the true power of the MLP model lies in its potential to influence populations via broad-scale policy change. MLPs strive to enact multilevel policy change by leveraging healthcare and legal expertise to improve local, state, and federal laws and regulations that impact the health and well-being of vulnerable populations.

The persistent barriers that prevent many vulnerable patients from receiving legal services warrants increased focus on policy-level advocacy, which impacts entire populations. To ensure the health of vulnerable patients at a population level, MLPs offer special expertise and experience in working with other community groups to promote external system change through (1) ensuring compliance with existing health-promoting laws, (2) supporting enactment of new or amended health-promoting laws and regulations, and (3) opposing enactment of health-harming laws and regulations.

A unique advantage of MLP in the policy realm is the foregrounding of the clinical stories, experiences and perspective in debates regarding laws, rules, regulations and practices—often allowing for strategies outside the traditional litigation model and maintaining a critical focus on how policy will impact health and well-being of real people.

From Practice to Policy
Sample of MLP Policy Activities

Attorneys and frontline healthcare providers from MLP programs have:

- Submitted joint medical-legal comments to the Social Security Administration regarding disability eligibility requirements (Chicago)
- Published Child Health Impact Assessments of housing and fuel assistance programs (Boston)
- Coordinated passage of a city government resolution supporting U visas, a form of immigration relief available to some immigrant survivors of domestic violence and other crimes (Cleveland)

See Chapter 16 for detailed discussion of MLP policy opportunities and analysis.

Transforming Medicine and Law

With its three core components and activities, MLP distinguishes itself as a unique model of care that redefines the scope of activities of the healthcare team and facilitates upstream, preventive legal interventions (see Figure 3.3). This means that legal problems are identified and addressed, thereby preventing subsequent legal health crisis (e.g., eviction, child abuse, asthma hospitalization, etc.).

Figure 3.3 Shifting Paradigms in Healthcare and Law

	PREVAILING MODEL	MLP MODEL
LEGAL ASSISTANCE	• Service is crisis-driven • Individuals are responsible for seeking legal assistance • Primary pursuit is justice	• Service is preventive, focuses on early identification of and response to legal needs • Healthcare team works with patients to identify legal needs and makes referrals for assistance • Aims include improved health and well-being
HEALTHCARE	• Adverse social conditions affect patient health but are difficult to address • Healthcare team refers patients to social worker/case manager for limited assistance • Advocacy skills are valued, taught and deployed inconsistently	• Adverse social conditions with legal remedies are identified and addressed as part of care • Healthcare, social work and legal teams work together to address legal needs, improve health and change systems • Advocacy skills are prioritized as part of the standard of care

Building Capacity in the Healthcare Team

The medical community has long recognized the broad scope of the physician's role, which extends beyond the administration of medicine and treatment of disease to protecting the ongoing health and well-being of the patient. In 1848, Rudolf Virchow, considered the founder of modern pathology, described medicine as a social science: "the physicians are the natural attorneys of the poor, and social problems fall to a large extent within their jurisdiction."[7] More recently, a number of prominent medical societies in the United States and Europe joined together to compose a consensus statement on the professional responsibilities of the modern day physician. The Charter on Medical Professionalism defined the three fundamental principles of the physician's charge as (1) the primacy of the patient's welfare, (2) patient autonomy and (3) social justice.[8]

With growing evidence of how social conditions impact health outcomes and the widely acknowledged view that clinicians' duties encompass more than medical treatment, the rationale for giving the healthcare team a central role in screening for, identifying and triaging legal problems is compelling.

Despite prominent and historical endorsements of the physician's role in addressing social problems, most trainees in medicine are not routinely educated on how specific social influences may cause or contribute to their patients' medical problems.[9] In prevailing healthcare models, the skills needed to address the social determinants of health are not taught, deployed or valued consistently.

There are many possible reasons behind this reluctance to embrace advocacy as a part of standard medical practice. Arguments against clinician inquiry into a patient's social and environmental conditions include a lack of time, as well as a fear of opening Pandora's box.[10] In this context, the Pandora's box reference anticipates a harrowing array of deeply rooted social problems that the frontline provider has neither the tools nor training to address. Without interventions to help mitigate the effects of nonmedical influences, healthcare providers fear uncovering a problem they cannot address. Others have suggested that providers should consider how closely an individual factor or circumstance (such as health insurance or homelessness) has been linked to a specific health outcome when determining whether it is within the realm of their professional responsibility.[11]

Over the past few decades a number of factors have diminished provider reticence to greater investigation of a patient's social milieu. From a scientific perspective, specific aspects of the social environment have become critical as part of modern genomics for complex diseases. Physical and social environments have been shown to trigger gene changes (epigenetics) that contribute to the development of many diseases. On a very practical level, though most clinical teams lack the training necessary to identify and address nonmedical barriers to health, the medical community has embraced a holistic approach to patient care as demonstrated by incorporating nurses, social workers, patient navigators, case managers and other professionals into the patient-centered medical home and other coordinated care models.

As medical homes develop in health settings across the country, MLPs bring an additional set of skills and legal expertise to the table. MLP is built on the idea that having an attorney as part of the team enables and encourages frontline healthcare providers to ask the difficult questions about their patients' social and environmental conditions, knowing that legal help is available if needed. Under the MLP model, clinicians with appropriate training and connection to MLP identify patients with legal needs and refer them to MLP attorneys, thus having a robust effect on health influences previously thought irremediable in the healthcare setting. The increasing presence of skilled legal professionals on the healthcare team thus introduces a set of interventions that can address risk factors related to unmet legal needs.[12]

Evaluations of MLPs as part of medical home and other comprehensive care programs have demonstrated their ability to achieve important legal outcomes[13] and their effects on health outcomes are promising. Table 3.1, from a recent Geiger Gibson/RCHN study, describes the advantages of integrating social workers, patient navigators and MLP attorneys into the healthcare team.

MLPs, like other interdisciplinary team-oriented models, can help relieve the burden on clinical staff by reducing the gap between what vulnerable patients need and the resources that are available to them.

A Preventive Approach to Legal Services

As MLP reshapes and enhances clinicians' roles in patient care, the MLP model has equally significant implications for attorneys and the legal system. The legal profession has a long history of dedicating resources to addressing the needs of low-income, otherwise vulnerable people (see Chapter 2 for a historical and current perspective on legal services access and resources).

Multiple studies repeatedly conclude that vital legal services are not reaching the people who need them. According to the Legal Services Corporation, 80 percent of legal needs experienced by low-income Americans are not being met (see Figure 3.4).[14] Today, the supply-demand gulf between legal aid programs and the low-income people who need their services remains distressingly large. Although complementary legal resources have emerged in the private bar community (pro bono volunteerism) and the non-federally funded advocacy arena, those resources are not sufficient to meaningfully impact the current supply-demand gap.

In the United States, free or low-cost legal services are provided by a range of federally or state-funded legal aid agencies. However, these organizations are chronically underfunded

Table 3.1 Key Attributes of Patient Navigators, Social Workers, and MLPs

	Social Workers	Patient Navigators/Community Health Workers	Medical-Legal Partnership
Services Provided	Psychosocial, emotional support, including grief counseling.	General patient support and health system coordination of services.	Medical and legal assistance with chronic conditions, abuse and other issues preventing health and wellness.
Required Education and Training	A master's of social work (MSW) or bachelor's degree is often required.	No degree or training requirements for lay navigators who are often former patients/survivors of cancer or other diseases and go through onsite training. Can also be registered nurses (RN).	Attorneys, paralegals, healthcare providers, including doctors, nurses and hospital staff can be involved and trained. Some MLP activities are accredited.[a]
Budgets/Salary	Generally paid by hospital/care center as grief counselor or patient services and not a separate program. Median annual wages were $46,650 in May 2008.[b]	Can be paid entirely by hospital/care center or costs can be shared with grants from the American Cancer Society or other groups. 64% of the positions paid new hires less than $13/hour.[c]	42% of MLP sites surveyed had an annual budget between $101,000 and $250,000.[d]
Specific Prevention Groups	Cancer, chronic disease, trauma, and specifically trained for terminal diseases and family support.[e]	General services but most notable for oncology, particularly colorectal and breast cancer.	Began in pediatric setting, but expanded to other low-income patients and their families.
Benefits and Intervention Focus	Organize support for emotional and family needs, especially with chronic and terminally ill patients and their families.	Guide patients through entire process, e.g., cancer screenings, treatment and recovery; navigate patients through combination of insurance and care providers; arrange transportation to medical care; point person for patient through process.	Legal assistance with income supports and benefits like Medicaid; housing assistance to alleviate chronic disease (e.g., mold in home); and family law, including domestic abuse and custody.

Source: Peter Shin, Fraser Rothenberg Byrne, Emily Jones, Joel Teitelbaum, Lee Repasch, and Sara Rosenbaum, *Medical-Legal Partnership: Addressing the Unmet Legal Needs of Health Center Patients,* Geiger Gibson/RCHN Community Health Foundation Research Collaborative (May 2010).

Notes: [a] Ed Paul, Danya Fortess Fullerton, Ellen Cohen, et al., "Medical-Legal Partnerships: Addressing Competency Needs Through Lawyers," *Journal of Graduate Medical Education* 1, no. 2 (2009): 304–9. Available at: www.medical-legalpartnership.org/sites/default/files/page/MLPs%20-%20Addressing%20 Competency%20Needs%20Through%20Lawyers.pdf; [b] U.S. Bureau of Labor Statistics, "Occupational Outlook Handbook, 2010–11 Edition," available at www.bls.gov/oco/ocos060.htm, accessed April 20, 2010; [c] Department of Health and Human Services, Human Resources and Services Administration, Bureau of Health Professions, "Community Health Worker National Workforce Study," last modified March 2007, available at http://bhpr.hrsa.gov/healthworkforce/chw/; [d] Marissa Wise, Kate Marple, Ed De Vos, Megan Sandel, and Ellen Lawton, "Medical-Legal Partnership Network Annual Partnership Site Survey" (2009); [e] U.S. Bureau of Labor Statistics, "Occupational Outlook handbook."

Figure 3.4 Civil Legal Needs of Low-Income Americans

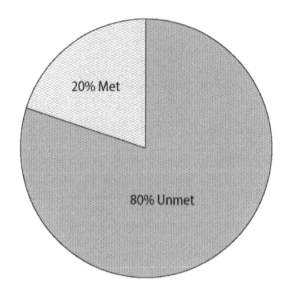

Source: Legal Services Corporation, *Documenting the Justice Gap in America: The Current Unmet Civil Legal Needs of Low-Income Americans* (September 2009).

and cannot meet the needs of clients needing legal assistance. In fact, as of June 2007, one out of two persons seeking assistance from a federally funded legal services organization was turned away.[15]

Across the board, there is a shortage of legal aid attorneys and resources to meet the demand for low-cost legal services. In 2002, for example, there was an average of one legal aid attorney for 6,861 low-income persons, compared to one attorney per 525 people in the general population.[16]

High rates of legal need among low-income populations, coupled with a demand for services that exceeds available resources, contribute to the reality that thousands of low-income individuals and families struggle with unmet legal needs.

This is true both because of limited resources and the fact that many living in poverty are not aware of programs designed to help them. A study of MLP found that 85 percent of participating families who received legal services through their healthcare provider had not used legal resources before, and 78.8 percent were not aware of legal resources prior to MLP intervention.[17]

Moreover, in prevailing legal services models, it is often the case that by the time an individual reaches a legal service provider, his or her legal issue has become a crisis, such as imminent eviction, escalating domestic violence or termination of SNAP (Supplemental Nutrition Assistance Program) benefits.

By placing legal services in the healthcare setting, MLP addresses a multitude of problems facing the current justice system. MLP brings legal assistance to the client, rather than waiting for the client to seek help, often when it is too late. By training frontline clinicians to detect unmet legal needs that are impacting patients' health — no matter how severe — MLP promotes the early identification of legal needs and allows for timely, preventive legal intervention.

MLP attorneys practice preventive law, whereby attorneys work with healthcare providers and patients to (1) identify the root causes (antecedents) of problems that generate needs; (2) understand the broad context in which legal needs arise; and (3) work proactively toward legal or nonlegal interventions that disrupt harmful tendencies or strengthen resiliency within the systems in which the client operates.

First developed by Louis M. Brown, a California lawyer and educator during the second half of the twentieth century, preventive law calls for a restructuring of the risk analysis that attorneys usually conduct to ascertain legal strategies and instead encourages lawyers and their clients to undertake interventions that will "disrupt pathways or environments that are potentially harmful."[18]

In recent decades, many legal services organizations have embraced preventive law principles (operationally if not explicitly) by investing more in outreach to and education of potential clients on a comprehensive menu of legal issues—all in the hope of enhancing self-advocacy and averting the escalation of legal needs.

MLP is a natural opportunity to extend preventive law practice to the healthcare setting on behalf of low-income, medically vulnerable patients.[19] Through MLP, the healthcare setting becomes "a gateway to preventive law for the legal services population."[20]

Questions for Discussion

1. Describe the "Pandora's box" effect as it relates to why some physicians are hesitant to inquire into patients' social and environmental conditions. How does MLP overcome their concerns?

2. How does MLP differ from the traditional social service delivery model in hospitals and clinics? What are some limitations of prevailing models of healthcare and legal services?

3. In what way does MLP reorient legal service delivery toward preventive law?

The Multilevel Impact of MLP

Significant strides have been made to demonstrate the multilevel impact of the MLP model. MLPs seek to impact patients, providers and populations by improving health and well-being, transforming institutions and practices within law and medicine, and improving laws and policies that affect the health of vulnerable communities (see Figure 3.5). Although research gaps exist, pilot studies reveal promising results in each of these domains. For more detailed information about evaluation of different levels of MLP impact, see Chapter 18.

Improved Health and Well-Being

The negative ways adverse social conditions influence health are well documented. For instance, suboptimal urban housing conditions with high levels of mold,[21] dust mites,[22] and cockroach antigen[23] have well-established links to poorer health outcomes in children with asthma. Substandard housing and homelessness also have been linked to higher rates of diarrheal illness, ear infections[24] and lead poisoning.[25] A troubling and widespread "heat-or-eat" phenomenon, in which low-income children who live in cold climates experience impaired growth in the winter because family finances are diverted to heat the home, has been documented.[26] Inadequate school services for children with learning and

Figure 3.5 Multilevel Impact of the MLP Model

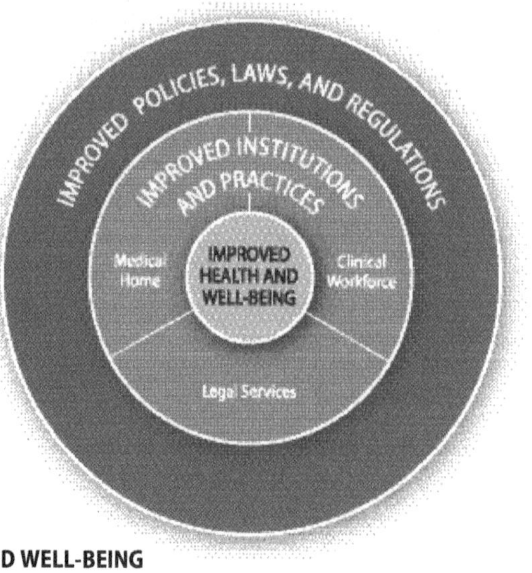

IMPROVED HEALTH AND WELL-BEING
• Less severe chronic disease
• Fewer emergency room visits, shortened hospital stays
• Decreased stress, improved coping

IMPROVED MEDICAL HOME AND INSTITUTIONS
• Cost-effective care and improved healthcare reimbursement
• Better patient compliance
• Improved patient and provider satisfaction

IMPROVED CLINICAL WORKFORCE SKILLS
• Improved provider satisfaction
• Improve capacity to address non-medical determinants of health
• Improved provider communication and screening skills

IMPROVED LEGAL SERVICES AND INSTITUTIONS
• Improved access to health promoting legal services
• Reduction in severe legal needs through early detection
• Cost-effective delivery of legal services

IMPROVED POLICIES, LAWS AND REGULATIONS
• More effective enforcement of laws and regulations that protect vulnerable populations
• Increased alignment of public policy activities with healthcare priorities
• Improved capacity to identify policy gaps and opportunities

behavior issues can lead to school failure,[27] which has been connected with poor health behaviors and poorer health as an adult.[28]

By removing the adverse social factors in patients' lives through preventive legal interventions at both the patient and system level, MLPs likely reduce the risk for illnesses and conditions that are exacerbated by these factors, thereby improving patient health and well-being.

The patient is always at the heart of MLP, and the ultimate goal of these programs is to help low-income individuals, families, and populations get and stay healthy. Although long-run health outcomes are difficult to measure, several pilot studies show that people reported improved general health, less stress, and feeling more empowered after MLP intervention.[29]

Empowering Patients and Clients

MLP provides patients and their families the opportunity to become better informed and to become successful advocates for themselves. In line with the preventive nature of MLP, lawyers educate clients about ways to advocate on their own behalf with administrative agencies, employers, and in private disputes (such as with landlords) before a problem escalates into a crisis. For example, a healthcare provider may refer a female HIV patient to the MLP lawyer about concerns that she may be wrongfully terminated from her job based on absences associated with treatment. The MLP lawyer will educate her about her rights under the Family and Medical Leave Act and the Americans with Disabilities Act. When the patient returns to work, she will be armed with information about her rights. She may also pass on the information she has learned from the MLP lawyer to others in her community who may be struggling with HIV and their rights in the workplace.

Improved Legal Services and Institutions

As mentioned earlier, MLP transforms legal institutions and practices by bringing legal services to the client (as opposed to requiring the reverse) and creating a multidisciplinary advocacy team that can respond to clients' varied needs. By providing legal support to patients in the healthcare setting and partnering with frontline providers, a number of efficiencies geared toward prevention are attained. First and foremost, lawyers practicing in this context are more likely to come into contact with a family when its legal concerns have not yet caused a legal and health crisis, thereby increasing the likelihood that those concerns can be addressed without engaging in stressful and time-consuming litigation.

This preventive stance is representative of the types of legal interventions MLPs carry out in a variety of legal contexts; some programs intentionally prioritize interventions occurring in a preventive context, in the hope of eliminating the likelihood of a future emergency, whether health or legal. For example, housing evictions constitute legal — and health — emergencies, that frequently could have been avoided "upstream" with the right intervention earlier in time. But it takes a reallocation of legal resources toward preventive activities to have a meaningful, sustained preventive impact.

A case example illustrates how prevailing healthcare and legal models often miss crucial opportunities to intervene when health and legal problems arise, and how MLP can help patients avoid crises situations through preventive measures.

Lawyers practicing in this context are also better able to tap healthcare professionals for their expertise as needed over the course of the legal intervention, thereby enhancing service delivery to the client. As an initial matter, lawyers working within MLPs have an advantage in gaining access to crucial medical evidence, whether it is used in testimony for a Supplemental Security Income (SSI) appeal hearing or an affidavit for a special education case or domestic violence-based immigration case. Indeed, the partnership is structured such that the referring provider is part of the advocacy team from the moment of referral to MLP (subject to all relevant confidentiality and ethics constraints). This immediate relationship with the healthcare team allows the lawyers to better evaluate the strength of a client's legal position at the time of referral.

Case Example: How MLP Prevents Legal Needs from Exacerbating Health Problems

Claudia, single mother of 2 children, is diagnosed with stage 2 breast cancer. She needs multiple healthcare visits for diagnosis and staging.

Claudia gets a lumpectomy and starts bi-weekly radiation treatments. She misses a lot of work and loses her job.

MLP could have helped Claudia avoid losing her job by advising her about eligibility for Family Medical Leave Act and other employment protections.

6 months later

Separate from the enhanced availability of clinical evidence, lawyers working in this model benefit from operating in a multidisciplinary context when a client's existing or emerging medical needs (often mental health- or substance abuse-related) intensify, requiring a medical response. In the same way that the clinicians can be assured that a legal professional is available to respond to a patient's legal needs, the lawyers can be assured that healthcare professionals are available to respond to a client's medical needs.

The "one-stop shopping" dimension of MLP provides two complementary benefits to patients with legal questions or concerns—they are able to access legal services in the same location where they receive medical care, and their medical team is more knowledgeable and effective in addressing issues, thereby increasing the available capacity of professionals who can help solve problems. The Geiger Gibson/RCHN study on how MLPs address the unmet needs of vulnerable populations found that MLP empowers patients to speak with their physician about health-related legal problems and access the services they need (see Figure 3.6).

Improved Clinical Workforce

MLP transforms the practice of law and medicine for healthcare and legal professionals. While doctors and other healthcare providers are important advocates for their patients, they may lack the specific knowledge or resources to address social and legal needs.[30] Partnering with lawyers can help healthcare providers address the root social and legal causes of patients' illnesses, thus improving their ability to help their patients.

MLPs promote a culture of advocacy within the healthcare profession by demonstrating how joint efforts among providers who care for the poor can result in long-lasting improvements to institutions, policies and laws. MLPs are premised on the belief that formalizing a culture of advocacy within the healthcare profession will improve the health and well-being of vulnerable populations. In other words, the partnership encourages and empowers clinicians to view and treat their patients in a broader socioeconomic-environmental context, and this will result in better patient care and medical outcomes.

After losing her job, Claudia has no income and she and her children are evicted, become homeless and live doubled up with friends.

MLP could have advised Claudia about eligibility for disability benefits during her illness, as well as other safety net services to avoid homelessness.

Claudia is denied health coverage because she doesn't have a permanent address and stops radiation treatments.

MLP could have helped Claudia provide sufficient documentation to meet application requirements so that she gets health insurance and continues radiation treatments.

12 months later

16 months later

Figure 3.6 The Impact of MLP in Health Centers

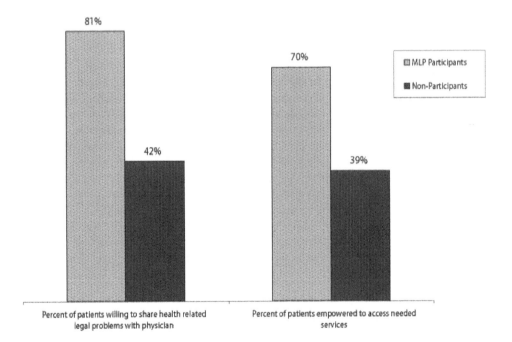

Source: Peter Shin, Fraser Rothenberg Byrne, Emily Jones, Joel Teitelbaum, Lee Repasch, and Sara Rosenbaum, *Medical-Legal Partnership: Addressing the Unmet Legal Needs of Health Center Patients,* Geiger Gibson/RCHN Community Health Foundation Research Collaborative (May 2010). *Data Source:* AHRQ Health Care Innovations Exchange, *Provider-Lawyer Partnerships Increase Access to Health-Related Legal Services and Improve Well-Being for Low-Income Children and Families* (November 2010).

On the legal side, attorneys who work alongside clinicians in healthcare settings have unparalleled access to populations who may benefit from their services. Although many low-income Americans remain unaware of free legal services, most will require and seek medical care in a health institution at some point in their lives. By linking with clients via the healthcare setting in a team-oriented integrated referral system, lawyers reach clients earlier and focus on preventive action to avoid the escalation of legal problems.

Thus, MLP offers both lawyers and healthcare providers a more preventive way to practice: social and legal problems are identified early in the healthcare setting and may be addressed through joint medical and legal intervention.

Improved Medical Homes and Institutions

The Role of Legal Services in the Medical Home

The integration of legal services into the medical home can provide important support to vulnerable patients. Alongside social workers, patient navigators, healthcare providers and other professionals who coordinate their services within the medical home, legal professionals can help ensure that patients' basic needs are met. Incorporating legal professionals within the medical setting is an important pillar of advocacy, because too often legal needs that remain unaddressed evolve into health crises.

MLPs emphasize the interconnectedness of issues impacting the health of low-income patients. Rather than focus on the particular health or legal issue presented by the patient, healthcare providers and lawyers ask questions that help identify the multiple social, environmental and economic factors that may affect patients' and their families' health and well-being.

Additionally, by partnering healthcare providers and lawyers in an interdisciplinary team, MLPs help patients avoid communication problems that often occur when they must rely on multiple service providers at different organizations. MLP serves as both the medical and legal home for patients and their family. The one-stop shopping approach can be enormously helpful to patients who may have a difficult time with transportation, cannot take time from work or school for appointments, or are coping with multiple stressors. MLP serves as more than just a referral from one provider to another; rather, MLP lawyers and healthcare providers collaborate to problem solve and offer patients high-quality, comprehensive and coordinated care. For example, in the Kansas City MLP, a grandmother's Section 8 certificate was terminated after her grandson, who had sickle cell disease, came to live with her. The MLP lawyer relied on the hematology clinic to help expedite the paperwork the grandmother needed to sign, since she was at the hospital so frequently.

Return on Investment for Healthcare Institutions

Multiple pilot studies demonstrate that MLPs provide a positive return on investment for health institutions. Through successful appeals of improperly denied Medicaid or Social Security disability benefits, MLP attorneys can bring new funds to partner health institutions. A study in Health Promotions Practice evaluated the effectiveness of a legal assistance and community healthcare center partnership program in Carbondale, IL. The study found that the partnership was cost-effective and therefore sustainable.[31] It found that in the particular program explored, the healthcare institution received a return on investment that was 149 percent more than the amount it had originally invested in the MLP, largely through Medicaid and other insurance reimbursements. Figure 3.7 provides a tracking model that summarizes the known processes and impacts of the MLP program.

Separately, active and nascent MLP programs are examining pilot qualitative data that reveal the cost reductions that flow from MLP interventions that improve health, including reduction of emergency department visits, increased adherence to clinical regimens for chronically ill patients and more rapid discharge for patients with historically unstable housing situations.

Improved Policies, Laws, and Regulations

MLPs have taken important steps to influence policies, laws and regulations that protect vulnerable populations across the country. Through joint testimony given by health and legal professionals and other coordinated policy efforts, MLPs have petitioned to see an increased alignment of public policy activities with healthcare priorities, and more effective enforcements of laws and regulations that affect the health of low-income people. Examples include improved disability eligibility requirements, housing and fuel assistance programs and immigration relief visas.

See Chapter 16 for a more detailed account of how MLPs are powerful voices in impacting external systems, laws and policies that influence the health and well-being of vulnerable patient populations.

Questions for Discussion

1. MLP was first initiated in pediatric settings and in the area of HIV/AIDS. Why do you think MLP first developed in these settings? Are there similarities between pediatric patients and HIV/AIDS patients that make them particularly susceptible to the benefits of MLP?

2. How does MLP change the way that healthcare providers and lawyers practice?

3. What is meant by the "medical home"? How does MLP fit within it?

4. What is meant by "Institutions and Practice Transformation" and "Policy Change"? Give examples of how MLP may achieve these.

MLP in Practice

A doctor gets very tired of this kind of thing: sending a child with asthma home to an apartment full of roaches and mold; telling the parents of an anemic toddler to buy more and healthier food when they clearly do not have a cent; seeing babies who live in unheated apartments come in again and again with lung ailments. At Boston Medical Center, the hospital that treats more poor people than any other in Massachusetts, pediatricians got so tired of it that they decided to try a radical solution: getting their own lawyers.

New York Times, May 21, 2001.

Figure 3.7 Known Processes and Impacts of an MLP

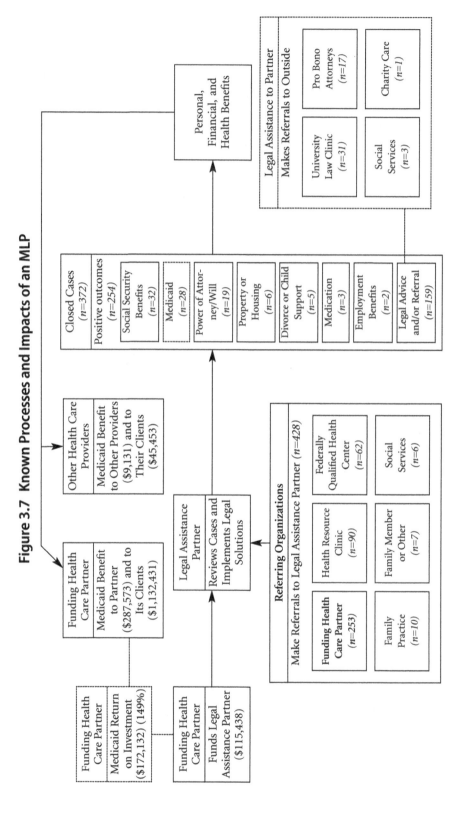

Source: James Teufel, Stephen Brown, Woody Thorne, Diane Goffinet, Latesha Clemons, "Process and Impact Evaluation of a Legal Assistance and Health Care Community Partnership," *Health Promotions Practice*, 10, no. 3 (2009): 378–85.

MLP: A Growing Network

The MLP model was founded in the pediatrics department at Boston Medical Center in 1993. Since then, the idea of bringing legal teams into healthcare settings to address health-related legal needs has spread throughout the United States.

In 2005 there were fewer than twenty MLP programs in the country. Motivated by an article in the *New York Times* in 2001, word of mouth, and a few small academic publications, legal and healthcare professionals passionate about the opportunity to join forces in their community began to take initiative to set up their own MLP programs.

Just five years later, eighty-seven MLP programs were in full gear, serving patients in 225 hospitals and health centers in thirty-eight states across the nation (see Figure 3.8). In 2010 alone, programs in the MLP Network (a voluntary affiliation of MLPs nationwide) provided legal assistance to 13,000 patients and their families and trained 10,000 healthcare providers to recognize the connections between unmet legal needs and health.

Figure 3.8 MLP Network at a Glance (2010)

87 MLP programs in 225 hospitals and health centers	122 community health centers 34 children's hospitals 40 DSH hospitals 29 public hospitals 68 teaching hospitals 80 legal aid agencies 38 law schools 28 medical schools 46 residency programs 46 pro bono law firms

Data Source: National Center for Medical-Legal Partnership, *Annual MLP Site Survey* (2009).

Though most MLP programs all engage in some version of the fundamental components and activities of the model across a continuum of effectiveness, MLPs are diverse. For additional information from the *Annual MLP Site Survey* see Appendix 3.1. Many have grown organically to meet the unique needs of their patient populations and communities. Across the country, MLPs serve children, the elderly, adults with disabilities, the formerly incarcerated and other underserved populations in a variety of health settings. MLP programs have been successfully integrated within a variety of medical specialties, including family and internal medicine, behavioral health and cancer care.

MLPs also partner with a multiplicity of groups and organizations, including health insurers, pro bono attorneys, law and medical schools and state health departments (see Figure 3.9).

In recent years, a number of professional health and legal organizations have publicly supported the MLP model as a best practice. The American Bar Association was an early leader in promoting the MLP model, adopting a resolution in 2007, followed by the American Academy of Pediatrics; in 2010 the American Medical Association issued a call to action encouraging physicians to develop MLPs and physician groups to educate providers on the health impact of unmet legal needs. See Appendix 3.2.

Best Practices and Advocacy Strategies for Medical-Legal Partnership

The National Center for Medical-Legal Partnership is the parent organization to MLP programs around the country. The National Center supports the expansion and

Figure 3.9 MLP Stakeholders

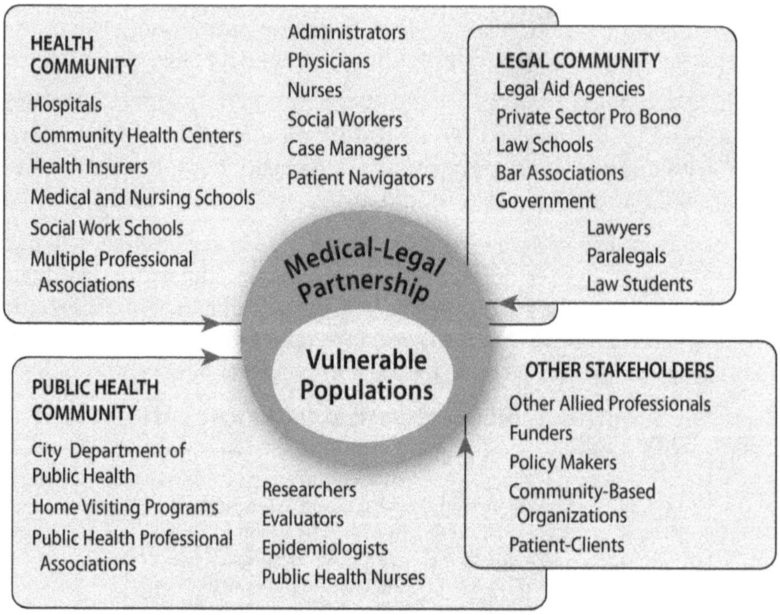

	Administrators	
HEALTH COMMUNITY	Physicians	**LEGAL COMMUNITY**
	Nurses	Legal Aid Agencies
Hospitals	Social Workers	Private Sector Pro Bono
Community Health Centers	Case Managers	Law Schools
Health Insurers	Patient Navigators	Bar Associations
Medical and Nursing Schools		Government
Social Work Schools		Lawyers
Multiple Professional		Paralegals
Associations		Law Students

Medical-Legal Partnership

Vulnerable Populations

PUBLIC HEALTH COMMUNITY		**OTHER STAKEHOLDERS**
City Department of Public Health		Other Allied Professionals
		Funders
Home Visiting Programs	Researchers	Policy Makers
Public Health Professional	Evaluators	Community-Based
Associations	Epidemiologists	Organizations
	Public Health Nurses	Patient-Clients

advancement of MLP by providing technical assistance to MLPs, promoting leadership in law and medicine, coordinating national research and policy activities, facilitating the national MLP Network and disseminating best practices. The National Center has found that many of the most successful MLPs incorporate the following key elements into their programs (see Figure 3.10):

- Joint Planning: Health and legal partners are committed to working together, from the earliest stages of program development, through implementation and expansion.

- Feedback Loop: MLP partners engage in constant communication and keep each other informed of health and legal outcomes. To respect the confidentiality of clients and adhere to ethical guidelines, many MLPs use consent forms during their patient-client intake.

- Metrics: To promote sustainability and raise awareness of the MLP model, MLPs are continually conducting research and evaluation on internal and external impact, quality and effectiveness. Programs across the network have created different tools to guide them in the process of collecting and evaluating data. Each program decides which data points to collect and translate that data to show the impact of MLP on the community.

- On-Site Legal Team: For an MLP to achieve true integration, a lawyer is on site at the health institution as a member of the clinical team.

- Start Small and Set and Align Priorities with the Healthcare Partner: MLPs often focus on a single legal issue area in which the legal team has the most expertise, and stage their intervention in a single clinic or population, expanding to new issues and populations as they grow; successful MLPs align their legal priorities with healthcare partner priorities, from addressing health disparities to reducing unnecessary emergency department visits or improving asthma outcomes.

Figure 3.10 MLP Foundation and Expansion Framework

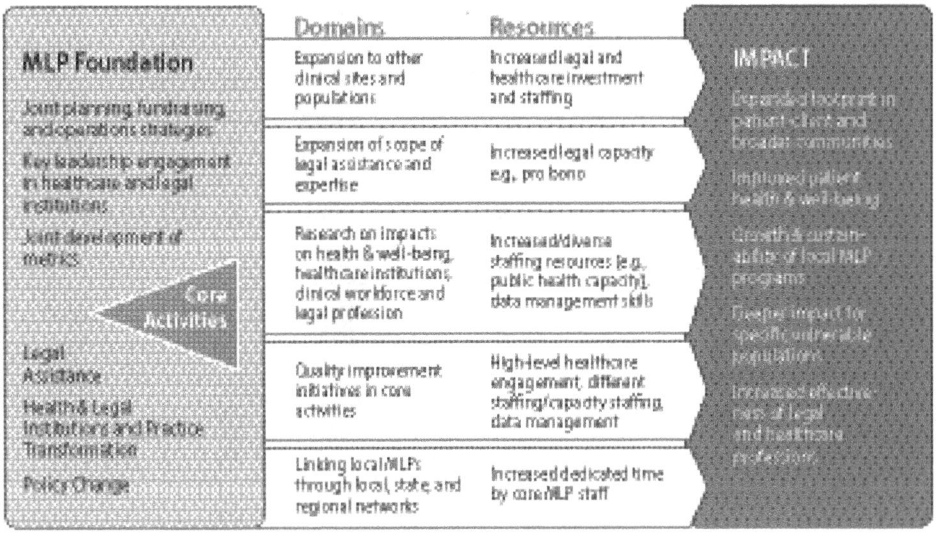

- Systems Improvement: MLP staff dedicate time and resources not only to the direct service aspects of their program but also to improving internal and external systems that can positively impact patients on a population level.

Many existing clinical systems and work flow models enable MLP teams to effectively triage legal issues. To better identify and "treat" legal needs that impact health, advocacy tools can be developed to better leverage those systems, such as:

- Electronic health record (EHR) prompts that direct providers to screen for unmet legal needs.

- Formatted letters in EHRs addressing clinical implications of noncompliance with laws (e.g., housing code violations for asthmatic patients).

- "Calculators" to help pediatricians stay on top of school timelines when advising families of children with special needs about compliance with the Individuals with Disabilities Education Act.

- Policies and protocols for partner healthcare institutions (in collaboration with the office of general counsel) that support provider engagement with safety net protections connected to health (for example, in Massachusetts, only certain healthcare providers can certify that a household qualifies for protection from utility service shutoff due to medical reasons).

MLP and Healthcare Reform: The Next Ten Years

The emerging consensus in the United States on the role of social determinants in impacting health can be coupled with more recent acknowledgment of the potential for legal intervention to address adverse social conditions. Together, this recognition highlights the value of the MLP model in the current healthcare landscape. The advent of healthcare reform in its multiple facets—within the healthcare system as well as at the state and federal level—will provide further impetus to patient- and family-centered healthcare solutions. As payment reform increases its focus on patient outcomes (which will be worse for low-income individuals and families, given the dynamics described), healthcare institutions and professions will require new and effective strategies beyond traditional medical care.

In the wake of healthcare reform, national attention is focused more than ever on the 1,800 community health centers and 1,600 disproportionate share and children's hospitals where America's neediest individuals and families get their healthcare. At the same time, the massive restructuring of the healthcare system that will take place over the next ten to twenty years will value innovative interventions that improve the health of everyone, especially vulnerable (and costly to serve) children and adults. MLP is poised to take advantage of this shift at multiple levels of the healthcare system—from clinical care, to workforce development, to quality improvement. The importance of these tasks is now recognized by government entities that oversee health and legal services delivery, academic institutions, professional associations and national advocacy groups, which are each highly attuned to the opportunities that MLP presents. See Chapter 19 for further discussion of MLP in the context of healthcare reform.

As the MLP model becomes institutionalized in healthcare settings, MLP will be an important tool in implementing disease prevention strategies and delivery system changes envisioned by the 2010 healthcare reform law. MLPs transform the way health is understood, the way medicine is practiced, and the way the healthcare system responds to the needs of vulnerable populations.

---

1. Megan Sandel, Mark Hansen, Robert Kahn, et al., "Medical-Legal Partnerships: Transforming Primary Care by Addressing the Legal Needs of Vulnerable Populations," Health Affairs, 29, no. 9 (2010): 1697–705.

2. Consortium on Legal Services and the Public, "Legal Needs and Civil Justice: A Survey of Americans," American Bar Association (1994).

3. Ibid.

4. Legal Services Corporation, *Documenting the Justice Gap in America*, preface (June 2007); Mark Hansen, Ellen Lawton, "Between a Rock and a Hard Place: The Prevalence and Severity of Unmet Legal Needs in a Pediatric Emergency Department Setting," Medical-Legal Partnership for Children (revised April 10, 2008), http://www.medical-legalpartnership.org/sites/default/files/page/Between%20a%20Rock%20and%20A%20Hard%20Place(2).pdf.

5. Schulman, Ronca & Bucuvalas, "Massachusetts Legal Needs Survey: Findings from a Survey of Legal Needs of Low-Income Households in Massachusetts," Massachusetts Legal Assistance Corporation (May 2003).

6. See http://www.cbpp.org/cms/index.cfm?fa=view&id=2226.

7. Ian F. McNeely, *"Medicine on a Grand Scale": Rudolf Virchow, Liberalism, and the Public Health* (London: Welcome Trust Centre for the History of Medicine at University College London, 2002), Occasional Publication, no. 1.

8. Linda Blank, Troy Brennan, Jordan Cohen, et al., "Medical Professionalism in the New Millennium: A Physician Charter," *Annals of Internal Medicine*, 136, no. 3 (2002): 243–46.

9. Chen Kenyon, Megan Sandel, Michael Silverstein, Alefiya Shakir, Barry Zuckerman, "Revisiting the Social History for Child Health," *Pediatrics*, 120, no. 3 (2007): e734–38.

10. Nancy Kathleen Sugg, Thomas Inui, "Primary Care Physicians' Response to Domestic Violence: Opening Pandora's Box," *Journal of the American Medical Association*, 267, no. 23 (1992): 3157–60.

11. Russell L. Gruen, Steven D. Pearson, Troyen A. Brennan, "Physician-Citizens—Public Roles and Professional Obligations," *Journal of the American Medical Association,* 291, no. 1 (2004): 94–98.

12. Barry Zuckerman, Megan Sandel, Lauren Smith, Ellen Lawton, "Why Pediatricians Need Lawyers to Keep Children Healthy," *Pediatrics,* 114, no. 1 (2004): 224–28.

13. See http://www.medical-legalpartnership.org/impact/research-and-evaluation.

14. Legal Services Corporation, *Documenting the Justice Gap in America,* Preface (June 2007).

15. Ibid.

16. Ibid.

17. Dana Weintraub, Melissa A. Rodgers, Luba Botcheva, et al., "Pilot Study of Medical-Legal Partnership to Address Social and Legal Needs of Patients," *Journal of Health Care for the Poor and Underserved,* 21 (2010): 157–68.

18. Samantha Morton, Thomas Barton, Jack Maypole, "Advancing the Integrated Practice of Preventive Law and Preventive Medicine," in Preventive Law and Problem Solving: Lawyering for the Future, ed. Thomas Barton (Lake Mary, FL: Vandeplas Publishing, 2009).

19. Lisa Pilnik, "Practicing Preventative Law: A Day in the Life of a Medical-Legal Partnership Attorney," *Health Matters,* 27, no. 1 (2008); Evan George, "Legal Aid Clinics Are Just What the Doctor Ordered: Joint Medical-Legal Efforts Help Patients Deal with Inevitable Health-Related Issues," *Daily Journal Newswire,* September 24, 2008.

20. Ellen Lawton, "Medical-Legal Partnerships: From Surgery to Prevention?," *Management Information Exchange Journal* (2007).

21. George T. O'Connor, Michelle Walter, Herman Mitchell, et al., "Airborne Fungi in the Homes of Children with Asthma in Low-Income Urban Communities: The Inner-City Asthma Study," *Journal of Allergy and Clinical Immunology,* 114, no. 3 (2004): 599–606.

22. B. Ehnert, S. Lau-Schadendorf, A. Weber, et al., "Reducing Domestic Exposure to Dust Mite Allergen Reduces Bronchial Hyperreactivity in Sensitive Children with Asthma," *Journal of Allergy and Clinical Immunology,* 90, no. 1 (1992): 135–38.

23. David L. Rosenstreich, Peyton Eggleston, Meyer Kattan, et al., "The Role of Cockroach Allergy and Exposure to Cockroach Allergen in Causing Morbidity among Inner-City Children with Asthma," *New England Journal of Medicine,* 336 (1997): 1356–63.

24. David L. Wood, R. Burciaga Valdez, Toshi Hayashi, Albert Shen, "Health of Homeless and Housed Poor Children," *Pediatrics,* 86, no. 6 (1990): 858–66.

25. James D. Sargent, Madeline Dalton, Eugene Demidenko, et al., "The Association between State Housing Policy and Lead Poisoning in Children," *American Journal of Public Health,* 89, no. 11 (1999): 1690–95.

26. Deborah A. Frank, Nicole B. Neault, Anne Skalicky, et al., "Heat or Eat: The Low Income Home Energy Assistance Program and Nutritional and Health Risks among Children Less than 3 Years of Age," *Pediatrics,* 118, no. 5 (2006): e1293–302.

27. David A. Kube, Bruce K. Shapiro, "Persistent School Dysfunction: Unrecognized Comorbidity and Suboptimal Therapy," *Clinical Pediatrics,* 35, no. 11 (1996): 571–76.

28. James F. Fries, "Reducing Disability in Older Age," *Journal of the American Medical Association,* 288, no. 4 (2002): 3164–66.

29. See MLP research and evaluation landscape, http://www.medical-legalpartnership.org/impact/research-and-evaluation; Anne Ryan, "Connecting the Dots: Stress, Health Disparities and Legal Interventions," presentation at 2010 Medical-Legal Partnership Summit, Arlington, VA (March 25, 2010); Diana Hernandez, "Legal Needs Study Executive Summary," National Center for Medical-Legal Partnership and Cornell University, Boston (2008); Weintraub et al., "Pilot Study of Medical-Legal Partnership."

30. Zuckerman et al., "Why Pediatricians Need Lawyers."

31. James Teufel, Stephen Brown, Woody Thorne, Diane Goffinet, Latesha Clemons, "Process and Impact Evaluation of a Legal Assistance and Health Care Community Partnership," *Health Promotions Practice,* 10, no. 3 (2009): 378–85.

Part II

Working Together: Lawyers and Healthcare Providers as Partners

Chapter 4

Bridging the Health and Legal Professions through Education and Training

Elizabeth Tobin Tyler, JD, MA
Melissa A. Rodgers, JD, MEd
Dana L. Weintraub, MD

As discussed in Chapter 3, medical-legal partnerships (MLPs) allow medical and legal professionals to address the health, social and legal needs of individual families and identify and advocate for policy changes that improve the health of vulnerable populations. An effective interdisciplinary partnership, however, can be difficult, requiring substantial commitment of time and energy to reach across disciplines. Although MLP healthcare providers and lawyers may have shared goals—providing better access to justice and improving health for vulnerable clients and patients—the differences between the professions can make collaboration daunting.

In addition to the common challenges of any interdisciplinary partnership—different objectives, perspectives, training and approaches to problems—healthcare providers and lawyers have historically faced barriers to effective collaboration and have been seen (largely as a by-product of medical malpractice litigation) as adversaries rather than allies. MLPs offer an opportunity for healthcare providers and lawyers to overcome misconceptions and work together toward common goals. But first, they must address the cultural differences that make collaboration difficult.

Effective interdisciplinary education and training is fundamental to successful partnership. From their inception, MLPs have incorporated interdisciplinary training for healthcare providers to help them understand the legal issues faced by their patients and how to work effectively with legal partners. More recently, medical and law schools have adopted a range of opportunities for interdisciplinary medical-legal education. These opportunities include hands-on and classroom experiences that teach the next generation of healthcare providers and lawyers about social and legal determinants of health and practical skills in collaborative advocacy. Because early efforts in medical-legal education have focused primarily on bringing medical and law students together for interdisciplinary opportunities, this chapter focuses primarily on the challenges and benefits of that model. However, as MLPs continue to expand to include multidisciplinary partners involved in healthcare, educators should also work to incorporate nursing, social work, public health and other critical disciplines. Opportunities to include these disciplines in interdisciplinary medical-legal education are discussed at the end of the chapter.

Bridging Two Cultures: Improving Medical-Legal Communication

"Culture is the collective programming of the human mind that distinguishes the members of one human group from those of another. Culture in this sense is a system of collectively held values." — *Geert Hofstede*[1]

No better window exists into the process of shaping the medical and legal cultures than the classroom, where future doctors and lawyers are being "programmed," as it were, to join the ranks of their profession. In medical and law school, one learns not only how to practice medicine and law but how to *be* a doctor or lawyer. The process of shaping cultural cohesion in each profession also creates a cultural divide between professions based on distinctive values and thinking. Bridging these cultures is the underlying objective of medical-legal education and a precondition to collaborative work.

Finding Common Ground and Shared Values

It is no secret that doctors and lawyers have a history of antipathy derived primarily from the role of lawyers in medical malpractice lawsuits. Some of the mistrust, however, comes from perceptions on both sides that the other profession is focused more on self-interest than fidelity to the patient or client.

> Many attorneys, particularly members of the plaintiffs' personal injury bar, continue to characterize too many physicians as avaricious business people more intent on maximizing personal profits than faithfully serving vulnerable people. Conversely, many physicians envision the legal environment within which they are compelled to function as one made unduly precarious, both for the physicians and their patients, by a legal profession too expansive in numbers and too deficient in adherence to professional ethics and public service. The pejorative perceptions enduringly (perhaps today even more intensely than ever) held by members of the legal and medical professions regarding each other, and the resulting psychological tensions and adversarial political and cultural battles in which the respective professions engage, exert important tangible consequences.[2]

Although it is important to acknowledge these existing tensions, the medical and legal professions have, in fact, many shared goals and values. "Both professions have ethical aspirations and legal obligations to provide services to the community and individuals who cannot afford to pay them."[3] In the increasingly complex systems in which doctors and lawyers practice, collaboration is not only desirable, it is essential for achieving better outcomes for patients and clients. As discussed, addressing health problems requires multidisciplinary solutions, including legal interventions.

Collaboration is only effective and beneficial for practitioners, as well as patients and clients, if healthcare providers and lawyers are trained to understand the goals, values and challenges of the other profession. Healthcare providers and lawyers who work in MLPs indicate a greater satisfaction with their ability to address patients' and clients' needs with their practice. One doctor describes how MLP changes his practice:

> Before [joining the MLP] … I might have sent [patients] to legal aid or to a lawyer down the street who I knew. I felt like I was just giving people a phone number and an address and pushing them out into the ether. The patient might not be back for two months, and I'd have no idea what happened.

This is a way where we can actually take care of it in-house, and it just feels a lot more secure. I'm not afraid to go out and look for these issues and look for the social determinants of health, because I know I can do something more proactively about it. Rather than commiserate and gnash our teeth, we can actually make a difference and make positive change for individuals and families.[4]

The Cultural Challenge

Many healthcare providers and lawyers are not well-prepared for interdisciplinary collaboration.[5] Collaboration can be challenging due to differences in professional training, culture and language.

As early as the first year of medical and law school, future doctors and lawyers are taught to pay attention to different things. Both disciplines focus on the particularities of individual experience and the general rules that govern them, but the similarities end there. Medical students assimilate a massive amount of factual information. In the preclinical years, core courses may include anatomy, genetics, microbiology and biochemistry. Law students learn to parse the meaning of words and the logical structure of arguments. First-year law school courses focus on understanding foundation concepts of torts, contracts, property and civil procedure, among other topics. Skills-based and community-based courses in both disciplines attempt to broaden the curricular scope. Nonetheless, working together during and after school requires overcoming the challenges of these "cultural" differences.

Just as establishing and sustaining an MLP can be difficult, interdisciplinary practice can present challenges. Medical and legal education have each traditionally stressed "the professional as an autonomous expert."[6] Each profession has its own specialized jargon. (See *Jargon and Other Language Barriers*.) Even practitioners with the best of intentions about working collaboratively to address the social determinants of health may struggle with effectuating MLP goals in practice. Many of the challenges that are present in MLP practice may be mitigated through thorough, up-front training and planning among the partners.

Finally, doctors and lawyers interact with patients and clients on different schedules and in different timeframes. Doctors may spend on average 20 minutes with a patient,[7] whereas lawyers might spend 30–90 minutes conducting an intake interview. Doctors see patients for regular preventive or monitoring check-ups; for example, pediatricians see patients as frequently as every two to three months in the first year of life, whereas legal services generally see clients only when they are in crisis.

Lack of Background in Other Disciplines

To work together, doctors and lawyers must know enough about each other's profession to understand its value for their own work. With the exception of students who pursue an MD/JD degree, medical-legal courses may be each student's first introduction to the other discipline. Because doctors and lawyers typically lack background in the other's field, they are unfamiliar with the impact of medical or legal conditions on individuals and the potential for interventions from either field to help. For example, doctors may not consider how lawyers can be important allies in policy advocacy around health issues, and lawyers may not recognize how medical data or the involvement of doctors can advance their cause.

Ethical considerations and misunderstandings about the requirements that bind each profession can also cause rifts. For example, requirements for preserving confidentiality and reporting child abuse differ between the professions, and that difference can create misunderstanding if it is not fully explored and explained. See Chapter 6 for a detailed discussion of the different obligations of doctors and lawyers regarding the reporting of child abuse.

Jargon and Other Language Barriers

The medical and legal professions rely heavily on jargon as shorthand. Each profession uses terms that have specific significance within the discipline but evoke a different meaning outside (for example, the word "reasonable" in law or "unremarkable" in medicine). In addition, lawyers may use "legalese" even in casual conversation or email, using words like "hereinafter." Doctors similarly use "medspeak," for example, "erythema" rather than "red." Both professions rely heavily on Latin and Latin abbreviations, such as *ex parte,* meaning "without the other party present" or "bid" (*bis in die*) for "twice daily." Figures 4.1 and 4.2 depict the comical side of doctors and lawyers overusing jargon.

As a result, advocacy tip sheets written by lawyers for their colleagues may not be easily understood by doctors. Similarly, lawyers may have trouble deciphering doctors' notes in a client's medical records. By creating a front-end barrier to communication, jargon interferes with collaboration.

In addition to having different jargon, medical and legal professionals may also define the same term differently based on their specific professional orientation. For example, the term "disability" has different meanings within each profession. Lawyers construe the meaning of disability based on legal definitions provided by federal and state law—and this meaning changes from one area of law to another. For example, a person with a

Figure 4.1 Medical Jargon Snapshots

Translation: "You have a bruised rib."

Figure 4.2 Legal Jargon

"HAVE I LAPSED INTO LEGALESE?"

spinal cord injury who uses a wheelchair and has a full-time job could be considered disabled for purposes of the Americans with Disabilities Act but ineligible for disability-based benefits from the Social Security Administration.

The American Medical Association defines disability as "an alteration of an individual's capacity to meet personal, social, or occupational demands because of impairment."[8] A patient deemed disabled by a doctor, therefore, may or may not meet the legal definition of disability. Conversely, a healthcare provider may not view a patient who meets the legal definition of disability as disabled.

On the most basic level, before doctors or medical students and lawyers or law students can work together, they must understand each other's language and terminology. During medical-legal course work and in professional trainings, speakers and trainees are encouraged to avoid use of medical and legal jargon. When unfamiliar terms and concepts appear, speakers and trainees are encouraged to ask for definitions. As a first step toward reaching a common understanding, a medical-legal glossary is included at the end of this book.

Questions for Discussion

1. Are cultural differences between doctors and lawyers unique? Why or why not?

2. To what extent should doctors and lawyers learn each other's jargon? How far should this interdisciplinary education reach before it means teaching doctors law and lawyers medicine?

3. What other disciplines might be additional partners in serving underserved patients and families? What cultural challenges would emerge in these interdisciplinary collaborations?

Culture Bridging Across the Professions

"In addition to becoming aware of the legal resources ... the introduction into the culture of law itself was an invaluable insight. Seeing how lawyers prioritize components of a patient case differently than doctors gave me a new perspective on how I might approach a patient." — Medical Student

Early communication between doctors and lawyers during their education helps dispel many misconceptions each profession may have of the other. For instance, a doctor may become nervous when contacted by a lawyer regarding a patient, anticipating an adversarial interaction. Likewise, the legal profession may find medical professionals to be uncooperative. Early collaboration can help dispel myths about the other profession, allowing future doctors to view lawyers as colleagues in aiding a patient, and teaching future lawyers to navigate the medical system and work with (rather than against) doctors.

Improved communication between the professions allows for rapid solutions to common problems. For instance, a lawyer working on a case of a Supplemental Security Income (SSI) denial for a disabled patient may contact a doctor to help write a letter for the client. A doctor unfamiliar with legal advocacy may be hesitant to return a lawyer's phone call or be uncomfortable writing a letter on behalf of a patient because of a concern about whether the patient truly is entitled to disability benefits. In contrast, a doctor trained in medical-legal advocacy would perceive the lawyer as a colleague who can help advocate for the patient. The doctor may better appreciate the multiple ways the SSI benefit might help the patient in question (for example, providing extra cash to replace lost earnings and creating a link to Medicaid). In addition, the doctor would see the lawyer as an important resource in writing an accurate letter that incorporates needed medical information and reference to appropriate legal standards. In this way, the medical-legal team can ensure an eligible patient receives needed benefits.

The purpose of medical-legal education, as described, is to not only teach the connections between health and law but also provide students and practitioners with skills in interdisciplinary, collaborative problem solving. To achieve this goal, medical and legal professionals and students need to work together to fully understand and appreciate the other profession.

Questions for Discussion

1. What are the most effective ways to overcome cultural divides between lawyers and doctors?

2. How can lessons learned from MLP be translated into improving relationships between lawyers and doctors beyond MLP?

Case for Medical-Legal Partnership

Dr. Long has never attended an MLP training but heard from a pediatrics colleague that the partnership had helped resolve a housing situation that was causing his patient's asthma to flare up. Dr. Long decides to refer the family of her seven-year-old patient, A, to the MLP for help with his housing situation, which is contributing to A's asthma. During intake, the MLP lawyer assesses the housing case and determines that although the landlord is partly at fault for unsanitary housing conditions, overcrowding in the home is also a contributing factor, one that would put the family at risk of losing its housing altogether if it came to the landlord's attention. The lawyer asks A's mother if moving is an option and learns that A is also about to lose the SSI benefit he had been receiving due to his asthma. (For more information about SSI, see Chapter 7.) The Social Security Administration reviewed A's case and determined that he was no longer disabled.

The MLP lawyer asks Dr. Long to write a letter in support of A's SSI appeal, establishing that the boy remains disabled. Dr. Long is reluctant to write the letter. She does not perceive A as being disabled and is uncomfortable with getting involved in an appeal—especially an attempt to get a monthly payment for a child. The MLP lawyer faxes Dr. Long a copy of the SSI listing for asthma and tells Dr. Long that all she needs to do is read the listing and write a letter explaining that A's asthma rises to the standard of the listing. Feeling pressed, Dr. Long agrees, and the next day faxes the lawyer a handwritten letter that reads: "A has been my patient for three years. He has persistent asthma aggravated by his housing situation. Continued monitoring of his asthma plan recommended." On reading the letter, the MLP lawyer tells a colleague, "I can't believe this doctor doesn't want to help her patient." Meanwhile, Dr. Long tells her colleague, "I guess you need to know those lawyers before they'll help your patient; I'm not getting any follow-up on my referral."

Questions for Discussion

1. What issues did the doctor and lawyer think were the most important for A? What explains their different perspectives?

2. How might the lawyer have helped Dr. Long understand the significance of the SSI case for A and the role her letter would play? What would you have included in an SSI training for the medical team that might have preempted this frustrating experience?

3. Should the lawyer have drafted the letter for Dr. Long to sign?

Educating Professionals to Collaborate with Interdisciplinary Partners

Teaching doctors and lawyers to work collaboratively occurs at two stages in professional development: in medical and law school curricula, when students train for their respective professions, and in legal advocacy training for practicing doctors. The latter includes training for medical residents—medical school graduates who are completing training in their field of practice. Figures 4.3 and 4.4 depict the trajectory of medical and legal education. Also see Appendix 4.1 (Medical Education Competencies) and 4.2 (Preparation for the Practice of Law).

Medical-legal partners have developed diverse models of interdisciplinary education. For medical and law students, these include:

1. the fieldwork model, including externships, advocacy rotations and pro bono opportunities;

2. the law school clinic model, generally affiliated with a medical-legal practice, in which law students work with patients referred by healthcare providers;

3. the mini-seminar model, in which law and medical students participate together in a weekly seminar during a portion of the semester;

4. the integrated course model, in which medical students join law students for a portion of a full semester-long course; and

Figure 4.3 Medical Education

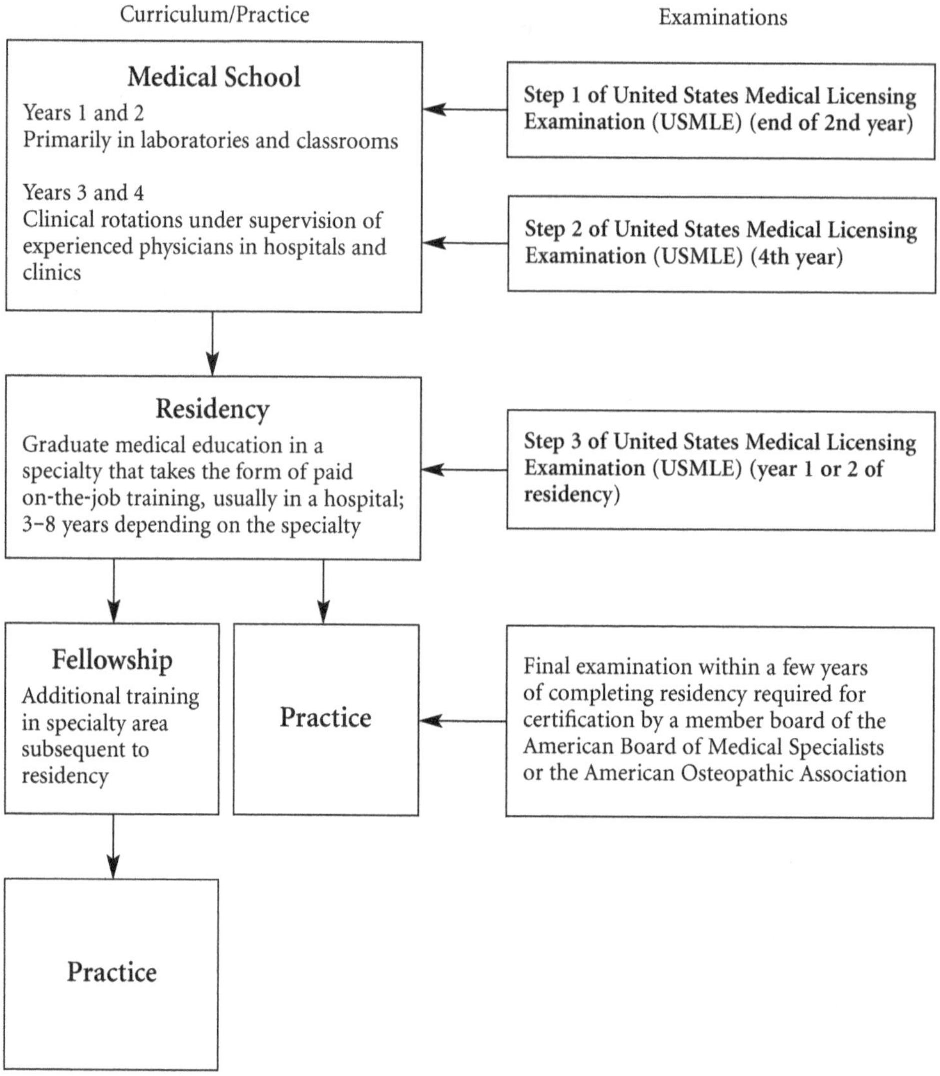

Curriculum/Practice   Examinations

Medical School	Step 1 of United States Medical Licensing Examination (USMLE) (end of 2nd year)

Medical School

Years 1 and 2
Primarily in laboratories and classrooms

Years 3 and 4
Clinical rotations under supervision of
experienced physicians in hospitals and
clinics

Step 1 of United States Medical Licensing Examination (USMLE) (end of 2nd year)

Step 2 of United States Medical Licensing Examination (USMLE) (4th year)

Residency

Graduate medical education in a
specialty that takes the form of paid
on-the-job training, usually in a hospital;
3–8 years depending on the specialty

Step 3 of United States Medical Licensing Examination (USMLE) (year 1 or 2 of residency)

Fellowship

Additional training
in specialty area
subsequent to
residency

Practice

*Final examination within a few years
of completing residency required for
certification by a member board of the
American Board of Medical Specialists
or the American Osteopathic Association*

Practice

---

5. the joint course model, in which both medical students and law students are
    enrolled in a semester-long course that includes fieldwork or a clinic, co-led by
    a doctor and a lawyer.

During residency, MLP advocacy training may include (1) individual trainings of residents,
including rotations with the legal team; (2) group trainings through morning reports,
noon conferences and grand rounds; (3) curbside consultations; and (4) individual and
group training in media and legislative advocacy. This type of training is discussed in
more detail in Training Healthcare Providers about Their Patients' Legal Rights.

The following section sets forth the goals, benefits, challenges and best practices in
teaching medical and law students together. It provides a guide in the development of
medical-legal courses to improve on existing models and propel medical-legal education
forward.

Figure 4.4 Legal Education

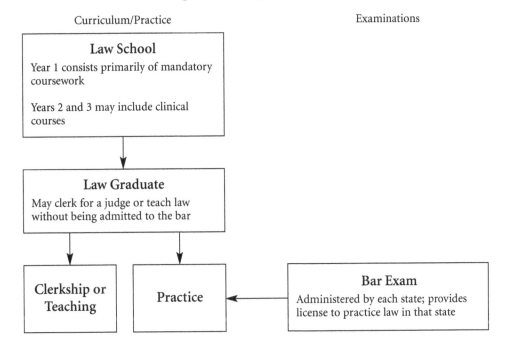

Curriculum/Practice   Examinations

Law School
Year 1 consists primarily of mandatory coursework

Years 2 and 3 may include clinical courses

Law Graduate
May clerk for a judge or teach law without being admitted to the bar

Clerkship or Teaching

Practice

Bar Exam
Administered by each state; provides license to practice law in that state

Teaching Medical and Law Students Together

Goals

The need for interdisciplinary medical-legal education has been recognized since the early twentieth century.[9] Historically, interdisciplinary medical-legal teaching has generally focused on bioethics, professionalism, healthcare systems and policy.[10]

More recently, interdisciplinary education has increased in popularity in medical and law schools as a way to instill skills of collaboration, communication and complex problem solving. Among the many goals of interdisciplinary education cited by its proponents are generating respect and appreciation among the disciplines; teaching teamwork and collaboration; developing a knowledge base about other disciplines; teaching communication among disciplines; and teaching other disciplines' rules, beliefs and ethical principles.[11]

The goals of teaching medical and law students together about MLP include the following: to foster collaboration between the two professions; to develop doctors' and lawyers' complementary skills outside the traditional bounds of their field to address individual problems or social policy; to reduce the "atmosphere of distrust, fear, and antagonism" that stereotypically characterizes attitudes of the professions toward each other; and to encourage and prepare future doctors and lawyers to advocate for underserved populations.

Skills in Collaboration, Problem Solving and Professionalism

Recent reports from the Carnegie Foundation for the Advancement of Teaching, *Educating Lawyers: Preparation for the Profession of Law*[12] and *American Medical Education 100 Years after the Flexner Report*,[13] suggest that both legal and medical education have focused too narrowly on knowledge-based learning and not enough on context-based problem solving, professionalism and ethical decision making. Legal educators have noted the importance of interdisciplinary education for helping students learn the skills necessary to become collaborative problem-solvers:

> Legal problems are like elephants: examining them from only one perspective gives a distorted image of the whole. In order to understand legal problems, lawyers often need to examine them from the perspective of multiple disciplines. Likewise, successful legal problem-solving sometimes means that lawyers need to be able to collaborate with other professionals in order to address a client's problems.[14]

Like their peers in legal education, medical educators agree that interdisciplinary education provides medical students with important skills in collaboration and communication and broadens their understanding of the complexities of their patients' healthcare needs. "Patient needs are interdisciplinary, and improving healthcare is an interdisciplinary effort. Working as part of an interdisciplinary team to provide and improve healthcare is a skill; like other skills it is best learned *during* training, not after."[15]

Reducing Antagonism and Fostering Respect for Other Disciplines

Teaching law and medical students together helps break down barriers between the professions, providing an alternative vision of doctor-lawyer relationships, distinct from the adversarial one most prominently portrayed in U.S. culture. As one educator has noted, "Medicolegal education in law and medical schools can give students a chance to discover 'that the other group did not come congenitally equipped with either horns or pointed tails.'"[16] Teaching law and medical students about the challenges faced by the other profession and how to work together as partners helps overcome the initial antagonism that sometimes exists.

Advocating for the Underserved

Advocacy training for doctors is incorporated into both medical school curricula and residency training; however, "advocacy" is not clearly defined. "Despite widespread acceptance of advocacy as a professional obligation, the concept remains problematic within the profession of medicine because it remains undefined in concept, scope, and practice."[17] We adopt the definition proposed by M. A. Earnest and colleagues: "action by a physician to promote those social, economic, educational, and political changes that ameliorate the suffering and threats to human health and well-being that he or she identifies through his or her professional work and expertise."[18] Law students, on the other hand, are schooled throughout their education in the notion of "zealous advocacy"—that it is their duty to represent the client's interests zealously within the bounds of law.

In addition to teaching advocacy, there has been heightened awareness in both medicine and law of the need to instill in students a sense of professional responsibility for the poor and disenfranchised. In the medical profession, the focus has been on health disparities by race, ethnicity and socioeconomic status. In the legal profession, attention has focused on unmet legal needs, specifically those of unrepresented parties, and recognition that access to the justice system is severely restricted by inability to pay. Both medical and law schools offer opportunities for students to learn about the needs of low-income populations and service models designed to address these needs. The Association of American Medical Colleges (AAMC) and the Accreditation Council for Graduate

Medical Education (ACGME) have developed core competencies for medical students and residents, respectively, that emphasize professional responsibility and engagement with issues of social inequity and advocacy. MLP helps fulfill the six competencies set forth by the ACGME for all residency programs as well as the specific requirement for pediatric residency programs to prepare residents "for the role of advocate for the health of children in the community."[19]

Law schools provide their students the opportunity to serve underrepresented clients through clinical legal education under faculty supervision, supervised externships, and pro bono placements at nonprofit legal organizations or government agencies. Medical-legal education offers a unique opportunity for students to grapple with issues of social justice and disparities and is, in and of itself, an interdisciplinary strategy for addressing these concerns.

Benefits

"Medicine is often not enough to treat disease and illness. Working with patients, especially underserved and uninsured populations, requires an understanding of the socioeconomic factors that affect health. Physicians need to advocate on behalf of their patients and to be able to work with and within the legal and social arena to address health from a multifaceted approach." — Medical Student

"Encouraging earlier interdisciplinary cooperation will benefit later professional relationships. Additionally, the empathy realized by exposing one profession to the structure and nuances of the other will have a dramatic effect on attitudes in the next generation of professionals. Fear of the unknown still pervades medicine's perception of lawyers, and vice versa. Ultimately, the indirect effects of cooperation and understanding between medical and law students may have widespread consequences." — Law Student

MLP has educational benefits that translate into professional synergy, as already described. In the classroom, bringing students from two disciplines together generates energy and curiosity that enriches the learning experience. Students—many of whom may have considered medical school instead of law school, and vice versa—are stimulated by the presence of peers who participate in a different educational experience but have overlapping interests. In addition, students accustomed to typical medical or law school assignments (in general, textbooks for medical students and cases for law students) are challenged to read outside of their field and escape the routine of their educational milieus.

As students apply their knowledge to classroom discussions and problem solving, they expand their understanding to encompass new ways of framing and analyzing issues, as well as different methodologies for reaching conclusions. Future doctors learn about how to spot legal issues for their patients, develop a basic understanding of law and policy as pertinent to patient health and understand when and how to refer a patient for legal help. Future lawyers learn about medical issues that may impact their clients' well-being and how collaboration with doctors can support client advocacy and develop skills to navigate the medical world both culturally and linguistically. Both types of students are taught to focus on prevention or upstream interventions that address the social determinants of health. Medical students learn ways to connect with lawyers and other professionals to help address conditions that may cause or exacerbate patients' health problems. Law students learn that legal advice and assistance may be most effective when problems are detected early, rather than when a client is already in crisis.

As discussed, long-term benefits of medical-legal education include improved knowledge, skill development, and cross-professional relationships. But perhaps the greatest benefit of medical-legal education may be how much fun it is for the students and professors. Anecdotal evidence suggests that medical and law faculty enjoy the interdisciplinary process of curriculum development and teaching, and students enjoy the break from their more typical course experience. Because MLP courses are still relatively uncharted territory, all aspects of course development have great creative potential. Students have the additional benefit of experiencing, in the classroom itself, a medical-legal collaboration in action.

Challenges

The challenges of medical-legal education range from administrative to cultural. Overcoming obstacles to implement a joint medical-legal course requires extensive planning.

Administrative Barriers

A law or medical school that wishes to offer a medical-legal course may not have a partner institution, or, if it does, the two programs may not be on the same academic calendar. Moreover, if it is not carefully conceptualized, the registration process may become an obstacle that dissuades interested students from enrolling. Medical and law schools may cross-list the course, or list it at one school only and require medical or law students to cross-register. Cross-registration requirements can generate confusion. Moreover, medical students may prefer to have a medical school course rather than a cross-registered course on their transcript. There may also be limits to the number of credits students may take within and outside of their programs.

Ensuring that the interdisciplinary course is offered at a time that does not conflict with mandatory or high-demand courses at both the medical school and the law school presents additional challenges. After their first year, law students have a great deal of flexibility in choosing courses, and the curriculum is mostly elective. The greatest challenge for law students is to ensure that a medical-legal course does not conflict with other "public interest" courses, particularly clinical offerings and the seminars that go along with them.

For medical students, scheduling is far more challenging. In general, medical school curricula are divided into preclinical (years one and two) and clinical years (years three and four). Preclinical years are primarily dedicated to mandatory coursework with a full required courseload. Clinical years are primarily dedicated to patient care; the medical student is integrated into the clinical team, taking care of patients in a hospital or clinic. Hours are usually from early morning to early evening and often include overnight call, thereby rendering participation in electives during these years challenging, if not impossible. Therefore, traditional seminar or semester-long coursework may need to be directed at the preclinical medical student, usually during a lunch or late afternoon time slot that may not interfere with other coursework. Some medical schools have developed advocacy, ethics or public health concentrations for students, requiring elective coursework in these concentrations. In these schools, it is important to work with faculty directors in respective concentrations to ensure that the medical-legal course can be counted toward graduation requirements. Other potential conflicts include competing electives, particularly those that include patient care, that may attract medical students in their preclinical years.

Curricular and Learning Style Differences

Beyond administrative barriers, there are differences in the structure and content of medical and legal education that make it difficult to offer a joint medical-legal course. Related to the point about scheduling, the amount of flexible time that medical students have for electives is much less than that of law students. After the first year, law students get most of their credits from electives, whereas—as mentioned—medical students do not. The challenge is magnified when joint medical-legal courses require students to participate in a service learning project practicum as well as a seminar.

Successful course development requires flexibility so that requirements for medical and law students match the educational expectations of their fields. For example, typical law school classes often have paper length requirements, whereas medical school courses do not. It is helpful to address the differences in curricula up front with all students to preserve the collaborative environment.

Medical and law students enrolled in an interdisciplinary course are often at different stages in career development. As noted, first- and second-year medical students—who are the ones most likely to be able to fit a medical-legal course in their schedule—have had limited clinical experience, whereas second- and especially third-year law students may have significant practical experience.

Medical and law students are trained using different pedagogical and learning styles and may prefer information presented in different formats. For instance, the Socratic method that dominates law schools favors argument and expects participation, whereas medical students in preclinical years are accustomed to lectures, supported with slide visuals, with clear take-away points. Medicine and law use facts to different ends: medical schools train students to analyze evidence to reach a diagnosis, whereas law schools train students to marshal evidence in favor of an argument. Medical-legal courses must therefore incorporate multiple teaching strategies that engage all students and build on their different developing skill sets.

Selecting appropriate readings can be tricky as well. Avoiding simplistic or superficial material while also allowing for students' vastly different subject matter background requires thoughtful syllabus development. Does one alternate between medical readings (e.g., medical journal articles) and legal readings (typically cases and statutes), or should the readings sit somewhere in the middle, encompassing legal issues as addressed in medical publications (examples in the journal *Pediatrics* abound), as well as material drawn from the fields of public health and public policy? Similarly, when students engage in fieldwork outside the classroom, determining the proper role for students also poses challenges. What is the role of the medical student when the medical-legal team meets with a patient-client for legal intake? What is the respective role of each student when they engage in advocacy? Do both kinds of students learn as much from the experience? Clarity on roles and instructional goals is essential.

Institutional Responsibility

A final challenge is institutional responsibility for the course. Instructors for medical-legal classes may be on the faculty of the law or medical school or may teach as adjuncts. If the course is taught by regular faculty, the institutional issues are not as complex. Generally, the institution will support the faculty member's time and salary. If instructors are adjuncts, the team should consider in advance whether the law school or medical school—or both—will take financial responsibility for the course.

Best Practices and Advocacy Strategies for Medical-Legal Partnership

Because medical-legal courses have many different approaches and designs, three examples are offered here to illustrate these variations.

Medical-Legal Issues in Children's Health (Stanford University)

Medical-Legal Issues in Children's Health (at Stanford's Medical School and Law School) was developed in 2007 by Dr. Dana Weintraub and Melissa Rodgers, three years after their development of the Peninsula Family Advocacy Program (FAP), an MLP between Lucile Packard Children's Hospital at Stanford University and the Legal Aid Society of San Mateo County. The idea for the course was first developed at the recommendation of then Chief of Staff of Lucile Packard Children's Hospital, Dr. Harvey Cohen, who serves on the advisory committee for the partnership. He encouraged the MLP to expand its training to medical and law students rather than focus solely on practitioners. The course has subsequently expanded to include social work interns, pediatric residents, nurse practitioners and graduate students from the schools of education and journalism.

The course is cross-listed at the medical and law school as an experiential learning seminar open to medical and law students interested in exploring the link between poverty and children's health and in learning how the professions can work together to improve health outcomes for low-income children. The course consists of four components: (1) weekly class meetings with discussions on a series of medical-legal issues (such as asthma, immigration and health insurance) with guest lecturers from the medical and legal fields who are selected for their expertise on each topic; (2) case advocacy work with patient families from FAP; (3) a group project focused on a local or state-level medical-legal policy issue (such as obesity prevention); and (4) a final paper.

Requirements for medical and law students vary based on curricular differences. All enrolled students are expected to participate in weekly two-hour seminars and complete required reading. The first hour of each seminar is an expert-led discussion on the week's topic. A doctor and lawyer specializing in each week's topic are invited to lead the discussion. Topics include poverty, public benefits, health insurance, obesity, immigration, asthma and habitability, employment law, special education and domestic violence. The second half of the class is a student-led discussion of the cases and policy work, which make up the service learning component of the course. Law students are required to participate in both the client case and policy work components of the service learning curriculum, which require on average five additional hours of work weekly. Medical students may elect to either take the course for two credits (participation in seminar portion only) or receive additional credits for participation in the case and/or policy work. Client case work is done in teams of two students, ideally students from different disciplines. Student teams work collaboratively with the lawyers at the Legal Aid Society on one or two cases per semester and, during the second half of class, present a case analysis of the medical-legal issues they identified. For the policy work, the instructors work with students to select a medical-legal policy issue that the entire class works on together.

Medical-Legal Partnership and the Social Determinants of Health (University of California)

The Medical-Legal Partnership course (at the University of California, Berkeley, School of Law and the Joint Medical Program of the University of California, San Francisco, and

University of California, Berkeley, School of Public health) was developed in 2009 by Melissa Rodgers with Dr. Gena Lewis, ambulatory pediatrician at the Children's Hospital & Research Center Oakland and the medical director of the East Bay Medical-Legal Partnership. The course is open to law students and medical students, with the possibility of opening enrollment in the future to public health, public policy and social welfare students. The course also received inception funding from the Berkeley Engaged Scholarship Initiative and incorporates in its design concepts of engaged scholarship—"connecting the rich resources of the university to our most pressing social, civic and ethical problem."[20]

The course consists of three components that include service and empirical research with the goal of students contributing to critical societal issues: (1) a weekly seminar with invited medical and legal guest experts presenting the social determinants of health from a medical-legal perspective (e.g., the link between environmental conditions and asthma, immigration policies and health status, and so on); (2) a practicum wherein students join one of several community-oriented team projects focused on a local, state or federal medical-legal policy issue (e.g., obesity prevention); and (3) an engaged scholarship paper, preferably co-written by law and medical students, that presents the issue each team of students addressed in the practicum, grounds it in empirical findings including a literature review, explains the students' approach to the issue (including goals, outcomes and barriers), and makes recommendation for future research and action. At the end of the semester, students formally present their practicum work and findings to an audience of university faculty and staff, community-based organizations and their peers.

For the seminar, guest speakers are invited on a biweekly basis to give the medical and legal perspective on each topic. Topics include asthma paired with environmental justice law, obesity paired with public health law, prematurity paired with family leave law, developmental disability paired with special education law, and infectious disease paired with immigration law. For the practicum, teams of students (ideally one medical and one law student) choose placements with community-based organizations that have tailored projects to medical-legal student teams. Students devote 4 hours a week on average to the practicum, with the option of receiving credit for up to 12 hours per week of work. Projects range from drafting material for advocacy toolkits, to creating client profiles and preparing clients to testify in the context of an organization's legislative advocacy strategy, to drafting a model municipal ordinance based on empirical research. The greatest challenge for the course is structuring the practicum component in such a way that medical students, who may not have time to participate as fully as the law students, can nonetheless contribute to a policy initiative.

Poverty, Health and Law: The Medical-Legal Partnership (Roger Williams University and Brown University)

Poverty, Health and Law: The Medical-Legal Partnership, a joint medical-legal course at Roger Williams University School of Law and the Warren Alpert Medical School at Brown University, was designed by Liz Tobin Tyler with Brown University Medical School faculty Dr. Alicia Monroe, Dr. Jay Baruch, and Dr. Patricia Flanagan in 2002, in conjunction with the development of the Rhode Island Medical-Legal Partnership for Children (RILMPC) at Hasbro Children's Hospital in Providence, Rhode Island. In addition to the joint medical-legal course, the faculty initiated on-site legal externships and medical clerkship rotations at the hospital for law and medical students to gain hands-on experience in the MLP model.

This course focuses on helping law and medical students develop skills in interdisciplinary problem solving, while exploring the connections between the social determinants of health and access to justice. The course also engages students with questions about professional roles and boundaries and in ethical dilemmas that may arise when working in interdisciplinary practice and with vulnerable patients and clients.

Second- and third-year law students take a full semester seminar, which meets weekly for two hours; six of those sessions are held jointly with Brown Medical School students who enroll in a preclinical elective. Class sessions alternate between the law school and the medical school. Because the law students take a full-semester course, they write reflective essays, complete short case analyses, and work collaboratively with partners to complete a course project that involves creation of a legal education workshop and materials for healthcare providers on issues pertinent to poor families. These projects are provided to RIMLPC for use in its work with healthcare providers and clients at Hasbro Children's Hospital. Medical students complete a reflection paper at the conclusion of each class.

The joint class sessions consist of simulations focused on substantive issues in which health and law intersect, such as poverty and asthma, substandard housing and childhood lead poisoning, educational rights of children with disabilities, and family violence and mandatory reporting. One of the initial classes on poverty is taught using a "poverty simulation," which exposes students to the budgetary constraints of a poor family through a simulated role-play. To prepare for the case simulations on substantive topics, students read interdisciplinary materials that represent the topics from both medical and legal perspectives. In addition, community guests speak about these topics from a variety of perspectives. These include doctors, nurses, lawyers, social workers, community advocates, and patients or clients willing to share their stories. For the case simulations, students are assigned to medical-legal groups that work together to develop an interdisciplinary approach to the problems presented.

The course culminates with a "clinic" at Hasbro Children's Hospital focused on utility challenges. Prior to the clinic, students are taught about the connections between health problems and utility shut-offs (the so-called "heat or eat" dilemma, discussed in Chapter 8) as well as the documented health problems, particularly for children, caused by insufficient heat. At the clinic, pairs of law and medical students advise low-income families facing a utility shut-off for failure to pay about potential budget plan options. The teams also help determine whether someone in the household may qualify for protected status based on health or other considerations under state regulations.

Questions for Discussion:

1. How does medical-legal education prepare doctors and lawyers to address the needs of low-income populations?

2. What are the greatest challenges for medical-legal teaching? What strategies can be used to overcome these challenges?

3. What topics should medical-legal courses cover?

Training Healthcare Providers about Their Patients' Legal Rights

MLPs depend on educating healthcare providers about patients' legal rights so that they know when to make an appropriate referral to the MLP lawyer. Although doctors and other healthcare providers also participate in training lawyers on medical-legal cases, the focus of this section is on training healthcare providers by lawyers or by a medical-legal team.

Types of Trainings

The first model of practitioner training—in which lawyers provide resident doctors (typically interns) with in-depth one-on-one training—bridges the world of medical student education and practitioner education. The goal of these trainings is to alert the new doctor to the medical-legal partnership model, provide examples of the types of issues that may arise in medical practice, and encourage doctors to engage in collaborative practice.

Goals of MLP Training

- To raise awareness among healthcare providers that social determinants of health may have legal remedies

- To enable healthcare providers to identify and address those issues as part of patient care

- To provide healthcare providers with a basic knowledge of potential legal remedies and resources

Intended Outcomes of Training

Healthcare providers will be able to:

- Screen for social determinants of health that have legal remedies

- Triage appropriate legal issues with legal partners

- Treat patients with preventive health and legal care

The most prevalent forms of trainings for doctors are group trainings and curbside consultations. In the former, a lawyer—or ideally a doctor-lawyer team—trains a group of doctors or other healthcare providers on a legal topic relevant to patients' health. Ideal opportunities for provider education are during established educational conferences, such as daily noon conferences that occur in most academic training programs for doctors. Examples of trainings may follow the IHELP acronym discussed in Chapter 3: Income Supports (e.g., access to public benefits); Housing (e.g., habitability conditions as related to asthma); Education (e.g., special education needs); Legal Status (e.g., immigration issues); and Personal Safety (e.g., domestic violence).

A second opportunity for training arises in daily morning reports during which residents or medical students present current cases and attendees work through the case together to establish a diagnosis and treatment plan. This is an excellent forum for demonstrating the impact of medical-legal issues on a patient's health. Finally, grand rounds, a weekly presentation to doctors, residents and medical students, is an ideal opportunity for doctors to increase their knowledge about MLPs and legal issues that may impact the health of the broader medical community.

The curbside consultation involves an issue-specific conversation between a doctor and a lawyer, modeled after specialist consultations routinely used in the medical profession.

Other healthcare providers, including social workers and nurses, also use the MLP curbside consultation model. For example, a doctor may call a lawyer to ask about the requirements for a child to qualify for special education on the basis of autism or whether the family of a U.S. citizen child with undocumented immigrant parents would qualify for public housing. The goal of the curbside consultation is to answer the doctor's immediate question and educate him or her about the issue, identify legal referral needs and also build the doctor-lawyer relationship. It is important to recognize that the goal of the curbside consultation is never to provide patient-specific legal advice through the doctor. Not only would that expose doctors to unauthorized practice of law claims, it would also create legal malpractice risks for lawyers. See Chapter 6 for discussion of these professional ethical concerns in medical-legal partnership. If a patient needs specific legal advice, the appropriate next step is a legal referral. Table 4.1 provides examples of types of MLP trainings.

Table 4.1 Examples of MLP Trainings

Training Venue	Structure
Curbside Consultation	One-on-one conversation between a healthcare provider and lawyer to educate him or her about a legal issue
Noon Conference	One-hour noon lecture offered daily for residents
Grand Rounds	One-hour didactic lecture each week for faculty and residents
Morning Report	One-hour case-based teaching conference for residents
Staff Meetings	One- to three-hour in-service training for a range of hospital or clinic staff
Intern Orientation	One-morning session during intern orientation for new residents
Advocacy Boot Camp	Two- to three-hour intensive MLP training for physicians and allied health professionals; can be CME and CEU accredited

In addition to training doctors, MLPs may also train social workers, nurses, nurse practitioners, case managers and receptionists at staff meetings. Many MLPs offer tools to more easily identify patient needs and find needed resources. The advocacy code card, first developed at Boston Medical Center, parallels a code card used by doctors delineating decision chains to follow in medical emergencies. The advocacy code card instructs the practitioner on steps to take to find housing for a family facing eviction or a food bank for a family without enough food. Some MLPs also use screening tools to identify patients' legal needs before they meet with the doctor. For additional discussion of screening tools, see Chapter 3.

Designing Effective Trainings

Goals

The goal of training healthcare providers is to present them with sufficient knowledge about legal issues affecting health so that they will ask relevant questions, engage in advocacy when needed, and make referrals for legal assistance when appropriate.

The goals of medical-legal education, as discussed, also apply to training. When healthcare providers learn about the importance of legal advocacy in improving health and develop collaborative relationships with lawyers to address the needs of their patients, they change the way they practice medicine and understand health. They not only expand the resources they bring to their individual patients, they also learn how to collaborate to resolve complex policy issues requiring interdisciplinary solutions.[21]

Benefits

"I really appreciate knowing about the MLP and having this as a resource to offer my patients and families." — Pediatric Resident

Training healthcare providers about legal issues that impact health helps remove barriers to addressing the social and legal needs of their patients and their patients' families. Healthcare providers may be hesitant to ask about legal issues due to lack of time or knowledge about resources or because they do not want to make the patient uncomfortable or nervous. MLPs provide needed training in how to ask effectively about these issues and act as a referral resource when issues arise. The partnership between the healthcare provider and lawyer also allows for case-by-case education. For example, after working on a special education case with a lawyer, a healthcare provider can more effectively advocate for future patients.

Trainings also promote the partnership between healthcare providers and lawyers. A practitioner who attends a training on Social Security program requirements will have a better understanding of the importance of his or her role in establishing eligibility for benefits in the future. In addition, face-to-face time with legal experts can give providers confidence that their referrals will be handled well. With interdisciplinary collaboration comes access to the expertise of colleagues who can help make the case for a patient-client's needs — be it safe and sanitary housing, income support, educational services or safety from violence.

At the policy level, provider trainings create an opportunity for dialogue between healthcare providers and lawyers about how to pool resources to address a shared challenge: making a case for pollution reduction in chronic disease "hot spot" neighborhoods, changing school lunch policies across a district or advocating for increased affordable housing units across a state.

Challenges

Training healthcare providers about legal issues is not inherently more challenging than training other nonlawyer groups. However, there are challenges unique to medical-legal training. The greatest challenge for MLPs, perhaps, involves going beyond "preaching to the choir" — in other words, accessing providers who would not ordinarily attend an advocacy training because they do not see its value or connection to their practice. As noted, by integrating medical-legal trainings into existing educational training, more healthcare providers can be reached.

Striking the Right Balance

For lawyers, the challenge in training healthcare providers is striking the right balance between superficial overview and overwhelming detail. Legal analysis focuses on fine point distinctions, and legal practice grounds itself in the able application of detailed legal rules to varying factual situations. As a result, typical legal trainings are rife with nuanced practice tips and feature lengthy handouts ill-suited to the purpose of giving healthcare providers the competencies they need to begin addressing the issues covered in the training with their patients. Medical trainings, by contrast, are designed around a discrete number of "take-home points." Lawyers may need assistance designing appropriate trainings and can benefit from guidance from an MLP's medical director. In addition, we highly recommend having a medical champion present at every training to ensure clinical relevance of the presentation and to point out clinical take-home points.

Understanding Team Members' Roles

Another challenge entails referrals, and specifically the question of whether a patient requires a legal referral or a social work referral. As already explained, one training goal focuses on encouraging healthcare providers to refer their patients to a lawyer for legal assistance, when appropriate. An essential component of these trainings is ensuring that trainees understand the types of problems that implicate legal issues. Involving social workers in trainings can be an important way to explore appropriate legal and social work referrals.

Beyond the Training

Additionally, although institutionalizing referrals from healthcare providers to lawyers is critical, the relationship should not end there. One challenge in MLP is ensuring that true collaboration and follow-up communication occurs between the health and legal staff. This is sometimes difficult when both the healthcare providers and lawyers may have significant demands on their time.

Finally, evaluating training effectiveness presents its own set of challenges. To measure the success of trainings, it is important to evaluate the impact on provider knowledge and practices. Across MLPs, evaluations have included measures of provider knowledge, comfort with legal and social issues and referral patterns.

Best Practices and Advocacy Strategies for Medical-Legal Partnership

Effective medical-legal training should be designed with clear objectives and goals, thoughtful attention to how information is conveyed across disciplines and opportunities for evaluation. Best practices include:

- State learning objectives.
- Develop curricula based on the types of needs that present in the providers' patient population.
- Be careful not to provide too much information about the law, but stress a few relevant points.
- Steer clear of legalese or jargon that is inaccessible to healthcare providers.
- Present problems that patients may face along with straightforward remedies and tools.
- Use an interactive learning environment that engages participants.
- Offer relevant case studies that provide practice in identifying medical-legal solutions.
- Address issues of cultural competency.

Evaluation of training methods and goals is critical. Trainers should collect pre- and post-survey data from participating healthcare providers. Data collection not only helps trainers improve their delivery of information, but also helps them assess if the training is likely to change healthcare providers' practice. Table 4.2 provides examples of trainings and evaluation methods from four MLPs: LegalHealth, Legal Assistance to Medical Patients (LAMP), MLP | Boston and Peninsula Family Advocacy Program (FAP).

Questions for Discussion

1. What skills do the various training models for healthcare providers build, and what needs do they meet?

2. Where, when and how might MLP training be incorporated into the medical school curriculum and residency training?

Case for Medical-Legal Partnership

Dr. Gold participated in a medical-legal training during a noon conference on government benefits conducted by an MLP lawyer. He found the training a bit overwhelming and got lost in the lawyer's level of detail about eligibility requirements for different government programs. He is nonetheless intrigued by the idea of the MLP. The next day Dr. Gold sees a patient, Ms. S., a 60-year-old woman who has diabetes. While taking the social history, he asks her if she has any trouble paying her bills or buying food. Ms. S. replies that she usually runs out of money the last week of the month and has to skip meals and sometimes has to cut her medication in half. Dr. Gold is not sure whether to refer this case to the MLP or the hospital social worker.

Questions for Discussion

1. What types of questions should Dr. Gold ask to determine whether the MLP lawyer might be helpful to Ms. S.? Might the social worker and lawyer each play a role in caring for Ms. S.? How?

2. What were the strengths and weaknesses of the training Dr. Gold received? How might it be improved?

Beyond Doctors and Lawyers: Opportunities for Interdisciplinary Medical-Legal Education and Training

MLPs integrate nurses, social workers and public health workers as part of the medical-legal team. Some also incorporate students from these fields through internship and volunteer programs. Because professionals from these disciplines bring important skills and perspectives to multidisciplinary problem solving, they strengthen and improve the MLP model. Accordingly, educating students and professionals from these disciplines is important to further broaden the benefits of MLP. Although the challenges of bringing two disciplines—medicine and law—together in the classroom may be compounded by adding other disciplines, so are the benefits. The varying perspectives and approaches to problem solving that are illuminated by multiple disciplines in the classroom widen the lens of all participating students. For example, nursing students may bring a different understanding of patient care than medical students do; social work students may illuminate community barriers faced by clients that law students are not aware of. Identifying shared goals can help students with differing perspectives develop collaborative problem-solving skills and a deeper understanding of patient-client needs.

Table 4.2 Description of Selected Medical-Legal Partnership Programs

Types of teaching methods	MLP programs using these types of methods	Examples of topics covered	Types of educational settings	Evaluation Methods	Lessons Learned
Didactic sessions	Legal Health	Bring advocacy to practice	Grand rounds	Pre-post test evaluations	Important to have take-home messages clear
	Legal Assistance to Medical Patients (LAMP)	Forms 101 (disability, others)	Resident conferences		Case-based learning essential
	Medical Legal Partnership | Boston (MLP | Boston)	Improving your patient's housing	Rotation block conferences		
	Peninsula Family Advocacy Program (FAP)	Your patient and the workplace / Immigrants and healthcare system / **Health and legal decision making**	Staff meetings	CME/advocacy Boot camps	
Direct one-on-one teaching around cases	Legal Health / Legal Assistance to Medical Patients (LAMP)	Income supports / Housing and utilities	Continuity clinics / Primary care outpatient blocks	Qualitative evaluations	Feedback as crucial teachable moments
	Medical Legal Partnership | Boston (MLP | Boston)	Employment and education	Inpatient wards		
	Peninsula Family Advocacy Program (FAP)	Legal status (i.e., immigration) / Personal stability (i.e., advanced directives, guardianship)			
Block courses or rotations (required or elective)	Medical Legal Partnership | Boston (MLP | Boston)	Learn social disparities in health	Electives	Pre-post evaluation	Model grids essential
	Peninsula Family Advocacy Program (FAP)	Learn legal topic knowledge above	Required courses	Qualitative evaluation	Project examples helpful
		Apply knowledge for use in project around legal solutions to disparities	Poverty simulations	Project evaluation	

Source: Ellen Cohen, et al., "Medical-Legal Partnership: Collaborating with Lawyers to Identify and Address Health Disparities," *Journal of General Internal Medicine* 25 (Supp. 2) (2010): 136–39.

Following is a discussion of ways the disciplines of nursing, social work and public health may offer opportunities for interdisciplinary education focused on MLP for vulnerable patients and populations.

Nursing

The American Nursing Association defines nursing as "the protection, promotion, and optimization of health and abilities, prevention of illness and injury, alleviation of suffering through the diagnosis and treatment of human response, and advocacy in the care of individuals, families, communities, and populations."[22] Because nurses are often the first providers to assess the needs of a patient and his or her family, they are important partners in MLP. As the Institute of Medicine notes, nurses are particularly poised to identify social and environmental conditions that affect health: "The close interaction of nurses with patients and the 'on-site' aspects of nursing care provide tremendous opportunities for nurses to detect previously unrecognized health problems, including those related to environmental exposures, and to initiate appropriate interventions."[23] Nurses are natural allies in MLPs because of their orientation toward a broader understanding of the social context of patient health, problem solving and partnership with other professionals.

Like other members of the healthcare team, nurses need to be exposed early in their education to interdisciplinary collaboration.

> For effective teamwork, the educational preparation of all health professionals— nurses, physicians, and allied health professionals—needs to place a greater emphasis on skills needed for interprofessional collaboration, such as negotiation, critical thinking, and mutual problem-solving. In addition, there must be opportunities for interdisciplinary interaction throughout professional education and clinical practice, and existing barriers to interdisciplinary practice must be removed.[24]

Because nurses may be educated on different tracks, MLPs and their academic partners will need to develop flexible models for incorporating nursing students into interdisciplinary courses and other educational opportunities.

Social Work

Just as nurses are important partners in developing an effective healthcare team that can address the social determinants of health, social workers are critical allies in MLPs. With the profession's emphasis on addressing and advocating for the basic needs of vulnerable individuals and populations, social workers brings skills and resources to the partnership. Consider the preamble to the National Association of Social Workers Code of Ethics:

> The primary mission of the social work profession is to enhance human well-being and help meet the basic human needs of all people, with particular attention to the needs and empowerment of people who are vulnerable, oppressed, and living in poverty. A historic and defining feature of social work is the profession's focus on individual well-being in a social context and the well-being of society. Fundamental to social work is attention to the environmental forces that create, contribute to, and address problems in living.[25]

Social work involves a range of activities that are important to improving interdisciplinary approaches to complex problems. These include direct service to individuals, including providing counseling, helping clients navigate a range of government and nongovernment agencies, community organizing, education and outreach and policy development and implementation.

In the healthcare context, social workers may be specially trained as medical or public health social workers who focus specifically on the needs of patients and their families. Typically, medical or public health social workers address the needs of particular patients and populations, such as those with chronic or terminal illness, but may provide services to patients and their families in a range of healthcare settings. They advise and support patients and caregivers and help connect families with needed resources outside the healthcare setting.[26]

Because social work education includes both classroom and significant field placement hours, it offers excellent opportunities for incorporating both medical-legal education and internship placements. Including social work students in medical-legal courses not only brings a different orientation and perspective about the problems faced by patient-clients and their families, it also helps students from the different professions to better understand their own roles and boundaries. For example, although a social worker may be critical in helping a family navigate a state bureaucracy when they apply for the Supplemental Nutrition Assistance Program, a lawyer may be needed if the family is unlawfully denied benefits and seeks to appeal the denial.

Public Health

Public health professionals analyze a range of issues affecting population health, such as "improving access to healthcare, controlling infectious disease, and reducing environmental hazards, violence, substance abuse, and injury."[27] The preventive orientation of public health interventions—addressing health problems "upstream"—fits closely with the goals of MLP: to identify and intervene early before problems escalate. Although traditionally public health has focused on broad interventions such as immunization or emergency response during epidemics, public health educators and practitioners increasingly focus on interventions directed at specific, vulnerable populations and at addressing health disparities.

The Association of Schools of Public Health MPH Core Competencies reflect a focus on incorporating the social determinants of health and development of interventions to address health disparities into the curriculum. They define competencies based on "social and behavioral sciences" as:

> The social and behavioral sciences in public health address the behavioral, social, and cultural factors related to individual and population health and health disparities over the life course. Research and practice in this area contribute to the development, administration, and evaluation of programs and policies in public health and health services to promote and sustain healthy environments and healthy lives for individuals and populations.[28]

The broader focus of public health students on systems and upstream interventions brings a critical discussion to the medical-legal classroom or partnership. Although lawyers and law students may be taught to think about public policy and systems change, they are generally not trained to understand the use of data in formulating and influencing policy. Because of their expertise in analyzing data and policy, public health practitioners are important partners in efforts to change systems both within and outside the healthcare system—an important component of the MLP model.

Best Practices and Advocacy Strategies for Medical-Legal Partnership

The Health Law Partnership in Atlanta (HeLP) offers externship opportunities for graduate students in law, public health, nursing and social work to work on site at their MLP locations. Participants assist with client representation and thereby gain an understanding of the multiple determinants of children's health, experience interdisciplinary approaches to problem solving and develop experience in dealing with the health issues of low-income children and their families. By offering experiential educational opportunities to students from multiple disciplines, HeLP offers students the opportunity to learn from the perspectives and professional orientation of other disciplines while also building capacity for future MLP practitioners.

Case for Medical-Legal Partnership

Sam has been referred to a public health clinic that specializes in serving low-income HIV-positive adults. He is 24 years old, is HIV-positive, and was recently released from prison, where he served 1 year for drug possession. When he was released he moved in with his brother and his family. This living arrangement is causing tension between Sam and his brother's wife, and he is afraid that soon he will be homeless. He has no health insurance coverage. He recently applied for the state's Medicaid program but was denied.

The clinic has an MLP. The MLP team includes partnering doctors and nurses, as well as a social worker and a lawyer. Additionally, the clinic is partnering with the public health program at the local university to identify the health and social challenges faced by HIV-positive adults. An MPH student from the program is working on site with the MLP team.

Questions for Discussion

1. Describe the role of each professional in the MLP team in addressing the problems Sam faces.

2. How can Sam's situation help the public health student identify systemic issues affecting the HIV-positive population served by the clinic? What strategies might the team identify to prevent poor health outcomes for this population?

Conclusion

Just as MLP has the potential to transform the healthcare delivery model, medical-legal education may help shape the way that healthcare teams, including doctors, nurses, social workers, public health workers and lawyers are trained in their professions. The complex problems faced by low-income and vulnerable patients and populations require professionals who understand the importance of comprehensive and interdisciplinary solutions. Infusing skills in collaboration and interdisciplinary problem solving early in professional training will produce more thoughtful and effective practitioners and policy makers who understand the connections between social conditions, the law and health.

Notes

Elizabeth Tobin Tyler would like to thank Dr. Patricia Flanagan, Dr. Alicia Monroe and Dr. Jay Baruch for their collaborative spirit and willingness to take risks in creating

"Poverty, Health and Law," as well as the many medical students from Brown University and law students from Roger Williams University who continue to inspire us as teachers and learners. Melissa Rodgers would like to thank her clients at the Legal Aid Society of San Mateo County and her medical colleagues at Lucile Packard Children's Hospital at Stanford, especially Dr. Dana Weintraub, for inspiring the creation of the Peninsula Family Advocacy Program and "Medical-Legal Issues in Children's Health"; Dr. Gena Lewis at Children's Hospital and Research Center Oakland and the East Bay Medical-Legal Partnership for crafting and co-teaching "Medical-Legal Partnership and the Social Determinants of Health" with her at UC Berkeley; and finally the many funders whose generous support made her work possible. Dana Weintraub thanks Melissa Rodgers for her partnership in developing the Peninsula Family Advocacy Program and "Medical-Legal Issues in Children's Health" at Stanford University's Medical and Law Schools, and Brooke Heymach, for her ongoing leadership of these programs, along with all the attorneys and staff of Legal Aid Society of San Mateo County for their ongoing commitment to justice for all; the outstanding medical, law, social work, nursing and other graduate students who continue to learn from, teach and inspire each other and their professors; Brandon-Luke L. Seagle for his outstanding research on the history of medical-legal education; and the families who inspire us in our work.

1. Geert Hofstede, *Cultures and Organizations: Software of the Mind* (New York: McGraw-Hill, 1991).

2. Marshall B. Kapp, "The Hundred-Plus-Year War between Physicians and Attorneys: Peace in Our Time?" *Annals of Health Law, Florida State University*, Research Paper no. 424 (2010).

3. Peter D. Jacobson, Gregg M. Bloche, "Improving Relations between Attorneys and Physicians," *Journal of American Medical Association*, 294, no. 16 (2005): 2083–84.

4. Charles Vega, Residency Program Director, University of California, Irvine, Department of Family Medicine. Interview with the National Center for Medical Legal Partnership (2010).

5. Elizabeth Tobin Tyler, "Allies not Adversaries: Teaching Collaboration to the Next Generation of Doctors and Lawyers to Address Social Inequality," Journal of Healthcare Law & Policy, 11 (September 2008): 249–94.

6. Edgar Schein, Diane W. Kommers, *Professional Education: Some New Directions* (New York: McGraw-Hill, 1972), 36–39.

7. Lena M. Chen, Wildon R. Farwell, Ashish K. Jha, "Primary Care Visit Duration and Quality: Does Good Care Take Longer?" *Archives of Internal Medicine*, 169, no. 20 (2009): 1866–72.

8. L. Cocchiarella, G. B. J. Anderson, eds., Guides to the Evaluation of Permanent Impairment, 5th ed. (Chicago: American Medical Association, 2001).

9. Abraham Flexner, *Medical Education in the United States and Canada, A Report to the Carnegie Foundation for the Advancement of Teaching*, Bulletin no. 4 (New York: Carnegie Foundation for the Advancement of Teaching, 1910). Jerome Frank, "Why Not a Clinical Lawyer-School?" *University of Pennsylvania Law Review and American Law Register*, 81, no. 8 (June 1933): 907–23.

10. Tobin Tyler, "Allies not Adversaries." David B. Wilkins, "Redefining the 'Professional' in Professional Ethics: An Interdisciplinary Approach to Teaching Professionalism," *Law and Contemporary Problems*, 58, no. 241 (Summer 1995). Linda Morton, "Teaching Creative Problem Solving: A Paradigmatic Approach," *California Western Law Review*, 34 (1998): 375–79. Linda Morton, "A New Approach to Healthcare ADR: Training Law Students to be Problem Solvers in the Healthcare Context," *Georgia State University Law Review*, 21 (2005): 965, 971–72, 975–77. Benjamin J. Naitove, "Note and Comment: Medicolegal Education and the Crisis in Interprofessional Relations," *American Journal of Law & Medicine*, 8 (1982): 293–304 (quoting Frederic K. Spies et al./ "Teaching Law Students in the Medical Schools," *Surgery*, 77 [1975]: 793–95). Frank, "Why Not a Clinical Lawyer-School?" Wadlington, "The Law-Medicine Center 50th Anniversary Symposium: The Field of Health Law: Its

Past and Future: Some Reflections on Teaching Law and Medicine in Law School Since the '60s," *Health Matrix,* 14 (2004): 231. Martin Lloyd Norton,"Development of an Interdisciplinary Program of Instruction in Medicine and Law," *Journal of Medical Education,* 46 (1971): 405. Eric S. Janus, Maureen Hackett, "Justice, Ethics, and Interdisciplinary Teaching and Practice: Establishing a Law and Psychiatry Clinic," *Washington University Journal of Law & Policy,* 14 (2004): 209. Christopher Peabody, Alison Block, Sharad Jain, "Multi-Disciplinary Service Learning: A Medico-Legal Collaboration," *Medical Education,* 42, no. 5 (2008): 533. William M. Sage, "Physicians as Advocates," *Houston Law Review,* 35 (1999): 1548–50. J. J. Whyte, "Mock Ethics Trial for Medical Students and Law Students," *Academic Medicine,* 68 (1993): 844.

11. Anita Weinberg, Carol Harding, "Interdisciplinary Teaching and Collaboration in Higher Education: A Concept Whose Time Has Come," *Washington University Journal of Law & Policy,* 14 (2004): 15–22.

12. William M. Sullivan et al., "Educating Lawyers: Preparation for the Profession of Law," *Carnegie Foundation for the Advancement of Teaching* (2007): 191–92.

13. Molly Cooke et al., "American Medical Education 100 Years after the Flexner Report," *New England Journal of Medicine,* 355 (2006): 1341.

14. Kim Diana Connelly, "Elucidating the Elephant: Interdisciplinary Law School Classes," *Washington University Journal of Law & Policy,* 11 (2003): 13–14.

15. Linda A. Headrick et al., "Continuous Quality Improvement and the Education of the Generalist Physician," *Academic Medicine,* 70 (Supp. 1) (1995): S104–8 (emphasis in original).

16. Naitove, "Medicolegal Education and the Crisis."

17. M. A. Earnest, S.L. Wong, S. G. Frederico, "Perspective: Physician Advocacy: What is It and How Do We Do It?" *Academic Medicine,* 85, no. 1 (2010): 63–67.

18. Ibid.

19. E. Paul, D. F. Fullerton, E. Cohen, et al., "Medical-Legal Partnerships: Addressing Competency Needs through Lawyers," *Journal of Graduate Medical Education,* 2, no. 4 (December 2009): 304–9. Accreditation Council for Graduate Medical Education, *Pediatrics Program Requirements* (last modified January 5, 2011), http://www.acgme.org/acWebsite/RRC_320/320_prIndex.asp.

20. E. Boyer, "The Scholarship of Engagement," *Journal of Public Outreach,* 1, no. 1 (1996): 11–20.

21. M. Sandel, M. Hansen, R. Kahn, et al., "Medical-Legal Partnerships: Transforming Primary Care by Addressing the Legal Needs of Vulnerable Populations," Health Affairs, 29, no. 9 (September 2010): 1697–705.

22. American Nurses Association, *ANA Definition of Nursing* (last modified January 5, 2011), http://www.nursingworld.org/EspeciallyForYou/StudentNurses.aspx.

23. Institute of Medicine, Nursing, Health and the Environment, *Executive Summary* (1995), http://www.nap.edu/openbook.php?record_id=4986&page=2.

24. Ibid.

25. National Association of Social Workers, *Code of Ethics* (Washington, DC: National Association of Social Workers, 1999).

26. United States Dept. of Labor, Bureau of Labor Statistics, *Occupational Outlook Handbook, 2010–2011 Edition, Social Workers,* 2010, http://www.bls.gov/oco/ocos060.htm.

27. Association of Public Health Schools, *What Is Public Health? Frequently Asked Questions* (last modified January 5, 2011), http://www.whatispublichealth.org/faqs/index.html#career_faqs3.

28. Association of Schools of Public Health, *Schools of Public Health Goals toward Eliminating Racial and Ethnic Health Disparities* (2008).

Chapter 5

Client and Patient Relationships: Understanding Cultural and Social Context

Lisa Bliss, JD
Sylvia Caley, JD, MBA, RN
Robert Pettignano, MD, FAAP, FCCM, MBA

Effective interdisciplinary collaboration and problem-solving in a medical-legal partnership (MLP) require sensitivity to and understanding of the context of patients' and clients' lives. Because the MLP is premised on problem-solving, it is important to understand the client/patient's social context in a broad sense, not solely based on the presenting medical or legal problem. Moreover, MLPs provide services for the most vulnerable populations — low-income families, immigrants, children and the elderly. Developing an understanding of the relationship between living conditions, socioeconomic status, culture and health is critical to effective problem solving on behalf of such populations.

Successful medical-legal advocacy results from a shared understanding of the complex cultural and social factors that influence the patient's health problems. In addition, cultural context influences relationships between healthcare provider-patient, lawyer-client as well as healthcare provider-lawyer. Interdisciplinary approaches to problem solving are most effective when the client/patient relationship is central, and practitioners engage with the patient or client's personal "narrative." This chapter begins by describing the practice of narrative listening and becoming attuned to what client and patient stories tell us. It then addresses the role of cultural differences in relationships between professionals and clients/patients, what it means to be culturally competent, and approaches to cultural competence education. Finally, it addresses best practices for culturally competent client and patient practice in an MLP. Although this chapter focuses primarily on relationships between doctors and patients and lawyers and clients, the key issues raised apply to the many professionals involved in MLP, including nurses, social workers and others engaged in service delivery.

Narrative Listening: What Client and Patient Stories Tell Us about Justice and Health

Both medical and legal professionals are trained to obtain and rely on information provided by the patient or client to define, clarify and craft a solution to a problem. Although the methods of obtaining and using information may differ between these fields, both professions rely on questioning and listening skills to obtain accurate, relevant and complete stories from patients and clients. Each has its own unique structure, hierarchy, technical expertise and highly stylized language, and each ultimately has the responsibility to act in the best interest of the patient or client.

Professional Training: How Well Are Doctors and Lawyers Taught to Listen?

Medical Education

The signature pedagogy of medical education is marked by bedside teaching and clinical rounds, where medical students and residents learn their profession by working directly with patients. This clinical experience in medical school generally takes place after two years of training in basic science.[1] Thus, the culture of medicine is to school physicians "on the job." Residents treat patients who have real health issues under the close supervision of attending physicians. Accordingly, medical students become very familiar with the environment and the issues that they will face as practicing physicians. A piece of that familiarity for medical students is direct experience in working with patients from different cultures. They are influenced by the approach and preferences of the attending physician, which inculcates the culture of doctoring. The apprenticeship is an experience of socialization into the overt and hidden culture of medical practice.

Doctors are in the business of translating stories and interpreting scientific data to diagnose illness in individual patients. To translate a patient's story of illness effectively requires empathetic listening. Teaching empathetic responses is a goal of many medical school curricula.[2] Scholars of narrative medicine theorize that the key to empathetic communication is the ability to elicit, interpret, and translate a patient's illness story.[3]

Obtaining essential information from patients entails encouraging, supporting and listening carefully to their narratives. Deciphering important information is fundamental to problem solving. Despite medical schools' commitments to training students to listen to patients, even the best physicians sometimes jump to diagnosis without fully listening to what the patient deems important. Honoring the role of the narrative in the development of the doctor-patient relationship promotes trust and helps establish good rapport from the outset.

Legal Education

Legal scholars have recognized that legal training and culture impact the attorney-client relationship. Lawyers are trained to "spot legal issues" from the facts presented by the client and may therefore be predisposed to sort clients and their stories into predetermined narratives or "stock stories" that are familiar to them.[4] The danger is that the lawyer then becomes the owner of the story, and the client narrative is diminished. If he or she is not careful, a lawyer's "translation" of a client's case may visit another injustice on a client.[5] To be an effective, patient-centered advocate, a lawyer must not only listen carefully to a client's story, but take care in the "retelling." For example, a low-income client may not self-identify as "poor," even though he or she may fall within the federal poverty guidelines for income. A lawyer, in an effort to portray such a client as sympathetic, may use the word *poverty* or other descriptions in legal documents, which could inadvertently cause the client shame or distress.

Many law students do not initially appreciate the significance of the client as the source of important factual information or that some information can only be learned by listening carefully to the client. Identifying the client's perceptions, opinions, and concerns as well as his or her strengths and resources, is vital to developing a legal strategy and a solution that will achieve success as the client defines it.[6] To improve sensitivity to the client narrative as well as cultural differences, some scholars have advocated the implementation of a cultural competence curriculum for law schools.[7] Some law students may be exposed to cultural competence training in clinics or other courses that focus on the work of the lawyer and the lawyer-client relationship, but such exposure is entirely dependent on the interests of the professor. Cultural competency training for healthcare providers and lawyers is discussed later in the chapter.

Eliciting and Translating the Narrative: Challenges in Practice

The Medical Interview

A physician (or other healthcare provider) gathers information about the problem at hand by soliciting a patient's narrative during the process of taking his or her history. The history follows a prescribed path of questions related to the health complaint, history of the present illness, past medical history, family history, social history and a review of systems, all designed to elicit information about the problem. Physicians then use the physical exam and various tests and procedures to verify, confirm or refute the patient's description of the problem. Effective diagnosticians emphasize the role and importance of the patient history in uncovering the medical problem.[8] Thus, the patient's description of the problem, the physician's observations of the patient and the clinical findings are each key components of problem solving. Table 5.1 shows the types of information gathered during a patient history and physical exam. See Appendix A for an example of the information contained in a medical record.

Table 5.1 The Patient History and Physical Examination

History	Physical
• Patient identification information • Chief complaint • History of present illness • Past medical history • Family history • Psychosocial history • Review of systems	• General state of the patient • Vital signs • Skin • Lymph nodes • Head, eyes, ears, nose and throat • Neck • Chest • Heart • Breast • Abdomen • Male genitalia/pelvic • Rectal • Musculoskeletal • Peripheral vascular • Neurologic

When patients schedule a visit with a physician, they bring two stories with them — their oral narrative and the story revealed by their bodies. Physicians explore both to develop a diagnosis and care plan. The patient provides a narrative that subsequently is "doctored up"[9] to provide a tight, formulaic description of the illness. The patient's experiences and story, however, may become lost in this translation. When the doctor's version of the narrative is reduced to writing, the memorializing of the subjective and objective findings followed by the assessment and plan further reduce the profile of the patient's story. Yet as one doctor describes, taking the time to penetrate the patient's narrative may provide important insight that will inform the plan for care:

> [I] tell [my patient] I have to learn as much as I can about his health. Could he tell me whatever he thinks I should know about his situation? And then I do my best not to say a word, not to write in his chart, but to absorb all that he emits about his life and his health. I listen not only for the content of his narrative, but for its form—its temporal course, its images, its associated subplots, its silences, where he chooses to begin in telling of himself, how he sequences symptoms with other life events. I pay attention to the narrative's performance— the patient's gestures, expressions, body positions, tones of voice.[10]

Interpreting the Narrative: Non-Compliance

A 45-year-old patient is seen in the diabetes clinic. A review of his medical record reveals numerous notations in the progress notes that the patient is noncompliant. The MLP team is frustrated. The notations of noncompliance may have contributed to the denial of the patient's application for Supplemental Security Income (SSI) benefits.

Members of the health team, noting that a patient has failed to follow the care plan—missing appointments, failing to take prescribed medications, failing to consent to treatments and procedures, failing to follow a diet or resisting certain behaviors—frequently label the patient as noncompliant. This is often noted in the chart without regard to the reasons for noncompliance. For subsequent caregivers who read the notes, this label is accepted as accurate, and if not true is very difficult to overcome.

Although it may serve as a protective measure for a healthcare provider, applying the label that a patient is noncompliant has consequences.[a] A blanket determination of noncompliance may tarnish the relationships the patient may need to establish with subsequent healthcare providers. The label becomes permanent. Discerning the underlying reasons making adherence to the care plan difficult or impossible may improve outcomes and reduce otherwise preventable and expensive care. The legal members of the team can address issues that surface during a thorough patient narrative. The care team should explore reasons for a patient's noncompliance, which may include inadequate funds to purchase prescribed medication, insufficient patient or parent education to implement the care plan, and fear or lack of understanding. For example, when patients and families are advised to apply for public benefits but fail to act, it is often because of concern that the application may threaten their chances for citizenship at some point in the future.

Questions for Discussion

1. What kinds of questions might the MLP team ask the patient in this case scenario to determine why the treatment plan has not been followed?

2. What is the role of the healthcare provider in assessing the reasons for non-compliance? What is the role of the lawyer?

Note: [a] Fitzhugh Mullan, Ellen Ficklen, and Kyna Ruban, eds. *Narrative Matters: The Power of the Personal Essay in Health Policy* (Baltimore: Johns Hopkins University Press, 2006), 211.

The ultimate goal of the doctor-patient relationship is patient-centered care. This type of care considers the patients' culture, their personal preferences and values, their family situations and their lifestyles in the medical decision-making process. It also involves ensuring that appropriate, high-quality and cost-effective care is delivered with the patient and/or family members as an integral part of the care team. Unfortunately, development of this relationship may be rushed in the emergency department and also in primary care settings where physicians must book patients in rapid sequence and see many people during a normal workday.[11] The fast pace in these environments challenges the professional to discover and understand the whole patient in a short period of time.

The professional's drive for efficiency may impede his or her ability to listen effectively to the patient's narrative and pick up important details. A study of the healthcare provider's role in soliciting and developing patients' concerns[12] found that doctors often interrupt patients frequently and do not give patients a chance to tell their story:

> Because of that "facts only" attitude, doctors frequently interrupt patients before they get to tell their full story. In recordings of doctor-patient encounters, where both doctor and patient knew they were being taped, the doctor interrupted the patient in his initial description of his symptoms over 75 percent of the time. And it didn't take too long either. In one study doctors listened for an average of sixteen seconds before breaking in — some interrupting the patient after only three seconds. And once the story was interrupted, patients were unlikely to resume it. In these recorded encounters fewer than 2 percent of the patients completed their story once the doctor broke in.[13]

Despite the time constraints and challenges of contemporary medical practice, healthcare providers should work to balance efficiency with listening to the patient narrative.

The Legal Interview

Unlike the standard history and physical exam in medicine, in which medical students and residents are trained, there is no standardized client interview process from which a lawyer develops knowledge and understanding of a client's problem(s). Many MLP lawyers have developed a "legal checkup" designed to screen for multiple legal problems. Other law practices have developed tools for use in screening and interviewing. A thorough interview may reveal that a client has multiple legal issues. A client's problems generally fall into three categories: (1) legal problems that clients are aware of and articulate; (2) problems clients are unaware of or do not articulate; and (3) nonlegal problems that affect a legal matter.[14] See Appendix B for an example of a legal intake. Nonetheless, like physicians, lawyers rely on oral communication and engage in questioning to develop a narrative of the problem(s) from the client's perspective. However, it has been observed that lawyers often interview prospective clients with a view to what is important to the lawyer, and most interview forms are focused on seeking answers to legal questions rather than on actually *listening* to the client. The ability to listen carefully is one of the most important skills an attorney can develop.[1]

The Story Comes First

After the initial introductions, the client is asked by the lawyer what happened. The client begins to narrate.

Client: Several years back I was in a car accident ...

Lawyer: Where?

Client: What? Oh, here in town. Fifth Street. By the old off-ramp.

Lawyer: When was that?

Client: Uh, 1999 I think.

Lawyer: You think? Don't you know? This is very important! Your statute of limitation might already have passed!

Client: My statute of what?

Lawyer: Your statute of limitation. Tell me as best you can when the accident occurred.

Client: Uh, 1999, but, and I was just gonna get to this, the accident is where I first hurt my back, but that isn't what caused me to be in this wheelchair.

Lawyer: Well, what did?

Client: I was getting to that ...

The lawyer's interruption on a point immaterial to the overall story erected a communications wall between the attorney and the client. The attorney is clearly focused on what is important to him, not on what is important to the client. The attorney begins by talking about legal issues that he has not even broached with the client because he fails to understand that this interview is about the client, not about the law. The law can come later. The story has to come first.

Source: Excerpted from Anthony L. DeWitt. "Therapeutic Communication as a Tool for Case Theming." *American Journal of Trial Advocacy*, 29 (2005): 401–2.

In law school, listening may be undervalued when the framework for instruction is the Socratic method and a great deal of energy is devoted to preparing oral arguments. (See Chapter 4 for discussion of how law students are taught using the Socratic method.) For lawyers, a great premium is placed on speaking well. Generally, lawyers want to use their technical skills and expertise to solve a problem, correct a wrong or protect a right and would prefer to avoid the emotional or psychological issues affecting their clients. Law students have historically learned that law is rational and logical, based on generic conceptual rules that are devoid of religious, ethical, political or other underpinnings. Thus, legal education generally tends to focus on what is "legally important" or relevant and filters out a broad range of other factors that can affect the client and the case.[16] Just as doctors may reduce the patient's story to a diagnosis, lawyers run the risk of reducing the client's narrative to a cause of action. The manner in which lawyers make a statement or ask questions affect the response to or the quality of the information provided by the client.

The ultimate goal in creating a lawyer-client relationship is to solve the client's problem using a client-centered approach to representation. This perspective acknowledges that legal problems typically raise both legal and nonlegal concerns for clients, that attorney-client collaboration will maximize effective problem solving and that clients are in the best position to make important decisions affecting their own lives.[17] A client-centered approach can be hampered in the name of efficiency by failing to obtain all pertinent information from the client or rushing to judgment on the nature of the problem.

Go in with the Right Attitude

- *Focus all of your attention on the client.* Do not tap a pencil, doodle or look away from the client when the client speaks.

- *Review case intake material before the meeting.* Organize in advance relevant medical records, articles, letters and synopses of events. Being prepared helps you ask better questions.

- *Avoid distractions and interruptions.* Do not allow others to interrupt the meeting. Seat yourself appropriately close to the speaker and conduct the interview in a location where you will not be distracted (e.g., not in the conference room overlooking the thirteenth hole).

- *Acknowledge the client's emotional state.* Be prepared with tissues for clients who will break down while telling their story. Be patient; do not rush the client.

- *Set aside your opinions about the case.* You are there to find out what the client knows. The client already thinks you know plenty about the law, and in most cases, you will not have to convince him.[a]

Note: [a] Anthony L. DeWitt. "Therapeutic Communication as a Tool for Case Theming." *American Journal of Trial Advocacy*, 29 (2005): 401–2.

Questions for Discussion

1. How well are medical and law students taught to listen to their patients' and clients' story? Should training in how to listen be part of learning to be a healthcare provider or lawyer?

2. Can you recall a time when you visited a professional whom you felt did not listen to you? How did you feel? What contextual or cultural factors do you think may have interfered with the professional's ability to listen?

Listen and Notice: Stories Revealed

Receiving the Narrative: A Broader Understanding of Health and Justice

Even in the absence of additional differences between the professional and the patient-client, the professional's work culture and communication style are frequently discordant with that of the patient-client. Professionals are accustomed to providing and receiving information in a structured manner, with both oral and written communication containing a beginning, middle and end. Most professionals want to be able to get straight to the point. All too often, patients/clients do not follow this structured form of storytelling and instead weave a circuitous path to the point of the story. Frequently, patients and clients focus on the part of the story causing the greatest emotional stress, even though this may have little or no bearing on the medical or legal problem for which the person is seeking assistance.[18]

The patient's perception of an illness may be quite different from a doctor's interpretation of disease. For instance:

> *Disease* is taken to refer to the medical definitions of sickness by professionals, and is explained from the perspective of biological and physiological etiology, patterned clinical manifestations, course, and outcome. Disease is considered objective and universally similar in nature. In contrast, *illness* refers to the patient's psychological construct of the perception, experience, and understanding of suffering. Illness is subjective and open to cultural impact.[19] These two concepts may or may not overlap in some way, but in many ways they are different. From a cultural point of view, a physician needs to know and comprehend the whole situation—not just the medically oriented concept of the disease, but also the patient's and his family's perception of the illness.[20]

If a clinician fails to listen effectively, the patient may not tell the whole story, ask the most frightening questions or feel acknowledged. These gaps could result in a diagnostic work-up that may miss the correct diagnosis, cost more than it needs to, and create other risks to the therapeutic relationship, such as noncompliance.[21] Narrative medicine scholars have quoted Hippocrates: "It is far more important to know what person the disease has than what disease the person has."[22]

A person's race, ethnicity or other cultural characteristics may also influence the information provided to the professional. Patients may filter descriptions of symptoms because to talk about them would be unseemly in the presence of a person of the opposite sex. Similarly, clients may not be forthcoming with crucial facts because to do so might be embarrassing. A lawyer may contribute to the impaired communication by overtly or covertly devaluing the client. How one listens to the patient's or client's story is critical to helping them be forthcoming with important details.

Active Listening

Calibrating the senses—eyes, ears, touch and intuition—to hearing the stories of culturally diverse patients and clients requires developing good listening skills. Despite the fact that listening is critical to almost all interactions, few do it well. Another truism may be that we fail to hear or see what we don't believe.[23] Most people use helpful gestures and verbal prompts, such as head nodding, maintaining eye contact and encouragingly offering "go on" to nurture an interview with a reluctant speaker. Few professionals regularly practice the art of active listening. Figure 5.1 illustrates different types of listening used by professionals.

Active listening involves not only listening to the patient-client's spoken words but also paying attention to body language and providing feedback through paraphrasing what is heard and observed. Paraphrasing requires the listener to restate the essence of the speaker's communication. The act of paraphrasing honors the speaker, provides the opportunity to ensure that the listener heard what the speaker intended, and acknowledges the emotional context of the dialogue. Active listening requires participation in the conversation and takes practice and commitment. Initially, the process feels awkward and perhaps annoying both to the speaker and the listener. Incorporating the principles of active listening as a standard practice in oral communication provides the speaker with the opportunity to refine and correct understanding and facilitates relationship and trust building.

Figure 5.1 Types of Listening

- *Passive* → no feedback → listener learns only what the patient/client decides to disclose
- *Acknowledgment* → some encouragement → begins the process of building rapport facilitates a comfortable atmosphere
- *Active* → participation by reflecting → patient/client aware of listener's participation and feels central to the conversation, builds trust and confirmation, gleans more details and permits clarification of the narrative → a more complete and accurate patient/client narrative

Source: Stephan H. Krieger & Richard K. Neumann, R, Essential Lawyering Skills, 3rd ed., (Wolters Kluwer, 2007): 83–87.

Best Practices and Advocacy Strategies for Medical-Legal Partnership

Creating a structure for conversations with patients/clients that incorporates open-ended questions, targeted questions and summary questions and uses active listening throughout improves the likelihood of gleaning necessary information and creates the opportunity for the listener to demonstrate empathy. Displaying empathy and incorporating active listening in communications improves understanding and facilitates good decision making. Next are some helpful practices for patient-centered and client-centered listening.

Patient-Centered Doctoring

Although a healthcare provider may think that patient nodding is a sign of comprehension, it could be simply a sign of politeness. In 1978, Arthur Kleinman developed a communication tool still used today to elicit health beliefs during a clinical encounter. This is known as the explanatory model of illness, in which the practitioner explores how the patient views his illness and its causes.[24] Another tool is the mnemonic LEARN, developed by Berlin and Fowlkes, to guide culturally sensitive care: (1) the provider *listens* to the patient's perception of the problem, (2) he or she *explains* his or her perception of the problem, (3) *acknowledges* and discusses with the patient the differences and/or similarities of the providers and patient's perception of the problem, (4) *recommends* the treatment, and (5) *negotiates* agreement.[25] Despite the fact that these approaches were initially created for the medical profession, they can be applied with targeted modification to other professions.

Client-Centered Lawyering

Legal scholars have developed approaches comparable to those discussed above for practicing client-centered lawyering. For example, Binder, Bergman and Price stress that client problems have both legal and nonlegal dimensions. A client-centered approach includes these steps: (1) the lawyer helps identify problems from a client's perspective, (2) the lawyer actively involves the client in the process of exploring potential solutions, (3) the lawyer encourages a client to make those decisions that are likely to have a substantial legal or nonlegal impact, (4) the lawyer provides advice based on a client's values, (5) the lawyer acknowledges a client's feelings and recognizes their importance, and (6) the lawyer repeatedly conveys a desire to help.[26]

Case for Medical-Legal Partnership

A seven-year-old boy diagnosed with autism spectrum disorder should be followed regularly in the clinic. The child is well known to the medical team. The team is frustrated by frequently missed appointments, the lack of continuity in caregivers and the child's lack of progress. The boy needs structure, a predictable routine, and understanding. Unfortunately, his home situation is complicated and chaotic. His parents were very young when he was born and never wed. Since the child's birth, their relationship has deteriorated to the point where civil conversation concerning their child appears to be impossible. Both parents have engaged in self-destructive behavior, including substance abuse; at various times during the child's life both parents have been sentenced to serve prison time. The medical team has not seen either parent in some time. The most consistent figure in the child's life is his paternal grandmother. From the medical team's perspective, the paternal grandmother should seek custody of the child. On several occasions, team members have suggested to the paternal grandmother that she consult with the on-site MLP law office to discuss obtaining legal custody of the child. The paternal grandmother consistently responds by saying she wants her son to "step up to the plate."

The MLP law office is located within the hospital in a busy patient area. Direction signs to the law office are visible and printed information about the law offices is located throughout the hospital. One afternoon, the child's father arrives unannounced at the law office door. He says that he has taken the necessary steps to be recognized as the legal father of the child, and now he would like help obtaining legal custody. He also reports that the child has been living with him and his wife (not the mother of the child) for the past year. He reports that due to his work schedule, his mother has been helping by taking the boy to his various doctor and treatment appointments. The lawyer wants to do a full case intake, including a legal check-up, but the father states he knows what he wants, he doesn't have time to sit and answer a bunch of questions, and if the lawyer won't help he will get custody on his own.

Questions for Discussion

1. How could medical team members have improved communication with the family concerning the care and well-being of the child?

2. What steps could the medical team have taken to facilitate referral of the case to the legal team?

3. Should the legal team assist the father in obtaining legal custody of the child? Is there information that both the MLP teams have failed to obtain?

Cultural Competence in Law and Medicine

Understanding "Culture": The Melting Pot versus the Multicultural Mosaic

At the beginning of the twentieth century, Israel Zangwill wrote a play titled *The Melting Pot*, describing the promise that all immigrants can be transformed into Americans, a new alloy forged in a crucible of democracy, freedom and civic responsibility.[27] But some argue that as we move into the twenty-first century, immigrants may be following a different path:

> The United States is experiencing its second great wave of immigration, a movement of people that has profound implications for a society that by tradition pays homage to its immigrant roots at the same time it confronts complex and deeply ingrained ethnic and racial divisions. The immigrants of today come not from Europe but overwhelmingly from the still developing world of Asia and Latin America.[28]

The notion of a single American culture, if ever true, is certainly challenged by the current waves of immigrants who may be less likely to melt into the American way and more likely to retain their cultural identity and unique social norms, resembling a cultural mosaic within the larger community. This growing population of non-Western European immigrants is gaining critical mass, increasing their influence and perhaps generating a trend toward immigrants retaining their social norms, rather than abandoning them to the "melting pot." Rather than wholesale assimilation and full integration, recent immigration waves appear to be retaining behavioral, cultural and structural norms, moving along a continuum of acculturation, and in the process, influencing traditional American culture.

To the extent that assimilation occurs within recent waves of immigration, it may be very slow. One explanation is the marked difference in cultures and social norms. Retention of an immigrant group's culture and norms facilitates inclusion of new immigrants who need the support of their cultural group.[29] Like a home away from home, this familiar culture helps new immigrants form a basis on which to develop socioeconomic standing in America: build relationships, find housing and obtain work. As such, some immigrant communities may become insular and member-reliant.[30] Also, anti-immigrant sentiment may make certain groups feel less welcome and thus encourage reliance on and within their own cultural communities. Additionally, the legal and healthcare systems and the roles of legal and medical professionals in the United States may be very different than in immigrants' home countries.[31]

Too often, culturally diverse groups, such as immigrant groups, seek medical or legal assistance when the situation has become so dire that they are forced to engage with the system. Delay may result from poor understanding of the pathways to and through a system, inability to speak English, lack of legal status, lack of a payment stream to cover the cost of services, or the absence of trust in the system. Frequently, seeking assistance once the problem has become serious is the most expensive way to obtain services. It also creates the most stressful circumstances under which to develop relationships of trust, to listen, to understand and to accept different culturally-based viewpoints. In addition to the obvious differences such as language,[32] there also may be cultural differences with regard to understanding of autonomy, decision-making and respect. These more subtle nuances may be more difficult for the practitioner to discern when events have reached crisis proportions. (See Chapter 10 for further discussion of immigrants' experiences in the health and legal systems and the ways in which medical and legal professionals can be responsive to their concerns.)

Is Race Still a Factor?

For some members of the millennial generation (those born after 1981), the United States has become a postracial society.[33] Many of this generation espouse the ideal that racism no longer exists—it has been vanquished—and all systems are fair. Everyone, irrespective of color, faith or ethnic origin may expect equal treatment or at least equal opportunity. For others, "no aspect of diversity creates challenges as intractable as that of race. Race in America is the most salient, the most toxic of all areas of difference."[34] In some instances resulting bias, prejudice and stereotyping may result in labeling and differences in care and service.[35]

> The first step in addressing the problem is the recognition that race plays a role in what both the counselor and the client bring to the relationship. In the context of the climate of racism that has historically and currently permeates American society, the culturally different client is inclined to anticipate assistance from a member of the majority culture with a significant dose of skepticism.[36]

Although for some it may seem that U.S. society has moved beyond its sordid racist past, the legacy of racism must be confronted openly. Figure 5.2 illustrates the changing demographics and concepts of race and ethnicity in the United States.

Figure 5.2 Understanding Cultural Diversity

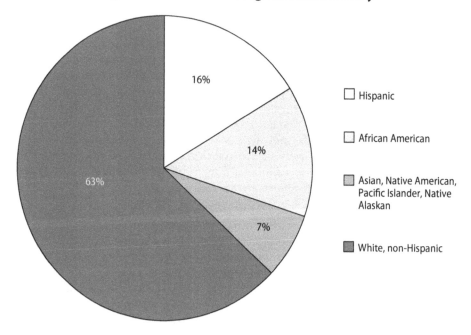

Source: U.S. Department of Commerce, U.S. Census Bureau, U.S. Summary 2009. Available at: http//www.census.gov/popest/national/asrh/NC-EST2009-srh.html. Accessed May 2010.

Understanding Cultural Diversity

The United States is a culturally and ethnically diverse nation composed of groups that contribute positively to our growth and development.

Changing Demographics

Minority populations continue to grow steadily. According to 2009 Census Bureau estimates, one-third of the U.S. population is identified as minority (see Figure 5.2).

Changing Concepts of Race and Ethnicity

Race is defined by some as a social category referring to groups often sharing cultural heritage and ancestry. Others define race as a classification of people on the basis of biological and genetic characters. Ethnicity typically identifies selected cultural and sometimes physical characteristics used to classify people into groups.

Sources: U.S. Department of Commerce, U.S. Census Bureau, U.S. Summary 2009. Available at: http//www.census.gov/popest/national/asrh/NC-EST2009-srh.html. Accessed May 2010; Nancy A Krieger, "A Glossary for Social Epidemiology." *Journal of Epidemiology Community Health,* 55 (2001): 693–00; *The American Heritage Science Dictionary.* (New York: Houghton Mifflin, 2005).

Different perspectives about race and racism raise challenges and opportunities for intergenerational and interracial communication. How does the practitioner or the student prepare for interactions with patients/clients who are younger, older, or from a different racial or ethnic group? How does the practitioner respectfully display empathy, actively listen, show respect and effectively address the client/patient's needs?

Clinicians, medical or legal, are first responders—at the bedside and in the law clinic or office. As professionals focused on accomplishing our goals, we may impose our cultural norms on our patients and clients without even realizing we are doing so. Acknowledging that cultural and racial differences factor into the development of an effective and respectful professional relationship is a critically important first step in developing cultural competence. As will be described, cultural competence exists on a continuum—moving from awareness and sensitivity to cultural difference toward skillful and adept interpretation of the cultural significance of a patient/-client encounter and responding appropriately and respectfully.

Defining Cultural Competence

There are many ways to define "cultural competence." Generally, these definitions describe the process by which people have greater understanding of and become more attuned to the breadth of sociocultural diversity that exists in and enriches society. Consider these definitions:

- *linguistic and cultural competence*: "a set of congruent behaviors, attitudes, and policies that come together in a system, agency, or among professionals that enables effective work in cross-cultural situations."[37]
- *culture*: "integrated patterns of human behavior that include the language, thoughts, communications, actions, customs, beliefs, values, and institutions of racial, ethnic, religious, or social groups."[38] Culture can also be associated with social groups such as the family, an organization or those created by disability, class, nationality, age, language, sexual orientation and other characteristics.[39]

- *competence*: "having the capacity to function effectively as an individual [and/or] an organization within the context of the cultural beliefs, behaviors, and needs presented by consumers and their communities."[40]

More simply, cultural competence is the recognition of specific cultural attributes and the appropriate response to them. The Institute of Medicine has identified it as one of the main factors in addressing health disparities among minority and low-income populations.[41] It is also critical to effective legal advocacy. Cultural competency is not static, but develops and evolves over time molded by experiences and ever-increasing awareness. Within the healthcare field, great emphasis is placed on developing both organizational and individual cultural competence.[42] By contrast, the legal field has not yet developed definitions of cultural competence, nor is there a shared understanding about the need for and type of cultural competence to be developed. However, this area is of continuing interest to legal scholars.[43]

Cultural Competence Education in Law and Medicine

There is growing recognition that competence in cultural differences is needed to improve understanding and delivery of services in professions such as medicine and law that involve important relationships between providers and those they serve. Culturally skilled professionals are aware of their heritage and value that of others; they recognize their values and beliefs and how these may affect others; they accept difference, such as race and beliefs; and they acknowledge and own their attitudes, beliefs and feelings.[44] In both medical and legal education, cultural competence should be an important component of professional training as students prepare to serve increasingly diverse patient and client populations.

Medical Education

In medical education, the Liaison Committee on Medical Education (LCME) established standards in the United States and Canada for faculty and students to learn and understand how people of different cultures perceive health and illness. These standards are also meant to foster understanding of how to respond to diverse symptoms, diseases and treatments.[45] In 2001, the Association of American Medical Colleges (AAMC) launched a project commissioning papers to establish the domains of cultural competence and created an expert panel to develop a tool for assessing training in the medical school curriculum.[46] The ultimate purpose of the project was to support the standards, promote their use and broaden their scope of influence as outlined by LCME.

As a result, many healthcare institutions and medical schools have implemented some kind of cultural competence training. Cultural competence educational initiatives in medical education vary widely and include language training, lectures and interactive sessions, workshops, elective courses, immersion programs, components within residency curricula and more.[47]

For example, the state of New Jersey requires cultural competence training in accordance with AAMC guidelines in all colleges of medicine as a condition of receiving a diploma. Any physician licensed prior to June 29, 2007, who did not receive cultural competence training during medical school, is required to complete a continuing medical education (CME) program of at least six hours' duration prior to license renewal. The specific CME content requirements are outlined by the State Board of Medical Examiners. State policy requires CME programs on cultural diversity offered to meet license renewal requirements be developed in accordance with the AAMC guidelines or another nationally recognized organization, which reviews medical school curriculum.[48]

Medicine leads other professions in cultural competence education and training. The reason may have less to do with altruism and more to do with federal mandates that require cultural competence training as a condition of cost reimbursement from payers.[49] On the other hand, the diverse nature of the healthcare workforce may have compelled healthcare organizations to help employees develop the skills necessary to bridge cultural differences, such as improving communication and understanding personal interactions.

Legal Education

In legal education, cultural competence training has not been offered in a systematic manner. Some legal scholars have addressed the need for this kind of training and suggested models for incorporating it.[50] For example, *Best Practices in Legal Education* cites "sensitivity and effectiveness with diverse clients and colleagues" as a core value that should be addressed during law school.[51] Despite this recommendation, there is no requirement that cultural competence training be offered in law school or continuing legal education. As cultural competence training becomes institutionalized in business, education and healthcare settings, legal education may follow suit.

Increasing Diversity in the Health and Legal Professions

Underrepresentation of minorities is a concern in both the health and legal professions. The Association of American Medical Colleges reports that in 2004 the physician workforce was 3.3% black, 2.8% Hispanic/Latino and 5.7% Asian.[a] Similarly, a 2010 report by the American Bar Association on diversity in the legal profession, notes that "Despite decades of reports, task forces, and goals, in 2000 the legal profession remained about 90% Caucasian, with the national population at that time being about 70% Caucasian. Demographic projections for the legal profession for 2010 are not suggesting that much progress has been achieved."[b]

A 2004 report by the Institute of Medicine entitled, "In the Nation's Compelling Interest: Ensuring Diversity in the Health Care Workforce,"[c] provided multiple recommendations for increasing diversity. Four of those recommendations are listed here:

- Health Professions Educational Institutions (HPEIs) should develop, disseminate and utilize a clear statement of mission that recognizes the value of diversity in enhancing its mission and that of the relevant health care professions.

- Health professions education accreditation bodies should develop standards and criteria that more effectively encourage health professions schools to recruit URM (underrepresented miniority) students and faculty, to develop cultural competence curricula, and to develop an institutional climate that encourages and sustains the development of a critical mass of diversity.

- HPEIs should develop and regularly evaluate comprehensive strategies to improve the institutional climate for diversity. These strategies should attend not only to the structural dimensions of diversity, but also to the range of other dimensions (e.g., psychological and behavioral) that affect the success of institutional diversity efforts.

- HPEIs should be encouraged to affiliate with community-based health care facilities in order to attract and train a more diverse and culturally competent workforce and to increase access to health care.

The American Bar Association cites four rationales for the need to increase diversity in the legal profession:

- *The Democracy Rationale*: Lawyers and judges have a unique responsibility for sustaining a political system with broad participation by all its citizens. A diverse bar and bench create greater trust in the mechanisms of government and the rule of law.

- *The Business Rationale:* Business entities are rapidly responding to the needs of global customers, suppliers and competitors by creating workforces from many different backgrounds, perspectives, skill sets and tastes. Ever more frequently, clients expect and sometimes demand lawyers who are culturally and linguistically proficient.

- *The Leadership Rationale:* Individuals with law degrees often possess the communication and interpersonal skills and the social networks to rise into civic leadership positions, both in and out that law schools serve as the training ground for such leadership and therefore access to the profession must be broadly inclusive.

- *The Demographic Rationale:* Our country is becoming diverse along many dimensions and we expect that the profile of LGBT lawyers and lawyers with disabilities will increase more rapidly. With respect to the nation's racial/ethnic populations, the Census Bureau projects that by 2042 the United States will be a "majority minority" country.[d]

Notes: [a] Association of American Medical Colleges, "Diversity in the Physician Workforce: Facts and Figures, 2006," 15; [b] American Bar Association, Diversity in the Legal Profession: The Next Steps (ABA Presidential Initiative Commission on Diversity, April 2010); [c] Institute of Medicine, "In the Nation's Compelling Interest: Ensuring Diversity in the Health Care Workforce," (2003); [d] ABA, "Diversity in the Legal Profession," 5.

Questions for Discussion

1. Should cultural competence training be required for medical and law students? Should it be required for continuing education for lawyers, physicians and others on the MLP team?

2. Do you have a personal experience with a situation involving cross-cultural communication or practices? How did noticing such differences impact your ability to communicate and understand? To empathize?

3. Do you have an example of a situation in which you made a negative inference about a person which later turned out not to be true? How did you feel about your mistake?

4. Why is a diverse workforce important to the health and legal professions? To patients and clients?

Why Must Professionals Strive for Cultural Competence?

The goal of striving for cultural competence is to remove barriers to access. Barriers based on cultural differences may impede communication and trust between a patient or client and a provider, thus hampering access to important medical and legal services. Overcoming cultural barriers may improve outcomes by enabling the professional to better understand the patient-client's expectations and the incidence of problems or disease.[52]

The values, beliefs and customs of a group are all part of its culture. Knowing which of these factors has the most direct or indirect influence over a patient-client is important because it can impact the approach to health or problem solving. From a cultural point of view, three aspects of interpersonal behavior influence interactions between patients-clients and the professionals serving them: social environment, cultural environment and belief orientation.

The Impact of Culture

- Events may be viewed differently
- Importance of roles, hierarchy or personal relationships may differ
- Priorities may differ as to the rights of the individual versus the group
- Conflict may be resolved differently
- Emotion and displays of emotion may be viewed differently
- Discussion of intimate or embarrassing issues may be constrained
- Reliance on inference and implication in communication may be required

---

Social Environment

It is critical that service providers understand the patient-client's social environment so that appropriate services can be provided. "Social environment" refers to one's life experiences and includes factors such as socioeconomic status, household size, and access to safe housing, education and adequate food sources. Such social determinants of health may directly affect a patient-client's ability to access care, follow a care plan or meet legal deadlines, which can impact health outcomes and overall well-being. For example, professionals should actively solicit information regarding a patient-client's access to transportation because without reliable transportation he or she may miss medical appointments or important legal meetings. Inquiries into the patient-client's awareness of available services and his or her support system will help professionals determine the client-patient's ability to navigate complex medical and legal systems and identify areas where additional assistance may be warranted. A practitioner should not wait passively for a patient-client to offer up challenges, but should be proactive in identifying those challenges.

Additionally, knowing a patient-client's stressors will make practitioners more sensitive to the patient-client's needs and his or her capacity for accessing services and following-through on suggested action steps. Is the patient working? Is the client's income sufficient to meet his or her needs? Does the family have health insurance? Alternatively, does the patient feel good about his or her ability to resolve the situation or problem because of strong family support or active involvement in a religious or other organization that will provide additional support?

Cultural Environment

In addition to understanding social environment, professionals should be attuned to the patient-client's cultural environment as well. Cultural environment affects how a patient-client takes in, interprets and responds to information. Familiarity with these influences helps professionals avoid misunderstandings and informs decision making. Consider the following example from the medical context:

> The doctor can give offense. "For Latinos, there's a big emphasis on *respeto*, which means 'respect,' and *fatalismo* which is 'fatalism,' said Dr. Glenn Flores, co-director of the Pediatric Latino Clinic at the Boston Medical Center. This can set up a cultural clash between the Latino parent and the "harried, hurried medical care provider …" If you feel that you've been slighted, you're not going to follow through with therapy, you're not going to come back for a return visit, and that will affect your health.[53]

In addition to perceptions based on cultural differences, family hierarchy may be an indirect cultural influence as well. Understanding familial hierarchy and its relationship to a particular culture may help a caregiver determine who in the family holds the role of decision maker. For example, even though a patient-client comes to the doctor or lawyer with his or her spouse, it may be an elder or another family leader that will make the ultimate decision about how medical care or the legal problem will be addressed.

Similar to healthcare, law and legal assistance for the poor, the culturally diverse and immigrant populations is rooted in culture.[54] Although practitioners appreciate that law evolves (slowly), clients bring their culturally based experiences with them when they confront the legal system. Many perceive the law as the enemy and fear lawyers and the justice system.[55] Determining a client's understanding of what it means to engage with lawyers and the legal system can help the lawyer determine the client's degree of acculturation and thus adopt strategies for developing a trusting relationship.

Acculturation is how and to what extent a particular member or family has adopted the beliefs, social patterns, and behaviors of the group, area or country in which they live.[56] See Table 5.2. Acculturation is important because healthcare and legal providers must know the degree to which the patient-client is acculturated to understand the extent to which the patient-client's culture will influence the interaction and the outcomes. In the lawyer-client context, the degree of acculturation may be a factor that affects the relationships between a lawyer and the client.

Table 5.2 Factors That Affect Acculturation

Education	Time in country of residence
Living environment—neighborhood	Family involvement
Community of residence	Primary language in home
Employment	Age at immigration

The influence of culture on a patient's ability to access healthcare has been long recognized by the medical community. For example, the Culturally and Linguistically Appropriate Services (CLAS) standards were created in response to Title VI of the Civil Rights Act of 1964.[57] These standards are included as Appendix 5.1. The standards are divided into those relating to culturally competent care, access to language services, and how an organization should support cultural competence. The standards are further divided into those that are mandated (standards 4–7), recommended (standards 1–3, standards 8–13) and suggested (standard 14). Mandated standards must be addressed in all healthcare entities receiving federal funds. Although created for healthcare organizations, the standards are clearly applicable to other professions, particularly the legal profession, in which both organizations (legal services offices and law firms) as well as individual practitioners serve a diverse population.

Acculturation as a determinant is not limited to doctor-patient and lawyer-client relationships. Organizations such as hospitals, law offices and academic institutions have cultural environments. People working in these environments acculturate to one degree or another. From an organizational point of view, acculturation is a socialization process through which new employees learn, adjust and internalize the corporate culture. Progressive organizations allow sufficient transition time, help newcomers through orientation sessions and facilitate learning.[58] Employees who acculturate are more likely to experience success within the organization. This may be especially important to recognize in the context of MLPs in which medical and legal professionals must "acculturate" to one another's different perspectives and problem-solving orientation.

Belief Orientation

Another consideration in medicine is the patient-client's perception of the cause of an event or illness. This includes the broader beliefs concerning how, in terms of medicine, the body works, and in terms of other professions, how the system works. It also includes the general factors that influence a person's fate. Anthropologist Arthur Kleinman suggested that by using what he called the "explanatory model" of illness, we can better understand our patients and their families.[59] The explanatory model focuses on the patient's belief of what causes illness and is particular to individual cultures. The cause will often directly relate to a "cure." Patients may believe that their god, a spirit, a curse, a sin or an emotional imbalance causes the illness.[60] For example, the Hmong believe that the most common cause of illness is "soul loss."[61] The "cure" in these instances may not be the medicine prescribed but instead prayer, making a sacrifice or meditating to rebalance the disharmony in the patient's life. Similarly, a patient's religious beliefs, such as being a member of the Jehovah's Witness faith, may significantly affect his or her perception of illness, whether to seek care and with whom, as well as acceptance of and adherence to the plan of care as prescribed.[62]

Likewise, a patient-client's beliefs about the justice system, the role of lawyers and the availability of remedies creates expectations that may be difficult to realize. Some beliefs relate to concepts of fairness and the power of judges and lawyers to achieve particular results. A common belief is that lawyers have the power to "fix" legal problems quickly. However, systemic factors often make immediate resolution unrealistic. Additionally, clients may believe that having a "day in court" will satisfactorily resolve his or her problem. Clients have a tendency to underestimate the financial and personal costs associated with adversarial court intervention. Moreover, a client's belief orientation or expectations about the law may be based on his or her experiences in another country. For example, the role of a lawyer in some countries is one of "fixer" or person in charge, which differs from the client-centered model of U.S. lawyers.[63]

Questions for Discussion

1. How do social environment, cultural environment and belief orientation affect patients' and clients' perceptions of the healthcare and legal systems? What is the role of healthcare providers in helping culturally diverse patients to navigate the

healthcare system? What is the role of lawyers in helping them to navigate the legal system?

2. Apart from simply understanding that there may be differences in cultures, in what ways could an MLP ensure that its interventions are culturally competent?

What Does It Mean to Be a "Culturally Competent" Professional?

The question "What is cultural competence and how can it best be achieved?" remains unanswered. Can we really be "culturally competent"? Is the best we can hope for to be educated, aware or sensitive? *Cultural awareness* is an appreciation of diversity and acknowledgment that people have external cues distinguishing them from one another— for instance, the clothes they wear or the food they eat. *Cultural sensitivity*, on the other hand, is "awareness plus": awareness that there are differences between cultures *and* without assignment of value to those differences. Often, in efforts to acknowledge diversity and be respectful, professionals get lost in semantics. Should we be working toward cultural competence or developing cultural competencies?[64] Programs focus on developing cultural sensitivity, but should the emphasis be placed on exercising cultural effectiveness?[65] Should cultural humility also be placed on the continuum to competence?[66] Attaining cultural competence is an ongoing process requiring a long-term educational commitment. One does not "become competent" at any one point. Instead, he or she becomes more knowledgeable, aware and sensitive in an attempt to reach competence.

As one works toward cultural competence, it is helpful to remember that in the absence of any guidelines or knowledge in a given situation, the best approach for providers is to ask permission or explain intent. A provider should avoid making assumptions that a patient-client knows his or her intentions, even if those intentions seem obvious. One should respectfully ask patients and clients if they are comfortable with a procedure or process and ensure that they understand what is being asked of them.

A lawyer may want to ask probing questions about difficult personal topics, and may be unsure of the client's feelings or reactions. An example of how to proceed in a culturally sensitive manner is to announce one's intention: "I would now like to ask you some questions about the incident when your husband struck you. I need this information so that we can seek a protective order for you. Is that okay with you?" Another example, from the medical side: "I need you to disrobe so that I can examine your bruises. We need to check your injuries to make sure that you are okay and document what has happened to you. Is that okay with you?" In some cases, respectfully asking a patient's preference for physician gender, for example, rather than making assumptions about what a patient may prefer helps prevent uncomfortable situations.[67] The best way to avoid pitfalls in cross-cultural communication is to go in with the expectation that the professional does not have all the answers and is not the situational expert. The patient-client is the expert, and the physician or lawyer is there to learn his or her story.

Frameworks for Understanding Cultural Competence

There are several frameworks for theorizing the practice of cultural competence and for measuring it in medical and legal practices. In legal education, one model teaches five professional habits: (1) recognizing "degrees of separation and connection" with clients; (2) understanding the "rings of similarity and difference" among lawyers, clients and decision makers; (3) accepting that clients may operate within "parallel universes" (in different environments rewarding different motives); (4) understanding "pitfalls, red flags, and remedies" to cultural differences; and (5) "the camel's back" involving habits of mind.[68] This model for training educators teaches the "hidden rules" of class and culture.[69] These five habits are discussed in detail below.

The Five Habits: Building Cross-Cultural Competence

Habit 1: Degrees of Separation and Connection

Analyze how similarities and differences between the lawyer and client may influence lawyer-client interactions, particularly in the information-gathering process. The process of identifying differences reveals the possibility that cultural misunderstanding, bias and stereotyping may occur. Identifying similarities shows shared connections.

Habit 2: The Three Rings

Analyze the effects of similarities and differences on the three rings: the client, the legal decision maker and the lawyer. This process includes considering what a successful client may look like to the legal decision maker, and how the client is similar or different to this successful prototype, and what implicit cultural values and norms in the law will be applied to the client.

Habit 3: Parallel Universes

Encourages the lawyer to consider multiple interpretations and imagine alternative explanations when judging a client or client's actions negatively. Engaging in parallel universe thinking reduces the likelihood of making incorrect assumptions about reasons for a client's behavior.

Habit 4: Pitfalls, Red Flags and Remedies

Encourages culturally sensitive exchanges with clients and conscious attention to the process of lawyer-client communication. This habit includes consideration of culture, scripts and rituals that could impact communication and invites lawyers to look for "red flags" that indicate miscommunication may have occurred. A part of preparation is planning for red flags as well as corrective measures.

Habit 5: The Camel's Back

Encourages self-reflection to bring awareness to factors outside factors, including stress, that may interact with bias and stereotype to negatively influence attorney-client interaction.[a]

Note: [a] Susan Bryant. "The Five Habits: Building Cross Cultural Competence." *Clinical Law Review*, 8 (2001): 33–107.

Another model is based on the awareness-knowledge-skill model, using a structural framework as follows:

- Communication (speaking and listening)
- Cognition (thinking)
- Reference (what is known and shared)
- Resources (what is drawn on individually)

- Relationships (how we interact with others)[70]

In the medical field, the concept of cultural humility has been distinguished from cultural competence. This concept is a process that requires humility, continual self-reflection and self-critique by lifelong learners and reflective practitioners. It requires humility in how physicians check the power imbalances that exist in the dynamics of physician-patient communication by using patient-focused interviewing and care.[71]

Language Differences and Translation in Client/Patient Relationships

The number of non-English speakers continues to increase. Data from the 2007 American Community Survey (ACS) analyzed by the U.S. Census Bureau show the number of people five years of age and older speaking a language other than English at home has more than doubled in the past three decades.[72] From 1980 to 2007, the percentage of non-English language speakers grew by 140 percent, while the nation's overall population grew by only 34 percent. The states with the highest concentrations of the most commonly spoken non-English languages are: Texas, California and New Mexico (Spanish); Louisiana and Maine (French); North Dakota and South Dakota (German); Illinois, New York, New Jersey and Connecticut (Slavic languages); California, New York, Hawaii and Massachusetts (Chinese); and Hawaii, California, and New Jersey (Korean).[73]

These data highlight the need to consistently provide interpreter services for non-native speakers to access care and services.[74] (See Chapter 10 for additional discussion of the importance of interpretive services for patients and clients with limited English proficiency.) In addition to being bilingual, interpreters should ideally be bicultural, meaning that they have an understanding of the cultural concerns that may arise in the interaction. In addition, interpreters should have a full understanding of medical/legal vocabulary, understand the significance of the problems being addressed, and above all maintain confidentiality.

In 2006 the Joint Commission, the agency that accredits hospitals, created standards related to the provision of culturally and linguistically appropriate healthcare as specific issues that must be addressed, in addition to compliance with CLAS standards, for hospital accreditation.[75] However, using an interpreter does not relieve the provider of his or her interpersonal responsibilities. For example, learning the greeting of the most frequently encountered cultures and using it in a discussion conveys a sign of respect and willingness to understand an individual's culture. During the conversation, providers should maintain eye contact with the patient-client, not the interpreter. Information should be reinforced with materials written in the patient-client's native language, if possible.

Attention to nonverbal communication is important as well, because communication styles also differ from culture to culture. Because 60 percent of all communication is nonverbal in any culture, both the interpreter and the provider should be aware of the types of interaction and the appropriateness of the response. Understanding whether to make eye contact, use hand gestures or engage in or avoid personal contact are essential in effectively communicating with the patient-client.

Cultural awareness, sensitivity and competence involve valuing the differences and similarities among people. In an increasingly culturally diverse world, practitioners need to become as informed as possible about the cultures of those with whom they deal on a daily basis. Professionals must remain open to learning about new and different cultures

Figure 5.3 Contextual Factors That Influence the Relationships between MLP Practitioners and Their Patient-Clients

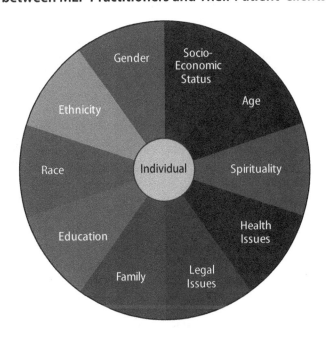

and responding in a respectful manner. Though this part of the chapter focused on individual competence, to be effective, the concepts of cultural awareness, sensitivity and competence must permeate an organization as well. Figure 5.3 illustrates the range of contextual factors that come into play in an MLP.

Professional Cultures and Communication across Disciplines

The form of language used by both the medical and legal professions is a cultural difference that can unintentionally exclude others. Lawyers are often guilty of using legal jargon ("legalese") when writing and talking, which may include Latin phrases or extra words that obscure meaning or make meaning difficult to discern for laypersons. The tendency to use legalese is a subject addressed in the context of improving client interviewing and counseling.[76] Similarly, physicians and other healthcare providers have their own jargon ("medspeak"), which involves unfamiliar medical terms ("myocardial infarction" instead of "heart attack," for example) and abbreviations or initials that are not familiar to laypersons or other professionals. Use of jargon around those who are not inculcated to that language can be alienating or confusing and communicates "insider" status and elitism based on education. Both professions should take note of their use of language when working with one another as well as with patients and clients. For further discussion of medical and legal jargon, see Chapter 4.

Context can affect the culture of the MLP itself. Each partnership forms its own joint culture, borne of the unique circumstances that led to its formation. MLPs may have many stakeholders: doctors, lawyers, social workers, nurses, hospitals, health clinics, medical schools, law schools, students from different disciplines, legal services providers, nonprofit agencies and more. MLPs may also be located at multiple locations. Physical location can influence operations and power sharing. Funding sources may impact the administrative roles played by each partner and how they interact and view one another. All of the participants must develop skills to effectively work across disciplines and professional cultures. Thus, it is important for each stakeholder to understand the needs and goals of the MLP as a whole as well as the needs and goals of its individual members. Moreover, as the MLP matures, needs and goals evolve with it, so the process of seeking mutual understanding must continually evolve. (For additional discussion of the challenges inherent in the MLP model, see Chapter 3.)

Best Practices and Advocacy Strategies for Medical-Legal Partnership

The following is a list of best practices that can be implemented by healthcare and legal institutions that serve vulnerable populations to provide culturally competent services to patients and clients.

Develop Awareness. To become effective cross-cultural professionals, practitioners must first become aware of the significance of their own cultural values, attitudes and norms of behavior. During daily interactions, professionals may unconsciously attach culturally based meaning and make assumptions or judgments about the meaning of a patient or client's behavior.[77] A culturally sensitive professional is aware of how his or her personal culture may shape perception of a client or patient's problem and how this may influence his or her advice. Likewise, culture shapes a client's decisions and responses to the professional.[78] Thus, effective professional services require an effort to minimize harmful attributions or assumptions and to understand clients within their cultural contexts.[79]

Provide Training. Institutions should provide training in cultural competence as part of their educational curriculum. Participants may include all hospital or clinic staff, medical trainees and faculty learners. Training should be offered on a predictable ongoing schedule to accommodate providers' schedules, capture newcomers and reinforce cultural competence skills.

Institute Protocols. Institutions should consider developing a protocol for cross-cultural exploration, such as the series of questions developed by Kleinman, Eisenberg and Good (discussed earlier in this chapter).[80] Such questions can serve as guidelines for exploring the patient's belief of the causes of his or her illness or legal problem, and the patient's agenda. Such a model also addresses the social context in which the patient-client presents. Following a protocol assists individuals in becoming attuned to sociocultural aspects associated with presenting problems and helps individuals identify their own cultural blind spots.

Provide Interpreter and Translator Services. Health and legal institutions should have written policies and procedures for serving individuals who speak little or no English, are hearing impaired, or have other needs that may impede communication. It is important to remember, however, that language fluency alone does not guarantee cultural competence. It is preferable to use in-person interpreter services whenever possible. In some instances, a phone interpreter must be used, and in those situations the care provider may have to balance the need to build a personal connection and rapport with the need for accurate information. All members of an organization should be trained to use translation services.

Promote Diversity. Institutions should reflect and promote diversity in the healthcare and legal services leadership and workforce.[81] They should actively recruit employees and volunteers who reflect culturally diverse backgrounds and the communities they serve. All print and online program awareness materials should likewise reflect the communities served.

Table 5.3 A Framework for Best Practices for Cultural Competence Development in MLP

Organizational
• Acknowledge and model cultural competence as a core value • Offer training in cultural competence • Ensure MLP staff reflects the makeup of the community it serves
Structural
• Use evaluation to seek feedback from constituents • Provide access to certified interpreters who have cultural training • Provide training for native speakers on how to effectively use interpreters (for example, make eye contact with the person with whom they are speaking, rather than the interpreter)
Clinical
• Treat the client/patient as an active partner in resolving the problem rather than viewing MLP partners as legal and medical prescribers of solutions • Provide lecture series or other events that encourage conversation about cultural competency • Provide reminders in the physical environment of the importance of cultural competency using posters, flyers, displays, and other materials • Use humility in treatment of patients/clients, and remember that clients are the experts on their own lives
Professional
• Ensure that partners are familiar with the community and the history of the healthcare system • Create systems and protocols that help the MLP be attuned to the sociocultural aspects of patient and client problems

Best practices focused on cultural competency that are particularly important for MLPs include the following (also see Table 5.3).

Acknowledge Context. It is essential that professionals understand the broader context surrounding a patient-client's health problem or legal issue. Often, patient-clients in an MLP setting are enduring multiple crises simultaneously. Understanding the various factors contributing to the situation allows participants in the MLP to care for the whole patient-client.

Model Cultural Competence. MLPs are in a unique position to model cultural competence as a value. Partnerships should explicitly state a value of confronting and eliminating bias, discrimination and racism in the healthcare and legal systems. Partnerships may demonstrate this value by undertaking cross-cultural skills training and research, such as the health disparities lecture series provided by the Health Law Partnership (discussed shortly). This value can also be demonstrated by creating informal opportunities for learning cross-cultural competence through library displays, speaker events, volunteer opportunities, interdisciplinary book clubs and other work groups.

Practice Client/Patient-Centeredness. MLPs should actively articulate a commitment to consider patients and clients as active partners in resolving the problem to be addressed, rather than viewing the professionals as legal and medical prescribers of solutions. This articulation of commitment is reinforced with action in the form of active listening and client/patient centered counseling and decision-making.

Hold Interdisciplinary Case Conferences. MLPs should hold regular shared case conferences so that the team consistently engages in holistic problem solving for each patient-client. Through regular meetings to discuss cases, each profession has the opportunity to educate the other and to share opportunities to impact the case and the outcome of the patient-clients under discussion. This creates a culture of cooperation and collaboration.

Promote Interdisciplinary Education. MLPs should hold joint classes and training sessions for students in the professions represented in the MLP. Interdisciplinary education allows for the exploration of similarities and differences among the professions in addressing patient-client issues and continues to foster development of cooperation and collaboration among the professions. (For discussion of joint medical-legal education, see Chapter 4.)

Seek Feedback. MLPs should develop mechanisms for feedback and evaluation. The partnership should offer opportunities for its communities to influence the direction of the provision of healthcare and public health legal services. Such feedback can include conducting listening tours, community assessments, implementing systems for patient racial/ethnic and language preference data collection, developing quality measures for diverse patient populations, and ensuring culturally and linguistically appropriate health education materials and health promotion and disease prevention interventions, as well as legal interventions.[82]

Consider Space. Seating arrangements or office location can have an impact on cross-cultural communication. The office environment should be comfortable, accessible and welcoming. Strive to create spaces where patients and healthcare providers or lawyers can interact in a physical layout that communicates equality rather than dominance by one individual over another.

From Practice to Policy

To encourage understanding of health disparities and develop awareness of cultural differences to enhance patient care, one MLP implemented training specifically designed to address this component of its services. The Health Law Partnership (HeLP), an MLP comprised of Children's Healthcare of Atlanta, Georgia State University College of Law and Atlanta Legal Aid Society, received a grant from the Georgia Department of Community Health to accomplish these goals. This Health Equity Grant funded expansion of HeLP's established educational programming by incorporating new and focused educational programs about health disparities among low-income and minority children. At Children's at Hughes Spalding, one of the partnering hospitals, a professional healthcare disparities instructor collaborated with the law faculty at Georgia State University College of Law and with the physician champion for HeLP to provide culturally relevant and appropriate educational programming on the root causes of health disparities in the patient population and methods for reducing and eliminating them. The Cultural Diversity and Healthcare Disparities Class Series, presented as a part of the grant, included five different class sessions presented over a five-month period.[83] This educational series was directed toward house staff and faculty.

Children's Healthcare of Atlanta at Children's at Hughes Spalding is located in close proximity of Georgia State's College of Law in downtown Atlanta. The medical faculty, residents and students from Morehouse and Emory medical schools provide services and receive training at Children's at Hughes Spalding. HeLP and the HeLP Legal Services Clinic also provide educational programming and public health legal services on site. The health disparities education program provided a forum and a framework for discussion and learning about health disparities and the exploration of cultural difference in the healthcare setting for all of these constituents. The focus on health disparities and the class series were complemented by the contemporaneous hiring of a lawyer who served as the Health

Disparities Fellow, a position also supported by the grant. The fellow was responsible for addressing legal needs at the Children's at Hughes Spalding hospital location.

The Health Equity Grant project was an innovative approach to addressing health disparities. The program was evaluated as part of HeLP's ongoing research and evaluation component. Attendees were given a pre- and post-Cultural Competence Self-Assessment tool.[84] The project design and implementation was a positive beginning in creating an environment of cultural awareness and enhancing cultural competence as part of the goals of an MLP. Based on the evaluations as well as anecdotal reports, the health disparities programming was an important step in strengthening the long-term effectiveness of HeLP's public health legal services. The training helped legal and healthcare professionals better understand the socioeconomic factors and cultural factors that impact the provision of healthcare and public health legal services. HeLP continues to engage in research and evaluation to demonstrate the benefits of its services in reducing factors that contribute to health disparities and the impact of its educational programming on the professional and patient populations as well as positive patient and family outcomes. The positive effect of this and other HeLP programming has been recognized by the Joint Commission as "best practice" in the 2010 survey of Children's Healthcare of Atlanta at Hughes Spalding.

Case for Medical-Legal Partnership

Mr. and Mrs. Z. have a 12-year-old daughter who is developmentally delayed, and she exhibits behavioral issues that her parents, the school and the medical team find challenging. She is followed in a specialty clinic at the hospital. Mr. Z. consistently is the parent who brings the child to appointments and holds the conversations with the medical team about the plan of care. In fact, the medical team has never met Mrs. Z. The medical team has asked Mr. Z. to bring his wife to the clinic appointments, but she has never come. They also have asked to speak to her on the phone, but Mr. Z. always has some excuse to explain why this is not possible. The family immigrated to the United States from Southeast Asia when the girl was an infant, locating first in New Orleans. In the aftermath of Hurricane Katrina, the family moved to your city. Last year, an apartment complex fire destroyed all of the family's belongings, including important documents.

For many weeks, the medical team has been urging Mr. Z. to apply for Medicaid on behalf of his daughter. A new behavioral treatment program is available that may benefit the child; however, the program is open only to Medicaid members. The team has been trying for months to enroll the girl in the program, and they can't understand why she is not yet covered by Medicaid. The social worker has met with Mr. Z. several times to discuss the process for applying for Medicaid. During the clinic visit earlier today, the team asks Mr. Z. again about the status of the Medicaid application. Mr. Z. responds by saying he has told his wife to apply for Medicaid. In complete frustration, the physician asks the social worker to refer Mr. Z. to the MLP law office.

The social worker escorts Mr. Z. to the MLP law office. A member of the legal team does a complete intake, including a legal check-up to spot issues that may not have come up during the interview. Mr. Z. says that he has told his wife to go to the Medicaid office to apply, but something always seems to be missing from their application. He says that he worries about using Medicaid because the family wants to apply for citizenship. Everything has been complicated by the fact that they lost their documents in the apartment fire. Although Mr. Z. thinks it would be nice for his daughter to attend the special behavioral clinic, he appears to be preoccupied with papers he got from the bank. He does not have the papers with him, and when asked about them, he provides few details. He admits that he has not read the papers. The lawyer wonders about Mr. Z.'s reading skills and his command of English. Mr. Z. reports that he is current on his rent and utilities, owns his van, and he does not owe anyone any money. He proudly states that he works hard to support his family and that he never has taken a handout. Later in the afternoon Mr. Z. faxes the papers from the bank. The faxed documents are associated with a lawsuit filed against Mrs. Z. for bank credit card debt in the amount of $22,000. In a follow-up phone conversation, Mr. Z. denies that he or his wife has a bank credit card. He also says that his wife is not available to discuss the matter.

Questions for Discussion

1. Discuss how the medical team could improve communication with Mr. Z. Are cultural differences interfering with the flow of information?

2. What steps should both the medical team and the legal team take to address challenges facing Mr. and Mrs. Z. and their daughter?

3. Is it necessary to have Mr. and Mrs. Z. both attend meetings with the medical and legal teams? Is this a reasonable request in this instance? What are some ways to approach Mr. or Mrs. Z in a culturally respectful manner?

Conclusion

Because MLPs are premised on understanding health and well-being within the social context of a patient or client's life, the relationship and communication between the professional and the patient-client is critical. MLPs should promote effective listening to the patient-client narrative as well as cultural awareness and sensitivity by all of its team members. Open acknowledgment that cultural differences exist and attempts to appreciate how such differences may impact the lawyer-client and healthcare provider-patient relationship can contribute to better understanding among all parties and better outcomes.

The medical profession has recognized that to understand and eliminate racial and ethnic disparities in healthcare requires an understanding that bias, stereotyping and prejudice contribute to healthcare disparities. In fact, when sociocultural differences are not appreciated, explored, understood or communicated in the medical encounter, the result is patient dissatisfaction, poor adherence, poorer health outcomes and racial/ethnic disparities in care. Similarly, the legal profession has acknowledged the importance of cultural sensitivity and competency by lawyers. In lawyer-client interactions, lawyers may make assumptions about a client's situations or choices, which can inhibit communication. Lack of complete understanding between lawyer and client can, at best, limit options, and at worst, foreclose them.

By creating an expectation that those operating within professional environments are conscious of social context and cultural differences, professionals come to understand that differences can lead individuals to alternative interpretations of situations and conclusions based on the same set of facts. This understanding ultimately improves outcomes because it encourages both respect as well as flexible thinking. Although healthcare providers and lawyers may receive education in cultural competence as part of their professional training, cultural competence and awareness are practiced skills that evolve over time and with experience.

1. See Chapter 4 for discussion of medical education.

2. Sayantani DasGupta and Rita Charon. "Personal Illness Narratives: Using Reflective Writing to Teach Empathy." *Academic Medicine*, 23, no. 4 (2004): 351.

3. Ibid.

4. Christopher P. Gilkerson. "Poverty Law Narratives: The Critical Practice and Theory of Receiving and Translating Client Stories." *Hasting Law Journal*, 43 (1992): 904, 912.

5. *See* Clark D. Cunningham. "Lawyer as Translator, Representation as Text: Towards an Ethnography of Legal Discourse." *Cornell Law Review*, 77 (1992): 1298–87.

6. V. Pualani Enos and Lois H. Kanter. "Who's Listening? Introducing Students to Client-Centered, Client-Empowering and Multidisciplinary Problem-Solving in a Clinical Setting." *Clinical Law Review*, 9 (2002): 85.

7. *See* Susan Bryant. "The Five Habits: Building Cross Cultural Competence." *Clinical Law Review*, 8 (2001): 33–107; Susan L. Brooks and Robert G. Madden. *Relationship-Centered Lawyering: Social Science Theory for Transforming Legal Practice* (Durham, NC: Carolina Academic Press, 2010), 277.

8. Lisa Sanders. *Every Patient Tells a Story* (New York: Broadway Books, 2009), 6–7.

9. Ibid., 24.

10. Rita Charon. "Narrative and Medicine." *New England Journal of Medicine*, 350 (2004): 862.

11. David Margolius and Thomas Bodenheimer. "Transforming Primary Care: From Past Practice to the Practice of the Future." *Health Affairs*, 29, no. 5 (2010): 779, 781.

12. Howard B. Beckman and Richard M. Frankel. "The Effect of Physician Behavior on the Collection of Data." *Annals of Intern Medicine*, 101, no. 5 (1984): 692–96. Of the recorded office visits, the physician interrupted the patient's statements during 51 encounters (69 percent). The mean time it took for the physician to interrupt was 18 seconds. Of the patient statements that were completed, no statement took longer than 150 seconds. See also Kim Marvel et al. "Soliciting the Patient's Agenda: Have We Improved?" *Journal of the American Medical Association*, 281, no. 3 (1999): 283–87. Physicians redirected patients' opening statements after 23.1 seconds on average.

13. Sanders, "Every Patient Tells a Story," 6–7.

14. Robert M. Bastress and Joseph D. Harbaugh. *Interviewing, Counseling and Negotiating Skills for Effective Representation* (New York: Aspen Law and Business, 1990), 63–64.

15. Anthony L. DeWitt. "Therapeutic Communication as a Tool for Case Theming." *American Journal of Trial Advocacy*, 29 (2005): 401–2.

16. Liwen Mah. "The Legal Profession Faces New Faces: How Lawyers' Professional Norms Should Change to Serve a Changing American Population." *California Law Review*, 93 (2005): 1728.

17. David A. Binder et al. *Lawyers as Counselors: A Client-Centered Approach*, 2nd ed. (Eagen, MN: West Publishing, 2004), 5.

18. Sanders, "Every Patient Tells a Story," 27.

19. Tseng Wen-Shing and Jon Stretzler. *Cultural Competence in Health Care, A Guide for Professionals.* (New York: Springer Science + Business Media, 2008), 4.

20. Ibid.

21. Rita Charon. "Narrative Medicine: A Model for Empathy, Reflection, Profession and Trust." *Journal of the American Medical Association*, 286, no. 5 (2001), 1899.

22. Megan Alcauskas and Rita Charon. "Right Brain: Reading, Writing, and Reflecting: Making a Case for Narrative Medicine in Neurology." *Neurology*, 70, no. 11 (2008), 893.

23. "Race and Empathy Matter on a Neural Level." ScienceDaily, Northwestern University, http://www.sciencedaily.com/releases/2010/04/100426182002.htm.

24. Arthur Kleinman, Leon Eisenberg, and Byron Good. "Culture, Illness, and Care: Clinical Lessons from Anthropologic and Cross-Cultural Research." *Annals of Internal Medicine*, 88, no. 2 (1978), 251–58.

25. Elois Ann Berlin and William C. Fowkes. "A Teaching Framework for Cross-Cultural Healthcare: Application in Family Practice." *Western Journal of Medicine*, 139, no. 6 (1983), 934–38.

26. Binder et al., "Lawyers as Counselors," 2–11.

27. William Booth. "One Nation, Indivisible: Is It History?" *Washington Post,* February 22, 1998, A1.

28. Ibid.

29. Mah, "The Legal Profession Faces New Faces," 1736.

30. Ibid., 1739–44.

31. Ibid., 1745.

32. 19.7 percent of population five years of age and older speaks a language other than English at home. "One-in-Five Speak Spanish in Four States," September 23, 2008, http://www.census.gov/newsroom/releases/archives/american_community_survey_acs/cb08-cn67.html.

33. See Lynne C. Lancaster and David Stillman. *The M-Factor* (New York: HarperCollins, 2010), 2–285. Lynne C. Lancaster and David Stillman. *When Generations Collide* (New York: Harper Business 2005), 3–335.

34. Marjorie A. Silver. "Emotional Competence, Multicultural Lawyering and Race." *Florida Coastal Law Journal*, 3 (2002): 231.

35. Mullan, Ficklen, and Rubin, *Narrative Matters*, 205.

36. Ibid., 235.

37. "What Is Cultural Competency?" Office of Minority Health, U.S. Department of Health and Human Services, last modified October 19, 2005, http://minorityhealth.hhs.gov/templates/browse.aspx?lvl=2&lvlid=11.

38. Ibid.

39. Rose Voyvodic. "Lawyers Meet the Social Context: Understanding Cultural Competence." *Canadian Bar Review*, 563 (2005), 569–70.

40. "What Is Cultural Competency?"

41. Smedley, Stith, and Nelson, "Unequal Treatment," 126.

42. "The Compelling Need for Cultural and Linguistic Competence," Georgetown University National Center for Cultural Competence, http://nccc.georgetown.edu/foundations/need.html. The National Center for Cultural Competence identifies six compelling reasons for establishing mechanisms for developing cultural and linguistic competence in the healthcare setting. Important among them are to respond to the changing demographics in the United States; eliminate long-standing health disparities experienced by people of diverse racial, ethnic and cultural backgrounds; and improve the quality of services and health outcomes.

43. See Ascanio Piomelli. "Cross-Cultural Lawyering by the Book: The Latest Clinical Texts and a Sketch of a Future Agenda." *Hastings Race & Poverty Law Journal*, 4, no. 131 (2006), 131–79.

44. Silver, "Emotional Competence, Multicultural Lawyering and Race," 238. Silver adapts Sue and Sue's prescription for the "culturally skilled counselor" as goals for the "culturally skilled lawyer." Derald Wing Sue and David Sue. *Counseling the Culturally Different: Theory and Practice*, 2nd ed. (Hoboken: John Wiley & Sons, 1990), 167–69.

45. Liaison Committee on Medical Education (LCME), http://www.lcme.org.

46. Joseph R. Betencourt. "Cross-Cultural Medical Education: Conceptual Approaches and Framework for Evaluation." *Academic Medicine*, 78, no. 6 (2003), 560–69. Melonie Tervalon, "Components of Culture in Health for Medical Students Education." *Academic Medicine*, 78, no. 6 (2003), 570–76. Marjorie Kagawa Singer and Shaheen Kassim-Lakha. "A Strategy to Reduce Cross-Cultural Miscommunication and Increase the Likelihood of Improving Health Outcomes." *Academic Medicine*, 78, no. 6 (2003), 577–87. "Tools for Assessing Cultural Competence Training," Association of American Medical Colleges, http://www.aamc.org/meded/tacct/start.htm.

47. Sonia J. Crandall et al. "Applying Theory to the Design of Cultural Competence Training for Medical Students: A Case Study." *Academic Medicine*, 78, no. 6 (2003), 589. George Rust. "CRASH-Course in Cultural Competence." Lecture to Grady Health System Ethics Committee, National Center for Primary Care at Morehouse School of Medicine, Atlanta, GA, December 2009. Dr. Rust raises

the issue of the risks associated with cultural competence training. Training may confer false confidence, reinforce stereotypes, focus on the exotic rather than the important, emphasize across-group difference over within-group heterogeneity, or diminish the need for culturally representative health care teams.

48. N.J.A.C. § 13.35-6.25; "New Jersey Division of Consumer Affairs," *New Jersey Register*, 40, no. 7 (2008), http://www.nj.gov/lps/ca/adoption/bmeado47.htm.

49. For example, Medicaid regulations require Medicaid providers and participating agencies, including long-term care facilities, to render culturally and linguistically appropriate services. The Health Care Financing Administration, the federal agency that oversees Medicaid, requires that states communicate both orally and in writing "in a language understood by the beneficiary" and provide interpretation services at Medicaid hearings. Medicare addresses linguistic access in its reimbursement and outreach education policies. Medicare "providers are encouraged to make bilingual services available to patients wherever the services are necessary to adequately serve a multilingual population." Medicare reimburses hospitals for the cost of the provision of bilingual services to patients. "Laws," Office of Minority Health, last modified September 8, 2008, http://minorityhealth.hhs.gov/templates/browse.aspx?lvl=3&lvlid=18.

50. *See* Silver, "Emotional Competence, Multicultural Lawyering, and Race"; Bryant, "The Five Habits"; Michelle S. Jacobs, "People From the Footnotes: The Missing Element in Client-Centered Counseling." *Golden Gate University Law Review*, 27 (1997), 345–412.

51. Roy Stuckey et al. "Best Practices for Legal Education: A Vision and a Road Map." *Clinical Legal Education Association* (2007), 88.

52. Smedley, Stith, and Nelson, "Unequal Treatment: Confronting Racial and Ethnic Disparities in Health Care," 562–72.

53. David Shipler. *The Working Poor: Invisible in America* (New York: Knopf, 2004), 210.

54. Kris Shepard, *Rationing Justice: Poverty Lawyers and Poor People in the Deep South* (Baton Rouge: Louisiana State University Press, 2007), 14.

55. Ibid., 15.

56. "Acculturation: Definition," Hispanic Health, http://www.rice.edu/projects/HispanicHealth/Acculturation.html.

57. "National Standards for Culturally and Linguistically Appropriate Services in Health Care," U.S. Department of Health and Human Services, Office of Minority Health, March 2001, http://minorityhealth.hhs.gov/assets/pdf/checked/finalreport.pdf; 42 U.S.C. § 2000d, 45 C.F.R. § 80.1.

58. Kleinman, Eisenberg, and Good, "Culture, Illness and Cure," 251–58.

59. Ibid.

60. *See* Anne Fadiman. *The Spirit Catches You and You Fall Down* (New York: Farrar, Strauss, Giroux, 1997).

61. Ibid., 10.

62. For example, Jehovah's Witnesses do not believe in blood transfusions. This can cause an ethical dilemma for a healthcare provider who wishes to respect the patient's religious beliefs, while at the same time providing appropriate health care.

63. Bryant, "The Five Habits," 74.

64. Rust, "CRASH-Course in Cultural Competence."

65. Ibid.

66. Ibid.

67. J. Emilio Carillo, Alexander R. Green, and Joseph R. Betancourt. "Cross Cultural Primary Care: A Patient Based Approach." *Annals of Internal Medicine*, 130, no. 10 (1999), 829.

68. Bryant, "The Five Habits," 33–107.

69. Nelson P. Miller, et al. "Equality as Talisman: Getting Beyond Bias to Cultural Competence as a Professional Skill." *Thomas M. Cooley Law Review*, 25 (2008), 110.

70. Ibid., 115.

71. Melanie Tervalon and Jann Murray-Garcia. "Cultural Humility versus Cultural Competence: A Critical Distinction in Defining Physician Training Outcomes in Multicultural Education." *Journal of Health Care for the Poor and Underserved*, 9, no. 2 (1998), 118.

72. "New Census Bureau Report Analyzes Nation's Linguistic Diversity," U.S. Census Bureau, http://www.census.gov/newsroom/releases/archives/american_community_survey_acs/cb10-cn58.html.

73. Hyon B. Shin and Robert A. Kominski. "Language Use in the United States: 2007." American Community Service Reports, U.S. Census Bureau, http://www.census.gov/prod/2010pubs/acs-12.pdf.

74. "2006 Hospital Requirements Related to the Provision of Culturally and Linguistically Appropriate Health Care," Joint Commission, http://www.wssdvs.org/Documents/hl_standards.pdf.

75. Ibid.

76. *See* Gay Gellhorn, Lynne Robins, and Pat Roth. "Law and Language: An Interdisciplinary Study of Client Interviews." *Clinical Law Review*, 1 (1994), 245–95.

77. This process of making assumptions has been described as the "ladder of interference" to illustrate how our brains take in data and formulate conclusions. This process follows several steps up the ladder: Step 1: our brain takes in observable data and experiences. Step 2: from what we observe the data in step 1, we start to filter and select specific pieces of it. Step 3: we start to add meaning to the data, based on our personal and cultural experiences and beliefs. Step 4: we draw conclusions from the meaning we have added to the data. Step 5: we adopt beliefs of the world. Step 6: we take action based on those beliefs or judgments. Rick Ross. "The Ladder of Inference," Society for Organizational Learning, http://www.solonline.org/pra/tool/ladder.html. Bryant, "The Five Habits," 42, 56.

78. Miller et al, "Equality as Talisman," 105.

79. Ibid., 106.

80. Kleinman, Eisenberg, and Good, "Culture, Illness and Care," 251–58.

81. Racial and ethnic diversity in the workforce has been correlated with the delivery of quality of care to diverse patient populations. Additionally, there is anecdotal evidence that suggests that lack of diversity in the leadership and workforce of healthcare organizations results in structural policies, procedures, and delivery systems inappropriately designed or poorly suited to service diverse patient populations. *See* Joseph R. Betancourt et al. "Defining Cultural Competence: A Practical Framework for Addressing Racial/Ethnic Disparities in Health and Health Care." *Public Health Reports,* 118 (July–August 2003), 296.

82. Joseph Betancourt, Alexander Green, and J. Emilio Carrillo. "Cultural Competence in Health Care: Emerging Frameworks and Practical Approaches." *Commonwealth Fund* (2002), ix.

83. The five-part series progressed as follows: Class 1: Introduction to Cultural Competence in Health Care; Class 2: Characteristics of Cultural Competence in Health Care; Class 3: Strategies for Cultural Competence in Health Care; Class 4: States of Cultural Competence in Health Care; and Class 5: Adoption and Assessment of Cultural Competence in Health Care.

84. Tools for cultural competence training and assessment are available from the National Center for Cultural Competence at the Georgetown University Center for Child and Human Development, http://nccc.georgetown.edu/index.html.

Chapter 6

Ethical Issues in Medical-Legal Partnership

Paula Galowitz, JD, MSW
Jerome Tichner, JD
Paul R. Tremblay, JD
Steven D. Blatt, MD

Successful medical-legal partnerships (MLPs) typically involve many participants with different qualifications, roles and responsibilities. MLP teams are usually made up of a combination of lawyers, paralegals, physicians, psychologists, nurses, social workers and other clinical providers all working to champion the needs of patients. The ability of these participants and patients—the most important MLP participants—to effectively communicate and collaborate is at the heart of the MLP process. Developing a framework for promoting communication and collaboration between MLP participants is sometimes difficult, however, as ethical rules, laws and related principles sometimes establish barriers against sharing information about the patient's health or legal developments. To better understand the communication-related challenges of an interdisciplinary MLP model, it is important to understand the structure of how MLPs generally work and the various points of communication and collaboration.

The standard life cycle of a relationship between an MLP and a patient-client generally involves at least six steps (see Figure 6.1):

1. healthcare provider identification of a patient's potential legal issue;

2. healthcare provider referral of the patient to the MLP legal staff;

3. MLP legal staff's evaluation of the patient's need for legal representation (and the ability of the legal staff to provide such representation);

4. MLP legal staff's notification to the patient as to whether it will take the patient as a client;

5. if representing the patient, the provision of legal services that may require interaction with healthcare providers and/or other third parties (e.g., translators); and

6. communication with the healthcare provider regarding the status and outcome of the patient's legal matters.

Figure 6.1 The Life Cycle of a Relationship between MLP and a Patient

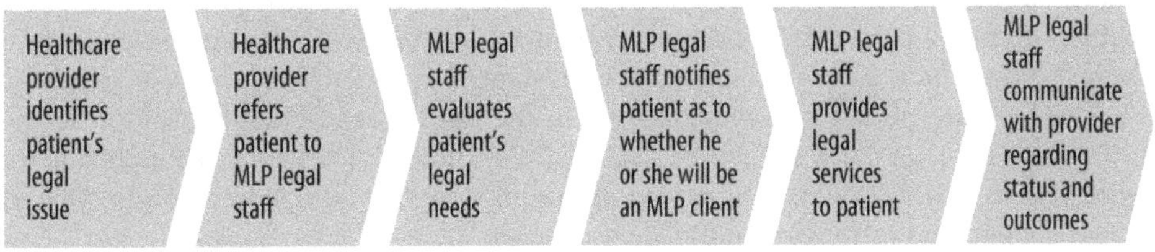

Healthcare provider identifies patient's legal issue → Healthcare provider refers patient to MLP legal staff → MLP legal staff evaluates patient's legal needs → MLP legal staff notifies patient as to whether he or she will be an MLP client → MLP legal staff provides legal services to patient → MLP legal staff communicate with provider regarding status and outcomes

Each step serves a critical function to the MLP's success and also provides challenges with respect to issues such as conflicts of interest, confidentiality and attorney-client privilege which must be considered carefully. From the moment a healthcare provider identifies a patient's potential need for legal assistance, the treating provider and any involved MLP legal staff must engage in the delicate balancing act of promoting the success of the MLP relationship while preserving the protections and rights of the patient. In particular, the interactions between healthcare provider, lawyer and patient need to enable the lawyers to determine and establish the scope (if any) of the legal staff's representation, to provide the lawyer sufficient access to patient information while at the same time preserving the patient's confidentiality and attorney-client privilege. In addition, to increase healthcare provider satisfaction and buy-in to the MLP model, legal staff may need to share some case status information with the healthcare provider whenever permissible. It is important to note that the nature of the interdisciplinary collaboration can influence the ethical issues that need to be addressed in MLPs;[1] the ethical issues are more pronounced where the extent of collaboration is greater.

In this chapter we discuss some of the laws, ethical principles and considerations that affect an MLP's ability to achieve these sometimes conflicting objectives. Although our discussions focus primarily on lawyer-physician-patient involvement and interaction, it is important to recognize that the involvement of nurses, social workers, psychologists and other clinicians in the MLP, who are subject to their own ethical and professional rules, may affect the manner in which information can be shared. We discuss the basic ethical principles guiding lawyers and clinicians, including professional autonomy. We then summarize how lawyers and physicians are both bound by confidentiality and describe certain key sources for these obligations (e.g., ethical rules, privacy provisions under the Health Insurance Portability and Accountability Act (HIPAA) and attorney-client privilege). Next we address the complex issues of confidentiality and conflicts of interest that arise in the unique context of MLPs. We also cover a number of other discrete subjects related to ethics and confidentiality that arise in the context of the MLP model, including mandatory reporting requirements for abuse and neglect.

Ethical Guidelines for Healthcare Providers and Lawyers

We begin this chapter by introducing you to some of the sources of guidance on ethical issues for some of the professional worlds involved in the MLP enterprise. We start with the legal side and then address the medical side. This background should be helpful as we move into a discussion of ethics topics in the later sections.

Lawyers' Ethics Rules, Model Rules and "Law of Lawyering"

Legal education focuses on teaching a combination of substantive law, skills education, and the inculcation of professional values. As part of that last prong, law students are required to pass a course that discusses legal ethics, whether an independent course or a pervasive one. Each student must receive substantial instruction in the history, goals, structure, value, rules and responsibilities of the legal profession.[2] In addition to the course, all but four states require passage of the Multistate Professional Responsibility Examination (MPRE), which focuses on ethical standards, to gain admission to the bar; the acceptable pass rate is determined by each state.[3]

The ethical rules of the legal profession come from a variety of sources. One is the rules of professional conduct adopted by the jurisdiction in which the lawyer is practicing. The American Bar Association (ABA), a voluntary professional association with over 400,000 members, adopted a revised set of model rules of professional conduct in 1983,[4] the Model Rules of Professional Conduct. The ABA Model Rules and the ethics opinions that interpret them are advisory and act merely as models for the rules enacted by each state.

All states (except California) have professional conduct rules that follow the format of the ABA Model Rules.[5] That format is a preamble, a definition section and eight major categories. Those eight categories are:

- Client-Lawyer Relationship
- Counselor
- Advocate
- Transactions with Persons Other than Clients
- Law Firms and Associations
- Public Service
- Information about Legal Services
- Maintaining the Integrity of the Profession

Within these categories, there are 57 specific rules. In many jurisdictions, a rule is split into rules and comments. The rules are more law-like, with codes of conduct, and the comments are intended to guide interpretation of the rules.[6] Many of the rules are phrased as imperatives (i.e., Model Rule 1.1 provides that "a lawyer shall provide competent representation"), and some are permissive or discretionary (i.e., Model Rule 1.16(b) states that "a lawyer may withdraw from representing a client if ...").

In addition to the state ethical rules, additional sources govern the conduct of lawyers, including constitutional, statutory or common-law rules that relate to the ethical obligations of lawyers. Also relevant are decisions in court cases that may interpret the ethics rules, as well as court rules and statutes (both state and federal). As stated in the Scope section of the Model Rules, "the Rules presuppose a larger legal context shaping the lawyer's role. That context includes court rules and statutes relating to matters of licensure, laws defining specific obligations of lawyers and substantive and procedural law in general."[7]

Guidance in applying and interpreting the rules of professional conduct is also found in ethics opinions, which typically are responses to questions from lawyers about the application of the ethics rule to a particular situation. The ABA issues opinions on many aspects of the Model Rules; many state and local bar associations have ethics committees that also issue opinions. These opinions are not binding but can be very helpful resources and may be persuasive. However, the ethical rules, cases, and relevant statutes (as well as opinions) don't give all of the answers. Some of the decision making on ethical issues also depends on an individual lawyer's moral and philosophical compass.

In most states, the rules governing the authority to practice law and professional responsibility are enacted by the highest court in that state. Each state has its own procedure to enforce the ethical rules. Violating provisions of the ethical rules can result in professional discipline by the state, including fines, public and private reprimands, suspension from practice and disbarment.

Medical Ethics

Although medical and legal professionals regard ethical considerations with great importance, the way the two professions approach ethical challenges is considerably different. The American Medical Association (AMA) first articulated its Code of Medical Ethics in 1847. The preamble of the current code (2001) states: "the medical profession has long subscribed to a body of ethical statements developed primarily for the benefit of the patient."[8] The code addresses a wide variety of ethical issues, including social policy issues (abortion, end of life, torture, capital punishment), economic and practice issues, hospital relations, and medical records.

Despite its preeminence in the public eye, membership in the AMA and participation in any of its activities, including adherence to the Code of Medical Ethics, is voluntary. In fact, although it is the largest physician organization in this country, fewer than 20 percent of all practicing physicians are members of the AMA. The Code of Medical Ethics is not associated with any specific statutes. The principles from the Code of Medical Ethics are found throughout medicine and medical education, but participation by physicians is largely voluntary.

In addition to ongoing efforts of the AMA's Council on Ethical and Judicial Affairs to develop and promote ethical behaviors for physicians, most specialty organizations have similar efforts for their membership. Recently, many hospitals, medical schools and even states have taken a more proscriptive approach to undue influence on physician behavior from relationships with the pharmaceutical and medical manufacturing industries. The pervasive practice of physicians receiving gifts, trips to conferences and honoraria are being scrutinized as compromising physicians' objectivity in patient care.

More recently, in 2007, the Accreditation Council of Graduate Medical Education (ACGME) defined six core competencies which all medical residents (physicians in training) must demonstrate. See Appendix 4.1. Under the heading of Professionalism, the ACGME statement declares: "Residents must demonstrate a commitment to carrying out professional responsibilities and an adherence to ethical principles."[9] Not listed in the competencies is any further definition of what those ethical principles are. Thus, the primary accreditation agency for physician training has not defined for its members what medical ethics entails.

As with professional ethics in other fields, medical ethics has long been the subject of study by its practitioners and taught to its trainees. As with lawyers and legal ethics, physicians are taught the tenets of medical ethics and how to apply them to their daily practice (See Medical Ethics in Everyday Practice). However, the application of medical ethics to a practitioner's daily practice is dependent on multiple factors. Often state or federal statutes become paramount in medical decision making. HIPAA, reproductive rights, consent and confidentiality are areas within medical ethics that have specific laws governing professional behaviors. Large hospitals have developed bioethics committees to help guide the staff in all areas of ethics as they relate to patient care.[10]

Medical Ethics in Everyday Practice

Relationships with Pharmaceutical Industry

HIPAA and Communication Issues

Clinical Research

Clinical Research with Vulnerable Populations

Conflicts with Physician Monetary Interests (e.g., unnecessary procedures, fee for service)

Consent to Treatment for Minors

Confidentiality for Minors

Abortion and Right to Life

Sexuality (including Abortion and Right to Life) and Minors

End-of-Life Issues and Patient Decision Making

Medical Documentation Not Accurately Reflecting the Care Delivered

Mandatory Reporting of Suspected Child Abuse/Elder Abuse

Physicians often think of medical ethics in two ways. First, "did I do (or am I about to do) something wrong to the patient?" For example, a patient may have a bad or unexpected outcome and the physician is concerned about malpractice. The physician may be concerned about inadvertently or intentionally breaking confidentiality while caring for the patient. These situations often involve specific statutes which might be breached. When faced with these kinds of concerns, physicians often seek legal advice from their personal or practice counsel or consult with the hospital's or malpractice company's risk management professionals.

The second type of situation in which medical ethics comes to the forefront for a practicing physician is when difficult and complex medical decisions must be made. End-of-life decisions for the terminally ill and termination of pregnancy are very difficult for physicians and patients. State and federal laws do not always offer clarity. Lawyers and risk managers may provide some guidance and advice, but it is frequently not sufficient. Any member of the healthcare team caring for a patient in the hospital can seek guidance from the hospital's Medical Ethics Committee, made up of physicians, nurses, clergy, social workers and laypeople. Some physicians choose not to access these committees and prefer to rely on their own decision-making abilities to guide care. Physicians caring for patients outside of the hospital typically do not have such resources readily available. Medical societies and other professional groups usually do not provide these services. In these circumstances, physicians usually are without formal guidance from those with expertise.

Professional Autonomy

One of the valuable aspects of medical-legal collaborations is bringing together the different professions, with their independent values, roles, professional judgments and moral sensibilities. There are commonalities in these professions. As described by Jacobson and Bloche, there is a "shared set of core social and ethical values, interests, and experiences that help define physicians and attorneys as professionals. The two professions share respect for the individual and commitment to reason, professional judgment, and experience as a basis for decision making."[11]

While recognizing the similarities, it is also important to acknowledge and to celebrate the different values, professional roles, skills and problem-solving approaches that each profession brings to the collaboration.[12] These differences need not be barriers to collaboration but can instead enhance it and the services provided to the patient-client.

One difference that can affect the collaboration is the lawyer's professional independence, which is one of the legal profession's guiding principles/core values. ABA Model Rule 5.4, entitled, "Professional Independence of a Lawyer," has several provisions that relate to

MLPs. For example, Model Rule 5.4(c) provides that "a lawyer shall not permit a person who recommends, employs, or pays that lawyer to render legal services for another to direct or regulate the lawyer's professional judgment in rendering such legal services." The rule prohibits a third party directing or regulating a lawyer's professional judgment in the representation of a client.[13] This principle can affect what (if any) influence the physician may have on what the MLP and the lawyer can do for clients. Other autonomy provisions relate to the prohibition on a lawyer forming a partnership with a nonlawyer if any of the partnership consists of the practice of law[14] and limitations on a lawyer sharing legal fees with a nonlawyer.[15]

There are many ways a lawyer's professional independence can be challenged in an MLP. For example, a lawyer's advice to a client (or the direction of the representation) might be different from what the physician wants for the patient. Similarly, the institutional interest of a healthcare provider might not be consistent with how the client or lawyer sees the client's interests. Additionally, successful partnerships — in which physicians and lawyers work closely together — could result in the professionals merging their advice without informing clients that they might have different approaches.[16] Of course, the patient ultimately gets to decide all important questions, but he or she will be informed (and usually influenced) by advice from professionals. Therefore, the different orientations of the professions might matter to the patient.

Each of the professionals needs an opportunity to understand and appreciate what each professional culture and problem-solving approach brings to the collaboration; similarly the "roles, boundaries, and limits of each team member as they relate to the purpose of the MDP [multidisciplinary practice]"[17] must be addressed. By having initial discussions among the partners in the collaboration about the roles and values of each of the partners, a framework can be established about the parameters of the relationship. The discussion about the relevant issues is not just to learn from each of the professions but also to share the underlying principles. A key piece of the collaboration is to help the "other" understand and appreciate the approaches and values of the professional partners. The collaboration can also result, where appropriate, in the various professional partners embodying those varying approaches and values in their own practices. (See Chapter 4 for further discussion of these issues.)

Ethical concerns and other issues that logically arise should be addressed before the collaboration begins, such as different approaches to confidentiality (discussed later), which cases are appropriate for referral for legal assistance, and what happens when there is a difference of opinion about the appropriate approach. It is important that these issues are unearthed, discussed and addressed before the formal initiation of the collaboration. As stated by commentators in one article about the ethical issues in MLPs:

> When professionals who are educated and trained differently, practice different trades, and follow different ethical codes combine efforts to provide one holistic remedy, each may be required to compromise some of the professional autonomy that each practitioner typically exercises. These clashes of professional independence may arise in determining what cases are appropriate for MLP intervention, what level of intervention is necessary, and what intervention is most suitable for a particular case. This situation begs the question of whose voice reigns supreme in resolving these matters.[18]

The issue, however, is not which voice reigns supreme. The patient-client's voice is the most important; it is critical to make sure that all of the voices get heard by the patient-client, recognizing that each of the professionals is part of an interdisciplinary approach. As noted in an article about a long-standing MLP:

It is true that the lawyers' allegiance to the mission of the MDP, and the lawyers' respect for the other members of the MDP team, may well influence some choices he or she makes in practice regarding the professional relationships with the clients. These choices include which clients to represent and which clients to decline to represent, whether to limit the scope of representation to matters that do not conflict with the mission of the MDP, whether to limit the means of pursuing the clients' objectives to those that are consistent with the philosophy of the MDP, and whether to counsel clients to conduct themselves in a manner that advances the MDP mission. Nevertheless, all of these choices are within the bounds of the ABA Model Rules, although they may require disclosure, and in some instances, informed consent from the client.[19]

Best Practices and Advocacy Strategies for Medical-Legal Partnership

Transparency and communication are critical to successful interdisciplinary partnership. In many cases, it is beneficial for the participating healthcare providers and lawyers (generally through their respective organizations) to enter into a memorandum of understanding, agreement or other relationship-defining documents that help clarify the various roles and responsibilities of the participants and their approaches to ethical issues.[20] In addition, protocols need to be developed that recognize the lawyer's professional independence, even when his or her advice to the client differs from or conflicts with that of the physician, hospital administration or other professionals involved in the collaboration. An organizational structure needs to be developed that "formalizes their relationships and addresses the complexities of responding to ongoing client needs in a manner that both maximizes efficiency of effort and minimizes ethical pitfalls."[21]

In addition to the protocols, there needs to be training, supervision, an ongoing structure[22] and continued communication among the professional partners. One MLP, in which the University of New Mexico School of Law's Child Advocacy Clinic is the legal partner, developed and implemented a formal curriculum to build trust and understanding among the team members; "when trust and understanding is established, differences in professional problem-solving can be turned from a liability into a strength."[23] Attention to structures and ongoing communication helps ensure a collaboration that is more successful for the clients/patients and the professional partners.

Case for Medical-Legal Partnership

Dr. Sanders referred Ms. Greene to see the lawyer about the educational needs of her eight-year-old son, Gabriel. Gabriel has been acting out in school, has difficulty paying attention and is not able to keep up with the classwork. Dr. Sanders wants Ms. Greene to start the process of having the boy evaluated for consideration of an Individualized Education Program (IEP) and has asked the lawyer to help with coordination of the evaluation (see Chapter 9).

When Ms. Greene meets with the lawyer, she explains to him that she has reservations about the testing, because she fears her son will be placed in a special education class. Her daughter had been in a special education class at the same school, and Ms. Greene felt that the experience was quite negative. The legal ethical rules tell us that in counseling Ms. Greene, the lawyer could mention Dr. Sanders's opinion and refer to any relevant moral, economic, social and political factors.[24] However, the ethical rules also tell us that the lawyer shall abide by the client's decision about the objectives of the representation (ABA Model Rule 1.2(a)), even if they are different from what the physician wants.

Questions for Discussion

1. What would you do if you were the lawyer? How would you advise Ms. Greene? How would you collaborate with the physician?

2. What would you do if you were the physician? What does your professional role require here?

This example shows one of the many ways that there can be conflicts between the lawyer's professional autonomy and the approaches of other partners to the collaboration. This example also shows how addressing these questions before the partnership begins can improve the service each professional brings to the collaboration.

Confidentiality for Healthcare Providers and Lawyers

Confidentiality Rules, Principles and Laws

As we already noted, both lawyers and healthcare providers are bound by ethical responsibilities regarding their work with their clients/patients, and both professions emphasize strong protection for confidentiality. However, though confidentiality is prized by the various professions, their separate and disparate confidentiality codes can pose challenges for an MLP.

For lawyers, the strongest protections come from Rule 1.6 of the ABA Model Rules. That rule requires attorneys to maintain the confidentiality of all of the information learned in the representation of a client, unless the client consents or some narrow specified exception (like prevention of reasonably certain death or substantial bodily harm[25]) applies. There is also a related but more narrow protection known as the attorney-client privilege.

For physicians and medical professionals, the confidentiality protection for patients comes from various places. The voluntary code of ethics of the AMA (already discussed) asks physicians to respect the confidentiality of their patients. Perhaps more important, a strong, comprehensive federal law known as the Health Insurance Portability and Accountability Act of 1996 (HIPAA) mandates strict protection except which the patient consents to disclosure or when the legitimate needs of the medical facility requires disclosure.

Table 6.1 provides a summary of the sources of protection of confidentiality discussed in more detail shortly.

Rule 1.6: The Basics of Lawyer Confidentiality

ABA Model Rule 1.6, whose basic principles have been adopted by almost every state, imposes a broad confidentiality obligation on lawyers. According to that rule, all information related to a lawyer's representation of a client must be kept confidential; unless the client provides informed consent, the disclosure is impliedly authorized by the representation (which is a version of informed consent), or unless one of the exceptions to Rule 1.6 applies. The scope of the coverage is broad. It does not matter whether some other persons know the information, or whether the information might be located in a public record

Table 6.1 Confidentiality Provisions

Source	Applies To	Broad or Narrow	Waivable?	Exceptions?
ABA Model Rule 1.6	Lawyers	Very broad	Yes, with informed consent[a]	Few
Attorney-client privilege	Lawyers	Narrow	Yes; sometimes inadvertently	Many
HIPAA	Healthcare professionals and lawyers if "business associates"[b]	Broad	Yes, with written consent	Some
AMA Code of Medical Ethics	Physicians, voluntary	Broad	By implication	By implication

Notes: [a] Informed consent is discussed in the section on confidentiality; [b] Business associates are discussed in the section on HIPAA.

or filing. If the lawyer learned about it as a result of representation, then he or she must not share that information with anyone without the client's informed consent.

Later we discuss the definition of informed consent and how a lawyer might obtain it from a client. (See our example and its discussion to follow.) We see there that the client must understand the risks and benefits of disclosure for the consent to be valid. There are some situations in which a lawyer will share information properly because of the "impliedly authorized" principle. Here's a simple example: If a client comes to a lawyer with a lawsuit filed against him and asks the lawyer for assistance in the matter, the lawyer violates no rule if she files an answer in court to the lawsuit before the deadline expires. Even though her answer to the lawsuit certainly reveals information learned from the client related to the representation, and therefore information plainly covered by Rule 1.6, the lawyer is impliedly authorized to make that disclosure by the nature of the representation.

Sometimes a lawyer may disclose protected information because one of Rule 1.6's exceptions applies. See Table 6.2 for four of the exceptions most relevant to MLP practice.

Table 6.2 Exceptions to Lawyer Confidentiality

Exception	How It Works	Source
To prevent death or bodily harm	The lawyer must "reasonably believe" that action is necessary to prevent "reasonably certain" death or substantial bodily harm.	Rule 1.6(b)(1)
To prevent or rectify fraud by the client	The lawyer must "reasonably believe" that action is necessary to prevent or rectify fraud causing "reasonably certain" substantial financial harm, but only if the lawyer's services were used.	Rule 1.6(b)(2), (3)
To prevent or rectify perjury	The lawyer must "know" that a client or witness has offered or intends to offer false material information to a court or a hearing officer.	Rule 3.3(a)(3), (b)
To protect a person with diminished capacity	The lawyer may reveal secrets if a client's ability to make considered decisions is impaired, and the client faces substantial physical, financial or other harm.	Rule 1.14(b), (c)

Lawyers seldom need these exceptions, but sometimes they are necessary. It is important to realize that most of these exceptions are *discretionary*. A lawyer may reveal information subject to the exceptions, but need not reveal it if the circumstances warrant maintaining secrecy. In the case of perjury, however, the lawyer *must* take reasonable remedial measures, including, if necessary, disclosure of the intended or completed fraud on a court or tribunal; the obligation is mandatory in that setting.

Healthcare Provider Involvement and the Attorney-Client Privilege

Although healthcare providers and lawyers have obligations with respect to confidentiality, lawyers also seek to protect the attorney-client privilege of their communications with clients, which protects such information from being admissible in court or other legal proceedings. Healthcare providers participating in the MLP model need to understand that depending on their involvement in the MLP process, they may be in a position to affect the attorney-client privilege of a patient's communications. First, healthcare providers who participate in meetings with a patient and the patient's MLP lawyer may jeopardize the privileged nature of the conversation if the healthcare provider is viewed as an independent third party not involved in the legal representation of the client. Many state courts take the position that the presence of independent third parties during an otherwise privileged conversation between lawyer and client acts as a waiver of the attorney-client privilege. As a result, healthcare providers should generally not participate in attorney-client meetings.

If the MLP lawyer, the client and the healthcare provider want the healthcare provider to play a more active role, MLP legal staff could request that the healthcare provider actively participate as a member of the client's legal team at least during the course of the meeting. This could be memorialized through the use of a form developed by the MLP legal staff discussing the role of the healthcare provider with the legal team. For example, the form could indicate that the healthcare provider would be present to help the lawyers identify what health conditions could be exacerbated by social issues (e.g., poor living conditions, lack of utilities). Establishing such a relationship would also help protect healthcare provider notes regarding a patient's legal issues that are included in the patient's medical records from being subject to subpoena. Even where a healthcare provider agrees to act as part of the MLP's legal team, MLPs should still be cautious about including healthcare providers in any conversations or meetings with clients, unless the client has given informed consent to waive the privilege. The impact of a healthcare provider's presence in this context when there has not been informed consent by the client has not been tested in the courts and could pose a serious risk of waiver of the attorney-client privilege.

Healthcare providers and MLP lawyers should anticipate that due to the fact that the patient is pursuing legal remedies, medical records of the patient will likely be subpoenaed. Consequently, healthcare providers involved in the MLP model should segregate any legal information obtained regarding a patient from the remainder of the patient's medical records so that such information could be easily redacted if appropriate and necessary.

Health Insurance Portability and Accountability Act of 1996

Overview

The primary federal laws addressing healthcare provider disclosure of patients' health information are found in the Health Insurance Portability and Accountability Act of 1996 and various regulations and recently enacted statutes addressing and clarifying that act (collectively, HIPAA).[26] HIPAA establishes a framework under which most physicians and other health care industry participants (so-called covered entities[27]) are permitted to freely use and disclose individually identifiable health information protected under the law (protected health information) for certain purposes integral to patient care while at the same time generally restricting the use or disclosure of protected health information for other purposes without the express written authorization of the patient (or the patient's authorized representative). Specifically, HIPAA permits covered physicians to use and disclose protected health information for "treatment," "payment" and "healthcare operations" purposes without patient authorization.[28] HIPAA also permits use and disclosure of protected health information without authorization for certain purposes generally related to public health and safety. For example, the law allows the use and disclosure of information without authorization for law enforcement purposes, such as responding to warrants or subpoenas, and public health activities (e.g., required reporting of births, deaths, diseases, or child or elder abuse).[29] For most other purposes, a written authorization is oftlinerequired.[30]

Organizations interacting with physicians and practices covered by HIPAA also need to be aware of the requirements. In particular, individuals or entities qualifying as business associates of covered entities are required to comply with various aspects of HIPAA, such as the security-related requirements for electronic health information, and are subject to potential liability for noncompliance. Business associates include those organizations and individuals who are not a part of the covered entity's workforce and who perform a function on behalf of the entity involving the use of individually identifiable patient information.[31]

Providing legal services to patients will not generally lead to an MLP qualifying as a business associate because the MLP generally acts as an independent organization providing legal services on its own behalf. In some cases, however, MLPs agree to provide direct services to healthcare provider partners, which could result in the organization qualifying as a business associate. Examples of activities that could result in an MLP qualifying as a business associate may include agreeing to pursue payments from payors (e.g., Medicaid) on behalf of a clinical partner or performing healthcare quality-related services for the healthcare provider.

Penalties for violating HIPAA depend on the circumstances surrounding noncompliance and can range from significant civil fines to potential criminal penalties for intentional violations, which may include imprisonment.

Consideration of State Privacy Laws

Healthcare providers, MLPs and other organizations considering the impact of HIPAA must also consider potentially applicable state laws. HIPAA preempts state laws that are less protective of individual's rights but does not eliminate any state requirements that are more protective of patients.[32] As an example of this, where a state law requires that an authorization to disclose protected health information include specific elements not required by HIPAA, such elements must be included along with the elements of a standard HIPAA authorization.

HIPAA's Impact on the MLP Model

For healthcare providers to disclose protected health information to the members of the MLP team, HIPAA requires that such disclosures be made only after the healthcare provider obtains a signed HIPAA-compliant authorization. Although this can interrupt the flow of information during the patient referral process and during the MLP attorney's investigation and management of the patient's legal issues (which often requires that additional information be obtained from healthcare providers), it is relatively easy to avoid any obstacles and risk by developing and using a template HIPAA-compliant (and state law-compliant) authorization form permitting the disclosure of protected health information. MLPs using this approach commonly have the patient sign a pre-prepared authorization provided to the clinical partner at the time the healthcare provider asks the patient if he or she would be interested in a referral to the MLP. During the course of the intake and case management process, the MLP may determine that it needs additional information from healthcare providers potentially not addressed by the initial authorization (e.g., HIV/AIDS information or psychotherapy information). In such cases, the MLP can complete an additional authorization to be presented to the healthcare provider or clinical partner specifically addressing the additional information needed.

In the instances in which an MLP acts as a business associate of a clinical partner, it is still likely that an authorization would be needed to allow the clinical partner to disclose information needed to pursue the patient's legal issues. This is because business associates are restricted from using protected health information for purposes outside of the scope of their duties as a business associate, and it is unlikely that these duties will include the MLP's legal representation of patients (generally healthcare provider partners try to avoid acting in an oversight capacity with respect to legal representation). In addition, MLPs qualifying as business associates will have significant responsibilities under HIPAA with respect to the privacy and security of protected health information and will need to develop substantial policies, procedures and safeguards addressing these requirements. For example, business associates need to appoint a security officer; implement physical, administrative and technical safeguards (e.g., locking devices, encryption technology, password access and disaster recovery protocols); and take other measures.

HIPAA and Medical Practice

Excellent patient care is congruent with ethical decision making. However, at times physicians are faced with tension between ethics and achieving a better patient outcome. For example, when dealing with an elderly patient, the healthcare provider may wish to discuss details with a family member but is prohibited because of patient confidentiality. Similarly, teenagers in many states have rights to confidentiality, yet the healthcare provider may want to involve parents in decision making. In these types of circumstances, it is clear that patient confidentiality must be maintained.

In specific contrast to these situations, it is often necessary for physicians to discuss patients with one another even in the absence of written permission from the patient. Fortunately, HIPAA provides for these cases. For example, an internist can readily discuss a patient suffering from chronic lung disease with a pulmonologist in the physician's practice facility. Almost all physicians rely on other physicians for patient referrals, consultations or specialized testing. Physicians are accustomed to working with a team of professionals to provide care for their patients, and HIPAA allows for a team of healthcare professionals to achieve this without written permission. In the medical setting, this communication is essential to providing timely and appropriate patient care. That same internist who readily consults the pulmonologist may incorrectly assume that it is equally allowable to discuss, without written authorization, the substandard living conditions of the same patient with an MLP lawyer. Healthcare providers may not make the distinction that the MLP lawyer is not considered part of the healthcare team. Healthcare providers may have erroneous views of initiating confidential discussions without prior authorizations, and providers often have unrealistic expectations on receiving confidential information from professionals beyond the healthcare team. Clinical best practices dictate that the physician who refers the patient to the pulmonologist has an expectation that after consultation, the pulmonologist will send a detailed note describing the encounter to the originating physician. This consultation note reassures the physician that the patient did get to the appropriate office and was assessed. Furthermore, it provides the physician with specific guidance as how to care for the patient.

Physicians in an MLP must recognize that the open communication they enjoy with their medical colleagues cannot exist to the same degree with their legal partners. Providers must recognize that they cannot routinely receive or release communication with the legal team as if they were a medical entity. That is, in most instances the attorney will not be considered as part of the medical team and will need specific, explicit consent for communication. Developing appropriate releases of information between the medical and legal teams and establishing clear protocols for all forms of communication is crucial to avoiding misunderstandings and maximizing communication opportunities.

Questions for Discussion

1. If you are a lawyer, and your client is aware that your program is part of an MLP, what would you do if your client wanted the physician to participate in the initial interview?

2. Do you agree with the proposition, found in ABA Model Rule 1.14, that a lawyer may reveal otherwise confidential information to others if necessary to protect a disabled or mentally ill client from suffering serious harm? What safeguards would you establish to protect your clients' rights of autonomy and privacy?

3. How might a lawyer "know" that a client's actions qualify as likely to cause substantial bodily harm or fraud on a tribunal?

Confidentiality in the Medical-Legal Partnership

The MLP model is grounded in an appreciation for the *collaborative*, interdisciplinary quality of the professionals' work with a patient-client. Sometimes, however, the rules governing lawyers' practice make the collaboration a bit delicate. We explore this using the following example.

> Carol Parsons brings her two sons, ages five and seven, into the pediatric clinic because their chronic asthma continues to worsen. The pediatrician, Dr. Alba Dominguez, asks questions about the apartment where Ms. Parsons and her family live, and learns of a severe mice and cockroach infestation. Without some effective advocacy efforts about the family's living conditions, Dr. Dominguez will not have much success in treating the children's asthma. The family needs a lawyer, she concludes.[33]

Using this example, let's consider some of the confidentiality nuances that arise. For purposes of the discussion, assume for the moment that the MLP collaborators *have not* created a comprehensive memorandum of understanding (or some other agreement that addresses these issues). That assumption should help us appreciate the benefits of having such an agreement in advance.

Referrals

Dr. Dominguez understands the benefits of involving a legal team in her treatment of the Parsons children. If she sends an email to the MLP legal office affiliated with her health clinic, describing the family and its situation without asking the Parsons about doing so, she has likely violated her duties to the parent and the children, even if her motives are entirely noble.[34] She needs permission from her patients under HIPAA. Because the children are minors, Dr. Dominguez may rely on the informed consent from their mother.[35] Because that consent may be oral, Dr. Dominguez may simply ask Ms. Parsons if she is willing to talk to a lawyer or paralegal about the infestation issues in her apartment and ask her for permission to make a referral.

Let us assume that Dr. Dominguez asks Ms. Parsons for that authorization, gets it, and makes a referral to the MLP cooperating legal office, including the contact information for Ms. Parsons. The MLP legal office arranges a meeting between Dominic Greene, an MLP paralegal, and Ms. Parsons. Once Ms. Parsons meets with the paralegal, the same kind of confidentiality obligations that applied in the medical clinic protect the information she shares with the legal team. Mr. Greene may not report back to Dr. Dominguez anything about interactions between the legal team and Ms. Parsons without the client's permission. The fact that Dominic Greene is a paralegal does not make the communications any less protected, as long as he is working within a law firm environment, as he is here.[36]

All three of the participants—Carol Parsons, Alba Dominguez, and Dominic Greene—might treat their collaboration as one where information may be shared freely, given the way the referral took place. That assumption *might* be true, as long as Ms. Parsons does not mind that the medical and the legal teams discuss their common goals and share what each knows about the family. But it is risky for the medical and legal teams to *assume* it is true. The oral consent Dr. Dominguez obtained from Ms. Parsons to call the MLP legal office surely covered that referral and the information necessary to affect it, but did it also include permission to disclose everything about the children's health and family issues previously disclosed to the clinic? Seemingly not. Similarly, although Mr. Greene might infer reasonably that he may speak with Dr. Dominguez about the infestation issues given the connection between the physician's work and the legal team's mission, even if he is right about that, does he have permission to report to Dr. Dominguez everything he learns from Ms. Parsons? The answer is "no"—he does *not* have permission, unless he obtains the informed consent of the client (discussed in the next section).

This example shows the delicacy of interdisciplinary collaborations given the important commitment the various professions exhibit to protecting confidences. We review the steps the legal team might take to ensure that any sharing of information has proper authorization.

Informed Consent

Recall that Mr. Greene would like to discuss his legal work with Dr. Dominguez, both to keep her informed for her own clinical purposes and perhaps to use her medical expertise in the advocacy efforts needed to make the Parsons' apartment more safe and habitable. We just saw how risky it would be for him to do so based only on a conversation he has had with Ms. Parsons in his office. A more responsible practice would be for Mr. Greene to obtain written informed consent to his communications with Dr. Dominguez and her staff.

Although Mr. Greene's office likely stocks standard, boilerplate waiver or consent forms for use in a situation like this, we review what ought to be in such a form and how the legal team ought to review it with Ms. Parsons. We assume for this discussion that in the state where this story takes place Ms. Parsons has the direct legal right to make such informed consent decisions for her children. If that jurisdiction has adopted the ABA Model Rules, then Mr. Greene would rely on Rule 1.6(a) of that authority, which states the following: "A lawyer shall not reveal information relating to the representation of a client unless the client gives informed consent, the disclosure is impliedly authorized in order to carry out the representation, or the disclosure is permitted by [one of the exceptions listed in 1.6(b)]."

ABA Model Rule 1.0(e) defines the kind of consent Mr. Greene would need to obtain from Ms. Parsons as follows: "'Informed consent' denotes the agreement by a person to a proposed course of conduct after the lawyer has communicated adequate information and explanation about the material risks or and reasonably available alternatives to the proposed course of conduct."[37]

Given the strictures of the rules governing the law firm's business, Mr. Greene must do more than just ask Ms. Parsons to sign a form that gives the MLP team the right to discuss her children's matters with the health clinic and Dr. Dominguez. A more adequate informed consent discussion between Mr. Greene and Ms. Parsons would include the following factors.

- *The Scope of the Waiver*: Dominic Greene should explain to Carol Parsons the scope of the information he will — and, importantly, he will not — share with the health clinic. He should create a document that explains what Ms. Parsons believes is safe to share, and what she would prefer that he not share.[38]

- *The Costs and Benefits of the Sharing of Information*: ABA Model Rule 1.6(a) as interpreted by Rule 1.0(e) requires that the MLP legal staff inform Ms. Parsons about why she might want to share information with Dr. Dominguez and her team, and why she might not. If there is any risk that the MLP legal team will disclose to Dr. Dominguez, advertently or otherwise, any information that the physician would be required to report to the state's child protective services officials, Ms. Parsons must know about that risk.

- *The Right to Revoke the Consent at Any Time*: Waiver is always a voluntary action, and it is always revocable. This fact has several implications for a written consent document prepared by the MLP legal office. Here are some of them:

  Ms. Parsons has the right to end the sharing of information and revoke the participants' permission to speak about her children's health and legal matters. If she does so, each professional would need to discuss with her how that revocation affects the ongoing legal and medical services provided to the family.

  Alternatively, Ms. Parsons has the right to discontinue the sharing of any new information but permit ongoing discussions among the professionals regarding information already shared. That choice may also have some implications for the collaboration, and Ms. Parsons needs to understand those implications.

  Most complicated, and most worrisome, is this option: Ms. Parsons has the right to withhold permission to share discrete items of information, while otherwise permitting the collaborative discussions about her children's health and her tenancy. This means that conceivably Dominic Greene will know something about his clients that he will not disclose to Dr. Dominguez and, critically, whose nondisclosure he will *not* be able to reveal to Dr. Dominguez. This kind of limited exception to the waiver might tempt the MLP legal team to conclude that it cannot adequately represent the family with that constraint, in which case Mr. Greene might consider counseling Ms. Parsons about the possibility that the law firm would withdraw from the matter. It is doubtful that the law firm could withdraw for that reason,[39] and the threat to do so undercuts any claim that Ms. Parsons's consent would be voluntary.

Both the MLP legal team and Dr. Dominguez must recognize that the collaboration will be subject to this ongoing and inevitable uncertainty. Each professional will necessarily harbor some doubt about whether the other knows some important information but cannot share it. That uncertainty is a constraint on the collaboration, but it is unavoidable.[40]

For the MLP legal team to collaborate with Dr. Dominguez while respecting the confidentiality rights of Ms. Parsons and her children, it should draft a document for Ms. Parsons to sign outlining the scope of the waiver as just described. The MLP legal team must also explain to her the meaning of the waiver. The document prepared for the client's signature need not (and likely will not) cover all the permutations of the revocation options just described. No one will know at the beginning of the relationship whether any of those scenarios will arise, and the odds are that none will. But both the form and the conversation should alert Ms. Parsons of her rights to limit or change the consent as she sees fit. And of course, the MLP team and Dr. Dominguez should discuss the effects and the necessary limitations of this waiver of confidences.

Best Practices and Advocacy Strategies for Medical-Legal Partnership

An effective MLP partnership considers some of the following practices in its effort to serve its patients/clients well, honor the letter and spirit of the ethical considerations at stake and protect both the medical and the legal institutions from liability and mistakes.

- *Memoranda of Understanding (or Other Agreements) and Protocols*: Many of the more intricate confidentiality concerns may be anticipated by the MLP collaborators. Healthcare providers and legal providers should consider entering into Memoranda of Understanding (or other agreements) and protocols that establish the roles and responsibilities of each participant and clarify how each professional will operate to protect confidential patient-client information.

- *Effective Waiver and Consent Forms*: Every organization, whether medical or legal, will use waiver forms. The waiver and consent forms should be carefully tailored to cover only the information necessary to achieve the objectives desired by the professionals and the patient-client. Revisit forms signed in the past to ensure that the details of the consent are still appropriate. Ensure that all of the forms comply with HIPAA rules and regulations.

- *Transparency, Conversation and Informed Consent*: Patients and clients have a legal and a moral right to confidentiality. Although it is often in their interest to permit some disclosure to achieve their objectives, the patients/clients should never feel that their consent is anything less than fully voluntary and the result of their own free election. In addition to forms, frank and open conversations about the waiver request are essential to ensure that any waiver is based on informed consent by the client. Similarly, the collaborating professionals need to be as clear as possible with each other about the scope and the protocols for sharing information.

- *Protocols for Protecting Attorney-Client Privilege*: Collaborating professionals need to take great care to ensure that an individual's attorney-client privilege does not become waived because of the presence of an unnecessary person during a communication involving a member of the legal team. The professionals must remain attentive to the nature of the conversations and the participants. Collaborating medical and legal teams must establish strict protocols, including shadow files and firewalls, to protect records of legal communications from becoming part of the medical records.

Conflicts of Interest for Lawyers and Physicians

Legal Conflicts of Interest in an MLP Setting

When a lawyer represents a client, the work the lawyer does might deprive another person of some rights or affect that other person's interests in a harmful way. Generally speaking, that principle does not apply to healthcare providers — healing one patient seldom causes ill health in another person. But lawyering is not a victimless pastime,[41] so lawyers must make sure that those who might be harmed by their work are not also their clients. Lawyers therefore regularly engage in protocols to anticipate, avoid and react to conflicts of interest, whether actual or potential.

In this section we address conflicts of interest in the MLP setting. We do not canvass the typical conflicts protocols law firms generally use; as a law office, an MLP practice honors all of the usual strictures regarding attending to conflicts involving present clients[42] and former clients,[43] as well as those limitations arising from commitments among lawyers sharing a law practice.[44] Instead, we identify a few instances in which an MLP practice might implicate special conflicts concerns arising from the fact of the collaboration among the professions.

Before we address a few examples, we highlight the basic principles governing conflicts of interest in the attorney-client relationship. Table 6.3 explains the basic rules.

Table 6.3 Conflict of Interest Rules Governing Lawyers

ABA Model Rule	Explanation[a]
1.7(a)(1)	A lawyer may not accept a matter that is opposed to another ongoing client. Usually not waivable even with client consent.
1.7(a)(2)	A lawyer must ensure that other allegiances or interests do not interfere with his or her commitment to a client. Might be waivable if the affected client gives informed consent, confirmed in writing.
1.9(a)	A lawyer may not oppose a *former* client if the new matter is substantially related to the prior matter. Waivable with informed consent of *both* clients, confirmed in writing.
1.9(b)	A lawyer may not work on a matter opposing a client of the lawyer's *former law practice,* but only if the lawyer has information about the previous matter.
1.10(a)	In general, if one lawyer in a practice is forbidden to work on a matter, *all lawyers* in that practice will be forbidden as well, with some narrow exceptions.

Note: [a] The explanations are simplified; in fact, their application is typically far more complex and nuanced than the table implies.

Conflict Concerns Triggered by Referrals

A centerpiece of a successful MLP practice is the flow of referrals from healthcare providers to the legal staff. The elegance of the MLP model rests on the fundamental truth that medical problems often need legal intervention for successful solution. Just as a physician might refer a patient to a cardiac specialist if necessary to resolve a serious heart disease problem, so might that physician refer an AIDS patient to a legal specialist if the patient needs assistance to sustain health.

Imagine, then, the following scenario:

> Dr. Adrienne Koh has been treating Alex Jones, an HIV-positive patient who has been suffering from serious mental health reactions to the news of his infection with the AIDS virus.[45] Dr. Koh knows that Mr. Jones's health might benefit from an HIV legal check-up,[46] so she makes her typical referral to the affiliated MLP program. With Mr. Jones's consent, she describes to the MLP staff the reasons for the referral. At the MLP office, Dominic Greene, a paralegal, quickly recognizes Mr. Jones's name and address. Greene has been working with a client, Stephanie Martin, on legal issues relating to her having been a recent victim of severe domestic violence. Mr. Jones is Ms. Martin's former lover and her assailant.

We see here how the otherwise proper referral of Alex Jones's matter from the healthcare provider to the MLP legal team has created a possible conflict of interest problem for the MLP. The MLP owes a limited duty of confidentiality and fidelity to its prospective clients, including Alex Jones.[47] The staff may not reveal any information arising from the intake screening, as that information is protected as confidential under ABA Model Rule 1.6, and neither may the staff use the information in its representation of another client.[48] Nor may the legal team represent a client with interests adverse to Alex Jones in a matter related to the subject mater of the intake screening.[49] The MLP staff therefore has a worry that it may not be able to continue to represent Ms. Martin against Mr. Jones as a result of this call.[50]

Even if the MLP is not disqualified from continuing to represent Ms. Martin, it wants to avoid this worry and the risks such a referral might create. It therefore needs to establish screening protocols by which the healthcare provider and the legal team identify possible conflicts before the healthcare provider transmits any personal information. It will establish a screening mechanism where only the name gets disclosed, without any reference to the nature of the legal need or any other factual information. If the name does not trigger any problems, then the healthcare provider may share whatever limited facts it has authorization to disclose. With the name and the limited information (including, if relevant, the names of any persons involved with the prospective client whose interests might be adverse to him), the MLP staff may then determine whether any likely conflict will arise. If not, the staff may decide, using its standard intake procedures, whether the referral warrants acceptance of the new legal matter.

Conflicts Triggered by Inconsistent Allegiances

The collaborative nature of the MLP arrangements might lead to an awkward clash of allegiances. From the perspective of the MLP legal team, its allegiances may be tracked carefully and explicitly through conventional and MLP-specific (as just described) conflict-checking designs. But the close work between the MLP law firm and the institutional healthcare provider might lead to conflict-like situations, even if they do not rise to the level of an actual, formal conflict of interest for the lawyers or the law firm.

Imagine, for instance, the following scenario:

> Carol Parsons brings her two sons, ages five and seven, into the pediatric clinic because the children's chronic asthma continues to worsen. The physician, Alba Dominguez, asks questions about the apartment where Ms. Parsons and her family live and learns of severe mice and cockroach infestation. Without some effective advocacy efforts about the family's living conditions, Dr. Dominguez will not have much success in treating the children's asthma. The family needs a lawyer, she concludes.

> The MLP clinic accepts the Parsons family as a client and files an aggressive lawsuit against the landlords, Jeffrey and Elaine Lidman. The Lidmans own the aging three-decker where the Parsons live and have never been clients of the MLP law firm, so no conflict of interest arises for the lawyers.

> But Elaine Lidman is a long-standing patient of the medical clinic where Dr. Dominguez practices. Although Dr. Dominguez is not her physician, Ms. Lidman sees Dr. Dominguez's colleague, Dr. Albert Kisambiro, for treatment of serious, malignant breast cancer. Dr. Dominguez knows that the litigation against the Lidmans has two significant side effects for the landlords—it exhausts and weakens Elaine, leaving her much sicker, and it depletes the family's finances, an important source of payment for Elaine's healthcare treatment. Because of the institutionalized MLP arrangement at the medical clinic, Dr. Kisambiro regularly works with the lawyers and paralegals from the MLP law firm.

The story just described is not likely to arise in a law firm's conventional practice. The close work between the healthcare providers and the lawyers in an MLP setting, however, leads to complicated allegiances among the clients of the lawyers and the patients of the physicians, of which the example is one, perhaps somewhat exaggerated example.

From a conventional legal ethics perspective, the situation seemingly does not qualify as a worrisome conflict of interest for the MLP legal team. The Lidmans are, ethically speaking, "strangers" to the lawyers, whose clients, the Parsons family, are entitled to their undivided loyalty, regardless of the harm to the landlords.[51] The fact that the physician has allegiances to the landlord does not interfere directly with the lawyer's work. But seen as an organic whole, the institution of the MLP *does* have conflicting allegiances, and the participants must negotiate those tensions.

Those negotiations have two implications. First, the healthcare providers and the legal providers must understand the limits of each other's professional role when each chooses to engage in an MLP arrangement. The lawyers must understand that healthcare providers might display a wider swath of caring connections than the legal providers are accustomed to. The healthcare providers must understand that any such wider swath of caring connections may not be relevant for the more focused and isolated work of the legal team. The second implication follows from the first one. Because of these understandings, the *clients* in an MLP arrangement might be entitled to some fair warning that their lawyers practice within a setting where the caring connections are more diffuse than in a conventional law firm. Put another way, the MLP lawyers' practice may be *different* from that of conventional lawyers because of the collaboration. Those lawyers might practice law with a greater concern for how their legal tactics affect other persons, more so than lawyers trained in the traditional fashion. If this reflects differences from typical law practice, the MLP clients deserve to know about the quality of those differences.

Institutional Conflicts

The final set of conflicts noted here are both the most obvious ones emanating from an MLP practice and the most easily accounted for. They concern the institutional interests of the healthcare providers and the legal providers. We separate these institutional conflicts into two types, direct and indirect.

Direct Institutional Conflicts

The clients of MLP lawyers must know that the lawyers may not represent the clients on matters directly adverse to the medical clinic, hospital or other institutional provider of healthcare services. A truly independent lawyer would not be so limited, and could pursue, say, a medical malpractice claim against the patient's medical provider as part of the representation. An MLP lawyer may not do so, and the clients must know of that limitation in advance. Although the MLP lawyer may not file a claim against the collaborating medical providers, it would not be improper for that lawyer to recognize the possibility of such a claim and refer the client to an appropriate lawyer or bar referral service. A responsible MLP structure permits that referral, notwithstanding its slight disloyalty to the medical provider, and the substantive law of malpractice likely requires it.[52]

Indirect Institutional Conflicts

Because the MLP arrangements have institutional history and collective investments of time and experiences, the participants naturally develop allegiances. One possible result of these allegiances is an unwillingness on the part of the MLP lawyers to antagonize the collaborating healthcare providers. This felt responsibility might, in certain settings, create some subtle (or not-so-subtle) influences on the tactics of the MLP legal team. Those influences might rise to the level of a conflict of interest, which the legal team must ethically address.

The key issue for an indirect conflict is whether there exists "a significant risk that the representation [of the client] will be materially limited by the lawyer's responsibilities to" the healthcare provider (ABA Model Rules 1.7(a)(2)). In other words, an indirect conflict might arise if the client's representation leads the lawyer to want to take actions that the lawyer fears will displease the collaborating healthcare providers. The example from the previous section, where the lawsuit against the landlord leads the landlord's physician to oppose the action, is one such case. Another might be a strategy by which the MLP legal team sues a different healthcare provider on behalf of the client. The fundamental point is that because of its allegiances, the MLP legal team is different from a typical unfettered lawyer, and the team must ensure that its allegiances do not interfere with the duties owed to its clients.

Questions for Discussion

1. How might a lawyer's commitment to the healthcare institution or the providers with whom the lawyer works create divided allegiances? If there are any, should prospective clients be warned about that? If so, how? How should the lawyer deal with any divided allegiances?

2. Do healthcare providers face similar conflicts of interests as lawyers? What might those be?

Identifying the Lawyer's Client in an MLP Setting

Who Is the Client and What Is the Scope of the Attorney-Client Relationship?

Physician-Patient and Attorney-Client Relationships

Although lawyers are familiar with conflicts, most physicians have no experiences with them. In fact, the ethics involving physicians accepting patients are very different from lawyers accepting clients. At most hospitals, physicians take turns accepting patients who are seen through the emergency department and do not have their own physician. For example, a patient arriving at the emergency department with appendicitis will be assigned to a surgeon unless he or she has an established relationship with a different surgeon. Once a physician has provided any type of care to a patient, the physician-patient relationship is established and can only be disrupted through specific procedures. Without appropriate education, the physician may become puzzled or even upset by a conflict resulting in the MLP lawyer not accepting a case.

Although the attorney-client privilege is a concept that all physicians profess familiarity with, many may erroneously equate it with the physician-patient relationship and do not fully understand its implications. For example, an adult child may accompany his elderly parent to the physician. During the encounter, the adult child may participate and share the family's concerns with the physician. In this case, the elderly patient allows the child to participate in the encounter. Usually, this is done in an informal way by the physician asking, "Mrs. Jones, do you want your son to stay while I talk with you?" Patients are often encouraged to bring family members to the visit to share information with the physician, clarify concerns and participate in important decisions.

Conversely, third parties are seldom included into the attorney-client arena. As this chapter described earlier, doing so could invalidate privilege and confidentiality. Exclusion of family members or even the physician from the "team approach" or the lack of open communication with the MLP lawyer is often puzzling and frustrating to the physician. The requirement for written releases, exclusion from substantive discussions and lack of progress updates are significantly different from the typical medical model. In establishing the partnership, these issues must be clarified with the medical team.

Patient versus Client

Both medical and legal professionals must recognize that even after the logistics of navigating the ethical differences between the two teams have been established, the patient may need clarification of everyone's role. It is not uncommon for anyone, especially people in the midst of medical or legal situations, to be confused about the role of each professional, advice given or strategies discussed. Therefore, during an MLP case it would not be unlikely for the patient to contact the healthcare provider's office for an answer to a legal question or approach the lawyer to address a medical issue.

It is crucial for the MLP legal staff, the client and the client's representatives and relatives that the MLP legal staff clearly establish and communicate who will provide the legal services, who is entitled to receive the legal services and what the scope of legal services will include. By way of example, imagine the following scenario:

> Jane Doe, a minor with autism, is accompanied by her mother and father to a pediatric visit at a local clinic that participates in an MLP program. The purpose of the visit is to evaluate Jane's general physical condition. During the course of the visit, the treating pediatrician learns that Jane's school has repeatedly failed

to provide her with any special education supports. During the course of the clinical evaluation, the pediatrician recognizes that the MLP legal staff may be able to assist the family in pressuring the school to provide needed support. After receiving a signed authorization, the healthcare provider introduces the family to the on-site MLP lawyer and an evaluation/intake meeting is held.

During the course of the meeting, after receiving preliminary information from the family, the lawyer explains orally that she will represent the child and attempt to force the school to provide the necessary support. The lawyer is participating in a new MLP program and does not formally provide an engagement letter to the family. A week later, the mother calls the lawyer and indicates that the father spent their rent money and, when confronted, assaulted the mother. She requests assistance in securing a restraining order against the father and having him removed from the apartment. At the same time, the father calls the pediatrician who made the referral and states that the mother is irrational and is endangering their daughter. He asks the healthcare provider for the lawyer's assistance in securing custody of the child.

The predictable chaos that would likely occur after such a series of events, which could involve the lawyer and the clinical partner having to defend their roles, could be easily avoided. The healthcare provider should reinforce orally and in writing (through use of standard forms developed in conjunction with the MLP) that the healthcare provider is not offering and will not provide legal advice and that all legal questions should be addressed to the MLP legal staff. Similarly, the MLP legal staff should develop and use a written engagement letter specifically identifying whom it will represent (e.g., Jane Doe) and should inform the patient that the MLP will not be representing any other individuals or family members without a new engagement agreement. In addition, the engagement letter should describe the specific matter(s) for which the MLP legal staff will provide representation. The use of forms by the healthcare provider and the MLP will greatly assist in setting appropriate boundaries with the Doe family. Such forms will also hopefully have the effect of clarifying the role of the MLP legal staff and the healthcare provider for family members who may have never had someone (much less a team of people) fighting on their behalf.

Best Practices and Advocacy Strategies for Medical-Legal Partnership

Conflicts of interest are inevitable in any law practice, and the collaboration between the healthcare providers and the legal team increases the likelihood of some kinds of conflicts coming up. An effective MLP collaboration will understand this likelihood and take thoughtful measures to respond to the actual and potential conflicts that appear. Those measures may include the following:

- *Engagement Letters*: In the world of conflicts of interest, it is essential for the legal team to identify those who are indeed "clients," for the client relationship triggers the most direct conflict worries. The legal team should have explicit client retainer agreements or engagement letters identifying the client and articulating the scope of the relationship.

- *Conflict-Checking Databases*: Every law firm must maintain a searchable list of its present and former clients to check for conflicts in advance of accepting a new matter.

- *Memorandum of Understanding (or Other Agreement), Indirect Institutional Conflicts*: In an MLP collaboration, the interests of the healthcare providers and the scope of its "caring community" will not be identical to those of the legal team. As described, those differing interests do not necessarily represent serious conflicts of interest, but they may affect the working relationship between the professionals. The MLP collaborators should identify any such considerations explicitly and negotiate a Memorandum of Understanding (or other agreement) articulating how each member of the collaboration will respond to them.

- *Memorandum of Understanding (or Other Agreement), Direct Institutional Conflicts*: In an MLP, the lawyers are usually prohibited from representing their clients in matters directly adverse to the healthcare providers. The MLP collaborators should acknowledge the scope of this limitation through a Memorandum of Understanding (or other agreement) at the commencement of their relationship, and, of course, clients of the MLP legal team must understand this restriction on the lawyers' representation scope as well.

- *Effective Waiver Templates and Execution*: Many of the conflicts of interest arising in an MLP setting will be *waivable*—the affected client or clients may waive the conflict through a process of informed consent. The MLP legal team must document any such waiver through an effective form or document memorializing the election of the client. Although a practice will rely on stock forms to state this process, the waivers should never be boilerplate. A template is essential for starters, but any template must reflect the specific circumstances of an individual's waiver.

- *Protocols:* The MLP collaborators should develop protocols to address anticipated issues that arise in such a collaboration. Issues that should be addressed include how referrals will be made and the nature of the interaction between the healthcare referring source and the lawyer.

- *Transparency and Conversations*: As with the Best Practices for Confidentiality, the conflict worries in a fluid, multilayered interdisciplinary MLP practice deserve a lot of open and frank conversation, among the healthcare providers, the legal team and the patient-clients. Memoranda of Understanding, protocols and waiver forms are essential to good practice, but they do not and cannot replace open, honest conversation about the nature of the MLP collaboration and its implications for the participants.

Case for Medical-Legal Partnership

Mr. Wilson, a 75 year-old man, was admitted to the hospital for a heart valve replacement. His physician, Dr. Johnson, refers Mr. Wilson to the MLP lawyer so that Mr. Wilson can complete advanced directives (including a Health Care Proxy and Power of Attorney).

When Mr. Wilson meets with the lawyer, he also mentions that he wants legal assistance because he is not happy with the hospital's plans for his discharge. Mr. Wilson tells the lawyer that the social worker said she was discharging him in two days to a nursing home, whereas Mr. Wilson believes that he needs an inpatient rehabilitation facility, as the nursing home does not have a rehabilitation program that he considers adequate to assist in his postsurgery recovery. Mr. Wilson was informed by his social worker that he needed to be discharged because his medical insurance would not cover any additional days in the hospital and only the nursing home had room for him at this time.

Questions for Discussion

1. Assuming that the memorandum of understanding in this MLP did not prohibit legal representation in this type of situation, should the lawyer help advocate for Mr. Wilson, even though it was contrary to the apparent interests of the hospital?

2. If you were Mr. Wilson's lawyer what would you say to him in response to his complaints about the hospital's discharge plan? What is your role in this situation?

3. If you were Dr. Johnson, how would you think about this situation? What is your role in this situation?

Other Ethical Concerns in MLP Practice

Mandatory Reporting of Abuse and Neglect

The Mandatory Reporting Challenges in an MLP Practice

Mandatory reporting is one issue in MLPs that affects collaboration and highlights the issues surrounding professional autonomy, confidentiality and conflict of interest, particularly in those based in pediatric or geriatric settings. Most states require physicians and other professionals, such as nurses, psychologists, social workers and teachers, to report all cases of suspected child abuse[53] or neglect;[54] most also require mandatory reporting of elder abuse or neglect to the appropriate state agency.[55] Even if there is no conclusive evidence that child abuse or neglect has occurred, the suspicion of abuse or neglect is sufficient to mandate reporting to a governmental agency. Failure to do so can have professional, civil and even criminal implications. In many states, healthcare providers are required to undergo mandatory training about child abuse.[56] Most states do not include lawyers in the statutory list of professionals who are required to report.[57] Moreover, the ethical codes applicable to lawyers in many states would probably bar them from making such a report, except in imminent emergencies. See Chapter 11 for further discussion of mandatory reporting.

It is possible to have an MLP patient-client who has abused or neglected a child. If the healthcare provider suspects that this has occurred, then a report to a governmental agency is required. Were the lawyer to become aware of the abuse or neglect by the client, the attorney would likely be specifically prohibited from disclosing this information. These differing reporting requirements can lead to discord between the medical and legal professionals. Following their profession's ethical tenets may lead to opposite actions. Following is an example that highlights these issues:

> Dr. Wilson, an internist, has referred her patient, Carla Simons, to the MLP legal team because Ms. Simons's public assistance benefits have been terminated. In the course of the legal interview, the lawyer learns that Ms. Simons has been keeping her 12-year old son out of school the last two months so that he can help her care for her twin daughters, who were born two months ago. Ms. Simons has been overwhelmed by caring for her newborns. Keeping her son out of school might well be considered neglect, something the internist might be required to report to the appropriate state agency; the lawyer has no such reporting requirement. What would you do if you were the lawyer? What if you were the physician?

Lessons Learned from Collaborations between Social Workers and Lawyers

Similar concerns about the impact of mandated reporting have arisen in collaborations between lawyers and social workers; these experiences are relevant in collaborations between lawyers, physicians and other clinical providers. Many legal services and clinical programs have taken the position that social workers and social work students who are part of the program's legal representation of clients come under the rubric of law office personnel and are therefore bound by the attorney-client rules of confidentiality.[58] ABA Model Rule 5.3 (and comment 1) requires that lawyers make reasonable efforts to ensure that any nonlawyer who is employed, retained or associated with the lawyer conduct him- or herself in ways that are compatible with the professional obligations of the lawyer, including the requirement of maintaining confidentiality. Others have concluded that if a social worker's obligations are defined by his or her role as a member of the law firm, then the social worker, like the lawyer, is obligated not to report and a court would conclude that "a social worker employed within a law firm ought to be treated as a member of a legal team and not as part of a free-standing social worker"[59] as long as the social worker is part of the interdisciplinary team that is representing the client.

Although this may help in some situations, it does not resolve the dilemma when the other professional has independent obligations under the relevant code of ethics or laws. It also does not resolve the dilemma when the setting is not a legal office but another setting, such as a hospital or healthcare facility.[60]

One way to overcome the ethical dilemmas is to follow a general rule that the confidentiality requirements of the primary service provider should prevail.[61] Thus, if the primary service provider is the legal services office or if the primary objective is legal representation, then the social worker or mental health professional will come under the lawyer's confidentiality umbrella and will be prohibited from revealing privileged information. If the professional goal is therapy, then the mental health professional's privilege and confidentiality rules apply. Similarly, if the primary service provider is the physician or healthcare provider, then the requirements of the physician or healthcare provider prevail for those professionals; however, the lawyer still has to follow the confidentiality rule for lawyers.

Another approach to minimizing difficulties is to have a limited relationship between the two professionals in which each area is given discrete tasks. Clients are given advance notice of the relative lines of authority of the professionals as well as the legal reporting obligations of the physicians and social workers (such as the duty to report). Under this approach, the attorney would probably share less information and would not give the physician or social worker access to the client's file.

For both ethical and role issues, it is useful to identify and discuss possible conflicts at the beginning of the relationship.[62] If the lawyer and social worker work in the same agency, it is critical that it be decided whether (and, if so, when and how) they will share information;[63] even when the lawyers and social workers are in different agencies, it is extremely useful for role issues to be clarified in writing at the beginning of the relationship. Another approach is to build a "confidentiality wall" that limits access to protected client information, such as information about possible abuse or neglect.[64] Although the wall does limit some of the free flow of information (and the free flow is important for interdisciplinary collaborations), it does provide a way for professions to collaborate on other issues while avoiding the possible ethical conflicts resulting from mandatory reporting rules.[65]

Another means to avoid or resolve potential conflicts is for the professions to address the subject of interprofessional conflicts explicitly; this could be done with an ethical opinion by each profession's ethics committee.[66] Alternatively, the state legislatures could adopt a new confidentiality statute that would apply consistently to lawyers, social workers, physicians, psychologists and other healthcare providers.[67] The obvious advantage of such a uniform statute is that "the professionals would have a clear understanding of their obligations to the state, and the professionals could provide their clients a clear definition of confidentiality and its exceptions."[68] The uniform statute would thus make treatment and representation of clients/patients easier and would improve the collaboration.[69]

Best Practices and Advocacy Strategies for Medical-Legal Partnership

Until there are changes in state rules and/or ethical opinions that modify and clarify the confidentiality and mandated reporting issues, there are best practices that MLPs can follow. The list below includes some of these practices:

- *Agreements and Protocols:* There should be discussion among the MLP partners about the issues surrounding mandatory reporting and agreements (whether in the Memorandum of Understanding or other documents) of the nature of the conflicts and how they will be resolved. Protocols should be developed by and shared with the appropriate staff.

- *Training:* There should be training of all the staff on the ethical responsibilities of each of the partners to the collaboration. "Such training engenders better understanding among staff, enhanced services to clients, and fewer ethical crises."[70] There also needs to be ongoing communication and training built in to the collaboration, once it begins.

- *Forms:* Another issue for which protocols and documents need to be created is the communication with the client and the process for obtaining informed consent from the client (if consent can ethically be obtained).[71] It has been suggested that the retainer that the client signs should include provisions that describe the unique parts of the multidisciplinary practice, as well as a separate release that allows the lawyer to talk with nonlawyers about relevant parts of the case; the lawyer should advise the client that physicians and other professionals are mandated reporters and may have a statutory duty to report if the client gives consent to share information.[72]

Conclusion

The rules governing lawyers' ethics and practice, as they have developed over the years, have tended to assume a rather traditional service delivery setting, with a self-contained law firm and its discrete clients. The principles governing medical ethics and that of other healthcare professionals, although more flexible than that in law, still tend to envision a delivery system that remains intradisciplinary, rather than interdisciplinary. The MLP model, with its creative approach to multidisciplinary service, therefore sometimes bumps into traditional ethical concepts in an awkward way, as we have seen here. Practitioners using the MLP model may nevertheless succeed, if they are intentional, caring and careful, in offering high-quality service to their clients and patients while at the same time respecting the rules, principles and commitments reflected in the respective ethics regimes.

---

1. J. Michael Norwood and Alan Paterson, "Problem-Solving in a Multidisciplinary Environment? Must Ethics Get in the Way of Holistic Services," *Clinical Law Review* 9 (2002): 346; Jacqueline St. Joan, "Building Bridges, Building Walls: Collaboration between Lawyers and Social Workers in a Domestic Violence Clinic and Issues of Client Confidentiality," *Clinical Law Review* 7 (2001): 430–38.

2. Standard 302 (a) (5) of the ABA Section of Legal Education and Admission. *See* http://www.abanet.org/legaled/standards/2009-2010%20StandardsWebContent/Chapter3.pdf.

3. Information about the MPRE is available on the National Conference of Bar Examiners website: http://www.ncbex.org/multistate-tests/mpre/.

4. ABA Commission on Ethics 20/20 available at http://www.abanet.org/ethics2020/chairs.html.

5. Links to the rules for each state can be found at http://www.abanet.org/cpr/links.html#States (last visited June 23, 2010).

6. ABA Model Rules of Professional Conduct, Preamble [21].

7. ABA Model Rules, Scope, ¶ 15(available at http://www.abanet.org/cpr/mrpc/preamble.html).

8. American Medical Association, "AMA Code of Medical Ethics," last revised June 2001, http://www.ama-assn.org/ama/pub/physician-resources/medical-ethics/code-medical-ethics/princi-ples-medical-ethics.shtml.

9. Accreditation Council for Graduate Medical Education, "Common Program Requirements: General Competencies," last revised February 13, 2007, http://www.acgme.org/outcome/comp/GeneralCompetenciesStandards21307.pdf.

10. Amy T. Campbell, et al., "How Bioethics Can Enrich Medical-Legal Collaborations," *Journal of Law, Medicine & Ethics* 38 (2010): 847–62.

11. Peter D. Jacobson and M. Gregg Bloche, "Improving Relations between Attorneys and Physicians," *Journal of the American Medical Association* 294 (October 26, 2005): 2083–85.

12. For a discussion of these differing approaches, see, e.g., Norwood and Paterson, "Problem-Solving in a Multidisciplinary Environment?" 362; Marcia M. Boumil, Debbie F. Freitas and Cristina F. Freitas, "Multidisciplinary Representation of Patients: The Potential for Ethical Issues and Professional Duty Conflicts in the Medical-Legal Partnership Model," *Journal of Health Care Law & Policy*, 13, no. 1 (2010): 122–25.

13. Comment [2] to ABA Model Rule 5.4 provides: "this Rule also expresses traditional limitations on permitting a third party to direct or regulate the lawyer's professional judgment in rendering legal services to another."

14. ABA Model Rules, R. 5.4(b).

15. ABA Model Rules, R. 5.4(a).

16. "While an MDP may allow a lawyer to better counsel her client as to all legal and non-legal options available (as required by the rules of professional conduct), the MDP may also heighten the risk that a group of professionals discussing the courses of action available to a client will fail to relay all options to a client and, in effect, make the decision for the client." Stacy L. Brustin, "Legal Services Provision Through Multidisciplinary Practice — Encouraging Holistic Advocacy While Protecting Ethical Issues," *University of Colorado Law Review*, 73 (2002): 819–36.

17. Norwood and Paterson, "Problem-Solving in a Multidisciplinary Environment?," 362.

18. Boumil, Freitas, and Freitas, "Multidisciplinary Representation of Patients," 123–24.

19. Norwood and Paterson, "Problem-Solving in a Multidisciplinary Environment?," 360–61.

20. For an example of a memorandum of understanding used by an MLP, visit http://www.medical-legalpartnership.org/.

21. Norwood and Paterson, "Problem-Solving in a Multidisciplinary Environment?," 357.

22. Ibid., 365–71.

23. Ibid., 363. The curriculum included actual case simulations, followed by critique and discussions. Ibid., 363–64.

24. ABA Model Rule 2.1, titled "Advisor," provides that "in representing a client, a lawyer shall exercise independent professional judgment and render candid advice. In rendering advice, a lawyer may refer not only to law but to other considerations such as moral, economic, social and political factors, that may be relevant to the client's situation."

25. ABA Model Rules, 1.6(b)(1). Other exceptions include prevention or rectification of fraud where the lawyer's services were used (Rules 1.6(b)(2) and (3)), or to comply with a law or a court order (1.6(b)(6)).

26. The HIPAA statute is found at P.L. 104-191, and related regulations addressing privacy and security are located within 45 CFR Parts 160, 162, and 164. The Health Information Technology for Economic and Clinical Health Act (HITECH) which also addressed and in some cases expanded HIPAA's impact was enacted under Division A, Tile XIII of Pub. L. 111-5, the American Recovery and Reinvestment Act of 2009.

27. Providers (e.g., hospitals, clinics, individual healthcare providers and medical groups) covered by HIPAA include all providers transmitting health information electronically and in connection with a HIPAA-covered transaction. A vast majority of healthcare providers qualify as HIPAA covered entities.

28. These terms are defined within 45 CFR § 154.501.

29. Additional purposes for which protected health information may be disclosed without authorization are described within 45 CFR § 164.512.

30. Additional elements of HIPAA-compliant authorizations are described in detail at 45 CFR § 164.508.

31. The term *business associate* is defined at 45 CFR § 160.103. The HITECH Act resulted in the application of HIPAA directly to business associates.

32. See 45 CFR Part 160 Subpart B.

33. We borrow this story from a recent article addressing ethical issues in the MLP setting. *See* Boumil, Freitas, and Freitas, "Multidisciplinary Representation of Patients," 124.

34. See, for example, *Rosen v. Montgomery Surgical Center*, 825 So.2d 735, 738 (Ala. 2001) ("physician has a general duty to not disclose a patient's medical information" because the "unauthorized disclosure of intimate details of a patient's health may amount to unwarranted publicization of one's private affairs ... such as to cause outrage, mental suffering, shame, or humiliation").

35. See, for example, *Belcher v. Charleston Area Med. Center*, 422 S.E.2d 827, 838 (W.Va., 1992) (state law requires the consent of a parent to medical treatment on a minor, "except in very extreme cases"); 45 C.F.R. 164.502(g)(1)(3)(i) (HIPAA regulation stating "if under applicable law a parent, guardian, or other person acting in *loco parentis* has authority to act on behalf of an individual who is an un-emancipated minor in making decisions related to health care, a covered entity must treat such person as a personal representative").

36. See ABA Model Rule 5.3 (2010); *Hanover Ins. Co. v. Rapo & Jepsen Ins. Services, Inc.*, 870 N.E.2d 1105 (Mass. 2007) (attorney-client privilege protects statements by client when made to or shared with necessary agents of the attorney); *Ellingsgard v. Silver*, 223 N.E.2d 813, 817 (Mass. 1967) ("attorney-client privilege may extend to communications from client's agent or employee to the attorney").

37. Comment 7 to Rule 1.0(e) offers some further clarification relevant to Mr. Greene: "In general, a lawyer may not assume consent from a client's or other person's silence. Consent may be inferred, however, from the conduct of a client or other person who has reasonably adequate information about the matter."

38. See Paul R. Tremblay, "Shadow Lawyering: Nonlawyer Practice within Law Firms," *Indiana Law Journal*, 85,(2010): 653–98.

39. ABA Model Rule 1.16 governs withdrawal from representation. None of the provisions of Rule 1.16 allowing for permissive withdrawal would apply comfortably to this situation.

40. See Pamela Tames, et al., "The Lawyer Is In: Why Some Doctors Are Prescribing Legal Remedies for Their Patients, and How the Legal Profession Can Support This Effort," *Boston University Public Interest Law Journal*, 12,(2003): 505–27.

41. We owe that observation to David Luban. *See* David Luban, *Lawyers and Justice: An Ethical Study* (Princeton: Princeton University Press, 1988), 286. ("law practice is not a victimless pastime").

42. The baseline considerations regarding conflicts involving present clients may be found in ABA Model Rule 1.7.

43. The baseline considerations regarding conflicts involving former clients may be found in ABA Model Rule 1.9.

44. The baseline considerations regarding conflicts involving law firms may be found in ABA Model Rule 1.10.

45. We borrow the Alex Jones story, with many changes for our present purposes, from a recent article on MLP ethics. *See* Boumi, Freitas, and Freitas, "Multidisciplinary Representation of Patients."

46. The Centers for Disease Control and Prevention have issued guidelines recommending such checkups. *See* CDC, "HIV-Related Knowledge and Stigma, United States, 2000," *Morbidity & Mortality Weekly Report,* 49, no. 1062 (Dec. 1, 2000), available at http://www.cdc.gov/mmwR/PDF/wk/mm 4947.pdf (accessed June 29, 2010).

47. See ABA Model Rules 1.18.

48. Ibid., 1.18(b); 1.9(c)(1).

49. Ibid., 1.18(c).

50. See Ibid., 1.18(d).

51. See, for example, Charles Fried, "The Lawyer as Friend: The Moral Foundations of the Lawyer-Client Relations," *Yale Law Journal,* 85 (1976): 1060–89; Stephen Ellmann, "Empathy and Approval," *Hastings Law Journal,* 43 (1992): 991–1015; Stephen Ellmann, "The Ethic of Care as an Ethic for Lawyers," *Georgetown Law Journal,* 81,(1993): 2665–726; and the legal profession's rules permit it, *see* ABA Model Rule 2.1.

52. See, for example, *Togstad v. Vesely, Otto, Miller & Keefe,* 291 N.W. 2d 686 (Minn. 1980) (malpractice verdict affirmed against lawyer who failed to refer a client to a lawyer who would pursue a claim).

53. Child Welfare Information Gateway, "Mandatory Reporters of Child Abuse and Neglect: Summary of State Laws," revised April 2010, http://www.childwelfare.gov/systemwide/laws_policies/statutes/manda.pdf.

54. States are required to have some form of a mandatory child abuse and neglect reporting statute to qualify for funding under the Child Abuse Prevention and Treatment Act, 42 U.S.C. §5101 et seq.

55. See Lori Stiegal and Ellen Klem, "Reporting Requirements: Provisions and Citations in Adult Protective Services Laws, by State" (current as of December 31, 2006) http://www.abanet.org/aging/docs/MandatoryReportingProvisionsChart.pdf.

56. Ibid.

57. ABA Commission on Domestic Violence, "Mandatory Reporting of Child Abuse" (June 2009) http://www.abanet.org/domviol/pdfs/mandatory_reporting_statutory_summary_chart.pdf.

58. Paula Galowitz, "Collaboration between Lawyers and Social Workers: Re-examining the Nature and Potential of the Relationship," *Fordham Law Review,* 67 (1999): 2138.

59. Alexis Anderson et al., "Professional Ethics in Interdisciplinary Collaboratives: Zeal, Paternalism and Mandated Reporting," *Clinical Law Review,* 13 (2007): 700–01.

60. Ibid., 693.

61. Gerard F. Glynn, "Multidisciplinary Representation of Children: Conflicts over Disclosure of Client Communications," *John Marshall Law Review,* 27 (1994): 651–52.

62. Ibid., 629–30.

63. See Randye Retkin et al., "Attorneys and Social Workers Collaborating in HIV Care: Breaking New Ground," *Fordham Urban Law Journal,* 24 (1997): 541.

64. St. Joan, "Building Bridges, Building Walls," 430–38.

65. Ibid., 458–59.

66. Glynn, "Multidisciplinary Representation of Children," 651–52.

67. Ibid., 653.

68. Ibid., 656.

69. See Heather A. Wydra, "Keeping Secrets within the Team: Maintaining Client Confidentiality while Offering Interdisciplinary Services to the Elderly Client," *Fordham Law Review,* 62 (1994): 1533–39.

70. Brustin, "Legal Services Provision Through Multidisciplinary Practice," 839.

71. Ibid., note 15, that it may not be ethical to obtain consent.

72. Ibid., 841–42. Boumil, Freitas, and Freitas, "Multidisciplinary Representation of Patients," 122.

Part III

Addressing the Social Determinants of Health through Legal Advocacy

Chapter 7

Income and Health: Dynamics of Employment and the Safety Net

Anne M. Ryan, JD
Cristina Dacchille, JD
Debra J. Wolf, JD
Ellen Lawton, JD
Edward G. Paul, MD

The correlation between poverty and adverse health effects is significant and well documented, as detailed in Chapter 1 and throughout this book. Reports from the Institute of Medicine, the Robert Wood Johnson Foundation, the U.S. Department of Health and Human Services, and multiple other government and nongovernmental agencies describe the connection between chronic diseases, health problems and a wide variety of nonmedical conditions, such as hunger and unsafe housing. Prevention of and recovery from any illness is greatly impeded in the absence of adequate food or sufficient income to meet basic human needs.

This chapter builds on the foundations established in Chapter 1 regarding the connections between poverty and health and explores the dynamics of employment, disability and the public safety net for low-income communities, with a focus on individual and family ability to generate income.

"Employment, Health and Poverty" describes health dynamics and key protections for low-wage workforce, including the Fair Labor Standards Act, the Family and Medical Leave Act, Unemployment and Worker's Compensation. "Disability, Health and Income" describes the health and legal landscape of disability, with a focus on facets of the Americans with Disabilities Act and the Supplemental Security Income and Social Security Disability Income programs. "Health-Promoting Programs in the Safety Net" describes several key health-promoting public benefits and services, including nutrition programs, the earned income tax credit (EITC), and Transitional Assistance for Needy Families (TANF) (federal welfare benefits). Healthcare coverage and access, a critical component of the safety net, is described in detail in Chapter 2 as well as in the "Medical-Legal Partnership for Special Populations" section of the book.

Each section briefly describes the range of health dynamics, such as chronic conditions that interfere with employment, and offers a summary of public benefit programs designed to ease facets of economic vulnerability for those who cannot earn sufficient income due to disability or other intervening circumstances. Chapters 12, 13 and 14 contain additional discussion and more specific applications of Social Security Disability Insurance and Supplemental Security Income as well as other job-related protections such as the Family and Medical Leave Act.

Finally, this chapter explores ways medical-legal partnerships (MLPs) support access to health-promoting public benefits and available workplace protections for vulnerable populations and transform the way poverty and health are understood in the healthcare and legal systems.

Poverty and Health

We recognize that income and education are two of the most critical factors for enabling improvements in health and reducing health disparities ... until we reduce poverty, particularly child poverty, and improve overall educational attainment and quality, America cannot and will not be as healthy as it should be. Where people live, learn, work and play affects how long and how well they live — to a greater extent than most of us realize ... [income is] an essential contributor to health.

Higher income can make it easier to pay for medical care, nutritious foods, quality child care, housing free of hazards, and neighborhoods with good schools and recreational facilities. Limited economic means can make everyday life a struggle, leaving little time or energy to adopt healthy behaviors and crushing motivation. Chronic stress associated with financial insecurity can seriously damage health, causing wear and tear on the heart and other organs and accelerating aging. — RWJ Commission on Building a Healthier America (2009)

Trends and Challenges
Chronic Illness

The prevalence of chronic illness in the United States is stark. Almost half of all Americans — 145 million people in 2009 — live with a chronic condition.[1] Figure 7.1 depicts the percentage of people with specific chronic conditions across all ages.

What Are Chronic Conditions and Activity Limitations?

Chronic conditions is a general term that includes chronic illnesses and impairments. It includes conditions that are expected to last a year or longer, limit what one can do, and/or may require ongoing medical care.

Serious chronic conditions are a subset of chronic conditions that require ongoing medical care and limit what a person can do.

Chronic illnesses are conditions that are expected to last a year or more and require ongoing medical care.

Activity limitations are functional limitations and disabilities that restrict a person from performing normal activities without assistance — such as walking, dressing and bathing — or affect a person's ability to work or attend school.

Source: Gerard Anderson, "Chronic Care: Making the Case for Ongoing Care," Robert Wood Johnson Foundation (2010).

Chronic health conditions not only impede daily activities for many vulnerable individuals and families, they also impact family economic stability. For example, a con-

Figure 7.1 Percentage of Noninstitutionalized People with Specific Chronic Conditions, All Ages

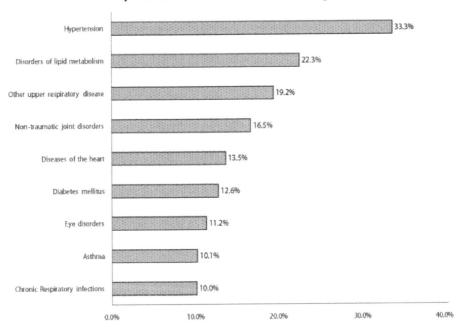

Source: Gerard Anderson, "Chronic Care: Making the Case for Ongoing Care," Robert Wood Johnson Foundation (2010). *Data source:* Medical Expenditure Panel Survey, 2006.

struction worker diagnosed with a chronic heart condition may no longer be able to perform the requisite physical labor for his job and may not have the job training to seek another comparably paid position. As detailed in Chapter 1, the burden of chronic health conditions is also disproportionately borne by racial and ethnic minorities in the United States.

Stress and Health

As detailed in Chapter 1, stress and health are interconnected and linked with exposure to social determinants. Stress can trigger the body to release hormones that can damage immune defenses and vital organs and lead to serious chronic illnesses.[2]

Unnatural Causes, the acclaimed 2008 PBS series on the root causes of socioeconomic and racial disparities in America, vividly depicts the real-life experiences that produce "toxic" stress for many low-income Americans. Unemployment, racism, and neighborhood violence are among the triggers for the biologic stress response.[3]

A 2010 review of stress research in the *Journal of Health and Social Behavior* highlighted the following findings:

- The damaging impact of stressors on physical and mental health are substantial.
- Differential exposure to stressful experiences is a primary way that inequities, such as racial-ethnic and social class, in physical and mental health are produced.
- Minority group members are additionally harmed by discrimination stress.

- Stressors proliferate over the life course and across generations, widening health gaps between advantaged and disadvantaged populations.

- The impact of stressors on health and well-being are reduced when people have high levels of mastery, self-esteem and/or social support.[4]

As healthcare providers and researchers expand their understanding of the impact of stress on patient and population health, they require new tools and interventions to support individuals and communities to not only cope with health-harming stressors but interrupt and/or eliminate their root causes. The finding that social inequality and economic instability are key stressors means that addressing these social determinants is a crucial step in reducing health disparities.

Healthy Choices

The rapidly accumulating research on the social determinants of health also explores the dynamics of healthy behaviors for all Americans, especially regarding exercise and nutrition (see Chapter 17). Although decisions to engage in risky health behaviors, such as use and abuse of tobacco, alcohol and drugs, are partly a matter of individual choice, research demonstrates that many social, economic and environmental pressures make it more likely that some people will pursue risky health behaviors, and such patterns are closely linked to educational background, race/ethnicity and income. For example:

- People with less than a college degree are more than twice as likely to smoke cigarettes as are college graduates.

- Blacks and Hispanics are more likely to live in areas with a high concentration of tobacco and alcohol outlets and are more likely to be targeted by advertising and marketing of these products.

- Unemployed adults are more likely to engage in illicit drug use than are those fully employed (18 percent vs. 8 percent).[5]

Understanding individual health choices in the context of the social environment in which people live is critical to conceptualizing and deploying effective interventions.

Understanding and Measuring Poverty

In 2009, the number of Americans in poverty increased to 42.9 million.[6] See Figure 7.2 for a map of the percentage of people living in poverty in the United States.

The United States measures poverty using two different calculations: the poverty threshold and the poverty guidelines. The *poverty thresholds* are the original version of the federal poverty measure, and are updated annually by the Census Bureau. Devised in 1963 based on household spending patterns at that time, the thresholds purport to calculate the material well-being of low-income Americans by comparing a family's income to the amount believed necessary to meet a minimum standard of living.

The thresholds are used mainly for statistical purposes — for instance, preparing estimates of the number of Americans in poverty each year. Updated yearly for inflation based on the Consumer Price Index, the poverty thresholds nevertheless understate the cost of meeting basic needs, because they fail to account for geographic differences, work-related expenses, dramatic fluctuations and increases in housing costs and other expenses borne by individuals and families in the current economy.[7]

Figure 7.2 Percentage of People in Poverty in the Past 12 Months by State and Puerto Rico, 2009

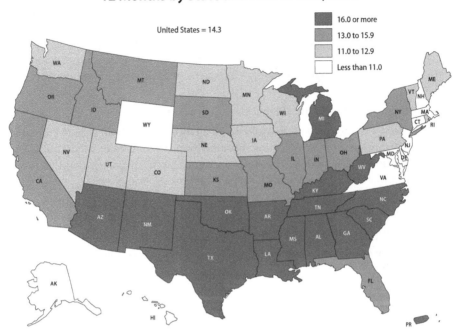

Source: Alemayehu Bishaw and Suzanne Macartney, "Poverty: 2008 and 2009," American Community Survey Briefs (2010), http://www.census.gov/prod/2010pubs/acsbr09-1.pdf.

Federal Poverty Guidelines

The *poverty guidelines* are the other version of the federal poverty measure. Issued each year in the *Federal Register* by the Department of Health and Human Services (DHHS), the guidelines are a simplification of the poverty thresholds used for administrative purposes — for instance, determining financial eligibility for certain federal programs (see Table 7.1).[8]

Table 7.1 The 2010 Poverty Guidelines for the 48 Contiguous States and the District of Columbia

Persons in Family	Poverty Guideline
1	$10,830
2	14,570
3	18,310
4	22,050
5	25,790
6	29,530
7	33,270
8	37,010

Note: For families with more than 8 persons, add $3,740 for each additional person.
Source: U.S. Department of Health & Human Services, http://aspe.hhs.gov/poverty/10poverty.shtml.

Changing Current Poverty Measures

Revision of the federal poverty threshold and guidelines has political and economic ramifications, because any change would mean that the number of people in poverty would go up or down and relative poverty rates may change among age, racial, and ethnic groups and between states. Any changes in the definition of thresholds or the measurement of poverty raise the possibility of changes in government funding allocation or program eligibility.[9]

Suggested alternatives to the current measure include:

1. a relative standard, which would count all those below a percentile of the income distribution as poor or count those below a percentage of median income or consumption as poor.[10] A common critique of a relative measure is that it relates information about inequality, not about basic economic need.

2. a consumption measure, under which spending on specific goods and services, rather than income, would be compared to a poverty threshold.[11]

3. a well-being measure, which would track well-being indicators such as health and life expectancy, food insecurity or hunger, living conditions and the absence of other life necessities.[12]

Questions for Discussion

1. How effectively do the poverty threshold and the poverty guidelines measure poverty in the United States? Should the United States change the way it measures poverty? If so, what should the criteria be?

2. What would a budget for a low-income family of three include?

3. How would you describe the connection between poverty and health to a policymaker?

Employment, Health and Poverty

According to the U.S. Department of Labor, in 2010 the unemployment rate was approximately 9.8 percent, representing about 15 million Americans.[13] Rates of unemployment reflect the same racial/ethnic stratification mirrored in other domains, with the unemployment rate for black workers at 16 percent, roughly twice the rate for white workers (8.9 percent).

Income and economic stability strongly impact on the level of education achieved for children and the employment opportunities that follow in adulthood, creating a cycle of poverty.[14] Children who grow up in poverty have diminished early life environments and poor educational opportunities that lead to limited employment opportunities.[15]

Over the past 75 years, the federal government, working in tandem with states, has devised a range of public programs that provide an individual or family with cash assistance when employment is not an option due to economic, health or other reasons.[16] Key programs that protect workers and their families include worker's compensation, the Fair Labor Standards Act, the Family and Medical Leave Act, Unemployment Insurance, Social Security Disability Insurance (SSDI), Supplemental Security Income (SSI) and Temporary Assistance for Needy Families (TANF).

Low-Wage Workers and Health

In 2007, 7.5 million adults were classified as "working poor," defined as "individuals who spent the last 27 weeks in the labor force (working or looking for work), but whose incomes fell below the official poverty level."[17] Although approximately 66 percent of the working poor have full-time employment, the vast majority work in low-wage service jobs. Low-wage workers also often cycle in and out of involuntary unemployment or can only find part-time work. Even for those working full-time, it is difficult to afford basic services and resources that promote healthy lives, including health insurance.[18]

The rapid expansion of "contingent work," including part-time, contracted or time-limited jobs that provide poorer training, less safety oversight and diffused responsibility for enforcing safety, creates pervasive unsafe working conditions for the working poor. Substantial research also shows that stress at work related to job insecurity, demanding labor and the inability to control the pace and content of work also increases the risk of poorer health for workers. Such stressors often define the jobs held by many of the working poor.[19]

Beyond the poverty endemic in low-wage jobs and the concomitant health effects detailed throughout this chapter and elsewhere, low-income workers and their families confront additional healthcare challenges related to their employment in two key ways: (1) exposure to dangerous or unhealthy working conditions, and (2) interrupted or inconsistent healthcare access due to inflexible, remote, or poorly remunerated working conditions.

Time pressures, lack of health insurance and other barriers can lead low-wage workers and their families to seek nonemergent care for problems such as respiratory infections or minor injuries in an emergency room setting. This care-seeking pattern results in episodic, noncontinuous care that is expensive for the healthcare system. Failure to access primary care means that low-wage workers and their families miss out on preventive medical interventions and opportunities for coordinated care, especially for chronic conditions such as asthma or hypertension. Even illnesses requiring only short-term follow-up may become complicated due to lack of follow-up or continuity of care. Although provisions in the 2010 healthcare reform legislation will address many of these challenges, they remain pervasive.[20]

The Working Family in Poverty

The barriers many working-poor parents currently face in the United States make it difficult for them to succeed at work while taking basic care of their own and their families' needs. The normal challenges and expenses of childcare, transportation and other essentials for successful work can be daunting under the best of circumstances. Beyond these obstacles, low-income earners often have limited employment leave and are forced into crisis when unanticipated complications, such as a sick child or parent, arise. Critical questions related to work and health for families in poverty include:

- Who regularly cares for preschool and out-of-school children when parents work outside the home?
- Who provides routine care for elderly parents who can no longer care for themselves?
- What happens when children and the elderly get sick and need care at unanticipated times?
- What happens when children with special healthcare needs or educational problems need a parent's assistance during work hours?

Working poor families are caught between their financial vulnerability on one hand and the combination of a demanding workplace culture, outdated social institutions and inadequate public policies on the other hand. This forces families to make hard choices, between paying for food or electricity, or working instead of bringing their child to the doctor.[21] Although the public benefit safety net described later addresses some of these needs, it is clear that families in poverty struggle not only to move ahead but to simply maintain their everyday lives.[22]

Job Protections and Job-Related Income Supports

Federal and state legislation establishes standards and programs for basic employment conditions, as well as job and income protections for ill, injured and disabled workers, including those who need time off to care for a family member in certain health-related circumstances. Finally, the unemployment insurance system offers temporary critical income supports in certain job-loss situations.

Worker's Compensation

Worker's compensation is a state-mandated insurance program that provides compensation to employees who suffer job-related injuries and illnesses. Although the federal government administers a worker's compensation program for federal and certain other types of employees, each state has its own laws and programs for worker's compensation. In general, an employee with a work-related illness or injury is eligible for worker's compensation benefits—typically regardless of who was at fault, the employee, the employer, a co-worker, a customer or some other third party. In exchange for these guaranteed benefits, employees relinquish the right to sue the employer in court for damages for those injuries.[23]

Unfortunately, research data reveal that the worker's compensation program falls well short of its aims where low-income workers are concerned. A recent landmark survey of over 4,000 workers in low-wage industries in Chicago revealed that 20 percent of injured workers in the sample experienced an illegal employer response to news of their injury (including being told not to file a WC claim), only 9 percent filed a claim, and only 3 percent had their medical expenses covered in whole or in part by the program.[24]

In the United States, the rate of fatal work injuries among self-employed workers is more than twice the national average. In a 2004 survey of day laborers—the majority of whom were undocumented immigrants—19 percent reported work-related injuries that required medical attention in the past year, compared with less than 5 percent in all private industries and approximately 6 percent in construction.[25] MLPs can play a pivotal role for underrepresented workers by sensitizing front-line healthcare providers to this pervasive problem so that they can respond to patient health needs using the appropriate tools, strategies and referrals.

Fair Labor Standards Act

The Fair Labor Standards Act (FLSA) establishes minimum wage, overtime pay, record-keeping and child labor standards affecting full-time and part-time workers in the private sector and in federal, state and local governments. Under the FLSA, covered nonexempt workers are entitled to a minimum wage of not less than $7.25 per hour, and overtime pay at a rate of not less than one and a half times their regular rates of pay is required after 40 hours of work in a work week.[26]

Low-wage workers are frequently subjected to wage and hour violations, such as being required to work longer hours without proper compensation or being paid less than the minimum wage. Though any employee has the right to bring a wage and hours violation charge against an employer, it is particularly challenging for such workers to seek redress, given their other life priorities and lack of access to advocacy and assistance. Multiple studies by both governmental and nongovernmental agencies detail the prevalence of workplace violations borne by low-income workers, with concomitant health impacts ranging from stress-induced hypertension to unsafe working conditions. Immigration status in particular places low-wage workers at risk for wage and hours violations.[27]

Family and Medical Leave Act

The federal Family and Medical Leave Act of 1993 (FMLA) provides up to 12 weeks of unpaid, job-protected leave to qualified employees for a range of health-related circumstances. An employee under FMLA protection is guaranteed restoration to the same position on return to work. If the same position is unavailable, the employer must provide the worker with a position that is substantially equal in pay, benefits and responsibility. An employee is also protected from retaliation by an employer for exercising rights under the Act.

FMLA leave is permissible under the following circumstances:

- to care for a new child, whether for the birth of a son or daughter or for the adoption or placement of a child in foster care;
- to care for a seriously ill family member (spouse, child, or parent);
- to recover from a worker's own serious illness;
- to care for an injured service member in the family; or
- to address qualifying circumstances arising out of a family member's deployment.[28]

Covered employers include public agencies, including state, local and federal employers; local education agencies (schools); and private sector employers who employ 50 or more employees in 20 or more work weeks in the current or preceding calendar year.[29]

Basic Facts of FMLA

- FMLA protects the job of an employee who needs to take time off from work to care for themselves or a qualified family member.
- Provides unpaid leave with job protection for up to 12 weeks; can use accrued sick or vacation days for paid leave.
- Applies to employers with 50 or more employees.
- Employee must have worked at least 12 months and for 1,250 hours during the previous year.
- Provides for intermittent leave for planned medical appointments or treatment when sick leave is exhausted.
- During time off under FMLA, an employer must maintain all benefits and insurance, although employees must continue to pay any required contribution.

For the specific FMLA requirements, see http://www.dol.gov/whd/fmla/index.htm.

The federal Americans with Disabilities Act (ADA) (discussed in more detail later in this section) also requires an employer to grant additional time off as a reasonable accommodation under certain circumstances:

> An otherwise qualified individual with a disability is entitled to more than 12 weeks of unpaid leave as a reasonable accommodation if the additional leave would not impose an undue hardship on the operation of the employer's business. To evaluate whether additional leave would impose an undue hardship, the employer may consider the impact on its operations caused by the employee's initial 12-week absence, along with the undue hardship factors specified in the ADA.[30]

See Chapters 12 and 13 for additional discussion of the FMLA and the ADA.

Unemployment Insurance

Created in 1935, the jointly managed federal-state unemployment insurance system provides temporary, partial income replacement for workers who have lost their jobs through no fault of their own. Although a few federal regulations apply and the system is overseen by the Department of Labor, states provide most of the funding for the program and all the actual worker benefits. Eligibility and benefit levels are generally under state control and vary across the country. The basic benefit typically amounts to about half of a worker's prior wages, up to a maximum benefit amount, for a period up to 26 weeks. Each state has its own requirements, but to qualify, the worker must certify that he or she is able to and actively seeking work.

Although the state and federal programs described in this section provide protection and support for millions of workers every year, millions more are unaware of their rights, reluctant to assert them for fear of adverse consequences, or simply lack the ability to advocate for themselves or to navigate government systems and application processes. In addition, standards violations (such as harassment of a worker who asks for time off to care for an ill relative), unfair treatment (such as when a worker is undeservedly fired and thus deprived of unemployment benefits), or even retaliation against a worker who has asserted his or her rights can be hard to prove. The reality for many low-wage workers in an employment crisis is that enforcement of employment rights and access to the safety net is out of reach.[31]

Given the connection between employment and health for vulnerable populations and the multiplicity and complexity of public programs targeting workers, the opportunity and need for MLP intervention in this area is vast.

Military Service and Veteran's Benefits

In 2009, over 1.4 million men and women were serving in all four branches of the military. Both active-duty and veteran soldiers are eligible for a range of government benefits and services in recompense for their commitment and service to their country. Governed by the Department of Veteran Affairs at both the federal and local level, veterans' services are comprehensive and include pension, insurance and healthcare.

The Veterans Health Administration operates the largest integrated health system in the United States, serving over 8 million active-duty and veteran soldiers in 2010. Protecting the health and well-being of veterans who have served in the armed forces is a central priority for the Department of Veteran Affairs, one that is intimately connected with the dangerous nature of military service. For example, over 3.2 million veterans receive disability compensation stemming from a disability that occurred while serving in the military.

Like other government benefits and services, accessing veterans' benefits can present administrative challenges for recipients, especially those who are disabled. Advocacy services for low-income veterans are common throughout the United States and are frequently connected to local, state or national bar associations, who provide free or reduced-fee services to veterans seeking assistance in securing accurate pension or other benefits. Law schools, legal aid agencies and local social service organizations also provide services for veterans. As with the broader population, legal need vastly outstrips the services available.

Source: National Center for Veterans Analysis and Statistics, "VA Benefits & Health Care Utilization" (last revised November 19, 2010) and Sidath Viranga Panangala, "Veterans' Health Care Issues in the 109th Congress," Congressional Research Service (last revised October 26, 2006).

Questions for Discussion

1. What types of health risks do low-income workers face? How can healthcare providers help prevent or more effectively treat these health risks?

2. What kinds of healthcare provider advocacy might be effective in addressing the health concerns of low-income workers?

3. What can MLP lawyers do to protect low-income workers in the workplace and to reduce health risks?

Best Practices and Advocacy Strategies for Medical-Legal Partnership

MLP has a special role to play in (1) ensuring healthcare teams have the knowledge and training to identify, screen, and refer employment-related questions and problems; and (2) educating workers as to their employment rights, with the goal of avoiding termination or discrimination as a result of their health status or disability.

During a medical examination, patients are often hesitant to discuss intolerable or illegal work conditions that affect their health due to concerns of job security. Physicians are ideally situated to raise this topic but need to do so with an understanding of the landscape of protections and risks. To optimize patient-client access to employment-related protections, New York-based MLP LegalHealth offers healthcare setting-based trainings by MLP legal teams for both patients and healthcare providers.

- For *patient-clients*, trainings focus on a review of legal protections for active workers and those considering a health-related leave, as well as disabled individuals seeking to return to work.

- For *healthcare providers*, trainings teach them to identify the work-related concerns of their patients, make referrals to the legal team and effectively advocate on behalf of patients.

The LegalHealth team helps patient-clients "behind the scenes" to understand and resolve any workplace issues and avoid the stress that can affect their health. Activities can include drafting a letter requesting reasonable accommodations, securing medical letters of support and reviewing FMLA or disability forms.

Joint medical-legal goals are to (1) assist individuals who can work to pursue the necessary medical leave or accommodation that will ensure their continued employment, (2) help workers know when either an accommodation or medical leave may be necessary, and (3) ensure that, should their physician recommend that they stop work, they successfully pursue all benefits and protections they are entitled to as a disabled person who is unable to work.

Case for Medical-Legal Partnership

Margaret has multiple sclerosis. She is capable of working, but her treatment includes weekly injections of interferon, which often cause her to have flu-like symptoms for a day following her injections. She works six days a week (Monday through Saturday) at a grocery store. Her shifts are generally eight hours long.

Questions for Discussion

1. Should Margaret decide to request a reasonable accommodation or FMLA leave?

2. What is Margaret's healthcare provider's role in helping her with her employment issues? What role should the MLP lawyer play in collaborating with the healthcare provider and in helping protect Margaret's rights?

Disability, Health and Income

Today more than 54 million Americans (one in five) live with some kind of disability. About 52 million live in their community, and about 2 million live in nursing homes and long-term care facilities.[32] The percentage of people impacted by family members with disabilities is correspondingly significant, with virtually every American touched by the experiences of a disabled person in their family or extended community.

Different definitions of disability abound, especially within the laws and regulations related to disability programs, benefits and services. There is no single, encompassing medical definition. The surgeon general has defined disability broadly, stating, "in general, disabilities are characteristics of the body, mind, or senses that, to a greater or lesser extent, affect a person's ability to engage independently in some or all aspects of day-to-day life."[33]

The definition of disability for both children and adults has evolved and expanded over the past 30 years. The Americans with Disabilities Act of 1990, the landmark legislation that secured a broad range of protections and rights for the disabled community, contains the following statutory definition: "A physical or mental impairment that substantially limits one or more of the major life activities of such individual; a record of such impairment; or being regarded as having such an impairment" (P.L. 101-336).

For children with disabilities, a key defining facet is the unique educational needs of the child. The Individuals with Disabilities Education Act includes the following definition of *disability*:

> Child with a disability means a child ... having mental retardation, a hearing impairment (including deafness), a speech or language impairment, a visual impairment (including blindness), a serious emotional disturbance (referred to in

this part as "emotional disturbance"), an orthopedic impairment, autism, traumatic brain injury, or other health impairment, a specific learning disability, deaf-blindness, or multiple disabilities, and who, by reason thereof, needs special education and related services. (20 U.S.C. § 1400 *et seq.* (1990)).

Table 7.2 shows the incidence of disability among children over age five years through adulthood.

Table 7.2 Population by Age and Disability

Characteristic	Total	Total %
Population, age 5 and over	257,167,527	100.0
With any disability	49,746,248	19.3
Population, ages 5–15	45,133,687	100.0
With any disability	2,614,919	5.8
Sensory	442,894	1.0
Physical	455,461	1.0
Mental	2,078,502	4.6
Self-care	419,018	0.9
Population, ages 16–64	178,687,234	100.0
With any disability	33,153,211	18.6
Sensory	4,123,902	2.3
Physical	11,140,365	6.2
Mental	6,764,439	3.8
Self-care	3,149,875	1.8
Difficulty going out	11,414,508	6.4
Employment disability	21,287,570	11.9
Population, age 65 and over	33,346,626	100.0
With any disability	13,978,118	41.9
Sensory	4,738,479	14.2
Physical	9,545,680	28.6
Mental	3,592,912	10.8
Self-care	3,183,840	9.5
Difficulty going out	8,795,517	20.4

Source: U.S. Census Bureau, Census 2000 Summary File 3.

Clinical Implications for Disabled Adults and Children

The Surgeon General's 2005 Call to Action to Improve the Health and Wellness of Persons with Disabilities was based on a central principle that "good health is necessary for persons with disabilities to have the freedom to work, learn and engage actively in their families and their communities."[34] The report noted that people with disabilities are often treated by health care providers on the basis of their disability and called for (among other improvements) healthcare providers to receive increased training on disability, citing particular challenges that disabled people have in getting the healthcare and wellness services they need. Other findings include:

- Persons with disabilities of all kinds share similar challenges as those without disabilities when it comes to their own health and well-being, including needing the tools and the knowledge—and the knowledgeable healthcare professionals—to help them enjoy and maintain full, healthy lives;

- Only 28.4 percent of persons with disabilities report their health to be excellent or very good compared to 61.4 percent of nondisabled persons.[35]

- Although at risk for the same ailments and conditions as people in the general population (e.g., injury, obesity, hypertension and the common cold), persons with disabilities also are at specific risk for secondary conditions that can damage their health status and the quality of their lives.

Additional challenges include insufficient knowledge and awareness of disability by the public across all sectors, including healthcare and wellness service providers, educators, government agencies, the media and so on.[36]

The role of physicians and other providers in providing primary care to disabled persons is to recognize, treat and provide subspecialty referral for the unique medical conditions and needs associated with the disability and also attend to usual preventive care. Most primary care providers have received little training and exposure to patients with disabilities, and disabled persons therefore struggle to find providers who are knowledgeable and experienced. In the largest national poll of persons with disabilities:

- 18 percent indicated they did not get needed health care on at least one occasion in the last year, compared to 7 percent of the nondisabled population; and

- 26 percent had trouble finding a doctor who understood their personal health care needs, compared to 10 percent of nondisabled persons.[37]

Like many adults, children with disabilities often require substantial clinical and social services to thrive, beyond basic preventive and primary care. The American Academy of Pediatrics recommends that children with special healthcare needs in particular have access to coordinated care from multiple providers.[38] Primary care providers who care for disabled children are ideally part of a multidisciplinary team familiar with identifying the medical and social needs of the disabled child and family as well as the myriad resources available for disabled children in the local community, school districts, community health agencies and through case managers, as well as healthcare resources through the state and region. Disabled children are often referred to such care teams that are usually present in pediatrics departments of academic centers or in large, urban hospitals. Families of disabled children in rural areas must often face the reality of traveling to larger centers for specialized care related to the disability and coordinating routine pediatric care with a local provider. See Chapter 9 for discussion of the educational rights of children with disabilities.

Questions for Discussion

1. Many healthcare providers lack training to care effectively for disabled persons. What kinds of challenges might exist for a disabled person seeking healthcare?

2. Consider a disabled firefighter with chronic pain due to a back injury or an obese person disabled from arthritis who gets around with an electric scooter. What assumptions or judgments might practitioners make about these patients? Are you aware of any personal biases about people who are disabled? How might these biases be overcome?

Legal Protections for People with Disabilities

The Americans with Disabilities Act of 1990

The Americans with Disabilities Act of 1990 (ADA) is the cornerstone of modern public laws designed to protect and support disabled adults, children and their families. With a broad mandate to prohibit discrimination on the basis of disability in employment, state and local government, public accommodations, commercial facilities, transportation and telecommunications, the ADA crisscrosses 10 different federal agencies, including Health and Human Services, the Federal Communications Commission, and the Department of Labor. The Equal Employment Opportunity Commission (EEOC) is empowered to enforce the ADA and has proscribed rules of compliance as well as rights of enforcement.[39]

Although this particular section focuses on ADA workplace protections and accommodations for the disabled, the ADA has multiple implications for vulnerable disabled individuals and their families across the United States and consequently for the health and legal professionals who serve them.

The Americans with Disabilities Act Amendments Act of 2008 (ADAAA) was enacted to expand the definition of disability and increase protections to reach more individuals with less severe conditions or conditions that may go into remission, such as multiple sclerosis or cancer. The ADAAA also includes coverage for conditions that have medications available to mitigate impairments, such as diabetes or high blood pressure. As a result, the ADAAA expands the protections offered under the ADA to a larger group of workers.[40] See Chapter 12 for expanded analysis of ADA protections and cancer.

How Does a Person Qualify for Protection under the ADA?

A disabled person is eligible for protection under the ADA if he or she:

- has a physical or mental impairment that substantially limits a major life activity;
- has a history of such a disability, such as cancer now in remission;
- is regarded as having a disability (even if they don't). If an employer erroneously assumed an employee had a medical disability and took adverse action such as firing or demoting the employee based on the disability, the employee may be "regarded as" having a disability and covered under the ADA, even if they are not actually ill or disabled.

A substantial impairment is one that significantly limits or restricts a major life activity, such as hearing, seeing, speaking, walking, breathing, performing manual tasks, caring for oneself, learning or working.

Employees seeking ADA protection must be:

- qualified to perform the essential functions or duties of their job, with or without a reasonable accommodation; and
- able to satisfy the employer's requirements for the job, such as education, employment experience, skills or licenses.

The ADA allows an employee who can perform the essential functions of his or her job to request a reasonable accommodation for a disability. For example, an office worker suffering from nausea in the morning due to side effects of medication may request to modify work hours for a later start in the morning. Other possible accommodations include an extra break to rest due to fatigue, an ergonomically correct chair or, depending on one's job duties, even working at home on occasion as long as the worker can perform the essential functions of the job from home. An employer is required to either grant the accommodation request or, if not feasible, engage in an interactive process with the employee to determine what form of accommodation will meet the needs of both employer and employee.[41] An employer does not have to grant the accommodation if it will pose an undue hardship.

Whether an accommodation is an undue hardship for the employer is determined by balancing:

- the nature and cost of the accommodation needed;
- the overall financial resources of the facility making the reasonable accommodation; the number of persons employed at this facility;
- the effect on expenses and resources of the facility;
- the overall financial resources, size, number of employees, type and location of facilities of the employer (if the facility involved in the reasonable accommodation is part of a larger entity);
- the type of operation of the employer, including the structure and functions of the workforce, the geographic separateness, and the administrative or fiscal relationship of the facility involved in making the accommodation to the employer; and
- the impact of the accommodation on the operation of the facility.[42]

Employees seeking accommodations typically specify the types of modifications that will help them perform their job successfully and provide documentation of their needs where possible. A crucial component of triggering legal protections under ADA, FMLA or other regulatory frameworks designed to protect people who are disabled is to ensure that sufficient, accurate clinical and diagnostic evidence is available to document the employee's needs.

MLP teams are ideally situated to facilitate and expedite disability benefit access for eligible patient-clients by streamlining information sharing across legal and medical domains, eliminating applications unsupported by medical diagnosis or criteria and improving communication regarding appropriate pathways to benefits and protections. If the treating physician believes a patient is capable of working, this critical assessment will—and should—impact the MLP legal team's advice regarding suitability of certain public programs.

ADA Accommodations or FMLA Leave

When an employee is able to work but may require an accommodation or intermittent leave under FMLA, he or she requires both a legal assessment as to eligibility for benefits as well as a medical assessment as to the diagnosis and prognosis specifically related to work.[43] Once the employee's legal rights and work abilities are established, the MLP team can:

- assist the patient-client in developing the appropriate supporting documentation and request;
- advise the MLP medical team on appropriate strategies for effectively documenting disability and medical status to trigger eligibility; and

- ensure required deadlines are met to avoid delay or denial of benefits and protections.

Model Physician Letter for ADA Reasonable Accommodation Request

Jennifer Jones, MD
Hospital Center for Multiple Sclerosis
111 Main Street
Boston, MA

To whom it may concern:

I am a board-certified neurologist who specializes in treating patients with multiple sclerosis. Margaret Doe has been my patient for the past seven years as a result of her diagnosis of multiple sclerosis. Ms. Doe is able to perform all of the essential functions of her job as a grocery store clerk but requires a reasonable accommodation. Her treatment includes monthly injections of interferon, which often have a side effect the next day of flu-like symptoms, including fatigue and malaise. Ms. Doe has requested that during the week she has her injection, her scheduled day off is the day following her injection. This request is medically necessary.

It may also be necessary, on an as-needed basis, for Ms. Doe to have additional break time so she can rest.

Thank you for your assistance with this matter.
Jennifer Jones, MD

Income for Disabled Persons: Short- and Long-Term Disability Insurance

There is no question that disability, especially long-term disability, impacts economic stability for many Americans. The link between disability and poverty is tragic and clear: where people with disabilities are unable to work due to either disability or lack of access to employment as a result of discrimination or other structural problems, they must rely on government-funded disability insurance programs, principally those administered by the Social Security Administration.

The pathway to federal disability benefits is complex and restricted to those with serious disabilities that interfere with major life functions. As described in Chapters 12 and 13, people with chronic illnesses often need short-term disability. Short-term disability programs provide cash assistance for approximately one to six months, which can be critical income supports because SSDI and most private long-term disability plans apply a waiting period before any benefits are payable. Employers frequently provide short-term disability plans (mandated in five states), but private short-term disability policies can also be purchased individually.[44]

Federal Social Security Benefits for Adults and Children with Disabilities

The Social Security Administration (SSA) administers several federal programs that provide income support to aged, disabled or blind individuals and eligible family members, including retirement benefits,[45] dependent or survivor benefits[46] and disability benefits.[47] Two programs, SSDI and SSI, provide critical cash assistance based on federal disability criteria.

Defining SSDI and SSI

Social Security Disability Income was established by Title II of the Social Security Act and provides benefits to disabled or blind individuals who are "insured" by workers' contributions to the Social Security trust fund. The claimant or a qualified family member must have worked a specified number of quarters with payment into the trust fund through payroll or self-employment taxes. SSDI originally covered only disabled workers ages 50–64 years but was expanded in 1960 to cover qualified disabled workers of any age and specified family members.

Supplemental Security Income was established by Title XVI of the Social Security Act and provides benefits to disabled, blind or aged (65 years or older) individuals with limited income and resources. There is no prior work history requirement.

Source: Jenny Kaufmann, "An Introduction to Old-Age, Survivors, and Disability Insurance and Supplemental Security Income," in *Poverty Law Manual for the New Lawyer* (Chicago: Sargent Shriver National Center on Poverty Law, 2002), 92–103.

Disabled individuals can be concurrently eligible for both programs, and the SSA uses the same criteria to determine if an individual is disabled once the categorical eligibility is met. Key eligibility requirements and benefits for both programs are summarized in Table 7.3.

Table 7.3 Comparison of Key Provisions of SSDI and SSI

SSDI	SSI
Must meet SSA definition of medical disability or blindness	Must meet SSA definition of medical disability or blindness or be age 65 or over
U.S. citizen or "qualified alien"	U.S. citizen or "qualified alien"
No income or resource restrictions	Stringent income and resource restrictions
Minimum time worked required (of disabled person or qualified family member) with payments into SSDI trust fund	No work history requirement
Monthly benefit based on worker's lifetime average earnings	Uniform base monthly benefit set by federal government and supplemented by some states ($674/month 2010)
Benefits also available to some family members	No family benefits
Eligible for Medicare at age 65 or 24 months after entitlement to disability benefit payments (no waiting period for end-stage renal disease or amyotrophic lateral sclerosis)	Not eligible for Medicare unless also eligible for SSDI
May also be eligible for Medicaid depending on income level	Automatic Medicaid eligibility in most states

Eligibility for SSDI and SSI

Once the SSA determines that all nonmedical eligibility criteria are met for SSDI or SSI (e.g., income, resources, work history, citizenship or qualified alien status), applications are reviewed by the state Disability Determination Services (DDS). DDS offices are fully funded by the federal government and are responsible for developing medical evidence and making the initial determination whether a claimant is disabled or blind under the regulations. To make that determination, DDS disability specialists gather medical evidence from all reported sources of medical treatment, including doctors, clinics and hospitals. If sufficient information is not available from the claimant's medical providers, DDS can also arrange and pay for consultative medical examinations by an independent health provider.

To be considered medically disabled under either SSI or SSDI, adults (age 18 or over) must demonstrate that they are unable to engage in any "substantial gainful activity" by reason of any medically determinable physical or mental impairment or combination of impairments that has lasted or can be expected to last for a continuous period of not less than 12 months or result in death.[48] The disability standard for a child under age 18 is similar, but instead of evaluating ability to work or substantial gainful activity, SSA evaluates whether the impairments cause "marked and severe functional limitations." The duration requirement (12 months or expected to cause death) is the same under the tests for both adults and children.[49]

DDS uses a sequential evaluation process to determine whether a claimant meets the disability test. For adults, this process includes review of the claimant's current work activity, the severity of any impairment(s), a determination of whether the impairment(s) meets or equals the criteria in an adult "Listings of Impairment,"[50] the claimant's residual functional capacity, any past work experience, and other factors, including age and education. An example from the Listings of Impairment is provided in *SSA Listing for Chronic Heart Failure*.

SSA Listing for Chronic Heart Failure

4.02 *Chronic heart failure* while on a regimen of prescribed treatment, with symptoms and signs described in 4.00D2. The required level of severity for this impairment is met when the requirements in *both A and B* are satisfied.

A. Medically documented presence of one of the following:

1. Systolic failure (see 4.00D1a(i)), with left ventricular end diastolic dimensions greater than 6.0 cm or ejection fraction of 30 percent or less during a period of stability (not during an episode of acute heart failure); or

2. Diastolic failure (see 4.00D1a(ii)), with left ventricular posterior wall plus septal thickness totaling 2.5 cm or greater on imaging, with an enlarged left atrium greater than or equal to 4.5 cm, with normal or elevated ejection fraction during a period of stability (not during an episode of acute heart failure);

AND

B. Resulting in one of the following:

1. Persistent symptoms of heart failure which very seriously limit the ability to independently initiate, sustain, or complete activities of daily living in an individual for whom a medical consultant (MC), preferably one experienced in the care of patients with cardiovascular disease, has concluded that the performance of an exercise test would present a significant risk to the individual; or

2. Three or more separate episodes of acute congestive heart failure within a consecutive 12-month period (see 4.00A3e), with evidence of fluid retention

(see 4.00D2b (ii)) from clinical and imaging assessments at the time of the episodes, requiring acute extended physician intervention such as hospitalization or emergency room treatment for 12 hours or more, separated by periods of stabilization (see 4.00D4c); or

3. Inability to perform on an exercise tolerance test at a workload equivalent to 5 metabolic equivalents (METs) or less due to:

a. Dyspnea, fatigue, palpitations, or chest discomfort; or

b. Three or more consecutive premature ventricular contractions (ventricular tachycardia), or increasing frequency of ventricular ectopy with at least 6 premature ventricular contractions per minute; or

c. Decrease of 10 mm Hg or more in systolic pressure below the baseline systolic blood pressure or the preceding systolic pressure measured during exercise (see 4.00D4d) due to left ventricular dysfunction, despite an increase in workload; or

d. Signs attributable to inadequate cerebral perfusion, such as ataxic gait or mental confusion.

Source: Social Security Administration, "Disability Evaluation under Social Security: 4.00 Cardiovascular System — Adult" (last revised October 2008), http://www.ssa.gov/disability/professionals/bluebook/4.00-Cardiovascular-Adult.htm#4_02.

For children applying for SSI, the process requires sequential review of the child's current work activity (if any), the severity of impairment(s) and an assessment of whether the impairment(s) results in "marked and severe functional limitations." If DDS determines that the claimant is disabled at any step in this process, the evaluation does not continue. Criteria for each step in the evaluation process are summarized in Figure 7.3.

SSA Administrative Appeals Process

SSA generally decides claims for disability benefits using an administrative review process that consists of four levels: initial determination, reconsideration, ALJ (administrative law judge) hearing and Appeals Council review (20 CFR 404.900 and 416.1400).

Applicants who are denied at the initial determination stage may generally request reconsideration,[51] at which time the prior case record as well as any new evidence is reviewed by individuals who were not involved in the initial decision, and a new decision is issued (20 CFR § 404.913). If applicants disagree with the decision at the reconsideration stage, they may request a hearing with an ALJ. At this stage, applicants may call witnesses that will support the claim of disability and cross-examine any witnesses the agency calls (20 CFR § 404.950).

If claimants are denied at the ALJ hearing level, the next level of appeal is the Social Security Appeals Council. The Appeals Council may undertake review on its own initiative or exercise discretion as to which cases they will review on request (20 CFR § 404.967 et. seq.). If the Appeals Council believes that the ALJ's decision was correct, they generally will not grant review. Applicants may file a lawsuit in federal district court if the Appeals Council denies a request of review or if they disagree with the Appeals Council's decision (20 CFR § 404.981).

Figure 7.3 Disability Determination Process for Adults

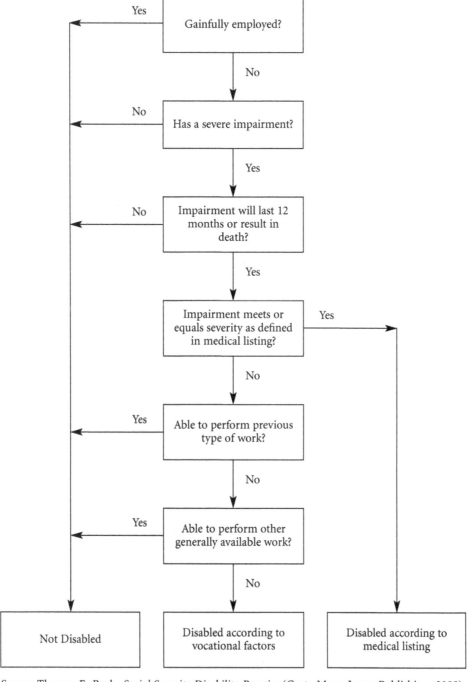

Source: Thomas E. Bush, *Social Security Disability Practice* (Costa Mesa: James Publishing, 2008), www.jamespublishing.com.

Processing delays of federal disability claims create significant hardships for disabled claimants. The average processing time nationally in 2010 from date of claim filing to initial determination was 111 days; approximately 9 months from filing until decision on request for redetermination; and over 2 years from initial claim filing until decision at the ALJ hearing level (see Figure 7.4).[52] At the end of 2009, over 770,000 cases were pending nationally for initial determination of disability, an increase of 38 percent over 2008.[53]

Figure 7.4 Average Processing Time for SSDI Claims

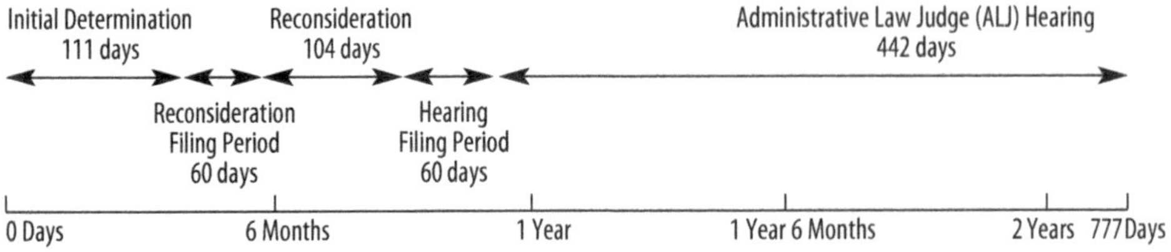

Initial Determination — 111 days

Reconsideration — 104 days

Administrative Law Judge (ALJ) Hearing — 442 days

Reconsideration Filing Period — 60 days

Hearing Filing Period — 60 days

0 Days   6 Months   1 Year   1 Year 6 Months   2 Years 777 Days

Notes: Data are for FY 2010 through February 2010. Processing times do not include time needed to file appeals. However, the timeline includes the 60 days claimants have to file appeals. Average processing time for reconsideration includes only Title II claims.
Source: Congressional Research Services. Data provided by the SSA.

The hardship to disabled claimants from lengthy delays was documented by a study conducted by the SSA in 2009, which found that "80 percent of the claimants ... surveyed believed that their finances were impacted by the wait for a disability decision, 30 percent believed that their access to medical care was impacted, and 42 percent believed that their relationships were impacted."[54] Study participants reported that due to the delay, they were unable to pay their rent, utilities, grocery bills, medical expenses or meet other critical needs.[55] Although the SSA has taken a number of steps to address delays, including redesigning facets of the determination and appeal processes, claimants and the healthcare providers who are key repositories of patient health data still find the disability process inordinately challenging.

Reassessment and Work Incentives

After disability benefits are awarded, the SSA reassesses continued eligibility periodically, based on the anticipated duration of the impairments. The SSA also continually reassesses financial eligibility for SSI. For low-income families with a disabled sibling or parent who receives SSI, maintaining financial eligibility for SSI while also supplementing SSI income through paid work by a nondisabled parent or sibling can be challenging.[56]

The SSA also has incentives designed to encourage and help disability recipients test their ability to return to work without losing monthly benefits. The incentives and requirements vary for SSI and SSDI but may provide continued full or reduced cash benefits while working during trial periods or for earnings lower than specified levels, continued help with medical bills, help with work related expenses and vocational training.[57]

Questions for Discussion

1. You are meeting with the congressional delegation from your district to discuss the waiting times for determination of medical disability on SSI and SSDI in your state. What would you say? How would you connect health to the discussion?

2. What is an acceptable amount of time for administrative decisions on disability claims? What are the key factors that must be considered in development of any plan to improve the efficiency of initial determinations and administrative appeals for SSI/SSDI disability claims? What weight should be given to each of these factors?

Best Practices and Advocacy Strategies for Medical-Legal Partnership

MLPs offer a unique opportunity to help disabled individuals obtain critical income supports through monthly Social Security disability benefits. The process of applying for or appealing a denial of SSI or SSDI benefits is overwhelming for many, and is particularly challenging for someone with severe medical impairments. Effective physician participation and advocacy in the disability process is crucial for success. Treating physicians are in the best position to know and convey a complete medical picture about their patients. Working together as part of an MLP team can ensure that detailed documentation of all medical impairments is accurate and appropriately submitted to SSA for review. This is particularly critical because a qualified treating physician's opinion on the nature and severity of medical impairments can be given "controlling weight" in the SSI/SSDI review process.[58]

MLP teams can also ensure that all applicable legal arguments supporting the claim are advanced and that successful claimants receive the maximum amount of benefits to which they are entitled. By partnering, MLP healthcare providers and lawyers can offer invaluable assistance to their patients-clients in the disability process.

MLPs in Tucson, Arizona, and New York (see Table 7.4) are examples of programs with a strong Social Security disability advocacy component.

Table 7.4 Comparison of Two MLPs

Tucson Family Advocacy Program (TFAP)	LegalHealth SSI/SSDI Application Assistance Project
Attorney on site full-time in University of Arizona primary care clinic, Dept. of Family and Community Medicine	Legal team on site weekly in multiple hospitals and health centers in New York City
Attorney and physician train residents and faculty annually on disability dynamics, including: • SSA disability definitions and evaluation process • Medical and legal advocacy strategies to support disabled patients, including how to write effective medical letters in SSI/SSDI claims • Small group discussion to identify and address barriers to healthcare provider advocacy for disabled patients	Attorneys train healthcare team members on disability dynamics, legal referral strategies Paralegal provides holistic application assistance to patients, coordinating medical record submission, development of healthcare provider assessments and evaluations, interactions with SSA staff and orientation to benefit receipt for new awardees
30% of TFAP referrals were for SS disability claims; training led to increased screening and triage of cases referred for legal advice or representation as part of medical treatment plan	Comprehensive legal assistance to patients of partner hospitals seeking advocacy, advice, or representation on legal matters

From Practice to Policy

Emergency Medicaid for Non-Citizens

For six weeks, two-year-old Nallely R. endured what no child should have to endure. Hospitalized for severe respiratory distress, Nallely suffered more than 100 seizures per day and could not be discharged from the hospital due to risk of aspiration. Nallely spent four days in the Pediatric Intensive Care Unit (PICU), and then was moved to a pediatric floor.

Nallely came to the U.S. one year earlier to join her father, who is a legal resident. Nallely's family is low-income and her father's employer does not provide health insurance. Ineligible for Medicaid because she does not fit into the qualified immigrant categories, Nallely could receive emergency medical services only.

Nallely's doctor determined that she was in a medically unstable emergency condition throughout her six-week hospitalization. Still, the state agreed to cover only the four days that Nallely spent in the PICU—not the services she received while on the pediatric floor. Nallely's case was referred to medical-legal partnership (MLP) program at the hospital.

With clinicians' support and medical documentation on the emergency nature of Nallely's conditions, MLP attorneys appealed the state's denial of Medicaid. The attorneys cited federal Medicaid law, which defines emergency medical conditions by the risks involved—not the location of treatment. Together, clinicians and attorneys secured insurance coverage for Nallely throughout the duration of her hospital stay.

Drawing upon their success, the MLP team pursued a broader commitment from the state in order to help others like Nallely. At the MLP's urging, the state agreed to issue a new policy consistent with federal law, guaranteeing full coverage for all emergency conditions, regardless of whether patients are transferred to a hospital floor.

Case for Medical-Legal Partnership

Ms. Ahmad, a 56-year-old political refugee from Iraq, comes to her family doctor visit for follow-up with hypertension. She reports having severe back and knee pain, causing difficulty with walking and other activities of daily living. Ms. Ahmad also reports that she has nightmares almost every night that disturb her sleep. She also suffers from panic attacks during the day secondary to trauma and events in her country of origin prior to immigrating to the United States last year. She states that she cannot work because of constant pain, fear of strangers and limited English proficiency. Ms. Ahmad asks what she should do.

Questions for Discussion

1. What else do you need to know to help Ms. Ahmad? What more do you need to know about her health conditions? What additional questions will you ask to determine what legal rights she may have?

2. What type of evidence would be necessary to show that the patient is disabled?

3. How can a medical-legal team work together to help this patient?

Health-Promoting Programs in the Safety Net

Even with employment, low-income individuals and families still struggle to meet basic needs. "The safety net" refers to the myriad public and community programs that exist to provide for the multiple needs of low-income individuals and families outside of earned income.

From housing subsidies issued by federal housing agencies to nutrition programs administered by public health departments, government programs are designed to supplement family budgets that are insufficient due to unemployment, disability or simply insufficient wages despite gainful employment. Research clearly shows that public benefits programs reduce poverty, especially among the elderly (see Figure 7.5).[59]

Figure 7.5 Public Benefits Reduce Poverty by Nearly Half

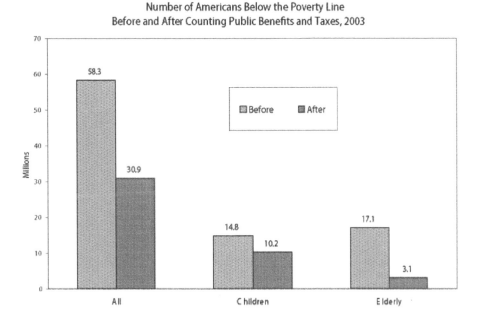

Number of Americans Below the Poverty Line
Before and After Counting Public Benefits and Taxes, 2003

Note: Poverty status is based on family disposable income (after taxes and counting near-cash benefits).
Source: Center on Budget and Policy Priorities tabulations of March 2004 Current Population Survey.

This section reviews two key domains where public benefits programs promote health for America's low-income communities—nutrition support programs and TANF/welfare.

Nutrition Support Programs

As detailed in Chapter 1, food insecurity and hunger persist in the United States, affecting over 50 million people in 2008.[60] Millions of American children do not receive adequate nutrition, which jeopardizes their health and normal development, and adults in food-insecure households were significantly more likely to rate their health as poor/fair and scored significantly lower on commonly accepted physical and mental health scales.[61] There is a well-documented link between being low-income, poor nutrition and being overweight.[62] Finally, for older adults, adequate nutrition is particularly important for health because of their increased vulnerability to disease and conditions that may impair functionality (the ability to live or cook at home).[63] Inadequate diets may contribute to or exacerbate disease, quicken the advance of age-related degenerative diseases and delay recovery from illnesses.[64]

Supplemental Nutrition Assistance Program (Food Stamps)

With nearly one in five households reporting that they lacked the money to purchase needed food in 2009, federal and state nutrition programs are more critical than ever to maintaining the health and well-being of low-income children and families.[65] The Supplemental Nutrition Assistance Program (SNAP)[66] is a federal benefits program that assists more than 38 million people nationwide in affording nutritionally adequate food (see Table 7.5 for maximum benefits).[67] Originally conceived in 1939 as a means of encouraging the purchase of unmarketable farm surpluses by low-income urban populations, SNAP is today considered the nation's leading antihunger initiative.[68]

Table 7.5 Maximum Monthly Food Stamp Benefits

April to October 2009 (includes benefit increase from Economic Recovery Act)	
Household Size	Maximum Benefit
1	$200
2	$367
3	$526
4	$668
5	$793
6	$952
7	$1052
Each additional	$150

Source: Center on Budget and Policy Priorities, "Policy Basics: Introduction to the Food Stamp Program" (last revised December 21, 2010).

A significant gap remains between the number of eligible individuals and the number of SNAP participants. Across states, overall participation in food stamps in FY 2006 ranged from just 50 percent of eligible persons to over 95 percent, indicating that some states could do much more to reach the target population.[69]

Basic Facts about Food Stamps

Who administers and pays for SNAP? The federal government pays the full cost of SNAP benefits and splits the cost of administering the program with the states. In fiscal year 2008, the federal government spent approximately $39 billion on SNAP, with 90 percent of those funds going directly to low-income households to purchase food. The Department of Agriculture's Food and Nutrition Service administers SNAP at the federal level. State agencies administer the program on a local level; this includes community outreach, nutrition education, eligibility determinations and distribution of benefits.

What benefits are provided by SNAP? Households that qualify for SNAP benefits receive a set dollar amount per month for the purchase of food and food-bearing seeds. A family of four with $900 in net monthly income would receive the maximum benefit ($668) minus 30 percent of its net income ($270), or $398. In most states, a family's net income is calculated by subtracting certain deductions (e.g., the cost of childcare, housing and utilities) from gross monthly income.

Who is eligible for food stamps? SNAP is available to almost all low-income individuals with qualified immigration status or citizenship. Many states have expanded eligibility for SNAP to include working families who struggle to afford food. Although categorical eligibility for SNAP is very broad, only certain groups of legal immigrants are eligible for SNAP benefits.

How is a family's benefit amount calculated? The benefit formula is based on the cost of the "Thrifty Food Plan," a low-cost nutritionally adequate diet established and updated annually by the USDA. The formula estimates that families will spend approximately 30 percent of their net income on food each month. As such, SNAP benefits provide the difference between that 30 percent contribution and the cost of the Thrifty Food Plan. As a result, a household with no net income will receive the maximum SNAP benefit, which generally equals the cost of the Thrifty Food Plan for a household of its size.

How do families apply for and use their benefits? Though SNAP is a federal benefit, states are charged with the distribution of SNAP funds. As such, application and distribution processes vary by state.

After receiving an application, the local SNAP office may request documentary evidence of the applicant's eligibility for the program, such as pay stubs or government-issued identification. The applicant will also be required to complete an interview (either in-person or by phone) with a local SNAP officer to make sure they understand their legal rights and responsibilities as a SNAP recipient.

Once an individual's application for food stamps is approved, the head of the household will be issued an Electronic Benefits Transfer (EBT) card and asked to set up a personal identification number. This card, developed to help track SNAP purchases and eliminate the stigma associated with paper stamps/coupons, works similarly to a bank card. Each month, the household's SNAP benefits are deposited into its personal account. The household may then use its EBT card at any authorized location (which includes all major grocery chains, many local stores and in some states local farmers' markets) to purchase food.

Source: Center on Budget and Policy Priorities, "Policy Basics: Introduction to the Food Stamp Program" (last revised December 21, 2010); Supplemental Nutrition Assistance Program, "Frequently Asked Questions," U.S. Department of Agriculture Food and Nutrition Service (last revised November 2, 2010).

Special Supplemental Nutrition Program for Women, Infants and Children

The Special Supplemental Nutrition Program for Women, Infants and Children (more commonly known as WIC) is a federal program designed to safeguard the nutritional health of pregnant or nursing women, infants and children under age five.[70] Piloted in 1972 and adopted permanently in 1974, WIC, like SNAP, is administered by the Department of Agriculture's Food and Nutrition Service.[71] To be eligible for WIC, individuals must be:

- A resident in the state in which they are applying,
- A pregnant or nursing woman, or a child under the age of five,
- Low-income, and

- At risk for poor nutrition.[72]

Some of the eligibility requirements for WIC—such as the categorical requirement that the recipient be a qualifying woman, infant or child—are strictly defined by federal regulation. Others, however, particularly income and nutritional requirements, are determined at the state level.[73] States can choose, for example, to set the income limit for WIC anywhere between 100 percent and 185 percent of the FPL, or determine how much proof of nutritional risk to require from applicants. Finally, WIC has no immigration restrictions, so it is widely available to all individuals regardless of citizenship status as a critical nutrition support.

The WIC program serves half of all American infants, and a quarter of all children ages one to four.[74] WIC food packages differ by population and are chosen by medical and nutrition specialists. An infant's package, for example, may include access to formula, whereas a toddler's package would include vouchers for cereal, milk or fresh produce.[75] WIC participants also receive nutrition counseling and healthcare referrals. WIC serves an important role in promoting breastfeeding among low-income mothers, who are less likely to breastfeed their infants than their higher-income counterparts. WIC participation has been demonstrated to improve birth outcomes and reduce illness among children in participating low-income families. In 1992, the General Accounting Office (now the Government Accountability Office) estimated that for every dollar spent on WIC, the federal government saves up to $3.50.[76]

The Earned Income Tax Credit

What Is It?

The Earned Income Tax Credit (EITC) is a federal tax credit for low- and moderate-income working people.[77] It is designed to encourage and reward work as well as offset payroll and income taxes. The EITC is "refundable," which means that if it exceeds a low-wage worker's income tax liability, the IRS will refund the balance.[78] Twenty-four states have established their own EITCs to supplement the federal credit.[79]

How Does It Work?

The EITC has two core goals: (1) encourage and reward work, and (2) reduce poverty. Beginning with the first dollar, a worker's EITC grows with each additional dollar of wages until it reaches the maximum value (see Figure 7.6), creating a work incentive that studies show has been successful. The Committee for Economic Development, an organization of 250 corporate executives and university presidents, concluded in 2000 that "the EITC has become a powerful force in dramatically raising the employment of low-income women in recent years."[80]

How Does EITC Impact Poverty?

In 2009, the EITC lifted an estimated 6.6 million people out of poverty, including 3.3 million children.[81] The poverty rate among children would have been nearly a third higher without the EITC. The EITC lifts more children out of poverty than any other single program or category of programs. One way the EITC reduces poverty is by supplementing the earnings of minimum-wage workers. There is broad bipartisan agreement that a two-parent family with two children with a full-time, minimum-wage worker should not have

Figure 7.6 The Federal Earned Income Tax Credit in Tax Year 2009

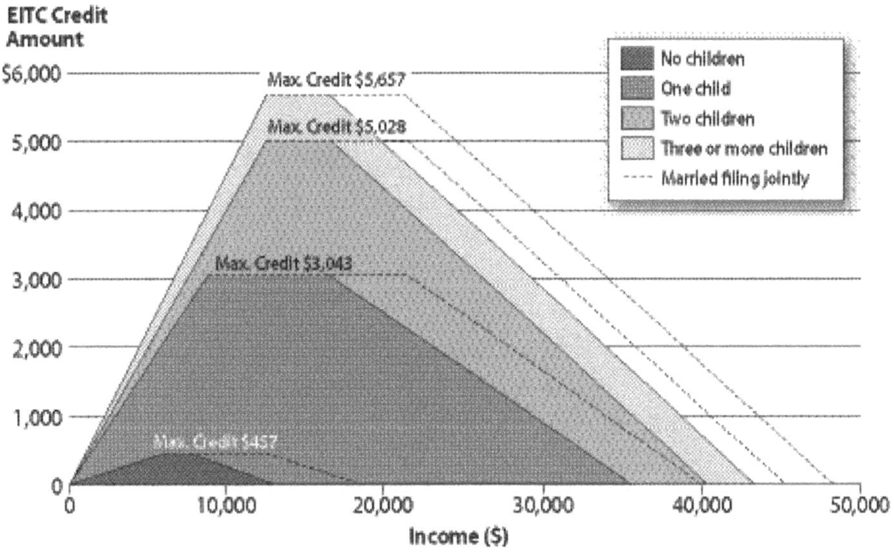

Note: Married couples with income in the phaseout range qualify for a higher credit than singles (shown by dashed lines).
Source: Center on Budget and Policy Priorities, "Policy Basics: The Earned Income Tax Credit" (last revised December 4, 2009).

to raise its children in poverty. At the minimum wage's current level, such a family can move out of poverty only if it receives the EITC as well as food stamps.[82]

Temporary Assistance for Needy Families

The modern notion of providing cash assistance to individuals and families who were not earning wages in the workforce emerged in 1911 with the development of the "mother's pension" program, which provided aid to needy children who were without fathers in an effort to keep the children's mothers from working outside the home.[83] With the onset of the Great Depression and the corresponding 800 percent increase in unemployment (from 1929 to 1933), the federal government expanded its welfare system by enacting the Social Security Act of 1935.[84] Although the Act primarily focused on aiding unemployed and disabled workers and creating public jobs, it also created Aid to Dependent Children (ADC). ADC required states to provide assistance to children of divorced, separated, widowed or unwed mothers so that the mothers could remain home to care for their children.[85]

The onset of the civil rights movement in the 1950s and 1960s led to a legal and legislative campaign to broaden and improve access to ADC—renamed Aid to Families with Dependent Children (AFDC)—as a strategy to alleviate the impact of poverty on families. By the 1970s and 1980s, the so-called welfare program was at the forefront of heated national debates, with many political leaders calling for an overhaul of a system deemed fraught with fraud. Political rhetoric and shifting cultural attitudes provoked a national controversy that culminated in 1996 with the passage of the Personal Responsibility Work Opportunity and Reconciliation Act (PRWORA). Under the new law, AFDC was replaced by Temporary Assistance to Needy Families (TANF), in which Congress conditioned funding on strict work requirements, time limits and other restrictions.[86]

TANF (more commonly referred to as "welfare") is a federally funded public assistance program that provides a variety of benefits, including cash and rental assistance, job training, childcare and education, to low-income families. TANF has four objectives:

(1) Provide assistance to needy families so children may be cared for in their own homes or homes of relatives.

(2) End the dependence of needy parents on government benefits by promoting job preparation, work, and marriage.

(3) Prevent and reduce the incidence of out-of-wedlock pregnancies and establish annual numerical goals for preventing and reducing the incidence of such pregnancies.

(4) Encourage the formation and maintenance of two-parent families. (45 CFR § 260.20)

Under the current TANF structure, the federal government provides block grants to states, which are given the discretion to use the money for their own programs as long as such programs further one or more of the objectives.[87]

PRWORA imposed stringent work requirements that states must adhere to or risk losing TANF funding. States are required to provide appropriate job training, education and/or placement programs for TANF recipients. States are also required to ensure that a certain percentage of their adult-headed TANF cases (50 percent generally, 90 percent for two-parent households; 45 CFR §§ 261.21, 261.23) participate in allowable work activities for a minimum number of hours each week.[88] The number of hours per week each family is required to work depends on the family composition. For example, households with two parents must complete 35 hours of work activities per week, while a household headed by a single custodial parent must complete 20 hours of work activities per week (45 CFR §§ 261.31, 261.35). Examples of allowable work activities include: employment, job training, job search, community service, vocational training and attendance at a secondary school or GED course (45 CFR § 261.30). Prior to 2006, there were very few exceptions to the work requirements, but with the passage of the Deficit Reduction Act of 2005, states were permitted to exempt certain groups, including disabled parents and parent of caretaker of a disabled person.[89]

In addition to work requirements, receipt of TANF benefits is conditioned on several other federal mandates. First, single parents have an obligation to assign any right to collect child support to the state (45 CFR § 301.1, et seq.). This gives states the right to pursue absent parents for child support to help offset the costs of the TANF program. Second, states are held to a strict time limit regarding how long a family may receive benefits; families are subject to a lifetime cap of five years of TANF cash assistance (45 CFR § 264.1). Finally, the federal regulations impose rigid restrictions on eligibility of legal immigrants for assistance. (For a more detailed discussion of immigrants' eligibility for public benefits, see Chapter 10.)

It makes sense that families with reduced or no income would suffer hardships, and several studies have demonstrated that the impact of welfare termination has implications for poor child health. For example, one study showed that children in families whose cash assistance was terminated or reduced because of sanctions were more likely to be food insecure and be hospitalized. Food stamp receipt did not offset the negative impact of loss of cash assistance.[90] More broadly, policy makers and others have cited lower rates of welfare receipt in recent years as evidence of the success of PRWORA in reorienting this safety net benefit to emphasize transition to employment, but researchers and critics continue to question whether stringent requirements are simply keeping vulnerable families from accessing crucial income supports when in crisis.

Questions for Discussion

1. The passage of PRWORA created numerous conditions for TANF eligibility. If you were tasked with redesigning the welfare system, which of these conditions would you keep or eliminate? Are there any conditions missing from the discussion that you would add?

2. Does the current TANF law do an adequate job of addressing the connections between poverty and health? If not, how could the system be changed to make health a priority?

Best Practices and Advocacy Strategies for Medical-Legal Partnership

As the most common public program serving low-income communities, SNAP is a critical intervention for front-line healthcare providers to understand, screen for and encourage patients to access. People (especially the elderly) often need encouragement to apply for SNAP benefits because the application process can be daunting. But SNAP eligibility can trigger access to other critical income supports like the Low Income Heating and Energy Assistance Program. MLP legal expertise is especially critical to back up frontline healthcare providers who are serving immigrant communities, where eligibility for SNAP benefits may be confusing, and the need for healthcare provider support and encouragement is at a premium. Because the application process is relatively swift compared to other benefits and services, MLP teams that prioritize ensuring that low-income patients get access to SNAP benefits can show rapid results — for patients, providers and legal advocates.

From Practice to Policy

Medical-Legal Partnership | Boston began prioritizing food stamp and utility access — "heat and eat" clinics — at Boston Medical Center in 2006, where 70 percent of the patient population was eligible for SNAP benefits. After several years of handling hundreds of food stamp cases for eligible patients who had not gotten their benefits, hospital and physician leadership, together with MLP | Boston legal leadership, invited the state SNAP office to open a satellite application center in the hospital to improve access for patient-families and facilitate problem solving for complex applications. The pilot SNAP office led to other such offices in hospitals and clinics across Massachusetts and changed how healthcare providers understood the SNAP benefits and what they mean for patients.

Case for Medical-Legal Partnership

Sarah is a 23-year-old mother of two children ages six and two and a half. She did not finish high school and has worked primarily in service jobs paying minimum wage. She was fired six months ago from her job because of absenteeism. She receives sporadic child support from the children's father. Sarah is diabetic. She has a history of problems controlling her glucose levels because she often misses her medication. She has no health insurance. With the recession, she has not been able to find a job and has been receiving cash assistance (through the state's TANF program) and SNAP benefits for the past six months. Last week she received a termination letter from the Department of Human Services stating that she is no longer eligible for cash assistance.

Questions for Discussion

1. Medical: How might you learn of Sarah's situation? How might you address her health concerns? What should you do when she tells you about the letter terminating her cash assistance?

2. Legal: What questions will you need to ask Sarah to determine whether the denial of cash assistance can be challenged? Will loss of cash assistance affect her food stamps?

3. How might healthcare providers and lawyers work together to most effectively support the health and well-being of Sarah and her children?

Conclusion

Over the past 75 years, policy makers have implemented a range of programs and benefits that, taken together, will help the least fortunate in our communities—underserved low-income minorities, the disabled, children and elderly—maintain a basic standard of living and meet their basic needs. As the deep connections between social determinants and health are cemented in research and in the public eye, these public programs, from SSDI to SNAP, take on new urgency, as not simply antipoverty programs but key interventions in addressing and promoting health for our most vulnerable individuals and families.

Notes

Anne Ryan would like to acknowledge Stephanie Altman from the Chicago Medical-Legal Partnership for Children, Health and Disability Advocates, and Shanah Tirado from LegalHealth, New York Legal Assistance Group, for their contributions; Cristina Dachille would like to thank Britt Backhaus, a JD candidate at Northeastern University School of Law, and James Racine, a JD candidate at Boston College Law School, for their assistance with the chapter.

1. Gerard Anderson, "Chronic Care: Making the Case for Ongoing Care," Robert Wood Johnson Foundation (2010), http://www.rwjf.org/files/research/50968chronic.care.chartbook.pdf (accessed December 29, 2010).

2. Susan Egerter, Paula Braveman, Catherine Cubbin, et al., "Reaching America's Health Potential: A State-by-State Look at Adult Health," Robert Wood Johnson Foundation (2009), http://www.commissiononhealth.org/Documents/AdultHealthChartbookFullReport.pdf.

3. Holly Avey, "How U.S. Laws and Social Policies Influence Chronic Stress and Health Disparities," Politics of Race, Culture, and Health Symposium, Ithaca College (2002), http://www.unnaturalcauses.org/assets/uploads/file/Avey-Chronic_Stress_and_Health_Disparities.pdf.

4. Peggy A. Thoits, "Stress and Health: Major Findings & Policy Implications," Journal of Health and Social Behavior, 51, no. 1 (2010): S41–53.

5. Egerter et al., "Reaching America's Health Potential."

6. Alemayehu Bishaw, Suzanne Macartney, "Poverty: 2008 and 2009," American Community Survey Briefs (2010), http://www.census.gov/prod/2010pubs/acsbr09-1.pdf.

7. Nancy K. Cauthen, Sarah Fass, "Measuring Poverty in the United States," National Center for Children in Poverty (last modified June 2008), http://www.nccp.org/publications/pub_825.html.

8. U.S. Census Bureau, "How the Census Bureau Measures Poverty" (last modified December 18, 2010), http://www.census.gov/hhes/www/poverty/about/overview/measure.html.

9. Arloc Sherman, "Public Benefits: Easing Poverty Report and Ensuring Medical Coverage," Center on Budget and Policy Priorities (last modified August 17, 2005), http://www.cbpp.org/cms/?fa= view&id=508.

10. Rebecca M. Blank, Mark H. Greenberg, "Improving the Measurement of Poverty," Brookings Institute: Discussion paper under the Hamilton Project (2008), 1–35.

11. Ibid., 13.

12. Douglas Besharov, Peter Germanis, "Reconsidering the Federal Poverty Measure," University of Maryland School of Public Policy, Welfare Reform Academy (2004), 1–24.

13. U.S. Department of Labor, Bureau of Labor Statistics, "Employment Situation Summary" (last modified January 7, 2011), http://www.bls.gov/news.release/empsit.nr0.htm.

14. Martin N. Marger, Social Inequality: Patterns and Processes (New York: McGraw-Hill, 2010).

15. George A. Kaplan, "The Poor Pay More: Poverty's High Cost to Health," Robert Wood Johnson Foundation (last modified September 1, 2009), http://www.rwjf.org/files/research/thepoorpaymore 2009.pdf.

16. Sherman, "Public Benefits."

17. Bureau of Labor Statistics, "A Profile of the Working Poor, 2000," U.S. Department of Labor (last modified March 2002), http://www.bls.gov/cps/cpswp2000.htm.

18. Joseph S. Ross, Susannah M. Bernheim, Elizabeth H. Bradley, Hsun-Mei Teng, William T. Gallo, "Use of Preventive Care by the Working Poor in the United States," Preventive Medicine, 44 (2007): 254–59.

19. Nancy E. Adler, Katherine Newman, "Socioeconomic Disparities in Health: Pathways and Policies," Health Affairs, 21, no. 2 (2002): 60–76; Maria Melchior, Nancy Krieger, Ichiro Kawachi, et al., "Work Factors and Occupational Class Disparities in Sickness Absence: Findings from the GAZEL Cohort Study," American Journal of Public Health, 95, no. 7 (2005): 1206–12.

20. Robin Weinick, John Billings, Helen Burstin, "What Is the Role of Primary Care in Emergency Department Overcrowding?," Publications of the Council on Health Care Economics and Policy, http://www.kaisernetwork.org/healthcast/uploadedfiles/WeinickED.pdf.

21. Child Health Impact Working Group, "Unhealthy Consequences: Energy Costs and Child Health" (2007), http://www.hiaguide.org/sites/default/files/ChildHIAofenergycostsandchildhealth.pdf.

22. Arloc Sherman, Danilo Trisi, Robert Greenstein, Matt Broaddus, "Census Data Show Large Jump in Poverty and the Ranks of the Uninsured in 2009," Center on Budget and Policy Priorities (last modified September 17, 2010), http://www.cbpp.org/cms/index.cfm?fa=view&id=3294.

23. NOLO Law for All, "Workers' Compensation Benefits FAQ," http://www.nolo.com/legal-encyclopedia/faqEditorial-29093.html.

24. Nik Theodore, Mirabai Auer, Ryan Hollon, Sandra Morales Mirque, "The Breakdown of Workplace Protections in the Low-Wage Labor Market," Center for Urban Economic Development, http://www.urbaneconomy.org/sites/default/files/Unregulated%20Work%20inChicago%204_7_210%20FINAL%20REPORT_0.pdf.

25. Kristin J. Cummings, Kathleen Kreiss, "Contingent Workers and Contingent Health," Journal of the American Medical Association, 299, no. 4 (2008): 448–50.

26. U.S. Department of Labor, Wage and Hour Division, "Compliance Assistance—Fair Labor Standards Act (FLSA)," http://www.dol.gov/whd/flsa/.

27. Theodore et al., "The Breakdown of Workplace Protections."

28. U.S. Department of Labor, Wage and Hour Division, "Fact Sheet #28: The Family and Medical Leave Act of 1993" (last modified February 2010), http://www.dol.gov/whd/regs/compliance/whdfs28.htm.

29. The Department of labor oversees FMLA compliance. See http://www.dol.gov/whd/fmla/index.htm.

30. See 29 C.F.R. § 1630.2(p). See also, "EEOC Fact Sheet The Family and Medical Leave Act, the Americans with Disabilities Act, and Title VII of the Civil Rights Act of 1964," http://www.eeoc.gov/policy/docs/fmlaada.html.

31. Theodore et al., "The Breakdown of Workplace Protections."

32. U.S. Department of Health and Human Services, Office on Disability, "Disability and Aging," http://www.hhs.gov/od/about/fact_sheets/disabilityaging.html (accessed January 19, 2011).

33. U.S. Department of Health and Human Services, "The 2005 Surgeon General's Call to Action to Improve the Health and Wellness of Persons with Disabilities: Calling You to Action," Office of the Surgeon General (last modified 2005), http://www.surgeongeneral.gov/library/disabilities/calltoaction/whatitmeanstoyou.pdf.

34. Ibid.

35. Ibid.

36. Ibid.

37. National Organization on Disability, Harris Poll, 2004.

38. Bonnie Strickland, Merle McPherson, Gloria Weissman, Peter van Dyck, Zhihuan J. Huang, Paul Newacheck, "Access to the Medical Home. Results of the National Survey of Children with Special Health Care Needs," *Pediatrics,* 113, no. 5 (2004): 1485–92.

39. EEOC Policy Compliance Manuals can be found at http://www.eeoc.gov/laws/guidance/ index.cfm.

40. See http://www.eeoc.gov/laws/statutes/adaaa_info.cfm.

41. *Barnett v. U.S. Air, Inc.* (228 F3d 1105, 1116 [9th Cir 2000, en banc], *vacated on other grounds,* 535 US 391 [2002]).

42. Enforcement Guidance: Reasonable Accommodation and Undue Hardship Under the Americans with Disabilities Act. See 42 U.S.C. § 12111(10) (B) (1994); 29 C.F.R. § 1630.2(p) (2) (1997); 29 C.F.R. pt. 1630 app. § 1630.2(p) (1997); TAM, supra note 49, at 3.9, 8 FEP Manual (BNA) 405: 7005–7.

43. Stewart B. Fleishman, Randye Retkin, Julie Brandfield, Victoria Braun, "The Attorney as the Newest Member of the Cancer Treatment Team," *Journal of Clinical Oncology,* 24, no. 13 (2006): 2123–26.

44. Cancer Legal Resource Center, "Disability Insurance," Disability Rights Legal Center and Loyola Law School Los Angeles (last modified December 2010), http://disabilityrightslegalcenter.org/about/documents/NationalDisabiiltyInsurance_2010.pdf.

45. Social Security Act Title II § 202.

46. Ibid.

47. Social Security Act of 1935, P.L. No. 74-271, 49 Stat. 620 (codified as amended at 42 U.S.C. §§ 301–1399 (2000)). SSDI at 42 U.S.C. § 401; 20 C.F.R. §§ 404 et seq.; SSI at 42 U.S.C. § 1381 et seq.; 20 C.F.R. § 416 et seq. SSA Program Operations Manual System (POMS), http://policy.ssa.gov/poms.nsf/aboutpoms.

48. Social Security Administration, "507. Definition of Disability for Disabled Worker's Benefits," Social Security Handbook (last modified November 16, 2010), http://www.ssa.gov/OP_Home/handbook/handbook.05/handbook-0507.html.

49. Social Security Administration, "Benefits for Children with Disabilities," SSA Publication no. 05-10026 (January 2011), ICN 455360 (last modified January 2011), http://www.ssa.gov/pubs/10026.html#ssi-benefits.

50. The Listing of Impairments describes impairments for each major body system that are considered severe enough to automatically meet the medical disability test. The SSA has developed separate listings for adults and children: http://www.ssa.gov/disability/professionals/bluebook/AdultListings.htm and http://www.ssa.gov/disability/professionals/bluebook/ChildhoodListings.htm.

51. The SSA has eliminated the reconsideration step in 10 "prototype states" in an effort to decrease time delays for administrative appeals. Modifications to the Disability Determination Procedures;

Disability Claims Process Redesign Prototype, 64 *Federal Register,* 47,218 (Aug. 30, 1999). 20 C.F.R. 404.906 and 416.1406.

52. Congressional Research Service, "Average Processing Times for Social Security Claims" (2010), http://waysandmeans.house.gov/Hearings/hearingDetails.aspx?NewsID=11143.

53. Testimony of Patrick P. O'Carroll Jr., Inspector General, Social Security Administration before the U.S. House of Representatives, Committee on Ways and Means, Subcommittees on Social Security and Income Security and Family Support (April 27, 2010), http://www.ssa.gov/oig/communications/testimony_speeches/04272010testimony.htm.

54. Inspector General, "Impact of the Social Security Administration's Claims Process on Disability Beneficiaries," Congressional Response Report, SSA IG Report A-01-09-29084, Sept. 2009.

55. Ibid., 4–10.

56. SSI recipients must report all changes in income and resources to the SSA. Failure to report this information in a timely way can result in over- or under-payment of monthly benefits and subsequent reduction of future benefits.

57. For more information about work incentives, see "A Summary Guide to Employment Support for Individuals with Disabilities under the Social Security Disability Insurance and Supplemental Security Income Programs," http://www.socialsecurity.gov/redbook/index.html.

58. 20 C.F.R. 404.1527(d)(2), Social Security Rulings SSR 96-5p, 96-6p, and 96-2p.

59. Sherman, "Public Benefits."

60. Mark Nord, Margaret Andrews, Steven Carlson, "United States Department of Agriculture, *Economic Research Report* 83 (2009): 15.

61. Janice E. Stuff, Patrick H. Casey, Kitty L. Szeto, et al., "Household Food Insecurity Is Associated with Adult Health Status," *Journal of Nutrition,* 134, no. 9 (2004): 2330–35.

62. Centers for Disease Control, "National Health and Nutrition Examination Survey" (November 2007), http://www.cdc.gov/nchs/nhanes.htm. Centers for Disease Control, "About BMI for Adults" (May 22, 2007), http://www.cdc.gov/nccdphp/dnpa/bmi/adult_BMI/about_adult_BMI.htm.

63. Administration on Aging, "Fact Sheet: The Older Americans Act Nutrition Programs (Elderly Nutrition Program)," U.S. Department of Health and Human Services (2002), http://www.aoa.gov/nutrition/OAANP-FS.pdf.

64. Jon P. Weimer, "Many Elderly at Nutritional Risk," *Food Review,* January–April (1997): 42–48.

65. Jason DeParle, "One in Five Report Hunger," *New York Times,* January 27, 2010, A16.

66. Effective October 1, 2008, the 2007 federal farm bill renamed the Food Stamp Program the Supplemental Nutrition Assistance Program (SNAP).

67. DeParle, "One in Five Report Hunger."

68. U.S. Department of Agriculture Food and Nutrition Service, "A Short History of SNAP" (last modified April 30, 2009), http://www.fns.usda.gov/snap/rules/Legislation/about.htm.

69. Dottie Rosenbaum, "The Food Stamp Program is Effective and Efficient," Center on Budget and Policy Priorities (last revised June 29, 2005).

70. U.S. Department of Agriculture Food and Nutrition Service, "WIC at a Glance" (last modified March 8, 2010), http://www.fns.usda.gov/wic/aboutwic/wicataglance.htm.

71. Ibid.

72. Ibid.

73. Ibid.

74. Victor Oliveira, Elizabeth Racine, Jennifer Olmsted, Linda M. Ghelfi, "The WIC Program: Background, Trends, and Issues," Food and Rural Economics Division, Economic Research Service, U.S. Department of Agriculture, *Food Assistance and Nutrition Research Report* 27 (2002).

75. U.S. Department of Agriculture Food and Nutrition Service, "WIC Food Packages" (last modified April 21, 2010), http://www.fns.usda.gov/wic/benefitsandservices/foodpkg.htm.

76. U.S. General Accounting Office, "Early Intervention: Federal Investments Like WIC Can Produce Savings," Report to Congressional Requesters (April 1992), 4.

77. Center on Budget and Policy Priorities, "Policy Basics: The Earned Income Tax Credit" (last modified December 4, 2009), available at http://www.cbpp.org/cms/index.cfm?fa=view&id=2505.

78. Ibid.

79. Ibid.

80. Ibid.

81. Ibid.

82. Ibid.

83. Mara Lindsay Schoen, "Working Welfare Recipients: A Comparison of the Family Support Act and the Personal Responsibility and Work Opportunity Reconciliation Act," *Fordham Urban Law Journal,* 24 (1997): 635–62.

84. Tammi D. Jackson, "Free Social Services: Where Do I Enroll? The True Cost Welfare Recipients and Undocumented Immigrants Have on the U.S. Economy," *Public Interest Law Reporter,* 13 (2008): 271–74.

85. Lucy A. Williams, "Race, Rat Bites and Unfit Mothers: How Media Discourse Informs Welfare Legislation Debate," *Fordham Urban Law Journal,* 22 (1995): 1159–96. Jonathan Zasloff, "Children, Families and Bureaucrats: A Prehistory of Welfare Reform," *Journal of Law and Policy,* 14 (1998): 225–317.

86. Schoen, "Working Welfare Recipients," 649.

87. Liz Schott, "Policy Basics: An Introduction to TANF," Center for Budget and Policy Priorities (last modified March 19, 2009), http://www.cbpp.org/cms/?fa=view&id=936.

88. Yoanna X. Moisides, "I Just Need Help … TANF, the Deficit Reduction Act, and the New 'Work-Eligible Individual,'" *Journal of Gender Race and Justice,* 11 (2007–2008): 17–46.

89. Center on Budget and Policy Priorities and Center for Law and Social Policy, "Implementing the TANF Changes in the Deficit Reduction Act: 'Win-Win' Solutions for Families and States" (last modified February 2007), http://www.clasp.org/admin/site/publications/files/0339.pdf.

90. John T. Cook, et al., "Welfare Reform and the Health of Young Children," Archives of Pediatrics & Adolescent Medicine, 156 (2002): 678–84.

Chapter 8

Housing: The Intersection of Affordability, Safety and Health

Elizabeth Tobin Tyler, JD, MA
Kathleen N. Conroy, MD, MSc
Chong-Min Fu, BA
Megan Sandel, MD, MPH

The shortage of safe, affordable housing in the United States is directly correlated to adverse health outcomes, particularly for children.[1] The unavailability of affordable housing affects health in at least two significant ways: (1) a high percentage of income devoted to rent may mean cutting back on other necessities, notably food and medical expenses; and (2) tenants may accept substandard and unhealthy housing conditions when safe, affordable housing is unavailable. Addressing the connections between housing and health requires a multidisciplinary and holistic approach. A strategy should include preventive legal protections for tenants, accessible resources and supports for families and effective health management. This chapter begins by describing the health consequences of the lack of affordable and healthy housing for low-income individuals and families. It then outlines available legal protections for low-income families facing housing problems. Finally, it explores different contexts in which poverty, housing and health converge and ways a medical-legal partnership can provide preventive protections for individuals and families.

Affordable Housing and Its Effects on Family Health

Even prior to the mortgage crisis and economic recession of 2008, the lack of safe, affordable housing had reached crisis levels in the United States. From 2000 to 2006, the number of low-income renter households whose housing costs exceeded 50 percent of their income (a group the U.S. Department of Housing and Urban Development categorizes as having "severe housing cost burdens") increased by 2 million, or 32 percent.[2] Figure 8.1 shows how the percentage of income spent on housing decreases by income level. In 2007, it was estimated that 9.0 million households were competing for 6.2 million affordable housing units. In 2009, to afford a two-bedroom unit at the average national rent, a household had to earn the equivalent of $17.84 per hour full-time, nearly three times the federal minimum wage.[3]

Housing and Health

The high cost of housing affects health in several ways. Paying a disproportionate percentage of household income for housing reduces available income for other necessities, such as food, medical care and utilities. For example, low-income families with high

Figure 8.1 The Percentage of American Families Who Spend More Than 30% of Their Income on Housing by Income Level

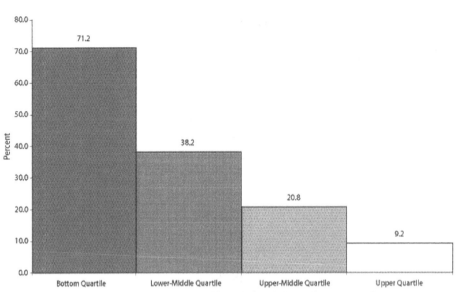

Source: Craig Pollack, Susan Egerter, Tabashir Sadegh-Nobari, Mercedes Dekker, and Paula Braveman, *Issue Brief 2: Housing and Health.* Washington, DC: Robert Wood Johnson Foundation Commission to Build a Healthier America, September 2008. Based on analyses from the Joint Center for Housing Studies at Harvard University, *State of the Nation's Housing, 2008.*
Copyright 2008. Robert Wood Johnson Foundation Commission to Build a Healthier America. Used with permission from the Robert Wood Johnson Foundation.

housing and utility costs spend less on food, especially in the winter when utility costs are at their highest.[4] Children in families that are eligible for but do not receive rent subsidies are significantly more likely to present with malnutrition and stunted growth and have an increased risk of infection compared to those who receive subsidies.[5]

With a lack of affordable housing options, families may also be faced with the choice between substandard housing and no housing at all. Figure 8.2 shows the relationship among affordability, housing conditions and health. Low-income children living in substandard housing have disproportionately higher rates of lead poisoning, asthma and injuries resulting from deteriorating lead paint; asthma triggers such as rodents and mold; and missing smoke detectors and window guards.[6] Rising utility prices force families to choose whether to "heat or eat," leading to malnutrition and/or exacerbation of health problems from lack of sufficient heat or cooling.[7]

For families who become homeless, child health consequences are even more severe. One study found that homeless children have diarrhea five times as often as low-income children who live in homes. Homeless children are twice as likely to suffer from respiratory infections and seven times more likely to have iron deficiency and malnutrition than housed children. They are also at risk for interrupted primary care, inadequate immunizations, developmental delays and poor school performance.[8]

Figure 8.2 Housing Influences Health in Many Ways

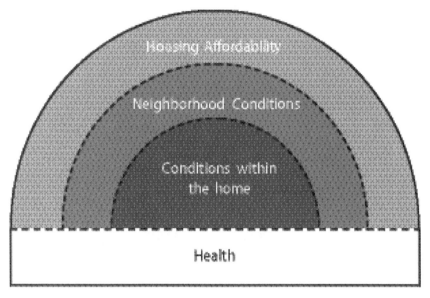

Source: Craig Pollack, Susan Egerter, Tabashir Sadegh-Nobari, Mercedes Dekker, and Paula Braveman, *Issue Brief 2: Housing and Health.* Washington, DC: Robert Wood Johnson Foundation Commission to Build a Healthier America, September 2008.
Copyright 2008. Robert Wood Johnson Foundation Commission to Build a Healthier America. Used with permission from the Robert Wood Johnson Foundation.

Questions for Discussion

1. What is the connection between access to affordable housing and the safety of housing? Why would addressing affordability of housing potentially increase the health and safety of children?

2. The data indicate that homeless children and children whose families are eligible but do not receive rent subsidies have worse health outcomes than other children. What may explain these findings?

Housing and Legal Rights

Many low-income people struggle daily to secure safe, affordable housing. Families who have a difficult time paying rent are said to have housing insecurity: they may be forced to move frequently, or they may face disruptive eviction proceedings. Although under current law there is no universal right to housing in the United States, tenants do have rights to habitable conditions in the homes they rent.[9] Many low-income tenants have a difficult time exercising these legal rights because they lack access to legal assistance. Yet safe, affordable housing is fundamental to health. To address poor health outcomes associated with substandard housing conditions or instability, lawyers are critical to efforts to protect family health.

Housing Assistance

There are federal and state housing assistance programs for low-income families and individuals (see Figure 8.3), but it is estimated that only one third to one fifth of those

Figure 8.3 Who Lives in Public Housing?

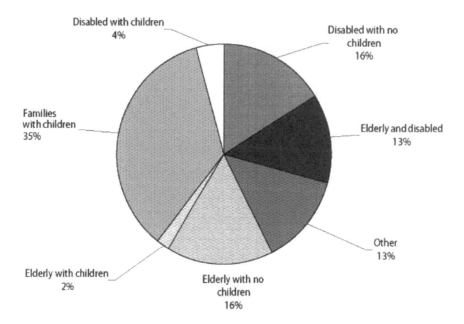

Source: Barbara Sard and Will Fischer, *Preserving Safe, High Quality Public Housing Should Be a Priority of Federal Housing Policy,* Center on Budget and Policy Priorities (October 8, 2008).

who qualify for housing assistance actually receive it.[10] From 2003 to 2005, the proportion of extremely low-income renters without housing assistance increased from 66 percent to 72 percent.[11] Many states have lengthy waiting lists for public housing units and Section 8 vouchers (which allow low-income families and individuals to find rentals in the private market).[12] The unavailability of subsidized housing options as well as affordable housing in the private market renders many low-income families with few housing choices and in a poor bargaining position when they try to negotiate terms with a landlord. This position may affect the quality and safety of housing options, sometimes forcing families to choose housing in poor condition.

Basic Facts about Public Housing

• **How many public housing units are there?** There are 1.16 million units, located in close to 14,000 developments spread throughout every state and in several territories. About 1.04 million units are currently occupied. The remainder are undergoing renovation or are vacant for other reasons.

• **Who owns and administers public housing?** Public housing units are owned by more than 3,100 housing agencies. Most of these are semi-independent housing authorities, but some are agencies of local or state governments. Most agencies are small: half own fewer than 100 public housing units; 88 percent own 500 or fewer units. The Department of Housing and Urban Development (HUD) oversees public housing at the federal level.

• **Is public housing the same as Section 8?** Public housing is a separate program from the Section 8 housing voucher program (which helps tenants rent units of their choice in the private market), although 47 percent of the agencies that administer public housing also run voucher programs. Public housing is also distinct from "project-based" Section 8 and other federal programs that directly subsidize private affordable housing owners.

• **When was public housing created?** The public housing program began in 1937. Nearly all of today's developments were built before 1985. No funds have been provided to build new public housing since the mid-1990s (except to replace other public housing that was demolished or otherwise removed from the program).

• **Who is eligible to live in public housing?** A family must be "low-income" — meaning that its income may not exceed 80 percent of the local median income — to move into public housing. At least 40 percent of the new families an agency admits each year must be "extremely low income," with incomes at or below 30 percent of the local median. But on average agencies exceed this 40 percent requirement by a wide margin.

• **How much rent do tenants pay?** Most tenants pay 30 percent of their income (after certain deductions are taken out) for rent and utilities. Tenants also have the option to pay "flat rents" that are set based on local market rents regardless of the tenant's income.

• **How is public housing funded?** The federal government provides three funding streams for public housing: (1) the Public Housing Operating Fund, which makes up the difference between the rent revenues tenants pay and operating expenses, such as utilities, security and maintenance; (2) the Public Housing Capital Fund, which funds renovation of developments and replacement of appliances and systems; and (3) HOPE VI, a competitive grant program that supports revitalization of the most distressed developments. In 2008, Congress provided $6.7 billion from these three sources. In addition, some agencies receive supplemental resources from states or localities or from other federal funding streams like the Low-Income Housing Tax Credit.

Source: Barbara Sard and Will Fischer, *Preserving Safe, High Quality Public Housing Should Be a Priority of Federal Housing Policy,* Center on Budget and Policy Priorities (October 8, 2008).

Protections from Housing Discrimination

Federal, state and local fair housing laws are intended to prevent landlords from discriminating against tenants, including those who may have the most difficulty securing housing (poor families). Some landlords attempt to avoid their obligations under lead safety laws, for example, by refusing to rent to families with children under the age of six. Fair housing laws are one avenue to enforce the rights of low-income families to access housing options. Remedying discrimination not only helps an individual or family secure housing, it also sends a message to private landlords that discrimination may not be used to avoid compliance with laws and policies designed to make safe and affordable housing available.

The Federal Fair Housing Act of 1968

Congress passed the Federal Fair Housing Act as part of the Civil Rights Act of 1968. It has been amended several times to extend the categories of protected individuals. The

Table 8.1 Protections under the Federal Fair Housing Act

Protected Classes	Property Covered	Property Exempt	Prohibited Activities
Race Sex Color National Origin Religion Handicap Familial Status: (Child under 18 lives with): • A parent • A person who has legal custody of the child or children • The designee of the parent or legal custodian • Includes pregnant women	Most Residential Property	Single family property sold or rented without use of a broker Owner-occupied housing with no more than four units Private housing operated by organization or club that limits occupancy to members Housing specifically designed for older persons is exempt from the prohibition against familial status discrimination	Refuse to rent or sell housing Refuse to negotiate for housing Make housing unavailable Deny a dwelling Failure to make a reasonable accommodation Set different terms, conditions or privileges for sale or rental of a dwelling Provide different housing services or facilities Falsely deny that housing is available for inspection, sale, or rental For profit, persuade owners to sell or rent (blockbusting) or Deny anyone access to or membership in a facility or service (such as a multiple listing service) related to the sale or rental of housing

Act protects individuals "in the sale, rental, and financing of dwellings, and in other housing-related transactions, based on race, color, national origin, religion, sex, familial status (including children under the age of 18 living with parents or legal custodians, pregnant women, and people securing custody of children under the age of 18), and handicap (disability)."[13] See Table 8.1 for the protections and exemptions provided under the Act. The law is administered by the U.S. Department of Housing and Urban Development (HUD).

State and Local Fair Housing Laws

Though similar in scope, some state and local laws provide wider protections than the federal Fair Housing Act. Some states, for example, cover other classifications such as marital status, sexual orientation or receipt of a housing voucher as protected under the fair housing law.[14] Fair housing laws are enforced at the local, state and federal levels. An individual who believes he or she has been discriminated against can file a complaint with his or her state or local fair housing agency[15] or file a complaint with HUD. An individual may also file a lawsuit in federal court. Complaints may be filed in all three venues.[16]

Questions for Discussion

1. You are meeting with the congressional delegation from your district to discuss a proposal for additional funding for public housing. What would you say? How would you connect health to the discussion?

2. What types of housing discrimination might occur based on health-related conditions? How helpful are fair housing laws in addressing these types of discrimination?

The Right to Safe and Sanitary Housing

The laws and regulations governing the construction and conditions of residential housing are governed by state and local housing codes. Nearly all state and local codes include provisions to ensure correction of substandard housing conditions that can lead to health problems. Tenants have the right to complain to state and local code enforcement agencies when landlords do not address code violations. Enforcement officials should respond to complaints by scheduling a time to inspect the property, documenting the condition of the property, including any code violations, and notifying the property owner of the needed repairs.

State and Local Protections for Healthy Housing

Housing Code

State and local housing codes govern the condition of residential housing to ensure that the property remains safe for occupants. Codes set requirements for proper owner maintenance of structural elements, heat and hot water, kitchen facilities, and rodent and pest extermination. Housing codes are generally quite detailed and should serve as a "checklist" for property owners and tenants.[17] Landlords must abide by the provisions of both the state and local housing codes. Generally, local housing codes are more detailed than state codes.

Implied Warranty of Habitability

The implied warranty of habitability derives from the common law (law developed through court decisions, not legislatures). It requires that a landlord must maintain a property in exchange for receipt of rental payments from the tenant. In other words, it is implied that when a tenant agrees to pay rent to the landlord in exchange for use of the property, the landlord must keep the rental unit in a sanitary and safe condition to make it habitable. A tenant may bring an action against a landlord who fails to maintain the property in a habitable and safe condition.[18]

Landlord-Tenant Act

Most states have statutes governing the rights and responsibilities of tenants and landlords. These statutes regulate issues that may arise with regard to rental payments and security deposits, notice of termination of tenancy, eviction procedures and tenants' remedies for violation of the housing code. Although a lease (a written agreement between a landlord and tenant) may cover many of these issues, a tenant may not sign away his or her rights provided by statute.[19] It is important to note that a lease may provide longer-term protections for a tenant. For example, most state landlord-tenant acts provide that a tenant who does not have a lease may be evicted without cause as long as appropriate notice is given. Generally, a tenant who pays rent on a monthly basis may be evicted with just 30 days' notice.

Nuisance Law

State and local nuisance laws provide local governments with the authority to address conditions that may be hazardous to public health and safety. Local enforcement agencies may cite multiple violations of the housing code as a nuisance.[20] For example, a landlord who fails to address a significant pest problem, such as rats, may jeopardize the health and safety of residents of the neighborhood, not just the tenants who occupy the property. This type of code violation may be addressed through nuisance laws.

Enforcement of Housing Protections

Though many landlords meet their legal obligations to maintain their rental property, there are multiple ways they may violate tenants' rights or that inspection agencies may fail to enforce tenants' rights. For example, some landlords avoid their responsibilities to maintain their property until they receive a phone call or letter from a lawyer outlining the tenant's complaints and needed actions. Others respond only to threat of litigation. Additionally, the agency charged with responding to tenant complaints can be unresponsive and fail to meet their obligation to inspect and issue a notice of violation to property owners.[21]

Many low-income tenants are unaware of their rights regarding safe housing. Landlord-tenant relationships and city bureaucracies, like code enforcement agencies, are often difficult for people to navigate without assistance. Collaboration between a healthcare provider and lawyer, such as through a medical-legal partnership (MLP), may be very effective in documenting and addressing the health effects of substandard housing and the actions required for the landlord to comply with state and local laws.

Protections Against Eviction

In addition to unsafe and unhealthy housing, many low-income tenants struggle with insecure housing. As already described, finding an affordable unit can be difficult, and families may constantly be at risk of falling behind in rent. In addition, because many low-income tenants do not have a lease giving them longer-term security in their rental housing, they may be particularly vulnerable to eviction. A 2007 study by the Brennan Center for Justice found that 67 percent of the potential evictees in New York City had annual incomes of less than $25,000, 61 percent lived with children under the age of 18, and only one in four tenants facing eviction had legal representation.[22]

Additionally, with the recent mortgage lending crisis, many tenants are vulnerable to eviction when their landlord experiences foreclosure. Although state laws generally regulate the relationship between landlords and tenants, including during foreclosure, Congress stepped in with passage of the Protecting Tenants at Foreclosure Act of 2009 (PTFA) to provide some limited protections for tenants. The law requires that certain tenants must receive a 90-day notice before they can be evicted when the rental property is in foreclosure. The PTFA does not preempt state laws that provide additional protections. New Jersey, for example, provides strong protection for tenants from eviction on foreclosure. For example, New Jersey law "requires a purchaser of foreclosed residential properties to provide to tenants written notice in English and Spanish within ten days after the purchaser takes ownership."[23]

Housing insecurity is tied to substandard housing in that a tenant may accept substandard housing conditions to preserve *any* housing. Low-income tenants may fear that if they seek to enforce their rights under the law, their landlord may evict them. For poor families, eviction "is identifiable as the singular point in time at which they either become homeless, or are at the greatest danger of becoming homeless. Many families have no place to go after losing their homes from eviction."[24] Most states provide protection for tenants against retaliatory action by a landlord when a tenant seeks to enforce the right to safe housing under the state's housing code or other state laws governing housing standards. The retaliatory eviction statute from North Carolina is an example of a state law designed to protect tenants who assert their rights to safe, sanitary housing under state and local laws.

Protections Against Retaliatory Eviction

North Carolina Article 4A, § 42-37.1. Defense of retaliatory eviction.

(a) It is the public policy of the State of North Carolina to protect tenants and other persons whose residence in the household is explicitly or implicitly known to the landlord, who seek to exercise their rights to decent, safe, and sanitary housing. Therefore, the following activities of such persons are protected by law:

(1) A good faith complaint or request for repairs to the landlord, his employee, or his agent about conditions or defects in the premises that the landlord is obligated to repair under G.S. 42-42;

(2) A good faith complaint to a government agency about a landlord's alleged violation of any health or safety law, or any regulation, code, ordinance, or State or federal law that regulates premises used for dwelling purposes;

(3) A government authority's issuance of a formal complaint to a landlord concerning premises rented by a tenant;

(4) A good faith attempt to exercise, secure or enforce any rights existing under a valid lease or rental agreement or under State or federal law; or

(5) A good faith attempt to organize, join, or become otherwise involved with, any organization promoting or enforcing tenants' rights.

(b) In an action for summary ejectment pursuant to G.S. 42-26, a tenant may raise the affirmative defense of retaliatory eviction and may present evidence that the landlord's action is substantially in response to the occurrence within 12 months of the filing of such action of one or more of the protected acts described in subsection (a) of this section.

Protections against retaliatory eviction, however, are only effective if a tenant can show that he or she has tried to enforce his or her right to safe housing through the appropriate measures, such as notifying the landlord in writing of the repairs needed or calling the local code enforcement office to complain. Many low-income tenants find themselves unprotected, particularly if they do not address the issue of unsafe housing conditions until they are faced with eviction. As is demonstrated in *Remedor v. Massachusetts Department of Housing & Community Development*, health problems exacerbated by substandard housing conditions can lead to a downward spiral for a tenant who does not receive preventive legal help. Given that many low-income renters are not well educated about their rights and may face barriers to education, such as limited English proficiency, MLPs can play an important role in preventing evictions by educating residents of their rights and responsibilities before problems escalate.

Superior Court of Massachusetts.

Clarisse REMEDOR
v.
MASSACHUSETTS DEPARTMENT OF HOUSING &
COMMUNITY DEVELOPMENT
No. 03-3803.
Sept. 9, 2004.

Ms. Remedor worked as a certified nurse's aide and lived in an apartment in Waltham for approximately four years prior to 2002. She had always paid her rent on time. She has suffered from multiple ailments, including asthma, high blood pressure, obesity, and diabetes. In February 2002, she lost her job because her health prevented her from working. She continued to pay her rent in full through August 2002 when she depleted her savings. She maintains that conditions in the apartment were substandard, violated the warranty of habitability, exacerbated her illnesses, and endangered her health.

In September of 2002 Remedor's landlord terminated her tenancy for failure to pay rent.... With the assistance of counsel, Remedor negotiated a settlement.... Remedor agreed to vacate the premises by January 10, 2003, and "acknowledge[d] and agree[d] that the [landlord] [was] entitled to outstanding rent" and "use and occupancy" charges for the months of July through January. However, as part of the agreement, the landlord agreed to waive the claim to those amounts if Remedor vacated the apartment by January 10. Finally, Remedor released any and all claims against the landlord arising from her tenancy in the premises.

Remedor applied to the Waltham Housing Authority (WHA) for placement in public housing on November 22, 2002, and sought "emergency case status" through the WHA's emergency case plan. Emergency case status places an applicant ahead of other "standard" applicants awaiting public housing. WHA's plan conferred emergency case status upon individuals who were "homeless," as defined in 760 CMR 5.03, and whose homelessness was the result of "causes other than the fault of the applicant." The regulation defines the second criterion as "causes outside of the [applicant's] reasonable control, including but not limited to substandard housing conditions which directly and substantially endanger or impair the health, safety, or well-being [of the applicant], and other circumstances as determined by the [Local Housing Authority]." On February 26, 2002, WHA approved her application for public housing but denied her application for emergency case status. It found that she had a history of nonpayment of rent.

The WHA director affirmed the decision. He found that Ms. Remedor had become homeless as a result of her own doing. He cited the terms of the agreement for judgment: Remedor's admission of liability for rent and her waiver of all claims against the landlord.... He reasoned that "it cannot be inferred from the agreement that [her allegations were] true." He noted that Ms. Remedor "also claims that she was not evicted but rather reached an agreement to vacate her apartment owing nothing to the landlord." He concluded as follows: "The applicant cannot have it both ways. She vacated the apartment because she owed money she couldn't or wouldn't pay or she left voluntarily. In either case, she is 'not homeless at no fault.'"

Ms. Remedor appealed that decision to DHCD. She was the only witness. The agency affirmed the denial of emergency care status. Its decision included its reasoning.

"The 'homeless' property under the Emergency Case Plan is only available to applicants who lost their housing for reasons that were beyond [their] control. Although the Applicant claimed there were defects in the premises that negatively affected her health, she did not pursue available ways to prevent or avoid any safety or life threatening situation by seeking assistance through the courts or appropriate administrative or enforcement agencies.... There is no indication that the Applicant would have vacated the premises but for the eviction action brought against her for failing to pay rent. Because the Applicant's housing situation does not meet the requirements of an Emergency Case ... she cannot be offered housing ahead of other equally needy applicants on the waiting list."

Questions for Discussion

1. What is the relationship between Ms. Remedor's health, her ability to pay rent and her access to safe housing?

2. What agreement did Ms. Remedor make with her landlord when he sought to terminate her tenancy (evict her) for failure to pay rent?

3. Whose "fault" is it that Ms. Remedor became homeless? Do you agree with the WHA director that she became homeless "by her own doing?" Would earlier legal assistance have made a difference in her case?

4. How can healthcare providers ensure that homeless individuals and families and those living in unhealthy housing are identified? What types of questions should practitioners ask families to identify these problems?

5. What is the role of doctors in addressing housing issues for individual patients and families? For their larger patient population?

Preventing Injuries to Health from Substandard Housing

Medical-legal partnership offers the opportunity to identify unhealthy housing problems before a family faces a crisis, such as the threat of eviction (see Figure 8.4). By working together, doctors and lawyers can support a low-income tenant to enforce her rights under the law and preserve her housing. A healthcare provider is often the first professional to identify substandard housing as an issue for a family. By collaborating with lawyers, they can help access preventive legal services for the family as well as support legal action by offering important information regarding the effects of housing violations on family

Figure 8.4 Preventive Legal Advocacy in the Housing Context

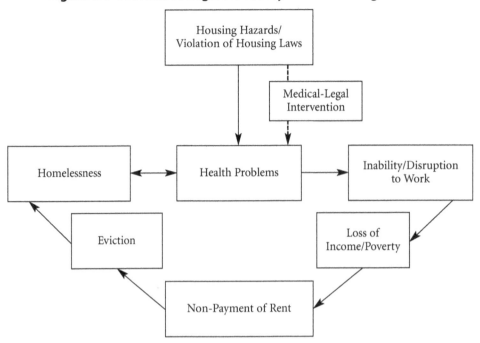

health. Preventive legal action in housing cases often involves nontraditional, hands-on problem-solving approaches that partner healthcare professionals and legal professionals to challenge unresponsive systems or property owners.

Best Practices and Advocacy Strategies for Medical-Legal Partnership

Medical Legal-Partnership for Children | Boston (MLP | Boston) recommends the following protocol to address unhealthy housing conditions and to prevent resulting health problems.

Representation of Tenants Who Report Substandard Housing
Sample Protocol

First, the lawyers should visit the tenant's unit. Rather than relying solely on the client's description, the lawyer must have firsthand knowledge of the conditions of the apartment before contacting the landlord.... During the first visit, the lawyer should assess the problem, and explore with the tenant whether the tenant can do anything to alleviate it. After inspecting the apartment, the lawyer should contact the landlord.

The next meeting with tenant, lawyer, and landlord present should occur at the apartment, so that the tenant and lawyer can point out each problem to the landlord. The lawyer or tenant should submit to the landlord a written description of each problem, particularly if the tenant is withholding rent because of substandard conditions. If the landlord agrees to take remedial action, then the lawyer, or someone on her staff, should coordinate the scheduling of all work appointments for the landlord to access the unit....

If, despite the lawyer's participation in the process, the landlord does not adequately remedy the unit, then the tenant should contact the inspectional services office and request a residential inspection. The product of the inspection is a list, which is served on the landlord, of the sanitary code violations. Once served with that report, the landlord is under a legal duty to remedy the conditions of disrepair....

The thoroughness of the report is critical; what is stated in the report is an objective finding that can help support a tenant's claim of housing problems in a civil or criminal case. Part of the lawyer's role during the inspection therefore is to ensure that the inspecting agency records every single violation.... Ideally, the landlord is also present during the initial inspection.... Having all parties present to discuss each violation and its appropriate remediation increases the likelihood that the landlord will do a better job at remediation and makes it easier to hold the landlord accountable.... The lawyer should be forceful in requesting that the inspector order the landlord to address the problem more globally, such as having the entire building exterminated....

The lawyer should also hold the inspector accountable for returning to the unit and ensuring that all parties are notified of reinspection and are present. When this level of oversight does not occur, inspectors often do not return for reinspections either because of poor communication with the tenant or because of their own negligence. The lawyer must ensure that neither the landlord nor the inspectional services department is exonerated of its obligations toward the tenant until all violations are appropriately eliminated.[25]

From Practice to Policy

The MLPs in northern California organized a regional policy initiative to investigate the housing code inspection practices in the San Francisco Bay area. Medical students researched the link between inadequate housing and poor health, and medical partners documented the health connection. A policy brief was written and disseminated in September 2009 with recommendations to improve access to healthy housing. Some of those recommendations are excerpted here.

Policy Changes and Changes to the Law
State-Level Changes

For maximum effect and efficiency, policy change around code enforcement should be executed first and foremost at the state level. In almost every locality surveyed, the local ordinances cited to the California Health and Safety Code as authority for code enforcement powers. Therefore, a change at the state level would affect each individual locality. Several broad, statewide policy suggestions are as follows:

1. *Establish a Statewide Coalition.* To build broad support for amending the current Health and Safety Code to better protect tenants with habitability problems, establish a statewide coalition. This coalition should include public health and legal experts as well as residents who are facing or have faced habitability issues.

2. *Examine Best Practices Around the State.* Within the coalition, disseminate code enforcement findings from the [area] and compare and contrast them with anecdotal stories of other coalition partners. Follow up on any jurisdictions with potential best practice models.

3. *Develop Policy Goals and Framing.* Within the coalition, develop policy change goals with an eye toward on-the-ground enforcement. Make strategic decisions about the scope of the change and how to frame and present policy change priorities. Develop an action plan for passing these policies.

Local-Level Changes

Tenant Education

While change on the state level may be more efficient and effective, there is also a great deal that local jurisdictions can do to improve code enforcement, even absent any change on the state level. First and foremost, there is a need to raise awareness of code enforcement activities. Many cities remarked that there are many residents who are not aware of code enforcement services, thus leading to their underutilization. However, as code enforcement staff positions are eliminated, additional strain or demand on the municipality may cause unprecedented delays in service and potentially less effective inspections, reports, or enforcement.

Assuming the best for the future, as a part of an effort to raise awareness, tenants should be better educated about their rights and about how code enforcement works in their local jurisdictions. Some interviewees noted that the way in which a complaint is made can impact the breadth of the inspection that follows, and therefore the results of the code enforcement process. Tenants and their advocates should be informed that their complaints will be more effective if they mention the causes of problems (e.g., water leak, lack of ventilation, broken bathroom fan) rather than just the effects they can see or smell (e.g., mold spots).

Outreach and Advocacy

A related local-level change that could increase the effectiveness of code enforcement, even without changes in law or policy, is the implementation of more outreach programs such as the CEOP program in San Francisco. The experience in San Francisco has shown that advocates appreciate the ability to work alongside code enforcement staff, and are able to communicate with tenants and to work with the landlord group to more quickly and effectively resolve habitability problems. Such outreach programs give all parties involved in the code enforcement process access to additional information and help in navigating the process. Having advocates available to facilitate the process allows the code enforcement staff to focus on conducting inspections and enforcing notices of violation. Replicating this program in other jurisdictions could serve as a useful tool to increase the efficacy of existing code enforcement activities.

In addition to state and local policy initiatives such as those in California, there have been significant efforts at the federal level to address healthy housing.

The Healthy Housing Initiative (HHI). Congress established the HHI to "develop and implement a program of research and demonstration projects that would address multiple housing-related problems affecting the health of children." Begun in 1999, this HUD initiative strives both to identify multiple housing deficiencies that affect health, safety, and quality of life and to take actions to reduce or eliminate the health risks related to poor-quality housing. HHI supports interventions (executed through competitively awarded agreements, contracts with private and public agencies, and interagency agreements) in four areas: excess moisture, dust, ventilation and control of toxins, and tenant education in high-risk housing areas. Approximately $48.5 million was spent on these programs from 1999 to 2005.[26, 27]

Case for Medical-Legal Partnership

Mary was recently evicted from her apartment. She is currently living with her three children, Sam (10), Beth (6) and Michelle (3) in a homeless shelter until she can find a suitable, affordable apartment. Michelle suffers from repeated upper respiratory infections and is not gaining weight; Sam is having major behavioral problems in school. Mary has been desperately looking for an apartment but has not been able to find one that she can afford. Yesterday, she found apartments listed in the newspaper in her price range at a building that is close to Sam and Beth's school. When she called to inquire, the rental agency representative asked her whether she has children. When Mary responded that she has three children, the person on the phone told her that the apartments have all been rented.

Questions for Discussion

1. What questions will you ask Mary?

    Medical: What will you ask Mary about her and her children's health?

    Legal: What questions will you ask Mary regarding her search for housing?

2. Does Mary have any recourse with the rental agency?

3. Are there ways that you can help Mary find permanent housing?

Housing and Health in Context

The following sections explore the specific health and housing problems of lead poisoning, asthma and "heat or eat," or the choice between utilities and food. These problems expose the important connections between poverty, health and law and the ways MLP can provide a uniquely preventive approach and solution. As already discussed, federal and state laws exist that should protect poor tenants from unhealthy housing; however, the enforcement of those laws is often lacking. The advocacy of healthcare providers, lawyers and other professionals in promoting housing stability and healthy conditions can prevent or minimize the health insults of poor conditions.

Childhood Lead Poisoning: A Preventable Yet Persistent Child Health Problem

Although numerous public health and policy interventions have been undertaken over the past decade to address childhood lead poisoning, the condition still impacts over 8,000 children each year;[28] poor children are at increased risk of encountering lead in their environment.[29] The ongoing incidence of lead poisoning is largely due to inadequate enforcement of existing screening and abatement laws.[30] Weak enforcement is partly the result of differing views of responsibility for the problem. Because lead abatement is expensive, state and local officials are often reticent to place too large a burden on individual property owners. Yet government has not accepted the responsibility for funding wide scale or systematic lead abatement. Often, the burden falls on individual families to protect their children.

One lesson from the response to lead poisoning is that action and advocacy need to be taken at the individual family level as well as at the local, state and federal levels. Laws should focus on a *primary prevention approach*—clearly articulating lead safety standards and duties of property owners *before a child is poisoned*. Healthcare providers and lawyers should partner to prevent childhood lead poisoning by ensuring that laws are enforced in a timely manner.

Disease Overview: Why Does Lead Cause "Poisoning?"

Lead exposure is known to cause a multiplicity of health problems, including neurological problems, anemia, kidney and bone problems. Humans have come in contact with lead throughout the ages; due to the convenience of its low melting point and easy malleability, it has been mined since 6500 BCE.[31] Its health effects have also long been recognized— Greek physicians documented an understanding of "lead poisoning" as far back as 100 BCE, and some have postulated that lead poisoning contributed to the fall of the Roman Empire.[32] Lead poisoning is particularly important to include in our discussion on housing; 50 percent of lead exposure in the United States currently is from sources in the home, and low-income children bear the brunt of this residential lead poisoning.[33]

Lead is absorbed into the body through both gastrointestinal and respiratory routes and causes damage because it competes with other divalent cations (molecules carrying two positive charges), including calcium and magnesium.[34] It prevents red blood cells from constructing the iron structure (called heme) for carrying oxygen; causes death of brain cells by uncoupling mitochondrial oxidative phosphorylation in the central nervous system; damages kidneys (causing interstitial nephritis); and can decrease bone growth. Lead can be stored in the blood, in soft tissues and in bone with different half-lives in each type of tissue; bone stores lead for the longest period of time—up to decades in some cases (see Figure 8.5).

Children suffer the greatest effects of lead poisoning. Their gastrointestinal systems are more efficient at absorbing lead,[35] and, due to increased "hand-to-mouth" behavior, young children are also more likely to expose themselves to lead if it is in their environment.[36] Children experience more linear growth than adults, and therefore are more likely to store lead in their bones.[37] Finally, the membrane separating blood and neural cells in the brain is more permeable in young children, allowing more lead to enter the brain and cause neurological damage.[38]

The presentation of children with lead poisoning can range from severely affected to "asymptomatic," though a deepening understanding of the impact of lead on the body has revealed that no level of lead is completely safe.[39] Children with very high lead levels can display acute encephalopathy (or profound confusion/coma), seizures, kidney failure and heart block. Children with more moderate levels of lead exposure are likely to suffer from fatigue, constipation, abdominal pain and difficulty concentrating. Children with lower levels of poisoning experience decreased learning and memory, may display hyperactivity and suffer from impaired speech and hearing. They also suffer IQ loss in direct proportion to their level of exposure (see Figure 8.5).[40] Often, these developmental concerns or impacts on IQ are considered to be the child's baseline state, and lead is not recognized as the culprit.

Lead exposure in patients is measured via blood lead levels (BLLs) in micrograms per deciliter (µg/dL). As the medical understanding of lead's effects has improved, the "acceptable" level for BLL has continued to drop. In 1991, the lead intervention level was set at 10 µg/dL.[41] Subsequently, evidence has demonstrated that children with even lower levels of blood lead can also demonstrate IQ losses, and, indeed, that the rate of neurological decline per 1-point increase in BLL is higher between 0–10 µg/dL than it is at 10–20 µg/dL.[42]

Epidemiology and Disparities in Lead Poisoning

The twentieth century saw much change in the availability of lead in the environment. Lead was added to gasoline early in the 1900s to counter engine knock. Leaded gasoline

Figure 8.5 Toxicity of Blood Lead (μg Pb/dL) Concentration in Children

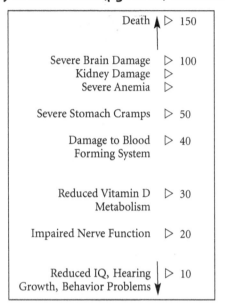

Source: President's Task Force on Environmental Health Risks and Safety Risks to Children. *Eliminating Childhood Lead Poisoning: A Federal Strategy Targeting Lead Paint Hazards* (February 2000).

was eventually taken off the market in 1986 due to its lack of compatibility with catalytic converters; an unintended benefit of this market change was a fivefold reduction in average childhood blood lead levels.[43]

Lead paint has since become the major source of environmental lead. Known for its attractive sheen and durability, lead paint was widely used in the United States until the early 1970s, despite a proposed ban by the League of Nations in 1922 due to concern for children's health.[44] Homes painted before 1978 are thought to be at high risk of containing lead paint, and data demonstrate that children who live in or frequently visit homes/day care centers built before 1950 are at increased risk of lead poisoning.[45] Children come into contact with lead most often through paint dust found on the ground;[46] the highest risk zones are near windows, where paint is mechanically disrupted during opening and closing. Leaky pipes or ceilings also contribute to lead paint exposure when these leaks cause cracking or peeling in paint, thus increasing the likelihood of chipping and dust formation.

In addition to containing lead paint, older homes may also be more likely to contain lead pipes or have lead joints that connect nonlead pipes. Though municipal water sources are tested for lead content, water that has passed through pipes in the home to the tap is rarely tested, and therefore can contain an unknown quantity of lead. Finally, soil—which, like lead paint, is more likely to be ingested by children—can also be a source of lead, particularly if car repair work is done in the yard or if the child lives near industrial sites where lead is processed.[47] Food grown in lead-containing soil can also be a source of lead poisoning.[48]

Given the reductions in lead in paint, gasoline and pipes, the average BLL of children has dropped substantially in the past 20 years.[49] However, these decreases have not been experienced equally by all children. In 2000 in the United States, approximately 2.2 percent of children age 1 to 5 (about 440,000 children) had BLLs > 10 μg/dL.[50] However, African

American children were three times more likely to have elevated BLLs than white children. Mexican American children also experienced higher rates of lead poisoning, even when these groups were stratified by age of housing.[51] Figure 8.6 shows persistent racial disparities in lead poisoning despite improvements over time in the overall rates of poisoning. Within each racial group, low-income children are also more likely to experience lead poisoning.

These disparities are driven by several mechanisms. To begin with, low-income children are more likely to live in housing experiencing disrepair. Although this does not necessarily mean that low-income children live in older housing, it does mean that if lead paint is present in the house, it is more likely to produce dust. Overlaps between housing needs and food needs may also be at the root of the disparity. Deficiencies in both iron and calcium are thought to result in increased absorption of lead from the gut. Low-income children are more likely to experience food insecurity, and thus anemia and calcium deficiencies, which may increase their lead uptake.[52]

The impact of these disparities is significant. Not only do low-income children have higher risks of acute, life-threatening iron deficiency, they also bear the brunt of harmful BLLs, which can lead to IQ loss. Although the loss of a few IQ points may not affect the life outcomes of a given individual, it has profound population effects. IQ is rated on a standardized scale, with a population mean of 100 and a standard deviation of 15. Accordingly, 2.5 percent of the general population has an IQ < 70, and is considered mentally retarded (an equal number of individuals have an IQ > 130 and are considered

Figure 8.6 Percentage of Children Aged 5 and Under with Blood Lead Levels ≥ 10 µg/dL

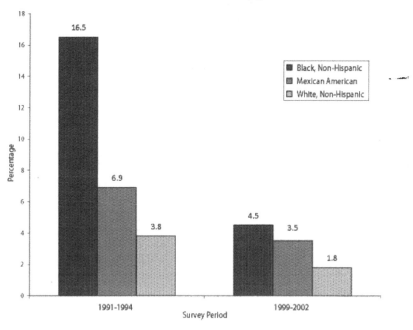

Source: CDC, "Blood Lead Levels—United States, 1999–2002," *MMWR 54*, no. 20 (May 2005): 513–516.
Data Source: National Health and Nutritional Examination Surveys, United States, 1991–1994, 1999–2002.

"gifted"). A decrease in average of IQ in a population by as little as 5 percent, or 5 points (equivalent to a shift of < 5 mg/dL of BLL) would result in a profound increase in the number of individuals with an IQ < 70, which takes a major toll on a community.[53] Iron deficiency anemia has also been shown to impact IQ and to be more prevalent in low-income children.[54] When combined with decreased school and job opportunities in low-income communities, these cognitive losses can multiply to reduce the academic and economic success of an overall community.

Clinical Implications: Prevention and Treatment of Lead Poisoning

Chelation (a process of cleaning lead from the blood) for lead poisoning is available and effective for children with levels > 45 mg/dL. Chelation is complicated by the effects of its own toxicities and also by the fact that it only targets lead stores in the blood, rather than the bone, and therefore lead can leak from the bone after chelation, exerting its neurotoxic effects once more.[55]

For children with lead levels between 10 and 45 mg/dL, chelation does not seem effective in lowering levels (compared to no chelation) and can cause risks to other organs.[56] Multiple researchers have tested the impact of residential lead hazard control efforts for children with elevated lead levels. Unfortunately, there is no good evidence that these measures result in sustained decreases in blood levels. Furthermore, there are no studies linking residential lead hazard control efforts and neurocognitive outcomes.[57]

Prevention of lead poisoning is therefore paramount. In 2007, the Centers for Disease Control and Prevention (CDC) released new guidelines for assessing and managing lead poisoning, and stressed that clinicians should focus on preventing lead poisoning through "anticipatory guidance" and should take careful environmental histories to identify potential lead sources in their young patients' homes.[58] (There is, however, no evidence that physicians can accurately identify these sources, or that giving parents advice on ways to reduce exposure to lead changes the family's behaviors regarding potential sources of lead.) Screening via blood testing could theoretically play a role in identifying lead poisoning before it becomes severe. Current recommendations to clinicians is that all Medicaid patients be screened at 12 and 24 months and other children be screened on a "targeted" basis, determined by geographic residence in an area with high lead prevalence or due to information obtained in the environmental history.

Questions for Discussion

1. Why are children so much more susceptible to lead poisoning than adults?

2. Why is routine screening for lead poisoning so critical for young children? Why do policies stress prevention rather than treatment of lead poisoning?

3. Why are there disparities in the rates of lead poisoning among children by socioeconomic status and race? What do these disparities mean for strategies to prevent or reduce lead poisoning?

Laws Intended to Prevent Childhood Lead Poisoning

As discussed, screening children for elevated BLLs is critical to detect and address lead hazards. Additionally, healthcare providers can play an important role in educating parents about the potential for lead exposure in housing. Nonetheless, many low-income tenants may not be able to address lead hazards on their own. To prevent childhood exposure to lead in the first place, the best approach is to ensure that property owners maintain their properties in a lead-safe condition. Over the past two decades, federal, state and local laws have been passed in an effort to reduce the lead hazards originating in housing and to hold property owners more accountable for childhood lead poisoning.

Federal Law

Title X: The Residential Lead-Based Paint Hazard Reduction Act of 1992

In 1992, in response to growing concern about the number of children poisoned each year by lead paint in their homes, Congress passed the Residential Lead-Based Paint Hazard Reduction Act (RLBPHRA). In its findings, Congress noted that lead poisoning "is widespread among American children, afflicting as many as 3,000,000 children under age 6, with minority and low-income communities disproportionately affected." It acknowledged that "the Federal response to this national crisis remains severely limited" and that "the Federal Government must take a leadership role ... necessary to ensure that the national goal of eliminating lead-based paint hazards in housing can be achieved as expeditiously as possible" (48 USCA § 4851).

The stated goals of RLBPHRA are:

(1) to develop a national strategy to build the infrastructure necessary to eliminate lead-based paint hazards in all housing as expeditiously as possible.

(2) to reorient the national approach to the presence of lead-based paint in housing to implement, on a priority basis, a broad program to evaluate and reduce lead-based paint hazards in the nation's housing stock.

(3) to encourage effective action to prevent childhood lead poisoning by establishing a workable framework for lead-based paint hazard evaluation and reduction and by ending the current confusion over reasonable standards of care.

(4) to ensure that the existence of lead-based paint hazards is taken into account in the development of government housing policies and in the sale, rental, and renovation of homes and apartments.

(5) to mobilize national resources expeditiously, through a partnership among all levels of government and the private sector, to develop the most promising, cost-effective methods for evaluating and reducing lead-based paint hazards.

(6) to reduce the threat of childhood lead poisoning in housing owned, assisted, or transferred by the federal government.

(7) to educate the public concerning the hazards and sources of lead-based paint poisoning and steps to reduce and eliminate such hazards (48 USCA § 4851a).

Table 8.2 shows some of the responsibilities of HUD and the Environmental Protection Agency (EPA) under Title X.

Disclosure to Tenants and Buyers

One important provision of the RLBPHRA is the disclosure rule. The law requires property owners of housing constructed before 1978 to disclose the presence of any known lead-based paint or lead-based paint hazards on their property before obligating a lessee or purchaser under a contract for sale or lease. The Act calls for property owners to:

- Give the purchaser or lessee a pamphlet, titled *Protect Your Family from Lead in Your Home,* approved by the EPA.

- Disclose the presence of any known lead-based paint or lead-based paint hazards.

- Give the purchaser or lessee copies of all available reports or records concerning lead-based paint or lead-based paint hazards at the property.

- Attach to the contract or lease (or include in the lease itself) a lead warning statement and confirmation that the seller or lessor has complied with all notification requirements.

- Secure written confirmation from the purchaser or lessee that he or she received the EPA-approved pamphlet and all information required under the Act.[59]

Table 8.2 Title X: The Residential Lead-Based Paint Hazard Reduction Act of 1992 Primary Agency Responsibilities

Agency	Duties
Department of Housing and Urban Development (HUD)	• Principal implementation agency • Oversees grants to state and local governments for lead programs • Assesses all federal housing units • Estimates the number of low-income units with lead-based paint
Environmental Protection Agency (EPA)	• Studies exposure for workers working in lead reduction, and renovation • Revises regulations to ensure worker protection from lead poisoning • Requires state programs to address lead • Develops state model programs
HUD & EPA	• Disclosure and property exchange guidelines for private and federally owned real property

Source: Jeanita W. Richardson, *The Cost of Being Poor, Poverty: Lead Poisoning and Policy Implementation* (Westport, CT: Praeger, 2005), 60–63.

Unfortunately, because many tenants and buyers (and some property owners) are not educated about their rights under the disclosure rule, it is often not followed. Additionally, because the law only requires disclosure of *known* lead hazards, and many property owners have not inspected their property for lead, tenants and buyers may receive little if any information about the safety of the property.[60]

HUD and the EPA enforce the law by bringing civil complaints against violators and obtaining consent decrees in which owners and property managers must complete lead abatement activities. In addition, the law provides that the purchaser or lessee has the right to enforce the Act through a private lawsuit for damages.[61] For example, potential damages that may be awarded to a tenant are: rent paid, abatement of future rent, displacement or relocation costs, apartment application or "finder's" fees, and blood-screening costs. In addition to the federal disclosure law, some states have complementary disclosure laws that may provide plaintiffs an additional means of enforcing their right to lead-safe housing.

Questions for Discussion

1. Did Title X go far enough in creating a federal response to childhood lead poisoning? Should the federal government play a more active role in addressing

lead hazards in housing or does Title X create the appropriate balance in federal, state and local roles?

2. How effective is the Lead Hazard Disclosure Rule in preventing lead poisoning? Why do you think it is often unenforced? Should federal law create stronger rules regarding lead safety when housing is transferred by sale or rental?

State and Local Law

Many states and localities have laws that regulate lead hazards in housing. Most state laws implement the EPA guidelines for lead-safe levels, inspections and safe work practices. As the National Center for Healthy Housing notes, "an 'ideal' LBP [lead-based paint] law would require permanent elimination of all LBP using lead-safe work practices; however, such a law is viewed as impracticable, since the cost of such work would exceed the value of many lead-contaminated properties."[62] In writing lead safety laws, state legislatures have balanced a variety of constituent interests, including property owners, insurance companies and families affected by lead poisoning.

The primary concern is cost. If lead safety standards are strict, for example, a "lead-free" standard requiring that all lead paint be removed before a child moves in, the cost burden on the property owner is quite high. On the other hand, if the standard is low, for example, a "coverage" standard requiring only that lead-based paint be intact, there may be a danger that if paint deteriorates, a child will be poisoned. Some have raised concerns that comprehensive enforcement of lead safety laws may actually hurt low-income families by making affordable housing less available because property owners would simply pass the costs of abatement onto tenants. Others have rejected the premise that aggressive enforcement would have this impact.[63]

Some states have attempted to move away from a secondary prevention approach — only requiring inspection of a property for lead hazards after a child has been poisoned — to a primary prevention approach, holding property owners to lead safety standards and allowing for inspections on tenant complaint. For example in Rhode Island, the legislature passed the Lead Hazard Mitigation Act of 2002 in an attempt to strengthen compliance by landlords with lead safety standards. However, as with the federal disclosure rule, a preventive approach is only successful if tenants are informed of their rights and enforcement agencies systematically inspect and hold property owners accountable.

Rhode Island Lead Hazard Mitigation Act of 2002

§ 42-128.1-8 Duties of property owners of pre-1978 rental dwellings.

(a) Property owners of pre-1978 rental dwellings, which have not been made lead safe or have not been lead hazard abated shall comply with all the following requirements:

(1) Learn about lead hazards by taking a lead hazard awareness seminar, himself or herself or through a designated person;

(2) Evaluate the dwelling unit and premises for lead hazards consistent with the requirements for a lead hazard control evaluation;

(3) Correct identified lead hazards by meeting and maintaining the lead hazard mitigation standard;

(4) Provide tenants: (i) basic information about lead hazard control; (ii) a copy of the independent clearance inspection; and (iii) information about how to give notice of deteriorating conditions;

(5) Correct lead hazards within thirty (30) days after notification from the tenant of a dwelling unit with an at risk occupant, or as provided for by § 34-18-22.

Questions for Discussion

1. In drafting the Lead Hazard Mitigation Act, the Rhode Island legislature intentionally tried to strike a balance between holding property owners accountable for addressing lead hazards while not imposing too stringent a financial burden on them. How do you assess the relative burdens between the property owner and the tenant?

2. If tenants are not aware of their right to safe housing or if enforcement agencies are not responsive to tenant complaints, how effective are laws like the Lead Hazard Mitigation Act?

3. What role can MLPs play in ensuring enforcement of lead safety legislation such as the RI Lead Hazard Mitigation Act?

Who Is to Blame? Liability for Lead Poisoning

In addition to federal, state and local laws governing lead safety in housing, parents and guardians of lead-poisoned children also have the right under state laws to sue negligent landlords and recover damages for the injuries sustained by the child. Because lead poisoning can damage a child's long-term health, intellectual capacity and behavioral development, the cost of services required may be devastating, particularly for a low-income family. If a parent believes that a landlord's negligence has exposed a child to lead poisoning, they may seek financial compensation for the medical, psychological and educational needs of their children. In addition, lead poisoning may limit a child's future potential and productivity.[64] Some states and localities have sought recovery from lead paint manufacturers for the public health, education and housing costs assumed by the government when a substantial number of children are poisoned.[65]

To find a landlord liable for a child's injuries from lead poisoning, the plaintiff must show that the landlord was negligent. To be negligent, a landlord must have breached his duty to a tenant by failing to meet his or her responsibilities. States have interpreted a landlord's breach of duty differently. Some courts only require that the plaintiff show the landlord has violated the state or local regulations governing lead safety. Other courts assess whether the landlord's behavior was reasonable in his or her efforts to maintain the property in a lead-safe condition, including efforts to comply with lead safety regulations.

Demonstrating the extent of a child's injury from lead poisoning can prove difficult. The health and cognitive consequences of poisoning may take time to manifest. Defendants often raise doubts about not only the significance of the child's injuries but also the cause. Some defendant landlords argue that a child's low IQ or behavioral issues result not from lead poisoning but from heredity or family environment. It is not unheard of for a landlord defendant to subpoena employment and school records of parents, and even request IQ testing of siblings to discount the plaintiff's argument that a child's diminished capacity is the result of lead poisoning.[66]

Polakoff v. Turner demonstrates some of the issues that courts address in negligence actions brought against landlords when children are lead poisoned.

Court of Appeals of Maryland

LAWRENCE POLAKOFF, ET AL.

v.

JASMINE TURNER

385 Md. 467; 869 A.2d 837; 2005 Md. LEXIS 108

March 11, 2005

In March of 1985, Lelia Whittington ("Lelia") and her daughter, Crystal Whittington ("Crystal"), moved into a residential rental property located at 17 North Bentalou Street. 17 North Bentalou is a row house located in Baltimore City. It was built prior to 1950 and was later determined to contain lead-based paint. While residing at the property, Crystal gave birth to Jasmine on April 3, 1990. The women lived in the home for nine years until August of 1994 when Polakoff asked them to move out.... While under his ownership, Polakoff hired a property manager to handle day-to-day management and maintenance....

Prior to Jasmine's birth, a workman painted the two windowsills in the living room. The paint was applied again over top of the chipping and flaking paint without removing the old paint. According to testimony, the paint continued to chip. Other than the one time the windowsills were painted, no other painting or repairs to the chipping and flaking paint were made during the nine-year tenancy....

In early 1993, when Jasmine was almost three years old, a routine physical revealed that she had elevated levels of lead in her blood.* Doctors placed Jasmine on a special diet and gave her iron to treat the poisoning. Crystal was also instructed to remove anything from the home that could contribute to Jasmine's lead levels, e.g., lead containing dust....

Section 702(a) [of the state housing code] provides that "every building and all parts thereof used or occupied as a dwelling shall, while in use or at any time when the lack of maintenance affects neighboring property, be kept in good repair, in safe condition, and fit for human habitation." Section 703(b)(3) provides that "good repair and safe condition" includes a requirement that "all walls, ceilings, woodwork, doors, and windows shall be kept clean and free of any flaking, loose, or peeling paint and paper." The Code places the duty on the owner or operator of the property to keep it in compliance with all provisions of the Code....

Based on the language of the Code, we concluded that the landlord's duty to keep the property in compliance is continuous. "The landlord must take whatever measures are necessary during the pendency of the lease to ensure the dwelling's continued compliance with the Code." *Brooks, 378 Md. at 84, 835 A.2d at 624.* Consequently, because the Code prescribes the property owner's duty to keep the property continuously free of any flaking, loose, or peeling paint, the failure to keep the property in such a condition is itself evidence of negligence....

Liability will depend on the reasonableness of the landlord's efforts to remain in compliance with the statute; therefore, it is incumbent upon the landlord to take such reasonable steps as may be necessary. One surefire way of avoiding lead-paint poisoning liability is to remove lead paint from the rental property.

We recognize, however, that the current law does not require this action. Less extreme options may include: notifying the tenant in writing and orally of the possible presence of lead paint in the property and its potential danger; asking the tenant to notify the landlord or property manager immediately if flaking, loose, or peeling paint occurs; and inspecting the property at the inception and at regular intervals throughout the tenancy to ensure that there is no flaking, loose, or peeling paint. This list is by no means exhaustive nor is it a guarantee that a jury will find the landlord's actions reasonable. Our point is simply to show that there are reasonable ways of attempting to satisfy one's duty pursuant to the Code....

If a landlord of property located in Baltimore City fails to maintain the premises in a safe condition and someone whom the Code was designed to protect, i.e., a resident child, is injured as a result of the landlord's failure to maintain the premises, the plaintiff will have successfully established a *prima facie* case of negligence. It will then be incumbent upon the finder of fact [the jury or judge] to determine whether the landlord's actions were reasonable under all of the circumstances....

* Jasmine's blood lead level was 22 mg/dl. A child is considered to have "elevated" blood lead levels at 10 mg/dl. mg/dl is an abbreviation for micrograms per deciliter. It indicates that the child has 22 micrograms of lead per every deciliter of blood.

Questions for Discussion

1. The court in *Polakoff* acknowledges that there is no requirement that a property owner remove lead paint and that removal is the only way to ensure that there is not a danger to children. Are the other options presented by the court — for example, notifying the tenant of potential hazards, asking the tenant to notify the landlord if paint begins to chip — satisfactory in preventing childhood lead poisoning?

2. Does holding a landlord accountable *after* a child is poisoned provide sufficient incentive for him or her to address hazards? How might laws and policies be drafted to create a stronger likelihood that landlords take action *before* a child is poisoned on his or her property?

3. What role might a healthcare provider play in helping establish that a child has been poisoned as the result of exposure to lead hazards in the home?

Best Practices and Advocacy Strategies for Medical-Legal Partnership

MLP offers a unique opportunity to both prevent lead exposure and to ensure that lead-poisoned children receive appropriate healthcare and services. Pediatricians and other healthcare providers can identify potential lead hazards by asking parents about the condition of their home and referring families for preventive legal assistance. Healthcare providers are also well positioned to ensure that when a child has been poisoned that the child and family receive services that, to the extent possible, ameliorate the harmful effects of lead poisoning on the child and family.

The MLP team can work together to both prevent lead poisoning and address the needs of affected children and their families.

Preventive Advocacy

- Identify children who are most vulnerable to lead poisoning

- Educate healthcare providers and community officials about the health implications of lead exposure for child health and the importance of enforcement of lead safety and housing code provisions

- Conduct culturally appropriate educational programs for families and service providers in community-based settings about tenants' rights to lead-safe housing

- Ensure that lead safety and housing code provisions are enforced and that property owners are held accountable for remediating lead hazards in compliance with federal, state and local laws

- Work with housing authorities to ensure that systematic inspections are conducted to meet federal and state lead safety standards in public housing units

- Hold code enforcement and other agencies charged with enforcement of lead safety standards accountable for promptly responding to complaints by tenants and service providers about lead hazards

Address the Needs of Lead-Poisoned Children and their Families

- Work with the family and the property owner to ensure that lead hazards are immediately remediated so that the child may remain in the home or help identify alternative housing

- Ensure that a poisoned child receives public benefits for which he or she may be eligible, such as Medicaid/EPSDT and SSI

- Connect parents to early intervention and case management services and continue to help them navigate the systems that administer those services

- Advocate for the rights of poisoned children in the school system to special education services under state and federal law and to Section 504 accommodations

- Provide referrals to families seeking to hold a negligent property owner liable for lead poisoning

From Practice to Policy

To prevent childhood lead poisoning, enforcement policies must be proactive. Identifying and addressing lead hazards *before* a child is poisoned is critical to efforts to reduce the number of children harmed by lead. Code enforcement agencies can and should play a proactive role in preventing lead poisoning. In the excerpt that follows, the Alliance to End Childhood Lead Poisoning identifies critical policies and practices for code enforcement agencies that can prevent lead poisoning.

Preventing Childhood Lead Poisoning through Code Enforcement: Ten Effective Strategies

Code enforcers can play a critical role in fighting childhood lead poisoning, due to the strong link between poor housing conditions and the increased risk of lead exposure. By including lead among the hazards they address and focusing on effective enforcement of housing code standards in communities at highest risk, code enforcers can significantly increase the identification and control of lead hazards and prevent the needless poisoning of children.

Strategies

1. Require owners to secure a license for rental property.

2. Conduct routine, periodic inspections.

3. Enforce chipping and peeling paint violations.

4. Include lead-based paint and dust hazards as prosecutable offenses in housing codes.

5. Train and require code enforcers to conduct visual inspections for potential lead hazards in all pre-1978 housing and, where appropriate, sample household dust.

6. Ban unsafe work practices, and require property owners to conduct repair work in a lead-safe manner and to undergo postwork clearance testing to ensure the absence of hazards.

7. Develop self-sustaining, effective enforcement programs.

8. Target intensive enforcement efforts to high-risk units and neighborhoods and recalcitrant landlords.

9. Use lead hazard data gathered by code enforcers to prevent lead poisoning and neighborhood decay.

10. Collaborate with agencies working on environmental health and housing issues.[67]

Case for Medical-Legal Partnership

A lab result shows that Jason, a two-year-old boy, has a BLL of 32 μg/dL. The nurse has left three messages for Jason's mother, Karen, about the lab results, asking her to come to the primary care clinic at the hospital as soon as possible. After a week and a half, Karen and Jason come to the clinic. Karen is upset because she believes that the clinic has turned her landlord in to the Department of Health. The Department of Health sent an inspector to her apartment to conduct an inspection for lead paint hazards and put the landlord on notice that he must address the hazards. Now the landlord is angry at Karen and is threatening to evict her.

Questions for Discussion

1. What additional information do you need to help Karen?

2. How will you discuss this issue with Karen?

   Medical: What will you say about Jason's BLL? How will you help Karen understand the seriousness of lead poisoning?

   Legal: How will you address Karen's concerns about being evicted?

3. What course of action will you pursue?

   Medical: How will you ensure that Jason's BLL does not continue to rise?

   Legal: How will you work with Karen to make sure that her housing is safe?

4. What are your professional ethical obligations in this case?

Asthma: A Multifactor Disease with an Interdisciplinary Solution

Asthma is an inflammatory disease of the lung, which leads to episodic periods of wheezing and severe respiratory compromise. Twenty-three million adults and children in the United States suffer from asthma; overall, 12 percent of children have a diagnosis of asthma at some point in childhood.[68] Asthma prevalence has doubled in the past two decades, and asthma accounts for over 10 million office visits, 400,000 hospitalizations, and 10 million missed days of work each year.[69, 70] Both the development of asthma and the severity of asthma are thought to be related to environmental "triggers", such as mold, cockroaches, dust mites and mouse/animal dander. Given the correlation between these environmental triggers and poor housing conditions, addressing the quality of housing is essential in preventing and limiting the severity of asthma. As with lead poisoning, addressing asthma as a health problem requires an interdisciplinary approach which brings together doctors, public health officials, lawyers and policy-makers. And, like lead poisoning, asthma requires both individual and systemic advocacy.

Figure 8.7 Percent of Children with Asthma Problems, 2007

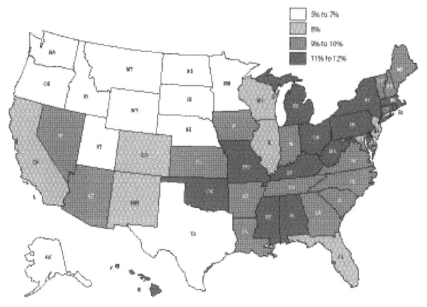

Source: National KIDS COUNT Program, Annie E. Casey Foundation. *Data Source:* Child Trends analysis of data from the U.S. Department of Health and Human Services, Health Resources and Services Administration, Maternal and Child Health Bureau, National Survey of Children's Health.

Disease Overview: What Does It Mean to Have Asthma?

Asthma is characterized by periodic "exacerbations" in which the small airways of the lung become narrowed and fill with mucus, leading to air trapping and "wheezing." Most (but not all) asthma begins in childhood and generally wanes as the individual ages. However, there are also cases of adult-onset asthma and individuals who have asthma across their lifetime.

There are many different subtypes of asthma, distinguished by what factors trigger the attacks. The narrowing of the airways can be caused by substances to which the patient is allergic, most commonly airborne substances like dust, animal dander, pollen and mold. Viruses and bacteria causing colds, ear infections or pneumonias can also precipitate asthma exacerbations. Finally, for some people attacks can be caused by exercise, cold air or changes in weather.

The most recent guidelines for managing asthma distinguish between asthma severity, which is the intrinsic intensity of the disease, and "control," which is how frequently a patient has symptoms. Individuals with very severe disease (such as people who have many allergies and the potential for life-threatening asthma attacks) can have good control of their symptoms and feel well from day to day. Likewise, people who have very mild disease can be in poor control and have daily wheezing.

There are two broad categories of actions patients may take that can reduce their symptoms (i.e., improve control of their disease). First, patients do best when they avoid their triggers. The steps involved in trigger avoidance are different for each patient, depending on whether they have allergically mediated asthma and what they are allergic to. For some people, this means reducing exposure to cold air; to others, especially those that have common allergic triggers, this means substantially addressing the indoor air quality of the home. Second, patients can adhere to medication regimens, including preventive or controller medications. These medications, generally taken every day, blunt the inflammatory response, meaning that exposure to triggers is less likely to result in an asthma attack. The types of medication used in asthma—in both a preventive and "rescue" approach—are summarized in Table 8.3.

Table 8.3 Medication Types Used in Asthma

Medication	Types Examples
Controller Medications: Taken on a daily basis to blunt inflammation or prevent allergic response	*Inhaled corticosteroids:* reduce inflammation in the airways to reduce the possibility of narrowing and wheeze *Leukotriene Inhibitors:* stabilize mast cells (a type of allergic cell), preventing allergic responses *Combination medications:* contain both an inhaled corticosteroid and a beta agonist (see below), but are taken in a preventive approach
Rescue Medications: Taken when the patient has shortness of breath or wheezing	*Beta-agonists:* Taken as inhaled medications to relax the smooth muscle of the lung and allow air to escape from the lung *Magnesium:* A medication given intravenously in an emergency room in order to relax the smooth muscles of the lung

Epidemiology and Disparities in Asthma: A Focus on Housing

Although asthma affects people of all ages, ethnicities and geographical locations, it has long been understood to have both ethnic and income disparities, with poor children experiencing higher rates of asthma across all ethnic groups and black children experiencing higher rates of asthma than white children.[71] Figure 8.8 shows the percentages of asthma in children by poverty status. In addition to disparities in the incidence of asthma, low-income and racial minorities also have more severe asthma than their white, nonpoor peers. A discussion of the current knowledge of the causes of asthma as well as the factors that drive asthma may help explain these disparities and suggest how enforcement of environmental and housing-related laws can serve a preventive and therapeutic approach for people with asthma.

Asthma incidence is higher in developed countries than nondeveloped countries, and is thought to have been on the rise in developed countries during the later part of the

Figure 8.8 Percentages of Asthma in Children under 18 Years of Age by Poverty Status in 2007

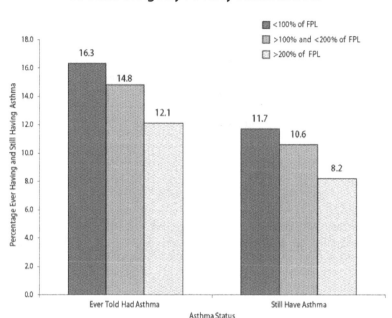

Source: CDC, "Summary Health Statistics for U.S. Children: National Health Interview Survey, 2007," *Vital and Health Statistics 10*, no. 239 (2007).

twentieth century.[72] There have also been repeated observations that children growing up in rural areas, particularly on farms, have lower incidence of asthma and allergic disease than children growing up in cities.[73] This farm-protective effect, along with findings that a larger number of siblings is found to be protective against asthma and allergic disease, has prompted the so-called hygiene hypothesis.[74] According to this hypothesis, exposure to microbes (perhaps parasites or other microbes related to livestock) early in life may favor the development of the immune system in a way that is protective against autoimmune conditions like asthma or seasonal allergies.

The hygiene hypothesis would explain why children growing up away from livestock and farm influences—all urban children—might have higher risks of asthma and allergic diseases, but fails to explain why lower-income children living in cities have higher risk of asthma than upper-income children who are also urban dwellers. For poor children with a family history of asthma, certain indoor allergens are influential in the development of asthma and allergic disease.[75] In the Northeast, cockroaches, which are more likely to be present in homes that are deteriorating,[76] have been shown to cause changes in the immune system that can promote the development of asthma and, if they continue to be present, lead to increases in asthma symptoms among those sensitized.[77] Dust mites and mold are also culprits in the development and exacerbation of asthma. Children with demonstrable sensitization to dust mites appear more likely to develop asthma, and the frequency of exposure to dust mites is such that some believe that they are an exacerbating factor in over 60 percent of pediatric asthma cases in the United States.[78] Alternaria mold similarly appears to be important for the development of asthma and, interestingly, seems to be more common in areas where dust mites are less common, specifically in the Midwest and Western parts of the United States.

An additional "environmental" risk factor for both asthma incidence and morbidity in children is secondhand tobacco smoke exposure. Children exposed to cigarette smoke in the first year of life have higher rates of asthma, and children among lower socioeconomic groups are more likely to be exposed to cigarette smoke.[79]

In addition to the physical conditions of housing, housing insecurity—earlier defined as difficulty paying for current housing, leading to a risk for eviction or a need to move—can contribute to worsening of asthma conditions through the generation of stress. Although little research has examined the independent role of housing stress on asthma outcomes, many studies have shown that those facing increased stress have worse asthma outcomes.[80] In addition, families struggling to pay for housing may be forced to choose housing in less safe neighborhoods; they may then have increased risk of exposure to violence. In the foundational Inner City Asthma Study, conducted in the early 2000s, researchers saw an association between exposure to violence and stress and exposure to violence and asthma symptoms, even after accounting for other sources of stress.[81] Figure 8.9 summarizes several of these relationships.

Figure 8.9 Theoretical Model for Housing Quality, Housing Stress and Asthma Risk

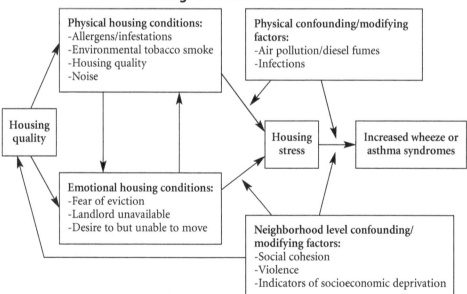

Source: Megan Sandel and Rosalind J. Wright, "When home is where the stress is: expanding the dimensions of housing that influence asthma morbidity," *Archives of Disease in Childhood 91*, no. 11 (2006): 942–48.

Clinical Implications: Treatment of Asthma and Prevention of Exacerbations

For low-income asthmatics, both access to medications and avoidance of asthma triggers can be challenging, leading to increased ER visits and hospitalizations over their higher-income asthmatic counterparts.

As already discussed, housing conditions are often a major source of triggers for low-income asthmatics, and many studies have been done to examine whether low-tech interventions, like mattress covers to protect against dust mites, or high-tech interventions, like pest control, can reduce asthma exacerbations in this population. Unfortunately, most studies that examine only a single intervention have shown very little impact on disease. However, a few studies have combined moisture control, pest control, mattress dust covers, vacuum cleaners with HEPA filters as well as education for family members about allergen reduction and have improved asthma symptoms in those known to be allergic to triggers in the home. Sadly, although these programs have been effective, they have not been rolled out on a widespread basis. This is likely due to the high costs of these interventions and, as of current practice, no or low reimbursement for such services from health insurance companies.[82] Fortunately, as we explore in the law section, many of the housing conditions known to exacerbate asthma are prohibited in sanitary code laws. Thus, the funding for this type of trigger reduction for asthmatic tenants may actually flow from the landlord and not the tenant.

In addition to experiencing more asthma triggers in the home, low-income asthmatics face greater barriers to adhering to controller medications. Studies demonstrate that upward of 50 percent of asthmatic children who should be on controller medications are not receiving them,[83] and other researchers have shown that low-income families who are concerned about competing household issues are less likely to follow medication regimens.[84] Thus, even for families whose physical housing conditions are not a problem, concerns about continuing to pay rents that are not affordable may create barriers to adhering to medications. Although a few studies have demonstrated that the intervention of a social worker can improve asthma outcomes, no studies have directly related housing subsidies to asthma outcomes.

Questions for Discussion

1. What are the risk factors for childhood asthma?

2. What explains the disparities in the rates of asthma for low-income urban children?

3. What medical interventions can prevent or alleviate asthma? How effective are these interventions? What is needed to fully "treat" poor children with asthma?

Legal Options for Addressing Asthma

To be effective, medical treatment of asthma must include an assessment of a patient's home environment to determine if it contains asthma triggers, such as mold, cockroaches and dust. Even when a healthcare provider is careful to discuss asthma triggers with a patient or a patient's caregiver, however, this may not be enough if the patient cannot control some parts of the home environment. For example, a low-income tenant living in an apartment with water leaks that lead to mold or with a widespread problem with insects or vermin may not be able to enforce his or her right to safe and healthy housing on his or her own. Some landlords fail to meet their obligations under state and local housing codes. In these cases, legal advocacy becomes an important avenue of ensuring better health.[85] In addition, people with asthma are also protected under antidiscrimination and accommodations laws that protect people with certain disabilities. These laws may support a patient seeking to enforce his or her right to safe and healthy environments at home, work or school.

Federal Law

Although there is no equivalent comprehensive federal law that regulates asthma triggers the way that Title X regulates lead hazards, there are legal protections for some individuals with asthma who live in federally subsidized housing under the Fair Housing Act and under federal disability laws. These protections help ensure that an individual is not discriminated against due to disability and that appropriate accommodations or modifications are made to ensure that he or she has appropriate access to housing. In the case of asthma, these laws may help people ensure that their housing does not exacerbate asthma symptoms.

Section 504 of the U.S. Rehabilitation Act of 1973 and the Americans with Disabilities Act of 1990 (ADA)

Section 504 states that "no qualified individual with a disability in the United States shall be excluded from, denied the benefits of, or be subjected to discrimination under" any program or activity that either receives federal financial assistance or is conducted by any executive agency (29 U.S.C. § 794). The ADA prohibits discrimination on the basis of disability in employment, state and local government, public accommodations, commercial facilities, transportation and telecommunications (42 U.S.C. § 12101 et sec.). Section 504, therefore, covers federally funded housing. The ADA covers housing that receives funding from a local government. A private landlord who accepts a Section 8 voucher, however, is not covered by either Section 504 or the ADA.

Both Section 504 and the ADA define a person with a disability as an individual who has a physical or mental impairment that "limits one or more major life activities, has a record of such an impairment, or is regarded as having such an impairment" (29 U.S.C. § 794; 42 U.S.C. § 12102). If an individual is deemed disabled under Section 504 or the ADA, he or she may not be discriminated against by a publicly funded housing program. In addition, the housing program must ensure that units are accessible to and usable for a person with a disability and provide reasonable accommodations or modifications to make it possible for that person enjoy the facility. A person with asthma may qualify as disabled if he or she can show that asthma limits a major life activity.[86] Notably, criteria for determination of "disability" for protections under Section 504 and the ADA are different from eligibility criteria for receipt of Supplemental Security Income (SSI). (See Chapter 7 for discussion of eligibility criteria for SSI.) Therefore, some patients may qualify as disabled for purposes of housing protections but not for SSI.

Once a person with asthma demonstrates that he or she is disabled under either Section 504 or the ADA, he or she may request a reasonable accommodation or modification if his or her housing unit exacerbates asthma symptoms. For example, a modification might include removal of carpeting; an accommodation might include requesting a transfer to a different unit that does not contain carpet.

State and Local Laws

Housing Code Violations

Unlike the problem of lead poisoning, for which many states and localities have passed laws that specifically address lead hazards in housing, there has been no equivalent widespread legislative effort to specifically address housing conditions that may cause or exacerbate asthma.[87] In most states, when a client or client's child is suffering from asthma triggers, a lawyer may bring an affirmative civil action against a landlord for violation of the state and/or local housing code. If successful, this type of action requires a landlord, for example, to make specific repairs that may prevent asthma triggers, such as fixing a leaky pipe that leads to excessive moisture and mold. Additionally, an action may be brought against a landlord for breaching the implied warranty of habitability for failing to maintain the premises and endangering the tenants' health and safety.[88]

Asthma and Advocacy: A Role for Healthcare Providers

A healthcare provider can play a very important role in helping enforce the rights of a patient with asthma to healthy housing by documenting the effects of housing problems on the patient's health. By drafting effective letters to housing authorities and private landlords, healthcare providers can help build a legal case where necessary to enforce housing laws that protect the health of tenants. Table 8.4 provides some tips on the key components in a letter to support a patient enforce his or her rights.

Table 8.4 Key Components of Letters on Behalf of Patients

Letter to a Public Housing Entity Seeking Accommodation Under Section 504 and/or the ADA	Letter to a Private Landlord Seeking Repairs Under a State or Local Housing Code
1. Documents that patient has a qualifying disability due to asthma	1. Documents the nature of the housing problem(s) (i.e mold, pests)
2. Documents the nature of the housing problem that exacerbates asthma symptoms	2. Documents the rule under the state or local code and how it has been violated (i.e. failure to address moisture or pest problems)
3. Requests specific accommodation or modification to address the housing problem	3. Applies the housing rule to the patient's asthma and spells out the link between the housing exposure and its health consequences

Questions for Discussion

1. What type of evidence would be necessary to show that a patient is disabled by asthma and requires an accommodation under Section 504 or the ADA?

2. Some studies have shown that asthma rates are higher for those who live in public housing than for the general population.[89] If you were able to document that asthma rates were higher in your local public housing facility than for the comparable population, what types of legal and policy strategies would you recommend be used to address this problem?

3. How can an MLP work together to build a case against a landlord who has failed to address housing violations that may exacerbate a patient's asthma symptoms?

Best Practices and Advocacy Strategies for Medical-Legal Partnership

The Breathe Easy at Home program is a collaboration among several city agencies, including Inspectional Services (code enforcement), the Boston Public Health Commission, and healthcare providers, including Boston Medical Center. The program is designed to improve communication between medical homes for children with asthma and public health and housing agencies within the city of Boston. Doctors, nurses and other healthcare professionals refer patients with asthma for housing inspections through a shared website if they suspect that substandard housing conditions are triggering a patient's asthma.

Inspectors are trained to specifically identify asthma triggers which are covered through the housing code, including mold and chronic dampness, leaks, pest infestations, drafty doors & windows, no heat, poor ventilation and damaged carpeting. *Breathe Easy at Home* inspectors then work with the property owners to address these conditions.

The collaboration allows healthcare providers to ensure that inspections are performed and housing code violations are resolved quickly. Because the program allows for tracking of the inspection and enforcement process for an individual family, healthcare providers are informed of efforts to address the housing conditions affecting a patient's health.[90]

From Practice to Policy

One question that some health advocacy groups are beginning to ask is: Are housing codes and the courts that enforce them sufficient to address housing conditions that trigger asthma? For example, a report by the Coalition for Asthma-Free Homes suggests that low-income New Yorkers with asthma have had difficulty enforcing housing code provisions focused on asthma triggers such as mold and pest infestation. The report concludes that asthma triggers are "seldom classified as serious housing violations, Class C violations, which present an immediate threat to the health of tenants."[91] To remedy this problem, the report supports proposed legislation, the Asthma Free Housing Act, to improve the existing code enforcement system to reduce indoor allergen hazards that trigger asthma in dwellings where "susceptible persons" reside. The bill was introduced by New York City Council members on April 28, 2008, but has yet to be passed. Proposed New York City Asthma Free Housing provides some key provisions of the bill.[92]

Proposed New York City Asthma Free Housing Act

- Requires landlords to inquire whether a person susceptible to asthma ... resides in the dwelling, and if so, conduct an inspection on an annual basis for indoor allergen hazards, including mold and pest infestation.

- Requires landlords to correct allergen hazards, including underlying conditions that may cause these hazards, such as water leaks and holes that allow for pest infestation.

- In response to complaints from tenants, requires that a city inspector inspect for indoor allergen hazards and issue a notice of violation to the landlord.

- Classifies indoor allergen hazards as Class C violations (immediately hazardous) when a susceptible person resides in the dwelling. The landlord is given 21 days to make repairs.

Case for Medical-Legal Partnership

Juan, a 32-year-old man, lives with his wife, Carla, and their two children in a two-bedroom rental apartment. Carla, age 30, suffers from severe asthma and has been to the emergency room twice in the past six months for asthma attacks. Due to a problem with water leakage, there is mold in Carla and Juan's bedroom. They have tried to clean the mold themselves, but because of the leak, it keeps coming back. They have also had a problem with rats and roaches in the apartment. They have put out traps, but because their apartment is in a three-decker with two others, the traps do not help. At the end of last winter the boiler broke, and when Juan asked the landlord to fix it, he said that he does not have the money. He is afraid they may not have heat this winter. They are afraid to push their landlord too hard for fear that they may lose the apartment. They do not have a lease. They have looked around for other apartments, but the rents are beyond their means.

Questions for Discussion

1. What additional information do you need to gather to help this family?

    Medical: What more do you need to know about Carla's health? The health of other members of the family?

    Legal: What additional questions will you ask to determine what rights this family may have?

2. What types of legal protections may be available to the family?

3. What will be your course of action to assist this family to improve Carla's health and ensure that her family has healthy housing?

Heat or Eat? Preventing Utility Shut-Offs to Protect Health

In a landmark investigation performed in 1996, researchers in Boston noted that children seeking emergency care in the three months immediately following the coldest months of the year were more likely to be small for their age than at any other time during the year. Families who reported that the utility company had threatened to turn off their service for failure to pay were also more likely to have a child who was small for his or her age than those who had not faced utility shut-off. The researchers theorized that low-income families face a budget trade-off between food and fuel—the "heat or eat" dilemma—that becomes most critical during the cold winter months.[93] This food and fuel trade-off mirrors a health trade-off between undernutrition and the health hazards of excessive cold or alternative heat sources. State regulations may provide protection for families against shut-off or offer alternative payment options to make utility costs more manageable. However, families are often unaware of these utility resources or need help in negotiating with utility companies to gain access to these benefits. Doctors and lawyers can be key players in helping families navigate the systems, thus preventing health problems and housing instability and safety.

Disease Overview: Understanding Failure to Thrive and the Health Hazards of Utility Shut-Off

Weight is a fundamental vital sign when evaluating the health of young children. It is both a reflection of the current health of the child as well as a predictor of future health outcomes. "Failure to thrive" is a broad term used to describe children who weigh less than the fifth percentile for their age, or who demonstrate a chronic pattern of poor weight gain (such as daily weight gain less than that expected for age, or a growth curve demonstrating that weight for age is decreasing over time).[94] Failure to thrive has many different causes, including chronic diseases (such as heart disease or respiratory disease, which increase the caloric requirements for a child on a daily basis) and social factors, such as inadequate food availability or dysfunctional feeding patterns, that lead to poor caloric intake. Poverty is, of course, a critical risk factor for failure to thrive. Children with failure to thrive have weakened immune systems that can increase their chance of and severity of infection; these children also are at risk for persistent short stature (i.e., they never attain proper adult height) and permanent neurological delays.[95] Correcting failure to thrive is necessary to improve immune function in the short term and prevent neurological delays and short stature in the long term.

Although poor pediatric nutrition should be avoided, utility shut-off itself can have significant health impacts on the growing child. Prolonged exposure to cold temperatures puts individuals at risk for hypothermia, which can cause weight loss and neurological damage. In the early stages of hypothermia, the body naturally increases metabolic rate and shivers to restore normal body temperature. Both of these strategies require energy in the form of calories—thus increasing caloric requirements for the individual. Young children have increased body surface area relative to their mass, and thus have been theorized to lose more heat than adults when exposed to cold temperatures. Children thus require more calories relative to their mass to stay warm under a cold stress.[96] Ironically, malnutrition and its poor sequelae are the final common pathway of both food insecurity and utility insecurity.

Inadequate heating during the winter can also create health risks when families choose alternative heat sources for warmth, such as cooking stoves, wood-burning stoves and space heaters. Although not frequently a choice in urban homes, wood-burning stoves have been associated with increased numbers of both burns and respiratory illnesses in young children.[97] Space heaters—of the kerosene and gas variety—increase levels of air pollution in the home (nitrogen, sulfur and carbon monoxide particles) and are associated with increased respiratory illness and burns in children and adults when compared to conventional heating sources. Finally, candle use in homes where the power has been shut off contributes to home fires; young children are the most likely to die in such fires.[98]

Epidemiology and Disparities in Heat or Eat

Families facing this heat or eat dilemma are called "energy insecure," meaning that the utility company has either threatened to turn off service, or has, in fact, terminated service for some portion of the prior 12 months. Energy insecurity has been linked to poor health, increased numbers of hospitalizations and developmental delay for the multiple reasons already explored.[99] Low-income households are understandably more likely to experience energy insecurity. The affordability standard for utilities is capped at 6 percent of family income, but the average low-income family spends 13.5 percent of their income on utilities, forcing budget trade-offs.[100] Figure 8.10 shows the percentage of total average expenditures spent on food and energy. Consequently, whereas all families living in cold climates spend more on fuel during the winter, only poor families have been found to spend less money on food during the winter and to decrease their calorie intake by up to 10 percent.[101]

Although no hard data exist to determine the number of Americans who experience energy insecurity in an average year, the Low Income Home Energy Assistance Program (LIHEAP)—a federal program that assists families with heating and cooling costs—estimated that there were 34 million households eligible for fuel assistance in 2007 (of whom only 16 percent received benefits).[102] Given that children of color are more likely to live in low-income households, they are also more likely to experience the health consequences of utility and food insecurity than their white peers.

Figure 8.10 Percentage of Total Average Expenditures Spent on Food and Energy in 2007

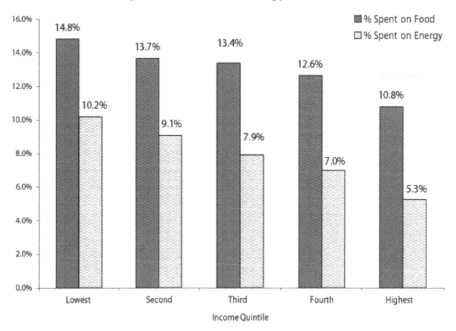

Source: United States Department of Labor, Bureau of Labor Statistics, *Consumer Expenditure Survey* (2007).

Clinical Implications: What Is the Role of Healthcare Providers in Intervention?

Primary care providers are asked to screen for a variety of potential health risks in their patients. Screening is considered most useful when (a) the condition might be overlooked if not systematically examined for, (b) there is a clinically useful tool for identification of the condition and (c) identification of the condition in question can improve outcomes.

Researchers have developed useful questions that can help healthcare providers identify individual families who are at risk.[103] (See Identifying Household Energy Insecurity.) However, identifying energy insecurity is only useful if there are existing programs that help support a family with energy needs. As will be described in greater detail, financial support for fuel assistance is provided through LIHEAP. However, this funding is not sufficient to cover all families in need, and the funding has not kept up with increases in fuel costs, creating what has been called the "home energy affordability gap."

Whereas financial assistance may be difficult to obtain, protection against utility shut-off is relatively available to low-income families, through documentation of their low-income status and, in some cases, certification of a chronic or serious illness by a healthcare provider. In states where shut-off protection is available, healthcare providers have a responsibility to screen for energy insecurity, as they will be instrumental in protecting families against shut-off. This is consistent with the first principle of screening—that early identification can be protective—as it is easier in many cases to prevent shut-off (which can be done for free) than to turn utilities back on (which often requires a fee and/or paying a portion of the bill). (As already discussed, the existence of clinically useful screening tools for energy insecurity, as well as the existence of an effective shut-off protection law thus complete principles 2 and 3 of optimal conditions for screening.)

Because of the limited resources available to help families with energy insecurity, supplementing the family through other types of programs may allow them to shift income toward the fuel budget. Fortifying food resources—which are much more abundant that fuel resources—can protect children in the family from nutritional deficiencies and could also allow the family to spend more of their finances on fuel. Thus, to become effective advocates for families facing energy insecurity, healthcare providers and lawyers need to become experts in identifying available food resources for families.

Identifying Household Energy Insecurity

1. Since [current month] of last year, has the [gas/electric] company sent [you/the primary caregiver] a letter threatening to shut off the [gas/electricity] in the house for not paying bills?

2. In the last 12 months since last [current month], [have you/has the primary caregiver] ever used a cooking stove to heat the [house/apartment]?

3. Since [current month] of last year, were there any days that the home was not [heated/cooled] because [you/the primary caregiver] could not pay the bills?

4. Since [current month] of last year, has the [gas/electric/oil] company [shut off/refused to deliver] the [gas/electricity/oil] for not paying bills?

Source: John T. Cook, Deborah A. Frank, Patrick H. Casey, et al., "A Brief Indicator of Household Energy Security: Associations with Food Security, Child Health, and Child Development in US Infants and Toddlers," *Pediatrics* 122, no. 4 (2008): 867–75.

Questions for Discussion

1. What do the studies correlating failure to thrive in children with the threat of utility shut-off suggest about the relationship between health and poverty?

2. Although the research has focused on the effects of utility shut-off on children's health, what types of health-related consequences might exist for adults facing shut-off or utility bills they cannot afford?

3. Describe the heat or eat dilemma. If insufficient income is the primary cause of the dilemma, why is this a legal or medical problem?

Laws and Programs that Address High Energy Costs for Low-Income Families

Federal Assistance: LIHEAP

In response to the energy crisis of the late 1970s, Congress created a program to provide funding for home heating, medically necessary home cooling and weather-related supply shortage emergencies.[104] In 1982, the program was named the Low Income Home Energy Assistance Program (LIHEAP).[105] The stated mission of LIHEAP is to "assist low income households, particularly those with the lowest incomes that pay a high proportion of household income for home energy, primarily in meeting their immediate home energy needs."[106] LIHEAP funds are available as block grants to states and programs are administered at the designated state agency.[107] The appropriation for LIHEAP in 2009 was $4.5 million, with additional funds made available for emergency situations. Funds may be used for reduction of utility debts, to help restore utility service that has been shut off, or for home weatherization projects.

For a family to be eligible for LIHEAP assistance, the household income cannot exceed 150 percent of the federal poverty level ($33,075 for a family of four) or 75 percent of the state median income.[108] By statute, certain households are targeted as a higher priority for receipt of funds if they are considered "vulnerable" households or have a high energy burden (see Priority Low-Income Households for LIHEAP Funds).[109]

Historically, the LIHEAP program has not provided sufficient funds to serve all of the households that are eligible, and funding has not increased with the recent rise in energy costs.[110] Some states run out of funding early in the winter months. Many eligible families are not aware of the program. A 2008 study of state outreach efforts to raise awareness among eligible households found that some state agencies that administer LIHEAP funds are reluctant to conduct aggressive outreach because funds are insufficient to meet need.[111]

Priority Low-Income Households for LIHEAP Funds

Vulnerable Households

    Frail individual (such as an elderly person)

    A young child under the age of six

    Disabled person

High-Burden Households

    Pays a high percentage of household income for utilities (not defined by LIHEAP statute)

Questions for Discussion

1. From what you read about the LIHEAP program, does it seem adequate to address the heat or eat dilemma? Can you think of other ways to address it?

2. Does the list of priority households for LIHEAP funds adequately address concerns about the correlations between poor health and utility shut-off? Are there others that you would add based on health considerations?

State Laws and Regulations Governing Utility Payment and Shut-Offs

At the state level, utility companies (such as gas, electricity, water and telecommunications) are regulated by public utility commissions. These commissions regulate utility rates to ensure that they are fair and reasonable. They also draft regulations that address utility payment by vulnerable and low-income households as well as regulations that stipulate how and when utilities may be shut-off for nonpayment.[112]

Utility regulation varies by state, but some general principles apply. First, before utilities may be shut off for nonpayment, proper notice must be given to allow for the family or individual to make a payment or negotiate a payment plan. Second, there are often protections from shut-off for households in which an individual with an illness resides. In some states, there are protections from shut-off for households with a young child. Third, if a family or individual believes that their utilities have been shut off in violation of state regulations, they have the right to appeal the utility company's decision to a hearing officer at the state commission. Some states also have moratoriums on utility shut-offs during winter months. Some sections of Connecticut's law governing utility shut-offs are highlighted in Protections from Utility Shut-off for Low-Income Households.

Protections from Utility Shut-Off for Low-Income Households

Connecticut General Laws Chapter 283, Section 16

Moratorium Period

From *November first to April fifteenth*, inclusive, no electric or electric distribution company … no electric supplier and no municipal utility furnishing electricity shall terminate or refuse to reinstate residential electric service in hardship cases where the customer lacks the financial resources to pay his or her entire account. From November first to April fifteenth, inclusive, no gas company and no municipal utility furnishing gas shall terminate or refuse to reinstate residential gas service in hardship cases where the customer uses such gas for heat and lacks the financial resources to pay his or her entire account. (Section 16-262c(b)(1))

During any period in which a residential customer is subject to termination … [the company] … shall provide such residential customer whose account is delinquent an *opportunity to enter into a reasonable amortization agreement* with such company, electric supplier or utility to pay such delinquent account and to avoid termination of service. (Section 16-262c(b)(2))

Protection for Illness

No such company, electric supplier or municipal utility shall effect termination of service for nonpayment during such time as any resident of a *dwelling to which such service is furnished is seriously ill, if the fact of such serious illness is certified to such company, electric supplier or municipal utility by a registered physician* within such period of time after the mailing of a termination … provided the customer agrees to amortize the unpaid balance of his account over a reasonable period of time and keeps current his account for utility service as charges accrue in each subsequent billing period. (Section 16-262d(b))

Notice Prior to Termination

No … [company] … may terminate such service to a residential dwelling on account of nonpayment of a delinquent account unless such company, electric supplier or municipal utility *first gives notice* of such delinquency and impending termination by first class mail addressed to the customer to which such service is billed, at least thirteen calendar days prior to the proposed termination…. (Section 16-262d(a))

Right to Appeal and Continuance of Service during Appeal

Any customer whose complaint or request for an investigation has resulted in a determination by a company, electric supplier or municipal utility which is adverse to him *may appeal such determination to the Department of Public Utility Control or a hearing officer* appointed by the department. (Section 16-262d(e)) No such company, electric supplier or municipal utility *shall effect termination of service to a residential dwelling for nonpayment during the pendency of any complaint, investigation, hearing or appeal*, initiated by a customer within such period of time after the mailing of a termination notice.... (Section 16-262d(c))

Interpreting regulations such as those highlighted in the box can be difficult and confusing, particularly for physicians who may be asked to certify that a patient has an illness that should preclude utility shut-off. Healthcare providers may not know what qualifies as a "serious illness" for purposes of certifying that a patient should be protected from shut-off or may not understand the criteria for "financial hardship." MLP lawyers may be helpful in educating healthcare professionals about the requirements as well as assisting families when they seek energy assistance.

Questions for Discussion

1. What is the role of the healthcare provider in helping families who may be facing imminent utility shut-off?

2. What options do advocates have for preventing utility shut-offs for vulnerable individuals and families? Are laws such as Connecticut's sufficient?

3. Should utility advocacy by healthcare providers and lawyers be focused solely on prevention of shut-offs? What types of issues should be considered when helping low-income individuals and families have more energy security?

Best Practices and Advocacy Strategies for Medical-Legal Partnership

The Medical-Legal Partnership Project (MLPP), a project of the Center for Children's Advocacy in Connecticut, hosts utilities clinics within Connecticut Children's Medical Center and Saint Francis Hospital and Medical Center. Low-income clients meet with pro bono volunteers for a private budget counseling session and to assess whether they may be eligible for protections from utility shut-off under the state regulations. These volunteers, who include attorneys, law students, paralegals and also hospital medical residents and nurses, talk with the clients about their spending habits, identifying how much the client is paying for food, energy, shelter, medicine and other expenses. After completing a review of the client's budget, the volunteers help the client develop a budget plan that prioritizes the expenses that are most important to him or her. MLP staff also review the client's budget to determine if the client is eligible for income supports or other public benefits, such as food stamps and WIC.

Utility company representatives, community action agencies and other human services programs are also present at the clinics to offer assistance. The utility companies are an essential component of the clinic, because they can meet with clients in person to enroll them in the utility company's special programs, such as budget plans. For the utility companies, the clinics provide an opportunity to give customers who are behind in their payments an opportunity to make payments. For the client, the clinics offer the help of a legal advocate who can help to negotiate an affordable budget.

The clinics, which average attendance of about 60 families and take place in a large meeting room at the hospital, are also a chance for local businesses to donate food in return for free publicity. For the volunteers, the time commitment is manageable. They receive a two-hour training and commit to helping at a four-hour clinic. The MLP is able to substantially increase its capacity to address utility insecurity through the use of trained volunteers.

From Practice to Policy

To maximize utility access for patients while simplifying the role of the clinician, the pediatrics clinic at Boston Medical Center partnered with MLP | Boston on the issue of shut-off protection. What began with training and direct service evolved into a campaign for institutional and regulatory change, which ultimately helped thousands of low-income families and individuals meet their energy needs. After providing trainings to healthcare staff regarding letter writing and facilitating improvements in the clinic system that minimized burdens in generating these letters, MLP | Boston saw an increase in utility letters written. The increase revealed a set of significant barriers in the existing regulation governing shut-off protection; MLP | Boston responded by bringing the testimony of healthcare providers to hearings at the Department of Public Utilities (DPU), which governs the utilities. This testimony resulted in powerful changes to the regulations that increased the duration of shut-off protection for families and cut in half the overall number of letters that were required.

As one advocate notes, "When you create systemic solutions in any state, you can protect literally thousands, if not tens of thousands, of people from losing their utility service. If you're changing the rules, you make sure all customers will get the benefit of what otherwise only an individual with a good advocate would get." Figure 8.11 shows how MLP | Boston's work with individual healthcare providers and patients led to systemic changes that improved health for larger populations.

Figure 8.11. The Evolution of MLP | Boston Advocacy

Source: National Center for Medical-Legal Partnership and Medical-Legal Partnership | Boston, *Utilities Access and Health: A Medical-Legal Partnership Patients-to-Policy Case Study* (June 2010).

Case for Medical-Legal Partnership

Joe is 54 years old and earns $875 a month as a part-time plumber. He has a Section 8 housing voucher and pays $300 per month for rent. He has emphysema and hypoglycemia. Until last year, Joe was able to afford his utility costs, but with the rise in energy costs, he is struggling to pay his bills without cutting back on other expenses, such as medicine and food. Because he currently owes $552 to the gas company, they are threatening to shut off his gas. He is worried about not having heat for the winter.

Questions for Discussion

1. What questions will you ask Joe?

    Medical: What more do you need to know about Joe's health to help him with his utility problem?

    Legal: What information do you need to gather from Joe? What information do you need from your partnering healthcare provider?

2. What protections might be available to Joe to prevent his gas from being shut off?

3. What advice will you give Joe to help him deal with his current arrearage (the money he owes to the gas company) and to help him avoid accumulating debt to the utility companies in the future?

Conclusion

The medical literature clearly documents the links between high-cost housing, substandard housing, utility shut-offs and poor health outcomes. Yet despite these well-understood links, many individuals and families continue to endure housing insecurity, unsanitary and unsafe housing conditions, and the threat of utility shut-offs. Legal protections designed to ensure that housing is safe are often not adhered to by property owners or enforced by government agencies. Access to safe housing requires not just enforcement of existing laws but also policies that make more affordable housing options available. Lawyers and healthcare providers can partner to not only advocate for individuals and families but also play a critical role in educating policy makers about the links between health and housing and in advocating for more affordable housing options for families.

---

1. Joseph Harkness and Sandra J. Newman, "Housing Affordability and Children's Well-Being: Evidence from the National Survey of America's Families," *Housing Policy Debate* 16, no. 2 (2005): 223–55.

2. Douglas Rice and Barbara Sard, "Decade of Neglect Has Weakened Federal Low-Income Housing Programs: New Resources Required to Meet Growing Needs," Center on Budget and Policy Priorities (2009).

3. National Low Income Housing Coalition, *Out of Reach* (2009).

4. Megan Sandel and Joshua Sharfstein, "Not Safe at Home: How America's Housing Crisis Threatens the Health of Its Children," Docs4Kids Project (1998).

5. Alan Meyers, Diana Cutts, Deborah Frank, et al., "Subsidized Housing and Children's Nutritional Status," *Archives of Pediatrics & Adolescent Medicine* 159, no. 6 (2005): 551–56.

6. Sandel and Sharfstein, "Not Safe at Home."

7. John T. Cook, Deborah A. Frank, Patrick H. Casey, et al., "A Brief Indicator of Household Energy Security: Associations with Food Security, Child Health, and Child Development in US Infants and Toddlers," *Pediatrics* 122, no. 4 (2008): e867–e875.

8. Sandel and Sharfstein, "Not Safe at Home."

9. Maria Foscarinas, "The Growth of a Movement for a Human Right to Housing in the United States," *Harvard Human Rights Journal* 20 (2007): 35–40.

10. National Low Income Housing Coalition, "Recent Data Shows Continuation, Acceleration of Housing Affordability Crisis," 1, no. 3 (2006), available at http://www.nlihc.org/doc/RN06-05.pdf. Cited in Foscarinas, "The Growth," 36.

11. Ibid.

12. Fred Fuchs, "Overview of Public Housing, HUD Federally Subsidized Housing, and Section 8 Housing Voucher Programs," in *Poverty Law Manual for the New Lawyer,* Sargent Shriver National Center on Poverty Law (2002) 109–25; see also The U.S. Department of Housing and Urban Development, *Waiting in Vain: An Update on America's Rental Housing Crisis* (Washington DC, 1999).

13. See http://www.civilrights.org/fairhousing/laws/federal.html (summarizing 42 USCA § 3601 et seq. (3604); Ch. 45, Fair Housing).

14. For example, see MA ST 151B § 4 et seq. (4.6), Chapter 151B: Unlawful Discrimination Because of Race, Color, Religious Creed, National Origin, Ancestry or Sex; West's Ann.Cal.Gov.Code § 12900 et seq.

15. National Fair Housing Advocate On-line provides a list of state and local fair housing agencies: http://fairhousing.com/index.cfm?method=Agency.list&new=1 (accessed June 2, 2010).

16. Alliance for Healthy Homes, "Fair Housing Laws and Discrimination against Families," *Alliance for Healthy Homes,* http://www.cehrc.org/res/res_pubs/disclosure_Fair_Housing.pdf; see also Housing Discrimination, U.S. Department of Housing and Urban Development, http://portal.hud.gov/portal/page/portal/HUD/topics/housing_discrimination.

17. Jean Zotter and Megan Sandel, "How Substandard Housing Affects Children's Health," *Contemporary Pediatrics* 17, no. 10 (2000).

18. Monisha Cherayil, Denise Oliveira, Megan Sandel, et al., "Lawyers and Doctors Partner for Healthy Housing," *Clearinghouse Review Journal of Poverty Law and Policy 3* (2005): 65–72.

19. Ibid.

20. Ibid.

21. Ibid.

22. Brennan Center for Justice, "Results from Three Surveys of Tenants Facing Eviction in New York City Housing Court, Executive Summary" (February 14, 2007).

23. Creola Johnson, "Renters Evicted En Masse: Collateral Damage Arising from the Subprime Foreclosure Crisis," *Florida Law Review* 62 (2010): 975.

24. Madeleine R. Stoner, *The Civil Rights of Homeless People: Law, Social Policy, and Social Work Practice* (Aldine De Gruyter, 1995).

25. Cherayil et al., "Lawyers and Doctors Partner for Healthy Housing," 69–70.

26. Medical-Legal Bay Area Coalition of the San Francisco Bay Area, *Code Enforcement and Healthy Homes: An Analysis of Practices in Four Bay Area Counties, Recommendations for Next Steps* (2009).

27. Robert Wood Johnson Foundation, Commission to Build a Healthier America, "Issue Brief 2: Housing and Health" (2008): 3.

28. Pamela A. Meyer, Timothy Pivetz, Timothy A Dignam, et al., "Surveillance for Elevated Blood Lead Levels Among Children—United States, 1997–2001," *Morbidity and Mortality Weekly Report,* 52 (2003): 1–20.

29. "Blood Lead Levels—United States, 1999–2002," *Morbidity and Mortality Weekly Report* 54, no. 20 (2005): 515–16.

30. Gary Rischitelli, Peggy Nygren, Michelle Freeman, Christina Bougatsos, and Mark Helfand Bougatsos, "Screening for Elevated Lead Levels in Childhood and Pregnancy: An Updated Summary of Evidence for the U.S. Preventive Services Taskforce," *Pediatrics,* 118 (2006): 1867–95. See Elizabeth Tobin Tyler, "Safe and Secure: Enforcing the Right of Low-Income Tenants and Their Children to Lead-Safe Housing," Children's Friend and Service & the HELP Lead-Safe Center (Providence, RI: 2002).

31. Jerome O. Nriagu, "Occupational Exposure to Lead in Ancient Times," *Science of the Total Environment,* 31, no. 2 (1983): 105–16.

32. Jerome O. Nriagu, "Saturnine Gout among Roman Aristocrats. Did Lead Poisoning Contribute to the Fall of the Empire?" *New England Journal of Medicine,* 308, no. 11 (1983): 660–63.

33. M. Masquood Ahamed and Kaleem Javed Siddiqui Mohd, "Environmental Lead Toxicity and Nutritional Factors," *Clinical Nutrition,* 26, no. 4 (2007): 400–408.

34. G. D. Miller, T. F. Massaro, and E. J. Massaro, "Interactions between Lead and Essential Elements: A Review," *Neurotoxicology*, 11, no. 1 (1990): 99–119.

35. E. E. Ziegler et al., "Absorption and Retention of Lead by Infants," *Pediatric Research*, 12, no. 1 (1978): 29–34.

36. Bruce P. Lanphear, Richard Hornung, Mona Ho, Cynthia R. Howard, "Environmental Lead Exposure during Early Childhood," *Journal of Pediatrics*, 140, no. 1 (2002): 40–47.

37. P. S. Barry, "A Comparison of Concentrations of Lead in Human Tissues," *British Journal of Industrial Medicine*, 32, no. 2 (1975): 119–39.

38. Theodore I. Lidsky and Jay S. Schneider, "Lead Neurotoxicity in Children: Basic Mechanisms and Clinical Correlates," *Brain*, 126, no. 1 (2003): 5–19.

39. H. J. Binns, C. Campbell, and M. J. Brown, "Interpreting and Managing Blood Lead Levels of Less than 10 microg/dL in Children and Reducing Childhood Exposure to Lead: Recommendations of the Centers for Disease Control and Prevention Advisory Committee on Childhood Lead Poisoning Prevention," *Pediatrics*, 120, no. 5 (2007): 1285–98.

40. Richard L. Canfield, Charles H. Henderson, Deborah A. Cory-Slechta, et al., "Intellectual Impairment in Children with Blood Lead Concentrations Below 10 microg per deciliter," *New England Journal of Medicine*, 348, no. 16 (2003): 1517–26.

41. *Preventing Lead Poisoning in Young Children* (Atlanta: Centers for Disease Control and Prevention, 1991).

42. Canfield et al., "Intellectual impairment."

43. Binns et al., "Interpreting and Managing Blood Lead Levels." Herbert L. Needleman, "The Removal of Lead from Gasoline: Historical and Personal Reflections," *Environmental Research*, 84, no. 1 (2000): 20–35.

44. S. G. Gilbert and B. Weiss, "A Rationale for Lowering the Blood Lead Action Level from 10 to 2 microg/dL," *Neurotoxicology* 27, no. 5 (2006): 693–701.

45. *Screening for Elevated Blood Levels in Children and Pregnant Women* (Washington DC: U.S. Preventive Services Task Force, 2006).

46. Ahamed et al., "Environmental Lead Toxicity."

47. James A. Ryan, Kirk G. Scheckel, William R. Berti, et al., "Reducing Children's Risk from Lead in Soil," *Environmental Science Technology*, 38, no 1. (2004): 18A–24A.

48. Martha Keel and Janice McCoy, "Sources of Lead in Food," Tennessee Department of Health, http://www.utextension.utk.edu/publications/spfiles/SP605-G.pdf.

49. Gilbert et al., "A Rationale for Lowering the Blood Lead Level."

50. Ibid.

51. Ibid.

52. Ahamed et al., ''Environmental Lead Toxicity."

53. B. Weiss, "Neurobehavioral Toxicity as a Basis for Risk Assessment," *Trends in Pharmaceutical Science*, 9, no. 2 (1988): 59–62.

54. Sarah E. Cusick, Zuguo Mei, Mary E. Cogswell, "Continuing Anemia Prevention Strategies Are Needed throughout Early Childhood in Low-income Preschool Children," *Journal of Pediatrics*, 150, no. 4 (2007): 422–28.

55. Alan D. Woolf, Rose Goldman, David Bellinger, "Update on the Clinical Management of Childhood Lead Poisoning," *Pediatric Clinics of North America*, 54, no. 2 (2007): 271–94.

56. Walter J. Rogan, Kim D. Dietrich, James H. Ware, et al., "The Effect of Chelation Therapy with Succimer on Neuropsychological Development in Children Exposed to Lead," *New England Journal of Medicine*, 344, no. 19 (2001): 1421–26.

57. Binns et al., "Interpreting and Managing Blood Lead Levels."

58. Ibid.

59. Gregory D. Luce, Anne M. Phelps, "Using the Federal Lead Hazard Disclosure Rule's Private Right of Action for Compensatory Damages and Broad-Based Injunctive Relief," *Clearinghouse Review Journal of Poverty Law and Policy* (May–June 2005) (summarizing 42 USCA § 4852d).

60. Maria Rapuano and Anne M. Phelps, "Leveraging the Federal Lead Hazard Disclosure Law to Improve Housing Conditions," *Clearinghouse Review Journal of Poverty Law and Policy* (May–June 2005).

61. Luce and Phelps, "Using the Federal Lead Hazard Disclosure Rule's Private Right of Action."

62. Stephanie P. Brown, "Guide for Developing State and Local Lead-Based Paint Enforcement Bench Books," *National Center for Healthy Housing* (2008): 1–37, 14.

63. Rafael Mares, "Enforcement of the Massachusetts Lead Law and Its Effect on Rental Prices and Abandonment," *Journal of Affordable Housing*, 12, no. 3 (Spring 2003).

64. Jeanita W. Richardson, *The Cost of Being Poor, Poverty: Lead Poisoning and Policy Implementation* (Westport, CT: Praeger, 2005), 60–63.

65. Aileen Sprague, Fidelma Fitzpatrick, "Getting the Lead Out: How Public Nuisance Law Protects Rhode Island's Children," *Roger Williams University Law Review*, 11, no. 603 (2005–2006): 603–49

66. Ibid., 63–64.

67. *Preventing Lead Poisoning through Code Enforcement: Ten Effective Strategies, Alliance to End Childhood Lead Poisoning* (2005), available at www.hud.gov/offices/lead/lbp/startup/CodeEnforcementStrategies.doc.

68. "Summary Health Statistics for U.S. Children: National Health Interview Survey," *Vital Health Stat*, 10, no. 221 (2004): 1–78.

69. Ibid.

70. Paul W. Newacheck, Neal Halfon, "Prevalence, Impact, and Trends in Childhood Disability due to Asthma," *Archives of Pediatric and Adolescent Medicine*, 154 (2000): 287–93.

71. Michael Weitzman, Steven Gortmaker, Arthur Sorbol. "Racial, Social, and Environmental Risks for Childhood Asthma," *American Journal of Disease Childhood*, 144 (1990): 1189–94. J. Schwartz, D. Gold, D. W. Dockery, et al., "Predictors of Asthma and Persistent Wheeze in a National Sample of Children in the US: Association with Social Class, Perinatal Events and Race," *American Review of Respiratory Disease*, 142 (1990): 555–62.

72. Jennifer K. Peat, Ree H. van der Berg, Wesley F. Green, et al., "Changing Prevalence of Asthma in Australian Children," *British Medical Journal*, 308 (1994): 1591–96. R. K. Ninan, G. Russell, "Respiratory Symptoms and Atopy in Aberdeen Schoolchildren: Evidence from Two Surveys 25 Years Apart," *British Medical Journal*, 3–4 (1992): 873–75. M. I. Asher, S. Montefort, B. Bjorkesten, et al., ISACC Phase Three Study Group, "Worldwide Time Trends in the Prevalence of Symptoms of Asthma, Allergic Rhoniconjuntivitis, and Eczema in Childhood," *Lancet*, 368 (2006): 733–43.

73. O. S. VonEhrenstein, E. Von Mutius, S. Illi, et al., "Reduced Risk of Hay Fever and Asthma among Children of Farmers," *Clinical Exposure Allergy*, 30 (2000): 187–93. C. Braun-Fahrlander, M. Ganner, L. Grize, et al., "Prevalence of Hay Fever and Allergic Sensitization in Farmer's Children and Their Peers Living in the Same Rural Community," SCARPOL team, Swiss Study on Childhood Allergy and Respiratory Symptoms with Respect to Air Pollution, *Clinical Exposure Allergy*, 29 (1999): 28–34. J. Riedler, C. J. Braun-Fahrlander, W. Eder, M. Schreurer, "Exposure to Farming in Early Life and Development of Asthma and Allergy: A Cross-Sectional Survey," *Lancet*, 358 (2001): 1129–33. Pierre Ernst and Yvon Cormier, "Relative Scarcity of Asthma and Atopy among Rural Adolescents Raised on a Farm," *American Journal of Respiratory Critical Care Medicine*, 161 (2000): 1563–66.

74. S. R. Strachan, "Hay Fever, Hygiene, and Household Size," *British Medical Journal*, 299 (1989): 1259–60. E. Von Mutius, F. D. Martinez, C. Fritzsch, et al., "Skin Test Reactivity and Number of Siblings," *British Medical Journal*, 308 (1994): 692–95.

75. T. A. Platts-Mills, "How Environment Affects Patients with Allergic Disease: Indoor Allergens and Asthma," *Annals of Allergy*, 72 (1994): 381. J. E. Brussee, H. A. Smit, R. V. Van Strein et al., "Allergen Exposure in Infancy and the Development of Sensitization, Wheeze, and Asthma at 4 Years," *Journal of Allergy and Clinical Immunology*, 115 (2005): 946.

76. Virginia A. Rauh, Ginger R. Chew, Robin S. Garfinkel, "Deteriorated Housing Contributes to Higher Cockroach Allergen Levels in Inner-city Households," *Environmental Health Perspective*, 110, suppl 1–2 (1994): 323–27.

77. Robert S. Call, Thomas F. Smith, Elsie Morris, et al., "Risk Factors for Asthma in Inner-city Children," *Journal of Pediatrics*, 121 (1992): 862. Bann C. Kang, Jesse Johnson, Chris Veres-Thorner,

"Atopic Profile of Inner-City Asthma with a Comparative Analysis on the Cockroach-Sensitive and Ragweed-Sensitive Subgroups," *Journal of Allergy and Clinical Immunology*, 92 (1993): 802–11. David Rosenstreich, Peyton Eglleston, Meyer Kattan, et al., "The Role of Cockroach Allergy and Exposure to Cockroach Allergen in Causing Morbidity among Inner-city Children with Asthma," *New England Journal of Medicine*, 336 (1997): 1356–63.

78. Celeste Porsbjerg, Marie Louise von Linstow, Charlotte S. Ulrick, et al., "Risk Factors for the Onset of Asthma: A 12 Year Prospective Follow-up Study," *Chest*, 129 (2006): 309–16. R. Sporik, M. D. Chapman, T. A. Platts-Mills, "House Dust-mite Exposure as a Cause of Asthma," *Clinical Experimental Allergy*, 22 (1992): 897–906.

79. W. B. Weiss, P. J. Gergen, D. K. Wagener, "Breathing Better or Wheezing Worse? The Changing Epidemiology of Asthma Morbidity and Mortality," *Annual Review of Public Health*, 14 (1993): 491–513. Michael Weitzman, Steven Gortmaker, Deborah Walker, "Maternal Smoking and Childhood Asthma," *Pediatrics*, 85 (1990): 505–11. Fernando d. Martinez, Martha Cline, Benjamin Burrows, "Increased Incidence of Asthma in Children of Smoking Mothers," *Pediatrics*, 89 (1992): 21–26. D. P. Strachan, D. G. Cook, "Health Effects of Passive Smoking: 1," *Thorax*, 52 (1997): 905–14. D. P. Strachan, D. G. Cook, "Health Effects of Passive Smoking: 6," *Thorax*, 53 (1998): 204–12.

80. Rosalind J. Wright, Sheldon Cohen, Vincent Carey, et al., "Parental Stress as a Predictor of Wheezing in Infancy," *American Journal of Respiratory Critical Care Medicine*, 165 (2002): 358–65.

81. Rosalind J. Wright, Herman Mitchell, Cynthia M. Visness, et al., "Community Violence and Asthma Morbidity: the Inner-City Asthma Study," *American Journal of Public Health*, 94 (2004): 625–32.

82. M. Kattan, S. C. Stearns, E. Crain, et al., "Cost-Effectiveness of a Home-Based Envioronmental Intervention for Inner-City Children with Asthma," *Journal of Allergy and Clinical Immunology*, 116 (2005): 1058–63. Wayne J. Morgan, Ellen F. Crain, Rebecca S. Guchalla, et al., "Results of a Home-Based Environmental Intervention among Urban Children with Asthma," *New England Journal of Medicine*, 351 (2004): 1068–80. Meyer Kattan, Ellen Crain, Suzanne Steinbach, et al., "A Randomized Clinical Trial of Clinician Feedback to Improve Quality of Care for Inner-city Children with Asthma," *Pediatrics*, 117 (2006): 1095–103.

83. C. S. Rand, "Non-adherence with Asthma Therapy: More than Just Forgetting," *Journal of Pediatrics*, 146, no. 2 (2005): 157–59.

84. Lauren A. Smith, Barbara Bokhour, Katherine H. Hohman, et al., "Modifiable Risk Factors for Suboptimal Control and Controller Medication Underuse among Children with Asthma," *Pediatrics*, 122, no. 4 (2008): 760–69.

85. Alina Das, "The Asthma Crisis in Low-Income Communities of Color: Using the Law as a Tool for Promoting Public Health," *NYU Review of Law and Social Change*, 31, no. 273 (2007).

86. See for example, *Hovarth v. Savage Mfg., Inc.*, 18 F. Supp. 2d 1296 (D. Utah 1998) (finding that the plaintiff established enough evidence that asthma is a disability under the ADA to withstand summary judgment); *Davidson v. Perry*, 133 F.3d 914 (4th Cir. 1998) (finding that plaintiff was disabled under the ADA based on her asthma).

87. Rebecca Miles, "Preventing Asthma through Housing Interventions: How Supportive is the U.S. Policy Environment?" *Housing Studies*, 20, no. 4 (2005): 589–603.

88. Das, "The Asthma Crisis."

89. Testimony of Susan Popkin, The Urban Institute, for the hearing on H.R. 1614 HOPE VI Reauthorization and Small Community Mainstreet Revitalization and Housing Act for the Committee on Financial Services, April 29, 2003. Lindsay Rosenfeld, Rima Rudd, Ginger L. Chew, et al., "Are Neighborhood-Level Characteristics Associated with Indoor Allergens in the Household?," *Journal of Asthma*, 47, no. 1 (2010): 66–75.

90. City of Boston, Breathe Easy At Home Program, http://www.cityofboston.gov/isd/housing/bmc.

91. *The Impact of Poor Housing Conditions on the Health of Asthmatic New Yorkers*, Coalition for Asthma-Free Homes (2008); "Report: Poor Housing Conditions Harming Asthmatic New Yorkers: Elected Officials, Health & Housing Advocates Urge City to Crack Down on Asthma Triggers," Press Advisory, Make the Road New York, May 20, 2009.

92. New York City Council, Int 0750-2008 (introduced April 16, 2008).

93. D.A. Frank, N. Roos, A Meyers, et al., "*Seasonal Variation in Weight-for-Age in a Pediatric Emergency Room*," Public Health Reporter, 111, no. 4. (1996): 366–71.

94. E. C. Perrin, C. H. Cole, D. A. Frank, et al., "Criteria for Determining Disability in Infants and Children: Failure to Thrive." *Evidence Report Technology Assessment*, 72 (2003): 1–5.

95. Ibid.

96. John T. Cook, Deborah A. Frank, Patrick H. Casey, et al., "A Brief Indicator of Household Energy Security: Associations with Food Security, Child Health, and Child Development in US Infants and Toddlers," *Pediatrics*, 122, no. 4. (2008): 867–75. Gregory S. Anderson, "Human Morphology and Temperature Regulation," *International Journal of Biometeorology*, 43, no. 3 (1999): 99–109.

97. R. E. Honicky, J. S. Osborne, "Respiratory Effects of Wood Heat: Clinical Observations and Epidemiologic Assessment," *Environmental Health Perspectives*, 95 (1999): 105–9.

98. M. Aherns, *Home Candle Fires* (Quincy, MA: National Fire Protection Association, 2005).

99. Cook et al., "A Brief Indicator."

100. *LIHEAP Home Energy Notebook for Fiscal Year 2007* (Washington, DC: U.S. Department of Health and Human Services, Administration for Children and Families, 2009).

101. Jayanta Bhattacharya, Thomas Deleire, Steven Haider, et al., "Heat or Eat? Cold-Weather Shocks and Nutrition in Poor American Families," *American Journal of Public Health*, 93, no. 7 (2003): 1149–54.

102. U.S. Department of Health and Human Service, Administration for Children and Families, Office of Community Services, Division of Energy Assistance, *LIHEAP Home Energy Notebook for FY 2007, Executive Summary* (June 2009), 12.

103. Cook et al., "A Brief Indicator."

104. Deborah A. Frank, Nicole B. Neault, Anne Skalicky, et al., "Heat or Eat: The Low Income Energy Assistance Program and Nutritional and Health Risks Amongst Children Less than Three Years of Age," *Pediatrics*, 118, no. 5 (2006): 1293–302.

105. Ibid.

106. U.S. Department of Health and Human Services, Administration for Children and Families, Low-Income Home Energy Assistance Program Factsheet, http://www.acf.hhs.gov/programs/ocs/liheap/about/factsheet.html.

107. Ibid.

108. Ibid.

109. Ibid.

110. Ibid., i.

111. DHHS, ACF, *Recipiency Targeting Analysis For Elderly and Young Child Households Final Report*, Department of Health and Human Services, Administration for Children and Families (December 2008), http://www.acf.hhs.gov/programs/ocs/liheap/targeting_report.html.

112. See National Association of Regulatory Utility Commissioners at http://www.naruc.org.

Chapter 9

Education: Connecting Health and Quality Learning Opportunities

Pamela Tames, JD
Mallory Curran, JD
Samuel Senft, JD, MPH
Robert Needlman, MD

Public schooling offers children a free education, primarily from kindergarten through grade 12.[1] By federal law,[2] such schooling must be available to all children, regardless of health, financial or legal status, race, religion, national origin or ethnicity. Multiple legal mandates, some under the guise of student testing and teacher accountability, strive for the provision of high-quality education to all children, including those with special needs.[3] Nonetheless, national and state-by-state data continue to show significant disparities in educational outcomes based on socioeconomic, geographic, racial and ethnic differences, as well as disability status.[4] Reading and math proficiency, high school graduation rates, the prevalence of juvenile delinquency, and enrollment and completion of higher education are a few of the many indicators.[5]

Some children and youth arrive at school with distinct social and/or economic disadvantages or hardships — inadequate food or nourishment, unstable or unhealthy housing or homelessness, exposure to violence or trauma and so on. Others suffer chronic diseases or physical, mental or emotionally disabling conditions. All of these factors influence a student's readiness to learn and ability to attend and participate in school. What help will a student need to succeed in school? What legal rights and protections does a student (and, in turn, a family) have to ensure those needs are met? What can a healthcare provider do to help a student access appropriate help? What can he or she do to help a student whose performance and/or behavior in school is lacking?

Conversely, the ability of a student to achieve mental, emotional and physical health as well as academic success may be adversely affected by disparate education and school discipline policies and practices. When schools do not abide by federal and state mandates and neglect to provide students with appropriate services and supports, student performance and well-being suffer. It then falls on individual families to assert and document violations and pursue remedies on behalf of their children. What legal rights do families have to address unlawful school policies and practices? What processes must a school have in place to ensure a lawful appeals process?

This chapter describes the interconnected relationship between health and education and the protections available to help students and families navigate relevant parts of the public school system. It also explores different contexts in which poverty, education and health converge and ways medical-legal partnerships (MLPs) can provide preventive protections for families.

The Connection between High-Quality Education and Health

Health and education are intimately connected. Educational underachievement in childhood commonly leads to poor physical health later in life; the link is mediated by economic disadvantage and a complex connection between low literacy and illness.[6] The link also runs in the opposite direction. Among children, any serious medical condition can disrupt school functioning and limit educational achievement. Life-threatening illnesses, such as leukemia or traumatic brain injury, clearly affect success in school. Less serious but far more common health conditions also regularly interfere with learning. Among these are asthma and allergies, attention deficit/hyperactivity disorder (ADHD), lead poisoning, sleep disorders, undernutrition, obesity and deficits in vision and hearing.

Medical conditions impair education in various ways. They may decrease school attendance, lower a child's general level of energy or ability to work, cause pain and anxiety that distract the child, or directly impair thinking, concentration and memory. Medications used to treat some conditions—epilepsy in particular—may impair learning as a side effect. It's common for children to have more than one ongoing medical condition, and these often act in a synergistic manner. For example, many obese children also have asthma and sleep apnea. These conditions exacerbate each other, and each interferes with attention and learning singly and in concert. In general, rates of illness are somewhat higher among economically disadvantaged children, contributing to reduced achievement.[7]

Mental Health and Learning

Among medical conditions that affect learning, ADHD, depression and anxiety disorders, and learning disabilities deserve special mention. Taken together, these mental health conditions affect 20–25 percent of children. These conditions interfere with functions that are crucial to school success—attention, self-control and learning—yet in other respects the child may seem thoroughly healthy. As a result, parents and teachers are apt to believe that the child is merely "being bad" or simply needs to try harder, and may fail to provide the medical and educational supports necessary for success. The children, in turn, may blame themselves. Unsupported, these children face an increased risk of school failure, suspension, dropout, occupational and often legal problems, as well as increased medical problems of all sorts once they reach adulthood. ADHD and learning disabilities are discussed in greater detail at the end of the chapter.

Environmental Causes of Chronic Illness and Their Effects on Learning

Many of the medical problems that interfere with learning coexist with and are themselves reinforced by environmental factors broadly associated with poverty. These include substandard housing and homelessness, air pollution, high levels of psychological stress and limited access to high-quality food and safe places to play. Homelessness has received special attention as a marker of more severe poverty and as a factor that has both direct and indirect effects on learning. (See Chapter 8, which details the connections between housing and health.) Parker and Zuckerman used the phrase "double jeopardy" to describe the synergistic effects of biomedical and psychosocial adversity on the educational and emotional development of children in poverty.[8]

Health risks associated with poor educational outcomes often begin before conception and continue throughout infancy and early childhood. These include (in roughly chronological order): young maternal age; poor maternal nutrition; prenatal exposure to environmental toxins such as lead and mercury, and to intentionally ingested toxins such as alcohol, cigarettes and various legal and illegal drugs; high levels of prenatal psychological stress (for example, the stress of being physically abused or abandoned); prenatal infections; preterm birth and low birth weight; prolonged treatment in a neonatal intensive care unit; serious infections in infancy, including vaccine-preventable diseases; undernutrition, particularly iron deficiency; lead exposure; recurrent ear infections; and injuries (often unintentional, but occasionally due to child abuse).[9] This list, though long, is not exhaustive.

Pediatric Approaches to Learning and Development

Pediatricians and other primary healthcare providers for children devote considerable time during health supervision visits (a.k.a. "well child care") trying to prevent and manage chronic health conditions that can impair educational outcomes. They administer formal screening tests and informal developmental surveillance (i.e., questioning and observation) to facilitate early intervention for developmental problems, such as language delays and autism. They may also intervene directly to promote educational well-being, for example, by advising parents on ways to support homework and engage in reading aloud or paired reading.

Once a child has been identified as having school problems, the healthcare provider has a role in sorting through the various possible medical, psychological and social causes, as mentioned. Although one or another cause may suggest itself up front, a thorough review often finds other concurrent contributing factors as well. The next step is to communicate this diagnostic formulation in a way that is understandable to the parents and the child and helps them begin to seek solutions. A medical professional may also communicate with a school nurse, teacher(s) and the principal, and may play a role in facilitating communication between the parent and the school. A clinician may assist the parents in understanding their child's educational rights, so that parents can advocate effectively with the school. If the school undertakes an evaluation to determine if special education and related services are warranted, the clinician may help the parent interpret the results of the evaluations.

Roles of Pediatric Health Providers in Children's Education

- Prevention
    - Optimal nutrition
    - Injury prevention
    - Immunizations
    - Support for cognitive stimulation and emotional well-being
- Early Detection and Referral
    - Developmental surveillance (questions and observations, over time)
    - Formal developmental and behavioral screening tests
    - Referral to appropriate therapies and early childhood education programs
- Assessment of Educational Problems
    - Identify contributing chronic illness (e.g., asthma, sleep disorders)

- º Identify and treat ADHD and other mental health conditions
- º Identify learning disabilities (chiefly dyslexia)
- º Assess possible environmental factors at home (e.g., family stress, domestic violence), and at school (e.g., bullying, physical insecurity, inappropriate classroom placement)
- Collaboration with Parents and Schools
  - º Educate parents and school personnel on the effects of chronic physical and mental conditions (e.g., why a child with dyslexia may appear to be undermotivated)
  - º Provide guidance on effective behavioral approaches (e.g., setting up regular homework routines)
  - º Provide medical treatment when possible (e.g., medication for ADHD), and assist parents and school in monitoring the effects
  - º Help parents establish positive working relationships with teachers, school principals, school psychologists and counselors, and other involved adults
  - º Help parents understand the local education authority (commonly referred to as the school system or school district) and laws that affect educational programming for children with chronic medical conditions and learning difficulties (very hard to do without training by and support of a legal provider)

Adapted from J. McAllister, "School Issues in Children with Chronic Illness," in *Pediatrics*, ed. L. M. Osborn, et al. (Philadelphia: Mosby, 2005), 873–76.

Early identification of health and learning problems and clinician advocacy are essential. School personnel often do not have the resources to recognize health problems; as a result, a child with a disability may be mislabeled as having a behavioral problem or simply being disruptive. Such children are at further risk for school dropout, suspension and expulsion.[10] In turn, educational failure is a very significant factor in predicting economic and occupational status in adulthood and health status throughout the life cycle.[11]

Questions for Discussion

1. Data indicate that three groups of children — those living in poverty, those who are African American or Latino, and those living with chronic diseases or disabilities — have worse education outcomes than other children. What might explain these findings?

2. What can healthcare professionals do to identify those children whose educational needs are not being met? What screening questions should practitioners ask families to identify education problems?

3. What is the role of the healthcare provider in addressing education issues for individual patients and families? What about for the broader community?

Education and the Law

There is a complex web of federal, state, and local laws, regulations, and policies governing public education and related services for children and youth.[12] They relate to, among other things, early intervention for infants and toddlers with disabilities,[13] elementary and secondary education,[14] special education,[15] rehabilitative services and civil rights protections for students with disabilities and chronic disease,[16] education of homeless students,[17] students in foster care, immigrant students,[18] and those with limited English proficiency,[19] adult education and literacy, and career and technical education.[20]

The overarching purpose of these laws is to ensure that public education is available to all children and youth, from elementary through high school. Special education laws seek to ensure that schools proactively identify students with disabilities and provide them with appropriate assistance or accommodations that will enable them to fully access and participate in their education. Unfortunately, many of these government mandates are neither fully funded nor well enforced. The states and, in turn, the local school districts are not given adequate resources to serve students with disabilities. Often it is left up to individual families to identify a child's unique learning barriers and advocate for services and/or supports to help them.

MLPs have proven to be a particularly effective way of identifying and addressing these barriers. Healthcare providers have a regular opportunity to ask families about a child's education, giving parents a forum to bring educational challenges to light. Healthcare providers, in turn, can help determine whether specialized assessment of a child's learning abilities may help address the problem. Given the complexity of the laws and the limited enforcement system, legal consultation and advocacy in the healthcare setting can be critical to ensuring that students' rights are not violated and their needs are met.

Training of clinicians in an MLP should raise awareness of all education-related issues that could benefit from advocacy. It also should build the capacity of clinicians to advocate on those issues most likely to arise. Providers working in MLPs are encouraged to screen broadly for unmet education-related needs.

Education of Children with Disabilities and Chronic Diseases

Two federal laws govern the identification, evaluation, eligibility, services and accommodations of children and youth suspected of developmental delays or risks, disabilities and chronic diseases that might impede learning and/or access to education. They are the Individuals with Disabilities Education Act (IDEA; 20 U.S.C. § 1400 et seq.) and Section 504 of the Rehabilitation Act of 1973 (29 U.S.C. § 701 et seq.).

Infants and toddlers (birth through age two) with disabilities and their families may qualify for early intervention services under IDEA Part C. Children and youth ages 3 through 21 may be eligible for special education and related services under IDEA Part B. All individuals with disabilities are protected from discrimination by Section 504 in programs and activities that receive federal financial assistance from the U.S. Department of Education.

Early Intervention

Part C of the IDEA[21] (Early Intervention or EI) authorizes the federal government to require states to provide a wide variety of support services to qualified infants and toddlers under the age of three. The goal of EI is to identify young children with physical or mental conditions that have affected or are at risk of affecting their development or impeding their education, and lessen the effects of the disability or delay. Services are designed to meet a child's needs in five developmental areas, including physical, cognitive, communication, social or emotional and adaptive development. Services are proven to be most effective when started as soon as the delay or disability is identified. Examples of conditions that might qualify a child for EI include cerebral palsy, autism spectrum disorders and communication disorders.

Data indicate that EI increases the developmental and educational gains for the child, improves functioning of the family and reaps long-term benefits for society. Specifically, longitudinal research indicates that effectively designed EI program show sizable benefits in "cognition and academic achievement, behavioral and emotional competencies, educational progression and attainment, child maltreatment, health, delinquency and crime, social welfare program use, and labor market success."[22]

Each state has its own eligibility criteria and methods of service provision. Some states include in their eligibility criteria children who are at risk of having substantial developmental delays if EI services are not provided;[23] others do not. Each state has a lead agency that is responsible for coordination and administration of EI. Services are delivered by a variety of providers under the central administration of the lead agency. The types of services provided to a child depend on the type and level of need as determined by the EI evaluation.

When a child is found to be eligible for EI, an Individualized Family Service Plan (IFSP) is developed by parents and program staff. The document details the services a child should receive and goals for that child. The IFSP is reviewed at least every six months.[24]

As a toddler ages, review of the IFSP should include a discussion of whether the child's disability is likely to continue beyond his or her third birthday, and, if so, whether it is likely to impede the child's learning. Part C of the IDEA requires that IFSPs provide for transition of children with ongoing needs to school-based services as early as age three, even if that is before the traditional age of enrollment in school.[25] Often, however, many families face difficulty in the transition of their children from EI to school-based services. The most common problem is a gap between the time when EI services end and school-based services begin. Such a gap can have detrimental health consequences on already vulnerable children. Healthcare providers should anticipate the ongoing needs of a child turning three, and inform and encourage parents to seek a school-based evaluation as early as two and a half years of age. Table 9.1 provides a basic overview of EI.

Both healthcare providers and legal partners should be aware of the importance of early intervention services and should develop competencies in navigating the EI system.

Questions for Discussion

1. Why is it important for infants and toddlers to receive Early Intervention?
2. What can a pediatrician do to help ensure that a child with a disability is identified early?
3. How can a pediatrician work with EI service providers to ensure that a child receives appropriate services?
4. What are some negative outcomes for children who do not promptly transition from EI to school-based services on turning three?

Case for Medical-Legal Partnership

Jaclyn, age two years, one month, comes with her mother to the pediatrician for a follow-up visit. She recently had her tonsils and adenoids removed and tubes inserted after experiencing chronic ear infections as an infant. During the visit, her mother, Mrs. Brown, expresses concern about Jaclyn's speech. Ms. Brown recalls that her older children were very verbal by age two, but Jaclyn is rather silent and often shies away from other children.

Table 9.1 Early Intervention: The Basics

Who can refer a child to EI?	Physicians, parents, other healthcare providers, daycare programs, local educational agencies and social service agencies (Comprehensive Child Find System, 34 C.F.R §303.321)
Who is eligible for EI?	Infants and toddlers who have developmental delays (including cognitive, physical, communication, social or emotional, or adaptive developmental delay), or who have a diagnosed physical or mental condition that has a high risk of resulting in developmental delay. States may define developmental delay. States also may include infants and toddlers who are at risk of having substantial developmental delays if EI is not provided.
What is the evaluation timeline?	After receiving a referral, an EI provider should complete the evaluation and hold an IFSP meeting within 45 days (34 C.F.R §303.321)
What is assessed in the evaluation?	Evaluations should include: • a review of medical records • evaluation of cognitive development • evaluation of physical development • evaluation of communication skills development • evaluation of social and emotional development • evaluation of adaptive development • an assessment of the unique needs of the child regarding his or her developmental functioning • a family assessment
What types of services are available through EI?	A wide range of services may be available through EI, including but not limited to: • Home visits and home therapy • Center-based individual visits • Community child groups • Parent groups and training • Physical therapy • Speech therapy • Occupational therapy • Case management (20 U.S.C. 1400.632)

Questions for Discussion

1. Should Jaclyn be referred for an EI evaluation?

2. What could the pediatrician do to help ensure that Jaclyn receives a timely and comprehensive evaluation and, if appropriate, services?

3. Assuming Jaclyn qualifies for EI services and her speech improves but is still considerably delayed, what should the pediatrician do to seek help for her beyond EI? How might the MLP lawyer help?

Special Education: The Individuals with Disabilities Education Act

Historically, millions of children and adolescents with disabilities were completely excluded from public school or provided with an inadequate education and isolated from their peers (20 U.S.C. § 1400(c)(2)). Since the 1970s, however, federal law (the Individuals with Disabilities Education Act, IDEA) has dictated that all students, including those with disabilities, are entitled to a free, appropriate, public education and, more recently, that those children meet high academic standards. The law has had several significant effects. More students with disabilities attend schools in their own neighborhoods—schools that may not have been open to them previously. Fewer students with disabilities are educated in separate buildings, separate programs or separate classrooms and instead are learning in classes with their peers. Finally, students with disabilities are increasingly completing high school, participating in postsecondary education and engaging in paid employment.[26]

Educating students with disabilities is quite challenging. Concerns range from how best to identify children who qualify for special education and related services to racial and ethnic disparities to budgets and funding. Understanding the protections provided by the IDEA and also some of the barriers to enforcement of its provisions is important for MLP practitioners.

The stated purpose of the IDEA is "to ensure that all children with disabilities have available to them a free appropriate public education that emphasizes special education and related services designed to meet their unique needs and prepare them for further education, employment, and independent living" (20 U.S.C. § 1400.601(d)(1)(A)). More than 13 percent of the students ages 3 to 21 attending public schools in the United States are identified as students with disabilities under the IDEA.[27] In 2008, this translated to approximately 6.6 million children with disabilities receiving special education and related services under the law.[28] IDEA makes clear that for children with disabilities, a free, appropriate public education must be provided in the "least restrictive environment" (20 U.S.C. § 1412(a)(5)) and must include an "individualized education program" (20 U.S.C. § 1414(d)) or individualized education plan (IEP) detailing services designed to meet the unique needs of each student. Table 9.2 details some of the key components of the IDEA.

Evaluation of Children for Special Education and Related Services

School districts are required to set up procedures to ensure that all children with disabilities residing within the district are identified, located and evaluated for special education and related services (20 U.S.C. § 1412(a)(3)). A referral for an evaluation can be made by the child's parent, a state or local educational agency or other state agency (20 U.S.C. § 1414(a)(1)(B)). In some states, such as Massachusetts, a broader range of individuals may initiate a referral (603 Mass. Code Regs. § 28.04(1)). Important deadlines for evaluation of students under the IDEA are outlined in Table 9.3.

Before a student can receive special education and related services, he or she must be evaluated by a multidisciplinary team through a multifactored evaluation. The IDEA details a number of different categories of disability under which a student may qualify for special education. For disability categories for school-age children under the IDEA, see Appendix 9.1.

Also, as young as age three, children may qualify for special education due to a "developmental delay" in one of several areas: physical development, cognitive development, communication development, social or emotional development, or adaptive development (Child With a Disability, 34 C.F.R. § 300.8(b)).

It is important to note that for both preschool and school-age children, having a medical diagnosis or chronic condition does not automatically qualify a student for special education and related services. As specifically stated in the definitions of most of the disability categories (see Appendix 9.1), *the disability must have an adverse effect on a student's educational performance.*

For example, a child who has been diagnosed with ADHD by a healthcare provider may or may not be eligible for special education and related services. A strong case can be made that a student whose ADHD has a negative impact on performance in school—

Table 9.2 The IDEA at a Glance

Evaluation	To qualify for special education and related services, a student must have an evaluation. An evaluation must include a variety of measures conducted by and collected from a number of different individuals (such as parents, teachers, school psychologists and speech-language pathologists) (20 U.S.C. §1414(b)(2)).
Referral	A referral for an evaluation can be made by the child's parent, a state or local educational agency or other state agency (20 U.S.C. §1414(a)(1)(B)).
Content	An evaluation often includes assessment of the following: • Intelligence (e.g., IQ testing) • Academic achievement • Speech-language skills • Social-emotional status • Classroom behavior • Vision • Hearing Other evaluative measures should be used as needed based on the student's areas of suspected disability.
Frequency	An evaluation must be conducted at least every three years, unless a parent and local educational agency agree it is unnecessary. It can be conducted more often if requested by parent, teacher or the school (20 U.S.C. §1414(a)(2)).
Individualized Education Program (IEP)	An IEP is the document that details the goals and services the student will receive. It must be rewritten and updated at least every 12 months. It may be amended at any time by the IEP team (20 U.S.C. §1414(d)).
Goals and objectives	IEP goals and objectives must be measurable (20 U.S.C. §1414(d)(1)(A)(i)(II)). Example objectives include: • Caroline will be able to identify 90/100 second-grade Dolch words. • David will subtract two-digit numbers with regrouping with 90% accuracy. • Avery will raise her hand and wait to be called on by the teacher before answering a question in the classroom on 9/10 trials.
Services	Documents the specialized services that will be provided to the child (20 U.S.C. §1414(d)(1)(A)(i)(IV)), for example: 100 minutes of direct speech therapy services per month according to the district calendar.
Least Restrictive Environment (LRE)	Students must be educated with nondisabled peers to the maximum extent possible (20 U.S.C. §1412(a)(5)). Each IEP must contain a statement of the LRE where the child will receive his or her special education and related services (e.g., speech room, in the regular education setting, in a separate facility, etc.) (20 U.S.C. §1414(d)(1)(A)(i)(V)).
Accommodations	An IEP outlines the accommodations that the student will receive, such as during testing (20 U.S.C. §1414(d)(1)(A)(i)(VI)). Common accommodations listed on an IEP include: • Tests given in a small-group setting, in a quiet room free from distractions • Extra time to complete assignments and tests • Tests read aloud • Instructions repeated
Discipline	Students who qualify, or should qualify, for special education are afforded additional due process protections when facing disciplinary action, including suspensions and expulsions (20 U.S.C. §1415(k)).

such as difficulty paying attention to the teacher during academic instruction, blurting out answers without waiting for the teacher to call on the student, poor performance on tests and quizzes, problems with peer interactions resulting in disciplinary action and trouble completing and turning in homework assignments—should qualify for services.

Table 9.3 Important Deadlines for Evaluating Students for Special Education under Federal Law

Action Taken	Relevant Deadline
Parent requests an evaluation in writing	School must initiate or refuse to conduct an evaluation and document their decision in writing. The amount of time the school has to do so varies by state.[a]
Parent signs permission for an evaluation to begin	School has no more than 60 days to complete the evaluation and convene a team to review it (20 USC §1414(a)(1)(C)).
Child found to qualify for special education and related services following completion of the evaluation and meeting of the team	School has no more than 30 days from the date the evaluation is completed and signed to complete and implement the Individualized Education Program (When IEPs Must be in Effect, 34 C.F.R. §300.323(c)).

Note: [a] There is a substantial amount of variance from state to state. For example, in Massachusetts, the school must respond within five days (603 Mass. Code Regs. 28.04(1)(a)). In Ohio, the school has 30 days. *Procedures and Guidance for Ohio Educational Agencies Serving Children with Disabilities: Evaluation 6.2 Request and Referral for Initial Evaluation* (October 2009).

However, a student with ADHD whose symptoms are generally well controlled with medication and other treatment, who is receiving good grades, and who is able to develop and maintain good relationships with peers and adults may have difficulty showing that the condition has an adverse effect on educational performance and might not need specially designed instruction. Nonetheless, such a student might benefit from and qualify for reasonable accommodations under a 504 Plan, discussed later in the chapter.

Further complicating matters for those trying to understand the special education framework is that often there is not a direct match between a healthcare provider's diagnosis and the categories of qualifying disabilities. For example, there is no medical diagnosis equivalent to "emotional disturbance." A child with a variety of mental health diagnoses, including anxiety or schizophrenia, might qualify for special education and related services under the broad category of "emotional disturbance."

Just as a healthcare provider does not make an "educational diagnosis," educators should not make medical diagnoses or demand that their students take medication. Educators can encourage a family to have a child evaluated medically for certain medical conditions, the symptoms of which manifest in the classroom, such as ADHD. However, it is not appropriate for an educator to tell a parent that a child "has ADHD and needs to be on medication" or "can't return to school until she is medicated." Medical diagnoses can be made only by a healthcare provider, and decisions about medication should be discussed among healthcare providers, parents, and, depending on age, the child in question.

Finally, no medical diagnosis is required for a child to qualify for special education and related services. For example, a student with a learning disability may be identified with that disability through the school's evaluation process; the first time a pediatrician might learn of the condition is at an office visit after an IEP is in place.

Challenges in Ensuring that Students Are Identified for Special Education

Although the IDEA provides clear guidelines for identifying students who qualify for special education, in practice, parents, schools and communities face many challenges in implementing the law. Although the academic literature has focused mainly on the issue of overidentification, some scholars have addressed concerns of underidentification or delay in identification for a number of groups of students, including kindergarten-age students,[29] students with cognitive disability/mental retardation,[30] students with emotional disturbance,[31] students with autism,[32] and English language learners.[33] Others note that racial and ethnic disparities—both over- and under-identification affecting students of all races and ethnicities—are complex and can vary greatly by location, type of disability and age of the student.[34]

As already discussed, for students with disabilities, the first step toward receiving special education is qualifying under at least one of the disability categories listed in Appendix 9.1 after having been evaluated through a multidisciplinary, multifaceted evaluation. In practice, many low-income families face difficult hurdles to getting their children evaluated. For them, a process that is supposed to take no more than three to four months can take many more months and even years longer. Some of the most commonly experienced barriers to evaluation are listed here.

Barriers Preventing Some Students with Disabilities from Being Evaluated

- Parents make request for evaluation verbally, rather than in writing.
- School psychologists are overwhelmed with requests for evaluations and are not adequately staffed to meet the need.
- Students with "invisible" disabilities (such as ADHD) may be written off by school staff as "lazy," "bad" or "apathetic."
- Children from low-income families experiencing housing instability may attend a different school each year or switch schools midyear, making it more difficult for an evaluation to be completed or for school staff to get to know the child.
- School staff may resist "labeling" a child, in part due to concern over history of overidentification of children of color and children living in poverty.
- If the parent of a child with a suspected disability had a negative experience in school, he or she may not feel comfortable or skilled at advocating for the child.
- If the parent of a child with a suspected disability has limited English proficiency, he or she may feel intimidated by or excluded from school referral systems.
- If the child is involved in the foster care system, there may be confusion over who is legally authorized to request an evaluation. This problem is magnified if the child moves frequently from one foster care placement and/or school district to another.

Questions for Discussion

1. What are some negative outcomes for students with disabilities who do not receive adequate support in school?

2. Are there any reasons a parent might choose not to share a medical diagnosis with a school district?

3. What role should a lawyer play in detecting education barriers and promoting education opportunities?

4. What are the challenges for schools simultaneously trying to avoid overidentification and underidentification of students with disabilities by economic status, race and gender?

Case for Medical-Legal Partnership

Austin is a six-year-old first-grade student. His mother, Ms. Gordon, shares Austin's first semester progress report with his pediatrician at his well child visit. The report shows poor grades, along with many tardy notices and several absences. Ms. Gordon also shares a letter from his teacher noting that Austin seems to have a lot of trouble paying attention. The teacher is recommending that the pediatrician evaluate Austin for ADHD. Verbally, she has encouraged Ms. Gordon to get him on medication to help him settle down.

Questions for Discussion

1. Might Austin qualify for special education?
2. How might the pediatrician handle the teacher's request that the child be evaluated for ADHD and prescribed medication?
3. How might the MLP lawyer assist Ms. Gordon in advocating for Austin in his school?

Accommodations in Schools: Section 504

Children and youth with chronic diseases and disabling conditions often need educationally-related services and reasonable accommodations to participate fully in school. Section 504 of the Rehabilitation Act of 1973 (Section 504) provides legal justification for related services and reasonable accommodations. It prohibits any discrimination based on disability within federal and federally assisted programs, like public schools. It seeks to ensure that students have an "equal opportunity to obtain the same result, to gain the same benefit, or to reach the same level of achievement, in the most integrated setting appropriate to the person's needs."[35]

Regulations promulgated by the U.S. Department of Education have broadly defined the persons covered by this Act, as well as the services that are to be provided. According to Section 504, all children must be provided with an appropriate education that "could consist of education in regular classes, education in regular classes with the use of supplementary services, or special educational and related services."[36] Psychological testing and evaluation, counseling, physical and occupational therapy, medical services, speech pathology, audiology and orientation mobility instruction are listed among the types of "developmental, corrective, and ... support services" that may be provided to qualified persons (34 C.F.R § 104).

Although Section 504 protects any child who qualifies for special education under IDEA, it also covers a broader range of students:[37] those who have, are regarded as having or have a prior record of having a physical or mental impairment that substantially limits one or more major life activities.[38] For children with disabilities and/or chronic diseases who do not qualify under IDEA but who need modifications and accommodations to be successful in their school experiences, Section 504 may apply. Section 504 provides that children with chronic diseases and disabling conditions are entitled to appropriate modifications within their educational program to accommodate their special needs, regardless of whether their classroom placement is considered regular education or special education. Table 9.4 lists some of the key differences between IDEA and Section 504.

Although some school systems develop flexible, function-oriented 504 or reasonable accommodation plans for students based on their needs, others are reluctant to make modifications and provide few services. Sometimes these school districts do not realize

Table 9.4 Some Key Differences between IDEA and Section 504

	IDEA	Section 504
Purpose	Provide free and appropriate public education	Prevent discrimination
Procedural safeguards	Explicit; parental notice, consent, timelines for evaluation, determination, implementation; right to an independent educational evaluation at public expense	Less defined; parental input and consent not required; no timelines; no provision regarding independent evaluation
Services	Specialized instruction, therapies and services	Reasonable adaptations and accommodations
Definition of disability	Narrower; 1 of 13 specific categories	Broader; wide group of students with physical or mental disabilities substantially limiting a major life function
Funding to implement services?	Yes	No
Placement	Provides "stay-put" provision until all proceedings are resolved; Change in placement requires 10-day notice to parent/guardian	No "stay-put" provision; notice required, but does not have to happen before change of placement
Dispute resolution	Each state must have procedures in place to address IDEA-related disputes and conflicts between parents/guardians and schools	Impartial hearing, parent participation and legal counsel permitted; however, states have discretion about all other details (for example, whether their IDEA hearing officers hear 504 issues)
	A parent/guardian can request mediation, file a complaint for investigation or file a complaint requesting a due process hearing	A complaint should be filed with the school's or district's Section 504 compliance officer, or with the Office for Civil Rights, which conducts compliance reviews and complaint investigations
	Enforced by U.S. Dept. of Education, Office of Special Education	Enforced by U.S. Dept. of Education, Office for Civil Rights

that children and youth with chronic or disabling medical conditions who function well in the standard classroom still need consideration for related services. For example, a school serving a child with severe food allergies should plan where life-saving anaphylaxis will be stored, where the students will eat lunches and snacks, whether allergens will be permitted on school premises (and if so, where) and how teachers, nurses and other school personnel will be trained to recognize food allergy symptoms. Issues of classroom modifications, curriculum adaptations, and training for and access to medications are common subjects of 504 plans.

A pediatrician or nurse can play a meaningful role here. With the parent's permission, he or she can serve as a referral source, document the child's needs in the medical records, or draft a letter or make a call to the school describing the child's conditions, how it affects his or her daily functioning, and what accommodations and/or services from which the child might benefit. He or she also can refer the child to a healthcare specialist if further medical evaluation will provide needed information or clarification.

The primary challenges are twofold: schools are not as familiar with 504 as they are with the IDEA, and the procedural provisions of 504 are not explicit, offering schools little guidance on how to proceed. It will be up to the parent or guardian and the child's healthcare provider to make a case for qualification and the appropriate accommodations and/or services.

Questions for Discussion

1. In what instances can students with disabilities or chronic diseases qualify for specialized instruction, related services and reasonable accommodations?

2. If a student misses many school days due to a disability or chronic disease, what remedies might a school offer?

3. What can parents and healthcare providers do to ensure that children with chronic diseases receive appropriate in-school services and/or reasonable accommodations? How can an MLP lawyer help?

Case for Medical-Legal Partnership

Josie is an 11-year-old student in the fifth grade. She has sickle cell anemia, a genetic disorder that causes her red blood cells to be shaped like crescents, or sickles. As a result, she has many health problems. She suffers frequent episodes of severe pain. She had a stroke and has mild learning impairments. Josie has missed many days of school due to frequent hospitalizations and is behind on her school work. She is often tired and needs to carry a water bottle to stay hydrated, but the school has told her that students may not carry drinks. She has been evaluated for special education by her school district but has been found ineligible. The principal says that her problems are "medical," and that the school is not required to offer services to her.

Questions for Discussion

1. Is Josie eligible for an IEP? Are there other mechanisms for her to receive supports? If so, what kinds of services might she benefit from?

2. What might the long-term consequences be for Josie if she does not receive services?

3. How might Josie's healthcare provider advocate for her? How might medical-legal partners work together to ensure that her needs are met and she has access to appropriate educational services?

Best Practices and Advocacy Strategies in Medical-Legal Partnership

There are many ways healthcare providers can integrate school-related advocacy into their clinical practice. Following are two examples of instruments that one MLP, the Community Advocacy Program, created to make such integration easier for clinicians in the pediatric practice at the MetroHealth System in Cleveland, Ohio.

Inspired by gestational calculators used to estimate a pregnant woman's due date, this special education calculator (see Figure 9.1) illustrates the steps and relevant timelines for requesting an evaluation. Healthcare providers can use this tool in the exam room with patient-families to help describe the evaluation process. Together, healthcare providers and patient-families can learn about the process and the timeline, determine whether the timeline has been violated and evaluate the remedies that exist.

Figure 9.1 Karody Special Education Calculator

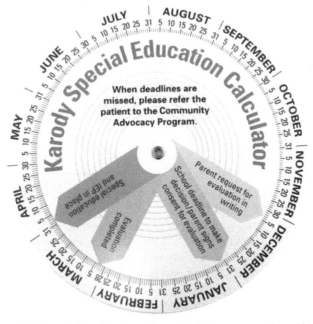

The Karody Special Education Calculator was developed by
Lucas Caldwell-McMillan, J.D., and Vijender Karody, M.D.,
and is the copyrighted property of The Legal Aid Society of Cleveland

To trigger many of the relevant timelines and protections under IDEA, a parent or guardian's request for an evaluation should be in writing. The parent should keep a copy for the family's own records, in the event that the original is misplaced by the school. Through use of a letter template in the electronic medical record, healthcare providers can quickly and easily assist parents in creating a written request for an evaluation. The letter should be saved as a part of the child's medical record. Request for Evaluation (Parent or Guardian) provides an example of a letter.

Request for Evaluation (Parent or Guardian)

January 3, 2011

Sharon Lance
Principal
Oakridge School

RE: **Request for Evaluation**
   Jane Smith (DOB 1/1/2003), Grade 2

Dear Principal Lance,

My child, Jane Smith, goes to your school. Jane is having problems in school, and she needs help.

I want the school to conduct an evaluation of Jane to see if she needs special education.

Jane is having difficulty with:

- reading
- writing
- speech-language
- attention, concentration and focus
- feeling anxious about going to school

I look forward to your written response to this request.
Sincerely,
/John Smith/
Parent of Jane Smith …

Healthcare providers who work with a significant population of children with chronic medical conditions may find it beneficial to hold an open meeting or training at the beginning of each school year, with the goal of teaching parents about the necessary steps to obtain reasonable accommodations. Such an initiative can empower families to communicate proactively with the school, while reducing the amount of time providers need to advocate with schools on behalf of individual patients. It also is helpful for providers to have standardized forms and/or letters for patient-families to submit to schools for assistance with 504 plans and reasonable accommodations. Request for Reasonable Accommodations (Healthcare Provider) illustrates a sample letter from a healthcare provider.

Request for Reasonable Accommodations (Healthcare Provider)

Re: Michael Adams, 6/23/10

To Whom It May Concern:

Michael Adams is followed by the Pediatric Hematology Program at City Medical Center. Michael has been diagnosed with sickle cell anemia, an inherited disorder of the red blood cell. Children with this diagnosis are at a high risk for serious infection, pain and pulmonary compromise.

It is crucial that all children with sickle cell anemia remain hydrated. They need to be allowed to drink fluids throughout the day, especially when it is warm outside or if the child is physically active. The child should constantly carry a water bottle and have easy access to the bathroom facilities throughout the day. The child should be appropriately dressed when going outside. Children with sickle cell disease also require door-to-door transportation to avoid getting too hot or cold. Prolonged exposure to the cold should be avoided (i.e., long wait outdoors, swimming in an unheated pool, etc.). Michael may participate in physical activities and field trips, but should be allowed to rest periodically at his discretion.

It is possible that children with sickle cell anemia will have multiple absences from school due to emergency department visits, hospitalizations and clinic visits. During this time, the school should be able to collect the child's academic assignments so they may work on them at home. All children with this disease require an extra set of textbooks for this purpose. Also, all children with sickle cell anemia are entitled to tutoring at home during periods of illness to ensure they do not fall behind in their studies.

A child with sickle cell anemia needs immediate medical attention if he has a fever above 101 degrees F, any neurological changes, respiratory distress or lethargy. A member of the hematology staff can always be reached through the answering service at 617.555.XXXX.

If you have any questions or concerns, please feel free to contact the Pediatric Hematology Division at 617.555.YYYY.

Sincerely,
The Staff of the Division of Hematology,
City Medical Center

From Practice to Policy

Improving the referral for evaluation system is one low-tech policy initiative that can be undertaken by medical and legal partners. As described, many low-income children face delays in being evaluated for special education; these delays can be minimized by healthcare provider intervention on a patient-by-patient basis. However, in trying to improve the referral system upstream, medical and legal providers can work with a local school districts or state educational agencies to create a uniform referral form for use within schools.

Currently, many schools do not have a dedicated form for a parent to request an evaluation. Medical and legal providers can meet with district special education directors to discuss the problems related to delayed evaluation, as presented in the clinical setting. Meeting with district staff could result in the implementation of such a form on a wide scale. Meeting with state officials could prompt the state educational agency to require use of the form throughout the state, to adopt the form as a "model" that districts can elect to use and/or to mandate use of the form by districts found to be out of compliance with evaluation or "child find" requirements. Improving the referral process upstream would help identify children with disabilities in a timely fashion. It also would reduce the need for patient-by-patient interventions by healthcare and legal service providers, empower parents to secure help for their children and make an adversarial climate less likely.

School Discipline

School discipline is necessary to ensure that students can learn. Respectful student-teacher relationships and reasonable rules ensuring safety of staff and students create an environment conducive to learning. However, under the current trend of zero tolerance, there is concern that school discipline may present a barrier to educational attainment for some students. Zero-tolerance policies are designed to punish *any* infraction of a school rule, without providing flexibility for administrators or consideration of extenuating circumstances. Therefore, these policies sometimes result in excluding students from school for long periods or permanently for behavior that does not warrant such extreme consequences. This response may cause negative mental health implications such as alienation, anxiety, rejection and the breaking of healthy adult bonds.[39]

Additionally, school discipline impacts certain groups more severely than others. According to the U.S. Department of Education's Office of Civil Rights, African American students are suspended at approximately 3 times the rate and expelled at 3.5 times the rate of Caucasian students, and Latino students are suspended at 1.5 times the rate and expelled at 2 times the rate of white students.[40] In addition, students who have mental and emotional disabilities, whether undiagnosed or those with an IEP, may be mislabeled as having a behavioral problem or as simply disruptive.[41] Studies have found that such children are at a higher risk of dropping out, suspension and expulsion;[42] children with IEPs are significantly more likely to be suspended or expelled than their nondisabled peers.[43]

Zero-Tolerance Policies and the School-to-Prison Pipeline

Zero-tolerance policies were developed in the 1980s as part of an attempt to reduce violence and drug use in public schools.[44] They call for little (if any) flexibility in punishment for certain infractions, especially violent offenses and those involving illegal substances, alcohol or weapons. Often, mitigating factors, including the severity or the context of the offense, are not taken into account.[45] Long-term suspensions (exclusions from school of more than 10 days) and expulsions (permanent exclusion) are not uncommon.

The Southern Poverty Law Center reported that between 1974 and 2006, suspension and expulsion rates (as measured by the proportion of the student population having experienced one of the two) — increased from 3.7 percent to 7.1 percent.[46] With stricter disciplinary policies, a significant number of students lose time in school. Approximately 46 percent of public schools reported imposing serious disciplinary action in the 2003–2004 school year. Seventy-four percent of actions reported were suspensions lasting five days or more; 5 percent were removals with no services; and 21 percent were transfers to specialized schools.[47] Dropping out of school is one consequence associated with zero tolerance. Suspension is a strong predictor for dropout; nationally over 30 percent of high school sophomores who drop out have been suspended.[48] Likewise, children who have been suspended are more likely to engage in criminal activity and end up incarcerated in adulthood.[49] Dropout is a very significant factor in predicting economic and occupational status in adulthood and health status throughout the entire life cycle.[50]

An increase in referrals to the juvenile justice system for infractions that were once handled by schools, known as the school-to-prison pipeline, is a further consequence. Here students (many of whom have disabilities) are pushed out of school and into the juvenile justice system through a combination of ineffective educational supports and harsh disciplinary policies. In fact, sometimes the pathway from school to the courts is direct, when overwhelmed and/or frustrated teachers and administrators turn students over to law enforcement authorities for acts committed in the school building.[51] Figure 9.2 illustrates the long-term consequences of harsh disciplinary policies.

The practice of zero tolerance is also questioned for its effectiveness. Authors of a 2006 report by the American Psychological Association reviewed 10 years of data and research to determine the efficacy of zero-tolerance approaches. They found that zero tolerance had not made schools safer, and among schools implementing such policies, discipline rates vary widely.[52] Some believe that zero tolerance has in fact *increased* the rate of suspension and expulsion without making an impact on school safety.

Federal Laws Pertaining to School Discipline

Federal guidance on school discipline law falls into two primary categories: case law establishing procedural due process protections for students threatened with suspension or expulsion, and a federal statute mandating one-year expulsion for students bringing a gun to school. The nature and severity of punishments for all other student infractions is left to the discretion of individual states.

Figure 9.2 Long-Term Consequences of Harsh School Discipline

Inadequate Assistance for Special Education

↓

Zero Tolerance Policies

↓

Suspension/Expulsion

↓

Lack of Economic Opportunities

↓

Criminal Activity

↓

Imprisonment

Procedural Due Process

In its 1975 decision in the case of *Goss v. Lopez* (419 U.S. 565), the Supreme Court determined that students facing exclusion from school should be provided with due process as required by the Fourteenth Amendment. The Court found that due process in the context of school exclusions includes oral or written notice of the charges leading to the exclusion, an explanation of the evidence if the student denies the charge, and an opportunity to be heard.[53]

The Court stopped short of requiring a formal hearing for short-term suspensions and did not guarantee the accused student the right to counsel or the right to cross-examine witnesses. The Court did state that normally the hearing shall precede suspension. However, it noted that in certain cases where the student poses "a continuing danger to persons or property or an ongoing threat of disrupting the academic process [the student] may be immediately removed from school. In such cases, the necessary notice and rudimentary hearing should follow as soon as practicable."[54]

The Court articulated the balance between school discipline and students' rights as follows:

> We do not believe that school authorities must be totally free from notice and hearing requirements if their schools are to operate with acceptable efficiency. Students facing temporary suspension have interests qualifying for protection of the Due Process Clause, and due process requires, in connection with a suspension of 10 days or less, that the student be given oral or written notice of the charges against him and, if he denies them, an explanation of the evidence the authorities have and an opportunity to present his side of the story. The Clause requires at least these rudimentary precautions against unfair or mistaken findings of misconduct and arbitrary exclusion from school.[55]

It is important to note that the Court in *Goss* addressed only suspensions lasting for 10 days or less. The Court acknowledged that "longer suspensions or expulsions ... may require more formal procedures."[56] The Court did not elaborate on what these formal procedures might be in practice, and no Supreme Court case has addressed the issue since this time, although lower courts have provided guidance in some jurisdictions.

Table 9.5 Key Terms and Procedures of IDEA on Student Discipline

10-Day Rule	Suspension of not more than 10 consecutive (or cumulative, if the offenses form a pattern) school days is not permitted, without employing special protections (Authority of School Personnel, 34 C.F.R §300.530(b)).
Manifestation Determination (MD)	Suspension of more than 10 days or a change in placement requires a school to conduct a manifestation determination. Did the student's actions result from, or have a "direct and substantial relationship to" his or her disability? Did the student's conduct result from the school's failure to implement the student's IEP? If the IEP team finds that the student's behavior was a manifestation of his or her disability, the school may not suspend the student (34 C.F.R. §§300.530(e) and (f)).
Continuation of Services	If the student's behavior is determined not to be a manifestation of his or her disability, the district still is required to provide educational services to the student. This may be in an interim alternative educational setting, such as in the home or an in-school suspension (34 C.F.R. §300.530(d)(i)).
Functional Behavioral Assessment	Students with disabilities who are suspended or whose placement is otherwise changed for 10 or more consecutive days must receive a functional behavioral assessment (FBA) (34 C.F.R. §§300.530 (d)(ii) and (f)(i)). The purpose of an FBA is to identify antecedents to target behaviors, target behaviors and consequences for these behaviors.
Behavior Intervention Plan	A school must draft and implement a behavior intervention plan based on the results of the FBA (34 C.F.R. §§300.530 (d)(ii) and (f)(i)).
45-Day Assessment	School personnel may place a student in an interim alternative educational setting for not more than 45 days, without regard to the results of the MD, if while at school, on school premises or at a school function the student: • Carries or possesses a weapon at school; • Knowingly possesses or uses illegal drugs, or sells or solicits the sale of drugs; or • Inflicts serious bodily injury on another person. (34 C.F.R. §300.530(g))

Special Protection for Students with Disabilities in Disciplinary Matters

Students with disabilities face higher rates of school discipline than their nondisabled peers. For example, of the 64,173 exclusions in Massachusetts during the 2006–2007 school year, 33 percent involved general education students and 67 percent involved special education students.[57] These data do not account for the discipline imposed on many students with unidentified disabilities.

Fortunately, the IDEA requires that school officials follow special procedures when disciplining students with disabilities (defined as students who have IEPs). Table 9.5 outlines the procedures required under IDEA.

The protections outlined in Table 9.5 apply not only to students with an IEP but also in cases in which the school knew or had reason to believe the student had a disability. A school is deemed to have such knowledge if the parent has expressed in writing to a teacher, principal or other administrator that the student needs special education; if the parent requested an evaluation; or if the teacher or other district personnel expressed specific concerns about a pattern of behavior displayed by the student.[58] For this reason, it is very important that parents and guardians put any concerns about their children in writing.

Healthcare providers can assist families by inquiring about school discipline issues and by informing them about protections that exist and how to access them. When caring for children with identified disabilities, providers should encourage parents to keep detailed records of any incidents. If a child has been disciplined repeatedly, a provider can submit evidence of disability at a manifestation hearing or may take the less formal approach of calling a school administrator directly.

State Laws Pertaining to School Discipline

In the absence of significant federal guidance regarding discipline of students who do not have disabilities, states have created their own disciplinary laws, which vary widely. In addition, many have granted considerable latitude to individual school districts in establishing disciplinary policies and procedures. Massachusetts is one example of a state that has enacted several statutes pertaining to school discipline. One statute requires a hearing prior to permanent exclusion (Mass. Gen. Laws, Ch. 76 § 17). Another requires that, on request, school committees issue a written statement describing the reason for denial of admission or exclusion of a public school student (Ch. 76 § 16). Massachusetts delegates most of the remaining school discipline authority to school districts.

Certain criminal allegations give Massachusetts school districts the authority to impose harsh measures on students. For example, districts are authorized to expel students for certain violations, including drug possession and violent behavior (Ch. 76 § 16). They also are authorized to suspend a student for an indeterminate period of time if the student has been charged with a felony or felony delinquency (Ch. 71 § 37H 1/2). The latter provision has resulted in a number of very long-term exclusions of students whose responsibility for a crime (often committed off school grounds) has not even been established.

Case for Medical-Legal Partnership

Jeffrey is a nine-year-old boy in the third grade. Up until this year, he had been doing well in school. When his dad brings him in for his annual check-up, his pediatrician asks how things are going in school. Jeffrey states, "School is stupid and I hate it." His dad, Mr. Packer, sighs and explains that although Jeffrey has always been "a little behind" in reading, this year he is really struggling. He seems to know the words but has difficulty comprehending what he has read. This has affected his grades in all subjects. His dad states, "He is a whiz at math — he can do 20 problems and get them all correct. But with the word problems … he's not doing so well." Jeffrey also has been getting into trouble for talking and occasionally getting into fights with other students during Language Arts. He has been suspended on three separate occasions.

Mr. Packer said that he's talked with Jeffrey's teachers and principal about whether there is extra help available for his son. He was told that there is a waiting list for testing and that kids with a lot more problems than Jeffrey are ahead on the list. The school advised Mr. Packer to ask again next year and to read to Jeffrey at home in the meantime.

Questions for Discussion

1. Is Jeffrey currently eligible to receive any special protections from repeated school discipline?

2. What role can a pediatrician play with regard to protecting Jeffrey from further school discipline?

3. Describe the health implications if Jeffrey's learning and discipline problems are not addressed in a timely manner.

Protections for Homeless Students

Homeless children are at an increased risk for adverse health and educational outcomes. Children experiencing homelessness are at higher risk than their housed peers for malnutrition, poor growth, developmental delay, infectious disease, asthma, lead poisoning and mental health problems. With respect to education, homeless students may have higher rates of school absence then their peers and also score lower on standardized academic assessments.[59] Healthcare providers play an important role in identifying homeless children and linking their families to services, including legal assistance.

With the passing of the McKinney-Vento Homeless Assistance Act, Congress created a framework which requires all public schools to provide homeless children with "equal access" to the free appropriate public education as is provided to all students (42 U.S.C. § 11431(1)). This law provides several important protections designed to stabilize the educational experience for children who are homeless.

McKinney-Vento Homeless Assistance Act

The McKinney-Vento Homeless Assistance Act provides special rights, protections and services for students who are homeless (see Figure 9.3). The key goals of McKinney-Vento are to identify students who are homeless, increase their ability to attend school and improve academic outcomes.

Figure 9.3 Purposes of the McKinney-Vento Homeless Assistance Act

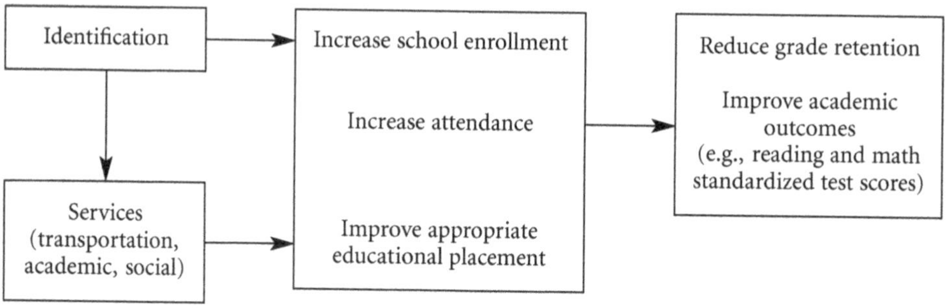

Source: Mary Cunningham, Robin Harwood, Sam Hall, "Residential Instability and the McKinney-Vento Homeless Children and Education Program: What We Know, Plus Gaps in Research," *Urban Institute* (2010): 1–13.

Homelessness is commonly thought to be limited to individuals living on the streets and in homeless shelters. In reality, homelessness is a much more multifaceted phenomenon, especially for homeless families with school-age children. Recognizing these complexities, McKinney-Vento uses a broad definition to identify students who are homeless, as illustrated in Students Considered Homeless under McKinney-Vento.

Students Considered Homeless under McKinney-Vento

Generally, "individuals who lack a fixed, regular, and adequate nighttime residence" are considered homeless under McKinney-Vento (42 U.S.C. § 11434a(2)(A)). This definition includes:

- Students living in emergency or transitional shelters (§ 11434a(2)(B)(i))
- Students living on the streets (§ 11434a(2)(B)(iii))
- Students sharing housing with others (including relatives) due to eviction, economic hardship, or similar situations (§ 11434a(2)(B)(i))
- Students living in motels or hotels (§ 11434a(2)(B)(i))
- Students who are considered "unaccompanied youth" (§ 11434a(6)) (e.g., students not living with a parent or other adult legal guardian, including children who have run away from home or who have been put out of their home by their parents or guardians)
- Students who are awaiting foster care placement (§ 11434a(2)(B)(i))

Once students are identified as homeless under McKinney-Vento, they are entitled to several important legal protections designed to improve academic stability. These include:

- The right to remain enrolled at the school they were attending when they became homeless ("school of origin"; 42 U.S.C. § 11432(g)(3)(G)) for the remainder of the academic year, even if they no longer live in the school's attendance boundaries (§ 11432(g)(3)(A)(i)).
- The right to receive transportation services so that they can remain in their school of origin for the remainder of the academic year (§ 11432(e)(3)(E)(i)(III)).
- The right to enroll in the school where they are residing while homeless, if they choose (§ 11432(g)(3)(A)(ii)).
- The right to enroll immediately in school, even if they do not have documents normally required for enrollment, such as previous school records, medical or immunization records, proof of residency, birth certificate, proof of guardianship or other documents (§ 11432(g)(3)(C)(i)).

Under this law, each public school district must identify a staff member who will serve as the district's McKinney-Vento liaison (§ 11432(g)(1)(J)(ii)). Larger school districts often have a special program or office to assist homeless students. For example, the Boston Public School District serves homeless students through the Homeless Student Initiative; in Cleveland, OH, the Cleveland Municipal School District serves homeless students through a program called Project ACT. Often, referring a student to these formal programs will result in the student receiving services to which he or she is entitled.

However, in some smaller school districts and in districts with less experience with homeless students, school district staff may be completely unfamiliar with McKinney-Vento and the rights afforded through it. For example, anecdotal evidence from the MLPs indicates that it is not uncommon for a school district staff member designated as the McKinney-Vento liaison to have no idea that he or she is the liaison or the responsibilities of that role.

McKinney-Vento provides homeless students with important tools to maintain some educational stability in the face of often chaotic living situations. Although these legal rights are valuable to homeless students, a number of important policy-related questions remain unanswered. How many homeless students are served by McKinney-Vento each year? How many homeless students and families are unaware of the protections available under McKinney-Vento? What are the best practices for school districts in identifying and serving homeless students?[60] MLPs are well positioned to improve services to homeless students. MLPs have an important opportunity to educate parents and advocate for individual homeless students with school districts. They also have an important policy voice and can play a critical role in improving the educational services provided to homeless students by local school districts.

Questions for Discussion

1. What are barriers to schools in identifying homeless students?
2. What can healthcare providers do to identify which of their patients are homeless?
3. What negative impacts can homelessness have on child health?
4. Why is it important for children to stay in the same school building for the entire academic year?
5. What barriers might prevent parents/guardians of homeless students from accessing help?

Case for Medical-Legal Partnership

Takesha is a 17-year-old senior who is doing well in high school and looking forward to graduating at the end of the school year. Over the summer, she and her family moved into a new apartment. Takesha's asthma started acting up, and by the end of September, she had an asthma exacerbation so severe that she had to stay in the hospital for three days. During this hospitalization, a health inspector found environmental hazards, including mold, which needed to be fixed by the landlord. While Takesha's mom worked with the landlord to fix the poor conditions in the apartment or to transfer to another housing unit, Takesha went to stay at her grandmother's house, about 10 miles away in another city.

When Takesha comes in for her asthma follow-up appointment, her pediatrician learns that she has been out of school for a week because she didn't have a way to get there from her grandmother's house.

Questions for Discussion

1. What additional information do Takesha's pediatrician and lawyer need to know to help her stay in school?
2. Can Takesha be considered homeless under the McKinney-Vento Act? If so:
   a. Which provisions of McKinney-Vento might be of assistance here?
   b. Who should Takesha's family notify to obtain assistance under McKinney-Vento?
3. Are there other, non-education-related legal issues impacting Takesha's health? What other questions might you ask her and her mother?

Education and Health in Context

The following sections explore the challenges faced by students with ADHD and learning disabilities (LDs). This section demonstrates the strong connections between the health, education and legal needs of students with these conditions, and the ways MLPs effectively ensure that students' needs are met and legal rights are enforced.

Attention Deficit/Hyperactivity Disorder and Learning Disabilities

ADHD and LDs are the medical conditions that most commonly interfere with children's school performance. ADHD and LDs also often co-occur in the same children and may be hard for parents, teachers and even doctors to distinguish. A well-known book on LDs and ADHD is titled *The Misunderstood Child*, and the title is apt. Children with ADHD and LDs are often treated by parents and teachers as though they are merely lazy or bad, and they often come to believe these negative judgments themselves. These misunderstandings also tend to prevent children with ADHD and LD from obtaining the assessments, treatments and accommodations that they need and deserve.

Defining Attention Deficit/Hyperactivity Disorder and Learning Disabilities

Attention Deficit/Hyperactivity Disorder

In the United States, between 5 and 10 percent of school-age children are diagnosed with ADHD, defined as decreased attention span, especially for dull or difficult tasks; increased physical activity or fidgetiness; and increased impulsivity (acting before considering the consequences). By definition, these problems are long-standing (at least six months), are present before age seven, and are severe enough to impair the child's ability to function in school, at home and with peers. A subset of children with ADHD has only inattentiveness (labeled as ADHD-inattentive subtype; previously called attention deficit disorder or ADD); a smaller subset appears to attend adequately but has severe overactivity and impulsiveness.[61]

Although the *Diagnostic and Statistical Manual of the American Psychiatric Association* (DSM-IV) sets forth specific criteria, there is still considerable room for subjectivity in the reports of the child's behavior provided by parents and teachers, and in the clinician's synthesis of those reports with direct observations of the child and other relevant information. Laboratory tests, including blood tests and brain scans, are not helpful. Not surprisingly, there are wide variations in the frequency of the diagnosis, both from region to region and from doctor to doctor. Boys are more likely to be diagnosed with ADHD; girls may be more likely to show the inattentive subtype and are more likely to remain undiagnosed because their behavior may not be obtrusive. Experts agree that ADHD is both over- and under-diagnosed. Poverty and minority status are not consistently linked to either over- or under-diagnosis.[62] Figure 9.4 shows the distribution of diagnosed cases of ADHD in the United States.

In addition to the core features of inattentiveness, hyperactivity and impulsivity, many children with ADHD have problems with oppositional and aggressive behaviors, anxiety, depression or various combinations of these traits; nearly half have an associated learning disability, most often for reading (i.e., dyslexia). Low self-esteem is common, especially among those who have experienced years of criticism at home and in school and often rejection by peers.[63]

Learning Disabilities

LDs are neurological conditions that interfere with a child's ability to master the skills necessary for academic success in elementary and secondary school. The definition excludes ADHD, emotional disabilities, vision and hearing deficits and general intellectual disability. The IDEA recognizes seven different LDs, including expressive and receptive

Figure 9.4 Percent of Youth Ages 4–17 Ever Diagnosed with ADHD, 2007

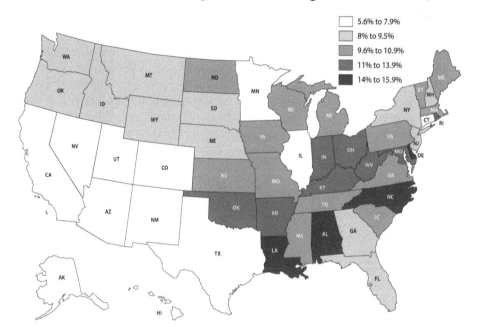

Source: National Survey of Children's Health, 2007, Centers for Disease Control, http://www.cdc.gov/ncb-ddd/adhd/prevalence.html.

language, math reasoning and calculation, written expression, reading comprehension and basic reading. Of these, basic reading accounts for 80 percent of the children who qualify as learning disabled under the IDEA. Approximately 8% to 10% of U.S. children have an LD.[64]

Although the definition of LDs invokes neurological processes, the public educational system has historically taken a different approach. Focusing on the exclusion of general intellectual disability (previously called mental retardation), state laws typically defined LDs as academic achievement that is significantly below general intelligence, also known as a "severe discrepancy" between intellectual ability and academic achievement. Depending on the state, the criteria for "significantly lower" required a gap of 1, 1.5 or 2 standard deviations between the child's scores on an IQ test and on an achievement test measuring a particular academic area, such as reading or math. Accordingly, children being assessed in public schools for possible LD received standardized tests of IQ and academic achievement.[65]

Most experts, however, reject this operational definition of LD on the grounds that many children who score low on IQ tests appear to have the same sorts of difficulty learning as children who score higher (and who thus qualify under the public definition, because their IQ-achievement gaps are sufficiently large). Furthermore, children with learning problems and lower IQ scores benefit from the same interventions as children with higher IQ scores. Nonetheless, many children with lower IQ scores have been excluded from LD services because the gap between their IQ and achievement scores did not meet the arbitrary state standards.[66]

In response to these concerns, the most recent federal regulations regarding the identification of learning disabilities requires that states broaden the ways in which a student may be identified as having a learning disability. Specifically, the regulations require that states:

1. Must not require the use of a severe discrepancy between intellectual ability and achievement for determining whether a child has a specific learning disability;

2. Must permit the use of a process based on the child's response to scientific, research-based intervention; and

3. May permit the use of other alternative research-based procedures for determining whether a child has a specific learning disability. (Specific Learning Disabilities, 34 C.F.R. § 300.307(a))

Despite these good intentions, the regulations have created confusion over what types of procedures must be used to identify a child as having a specific learning disability and sometimes lead to even longer delays in identification of children who desperately need special education and related services.

Etiology of Attention Deficit/Hyperactivity Disorder and Learning Disabilities

Attention Deficit/Hyperactivity Disorder

The causes of ADHD are not completely understood. A tendency to develop the disorder is inherited, with genetics accounting for roughly half of the overall variability. Many factors that may affect brain growth or neurological development are known to be associated with ADHD, including (among others) prenatal exposure to cigarette smoke or cocaine, lead poisoning, severe undernutrition and iron deficiency, brain infections and significant head trauma.[67] In any individual child, however, it is usually impossible to nail down a precise cause or set of causes. "Bad parenting" does not cause ADHD, although parents of children with ADHD often feel badly about their parenting skills.

Learning Disabilities

The causes of LDs are also various and poorly understood. Genetics plays an important role. However, genetics account for about half of the overall pattern (similar to the role of heredity in IQ and in ADHD). Although the precise causes are obscure, studies using various brain imaging techniques and measures of brain electrical activity have documented differences between the brains of children with LDs and those without. Consistent with the concept of neurological differences, many children with LDs also show special strengths, in creativity, for example, or visual-spatial skills.[68] Yet, as illustrated in Figure 9.5, the relationship between genetics and environment is quite complex. Early intervention, therefore, can make a significant difference in mitigating the impact of LD in a patient's life.

Clinical Implications and Treatment

Attention Deficit/Hyperactivity Disorder

By definition, children with untreated ADHD experience some degree of school failure, tense parent-child relationships, and social isolation. As a group, they are at increased risk of adverse long-term outcomes, including school dropout, substance abuse and law breaking. On the other hand, with effective treatment, many thrive socially and academically. By mid-adolescence, the symptoms of physical restlessness and impulsivity often wane, and about half of the children who required medication function well without it. For some, the traits of rapid thinking, high energy and creativity become positive assets

Figure 9.5 Interaction of Biological and Environmental Risk in Reading Failure

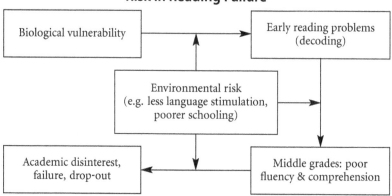

Source: R. Needlman, "Literacy's Cutting Edges," Grand Rounds presented at MetroNorth Medical Center, Cleveland, Ohio, November 12, 2010.

in the work world. For those continuing to struggle, medication is increasingly offered to older teens and adults.

The core symptoms of ADHD respond best to medication, although not all children with this disorder require medication. Moreover, a positive response to medication is not diagnostic of ADHD, in that children without the diagnosis may also become more focused and quiet on the medication. The first-line medications are the stimulants methylphenidate (Ritalin, Concerta, and other brand names) and amphetamine (Adderall and other brand names). These medications work by stimulating areas in the brain responsible for focusing attention and weighing alternatives. Behavior therapy (strategically applied rewards and punishments) is useful to decrease related problems such as oppositional behaviors and the development of low self-esteem and may reduce the need for medication dosage increases. Children with ADHD uniformly benefit from classroom adaptations that decrease distractions, increase adult attention and give prompt feedback for both positive (desired) and negative (undesired) behaviors.[69] Associated psychological problems (such as impaired social skills and learning problems) need to be addressed at the same time. Many alternative and complementary approaches have been suggested, including special diets, herbal medications, biofeedback, acupuncture and others, but so far none have proven to have much value for children with ADHD.[70]

Effective treatment relies on strong working relationships among parents, teachers, doctors and therapists. Medical-legal intervention may be helpful in establishing such re-lationships, or preventing strains in these relationships from undermining the child's treatment and education. It is important to remember that ADHD is a broad diagnosis, encompassing a wide range of impairments as well as strengths in multiple domains, and that treatment involves changes in the child's home, school and peer environment, not simply medication. An individualized approach is therefore critical to success.

Learning Disabilities

Treatments for learning disabilities depend on the particular brain functions that are deficient. For basic reading disability (also called dyslexia), the weak functions are most often those associated with phonological processing—the discrimination and manipulation of speech sounds. (Other problems, such as letter reversals and substitutions appear to be secondary, in most cases, to the phonological weakness.) Treatments for dyslexia therefore focus on extensive practice listening to, producing and manipulating speech sounds. Evidence-based remediation programs (such as Orton-Gillingham and Lindamood-Bell programs) focus on giving children many hours of such practice experiences. By contrast, therapies centered on eye training or the use of colored lenses (for example) have not been shown to be effective.[71]

In addition to educational therapy to treat the underlying cause of dyslexia, children benefit from accommodations that allow them to work around their disability. For example, a child who reads very slowly might be allowed extra time on tests; another might be allowed to audio-record homework assignments, or have required text books read aloud to him. Finally, when children have special skills in other areas (art, for example), they benefit from classes or tutoring to enhance these strengths, allowing them to experience genuine success.

Children with LDs are prone to being misunderstood. They may appear to have attention problems, although not in the subjects they excel in unless they also have ADHD as a related but separate problem. They may develop inappropriate classroom behaviors (clowning, for example) to draw attention away from the fact that they cannot do the work. Often they conclude, along with some less enlightened teachers, that they are simply lazy or stupid; neither of these attitudes is necessarily accurate nor helpful.

Medical-legal consultation can assist children with both ADHD and LDs at several points: to educate parents about their children's rights to an appropriate education; to ensure that children showing academic failure receive prompt, thorough assessments; to assist parents in advocating for appropriate treatment and educational programming for identified ADHD and LDs; and to help parents monitor their child's progress to ensure that educational interventions keep pace with the child's evolving skills and remaining deficits.

Legal Approaches to Support Students with ADHD and LDs

Children with ADHD and LDs face varying degrees of difficulty in the school environment. Services and supports that work well for one child may not be as helpful for another. Nonetheless, schools often use a "one-size-fits-all" approach to educating students with certain disabilities, including ADHD and LDs. Therefore, it is important that parents and professionals seek academic services and supports that are carefully tailored to meet the unique needs of each child. Because severity of symptoms vary dramatically for children with ADHD and LDs and because they are not always well understood, medical-legal advocacy may be critical for ensuring that children receive the supports and services they need to learn.

ADHD and LDs: Eligibility for Special Education

The IDEA authorizes parents and professionals to request a school-based evaluation of a child. A diagnosis is not necessary, although such information might be helpful to the evaluator and the team. If a healthcare provider diagnoses or suspects that a child has ADHD or a LD, he or she can play a critical role in helping the child's parents secure appropriate services at school. The first step may be to assist them in requesting an evaluation from the school to determine whether the child is eligible for special education services. Although the law does not require the request for an evaluation to be in writing,[72] parents are urged to document the request and to keep a record of it. Parents who make a request for an evaluation verbally, but not in writing, risk not being able to enforce the evaluation timelines. Furthermore, with respect to discipline, students not yet identified for special education and related services can receive the protection available to special education students only under certain circumstances. A parent's written request for an evaluation is among the most important of these factors.[73]

MLPs have developed template letters that healthcare providers can share with parents, making it easier for them to make formal requests to the school in a clear and timely manner. Template Letter for Parents to Request an Evaluation illustrates information that might be contained in a letter to school officials seeking an evaluation for a child experiencing school problems that indicate ADHD and LDs.

Template Letter for Parents to Request an Evaluation

Jason and Janet Doe
1234 Main Street
Springfield, KS 01111
(222) 555-5555

October 15, 2010

Principal Mary Barnes
Summit Elementary School
77 Pepperidge Lane
Springfield, OH 00000

RE: Charlie Doe, 1st Grader, DOB 2/2/2004

Dear Principal Barnes,

Our child Charlie Doe attends your school. He is having many problems in school and needs help.

We want the school to conduct an evaluation of Charlie to see if he needs special education.

Specifically, Charlie is having difficulty with:

- reading
- writing
- completing homework
- turning homework in
- staying organized
- paying attention
- concentration and focus
- impulsivity/acting without thinking of the consequences
- getting along with other students
- getting along with adults at school
- following classroom and school rules
- being suspended

We understand that the school must answer this request in writing within 30 calendar days; in this case by November 14, 2010. Our address and phone number are listed at the top of this letter.

We look forward to working with the school to improve our child's education.

Sincerely,
Jason and Janet Doe
Parents

Note that the IDEA does not identify an exact number of days in which a school must respond to a written request for an evaluation. Therefore, the amount of time varies from state to state. In Ohio, the school must respond within 30 days. By contrast, in Massachusetts, a school must respond to a request for an evaluation within five school days; that is, when an official consent form must be mailed to the family's home.

The IEP for a Child with ADHD and/or LDs

An IEP should contain measurable goals and objectives, specially designed services, accommodations and modifications. These should be designed to meet the unique needs of the student. For a student with ADHD and/or LDs, an IEP may include a range of modifications and accommodations that address, for example, ways to reduce distractions in the classroom or provide for extra time for assignments. Figure 9.6 provides sample sections of an IEP for a student with ADHD and LD.

ADHD and LDs: Implications for School Discipline

Because ADHD and LD may affect behavior at school that can trigger school disciplinary policies, school officials should be educated about the connections between the child's behavior and his or her ADHD or LDs. In addition, should there be a disciplinary problem requiring a Manifestation Determination Review, specific documentation from a healthcare provider of the relationship between the child's ADHD or LD and behavior will be critically important in order to prevent overly harsh disciplinary action. An MLP lawyer can help the parents advocate on behalf of the student and ensure that evidence is presented at the MDR.

Reasonable Accommodations: An Alternative to Special Education

As noted earlier, some children with disabilities and/or chronic diseases do not qualify for special education under the IDEA but do need modifications and accommodations in their school program to be successful students. A child with mild ADHD may not qualify for special education. Instead, the school may seek to meet his or her needs with a plan of reasonable accommodations pursuant to Section 504. For an excerpt of a Section 504 plan for a student with ADHD, see Sample Accommodations for Attention Deficit/Hyperactivity Disorder.

Sample Accommodations for Attention Deficit/Hyperactivity Disorder

Major Life Activity Affected: Learning, and Possibly Social Skills

- Provide appropriate staff training about ADHD.
- Place seat in close proximity to teacher; seat away from distractions.
- Provide the child with a peer helper for class work and projects.
- School personnel should understand the child's potential need for excessive movement; giving the child an opportunity to stand and/or move while working.
- School personnel should understand the child's tendency to be inattentive; establish nonverbal cues between teacher and child to get his attention and increase on-task behavior.
- Post classroom rules and review on a regular basis.
- Reinforce the child when he displays appropriate behavior.
- Give a five-minute warning for a change in activity, so the child can begin to disengage from the task.
- Provide supervision during transition times (switching from one activity to another; moving from one class to another).
- Ask the child to restate directions.
- Assist the child with organizational strategies.
- Allow tests to be completed in several short testing sessions.
- Provide extended time to complete assignments and tests.
- Train appropriate nursing staff to properly dispense medication and monitor for side effects (as needed).

Source: Excerpt from Linda Wilmshurt, Alan W. Brue, "Not All Roads Lead to Education Placement: The 411 on 504 Plans," in *A Parent's Guide To Special Education: Insider Advice on How to Navigate the System and Help Your Child* (New York: AMACOM Books, 2005).

Figure 9.6 Sample Sections of an IEP

IEP Individualized Education Program	CHILD'S NAME: Charlie Doe 2/22/2002	1234567

6 MEASURABLE ANNUAL GOALS

NUMBER: 1   AREA: Completing assignments

PRESENT LEVEL OF ACADEMIC ACHIEVEMENT AND FUNCTIONAL PERFORMANCE

The results of Charlie's MFE indicate that during the 2009-2010 academic year, Charlie was able to complete 30% of his classroom assignments during the time allowed during class. Charlie turned in 40% of homework assignments. When Charlie did turn in assignments, they were often not completed.

MEASURABLE ANNUAL GOAL	METHOD(S)
Charlie will fully complete 90% of classroom assignments given and turn in 90% of homework assignments.	b, c, g, i, j

METHOD FOR MEASURING THE CHILD'S PROGRESS TOWARDS ANNUAL GOAL

a. Curriculum Based Assessment   e. Short-Cycle Assessments   i. Work Samples
b. Portfolios   f. Performance Assessments   j. Inventories
c. Observation   g. Checklists   k. Rubrics
d. Anecdotal Records   h. Running Records

Select Display Mode   Objectives ▾

MEASURABLE OBJECTIVES   Add Objective

NUM	OBJECTIVE	
1.1	In the classroom setting, Charlie will repeat back to the teacher or classroom aide the instructions for a given assignment on 9/10 trials with 90% accuracy.	·
1.2	In the classroom setting, Charlie will correctly identify the school supplies needed (e.g., paper, pen, scissors, markers) for a given assignment on 9/10 trials.	·
1.3	When engaging in off-task behavior, Charlie will return to his given assignment following an agreed-upon nonverbal prompt from his teacher or classroom aide on 8/10 trials.	·
1.4	Charlie will turn in completed classroom assignments on 9/10 trials.	·
1.5	Charlie will put all homework assignments in his homework folder with 90% accuracy.	·
1.6	Given up to two verbal prompts by his teacher or classroom aide, Charlie will turn in completed homework assignments with 90% accuracy.	·

METHOD AND FREQUENCY FOR REPORTING THE CHILD'S PROGRESS TO PARENTS

☑ Written report
☐ Email   Reported every 1 weeks
☑ Phone call
☐ Journal entry
☑ The child's progress will be reported to the child's parents each time report cards are issued
☐ Other

IEP Individualized Education Program	CHILD'S NAME: Charlie Doe 2/22/2002	1234567

7 DESCRIPTION(S) OF SPECIALLY DESIGNED SERVICES

TYPE OF SERVICE	GOAL(s) ADDRESSED	PROVIDER TITLE	LOCATION OF SERVICES
SPECIALLY DESIGNED INSTRUCTION:			+
Charlie will receive instruction in a small group setting with an intervention specialist for Language Arts.	1, 2, 4.	Intervention specialist.	Intervention specialist's classroom.
BEGIN: 5/10/2010 END: 5/9/2011	AMOUNT OF TIME: 40 minutes		FREQUENCY: daily
Charlie will receive instruction from an intervention specialist and regular education teacher in the regular education classroom for math, social studies, and science.	1, 2, 3	Intervention specialist and regular education teacher.	Regular education classroom.
BEGIN: 5/10/2010 END: 5/9/2011	AMOUNT OF TIME: 100 minutes		FREQUENCY: daily
ACCOMMODATIONS:			+
1) 7) Charlie will have preferential seating near the teacher; 2) Charlie will be allowed to stand at a raised table instead of his desk to complete classroom work; 3) Charlie and his teacher will choose a non-verbal cue (e.g., shoulder tap) to be used to redirect Charlie as needed; 4) assignments of more than one page will be given to John one page at a time; 5) at least once per hour, Charlie will be allowed to take a break outside the classroom (e.g., get a drink of water, deliver note to office, etc.); 6) classroom teacher and other school staff will give Charlie a "five minute warning" before a transition to a new activity; 7) Charlie's homework folder will be checked at the end of the day by his classroom teacher or aide to ensure all assignments are included;		Classroom teacher, intervention specialist, classroom aide, adult school staff.	Throughout the school environment.
BEGIN: 5/10/2010 END: 5/9/2011	AMOUNT OF TIME:		FREQUENCY: daily
MODIFICATIONS:			+
1) Charlie will take tests, quizzes, and standardized assessments in a small-class environment to reduce distractions; 2) Charlie will be given twice the alloted time to complete tests and quizzes.		Classroom teacher, intervention specialist, classroom aide.	Classroom
BEGIN: Sep 1, 2010 END: Aug 31, 2011	AMOUNT OF TIME		FREQUENCY: daily
SUPPORT FOR SCHOOL PERSONNEL:			+
Principal, classroom teacher, intervention specialist, and classroom aide will participate in 90-minute training on ADHD conducted by pediatrician and psychologist at all-school staff meeting by October 15, 2010.		Principal, classroom teacher, intervention specialist, classroom aide	
BEGIN: Sep 1, 2010 END: Oct 15, 2010	AMOUNT OF TIME: 90 minutes		FREQUENCY:

Standards-Based Individualized Education Plan, (Columbus, Ohio: Ohio Department of Education, Office for Exceptional Children, 2010)

A plan of reasonable accommodations is not a substitute for an IEP, nor is it a first step to take on the road to assisting a student with a disability. However, when a student's condition does not fall within one of the disability categories under IDEA or the disability does not have an adverse effect on a student's educational performance, the condition may still satisfy Section 504 eligibility. A 504 or reasonable accommodations plan should be designed to give the student the help he or she needs to access and participate in the general education curriculum.

Questions for Discussion

1. Compare an IEP and a Section 504 plan. Describe three differences and the implications for a student's learning, behavior and health.

2. What are some disabilities or chronic diseases that are more likely to be served by a 504 plan than by an IEP?

3. Why might some parents prefer a 504 plan to an IEP? What are the advantages of each?

Best Practices and Advocacy Strategies for Medical-Legal Partnership

Gathering and documenting evidence is a key to successfully enforcing patients' rights in the education context, as it is in other venues. Because of the partnership between healthcare providers and lawyers in MLPs, they are uniquely positioned to document and present evidence to advocate for children with disabilities. Following are some strategies for evidence gathering related to ADHD and LDs.

- When children present with symptoms of ADHD or LD, the pediatrician should consider appropriate tools for screening and options for referral to a specialist. Although a primary care pediatrician should be able to conduct initial screening for ADHD and prescribe appropriate treatment, he or she might refer the child to a developmental and behavioral health specialist for a comprehensive evaluation, with documented findings about the nature and severity of the child's condition and implications for his or her education.

- Although a child does not need to have a diagnosis for his or her parents to request a school-based evaluation, including medical information related to the student's condition is preferable. Documentation of how the student's ADHD and/or LDs manifest in school and at home is particularly important in the special education context.

- Similarly, merely being identified as having an LD is not adequate. There are multiple types of learning disabilities—language-based, mathematics-based, sensory-related, nonverbal learning-based. Parents will need to know the specific type of LD to seek interventions and supports. The level and sophistication of this analysis might require the evaluation of a specialist, such as a developmental and behavioral health specialist.

- To ensure that the child's needs are being met as required by the IEP or 504 plan, tracking of school services and supports (type, frequency, etc.) and information about the credentials of each educational specialist working with the student is also important. Parents should seek to receive a log of services and communication about the student's progress on a regular basis (e.g., weekly). This will help an MLP lawyer to demonstrate that a child's rights are not being enforced.

MLPs play an important role in helping children with disabilities, like ADHD or LDs, that impact education. MLPs provide families with a framework for analyzing a child's education and/or school-related difficulties and can empower families to navigate complex school bureaucracies. MLPs also encourage early medical and legal intervention through an easily accessible consultation with or referral to a pediatric specialist combined with a similar engagement with a lawyer.

From Practice to Policy

The American Academy of Pediatrics Committee on School Health produced a policy statement regarding the role of pediatricians in helping schools identify the root causes of behaviors that lead to suspension and expulsion and in advocating for appropriate disciplinary policies. The committee's recommendations are as follows:[74]

1. Schools need to establish relationships with various health and social agencies in their communities so students with disciplinary problems who require assistance are readily referred and communication lines between these agencies and schools are established.

2. Students and their families should be encouraged by school staff members to access healthcare and social services, which can be accomplished if these important topics are included in health education and life skills curricula. It is also recommended that healthcare professionals provide information to children, youth and families on access to healthcare and social services.

3. As part of the school's or district's written policy on disciplinary action, schools should routinely refer a student to his or her primary healthcare professional for an assessment if there is a disciplinary action or a student is at risk of such action. Assistance with obtaining a medical home should occur in circumstances in which a student facing disciplinary action does not yet have one.

4. Pediatricians should advocate for practices and policies at the level of the local school, the school district and the state department of education to protect the safety and promote the health and mental health of children and youth who have committed serious school offenses.

5. Out-of-school placement for suspension or expulsion should be limited to the most egregious circumstances. For in-home suspension or expulsion, the school must be able to demonstrate how attendance at a school site, even in an alternative setting with a low ratio of highly trained staff to students, would be inadequate to prevent a student from causing harm to him or herself or to others.

6. Matters related to safety and supervision should be explored with parents whenever their child is barred from attending school. This includes but is not limited to screening parents by history for presence of household guns.

7. Pediatricians should advocate to the local school district on behalf of the child so that he or she is reintroduced into a supportive and supervised school environment.

8. Pediatricians are encouraged to provide input to or participate as members of school- or district-based multidisciplinary student support teams that can provide disciplined students with a comprehensive assessment and intervention strategies. Schools should help support the participation of pediatricians on multidisciplinary teams by arranging for participation at times and in formats (e.g., telephone) that are conducive to practicing healthcare professionals, by financially supporting time for school physicians or through other logistic considerations.

9. A full assessment for social, medical and mental health problems by a pediatrician (or other providers of care for children and youth) is recommended for all school-referred students who have been suspended or expelled. The evaluation should be designed to ascertain factors that may underlie the student's behaviors and health risks and provide a recommendation on how a child may better adapt to his or her school environment. A full history should be derived from the student, family members and school staff members once consent to exchange information is attained. Management options to consider include appropriate referrals to drug rehabilitation programs, social agencies, mental health professionals and other specialists who may assist with underlying problems. Pediatricians should routinely consider including school staff members as partners in the management of children and youth with school behavior problems, providing that privacy issues are respected as outlined in Health Insurance Portability and Accountability Act of 1996 (Pub. L. No. 104-191) regulations.

Conclusion

Education and health are inextricably connected. A child of ill health might find it difficult, if not impossible, to attend, participate fully in, or excel in school without special assistance or accommodations. Conversely, a child who misses school because of homelessness or other social factors, who performs poorly in school because of a disability, or who is repeatedly disciplined and excluded from school is more likely to be retained in grade and less likely to graduate high school, which in turn impacts economic, occupational and health status in adulthood.

MLPs bring together health and legal professionals to help families secure assistance and protections for their children in school. MLPs are in a unique position to identify a child who is experiencing health-related education problems, describe the connections between the child's education and his or her health, assist the child's family to address the problems, and identify and deploy legal remedies that might assist the child in accessing the help he or she needs to succeed in school.

---

1. The right to a free public education is not found in the U.S. Constitution. However, every state has a provision in its constitution, commonly called the education article, that guarantees some form of free public education, usually through the twelfth grade. This chapter addresses the nexus between law and health in the contexts of elementary and secondary school education; early education and postsecondary education are beyond the scope of this chapter.

2. 20 U.S.C. §§ 1701–1721. The Equal Education Opportunities Act of 1974 provides that no state shall deny equal educational opportunity to an individual on the basis of race, color, sex or national origin.

3. No Child Left Behind Act, Public Law 107-110, 107th Cong, 1st sess. (8 January 2002), sec. 1112 (B;1;iii–iv).

4. C. Chapman, J. Laird and A. KewlRamani, "Trends in High School Dropout and Completion Rates in the United States: 1972–2008," National Center for Education Statistics, Institute of Education Sciences, U.S. Department of Education, 2010, 1–54.

5. Ibid.

6. B. D. Weiss, et al., "Health Status of Illiterate Adults: Relation between Literacy and Health Status among Persons with Low Literacy Skills," *Journal of the American Board of Family Practice*, 5, no. 3 (1992): 257–64.

7. P. H. Wise, "Chronic Illness in Childhood," in *Nelson Textbook of Pediatrics,* 18th ed., eds. Robert Kliegman, et al. (Philadelphia: Saunders, 2007), 189.

8. S. Parker, S. Greer, and B. Zuckerman, "Double Jeopardy: The Impact of Poverty on Early Child Development," *Pediatric Clinician, North America,* 35, no. 6 (1988): 1227–40.

9. Ibid.

10. N. G. Murray, et al., "Coordinated School Health Programs and Academic Achievement: A Systemic Review of the Literature," *Journal of School Health,* 77, no. 9 (2007): 589–600.

11. Weiss et al., "Health Status of Illiterate Adults," 257–64.

12. This chapter focuses on students at the elementary and secondary levels. Different areas of law relate to adult and higher education and private schools.

13. Individuals with Disabilities Education Act, Part C, Sec. 631; 20 U.S.C. § 1431.

14. No Child Left Behind Act, Public Law 107-110, 107th Cong, 1st sess. (8 January 2002).

15. Individuals with Disabilities Education Act, 20 U.S.C. § 1400 et seq.

16. 29 U.S.C. § 701 et seq.

17. McKinney-Vento Homeless Assistance Act, 42 U.S.C. § 11431.

18. *Plyler v. Doe,* 457 U.S. 202 (1982).

19. Title VI of the Civil Rights Act of 1964 prohibits discrimination based on race, color or national origin. In *Lau v. Nichols,* 414 U.S. 563 (1974), the U.S. Supreme Court affirmed the Department of Education memorandum of May 25, 1970, which directed school districts to take steps to help limited-English proficient (LEP) students overcome language barriers and ensure that they can participate meaningfully in the district's educational programs.

20. Carl D. Perkins Vocational and Technical Education Act of 2006, Public Law 109-270, 109th Cong., 2nd sess. (7 January 2005); Title II, Adult Education and Family Literacy of the Workforce Investment Act of 1998, Public Law 105-220, 105th, 2nd sess. (27 January 1998). These laws stipulate that programs of adult education and vocational rehabilitation become salient and singular points of "workforce investment and education activities." They do not pertain to primary or secondary education, and thus are beyond the scope of this chapter.

21. 20 U.S.C. § 1431; regulations at 34 C.F.R § 303.

22. "Proven Benefits of Early Childhood Interventions," Rand Corporation, http://www.rand.org/pubs/research_briefs/RB9145/index1.html (accessed January 17, 2010).

23. Infants and Toddlers with Disabilities, 34 C.F.R § 303.16.

24. Procedures for IFSP Development, Review, and Evaluation, 34 C.F.R. § 303.342.

25. Content of an IFSP, 34 C.F.R § 303.344.

26. "Thirty Years of Progress in Educating Children with Disabilities through IDEA," U.S. Department of Education, http://www2.ed.gov/policy/speced/leg/idea/history30.html (accessed January 12, 2011).

27. "Number and Percentage of Children Served under Individuals with Disabilities Education Act, Part B, by Age Group and State or Jurisdiction: Selected Years, 1990–91 through 2007–08," National Center for Education Statistics, U.S. Department of Education Institute of Education Sciences, http://nces.ed.gov/programs/digest/d09/tables/dt09_052.asp (accessed July 23, 2010).

28. "Table 1-1. Children and Students Served under IDEA, Part B, By Age Group and State: Fall 2008," Data Accountability Center, http://www.ideadata.org/TABLES32ND/AR_1-1.htm (accessed July 23, 2010).

29. C. G. Litty, J. Amos Hatch, "Hurry Up and Wait: Rethinking Special Education Identification in Kindergarten," *Early Childhood Education Journal,* 33, no. 4 (2006): 203–8.

30. S. Cluett Redden, et al., "Head Start Children at Third Grade: Preliminary Special Education Identification and Placement of Children with Emotional, Learning, and Related Disabilities," *Journal of Child and Family Studies,* 8, no. 3 (1999): 285–303.

31. Ibid.

32. S. P. Safran, "Why Youngsters with Autism Remain Underrepresented in Special Education," *Remedial and Special Education,* 29, no. 2 (2008): 90–95.

33. J. F. Samson, N. K. Lesaux. "Language-Minority Learners in Special Education: Rates and Predictors of Identification for Services," *Journal of Learning Disabilities*, 42, no. 2 (2009): 148–62.

34. R. J. Skiba, et al., "Unproven Links: Can Poverty Explain Ethnic Disproportionality in Special Education?" *Journal of Special Education*, 39, no. 3 (2005): 130–44.

35. U.S. Commission on Civil Rights, "Equal Educational Opportunity and Non Discrimination for Students with Disabilities: Federal Enforcement Section 504" (1997): 94.

36. Rehabilitation Act of 1973, Public Law 93-112, 93rd Cong., 1st sess. (3 January 1973), § 504.

37. U.S. Commission on Civil Rights, "Equal Educational Opportunity and Non Discrimination" 94–95.

38. "Physical or mental impairment" means (A) any physiological disorder or condition, cosmetic disfigurement, or anatomical loss affecting one or more of the following body systems: neurological; musculoskeletal; special sense organs; respiratory, including speech organs; cardiovascular; reproductive, digestive, genito-urinary; hemic and lymphatic; skin; and endocrine; or (B) any mental or psychological disorder, such as mental retardation, organic brain syndrome, emotional or mental illness, and specific learning disabilities. 34 C.F.R. § 104.3(j)(2)(i) (2008). "Major life activities" means functions such as caring for one's self, performing manual tasks, walking, seeing, hearing, speaking, breathing, learning, and working. 34 C.F.R. § 104.3(j)(2)(i)(ii).

39. C.R. Reynolds, et al., "Are Zero Tolerance Policies Effective in the Schools?," *American Psychologist*, 63, no. 9 (2008): 856.

40. R. Brownstein, "Pushed Out," *Teaching Tolerance* (Fall 2009).

41. Ibid.

42. Ibid.

43. Ibid.

44. American Psychological Association, "Zero Tolerance Policies Are Not as Effective as Thought in Reducing Violence and Promoting Learning in School, Says APA Task Force," press release, August 9, 2006, http://www.apa.org/releases/zerotolerance.html (accessed January 12, 2011).

45. Reese L. Peterson, Brian Schoonover. "Fact Sheet #3: Zero Tolerance Policies in Schools," Consortium to Prevent School Violence (2008), 2, http://www.preventschoolviolence.org/resources_assets/CPSV-Fact-Sheet-3-Zero-Tolerance.pdf.

46. Brownstein, "Pushed Out."

47. P. Guerino, et al., "Crime, Violence, Discipline and Safety in U.S. Public Schools: Findings from the School Survey on Crime and Safety: 2003–04," National Center for Education Statistics, U.S. Department of Education (2006), 10.

48. Harvard University Advancement Project, "Opportunities Suspended: The Devastating Consequences of Zero Tolerance and School Discipline," Civil Rights Project Harvard University (2000), 11.

49. NAACP Legal Defense and Education Fund, "Dismantling the School to Prison Pipeline," http://www.naacpldf.org/content/pdf/pipeline/Dismantling_the_School_to_Prison_Pipeline.pdf (accessed January 12, 2010).

50. J. H. Tyler and M. Lofstrum, "Finishing High School: Alternative Pathways and Dropout Recovery," *Future of Children*, 19, no. 1 (Spring 2009): 77–103.

51. NAACP Legal Defense and Education Fund, "Dismantling the School to Prison Pipeline."

52. Reynolds et al., "Are Zero Tolerance Policies Effective in the Schools?," 854.

53. "We do not believe that school authorities must be totally free from notice and hearing requirements if schools are to operate with acceptable efficiency. Students facing temporary suspension have interests qualifying for protection of the Due Process Clause, and due process requires, in connection with a suspension of 10 days or less, that the student be given oral or written notice of the charges against him and, if he denies them, an explanation of the evidence the authorities have and an opportunity to present his side of the story. The Clause requires at least these rudimentary precautions against unfair or mistaken findings of misconduct and arbitrary exclusion from school." *Goss v. Lopez*, 419 U.S. 565 (1975).

54. Ibid.

55. Ibid., 581.

56. Ibid., 584.

57. Massachusetts Advocates for Children, "An Act to Help Students Stay in School H.3435," http://www.massadvocates.org/documents/Stay-in-School-Fact-Sheet.pdf (accessed January 12, 2011).

58. Protections for Children Not Determined Eligible for Special Education and Related Services, 34 C.F.R § 300.534(b).

59. M. Cunningham, R. Harwood, S. Hall, "Residential Instability and the McKinney-Vento Homeless Children and Education Program: What We Know, Plus Gaps in Research," Urban Institute (2010), 1–13.

60. Ibid., 10–11.

61. M. D. Rappley, "Attention Deficit-Hyperactivity Disorder," *New England Journal of Medicine*, 352, no. 2 (2005): 165–73.

62. American Academy of Pediatrics, "Clinical Practice Guidelines: Diagnosis and Evaluation of the Child with Attention-Deficit/Hyperactivity Disorder," *Pediatrics*, 105, no. 5 (2000): 1158–70.

63. Rappley, "Attention Deficit-Hyperactivity Disorder."

64. M. Altarac and E. Saroha, "Lifetime Prevalence of Learning Disability Among US Children," *Pediatrics*, 119, no. 1 (2007): S81.

65. W. B. Carey et al., eds., *Developmental-Behavioral Pediatrics* (Philadelphia: Saunders/Elsevier, 2009), 811–27. Marianne S. Meyer, "The Ability-Achievement Discrepancy: Does it Contribute to an Understanding of Learning Disabilities?," *Educational Psychology Review*, 12, no. 3 (2000): 315–37.

66. B. A. Shaywitz, et al., "Discrepancy Compared to Low Achievement Definitions of Reading Disability," *Journal of Learning Disabilities*, 25, no. 10 (1992): 639–48.

67. Rappley, "Attention Deficit-Hyperactivity Disorder."

68. G. Reid Lyon, "Learning Disabilities," *Future of Children*, 6, no. 1 (1996): 54–76.

69. R. T. Brown, et al., "Treatment of Attention Deficit/Hyperactivity Disorder: Overview of the Evidence," *Pediatrics*, 115, no. 6 (2005): 749–57.

70. E. Chan, L. A. Rappaport, K. J. Kemper, "Complementary and Alternative Therapies in Childhood Attention and Hyperactivity Problems," *Journal of Developmental and Behavioral Pediatrics*, 24, no. 1 (2003): 4–8.

71. T. Oakland, et al., "An Evaluation of the Dyslexia Training Program: A Multisensory Method for Promoting Reading in Students with Reading Disabilities," *Journal of Learning Disabilities*, 31, no. 2 (1998):140–47.

72. 20 U.S.C. § 1414(a)(1)(B); Initial Evaluations, 34 C.F.R. § 300.301(b).

73. 20 U.S.C. § 1415(k)(5)(B)(i); Protections for Children Not Determined Eligible for Special Education and Related Services, 34 C.F.R. § 300.534(b)(1) and (2).

74. American Academy of Pediatrics, "Out-of-School Suspension and Expulsion," *Pediatrics*, 112, no. 5 (2003): 1208.

Chapter 10

Legal Status: Meeting the Needs of Immigrants in the Healthcare Setting

Samantha Morton, JD
Megan Sprecher, JD
Lynda Shuster, MSW, LICSW
Ellen Cohen, MD

The immigrant population in the United States has tripled in less than three decades. Between 1980 and 2007, the number of immigrants increased from 14 million to 38 million. During this time period, the number of children (ages 0 to 17) with immigrant parents increased from 6.2 million to 16.3 million.[1] As Figure 10.1 indicates, immigrant populations in metropolitan areas have increased dramatically since 1980. The immigrant population in the United States has a consistently higher poverty rate than the native-born population (see Figure 10.2). Children of immigrant parents are more likely to be poor than children of native-born parents. In 2007, 20 percent of children of immigrants were poor, whereas 16 percent of children with native-born parents were.[2]

The low-income immigrant community faces many barriers to good health. Some of these barriers, such as the inaccessibility of healthy food and reliable transportation, are similar to those faced by other vulnerable populations served by medical-legal partnerships. Others, such as limited English proficiency and legal status, are unique to the immigrant community. This chapter begins with an overview of the barriers immigrants to the United States face in accessing healthcare. It continues with a discussion about chronic illness within the immigrant community and its collateral effects on the immigration process. It concludes with details about the health and legal implications of domestic violence (and other crimes) against immigrants. Throughout the chapter we address the roles medical and legal practitioners can play in assisting immigrants to overcome these barriers.

Barriers to Health Faced by Immigrants

Immigrants face particular barriers to health and healthcare based on their unique experiences and legal status. Medical-legal partnerships (MLPs) are well situated to identify and address some of these barriers because of their preventive and comprehensive approach to caring for vulnerable populations.

Healthcare: Social and Cultural Barriers

Immigrants face many barriers when trying to access healthcare. Figure 10.3 illustrates nine common barriers prevalent in the immigrant community. Lack of preventive care

Figure 10.1 Top 100 Metros with Immigrants and Their Children by Size of Immigrant Population, 1980–2007

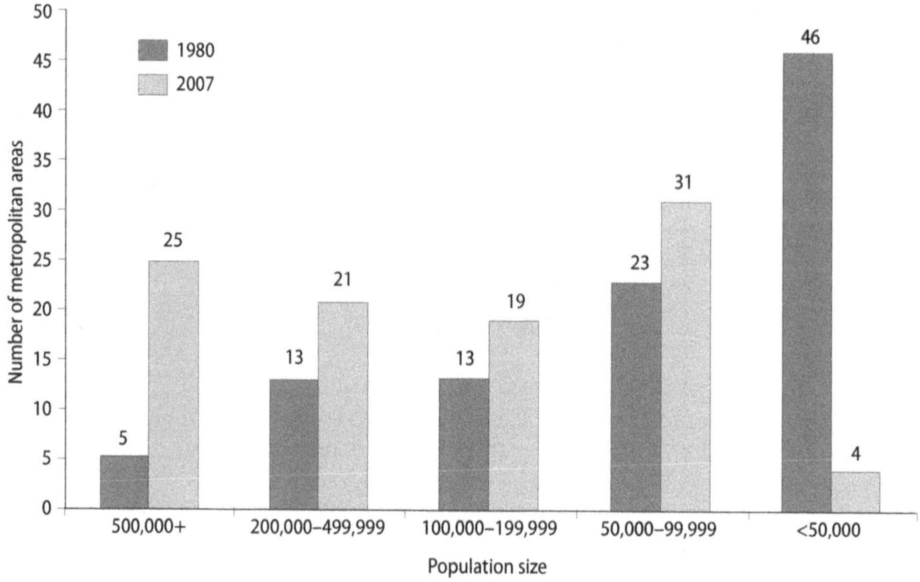

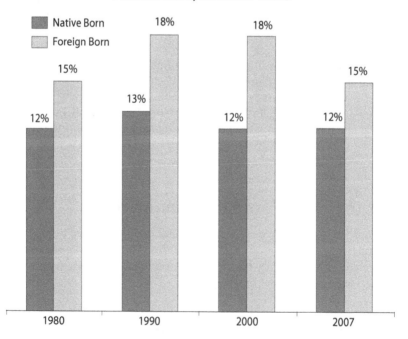

Source: Urban Institute tabulation from the IPUMS datasets drawn from the 1980 U.S. Census of Population and Housing, 5 percent sample, and the 2007 American Community Survey.

Figure 10.2 Poverty Rates for Immigrants versus Natives, United States, Selected Years

Source: Urban Institute tabulation from the IPUMS datasets drawn from the 1980 U.S. Census of Population and Housing, 5 percent sample, and the 2007 American Community Survey.

Figure 10.3 Barriers to Healthcare for Immigrants

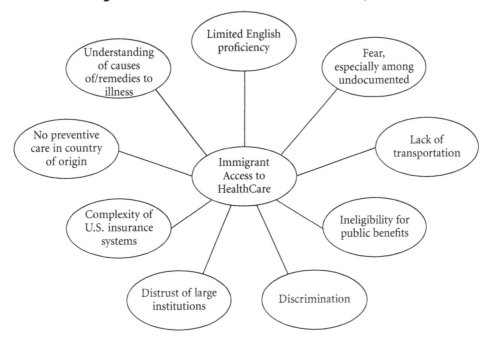

in the country of origin may affect the patterns of healthcare usage of immigrants even after moving to the United States.

These barriers lead to decreased access to healthcare; as a result, immigrants are significantly less likely than native citizens to visit a physician for preventive or emergency care, as illustrated by Figures 10.4 and 10.5.

The result of impeded access to healthcare and underutilization of medical services is "lateness to care," which means:

- patients are presenting sicker;

- more emergent, or complex, care is required;

- healthcare is often more costly, posing a greater financial burden on the patient and/or the healthcare system; and

- potentially preventable complications of chronic diseases arise due to delayed diagnosis and intervention and severe limitations in access to treatment and medical follow-up.

One of the most troubling and adverse aspects of this "lateness to care" is the very prevalent phenomenon of delayed and/or absent prenatal care among pregnant undocumented women, with all of the associated complications that may ensue. This is particularly tragic in light of the fact that the majority of these women are eligible for emergency Medicaid benefits (discussed later) but are either mistrustful of registering for care or are wrongfully denied those benefits.

Figure 10.4 Percent of Low-Income Nonelderly Adults Who Did Not Receive Preventive Care, 2004–2005

Percent of Low-Income Nonelderly Adults with an Emergency Room Visit in the Past Year, 2004–2005

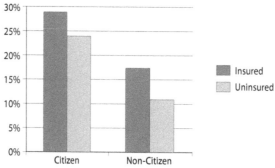

Note: "Nonelderly adults" includes all individuals age 18–64. Low-income is defined as twice the federal poverty level, which was $2,600 per month for a family of three in 2005.
Source: Samantha Artiga and Karyn Schwartz, "Health Insurance Coverage and Access to Care for Low-Income Non-Citizen Adults," Kaiser Commission on Medicaid and the Uninsured (2007): 1–5. KCMU analysis of 2004–2005 NHIS data. Data analyzed using multiple imputation methodology.

The Legal Perspective: Access to Income and Health-Promoting Public Benefits

Immigrants constitute a substantial part of the U.S. workforce. In 2009, there were 23.9 million foreign-born labor force participants in the United States, which was 15.5 percent of the civilian labor force.[3] Immigrants are more likely to work in low-wage jobs: one in five low-wage workers is an immigrant.[4] In 2009, the median weekly earnings of foreign-born, full-time employees were 79 percent of those of native-born employees. The unemployment rate for foreign-born workers was also higher than that of native-born workers by 0.5 percent.[5]

The majority of foreign-born workers have some kind of status that enables them to work legally in the United States. Of the approximately 9.3 million undocumented individuals representing 26 percent of the foreign-born population, approximately 6 million are in the workforce (which translates into approximately 5 percent of the U.S. labor force).[6]

As discussed in Chapter 7, income supports and access to public benefits play an integral role in promoting health in vulnerable low-income populations. Public benefits are an

Figure 10.5 Percent of Low-Income Children Who Did Not Receive Preventive Care, 2004–2005

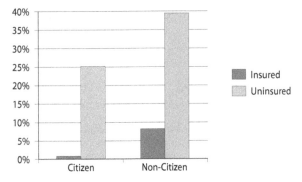

Percent of Low-Income Children with an Emergency Room Visit in the Past Year, 2004–2005

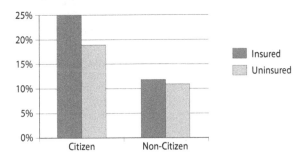

Source: Samantha Artiga and Karyn Schwartz. "Health Insurance Coverage and Access to Care for Low-Income Non-Citizen Adults," Kaiser Commission on Medicaid and the Uninsured (2007), 1–5. KCMU analysis of 2004–2005 NHIS data. Data analyzed using multiple imputation methodology.

even more essential tool in health promotion for certain immigrant groups, such as refugees, who typically have a less robust support system than other immigrant groups.

Yet low-income immigrants face many barriers to health-promoting public benefits, such as SNAP (Supplemental Nutrition Assistance Program, formerly known as Food Stamps), SSI (Supplemental Security Income, a disability benefit), TANF (Temporary Assistance for Needy Families, a cash benefit), and Medicaid (government-funded health insurance). For a detailed discussion of these programs, see Chapter 7.

Ineligibility

One such barrier is the categorical ineligibility that applies to many classifications of immigrants. Even lawfully present immigrants are often ineligible for public benefits. Immigrant eligibility for public benefits involves a patchwork of federal and state laws. See Appendix 10.1 for information about immigrant eligibility for some government programs. In Table 10.1, we define several different designations under which immigrants may fall.

As a matter of federal law, simply being lawfully present in the United States is not sufficient to render a low-income immigrant eligible for a host of public benefits. Even assuming that an immigrant is eligible for a benefit, many government agency representatives lack specialized training in the U.S. immigration system and have difficulty

Table 10.1 Glossary of Immigration Terminology
Relevant to Benefits Eligibility

Qualified Immigrants	• Lawful Permanent Residents (LPRs) • Refugees, asylees, persons granted withholding of deportation/removal, conditional entry (in effect prior to April 1, 1980), or paroled into the United States for at least one year • Cuban/Haitian entrants • Battered spouses and children with a pending or approved (a) self-petition for an immigrant visa, (b) immigrant visa filed for a spouse or child by a U.S. citizen or LPR, or (c) application for cancellation of removal/suspension of deportation, whose need for benefits has a substantial connection to the battery or cruelty (parents/children of such battered child/spouse are also "qualified") • Victims of trafficking and their derivative beneficiaries who have obtained a T visa or whose application for a T visa sets forth a prima facie case. (A broader group of trafficking victims who are certified by or receive an eligibility letter from the Office of Refugee Resettlement are eligible for benefits funded or administered by federal agencies, without regard to their immigration status.)
Not Qualified Immigrants	All noncitizens who do not fall under the "qualified" immigrant categories.[a]
Lawful Permanent Residents (LPRs)	A Lawful Permanent Resident is someone who has been granted authorization to live and work on a permanent basis. As proof of that status, the person is granted a permanent resident card, commonly called a "green card." One can become a permanent resident several different ways. Most individuals are sponsored by a family member or employer in the United States. Other individuals may become permanent residents through refugee or asylee status or other humanitarian programs.[b]
Refugee	Refugee status may be granted to people who have a "well-founded fear of persecution"—on account of race, religion, nationality, membership in a particular social group, and/or political opinion—should they be forced to live in their home country. Refugee status is a form of protection that may be granted to people who meet the definition of refugee and who are of special humanitarian concern to the United States. Refugees generally are people outside of their country who are unable or unwilling to return home because they fear serious harm. One may seek a referral for refugee status only from outside of the United States.[c]
Asylee	A person who has been granted asylum. Asylum status is a form of protection available to people who: • Meet the definition of refugee (see above) • Are already in the United States when they are determined to meet that definition • Are seeking admission at a port of entry One may apply for asylum in the United States regardless of country of origin or current immigration status. With very limited exceptions, one must apply for asylum within one year of last entry into the United States.[c]
Withholding of Removal	An immigration remedy similar to asylum, but with a more exacting legal standard: applicants must demonstrate a "clear probability" that their "life or freedom would be threatened" if returned to the home country.
Parolee	A person temporarily allowed into the United States for "urgent humanitarian reasons" or where a grant would result in a "significant public benefit."[d]

Victim of Trafficking	Victim of: (1) Sex trafficking: the recruitment, harboring, transportation, provision or obtaining of a person for the purpose of a commercial sex act, in which a commercial sex act induced by force, fraud, or coercion, or in which the person is forced to perform such an act is under the age of 18 years; or (2) Labor trafficking: the recruitment, harboring, transportation, provision, or obtaining of a person for labor or services, through the use of force, fraud, or coercion for the purpose of subjection to involuntary servitude, peonage, debt bondage, or slavery.[e]
Derivative Beneficiaries	Some forms of immigration relief allow certain relatives of the alien to obtain status through the principal's application or petition.

Notes: [a] This includes migrants from Freely Associated States (or Compact of Free Association migrants). Under the 1996 Personal Responsibility and Work Opportunity Act, individuals lawfully residing in the United States in accordance with the Compacts of Free Association (agreements between the United States and the Federated States of Micronesia, the Republic of the Marshall Islands, and the Republic of Palau) were deemed "not qualified aliens." Because the compact agreements allow migrants from these nations to live and work in the United States without visas or other LPR requirements, they fall outside the "qualified immigrant" category and thus are deemed "not qualified." Compact of Free Association Act of 1985, Public Law 99-239, 99th Cong., 1st sess. (14 January 1986); Compact of Free Association Amendments Act of 2003, Public Law 108-188, 108th Cong., 1st Sess. (17 December 2003); [b] "Green Card (Permanent Residence)," U.S. Citizenship and Immigration Services, accessed November 24, 2010, from http://www.uscis.gov; [c] "Refugees & Asylum," U.S. Citizenship and Immigration Services, accessed November 24, 2010, from http://www.uscis.gov; [d] Immigration and Nationality Act, U.S. Code, vol. 8, sec. 1182(d)(5)(A); [e] Trafficking Victims Protection Act of 2000, Public Law No. 106-386, 106th Cong., 2nd sess. (28 October 2000).

confirming the immigrant's actual status and eligibility. Moreover, some immigrants, especially those who recently arrived in the United States, do not know that there are government programs to help them or, if they are aware of the programs, how to access them successfully.

Indeed, even qualified immigrants who secure benefits face other barriers to maintaining them, even when their underlying qualifications remain constant. Under current law, green card holders with documented serious disabilities risk losing their SSI benefits if they do not successfully naturalize (secure citizenship) within a limited period of time. (No such time limitations apply to U.S. citizens who are granted SSI benefits.) Unfortunately, many immigrants with green cards confront institutional delays in the citizenship application process (such as those relating to required background checks) and can face destitution while waiting for resolution. Only early screening of and advocacy for SSI-enrolled green card holders for naturalization eligibility can help ensure that they secure citizenship in time to allow for their benefits to continue uninterrupted. An early provider referral to an MLP lawyer for help with naturalization may save a patient from months or even years of interrupted SSI benefits.

Some states have expanded Medicaid coverage of income-eligible noncitizens who do not satisfy the federal immigration status requirements. Through Alien Emergency Medical Assistance (or similarly named) programs, treatment for certain types of emergency medical conditions (defined by state law) may be covered. Sample Definition of Emergency Medical Conditions offers one example of how such conditions may be defined. Limited access to coverage for preventive care may lead to an increase in future emergency coverage.

Sample Definition of Emergency Medical Conditions

Ohio Administrative Code 5101:1-41-20

(4) "Emergency medical condition" means after sudden onset, a medical condition, including labor and delivery, manifesting itself by acute symptoms of sufficient severity (including severe pain) such that the absence of immediate medical attention could reasonably be expected to result in placing the patient's health in serious jeopardy, serious impairment to bodily functions, or serious dysfunction of any bodily organ or part. An emergency medical condition does not include care and services related to either an organ transplant procedure or routine prenatal or postpartum care.

(5) "Emergency medical condition episode" is defined as the period of time that starts with the day on which the absence of immediate medical attention could reasonably be expected to result in placing the patient's health in serious jeopardy, serious impairment to bodily functions, or serious dysfunction of any bodily organ or part; and stops on the day on which the absence of immediate medical attention could no longer reasonably be expected to result in placing the patient's health in serious jeopardy, serious impairment to bodily functions, or serious dysfunction of any bodily organ or part. The emergency medical condition episode includes labor and delivery, but does not include ongoing treatment.

Other Forms of Inaccessibility

Language Barriers

The percentage of persons residing in the United States who do not speak English as their first language is growing rapidly. As of 2007, 20 percent of U.S. residents over age five speak a language other than English at home.[7]

Figure 10.6 shows the breakdown of how well those who spoke a language other than English at home speak English. Using a qualified interpreter when necessary is the first step to making healthcare truly accessible to the immigrant community. Title VI of the Civil Rights Act of 1964 requires agencies that receive federal funding (including welfare offices) to communicate with Limited English Proficient (LEP) clients in a language they understand. In most cases this means using an interpreter. An interpreter should be an impartial third party provided and compensated by the welfare office.

Despite this legal requirement, many welfare offices, especially during times of recession or tight budgets, do not provide interpreters for LEP applicants, creating another barrier to access to health-promoting benefits. This often leads the applicant to bring a friend or family member to interpret as best they can, even though that person likely has no training, expertise or impartiality. The worst-case scenario is that an applicant's minor child is given the onerous task of interpreting for his or her parent, knowing that the family's stability is resting on the ability to "say the right thing" when interpreting.

When a welfare office does not comply with the requirements under Title VI, one option for the legal practitioner is to file a complaint with the U.S. Department of Health and Human Services Office for Civil Rights (OCR). OCR is in charge of ensuring that county welfare agencies have adequate LEP plans and, more important, that agencies and

Figure 10.6 English Speaking Ability of Those Who Spoke a Language Other Than English at Home

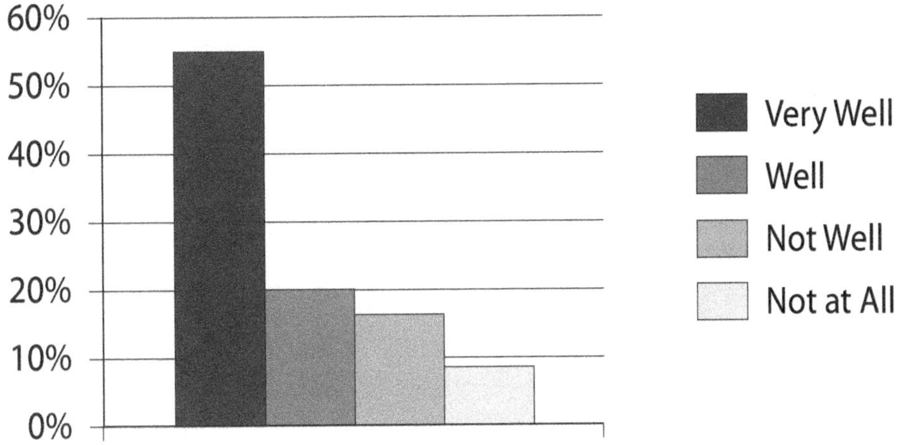

Source: Hyon B. Shin and Robert A. Kominski. "Language Use in the United States: 2007." American Community Service Reports, U.S. Census Bureau.

organizations comply with these plans. Instructions and forms relating to the complaint process can be found at OCR's website.[8]

Fear of Becoming a "Public Charge"

Many immigrants do not apply for public benefits, despite confirmation that they are eligible, for fear of becoming a "public charge." Since 1999, federal immigration authorities have defined "public charge" to mean an individual who is likely to become "primarily dependent on the government for subsistence, as demonstrated by either the receipt of public cash assistance for income maintenance, or institutionalization for long-term care at government expense."[9]

Immigration law provides that an individual seeking admission to the United States or to adjust status to lawful permanent residency is inadmissible if "at the time of application for admission or adjustment of status, [the person] is likely at any time to become a public charge."[10] Being inadmissible means the person is not allowed to enter the United States or become a lawful permanent resident (in other words, he or she cannot get a green card). Table 10.2 illustrates which benefits may qualify an individual as a public charge. Immigrants with questions or concerns about the risk of being labeled a public charge should be directed to an experienced immigration attorney for advice.

Table 10.2 Which Benefits Might Make Someone a "Public Charge?"

Benefits that Generally *Do* Make Someone a Public Charge	Benefits that Generally *Do Not* Make Someone a Public Charge
SSI Cash assistance from TANF State or local cash assistance programs for income maintenance ("general assistance" programs) Medicaid, to the extent it is used to support noncitizens who reside in an institution for long-term care, such as a nursing home or mental health institution	Medicaid and other health insurance and health services (including public assistance for immunizations and testing and treatment of symptoms of communicable diseases, use of health clinics, short-term rehabilitation services, prenatal care and emergency medical services) other than support for long-term institutional care Nutrition programs, including SNAP (Food Stamps); the Special Supplemental Nutrition Program for Women, Infants and Children (WIC); the National School Lunch and School Breakfast Program; and other supplementary and emergency food assistance programs Housing subsidies Child care subsidies Many others

Source: Michael A. Pearson, Executive Associate Commissioner, Office of Field Operations. "Field Guidance on Deportability and Inadmissibility on Public Charge Grounds." U.S. Department of Justice, Immigration and Naturalization Service, *Federal Register Publications*, 64 (1999): 28689.

Deeming of Sponsor's Income/Resources

The majority of immigrants seeking to adjust their status to lawful permanent residency must have a sponsor. In family-based cases, the sponsor is the individual petitioning for the immigrant (e.g., a U.S. citizen wife petitioning for her husband serves as his sponsor). To qualify as a sponsor, the individual must demonstrate that her income is at or above 125 percent of the federal poverty level for herself, her dependents and the immigrant(s) she is sponsoring. Sponsors on active duty in the U.S. Armed Forces who are petitioning for their spouse or child need only show they are at or above 100 percent of the federal poverty level. (See Chapter 7 for the federal poverty level.) If the sponsor does not earn enough money or have enough assets to support herself, her dependents and the immigrant seeking to adjust status, a co-sponsor may be necessary.

Importantly, under federal law, when someone who has secured a green card applies for public benefits, his or her sponsor's income and assets generally are taken into account when determining the person's financial eligibility for benefits. Depending on the sponsor's income status, this may make qualifying for public benefits much more difficult (or even impossible) for the green card holder—even if the sponsor does not provide any financial support to the green card holder's household.

It is critical to note that some categories of immigrants—such as refugees and asylees—do not need a sponsor to secure a green card. Financial qualification for public benefits is easier for those populations.

Questions for Discussion

1. Which barrier(s) to healthcare do you think is the most significant for immigrants? What are some strategies for overcoming them?

2. What role can a healthcare provider play to ensure that immigrant patients have meaningful access to public benefits?

3. What are the ethical concerns that arise when using a patient-client's family member to interpret?

Best Practices and Advocacy Strategies for Medical-Legal Partnership

Many immigrants, specifically refugees and asylum seekers, have experienced significant losses, including a view of the world as a safe and benevolent place. They often present with a distrust of authority figures, including medical and legal professionals. For some, doctors and government personnel were involved in perpetrating or supervising torture in their country of origin. Others who have uncertain legal status in the United States may believe that talking with medical or legal staff will lead to deportation if they are identified as experiencing medical or legal problems. Against this backdrop, it is important for medical-legal partners to:

- Allow time to establish rapport and trust

- Explain and emphasize confidentiality, consent, choice and control (including the roles of different professionals with respect to mandated reporting of suspected child or elder abuse, neglect or abandonment)

- Delineate the boundaries of the relationship so that the client knows what he or she can expect and will obtain from you (e.g., when are you available by phone and when are you not; what problems you can and will help the client with and the issues on which you cannot help the client, etc.)

- Explain everything (e.g., why you are asking certain questions) and be prepared to repeat information many times, as memory problems are common in those who have experienced or witnessed trauma

- Provide plenty of opportunities for the patient-client to ask questions, as some will come from cultures in which asking questions is not encouraged

- Understand that clients may openly show fear or hostility, which are characteristic responses to trauma and may have little to do with your interactions with them per se

- Allow for flexibility with appointment scheduling, as not all cultures are familiar with appointment systems and some clients may be experiencing anxiety, sleep or memory problems as result of past trauma, which can affect compliance

Both Medical-Legal Partnership | Boston (MLP | Boston) and the Tucson Family Advocacy Program have designed immigration-related advocacy curricula that include concrete suggestions for how to navigate these important issues when interacting with patient-clients. The Tucson Family Advocacy Program curriculum is targeted to the needs of refugees in particular, and the MLP | Boston curriculum is focused on supporting lawyers in providing trauma-informed advocacy to immigrant patient-clients.

From Practice to Policy

In August 2009, the Boston Housing Authority (BHA) was in the process of reforming its policies and procedures for providing equal opportunity to people with Limited English Proficiency (LEP). MLP | Boston worked with pro bono volunteers from law firm partner Ropes & Gray and clinicians from Dorchester House Multi-Service Center to submit written comments regarding the particular needs of Dorchester's specific immigrant populations and the relevance of LEP access to health and well-being. Although the implementation plan is still in draft form, the BHA was responsive to MLP | Boston's advocacy on behalf of populations who speak languages widely spoken in Dorchester other than those identified in the initial LEP plan (Spanish and Chinese). The BHA is planning to improve language access by affirmatively offering oral interpretation services to callers and visitors, and now offers that service on its VAWA (Violence Against Women Act) brochure in 10 languages, including Vietnamese, Haitian Creole and Portuguese. The BHA also plans to provide leases and other vital documents in more languages as well.

Case for Medical-Legal Partnership

Rosario, a 26-year-old from Honduras, is pregnant with her third child. She is 27 weeks pregnant and has received no prenatal care. She arrives at the emergency room alone complaining of nausea, headaches, racing pulse and pain in her side. She speaks no English and appears very frightened.

Questions for Discussion

1. What additional information do you need to gather to help this patient?

    Medical: What more do you need to know about Rosario's health?

    Legal: What questions will you ask to assess why Rosario has not accessed prenatal care?

2. How will you communicate with Rosario?

3. What barriers does Rosario face in addressing her health and the health of her baby? What would you do to try to remove those barriers?

4. How will you assist Rosario in accessing continuing prenatal care?

Immigrants, Chronic Disease and the Law

This section highlights the prevalence of certain chronic diseases in immigrant communities and addresses legal mechanisms that can help patients with chronic disease successfully navigate the immigration system. MLP is a critical tool in ensuring that chronically ill immigrant patients are able to adhere to often complex treatment and monitoring regimens — eliminating serious distractions like the threat of eviction or conflict with a school system regarding a child's educational needs can be crucial to promoting proper disease management. Importantly, this tool benefits not only the health of individuals and families but also public health more generally.

Chronic Diseases of Particular Relevance

Tuberculosis

Tuberculosis (TB) is a fastidious bacterial infection that, unlike most bacterial infections, typically has a long period of latency, during which the organism lies dormant before causing clinically apparent disease. During this period of dormancy, the only evidence of infection is often a positive tuberculin skin test, or PPD, which is routinely required for all immigrants and refugees entering the United States. Active TB, both pulmonary and extrapulmonary, has slowly decreased in its worldwide incidence since its peak in 2003. However, the incidence of newly diagnosed cases of TB remains the highest in sub-Saharan Africa (363/100,000 population), as well as India, China and Southeast Asia (all ≥ 100/100,000 population).[11] This is in sharp contrast to the typically low incidence rates (< 10/100,000) in developed countries like the United States. It is important to understand that the seriousness of TB infection in immigrants from these regions of the world is heightened by the very high rate of co-infection with HIV, particularly among those from sub-Saharan Africa. It is estimated that worldwide approximately 1 in 14 new cases of TB occurs in HIV-infected individuals, with the vast majority of them originating in Africa.[12] Unfortunately, the majority of patients diagnosed with TB in regions such as sub-Saharan Africa do not have HIV testing performed.

Within the United States, after a peak resurgence of TB infection in 1992 (> 150/100,000 population), there has been a gradual, sustained decline over the past two decades to an all-time low of 4.2/100,000. However, it is well recognized that the majority of cases (57 percent in 2006) of TB in the United States occur in foreign-born immigrants from countries with high TB rates. Indeed, according to the Centers for Disease Control and Prevention, in 2007, more than half (51.8 percent) of foreign-born TB cases were reported in persons from four countries:[13]

- Mexico (1,846)
- the Philippines (952)
- India (619)
- Vietnam (568)

In addition, in 2007, for the fourth consecutive year, more TB cases were reported among Latinos than any other racial/ethnic group. From 2006 to 2007, TB rates declined for all racial/ethnic minorities except for Asians (+0.8 percent) and Native Hawaiian or other Pacific Islanders (+42.9 percent).[14]

Of particular relevance to refugees and undocumented immigrants, a number of important clinical risk factors are well described as increasing the risk of TB (including multidrug-resistant TB). These include a number of common phenomena among immigrant (in particular refugee) populations, specifically:[15]

- Overcrowded and unsanitary living conditions
- Malnutrition and food insecurity
- Immunocompromise, including HIV infection
- Substance abuse, including alcohol and illicit drug use
- Lack of insurance and financial resources to access medical care

Because active pulmonary TB is highly contagious, it remains a basis for inadmissibility to the United States (see later discussion). As a result, some immigrants who demonstrate signs and symptoms potentially attributable to TB are reluctant to seek medical care. It is thus particularly important that clinicians and healthcare teams be sensitive to these concerns and aware that immigration status is a particularly strong determinant of healthcare avoidance behavior among foreign-born patients.

Psychiatric Disorders

Immigrants, particularly refugees and asylum-seekers, often have been exposed to physical and/or psychological violence on any of a number of levels, ranging from regional and national war to abuse of themselves and/or family members. Population-based studies have recently been conducted in areas of Africa that have seen persistent political disruption and military violence for decades. These studies describe extremely high rates of major depressive disorder (41–55.3 percent), anxiety (52.5 percent), and post-traumatic stress disorder (50.1 percent) among adults residing in the Congo and the Central African Republic.[16] It is critical that medical and mental health providers be aware of the prevalence and different forms of violence that may have impacted refugees and other immigrants and be keenly sensitive to the varied mental health sequelae as outlined here.

Events often experienced by immigrants in their countries of origin:

- War
- Human rights abuses, including sexual and other forms of physical abuse
- Persecution on grounds of political beliefs, national origin, religion, gender or ethnicity

The resultant losses:

- Country
- Culture
- Family
- Profession
- Language
- Friends
- Plans for the future

Challenges immigrants often face in their new home country:

- Multiple changes
- Psychological and practical adjustment
- Uncertain future
- Traumatic life events
- Hardship
- Racism
- Stereotyping by host community
- Unknown cultural traditions

Psychiatric disorders often associated with these types of life events can range from singular disruptions in daily living to major psychiatric problems that meet the criteria for an official psychiatric diagnosis.

It is helpful to be aware that different cultures express emotions and psychological problems in different ways. For many immigrants from the non-Western European countries, mental illness is an alien term; they are far more likely to talk about physical symptoms than seek treatment for psychological problems.[17] In response to the mental health field's growing awareness of and experience with such cultural differences as they relate to psychological presentations, the American Psychiatric Association has included in the current DSM IV-TR an appendix addressing this issue and providing a glossary of 25 "culture-bound syndromes and idioms of distress" from around the world that are commonly encountered by mental health providers in the United States treating foreign-born clients.[18]

The spectrum can vary from one or two symptoms to constellations of symptoms or an increase in the severity of a symptom to the extent that daily functioning is severely and negatively affected. Some symptoms that may be evident include:[19]

- Fatigue (changes in sleep)
- Weight loss/gain (changes in appetite)
- Worry
- Difficulty concentrating
- Difficulty remembering
- Nervousness
- Increased sensitivity/reactivity to external stimuli (sounds, sights, smells)
- Decreased reaction to external stimuli (numbing; flat affect; seeming nonreactive to pain)
- Panic attacks
- Hallucinations/flashbacks
- Suicidality
- Assaultiveness
- Substance abuse
- Denial/avoidance
- Anhedonia (inability to experience pleasurable emotions)

Disease and Immigration Law

Chronic disease (such as those already discussed) can impact the success of an immigrant patient's journey through the system in a number of important ways. This section focuses on two such manifestations—health-based grounds of inadmissibility and health-related barriers to successful naturalization—and suggests particular efficacies of MLP in addressing those challenges.

Naturalization is defined as "the conferring of nationality of a state upon a person after birth, by any means whatsoever."[20] At the end of the naturalization process, the applicant becomes a U.S. citizen with the same rights and responsibilities as natural-born citizens.

As background, Figure 10.7 depicts the various executive branch agencies that play a role in administering immigration law. Many types of immigration cases—including

Figure 10.7 Immigration Status Decision Makers

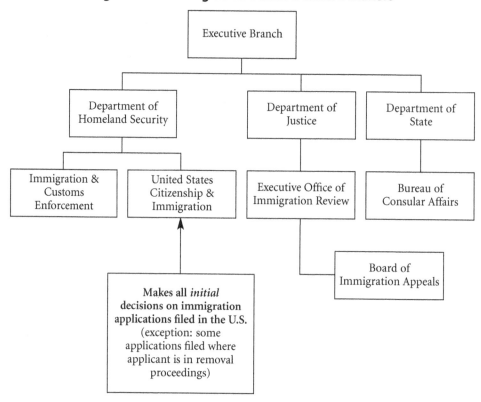

those discussed in this section—demand compelling medical evidence and can present particular cross-disciplinary challenges to immigration advocates.

Common case scenarios requiring (or enhanced by) clinical evidence include:

- medically based visa extension applications
- asylum and withholding of removal cases
- domestic violence-based relief (VAWA, U visa, T visa, certain Petitions to Remove Conditions on Residence)
- Special Immigrant Juvenile Status petitions
- adjustment cases (waivers)
- naturalization proceedings (medical waivers supporting exemptions from English and civics tests)
- medically based motions/requests for continuances

In the course of such cases, advocates might seek evidence in any combination of the following forms:

- medical records
- affidavits or letters
- forensic physical or mental evaluations
- live or telephonic testimony by clinicians in Immigration Court proceedings

- I-601 (Application for Waiver of Grounds of Inadmissibility)
- I-693 and Vaccination Supplement (medical examinations in adjustment context; to be completed only by Designated Civil Surgeons)
- N-648 (Medical Certification for Disability Exceptions)

Waivers of Health-Based Grounds of Inadmissibility

Generally, all green card applicants must demonstrate that they qualify for admission to the United States from a health perspective. Federal law still restricts immigration opportunities based on certain health-related grounds.

First, individuals with "communicable diseases of public health significance" are not eligible to enter the United States or obtain a green card.[21] The Department of Health and Human Services, in conjunction with the Centers for Disease Control and Prevention, is responsible for determining which diseases render a person inadmissible for immigration purposes. Currently, this list includes gonorrhea, leprosy (infectious), syphilis (infections stage) and tuberculosis.[22]

Second, persons may be deemed inadmissible who are shown to "have a physical or mental disorder and a history of behavior associated with the disorder that may pose or has posed a threat to the property, safety or welfare of the [individual] or others," or to have had such a disorder/behavior pattern previously that is likely to recur or lead to other harmful behavior.[23]

Third, a person determined to be a drug abuser or drug addict may be excluded.[24] MLPs can play an important role in helping immigrants with certain chronic medical conditions secure a waiver of health-related grounds of inadmissibility. As an example, individuals diagnosed with one of the above-listed communicable diseases must submit and receive a "waiver of inadmissibility" before they can be awarded a green card. A communicable disease waiver application requires (a) two forms (each of which must be signed by a doctor); and (b) three letters of support (one of which must be from the applicant's treating physician). The forms and letters of support serve to show the Citizenship and Immigration Services (CIS) that the applicant is receiving medical treatment for the communicable disease and the disease is not likely to be spread.

Overcoming Health-Related Barriers to Naturalization

Naturalization can be an important step for immigrants to take. A few of the many advantages to naturalizing are:

- becoming eligible for a range of public benefits
- being protected from deportation
- no longer having to worry about constituting a "public charge"
- having the ability to sponsor a wider range of family members for green cards
- having the ability to participate in U.S. civic life more fully (such as through voting)

Figure 10.8 shows the typical process for successful naturalization.

Importantly, during formal interviews, most green card holders applying for naturalization are evaluated for English proficiency (the ability to read, write and speak "simple words and phrases") and knowledge of U.S. history and government. Some immigrant populations, such as those over age 50 who have been LPRs for at least 20 years or those over age 55 who have been LPRs for at least 15 years, are categorically

Figure 10.8 Typical Process for Successful Naturalization

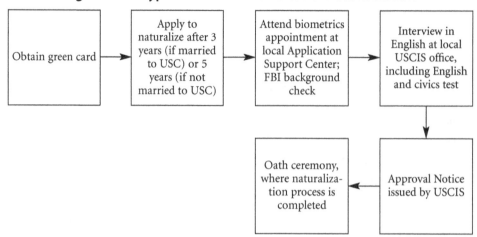

exempted from this testing requirement. However, other immigrants who are not categorically exempted from the English and civics exam requirements often have chronic physical, mental or developmental disabilities that prevent them from acquiring or demonstrating the required knowledge. For example, some torture survivors suffer from post-traumatic stress disorder, which in some cases can affect memory sufficiently to impact learning and retention. Under current law, to be exempted from the testing requirements, such persons must apply for an individual waiver of the testing requirement. Among other things, waiver applicants must demonstrate that the disability:

- is long-term (at least one year old, or expected to last for more than a year)
- is so severely debilitating that they are unable to meet the English or civics requirements
- must not have been caused by illegal drug use

The waiver application process requires submission of detailed medical evidence by a qualified clinician (via Form N-648, Medical Certification of Disability Exceptions). MLPs are uniquely positioned to assist immigrant patients with these types of waivers.

Best Practices and Advocacy Strategies for Medical-Legal Partnership

In 2009, MLP | Boston observed that many low-income immigrant patients were eligible to apply for naturalization, but needed advocacy to ensure the success of their applications — particularly those patients with medical conditions that rendered them eligible for waiver of the English/civics testing requirements.

Pro bono law firm partner Goodwin Procter piloted a representation project for MLP | Boston clients and has taken on many naturalization cases. MLP | Boston also has prepared and delivered to Goodwin Procter's volunteers a multipart advocacy training on naturalization.

From Practice to Policy

In January 2010, in response to a high volume of questions from clinicians treating immigrant patients with communicable diseases, MLP | Boston developed and disseminated a *Communicable Disease Waiver Toolkit for Medical Providers.* This toolkit offers practical tips and guidance for clinicians who assist immigrant patients in completing waiver applications and includes sample completed forms.[25] Integration of the toolkit into the Center for Infectious Diseases at Boston Medical Center increases the likelihood that medical eligibility for green card status will be successfully established on behalf of chronically ill and vulnerable patients, and also represents important advocacy capacity-building in healthcare partners.

Questions for Discussion

1. Should English-speaking ability be a requirement for naturalization? Why or why not?

2. What are some ways in which a healthcare provider or legal professional might change his or her practice to better serve the refugee and asylee community?

3. What is the healthcare provider's role in encouraging a patient-client to naturalize? What are some of the advantages to health in naturalizing?

Case for Medical-Legal Partnership

Liyongo came to the United States as a refugee from Burundi. He is 30 years old and has received SSI since he arrived because of a developmental disability. To keep receiving his benefits, Liyongo must naturalize. He only speaks Swahili and Kirundi.

Questions for Discussion

1. What additional information do you need to gather to help Liyongo?

   Medical: What aspects of Liyongo's medical condition might affect his eligibility for naturalization?

   Legal: How would you explain the importance of Liyongo naturalizing to his medical providers? How would you ask them to fill out the necessary waiver forms?

2. How will naturalizing positively affect Liyongo's health?

Immigrant Survivors of Abuse or Crime

This section discusses domestic violence and other crimes committed against immigrants and addresses legal mechanisms that can provide immigration relief to crime survivors.

Challenges Specific to Immigrant Survivors of Abuse

Empirical data on the prevalence of domestic violence among undocumented immigrants is limited by the inherently hidden nature of the problem within this population. (For a detailed discussion of the dynamics and prevalence of domestic violence in the United States, see Chapter 11.) However, in contrast to the 22.1 percent lifetime prevalence of domestic violence among the general population of women in the United States, a number of studies have described lifetime prevalence rates of physical and sexual abuse between

30 percent and 60 percent among immigrant women of Latina, South Asian and Korean origin.[26] This problem is thought to be particularly prevalent in undocumented women who are married to or otherwise dependent on citizen or legal permanent resident men, given the real or perceived notion that their ability to stay in the United States is dependent on remaining in relationships with these men.

For foreign-born women whose male partners are immigrants themselves, premigration exposure to violence is a potential risk factor for perpetration of domestic violence by the male partner. One study of 379 immigrant men largely of Caribbean, African and Central/South American origin in the Boston area found that 20 percent of these men reported premigration political violence exposure. Of the total study population, 17.9 percent reported perpetrating physical or sexual violence on their partner in the prior six months, with men who reported premigration exposure to political violence being more than twice as likely to be perpetrators of violence than those who did not report such exposure.[27] Thus, it is particularly important that healthcare providers caring for immigrants and refugees are sensitive to the risk of domestic violence, exercising at least as much care to screen for domestic violence as in the nonimmigrant population.

A number of features of the immigrant experience render noncitizen abuse victims uniquely vulnerable to isolation just when they need help the most. All domestic violence victims face barriers. Immigrants, especially ones without a stable legal status, face additional barriers. Figure 10.9 illustrates the layers of vulnerability faced by an immigrant survivor of domestic violence.

Figure 10.9 Immigrant Power and Control Wheel

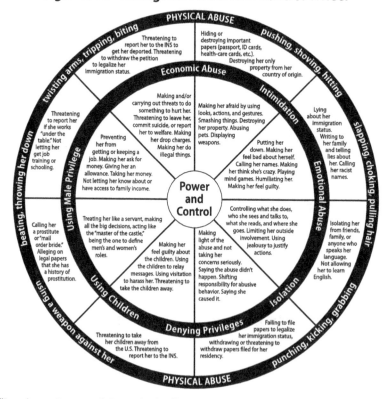

Source: "Immigrant Power and Control Wheel" (adapted from the original wheel by Domestic Abuse Intervention Project), National Center on Domestic and Sexual Violence, accessed November 21, 2010.

Immigration Remedies Available to Survivors of Abuse or Crime

Violence Against Women Act (VAWA)

Family-based immigration is the most common way for someone to gain lawful status in the United States. U.S. Citizens (USCs) and Lawful Permanent Residents (LPRs) may petition for certain family members (see Figure 10.10). There is a wait time between application and receipt of legal permanent status that is based on a combination of the immigrant family member's country of origin and their relationship to the USC or LPR.

Figure 10.10 Family Based Immigration

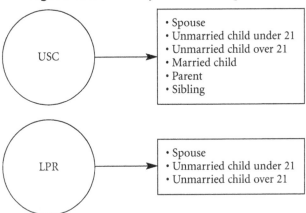

In situations where the USC or LPR is abusive to his or her family member, immigration status is used as a means of control. The abuser might threaten the victim with reporting him or her to immigration authorities if he or she seeks help from law enforcement.

The Violence Against Women Act (VAWA) (discussed in detail in Chapter 11) creates an alternative for immigrant survivors of domestic abuse: the self-petition. The VAWA self-petition essentially takes immigration-related control tactics away from the abuser by giving the survivor the ability to petition for him or herself. An approved VAWA self-petitioner is eligible to apply for permanent residency; when he or she is eligible to do so depends on the survivor's relationship to and the status of the abuser. VAWA Eligibility Basics outlines the eligibility requirements. VAWA is an eventual path to citizenship.

VAWA Eligibility Basics

Who Is Eligible to File a VAWA Self-Petition?

Despite the name of the Act, women are not the only ones eligible to file a VAWA self-petition. Men, women and children are all eligible, to the extent they are spouses or children of abusive USCs or LPRs, or parents of abusive USCs.

What Are the Requirements for a VAWA Self-Petition?

A VAWA self-petitioner must prove the following elements to qualify:

- Status of abuser as a USC or LPR
- Good faith marriage (for self-petition based on abusive marriage)
- Battery or extreme cruelty
- Good moral character of self-petitioner

U Visa

The U visa is a type of humanitarian immigration relief available to some victims of serious crimes. To qualify for a U visa, a person must show that he or she:

- Is the victim of designated criminal activity
- Suffered substantial physical or mental abuse as a result of the crime
- Possesses information about the crime
- Has been, is being or is likely to be helpful in the investigation and/or prosecution of the crime
- Is the victim of criminal activity that violated the laws of the United States or occurred in the United States

---

Designated Criminal Activities for U Visa Purposes

• Rape	• Being held	• Manslaughter
• Torture	hostage	• Murder
• Trafficking	• Peonage	• Felonious
• Incest	• Involuntary	assault
• Domestic	servitude	• Witness
violence	• Slave trade	tampering
• Sexual assault	• Kidnapping	• Obstruction of
• Abusive sexual	• Abduction	justice
contact	• Unlawful criminal	• Perjury
• Prostitution	restraint	• Attempt,
• Sexual	• False	conspiracy or
exploitation	imprisonment	solicitation to
• Female genital	• Blackmail	commit any
mutilation	• Extortion	of the above

Source: *Immigration and Nationality Act*, U.S. Code, vol. 8, sec 1101(a)(U)(iii).

After three years of U visa nonimmigrant status, the person is eligible to apply for permanent residency. The U visa is an eventual path to citizenship.

T Visa

The T visa is similar to the U visa. It is a type of humanitarian relief available to crime victims, though unlike the U visa, the T visa is only available to victims of human trafficking. This includes involuntary servitude, sex trafficking and labor trafficking.

The U.S. government estimates that between 14,500 and 17,500 persons are trafficked into the United States annually and there are currently 200,000 people in this country who have been trafficked. A large proportion of the victims are women and children, and many are domestic workers and farm workers.[28]

To qualify for a T visa, one must show that:

- He or she is or was a victim of trafficking, as defined by law
- He or she is in the United States, American Samoa, the Commonwealth of the Northern Mariana Islands or at a port of entry, due to trafficking

- He or she is complying with any reasonable request from a law enforcement agency for assistance in the investigation or prosecution of human trafficking (exceptions: he or she is under the age of 18 or is unable to cooperate due to physical or psychological trauma)

- He or she demonstrates that he or she would suffer extreme hardship involving unusual and severe harm if he or she were removed from the United States

(Readers probably noticed that trafficking is also one of the designated crimes for U visa eligibility. One advantage in applying for a T visa rather than the U visa is that T visa recipients qualify for more public benefits than U visa recipients.)

Trafficking victims often are kept sequestered by their captors from any form of social services or other assistance. Emergency medical care is often the only context in which a trafficking victim has contact with the outside world. It is especially important that healthcare providers be vigilant when treating someone who may be a trafficking victim; that one emergency medical visit may be the trafficking victim's only chance to escape.

Statements from Trafficking Survivors

• "I need support—emotional support—someone to listen to me. Someone who can listen to me without any judgment because sometimes when I talk to the wrong person, I got the impression that person would look down on me and my situation."

• "It was hard for me to learn about services while I was still there, because he kept me apart from other people, and he threatened to have me deported if I tried to leave."

• "I was ashamed to get help, because I thought I would be blamed as a bad person who deserved such bad treatment."

• "In INS [detention], I wasn't guilty person, but the ambiance and everybody treated me as I was guilty ... bunches of people, I think INS officers. Different people saying different things to different people."

• "I reported it to the police but they didn't believe me, they wouldn't arrest them."

Source: Lauden Y. Aron, Janine M. Zweig, and Lisa C. Newmark. "Comprehensive Services for Survivors of Human Trafficking: Findings from Clients in Three Communities." *Urban Institute Justice Policy Center* (2006): 11–12, 16, 28.

Special Immigrant Juvenile Status

Immigrant children under age 18 who are in the United States without a parent or guardian, or who have been abused, abandoned or neglected by one or both parents who are present here, may be eligible for Special Immigrant Juvenile Status (SIJS). SIJS requires a state court (probate or juvenile court) finding that the child has been abused, abandoned or neglected by one or both parents and a separate immigration application and determination.

Both of these steps are complicated; patients should consult with a lawyer before proceeding. The definitions of "abuse," "abandonment" and "neglect" are legally dense and vary by state, and have been interpreted to include everything from actual child abuse to a parent dying without leaving a guardian in place for the child.

Asylum

Asylum can be an option for a person who is unable or unwilling to return to his or her country of nationality (or last habitual residence in the case of a person having no nationality) because of persecution (or a well-founded fear of persecution) on account of race, religion, nationality, membership in a particular social group or political opinion.[29] Significantly, on entering the United States, a person seeking asylum has one year to file an application; the exceptions to this deadline are extraordinarily limited and do not include language challenges or lack of knowledge of the deadline.

For years, advocates have argued that women fleeing abusive relationships in their home countries should be granted asylum because this constituted gender-based persecution. Advocates argued that gender falls under the "social group" category of eligibility. In April 2009 the Obama administration put an end to long-standing ambiguity and controversy around gender-based asylum, when several senior attorneys in the Department of Homeland Security filed a legal brief on the issue in the case of Rody Alvarado-Pena, a Guatemalan woman who fled horrific abuse by her husband. The brief stated that in very severe cases, a battered woman might be eligible to obtain asylum.[30] Ms. Alvarado-Pena ultimately was granted asylum, but the criteria employed by the immigration courts in considering similar claims remain disputed.

Asylum applications are very heavily scrutinized. Therefore, it is very important for a potential asylum-seeker—especially one planning to base the application on a history of domestic violence in the home country—to consult an immigration attorney before deciding to file. Healthcare providers who screen immigrant patients for domestic violence and learn that a patient is (1) a survivor, and (2) in need of immigration support should contact their MLP legal colleagues immediately.

Questions for Discussion

1. Should a healthcare provider include information about a patient's immigration status in the medical record?

2. What should a medical or legal practitioner do if he or she suspects an immigrant patient-client is being abused at home?

3. What are strategies MLP practitioners can use to identify trafficking victims?

Best Practices and Advocacy Strategies for Medical-Legal Partnership

When working with immigrant victims of violence and crime, MLP professionals should embrace standard practices that have long guided effective trauma-informed medical and legal advocacy, such as:

- Interviewing the patient-client alone in a confidential space (guarding against influence of possible abuser or family member/friend with different interests)

- Incorporating safety questions into social history screening

- Managing expectations about what will happen during a particular conversation or interaction; reviewing and repeating this information; reinforcing through both verbal and written communication

- Expecting inconsistencies

- Establishing guidelines around contact; staying attuned to potential for vicarious trauma

Additionally, a notable best practice in MLP in this context is training healthcare providers to not only screen their immigrant patients for domestic violence (thus potentially identifying a possible pathway to lawful status) but also effectively document their patients' domestic violence histories. This in turn supports patients' applications for domestic violence-based immigration status. To the extent a legal advocate determines that a patient is eligible for VAWA, U visa or T visa, medical evidence will be a critical component of any successful application. The better prepared a clinician is to draft an accurate and compelling letter and affidavit, the more likely his or her patient is to be successful in the immigration case.

From the vantage point of the legal partner, effective legal advocacy in these instances means successfully interacting with medical partners on behalf of the client. Although this may appear straightforward (and often is), occasionally immigration advocates encounter difficulties in successfully communicating with healthcare partners, and thus in obtaining evidence crucial to the outcome of the legal case. Immigration lawyers can best serve clients by approaching interactions with healthcare providers with a recognition that although both lawyers and healthcare providers have the patient's best interests at heart, healthcare providers operate in a different professional arena than lawyers do, with unique pressures, constraints and expectations. Like any other dealings with third parties who hold valuable information about a client, communications with a client's healthcare providers (whether they are treating physicians or forensic experts) should be preceded by careful consideration and preparation and some degree of basic research.

When MLP immigration advocates contact clients' healthcare providers, they should keep in mind the following realities, which are not always intuitive:

- For a variety of reasons, many medical professionals may be accustomed to viewing lawyers as adversaries, not as partners with a common goal. Immigration lawyers have an opportunity to reframe such perceptions when dealing with clinicians on behalf of clients.

- Some healthcare providers (especially those treating low-income patients) have heard "horror stories" about immigration lawyers (or persons purporting to be such) from patients and colleagues who have had negative (if not unlawful) experiences with such persons. These providers, therefore, may react to immigration lawyers representing their patients with some skepticism or distrust. This can be overcome through a positive collaboration.

- Both legal and medical professionals are subject to stringent ethical and confidentiality obligations to their clients/patients; however, the principles governing each profession are not identical and communications between, for example, a patient's doctor and lawyer cannot be an unconditional two-way street. See Chapter 6 for a detailed discussion of the ethical issues involved in medical-legal communication. Lawyers are generally bound by more stringent confidentiality rules. Although maintaining these boundaries is essential, it is wise to invoke any such limits on information sharing with diplomacy and explanation, as appropriate.

- A healthy client is better able to participate in the legal advocacy being conducted on his or her behalf. Because clinicians are links to a variety of support services that lawyers are not trained to coordinate, developing a positive relationship with the client's clinical team makes the immigration lawyer's job easier.

From Practice to Policy

The U visa is a fairly new form of relief for immigrants. One important policy project is educating local law enforcement, legislators, immigrants and social service agencies on its existence. See the Cleveland City Council Resolution in Support of U Visas.

Before the Cleveland Community Advocacy Program, the local MLP, approached the city council about passing the resolution, none of the council members had heard of the U visa. After the resolution passed, all 18 council members and the mayor knew what the U visa was and why it was important for public safety.

Cleveland City Council Resolution in Support of U Visas

Res. No. 374-10
By Mayor Jackson and Council Members Westbrook and Sweeney
March 22, 2010

Whereas, in 2000, the U.S. Congress created the U Visa classification in the Victims of Trafficking and Violence Prevention Act (the "Act"), which allows foreign visitors and other non-US citizens who are victims of specified criminal activity, and who are needed to assist government officials in the investigation or prosecution of such criminal activity, to legally remain in the US for up to 4 years; and

Whereas, in passing the Act and creating the U Visa program, it was Congress' intent to strengthen the ability of local law enforcement agencies to detect, investigate or prosecute serious crimes committed against non-US citizens by providing them with legal status in this country when they assist local law enforcement agencies; and

Whereas, by creating the U Visa program, Congress also intended to offer "protection to victims of offenses in keeping with the humanitarian interests of the United States"; and

Whereas, information and assistance about serious crimes provided to law enforcement by foreign crime victims improves the safety and overall quality of life of a city's residents; and

Whereas, this resolution constitutes an emergency measure for the immediate preservation of public peace, property, health or safety, now, therefore,

Be it resolved by the Council of the City of Cleveland:

Section 1. That this Council supports the United States U Visa program, which is a temporary visa authorizing non-US citizen crime victims who assist law enforcement with crime investigations to remain in this country up to four years and urges the Cleveland Police Department to participate in the U Visa program when practicable.

Section 2. That this resolution is hereby declared to be an emergency measure and, provided it receives the affirmative vote of two-thirds of all the members elected to Council, it shall take effect and be in force immediately upon its adoption and approval by the Mayor; otherwise it shall take effect and be in force from and after the earliest period allowed by law.
Adopted. Yeas 18. Nays 0.

Educating the public also is an important area of policy advocacy. See the text of an op-ed piece coauthored by Cleveland MLP attorney Megan Sprecher and Cleveland Police Chief Michael McGrath.

Cleveland Plain Dealer Op-Ed Authored by Cleveland Community Advocacy Program and Police Chief McGrath

City takes important steps to ensure citizen safety
March 28, 2010

Megan Sprecher and Michael McGrath

Last year, because of cooperative work between the Legal Aid Society of Cleveland and the Cleveland Police Department, Rosa Gomez* was able to free herself and her young child from an abusive relationship.

Gomez and her baby lived in constant fear. The child's father, a U.S. citizen, was very abusive. He would yank Gomez to the ground by her hair. When she was pregnant, he pushed her down the stairs. After more than a year of daily insults, threats and assaults, Gomez sought help from the Cleveland Police Department. She wanted a better future for her child and safety and security for herself.

Thanks to Gomez's cooperation and assistance, the Cleveland Police Department detective assigned to her case quickly put together a strong case against the abuser. The detective promptly referred the evidence to the prosecutor's office.

The prosecutor swiftly charged Gomez's abuser with domestic violence and two other related crimes. Gomez faced her abuser in court, testifying against him for more than an hour. The prosecutor called Gomez "an ideal witness." Her testimony was so convincing that the abuser plead guilty to domestic violence. He received a jail sentence and probation.

Gomez then sought assistance from the Legal Aid Society of Cleveland. Gomez's cooperation with the investigation and prosecution of the crime made her eligible for a U Visa. The U Visa, a nonimmigrant visa, was created by Congress in 2000 for victims of serious crimes (including domestic violence and sexual assault). Congress created the U Visa with three goals in mind: encouraging the immigrant community to report crimes, strengthening trust between the immigrant community and law enforcement, and providing humanitarian relief to crime victims.

This relief is especially important for victims of domestic violence, who often are reluctant to press charges and who live in fear of retaliation from their abusers. Many victims remain with their abusers and do not seek the help of police for fear of deportation.

Gomez received the first known U Visa in Ohio.

One of the many requirements when applying for a U Visa is a form signed by law enforcement (usually police, prosecutor, or judge) certifying that the crime victim was, is or is likely to be helpful in the investigation and/or prosecution of the crime.

Eighteen months ago, the Cleveland Police Department issued a divisional notice outlining the procedure for signing these certification forms. With the help of this notice, several other crime victims in Northeast Ohio have obtained U Visas. Up to 10,000 individuals can receive a U Visa annually in the United States.

On March 22, City Council President Martin Sweeney and Councilman Jay Westbrook introduced a resolution in support of the U Visa and the Cleveland Police Department's involvement in signing certification forms. Council adopted the resolution, taking an important step to promote safety in our community. Additionally, with this action, City Council made clear that Cleveland is open to diversity and remains immigrant-friendly.

Police certification of U Visas is a powerful tool to build trust between immigrants and the Northeast Ohio community they now call home.

Cleveland City Council's recent attention to the importance of U Visas underscores the city's commitment to safety, immigrants and especially victims of domestic violence. However, our community cannot stop here—while the city has offered additional help and protection for victims of crime, we must continue to help our neighbors and encourage friends to get help from the police, Legal Aid and other service providers who are in positions to help.

* Gomez's name was changed to protect her identity.

Case for Medical-Legal Partnership

You suspect that Jutharat, a 19-year-old woman from Thailand, is being physically abused by her husband, John. Her physician notices in Jutharat's medical record that she has lost an unhealthy amount of weight in the past six months and has visited the emergency department twice for vague "accidents." Jutharat tells the social worker at her health clinic that she "feels scared" at home and that she and her parents are undocumented.

Questions for Discussion

1. What additional information do you need to gather to help Jutharat?

    Medical: What would you say to Jutharat when referring her to a legal partner?

    Legal: What additional questions would you ask Jutharat to determine what, if any, immigration remedies are available to her?

2. How would you create a safe environment in which Jutharat could communicate about safety issues and fears she might have about pursuing legal remedies?

Conclusion

MLP is an important strategy in efforts to protect and promote immigrant health because clinically facilitated legal advocacy can help eliminate barriers to healthcare access and support positive health outcomes. The unique challenges faced by immigrant patients, including chronic disease and exposure to violence, require sensitive responses. As discussion continues at both the state and national levels about reforms to immigration law and the treatment of immigrants in the United States, the work of MLPs serving these populations will bring an important perspective to the experience of immigrants in the healthcare and legal systems.

1. "Immigration Trends in Metropolitan America, 1980–2007," Urban Institute, accessed December 30, 2010, http://www.urban.org/publications/412273.html.

2. Ibid.

3. "Foreign-Born Workers: Labor Force Characteristics — 2009," U.S. Department of Labor, accessed December 30, 2010, http://www.bls.gov/news.release/forbrn.nr0.htm.

4. "Immigrants in the Workforce: Some Fast Facts," National Conference of State Legislatures, accessed December 30, 2010, http://www.ncsl.org/default.aspx?tabid=13120.

5. Ibid.

6. "Undocumented Immigrants: Facts and Figures," Urban Institute, accessed December 30, 2010, http://www.urban.org/publications/1000587.html.

7. Hyon B. Shin and Robert A. Kominski, "Language Use in the United States: 2007," American Community Service Reports, U.S. Census Bureau, accessed May 4, 2010, http://www.census.gov/population/www/socdemo/language/ACS-12.pdf.

8. "How to File a Complaint," U.S. Department of Health and Human Services, Office of Civil Rights, accessed November 24, 2010, http://www.hhs.gov/ocr/civilrights/complaints/index.html.

9. Michael A. Pearson, Executive Associate Commissioner, Office of Field Operations, "Field Guidance on Deportability and Inadmissibility on Public Charge Grounds," U.S. Department of Justice, Immigration and Naturalization Service, *Federal Register Publications*, 64 (1999): 28689.

10. *Immigration and Nationality Act*, U.S. Code, vol. 8, sec. 1182(a)(4)(A).

11. WHO, *Global Tuberculosis Control*. WHO/HTM/TB/2008.393. Geneva: World Health Organization, 2008.

12. Elizabeth Corbett et al., "Tuberculosis in Sub-Saharan Africa: Opportunities, Challenges, and Change in the Era of Antiretroviral Treatment." *Lancet* 367 (2006): 926–37.

13. "Trends in Tuberculosis — United States, 2007." *Morbidity and Mortality Weekly Report* 57, no. 11 (2008): 281–85.

14. Ibid.

15. Elizabeth Corbett, et al., "The Growing Burden of Tuberculosis: Global Trends and Interactions with the HIV Epidemic." *Archives of Internal Medicine*, 163 (2003): 1009–21.

16. Patrick Vinck and Phuong N. Pham, "Association of Exposure to Violence and Potential Traumatic Events with Self-Reported Physical and Mental Health Status in the Central African Republic." *Journal of the American Medical Association* 304, no. 5 (2010): 544–52; Kirsten Johnson et al., "Association of Sexual Violence and Human Rights Violations with Physical and Mental Health in Territories of the Eastern Democratic Republic of the Congo." *Journal of the American Medical Association*, 304, no. 5 (2010): 553–62.

17. Patricia Wen, "Culture Gap." *Boston Globe*, March 24, 2008, C1.

18. American Psychiatric Association, *Diagnostic and Statistical Manual of Mental Disorders, Fourth Edition Text Revision* (Washington, D.C.: American Psychiatric Publishing, 2000), Appendix I.

19. Ibid.

20. Immigration and Nationality Act, U.S. Code, vol. 8, sec. 1101(a)(23).

21. Immigration and Nationality Act, U.S. Code, vol. 8, sec. 1182(a)(1)(A)(i).

22. HIV was included on this list until January 4, 2010.

23. Immigration and Nationality Act, U.S. Code vol. 8, sec. 1182(a)(1)(A)(iii)(II).

24. Immigration and Nationality Act, U.S. Code, vol. 8, sec. 1182(a)(1)(A)(iv).

25. MLP | Boston, *Communicable Disease Waiver Toolkit for Medical Providers,* accessed at http://www.mlpboston.org/resources/trainings.

26. Barbara Moynihan, Mario Thomas Gaboury, and Kasie J. Onken, "Undocumented and Unprotected Immigrant Women and Children in Harm's Way." *Journal of Forensic Nursing*, 4, no. 3 (2008): 123–29.

27. Jhumka Gupta et al., "Pre-Migration Exposure to Political Violence and Perpetration of Intimate Partner Violence among Immigrant Men in Boston." *American Journal of Public Health*, 99, no. 3 (2009): 462–69.

28. "Fact Sheet: Distinctions between Human Smuggling and Human Trafficking 2006," U.S. Department of State, accessed November 21, 2010, http://www.state.gov/m/ds/hstcenter/90434.htm.

29. Immigration and Nationality Act, U.S. Code, vol 8, sec 1158(a).

30. "After Rody Alvarado's Victory, Obstacles Remain for Domestic Violence Victims Seeking Asylum," National Immigration Forum, http://www.immigrationforum.org/blog/display/after-rody-alvarados-victory-obstacles-remain-for-domestic-violence-victims/.

Chapter 11

Personal Safety: Addressing Interpersonal and Family Violence in the Health and Legal Systems

Betsy McAlister Groves, LICSW
Lisa Pilnik, JD
Elizabeth Tobin Tyler, JD, MA
Jane Liebschutz, MD, MPH
Megan Bair-Merritt, MD, MSCE

Family violence is disturbingly pervasive. It is estimated that 1 in 25 children in the United States are victims of child abuse or neglect and that one quarter of all women will experience intimate partner violence (IPV) during their lifetime.[1] Yearly, 15 million children witness IPV.[2] Children and adults who experience or witness family violence suffer a range of adverse physical and emotional health consequences, facing both immediate safety and health risks as well as longer term impacts on emotional functioning. Healthcare providers are often on the front lines of identifying and addressing family violence. They see adults and children in the emergency department, adult or pediatric primary care, and obstetrical care settings. Their regular contact and close relationships with people put them in a unique position to screen for and identify patients and families experiencing violence.

Once identified, victims of violence and abuse may intersect with multiple facets of the legal system. These include the child protection system, the criminal justice system, and juvenile and/or family courts. Responses to family violence in the medical and legal systems vary depending on the type and severity of the violence. It is important that healthcare and legal practitioners understand the dynamics of family violence, its effect on family members' health and how to access services to effectively address the needs of patients and clients. Medical-legal partnerships (MLPs) are uniquely positioned to address safety issues for families experiencing violence and ensure that they have access to legal and social services that help them to stay safe. These efforts are critical to optimizing victims' and children's health and well-being.

This chapter begins with an examination of IPV, focusing on the health and legal implications of IPV, and the strategies MLPs can use to most effectively screen for and address this kind of violence. It then focuses on child maltreatment and child exposure to IPV, examining the impact on child functioning as well as strategies for identifying and protecting children experiencing abuse or exposure to violence in their homes.

Definitions of Child Maltreatment and Family Violence

The phrases "child maltreatment" and "family violence" are used throughout this chapter. "Child maltreatment" includes both child abuse and child neglect. "Family violence" describes violence between family members, including violence between adults in the home, parental violence directed toward a child, elder abuse or violence between siblings. For the purposes of this chapter, we focus on three forms of family violence: child abuse and neglect, IPV and children's exposure to IPV. These types of violence are defined as follows:

Child abuse: The nonaccidental commission of any act by a caregiver on a child (in most states defined as a person under age 18) that causes or creates a substantial risk of physical or emotional injury; constitutes a sexual offense; or any sexual contact between a caregiver and a child under the care of that individual.[a]

Child neglect: Failure by a caregiver, either deliberately or through negligence or inability, to take those actions necessary to provide a child with minimally adequate food, clothing, shelter, medical care, supervision, emotional stability and growth, or other essential care; provided, however, that such inability is not due solely to inadequate economic resources or solely to the existence of a handicapping condition.[b]

Intimate partner violence (also called domestic violence): A pattern of purposeful coercive behaviors that may include inflicted physical injury, psychological abuse, sexual assault, progressive social isolation, stalking, deprivation, intimidation or threats. These behaviors are perpetrated by someone who is, was or wishes to be involved in an intimate or dating relationship with an adult or adolescent victim and aims to establish control over the other partner.[c]

Child exposure to IPV: A wide range of experiences for children whose parents are being abused physically, sexually or emotionally by an intimate partner. This phrase includes the child who actually observes his or her parents being harmed, threatened or murdered; who overhears this behavior from another part of the home; or who is exposed to the short- or long-term physical or emotional aftermath of the abuse without hearing or seeing a specific aggressive act. Children exposed to IPV may see their parents' bruises or other visible injuries, or bear witness to the emotional consequences of violence, such as fear or intimidation, without having directly witnessed violent acts.[d]

Source: [a] Department of Children and Families Regulations, 110 CMR, section 2.00; note that each U.S. state has its own definition of abuse and neglect; [b] Ibid; [c] B. M. Groves, M. Augustyn, D. Lee, P. Sawires, *Identifying and Responding to Domestic Violence: Consensus Recommendations for Child and Adolescent Health* (San Francisco: Family Violence Prevention Fund, 2002). [d] U.S. Department of Health and Human Services, Administration for Children and Families, Administration on Children, Youth and Families, Children's Bureau, *Child Maltreatment 2008* (Washington, DC: US Department of Health and Human Services, 2010).

Intimate Partner Violence

Intimate partner violence, also referred to as domestic violence, is a prevalent and persistent problem in the United States. In addition to the trauma it causes to victims and their children, it also contributes to a range of health problems. The Centers for Disease Control and Prevention (CDC) estimated in 2003 that the costs of IPV to the health and mental health systems exceed $4.1 billion per year.[3] Similarly, enormous resources are expended each year in the legal system as a result of IPV. It is estimated that IPV accounts for 15 percent of annual total crime costs.[4] To effectively address the needs of victims of IPV and their children, medical and legal practitioners must understand the unique dynamics of IPV as well as the risk factors and consequences for victims.

IPV in the Medical Context

We have provided a working definition of IPV, but definitions of IPV vary depending on one's professional perspective. In the legal system, it is defined primarily as physical violence, sexual violence, or the threat of such violence, which may lead to criminal or civil sanctions. The CDC defines it as "physical, sexual, or psychological harm by a current or former partner or spouse."[5] The public health system views violence victimization as a risk factor for morbidity and mortality, whereas the healthcare delivery system views it as a condition to screen for and a cause for presenting symptoms or a pathologic condition. Generally, IPV may be described as encompassing four forms of violence: physical violence, sexual violence, threats of physical or sexual violence, and psychological/emotional violence.

In assessing IPV, it is important that an MLP practitioner understand the differences between family or partner conflict or disagreement and the coercive, control-based intimidation or violence that characterizes IPV.[6] Figure 11.1 illustrates how physical violence is used as part of a larger scheme to exert power and control over the victim. Practitioners'

Figure 11.1 Power and Control in Physical and Sexual Violence

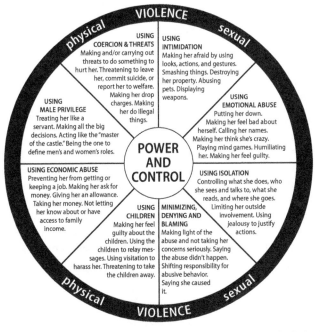

Source: Domestic Abuse Intervention Project, "Power and Control Wheel of Physical and Sexual Violence" (Duluth, MN: Domestic Abuse and Intervention Project).

responses and interventions must take the power dynamics of the relationship and the particular safety concerns of the victim into careful consideration.

Prevalence: Violence and Women's Health

One in five adult women report that they have experienced IPV at some point in the past.[7] Although men may be victims of IPV, it is far more common that women are victims. The U.S. Bureau of Justice Statistics reports that 4.3 per 1,000 women experience IPV per year compared to 0.8 per 1,000 men.[8] Although not every victim of IPV experiences morbidity related to this experience, it has been linked to a number of negative health outcomes for victims.[9] In addition, women experiencing IPV often increase healthcare usage during the period of violence.[10] Emerging evidence suggests that after cessation of IPV these healthcare costs decline, pointing to a causal effect of this violence on health and healthcare usage.[11] Thus, medical professionals interact frequently with victimized women and can play a role not only in treating medical outcomes but in recognizing and helping advocate for victims.

Risk Factors for IPV

Risk factors for IPV occur on multiple levels — individual, relationship and societal.

Individual Risk Factors

The individual risk factors include the following.

- Childhood exposure to violence, including witnessing parental violence, a commonly recognized risk factor for both violence perpetration (men) and victimization (women).[12]

- Marital status: single, separated or divorced women have higher prevalence of IPV in the United States.[13]

- Age: adults ages 18 to 24 have the highest risk for both perpetrating and experiencing IPV.[14]

- Race/ethnicity and poverty: a higher proportion of women of color experience violence, though this may be attributed to co-occurring poverty and not race per se.[15]

- Previous history of violence: many perpetrators of IPV have a history of prior violent behavior in the past. One study in Massachusetts showed that 45 percent of male perpetrators of homicide against a female partner had a prior history of violent crime; 19 percent had a history of a restraining order issued by a prior partner.[16] In addition, women whose partners abuse alcohol or use drugs are more likely to experience IPV at the hands of these partners than women whose partners do not abuse alcohol. Though in some analyses women who use alcohol appear more likely to be abused, this effect largely disappears when their partners' alcohol abuse is taken into consideration in the analyses. In addition, there is some evidence that women who are abused may turn to alcohol as a coping mechanism.[17]

Relationship Risk Factors

A common relationship risk factor for escalation of IPV is partner estrangement — either physical leaving or beginning legal separation.[18] These events have also been identified as risk factors for intimate partner homicide and serious injury.[19] Financial imbalance in the relationship, caused when only one partner is working, seems to be a risk factor for IPV.[20] Intense jealousy or suspicion on the part of the perpetrator is also a risk factor. The manifestations may include isolating the victim or stalking her every move,[21] both of which are coercive controlling behaviors, the hallmark of IPV.

Societal Risk Factors

Poverty[22] and homelessness[23] are particularly potent societal risk factors for intimate partner violence because the risk of poverty and the threat of homelessness may serve as deterrents to a woman's decision to leave an abusive relationship. Homelessness may be a direct consequence of escaping a violent relationship, and homeless women have been shown to have higher cumulative rates of violence, abuse and assault over their lifetimes compared to housed poor women. Immigrant women may have similar IPV prevalence compared to native-born persons; however, their immigrant status may increase vulnerability to the consequences of IPV.[24] An undocumented immigrant may fear reporting abuse to legal authorities because of the risk of deportation. (Legal protections for undocumented immigrant victims of IPV are discussed later in this chapter.) Language and cultural barriers, as well as lack of potential support systems, may increase an immigrant's risk for severe consequences of IPV.[25]

Physical Morbidity Associated with IPV

The physical morbidities associated with IPV range from death to minor injuries. In 2005, 329 men and 1,181 women were murdered by an intimate partner.[26] This does not count the homicide victims who died as a result of IPV, such as a new romantic partner of the targeted victim, children, other family members or even suicide by the homicide perpetrator.

IPV is the leading cause of *nonfatal* injury to women in the United States.[27] Injuries inflicted are diverse in nature, but many include the abdomen, breasts and genitals.[28] In addition, it has been demonstrated that injuries to the head and neck are more likely to occur through IPV than other mechanisms.[29] Traumatic brain injury — which can lead to chronic headaches and memory loss — is prevalent among women known to be abused;[30] the degree of brain injury may be related to the severity and frequency of head injury. Characteristic bruise patterns may be seen on a victim's arms if she has attempted to defend herself. However, despite these recognized patterns of injury, researchers have not identified a set of injuries that are sufficiently "predictive" of IPV to act as a screening tool.[31] As discussed later, it is generally recommended that medical practitioners take a universal approach to screening for IPV.

In addition to the direct injuries sustained during abuse, many chronic physical conditions have been linked to IPV. Pain and somatic complaints are particularly prevalent among abused or formerly abused women, who report high levels of headaches and neck pain, digestive disorders, pelvic pain, and overall low self-report of health-related quality of life.[32] As already discussed, numerous studies have shown an increase in healthcare utilization and costs associated with IPV. However, the relationship between women experiencing IPV and the healthcare system is not straightforward. As one scholar has noted, "Women who are abused are more likely to have unmet needs for care, as they do not always seek care for injuries or other health problems stemming from IPV."[33]

Adult Health Risk Behaviors Associated with IPV

Many high-risk health behaviors are associated with experiencing violence, including smoking, substance abuse and risky sexual behaviors.[34] The relationship between IPV and substance abuse is complex. In addition to evidence that substance use may place a person at risk for experiencing violence,[35] exposure to violence may increase subsequent substance use. One study of 3,000 women followed over two years showed that physical and sexual assault led to subsequent increases in both alcohol and drug use.[36] Other longitudinal studies have shown that IPV among low-income women translated into increased levels of intoxication.[37] High-risk sexual behavior is also associated with IPV. In a review of published literature on the topic, Coker and colleagues highlight studies that found significant association between IPV and sexual risk-taking behaviors, such as inconsistent condom use or multiple partners.[38] Sexually transmitted infections, a marker of high-risk sexual practices, has been associated with IPV.[39] Some of this increased risk taking may come from participation in relationships where women feel unable to negotiate condom use.[40]

Mental Health Morbidity Associated with IPV

IPV is associated with temporal increases in levels of stress, depression, anxiety and post-traumatic stress disorder (PTSD).[41] PTSD is a condition experienced after a traumatic event in which the individual experiences repetitive, intrusive flashbacks, nightmares and anxiety symptoms that evoke the initial trauma. PTSD is seen more commonly among abused versus nonabused women, and the risk of PTSD seems to increase with the severity of the abuse or with the presence of prior trauma.[42] IPV as a cause of depression has been difficult to research, because many women experiencing IPV have multiple risk factors for depression that are also risk factors for violence: a history of childhood abuse, multiple children, frequent housing changes and children with behavior problems.[43] However, studies have demonstrated that when violence in the relationship decreases, women are likely to have an improvement in their depression, suggesting a direct causal effect.[44]

The Adult Clinician's Role in Identifying and Responding to IPV

Both adult and pediatric healthcare providers are charged with identifying IPV taking place in the homes of their patients. This section focuses on the role of the provider treating an adult victim. (For more information about the pediatric provider's role in addressing IPV, see the section later in the chapter titled "Screening for and Addressing IPV in the Pediatric Setting.") Healthcare providers treating adult patients have the opportunity to play a significant role in identification of IPV, evaluation of medical and psychological problems associated with IPV, conducting a safety assessment, documentation of findings and referral to appropriate resources, including MLP legal assistance. Throughout the entire clinical encounter, a patient's personal safety should be the prime consideration.

Identification of IPV in individual patients can occur through disclosure (spontaneous or prompted) or through pattern recognition. Numerous assessment tools can be used in the clinical setting to screen for a history of IPV. One easy to use tool, STaT, can help identify lifetime IPV.

STaT: Screen for Lifetime Intimate Partner Violence

Have you been in a relationship where your partner has pushed and Slapped you?

Have you ever been in a relationship where your partner Threatened you with violence?

Have you ever been in a relationship where your partner has thrown, broken and punched Things?

1 positive response: 95 percent sensitivity and 37 percent specificity

2 positive responses: 85 percent sensitivity and 54 percent specificity

3 positive responses: 62 percent sensitivity and 66 percent specificity[a]

Source: [a] A. Paranjape and J.M. Liebschutz, "STaT: A Three Question Screen for Intimate Partner Violence," *Journal of Women's Health* 12, no. 3 (April 2003): 233–239; A. Paranjape, K. Rask K and J.M. Liebschutz, "Utility of STaT for the identification of recent intimate partner violence." *Journal of the National Medical Association* 98, no. 10 (2006): 1663–1669.

If a patient discloses IPV, the clinician should:

- Acknowledge and validate the abuse history.

- Conduct further assessment for comorbid conditions, including depression, PTSD, substance abuse and other health risk behaviors.

- Conduct a safety assessment for signs of danger or lethality. This assessment should include questions about homicide threats, history of serious injury, perpetrator's access to a gun and previous threat with a weapon, unemployment in the perpetrator and substance abuse in the perpetrator.[45]

- Offer to help the patient engage in safety planning (as discussed in more detail shortly).

- Provide education about IPV and refer for support, advocacy and shelter. At this point, a referral to an MLP lawyer should be discussed with the patient.

Documentation of IPV should include:

1. Patient's *report and direct statements* about the incidents resulting in injuries, including any details shared regarding abuser, relationship, location, time, weapons used and so on to the extent the patient is comfortable sharing and having recorded in the chart.

2. *Objective observations* of the patient's appearance, behavior and demeanor.

3. Detailed and accurate descriptions *of any injuries/wounds*, including shape, color, size, location and duration, using body maps and photographs (with patient consent).

4. A plan of care, recommendations for medical follow-up, and efforts to provide additional resources and referrals *without including details of work with advocates and safety planning* to provide the patient with maximum safety.

In addition to consideration of the care for an individual patient, the clinical environment should use an empowerment or trauma-sensitive care model, not one that trivializes or potentially escalates the violence. See Figure 11.2.

In summary, the healthcare provider should interview carefully, assess for danger and respect the patient's right for autonomy and decision making.

Figure 11.2 Empowerment in the Clinical Encounter

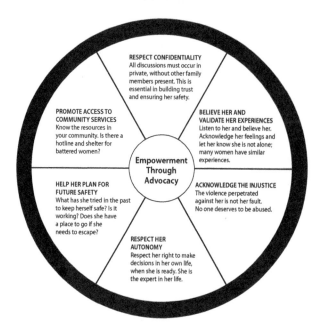

Source: Center for Health and Gender Equity, Population Reports, *Ending Violence Against Women,* Series L, no. 11, December 1999.

A Victim's Decision to Stay or Leave

Finally, it is important to understand that a victim's decision to leave a relationship is rarely easy. The seeming reluctance of some to end an obviously dangerous situation may frustrate healthcare providers, lawyers and other advocates. By definition, IPV occurs after the establishment of a romantic relationship, which may range from dating and living separately to marriage and owning property together. The physical or sexual violence is often intermittent whereas the psychological abuse tends to be continuous. Sometimes, the psychological abuse can make the victim believe that she is the cause of the problem and not the victim of abuse. The psychological abuse may, over time, reduce a victim's belief in self-efficacy; she may come to believe that she cannot escape. Sometimes the violence may come in short spurts with long periods of relative calm. It may take multiple violent events and interventions by family, friends, clergy, healthcare personnel or other advocates for her to recognize the abusive situation.

As noted, separation is often the most dangerous time for a victim of IPV. Many perpetrators threaten to kill the victim and/or her children if she leaves. Additionally, in many abusive relationships, the victim is isolated from friends and family and has little or no access to the family finances. Major concerns in leaving a relationship include children's welfare, housing, money, and, most important, personal safety. Psychological counseling as well as financial and legal planning may be necessary for a victim to safely and successfully leave an abusive relationship.

Best Practices and Advocacy Strategies for Medical-Legal Partnership

One of the most important parts of counseling a victim of IPV is to help her plan ahead to best protect herself from future violence. Following are safety planning strategies from the Center for Health and Gender Equity that medical and legal professionals can discuss with victims.

- Identify one or more neighbors you can tell about the violence, and ask them to seek help if they hear a disturbance in your home.

- If an argument seems unavoidable, try to have it in a room or an area that you can leave easily.

- Stay away from any room where weapons might be available.

- Practice how to get out of your home safely. Identify which doors, windows, elevator or stairwell would be best.

- Have a packed bag ready, containing spare keys, money, important documents and clothes. Keep it at the home of a relative or friend, in case you need to leave your home in a hurry.

- Devise a code word to use with your children, family, friends and neighbors when you need emergency help or want them to call the police.

- Decide where you will go if you have to leave home and have a plan to get there (even if you do not think you will need to leave).

- Use your instincts and judgment. If the situation is dangerous, consider giving the abuser what he is demanding to calm him down. You have the right to protect yourself and your children.

- Remember: you do not deserve to be hit or threatened.[46]

Questions for Discussion

1. How should healthcare providers identify victims of IPV?

2. What are the key elements of an effective interview and interaction with a patient who may be a victim of IPV?

3. What are the key elements of an *in*effective interview and interaction with a patient who may be a victim of IPV?

Legal Protections for Victims of IPV

The role of the law in responding to IPV has evolved significantly in the past 30 years. In the 1980s, battered women's advocates began to shift their focus from grassroots efforts, such as development of shelters and supportive programs for women and children leaving abusive partners, toward seeking protections from the state, which involved legal remedies and court involvement. These efforts included criminal sanctions for abuse, civil protection orders and recognition of past domestic violence in child custody determinations.[47] Developing and enforcing state laws designed to protect victims and their children have been a key strategy of advocates seeking recognition of family violence as a societal problem as well as an effective means for reducing its impact. Perhaps the most significant milestone in achieving these goals, however, was the passage of the federal Violence Against Women

Act (VAWA) of 1994 (which has been reauthorized and expanded by Congress twice, in 2000 and 2005).[48] As detailed next, VAWA has made enormous strides in supporting states to hold perpetrators of partner abuse accountable.

Even with these significant developments in the law, the legal system's response to IPV remains problematic and controversial. Many domestic violence advocates view the legal system as insensitive to the needs of victims and children.[49] Some legal protections, such as civil protective orders, they argue, are only as effective as those charged with enforcing them.[50] Perhaps most complex and problematic is the nexus between the child protection system, designed to protect children from abuse and neglect, and the legal and social systems focused on protecting victims from partner abuse. Although some state laws support victims and punish perpetrators in child custody determinations, other "failure to protect" laws may punish victims for exposing their children to partner abuse by removing children from the home.[51] These laws are discussed in detail shortly.

Given their place in the healthcare setting, MLPs play a critical role in responding to family violence, both by assessing the impact of violence on health and safety and by offering comprehensive on-site services, including legal assistance, to victims and their children. Because of the focus on interdisciplinary, multifaceted problem solving, MLPs are positioned to connect victims to a range of short- and long-term health, social service and legal supports.

Federal Law

The Violence Against Women Act (VAWA)

In 1994, Congress passed VAWA as Title IV of the Violent Crime Control and Law Enforcement Act. The Act represented the first comprehensive federal recognition of and response to the problem of violence against women. The Department of Justice, the federal agency responsible for implementing VAWA, describes the goals of the Act:

> VAWA requires a coordinated community response (CCR) to domestic violence, sexual assault, and stalking, encouraging jurisdictions to bring together players from diverse backgrounds to share information and to use their distinct roles to improve community responses to violence against women. These players include, but are not limited to: victim advocates, police officers, prosecutors, judges, probation and corrections officials, healthcare professionals, leaders within faith communities, and survivors of violence against women. The federal law takes a comprehensive approach to violence against women by combining tough new penalties to prosecute offenders while implementing programs to aid the victims of such violence.[52]

Some key provisions of VAWA include:

- Created a national domestic violence hotline.

- Provided $1.6 billion in grants to assist state and local governments and courts to develop and strengthen effective law enforcement and prosecution strategies to combat violent crimes against women and develop and strengthen victim services.

- Appropriated funds for civil legal assistance to victims of violence.

- Made it a felony to cross state lines with the intent to injure, harass or intimidate a spouse or intimate partner.

- Allowed "full faith and credit" for protective orders across state lines and prohibits the interstate violation of a state court's order of protection that involves protection against credible threats of violence, repeated harassment or bodily injury to the person or persons whom the order covers.

- Developed a mechanism for enabling battered immigrant women to obtain lawful immigration status without relying on the assistance of an abusive citizen husband.

- Provided a civil rights remedy for victims of gender-motivated violence, allowing victims of such violence to bring suits in federal court against perpetrators for violation of the victims' civil rights. (This provision was later deemed unconstitutional by the U.S. Supreme Court in 2000 in *United States v. Morrison.* The Court held that Congress did not have the power to enact this provision.[53])

VAWA 2000 and 2005: Reauthorization and Expansion

The Violence Against Women Act of 2000 (VAWA 2000) and the Violence Against Women and Department of Justice Reauthorization Act of 2005 (VAWA 2005) reauthorized the grant programs created by the original VAWA and also established new programs.

Key Provisions of VAWA 2000

- Strengthened protections under the 1994 Act for battered immigrants, sexual assault survivors and victims of dating violence.

- Enabled victims of domestic violence who flee across state lines to obtain custody orders without returning to jurisdictions where they may be in danger.

- Provided funding for supervised visitation and safe exchange programs for children whose parents are involved in domestic violence.

Key Provisions of VAWA 2005

- Provided that any civil legal assistance program funded by the Legal Services Corporation can assist any victim of domestic violence, regardless of immigration status.

- Increased focus on access to services for underserved populations, including culturally specific programs.

- Provided grants to help public and assisted housing programs respond to domestic violence and ensure tenant safety.

- Supported programs for children who have witnessed domestic violence and preventive interventions with men and youth.

- Provided for the training and education of medical students and other healthcare providers and strengthens the healthcare system's response to victims.

Source: P.L. 103-32; National Coalition Against Domestic Violence, *Comparison of VAWA 1994, VAWA 2000 and VAWA 2005 Reauthorization Bill* (Washington, DC: National Coalition Against Domestic Violence, January 16, 2006), http://www.ncadv.org/files/VAWA_94_00_05.pdf (accessed January 18, 2011).

VAWA has been critical in supporting state and local efforts in preventing and addressing domestic violence. Grants through VAWA often require or encourage multidisciplinary approaches to more effective law enforcement as well as services to victims and children. The 2005 provisions emphasizing the education of healthcare providers about IPV and supporting civil legal assistance to victims (without regard to immigration status) are important to MLPs. MLPs are well situated to train medical and legal professionals about appropriate responses to domestic violence and offer both preventive and responsive services to victims and children in the healthcare setting.

IPV and Homelessness:
Connecting Housing Laws and Policies to Family Violence

Domestic violence is estimated to be a leading cause of homelessness, particularly among women.[a] In VAWA 2005, Congress noted in its findings that:

- 92 percent of homeless women have experienced "severe physical or sexual abuse at some point in their lives."

- There were nearly 150 "documented eviction cases in the last year alone where the tenant was evicted because of the domestic violence crimes committed against her."

- As many as 100 persons were "denied housing because of their status as victims of domestic violence."

- Many domestic violence victims return to their abusers because they are unable to secure long-term housing.[b]

A study by the National Center on Homelessness and Poverty and National Network to End Domestic Violence found that 28 percent of housing denials by public and subsidized housing and private landlords were denials of domestic violence victims because of the violence against them. Reasons included:

- a victim's former residence was a domestic violence shelter,

- a victim had a history of obtaining a civil protection order from the court against the abuser,

- a victim had a record of calling the police several times at a former residence,

- a previous landlord stated that the applicant had experienced domestic violence.[c]

Source: [a] National Law Center on Homelessness and Poverty & National Network to End Domestic Violence, *Lost Housing, Lost Safety: Survivors of Domestic Violence Experience Housing Denials and Evictions Across the Country* (Washington, DC: National Center on Homelessness and Poverty National Network to End Domestic Violence February 2007); [b] Violence Against Women Act and Department of Justice Reauthorization Act of 2005, P.L. 109-162, §41401,119 Stat. 2960 (2005); [c] National Law Center on Homelessness and Poverty & National Network to End Domestic Violence, *Lost Housing, Lost Safety.*

State Law

Civil Protection Orders

Between 1976 and 1992, civil protection order legislation was enacted in all 50 states. Funding through VAWA vastly expanded civil legal assistance to victims to help obtain and enforce protection orders.[54] A civil protection order (or restraining order) is a court order protecting a victim of abuse (petitioner) from future abuse or harassment by an accused perpetrator of abuse (respondent). In seeking such an order, the petitioner files a request (petition) with the court stating the reasons he or she needs protection, the relationship he or she has with the perpetrator, and the type of remedies he or she is seeking. The petitioner's stated reasons must conform to the state statute's definition of domestic violence. For example, a state civil protection order statute may not recognize harassment as domestic violence and may require that the petitioner state that the respondent has a history of physical violence against him or her or has threatened imminent physical violence. Similarly, because stalking may not be covered by civil protection order statutes, some states have separate protections for victims of stalking. For example, in Ohio, victims who do not qualify for a protective order under the domestic violence statute may petition the court for a special protective order focusing on stalking and sexual violence, the Stalking or Sexually Oriented Offense Protection Order, for relief (Ohio Revised Code, Chapter 2903.214).

The Process for Obtaining a Civil Protection Order

There are generally two steps in obtaining a civil protection order. In the initial phase, the petitioner files a request for an *ex parte* order, meaning that the judge makes a decision on the petition without requiring the petitioner to notify the respondent of the request. The purpose of an *ex parte* order is that a survivor may need protection immediately and will be in danger if the assailant is notified of the request before an order is in place. Once the *ex parte* order has been issued, the court requires that the order be served on the respondent.

The second phase is a court hearing at which both the petitioner and the respondent may be represented by counsel and may present evidence, witnesses and testimony to support or refute the issuing of a final order. In some states, a hearing is not automatically scheduled unless the respondent requests it within a certain amount of time after being served with the *ex parte* order. If no hearing is requested, the *ex parte* order becomes the final order. In other states, the court automatically schedules a hearing after issuing an *ex parte* order and notice of that hearing date must be served on the respondent with the *ex parte* order.[55]

If, after the hearing, the court finds sufficient evidence of domestic violence to continue the order, state statutes usually grant broad discretion to judges regarding the types of relief that may be granted. This means that in addition to ordering the defendant to have no contact with the victim and the victim's children, the court may also order a range of other relief. For example, the order may require that the defendant vacate the family home, surrender a firearm, pay child support or attend counseling. Most states limit the duration of civil protection orders; most commonly they last one to four years, although some states allow a court to grant an order with an indefinite duration.[56]

Key Elements of Civil Protection Orders

- The petitioner must sign a sworn statement (affidavit) providing the reason she or he is seeking protection from defendant. This generally must include past physical violence or threat of physical violence.

- State statutes define a class of eligible applicants (generally the petitioner and defendant must be members of the same family or household).

- The order will specifically state how the defendant will be restricted from contact with the petitioner and, in some cases, the petitioner's children, as well as other types of protection to ensure safety.

- The defendant does not have to be present for a temporary order to be issued, but has the right to be heard at a hearing before a final order is issued (usually within a few weeks after the temporary order is granted).

- A petitioner may seek to modify or dismiss a final order at any time after it has been issued.

- The final order usually has a limited time period, most commonly between one and four years.

- If a defendant violates the protective order, he or she may be arrested. Violation of an order is a criminal offense in most states.

Source: Institute for Law and Justice, *Domestic Violence: A Review of State Legislation Defining Police and Prosecution Duties and Powers* (Alexandria, VA: Institute for Law and Justice, June 2004).

Civil protective order statutes vary by state with regard to how they define domestic violence, eligible relationships between the petitioner and the defendant, and the duration of the order of protection. Healthcare providers and lawyers should be familiar with how the key elements listed in the box are defined by their state law. Following is an example of how Massachusetts law delineates who may obtain a protective order and for how long.

Massachusetts General Laws 209A: Abuse Prevention

Section 1.

"Abuse", the occurrence of one or more of the following acts between family or household members:

(a) attempting to cause or causing physical harm;

(b) placing another in fear of imminent serious physical harm;

(c) causing another to engage involuntarily in sexual relations by force, threat or duress [...]

"Family or household members", persons who:

(a) are or were married to one another;

(b) are or were residing together in the same household;

(c) are or were related by blood or marriage;

(d) having a child in common regardless of whether they have ever married or lived together; or

(e) are or have been in a substantive dating or engagement relationship, which shall be adjudged by district, probate or Boston municipal courts consideration of the following factors:

(1) the length of time of the relationship; (2) the type of relationship; (3) the frequency of interaction between the parties; and (4) if the relationship has been terminated by either person, the length of time elapsed since the termination of the relationship [...]

Section 3.

A person suffering from abuse from an adult or minor family or household member may file a complaint in the court requesting protection from such abuse, including, but not limited to, the following orders:

(a) ordering the defendant to refrain from abusing the plaintiff, whether the defendant is an adult or minor;

(b) ordering the defendant to refrain from contacting the plaintiff, unless authorized by the court, whether the defendant is an adult or minor;

(c) ordering the defendant to vacate forthwith and remain away from the household, multiple family dwelling, and workplace. Notwithstanding the provisions of section thirty-four B of chapter two hundred and eight, an order to vacate shall be for a fixed period of time, not to exceed one year, at the expiration of which time the court may extend any such order upon motion of the plaintiff, with notice to the defendant, for such additional time as it deems necessary to protect the plaintiff from abuse. (MGL c. 209A, § 1, 3)

Enforcement of Civil Protection Orders

Any action by the defendant that is not in compliance with the order is a violation, even if the behavior does not involve violence or criminal conduct. If the order provides that the defendant not enter the home of the petitioner, he or she violates the order by entering the home. The petitioner's willingness to allow a violation of the order by the defendant generally does not undermine the enforceability of the order. Most states view the protective order as a matter for the court; therefore, the defendant may not disregard the terms of the order even with the invitation of the petitioner.[57]

Effectiveness of Civil Protection Orders in Stopping Abuse

Civil protection orders have been an important tool is providing safety for victims and their children. But as one commentator notes, "The utility of protection orders depends both on the specificity of the relief ordered and the enforcement practices of the police and the courts."[58] Studies have found that nearly 50 percent of civil protection orders are violated at least once.[59]

As discussed earlier in the chapter, healthcare providers may play a critical role in screening for domestic violence and serving as advocates for victims. Because of this role, an understanding of the process by which victims may seek orders of protection and the relationship between enforcement of protective orders and safety planning is important.

Although seeking a protective order may be an important first step in the road to safety, it does not, in and of itself, protect a victim and children from further violence or necessarily reduce a victim's fear. A 2009 study in Kentucky funded by the U.S. Department of Justice found that although protective orders did reduce some victims' fear, many were still fearful of future harm even six months after obtaining an order. Notably, rural women were more likely to remain fearful of future harm after receiving a protective order than urban women (see Table 11.1).[60] The study suggested that one reason rural women were more likely than urban women to remain fearful after obtaining a protective order was that IPV was treated as a lower priority for law enforcement in the selected rural areas than in the selected urban areas studied.[61]

Mandatory Reporting of IPV by Healthcare Providers

In a few states, healthcare providers are mandated reporters of adult IPV. For example in California, "any health practitioner who provides medical services for a physical condition

Table 11.1 Women Reporting They Are Somewhat or Extremely Fearful of Future Harm

Type of Fear	Rural (n = 93)		Urban (n = 77)	
	Baseline (Shortly After Receiving Order) (%)	Six Months After Receiving Order (%)	Baseline (Shortly After Receiving Order) (%)	Six Months After Receiving Order (%)
Threats and harassment	80	61	67	41
Physical injury	65	46	43	26
Control	74	53	57	32
Humiliation	84	55	59	37
Financial	74	48	59	21
Child interference or harm	82	59	52	34
Hurt others	75	49	33	29

Source: T. K. Logan, R. Walker, W. Hoyt, T. Faragher, *The Kentucky Civil Protective Order Study: A Rural and Urban Multiple Perspective Study of Protective Order Violation Consequences, Responses, & Costs* (Washington, DC: U.S. Department of Justice, September 2009).

to a patient whom he or she knows or reasonably suspects" is "suffering from any wound or other physical injury inflicted upon the person where the injury is the result of assaultive or abusive conduct ... shall make a report to local law enforcement" (Cal. Penal code §§ 11160). Mandatory reporting of adult IPV is controversial. Although proponents believe mandatory reporting will improve patient safety, opponents believe that it undermines patient confidentiality, will discourage victims from seeking healthcare and will put them at greater risk of retaliation from perpetrators.[62] In states where reporting is required, healthcare providers should take great care to work with victims to maximize patient autonomy and safety. See Elements of Responsible Practice in Reporting Adult IPV.

Elements of Responsible Practice in Reporting Adult IPV

In the few states that require healthcare providers to report adult IPV, practitioners should be careful to do so in ways that will be most likely to protect the victim's safety and preserve her autonomy. Following are elements of responsible reporting.

- Inform the patient of your responsibility to make a report to law enforcement.
- Learn how authorities respond to these reports in the local jurisdictions. Inform the patient of the likely response(s) of law enforcement.
- Inform the patient about what may happen to the report (check with your local law enforcement agency).
- Inform the patient that this report is to be kept confidential by the clinic and cannot be accessed by friends, family or other third parties without the patient's consent. Police may have to turn over a copy of the report to the abuser or his attorney but are required to delete information regarding the patient's whereabouts.

- Given the possibility of infringement on patient autonomy, maximize the role of the patient's input in future action; advocate for the patient's needs in communications with authorities/police.

- Address the risk of retaliation and need for precautions.

- Work with the patient and authorities to meet the patient's needs when handling the report (i.e., discuss the address where the patient can be safely contacted).

- Work with advocates and authorities to implement a process for responding to reports that enhance safety and autonomy.

Source: Ariella Hyman, "California's Domestic Violence and Mandatory Reporting Law: Requirements for Health Care Practitioners," San Francisco: Family Violence Prevention Fund, http://www.endabuse. org/userfiles/file/HealthCare/mandatory_calif.pdf (accessed January 18, 2011).

When a victim reveals IPV to a healthcare provider or lawyer, the immediate concern should be ensuring the safety of the victim and her children. Professionals should not underestimate the importance of their role in helping victims think about safety in both the short and long run. As discussed earlier, even if a victim is not ready to leave an abusive partner, it is important for her to engage in safety planning. In addition, MLP lawyers and healthcare providers should work together to connect victims with the resources they need, including legal remedies, such as protective orders or child custody orders, domestic violence programs, safe and secure housing, and income supports. They can also help victims navigate the legal and social systems they will inevitably encounter as they seek safety. IPV victims who are parents face particular safety concerns and legal issues with regard to their children. These issues are discussed in the next section in relation to child maltreatment and exposure to IPV and the role that MLPs play in addressing the needs of victims and children.

Best Practices and Advocacy Strategies for Medical-Legal Partnership

To assist healthcare providers in identifying and responding to IPV and to institutionalize screening, the Lancaster Medical-Legal Partnership for Families in Pennsylvania developed two resources: an Intimate Partner Violence Assessment Documentation Form and a wallet-sized Domestic Violence Resources Information Card. Both were produced in English and Spanish. The MLP lawyer from MidPenn Legal Services coordinates training for the entire health center staff at Southeast Lancaster Health Services—healthcare providers, dental staff, nurses, social workers, support staff, billing staff and administrators—about IPV assessment in the healthcare setting. Representatives from local domestic violence programs participate in the training.

The protocol following the training is that patients are screened by healthcare staff once a year, using the assessment form. The screening is always performed in private—in the absence of partners, relatives, friends, children older than 10 or anyone else who may be accompanying the patient to the appointment. The assessment forms are laminated, and the nurse completes the assessment with a dry erase marker. A negative assessment is noted in the patient's chart but not attached to the chart in hard-copy form. Positive assessments are attached to the chart in hard-copy form.

The assessment form was carefully designed to use simple language and clear, nonthreatening questions. The form includes a step-by-step analysis with instructions for the nurse conducting the assessment. Patients who disclose abuse or request assistance are offered a variety of services—information and resources, a safe place to call the local domestic violence shelter or police, social work support or legal consultation. The protocol also provides that domestic violence resource posters are hung in each patient exam room and restroom, and that a supply of wallet-sized domestic resource cards is readily available for patients.

Case for Medical-Legal Partnership

Susan, a 22-year-old patient, reveals during her annual exam that she is the victim of IPV. She tells her physician that she has not told anyone about the abuse and is terrified that if she does, her abuser will seriously harm or kill her. The physician practices in a state in which healthcare providers are mandated reporters of adult IPV.

Questions for Discussion

Medical

1. What additional questions should you ask Susan?

2. What steps will you take to help ensure Susan's safety?

3. If you decide you must report this case to authorities, what will you say to Susan?

Legal

1. What legal options does Susan have to try to protect herself?

2. What barriers might you face in trying to help Susan take advantage of legal protections?

3. How will you address those barriers? What kind of support and advice will you give Susan?

Child Maltreatment and Exposure to IPV

Healthcare providers may be the first point of contact for children who are abused or exposed to IPV. State laws mandate that healthcare providers report suspicion of child maltreatment (and in some states, childhood exposure to IPV) to Child Protective Services. In addition, healthcare providers must assess the safety of family members. Despite these mandates, family violence may be quite challenging for providers to identify, and management is often complicated. MLPs and other community agencies that provide ongoing services are valuable tools for safety assessments and referrals.

The Effects of Violence on Child Health

Epidemiology of Child Maltreatment and Childhood Exposure to IPV

In 2008, approximately 750,000 children were victims of abuse with the highest rates occurring in children less than three years of age.[63] Young children are also disproportionately represented in the group of children who suffered fatalities due to child abuse and neglect: 79.8 percent of these children were younger than four years of age.[64] Of all forms of child maltreatment, neglect is by far the most common; more than 70 percent of Child Protective Services investigations occur due to suspected neglect.[65]

Compared to their peers, children living in low socioeconomic households are more than three times as likely to be abused and about seven times as likely to be neglected than their higher income peers. Low socioeconomic status is also a risk factor for IPV, and child maltreatment and IPV commonly co-occur in the same families.[66]

Each year in the United States, over 15 million children are exposed to IPV. Approximately half of these children live in homes with severe IPV, which includes parents beating each other up or using a knife or gun against one another.[67] Childhood IPV exposure can be direct or indirect. *Direct* exposure generally refers to the child being in the room or overhearing the violence from a proximal room. For example, children may be in the room when IPV is occurring and may get "caught in the crossfire," literally caught in the middle of a violent argument between parents. *Indirect* exposure generally refers to changes in parental or parenting characteristics that are altered as a result of the IPV, such as maternal depression.

Healthcare providers are uniquely positioned to screen a wide age range of children for abuse and exposure to IPV. Sixty to seventy percent of school-age children visit pediatricians annually, and, because of the required visit schedule, infants and very young children go to a physician even more often.[68] Given that the rates of IPV and child maltreatment are highest in families with a child under age five, healthcare providers may be the only professionals to have dependable access to the children at highest risk of exposure to violence.[69]

Violence in the Home and Childhood Exposure

• 15.5 million children in the United States were exposed to IPV at least once in the past year; 7 million children were exposed to severe partner violence.[a]

• According to the Department of Justice, the majority of IPV incidents (two-thirds) in the United States occur at home. In 38 percent of homes in which these incidents occur, children under age 12 are residents.[b]

• In a single day in 2008, 16,458 children were living in a domestic violence shelter or transitional housing facility.[c]

Source: [a] C. L. Whitfield, R. F. Anda, S. R. Dube, V. J. Felitlle, "Violent Childhood Experiences and the Risk of Intimate Partner Violence in Adults: Assessment in a Large Health Maintenance Organization," *Journal of Interpersonal Violence*, 18, no. 2 (2003): 166–85; [b] S. Catalano, *Intimate Partner Violence in the United States* (Washington, DC: U.S. Department of Justice, Office of Justice Programs, Bureau of Justice Statistics, 2007); [c] The National Network to End Domestic Violence, *Domestic Violence Counts 2008: A 24-hour Census of Domestic Violence Shelters and Services* (Washington, D.C.: National Network to End Domestic Violence, 2009).

Impact of Maltreatment and IPV Exposure on Child Physical Health

The injuries that result directly from child maltreatment cause significant morbidity and mortality. Compared to children admitted to the hospital for accidental injuries, maltreated children are more likely to suffer from severe injury, be admitted to an intensive care unit and die as a result of their injuries.[70] In addition to direct injury, maltreatment has been associated with a host of additional adverse childhood physical health outcomes. Similarly, childhood exposure to IPV, even in cases in which children are not abused themselves, predicts poor health. Adverse childhood experiences, including family violence, appear to have a graded relationship with child physical health such that as the number of adverse experiences increases, health declines.[71] Specific childhood physical health outcomes that have been associated with child abuse or IPV exposure include asthma, failure to thrive, developmental delay and increased number of somatic complaints.[72] In addition to associations between family violence and poor childhood physical health, a history of child maltreatment or childhood exposure to IPV has consistently been linked with poor *adult* physical health, including increased rates of allergies, bronchitis, certain cancers and cardiovascular disease.[73]

Altered neuroendocrine stress response is one important mechanism linking maltreatment and IPV exposure to poor physical health (see Figure 11.4). When a person feels nervous or scared, the body generates a "fight-or-flight" response. Neurotransmitters and hormones are released that lead to short-term effects in the body, such as increased heart rate and increased blood glucose. Although these changes are adaptive in the short term, repeated activation of this stress response (especially in infancy or childhood) results in long-term pathologic changes in neurological and hormonal systems that do not enable the body to fully return to the prestress state after subsequent stressors. Thus, a child's traumatic experiences of maltreatment and IPV exposure "calibrate" the physiology of the stress response and can lead to a range of health risks over the course of a lifetime.[74]

Asthma is an example of an inflammatory health condition that is significantly impacted by childhood stress;[75] children exposed to IPV have a twofold greater risk of developing asthma than children who are not exposed.[76] This increased risk most likely occurs because altered stress physiology magnifies the body's response to allergens and irritants, leading to increased airway hyperreactivity and, ultimately, a diagnosis of asthma.

Figure 11.3 Stress and Its Impact on the Body

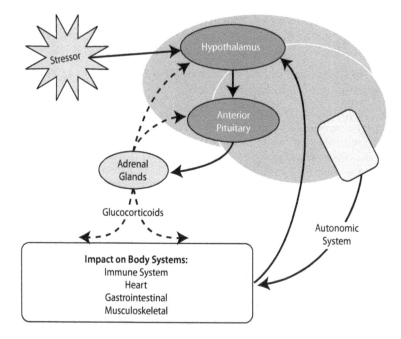

Changes in early brain development related to trauma help explain how maltreatment and/or IPV exposure lead to adverse emotional health outcomes. Children's developing brains are sensitive to traumatic experiences in the social environment, with child abuse and neglect representing one of the most toxic of all exposures. Imaging studies of the brains of children who have been severely abused or neglected reveal changes to the structure of the brain that may affect learning and regulation of emotions (see Figure 11.4). Infants and very young children are particularly vulnerable to these impacts because this time of life is considered to be a critical period for brain development.[77]

Figure 11.4 A Healthy versus an Abused Brain

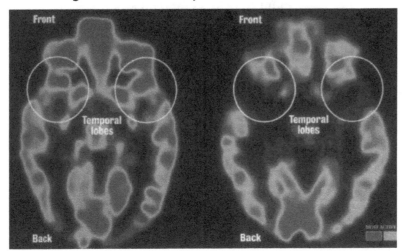

Healthy Brain: This PET scan of the brain of a normal child shows regions of high and low activity. At birth, only primitive structures such as the brain stem (center) are fully functional; in regions like the temporal lobes (top), early childhood experiences wire the circuits.

Abused Brain: This PET scan of a brain of a Romanian orphan, who was institutionalized shortly after birth, shows the effect of extreme deprivation in infancy. The temporal lobes (top), which regulate emotions and receive input from the senses, are nearly quiescent. Such children suffer emotional and cognitive problems.

Source: 14th National Conference on Child Abuse and Neglect: Gateways to Prevention, "Positron Emission Tomography Scan, Healthy Brain Abused Brain" (Washington, DC: U.S. Department of Health and Human Services, Administration for Children and Families, March 2003). *Data Source:* Centers for Disease Control and Prevention.

Impact of Maltreatment and IPV on Child Emotional Health and Social Functioning

In a survey of more than 10,000 children between the ages of 0 and 18 who sought trauma-related mental health services in the United States, the most commonly mentioned traumas were child abuse, sexual abuse and exposure to IPV.[78] Many of these children were exposed to multiple types of traumas, and the exposures began at an early age. The effects of multiple exposures to violence and abuse are cumulative, and these children have significantly greater rates of PTSD, other anxiety disorders and depression.

Children Exposed to IPV: The Hidden Victims

Numerous studies affirm that children who witness IPV are affected in similar ways to children who are direct victims of abuse.[79] This fact has been less well recognized, especially with younger children, who are assumed by many to be less vulnerable to the effects of exposure to violence because of their young age. Evidence suggests that exposure to domestic violence may be profoundly damaging for young children.[80] Children depend on their parents for emotional safety and protection. When parents are aggressive or victimized, they are less able to protect their children. Children show intense anxiety about their own safety and that of their parents. They begin to see their world as dangerous and unpredictable. In addition, they learn early and powerful lessons about the use of violence

Table 11.2 Symptoms/Behaviors Associated with Child Exposure to IPV by Age

Birth to Age 5	Ages 6 to 11	Ages 12 to 18
• Sleep or eating disruptions • Withdrawal/lack of responsiveness • Intense/pronounced separation anxiety • Inconsolable crying • Developmental regression, loss of acquired skills • Intense anxiety, worries or new fears • Increased aggression or impulsive behavior	• Nightmares, sleep disruptions • Aggression and difficulty with peer relationships in school • Difficulty with concentration and task completion in school • Withdrawal or emotional numbing • School avoidance or truancy	• Antisocial behavior • School failure • Impulsive or reckless behavior, such as: • School truancy • Substance abuse • Running away • Involvement in violent or or abusive dating relationships

Source: D. Wolfe, C. Crooks, V. Lee, et al., "The Effects of Children's Exposure to Domestic Violence: A Meta-Analysis and Critique," *Clinical Child and Family Psychology Review*, 16 (2003): 171–87.

in intimate relationships, and because children imitate adults, they use this violence in their social relationships.[81]

Numerous studies have documented the short- and long-term impact of child maltreatment and IPV on child/adolescent social and emotional development. Specific emotional health problems related to child maltreatment and IPV exposure differ depending on a child's age and development (see Table 11.2).[82]

Healthcare Use Patterns for Abused Children and Children Exposed to IPV

The American Academy of Pediatrics recommends that infants see their pediatric provider for well child visits at least five times within the first year of life, and two times in the second year of life.[83] After the second year, children generally are expected to attend well child visits annually. Compared to their peers, abused children and children exposed to IPV are less likely to have attended the recommended number of well child visits and also less likely to be fully immunized.[84] In addition, they are less likely to have continuity in the care they do receive,[85] which can complicate both the identification of abuse as well as the provision of care for any health or emotional problems that occur as a result of the maltreatment. Despite not keeping well child visits, families experiencing violence are more likely to bring their children to acute visits or to the emergency department (ED).[86]

This increased ratio of acute care and ED visits to well child visits is likely due to several factors. First, these children are at elevated risk for injury, which often necessitates ED visits. Additionally, EDs provide care 24 hours a day, 7 days a week, and do not require an appointment. Families experiencing violence may have difficulty making and keeping appointments, obtaining transportation to appointments or attending appointments during standard hours. Families in which child maltreatment is occurring may limit their care with a single provider in an attempt to hide the abuse. Finally, abused women also may be depressed, anxious or suffer from PTSD. This may translate into healthcare seeking for acute problems due to hypervigilance, misinterpretation of a child's symptoms or difficulty managing chronic conditions.[87]

Children who enter the foster care system are a particularly high-risk group for both health problems and poor continuity of care.[88] Care can be disrupted because the foster family lives far away from the child's primary provider, because of poor communication between child protection services and medical providers, or because the system mandates a change in the provider.

These altered healthcare use patterns cost the system money and reduce the quality of care. Patient advocates in both the medical and legal systems must work together to find ways to ensure that abused children and children exposed to IPV have access to a patient-centered medical home that provides comprehensive, longitudinal care.

The Role of Healthcare Providers in Identifying and Addressing Child Maltreatment and Exposure to IPV

Although healthcare use patterns of abused children or children exposed to IPV differ from their peers, nearly all of these children see their pediatric providers with some frequency, particularly in the first years of their lives. These professionals, therefore, are on the front lines of learning about child or family traumatic experiences and serve as sentinel professionals in the effort to provide early identification and intervention for the childhood traumas of child abuse, neglect or IPV. Because children depend almost exclusively on their parents for emotional support and protection, many experts believe that an essential strategy for helping the young child affected by abuse or trauma is to help the parent by providing advocacy and support.[89] These supports may be offered by MLPs through legal advocacy, assistance with obtaining an order of protection and/or safety planning for victims of IPV.

Screening for and Addressing Child Abuse and Neglect

Pediatric healthcare providers should conduct a thorough social history at *all* well child visits. This social history should include questions about who lives with and cares for the child, and should assess for stressors such as maternal depression, financial difficulty and substance abuse. If any of these stressors are detected, providers should offer assistance in connecting families with local resources. Comprehensive screening, advocacy and intervention may allow providers to address some of the social determinants of maltreatment and IPV, which may in turn help prevent family violence.

All children should have an *unclothed* exam that allows the provider to examine the child for any skin (bruising, burns, scars) or bony (areas of tenderness or redness) abnormalities. Any abnormalities should be accurately and complete documented. If a child presents with an injury that is concerning for maltreatment, the caregiver should be asked open, nondirective questions about the chronological details leading up to the injury, including how, when and where events occurred and who was present. This history, using quotations when possible, and a thorough physical exam with photographs as appropriate should be completely documented. Suspicion of child maltreatment should be reported to Child Protective Services.[90]

Screening for and Addressing IPV in the Pediatric Setting

Pediatric healthcare providers play a key role in assessing families for IPV. Because of the significant overlap between child abuse and IPV, the American Academy of Pediatrics recommends routine screening of caregivers for IPV, stating that screening female caregivers for IPV may be one of "the most effective means by which to prevent child abuse."[91] Screening caregivers for IPV in a pediatric setting, however, offers unique challenges.[92]

Research suggests that abused women may be reluctant to discuss IPV when a child over the age of three is present.[93] In one study, women expressed concern that these verbal children may relay the conversation to a perpetrator; they also expressed concern that the discussion might traumatize the children.[94] If an older child is present, providers can use more general screening questions, such as "How do you and your partner handle conflicts: with no difficulty, some difficulty or a lot of difficulty?" or may attempt to screen the caregiver alone.[95] Second, because the medical record is the child's and not the woman's, the child's father has equal access to the records. If the father is the perpetrator, there is some concern that his obtaining records with a detailed account of the IPV may lead to increased harm. The provider should discuss options for documentation with the victim and should abide by her wishes.

When patient families reveal IPV to the pediatric provider, he or she should offer supportive statements that validate the victim, assess current safety and escalating violence, and offer local and national resource information. Pediatric providers, however, also must carefully assess for concurrent child maltreatment. It is helpful for healthcare organizations to have protocols for responding when the two forms of violence are co-occurring. Assuming that the mother is not the alleged perpetrator of child maltreatment, it may be helpful to suggest that she make the call to Child Protective Services and document ways she has been protective to her child. However, it is important for providers to know that in most states the parent report does not relieve them of their obligation to report as mandatory reporters of child abuse. Additionally, children exposed to IPV should be seen by their pediatric provider at regular intervals, and if they show concerning behaviors or symptoms, a referral to trauma-based mental health resources should be strongly considered.

Because laws in some states equate a child's exposure to IPV with child maltreatment, healthcare providers may be required to report incidences of exposure to Child Protective Services agencies. It is important that pediatric providers become familiar with the particular laws in their states about reporting child exposure to IPV. The legal definitions of child maltreatment and mandatory reporting duties of healthcare providers are discussed in greater detail next.

State Intervention in the Family When Violence Is Present

Criminal prosecutions for child abuse existed as early as the 1600s, and the first documented civil child abuse case took place in 1874.[96] Early child protection cases, like those litigated today, had to strike a balance between parents' constitutional rights to raise their children as they want to and the state's responsibility to protect children. Today, courts continue to balance parents' rights with children's needs, focusing on children's safety, health and well-being.[97]

Child maltreatment by family members is generally addressed in the civil courts, although more serious maltreatment may also result in a parallel criminal case being brought, depending on the severity of the maltreatment, state law, and whether the situation involves a basis for federal jurisdiction, such as crossing state lines or international borders. Except where specifically noted, this section of the chapter solely addresses civil child welfare interventions.

Federal Laws Governing State Intervention

Child Abuse Prevention and Treatment Act (CAPTA)

The first major stand-alone federal legislation on child abuse and neglect was the Child Abuse Prevention and Treatment Act (CAPTA), which was enacted in 1974 to fund state programs to identify and prevent child abuse and neglect. CAPTA has been amended many times over the years, including focusing more on children with special needs.

Whether a child is considered to be abused or neglected in any particular case will be determined by state law (discussed shortly), but CAPTA provides a minimum federal definition of child abuse and neglect:

- "Any recent act or failure to act on the part of a parent or caretaker which results in death, serious physical or emotional harm, sexual abuse or exploitation; or

- An act or failure to act which presents an imminent risk of serious harm."[98]

CAPTA also includes specific definitions for sexual abuse and withholding of medically indicated treatment (a form of medical neglect), but leaves definitions of other types of child maltreatment (e.g., physical abuse, emotional abuse, neglect) to state law. To receive funding through CAPTA, states must meet certain requirements, including having procedures for reporting, investigation of and response to child maltreatment as well as confidentiality protections and immunity provisions for those who report child maltreatment in good faith.[99] CAPTA also requires that states receiving funding must appoint a guardian ad litem (who can be an attorney or a trained volunteer) in all court cases involving child abuse or neglect.[100] The Act also helps guide the delivery of services for children who have been victims of child maltreatment, including requiring that children under age three who are the subject of a substantiated case of abuse or neglect and substance-affected infants receive referrals for early intervention screenings and services under Part C of the Individuals with Disabilities Education Act.[101] (See Chapter 9 for a discussion of the Individuals with Disabilities Education Act.)

Titles IV-B and IV-E of the Social Security Act

The Social Security Act has been the primary source of federal funding for child protection, foster care and adoption services since 1935. Many of the major federal laws regarding child welfare since then have simply been amendments of the Act, particularly Title IV.

In 1980, the Adoption Assistance and Child Welfare Act (AACWA; P.L. 96-272) amended Titles IV-B and XX of the Social Security Act in several important ways, including imposing the following requirements of states:

- States must make "reasonable efforts" to prevent children from being removed from their homes and to reunite children who have been removed with their families as quickly as possible.

- When children are removed from their homes, they must be placed in the least restrictive setting possible and in the closest possible proximity to their home.

- The court or social services agency must regularly review the status of children in state custody and determine a plan for the child's permanent status (e.g., adoption, return to parent) within set time frames.

Later revisions to Title IV-B put more resources into the prevention of abuse/neglect and preservation of families.[102]

In 1997 the Adoption and Safe Families Act (P.L. 105-89), another revision of Title IV-E, was enacted to increase the focus on child safety and health throughout the progress of child welfare cases, set timelines to prevent children from lingering in non-permanent homes (e.g., long-term foster care), and increase funding and support for adoption efforts.

A more recent major revision to Title IV of the Social Security Act was the Fostering Connections to Success and Increasing Adoptions Act of 2008 (P.L. 110-351). This law aims to improve child welfare practice in many ways, including:

- providing more support for relative caregivers;

- requiring better coordination and oversight of health matters for children in foster care;

- providing additional resources for reunification support for birth families, and for adoption;

- ensuring increased educational stability and sibling connections for children in foster care;

- supporting youth transitioning out of foster care; and

- allocating more direct support for Native Alaskan and American Indian children.

Indian Child Welfare Act

Under the Indian Child Welfare Act (P.L. 95-608), American Indian children and families involved in state child protective services agency interventions and judicial proceedings receive additional protections under federal law. These include specified minimum standards for when a child can be removed from the home and a set burden of proof for when parental rights can be terminated (for non-Indian families, these are determined by state law). States must also choose foster or adoptive homes for Indian children that reflect their culture.

Medicaid, CHIP (the Children's Health Insurance Program) and HIPAA (Health Information Portability and Accountability Act) also affect children who have been maltreated. Medicaid and CHIP provide access to healthcare for children whose families cannot afford it (see Chapter 7). Additionally, most children who are in foster care due to abuse or neglect are entitled to Medicaid. HIPAA protects the privacy of health information of all patients, including maltreated children, subject to relevant exceptions (see Chapter 6).

State Laws Addressing Child Maltreatment
Definitions of Abuse and Neglect

Although federal law provides a minimum definition of abuse and neglect, each state sets out a more detailed definition, which determines whether a child was abused or neglected in a particular case. The different types of child maltreatment covered generally include physical abuse, sexual abuse, emotional abuse and neglect. Some states also include abandonment, educational neglect, medical neglect or parental substance abuse as separate categories and/or define them separately.[103]

Some states do not define the different types of abuse or neglect separately and instead provide one definition that includes many types of maltreatment. For example, Iowa's statute (IA ST § 232.68) provides the following definition:

"Child abuse" or "abuse" means:

a. Any non-accidental physical injury, or injury which is at variance with the history given of it, suffered by a child as the result of the acts or omissions of a person responsible for the care of the child.

b. Any mental injury to a child's intellectual or psychological capacity as evidenced by an observable and substantial impairment in the child's ability to function within the child's normal range of performance and behavior as the result of the acts or omissions of a person responsible for the care of the child, if the impairment is diagnosed and confirmed by a licensed physician or qualified mental health professional....

c. The commission of a sexual offense with or to a child ... as a result of the acts or omissions of the person responsible for the care of the child ... the commission of a sexual offense under this paragraph includes any sexual offense referred to in this paragraph with or to a person under the age of eighteen years.

d. The failure on the part of a person responsible for the care of a child to provide for the adequate food, shelter, clothing or other care necessary for the child's health and welfare when financially able to do so or when offered financial or other reasonable means to do so. A parent or guardian legitimately practicing religious beliefs who does not provide specified medical treatment for a child for that reason alone shall not be considered abusing the child, however this provision shall not preclude a court from ordering that medical service be provided to the child where the child's health requires it....

e. The acts or omissions of a person responsible for the care of a child which allow, permit, or encourage the child to engage in acts prohibited pursuant to section 725.1.... acts or omissions under this paragraph include an act or omission referred to in this paragraph with or to a person under the age of eighteen years.

f. An illegal drug is present in a child's body as a direct and foreseeable consequence of the acts or omissions of the person responsible for the care of the child.

g. The person responsible for the care of a child has, in the presence of the child ... manufactured a dangerous substance ... or in the presence of the child possesses a product containing ephedrine, its salts, optical isomers, salts of optical isomers, or pseudoephedrine, its salts, optical isomers, salts of optical isomers, with the intent to use the product as a precursor or an intermediary to a dangerous substance.

h. The commission of bestiality in the presence of a minor ... by a person who resides in a home with a child, as a result of the acts or omissions of a person responsible for the care of the child.

i. Knowingly allowing a person custody or control of, or unsupervised access to a child or minor, after knowing the person is required to register or is on the sex offender registry....

Parental Substance Abuse

Parental substance abuse may lead to child maltreatment that fits into the definitions already discussed. In addition, most states' laws address parental substance abuse and/or children's exposure to drugs explicitly, either in the civil child protection statutes, the criminal code or both.[a] Some topics covered by state statutes include:

- Toxicology test results showing the presence of drugs in either the newborn or mother shortly before or after delivery, or symptoms or drug dependence or withdrawal in a newborn.[b]

- A medical diagnosis of fetal alcohol syndrome.[c]

- Allowing the child to be in an environment where drugs are kept, used, manufactured or sold.[d]

- Parental drug use that interferes with the parent's ability to properly care for the child.[e]

- Giving alcohol or controlled substances to a child for nonmedical reasons.[f]

Federal law also requires that states develop policies and procedures to address the needs of infants affected by substance abuse.[g] This includes a requirement that health professionals notify the appropriate child welfare agency.[h]

Source: [a] Child Welfare Information Gateway, U.S. Department of Health and Human Services, Administration for Children and Families, "Parental Drug Use as Abuse," (Washington, DC: U.S. Department of Health and Human Services Children's Bureau, May 2009); [b] Md. Crts. & Jud. Proc. Code Ann. §3-818; S.C. Code Ann. §63-7-1660(F)(1); Utah Code Ann. §76-5-112.5. Note that some states simply refer to illegal drugs, or controlled substances generally, whereas others name specific substances, such as cocaine, heroin or methamphetamine; [c] S.C. Code Ann. §63-7-1660(F)(1); S.C. Code Ann. §44-53-378; [d] N.M. Ann. Stat. §30-6-1(I)-(J). Mere presence/use of drugs around a child is primarily a concern with methamphetamine; [e] R.I. Gen Laws §40-11-2(1); N.Y. Soc. Serv Law §371(4-a); [f] Minn. Stat. Ann. §626.556; [g] CAPTA, 42 USCA §5106a; [h] Ibid.

Many states include exceptions in their laws, or carve-outs for specific acts that do *not* constitute abuse. Common examples include reasonable parental discipline[104] and failure to provide medical treatment to a child due to legitimate religious beliefs.[105] A number of states clarify that neglect charges should not apply to caregivers who fail or are unable to provide for their children due to poverty,[106] and at least one state requires that the child-rearing practices of the child's culture of origin be considered.[107]

Mandatory Reporting of Abuse and Neglect

Each state has laws and policies dealing with the procedures for reporting abuse and neglect. Most specify certain professionals who *must* report suspected abuse or neglect when acting in their professional capacity, such as physicians, nurses, teachers, social workers and child-care providers. Some also require reports by individuals who do not work directly with children but may be in a position to uncover child maltreatment through their jobs, such as film processors, substance abuse counselors and parole officers. Approximately 18 states require *any person* who suspects child abuse or neglect to report it.[108]

The level of suspicion or knowledge required to mandate a report also varies by state; for example, a state may require reporting when someone "has reasonable cause to suspect" (Alaska Stat. §§ 47.17.020), "reason to believe" (Utah Ann. Code § 62A-4a-403(1)(a)), or "knows or has reasonable cause to suspect" (Ohio Rev. Code § 2151.421) that abuse or neglect has occurred. Most states also specify whether physician-patient privilege, attorney-client privilege and other normally confidential communications relieve professionals of their responsibility to report,[109] although in some states tensions between different duties (e.g., attorney-client privilege and the duty to report abuse) may not yet have been resolved by legislation or case law.

Reports of child abuse or neglect are generally called in to a phone line run or overseen by the state or county, and the reporter will be asked to provide the child's and caregiver's names, address, age of the child, information about the child's injuries or situation, and information about other children in the home. In most states, reporters can remain anonymous.[110] All state laws require confidentiality protections for child abuse and neglect records, but many specify situations in which a reporter's identity can be shared (e.g., if there was an intentionally false report or if there is a compelling reason to disclose), and report information can be shared with other agencies or organizations specified in the law, generally those with a need for this information to carry out legal responsibilities to protect children from abuse and neglect.

Most states specify penalties for mandated reporters who fail to report abuse or neglect. Knowing and willful failure to report can be a civil violation, misdemeanor or felony depending on the state and the circumstances, and punishment can include fines and/or imprisonment. Intentionally making a false report is also prohibited in the majority of states, and it may be a civil or a criminal offense.[111]

Failure to Thrive: Poverty or Neglect?

Failure to thrive warrants a brief, specific discussion because it represents a medical condition for which an MLP may offer significant benefits for families. Defined simply, *failure to thrive* is due to a lack of nutrition that is sufficient for growth. A child is diagnosed with failure to thrive when he or she is tracking on a growth curve that is lower than the 5 percent compared to other children his or her sex and age, or when he or she has dropped two major growth percentiles (for example from the 75th percent to the 25th percent).[a] There are a variety of underlying etiologies for failure to thrive.[b] Traditionally, these etiologies have been divided into organic causes (there is an underlying medical condition) and nonorganic or psychosocial causes (there is not a diagnosed underlying medical condition). Most often, multiple causes coalesce to lead to poor nutrition and growth.

Poverty is perhaps the most common and significant risk factor for failure to thrive. Food insecurity (lack of availability or access to food) is prevalent in families who live in poverty. Low-income families of a child with failure to thrive may have limited access to food, limited social support or incorrect information about proper infant and child nutrition and feeding patterns. This may be compounded by a child's food refusal or aversion.[c]

Failure to thrive may be the result of child neglect, although it is often difficult to differentiate the independent influences of poverty versus overt neglect.[d] Some have posited that neglect is the underlying etiology for failure to thrive for only a small percentage of children and should be limited to those situations in which a caregiver overtly fails to provide proper nutrition.[e]

To achieve optimal outcomes, a multidisciplinary approach should be taken that includes medical care and family-based advocacy. MLPs may help support the families' efforts to secure an adequate food supply and create a more stable environment in which a child can thrive.

Source: [a] Agency for Healthcare Research and Quality, "Criteria for Determining Disability in Infants and Children: Failure to Thrive," *Evidence Report/Technology Assessment: Number 72,* Publication no. 03-E019 (2003), 13–14, http://www.ahrq.gov/clinic/epcsums/fthrivesum.htm (accessed January 21, 2011); [b] Block et al., "Failure to Thrive"; [c] M. M. Black, H. Dubowitz, P. H. Casey, et al., "Failure to Thrive as Distinct from Child Neglect," *Pediatrics,* 117 (2006): 145–48; S. D. Krugman, H. Dubowitz, "Failure to Thrive," *American Family Physician,* 68, no. 5 (2003): 879–84; [d] Black et al., "Failure to Thrive"; [e] Ibid.

State Child Protection Systems

Once a report of child abuse or neglect is made, the appropriate state or county agency determines whether allegations in the report meet the state's definition of abuse or neglect. If so, the report is "screened in" and the agency investigates further. If not, the report is "screened out" and no further action is taken. Some jurisdictions have different tracks that screened in cases may take, where cases involving more serious danger or harm receive a more traditional and adversarial investigation, whereas lower level neglect allegations receive a more family-centered and services-directed approach (possibly referred to as an "alternative" or "differential" response).

States set out different timelines by which the responsible agency must investigate and take action, depending on the circumstances. The agency charged with investigating is usually child protective services (sometimes called child welfare, child and family services, or some variant of those), although in some jurisdictions the law enforcement agency conducts the investigations, or the two agencies work together.

After an investigation of a screened-in case has been conducted, the report is either considered "unsubstantiated" or "unfounded," meaning there is not enough evidence of abuse or neglect for the agency to take further action, or is "founded" or "substantiated," and the agency generally continues its involvement with the family. The level of evidence to substantiate a report varies by state, from a "preponderance of the evidence" standard to simply having some "credible evidence" that child abuse or neglect occurred.[112] For reports that have been substantiated, one or more adults may be determined to be a "perpetrator" of the child maltreatment, and their names may be entered on a state registry or other database listing perpetrators of child abuse or neglect. Access to that data is generally restricted to child protective agency use as well as screening of adults for foster care, adoption or other child-care positions.

At this point, if the agency finds that the child cannot safely stay in the home, they may remove the child or seek authorization of a judge for the removal. In many states, there is law or agency policy to first seek to place a child with a relative, rather than use a conventional foster care placement.[113] If the child is removed from the home, typically the agency must quickly petition the court to (among other things) have a judge decide that further placement of the child is necessary. A petition to the court may also be made if the family is unwilling to cooperate with the agency, even if the agency does not feel the child needs to leave the home. Figure 11.5 presents an example of this process from Massachusetts.

Figure 11.5 Massachusetts Department of Children and Families: Response to Reports of Suspected Abuse/Neglect

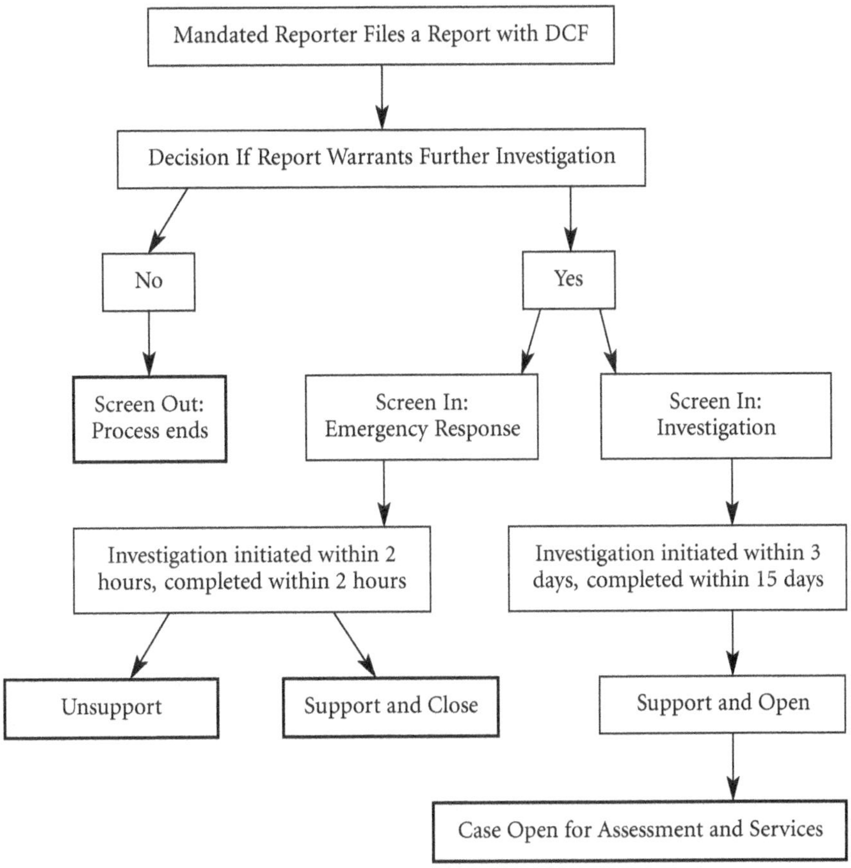

Source: Betsy McAlister Groves, Diagram for Healthcare Provider Trainings, 2009.

Juvenile or Family Court Process

The agency's petition to the court, which initiates a civil child protection action, lays out the facts that constitute abuse or neglect under the state statute. In emergency circumstances, the child may be taken out of the home before this petition is filed; in either case, there will be an initial hearing (also known as a shelter care, detention or emergency removal hearing) in court soon after the petition is filed.[114] The exact timeline for this and many other hearings varies by state. See Figure 11.6 for an example of the process and timelines in Wyoming's juvenile court. At the initial hearing, the judge will decide if it is safe for the child to live at home, and if not, where he or she should live. The judge will also decide if the agency met federal law requirements that it make "reasonable efforts" to keep the child in the home safely. In some states, the family and the agency may also use mediation, pretrial conferences or family group meetings to reach agreement and address some or all of the issues in the case.[115]

At the adjudication hearing, the judge considers sworn testimony and evidence submitted by the agency and the parents, and any evidence brought forward by the child's attorney or guardian ad litem, and make an official finding about whether the child was maltreated.

Figure 11.6 Wyoming Child Protection Act Timeline

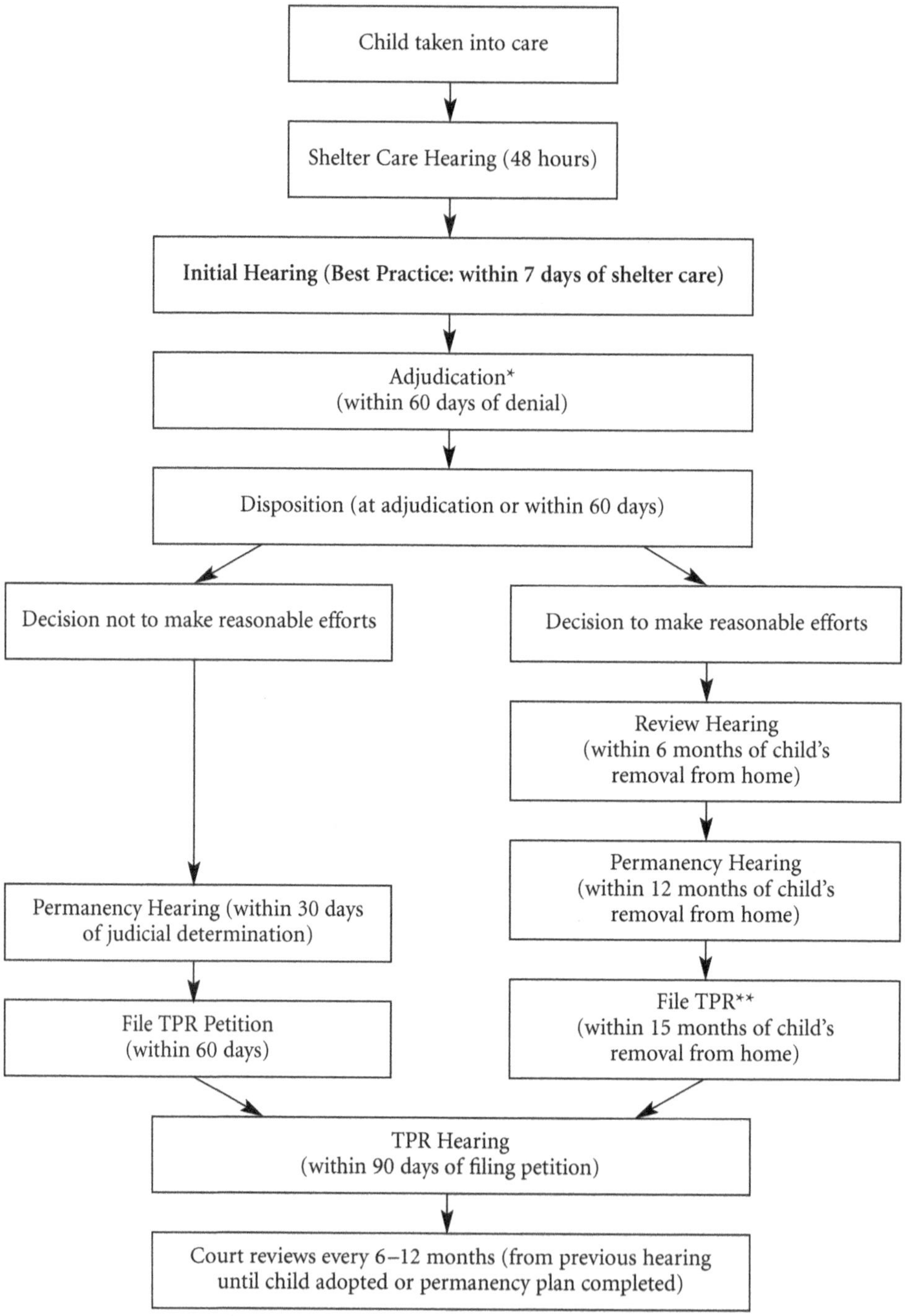

```
┌─────────────────────────────────────────┐
│           Child taken into care          │
└─────────────────────────────────────────┘
                     │
                     ▼
┌─────────────────────────────────────────┐
│      Shelter Care Hearing (48 hours)     │
└─────────────────────────────────────────┘
                     │
                     ▼
┌─────────────────────────────────────────────────────┐
│ Initial Hearing (Best Practice: within 7 days of shelter care) │
└─────────────────────────────────────────────────────┘
                     │
                     ▼
┌─────────────────────────────────────────┐
│              Adjudication*               │
│        (within 60 days of denial)        │
└─────────────────────────────────────────┘
                     │
                     ▼
┌─────────────────────────────────────────────────────┐
│    Disposition (at adjudication or within 60 days)   │
└─────────────────────────────────────────────────────┘
          │                              │
          ▼                              ▼
┌──────────────────────────┐   ┌──────────────────────────┐
│ Decision not to make      │   │ Decision to make          │
│ reasonable efforts        │   │ reasonable efforts        │
└──────────────────────────┘   └──────────────────────────┘
          │                              │
          │                              ▼
          │                   ┌──────────────────────────┐
          │                   │    Review Hearing         │
          │                   │ (within 6 months of child's│
          │                   │   removal from home)       │
          │                   └──────────────────────────┘
          │                              │
          ▼                              ▼
┌──────────────────────────┐   ┌──────────────────────────┐
│ Permanency Hearing         │   │  Permanency Hearing       │
│ (within 30 days of         │   │ (within 12 months of child's│
│ judicial determination)    │   │   removal from home)       │
└──────────────────────────┘   └──────────────────────────┘
          │                              │
          ▼                              ▼
┌──────────────────────────┐   ┌──────────────────────────┐
│ File TPR Petition          │   │       File TPR**          │
│ (within 60 days)           │   │ (within 15 months of child's│
│                            │   │   removal from home)       │
└──────────────────────────┘   └──────────────────────────┘
                    │              │
                    ▼              ▼
┌─────────────────────────────────────────────────────┐
│               TPR Hearing                             │
│       (within 90 days of filing petition)            │
└─────────────────────────────────────────────────────┘
                     │
                     ▼
┌─────────────────────────────────────────────────────┐
│ Court reviews every 6–12 months (from previous hearing│
│   until child adopted or permanency plan completed)   │
└─────────────────────────────────────────────────────┘
```

Notes: * Unless the court finds good cause to postpone the hearing, but no later than 90 days after the petition is filed.
** Unless child is being cared for by a relative or a compelling reason exists not to TPR.
Source: Reprinted with permission from *Wyoming Child Welfare Legal Resource Manual*, 2nd ed. (Washington DC: American Bar Association, 2008).

In the disposition hearing that follows, the court decides what needs to happen next and orders or approves services that must be provided and steps that need to be taken for the child to reunite with the parents. The agency and family are then supposed to work together to develop a detailed document called a case plan that outlines what is expected of each party, and this generally forms the basis for the court's disposition order.[116]

The court (and the agency itself) then hold review hearings (both administrative and judicial), and the case plan may be changed as well as the goals of the case, depending on how the family is doing. The goal may be changed from reunification with the parent(s) to something else, such as adoption, custody by a previously noncustodial parent or legal permanent guardianship with a relative. Sometimes, more than one of these goals will be pursued concurrently, with one being the first choice and the others as back-up options. Under federal law, no later than 12 months from when a child enters foster care, the court must hold a permanency hearing to determine definitively what the child's permanent placement goal should be (42 U.S.C. 671(16)).

If the agency believes, based on the severity of the maltreatment and the parents' failure to address the safety factors that led to the child's removal, that the child should never return to his or her parents, there will be a request for a termination of parental rights (TPR) hearing to determine if the child-parent relationship should be permanently and legally severed. After parental rights are terminated, the court continues to hold review hearings until the child is in a permanent living situation (e.g., adoption, legal guardianship, placement with a relative, or the child reaches the age at which foster care ends, called emancipation from care, which may be age 18 or extend to age 21 at the state's option).[117]

Poverty, Race and the Child Protection System

The proportion of African American children in out-of-home care (foster care or group home settings) is higher than for any other group and ranges from 3 to 10 times as high as for white children.[a] A 2002 study by the Administration for Children and Families[b] documented the perceptions of child welfare officials' from nine states about why African American children are overrepresented in the system. Some of the findings are excerpted here.

Poverty: Across all sites, an overwhelming majority of participants at all levels cited poverty, and poverty-related circumstances, as primary reasons for the over-representation of minority children in the child welfare system.

Need for services and lack of resources: Participants noted that despite their need for services, poor families were more likely to be living in resource-poor communities, many of which also were geographically isolated from other communities that might offer support and services.

Visibility of impoverished and minority families to other systems: Participants reported that because minority families are more likely to be poor and to lack access to resources, they are also more likely to use public services, including public healthcare (e.g., hospitals and clinics), and receive public assistance, including TANF and Medicaid. Participants felt that having more frequent contact with these systems made African American families more "visible" in terms of the problems they might be experiencing, including child abuse and neglect.

Over-reporting of minority parents for child abuse and neglect: Some theorists and researchers argue that the disproportionate number of minority children in out-of-home-care is a result of discriminatory practices within the larger society against minority (particularly African American) groups. According to participants in this study, in relation to the child welfare system, this differential treatment manifests itself most often in the over-reporting of minority parents for child abuse and neglect. The systems most frequently involved, at least as reported in this study, are the medical and school systems.

Lack of experience with other cultures: In many cases, participants felt that their colleagues (child welfare officials), across racial and ethnic groups and job categories, brought preconceived ideas or biases against minority groups, most often African Americans, to their position within the agency. Participants, most often African American participants, identified racial bias as a common problem that frequently interfered with good decision making. They felt that many staff, but Caucasian staff in particular, lacked exposure to cultures other than their own and had no context for understanding the cultural norms and practices of minority populations.

Source: [a] Dorothy Roberts, *Shattered Bonds: The Color of the Child Welfare System* (New York: Basic Civitas Books, 2002); [b] Susan Chibnall, et al., *Children of Color in the Child Welfare System: Perspectives from the Child Welfare Community* (Washington, DC: Department of Health and Human Services, Children's Bureau, Administration for Children and Families, December 2003).

Case for Medical-Legal Partnership

A six-month-old infant presents for well-child care. At birth, her weight was in the 25th percentile; at her four-month visit, her weight had dropped to the 10th percentile. At that point, her mother stated that she was drinking 28–30 ounces of a cow's milk-based formula each day (20 kcal/ounce). The pediatrician taught her mother how to mix the formula to increase the calories to 24 kcal/ounce and asked her to bring the infant back in for a weight check in two weeks. The mother missed the weight check appointment and, despite many attempts, the pediatrician was not able to get the family back in until today (two months later). Currently, the infant's weight is below the 5th percentile for her age. Her length and head circumference are following an appropriate growth curve in the 25th percentile. Her mother tearfully tells the doctor that she has had difficulty obtaining her WIC benefits. She also admits to feeling overwhelmed and says that sometimes she just feels "too tired" to get up and feed the baby. The infant has otherwise been well, with no illnesses. When her mother feeds her, she eats vigorously without any reported problems.

Questions for Discussion

1. How might an MLP benefit this family?

   Medical

1. What additional information do you need?

2. How will you assess whether you must report the family to child protective services? Will you?

3. What course of action should you pursue?

Legal

1. What legal issues might the mother have?

2. What legal strategies can you pursue to improve her situation and her ability to care for her child?

IPV and the Child Protection System

Historically, child protective services (CPS) and domestic violence service providers have not been collaborative in their approaches to family violence. Battered women's advocates saw CPS as insensitive to the needs of victims, and CPS workers viewed battered women's advocates as focusing on the safety of adult victims to the exclusion of children.[118] In recent years there have been efforts to address this conflict through training CPS workers to better understand the dynamics of IPV and the safety concerns of victims and through the development of programs focused on the specific effects of violence on children in domestic violence programs. Nonetheless, within the legal system, there remains ambivalence and conflict about how to address the harmful effects of IPV on children.

Defining Exposure to IPV as Child Maltreatment

Some state child abuse and neglect laws explicitly define exposure to IPV as child maltreatment (Alaska Stat. §47.17.290; 47.10.011(8)). In some states, police routinely report to CPS cases where children are exposed to IPV.[119] Some courts continue to equate failure to protect a child from exposure to IPV with child abuse and terminate the parental rights of the battered parent.[120] As the National Conference of State Legislatures notes, although some argue that expanding the definitions of child abuse and neglect to encompass exposure to IPV is necessary to protect children, child welfare and domestic violence advocates oppose this expansion for the following reasons:

- Defining exposure to domestic violence as child maltreatment per se is inappropriate because it fails to account for protective factors, such as resilience, which mitigate harm to children. In addition, overly broad definitions may incorporate less serious behaviors that are unlikely to result in demonstrable harm to children, even in the absence of identifiable protective factors.

- These laws increase the likelihood that victims of domestic violence will be blamed for failing to protect their children and that children will be removed from home at the very time they are most in need of their mother's care and emotional support.

- These laws may discourage women from seeking protection from the police and/or the courts out of fear that they will lose custody of their children.[121]

Courts have also begun to recognize that when CPS intervenes to remove children from a battered mother based on the child's exposure to IPV, this may unfairly blame and penalize the nonoffending parent. *Nicholson v. Williams*, a 2002 case brought by a class of battered women against the City of New York's CPS agency, illustrates this growing awareness.

Nicholson v. Williams

The evidence reveals widespread and unnecessary cruelty by agencies of the City of New York towards mothers abused by their consorts, through forced unnecessary separation of the mothers from their children on the excuse that this sundering is necessary to protect the children. The pitiless double abuse of these mothers is not malicious, but is due to benign indifference, bureaucratic inefficiency, and outmoded institutional biases.

This class action is brought on behalf of abused mothers and their children who are separated from each other because the mother has suffered domestic abuse and the children are for this reason deemed neglected by the mother. Three sometimes conflicting principles control: First, as a parent, a mother has rights to uninterrupted custody of her children and a child has rights to remain with parents; within wide limits, adults and children in a household are immune from state prying and intrusion. Second, domestic abuse—particularly if physical— of a mother or child will not be tolerated. Third, the state has the obligation to protect children from abuse, including, where clearly necessary to protect the child, the power to separate the mother and child. It is this third element that the defendants are misusing in unjustified reliance on the second and in violation of the first. The resulting denial of constitutional rights of both mothers and children cannot go unchecked....

The findings of fact may be summarized as follows:

1. ACS [New York City's child protective services agency] routinely prosecutes mothers for neglect and removes their children where the mothers have been the victims of significant domestic violence, and where the mothers themselves have done nothing wrong. ACS unnecessarily routinely does so without having previously ensured that a mother has access to the services she needs to protect herself and her children....

2. ACS caseworkers and case managers who make decisions about what services to provide and when to remove children do so without adequate training about domestic violence. ACS practice is to unnecessarily separate the mother from the child when less harmful alternatives involving non-separation are available....

As a matter of policy and practice ACS presumes that she is not a fit parent and that she is not capable of raising her children in a safe and appropriate manner because of actions which are not her own.... Applying this presumption violates constitutional rights. It desecrates fundamental precepts of justice to blame a crime on the victim.

Source: Nicholson v. Williams, 203 F.Supp.2d 153 (2002).

Criminal Sanctions for Failure to Protect

In addition to state child welfare laws that may be interpreted in ways that penalize battered parents, most states criminalize the failure to protect children from harm.[122] In cases involving domestic violence, the victim's failure to protect a child from abuse or from exposure to violence in the home may be interpreted by state officials as a criminal act.

Laws holding battered parents liable for failure to protect their children often ignore the context in which a battered parent must weigh short- and long-term safety considerations for herself and her children:

> These statutes allow for findings against the battered parent without considering her particular circumstances and the reasons for her inability to protect her child from harm. The underlying assumption on which these laws are based, that a good mother will always manage to protect her children from harm, fails to recognized that many battered parents lack resources to immediately escape from violent situations and feed, clothe, and house their children on their own; that attempts to escape a violent home may actually increase the battered parent's and the children's risk of being injured or killed; and that battered parents may, to protect their own and their children's lives in the long term, be compelled to endure abuse until they can develop a safe and effective plan to leave the violent situation.[123]

A balanced approach to protecting children from exposure to violence in the home focuses on supporting the abuse victim in creating a safe and stable environment for her children. MLP offers a unique opportunity to provide a more comprehensive response to family violence by addressing the social, legal and healthcare needs of victims of IPV and their children. This approach does come with challenges, however, when the ethical responsibilities of healthcare providers and lawyers conflict. For example, because healthcare providers are mandated reporters of child abuse and neglect and sometimes of adult IPV, collaboration with an MLP lawyer may be limited. (Ethical issues for MLPs related to mandatory reporting are discussed in Chapter 6.)

From Practice to Policy

In 2009, the Massachusetts Department of Children and Families formed a working group that included lawyers, domestic violence advocates, representatives from hospital child protection teams, child mental health providers and other community representatives to help draft guidelines for mandated reporters in cases involving a child's exposure to IPV. Excerpts from the guidelines that were adopted are shown here.

> Currently when some mandated reporters learn of domestic violence in families, they file a child abuse and neglect report without an assessment of the risk posed to the child(ren). Assessments of risk frequently cite a single factor, such as whether the child was in the room when the incident occurred, rather than examining the entire pattern of abuse. Mandated reporters are encouraged to carefully review each family's situation and to consider thoughtfully whether or not to file a report with the Department of Children and Families.... Mandated reporters should be aware that every circumstance involving domestic violence does not always merit intervention by the child protection system. Often, the caretaker is overwhelmed by the complexity of the home conditions, and is unable to take action. Filing in these circumstances can inadvertently penalize the caretaker for a perceived inability to keep the children safe.... [124]

A report is mandatory if the following circumstances are current concerns:

- The perpetrator threatened to kill the caretaker, children, and/or self and caretaker fears for their safety
- The perpetrator physically injured the child in an incident where the caretaker was the target

- The perpetrator coerced the child to participate in or witness the abuse of the caretaker

- The perpetrator used a weapon, made threats to use a weapon, and the caretaker believed that the perpetrator intended or has the ability to cause harm.[125]

Case for Medical-Legal Partnership

Ms. R. brings her 4-year-old son, Eddy, and her 12-year-old daughter, Jennifer, to an appointment with Dr. P., a primary care doctor at the ambulatory clinic. Ms. R. appears very nervous and agitated when she arrives. Jennifer is quiet and withdrawn. Eddy cannot sit still and is aggressive toward his mother, running into her and punching her legs. Ms. R. seems distracted and oblivious to the children.

Ms. R. only speaks Spanish. Through an interpreter, she tells Dr. P. that Eddy is "out of control." He is not eating and wakes up during the night. Yesterday, he punched another child at his day care and was sent home. When Dr. P. asks Ms. R. if anything has changed in his Eddy's life recently, she hesitates but finally reveals that "things have been very tense with my boyfriend lately." Ms. R. reveals that her boyfriend sometimes hits her and she knows that Eddy has seen that. When Dr. P. asks how her boyfriend treats the children, Ms. R. says that he is "sometimes pretty rough with them, especially with Eddy, because he is so hard to handle."

Questions for Discussion

1. What additional questions would you ask Ms. R.?

2. What are the ethical responsibilities of the healthcare provider? The lawyer?

3. What does Dr. P. need to know to make a decision about whether to report this family to CPS? What are the ramifications of reporting this case to the authorities? Of not reporting?

4. Working as an interdisciplinary team, what is your course of action?

The Family Law Context: Custody and Visitation Determinations in Cases Involving IPV

In addition to possible state intervention by CPS into a family experiencing IPV, victims with children often face prolonged involvement in the legal system when they seek legal separation or divorce. As discussed earlier, leaving an abusive relationship does not necessarily lead to safety for the victim; in fact, leaving may escalate the violence.[126] Leaving is even more complicated when the victim has children with the abuser. Whether the parties are married or cohabitants, if they have children in common, their separation will involve court intervention to determine custody, visitation and support for the children. Divorce and separation are emotionally difficult under any circumstance, but when domestic violence is part of the equation, appropriate legal advocacy for the victim and her children is critically important.

Consideration of IPV in Court Decision Making

As research continues to demonstrate the higher incidence of child abuse in homes where there is partner violence as well as the detrimental effects of children's exposure to this violence, state legislatures and courts have recognized a history of partner violence as an important factor in determining custody and visitation decisions.[127] Healthcare and legal advocates play an important role in ensuring that courts are aware of past violence, its effect on children and the way it may continue in the relationship, even after divorce or separation. It is not uncommon for the abusive partner to use the legal process to continue to harass, threaten and perpetrate violence against the victim.[128]

In determining the custody and visitation arrangement for children after divorce or separation, state family court judges' decision making is generally governed by the "best interests of the child" standard.[129] Generally, they must weigh a statutory list of factors to determine the frequency of contact between each parent and the child or children. State custody statutes vary in terms of the weight given to a history of domestic violence in the custody determination. Some include domestic violence as one factor to be considered along with other factors, such as the wishes of the child; the relationship of the child to his or her parents; the child's adjustment to his or her home, school and community; and the mental and physical health of the parents. Family court judges have a large degree of discretion in weighing these factors and some domestic violence advocates complain that judges often minimize the seriousness of domestic violence in custody determinations.[130]

In response to this concern, roughly half of the states have what is called a "rebuttable presumption" against awarding custody to the batterer.[131] In those states, once a court finds that there is a history of domestic violence, to overcome the presumption, the batterer must show, usually by clear and convincing evidence, that it is in the child's best interests to be placed with him.

Another important consideration in custody cases involving domestic violence are so-called friendly parent provisions. These provisions allow judges to give preference to the parent who is more likely to encourage contact with the other parent. More than half of state child custody statutes include friendly parent as a factor for judges to consider.[132] Because victims of domestic violence may seek to discourage contact between the children and the abusive parent out of fear for her own or the children's safety, these provisions may serve to penalize the victim. To address this concern, some states, such as New Jersey, Oregon and Virginia, make an exception to the friendly parent where there is a history of domestic violence.[133]

Examples of language from a state statute in which domestic violence and friendly parent are factors in custody decision making (Connecticut) and a statute in which there is a rebuttable presumption against custody with a batterer (Alabama) are shown here.

Connecticut General Statutes: Child Custody

Sec. 46b-56 (Orders re custody, care, education, visitation and support of children. Best interests of the child.) [emphasis added]

... (c) In making or modifying any order ... the court shall consider the best interests of the child, and in doing so may consider, but shall not be limited to, one or more of the following factors:

(1) The temperament and developmental needs of the child;

(2) the capacity and the disposition of the parents to understand and meet the needs of the child;

(3) any relevant and material information obtained from the child, including the informed preferences of the child;

(4) the wishes of the child's parents as to custody;

(5) the past and current interaction and relationship of the child with each parent, the child's siblings and any other person who may significantly affect the best interests of the child;

(6) the willingness and ability of each parent to facilitate and encourage such continuing parent-child relationship between the child and the other parent as is appropriate, including compliance with any court orders;

(7) any manipulation by or coercive behavior of the parents in an effort to involve the child in the parents' dispute;

(8) the ability of each parent to be actively involved in the life of the child;

(9) the child's adjustment to his or her home, school and community environments;

(10) the length of time that the child has lived in a stable and satisfactory environment and the desirability of maintaining continuity in such environment, provided the court may consider favorably a parent who voluntarily leaves the child's family home pendente lite in order to alleviate stress in the household;

(11) the stability of the child's existing or proposed residences, or both;

(12) the mental and physical health of all individuals involved, except that a disability of a proposed custodial parent or other party, in and of itself, shall not be determinative of custody unless the proposed custodial arrangement is not in the best interests of the child;

(13) the child's cultural background;

(14) the effect on the child of the actions of an abuser, if any domestic violence has occurred between the parents or between a parent and another individual or the child;

(15) whether the child or a sibling of the child has been abused or neglected, as defined respectively in section 46b-120; and

(16) whether the party satisfactorily completed participation in a parenting education program established pursuant to section 46b-69b. The court is not required to assign any weight to any of the factors that it considers.

Alabama Code: Rebuttable Presumption

Section 30-3-131: Determination raises rebuttable presumption that custody with perpetrator detrimental to child.

In every proceeding where there is at issue a dispute as to the custody of a child, a determination by the court that domestic or family violence has occurred raises a rebuttable presumption by the court that it is detrimental to the child and not in the best interest of the child to be placed in sole custody, joint legal custody, or joint physical custody with the perpetrator of domestic or family violence. Notwithstanding the provisions regarding rebuttable presumption, the judge must also take into account what, if any, impact the domestic violence had on the child.

Section 30-3-132: Factors court must consider.

(a) In addition to other factors that a court is required to consider in a proceeding in which the custody of a child or visitation by a parent is at issue and in which the court has made a finding of domestic or family violence the court shall consider each of the following:

(1) The safety and well-being of the child and of the parent who is the victim of family or domestic violence.

(2) The perpetrator's history of causing physical harm, bodily injury, assault, or causing reasonable fear of physical harm, bodily injury, or assault, to another person.

(b) If a parent is absent or relocates because of an act of domestic or family violence by the other parent, the absence or relocation may not be a factor that weighs against the parent in determining the custody or visitation.

Best Practices and Advocacy Strategies for Medical-Legal Partnership

The Child Witness to Violence Project at Boston Medical Center works with Medical Legal Partnership | Boston to ensure safety for parents and children who are affected by family violence and access to needed services. The project is a trauma-focused counseling program for young children and their parents who are affected by domestic or community violence. The program receives referrals from pediatricians in the hospital and also from the courts, law enforcement, domestic violence programs and other social services agencies. An MLP lawyer attends the clinical meetings of the program and hears cases that are presented by the mental health clinicians. In addition to the emotional risks of exposure to domestic or community violence, these cases frequently present advocacy challenges, such as a need for safe housing, a need for a restraining order or for advocacy in the family or probate court setting. The MLP attorney provides education for the staff on how to secure these services, or in some cases, meets directly with the family to obtain more information, secure a referral for legal assistance or write a letter on behalf of the family. In many of the cases, the counseling can't effectively begin until some of the basic needs for housing, safety or legal assistance are taken care of. This partnership with MLP has been effective in helping families address their legal and social needs so that they can make best use of the counseling services for their children.

Case for Medical-Legal Partnership

Two weeks ago, Susan left her abusive husband and moved into a battered women's shelter with her young son. She has been referred by the shelter to Dr. M. because of recurring severe headaches that the shelter staff believes may be the result of head injuries Susan endured during the abuse. In her visit with Dr. M., Susan reports that she is terrified that her husband will find her. He threatened to kill her and their child if she ever left him. He also said that he would seek custody of their son and make sure that she never gets to see him. She wants to seek a divorce but is terrified of seeing her abusive husband. She wants to move on with her life, but is unsure what she can do without resolving the custody issue.

Questions for Discussion

1. How can the medical-legal team work together to help keep Susan and her son safe and to escape the control of her abuser?

   Medical

1. What additional questions will you ask Susan?

2. How will her situation affect her healthcare?

3. How will you help Susan take steps to achieve safety and freedom from her abuser?

Legal

1. Should Susan worry that she will lose custody of her son to her abusive husband?

2. What kind of information and documentation will you need to help Susan?

3. How will you help Susan to take steps to achieve safety and freedom from her abuser?

Conclusion

Family violence remains a problem that demands enormous resources from both the healthcare and legal systems. Because victims of family violence—both adults and children—interact with the healthcare and legal systems and rely heavily on healthcare providers and lawyers, MLPs are particularly important in addressing this problem. Medical and legal professionals should be well trained in the dynamics of family violence and have an understanding of how their state systems function, including the child welfare and court systems. To respond effectively to victims' needs and to find solutions that can best ensure future safety, professionals must work together in interdisciplinary partnerships.

Notes

Lisa Pilnik's work on this chapter was supported in part by an Improving Understanding of Maternal and Child Health grant from the U.S. Department of Health and Human Services, Health Resources and Services Administration, Maternal and Child Health Bureau to the American Bar Association Center on Children and the Law.

1. U.S. Department of Health and Human Services, Administration for Children and Families, Administration on Children, Youth and Families, Children's Bureau, *Child Maltreatment 2008* (Washington, DC: US Department of Health and Human Services, 2010); P. Tjaden and Nancy Thoennes, National Institute of Justice and the Centers for Disease Control, "Extent, Nature and Consequences of Intimate Partner Violence: Findings from the National Violence Against Women Survey," (2000).

2. R. McDonald, E. N. Jouriles, S. Ramisetty-Mikler, R. Caetano, C. E.Green, "Estimating the Number of American Children Living with Partner-Violent Families," *Journal of Family Psychology,* 20, no. 1 (2006): 137–42.

3. Centers for Disease Control and Prevention, National Center for Injury Prevention and Control, *Costs of Intimate Partner Violence Against Women in the United States* (Atlanta: Centers for Disease Control and Prevention, 2003).

4. Nicky Ali Jackson, ed., *Encyclopedia of Domestic Violence* (New York: Routledge, 2007).

5. Centers for Disease Control and Prevention, *Intimate Partner Violence Surveillance: Uniform Definitions, and Recommended Data Elements* (Atlanta: Centers for Disease Control and Prevention, 2002); P. Tjaden and N. Thoennes, *Stalking in America: Findings from the National Violence Against Women Survey* (Washington, DC: U.S. Department of Justice, 1998).

6. R. Jewkes, "Intimate Partner Violence: Causes and Prevention," *Lancet,* 359, no. 9315 (2002): 1423–29.

7. J. McCauley, D. E. Kern, K. Kolodner, et al., "The 'Battering Syndrome': Prevalence and Clinical Characteristics of Domestic Violence in Primary Care Internal Medicine Practices," *Annals of Internal Medicine,* 123, no. 10 (1995): 737–46.

8. U.S. Bureau of Justice, "Victim Characteristics, Bureau of Justice Statistics," http://bjs.ojp.usdoj.gov/content/intimate/victims.cfm (accessed January 19, 2010).

9. J. C. Campbell, "Health Consequences of Intimate Partner Violence," *Lancet*, 359 (April 13, 2002): 1331–36.

10. A. E. Bonomi, M. L. Anderson, F. P. Rivara, R. S. Thompson, "Health Care Utilization and Costs Associated with Physical and Non-Physical Intimate Partner Violence," *Health Service Research*, 44, no. 3 (2009): 1052–67.

11. P. A. Fishman, A. Bonomi, et al., "Changes in Health Care Costs over Time Following Cessation of Intimate Partner Violence," *Journal of General Internal Medicine*, 25, no. 9 (2010): 920–25.

12. M. C. Ellsberg, R. Peña, A. Herrera, et al., "Wife Abuse among Women of Childbearing Age in Nicaragua," *American Journal of Public Health*, 89, no. 2 (1999): 241–44; R. Jewes, L. Penn-Kekan, J. Levin, "Risk Factors for Domestic Violence: Findings from a South African Cross-Sectional Study," *Social Science Medicine*, 55, no. 9 (November 2002): 1603–17.

13. S. Catalano, *Intimate Partner Violence in the United States* (Washington, DC: U.S. Department of Justice, Office of Justice Programs, Bureau of Justice Statistics, 2007).

14. Ibid.

15. C. M. Rennison, *Intimate Partner Violence, 1993–2001* (Washington, DC: Bureau of Justice Statistics, Crime Date Brief, February 2003).

16. Research and Policy Analysis Division in the Massachusetts Executive Office of Public Safety and Security, *Massachusetts Intimate Partner Homicide Review: An Overview of District Attorney Cases between 2005 and 2007* (Boston, MA: Research and Policy Division in the Massachusetts Executive Office of Public Safety and Security, June 2009).

17. D. Kyriacou, et al., "Risk Factors for Injury to Women from Domestic Violence," *New England Journal of Medicine*, 341, no. 25 (1999): 1892–98.

18. Jewkes, "Intimate Partner Violence."

19. J. C. Campbell, et al., "Risk Factors for Femicide in Abusive Relationships: Results from a Multi-site Case Control Study," *American Journal of Public Health*, 93, no. 7 (2003): 1089–97.

20. Jewkes, "Intimate Partner Violence."

21. Campbell et al., "Risk Factors for Femicide."

22. S. Catalano, "Intimate Partner Violence."

23. A. Brown, S. S. Bassuk, "Intimate Violence in the Lives of Homeless and Poor Housed Women," *Journal of Orthopsychiatry*, 67, no. 2 (1997): 261–78.

24. A. Raj, J. Silverman, "Violence Against Immigrant Women: The Roles of Culture, Context, and Legal Immigrant Status on Intimate Partner Violence," *Violence Against Women*, 18, no. 3 (2002): 367–98.

25. C. Menjivar, O. Salcido, "Immigrant Women and Domestic Violence: Common Experiences in Different Countries," *Gender and Society*, 16, no. 6 (2002): 898–920.

26. Bureau of Justice, *Homicide Trends in the U.S.: Intimate Homicide, Intimate Homicide Victims by Gender* (Washington, DC: Bureau of Justice Statistics, 2005), http://bjs.ojp.usdoj.gov/content/homicide/tables/intimatestab.cfm (accessed January 19, 2011).

27. Kyriacou et al., "Risk Factors for Injury to Women."

28. J. A. Grisso, D. F. Schwarz, N. Hirschinger, et al., "Violent Injuries among Women in an Urban Area," *New England Journal of Medicine*, 341 (Dec. 16, 1999): 1899–905.

29. R. L. Muelleman, et al., "Battered Women: Injury Locations and Types," *Annals of Emergency Medicine*, 28, no. 5 (1996): 486–92.

30. J.D. Corrigan, et al, "Early Identification of Mild Traumatic Brain Injury in Female Victims of Domestic Violence," *American Journal of Obstetrics and Gynecology,* 188, Issue 5 (2003): S71–76.

31. S. B. Plichta, "Intimate Partner Violence and Physical Health Consequences: Policy and Practice Implications," *Journal of Interpersonal Violence*, 19 (November 2004): 1296–323.

32. Ibid; Campbell, "Health Consequences."

33. Plichta, "Intimate Partner Violence."

34. J. E. Hathaway, L. A. Mucci, J. G. Silverman, et al., "Health Status and Health Care Use of Massachusetts Women Reporting Partner Abuse," *American Journal of Preventive Medicine*, 19, no. 4 (2000): 302–7; S. C. Lemon, W. Verhoek-Oftedhal, E. F. Donnelly, "Preventive Healthcare Use, Smoking, and Alcohol Use among Rhode Island Women Experiencing Intimate Partner Violence," *Journal of Women's Health and Gender-Based Medicine*, 11, no. 6 (2002): 555–62; A. L. Coker, P. H. Smith, L. Bethea, et al., "Physical Health Consequences of Physical and Psychological Intimate Partner Violence," *Archives of Family Medicine*, 9, no. 5 (2008): 451–57.

35. Kyriacou et al., "Risk Factors for Injury."

36. D. G. Kilpatrick, R. Acierno, H. S. Resnick, et al., "A Two-Year Longitudinal Analysis of the Relationships between Violent Assault and Substance Use in Women," *Journal of Consulting and Clinical Psychology*, 65 (1997): 834–47.

37. A. Coker, "Does Physical Intimate Partner Violence Affect Sexual Health? A Systematic Review," *Trauma, Violence, and Abuse*, 8, no. 2 (2007): 149–77.

38. Ibid.

39. Campbell, "Health Consequences of Intimate Partner Violence."

40. Plichta, "Intimate Partner Violence."

41. Campbell, "Health Consequences of Intimate Partner Violence."

42. J. M. Golding, "Intimate Partner Violence as a Risk Factor for Mental Disorders: A Meta-Analysis," *Journal of Family Violence*, 14, no. 2 (1999): 99–132; C. Silva, J. McFarlane, K. Socken, et al., "Symptoms of Post-Traumatic Stress Disorder in Abused Women in a Primary Care Setting," *Journal of Women's Health*, 6 (1997): 543–52.

43. M. Cascardi, K. D. O'Leary, K. A. Schlee, "Co-Occurrence and Correlates of Posttraumatic Stress Disorder and Major Depression in Physically Abused Women," *Journal of Family Violence*, 14, no. 3 (1999): 227–49.

44. J. C. Campbell, K. Socken, "Women's Responses to Battering over Time: An Analysis of Change," *Journal of Interpersonal Violence*, 14, no. 1 (1999): 21–40.

45. J. C. Campbell, D. W. Webster, N. Glass, "The Danger Assessment: Validation of a Lethality Risk Assessment Instrument for Intimate Partner Femicide," *Journal of Interpersonal Violence*, 24, no. 4 (2009): 653–74; Campbell et al., "Risk Factors for Femicide;" Dr. Jacqueline Campbell has developed a Danger Assessment with a 20-item screen, available online for free (http://www.dangerassessment.org/WebApplication1/pages/da/ (accessed January 20, 2011).

46. Center for Health and Gender Equity, "Ending Violence Against Women," Population Reports, Series L, no. 11 (December 1999).

47. J. Murphy, "Engaging with the State: The Growing Reliance on Lawyers and Judges to Protect Battered Women," *American University Journal of Gender, Social Policy & the Law*, 11 (2003): 499–501.

48. Ibid.

49. M. E. Bell, et al., "Battered Women's Perceptions of Civil and Criminal Court Helpfulness: The Role of Court Outcome and Process," Violence Against Women, 17 (2011): 71–88.

50. K. Tracy, "Building a Model Protective Order Process," *American Journal of Criminal Law*, 24 (1997): 475–78.

51. J. A. Fugate, "Note: Who's Failing Whom? A Critical Look at Failure-to-Protect Laws," *New York University Law Review*, 76 (2001): 272–308.

52. U.S. Department of Justice, *The Facts about the Violence Against Women Act* (Washington, DC: Office of Violence Against Women, 2005), http://www.ovw.usdoj.gov/ovw-fs.htm#fs-act (accessed January 18, 2011).

53. *United States v. Morrison*, 529 U.S. 598 (2000).

54. Murphy, "Engaging with the State."

55. C. Dalton and E. Schneider, *Battered Women and the Law* (New York: Foundation Press, 2001), 499.

56. C.V. Williams, "Not Everyone Will 'Get It' Until We Do It: Advocating for an Indefinite Order of Protection in Arizona," *Arizona State Law Journal*, 40, no. 1 (Spring 2008): 371.

57. Dalton and Schneider, *Battered Women and the Law*, 537.

58. Barbara Hart, "State Codes on Domestic Violence: Analysis, Commentary, and Recommendations," *Juvenile and Family Court Journal*, 3 (1992): 23–24.

59. Dalton and Schneider, *Battered Women and the Law*, 558.

60. T. K. Logan, Robert Walker, William Hoyt, Teri Faragher, *The Kentucky Civil Protective Order Study: A Rural and Urban Multiple Perspective Study of Protective Order Violation Consequences, Responses, & Costs* (Washington, DC: U.S. Department of Justice, September 2009).

61. Ibid, 4.

62. P. L. Culross, "Health Care System Responses to Children Exposed to Domestic Violence," *Future of Children*, 9, no. 3 (Winter 1999): 115.

63. U.S. Department of Health and Human Services, *Child Maltreatment 2008*.

64. Ibid.

65. Ibid.

66. A. Appel, G. Holden, "The Co-Occurrence of Spouse and Physical Child Abuse: A Review and Appraisal," *Journal of Family Psychology*, 12 (1998): 578–99.

67. R. McDonald, E. N. Jouriles, S. Ramisetty-Mikler, R. Caetano, C. E. Green, "Estimating the Number of American Children Living in Partner-Violent Families," *Journal of Family Psychology*, 20 (2006): 137–42.

68. G. Fairbrother, J. Stuber, S. Galea, B. Pfefferbaum, et al., "Unmet Need for Counseling Services by Children in New York City after the September 11th Attacks on the World Trade Center: Implications for Pediatricians," *Journal of Pediatrics*, 113, no. 5 (2004): 1367–74.

69. J. Fantuzzo, R. Boruch, A. Beriama, "Domestic Violence and Children: Prevalence and Risk in Five Major U.S. Cities," *Journal of American Academy of Child Adolescent Psychiatry*, 36 (1997): 116–22.

70. C. DiScala, R. Sege, G. Li, R. M. Reece, "Child Abuse and Unintentional Injuries: A 10-year Retrospective," *Archives of Pediatric Adolescent Medicine*, 154 (2000): 16–22.

71. E. G. Flaherty, R. Thompson, A. J. Litrownik, et al., "Adverse Childhood Exposures and Reported Child Health at Age 12," *American Academy of Pediatrics*, 9 (2009): 150–56.

72. S. F. Suglia, M. B. Enlow, A. Kullowatz, R. J. Wright, "Maternal Intimate Partner Violence and Increased Asthma Incidence In Children: Buffering Effects of Supportive Caregiving," *Archives of Pediatric Adolescent Medicine*, 163 (2009): 244–50; R. W. Block, N. F. Krebs, American Academy of Pediatrics Committee on Child Abuse and Neglect, American Academy of Pediatrics Committee on Nutrition, "Failure to Thrive as a Manifestation of Child Neglect," *Pediatrics*, 116 (2005): 1234–37; A. A. Scarborough, E. C. Lloyd, R. P. Barth, "Maltreated Infants and Toddlers: Predictors of Developmental Delay," *Journal of Developmental Behavioral Pediatrics*, 30, no. 6 (2009): 489–98; G. L. Carpenter, A. M. Stacks, "Developmental Effects of Exposure to Intimate Partner Violence in Early Childhood: A Review of the Literature," *Children and Youth Services Review*, 31, no. 8 (2009): 831–39.

73. V. J. Felitti, R. F. Anda, D. Nordenberg, D. F. Williamson, et al., "Relationship of Childhood Abuse and Household Dysfunction to Many of the Leading Causes of Death in Adults: The Adverse Childhood Experiences (ACE) Study," *American Journal of Preventive Medicine*, 14, no. 4 (1998): 245–58.

74. J. T. Shonkoff, W. T. Boyce, B. S. McEwen, "Neuroscience, Molecular Biology, and the Childhood Roots of Health Disparities: Building a New Framework for Health Promotion and Disease Prevention," *Journal of the American Medical Association*, 301, no. 21 (2009): 2252–59; Martin Teicher, "Wounds that Time Won't Heal: The Neurobiology of Child Abuse," *Cerebrum: The Dana Forum on Brain Science*, 2, no. 4 (2000): 50–67.

75. E. Chen, G. E. Miller, "Stress and Inflammation." E. Chen, L. S. Chim, R. C. Strunk, G. E. Miller, "The Role of the Social Environment in Children and Adolescents with Asthma," *American Journal of Respiratory Critical Care Medicine*, 176 (2007): 644–49.

76. Suglia et al., "Maternal Intimate Partner Violence."

77. J. Kaufman, D. Charney, "Effects of Early Stress on Brain Structure and Function: Implications for Understanding the Relationship between Child Maltreatment and Depression," *Development and Psychology*, 13 (2001): 451–71.

78. National Child Traumatic Stress Network, Core Data Set (2009). Unpublished data.

79. J. L. Edleson, "Children's Witnessing of Adult Domestic Violence," *Journal of Interpersonal Violence*, 14, no. 8 (1999): 839–70.

80. M. S. Scheeringa, C. H. Zeanah, "Symptom Expression and Trauma Variables in Children under 48 Months of Age," *Infant Mental Health Journal*, 1, no. 4 (1995): 259–69.

81. B. Groves, *Children Who See too Much: Lessons from the Child Witness to Violence Project* (Boston: Beacon Press, 2002).

82. D. Wolfe, C. Crooks, V. Lee, et al., "The Effects of Children's Exposure to Domestic Violence: A Meta-Analysis and Critique," *Clinical Child and Family Psychology Review*, 16 (2003): 171–87.

83. American Academy of Pediatrics, Committee on Practice and Ambulatory Medicine, "Recommendations for Preventive Pediatric Health Care," *Pediatrics*, 96 (1995): 373–74.

84. M. H. Bair-Merritt, S. S. Crowne, L.D. Burrell, D. Caldera, T. L. Cheng, A. K. Duggan, "Impact of Intimate Partner Violence on Children's Well-Child Care and Medical Home," *Pediatrics*, 121, no. 3 (2008): e473–80.

85. E. Y. Friedlaender, D. M. RubinE. R. Alpern, D. S. Mandell, C. W. Christian, E. A. Alessandrini, "Patterns of Health Care Use that May Identify Young Children Who Are at Risk for Maltreatment, *Pediatrics*, 116 (2005): 1303–8.

86. M. H. Bair-Merritt, C. Feudtner, A. R. Localio, J. A. Feinstein, D. Rubin, W. C. Holmes, "Health Care Use of Children Whose Female Caregivers Have Intimate Partner Violence Histories," *Archives of Pediatric Adolescent Medicine*, 162 (2008): 134–39.

87. Felitti, et al., "Relationship of Childhood Abuse and Household Dysfunction," 245–58.

88. M.D. Simms, H. Dubowitz, and M.A. Szilagy, "Health Care Needs of Children in the Foster Care System." *Journal of the Ambulatory Pediatric Association*, 106 (4 Supplement (2000)): 909–918.

89. H. MacMillan, C. N. Wathen, J. Barlow, D. M. Fergusson, J. M. Leventhal, H. N. Taussig, "Interventions to Prevent Child Maltreatment and Associated Impairment," *Lancet*, 373, no. 9659 (2009): 250–66.

90. N. D. Kellogg, The Committee on Child Abuse and Neglect, "Evaluation of Suspected Child Physical Abuse," *Pediatrics*, 119, no. 6 (June 2007): 1232–41.

91. American Academy of Pediatrics, "The Role of the Pediatrician in Recognizing and Intervening on Behalf of Abused Women," *Pediatrics*, 101 (1998): 1091–92; J. D. Thackeray, R. Hibbard, M. D. Dowd, American Academy of Pediatrics Committee on Child Abuse and Neglect & Committee on Injury, Violence and Poison Prevention, "Intimate Partner Violence: The Role of The Pediatrician," *Pediatrics*, 125, no. 5 (2010): 1094–100.

92. B. M. Groves, M. Augustyn, D. Lee, P. Sawires, *Identifying and Responding to Domestic Violence: Consensus Recommendations for Child and Adolescent Health* (San Francisco: Family Violence Prevention Fund, 2002).

93. T. Zink, J. Jacobson, "Screening for Intimate Partner Violence When Children Are Present," *Journal of Interpersonal Violence*, 18 (2003): 872–90.

94. Ibid.

95. Ibid.

96. D. Cicchetti and V. Carlson, *Child Maltreatment: Theory and Research on the Causes and Consequences of Child Abuse and Neglect* (Cambridge: Cambridge University Press, 1989), 43.

97. D.T. Kramer, ed., *Legal Rights of Children*, 2nd ed. (Colorado Springs, CO: Shepard's/McGraw-Hill, 1994), 5–10.

98. CAPTA, 42 U.S.C.A. §5106(g)(2), as amended by the Keeping Children and Families Safe Act of 2003.

99. Ibid., §5106(a).

100. Ibid.; CAPTA says that the guardian ad litem is appointed to represent the child "to obtain first-hand, a clear understanding of the situation and needs of the child; and to make recommendations to the court concerning the best interests of the child."

101. Ibid.; For more detail on CAPTA and other federal laws affecting children who have been maltreated, see Howard Davidson, "Federal Law and State Intervention When Parents Fail: Has National Guidance of Our Child Welfare System Been Successful?" *Family Law Quarterly*, 42 (2008): 481.

102. Family Preservation and Support Services Program Act of 1993 (P.L. 103-66).

103. Child Welfare Information Gateway, U.S. Department of Health and Human Services, Administration for Children and Families, *Definitions of Child Abuse and Neglect: Summary of State Laws* (Washington, DC: U.S. Department of Health and Human Services Children's Bureau, 2009).

104. D.C. Ann. Code § 16-2301(23)(B)(i); Ind. Ann. Code § 31-34-1-15.

105. Col. Rev. Stat. § 19-3-103; Fl. Ann. Stat. § 39.01(32)(f); N.M Ann. Stat. § 32A-4-2(E)(5). Note that some statutes that do not consider failure to provide medical treatment due to religious beliefs neglect may still allow courts to order medical treatment when necessary.

106. Kan. Ann. Stat. § 38-2202; Wash. Rev. Code § 26.44.020(13); D.C. Ann. Code § 16-2301(24).

107. Col. Rev. Stat. §§ 19-1-103(1)(b).

108. Child Welfare Information Gateway, US Department of Health and human Services, Administration for Children and Families, *Mandatory Reporters of Child Abuse and Neglect* (Washington, DC: U.S. Department of Health and Human Services Children's Bureau, 2008).

109. Ibid.

110. Child Welfare Information Gateway, US Department of Health and human Services, Administration for Children and Families, *How to Report Suspected Child Maltreatment*, (Washington, DC: U.S. Department of Health and Human Services Children's Bureau), http://www.childwelfare.gov/responding/how.cfm (accessed January 20, 2011).

111. Child Welfare Information Gateway, U.S. Department of Health and human Services, Administration for Children and Families, *Penalties for Failure to Report and False Reporting of Child Abuse and Neglect: Summary of State Laws* (Washington, DC: U.S. Department of Health and Human Services Children's Bureau, 2009).

112. "Preponderance of the evidence" is used as the standard in Missouri and New York: Missouri Department of Social Services, *Child Welfare Manual*: Section 2, Intake, Chapter 4, "Investigation Response" (Jefferson City: Missouri Department of Social Services, 2005); New York State Office of Mental Retardation and Developmental Disabilities, *Update on Child Abuse Reporting and Investigations* (Albany, NY: Office of Mental Retardation and Developmental Disabilities, November 2008): 4. Whereas the "credible evidence" standard that child abuse or neglect occurred is applied in the state of Illinois: Department of Children and Family Services, *Child Protection: Investigations* (Chicago: Department of Children and Family Services, 2009), http://www.state.il.us/dcfs/child/index.shtml#Investigations (accessed January 20, 2011).

113. R. Green, "The Evolution of Kinship Care: Policy and Practice," *Future of Children*, 14, no. 1 (2004): 131–48.

114. W. G. Jones, *Working with the Courts in Child Protection* (Washington DC: U.S. Department of Health and Human Services, 2006), 23–28.

115. Jones, "Working with the Courts in Child Protection," 27–29.

116. Ibid., 29–31.

117. 42 U.S.C. 671(16), 32–35; Fostering Connections to Success and Increasing Adoptions Act of 2008, P.L. 110-351.

118. J. E. Findlater, Susan Kelly, "Child Protective Services and Domestic Violence," *Future of Children*, 9, no. 3 (Winter 1999): 84–96.

119. S. Christian, "Children's Exposure to Domestic Violence: Is it Child Abuse?" *National Council of State Legislatures, State Legislative Reports*, 27, no. 1 (January 2002): 1–9.

120. Lemon et al., "Preventive Healthcare Use, Smoking, and Alcohol Use."

121. Christian, "Children's Exposure to Domestic Violence," 3.

122. N. Cahn, "Policing Women: Moral Arguments and the Dilemmas of Criminalization," *DePaul Law Review*, no. 49 (2000): 817.

123. M. A. Matthews, "The Impact of Federal and State Laws on Children Exposed to Domestic Violence," *Future of Children*, 9, no. 3 (Winter 1999): 57.

124. Cahn, "Policing Women."

125. Massachusetts Department of Children and Families, *Working with Families, Child Welfare and Domestic Violence: Promising Approaches* (Boston: Massachusetts Department of Children and Families, 2009).

126. M. E. Bell, L. A. Goodman, M. A. Dutton, "The Dynamics of Staying and Leaving: Implications for Battered Women's Emotional Well-Being and Experiences of Violence at the End of a Year," *Journal of Family Violence*, 22, no. 6 (2007): 413–28.

127. N.K. Lemon, "The Legal System's Response to Children Exposed to Domestic Violence," *Future of Children*, 9, no. 3 (Winter 1999): 67–83.

128. C. Shalansky, J. Ericksen, A. Henderson, "Abused Women and Child Custody: The Ongoing Exposure to Abusive Ex-partners," *Journal of Advanced Nursing*, 29, no. 2 (2001): 416–26.

129. Child Welfare Information Gateway, *Determining the Best Interests of the Child: Summary of State Laws* (Washington, DC: Administration for Children and Families, U.S. Department of Health and Human Services, 2010), http://www.childwelfare.gov/systemwide/laws_policies/statutes/best_interest.cfm (accessed January 21, 2011).

130. Bell et al., "Battered Women's Perceptions."

131. American Bar Association, Commission on Domestic Violence "Child Custody and Domestic Violence by State," American Bar Association, Commission on Domestic Violence, http://www.abanet.org/domviol/docs/Custody.pdf.

132. Ibid.; P.G. Jaffe, N. Lemon, S. E. Poisson, *Child Custody & Domestic Violence: A Call for Safety and Accountability* (Thousand Oaks, CA: Sage, 2003), 68.

133. Ibid.; M. K. Dore, "The 'Friendly Parent' Concept: A Flawed Factor for Child Custody," *Loyola Journal of Public Interest Law*, 6 (2004): 41–56.

Part IV

Medical-Legal Partnership for Special Populations

Chapter 12

Cancer Patients, Survivors and Their Families

Randye Retkin, JD
Kerry Rodabaugh, MD
Tenley Mochizuki, BA

Cancer affects more than 11.4 million people in the United States, and it is expected that in 2010 over 1.5 million new cancer cases will have been diagnosed.[1] Individuals diagnosed with cancer experience a host of medical, psychosocial, financial and legal issues. Receiving a cancer diagnosis can be devastating. When coupled with language and cultural barriers or financial difficulties, the navigation of the medical-legal issues can assume increasing precedence in a patient's life and may become overwhelming. This chapter explores some of the legal and financial issues experienced by people with cancer and the resolutions of these issues offered by the oncology-centered medical-legal partnership (MLP). It also touches on some of the psychosocial issues that arise in trying to address legal matters.

Prior to the MLP movement, as well as other shifts in legal service provision, legal services to people with cancer were often limited to assistance at the end of life, focusing on the drafting of health care proxies and wills. As this chapter outlines, legal services for people with cancer have evolved from this limited application and now serve patients throughout the continuum of care. As of this writing, approximately 33 legal programs across the country serve people with cancer, including 7 MLPs.[2] As people with cancer live longer, a number of important legal needs are being addressed. By resolving legal issues within the context of an MLP, it is anticipated that a person with cancer will experience greater access to care and improved quality of life for themselves, their family and the wider circle of loved ones impacted by the diagnosis.

Understanding Cancer in Medical, Social and Legal Contexts

Disease Overview: Many Diseases, Courses and Outcomes

Cancer, the second leading cause of death in the United States (one in four deaths),[3] is actually a larger category made up of many different diseases with multiple etiologies, courses and outcomes. There are approximately 80 types of malignant neoplasms currently reported, defined by their location and cell types. However, four sites account for approximately half of all cancer diagnoses: breast (15 percent), prostate (17 percent), lung (13 percent) and colon (8 percent) cancers accounted for 52 percent of all estimated new cancer diagnoses in 2006.[4] Figure 12.1 lists the 10 leading types for estimated new cancer cases and deaths.

Figure 12.1 Ten Leading Cancer Types for the Estimated New Cancer Cases and Deaths by Sex, 2010

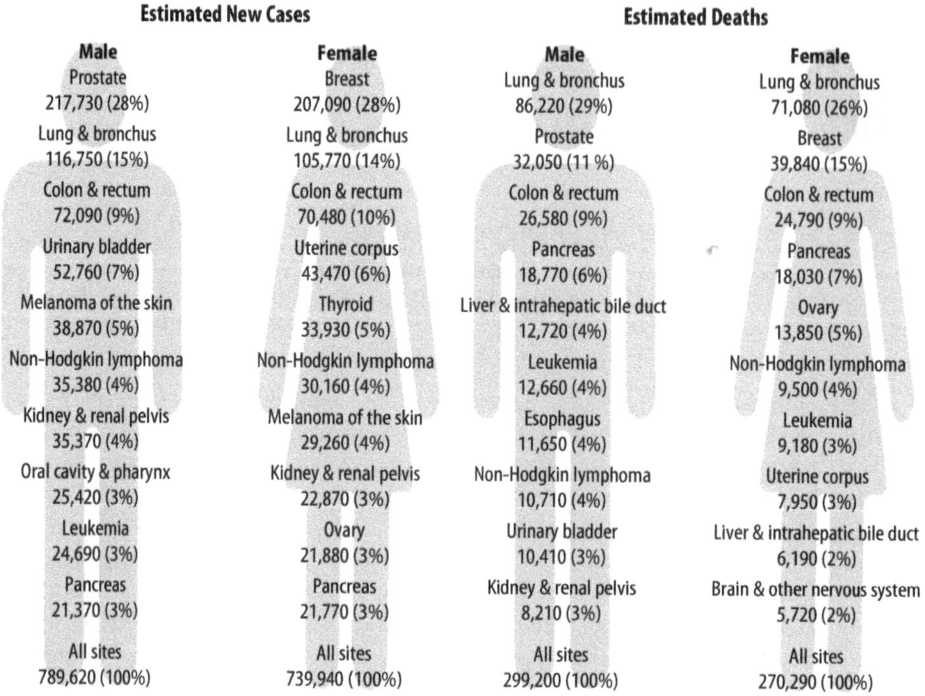

Estimated New Cases		Estimated Deaths	
Male	**Female**	**Male**	**Female**
Prostate 217,730 (28%)	Breast 207,090 (28%)	Lung & bronchus 86,220 (29%)	Lung & bronchus 71,080 (26%)
Lung & bronchus 116,750 (15%)	Lung & bronchus 105,770 (14%)	Prostate 32,050 (11%)	Breast 39,840 (15%)
Colon & rectum 72,090 (9%)	Colon & rectum 70,480 (10%)	Colon & rectum 26,580 (9%)	Colon & rectum 24,790 (9%)
Urinary bladder 52,760 (7%)	Uterine corpus 43,470 (6%)	Pancreas 18,770 (6%)	Pancreas 18,030 (7%)
Melanoma of the skin 38,870 (5%)	Thyroid 33,930 (5%)	Liver & intrahepatic bile duct 12,720 (4%)	Ovary 13,850 (5%)
Non-Hodgkin lymphoma 35,380 (4%)	Non-Hodgkin lymphoma 30,160 (4%)	Leukemia 12,660 (4%)	Non-Hodgkin lymphoma 9,500 (4%)
Kidney & renal pelvis 35,370 (4%)	Melanoma of the skin 29,260 (4%)	Esophagus 11,650 (4%)	Leukemia 9,180 (3%)
Oral cavity & pharynx 25,420 (3%)	Kidney & renal pelvis 22,870 (3%)	Non-Hodgkin lymphoma 10,710 (4%)	Uterine corpus 7,950 (3%)
Leukemia 24,690 (3%)	Ovary 21,880 (3%)	Urinary bladder 10,410 (3%)	Liver & intrahepatic bile duct 6,190 (2%)
Pancreas 21,370 (3%)	Pancreas 21,770 (3%)	Kidney & renal pelvis 8,210 (3%)	Brain & other nervous system 5,720 (2%)
All sites 789,620 (100%)	All sites 739,940 (100%)	All sites 299,200 (100%)	All sites 270,290 (100%)

Source: Cancer Facts & Figures 2010 (Atlanta: American Cancer Society, 2010).

The cancer continuum ranges from disease-free through preclinical early cancer to diagnosis, survivorship, and end of life and death, followed by bereavement of surviving family members. The National Institute of Cancer estimates that approximately 11.4 million Americans with a history of cancer were alive in January 2006. Some of these individuals were cancer-free, whereas others still had evidence of disease and may have been undergoing treatment.[5]

The populace affected by cancer ranges in age from the pediatric to the elderly and all ages in between. Cancer is the second most common cause of death among children between the ages of 1 and 14 years in the United States, surpassed only by accidents.[6] Over the past 25 years, there have been significant improvements in the 5-year relative survival rate for all of the major childhood cancers; rates improved from 58 percent for patients diagnosed between 1975 and 1977 to 81 percent for those diagnosed between 1999 and 2005.[7] At the other end of the spectrum, advancing age is a strong risk factor for cancer, with persons over 65 accounting for 60 percent of newly diagnosed malignancies and 70 percent of all cancer deaths.[8] Physical impairment due to cancer and its treatment is often present against a background of comorbidities and polypharmacy (use of multiple medications) in older patients. Cognitive impairment is common in the elderly, with Alzheimer's disease and other forms of dementia occurring especially frequently in those older than 85 years.[9] Dementia, depression and hearing impairment are significant barriers to the delivery of services to the elderly with cancer.

Epidemiology and Disparities: Cancer and Social Determinants

Although cancer can be the great equalizer, affecting people at every stage of life regardless of socioeconomic status (SES) or race, social determinants also play a role.

Social disparities in cancer incidence may be related to socioeconomic and demographic differences in cancer-related risk factors and behaviors, such as cigarette smoking, poor diet, physical inactivity, obesity, reproductive factors, human papillomavirus (HPV) infection and sun exposure.[10] Lung cancer mortality is strongly associated with tobacco use and social policies.[11] In fact, tobacco is the cause of more than one third of cancer deaths.[12] Individuals at lower levels of SES, particularly those with low educational attainment, are more likely than those with higher education or higher SES levels to be current smokers.[13]

Disparities in healthcare access and use, particularly in preventive health services such as cancer screening, may contribute to differentials in cancer stage distributions, especially in the late stage diagnosis.[14] Breast and colon cancer mortality is shaped by the distribution of screening in the population. Even though breast cancer incidence is more common in higher SES women, mortality is higher among lower SES women.[15] A 2004 study concluded that residents of poorer counties in the United States have a higher cancer death rate than residents in more affluent counties. The authors further concluded that even when poverty rates are accounted for, some racial groups (e.g., African Americans and American Indians/Alaskan Natives) have a lower survival rate than Caucasians.[16]

Lack of health insurance and other barriers prevents many Americans from receiving optimal healthcare. Uninsured patients and those from ethnic minorities are substantially more likely to be diagnosed with cancer at a later stage, when treatment can be more extensive and more costly.[17] In 1986, the American Cancer Society (ACS) issued a "Special Report on Cancer in the Economically Disadvantaged," which concluded that the disparate cancer outcomes in African Americans compared with white Americans is primarily related to lower SES in African Americans. The study further concluded that poor Americans, irrespective of race, have a 10–15 percent lower five-year survival rate.[18]

A follow-up report by the ACS in 1989, "Cancer in the Poor: A Report to the Nation,"[19] detailed the following:

- Poor people lack access to quality healthcare and are more likely than others to die of cancer.
- Poor people endure greater pain and suffering from cancer than other Americans.
- Poor people face substantial obstacles to obtaining and using health insurance and often do not seek needed care if they cannot pay for it.
- Poor people and their families must make extraordinary personal sacrifices to obtain and pay for healthcare.
- Cancer education and outreach efforts are insensitive and irrelevant to many poor people.
- Fatalism about cancer prevails among the poor and prevents them from gaining quality healthcare.

Practice to Policy

In 2001, the National Cancer Institute (NCI), which is part of the National Institutes of Health (NIH), established the Center to Reduce Cancer Health Disparities (CRCHD) to research and reduce the unequal burden of cancer in the United States. The CRCHD supports studies to advance the understanding of cancer-related health disparities and effective interventions in addressing those disparities. It also manages several programs and grants aimed at "addressing the cultural barriers and biases that racial and ethnic minorities encounter in obtaining appropriate and timely treatment, as well as financial and physical restraints that prevent underserved populations from obtaining quality health care." Finally, it encourages and trains students and researchers from diverse populations to pursue research focused on cancer and cancer health disparities.[20] MLPs directly address the social determinants of health, so they may be uniquely situated to participate in these broader policy initiatives aimed at reducing cancer health disparities by researching and promoting medical-legal interventions.

Addressing the Health, Social and Legal Needs of Patients and Survivors

The ACS reports that cancer death rates fell 21 percent among men and 12 percent among women between 1991 to 2006.[21] With these increased rate of survival comes an increased need to adapt to the intense financial, emotional, practical and health consequences associated with living with the illness.

When patients receive a cancer diagnosis, other concerns can take a back seat to their healthcare. Patients may give low priority to nonmedical needs in relation to medical issues. They may be reluctant to discuss those needs with their physician for fear of distracting the oncologist from the priority of treating the malignancy. Oncology specialists are often allocated only a few minutes to elicit toxicities from prescribed therapies, evaluate for evidence of disease progression or regression, and discern complications from the tumor. The provider must then interpret and explain this information as well as treatment plans to the patient in easily understandable language.

Providers must do all of this within the context of busy clinic schedules and often decreased face-to-face time with patients. It is therefore understandable that patients might be unable or unwilling to raise nonmedical needs. Furthermore, patients assume (often correctly) that their physician will not have the resources or answers to address nonmedical issues. MLPs can play a pivotal role in the care of patients with cancer by training healthcare providers about and encouraging them to raise legal issues common to a patient with a cancer diagnosis.

The cancer population is extremely heterogeneous, with a breadth of different types of cancers and patients, all with varied courses ranging from imminently terminal to potentially curable. For example, people diagnosed with advanced pancreatic cancer have a median survival of four to six months,[22] whereas men diagnosed with metastatic prostate cancer often measure their survival in years. Cancers diagnosed at an early stage have the potential for cure with surgery, chemotherapy or radiation therapy. Depending on the type of cancer and the prognosis, legal issues experienced by patients may be quite different.

The course traveled by a patient affected by cancer may also be quite episodic in nature. It is punctuated by the anxiety accompanying initial diagnosis and treatment that may encompass surgery, radiation or chemotherapy (or in some cases, all three). This is often followed by a relatively calm period of surveillance and then punctuated by the stress of a recurrence. There may be legal needs experienced by patients throughout the course of their disease, but during the times of stress and anxiety, those needs add to the stress that patients are already facing.

Additionally, the effects of illness and treatment—fatigue, pain, altered mental status and changes in physical functioning—all make it difficult for patients to follow up with service providers as required. The logistics of delivering legal care to the oncology population is also complicated when patients are bedridden, homebound, hospitalized for prolonged periods or in hospice or palliative care. Sometimes, a patient's life expectancy may be shorter than the lengthy waits for benefit eligibility to be determined (for example, SSI/SSDI, Medicaid and housing assistance). This obviates the necessity of being able to expedite cases in oncology patients, particularly those with terminal illnesses.

Cancer Survivors and Legal Need

Clinical experience reveals that patients and their families encounter many different legal issues during treatment for cancer. A number of investigations have explored legal needs among patients in general and, more specifically, among cancer patients.

- An early interview-based report examined service needs of cancer patients and identified three broad types of needs: physical, instrumental and administrative, with legally-related needs falling into the administrative category.[23]

- A majority of participants in a study examining factors that are important in end-of-life care cited a wide range of legally related issues they indicated were important.[24]

- A 2005 study reported the prevalence and significant impact of financial and employment-related needs among cancer patients and their families.[25]

- A retrospective study documenting the need for improved custody planning reported that only 50 percent of the single-parent patient families in the study population had developed successful custody plans for their children prior to the parent's death. Furthermore, in 40 percent of the cases the children were placed with family members to whom the deceased parents had been opposed.[26]

- A 2006 survey further detailed the barriers to care created for oncology patients by unresolved benefit and legal issues, most often affecting low-income clients.[27]

- A 2006 study documented the benefit of MLPs in oncology care in the *Journal of Clinical Oncology*. The article detailed the benefit of on-site legal assistance not only for patients and families but also for healthcare providers and institutions.[28]

- A 2007 survey found that providing legal services to people with cancer reduces stress.[29]

- A study published in 2007 empirically identified the types of legal needs of cancer patients, the extent to which these needs were currently addressed in cancer care, and the impact of these needs on the patient's quality of life. The focus group of cancer patients identified 30 medically related legal needs. These needs were then categorized into four medical-legal domains: healthcare-related, employment-related, financial and wills/estate-related. Participants rated these legal needs as having a significant impact on their quality of life and furthermore reported that these needs were not met by their current medical or supportive care.[30] These issues are detailed in Types of Legal Needs Reported by Patients. Figure 12.2 displays the mean ratings for the impact on quality of life of these issues and the degree to which they were addressed in current care.

As the studies suggest, the legal needs of cancer patients often go unaddressed. Nationally, over the past 10 years, MLPs have become an increasingly important model for delivering legal services to low-income people who become ill. The long-term objectives of MLPs developed around the oncology patient are to identify the legal needs of these patients and their families in the healthcare setting; establish a collaborative, interdisciplinary intervention program that provides the services and resources necessary to address these legal problems; and achieve potential resolution of identified legal needs, ultimately improving the quality of life for these individuals and their families.

Figure 12.2 Medically Related Legal Needs and Quality of Life

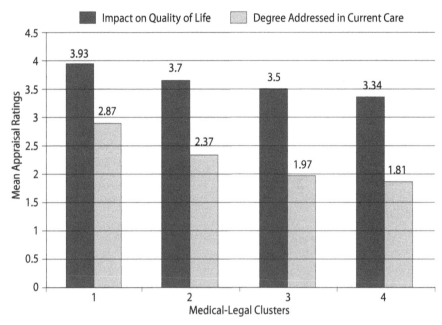

Notes: Mean ratings for the impact on quality of life and degree to which they are addressed in current care appraisal ratings for the four medical-legal needs clusters. Cluster 1: healthcare-related, cluster 2: employment-related, cluster 3: financial, cluster 4: wills/estate-related.
Source: M. A. Zevon, et al., "Medically Related Legal Needs and Quality of Life in Cancer Care: A Structural Analysis," *Cancer*, 109, no. 12 (2007): 2600–2606.

Types of Legal Needs Reported by Patients

Cluster 1 Healthcare-related
1   Healthcare proxy issues
2   Advance directives
3   Living will issues
4   Treatment implications — hydration/feeding
5   Do not resuscitate patient/family rights
7   Discharge rights
8   Skilled nursing facility regulations and laws
15   Rights of family members
30   Long-term care issues

Cluster 2 Employment-related
6   Employment rights — Family and Medical Leave Act
9   Insurance rights
16   Need for unbiased source of legal information
17   Education about legal issues
19   Unemployment issues
29   Disability issues

Cluster 3 Financial
13   Financial planning
18   Social Security issues
20   Pensions
22   IRS and tax implications
23   Stock and ownership issues
26   Veteran's benefits

Cluster 4 Wills/estate-related
10   Will and estate planning
11   Inheritance issues
12   Distributing property
14   Probate issues
21   Ownership issues — titles to auto/home, etc.
24   Bills pre- and post-death: who is responsible
25   Credit cards and responsibility for payment
27   Funeral home planning
28   Child custody issues

Note: Cluster number indicates the order in which patients placed the need by priority.
Source: M. A. Zevon, et al., "Medically Related Legal Needs and Quality of Life in Cancer Care: A Structural Analysis," *Cancer*, 109, no. 12 (2007): 2600–2606.

Improving the Quality of Life of a Person with Cancer through MLP

J.D. was a 43-year-old female diagnosed with recurrent cervical cancer and admitted to the hospital in the terminal phase of her illness for pain management. She experienced periods of mental fatigue. She was a single mother of two teenage children. She was concerned with what would happen to her children on her death and needed someone to pay her bills while she was in the hospital. A legal services consultation was requested by her oncology social worker, and she was referred to the on-site MLP.

She resided in an apartment that was partially funded through a federal housing subsidy. An inspection determined the apartment uninhabitable, and J.D. and her children were threatened with eviction and forced to find another apartment on short notice while she was hospitalized.

The MLP obtained a power of attorney to pay her bills. The attorney advocated for her with the federal housing program and assisted in obtaining suitable housing. If not for the legal intervention, she would have been placed on alternate level of care status in the hospital, awaiting either nursing home or hospice placement. The children would have been placed in foster care. With legal intervention, once a viable living space was secured, the patient was able to spend two weeks at home with her children prior to her death with hospice services and the assistance of her mother, thus keeping the family unit intact. The attorney assisted the grandmother with securing custody of the children following the death of the patient.

Questions for Discussion

1. What professionals should be part of the oncology team to effectively address the needs of cancer patients and their families?

2. How can an MLP adapt its service delivery model to address the episodic nature of cancer?

3. How should an MLP address its practice to be sensitive to the needs of cancer patients such as J.D. with the mental fog that often accompanies chemotherapy and other side effects of cancer treatment?

Best Practices and Advocacy Strategies for Medical-Legal Partnership

Because cancer patients, survivors and their families have a wide range of legal needs, training healthcare providers to identify these needs and to make appropriate referrals for legal assistance is critical. In addition to providing direct legal services to cancer patients and others with serious and chronic illness, LegalHealth, a division of the New York Legal Assistance Group, has developed a training curriculum for healthcare professionals tailored for oncology specialists. The trainings include:

- Forms 101: Completing the Forms Your Patients Bring You (SSI, SSDI)
- Improving Your Patient's Housing
- Decision Making in Health and Legal Matters
- Immigrants and the Health Care System
- Your Patient in the Workplace

MLP and Cancer: From Diagnosis to Treatment and Beyond

Given the diversity of the population affected by cancer, it is not surprising that the legal issues facing patients and their families are equally varied. From predictable disputes over insurance to perhaps less familiar conflicts over workplace accommodations, many areas of law are implicated in the broad context of cancer treatment. As such, the following sections trace the spectrum of matters—legal and emotional issues—that arise during the continuum of care: when a patient receives a definitive diagnosis, during treatment and in its aftermath.

For the sake of clarity, we present these issues chronologically to follow the continuum of care that informs medical practice. However, as Figure 12.3 illustrates, these issues

Figure 12.3 Legal Issues along the Cancer Trajectory

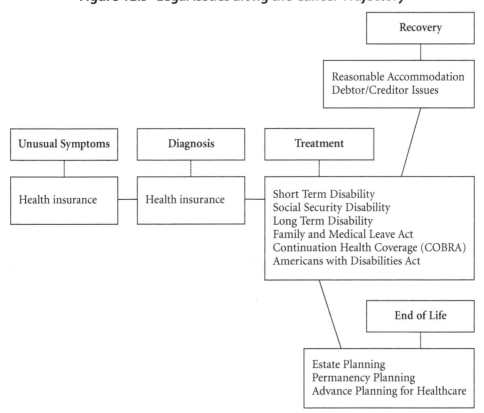

need not (and often do not) appear in the orderly fashion suggested by this chapter's structure. For example, a person might need reasonable accommodation under the Americans with Disabilities Act while undergoing treatment *and* on recovery. Likewise, there is no rule that confines a patient to consider estate planning only once death is imminent; some people, on discovering that they have a cancer diagnosis, want to do advance planning for health and financial matters as soon as possible, even though they may live for many more years. It is important to remember that the material presented here is meant to convey the continuum of a cancer diagnosis and the most common legal issues presented at a particular point in a patient's disease trajectory.

Health Insurance: Paying for Cancer Treatment

Once a physician diagnoses cancer, many patients immediately seek methods of financing treatments. Some patients or their family members will have insurance that will cover such costs. Others will have no such insurance and will need to find ways of financing their treatment. The following section provides a general overview of the many types of health insurance and the medical and legal issues that relate to these types of coverage, including both private health insurance and current government programs that help subsidize some costs for low-income individuals and families. Parts of this section were adapted with permission from the Cancer Legal Resource Center, *The HCP Manual: A Legal Resource Guide for Oncology Health Care Professionals* (2010).

Private Health Insurance: An Overview

There are several types of private health insurance; the basic distinction is between in-dividual and group plans. In the former, a person buys a policy directly from an insurance company; in the latter, a person is insured through an employer or other organization, such as a union. Group plans are further divided into insured and self-funded varieties. Most people obtain health insurance through their employers or their family members' employers.[31]

Private health insurance can also be classified by delivery model, of which there are three types: health maintenance organizations (HMOs), preferred provider organizations (PPOs) and point-of-service plans (POS plans). HMOs can be either independent physician organizations (IPAs) or stand-alone facilities. In an IPA, physicians provide care from their own offices to form a virtual organization. A stand-alone facility is a hospital that provides all services and care within its own system. In PPOs, a group of healthcare providers agree to see an insurer's members for a reduced rate. POS plans combine aspects of PPOs and HMOs so that members may choose what best serves their needs.[32] Table 12.1 summarizes the characteristics of the types of health plans.

Table 12.1 Types of Private Health Insurance

	Health Management Organization (HMO)	Preferred Provider Organization (PPO)	Point of Service Plan (POS Plan)
Who do patients see, and where do they go for care?	Participating doctors and hospitals; patient usually has a primary-care physician	Many healthcare providers and hospital choices	Can see providers in or out of network
How do patients select doctors or hospitals?	From within participating group	From all participating providers	From within or outside of network (costs more)
How much choice do patients have?	Limited: must stay in network	Lots	Lots, when patient so chooses
What is the cost?	Relatively low	Relatively high	In between HMO and PPO

Source: Cancer Legal Resource Center, *The HCP Manual: A Legal Resource Guide for Oncology Health Care Professionals* (2010), 30.

Regardless of the type of insurance in question, there are common factors that may give rise to specific legal issues. A healthcare provider working in an MLP should be familiar with these factors so that he or she can make a timely referral to an attorney if legal assistance is needed. First, every insurance plan has a unique summary of benefits (or terms of coverage). Whether a patient already has insurance or seeks to obtain insurance in light of changed circumstances, it is essential to know what the plan includes and excludes. Understanding the terms of coverage is necessary for the MLP to advocate effectively if there is a dispute about an aspect of coverage. Second, cost is an important consideration; based on monthly premiums, annual deductibles or co-payment requirements, certain plans may be beyond the reach of a particular individual or family. Third, one should keep in mind flexibility. For example, enrollment periods determine when a plan is available for new members and whether existing members may switch plans or make other changes to their current policies. An MLP may be able to advise clients as to whether and when they should apply for insurance or request to change their coverage. Finally, insurance holders or seekers should determine whether a particular plan has guaranteed renewability—does the insurance company automatically renew a person's policy because he or she made all payments on time? Guaranteed renewability does not "carry over" if a person switches insurance plans, nor does it prevent rate increases, but it is still a useful benefit.[33] An MLP lawyer could capitalize on this sort of provision to ensure that the patient remains covered throughout treatment.

Federal Protections for Private Health Insurance Coverage

The Consolidated Omnibus Budget Reconciliation Act

An important piece of federal legislation to address health insurance and employment is the Consolidated Omnibus Budget Reconciliation Act (COBRA).[34] This law requires employers to offer employees who leave a job for any reason (other than those fired for gross misconduct) the option of continuing as part of the group health insurance plan for up to 18 months.

Patients approved for Social Security Disability benefits who are taking time off from a job or became disabled within 60 days of leaving a job are eligible for an 11-month extension of COBRA coverage. He or she must provide a copy of the Social Security Disability award letter within 60 days of receipt to the plan administrator. Generally, to be eligible for COBRA an employer must have 20 or more employees.[35] However, some states have their own policies that require fewer than 20 employees; for example, New York extends COBRA coverage to employees with at least 2 employees.[36]

COBRA: Employee Responsibilities

There are a number of requirements that individuals must meet to keep their insurance through COBRA:

- The employee may be responsible for up to 102 percent of the premium formerly paid by the employer.
- The employee must be responsible for the full premium.
- The employee must elect COBRA within 60 days of being notified of his or her rights, and then has 45 days after electing coverage to pay the initial premium.

As stated, COBRA coverage is typically for 18 months but can last 29 months if the insured has a qualifying disability or 36 months if he or she meets certain qualifying events. Table 12.2 details coverage periods and qualifying events.

Table 12.2 COBRA Coverage Periods and Qualifying Events

Qualifying Event	Qualified Beneficiary/ies	Maximum Coverage
Termination of employment or reduction of hours	Employee, spouse, dependent child	18 months
Employee enrollment in Medicare	Employee, dependent child	36 months
Divorce or legal separation	Spouse, dependent child	36 months
Death of employee	Spouse, dependent child	36 months
Loss of dependent child status	Dependent child	36 months

Source: Employee Benefits Security Administration, Department of Labor, *An Employee's Guide to Health Benefits under COBRA*, http://www.dol.gov/ebsa/pdf/cobraemployee.pdf, 13–14.

The Health Insurance Premium Payment (HIPP) program provides an alternative means of obtaining COBRA coverage. If a person elects COBRA and is eligible for Medicaid (see discussion of Medicaid later in this chapter), HIPP will pay his or her premiums to maintain private health insurance.[37]

The Health Insurance Portability and Accountability Act

The Health Insurance Portability and Accountability Act (HIPAA; P.L. 104-191, 104th Cong., 2nd sess. (21 August 1996)) is another means by which employees may retain some form of health insurance, even in the face of changes in their employment status. Like COBRA, this law may be helpful to certain individuals with cancer who need health insurance but may not have access to it through an employer. HIPAA protects not only individuals who are moving from one group plan to another but also those who are changing from a group to an individual plan, known as a "HIPAA guarantee issue" plan.[38] By prohibiting discrimination against persons based on preexisting medical conditions, this law provides a federal right to individual health insurance. It is important to note that the HIPAA guarantee issue plan is not a specific plan but a right to purchase an individual plan. Although states have different laws, all ensure that those applying for such a policy will not be denied.[39]

To be eligible for a guarantee issue plan, applicants must be ineligible for Medicare, Medicaid (both discussed in the following section), or any other form of group coverage. Additionally, a person must have at least 18 months of creditable coverage or a period of insurance coverage that is not broken by 63 days or more. Finally, applicants must have exhausted COBRA or state COBRA insurance.[40] This last requirement highlights the fact that HIPAA and COBRA are very different in terms of coverage: under HIPAA, an individual must purchase new insurance, whereas COBRA allows an individual to maintain the same insurance obtained through employment.[41]

There are two means by which HIPAA protects individuals' right to health insurance. The first concerns the preexisting condition exclusion period (PECEP). A PECEP is when an insurer refuses to cover expenses relating to a preexisting condition for a period of time. HIPAA limits the PECEP to 12 months, and some states have extended the limit further.[42] The second method in HIPAA to protect individual health insurance is through creditable coverage. *Creditable coverage* refers to any period of insurance coverage that did not suffer a break of 63 days or more. The benefit to the insured is that it reduces the PECEP by the length of time a person had creditable coverage. Because nearly any type of coverage counts as creditable coverage—Medicare, Medicaid, COBRA, HIPAA or other group or individual plans—this policy, in many cases, effectively erases the PECEP.[43]

Importantly, the Patient Protection and Affordable Care Act (the Affordable Care Act or ACA) signed into law in 2010 phases out the PECEP insurance companies can impose on individuals. Under the new law, exclusion periods for children under the age of 19 are eliminated; by 2014, insurance companies are prohibited from enforcing a PECEP on all adults over 19 years old.[44] A second important provision of the ACA that is relevant for cancer patients focuses on high risk pools. For those unable to obtain insurance through COBRA or HIPAA, the ACA creates a Pre-Existing Condition Insurance Plan for individuals who have been uninsured for at least six months because of a preexisting condition.[45] This provision will be particularly helpful to patients with cancer who are uninsured.

Private Insurance Disputes

If a person has health insurance, disputes over medical bills are almost inevitable. The potential conflicts are endless: an insurer may dispute which services are covered, which treatments should be provided, which providers should be used or how much a service should cost. For a person with cancer, disputes may arise over the funding for experimental treatments. Again, it is preferable that patients try to minimize insurance disputes by taking preventive measures early on, such as ensuring that contact and other information is current and alerting all providers that he or she has insurance.

However, if and when a conflict arises, the insured should seek assistance from a lawyer. All companies are required to have an internal appeals process and must publish information about it to policy holders (29 CFR 2560.503-1 (h)). Consequently, it is advisable that patients and their families be familiar with the terms of their particular policy and keep in mind important deadlines. It is also a good idea to get any decisions or other communications from the insurance company in writing. An MLP lawyer can play a critical role in assisting a family with insurance disputes by explaining provisions in clear terms, helping the family maintain good documentation and advocating on behalf of the patient with the insurance company.

Additionally, some states have external appeals process by which patients or their families may contest an insurer's decision. Usually called external or independent medical review, this process involves a special organization evaluating the decisions made by insurance companies. Patients must first exhaust their insurer's internal appeals process, and there is no guarantee that they will win a reversal through this process.[46] Although independent review provides a useful resource, because of the complexities of state laws regarding insurance disputes, patients may be unable to capitalize on the information it provides. Thus, it is generally a good idea to enlist the services of an MLP for such appeals.

Healthcare Reform and Its Impact on People with Cancer

The ACS cites the following provisions of the ACA as beneficial to people with cancer:

- Insurance companies may no longer set lifetime dollar limits on coverage, ensuring that people with cancer have access to needed care.

- Annual dollar limits on coverage will be tightly restricted for most plans and will no longer be allowed as of 2014.

- Coverage will be guaranteed and out-of-pocket costs will be eliminated in new insurance plans for proven preventive services, giving people access to life-saving screenings for breast, cervical and colorectal cancer.

- By 2014, insurance companies will be required to issue plans to all applicants and prohibited from charging higher rates based on health status or gender.

- Health plans will be barred from dropping people from coverage when they get sick.

- Preventive services will be free for patients enrolled in Medicare.

- Health insurance will be made more administratively simple through a uniform set of rules for verifying eligibility and claims status and making payments.

- Preexisting condition exclusions will be eliminated for everyone with private insurance as of 2014.

- In 2014, waiting periods for coverage by employer provided coverage will be limited to 90 days.

Note: The effective dates for the provisions have been added by the chapter's authors. Unless otherwise noted, these changes are already in effect.
Source: Adapted from American Cancer Society, "The Affordable Care Act: How it Helps People with Cancer and Their Families" (2010).

Questions for Discussion

1. What are some of the issues that arise for privately insured patients when they are diagnosed with cancer?

2. What is the role of healthcare providers in helping patients navigate insurance issues?

3. What types of insurance disputes require the help of an MLP lawyer?

Federal Health Insurance Programs

Medicare and Cancer

As described in Chapter 2, Medicare is a federal health insurance program for those who (1) are 65 or older and eligible for Social Security retirement benefits; (2) are under age 65 and have received Social Security Disability benefits for 2 years; or (3) have end-stage renal disease (kidney failure).[47]

Because the Medicare program provides health insurance coverage to virtually all elderly Americans, it is a major source of financing for cancer care. According to the National Cancer Institute, Medicare accounted for about 45 percent of the estimated $72 billion spent on cancer treatment in 2004.[48] Likewise, cancer accounts for a large share of Medicare spending, with almost 1 in 10 Medicare fee-for-service dollars spent on cancer treatment or screening in 2006.[49]

There are four different parts to Medicare, each of which entail different types of services and coverage.

- Part A is available to anyone who qualifies for Medicare and is free unless an individual has insufficient work history. However, even those without adequate work history may obtain Part A insurance if they pay a monthly premium. This particular plan is often called "hospital insurance" because it covers in-patient stays, skilled nursing care and some home healthcare or hospice.[50]

- Part B is considered "medical insurance" because it covers physician services, outpatient hospital visits, tests and lab work, ambulance rides and other medical supplies and services. Those who qualify for Part A are automatically eligible for Part B, but must pay a monthly premium and annual deductible. Part B is, therefore, optional.[51]

- Part C was previously known as Medicare Plus Choice but is now referred to as Medicare Advantage Plans. It is usually administered with Parts A, B and D through a private Medicare HMO or PPO.[52]

- Since 2006, Medicare prescription drug plans have been available to all those who are eligible for Medicare. This particular benefit falls under Part D, which, like Part B, is optional. It is worth noting that plans differ depending on the state of administration.[53]

Some cancer screenings and other preventive health services are covered under Part B. Mammograms are covered annually for female beneficiaries over age 40, with a baseline mammogram for those ages 35–39.[54] Cervical cancer screening (Pap smear and pelvic exam) is covered once every 24 months and annually for certain high-risk women.[55] Annual prostate cancer screening (digital rectal exam and prostate-specific antigen test) is covered for male beneficiaries age 50 and older.[56] Colorectal screening is covered for all beneficiaries starting at age 50.[57]

Hospice care is limited to people with a terminal illness who are expected to live six months or less if the disease runs its normal course and who are willing to forgo curative treatment.[58] (Under the ACA, there are different standards for children.) Hospice benefits include pain relief, supportive medical and social services, physical therapy, nursing services and symptom management for a terminal illness.[59] Medicare also covers some short-term inpatient stays (for pain and symptom management) and inpatient respite care.

Part D is Medicare's prescription drug program, through which beneficiaries may enroll in a private prescription drug plan that contracts with Medicare. Although a standard benefit is defined in law, plans are permitted to vary the standard design and include more generous benefits.[60] For cancer patients considering Part D coverage options, a key concern is the adequacy of coverage for cancer-related drugs. Under Centers for Medicare and Medicaid Services guidance, Part D plans must list on formulary all (or substantially all) cancer-related drugs.[61] Accordingly, for 2009, oral anticancer drugs, including brand-name products, are covered by nearly all plans, although prior authorization or other utilization management requirements might limit access to some agents. Some cancer drugs, available at the pharmacy, are covered under Part B.[62]

Under Medicare Part C, or Medicare Advantage (MA), beneficiaries may choose to enroll in a private health plan that contracts with Medicare to provide benefits under Parts A and B or Parts A, B and D.[63] MA plans may also offer additional benefits, but beneficiaries who enroll in them may face a restricted choice of providers.[64] In 2008, about one in five Medicare beneficiaries was enrolled in an MA plan.[65] A patient may only enroll or unenroll from Part C at certain times of the year; therefore, it is important that the patient is sure the plan meets all of his or her needs.[66]

According to the ACS Cancer Action Network, recent amendments to Medicare recognize "the need to provide certain exceptions for cancer patients," including covering many cancer screening services, covering certain prescription drugs under Part B, requiring Part D plans to cover 'all or substantially all' anticancer drugs, and making coverage of anticancer off-label drug uses under Part D consistent with Part B."[67]

Medicaid and Cancer

Medicaid is another federal health insurance program through which many low-income people with cancer receive health insurance. In general, Medicaid is intended for the poor—those with low income and limited resources. To be eligible, applicants must meet income and asset eligibility requirements. The federal government requires that certain groups of people receive Medicaid, such as low-income families with children under age 19, and recipients of Supplement Security Income.[68]

States have the discretion to expand Medicaid eligibility beyond the minimum federal requirements. They can increase income limits or add eligibility groups or disease-specific waivers. (See Chapter 2 for a detailed discussion of Medicaid.) Many cancer patients can benefit from these state-by-state variations in eligibility. States also differ in their buy-in options. Under a buy-in program, individuals of any age who have a disability and are working can receive Medicaid by paying a monthly premium, which is determined by the applicant's income.[69]

Clinical Trials and Medicare and Medicaid

Medicare

If a patient takes part in an approved clinical trial, Medicare covers routine costs for items and services, such as:

- Room and board for a hospital stay that Medicare would cover even if the patient were not in a clinical trial
- An operation to implant an item that is being tested
- Treatment of side effects and problems caused by the new care

In most cases, Medicare does not cover:

- The experimental item or service being tested—unless Medicare would cover it even if the patient were not in a clinical trial
- Items and services the study provides the patient free of charge
- Items or services used only to collect data and not needed as part of the patient's direct healthcare, such as monthly CT scans for a condition that usually only requires one scan
- Co-insurance and deductibles

The patient will be responsible for the part of the charge that he or she would normally pay for Medicare-covered services.

Medicaid

Many state Medicaid programs cover all or some of the costs of clinical trials. Coverage is determined by each state, but many follow guidelines much like those listed for Medicare.

Source: "Clinical Trials: State Laws Regarding Insurance Coverage," http://www.cancer.org/Treatment/ TreatmentsandSideEffects/ClinicalTrials/StateLawsRegardingInsuranceCoverage/clinical-trials-state-laws-medicare-and-medicaid-coverage (accessed January 11, 2011).

Additionally, some states have a protection for people whose income is above the Medicaid limit. This is called Medicaid "spend down," and it works much like a medical deductible. Applicants "spend down" a portion of their income on medical care, and Medicaid pays the rest of their medical bills until the end of the month.[70] (For further discussion of the spend down option, see Chapter 14.) If a person with cancer needs permanent medical care but has more income or assets than allowed by Medicaid, he or she may choose to place income or assets in a created or pooled income trust to avoid a spend down of assets to qualify. A Supplemental Needs Trust (sometimes called a "Special Needs Trust") is designed to benefit an individual who has a disability, including people with cancer determined to be disabled (42 U.S.C. § 1396(d) (2010)). A Supplemental Needs Trust enables a person to have an unlimited amount of assets held in trust for his or her benefit. Those assets are not considered countable assets for purposes of qualification for certain governmental benefits, such as SSI and Medicaid.[71] The trust is then used to pay the patient's expenses (minus a fee the trust charges), while still allowing the patient to qualify for Medicaid.

Case for Medical-Legal Partnership

P.J. had a health insurance policy effective September 1, 2009, through his employment. Prior to that date he had been covered by Medicaid through July 25, 2009. He stopped working after he was diagnosed in February 2010 with an aggressive, malignant brain tumor. His insurance company denied coverage for his treatment based on a preexisting condition. His family has come to see the MLP attorney to discuss other coverage that may be available. The hospital is threatening to discontinue his treatment for lack of payment.

Questions for Discussion

1. Can PJ and his family challenge the insurance company's denial of coverage based on a preexisting condition?
2. Does the gap in insurance between July 25 and September 1, 2009, affect his claim?
3. What should the MLP do to advocate for P.J. with the insurance company?
4. Should the MLP team discuss advance planning options with P.J., and if so, how should they introduce them?

Working with Cancer: Employment Issues for Survivors

For many people, a cancer diagnosis does not mean that they can no longer work. Because of new and more effective treatments, individuals are living longer with a better quality of life and therefore are more likely to continue working. In one study of cancer survivors and work, approximately 13 percent of all survivors had quit working for cancer-related reasons within four years of diagnosis. More than half quit working after the first year. However, three quarters of those who stopped for treatment returned to work.[72] "Whether a survivor continues to work during treatment or returns to work after treatment—and if so, whether that survivor's diagnosis or treatment will result in working limitations—depends on many factors. They include the survivor's age, stage at diagnosis, financial status, education, and access to health insurance and transportation, as well as the physical demands of the job and the presence of any other chronic health conditions."[73]

In addition, treatment decisions that consider quality of life and the current shift toward providing cancer treatment in outpatient settings have contributed to the increasing number of survivors who can work during their treatment. For many people with cancer, work is a financial necessity because they need the income and access to employer-sponsored health insurance coverage. Work may also serve as an important source of self-esteem and social support.[74]

Employment-Related Legal Protections for Cancer Survivors

In the context of employment, there are several legal issues that may arise once a physician diagnoses cancer. Some are more obvious, such as potential discrimination against cancer patients, whereas others are more subtle, such as the right of family members to take time off from work to accompany loved ones to appointments. Even issues regarding disclosure of a person's diagnosis to an employer may raise legal issues.

The following sections describe some employment-related legal protections that are important and relevant for cancer survivors and their families.

Federal Protections for Cancer Survivors in the Workplace

The Americans with Disabilities Act

Conflicts in the workplace often stem from an employer's misunderstanding about the ability of a person with a disability to work. To combat these misperceptions and possible injustice, Congress passed the Americans with Disabilities Act (ADA) in 1990, which prohibits discrimination against a "qualified individual ... who, with or without reasonable accommodation, can perform the essential functions of [an] employment position" (42 U.S.C. § 12111(8)). The ADA is also discussed in Chapter 7.

Amendments to the Act in 2008 further strengthened protections for disabled employees, particularly those with cancer. This section focuses on those amendments and how an MLP can enforce ADA protections on behalf of cancer survivors.

Although there is no question that the ADA, as originally drafted, helped address discrimination in the workplace based on disability, many employee complaints under the law were unsuccessful because to prove disability a claimant had to show that they had "1) an impairment that substantially limits one or more major life activities; 2) a record of such an impairment; or 3) evidence of being regarded as having such an impairment" (42 U.S.C.§ 12102(1)). Under a narrow reading of the ADA, proving disability from cancer was particularly difficult. As such, the Amendments Act significantly affected cancer survivor's success in ADA litigation.

In *Cancer and Work: Protections Under the Americans with Disabilities Act,* Barbara Hoffman describes the four key changes provided by the ADA Amendments Act of 2008:

First, the Amendments Act adds the definition of "major life activities" to the statute itself and expands the list of covered activities. [It] broadens the definition of major life activity to include "the operation of a major bodily function, including but not limited to, functions of the immune system, normal cell growth, digestive bowel, bladder, neurological, brain, respiratory, circulatory, endocrine, and reproductive functions." Under the ADA, some cancer survivors could not prove that their cancer had an impact on one of the major life activities identified by the regulations. The far more expansive definition of major life activities in the Amendments Act provides practically all survivors the ability to identify a major life activity affected by their cancer.

Second, in 1999, the United States Supreme Court ruled that a court must consider whether an individual used mitigating measures, such as taking medication, in determining whether he or she had a disability. This rule created a Catch-22 for individuals whose impairments were quite disabling, but who could obtain some relief through medication.... The Amendments Act addressed this dilemma by stating: "The determination of whether an impairment substantially limits a major life activity shall be made without regard to the ameliorative effects of mitigating measures," which include medication, prosthetic devices, mobility devices, and oxygen therapy equipment and supplies. Under this language, a court could no longer consider how cancer treatment mitigated the effects of cancer on an individual....

Third, prior to the Amendments Act, a person whose impairment was episodic or in remission would be unlikely to prove that it substantially limited a major life activity. Therefore, a survivor whose cancer was in remission or whose cancer affected a major life activity only occasionally may not have been covered under the ADA. The Amendments Act overcame this hurdle by stating that an "impairment that is episodic or in remission is a disability if it would substantially limit a major life activity when active." This new language will benefit the large numbers of cancer survivors whose cancer is chronic, but often managed. Many survivors live for years or decades with their cancer, and at times are not substantially limited by their diagnosis.

Fourth, under the original ADA, an employee could be covered if his or her employer "regarded" him or her as having a disability if the employer believed that the employee had a disability. The Amendments Act no longer requires that the employer actually believe that the employee is substantially limited in a major life activity. Now the employee need prove only that "he or she has been subjected to an action prohibited under [the ADA] because of an actual or perceived physical or mental impairment whether or not the impairment limits or is perceived to limit a major life activity." Therefore, a survivor who is treated differently because of his or her cancer, regardless of whether his or her cancer substantially limits any major life activity, may be protected under the ADA.[75]

MLPs: Helping Patients Seek Accommodation and Enforce Their Rights under the ADA

- Healthcare providers should understand and become familiar with the rules and regulations governing an ADA request by their patients. For example, when explaining the side effects of treatment to a patient, a healthcare provider can alert him or her that he or she must file a request for accommodation as soon as possible, both to increase the chances that it will be made and to avoid disciplinary action.[a]

- The provider can also discuss the process of submitting a request, which often involves speaking with a supervisor or human resources representative, and documenting the request in writing.[b]

- If appropriate, the healthcare provider can request an accommodation on the patient's behalf, because the ADA is very lenient with regard to who can submit such requests.[c]

- The MLP can help to educate healthcare providers about the legal requirements imposed by the ADA so that he or she can write a successful request for accommodation.

- If the patient is denied, the healthcare provider should then refer the patient to the MLP lawyer so he or she can negotiate with the patient's employer to obtain the necessary accommodation, or, alternatively, to file a claim of discrimination.

- State and local laws may offer broader protections for people with cancer than the ADA; therefore, it is important to be familiar with the relevant laws of a particular jurisdiction.

Source: [a] Disability Rights Legal Center, *Healthcare Providers Manual* (Los Angeles: Disability Rights Legal Center (2010), 9; [b] U.S. Equal Employment Opportunity Commission, "EEOC Enforcement Guidance on Reasonable Accommodation and Undue Hardship Under the Americans with Disabilities Act, Number 915.002," http://www.eeoc.gov/policy/docs/accommodation.html (accessed January 19, 2011); [c] Ibid.

The Family and Medical Leave Act

Cancer patients are not the only ones for whom treatment may pose employment issues. Though patients certainly worry about job security if they must take time off for healthcare appointments or to recover from treatment, their family members and caregivers may also face the same concerns. The Family and Medical Leave Act (FMLA) of 1993 was the congressional response to this dilemma. This federal law requires employers with more than 50 employees (and all federal and state governments) to provide eligible employees up to 12 weeks of unpaid leave to take care of family and/or medical issues without the fear of losing their jobs (29 U.S.C. § 2611(4)(A)(i) (2010)). An employee may take time off to care for (1) a spouse, child or parent with a serious medical condition; (2) his or her own serious medical condition; (3) a newborn child; or (4) a newly adopted child (29 U.S.C. § 2612(a)(1)). The provisions of the FMLA are discussed in detail in Chapter 7. This section focuses on how the FMLA may provide extremely important employment protections for cancer survivors and their family members during treatment.

Cancer as a "Serious Health Condition"

An employee requesting leave for medical reasons—either for him or herself or for a family member—must prove that there is a legitimate "serious health condition." The FMLA defines this phrase as "an illness, injury, impairment, or physical or mental condition that involves (A) inpatient care in a hospital, hospice, or residential medical care facility; or (B) continuing treatment by a healthcare provider" (29 U.S.C. § 2611(11)). Generally, a patient undergoing treatment for cancer will meet this serious health condition test.[76]

FMLA also allows employers to demand that the employee provide certification from a healthcare provider that medical leave is necessary (29 U.S.C. § 2613(a)). Most employers have their own certification forms. Although this potential requirement (potential because it is merely an option for the employer and not a mandatory procedure) may seem strict, the definition of "healthcare provider" provides some wiggle room: not just a doctor but also a nurse practitioner, midwife, social worker or Christian Scientist practitioner may qualify as a healthcare provider (Definitions, C.F.R. § 825.800 (2010)).

For any such person asked to certify that the employee or employee's family member does, in fact, have a serious health condition, it is important to be aware of what information must appear in the certification. The bare minimum requirements include the date of onset, the probable duration of the condition and a statement that the employee is unable to perform one or more of the essential functions of the job because of the health condition (29 U.S.C. § 2613(b)). However, the provider need not disclose the specific condition or diagnosis for the employee or employee's family member.[77] For an employee requesting time off to care for a family member, though, the certification must explain why the health condition requires the employee to provide care, as well as estimate how long the employee will need to be on leave.[78] See Chapter 13 for discussion on FMLA in the context of HIV.

Procedural Requirements Imposed by FMLA

- Employees who want to take time off under the statute must provide reasonable advance notice, which has different timeframes depending on the circumstances.[a]

- The actual request must be in writing and contain sufficient information from which the employer can understand the situation.[b]

- The employer, on receipt of a request for medical leave, must notify the employee that a FMLA request has been filed and will be handled accordingly.[c]

- Finally, and with most relevance to medical and legal professionals, the complaint process requires that employees submit claims to Employee Standards Administration Wage and Hour Division of the Department of Labor, which will then investigate the matter.[d]

Source: [a] 29 U.S.C. § 2612(e)(2); Employee Notice Requirements for Foreseeable FMLA Leave, 29 C.F.R. §§ 825.302, 825.303 (2010); [b] Employer Notice Requirements, 29 C.F.R. § 825.300 (2010); [c] Designation of FMLA Leave, 29 C.F.R. § 825.301 (2010); [d] Filing a Complaint with the Federal Government, 29 C.F.R. § 825.401(a) (2010).

Comparing the Protections of the FMLA and the ADA

FMLA with the ADA are similar in their intent to preserve job security and benefits for employees who are disabled or dealing with a serious health condition. However, there are important ways in which FMLA provides employees with broader protections than the ADA. For example, FMLA allows employees to take up to three months off from work to care not just for themselves but also for family members, taken either all at once or intermittently (29 U.S.C. § 2612(a)(1)). Also, FMLA requires that employers allow employees to return to their original position (29 U.S.C. § 2614(a)); the ADA suggests employers should hold open employees' original positions unless doing so would constitute an undue hardship (42 U.S.C. § 12111).

It is also important to note that individual states may also have state laws that mirror and/or expand on the protections for workers under the ADA and FMLA. These state laws can provide important protections for people with cancer. MLP teams should be familiar with how these state provisions may apply to their patient-clients as well.

Best Practices and Advocacy Strategies for Medical-Legal Partnership

The MLP team can support patient-clients with cancer to enforce workplace protections by:

- Providing documentation of the cancer diagnosis and, as appropriate, documenting (e.g., in a letter to the employer) whether, in the provider's professional medical opinion, the patient is able to carry out the duties of his or her job.

- Advocating for their patients regarding reasonable accommodations (e.g., flexible daily work arrangements, leave flexibility) that will not interfere with (and which, in some cases, may be anticipated to improve) the worker's productivity without posing an undue burden on the employer.

- Providing an assessment for an individual cancer patient. For example, an MLP physician may be treating a patient who has difficulty concentrating at work in the afternoons and is making mistakes that the employer has observed. If the patient can avoid this problem, however, with the accommodation of taking two short breaks as needed to rest in the mid-afternoon instead of taking one long lunch break, the healthcare professional can document that the worker is able to do the job with the accommodation of these breaks.

- Providing the medical information needed by the person with cancer who wishes to take a leave under FMLA.

Working together as a team will result in less stress for patients and families and ultimately allow patients to focus solely on treatment and recovery instead of battling with employers over accommodations or other workplace issues.

From Practice to Policy

FMLA provides important job protections to patients with cancer and their family members. However, because the law only provides for *unpaid* leave for a serious health condition or to care for a family member, its effectiveness may be limited for low-income workers who cannot afford to take time off without pay. Since FMLA was enacted in 1993, family leave advocates have called for expansion of the law to require paid leave. Some states, such as California, have enacted paid leave schemes to protect workers during family or medical leave. Because MLPs serve low-income and vulnerable patient-client populations, they have an important role in advocating for expanded medical leave policies that will protect low-income cancer patients as well as those with other serious health conditions who may otherwise face job loss when they become ill. In addition to advocating for expansion of FMLA, MLP teams can work with other partners in their states to advocate for state paid leave policies.

Cases for Medical-Legal Partnership

Frank is a 44-year-old security guard who was recently diagnosed with colon cancer. Though his prognosis is good, he needs to take time off work to undergo treatment. After his first round of chemotherapy, Frank is released from the hospital to his wife Emily's care at home. At a subsequent visit to the doctor, Emily expressed her concern that she might be fired from her job because she had to spend so much time caring for her husband.

Questions for Discussion

1. What protections does the FMLA provide to Frank and/or Emily?
2. How might Frank's healthcare provider help him protect his job and reduce his stress during treatment?
3. How might an MLP lawyer help this family?

Maida was recently diagnosed with breast cancer, though she is still working in the maintenance department of an office with 20 employees. Unfortunately, she finds her work conditions nearly unbearable: her cubicle is in the basement of a building, where there is only one window that is always sealed, and she is surrounded by ventilation fans and garbage cans. Maida is uncomfortable and worried that these conditions could adversely affect her health, but she is afraid to speak with her supervisor.

Questions for Discussion

1. How might the MLP team advise or assist Maida?
2. What role might an attorney play in this situation?
3. What role might a healthcare provider play?

When a Survivor Cannot Work: Income Supports for Short- and Long-Term Disability

Types of Disability Insurance

Disability insurance covers people who have a temporary or permanent disability that prevents them from working. There are two varieties: short-term and long-term disability insurance. Short-term disability insurance provides benefits for a relatively brief period, ranging from six months to one year after the onset of disability. Long-term disability insurance, on the other hand, covers a period of more than one year; actual length of coverage varies by policy. Depending on the type of cancer, treatment program and prognosis, the patient should be directed to pursue the most appropriate claim.

Because it is a subset of private health insurance, disability insurance may be purchased by individuals or provided through employers. Consequently, the same concerns that arise with general health insurance—scrutinizing the terms of the policy, comparing costs of different plans, for example—also apply to disability insurance. However, healthcare providers and lawyers should draw patients' attention to certain elements unique to this type of insurance. Perhaps the most important is how an insurance company defines *disability*; the more inclusive the definition, the better for the patient and his or her family. Some companies may carve out "presumptive disabilities," such as blindness or deafness, which automatically trigger the payment of benefits, even if the person afflicted is still able to work. A cancer diagnosis may or may not be sufficient to trigger benefits. Patients should be urged to review any insurance policies they have, including life insurance policies, to see if they qualify for cash benefits.

Another important consideration is how long coverage lasts. The coverage period, of course, will be defined in specific terms, but there are other aspects of the policy that bear on it in more subtle ways. For example, whether there is a "qualifying period" between the onset of disability and the beginning of benefits will determine how soon a patient can start receiving payments from insurance. In some cases, the length of coverage is not as important as when it starts.

Before discussing federal disability insurance programs, a few words about state disability insurance programs are in order. Only five states and Puerto Rico have a disability insurance program, and they are dependent on length of employment and payment of state taxes. For example, California's State Disability Insurance covers employees for up to 52 weeks; New York covers up to 26.[79]

Supplemental Security Income

Supplemental Security Income (SSI) is the first type of long-term disability insurance offered by the government and is available to people sixty-five or older, the blind or the disabled, provided they meet the income requirements. The Social Security Administration's (SSA) complicated definition of disability is the fulcrum on which SSI benefits turn. At first glance, it does not seem so difficult: a "disability" is "a medically determinable physical or mental impairment" that prevents the affected person from doing "any substantial gainful activity," has lasted for or will last for a year or more (uninterrupted), and can result in death (42 U.S.C. §423(d)(1) (2010)). However, the test the SSA uses to determine the existence of a disability is considerably more complex (see Chapter 7).

One exception to the SSA's complicated test that is of particular importance to cancer survivors comes under the guise of Compassionate Allowances. Since 2008, this program identifies certain conditions — including many specific types of cancer — that automatically make an applicant eligible for Social Security benefits.

In the vast majority of cases, however, those seeking benefits will need to pass the rigorous five parts of the SSA's test to qualify as disabled. Additionally, all applicants, even an individual who is elderly (65 or older), blind or disabled must satisfy the financial eligibility requirements. In this area especially, a team effort between healthcare providers, patients and lawyers will be necessary. Aside from explaining the eligibility requirements for such benefits, a coordinated approach to filling out forms and submitting applications will yield the best result for the patient. For example, a physician may need to send notes or reports to document that an applicant is unable to perform any of the duties of his previous jobs. A lawyer overseeing the application for Social Security benefits would also want to check the SSA listing and verify that the final application meets the standard imposed by administrative law.

Social Security Disability Income

Social Security Disability Income (SSDI) is the other type of federal long-term disability insurance. The amount of benefits for which an applicant is eligible depends on his or her work history: how long she worked, how much she made and how much she paid in Social Security taxes. Applicants for SSDI are not subject to the strict financial need requirements of SSI applicants. The requirements are similar to those for SSI regarding the SSA process for determining whether an individual is disabled. But for SSDI, he or she must also be "insured," meaning the applicant worked 5 out of the past 10 years.[80] (Chapter 7 provides a comparison of SSI and SSDI.)

In determining the date of onset for cancer patients, the SSA focuses on the date of diagnosis, dates of discovered metastases, date of all attempts of resection (surgery) and the length and intensity of chemotherapy and radiation treatment. Supportive documentation such as biopsies and medical imaging should be provided, in addition to medical statements specifying the nature of the disease, prognosis of the patient and all residual effects of treatment.

Appealing an SSI or SSDI Denial

In an ideal world, every patient who qualifies and applies for Social Security benefits would receive them; but many patient-clients' initial applications for benefits are denied. (For discussion of the denial rate for SSI and SSDI applications, see Chapter 7.)

The MLP team should encourage cancer patients and their families to be persistent if their application is denied. First, they should alert patients that they have 60 days from the denial to write to the SSA and request a "reconsideration." If that request is denied again, healthcare providers and lawyers may need to participate more directly in the appeal. After the "reconsideration," applicants may ask for a hearing in front of an administrative law judge. At this hearing, the applicant may represent him or herself or may appear through a representative, who may be a lawyer. Unlike most appellate trials, the applicant may present new evidence, including testimony from healthcare providers.

If the judge upholds the SSA's original denial, the applicant may still try to obtain a reversal. Here, the services of both physicians and attorneys are clearly necessary. In the case of advanced cancer patients, most are approved early in the initial application process. However, for cancers that are not metastatic, are resected or resectable (otherwise known as an operable cancer), or have a positive prognosis with treatment, the case may still be denied.

SSI and SSDI do not require recipients to be unemployed for the entire benefit-paying period, though the SSA's definition of "disability" might suggest otherwise. Both programs have provisions that protect benefits while patients test whether they are ready to return to work.[81] For SSDI recipients, this trial work period may last up to 9 months out of a 60-month period. Once the trial period is over, a new 36-month period begins, during which beneficiaries may receive benefits for any month in which their earnings were not "substantial" (currently limited to $1,000 per month) and still maintain Medicare coverage. SSI recipients' benefits are reduced by a portion of their earnings, usually about 50 percent, and in some cases they are still able to maintain Medicaid coverage.[82] When discussing disability insurance options with patients and their families, healthcare providers and lawyers should keep this information in mind. This provision provides flexibility for the patient as he or she copes with the ups and downs of cancer treatment.

Advanced Cancer and Disability

When applying for disability benefits for claimants who have obvious disabilities, there are accommodations that can be made to expedite the processing of their claim. The discussion here is limited to such accommodations as they apply to claimants suffering from cancer. It is noteworthy to acknowledge that a diagnosis of cancer does not automatically qualify an individual to receive expedited processing. If the cancer has been completely resected or is resectable and the condition is not expected to result in death, then the claimant will be evaluated under the SSA listing (requirements for determining if a disability exists) for the body system that has been impacted by the disease and the residual functional capacity of the individual.

Accommodations made for quick processing of eligible claims go under many names, such as Terminal Illness (TERI), Compassionate Allowance (CAL), Presumptive Disability/Presumptive Blindness (PD/PB) and Quick Disability Determination (QDD). With regard to people with cancer, TERI and CAL are the most often used and are therefore discussed in this section.

Terminal Illness Cases (TERI)

Cases are marked as TERI when there has been an allegation made by the claimant, a friend or family member, a medical treating source, or his or her representative that the claimant's condition is terminal. A case can also be marked by the field officer or disability analyst should medical evidence sufficiently indicate that the condition is terminal. In those instances, the analyst would not assume that the claimant is aware of the terminal nature of the illness, and language used in any correspondence with the claimant would reflect that. The word *terminal* should not appear on any documents from Social Security that the claimant sees, especially if it was not the claimant who made the initial allegation of terminal illness. Another indication that makes a case eligible for TERI status is if the client is receiving hospice care as either an inpatient or an outpatient.[83]

Having the healthcare provider supply the claimant or the claimant's local Social Security office directly with a signed statement of the terminal nature of the disability can help ensure the expeditious processing of the case. Additionally, correspondence from the SSA may request that a Residual Functional Capacity Questionnaire be filled out by the treating doctor. At this point, especially if no prior opportunity was available, it would be appropriate to indicate the terminal nature of the illness. In general, the more medical documentation furnished, the more quickly the claim can be processed.

Although any claim that is terminal — untreatable and expected to end in death — can be processed as a TERI case, the following are the listings used by SSA to recognize such cases for people with cancer:

- Any malignant neoplasm (cancer) which is:
  - Metastatic (has spread);
  - Stage IV;
  - Persistent or recurrent following initial therapy; or
  - Inoperable or unresectable.
- An allegation or diagnosis of:
  - Cancer of the esophagus;
  - Cancer of the liver;
  - Cancer of the pancreas;
  - Cancer of the gallbladder;
  - Mesothelioma;

- ◦ Small cell or oat cell lung cancer;
- ◦ Cancer of the brain; or
- ◦ Acute myelogenous leukemia (AML) or acute lymphocytic leukemia (ALL).

This list is not intended to be all-inclusive but to serve as a guideline when trying to determine whether or not TERI status may be appropriate. Many aggressive cancers qualify.

Compassionate Allowance Cases (CAL)

Compassionate Allowance exists to identify cases where the claimant suffers from a disease or medical condition that invariably qualifies under the SSA's Listing of Impairments based on minimal but sufficient medical information. If the condition does not meet these strict criteria, it will not be designated as a CAL case. CAL cases are similar to TERI cases but do not necessarily require that the illness result in death.[84] See Conditions Identified by SSA as CAL Cases.

Conditions Identified by SSA as CAL Cases

The following is a list of some of the conditions for cancer identified by Social Security as CAL cases via a predictive model:

- Acute leukemia
- Adrenal cancer—with distant metastases or inoperable, unresectable or recurrent
- Anaplastic adrenal cancer—with distant metastases or inoperable, unresectable or recurrent
- Astrocytoma—Grade III and IV
- Bilateral Retinoblastoma
- Bladder cancer—with distant metastases or inoperable or unresectable
- Bone cancer—with distant metastases or inoperable or unresectable
- Breast cancer—with distant metastases or inoperable or unresectable
- Chronic Myelogenous Leukemia (CML)—blast phase
- Ependymoblastoma (child brain tumor)
- Esophageal cancer
- Gallbladder cancer
- Glioblastoma multiforme (brain tumor)
- Head and neck cancers—with distant metastasis or inoperable or unresectable
- Inflammatory Breast Cancer (IBC)
- Kidney cancer—inoperable or unresectable
- Large intestine cancer—with distant metastasis or inoperable, unresectable or recurrent
- Liver cancer
- Mantle Cell Lymphoma (MCL)

- Mucosal Malignant Melanoma
- Non-small cell lung cancer—with metastases to or beyond the hilar nodes or inoperable, unresectable or recurrent
- Ovarian cancer—with distant metastases or inoperable or unresectable
- Pancreatic cancer
- Peritoneal Mesothelioma
- Pleural Mesothelioma
- Salivary tumors
- Small cell cancer (of the large intestine, ovary, prostate or uterus)
- Small cell lung cancer
- Small intestine cancer—with distant metastases or inoperable, unresectable or recurrent
- Stomach cancer—with distant metastases or inoperable, unresectable or recurrent
- Thyroid cancer
- Ureter cancer—with distant metastases or inoperable, unresectable or recurrent

Note: This list is updated regularly through public outreach hearings held by the SSA.
Source: "Compassionate Allowances Initial List of Conditions." Last modified February 12, 2010: http://www.socialsecurity.gov/compassionateallowances/conditions.htm; "Social Security Adds 38 New Compassionate Allowance Conditions." Last modified December 28, 2010. http://www.social security.gov/compassionateallowances/newconditions.htm.

Often, a claimant may be unable to articulate the medical diagnosis. If the diagnosis is not clear at the time of application, the predictive model used to identify CAL cases will be unable to identify the claim. It is designed to identify particular keywords. For this reason, furnishing medical documents or a letter from a treating physician, which uses the appropriate language, can help ensure that the claim is properly identified as a CAL case.

Case for Medical-Legal Partnership

Jane was referred to an MLP through her social worker. She has breast cancer and has been living on Social Security retirement benefits in the amount of $356 monthly. Because she was denied SSDI, she turned to early retirement as an alternate source of income. If she were to successfully appeal and receive SSDI benefits, she would receive $781 per month. To successfully appeal the SSDI denial, she needs to show that her disability began prior to applying for retirement benefits.

Questions for Discussion

1. What role can Jane's healthcare provider play in assisting with her appeal? What kind of information will it be important for him or her to provide?

2. What types of evidence will the MLP lawyer need to present in the appeal hearing to ensure that Jane is awarded SSDI?

3. What benefit is there in having the social worker (who referred the case), Jane's healthcare provider and the MLP lawyer work together on this case?

Financial Concerns for People with Cancer

Even when treatment ends, the fight against cancer is far from over. In addition to medical concerns including the possibility of recurrence, there are a number of legal issues that may arise. In ways both subtle and obvious, these matters differ from those that appear during treatment. This section addresses the financial issues that a patient may experience at any time along the treatment continuum but often do not address until their immediate medical crisis is under control.

Even a cancer patient with private health insurance may end up paying for some portion of treatment through deductibles and co-pays. In addition, household bills that were manageable on a regular salary may become unmanageable if the patient needs to take time off from work for treatment and therefore experiences a loss in wages. Some patients lose their jobs and/or have to go on disability leave and must live on a fixed income and apply for Medicaid if they qualify. A spouse or partner may need to miss work to accompany the patient for care or stay home to take care of the patient. If the caregiver goes back to work, the patient may need to hire home care aides to help with meals, dressing, bathing or just tidying the house. The burden of these costs often falls on the patient and family, although some insurance plans may cover some of these expenses.

With all of these budgetary concerns it is not uncommon for a person with cancer to have his or her economic situation spiral out of control. According to a 2007 study by Harvard University researchers, 62 percent of all personal bankruptcies in the United States in 2007 were caused by health problems—and 78 percent of those filers had insurance.[85] Additionally, the share of personal bankruptcy attributable either to medical debt or significant financial loss due to illness and healthcare costs rose by 49.6 percent between 2001 and 2007, and the likelihood that bankruptcy was due to a health-related problem increased by 238 percent over the same period.[86]

Debtor/Creditor Issues for Cancer Survivors

An attorney's approach to debt is similar to that of a healthcare provider to health: prevention is the best policy. Patients and families should try to take whatever steps they can to avoid accumulating debt. If, however, they are facing a substantial debt, there are strategies to help them address their situation. This section focuses on medical bills but is generally applicable to other types of debt as well.

The first principle of debt management is that patients should always verify that the amount the hospital claims owed is correct. Medical bills may contain errors, and patients should review them carefully to ensure that the stated balance is accurate. As outlined in Cancer Legal Resource Center's Health Care Provider Manual, there are several ways to do so:

- The patient should request an itemized copy of the bill. If something seems wrong—such as 11 MRIs being listed rather than 1—the patient should alert the hospital or the insurer immediately.

- If the patient was billed for a service that resulted from the hospital's negligence, like a lost test result, the patient should contest that charge.

- It may be helpful to obtain a copy of the patient's medical record and/or pharmacy ledger. Especially in cases where a physician ordered and then canceled a particular medication, the patient should not have to pay for something he or she did not receive.

- If the billing hospital publishes standard rates for services (required by law in some states), the patient could compare them to the charges received.

The second principle of debt management follows from the first. The patient should never begin to pay a bill that he or she in some way disputes; after this initial commitment to pay, the patient assumes the obligation to pay the rest of the balance. Consequently, he or she loses the opportunity to challenge the charges later on.

If a patient wants to dispute a bill, he or she should contact the healthcare provider as well as the insurer. It may be that the hospital did not know the patient had insurance, or they may have billed incorrectly. The following section discusses insurance disputes in more detail. Assuming the charges are accurate, there are some options for patients facing large bills. Private financial assistance, such as those from charities and other organizations, may be available. Nonprofits and cancer-specific programs may also offer a potential source of funding. Many pharmaceutical companies have special programs that allow them to offer drugs at reduced rates. Alternatively, patients may inquire as to whether generic drugs are available for the medication prescribed.

MLP Role in Assisting with Debtor/Creditor Issues

If a patient is facing harassment from creditors, the MLP lawyer should advise him or her *not* to ignore the creditor. The MLP lawyer should:

- Work with the patient to obtain copies of all documentation (e.g., collection letters, original invoice, petition, judgment, etc.).

- Discuss possible defenses with the client (e.g., the claim exceeds the statute of limitations; identity theft, etc.).

- Prepare and execute action steps (e.g., letter to collection agency disputing debt; responding to lawsuit, contacting creditor attorney, etc.).

- For clients with income exempt from collection (SSI, SSD, pension income, etc.) write a "judgment proof" letter informing creditors of the protected status of the client's income.

Advance Planning Issues, Including for End of Life

End-of-life issues are not limited to patients with a poor prognosis; they affect everyone, from those who survive cancer to those fortunate enough never to have encountered a major disease. Because end-of-life issues cover a variety of topics, such as medical decision making and financial management, it is important that the MLP team broach the subject with patients and their families preventively to avoid problems later on. Although these matters may be difficult to discuss, a patient's failure to specify his or her wishes in advance could result in delay or a decision contrary to what he or she would have wanted. This approach neatly demonstrates the intersection of fundamental principles from both medicine and law: the former's preventive philosophy seeks to avoid future problems by focusing on present behavior, which overlaps with the latter's preference for precision that eliminates uncertainty by providing clear evidence of intent.

The following sections describe some of the many ways patients and their families working with an MLP may make their wishes known. Some focus solely on medical matters, whereas others concern finances and property, and still others address issues such as who will be responsible for caring for minor children after a parent dies. The final section discusses some of the issues unique to the bereavement phase, when those who survive the patient must face the aftermath of their loss. As with the other topics covered throughout this book, healthcare providers and lawyers as part of the MLP team have an important role to play in each of the following areas. Advance planning issues are also discussed in chapters 13 and 14.

Medical Decisions

Advance healthcare directives are the primary means by which patients may exercise control over their medical care. These written documents serve to alert medical professionals of an individual's wishes, should that person become incapable of communicating them directly. It is important to note that advance directives only take effect when a patient is unable to provide informed consent (often defined as understanding the nature, extent and probable consequences—risks and benefits—of treatment, and being able to communicate a decision to a healthcare provider) or loses capacity for decision making as determined by a physician.[87]

Types of Healthcare Directives

The healthcare proxy or power of attorney for healthcare decisions allows an individual to designate a specific person (and an alternate) to make medical decisions on his or her behalf if and when he or she is unable to do so. A patient may lose the ability to make such decisions on her own for many different reasons, such as dementia or coma. Regardless of the reason for the healthcare proxy taking effect, the appointed agent is limited to making medical decisions in accord with the patient's expressed wishes, either communicated before becoming incapacitated, or documented elsewhere or in the person's best interests.[a]

A living will is a separate document that records a patient's wishes regarding options for medical treatment.[b] The individual indicates what he or she would like done with regard to life-sustaining treatment[c] (actions that prolong life but do not cure the underlying condition, such as kidney dialysis), terminal conditions (conditions for which there is no cure, and, if left untreated, will result in a relatively quick death), and permanent unconscious state (a coma in which the patient is unaware of his or her situation, and recovery is unlikely).[d] A living will is particularly recommended for someone who does not have anyone to make healthcare decisions on his or her behalf.

Source: [a] King et al., *Rights of People with Disabilities*, 136–37; [b] American Cancer Society, "Advanced Directives," 3, http://www.cancer.org/acs/groups/cid/documents/webcontent/002016-pdf.pdf; [c] Ibid., 8; [d] Ibid., 4.

Overall, healthcare providers have a particular interest in promoting advance directives because the contents of such documents expressing specific wishes can avoid unnecessary complications and conflicts especially at the end of life. Consequently, physicians are able to provide care that meets with a patient's wishes, rather than relying on substituted judgment, which is someone else's best guess of what a person would have wanted. Although all states recognize the validity of these documents, the specific laws governing them vary across the country. Some states recognize properly executed advanced directives from other states.[88]

Nonmedical Matters

Depending on the circumstances, patients may need to make provisions for the management of their finances and other property if they cannot manage them any longer. In addition, even those with few assets will likely want to protect them so that they pass to relatives and friends of their choosing. In addition, it may be necessary to designate who will look after a patient's minor children if the person with cancer becomes unable to care for his or her children or dies. As with medical decision making, planning ahead with regard to both financial and family matters is one way to maintain the autonomy of a person with cancer, both during life and after death.

Power of Attorney

In the financial context, a power of attorney (POA) allows a designated agent to make decisions affecting a person's assets.[89] There are usually two types of POA: durable and springing. A durable POA goes into effect immediately—as soon as the document is signed and the agent can act on behalf of the patient. This authority lasts until the patient may make decisions for him or herself or until death. Once a POA is signed, it can be used by the agent, so it is important for patient-clients to name someone they trust.[90] A springing POA only becomes effective when the patient is deemed incapacitated or some other triggering event.

A power of attorney gives the person designated as agent broad powers to handle personal affairs during the person's lifetime, which may include powers to mortgage, sell or otherwise dispose of any real or personal property as well as handle banking and other important financial matters. Depending on the form used, these powers can continue to exist after the person becomes disabled or incompetent. A POA does not allow an agent to make medical decisions; those decisions have to be made by a healthcare agent designated in a healthcare proxy, sometimes called a medical power of attorney.[91]

It is worthwhile to note that if an individual does not complete an advance health directive and/or POA for financial matters, a court may step in and appoint someone to manage his or her affairs, both medical and financial. This type of proceeding is called a conservatorship or guardianship. It is best avoided because the court may not appoint the person the patient would have chosen, and it is also expensive, time-consuming and often contentious. MLP teams can play a very important role in preventing this problem by screening patients to see if they have directives in place and, if not, assisting in drafting them.

Wills

We have discussed decision making in a variety of contexts before an individual's death, but important matters arise after death as well. One way for a patient to maintain his or her autonomy is to draft a will. Wills allow individuals to designate who receives their property, rather than leaving the distribution of property to intestate succession, which are statutory laws in each state that dictate the order in which beneficiaries inherit. (Often, the spouse, if any, receives the bulk of the estate, followed by any children, grandchildren, parents and siblings.) Though most people are familiar with the general idea of wills, they may not fully understand what can and cannot be achieved through a will. Given the specificity of state laws regarding wills, it is important to solicit legal advice in the state the person resides when planning for after-death events.

Discussing the drafting of a will with a client provides an opportunity to talk about all assets that the person may wish for others to inherit on their death. The legal definition of a will is "a document by which a person directs his or her estate to be distributed upon death."[92] This description makes clear the asset-distributing function of wills, but there are subtle aspects that are important as well. A will does not cover everything; life insurance policies and retirement plans pass outside the will only if beneficiaries are named. Clients should ensure that beneficiary information for these instruments is kept up to date. In addition to stating how property is distributed after a person dies, a will also allows a person to state his or her wishes regarding a guardian for any children. The person designated in the will does not automatically have legal authority to act as a guardian, but a will provides evidence of a parent's wishes. (See the section on custody and guardianship later in this chapter.)

Though there are many options in terms of the form of a will—handwritten, fill-in-the-blank or attorney-drafted—not all will be valid in a given state. Fill-in-the-blank wills may be sufficient for those with small or uncomplicated estates; a lawyer should review whether such a document is valid in a particular state and that it actually mirrors the testator's wishes. Presumably, an attorney-drafted will would meet all of the above criteria. States vary on what they accept as a legally binding will.

Once an individual has a valid will—in whatever form—he or she may make changes to it through a codicil (a supplement to the will).[93] Like the original will itself, the codicil must also conform to state laws.[94] It is generally a good idea to review a will every few years to make sure that the information regarding assets is still current and the testator still wants the designated beneficiaries to inherit his or her property. Finally, when the time comes for the will to be carried out, the process called "probate" begins (discussed next). Wills are important not just for people with significant property and assets. Making one's wishes known is important for low-income as well as high-income individuals.

Probate Issues

Probate is the process by which a court determines that a will is legally valid.[95] Although the specific procedures vary across the states, probate is a time-consuming and expensive process everywhere, even under the best circumstances. During probate, the court oversees the payment of taxes and any outstanding debts, and then the distribution of the remaining property to the beneficiaries named in the will.[96]

If a person does not have a will, or has an invalid one, the process is even more complicated.[97] The court names an administrator of the will, who distributes property according to the laws of the particular state. This approach has several disadvantages. First, the executor may not act as the deceased would have liked. Second, state laws of "intestate succession," which creates default rules for who receives property from a person's estate (usually shares divided according to blood relation), may not match an individual's actual wishes. For example, most states provide that an estate should be divided equally among surviving relatives. If a person wanted his entire estate to go to his younger brother alone, though he had other living family members, his wishes would be ignored by the laws of intestate succession. Third, probate for intestate estates takes considerably longer than it does for an estate with a valid will, so beneficiaries have to wait to receive their portion of the deceased's estate. For all these reasons, MLPs should advise patients to make sure they have valid wills.

Custody and Guardianship

The preceding sections have covered the disposition of property, such as real estate, investments and other valuable items. However, there are often cases in which patients must address the future care and custody of their children—a task that encompasses both practical and financial, as well as more emotional considerations. It is important to remember that there is a variety of options for providing for one's children; the one a patient chooses will generally be a function of multiple factors, such as personal preference, the severity of illness and availability of trusted adults who could be named a guardian.[98]

First, a *guardian* is a person who has the right and duty to care for the personal and/or property interests of another person.[99] A guardian has a legal obligation to oversee all or some of the following: education, healthcare, finances and general upbringing. In this way, there are multiple kinds of guardianship. A full guardian is responsible for both the personal and financial interests of the child. A limited guardian has more limited powers:[100] a guardian "of the person" addresses more emotional issues, whereas a guardian "of the property" is in charge of monetary issues.[101]

These various definitions suggest that one of the fundamental issues regarding guardianship is who can or should be a guardian. In many cases, if the cancer patient is the parent (biological or otherwise) of a minor child, the surviving parent becomes the child's legal guardian. However, there may be reasons a patient would not want the surviving parent to become the guardian. In those and other situations, patients must consider a number of factors in selecting a guardian. The first and most important is whether the proposed guardian is willing to take on that responsibility. If there is more than one child at stake, does the patient want the children to stay together, and, if so, will the proposed guardian be able to accommodate all of them? Also, it may be important that the proposed guardian share the same values or beliefs as the patient.

Once a patient has decided on a guardian, it is advisable to name an alternate in case the designated guardian is unable to serve. It is generally not a good idea to name co-guardians unless the patient is relatively certain that the potential co-guardians would agree on all aspects of care and management of the child or children. If a married couple is designated as co-guardians, the patient should specify what he or she wants to happen if the couple divorces.

The other core issue is when to appoint a guardian. In short, a patient may designate a full or limited guardian, at any time, provided he or she has the consent of the other parent, if living. There are other factors to consider, however. For example, a patient with advanced cancer and a very poor prognosis might want to name a full guardian for his or her child, effective immediately, because he or she may be unable to care for the child. More likely, a patient will be able to continue caring for children throughout his or her illness, and thus a "standby guardian" would be more appropriate. A standby guardian steps in only when the parent-patient is mentally or physically unable to care for children.

Standby Guardianship

One of the more recent approaches to transferring custody is facilitated through standby guardianship laws.[a] Many states developed these laws specifically to address the needs of families living with HIV, other disabling conditions or terminal illnesses who desire to plan a legally secure future for their children.[b] Approximately 23 states and the District of Columbia have made statutory provisions for standby guardianships.[c] Standby guardianship is also discussed in Chapter 13 as it applies to patients and families living with HIV/AIDS.

Most standby guardian laws share these provisions:[d]

- A parent may designate a certain person to be guardian for his or her children.

- The guardianship may go into effect during the parent's lifetime and may continue in effect after the parent's death.

- The parent retains much control over the guardianship. He or she may determine when it can begin (although it may commence automatically if the parent becomes seriously ill or mentally incapacitated) and can withdraw the authority if the arrangement does not work to the parent's satisfaction.

- The parent shares decision-making responsibility with the guardian. During the parent's lifetime, the guardian is expected to be in the background, embrace responsibility when needed, and step back when the parent is feeling well.

- The court order for standby guardianship is supported by the authority of a court that has examined facts relevant to the particular family.[e]

Source: [a] In the adoption and Safe Families Act of 1997, Congress proposed that states adopt standby guardianship laws so that chronically ill parents could make future care and custody plans for their children; [b] National Abandoned Infants Resource Center, University of California Berkeley, "Guide to Future Care and Custody Planning for Children," 2005: 1–2, 5; http://aia.berkeley.edu/media/pdf/fccp_monograph.pdf; [c] "Standby Guardianship: Summary of State Laws," http://www.childwelfare.gov/systemwide/laws_policies/statutes/guardianship.cfm#one (accessed on January 11, 2011); [d] National Abandoned Infants Resource Center, University of California Berkeley, Guide to Future Care and Custody Planning for Children, 36–39. For a summary of state standby guardianship laws, see Children's Bureau, Dep't of Health and Human Services, *Standby Guardianship: Summary of State Laws* (2008), available at Child Welfare Information Gateway, 2008, http://www.childwelfare.gov/systemwide/laws_policies/statutes/guardianshipall.pdf; [e] For examples of state guardianship laws, see http://family.findlaw.com/guardianship/state-laws-examples-of-guardianships.html (accessed November 22, 2010).

The process of naming a guardian, standby or otherwise, is relatively straightforward. First, the individual documents in writing who he or she would like to serve as guardian and the conditions, if any, required for the guardianship to take effect. Special designation forms are used to name a guardian, and though a will can serve as strong evidence of a patient's wishes regarding guardianship, only the specially designated forms are legally binding. For standby guardians, a person may also petition the court, or ask a judge to approve his or her choice for guardianship.

We wish to emphasize the importance of naming a guardian. There are few other legal issues so emotionally laden for a terminally ill patient. Often, when guardianship or custody planning has been completed, the patient experiences a significant burden relief and is then able to focus on other critically important issues, such as spending quality time with his or her children. As is true in other areas, advance planning and specification of an individual's preferences reduces uncertainty and ensures that his or her true wishes will be honored. These advantages take on even greater significance in the context of childcare. Additionally, if a patient fails to specify a guardian or otherwise provide for children after death, he or she runs the risk that the child or children may end up in the foster care system. To prevent such outcomes, the MLP should encourage and assist patients and their families with all aspects of advance planning. All members of the team should screen cancer patients and their families to ask about advance planning.

Best Practices and Advocacy Strategies for Medical-Legal Partnership

The Nebraska Medical-Legal Partnership for Oncology provides legal assistance for cancer patients of the Nebraska Medical Center. Legal Aid of Nebraska works closely with oncology healthcare providers and social workers from the Medical Center to identify patients in need of assistance. In addition to providing help with legal issues such as access to public benefits, insurance coverage and financial concerns, the Nebraska MLP assists cancer patients and their families with a range of advance planning issues. These include:

- Healthcare directives
- Power of attorney
- Wills and probate issues
- Guardianship and custody of children

By working as a team, physicians, social workers and lawyers help relieve the stress patients and families experience while undergoing treatment for cancer.

Case for Medical-Legal Partnership

Blanca is a 67-year-old widow who has been fighting non-Hodgkin's lymphoma for the past several years. Thanks to her late husband's pension, she has been able to afford her healthcare, but the disease has spread and her outlook has darkened. In speaking with Blanca, the doctor learns that her primary concern is finding someone to care for her 13-year-old grandson, who has been living with her since the car accident that killed his mother and left his father disabled.

Questions for Discussion

1. How might the MLP team work with Blanca to alleviate her concerns?
2. How might an MLP lawyer assist with this and related issues, such as the disposition of her property?

Stress Concerns for MLP Partners

We must acknowledge that caring for patients with life-threatening and/or terminal illness is stressful for all involved in the care. The unique challenges of working closely with seriously ill patients and their families at highly emotional and stressful times in their lives as well as the frequent exposure to suffering and death can take a toll on healthcare providers, lawyers and social workers. Acknowledged components of burnout include emotional exhaustion, cynicism or depersonalization, and a low sense of personal accomplishment.[102] Recognition of this constellation of symptoms is primary to managing and preventing the stress accompanied by caring for critically ill patients. Several approaches have been proposed. These include self-awareness, self-reflection and self-monitoring,[103] as well as attention to physical well-being, which includes exercise, proper nutrition and rest.[104] Supportive professional relationships and interdisciplinary teams can be important in helping professionals cope with the difficult emotional toll inherent in cancer care.

It is important to remember that MLP lawyers and social workers are subject to the same burnout as the healthcare professionals and deserve the support of the team. Formal debriefing sessions with the team, either regularly scheduled or following a difficult case, can be an effective way to provide needed support to all team members.

Addressing the Stress of Working in an MLP Oncology Setting

MLPs can help address professional stress by:

- Soliciting help from psychosocial professionals who can discuss with team members what they experience when working with people who have advanced illness.

- Engaging in discussion about bereavement issues.

- Teaching team members how to set appropriate boundaries.

- Holding interdisciplinary meetings in which all members of the team discuss the strategies they employ to alleviate stress.

Conclusion

MLPs for oncology patients provide access to services and problem resolution that contribute to the economic, psychological and spiritual quality of life for people impacted by cancer. MLPs that focus on patients with cancer and survivors play an important role in alleviating the stress that accompanies this illness.[105] Healthcare providers have also noted that providing these services adds to the arsenal of tools they have to assist their patients with the nonmedical needs of their patients.

Dr. Stewart Fleishman, an oncologist states, "As a result of our partnership with the attorneys, our medical professionals are better able to identify the legal needs of their patients and make convenient referrals to the legal clinic attorneys onsite. Many of the obstacles that patients face in adhering to treatment have been overcome with the assistance of the dedicated attorneys who are familiar with the wide range of legal problems that can beset vulnerable cancer patients and complicate their care and recovery."[106] By relieving patients of their legal burdens, MLPs help cancer patients devote their potentially limited time to more important matters, such as concentrating on their health and spending time with loved ones.

Note

This chapter was written with assistance from LegalHealth, a division of the New York Legal Assistance Group, and Adam Templeton, student at the University of Virginia School of Law.

1. American Cancer Society (ACS), *Cancer Facts & Figures 2010* (Atlanta: American Cancer Society, 2010).

2. Survey conducted by the National Cancer Legal Services Network, 2010.

3. ACS, *Cancer Facts & Figures 2010*.

4. R. A. Hiatt, N. Breen, "The Social Determinants of Cancer: A Challenge for Transdisciplinary Science," *American Journal of Preventive Medicine*, 35, Suppl 2 (2008): S141–50.

5. ACS, *Cancer Facts & Figures 2010*.

6. A. Jemal, R. Siegel, J. Xu, E. Ward, "Cancer Statistics, 2010." *Cancer Journal for Clinicians*, 60, no. 5 (2010): 277–300.

7. M. J. Horner, L. A. G. Ries, M. Krapcho, et al., eds., *SEER Cancer Statistics Review, 1975–2006* (National Cancer Institute, 2009).

8. L. A. G. Ries, M. P. Eisner, et al., eds., *SEER Cancer Statistics Review, 1973–1998* (Bethesday, MD: National Institute of Health, 2000), 2789; R. Yancik, M. Holmes, *Exploring the Role of Cancer Centers for Integrating Aging and Cancer Research* (National Institute on Aging, National Cancer Institute, 2001).

9. W. B. Ershler, Cancer: a disease of the elderly. *Journal of Supportive Oncology* 1 (2003): (4 Suppl 2): 5–10.

10. L. X.Clegg, M. E. Reichman, B. A. Miller, et al., "Impact of Socioeconomic Status on Cancer Incidence and Stage at Diagnosis: Selected Findings from the Surveillance, Epidemiology, and End Results: National Longitudinal Mortality Study," *Cancer Causes Control*, 20, no. 4 (2009): 417–35.

11. G. K.Singh, B. A. Miller, B. F. Hankey, B. K. Edwards, "Area Socioeconomic Variations in U.S. Cancer Incidence, Mortality, Stage, Treatment and Survival, 1975–1999." NCI Cancer Surveillance Monograoh Series number 4, NIH Publication no. 03-5417 (2003).

12. H. P. Freeman, "Poverty, Culture, and Social Injustice: Determinants of Cancer Disparities," *Cancer Journal for Clinicians* 54, no. 2 (2004): 72–77.

13. Clegg et al., "Impact of Socioeconomic Status," 417–35.

14. Ibid.

15. Hiatt and Breen, "The Social Determinants of Cancer," S141–50.

16. E. Ward, A. Jemal, V. Cokkinides, et al., "Cancer Disparities by Race/Ethnicity and Socioeconomic Status, *Cancer Journal for Clinicians* 54, no. 2 (2004): 78–93.

17. ACS, *Cancer Facts & Figures 2010*; Freeman, "Poverty, Culture, and Social Injustice," 72–77.

18. H. P. Freeman, "Cancer in the Socioeconomically Disadvantaged," *Cancer Journal for Clinicians* 39, no. 5 (1989): 266–88.

19. ACS, *Cancer in the Poor: A Report to the Nation* (Atlanta, GA: American Cancer Society (1989)).

20. "Cancer Health Disparities," National Cancer Institute, http://www.cancer.gov/cancertopics/fact sheet/disparities/cancer-health-disparities (accessed January 20, 2011).

21. "Cancer Statistics," 2010, *Cancer Journal for Clinicians* (2010), http://caonline.amcancersoc.org/cgi/content/full/caac.20073vl.

22. "Pancreatic Cancer Survival Time: Different Stages of Cancer and the Different Types of Treatment," *Cancer Treatment Today*, http://www.cancer-today.com/Cancer/pancreatic-cancer-survival-time-different-stages-of-cancer-and-the-types-of-treatment/ (accessed January 20, 2011).

23. Edward Guadagnoli, Vincent Mor, "Daily Living Needs of Cancer Outpatients," *Journal of Community Health,* 16, no. 1 (1991): 37–47.

24. M. A. Zevon, S. Schwabish, J. P. Donnelly, K. J. Rodabaugh, "Medically Related Legal Needs and Quality of Life in Cancer Care: A Structural Analysis," *Cancer,* 109, no. 12 (2007): 2600–6.

25. R. B. Francoeur, "Cumulative Financial Stress and Strain in Palliative Radiation Outpatients: The Role of Age and Disability," *Acta Oncology,* 44, no. 4 (2005): 369–81.

26. L. Willis, M. Peck, S. Sells, K. J. Rodabaugh, "Custody Planning. A Retrospective Review of Oncology Patients Who Were Single Parents," *Journal of Pain and Symptom Management,* 21, no. 5 (2001): 380–84.

27. S. N. Wolff, C. Nichols, D. Ulman, et al., "Survivorship: An Unmet Need of the Patient with Cancer—Implications of a Survey of the Lance Armstrong Foundation (LAF)," *Journal of Clinical Oncology (Meeting Abstracts),* 23, Suppl 16 (2005): 6032, http://meeting.ascopubs.org/cgi/content/abstract/23/16_suppl/6032.

28. S. B. Fleishman, R. Retkin, J. Brandfield, V. Braun, "The Attorney as the Newest Member of the Cancer Treatment Team," *Journal of Clinical Oncology,* 24, no. 13 (2006): 2123–26.

29. R. Retkin, J. Brandfield, C. Bacich, "Impact of Legal Interventions on Cancer Survivors," *LegalHealth* (2007), http://www.bc.edu/phlsdocs.

30. Zevon et al., "Medically Related Legal Needs," 2600–6.

31. C. DeNavas-Walt, B. D. Proctor, J. C. Smith. "U.S. Census Bureau, Income, Poverty, and Health Insurance Coverage in the United States: 2009," U.S. Census Bureau (2010). (U.S. Census Bureau: In 2009, employment-based health insurance plans covered 55.8 percent of people.)

32. Cancer Legal Resource Center, *The HCP Manual: A Legal Resource Guide for Oncology Health Care Professionals* (2010), 29–30.

33. Ibid., 30.

34. The original health continuation provisions were contained in Title X of COBRA, P.L. 99-272, 99th Cong., 2nd sess. (7 April 1986).

35. "An Employee's Guide to Health Benefits under COBRA," Employee Benefits Security Administration, U.S. Department of Labor, http://www.dol.gov/ebsa/pdf/cobraemployee.pdf (accessed January 18, 2011).

36. Article 32 of the New York Insurance Regulation; New York State Insurance Dep't, Consumer Frequently Asked Questions, http://www.ins.state.ny.us/faqs/faqs_cobra.htm.

37. Social Security Act, 42 U.S.C. 1396e (2010). HIPP is only available in a few states, and each state has its own criteria to determine who qualifies for assistance. For a survey of states where HIPP is available see Phil Lebherz, "Foundation for Health Coverage Education," U.S. Directory of Health Care Options, http://www.coverageforall.org/pdf/USDirectory.pdf (accessed January 19, 2011).

38. *Guaranteed issue* means a requirement that health plans must permit you to enroll regardless of health status, age, gender, or other factors that might predict the use of health services. See Healthcare.gov, Glossary, "Guaranteed Issue," http://www.healthcare.gov/glossary/g/guaranteed.html.

39. Cancer Legal Resource Center, *The HCP Manual,* HIPAA Quick Tips, https://www.cms.gov/HealthInsReformforConsume/Downloads/HIPAA_Helpful_Tips_Rev_1.pdf.

40. Requirements for the Individual Health Insurance Market, 45 C.F.R. § 148.103; see also "Issues Related to Eligible Individual Status Under the Health Insurance Portability and Accountability Act of 1996," Department of Health and Human Services, https://www.cms.gov/HealthInsReformforConsume/downloads/HIPAA-99-02.pdf, (accessed January 18, 2011) 2–3.

41. Cancer Legal Resource Center, *The HCP Manual,* 33.

42. Ibid.

43. Ibid., 33–34.

44. "Provisions of the Affordable Care Act, By Year," http://www.healthcare.gov/law/about/order/byyear.html (accessed January 11, 2011).

45. Ibid.

46. Cancer Legal Resource Center, *The HCP Manual,* 37–38.

47. Center for Medicare and Medicaid Services, Dep't of Health and Human Services, *National Medicare Handbook: Medicare & You 2011* (2010):14, http://www.medicare.gov/publications/pubs/pdf/10050.pdf.

48. The National Cancer Institute estimates are cited in Cancer Action Network, *Cancer and Medicare: A Chartbook, 16,* chart 9 (Feb. 2009) ("The total Medicare costs [were] estimated by using cases from the SEER cancer registry—diagnosed from 1996–1999 and linked to Medicare claims for those years. These were updated to 2004 dollars using the medical care services component of the consumer price index. Details of the original estimation method are described in: Brown M.L., G.F. Riley, N. Schussler, and R.D. Etzioni. Estimating health care costs related to cancer treatment from SEER-Medicare data. *Medical Care,* 40 (2002): 104–17").

49. Cancer Action Network, *Cancer and Medicare: A Chartbook,* 1 chart 10.

50. "Am I Eligible for Premium-Free Part A if I Am over 65 and Medicare-Eligible?," last modified March 2, 2009, http://www.medicareinteractive.org/page2.php?topic=counselor&page=script&slide_id=621; "What Does Medicare Part A Cover?" last modified March 26, 2008, http://www.medicareinteractive.org/page2.php?topic=counselor&page=script&slide_id=178.

51. "What Does Medicare Part B Cover?," last modified August 16, 2010, http://www.medicareinteractive.org/page2.php?topic=counselor&page=script&slide_id=170. "What Do I Have to Pay for Services Covered under Medicare Part B?," last modified July 29, 2010, http://www.medicareinteractive.org/page2.php?topic=counselor&page=script&slide_id=552.

52. "Medicare Advantage," http://www.medicareadvocacy.org/InfoByTopic/MedicareAdvantage-AndHMOs/MAmain.htm#Comparision%20Chart (accessed November 20, 2010).

53. "What Is the Medicare Prescription Drug Benefit (Part D)?," last modified December 19, 2007, http://www.medicareinteractive.org/page2.php?topic=counselor&page=script&slide_id=1467; "Medicare Part D Prescription Drug Coverage. What Is Medicare Part D?," http://www.medicareadvocacy.org/InfoByTopic/PartDandPrescDrugs/PartDMain.htm#whatIsD (accessed November 20, 2010).

54. "Does Medicare Cover Mammogram Screenings?," last modified May 30, 2008, http://www.medicareinteractive.org/page2.php?topic=counselor&page=script&slide_id=199.

55. "Does Medicare Cover Pap Smears and Pelvic Exams?," last modified January 9, 2007, http://www.medicareinteractive.org/page2.php?topic=counselor&page=script&slide_id=200.

56. "Does Medicare Cover Prostate Cancer Screenings?," last modified June 18, 2009, http://www.medicareinteractive.org/page2.php?topic=counselor&page=script&slide_id=201.

57. "Does Medicare Cover Colorectal Cancer Screenings?," last modified June 18, 2009, http://www.medicareinteractive.org/page2.php?topic=counselor&page=script&slide_id=195.

58. "When Will Medicare Cover Hospice Care?," last modified May 27, 2009, http://www.medicareinteractive.org/page2.php?topic=counselor&page=script&slide_id=159.

59. "What Types of Care Will Medicare Pay for if I Have a Life-Threatening Illness and Elect the Hospice Benefit?," last modified February 11, 2009, http://www.medicareinteractive.org/page2.php?topic=counselor&page=script&slide_id=162.

60. "Medicare Part D Prescription Drug Coverage, The Standard Drug Benefit," http://www.medicareadvocacy.org/InfoByTopic/PartDandPrescDrugs/PartDMain.htm#standard (accessed November 20, 2010).

61. Medicare Prescription Drug Benefit Manual, Ch. 6, sec. 30.2.5, http://www.cms.gov/PrescriptionDrugCovContra/Downloads/Chapter6.pdf (accessed November 20, 2010).

62. Medicare Prescription Drug Benefit Manual, Appendix C, p. 57, http://www.cms.gov/PrescriptionDrugCovContra/Downloads/Chapter6.pdf (accessed November 20, 2010).

63. "What Is a Medicare Private Health Plan (Medicare Advantage)?," last modified October 28, 2010, http://www.medicareinteractive.org/page2.php?topic=counselor&page=script&slide_id=256.

64. "Medicare Part D Prescription Drug Coverage, Comparison Chart: Original Medicare and Medicare Advantage Options," http://www.medicareadvocacy.org/InfoByTopic/MedicareAdvantage-AndHMOs/MAmain.htm#Comparision%20Chart (accessed November 20, 2010). "What Is a Medicare Private Health Plan (Medicare Advantage)?"

65. "Medicare: Medicare Advantage/Private Plans," http://kff.org/medicare/choice.cfm (accessed November 20, 2010).

66. "Can I Change My Medicare Health Plan at any Time?," last modified November 4, 2010, http://www.medicareinteractive.org/page2.php?topic=counselor&page=script&slide_id=1064.

67. ACS, *Cancer and Medicare: A Chartbook* (2009), http://action.acscan.org/site/DocServer/medicare-chartbook.pdf?docID=12061.

68. "Mandatory Eligibility Groups," last modified December 14, 2005, https://www.cms.gov/Medicaid Eligibility/03_MandatoryEligibilityGroups.asp#TopOfPage.

69. "Medicaid Buy-In for Working People with Disabilities," last modified October 20, 2010, http://www.ssa.gov/disabilityresearch/wi/buyin.htm.

70. "Medically Needy," last modified December 14, 2005, http://www.cms.gov/MedicaidEligibility/06_ Medically_Needy.asp.

71. Kleo J. King, Suzanne A. Solomon, Association of the Bar of the City of New York, Committee on Legal Issues Affecting People with Disabilities, Steven H. Mosenson, Association of the Bar of the City of New York. *Rights of People with Disabilities,* 2nd ed. (New York: Association of the Bar of the City of New York, 1999), 140.

72. P. F. Short, J.J. Vasey, K. Tunceli, "Employment Pathways in a Large Cohort of Adult Cancer Survivors," *Cancer,* 103, no. 6 (2005): 1292–301.

73. Barbara Hoffman, "Cancer and Work: Protections Under the Americans with Disabilities Act," *Oncology Nurse Division,* 24, no. 4 (2010): 16.

74. Barbara Hoffman, "Cancer Survivors at Work: A Generation of Progress," *Cancer Journal for Clinicians,* 55 (2005): 271–80.

75. Hoffman, "Cancer and Work."

76. "Frequently Asked Questions about the Proposed Revisions to the Department's FMLA Regulations," http://www.dol.gov/whd/fmla/NPRMfaq.htm#QReason (accessed November 21, 2010); See also *Burnett v. LFW Inc.,* C.A.7 (Ill.) 2006, 472 F.3d 471.

77. Content of Medical Certification for Leave Taken Because of an Employee's Own Serious Health Condition or the Serious Health Condition of a Family Member, 29 C.F.R. § 825.306 (2010).

78. Ibid., § 825.306(a)(5).

79. "State Disability Insurance Benefits," http://employeeissues.com/state_disability.htm (accessed January 20, 2011).

80. "Annual Statistics Supplement, 2009," http://www.socialsecurity.gov/policy/docs/statcomps/supplement/2009/oasdi.html (accessed November 21, 2010); Also see Sections 213, 214a of the Social Security Act. "Title II — Federal Old-Age, Survivors, and Disability Insurance Benefits," last modified July 19, 2010, http://www.ssa.gov/OP_Home/ssact/title02/0200.htm.

81. Here the legislation points to the Social Security Act, 42 U.S.C. § 1320b-19 (2010).

82. See http://www.ssa.gov/disabilityresearch/wi/detailedinfo.htm.

83. SSA, "The Disability Interview — Identifying Terminal Illness (TERI) Cases," https://secure.ssa.gov/apps10/poms.nsf/lnx/0411005601 (accessed November 21, 2010).

84. SSA, "Compassionate Allowance (CAL) — DDS Instructions," https://secure.ssa.gov/apps10/poms.nsf/lnx/0423022015 (accessed November 21, 2010). "Compassionate Allowances," last modified November 8, 2010, http://www.socialsecurity.gov/compassionateallowances.

85. D. U. Himmelstein, D. Thorne, E. Warren, S. Woolhandler, "Medical Bankruptcy in the United States, 2007: Results of a National Study. *American Journal of Medicine,* 122, no. 8 (2009): 741–46, http://www.pnhp.org/new_bankruptcy_study/Bankruptcy-2009.pdf.

86. Ibid.

87. ACS, "Advanced Directives," last modified June 15, 2009, http://www.cancer.org/acs/groups/cid/documents/webcontent/002016-pdf.pdf.

88. Ibid.

89. LegalHealth, *Things to Consider if You Have a Serious or Chronic Illness* (New York: New York State Bar Association, 2004); See also ACS, "Advanced Directives," 5.

90. ACS, "Advanced Directives," 5.

91. May Clinic, "Living Wills and Advance Directives for Medical Decisions," http://www.mayoclinic.com/health/living-wills/HA00014 (accessed November 21, 2010).

92. *Black's Law Dictionary* (3rd Pocket Ed., 2006), 778.

93. Ibid., 109–10.

94. ABA Family Legal Guide, 2005, http://public.findlaw.com/abaflg/flg-18-4a-2.html.

95. *Black's Law Dictionary*, 558.

96. American Bar Association, Estate Planning FAQs, http://www.abanet.org/rpte/public/probate-process.html.

97. "Probate Without a Will," http://www.estateplancenter.com/probate-6/probate-without-a-will-58.html (accessed November 21, 2010).

98. For the sake of simplicity, we assume that guardians will be responsible for patients' minor children. This situation is most common, but there are cases in which a guardian looks after an incapacitated adult or someone otherwise unable to care for him or herself.

99. *Black's Law Dictionary*, 320.

100. *Matter of Guardianship of Hedin*, 528 N.W.2d 567 (Iowa 1995); "Uniform Guardianship and Protective Proceedings Act of 1982," National Conference of Commissioners of Uniform State Laws, http://www.law.upenn.edu/bll/archives/ulc/fnact99/1990s/ugppa97.pdf (accessed January 18, 2011).

101. For background on various types of guardianship, see George B. Fraser, "Guardianship of the Person," *Iowa Law Review*, 45 (1969): 239; See also *Children & the Law: Rights and Obligations* §7:24.

102. D. E. Meier, L. Beresford, "Preventing Burnout," *Journal of Palliative Medicine*, 9, no. 5 (2006): 1045–48; K. M. Swetz, S. E. Harrington, R. K. Matsuyama, T. D. Shanafelt, L. J. Lyckholm, "Strategies for Avoiding Burnout in Hospice and Palliative Medicine: Peer Advice for Physicians on Achieving Longevity and Fulfillment," *Journal of Palliative Medicine*, 12, no. 9 (2009): 773–77.

103. Meier and Beresford, "Preventing Burnout," 1045–48.

104. Swetz et al., "Strategies for Avoiding Burnout," 773–77.

105. P. Shin, F. R. Byrne, E. Jones, J. Teitelbaum, L. Repasch, S. Rosenbaum, *Medical-Legal Partnerships: Addressing the Unmet Legal Needs of Health Center Patients* (Washington, DC: Geiger Gibson/RCHN Community Health Foundation Research Collaborative, School of Public Health and Health Services, George Washington University, 2010), http://www.rchnfoundation.org/images/FE/chain207siteType8/site176/client/mlpfinal%20may4-2.pdf.

106. Informal Conversation with Stewart Fleishman, MD, Director of Cancer Supportive Services at Continuum Cancer Centers of New York and Associate Chief Medical Officer, Continuum Hospice Care.

Chapter 13

Patients and Families Living with HIV/AIDS

Alison Brock, BA
Deborah Weimer, JD
Ann Fisher, JD
Jayson Cooley, BA
Josiah D. Rich, MD, MPH

The history of HIV and AIDS has long been dominated by stigma, marginalization and discrimination. As noted by former World Health Organization official Jonathan Mann, individuals with HIV are more likely to be marginalized, and healthy individuals who are marginalized are more likely to contract HIV.[1] "In this regard," Mann writes, "HIV/AIDS may be illustrative of a more general phenomenon in which individual and population vulnerability to disease, disability, and premature death is linked to the status of respect for human rights and dignity."[2] Written in 1999, these words remain a call to examine disparities evident in the rates of infection and course of HIV among vulnerable populations. As this chapter discusses, the role of medical-legal partnership (MLP) in addressing and alleviating such disparities is critical.

HIV/AIDS was the first area in which lawyers and healthcare providers partnered to address the legal issues affecting a vulnerable population. Beginning in Los Angeles in the early 1980s, HIV legal services organizations developed close relationships with public healthcare providers to address particular legal issues affecting people with HIV/AIDS, including the need for future planning documents such as wills, medical power of attorney, guardianship and insurance beneficiary forms.[3] As these partnerships between the legal experts and healthcare providers deepened and funding increased, experts in HIV law identified other critical unmet needs in employment, public benefits, health, housing, family and immigration law.[4] Eventually, the HIV legal services programs in the Los Angeles area created a collaborative consortium and expanded their services to address the entire spectrum of legal needs of HIV/AIDS patients, which ultimately led to better health outcomes.[5]

This chapter first provides an overview of the HIV/AIDS epidemic in the United States and the specific ways HIV causes disease. Legal protections regarding testing and disclosure of HIV status is then discussed, followed by an examination of employment rights and protections for HIV-positive individuals. A subsequent discussion of the relationship between HIV, the social determinants of health and the law highlights relevant medical and legal issues for members of vulnerable populations, such as racial and ethnic minorities, women, the homeless, the incarcerated, children and adolescents. Legal issues addressed in this section include access to healthcare and income supports, housing protections, and state and federal laws pertaining to the HIV testing and treatment in prisons. Last, legal considerations specific to children and adolescents affected by HIV are discussed, including medication adherence, neglect, planning for the custody of children, incapacity and end of life.

Many of the topics discussed herein may come to the attention of providers when a patient or client is in crisis, a time in which effective MLP can ameliorate the detrimental effects of unmet legal needs as they are occurring. Effective advocacy for patients and clients living with HIV, however, also requires prevention. Just as preventive medicine involves screening and early treatment for illnesses that, left unaddressed, could lead to a medical crisis, preventive law[6] seeks to identify and address legal needs before they negatively affect a person's quality of life. Together with effective crisis management, preventive medicine and preventive law enable a proactive and comprehensive approach to advocacy for people living with HIV.

From Transmission to Treatment: A Medical Overview of HIV and AIDS in the United States

In June 1981, the U.S. Centers for Disease Control and Prevention (CDC) published a curious and concerning finding in the *Morbidity and Mortality Weekly Report*: clusters of previously healthy individuals were being diagnosed with rare and severe illnesses not typically seen in people with functioning immune systems. Although these illnesses were initially reported mainly among homosexual men in urban areas, physicians and epidemiologists soon recognized the same clinical syndrome among hemophiliacs, intravenous drug users and children born to mothers who used drugs. The syndrome, originally referred to as Gay-Related Immunodeficiency Disorder, was soon renamed Acquired Immunodeficiency Syndrome (see Table 13.1). In 1983, researchers isolated the cause of AIDS—a virus now known as Human Immunodeficiency Virus (HIV).[7]

Table 13.1 The AIDS Acronym

A	Acquired	In medicine, the word "acquired" implies "new" or "added." An acquired condition is "new" in the sense that it is not genetic (inherited) and "added" in the sense that was not present at birth.
ID	Immunodeficiency	The virus attacks a person's immune system and makes it less capable of fighting infections. Thus, the immune system becomes deficient.
S	Syndrome	AIDS is not one disease but presents itself as a number of diseases that come about as the immune system fails. Hence, it is regarded as a *syndrome.*

Source: AIDS.gov, "What is HIV/AIDS?" http://aids.gov/hiv-aids-basics/hiv-aids-101/overview/what-is-hiv-aids/#aids (accessed February 17, 2011).

Though HIV infection ultimately leads to AIDS, the terms are not synonymous. As clarified in Table 13.1 and discussed in the clinical overview, the diagnosis of AIDS is based on the syndrome or specific pattern of illnesses common to end-stage HIV infection.

HIV Prevalence

Most recent data suggest that more than one million Americans are currently infected with HIV, one in five of whom are unaware of their infection.[8] Each year, an estimated 56,000 Americans are newly infected with HIV.[9] Figure 13.1 demonstrates a sharp decline

Figure 13.1 Estimated Number of AIDS Cases and Deaths, United States, 1985–2005

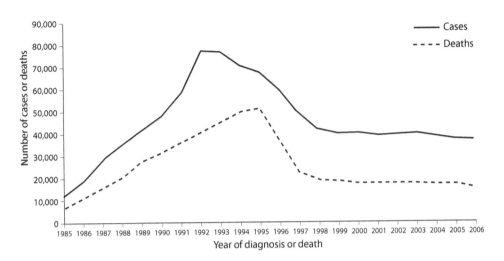

Source: A.S. Fauci, H.C. Lane, "Chapter 182: Human Immunodeficiency Virus Disease: AIDS and Related Disorders," in *Harrison's Principles of Internal Medicine*, eds. A.S. Fauci, E. Braunwald, D. L. Kasper, S. L. Hauser, D. L. Longo, J. L. Jameson, J. Loscalzo, 17 (New York: McGraw Hill, 2008). *Data Source:* Centers for Disease Control and Prevention, "HIV/AIDS Surveillance Supplemental Report: Deaths Among Persons with AIDS through December 2006," 14, No. 3 (2006): 21.

in both new AIDS diagnoses and AIDS-related deaths since their peak in 1995, but 18,000 Americans continue to die annually of AIDS-related causes.

Worldwide, an estimated 33.4 million people are currently living with HIV, and approximately 2 million people died in 2008 from AIDS-related causes.[10] Sub-Saharan Africa has long been considered the epicenter of the AIDS pandemic due to the region's particularly high rates of HIV infection and AIDS-related mortality, but the pandemic is not static. Rates of HIV are steeply on the rise in India and China, and Asia is projected to be the new epicenter of the global pandemic by 2020.[11]

Considered in light of its global impact, HIV/AIDS in the United States may appear to be a somewhat limited problem. However, subsets of the U.S. population, such as certain minority and urban populations, have prevalence rates rivaling those documented in Sub-Saharan Africa.[12] These data, represented in Figure 13.2, demonstrate the need for advocacy and intervention to address the disparities of HIV prevalence in the United States. As will be discussed, vulnerable populations are also more likely to encounter barriers when seeking healthcare, public benefits and basic needs such as adequate housing. Insofar as MLPs for HIV-infected people are designed to address these and other barriers to well-being, they are of critical importance within vulnerable communities.

Modes of Transmission

Compared to viruses such as the flu, HIV is surprisingly difficult to contract. It does not easily survive outside of the body. It is transmitted only through blood, semen, vaginal fluid and breast milk, not through saliva or through casual contact such as hugging,

Figure 13.2 HIV Prevalence in Adults from Selected Countries in Sub-Saharan Africa and Subpopulations in the United States

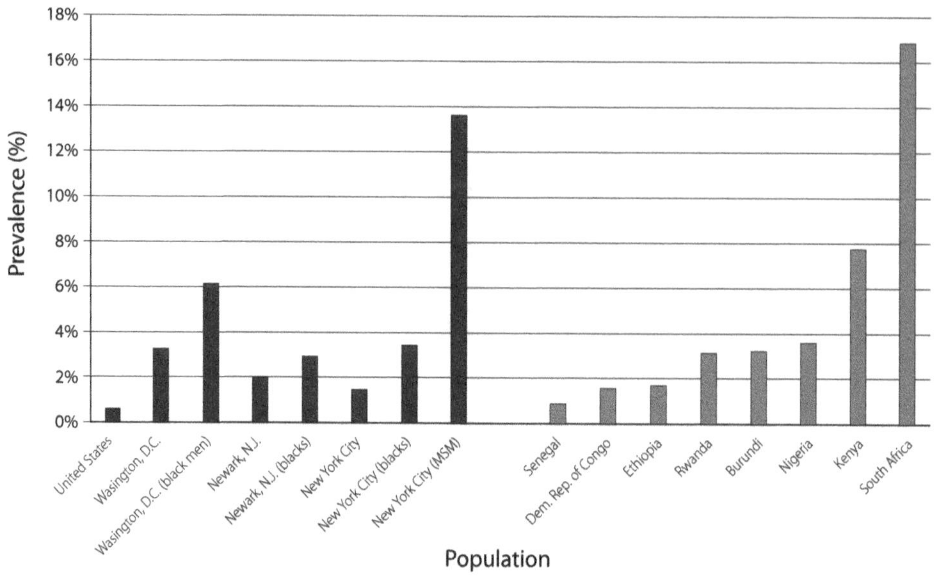

Note: MSM denotes men who have sex with men.
Source: W. M. El-Sadr, K. H. Mayer, S. L. Hodder, "Aids in America — Forgotten but Not Gone," *New England Journal of Medicine,* 362, no. 11 (2010): 967–70.

kissing, or sharing eating utensils or toilets. The most common forms of HIV transmission are as follows:

- unprotected sex
- mother-to-child transmission
- use of infected blood or blood products (such as blood transfusion)
- IV drug use via shared or nonsterile equipment

To become infected with HIV, three things must occur. (1) An individual must come into contact with contaminated body fluids, (2) a sufficient number of viruses must be present in the contaminated fluid to establish infection, and (3) the virus must cross into the bloodstream, usually through a mucous membrane or a break in the skin.[13] These things do not all happen with each high-risk encounter, so not every exposure to HIV results in contracting the virus. For example, the risk of a healthcare worker acquiring HIV from accidental exposure to contaminated blood via a needle stick is exceedingly low.[14] Because the risk is still present, however, individuals at risk for occupational exposure to HIV — including healthcare workers, first responders and teachers — are advised by the CDC to use gloves and goggles and other barrier devices whenever handling bodily fluids. Because this equipment can be useful (and even required) in other situations and conditions, this recommendation is referred to as using "universal precautions."[15]

Certain modes of virus transmission are more prevalent in some regions of the world than others. In the United States, approximately half of all cases of newly acquired HIV are transmitted by unprotected sexual contact between men.[16] Just as the epicenter of the pandemic is shifting, the predominant modes of transmission in the United States have changed over time, with an increase in transmission via high-risk heterosexual contact from 3 percent overall in 1985 to 31 percent in 2005.[17] As can be seen in Figure 13.3, the gender differences in mode of HIV transmission are striking; although most males acquire HIV through male-to-male unprotected sexual contact, the overwhelming majority of women acquire HIV through unprotected heterosexual contact.

Figure 13.3 Transmission Categories of Adults and Adolescents with HIV/AIDS Diagnosed during 2005 in the United States

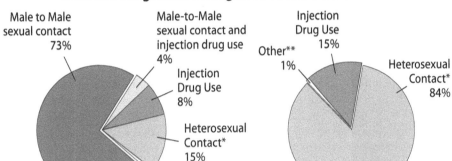

* Heterosexual contact with a person known to have, or to be at high risk for, HIV infection.
** Includes hemophilia, blood transfusion, perinatal exposure, and risk not reported or identified.

Source: A.S. Fauci, H.C. Lane, "Chapter 182: Human Immunodeficiency Virus Disease: AIDS and Related Disorders," in *Harrison's Principles of Internal Medicine*, eds. A.S. Fauci, E. Braunwald, D. L. Kasper, S. L. Hauser, D. L. Longo, J. L. Jameson, J. Loscalzo, 17 (New York: McGraw Hill, 2008). *Note:* Estimates based on data from 33 states with long-term, confidential, name-based HIV infection reporting. Data include persons with a diagnosis of HIV infection regardless of AIDS status at diagnosis. *Data Source:* Centers for Disease Control and Prevention, Basic Statistics: Diagnoses of HIV Infection by Transmission Category, 2008. Data Source: National Center for HIV/AIDS, Viral Hepatitis, STD, and TB Prevention, 2010.

Worldwide, mother-to-child transmission (MTCT) is the primary means by which children contract HIV.[18] The virus can be transmitted during pregnancy, the birth process, or through breastfeeding, and the rates of transmission increase with the levels of virus in the mother's blood and greatly decrease when she receives antiretroviral drugs. Though rates of MTCT are as high as 25 to 35 percent among untreated women in developing countries, these rates can be as low as one to five percent with the use of antiretroviral drugs during pregnancy and at the time of delivery.[19] Cesarean delivery can reduce exposure to HIV during the birth process, but the decision regarding whether to deliver this way is highly dependent on other aspects of the mother's health.[20] Avoidance of breastfeeding has been shown to reduce rates of transmission and is recommended in places where there is secure access to clean water and ability to pay for formula.

The Clinical Picture of HIV

Before examining factors increasing the prevalence and mortality from HIV and AIDS in vulnerable populations, it is necessary to have a basic understanding of how HIV works:

its structure, the specific way the virus enters and injures cells of the body, how it is detected, and the typical clinical course of infection. This understanding forms the foundation from which it will be possible to discuss why the medical and legal barriers encountered by some HIV-positive people—such as poor access to medication or public benefits, poor nutrition or substandard housing—can have severely detrimental effects on their health.

HIV and the Immune System

Viruses are often described as "obligate intracellular parasites"—small organisms incapable of surviving unless they invade a living cell.[21] Once inside, viruses make use of the cell's replication machinery to generate copies of themselves and subsequently infect more cells. Many different types of viruses exist, and different ones have particular affinities for different types of cells in the body.

As its name implies, HIV primarily targets cells of the immune system. The immune system can be defined as a collection of cells, tissues, and processes that work together in the body to fight off infection from bacteria, viruses and other invaders. Some immune cells are particularly good at guarding against invaders that enter cells (intracellular invaders), whereas others help defend against the invaders that cause damage outside of cells (extracellular invaders). The immune system can be described as a team, for which T-cells are the quarterback—they call the plays and direct the appropriate immune reaction in response to invaders.[22] HIV preferentially invades a subset of T-cells called helper T-cells (also called CD4 or Th cells). These cells are of particular importance in coordinating the fight against intracellular invaders such as viruses.

A key component to HIV's ability to cause serious disease rests in the virus's ability to evade antibodies. An *antibody* is a protein designed and produced by the immune system to help the body get rid of a specific invader. In the case of HIV, antibodies are unable to clear the invader completely because the virus mutates as it replicates, changing its appearance and therefore avoiding antibodies specifically designed to attack it.

Clinical Course

The course of HIV in an infected individual depends on many variables: the presence of other viruses or chronic illnesses, the baseline strength of the immune system, access to treatment and primary healthcare, nutrition status, and the characteristics of the particular strain of HIV with which a person is infected. That said, the clinical course presented here is a general timeline and series of events common to most untreated individuals infected with HIV.

Cell Entry

Once introduced into the bloodstream, HIV particles attach to and invade helper CD4 cells. Once inside, the virus integrates its genetic material into that of the host and uses the host cell's replication machinery to make copies of itself and assemble new particles. As can be seen in Figure 13.4, new viral particles leave infected CD4 cells through a process called *budding*, which damages and ultimately kills the cell. Each new particle goes on to infect another CD4 cell, and the cycle continues. As many as ten billion new virus particles can be produced daily.[23]

Figure 13.4 Transmission Electron Micrographic Image of HIV

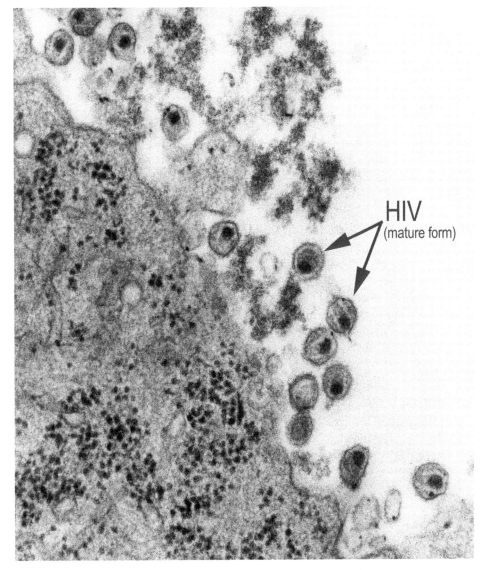

HIV
(mature form)

Note: This highly magnified transmission electron micrographic (TEM) image revealed the presence of mature forms of the *human immunodeficiency virus* (HIV) in a tissue sample under investigation.
Source: CDC, National Center for HIV, STD and TB Prevention—Division of HIV/AIDS Prevention.

Primary Infection

Primary HIV infection is marked by a peak in the level of virus in the blood—called the *viral load*—and a drop in the number of CD4 cells. The peak in viral load is due to intense and rapid replication of HIV once it enters a host. Because it takes the immune system time to sense and mount a response to HIV, early viral replication essentially occurs unchecked. Once the immune system begins to respond, however, one of its actions is to increase the number of CD4 cells produced to make up for those being killed during the replication cycle of HIV.

Clinical Latency

During the period of clinical *latency*—the period of time between initial infection and the symptomatic, clinical disease associated with AIDS—the rate of CD4 death due to viral replication is roughly equivalent to the rate of new CD4 cells being produced by the immune system. The rate of viral replication at this stage is relatively steady. Over time, however, the immune system is unable to keep pace with viral replication, and the CD4 cell levels drop. As this happens, the immune system weakens and becomes less able to fight off other infections. When an individual's CD4 cell count drops so low that he or she is at significant risk for developing opportunistic infections, he or she is clinically diagnosed with AIDS. The length of the clinical latency stage is estimated to be an average of 10 years in untreated patients.

Advanced HIV Disease: Opportunistic Infections and AIDS

Once a person's CD4 count falls below 200 cells/cubic millimeter (mm3) they are clinically diagnosed with AIDS. A person may also be diagnosed with AIDS if they have a CD4 count above 200 cells/mm3 but acquire one of 26 AIDS-defining illnesses characteristic of individuals in late-stage HIV disease.[24] As the CD4 count falls and the immune system weakens, the person eventually succumbs to opportunistic infections. These infections are caused by organisms that are generally harmless for people with normal immune systems. When given the opportunity to infect an individual with a weakened immune system, however, these organisms can cause severe illness and, in the case of end-stage AIDS, death.

Antiretroviral Drugs

Each stage in the life cycle of HIV is a potential target for antiretroviral (ARV) drugs, treatment for HIV-infected individuals designed specifically to attack the virus. The hallmark of HIV treatment is referred to as Highly Active Antiretroviral Therapy (HAART), and it has dramatically changed the course of HIV infection in individuals. By interfering with the life cycle of the virus and effectively lowering a viral load, HAART has increased the length of the latency stage and greatly extended the life expectancy of HIV-infected people who have access to treatment.[25] Though ARVs used to involve taking multiple doses of pills throughout the day and intolerable side effects, newer medications available today generally have far fewer side effects and can be taken once or twice a day.[26]

HAART may add years to the lives of many patients receiving treatment, but the development of new therapies and their increased availability and use raise the following concerns:

- *Adherence.* HAART is considered *combination therapy*, meaning that a doctor treats a patient's HIV with multiple drugs at once (usually three). This approach is employed because, as mentioned, HIV can mutate. Just as mutation enables viral particles to evade antibodies, it also allows HIV to adapt and become resistant to certain drugs. If a person does not take his or her medications as prescribed— such as might happen involuntarily, with the loss of health insurance, or voluntarily, due to depression—the virus in his or her body will have increased opportunity to develop resistance. Resistant strains of HIV are much harder to treat and thus decrease the effectiveness of HAART.[27]

- *The change in perception of HIV as a chronic disease.* The effectiveness and reduced side effects profile of newer ARVs have promoted the perception of HIV as a chronic disease only minimally impacting one's quality of life. For both infected and noninfected individuals, this shift in society's perception of the disease is potentially dangerous, as people may be less likely to take precautions to protect themselves from acquiring or transmitting a disease that, although treatable, ultimately remains fatal.[28]

Testing for HIV Infection

Though there are many tests that detect HIV infection, the cheapest and most readily available tests look for antibodies made by the body in response to the virus. As mentioned, antibodies are produced by the immune system in an attempt to clear HIV from the body. The presence of antibodies against HIV in a person's bloodstream thus serves as a footprint, indicating that HIV is present.[29]

The first three to six months during which a person is infected with HIV is referred to as the *window period*, representing the window of time between a person's initial infection with the virus and the time at which the presence of HIV can be detected by a blood test. This occurs because it takes time for the body to mount an antibody response to HIV; the process occurs simultaneously with the increase in CD4 cells in response to the high viral load during primary infection. Although most people seroconvert (generate HIV-specific antibodies) within one month of infection, it can take some people up to six months to generate enough antibodies to be detectable by a rapid HIV test. People who are HIV-positive therefore can test negative during the six-month window period if they have not yet seroconverted.

It is important to note that screening antibody tests do not *confirm* HIV infection. Individuals who have antibodies that are similar to those made in response to HIV, for example, may test positive for HIV on a screening antibody test when they are actually not infected with HIV. As a result, the false-positive rate for screening tests in some populations may be as high as high as 50 percent.[30] These can be ruled out or confirmed using more sophisticated tests (typically a Western blot). It is also important to acknowledge that among the general population, rapid HIV antibody tests are 98 percent accurate in detecting HIV infection.[31]

Questions for Discussion

1. What is the relationship between HIV and the immune system?

2. How does HAART work, and why is it so important for individuals with HIV to adhere to their medication regimen?

3. What is the window period for HIV testing, and why is it important for healthcare providers to consider it when testing individuals for HIV?

Legal Protections for People with HIV: Testing and Disclosure

Though in the early days of the HIV epidemic there were calls for mandatory testing and disclosure, people living with HIV/AIDS, healthcare providers and attorneys serving the communities most affected by the disease were able to persuade most policy makers that strong confidentiality and discrimination protections would better serve the public welfare. As effective treatment for HIV illness has become available, the goal of encouraging people to be tested has become more urgent. This is especially true for pregnant women, for whom, as mentioned, treatment can prevent transmission of HIV to the newborn.

HIV Testing

Although the CDC has established recommended guidelines for HIV testing in various settings and for various populations (e.g., in correctional facilities, for adults, for pregnant women),[32] testing rules are largely governed by state law. State laws vary as to the form of consent required, the training and qualifications of persons administering the test, the availability of anonymous testing, the age at which adolescents may consent to testing, and the extent and content of required pre- and/or post-test counseling.

As with any medical procedure, HIV testing should never be conducted without informed consent. However, the recognition that as many as 20 percent of people who are infected with HIV do not know they have it has prompted a move away from the need for written informed consent. In the most recent "Revised Recommendations for HIV Testing of Adults, Adolescents, and Pregnant Women in Health-Care Settings," the CDC defines *informed consent* as:

> A process of communication between patient and provider through which an informed patient can choose whether to undergo HIV testing or decline to do so. Elements of informed consent typically include providing oral or written information regarding HIV, the risks and benefits of testing, the implications of HIV test results, how test results will be communicated, and the opportunity to ask questions.[33]

Although the CDC strongly recommends opt-out testing — in which the patient is informed that HIV testing is done routinely and will be conducted unless they refuse — this does not mean that the provider does not need to discuss HIV testing with the patient. The requirement that patients be given an opportunity to ask questions means that even in opt-out settings there should be at least a brief discussion between the testing provider and the patient. This discussion should verify that the patient has received the pre-test information, knows he or she is going to be tested, and does not have any unanswered questions.

Despite the importance of informed consent, there are circumstances in which people with HIV may legally be tested without their consent and even without their knowledge. The most obvious exception is when blood or organs are being donated. Most states that have specific consent laws also have exceptions that apply when someone has been accused of sexual assault or a healthcare worker has been exposed to a patient's blood via a needle stick or other injury involving a break in the skin. Other exceptions may apply to insurance applicants, public safety officers or newborns whose mother's HIV status is unknown.

The revised CDC recommendations reflect a consensus in the public health community that HIV testing should be offered to all sexually active adults and adolescents, not simply to individuals perceived to be at risk for contracting HIV. Although the CDC recommends that testing be offered routinely in all healthcare settings, there is a special emphasis on STD clinics, correctional facilities and emergency rooms, all of which may see significant numbers of people who are uninsured and thus less likely to be receiving routine healthcare. In all settings, good medical practice and some state laws require careful attention to how results of preliminary positive screening tests are disclosed to the patient and charted in the medical record.[34]

Confidentiality

HIV is such a stigmatized disease worldwide that many high-risk individuals are reluctant to get tested or treated unless they can have complete confidence that their confidentiality will be protected.[35] Even with more than two decades of education and media attention, almost 40 percent of all Americans believe that HIV can be transmitted by kissing or ordinary household contact, and more than three-quarters report at least some level of discomfort with the idea of having a roommate with HIV.[36] These high rates of misunderstanding regarding the transmission of HIV, and the stigma and discrimination they facilitate, underlie the importance of protecting the confidentiality of people being tested or treated for HIV infection.

Protecting confidentiality protects not only against illegal discrimination—for example, against an employee of a fast-food restaurant who might be fired if her HIV status becomes known—but also against a wide range of private discrimination that is generally not illegal. There is no law, for example, that prevents a church from refusing to allow an HIV-positive child to attend Sunday school, or prevents a grandmother from insisting that her HIV-positive grandson use paper plates when he eats at her home. As one New York advocate so eloquently put it, the law

> does not stop your family members from never speaking to you again. It does not prevent your neighbor from forbidding her children to play with your children. It does not bar gossiping, slurs, religious curses or hostile stares and has very limited efficacy against menacing behavior. The law does not advise us not to blame people with HIV for their status. It does not stop people from assuming that you are gay or promiscuous or use drugs. For some things the law offers no protection and unfortunately these are the traumas that I most often hear recounted in my practice.[37]

One of the most important contributions an MLP can make is to ensure not only that confidentiality will be protected in both the clinic and legal settings but also that patients know about efforts made to protect their confidentiality and their own right to keep their HIV status confidential.[38]

As discussed in Chapter 6, the Health Insurance Protections Portability and Accountability Act (HIPAA) of 1996 is legislation designed to protect the confidentiality of medical records and ensure the continuity of care across all healthcare settings. The privacy protections of HIPAA of course provide important baseline protections against the disclosure of a patient's HIV status by "covered entities," which include insurance companies and healthcare providers.[39] HIPAA explicitly provides, however, that where there are more stringent state laws governing patient privacy, those laws remain in effect and are not preempted by HIPAA (45 C.F.R 160.203(b)). Almost 40 states have privacy laws that explicitly mention HIV/AIDS,[40] and some of these are clearly more stringent than HIPAA and may have enforcement mechanisms and penalties that are much stronger than those found in the federal law. In Illinois, for example, the AIDS Confidentiality Act goes far beyond HIPAA by providing that "no person" may disclose another's HIV status and by establishing minimum statutory penalties of $2,000 for a negligent and $10,000 for an intentional disclosure of an individual's HIV status, in addition to allowing for an award of attorneys fees in a civil suit brought under the act.[41]

Healthcare providers who are unfamiliar with the extent of HIV stigma may unwittingly disclose a patient's status in a situation where a disclosure of other health-related information might not cause as much concern. A common problem involves hospital staff members who mention a patient's HIV status in the presence of family members or other visitors (e.g., "your HIV doctor will be by to see you in the morning"). Seeing another patient's name on a sign-in sheet or hearing a name in a waiting room may also breach a patient's confidentiality and, equally important, may persuade other patients that they cannot trust the provider to protect confidentiality.

Partner Notification

There is wide variation among the states with regard to partner notification of HIV status and confidentiality. In New York, for example, a pregnant woman can be tested for HIV only if she signs a specific written consent. If she tests positive, her partner *must* be told unless there is a risk of domestic violence.[42] By contrast, in Illinois, all pregnant women are tested unless they refuse, but partner notification is voluntary.[43]

In nearly all states, the duty to inform sexual partners rests with the person with HIV. Many states have HIV criminal transmission laws that make it a felony for a person with HIV to have sex or share needles with another person without first disclosing his or her HIV status.[44] Providers should be familiar with their states' criminal transmission laws so that they can counsel patients about them. In addition, all states provide partner notification services, which work with the infected individual to identify partners and encourage them to get tested without disclosing the name of the infected individual. Providers should routinely refer newly diagnosed individuals for those services.

Generally state laws do not impose a duty to warn on healthcare providers but provide a right to disclose to some partners under some circumstances. In Illinois, for example, a physician (but not a nurse or other provider) may disclose to a spouse, although not to other partners (410 ILCS 305/9a). In Maryland, a physician may disclose to any sex or needle-sharing partners at his or her discretion (see Md. Code Ann § 18-336, 18-337). Neither state imposes a duty to notify partners, and both explicitly protect a physician who acts in good faith, whether or not the notification takes place. Because of the wide range of state law, healthcare providers are wise to avoid disclosing a patient's HIV status to sexual or needle-sharing partners unless they have first checked with their own risk management staff to ascertain the exact law in their state.[45]

Best Practices and Advocacy Strategies for Medical-Legal Partnership

1. MLP legal providers should educate healthcare providers about their jurisdiction's laws and regulations on specific confidentiality protections that may apply to patients with HIV/AIDS.

2. Healthcare providers should assure clients, verbally and in writing, that their confidentiality will be protected.

3. If files are routinely shared within a healthcare setting, or between parties in an MLP, providers should explain the purpose of the sharing and seek written consent during the first meeting with the patient.

4. Providers should never disclose a patient's HIV status outside of the healthcare setting except as required by law (e.g., public health reporting) without explicit written permission. This applies even if the referral is for the benefit of the patient, for example, to help locate housing that may be reserved for people with HIV/AIDS.

5. Providers should remember that even individuals who come to an appointment with a patient or visit him or her in the hospital may not know the patient's HIV

status. They should always have a private conversation with the patient first before continuing a discussion with another person present, and, if required by state law, have them sign a written consent that their information may be disclosed to that individual.

6. MLP partners should review clinic policies on matters such as sign-in sheets, brochures, business cards, fax protocol, signage and computer access from the viewpoint of a patient who is frightened to come to the clinic for fear his or her HIV status will be inadvertently disclosed. (If the clinic has a community advisory board, this is an excellent way in which they can contribute).

From Practice to Policy

The AIDS Legislative Committee in Maryland, composed of people living with HIV/AIDS, healthcare providers, public health experts and attorneys, came together to respond to legislative proposals that affected people living with AIDS. The committee advocated for informed consent for HIV testing, patient counseling and education, and support for needle exchange programs to stem the spread of the virus. It had a tremendous impact over a 12-year period on HIV-related legislation in Maryland. MLPs can be leaders in similarly bringing together healthcare providers, legal providers and other key allies to advocate for or oppose legislation that affects people with HIV and their families.

Case for Medical-Legal Partnership

Nineteen-year-old Tanya learned of her positive HIV status when she was tested during her pregnancy with her first child, born about six months ago. You are Tanya's healthcare provider. She tells you that the child's father is her current partner, and she has not yet disclosed her HIV status to him. The baby has been tested and is HIV-negative. She tells you the relationship with the child's father is not going well. She wants to move out but has no income and no place to go.

You counsel Tanya about the importance of disclosing HIV to her partner and offer to help her. She does not return for her next appointment with you.

Questions for Discussion

1. What is your next step in providing care for Tanya?

2. Do you have any responsibility to notify her partner of his possible exposure to HIV?

3. Would your responsibility change if Tanya informed you that her partner has been using heroin off and on for several years? What if she told you that her partner has been physically abusive to her?

Employment Rights and Protections

People with HIV who are able to work may face difficult questions regarding disclosure, job loss and discrimination. Lawyers knowledgeable about employment law working in collaboration with healthcare providers can help answer these kinds of employment-related questions. They can also train healthcare providers to be sensitive to employment-related legal issues their patients may encounter. This section discusses certain employment-related protections for patients with HIV under federal and state laws.

Protection from Employment Discrimination

The Americans with Disabilities Act

The Americans with Disabilities Act (ADA) offers protections for people living with HIV from discrimination in the workplace. When the Act was first passed in 1990, employers and healthcare providers challenged its applicability to people with HIV/AIDS. The ADA defined *disability* as a condition that impacts a "major life activity," and it was argued that people living with HIV/AIDS, particularly if they were asymptomatic, did not meet this definition. However, the Equal Employment Opportunity Commission (EEOC), the federal agency charged with enforcing the ADA, took the position that people living with HIV *were* covered by the Act.[46]

In 1995, a federal lawsuit was filed challenging the view that HIV/AIDS was not a disability under the ADA. That lawsuit, *Bragdon v. Abbott,* made its way to the U.S. Supreme Court in 1998, and the Court endorsed the EEOC's interpretation.[47] As an initial matter, the Court held that visible symptoms or illness were not a prerequisite to meeting the ADA's definition of disability, which was particularly important for those with stigmatic conditions such as HIV/AIDS.[48] The Court further held that because HIV substantially impacts the reproductive system, limiting such "major life activities" as procreation and sexual activity, the Act covered those living with HIV/AIDS.[49] Even after the Court's decision in *Bragdon,* however, legal challenges continued regarding whether Congress intended for HIV to be covered under the ADA. In response, Congress passed the ADA Amendments Act of 2008, which reinforced the decision in *Bragdon* that because HIV affects major life activities, it is covered by the ADA.[50]

When patients discuss fears or concerns about treatment by their employer with a healthcare provider, it is critical that an immediate referral be made to an MLP lawyer. Early legal assistance can sometimes help the patient avoid the loss of a job. For example, a lawyer can educate both the client about his or her rights under the ADA or the Family and Medical Leave Act of 1993 (FMLA) and the employer about his or her obligation to provide reasonable accommodations to an employee living with HIV. In this case, the practice of preventive law can directly avoid the crisis of job loss, its detrimental effects on the patient's quality of life and any adverse medical events that could potentially occur following the loss of health insurance. The following sections discuss two common fears and concerns that providers may encounter when interacting with patients or clients: workplace disclosure of HIV status and reasonable accommodation in the workplace.

Workplace Disclosure

It is illegal to discriminate against an employee based on his or her HIV/AIDS status; that is, employers cannot terminate, refuse to hire or demote employees solely because they have HIV or AIDS.[51] Although illegal, workplace discrimination is still common, and employees who disclose their status often face hostile work environments and, in some cases, termination. Because disclosing one's status at work is risky, it should be done only after speaking with a knowledgeable attorney so the employee is aware of his or her legal rights. Ultimately, the decision to disclose rests solely with an employee: he or she is *not* required to disclose his or her illness to current or potential employers.[52]

If an employee decides to disclose his or her HIV/AIDS status at work, the ADA provides strong protections against workplace discrimination and requires that this information be kept strictly confidential. For example, the ADA expressly prohibits employers from asking job applicants to submit to medical exams or answer any medical inquiries during the interview and application process (42 U.S.C. 12112(d)(2)). A direct inquiry about one's HIV status would therefore be illegal, as would a question about prior hospitalizations or medical problems that would make the job difficult.[53] An employer can, however, ask about one's ability to perform certain job duties—for instance, lifting heavy equipment.

Once an offer of employment has been made, however, an employer is permitted to request a medical examination, which—absent contrary state law—might include an HIV test or a health history questionnaire that asks about HIV.[54] When such an examination is requested, an employer must meet strict ADA requirements that include, among other things, that the same exam be given to all applicants and that results be kept confidential (42 U.S.C. § 12112(d)(3)). Most important, the results of an examination (including a positive HIV test) *cannot* be used to withdraw a job offer unless the results indicate that the individual is unable to perform the essential functions of the job (42 U.S.C. § 12112(d)(3)).

The ADA further provides that an employer may require current employees to submit to a medical exam but only if it is "job-related and consistent with [a] business necessity" (42 U.S.C. § 12112(d)(4)(A)). Medical examinations cannot be requested arbitrarily; an employer "must demonstrate that the examination is necessary to measure the employee's actual performance functions."[55] Such exams are unlikely to occur regularly but are a potential source of disclosure for HIV-positive individuals.

Reasonable Accommodation

In addition to protecting those with HIV or AIDS from workplace discrimination, the ADA also provides the right to "reasonable accommodation" at work. The Act requires employers with 15 or more employees to modify or adjust job requirements—for example, adjusting work schedules to accommodate medical appointments—to enable persons with disabilities to perform their job duties.[56] To receive reasonable accommodation, an employee must initiate the accommodation request and must inform the employer of the nature of the disability.[57] Such requests should be approached carefully, however, because they can lead to disclosure of HIV/AIDS status.

When an employee asks for reasonable accommodation, the employer may request medical documentation, which is usually a letter from the employee's doctor.[58] To avoid disclosing one's status, an employee may try to disclose the actual disabling condition— for example, fatigue.[59] However, for an employee who is HIV-positive and in good health but wants an accommodation to take time off to see the doctor regularly, it may be impossible to avoid disclosing HIV status.[60]

State Protections against Discrimination Based on HIV

Many states have analogous state laws that, like the ADA, provide protection from discrimination based on disability, whereas others have enacted laws that expressly relate to HIV/AIDS. Some states, like Rhode Island, have enacted both types and thus expressly prohibit discrimination based on disability and on HIV-status.

Under Rhode Island law, it is unlawful for any employer to "refuse to hire any applicant for employment because of his or her ... disability ... [or to] refuse to reasonably accommodate an employee's or prospective employee's disability" (R.I. Gen. Law § 28-5-7). Additionally, Rhode Island law provides that "no person, agency, organization, or legal entity may discriminate against an individual on the basis of an HIV test result … in … employment" (R.I. Gen. Law § 23-6.3-11). Thus, state laws like this may strengthen the protections under the ADA by specifically protecting workers who test positive for HIV. MLP practitioners should become familiar with workplace protections for patients with HIV under both federal laws such as FMLA and ADA, as well as state laws that may provide additional protections.

Protections for Health-Related Work Absence

The Family and Medical Leave Act

At times, serious health conditions render employees incapable of performing essential job duties and they must request leave from work. Prior to the passage of FMLA in 1993, employees could be denied medical leave for any reason and could be fired for taking family or medical leave. Today, FMLA requires certain employers to provide up to 12 weeks of unpaid leave per 12-month period for any employee with a "serious health condition" or an employee who is taking care of a sick family member (29 U.S.C. § 2612 (2009)). (For further discussion of FMLA, see Chapter 7. For discussion of FMLA protections for people with cancer and their families, see Chapter 12.)

Designed to protect workers who must miss work due their own or a family member's illness, FMLA is particularly important for people with HIV or AIDS. The law protects employees who need to miss work for intermittent medical treatment, such as a doctor appointment or hospital stay, by including inpatient hospital care, continuing treatment by a healthcare provider, periods of incapacity due to chronic serious health conditions and similar ongoing medical care in its definition of "serious health condition."[61] This is crucial because without such protections, individuals who attend regularly scheduled medical appointments during work hours could be subjected to discrimination and retaliation from employers.

However, although FMLA provides strong protections for those with HIV and AIDS, some provisions may cause concern. For instance, employers may require workers seeking leave to have their health condition certified by a medical provider (29 U.S.C. § 2613 (2009)). The law is somewhat unclear regarding exactly how much information an employer can demand, but FMLA says the certification must be "sufficient"; that is, it must include the date the condition commenced, the probable duration, and "appropriate medical facts" within the healthcare provider's knowledge (29 U.S.C. § 2613).

It is clear, however, that when a medical certification is requested, employers may only request information relating to the specific health condition for which leave is requested (29 U.S.C. § 2613). An employer may not request information beyond what is specified in the Department of Labor's sample certification form. Some employers include broad medical releases in their certification forms asking for access to an employee's full medical record and make signing the release a condition of taking leave. But FMLA provides that employees need *only* provide enough information to establish that a serious health condition exists (29 U.S.C. § 2613). Therefore, employees need not disclose all of their medical records to demonstrate a serious condition. Requiring such broad disclosure could have serious consequences for some employees, especially those with stigmatized health conditions such as HIV or AIDS.

Certain limitations imposed by FMLA might particularly affect those with HIV or AIDS. For example, an individual must be employed with an employer for one year and at least 1,250 hours during the previous year before he or she is eligible for FMLA protections (29 U.S.C. § 2611(2)(A) (2009)). If an individual is unable to work full-time or unable to commit a full year because of health complications, he or she will not satisfy these requirements and would not be covered. Moreover, because FMLA does not cover employers with fewer than 50 employees, those who work in small businesses would be denied coverage under FMLA unless the business offers it on its own discretion (29 U.S.C. § 2611(2)(B)(ii) (2009)). Finally, employers are not required to pay employees for medical or family leave, which could have an especially serious impact on low-income individuals with HIV or AIDS (29 U.S.C. § 2612(c) (2009)).

Employers are often unfamiliar with FMLA provisions or may be reluctant to abide by the Act's requirements. If healthcare providers are aware of patients being denied leave for medical appointments, illness or other health-related issues, they should refer them to a legal provider immediately to be informed of their rights.

Case for Medical-Legal Partnership

The adoptive mother of an HIV-positive 11-year-old patient was fired for taking too much time off to care for her son. She asked for leave to take him to medical appointments to monitor HIV medication and was told by her employer that FMLA is only for her medical needs and needs to be taken all at once (e.g., two weeks off for surgery and recovery). According to her employer, taking occasional days is too disruptive for the workplace.

Questions for Discussion

1. Does the mother of the patient have any legal recourse in this situation? What specific actions could a legal provider take?
2. What role might a healthcare provider play in facilitating this recourse?

HIV and Social Determinants of Health

The World Health Organization defines *social determinants of health* to be "the conditions in which people are born, grow, live, work, and age, including the health system."[62] Many determinants, such as housing, income and education, have been discussed in previous chapters and in the context of their relationship to health. Here, the discussion focuses specifically on the ways social determinants of health (such as poverty, race, gender, age, housing and access to treatment) can generate environments in which specific populations of people have an increased susceptibility to HIV infection.

It is important to acknowledge the complexity of confounding factors contributing to the disproportionate distribution of HIV infection and the inequity of greater mortality and illness between different HIV-infected populations. That said, the goal of this section is not to prove causation. There are, however, undeniable and evidence-based associations between the conditions into which people are born and live, their risk for HIV infection and the state of their health once they become infected. There is thus a dire need for legal interventions addressing social determinants of health, and medical practitioners caring for HIV-infected individuals are often well positioned to facilitate such interventions.

Just as the clinical course of HIV depends on a multitude of factors specific to the individual, legal considerations for people with HIV depend largely on each person's unique circumstances and needs as well as his or her social context. Additionally, legal concerns for HIV-positive individuals are inherently complicated by stigma and the specific ways unmet needs confound one another, such as may be the case for an individual whose job termination due to HIV-related issues results in housing instability, food insecurity and a lack of health insurance. Legal assistance can often prevent or ameliorate these detrimental effects.

In addition, teaching healthcare providers about the legal issues confronting their patients with HIV can help facilitate meeting those patients' basic needs and improve their health and well-being. For example, a doctor who is not familiar with how to document a patient's medical history to conform to Social Security Administration requirements for determining eligibility for disability benefits may lose an opportunity to assist a patient in improving his or her health. The discussion that follows highlights the connections between HIV, the social determinants of health and the law, and how partnership between healthcare and legal providers can most effectively meet the needs of people infected and affected by HIV.

Poverty

Physician and medical anthropologist Dr. Paul Farmer refers to the HIV/AIDS epidemic as a "biosocial phenomenon," one that is deeply rooted in both the biology of HIV and the social context of poverty.[63] Whether the relationship between HIV and poverty is one of association or causation, however, is a topic of great debate in the medical, economic and political realms. In Sub-Saharan Africa, research has resulted in conflicting data: both a positive correlation and an inverse relationship between a nation's poverty level and HIV prevalence have been found, the latter of which is largely attributed to the association between higher income, greater social mobility and an expanded network of sexual contacts.[64]

A recent CDC study focusing on inner-city heterosexuals in the urban United States, however, highlights the close association of poverty with HIV infection. Researchers found that 2.1 percent of heterosexuals living in deeply impoverished urban areas are infected with HIV, a prevalence nearly five times that of the general population.[65] Moreover, within this population, poverty was determined the strongest correlation with HIV infection. Although the U.S. epidemic has in the past been considered to be concentrated among high-risk groups such IV drug users and men who have sex with men, the high prevalence of HIV infection among inner-city heterosexuals meets UNAIDS criteria for a generalized epidemic,[66] saliently demonstrating that HIV/AIDS continues to be a major health threat in the United States.

Racial and Ethnic Minorities

Since the beginning of the HIV epidemic, the demographics of infected individuals have dramatically shifted. In 1985, less than 50 percent of reported AIDS cases in the United States were among members of minority populations. In 2007, minority populations comprised more than 70 percent of people newly diagnosed with HIV/AIDS in this country.[67] The following statistics demonstrate the disproportionate distribution of HIV infection among minorities in the United States:

- Though African Americans comprise only 12 percent of the general population, they accounted for approximately 50 percent of new HIV/AIDS diagnoses in 2007.

- Rates of HIV/AIDS diagnoses in African Americans are 10 times the rate of diagnosis in Caucasians. The rate of new AIDS diagnoses for Hispanic men is three times that of Caucasian men.

- Women account for nearly one quarter of all new HIV/AIDS diagnoses. Though together, African American and Hispanic women account for 24 percent of the general population, they comprised 80 percent of HIV/AIDS diagnoses among women in 2005 (Figure 13.5). The rate of AIDS diagnoses among African American women is 22 times that of Caucasian women; in 2004, HIV was found to be the leading cause of death in African American women aged 25 to 34 years.[68]

In addition to being more likely to contract HIV, members of minority populations also have poorer clinical outcomes than HIV-positive individuals from the general population. The disproportionate rates of infection and increased death rates due to HIV are two of the most significant factors contributing to the difference in life expectancy between African Americans and Caucasians.[69] One main component of this disparity in mortality appears to be poor or delayed access to HAART compared to nonminority populations.[70] HIV-positive individuals from a minority population are also less likely to receive primary care services,[71] a critical component of maintaining health, preventing opportunistic infections and monitoring the progression of HIV disease.

The disproportionate rate of new HIV/AIDS infections in the African American community, particularly among heterosexual women, is of great concern to providers and advocates. Although it is important to note that the factors contributing to this trend are

Figure 13.5 Race/Ethnicity of Adult or Adolescent Women with HIV/AIDS Diagnoses, 2005

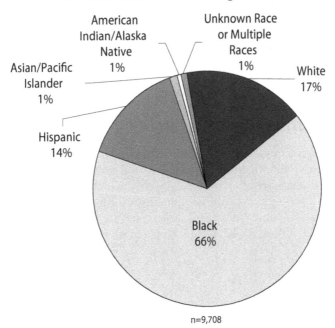

American Indian/Alaska Native 1%

Unknown Race or Multiple Races 1%

Asian/Pacific Islander 1%

White 17%

Hispanic 14%

Black 66%

n=9,708

Source: Centers for Disease Control and Prevention, *HIV/AIDS Surveillance Report, 2005,* 17, no. 1 (Washington, DC: U.S. Department of Health and Human Services, 2007): 1–54.
Note: Data from 33 states with confidential name-based HIV infection reporting.

controversial and continue to be studied,[72] they undoubtedly speak to the complex relationship between poverty, race and gender.

Recent Immigrants

Prior to January 2010, U.S. immigration law formally discriminated against people with HIV. It was illegal for anyone with HIV to even enter the United States, let alone immigrate, without being granted an HIV waiver. Although people entering as visitors were not tested for HIV, anyone applying for an immigrant visa, whether in their home country or adjusting their status (for example, by marriage) in the United States, was required to have an HIV test. Individuals who tested positive were then ineligible for resident status unless they met the very narrow exceptions for a waiver of the HIV ban. Since the ban was lifted as of January 4, 2010, prospective immigrants are no longer tested for HIV or even asked about their HIV status.[73]

Because the ban greatly limited the number of HIV-positive immigrants legally entering the United States, little evidence exists assessing the prevalence of HIV among immigrant populations. Researchers have called for a National HIV in Foreign-Born Registry, a database that would collect and make available data regarding disease prevalence among U.S. immigrants.[74]

Questions for Discussion

1. Why are the social determinants of health particularly relevant in the context of HIV/AIDS?

2. What factors place members of minority populations at an increased risk for contracting HIV? What might this mean for HIV prevention and treatment strategies within this population?

3. What are some examples of unmet legal needs that may be experienced by people living in poverty?

Accessing Healthcare and Income Supports

Given that HIV profoundly and disproportionately affects individuals living in poverty, access to government-funded healthcare and public benefits—which may alleviate some of the consequences of poverty—is critical to improving health outcomes and the well-being of people living with HIV. Because of disparities in access to HAART for minority and low-income individuals, ensuring timely access to healthcare is particularly potent in addressing healthcare disparities and outcomes for vulnerable populations.

Medicaid

As discussed in Chapter 7, Medicaid is a federal-state program that provides medical assistance to low-income individuals. Although eligibility and benefits vary from state to state, all require that applicants meet both income and categorical eligibility criteria to qualify. Although the Medicaid program is difficult to navigate for many people, there are distinctive aspects of the HIV epidemic that create particular problems that often necessitate legal assistance.

Barriers to Access for People with HIV

People with HIV need access to expensive medical care long before they meet the Medicaid disability standard. In nearly all states, Medicaid is only available to individuals who are "categorically eligible." In practice, this means that unless they over age 65 or in a family with minor children, people with HIV must establish that they are disabled before they can qualify for Medicaid. By federal law, states must use the same disability standard for Medicaid as is used for Social Security benefits based on disability, described shortly. The result is that many (perhaps most) people with HIV will not be eligible for Medicaid when they first come into care, and, paradoxically, getting care may prevent them from becoming so disabled that they would meet the Social Security definition and qualify for Medicaid.

HIV is no longer an inevitably progressive disease. As individuals newly diagnosed with HIV receive treatment, their health often improves. If they develop a co-occurring illness or must change their drug regimen, their health may decline for a period, but then improve after this interval. As a result, many people with HIV not only have good days and bad days, but good years and bad years. In the good years they may work. In the bad years they may need to rely on public benefits. Neither the Social Security system nor the Medicaid program is set up to adequately support individuals who transition in and out of the workforce.

Effective treatment of HIV often involves complex regimens of multiple drugs. Because of the flexibility given states in designing Medicaid programs, some may not provide prescription drug coverage adequate to cover the needs of people with HIV. Texas, for example, only covers three prescriptions per month, whether generic or brand name, with the result that many Texans with HIV must also enroll in the Texas AIDS Drug Assistance Program.[75]

Some of these points regarding Medicaid eligibility will change dramatically when the Medicaid provisions of the Patient Protection and Affordable Care Act (Pub. L. No: 111-148) go into effect on January 1, 2014. The Act abolishes the current "categorical eligibility" requirements of Medicaid and extends Medicaid coverage to all individuals (subject to financial and citizenship requirements) with annual incomes under 133 percent of the federal poverty level ("Bill Summary and Status"). Poor people with HIV will then be able to qualify for Medicaid regardless of whether they can prove disability or other categorical eligibility.

The AIDS Drug Assistance Programs (ADAP)

An important resource for individuals with HIV is AIDS Drug Assistance Programs. ADAPs are state administered programs funded in part by Title II of the Ryan White CARE Act (created in 1990 by Congress). These programs provide assistance in obtaining HIV medications to low-income, uninsured and underinsured individuals living with HIV/AIDS. The types of drugs provided and the eligibility criteria are determined by each state.[a]

For example, California requires that to be eligible, the individual:

- Is at least 18 years of age.
- Has an HIV diagnosis from a healthcare provider.
- Has limited or no prescription drug benefit from another source.

- Has a federal adjusted gross Income of not more than $50,000.[b]

Source: [a] National ADAP Monitoring Project Annual Report (May 2010), http://www.nastad.org/Docs/Public/InFocus/201053_2010%20National%20ADAP%20Monitoring%20Project%20Annual%20Report.pdf; [b] Ramsell Public Health Rx, "California AIDS Drug Assistance Program," http://www.publichealthrx.com/ca_adap.aspx.

Disability Benefits for People with HIV/AIDS

The effectiveness of HAART has dramatically changed the way HIV is managed as a chronic health problem. This means that some people living with HIV are able to successfully maintain full-time employment. However, many others may suffer side effects of medication and fatigue, and when those effects are considered along with co-occurring mental and physical illnesses, sustaining full-time employment can be very difficult, if not impossible. Because of the complexity of these situations, it is critical that legal and healthcare providers work together to assist patients who are unable to engage in substantial full-time employment to access income-supporting public benefits such as Supplemental Security Income (SSI) and Social Security Disability Insurance (SSDI).

Both SSI and SSDI are intended to provide income for those who may be too disabled to work or, in the case of children, income to support the family's care of a child who is disabled. The Social Security Administration (SSA) is responsible for determining whether an individual meets the eligibility requirements for SSI or SSDI. Although eligibility for both is based on the individual's disability, SSDI is based on the individual's work history and payment into the Social Security system, whereas SSI is based on need. (For a comparison of SSI and SSDI, see Chapter 7.) Federal law dictates that individuals applying for benefits based on disability must establish that they have a severe impairment that will last at least a year and that prevents them not only from doing work they have done in the past but also from doing any work in the future (20 CFR 404.1505 (2010)).

Establishing a Qualifying Disability for Patients with HIV

The SSA uses a screening tool called the Listing of Impairments (known as the Listings) to identify claimants who are so severely impaired that they clearly cannot work at all and thus immediately qualify for benefits. For claimants who do not meet the Listings criteria, the SSA requires additional, often extensive information about vocational capacity and other factors, such as work history, education and age, to decide on their claims. The Listings screen, therefore, provides many claimants with a rapid decision and saves SSA substantial administrative costs.

To establish a disability, a patient must show that he or she meets the requirements of the SSA Listings. When a patient cans do this, he or she is deemed disabled and unable to work. Under the Listings, HIV infection alone is not sufficient grounds for establishing that a person has a qualifying disability; the presence of an opportunistic or AIDS-defining illness, however, does result in an automatic finding of disability if properly documented.[76] The availability of effective treatment for HIV infection, however, has meant that many people living with HIV no longer suffer from severe opportunistic infections. As a result, for patients who do not meet the criteria of the Listings, establishing disability requires extensive and specific documentation of a patient's full health history, a task requiring clear communication and effective collaboration between physicians and lawyers.

Many patients with HIV also suffer from a range of coexisting health problems that may affect their ability to work, such as mental illness, hepatitis, asthma, diabetes or arthritis. In determining a patient's eligibility for disability benefits, SSA requires detailed medical evidence of the patient's health problems. Often, adult patients have health problems, such as severe back pain, that affect their ability to work but have not been able to see the appropriate specialist because of a lack of adequate health insurance. Patients, especially those emerging from prison, often have untreated mental health needs. The first step a legal provider must take in assisting a patient applying for SSI or SSDI or appealing a denial of benefits is to work closely with a healthcare provider to document the patient's health concerns. The lawyer's job is to establish that his or her client is disabled by a combination of impairments that make it impossible for him or her to engage in substantial gainful employment. This often requires a detailed description of the client's day-to-day ability to function, corroborated by a witness (for example, a family member who lives with the client).

As noted earlier, many people with HIV also suffer from substance abuse and addiction, so the issue of whether substance-abusing patients are eligible for disability benefits is important. Current law provides that applicants must establish that substance abuse or addiction plays no role in their disability.[77] If a patient with a substance abuse problem is relying on other impairments (particularly mental impairments) to establish disability, the patient must be able to establish that he or she is currently in treatment and/or is not using drugs or alcohol.[78]

Institute of Medicine Recommendations Regarding HIV and Disability

In September 2010, the Institute of Medicine released a report, "HIV and Disability: Updating the SSA Listings," which recommended that because the course of HIV illness has changed dramatically over the years, understanding of disability based on the disease should change. The committee that drafted the report concluded:

> The SSA claims process for people infected with HIV once reflected an early belief that HIV infection would result very quickly in an opportunistic infection or malignancy and lead to death over a short period. Medical advances and constant scientific progress have rendered those ideas out of date, as people infected with the virus can live longer, and more medically complicated, lives. Today, disability in HIV-infected claimants can be more precisely identified by clinical markers and specific sets of medical conditions. By updating the HIV Infection Listings to better reflect current clinical practice, SSA will be able to more accurately identify those people in need of Social Security disability benefits.

Based on the medical literature, the committee recommended that several categories of claimants be considered disabled:

- Claimants with CD4 cell counts (a common laboratory marker of disease stage for HIV/AIDS patients) less than or equal to 50 cells/mm3. Because CD4 counts can change in response to antiretroviral therapy, claimants allowed disability in this way should be regularly reevaluated.

- Claimants with several types of severe or fatal conditions that occur in connection with HIV infection should be considered permanently disabled.

- Claimants with severe HIV-associated conditions that are not included elsewhere in the Listing of Impairments should be allowed disability if the condition is found to limit functioning. Claimants allowed in this way should be regularly reevaluated.

- Claimants with severe HIV-associated conditions that are included elsewhere in the Listing of Impairments should be allowed disability if their conditions qualify under the other listing. Claimants allowed in this way should be regularly reevaluated.[a]

Source: [a] Institute of Medicine, "HIV and Disability: Updating the SSA Listings," Report Brief (September 2010).

Appeals Process

Each year, the SSA denies a substantial number of SSI and SSDI claims, particularly in the early stages of the application process. In 2008, for example, two thirds of the 2.5 million SSDI claims were denied at initial application or at the first level of appeal.[79] An applicant who disagrees with an SSA determination may request review under a three-step appeals process, as well as have any final determination reviewed in federal court. Because the SSA often denies applicants who in fact qualify for benefits, it is imperative that applicants are aware of their right to appeal and know what the appeals process entails. The SSA's appeals process provides an overview of the steps involved in filing an appeal. All appeals must be filed within 60 days of the prior denial.

The Appeals Process

Step 1: Reconsideration. If, after submitting an initial claim, an applicant has been denied benefits, he or she may request a complete review of his or her claim.[a] Known as reconsideration, this process is conducted by someone who had no role in the initial decision to deny SSI or SSDI benefits.[b] The SSA will reexamine all of the originally submitted evidence, as well as any additional supporting evidence, and send a notice of determination once it has reached a decision.[c]

Step 2: Hearing. This is the most important appeal and the only step in the administrative review process where the decision maker sees and speaks with an applicant.[c] The administrative law judge (ALJ) will question the applicant and any witnesses and may schedule experts to provide opinions on medical or vocational issues.[c] ALJs frequently overturn unfavorable decisions; therefore, an applicant who reaches this step in the appeals process has a relatively good chance of reversal.[c] Note that it may take months or even years after a request for hearing is filed before one takes place. Experienced advocates will work with healthcare providers during this stage to gather evidence which allows for a decision before a hearing is scheduled.[d]

Step 3: When the outcome of a hearing is unfavorable, an applicant may ask the Social Security appeals council to review the ALJ's decision, which is the final step in the administrative appeals process.[c] The appeals council denies most requests for review but, when granted, the council may uphold the decision, reverse the decision or remand the case to the ALJ for further proceedings.[c] A person appealing an ALJ's decision has the right to file a new application in the meantime and is generally wise to do so.

Step 4: Federal Court. An applicant may file a complaint for judicial review in federal court within 60 days of an adverse appeals council decision.[f] The court's jurisdiction is limited to reviewing the decision and record to determine whether errors of law exist or if the decision is contrary to substantial evidence.[c]

Source: [a] 80 The SSA's administrative appeals process is the same for all regions except Boston, which has used a modified appeals process since 2006. The Boston region encompasses Connecticut, Massachusetts, Maine, New Hampshire, Rhode Island and Vermont; [b] Social Security Administration, *Publication No. 05-100041: The Appeals Process* (Washington, DC: Social Security Administration, January 2008); [c] Linda Landry, et al., *An Advocate's Guide to Surviving the SSI System: Financial and Other Nondisability Criteria* (Massachusetts: Massachusetts Law Reform Institute, 2005), 64; 20 C.F.R. §§ 404.901, 416.1401; [d] Ibid, p. 64; [e] Ibid, p. 70; [f] Ibid, p. 71.

Case for Medical-Legal Partnership

Sarah is a 31-year-old woman who dropped out of school when she was 14 and her first child was born. She tells you she was flunking most of her classes anyway. She has a long history of IV heroin use, with intermittent periods of sobriety, including when she was in prison. Her children are in the custody of her mother, with whom she also lives when she's not on the street. Sarah has briefly worked a variety of menial jobs but has not been able to hold onto any one of them for more than a few months. She tells you she is fired because she misses too much work, blows up at a supervisor or makes too many mistakes.

She was diagnosed HIV-positive when her last child was born, about eight years ago, and with hepatitis C last year. She has had inconsistent healthcare but is currently in a methadone program and seems to be developing a trusting relationship with her primary care provider. She had developed resistance to several drug combinations because of her intermittent adherence but has been on her current regimen for six months with good results. Her major complaints are that the medication gives her diarrhea and she is tired all the time, but she thinks that may be because her children wear her out. She has never had any mental healthcare. She has no income.

Questions for Discussion

1. On what basis might Sarah qualify for SSI and Medicaid?
2. What impact will her substance abuse history have on her application, if any?
3. What further steps are necessary to appropriately manage Sarah's health concerns?
4. How might the MLP team work together to help stabilize this client's life?

Individuals Experiencing Homelessness

Though the relationship between poverty and poor health is well documented, the confounding variables that detrimentally affect the health of homeless individuals become most salient in the context of HIV. Homeless individuals are three to five times more likely than the general population to be infected with HIV, and those who are infected and homeless are more likely to be in poor health than housed individuals carrying the disease.[80]

Individuals experiencing homelessness confront a multitude of challenges that compromise both their physical health and ability to access quality healthcare. Of particular concern for this population is sexual risk behavior driven by economic need. In a study examining the relationship between homelessness, economic need, sex work and HIV risk behavior, female sex workers experiencing homelessness demonstrated increased levels of risky behavior compared to nonhomeless sex workers: a significantly greater proportion of the women used alcohol or crack daily, more frequently engaged in unprotected sex, and were more likely to engage in sex while under the influence of drugs or alcohol.[81] Moreover, behaviors associated with an increased risk for HIV infection occurred more frequently as economic need increased.[82] This trend, which greatly increases homeless individuals' risk for HIV infection, is seen in male as well as female sex workers. In a study among African American male sex workers, more than half of the participants indicated that they would take greater sexual risks when hungry or without housing.[83]

Once infected with HIV, any number of the adverse consequences of homelessness—poor nutrition due to food insecurity, poor access to primary healthcare, limited access to HAART, inadequate treatment for mental health conditions—can contribute to poorer health outcomes. Because poor nutrition can weaken an already compromised immune system, food insecurity among homeless individuals can have severe consequences on the rate of disease progression and adherence to treatment.[84]

Housing Protections for People with HIV/AIDS

Stable housing is an essential element of successful HIV/AIDS care. When HIV/AIDS patients are stably housed, they can more easily access comprehensive healthcare treatment and better adhere to complex drug therapies.[85] Stable housing provides "a place to store medication and food, a stable water supply, bathroom facilities, a secure place to rest, a dependable contact location, protection from harm, [and] emotional security and hope."[86] Unfortunately, many people living with HIV/AIDS are at risk of losing their housing due to rising medical and housing costs, reduced ability to work and discriminatory housing practices, among other factors.[87]

In many instances, however, taking advantage of assistance programs and/or invoking various legal protections can avoid housing loss. Fortunately, a variety of state and federal programs exist to address housing needs particular to those with HIV/AIDS. For instance, the Housing Opportunities for Persons with AIDS (HOPWA) program, a federal program managed by Housing and Urban Development, distributes funds to cities and states to address such housing issues.[88] Many of HOPWA's programs and projects provide short- and long-term rental assistance, operate community residences, or make use of other supportive housing facilities to address HIV/AIDS patients' housing concerns.[89]

Additionally, those with HIV/AIDS are often victims of discriminatory housing practices, which can affect housing stability. Federal law (and many state laws) makes housing discrimination illegal, and any suspected discrimination should be reported immediately. Under the Fair Housing Act, discrimination based on disability (which includes HIV/AIDS) is strictly prohibited.[90] Accordingly, landlords cannot refuse to rent to, evict or harass a person based solely on his or her HIV/AIDS status. Many state laws mirror the Fair Housing Act by prohibiting housing discrimination based on disability and/or HIV status. (For more information about federal and state fair housing laws, see Chapter 8.) Healthcare providers who learn that a patient may be threatened with homelessness or is experiencing discrimination based on his or her HIV status should refer the patient to a legal provider to explore options and/or recourse.

The Incarcerated

The United States has the highest rate of incarceration in the world. As of 2008, 2.3 million people are being held in jails or serving terms in prisons.[91] The demographics of incarcerated persons, however, do not reflect the general population.

Demographics of Incarcerated Persons

- Members of minority groups are overrepresented.[a]

  - African American men are seven times more likely to be incarcerated than Caucasian men. Hispanic men are incarcerated at more than twice the rate of Caucasians.

  - Although African Americans and Hispanic individuals account for 12 and 13 percent of the general population, respectively, together they comprise 58 percent of all incarcerated individuals.

- Mental illness is overrepresented.[b]

  - In a recent study, researchers found that although 65 percent of all American inmates meet medical criteria for substance abuse or addiction, only 11 percent are receiving the treatment they need.

  - More than 75 percent of convicted inmates with a history of three or more incarcerations have a substance abuse disorder.

  - One third of all U.S. inmates have been diagnosed with a mental health disorder, a rate more than three times that of the general population.

- Chronic and infectious diseases are overrepresented in this population.

  - The prevalence of HIV in federal and state prisons is five to seven times the rate of the general population, and the number of confirmed AIDS cases in prisoners is 2.5 times greater.[c]

  - Up to 25 percent of all individuals with HIV spend some time in a correctional facility, and one in seven HIV-positive Americans passes through a jail or prison each year.[d] Prisons are also one of the few settings in which the prevalence of HIV among women is greater than among men, with studies showing rates among women inmates as high as 12 percent in some states.[e]

  - It is estimated that 40 percent of people with active tuberculosis and 33 percent of individuals infected with hepatitis C cycle through the corrections system each year.[f]

Source: [a] W. J. Sabol, H.C. West, M. Cooper, *Bureau of Justice Statistics Bulletin: Prisoners in 2008* (Washington, DC: U.S. Department of Justice, 2009); [b] 93 The National Center for Addiction and Substance Abuse at Columbia University, *Beyond Bars II: Substance Abuse and America's Prison Population* (New York: National Center for Addiction and Substance Abuse at Columbia University, 2010); [c] 94 A. Spaulding, B. Stephenson, G. Macalino, W. Ruby, J. G. Clarke, T. P. Flanigan, "Human Immunodeficiency Virus in Correctional Facilities: A Review," *Clinical Infectious Disease*, 35, no. 3

(August 2002): 305–12. L. Maruschak, *HIV in Prisons, 2006, Report No.: NCJ-222179* (Washington, DC: U.S. Department of Justice, Bureau of Justice Statistics, 2008); [d] 95 S. Okie, "Sex, Drugs, Prisons, and HIV," *New England Journal of Medicine*, 356 (2007): 105–8; New Mexico AIDS Education and Training Center, *AIDS InfoNet, Fact Sheet 615: HIV in Prisons and Jails* (Arroyo Seco: New Mexico AIDS Education and Training Center, January 2010); A. C. Spaulding, R. M. Seals, M. J. Page, A. K. Brzozowski, W. Rhodes, T. M. Hammett, "HIV/AIDS among Inmates of and Releasees from US Correctional Facilities: Declining Share of Epidemic but Persistent Public Health Opportunity," *Public Library of Science*, 4, no. 11 (2006): e7558; [e] 96 Correctional Association of New York, Women in Prison Project, *Women and HIV/Hepatitis C Fact Sheet* (New York: Women in Prison Project, 2008); [f] 97 T. Hammett, M. Harmon, W. Rhodes, "The Burden of Infectious Disease among Inmates of and Releasees from U.S. Correctional Facilities, 1997," *American Journal of Public Health*, 92, no. 11 (2002): 1789–94.

The vulnerability of the incarcerated population due to the overrepresentation of minority groups, mental illness and infectious disease is exacerbated by prisoners' poor access to substance abuse treatment. One study found that only 24 percent of inmates in need of substance abuse treatment were receiving it, and many former prisoners who reenter the community continue to use drugs.[92] Active IV drug use (IDU) is a significant risk factor for HIV infection and is associated with less access to HAART, higher viral loads and subsequently an increased risk of transmitting HIV to others.[93] Together with the increased risk of homelessness and unemployment on release, formerly incarcerated individuals who are also substance abusers face multiple confounding risk factors for the contraction and progression of HIV. Although some communities have successful programs linking these individuals to healthcare and other social services,[94] such programs have yet to be widely replicated.

Because healthcare is required by law to be provided to all prisoners, the setting of incarceration is an excellent opportunity to screen for and provide care for individuals who may otherwise be unaware of their HIV infection or unable to access HAART or treatment for substance abuse. While poor funding and historically poor healthcare in correctional facilities pose barriers to effectively treating prisoners and protecting the communities to which they return, collaboration between healthcare and legal providers provides opportunities for effective advocacy on individual and institutional levels.

Laws Protecting the Incarcerated

The discretion given to prison officials combined with legal barriers that make it difficult to maintain litigation on behalf of inmates has historically permitted pervasive discrimination against HIV-positive prisoners. For instance, Mississippi segregated prisoners with HIV until 2010.[95] Alabama refused to allow HIV-positive prisoners to participate in work-release programs until 2009.[96] Alabama and South Carolina still segregate HIV-positive prisoners,[97] and Michigan still prevents HIV-positive inmates from working in food-service jobs.[98] There are many state and federal laws, however, designed to protect HIV-positive inmates from discrimination.

Federal Law Governing Testing and Care of Prisoners with HIV

The Eighth Amendment to the U.S. Constitution guarantees that prisoners will be free of "cruel and unusual punishment." The Supreme Court has held that "deliberate indifference" to inmates' "serious medical needs" constitutes cruel and unusual punishment and therefore violates the Eighth Amendment.[99] That does not mean, however, that prisoners are entitled to the highest standards of care or even that their care be free of malpractice. It does require that prisoners have access to care, receive the care that is ordered and have their care supervised by medical professionals.[100] The Department of Justice has the power to investigate allegations of unconstitutional penal conditions and enters into consent decrees that may mandate minimum standards of healthcare.[101]

State Laws Governing Testing and Care of Prisoners with HIV

The CDC recommends that jails and prisons conduct opt-out HIV testing of all new inmates. Although some states (e.g., Florida, Michigan, Mississippi) test all incoming inmates for HIV with or without their consent,[102] the practicalities of paying for testing and care mean that more often states test at the inmate's request or when it seems medically appropriate.[103] Often certain categories of sex offenders are required to be tested. Prisoners may also be tested if they get into an altercation with a correctional officer that poses a threat, however hypothetical, of infection. These laws and practices change frequently as states adopt the CDC recommendations, receive targeted prevention funding or face financial constraints.

Practical Issues Affecting Healthcare Access for Inmates with HIV

People with HIV who are incarcerated are most likely to face treatment interruptions at times of transition: when they are first arrested and booked, when they move from one unit to another within or between institutions and when they are discharged.

The first health screening at booking may not have sufficient privacy for a person to feel free to reveal his or her HIV status (although they should be strongly encouraged to do so). Inmates who disclose their status but do not know the exact names and dosages of all their medications may not be given any medication until the full regimen is established. Inmates who are being moved between police lock-ups, jails and courtrooms on a daily basis may not be given their medication on the theory that partial dosages are more likely to create resistance than a complete drug holiday until a regular schedule can be achieved.

Healthcare providers may receive calls from patients' family members that they are not being given their medications in jail. The most useful response in that situation is for the healthcare provider to contact the medical director or other responsible healthcare provider at the institution with a listing of the patient's current medications and dosages.

Another challenge commonly comes at the time of discharge. Although states are not required to terminate Medicaid benefits when an individual is incarcerated, in practice nearly all states do so, and federal law prohibits states from billing Medicaid for services provided to prisoners. The correctional system, on the other side, has a strong financial incentive to discharge inmates with the fewest possible days of medication. The result is that inmates will be discharged, after serving months or years in prison, with no immediate source of payment for their healthcare and frequently no provider with whom they have any prior relationship. Many states have systems that allow a benefits application to be initiated while someone is still incarcerated, and some providers have set up "continuity of care" clinics where patients are seen in the community by the same healthcare providers who treated them as inmates.[104]

Best Practices and Advocacy Strategies for Medical-Legal Partnership

MLPs can play a crucial role in protecting the rights and improving the health of particularly vulnerable populations affected by HIV/AIDS. Table 13.2 highlights some of the opportunities and special considerations for medical-legal partners who work with incarcerated and homeless individuals with HIV/AIDS.

Table 13.2 Opportunities and Special Considerations for MLPs Who Serve Incarcerated and Homeless Patients with HIV/AIDS

Population	Opportunities for MLP	Special Considerations
Incarcerated individuals	**Limiting treatment interruptions.** Medical providers in the community should encourage all HIV-positive patients, particularly individuals interacting with the justice system, to know the drugs in their treatment regimen. Because lawyers may be the first point of contact for prisoners or family members of prisoners concerned with poor or inadequate medical treatment, they can serve incarcerated individuals by communicating directly with healthcare providers, notifying prisoners of their rights or pursuing appropriate legal recourse. **Discharge and access to public benefits.** Discharge is a critical period for most prisoners and one in which MLP is of particular importance. It is critical that individuals eligible for public benefits on their release be enrolled at discharge, preferably before their release. Doctors can assist lawyers with establishing disability for eligible persons, and lawyers can screen for need and assist with public benefit applications and appeals, as necessary.	**Opt-out testing.** While the CDC recommends that all incoming prisoners undergo opt-out testing for HIV, many facilities test inmates only by request or when medically appropriate. Providers interacting with prisoners need to be aware that testing regulations vary by state and change frequently. **Substance abuse treatment.** The majority of individuals who are repeatedly incarcerated struggle with addiction or substance abuse disorders. Communication between medical and legal providers can facilitate the identification of a prisoner's need for mental health treatment, the possibility of receiving that treatment through alternative sentencing or drug court, and advocacy efforts to enhance mental health treatment in correctional facilities.
Homeless individuals	**Needs assessment and referrals.** Formal or informal needs assessments, distributed in the medical or legal setting, can be a critical tool for identifying unmet medical and legal needs. Communication between medical, legal and social service providers is essential to ensure that necessary referrals are made as needed.	**Sexual risk behavior.** Providers should be aware that patients or clients experiencing homelessness might be less able or willing to alter their sexual risk behaviors if those behaviors are driven by a need for housing, food or money.

From Practice to Policy

A number of states allow "medically needy" individuals to qualify for Medicaid even though their income exceeds eligibility requirements by "spending down" the excess income that makes them ineligible. The spend-down process is incredibly cumbersome, requiring individuals to bring bills and receipts to the state agency administering the Medicaid program, where they must be individually evaluated to determine if they will receive coverage. In the meantime, clients may be pursued by collection agencies or denied healthcare services because they cannot demonstrate Medicaid eligibility. In Illinois, advocates were able to persuade the state to adopt an optional pre-pay spend-down program, which allows individuals to centrally pre-pay their spend-down amount each month, much like an insurance premium, and be assured that they will be declared eligible for Medicaid so that coverage is not denied or interrupted. These provisions may be especially important for people with HIV/AIDS because it prevents interruptions to critical healthcare services while bills and receipts are being evaluated. MLP advocates can seek similar policy changes in their states to help their HIV clients avoid losing Medicaid coverage.

Case for Medical-Legal Partnership

Dominique, a woman who is HIV-positive with a long history of drug-related criminal charges, is picked up on what she calls "a drug deal gone bad." She has officially been charged with armed robbery. Her husband, from whom she contracted HIV, died of AIDS-related causes in 2000. She stopped her HAART eight months ago due to depression and is distressed to find out that in those eight months, her CD4 count has dropped from 750 to 250 and her viral load is no longer undetectable. Dominique is a former heroin addict who states that she was regularly using cocaine prior to her arrest.

Questions for Discussion

1. HAART therapy will likely be reinstated while Dominique is in prison. What other medical interventions would be appropriate at this time?

2. As her release date approaches, what challenges might Dominique encounter as she reenters the community? What needs to be considered to ensure that she can continue to adhere to her medication regimen?

   Medical: How will you counsel Dominique regarding her need to adhere to medication and continue treatment for her mental health conditions?

   Legal: What legal issues might Dominique encounter when she is released? How will you assess her needs?

Children and Adolescents Living with HIV

Transmission of HIV from mother to child has drastically decreased with the widespread availability of HAART in the United States. In 2003, only 59 cases of congenitally acquired HIV were reported to the CDC, and in 2007, children under the age of 13 comprised less than 1 percent of newly diagnosed cases of HIV/AIDS.[105] Children entering the United States from other countries, however, may have significantly higher rates of HIV infection. As discussed shortly, children and adolescents with HIV are at particular risk for mental health conditions and poor medication adherence.

In 2007, 4 percent of all new HIV/AIDS diagnoses occurred in adolescents aged 13 to 19.[106] In a recent survey of high school students nationwide, 34.2 percent of respondents reported being sexually active and nearly 40 percent of these reported not using a condom during their last sexual encounter.[107] Moreover, adolescents with mental health conditions are more likely to engage in sexual risk behaviors and struggle with substance abuse.[108] Mental illness also detrimentally affects the clinical course of HIV once children and adolescents become infected. The presence of a mental illness—estimated to be about 13 percent for children between the ages of 8 and 15[109]—is associated with decreased adherence to HAART and poorer medical and psychosocial outcomes overall.[110]

Independent of mental illness, HAART adherence is a significant issue of concern in adolescents. In one study examining the rate of adherence in a cohort of 114 HIV-positive adolescents, only 28.3 percent reported that they had taken all of their HIV-related medications in the previous month.[111] Poor medication adherence among this age group has been associated with adverse physical and psychological effects of taking the drugs daily, complications and irregularities in day-to-day routine,[112] and more advanced HIV disease.[113] In children, the responsibility for maintaining adherence most often belongs to parents, a fact that sometimes requires legal intervention and necessitates involving the entire family in the treatment planning process. This process can be further complicated by a family's concerns regarding when to disclose to a child that he or she is HIV-positive.[114]

Medication Adherence and Neglect

HAART treatment has greatly improved the quality of life for children and adolescents living with HIV. At the same time, however, it presents great challenges to families and providers because of the need for strict adherence to the medication regimen to avoid the development of resistance. This situation requires an unusually high level of communication and trust between the physician, child or adolescent patient, and family.[115]

On occasion, parents of children or adolescents living with HIV have faced charges of child neglect because of their perceived failure to achieve adherence to the child's medication regimen. (For a detailed discussion of child neglect law, see Chapter 11.) Often, the child welfare system is not well equipped to deal with cases involving perceived medical neglect. In addition, in some cases a neglect report may do more harm than good if the parent is trying but unable to achieve adherence by the child. Problems with medication adherence can result from a variety of factors such as a teenager's refusal to take medication because he or she does not want to be perceived as different from his or her peers or because of depression about the HIV diagnosis, a lapse in health insurance or a parent's work schedule interfering with the ability to oversee medication. In one case (*In re Nicholas E.*), the court found that a parent's refusal to approve HAART therapy for her four-year-old HIV-positive child was reasonable given her concerns about the drugs' side effects and uncertainty about their benefit.[116]

The exception to this is a situation is when a parent or caregiver is simply unable or unwilling to provide adequate parenting because of his or her own problems, such as untreated mental illness or substance abuse. The typical medical neglect case involves the failure or refusal of a parent to authorize a time-limited treatment for a child's medical need, such as surgery or chemotherapy. The central focus in these cases is an evaluation of the risks of the treatment compared to its potential for success.[117] In the case of HIV, mandated treatment must often be administered daily for years. In these cases, the court is faced with the difficult choice of having to place the child with another relative or in foster care to ensure the child receives treatment.

To avoid this difficult circumstance, it is critical that healthcare providers work closely with the family and child over an extended period to make appropriate medical decisions. The provider must consider whether it is essential that a child take antiretroviral drugs or whether treatment can be deferred. Developing an open and trusting relationship takes time and communication difficulties can be compounded by racial, ethnic and class differences. Providers must take time to hear the families' and/or patient's concerns and try to bridge the communication gap. Identifying barriers to adherence is critical and may require assistance from other providers, such as lawyers, social workers and mental health providers. Legal providers can help family members understand the legal issues involved in adherence to treatment and can help identify solutions to existing barriers to adherence, such as helping families access public benefits or addressing employment problems that may be causing family stress.

Disclosure of Medical Status and Confidentiality in Schools

Parents or others caring for a child with HIV are sometimes uncertain about whether the child's health status must be disclosed to his or her school. Ideally children living with HIV should gain support as a result of disclosing their status, but in reality the child may face fear and ostracism, an issue of particular concern among middle and high school students. As discussed next, disclosure is generally unnecessary unless it is needed to protect the welfare of the HIV-positive child, such as when medication must be administered during the school day. There are, however, a small number of states in which public health officials are required to disclose a child's HIV status to the school.[118]

Parents are not required to disclose their child's HIV status to school officials, and most states provide statutory protections against such disclosure. For instance, Vermont law explicitly provides that parents and students "are not required to disclose HIV status to any school personnel" (18 V.S.A. § 112 7(b)) and Wisconsin law makes such disclosure voluntary (Wis. Stat. § 252.15). In certain circumstances, however, a parent may determine that disclosure is necessary to protect his or her child's welfare and, if so, federal and state law requires that such information be kept strictly confidential.

The Family Education Rights and Privacy Act (FERPA), for example, requires federally funded educational institutions to keep all education records confidential (20 U.S.C. 1232g). FERPA defines "education records" as "those records, files, documents, and other materials" that "contain information directly related to a student"; and "are maintained by an educational agency or institution or by a person acting for such agency or institution," which would include any document that refer to a student's HIV status (20 U.S.C. 1232g(4)(B)).

Moreover, all states have laws that protect the confidentiality of private medical information and many have HIV-specific confidentiality laws. For instance, New Hampshire protects against disclosure of one's HIV/AIDS status in virtually every circumstance, stating that "all records and any other information pertaining to a person's testing for the [HIV] virus shall be maintained by the department, health care provider, health or social service agency, organization, business, school, or any other entity . . . as confidential and protected from . . . unwarranted intrusion" (N.H. Rev. Stat. § 141-F: 8).

Accordingly, when it is necessary for parents to disclose a child's HIV status to a school nurse or other school official, parents should be aware that state-specific confidentiality laws as well as federal protections require that all records and information related to their child's medical condition be kept strictly confidential by the school. In this instance, both healthcare and legal providers can play a critical role in informing families of their rights. Additionally, lawyers can assist in the education of school officials and healthcare providers regarding the protection of confidentiality in educational settings.

Questions for Discussion

1. What steps can providers take to provide support to families and children dealing with medication adherence challenges?

2. Does a child living with HIV have any need or obligation to disclose his or her HIV status to school officials?

3. What adverse actions might result from such a disclosure?

The Care and Custody of Children: Planning for the Future

Nearly 30 percent of people currently being treated for HIV infection in the United States have children under the age of 18.[119] This number is expected to increase along with the growing incidence of HIV infection among women of childbearing age.[120] Additionally, HIV-positive parents face unique challenges and stress. HIV-positive mothers may suffer from significant depression and social stigma, in addition to having difficulties performing daily tasks.[121] Forty percent of HIV-positive parents limit hugging, sharing utensils or other casual interactions with their children to minimize the risk of contracting an opportunistic infection or transmitting the virus (although, as previously discussed, HIV itself cannot be transmitted through saliva or casual contact).[122]

In the early years of the HIV epidemic, advocates realized there were many single parents living with HIV/AIDS who were at risk of dying and leaving their children with no caregiver. In addition, many single parents were ill and needed support in caring for their children as long as possible. To meet this need, the tool of *standby guardianship* was enacted by state legislatures in response to advocates in New York, Illinois, Maryland and other states. Standby guardianship enables a parent who is at risk of becoming disabled or dying to appoint a standby guardian who can assist with the care of his or her children. Fortunately, the need for standby guardianship is not as dramatic and widespread as it was in the early years of the epidemic, although it is still a useful planning tool for any parent with a serious health condition that could result in periods of incapacity. Though it does not substitute for the need to execute wills appointing guardian(s) for children in the event of parental death, standby guardianship can provide great peace of mind for parents and clear authority for substitute caregivers when needed.[123] (For further discussion of standby guardianship in the context of cancer, see Chapter 12.)

Third-Party Custody

If both parents are unable to take care of their child, for example, if one parent has died and the other is incarcerated for an extended period, a court may award custody to a third party. In most states, the standard used by courts in determining the placement of a child in the custody of a third party is whether such placement is in the "best interests of the child" (see, for example, Conn. Gen. Stat. Ann. § 46b-57).[124] For this purpose, the court considers such factors as the child's relationship to the person seeking custody, what the parent's wishes may have been and the third party's ability to meet the child's physical and emotional needs (Conn. Gen. Stat. Ann § 46b-56(c)).[125] If one parent has died and the other is unwilling to consent to custody to a third party, in most states the burden will be on the third party to establish that the parent is unfit or that extraordinary circumstances exist that warrant awarding custody. For example, in *Ross v. Hoffman* (280 Md. 172, 188 (1977)), the court found that sufficient extraordinary circumstances existed to place the child with a third party where the third party had already been caring for the child for an extended period.

When assisting a client in filing a guardianship or custody petition, a lawyer gathers evidence supporting a showing that the placement is in the best interest of the child. A pediatrician may be able to offer important support for a custody case, such as documenting that the caretaker has been responsible for bringing the child to appointments over a long period of time and has taken responsibility for the child's healthcare.

School Enrollment

When a family member or other caretaker steps in to care for a child after a parent has died or has become incapacitated by illness or drug use, the family member sometimes has difficulty enrolling the child in school, especially if the new school is in a different jurisdiction. Schools sometimes insist that the family member present a court order showing that he or she has legal custody before a child can be enrolled. This is an issue when the child is moving from a struggling school district to a more prosperous suburban area that is concerned about "school shopping" by families.

This issue has become so prevalent that some states have passed legislation to address it. Maryland, for example, enacted a statute that allows a relative who steps in due to a "serious family hardship"—which includes death, serious illness and incarceration, among other reasons—to sign an affidavit attesting to the family emergency. The affidavit permits the relative to enroll the child in the school system where the relative resides (Md. Code Ann § 20-105 (2009), "Relative Providing Informal Kinship Care to Child").[126]

Healthcare providers, legal providers and social workers who are aware of crises affecting families can provide invaluable assistance by simply informing families of the availability of these tools. Preventive legal assistance or advice is often all that is needed to avert a crisis.

Best Practices and Advocacy Strategies for Medical-Legal Partnership

Because the prognosis for HIV positive people is much better now than in the past due to effective drug therapies, planning for incapacity or end of life often is not viewed as urgent. Nonetheless, planning for the future is still critically important for people living with HIV/AIDS and their families. The details of estate planning, advance directives and guardianship are discussed further in Chapters 12 and 14. Here we discuss the particular concerns of people living with HIV/AIDS and ways in which MLPs can help to engage patient-clients in planning for the future.

- *Protecting unmarried partners.* State surrogate decision-making laws generally provide a statutory list of individuals who are authorized to make end-of-life decisions in the absence of a guardian or designated agent under a durable power of attorney. Any individual who, in the case of incapacitation or end of life, seeks to have their healthcare decisions made by someone other than a legal family member must be certain to designate an agent under a durable power of attorney for healthcare. Documenting end-of-life wishes is of particular importance among HIV-positive gay people with unmarried partners. Without proper documentation of power of attorney for healthcare, healthcare providers are legally bound to honor the requests of family members. As unmarried partners are not considered legally to be family, documentation is necessary to ensure that power of attorney for healthcare is granted to the partner. Similarly, if a patient owns a home that he or she wishes to pass on to an unmarried partner, it is essential that he or she obtain legal advice to review the ways that this can be accomplished.

- *Protecting minor children.* Every parent, regardless of HIV status, should have a will designating a guardian for children in the event of their death. Even when family members are in agreement about whom the guardian should be and no objections are anticipated, a will naming the guardian prevents future problems with enforcing the parent's wishes.

- *Ensuring that funeral wishes will be carried out.* Because of the stigma and discrimination associated with sexual orientation, drug use and HIV, a significant number of individuals with HIV are estranged from their family of origin. At the time of death, the family may want certain religious rites to be carried out or may want the person buried in a family plot in a hometown cemetery. They may also exclude partners or close friends from speaking at the funeral or attending. State laws may prohibit cremation over the objections of close family unless the individual has recorded his or her preference for cremation in ways that comport with state law. For all these reasons, people with HIV who have particular wishes regarding their funeral or the disposition of their remains must be sure to have those arrangements properly documented. Even for individuals who are not estranged from their family but who may have specific wishes that conflict with those of family members, documentation is necessary to ensure that funeral wishes will be carried out.

Medical-legal partners should work together to ensure that patients with HIV/AIDS plan for temporary incapacity and end of life in order to protect loved ones from undue emotional and financial burden. Healthcare providers can identify patients who may benefit from legal assistance in documenting their wishes. Physicians are particularly well positioned to identify situations in which mental incapacity or physical disability of a parent is likely, and to work with a patient to ensure that they prioritize consideration of guardianship decisions. Legal partners can then work with patients to articulate and document their wishes, including the following:

- Durable power of attorney for healthcare
- Advance directives
- A will documenting guardianship for children
- Funeral wishes
- Disposition of remains

From Practice to Policy

As discussed earlier in the chapter, in the early years of the HIV epidemic, healthcare providers caring for children with HIV or for their single mothers who were ill with AIDS were often faced with the question of who would be helping these patients care for their young children. These parents were understandably reluctant to relinquish custody while they were still able to be a part of their children's lives. The idea of standby guardianship grew out of this need to have an alternative caregiver and decision maker when the parent was medically unable to care for a child. Attorneys working with these healthcare providers were instrumental in developing this modification of the law that is now available to a parent facing a potentially disabling and/or terminal illness. The advantage of standby guardianship is that the parent can remain involved and in charge as long as possible, and the child has a standby guardian in place whenever needed. Standby guardianship also helped avoid the unnecessary placement of children in foster care. First in New York, and later in Maryland and other states, advocates came together to lobby for appropriate legislation at the state level.

Case for Medical-Legal Partnership

A 19-year-old perinatally infected patient with HIV has been caring for her 1-year-old son since his birth. The mother has not received healthcare for about a year and is not on HIV medication. She becomes very ill, is hospitalized and is in and out of consciousness during hospitalization. Her doctor is concerned that she will need help with her son when and if she is discharged.

Six months ago, the patient broke up with her boyfriend, the child's father, who since has visited his son only once. He has a new girlfriend, a part-time job, and is not paying child support. The doctor is aware that the patient was living with a friend who helped her with her son prior to hospitalization, and this friend has visited the patient during her stay at the hospital. The patient states that she would like for this friend to take care of her son if she is unable to do so.

Questions for Discussion

1. How can this patient make a plan for her son? Is there any reason to be in contact with her son's father?

2. Will standby guardianship work in this situation?

3. Are there any other documents the patient may wish to consider signing at this time?

4. What is the role of the healthcare provider in helping this patient? What is the role of a legal provider?

Conclusion

As this chapter has highlighted, the social implications and confounding factors contributing to poor health outcomes in people with HIV create an urgent need for effective MLP. Whether advocating for employment rights, serving the incarcerated population or documenting end-of-life care for families, healthcare and legal providers are uniquely positioned to improve health outcomes and the general well-being of those infected with and affected by HIV.

The best practices presented here demonstrate that clear and effective communication—essential to any MLP—is of critical importance in the context of HIV. In many cases, providers need simply to inquire about unmet legal needs or the social context of an individual's disease or current crisis. In all cases, an understanding of the protections and limitations of the law, in addition to the biological implications of unmet legal needs, enables healthcare and legal providers to provide holistic, comprehensive care for the HIV-positive community.

---

1. J. M. Mann, et al., *Health and Human Rights: A Reader* (New York: Routledge, 1999), 17.

2. Ibid.

3. HIV & AIDS Legal Services Alliance, "History," http://www.halsaservices.org/history.php (accessed January 7, 2011).

4. D. Schulman, et al., "Public Health Legal Services: A New Vision," *Georgetown Journal on Poverty Law & Policy*, 729, no. 15 (2008): 750–57.

5. Ibid.

6. E. Lawton, "Medical-Legal Partnerships: From Surgery to Prevention?" *Management Information Exchange Journal* (Spring 2007): 1–7.

7. T. Barnett, A. Whiteside, *AIDS in the Twenty-First Century: Disease and Globalization,* 2nd ed. (New York: Palgrave Macmillan, 2006), 30–31.

8. Centers for Disease Control and Prevention, "HIV and AIDS in the United States," CDC July 2010, http://www.cdc.gov/hiv/resources/factsheets/us.htm (accessed November 26, 2010).

9. Ibid.

10. Joint United Nations Programme on HIV/AIDS and World Health Organization, "AIDS Epidemic Update 2009," http://data.unaids.org:80/pub/Report/2009/JC1700_Epi_Update_2009_en.pdf (accessed January 7, 2011).

11. Ibid.

12. W. M. El-Sadr, K. H. Mayer, and S. L. Hodder, "Aids in America—Forgotten but Not Gone," *New England Journal of Medicine,* 362, no. 11 (2010): 967–70.

13. Barnett and Whiteside, *AIDS in the Twenty-First Century.*

14. Canadian Center for Occupational Health and Safety, "Needlestick Injuries," http://www.ccohs.ca/oshanswers/diseases/needlestick_injuries.html (accessed October 13, 2010).

15. Centers for Disease Control and Prevention, "Universal Precautions for Prevention of Transmission of HIV and Other Bloodborne Infections," http://www.cdc.gov/ncidod/dhqp/bp_universal_precautions.html (accessed October 13, 2010). "Universal precautions involve the use of protective barriers such as gloves, gowns, aprons, masks, or protective eyewear, which can reduce the risk of exposure of the health care worker's skin or mucous membranes to potentially infective materials."

16. Centers for Disease Control and Prevention, *HIV/AIDS Surveillance Report,* 2007, 15, no. 1 (Washington, DC: U.S. Department of Health and Human Services, 2009), 1–63.

17. A. S. Fauci, H. Clifford Lane, "Chapter 90, Human Immunodeficiency Virus Disease: AIDS and Related Disorders," in *Harrison's Principles of Internal Medicine,* 17th ed., eds. Dennis L. Kasper, Anthony S. Fauci (Berkshire: McGraw-Hill, 2004).

18. A. S. Sturt, E. K. Dokubo, T. T. Sint, "Antiretroviral Therapy (Art) for Treating HIV Infection in Art-Eligible Pregnant Women," *Cochrane Library,* 3 (2010).

19. Ibid.

20. European Collaborative Study, "Maternal to Child Transmission of HIV Infection in the Era of Highly Active Antiretroviral Therapy," *Clinical Infectious Disease,* 40, no. 3 (2005): 458–65; K. Luzuriaga, J. L. Sullivan, "Prevention of Mother to Child Transmission of HIV Infection," *Clinical Infectious Disease,* 40, no. 3 (2005): 466–67.

21. Fred Wang, Elliott Kieff, "Chapter 170, Medical Virology," in *Harrison's Principles of Internal Medicine,* 17th ed., eds. Dennis L. Kasper, Anthony S. Fauci (Berkshire: McGraw-Hill, 2004).

22. L. Sompayrac, *How the Immune System Works,* 3rd ed., (Malden: Blackwell, 2008), 8.

23. Barnett and Whiteside, *AIDS in the Twenty-First Century,* 34.

24. Additional information regarding AIDS-defining illness can be found at http://www.cdc.gov/mmwr/preview/mmwrhtml/00018871.htm (accessed January 8, 2011).

25. A.S. Fauci, H.C. Lane, "Chapter 182: Human Immunodeficiency Virus Disease: AIDS and Related Disorders," in *Harrison's Principles of Internal Medicine,* eds. A.S. Fauci, E. Braunwald, D. L. Kasper, S. L. Hauser, D. L. Longo, J. L. Jameson, J. Loscalzo, 17 e (New York: McGraw Hill, 2008).

26. T.W. Mahungu, A. J. Rodger, and M. A. Johnson, "HIV as a Chronic Disease," *Clinical Medicine* 9, no. 2 (2009): 125–8.

27. F. Clavel, A. J. Hance, "HIV Drug Resistance." *New England Journal of Medicine,* 350, no. 10 (2004): 1023–35.

28. http://journals.lww.com/aidsonline/Abstract/2001/02160/Sexual_risk_behaviour_relates_to_the_virological.; Nicole H. T. M. Dukers, et al., "Sexual Risk Behaviour Relates to the Virological and Immunological Improvements during Highly Active Antiretroviral Therapy in HIV-1 Infection," *AIDS,* 15, no. 3 (2001): 369–78.

29. Barnett and Whiteside, *AIDS in the Twenty-First Century,* 36.

30. N. M. Zacharias, I. D. Athanassaki, H. Sangi-Haghpeykar, M. O. Gardner, "High False-Positive Rate of Human Immunodeficiency Virus Rapid Serum Screening in a Predominantly Hispanic Prenatal Population," *Journal of Perinatology*, 24, no. 12 (2004): 743–47.

31. J. L. Greenwald, G. R. Burstein, J. Pincus, B. Branson. "A Rapid Review of Rapid HIV Antibody Tests." *Current Infectious Disease Reports*, 8, no. 2 (2006): 125–31.

32. Centers for Disease Control and Prevention, "Recommendations and Guidelines," http://www.cdc.gov/hiv/resources/guidelines/index.htm (accessed July 10, 2010).

33. Centers for Disease Control and Prevention, "Revised Recommendations for HIV Testing of Adults, Adolescents, and Pregnant Women in Health-Care Settings," *Morbidity and Mortalilty Weekly Report*, 55 (September 22, 2006): 1–17.

34. Greenwald et al., "A Rapid Review of Rapid HIV Antibody Tests."

35. Office of the United Nations High Commissioner for Human Rights and the Joint United Nations Programme on HIV/AIDS, "International Guidelines on HIV and Human Rights: 2006 Consolidated Version" (Geneva: UNAIDS 2006), http://data.unaids.org/Publications/IRC-pub07/jc1252-internguidelines_en.pdf (accessed January 7, 2011); J. Ogden, L. Nyblade, *Common at its Core, HIV-Related Stigma across Contexts* (Washington: National Center for Research on Women, 2005).

36. Lambda Legal HIV Project, "The State of HIV Stigma and Discrimination in 2007: An Evidence-Based Report," http://data.lambdalegal.org/pdf/stigmahiv.pdf (accessed January 7, 2011).

37. Ibid, 3.

38. Prior versions of the CDC testing guidelines recognized the importance of the partnership by recommending that individuals who were newly diagnosed be referred to legal services. Centers for Disease Control and Prevention, "Revised Guidelines for HIV Counseling, Testing, and Referral" *Morbidity and Mortality Weekly Report*, 50 (November 9, 2001): 1–58. ("Clients who test positive should be referred to legal services as soon as possible after learning their test result for counseling on how to prevent discrimination in employment, housing, and public accommodation by only disclosing their status to those who have a legal need to know.")

39. U.S. Department of Health and Human Services Office for Civil Rights, "HIPAA Administrative Simplification: Regulation Text," 45 CFR Parts 160, 162 and 164, http://www.hhs.gov/ocr/privacy/hipaa/administrative/privacyrule/adminsimpregtext.pdf (accessed January 7, 2011).

40. L. O. Gostin, "Legislative Survey of State Confidentiality Laws, with Specific Emphasis on HIV and Immunization," Electronic Privacy Information Center, 1996, http://epic.org/privacy/medical/cdc_survey.html (accessed January 8, 2011).

41. 410 Ill. Comp. Stat. Ann. 305/9 (West 2009); 410 Ill. Comp. Stat. Ann. 305/13 (West 2008).

42. New York State Department of Health, "HIV Reporting and Partner Notification Questions and Answers," http://www.health.state.ny.us/diseases/aids/regulations/reporting_and_notification/question_answer.htm#fiftyfive (accessed January 8, 2011).

43. 410 Ill. Comp. Stat. Ann. 305/9 (West 2009); 410 Ill. Comp. Stat. Ann. 335/10 (West 2008).

44. Lambda Legal HIV Project, "HIV Criminalization: State Laws Criminalizing Conduct Based on HIV Status," http://www.lambdalegal.org/our-work/publications/general/state-criminal-statutes-hiv.html (accessed January 8, 2011).

45. The National HIV/AIDS Clinicians Center maintains a useful Compendium of State HIV Testing Laws, which can be found at http://www.nccc.ucsf.edu/consultation_library/state_hiv_testing_laws (accessed January 8, 2011).

46. EEOC Interpretive Manual §902.4(c)(1), 902–12, cited in *Bragdon v. Abbott*, 524 U.S. 624, 647 (1998).

47. *Bragdon v. Abbott*, 524 U.S. 624, 647 (1998); Bennett H. Klein, et al., "Questions and Answers about the Supreme Court Decision in *Bragdon v. Abbott*," Gay & Lesbian Advocates & Defenders (Boston: GLAD), 3, http://www.glad.org/uploads/docs/publications/bragdon-abbott-qa.pdf (accessed January 8, 2011).

48. Klein et al., "Questions and Answers about the Supreme Court Decision in *Bragdon v. Abbott*."

49. *Bragdon*, 524 U.S. at 639–40.

50. ADA Amendments Act of 2008, Pub. L. No. 110-325, §3406 (2008).

51. AIDS Legal Council of Chicago, *HIV in the Workplace* (Chicago: AIDS Legal Council of Chicago, 2006), 4.

52. Ibid., 5.

53. GLAD, *HIV in the Workplace*, 5.

54. 42 U.S.C. § 12112(d)(3); GLAD, *HIV in the Workplace*.

55. GLAD, *HIV in the Workplace*.

56. 42 U.S.C. § 12112. The employer does not have to provide reasonable accommodation if it causes the employer an "undue hardship"; GLAD, *HIV in the Workplace*, 4.

57. GLAD, *HIV in the Workplace*.

58. Ibid.

59. Ibid.

60. Ibid.

61. 29 C.F.R. § 825.115(a)(2) (2009); 29 U.S.C. § 2612 (2009).

62. World Health Organization, eds., Erik Blas, Anand Sivasankara Kurup, *Equality, Social Determinants and Public Health Programmes* (Switzerland: World Health Organization, 2010).

63. P. E. Farmer, B. Nizeye, S. Stulac, S. Keshavjee, "Structural Violence and Clinical Medicine," *Public Library of Science Medicine*, 3, no. 10 (2006): e449.

64. S. Gillespie, S. Kadiyala, R. Greener, "Is Poverty or Wealth Driving HIV Transmission?" *AIDS*, 21, Suppl 7 (2007): S5–S16.

65. Centers for Disease Control and Prevention, "New CDC Analysis Reveals Strong Link Between Poverty and HIV Infection," http://www.cdc.gov/nchhstp/newsroom/povertyandhivpressrelease.html (accessed January 10, 2011).

66. Ibid.

67. CDC, *HIV/AIDS Surveillance Report*.

68. Ibid.

69. M. D. Wong, M. F. Shapiro, W. J. Boscardin, S. L. Ettner, "Contribution of Major Diseases to Disparities in Mortality," *New England Journal of Medicine*, 347, no. 20 (2002): 1585–92.

70. B. J. Turner, W. E. Cunningham, N. Duan, et al., "Delayed Medical Care after Diagnosis in a US National Probability Sample of Persons Infected with Human Immunodeficiency Virus," *Archives of Internal Medicine*, 160, no. 17 (2000): 2614–22; M. F. Shapiro, S. C. Morton, D. F. McCaffrey, et al. "Variations in the Care of HIV-Infected Adults in the United States: Results from the HIV Cost and Services Utilization Study," *Journal of the American Medical Association*, 281, no. 24 (1999): 2305–15.

71. Shapiro et al., "Variations in Care."

72. Some providers have raised concerns regarding men who have sex with men and women but who choose not to disclose their homosexual practices or other risk factors, such as IV drug use, to their female partners. Although there are conflicting data suggesting the extent to which these factors have contributed to the epidemic of HIV infection among African American women, these are certainly a concern and likely contributory.

73. U.S. Citizenship and Immigration Services, "Human Immunodeficiency Virus (HIV) Infection Removed from CDC List of Communicable Diseases of Public Health Significance," http://www.uscis.gov/portal/site/uscis/menuitem.5af9bb95919f35e66f614176543f6d1a/?vgnextoid=1a05cc5222ff5210VgnVCM100000082ca60aRCRD&vgnextchannel=68439c7755cb9010VgnVCM10000045f3d6a1RCRD.

74. H. B. Krentz, J. Gill, "Monitoring and Adjusting for Future Needs in Response to Changing HIV Policies," *Lancet Infectious Diseases*, 10, no. 10 (October 2010): 671–72.

75. These and all other data about state Medicaid programs comes from the Kaiser Family Foundation online database of Medicaid benefits, http://medicaidbenefits.kff.org/index.jsp (accessed January 8, 2011). Texas Department of State Health Services, "Texas HIV Medication Program: Frequently Asked Questions (FAQ)," http://www.dshs.state.tx.us/hivstd/meds/faq.shtm (accessed January 8, 2011).

76. Social Security Administration, Pub. No. 64-039, *BlueBook: Disability Evaluation Under Social Security. 14.00 Immune System Disorders—Adult* (Washington, DC: Social Security Administration, 2008).

77. 42 U.S.C.A § 423(2)(C); 20 C.F.R. § 404.1535.

78. Ironically, years ago, applicants for benefits could qualify as disabled because of their drug addiction/severe alcoholism. Social Security Administration, *Program Operations Manual System, Part 4, sections DI 2155-2155.35 and DI 00405.001ff,* http://www.ssa.gov/OP_Home/rulings/di/01/SSR82-60-di-01.html.

79. L. Yamamoto, "A Primer on Social Security Disability Insurance Law," *New Jersey Lawyer Magazine,* no. 256 (February 2009): 41–47.

80. National Coalition for the Homeless, *HIV/AIDS and Homelessness, NCH Fact Sheet #9* (Washington, DC: National Coalition for the Homeless, 2007).

81. H. L. Surratt, J. A. Inciardi, "HIV Risk, Seropositivity and Predictors of Infection among Homeless and Non-Homeless Women Sex Workers in Miami, Florida, USA," *AIDS Care,* 16, no. 5 (2004): 594–604.

82. Ibid.

83. T. T. Stephens, et al., "Homelessness and Hunger as HIV Risk Factors for African American Male Commercial Sex Workers," *Journal of African American Men,* 5, no. 1 (2000): 3–8.

84. S. D. Weiser, D. R. Bangsberg, S. Kegeles, K. Ragland, M. B. Kushel, E. A. Frongillo. "Food Insecurity among Homeless and Marginally Housed Individuals Living with HIV/Aids in San Francisco," *AIDS Behavior,* 13, no. 5 (2009): 841–48; A. Anema, N. Vogenthaler, E. A. Frongillo, S. Kadiyala, S. D. Weiser. "Food Insecurity and HIV/Aids: Current Knowledge, Gaps, and Research Priorities," *Current HIV/AIDS Reports,* 6, no. 4 (2009): 224–31.

85. "HIV/AIDS Housing, Housing and Urban Development," http://www.hud.gov/offices/cpd/aidshousing/ (accessed January 8, 2011).

86. John Song, *HIV/AIDS & Homelessness. Recommendations for Clinical Practice and Public Policy* (Nashville, TN: National Health Care for the Homeless Council, 1999); Housing and Urban Development, "HIV/AIDS Housing," http://www.hud.gov/offices/cpd/aidshousing/.

87. Ibid., n. 124.

88. Ibid.

89. Ibid.

90. 42 U.S.C. 3601. The Fair Housing Act exempts, in some circumstances, ownership-occupied buildings with no more than four units, single-family housing sold or rented without the use of a broker, and housing operated by organizations and private clubs that limit occupancy to members. 42 U.S.C. 3603, 3607; "Overview of Legal Issues for People with HIV" at 15, http://www.glad.org/uploads/docs/publications/ma-hiv-overview.pdf.

91. W. J. Sabol, H.C. West, M. Cooper, *Bureau of Justice Statistics Bulletin: Prisoners in 2008* (Washington, DC: U.S. Department of Justice, 2009).

92. S. Belenko, J. Peugh, "Estimating Drug Treatment Needs among State Prison Inmates," *Drug and Alcohol Dependence,* 77, no. 3 (March 2005): 269–81.

93. G. M. Lucas, L. W. Cheever, R. E. Chaisson, R. D. Moore, "Detrimental Effects of Continued Illicit Drug Use on the Treatment of HIV-1 Infection," *Journal of Acquired Immune Deficiency Syndrome,* 27, no. 3 (2001): 251–59.

94. Health & Disability Working Group, Boston University School of Public Health, "Case Study: Project Bridge," http://www.bu.edu/hdwg/pdf/projects/trainingfiles/ProjectBridge.pdf (accessed January 8, 2011).

95. American Civil Liberties Union, "Mississippi Stops Segregating Prisoners with HIV," March 17, 2010, http://www.aclu.org/prisoners-rights/mississippi-stops-segregating-prisoners-hiv (accessed January 8, 2011).

96. American Civil Liberties Union, "Alabama Department of Corrections Ends Ban of Prisoners from Work Release," August 13, 2009, http://www.aclu.org/hiv-aids_prisoners-rights/alabama-department-corrections-ends-ban-prisoners-hiv-work-release (accessed January 8, 2011).

97. N. Phillips, "S.C. Defends HIV Policy for Inmates," *State*, April 25, 2010, http://www.thestate.com/2010/04/15/1244440/sc-defends-hiv-policy-for-inmates.html (accessed January 8, 2011).

98. T. Heywood, "Department of Civil Rights: State's Ban on HIV Positive Inmates Working in Prison Food Service Violates Law," *Michigan Messenger*, April 24, 2009, http://michiganmessenger.com/17602/dept-of-civil-rights-states-ban-on-hiv-positive-inmates-working-in-prison-food-service-violates-law (accessed January 8, 2011).

99. *Estelle v. Gamble*, 429 U.S. 97, 103-04, 97 S.Ct. 285, 290–91 (1976).

100. W. J. Rold, "Thirty Years after *Estelle v. Gamble*: A Retrospective," *Journal of Correctional Health Care*, 14, no. 1 (2008): 11–20.

101. *United States of America vs. Cook County, Illinois et al., Ill.* Civil No. 10 C 2946, May 13, 2010, http://www.justice.gov/crt/split/documents/CookCountyJail_AgreedOrder_05-13-2010.pdf (accessed January 8, 2011).

102. M. Babineck,"HIV Testing of Inmates Clears Legal Hurdle," *Houston Chronicle*, February 1, 2007.

103. All data in this paragraph from the National HIV/AIDS Clinicians Center Compendium of State HIV Testing Laws, http://www.nccc.ucsf.edu/consultation_library/state_hiv_testing_laws. The Department of Justice Bureau of Justice Statistics also has a 2006 chart of state laws related to prisoner testing at http://bjs.ojp.usdoj.gov/content/pub/html/hivp/2006/tables/hivp06t10.cfm.

104. The Ruth M. Rothstein CORE Center in Chicago has a weekly continuity clinic staffed by the same healthcare providers who provide infectious disease services at the Cermak Health Care facility serving Cook County Jail. See http://www.corecenter.org/medical.html (accessed January 8, 2011).

105. CDC, *HIV/AIDS Surveillance Report*.

106. Ibid.

107. D. K. Eaton, L. Kann, S. Kinchen, et al., and Centers for Disease Control and Prevention, "Youth Risk Behavior Surveillance—United States, 2009," *MMWR Surveillance Summary*, 59, no. 5 (2010): 1–142.

108. J. G. Tubman, A. G. Gil, E. F. Wagner, H. Artigues, "Patterns of Sexual Risk Behaviors and Psychiatric Disorders in a Community Sample of Young Adults." *Journal of Behavioral Medicine*, 26, no. 5 (2003): 473–500. L. K. Brown, M. B. Danovsky, K. J. Lourie, R. J. DiClemente, L. E. Ponton, "Adolescents with Psychiatric Disorders and the Risk of HIV," *Journal of American Academy of Child Adolescent Psychiatry*, 36, no. 11 (1997): 1609–17.

109. National Institute of Mental Health, "Child and Adolescent Mental Health," http://www.nimh.nih.gov/health/topics/child-and-adolescent-mental-health/index.shtml (accessed June 15, 2010).

110. D. A. Murphy, M. Belzer, S. J. Durako, et al., and Adolescent Medicine HIV/AIDS Research Network, "Longitudinal Antiretroviral Adherence among Adolescents Infected with Human Immunodeficiency Virus," *Archives of Pediatric Adolescent Medicine*, 159, no. 8 (2005): 764–70.

111. D. A. Murphy, M. Sarr, S. J. Durako, et al., and Adolescent Medicine HIV/AIDS Research Network, "Barriers to HAART Adherence among Human Immunodeficiency Virus-Infected Adolescents," *Archives of Pediatric Adolescent Medicine*, 157, no. 3 (2003): 249–55.

112. Ibid.

113. Ibid., n. 159.

114. Committee on Pediatric AIDS, "Disclosure of Illness Status to Children and Adolescents with HIV Infection," *Pediatrics*, 103 (1999): 164–66. Although many parents have historically been reluctant to inform children of the fact that they are HIV-positive, the American Academy of Pediatrics notes that disclosing a child's HIV-positive status early in life, before he or she is even considering being sexually active, results in both increased self-esteem for the child and decreased depression for the parent.

115. D. J. Weimer, "Medical Treatment of Children with HIV Illness and the Need for Supportive Intervention: The Challenges for Medical Providers, Families, and the State," *Juvenile and Family Court Journal,* 54, no. 1 (2003): 1–16.

116. *In Re: Nicholas E.,* 720 A. 2d 562 (Maine Sup. Ct. 1998). "It is the obligation of the petitioning Department in this matter to prove by a preponderance of the evidence that [the mother's] deprivation of reasonable and effective health care for her son by now refusing to enter him into HIV/AIDS aggressive drug therapy constitutes an imminent threat of serious harm. The Department has proven that according to the current conventional medical wisdom in the relatively new and rapidly evolving art of treating children with certain elevated levels of HIV in the blood, that Nikolas would benefit from such treatment. However, it has not sufficiently prove [sic] what that benefit will likely be and that no significant injury or harm may ultimately befall the child if that therapy is now commenced.... With the relative uncertainty of the efficacy of the proposed treatment, it can only reasonably be left up to the parent to make an informed choice in this regard" (emphasis added).

117. 393 N.E. 2d 1009 (1979), "Matter of Hofbauer"; 379 N.E. 1053 (1978), "Custody of a Minor"; *Newmark v. Williams,* 588 A.2d 1108 (1991).

118. These include Illinois and South Carolina; S.C. Code Ann. § 44-29-135(e); Ill. Comp. Stat. 410 § 315/2a.

119. M. A. Schuster, D. E. Kanouse, S. C. Morton, et al., "HIV-Infected Parents and Their Children in the United States," *American Journal Public Health,* 90, no. 7 (2000): 1074–81.

120. M. A. Schuster, M. K. Beckett, R. Corona, A. J. Zhou, "Hugs and Kisses: HIV-Infected Parents' Fears about Contagion and the Effects on Parent-Child Interaction in a Nationally Representative Sample," *Archives of Pediatric Adolescent Medicine,* 159, no. 2 (2005): 173–79.

121. D. A. Murphy, W. D. Marelich, M. E. Dello Stritto, D. Swendeman, and A. Witkin, "Mothers Living with HIV/Aids: Mental, Physical, and Family Functioning," *AIDS Care,* 14, no. 5 (2002): 633–44.

122. Ibid., n. 174.

123. D. Weimer, "Implementation of Standby Guardianship: Respect for Family Autonomy," Dickinson Law Review, 100, no. 1 (1995): 65–102.

124. See, for example, Conn. Gen. Stat. Ann. § 46b-57.

125. Conn. Gen. Stat. Ann § 46b-56(c).

126. Md. Code Ann § 20-105 (2009), "Relative Providing Informal Kinship Care to Child."

Chapter 14

Elders and Their Caregivers

Eric J. Hardt, MD
Kate Mewhinney, JD

Older adults face an increasingly complex set of medical challenges as they age. In older persons, disease is more common, and illness often less well tolerated. The biological behavior of a disease may be different among older patients. Some diseases, like hip fracture and dementia, are far more prevalent among the elderly. Other conditions have atypical presentations in older adults and may lead to delayed diagnosis.[1] The impact of multiple interacting diseases can complicate a prognosis; multiple diseases also lead to numerous medications that may produce a burden of cost, toxicity and confusion. With the emergence of cognitive impairment, diagnostic and therapeutic decisions often become extremely subjective and complex. As elderly patients encounter multiple consultants and providers in different sites of care and residence, a consistent source of good primary care may be difficult to maintain. The best management plans are often made by those healthcare providers with knowledge of the relevant literature, longitudinal familiarity with the patient, and experience in making such judgments. Medical decision making should factor many elements into a cost-benefit estimate that makes sense from the patient's point of view.

Older adults also face numerous, often unmet legal needs. Some of the most common legal issues among older adults have an obvious connection to the medical world, such as Medicare and Medicaid rules, long-term care coverage, planning for medical and financial decision making and laws related to elder abuse. Others have important but perhaps more subtle impacts on health, such as laws related to housing subsidies and legal protections for debtors. Decisions solely based on either the legal or medical dimensions of a question are unlikely to result in the best outcomes for patients and families.

By partnering with lawyers who specialize in serving older clients, a healthcare team can better help elderly patients achieve their goals of independence and safety. Healthcare providers are in an excellent position to screen for legal vulnerabilities that could compromise future care; through MLP they have the opportunity to become better advocates for their patients.[2] Elder law practitioners can benefit from these partnerships by direct access to the patient's medical team and thus a better understanding of the patients' medical needs and concerns. Of course, caring for older people often requires the collaboration of many types of professionals, beyond lawyers and physicians. The goals of older people can best be achieved with an interdisciplinary approach. This collaboration is sketched out in Figure 14.1.

Before we proceed, it is important to note some particular complexities that arise when linking the medical and legal professions on behalf of elderly patients. First, this chapter addresses medical and legal concerns of older patients. It does not cover the legal rights of an older patient's family. Secondly, even when partnering on behalf of a patient, there may be times when a medical provider and a patient's legal adviser view a situation differently. For example, the lawyer may be less likely to take into consideration the views

Figure 14.1 Elder Law Paradigm

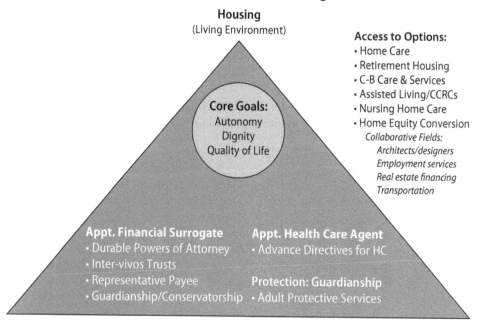

Housing
(Living Environment)

Core Goals:
Autonomy
Dignity
Quality of Life

Access to Options:
• Home Care
• Retirement Housing
• C-B Care & Services
• Assisted Living/CCRCs
• Nursing Home Care
• Home Equity Conversion
  Collaborative Fields:
  Architects/designers
  Employment services
  Real estate financing
  Transportation

Appt. Financial Surrogate
• Durable Powers of Attorney
• Inter-vivos Trusts
• Representative Payee
• Guardianship/Conservatorship

Appt. Health Care Agent
• Advance Directives for HC

Protection: Guardianship
• Adult Protective Services

Financial Well-Being
ADEA/Employment Issues
Pension & Other Retirement Benefits
Public Benefits:
• Social Security/Pensions
• Medicare & Medicare Rx Benefit
• Medicaid Planning
• Veterans Benefits, etc.

Special Needs Planning
Home Equity Conversion
Estate Planning:
• Wills & Trusts
• Property Transfers
• Medicaid Planning
• Special Needs Trusts
  Collaborative Fields:
  Healthcare
  Social work
  Gerontology
  Insurance
  Government administration

Health & Long Term Care
Private Benefits:
• Employer-based insurance
• Long-term care insurance

Public Benefits:
• Medicare
• Medigap
• Medicaid
• Veterans
  Collaborative Fields:
  Healthcare
  Social work
  Gerontology
  Insurance
  Government administration

Source: Charles P. Sabatino, "Elder Law: A Perspective on the Present and Future," *Experience Magazine,* 20, no. 1 (Winter 2009): 29.

of the older patient's family than a physician might. There are two main reasons lawyers generally "choose a side": first, decisions made under family pressure can sometimes be reversed by a court; second, professional ethical rules for lawyers are different from those for physicians and other healthcare providers. A lawyer can advise an older client to consider the family's input but ultimately owes a duty of loyalty only to the client.[3] (For further discussion of a lawyer's duty to the client under professional ethical rules, see Chapter 6.) With this framework in mind, we can now address the common medical and legal issues of older patients.

Healthcare for the Elderly Patient

Effects of Prognosis and Life Expectancy on Disease Management

The health status of older individuals depends more on the presence of disease than on chronological age. This may not be appreciated by patients, families and medical providers. For example, some might feel that a patient is "too old to have surgery." Research suggests that reasonably healthy elderly patients may have excellent surgical outcomes; age alone should not disqualify someone from potentially curative surgery or other treatment.[4] Such decisions may require a subtle assessment of the duration and quality of life of the individual.

Different Approaches to Disease Based on Age

Some diseases are approached very differently based on age of the patient. For example, prostate cancer is a leading cause of cancer deaths in American men; men over age 50 are often screened for this disease. Most patients with early disease are offered potentially curative surgery or radiation. On the other hand, screening for early cancer beyond age 75 does not appear to increase survival. This may relate to the biological nature of the disease or the reduced life expectancy at this age.[5]

Multiple Medical Problems in Elderly Patients

Elderly patients are more likely to have several active medical problems at the same time. These may interact and produce competing sources of morbidity and mortality. For some diseases, treatment may depend less on age than on the effects and risks of other problems. For example, surgical treatment of lung cancer might be considered too risky for a patient with severe emphysema. In such a case, decision making is relatively easy. In other cases, multiple conditions prompt evaluations by specialists requiring complex analysis. Often the geriatrician or another primary care provider familiar with the patient is in the best position to weigh all opinions and propose a treatment plan to the patient and family.

Quality of Life

With increases in age and disease burden, the goals of the patient often shift from life extension toward quality of life. Issues may include symptom management, limitation of out-of-pocket expenses, avoidance of institutionalization and matters of convenience and familiarity. For patients who are aware that they are approaching end of life, top priorities include:

- Avoiding "inappropriate" prolongation of life,
- Maintaining a sense of control over decision making,
- Relieving burdens from loved ones, and
- Strengthening relationships with loved ones.[6]

With extremes of age and illness, the focus of the patient may be more personal. More attention may be given to matters of family and other relationships, religion and spirituality, legacy and remembrance, and existential questions. These issues may be difficult for patients to discuss in a highly medicalized context; help from psychotherapists, social workers and pastoral counselors may be advisable. Patients may value most quality time spent with family, maintenance of dignity in the sick role, and the avoidance of hospitalization precipitated by aggressive therapy. Optimally, patients address these personal values when they consider advance directives. Counsel with or referral to an MLP lawyer can guide decisions about healthcare, finances and property and allow the patient to focus on other issues, such as relationships with family.

The advance care planning discussion can be facilitated by a healthcare provider[7] or an attorney or can be done by some patients on their own.[8] The importance of advance directives is emphasized in Medicare payment structures. A federal rule that went into effect on January 1, 2011, provided that Medicare would cover "voluntary advance care planning" to discuss end-of-life treatment, as part of the annual visit.[9] However, this new rule was undergoing reconsideration at the time of this writing.[10]

Consider this example: a grandfather may wish to leave savings for the education of his grandchildren rather than spend it on medical treatments. Feeling that the end of his life is approaching, he may choose conservative medical management over more aggressive care. Such a choice may be seen as a result of depression, lack of understanding of the disease or trust in the system, or even as evidence of financial exploitation. In most cases, these decisions could be rational, reasonable and consistent with the patient's previous behavior and values. This choice must be seen as valid and factored into plans for medical and legal management.

Medical, Legal and Ethical Criteria for End-of-Life Decisions

1. Patient's age

2. Possible side effects and risks of treatment, including pain and discomfort

3. Chance of temporary improvement or permanent cure

4. Likelihood that treatment will cause suffering

5. Patient's ability to cooperate with treatment without coercion or restraints

6. Patient's reactions to medical treatment of others in similar circumstances

7. Patient's religious beliefs

8. Consistent pattern of conduct by patient regarding prior medical decisions

9. Family views, if close-knit

10. Life expectancy with or without the contemplated interventions

11. Extent of the patient's physical and mental disability and dependency

12. Prior statements that expressed views on life-prolonging measures

13. The quality of the patient's life with or without the procedure

14. The physician's views

Medication and Pharmacy Issues

The presence of multiple chronic diseases often results in an expanding array of medications that can be a challenge to manage. Cost issues alone may threaten effective therapy.[11] Prices range widely from established generic drugs to newer brand-name medications. With complex Medicare drug benefits and other coverage, patients may be unable to navigate an array of regulations, preferred medications, restricted formularies, prior approval requirements and changing co-payments. Even experienced healthcare providers may be unaware of the costs of medication.

Geriatric patients are at high risk for adverse drug reactions and toxicity for many reasons: improper geriatric dosing, multidrug regimens predisposing a person to drug interactions and toxicity, and failure to recognize side effects.[12] Use of multiple prescribers and pharmacies increases the likelihood of these problems. Many elderly patients are reluctant to take too many medicines for too long. They may not be convinced that the value is worth the expense, inconvenience and risk of drug-related problems. Undiagnosed noncompliance is a common reason for medications to be poorly managed. Patients may not be candid about nonadherence for fear of judgmental reactions by prescribers.

Healthcare Coverage

Before we review healthcare programs for the elderly, it is important to recognize that most personal care of disabled older adults is provided for free by family.[13] Later in this chapter, we review what coverage is available for custodial care. First, we examine whether Medicare's focus on hospital and physician coverage provides the proper balance between acute level coverage and chronic care coverage.

Federal Healthcare Laws

Under federal law, most Americans aged 65 and older are eligible for Medicare coverage independent of income and health status.[14] Medicare helps pay for most major medical services, including hospital stays, physician visits, some preventive care, some medical supplies, prescription drugs and other services.[15]

Medicare is organized into four parts:

- Part A (Hospital Insurance) pays for inpatient care in hospitals, care in a skilled nursing facility (not custodial or long-term care), hospice care services and home healthcare. The vast majority of Medicare recipients pay no premium for Part A coverage.[16]

- Part B (Medical Insurance) pays for physician services, outpatient care, home health visits and some preventive services. In 2011, the monthly Part B premium was $96.40. Those with high annual incomes pay a higher premium.[17]

- Part C, the Medicare Advantage (MA) program, provides integrated coverage for hospital, physician and, in most cases, prescription drugs. About 25 percent of beneficiaries are in MA plans.[18] Premiums vary according to the policy one selects. An MA plan provides all of a person's Part A and Part B coverage.[19] However, a person typically pays a monthly premium to the MA plan in addition to the Part B premium.

- Part D is the prescription drug benefit, delivered through private plans. Monthly premiums averaged $39 in 2010, plus deductibles and cost sharing. Part D does not cover every dollar for the patient. After a deductible, the patient pays 25 percent of the cost of covered drugs, up to an initial coverage limit. Once that limit is reached, there's another deductible, known as the "donut hole" or "coverage gap." In that "hole," the patient pays the full costs of drugs until total out-of-pocket expenses reach the "catastrophic coverage" benefit. The donut hole is set to shrink starting in 2011 and be phased out by 2020. Subsidies are available for low-income beneficiaries.[20]

Medicare has no coverage for hearing aids, eyeglasses or dental care. Long-term care coverage is restricted to postacute care following a hospital discharge. For example, coverage in a skilled nursing facility is limited to 100 days and must follow a hospital discharge and a minimum hospital stay of 3 days.[21] Beneficiaries who need custodial care typically rely on family, friends and/or paid services, unless they qualify for Medicaid.[22] Unfortunately, many states are cutting home care services.[23]

Healthcare coverage for elders, most of whom are eligible for Medicare, is extensive; however, it is limited in some ways. In addition to the extremely limited coverage of in-home or custodial care, Medicare has no cap on beneficiaries' out-of-pocket expenses, co-pays and other deductibles.[24] Although most beneficiaries have additional coverage either through a Medicare supplement or an employer's plan, this is not the case with many low-income elders. The Medicare Savings Program (MSP) was enacted to provide low-income beneficiaries with assistance in meeting the out-of-pocket cost-sharing costs, but not payments for uncovered benefits.[25]

Cost-Sharing Requirements under Medicare Include

- Deductibles for hospitalizations ($1,132 in 2011)
- Monthly premiums for Part B
- 20 percent coinsurance for most Part B services
- Premiums, deductibles and co-payments for MA managed care plans and Part D drug plans

---

Medicaid and Seniors: Dual Eligibles

The poorest Medicare recipients, often also the sickest, also get help from Medicaid.[26] Unlike Medicare, Medicaid is a means-tested, needs-based program. (See Chapter 2 for a detailed discussion of Medicaid.) It often covers a range of healthcare services not covered by Medicare. Approximately 6 million seniors who are on Medicare (about 18 percent) also qualify for Medicaid;[27] these individuals are called "dual eligibles." Most dual eligibles also qualify for federal Supplemental Security Income (SSI) cash assistance because their incomes are low and assets limited. Many seniors become eligible for Medicaid after they have exhausted their financial resources paying for healthcare, a process sometimes referred to as "spending down" (see Chapter 13 for additional discussion of spending down). These beneficiaries receive assistance with Medicare premiums and co-payments and full Medicaid benefits, including nursing home care. Seventy percent of Medicaid beneficiaries who are aged 65 and older are women;[28] the vast majority of these women also have Medicare. For Medicare beneficiaries with income or resources just above the federal poverty level, Medicaid's assistance is more limited, primarily covering Medicare premiums.

The Affordable Care Act, the healthcare reform legislation passed by Congress in 2010, created an office within the Centers for Medicare and Medicaid Services (CMS) whose focus is dual eligibility.[29] This is in response to the underutilization of the dual eligible program and lack of full benefits given to those in the program.[30] (See Chapter 19 for more information about the Affordable Care Act.)

Not all low-income seniors on Medicare have Medicaid coverage. For many beneficiaries with savings or other property that exceeds $2,000 in value, the asset test disqualifies them from Medicaid eligibility, though this amount varies by state.[31] For others, the complex documentation requirements and administrative burdens of the eligibility process make enrollment difficult to complete.[32] This problem presents healthcare providers and lawyers in MLPs a concrete opportunity to collaborate to improve understanding of eligibility, to partner with those gathering data on dual eligibles who do not receive benefits from both programs and to seek changes in program administration.[33]

Questions for Discussion

1. Data indicate that many dually eligible seniors are not receiving all potential benefits. What might account for these findings?

2. What can healthcare professionals do to identify these elders?

3. What is the role of the healthcare provider in addressing the problems seniors have in understanding our complex coverage systems?

4. What role should lawyers play?

5. What types of systemic advocacy could MLPs explore to address the problem of underenrollment in the "dual eligible" program?

Case for Medical-Legal Partnership

States are cutting home healthcare programs for the elderly and disabled. A 2010 *New York Times* article described Ms. Afton England,[34] a woman who suffers from diabetes, spinal stenosis, degenerative disc disease, arthritis and other health problems that limit her walking or standing. Ms. England lives alone on $802 of monthly Social Security. Oregon was providing her with 45 hours of in-home help each month, but these services are at risk of being cut. Her case manager, Brandi Lemke, said she feared that Ms. England would "end up in the hospital because of the diabetes" and be in assisted living by the end of the year. "If she takes a fall," Ms. Lemke said, "she may require more than assisted living can handle." Nursing homes in Oregon cost the state an average of $5,900 a month; home- and community-based services cost $1,500 a month. "This is not saving any money," she said.

Questions for Discussion

1. The article hypothesizes that home care services for an elderly patient could prevent costly hospitalizations. How could MLPs advocate for maintaining funding for home-based care? What information could you gather to show that programs for the chronically ill save on expensive hospital stays?

2. In a campaign to promote coverage of home-based care programs, what community groups and allies might healthcare providers and lawyers partner with? What skills and knowledge might MLP partners bring to the table?

Medical Decision Making and Advance Care Planning

Consent for Treatment

The high incidence of acute and chronic illnesses among the elderly results in repeated episodes of complex medical decision making. The majority of such decisions are made in a nonurgent manner in the outpatient setting. Many choices to proceed (or not) with diagnostic studies, procedures and treatments are elective. For example, does a patient want immunizations like flu shots or health maintenance and screening studies like mammography and colonoscopy? Some decisions are more urgent, for example, acceptance of hospitalization for acute illness like pneumonia or for worsening of chronic illness like congestive heart failure. Other decision points can be anticipated, as in whether a patient with ALS (amyotrophic lateral sclerosis, or Lou Gehrig's disease) wishes to have a feeding tube or tracheotomy placed when the ability to swallow or breathe adequately is lost.

Most attention in the literature has focused on the more urgent decisions that occur in the inpatient setting, often referred to as "consent for treatment" decisions. In this context, the timeline is compressed. Patients who have been hospitalized are much more likely than other groups to have acute states of confusion superimposed on previously normal or less abnormal cognitive status.[35] The level of impairment may vary from day to day, even from hour to hour. A common observation is that a patient's consent may be considered valid and accepted when there is agreement with the management plan suggested by the medical team. The same patient's capacity to consent to treatment or decline it may be questioned when the decision is at variance with suggestions of the healthcare providers. Often the issue calls for evaluation of the degree of cognitive impairment related to medical, neurological or psychiatric disease.[36]

Legal Planning for Medical Decisions and Information

All adults should consider the possibility that they will one day be unable to make decisions. Physicians should address this possibility with patients of advanced age or who have progressive conditions that will lead to an inability to communicate. When the patient is already cognitively impaired, family members or designated alternative decision makers are typically involved. Preplanning with advance directives should be encouraged. When the patient can no longer provide consent and there is no decision maker, a guardian might be necessary.

Federal Laws

The Patient Self-Determination Act

Medical institutions must provide information to all adult patients about their state's laws on advance directives, such as living wills and healthcare powers of attorney. Such notice is required by the federal Patient Self-Determination Act (PSDA; 42 U.S.C. 1395cc (a)). The PSDA also protects patients from being required to sign advance directives.

The Health Insurance Portability and Accountability Act (HIPAA)

An older patient may want to allow a trusted family member to have access to medical information. Typically, an adult child comes to medical appointments to help explain a parent's symptoms and discuss future plans. The Health Insurance Portability and Accountability Act (HIPAA; 42 U.S.C. 1320d) allows the patient to sign a release, authorizing the relative to receive information. The same individual also might be listed as the patient's healthcare power of attorney, in which case he or she is authorized to make decisions if the patient becomes unable to do so. Providers may have their own institution-specific HIPAA release, but older people also should consider a blanket HIPAA form that can be used in the future with other providers. In general, confidential information may be given by doctors to lawyers only if a HIPAA authorization is signed. (See Chapter 6 for further discussion of patient privacy in the context of MLP.)

State Laws

Healthcare Power of Attorney or Healthcare Proxy

A healthcare power of attorney allows a person to choose a surrogate to make medical decisions in the event that the patient cannot do so personally. The person appointed is called the agent or healthcare proxy. Unless the document is drafted to be limited, the agent can make a wide range of decisions. This includes the choice of physicians, authorization for surgery or other treatment, and end-of-life decisions. The patient who signs the healthcare power of attorney can add or limit powers with specific directives related to issues like organ donation or anatomical gifts, mental health treatment, or religious and cultural preferences. Once signed, copies of advance directives should be given to family members and healthcare providers.

All states have statutory forms that should be easily available. People typically appoint a spouse or adult child as agent, but any adult can be appointed except for involved healthcare providers. Ethical principles and state laws generally exclude members of the patient's healthcare team from serving as the proxy, except when the patients are their own family members.[37]

Some patients choose not to sign advance directives for personal, religious or cultural reasons. Several studies show that minority group members are less likely to use these documents.[38] With an ongoing, trusting clinical relationship, patients may become more comfortable with documenting their wishes over time. Often patients are more willing to make these choices once they are back in their own homes with family support. Patients who are reluctant to designate a healthcare agent may do so once the act is seen as one that reduces potential stress, conflict and guilt among family members and others involved in the decisions.

Because state laws and family circumstances change, the views that are expressed by a patient in a healthcare power of attorney should be reviewed periodically. Priorities may change for personal reasons, including changes in health status, residence, available supports and needs of dependent family. For example, the patient who resisted cancer treatment for fear of nursing home placement may decide to accept treatment once placement has occurred. The parent or spouse who declined procedures to remain available to care for children or a sick spouse may accept them after the death of the spouse or once support for children is assured. A patient who initially declined hemodialysis may agree to it when symptoms of renal failure become more severe. Patients should be encouraged to have ongoing conversations with their families about the types of medical treatments they would or would not want.[39] Simply signing a document is not enough. Practitioners should encourage patients to think through what they believe is best in terms of quality of life.

The Living Will

A living will covers a narrower set of conditions than the healthcare power of attorney. It is a document that allows patients to specify preferences involving end-of-life medical decisions.[40] If the patient is competent when decisions need to be made, the living will would not come into play. Instead, the person would express his or her wishes, even if they are different than those expressed in a previously executed document. Once again, clinical status may be fluid. In these cases, the best course of action may be difficult to determine; ongoing contact between the agent, the healthcare team and the patient is important. Most states require a living will to be signed in the presence of a notary and may also require witnesses. Rules generally prohibit relatives or healthcare providers from serving as witnesses.[41]

Medical Decisions without an Advance Directive

The majority of Americans do not sign advance directives.[42] In these cases, some state laws prioritize a list of decision makers who can step in if the patient can no longer consent. A spouse and adult children are always included. In a growing number of states, a person who is close to the patient, such as a life partner or long-term friend, also can be the decision maker when no close relative is available.[43] Advance planning documents are critical for patients who do not want the people listed in surrogate decision making laws to make decisions for them.

Court decisions make clear that a person's wishes can be determined in ways other than a living will.[44] However, patients are more likely to have their wishes honored if they use the statutory advance directives. This is because these statutory forms give legal immunity (known as a "safe harbor") to providers who follow statutory advance directive forms. Medical providers often make decisions about life-sustaining medical treatment based on input from the patients' families. Prevailing medical ethical standards call for consideration of the patient's views and, if those are not known, an assessment of what would be in the patient's best interests.

Medical Orders on Scope of Treatment (MOST)

To improve patients' quality of life as they approach dying, several states have enacted laws that allow the patient and healthcare team to make choices in advance about a wide range of treatments. These expressed choices may be referred to as Medical Orders on Scope of Treatment (MOST), Physicians Orders on Scope of Treatment (POST), or Physicians Orders on Life-Sustaining Treatment (POLST). For simplicity, we refer to them as MOST. These orders allow the physician and the patient or his or her surrogate to discuss and spell out decisions about how aggressive medical care should be in a range of situations.[45] By collaborating in getting MOST statutes passed, healthcare providers and lawyers have improved end-of-life care for countless older patients.

Best Practices and Advocacy Strategies for Medical-Legal Partnership

Following are strategies for healthcare providers and lawyers in assisting patients with medical decision making and advance planning:

1. Healthcare providers should initiate conversations with patients about end-of-life preferences while the patients are still able to communicate.

2. Healthcare providers should encourage patients to consider healthcare proxies and alternates. They can also specify medical treatment they would or would not want. MLP lawyers can offer legal assistance around this issue.

3. MLP teams can provide information about their state's laws regarding advance directives; lawyers can help patients draft these advance directives.

4. MLP teams can encourage patients to discuss their preferences about medical care, especially end-of-life care, with family and close friends.

5. MLP teams can offer presentations to community groups, providing both medical and legal perspectives on the issue.[46]

6. Healthcare providers should review these decisions periodically with patients.

7. MLP teams can advocate for development of MOST and support organizations that are working to make these available (if they do not already exist in the state).

From Practice to Policy

Living wills have been criticized as addressing only a limited range of clinical options at the very end of life. As a result, healthcare providers and advocates for patients pushed for a more useful approach to end-of-life treatment decisions. MOST laws were enacted in several states, allowing patients to decline a wider range of treatment options than the typical living will addresses.

One example of a state law allowing the use of MOST is from West Virginia; the law specifies the types of end-of-life medical treatment that can be covered.

W. Va. Code § 16-30-25 [excerpts]. Physician Orders for Scope of Treatment form.

(b) Physician orders for scope of treatment forms shall be standardized forms used to reflect orders by a qualified physician for medical treatment of a person in accordance with that person's wishes or, if that person's wishes are not reasonably known and cannot with reasonable diligence be ascertained, in accordance with that person's best interest. The form shall be bright pink in color to facilitate recognition by emergency medical services personnel and other healthcare providers and shall be designed to provide for information regarding the care of the patient, including, but not limited to, the following:

(1) The orders of a qualified physician regarding cardiopulmonary resuscitation, level of medical intervention in the event of a medical emergency, use of antibiotics and of medically administered fluids and nutrition, and the basis for the orders;

(2) The signature of the qualified physician;

(3) Whether the person has completed an advance directive or had a guardian, medical power of attorney representative, or surrogate appointed;

(4) The signature of the person or his or her guardian, medical power of attorney representative, or surrogate acknowledging agreement with the orders of the qualified physician; and

(5) The date, location, and outcome of any review of the physician orders for scope of treatment form.

(c) The physician orders for scope of treatment form [...] shall be transferred with the person from one healthcare facility to another.

A second example of successful MLP policy advocacy is one that resisted the enactment of a law. In North Carolina, a coalition of physicians, hospice workers and lawyers was formed to oppose a bill in the state legislature that would have made it a felony to "assist in suicide." The coalition secured resolutions opposing the bill from the Elder Law and Health Law Sections of the North Carolina Bar Association (NCBA) and the NCBA Board of Governors. In letters, e-mails and visits to the legislature, the coalition expressed concern that good palliative care would be hampered due to the vague language of this proposed criminal law.[47]

Case for Medical-Legal Partnership

Mr. Trik is a clinic patient with severe congestive heart failure and mild memory loss. He is estranged from his children and ex-wife, but has an old friend, Joe, who is his primary support. Joe brings him to appointments, picks up prescriptions and helps Mr. Trik understand medical advice. His physician is concerned about how Mr. Trik's medical decision making will be handled in the future.

Questions for Discussion

1. What could Mr. Trik do to make his wishes about end-of-life care more likely to be honored? Could he appoint Joe, who is not related, to be a healthcare agent?

2. What would be the benefits of a HIPAA release allowing Joe to see Mr. Trik's medical information?

3. Mr. Trik's doctor talks with him about the poor prognosis of his condition. Mr. Trik says he agrees with the goals of a living will, but he is typically slow to make decisions. What information would still be helpful to include in his medical chart and why? Who else should have that information, and why?

4. Before the documents are finalized, Mr. Trik suffers a massive stroke, from which he is not expected to recover. One of his children comes to see him and insists that the hospital use all available medical technology to keep him alive. The MLP team asks the medical institution's Ethics Consultation Service for input on the right thing to do. What information should the MLP team provide to the ethics committee to consider?

Capacity and Competence

As many as half of all community-dwelling adults over age 85 suffer some degree of cognitive impairment.[48] When cognitive disabilities make it difficult to handle one's personal care, activities of daily living (ADLs), household functioning (sometimes called instrumental activities of daily living, or IADLs), finances or medical decisions, the result can be a cascade of legal problems. Family members are often affected financially and emotionally.

Disease Impact on Cognitive Function

Cognitive function can be adversely affected by virtually any disease. A relatively small subset of diseases produces the syndrome of dementia. Dementia involves deficits that are persistent rather than transient, acquired rather than present from birth, and irreversible. Dementia typically features a decline in memory and other cognitive functions severe enough to affect daily life. By definition, at least three of several domains are affected: memory, personality, language, visual-spatial function and so-called higher cognitive function. For most dementias, the course of the illness is marked by gradual onset and continued decline. Alzheimer's disease accounts for about 65 percent of dementias; vascular dementia or mixed forms account for an additional 20 percent; other diseases make up the rest.[49]

Alzheimer's disease itself may run its course over 10 years or more from the time of first symptoms to end-stage disease. Other degenerative dementias may kill a previously healthy person in a year or less. The vascular dementias tend to produce a "step-wise" decline in function as new strokes occur. Along with motor weakness, other functions may be affected like speech (aphasia) or the ability to perform certain motor tasks (apraxia). Differentiating between aphasic and demented patients may require sophisticated neurological examination. A single identifiable insult to the brain may produce a dementia. Traumatic brain injury or a period of anoxia may result in dementia that will typically be persistent but not progressive. Only occasionally is a reversible cause of dementia found in the course of an evaluation; however, it is critical that these be ruled out before dementia is assumed to be irreversible.[50]

In contrast to dementia, the syndrome of delirium is a potentially lethal but often reversible confused state, with acute onset, disturbed level of consciousness, disorganized thinking, classically a fluctuating course and often an identifiable underlying medical cause. Delirium is commonly superimposed on a preexisting dementia with uncertainty about how much cognitive impairment may improve over time. Occasionally recovery from hospital-acquired delirium may continue for weeks or months after discharge.[51]

The list of causes of delirium is long and includes:[52]

1. Medications of many types, either in excess or in appropriate doses

2. Intoxicants like alcohol and other drugs

3. Common infections like pneumonia or HIV/AIDS

4. Metabolic abnormalities

5. Failure of key organ function

Several screening tests for dementia exist, for example, the Folstein Mini-Mental Status Exam (MMSE), the Short Portable Mental Status Questionnaire, and the Mini-cog.[53, 54, 55] The MMSE is by far the most widely used, is validated in several languages, and is best suited to follow patients serially over time. The MMSE score varies with educational level, literacy, vision, cultural/language issues and other variables. The test is relatively insensitive at the high end of its range; patients with high educational levels may score in the normal range despite clinically significant impairment. Declining scores correlate roughly with advancing stages of dementia, as is seen in Figure 14.2.

Psychiatric Disease Affecting Cognitive Function

Geriatric patients may have underlying psychiatric illnesses that have been present for some time. Schizophrenia and other psychotic disorders may be quiescent or may be affecting the patient's ability to reason. Concerns involving major primary psychiatric disease are an indication for formal psychiatric consultation. As in the case of younger psychiatric patients, legal assistance may be required to authorize interventions like the use of antipsychotic medication. Some states have specific legal procedures to determine whether such medication can be administered against the patient's wishes.[56] On the other hand, depressive illness is highly prevalent in older populations and is generally managed by the primary care providers unless issues arise related to suicidal risk, psychotic behavior, need for complex management like electroconvulsive therapy, or legal questions.

In a particular patient, the elements of dementia and depression may be hard to untangle. In dementia, memory problems are usually more severe and associated with

Figure 14.2 Progression of the Symptoms of Alzheimer's Disease

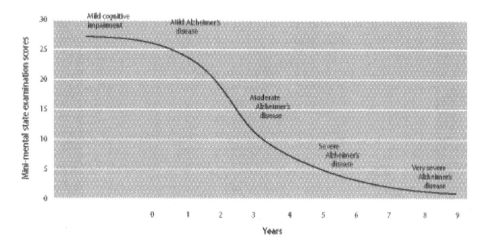

Mild cognitive impairment: Complaints of memory loss, intact activities of daily living, no evidence of Alzheimer's disease

Mild Alzheimer's disease: Forgetfulness, short term memory loss, repetitive questions, hobbies, interests lost, impaired activities of daily living

Moderate Alzheimer's disease: Progression of cognitive deficits, dysexecutive syndrome, further impaired activities of daily living, transitions in care, emergence of behavioural and psychological symptoms of dementia

Severe Alzheimer's disease: Agitation, altered sleep patterns, assistance required in dressing, feeding, bathing, established behavioural and psychological symptoms of dementia

Very severe Alzheimer's disease: Bedbound, no speech, incontinent, basic psychomotor skills lost

Source: Alistair Burns, Steven Iliffe, "Alzheimer's Disease," *British Medical Journal*, 338 (2009): 468.

problems in other areas (e.g., aphasia, apraxia). In depression, there may be a more pervasive depressed mood, excessive guilt and more often frank suicidal ideation. In either, patients might manifest flattened affect, poor sleep and appetite, decreased concentration and loss of interest in activities.[57]

Decisions regarding treatment or disposition are often made in the context of several interacting processes, some changing over time. Medical illness producing a fluctuating degree of delirium usually responds to treatment. The psychiatric components of the patient's illness may also respond to treatment, typically over a longer period of time. The tempo and trajectory of irreversible, progressive dementia can only be estimated.

Legal View of Capacity and Competence

Adults are presumed in the law to be competent, although impaired health can call this presumption into question. The medical tests and scales that disclose and measure mental impairments do not neatly match the legal standards of mental capacity. The legal standards for capacity vary according to the task to be done. Generally, the lowest standard of capacity is that required to sign a will, known as *testamentary capacity*. In most states, a person must simply understand the document to sign for an advance directive or financial power of attorney. These documents are considered contracts in the law. Unfortunately, the law does not set out an easily applied standard.

Lawyers may (but are not required to) obtain medical evaluations of a client before submitting documents for the client's signature; they generally do not. They should keep some record of why they believe the client had the capacity to understand what was signed. Some attorneys record the execution of a document, and, in some cases might refer the client to a geriatrician, a neurologist or a forensic psychiatrist for an evaluation. Before doing the evaluation, the physician should know the standard of capacity being used.

Just as in the medical setting where the patient must give informed consent to treatment, the requirements for capacity vary according to the complexity of the decision. In the medical setting, a decision about taking aspirin, for example, would require less mental ability than a decision choosing between multiple complex treatments. A practical approach that has been recommended in the legal context appears in Factors in Determining Capacity.

Factors in Determining Capacity

- Variability of choice

- Ability to understand consequences

- Ability to articulate reasons behind a decision

- Whether the decision is irreversible and extent of consequences

- Whether the transaction is substantively fair with respect to third parties and others

- Consistency with lifetime commitments[a]

Source: [a] Peter S. Margulies, "Access, Connection, and Voice: A Contextual Approach to Representing Senior Citizens of Questionable Capacity," *Fordham Law Review*, 62 (1994): 1073–99; American Bar Association, *Model Rules of Professional Conduct: Client-Lawyer Relationship Rule 1.14 Client with Diminished Capacity—Comment*, (Chicago: American Bar Association, 2010).

It is prudent for patients to plan for possible disability. This helps save money, avoid stress and empower the older person to make decisions about who will manage his or her money and how. MLP teams are very well positioned to discuss these issues and to assist older patients with planning. For most patients, a financial power of attorney should be considered while they are still able to understand these documents.

The Financial Power of Attorney

The person who signs the power of attorney, referred to as the *principal*, can designate a trusted individual to handle assets and income. This person is known as the agent or attorney-in-fact. In most cases, the agent does not take over the financial decision making but is available to step in if and when the older person is unable to handle these tasks. Most powers of attorney are referred to as durable because they specify that they will remain in effect if the principal becomes incapacitated. Others are referred to as springing powers of attorney; these only go into effect when the principal is incapacitated.[58] Many attorneys discourage clients from this type of power of attorney, because it may be difficult to determine when the principal has reached a point of mental incapacity.

Powers of attorney are usually written broadly to cover a wide range of assets, including real estate, investments, financial accounts and so forth. An alternate or a co-agent can be appointed. State laws require that the principal's signature be notarized, and some also require witnesses to the signature. To be honored by financial institutions, these powers of attorney need to be registered in a public office. Many states have laws that set out a basic power of attorney form, known as the statutory or short-form power of attorney. These forms, often found on the Internet, can be signed without a person consulting an attorney. However, they often are lacking in the options that experienced attorneys recommend.

Having a power of attorney generally allows a person to avoid court involvement in financial management in the event of incapacity. This court procedure is known as a guardianship or, in some states, conservatorship.[59] Most powers of attorney limit the agent's power to using the principal's assets for the principal's needs. However, there is an option that some patients may want to include, called a gifting provision. This authorizes the agent to give property away while the principal is alive, but not after death. This may provide a means by which a patient can provide for a spouse, children or grandchildren.

Older adults often want to leave property to family and may be fearful that nursing home costs will decimate their life savings and threaten home ownership. Medicaid rules do allow for some asset transfers while a person is still alive, but the rules are strict and vary from state to state. For example, it may be possible to retitle assets to one's disabled child (42 U.S.C. § 1396p(c)(2)(B)). Patients should be cautioned not to give away assets without consulting an experienced elder law attorney. MLPs that connect elder law attorneys to the geriatric practice can significantly reduce barriers for patients seeking legal counsel on such matters.

The Legal Check-Up for Older Patients

MLP teams should emphasize to patients that they and their families can avoid costs, stress, and court involvement by looking into these planning steps:

1. Financial power of attorney
2. Healthcare power of attorney or proxy
3. Living will
4. Release of confidential medical information (HIPAA)

Financial Management after Incapacity

If a patient suffers an acute health crisis and has not appointed a financial or medical decision maker, a guardian may be necessary as well as someone to handle the person's Social Security income. This section covers the basics of the legal process, referred to simply as "guardianship" or "conservatorship." Note that to handle the person's Social Security income, it is necessary to follow a separate process, described later.

Even in cases where there is a signed medical or financial power of attorney, there may still be a need for a court to appoint a guardian. For example, a guardian may be needed when the agent is unavailable or is mishandling the older person's assets, or the healthcare agent refuses to make medical decisions. The appointment of a guardian in these situations can trump or overrule the action (or inaction) of these agents.[60]

Federal Law: Representative Payees for Social Security

Federal laws regulate Social Security benefits. The primary income for many older adults is from Social Security payments.[61] The Social Security Administration (SSA) requires a special procedure if a beneficiary becomes unable to handle payments or directs someone to handle them.[62] Usually a family member is appointed by the SSA, but it can also be a nursing facility or certain agencies. The person or agency appointed is called a *representative payee*, "rep payee" or just "payee." The payee manages the beneficiary's Social Security or SSI benefits with an eye to providing for all the patient's needs. Even if the incapacitated beneficiary has a power of attorney, the SSA requires that a representative payee be designated to handle the benefits; in some cases, the agent is the same for both roles.[63]

The payee must first provide for the beneficiary's day-to-day needs of food and shelter. Extra money must be used for clothing, recreation and other benefits, such as medical/dental expenses that Medicare/Medicaid do not cover. For beneficiaries in nursing homes, the benefits are used to pay for the usual costs, and $30 per month is permitted to be set aside for personal needs for individuals on Medicaid.[64]

State Laws: Guardianships for Financial and Medical Management

State laws regulate guardianship, which is the legal mechanism by which a person is declared incompetent. The court appoints a guardian to handle assets and/or make medical and housing decisions for him or her, often resulting in a complete loss of rights. Where incompetency is developing or suspected, the older patient should be encouraged to see a lawyer because he or she might still have the capacity to designate a surrogate.

Grounds for Guardianship

State laws generally define an incapacitated person as one who lacks the ability to make good decisions about his or her care or property.[65] Functional limitations are more important than a list of diagnoses. Healthcare providers should give complete evaluations or state what further evaluations are needed, so that courts can understand the patient's deficits and their impact on daily living.

Medical Evidence

Medical information is usually required for such a court action, so understanding common medical and legal terminology is useful. When a provider is asked for information about possible guardianship, the court should be informed about what abilities the patient retains. This reflects the legal principle of least restrictive alternative and the ethical principle of respect for the autonomy and dignity of impaired people. Some states encourage limited guardianships allowing impaired adults to retain some rights.[66] Some are trying to keep competency disputes out of the courts.[67]

If the patient does not consent to allow his or her personal health information to be disclosed to family, the healthcare provider may need to get legal advice as to whether federal HIPAA rules prohibit giving out the information without a court order. Many cases are initiated by family members with only their written summaries of behaviors that, in their opinion, show mental incapacity. Once the case is filed, courts generally allow the parties to submit a letter or sworn affidavit from the physician, with more details. Generally, the physician is not required to appear in court. Some jurisdictions provide written formats designed to increase the quality of the evidence on which the court bases its decision.

The Court Process

First, a concerned party files a court action or petition, as it is called in some states. Many states provide simple forms requiring little more than the person's name, age, condition and assets, along with the name of a recommended guardian. A copy of this is served on the respondent (or alleged incapacitated person), and a time limit is given to respond. Relatives and other interested parties also get a copy of the papers. A relative, neighbor, banker or other interested party can initiate the process. In most states, even the person's attorney could initiate it to protect the older person in an extreme situation.[68]

A court then appoints either a court visitor or a guardian ad litem (a guardian for the duration of the litigation) to gather information. Some states provide both, one to serve as an investigator for the court and the other as an advocate for the respondent. The guardian ad litem is usually an attorney, who might also be required to determine what the respondent wants done and then communicate this to the court at the hearing.[69] If the health or property of the respondent is at great risk, more immediate court intervention may be possible.

The parties are given a period of time to investigate the facts, gather documents and interview witnesses, taking a few weeks to a few months. At the hearing, the respondent may appear but often does not. Nevertheless, a hearing is held and a decision rendered. The hearings often are less formal than other court proceedings, allowing for letters or other sworn statements in lieu of live testimony with cross-examination. Figure 14.3 provides a detailed outline of the guardianship process.

State laws prefer family members as guardians but, lacking a suitable person, can appoint government and nonprofit agencies to serve as guardian. For property management, the courts appoint a relative, an agency or a public guardian who manages the assets of numerous wards.[70]

The Guardian's Power

A guardian with authority to make medical decisions generally can address the full range of decisions from minor ones to end-of-life choices. Because state laws differ, the best way to determine the scope of a guardian's power is to read the court order appointing the guardian or seek legal advice. Even where the person has been declared incompetent, guardians are generally required by law to consider the person's wishes.[71] A healthcare provider can and should attempt to communicate with the ward as well as with the guardian.

Ending a Guardianship

When patients under guardianship have recovered enough to make good decisions, the medical provider should inquire of the guardian or court about removing the guardianship. The patient also has the right to ask to have the guardianship removed, but practically speaking may need a lawyer's help. Generally, guardianship remains in place until the person dies.

Figure 14.3 Guidelines to the Guardianship Process

Note: The following chart was developed by the American Bar Association (ABA) to provide a basic outline of the guardianship process. Lori Stiegel, assistant staff director at the ABA's Commission on Law and Aging, cautions that actual terminology and requirements regarding guardianship will differ slightly from state to state. Local courts within the same state also may have their own legal nuances.

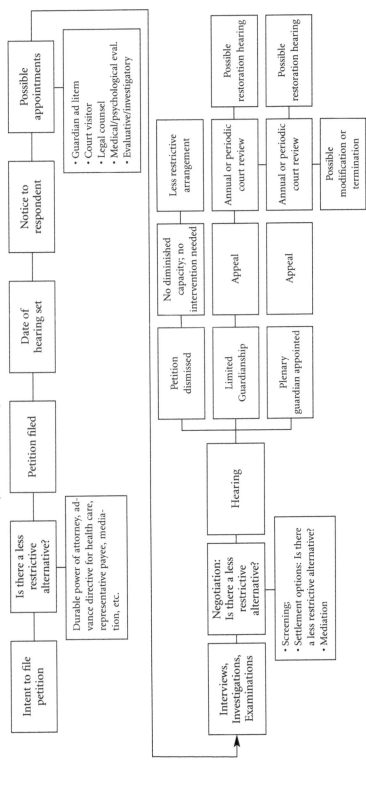

Source: American Bar Association, Commission on Law and Aging and Young Lawyers Division Committee on the Delivery of Legal Services to the Elderly, February 1990, Washington, DC. Updated 2010 (Erica Wood, ABA Commission).

North Carolina defines an incompetent adult as "an adult or emancipated minor who lacks sufficient capacity to manage the adult's own affairs or to make or communicate important decisions concerning the adult's person, family or property whether the lack of capacity is due to mental illness, mental retardation, epilepsy, cerebral palsy, autism, inebriety, senility, disease, injury or similar cause or condition" (N.C. Gen. Stat. 35A-1101(7)).

In New Hampshire, "incapacity" means:

> [A] legal, not a medical, disability and shall be measured by functional limitations. It shall be construed to mean or refer to any person who has suffered, is suffering or is likely to suffer substantial harm due to an inability to provide for his or her personal needs for food, clothing, shelter, healthcare or safety or an inability to manage his or her property or financial affairs. Inability to provide for personal needs or to manage property shall be evidenced by acts or occurrences, or statements which strongly indicate imminent acts or occurrences. All evidence of inability must have occurred within 6 months prior to the filing of the petition and at least one incidence of such behavior must have occurred within 20 days of the filing of the petition for guardianship. Isolated instances of simple negligence or improvidence, lack of resources or any act, occurrence or statement if that act, occurrence or statement is the product of an informed judgment shall not constitute evidence of inability to provide for personal needs or to manage property. (NH Rev. Statute 464-A: 2 XI).

From Practice to Policy

In the past, older people have sometimes been declared incompetent based on perfunctory letters from physicians. Although not an actual example, this is the type of letter that might have sufficed: "Mrs. Eileen McGillicuddy is a lovely 82-year-old widow who is getting senile and would benefit from having a guardian." To protect people from losing their rights through inappropriate guardianships, some states have reformed their laws, some requiring that medical statements be made on certain forms. In Massachusetts, a Medical Certificate for Guardianship or Conservatorship details what limitations the person has, the prognosis, what abilities he or she retains, and other information for courts to consider.[72] These reforms make the process more protective, but also more costly and time-consuming.[73] MLPs can propose ways to standardize and refine forms, address procedures for calling medical witnesses and provide a guardianship system that is fair, cost-effective and efficient. Legislatures have to weigh competing interests of healthcare professionals, disempowered older adults and the limited resources of courthouse personnel.

Case for Medical-Legal Partnership

Mack Smith, a quirky 80-year-old widower, has been a patient for several years at the geriatric practice, and the MLP has helped in the past. He has been befriended by a pleasant 56-year-old woman who stays with him at times and comes with him to appointments. They have traveled together over the past few years. He appears to be well cared for and content, but admits that his memory is somewhat impaired, mainly affecting his ability to handle financial decisions. He uses bank drafts to pay bills. Mr. Smith's adult children have filed a guardianship to have him declared incompetent. They call the MLP lawyer's office and refer to "that woman" as a "gold digger." Assume they obtain the necessary court papers to get your written evaluation.

Questions for Discussion

1. Your state's law is similar to the New Hampshire statute. What information would you consider important to obtain and include in your medical report to the court?

2. What information would Mr. Smith's court-appointed advocate want to gather to show that he does not meet the standard set out in the law?

3. What factors, in your opinion, should the law consider before it steps in to "protect" older people from making choices on their own?

Financial Stress and Older People

Financial and healthcare problems affect increasing numbers of older people, even though Medicare coverage and Social Security income provide a baseline of protection. Over 3.4 million older adults live in poverty in the United States.[74] Unemployment, uninsured medical costs, housing and transportation costs and normal living expenses put a strain on many older adults. The states with the highest poverty rates for older adults are Mississippi, Louisiana, New York, California, Massachusetts and New Jersey, as well as the District of Columbia.[75] Financially distressed seniors often are not aware of the legal protections that could be of help to them. This section touches on some of these protections but does not attempt to cover all the laws that might be applicable. Healthcare providers should inquire about financial concerns and refer patients for legal assistance when appropriate.

Women outnumber men in higher ratios in older age groups;[76] they often struggle with limited incomes and no caregiver in the home. The increase in the "old-old" cohort (those over age 80) means that increasing numbers of older citizens will need long-term care, especially those with cognitive impairment. Paying for this care is problematic, as Medicare covers very little of it. Medicaid rules are difficult to understand and change frequently. Older homeowners may be "house rich but cash poor" and frequently are burdened by property tax bills and the inability to sell homes in a down market. Adapting homes and finding transportation to accommodate physical limitations are other challenges that older people face.

Even before the economic downturn that started in 2008, financial difficulties were increasing for older people. For example, the rate of bankruptcy filings among those 65 and older more than doubled between 1991 and 2007. Among those ages 75 to 84, the rate of filing personal bankruptcies soared 433 percent. Elderly poverty is particularly acute for minority populations. In 2004, 7.5 percent of white elderly were below the federal poverty level, compared to 23.9 percent of elderly African Americans and 18.7 percent of elderly Hispanics. Elderly women had a higher poverty rate (12 percent) than elderly men (7 percent) (see Figure 14.4).[77]

Figure 14.4 Poverty Rates for Older Americans by Sex and Race/Ethnicity

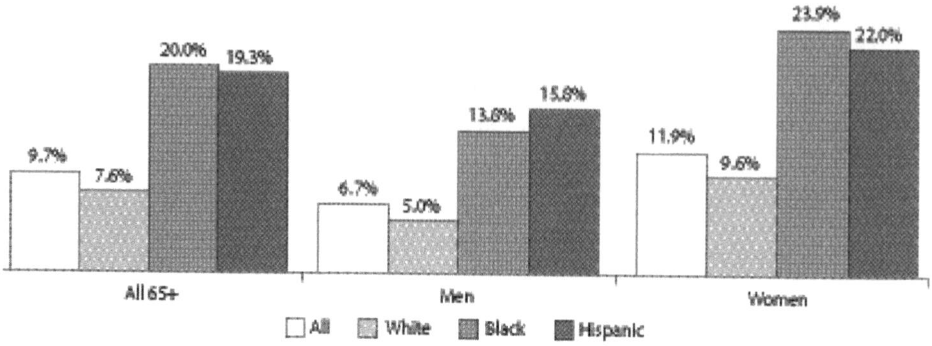

Source: Ellen O'Brian, Ke Bin Wu, and David Baer, "Older Americans in Poverty," AARP Public Policy Institute, April 2010, http://assets.aarp.org/rgcenter/ppi/econ-sec/2010-03-poverty.pdf. Graph reproduced with permission. Data Source: AARP Public Policy Institute estimates based on the Current Population Survey, 2009 Annual Social and Economic Supplement. *Note:* "Hispanic" includes people of any race. "White" includes people who are not Hispanic who report only one race or who report more than one race (e.g., white and black, white and Asian); "Black" includes people who are not Hispanic who report only one race or who report black and any other race except white.

Less Money Means Less Food

In 2008, 8.1 percent of households with an adult age 65 or older experienced food insecurity during the year. Another 10 percent had "very low food security." This means that they not only had limited or uncertain availability of food, but they ate less than they felt they could, cut the size of meals, or skipped meals in three or more months that year. These numbers increased from 2006 to 2008.

Source: Ellen O'Brien, Ke Bin Wu, David Baer, *Older Americans in Poverty: A Snapshot* (Washington, DC: American Association of Retired Persons Public Policy Institute, April 2010), 12.

Increasing numbers of older people lack retirement income security.[78] Many pension plans and benefits have been abandoned by employers. Employer pensions comprise 20 percent of all sources of retirement income, and less than one-half of all employees have coverage. Minorities and women are the least likely to get employer pensions, and when they do receive pensions they get the lowest benefit amounts of those getting pensions.[79] Social Security is the principal source of income for most individuals over 65, but is the source of 90 percent or more of the income for more than three-quarters of single and minority older women (see Figure 14.5).[80]

Figure 14.5 Sources of Income by Quintile for Married Couples and Nonmarried People Age 65 and Older (2008)

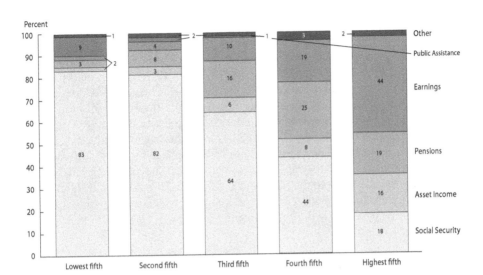

Source: "Older Americans 2010: Key Indicators of Well Being," Federal Interagency Forum on Aging-Related Statistics, http://www.agingstats.gov/agingstatsdotnet/Main_Site/Data/2010_Documents/Docs/OA_2010.pdf. *Data Source:* U.S. Census Bureau, Current Population Survey, Annual Social and Economic Supplement, 2009. *Note:* A married couple is age 65 and over if the husband is age 65 and over or the husband is younger than age 55 and the wife is age 65 and over. The definition of "other" includes, but is not limited to, public assistance, unemployment compensation, worker's compensation, alimony, child support, and personal contributions. Quintile limits are $12,082, $19,877, $31,303, and $55,889 for all units; $23,637, $35,794, $53,180, and $86,988 for married couples; and $9,929, $14,265, $20,187, and $32,937 for nonmarried persons. These data refer to the civilian noninstitutionalized population.

Federal Laws That Offer Protection to Debtors

Protection of Social Security and Property

Although most laws relating to creditors' and debtors' rights are state laws, some laws from the federal government relating to debts should be noted. Older people can be reassured that federal law generally protects Social Security income, veterans' benefits and black lung benefits from creditors (42 U.S.C. Sec. 407). Some of the limited exceptions to this law are when the creditor is the federal government itself, as is the case with the collection of taxes and Social Security overpayments.[81] It may be advisable for the older person to change banking institutions if Social Security checks are being deposited into an institution to which the person owes money.

A person with debt problems sometimes can benefit from filing bankruptcy in federal bankruptcy court. A certain amount of property is protected in bankruptcy, although this varies from state to state. If the person's property exceeds the limits, then some of his or her creditors may have to be paid, in full or in part. In one type of bankruptcy, debts are paid over a three- to five-year period. In another type of bankruptcy, the debts are wiped out ("discharged" is the term used in the law). Even without filing bankruptcy, debtors have other protections. Federal law prohibits debt collectors from harassing debtors, making false statements or threatening illegal action in a wide variety of circumstances.[82]

Debt Relief for Homeowners

Homeowners facing possible foreclosure may be eligible for a federal loan modification program called Home Affordable Modification Plan or HAMP.[83] Another option is known as the reverse mortgage or home equity conversion mortgage. This can offer some additional income and a line of credit for expenses like long-term care costs or major home repairs. The reverse mortgage is a form of loan that does not require monthly payments or good credit. It is available to homeowners aged 62 or older who live in a home that is fully or almost completely paid off. The mortgage lender offers different options, such as monthly payments for a term or for life, and/or a line of credit. The amount available to the homeowner varies according to the age of the borrower and the value of the home. Before homeowners can take out such a mortgage, they must see an independent financial counselor who is approved by the government.[84]

State Laws That Offer Protection to Debtors

Debt Collection Practices

Debt collection practices are also regulated by state laws.[85] Under state laws, wage garnishment of non-Social Security income is either strictly limited or unavailable to creditors.[86] Even where debts are secured by liens or mortgages, older debtors should be encouraged to clarify the timetable for collections. Protections exist for them despite defaulting or being late on payments. MLP lawyers can help ensure that their rights are not violated under these protections.

Property Tax Relief and Special Purpose Loans

Elderly homeowners often lack the ability to pay rising property taxes or make expensive repairs to their homes. To address this, some states and localities have programs that provide for low- or no-interest home improvement loans. Older patients who express concerns about their ability to pay property taxes may be able to benefit from these programs and use limited incomes for more immediate living expenses.

Best Practices and Advocacy Strategies for Medical-Legal Partnership

Because financial stresses impact the health of low-income older patients, MLP teams that serve low-income elders should have some familiarity with local programs that address these issues. These programs include nonprofit consumer credit counseling organizations, local property tax offices, the Social Security Administration and state attorneys general that have consumer protection divisions.

Understanding that many older people are in financial distress, healthcare providers should ask these patients questions and make appropriate referrals to the MLP lawyer or other agencies:

- Are you worrying about your financial security?
- Do you cut back on food due to money problems?

- Are you concerned about what creditors might do if you get behind on payments?
- Have creditors been bothering you?

Emphasize to financially stressed elders that:

- Laws exist to protect Social Security income from virtually all creditors.
- Even people who cannot pay their debts have legal protection of a certain amount of property.
- Debt collectors cannot violate certain laws in trying to collect payment.
- The MLP lawyer can explain their rights, and a credit counseling agency can often provide relief and resources.
- Food stamps and heating assistance programs might be available through county social services departments.

From Practice to Policy

Income insecurity causes a wide range of health problems for older patients. It affects their mental health, determines whether they can afford to pay for medications and healthy foods, and whether they can live in safe and age-appropriate housing. Healthcare provider organizations and legal advocacy groups work together in the Leadership Council on Aging Organizations to find common ground and encourage positive legislative change. Fifty-six national not-for-profit organizations collaborate to advance national policies to improve the lives of senior citizens. The groups include the American Geriatrics Society the American Public Health Association and the Visiting Nurses Association of America.

Questions for Discussion

1. Review the list of recent legislative priorities of the Leadership Council of Aging Organizations online at http://www.lcao.org/default.htm. You have been called to testify before Congress on this list of recommendations, because one of the U.S. senators from your state is on the Senate Special Committee on Aging. Select four items that you feel should be priorities for improving the lives of your older, low-income patients. Why did you select these? You should address one item from each of these categories: Community Services, Healthcare, Income Security, and Long-Term Care. You can consult AARP's *Older Americans in Poverty: A Snapshot*, by Ellen O'Brien, Ke Bin Wu, David Baer (April 2010).

Case for Medical-Legal Partnership

When her healthcare provider asks if she has been in good spirits, an 80-year-old patient tears up. She confides that she just doesn't understand why the bills keep growing, even though she sends in the minimum monthly payment. Unfamiliar with interest rates, late charges and penalties on credit cards, she has used her only charge card to cover the cost of food and heating oil. If she is late in paying by a few days, the company representatives call at all hours and threaten that her Social Security will be garnished (a portion taken by court order).

She owns her home but is determined not to take out a mortgage on it for fear that she couldn't make the monthly payments.

Questions for Discussion

1. Should the healthcare provider refer this patient to the MLP lawyer? How might the lawyer be able to help?

2. How can the MLP team work together to connect this patient with resources that might help her keep her home and work through her debt issues?

3. Develop a short checklist of issues and possible referrals for income insecurity concerns among older patients.

Living in the Community

Many of the housing concerns facing younger people and families are also issues for older people. Laws requiring that landlords properly maintain property are equally if not more important to older people whose health may be threatened unless they have housing that is free of leaks, unsafe stairs and handrails, inadequate heating or cooling, poor security, and other hazards. (See Chapter 8 for a detailed discussion of housing conditions and health.) There are some housing issues that disproportionately or only affect older people. Familiarity with these can go a long way toward ensuring the health and well-being of the older person.

Housing and Residential Options

Medical illness, financial pressure and changing levels of family and community support often raise the issue of a change in living situation. These may arise acutely for the hospitalized patient with recent decline in functional ability, or less acutely in the outpatient who is not doing well. The landscape of options is full of detail and may vary by geographic location. We provide a general overview of options.

Subsidized housing for the elderly or disabled offers housing in which rents are set according to income. But there are often long waiting lists, especially for handicapped-accessible units. Many communities have federally subsidized public housing for older adults where the rents are considerably lower than the open-market rent. Supportive services may be available to the tenants providing social services, meal sites, common room areas, laundry facilities, recreational opportunities and other assistance.

Assisted living facilities (ALFs) typically provide personal care if needed, supervision of self-administered medication, meals, laundry services, housekeeping and a variety of options like in-house social work support, exercise programs and recreational activity. A reasonable degree of independent mobility is usually required. The high end of such facilities may be prohibitively expensive, but a variety of state and local programs may provide financial support.

Adult foster care, often state-sponsored, may be available for patients needing more support than an ALF provides but wishing to avoid nursing home placement. Such programs may offer a home-like environment that provides supports similar to those found in an ALF.

Adult day health programs provide recreation and supervision for the patient and respite for the caregiver during daytime hours. Although not strictly a residential option, they often provide the structure and support needed for an elder to remain in the community.

Some are specialized for people with dementia, blindness, and so on. Some are customized for particular linguistic and cultural groups.

Community Supports

Here is a list of community supports that may help elders stay in their homes:

- A licensed home health agency may provide a visiting nurse for a limited period of time.
- Home health aides or personal care attendants help with activities of daily living like bathing, dressing and toileting.
- Homemaking services help with shopping, cooking and light household chores.
- Physical therapists, occupational therapists, speech therapists, medical social workers, and other skilled resources may be provided by a home health agency under the direction of the visiting nurse.
- Case management services are provided either via public agencies or paid for privately by the patient.

Disability Discrimination

The goal of aging in place is sometimes achieved by asserting a person's right to get reasonable modifications made to housing or to a landlord's normal rules. State and federal laws, particularly the Americans with Disabilities Act (ADA) and the Fair Housing Amendments Act, ban disability discrimination. Discrimination based on disability or perceived disability is prohibited in any program that receives federal funding, pursuant to Section 504 of the Rehabilitation Act of 1973. (See Chapter 8 for discussion of these laws in relation to housing protections.) These laws can be invoked to help older people remain in the community.

All housing subsidized by the government and most private landlords is subject to disability discrimination laws.[87] For older people who have mental or physical disabilities, these laws offer protection and some entitlement to reasonable accommodation of their disabilities. Minor illnesses or disabilities are not covered by these laws (42 U.S.C. §3604(f)(3)(b)). A person is considered to have a disability if he or she has a physical or mental impairment that substantially limits a major life activity (42 U.S.C. §3602(h)). The ADA also protects a person who has a history of such a disability and, if a landlord believes that the person has such a disability, even if they do not (42 U.S.C. §3602(h)(3). The landlord may not bar applicants who are considered to be at risk because of disability. A landlord may not refuse to rent to an individual with a disability because that person requires occasional supports or services to live independently.[88] A landlord may not evict a tenant who requires more time and effort than other tenants due to mild cognitive impairment or minor psychiatric illness.[89]

Rules that apply to other tenants may have to be adjusted, as long as doing so does not result in a fundamental alteration of the program. For example, a landlord must make modifications or policy adjustments that allow the disabled applicant or tenant to live there. When the applicant or tenant is a direct threat to the health and safety of others even after an accommodation has been attempted, he or she is not entitled to demand further accommodation.

Best Practices and Advocacy Strategies for Medical-Legal Partnership

Following are strategies that MLPs can use to assist older patients with housing issues:

- Provide older patients with a list of local subsidized housing options.
- Work with patients who have unfit housing conditions to acquire an inspection from the local code enforcement department and ensure that their rights are enforced.
- Document in a letter to the landlord how the unfit conditions are affecting the patient or putting the patient at risk; provide a copy for the patient to use at the code enforcement office.
- Include a checklist of ways that the patient's housing is affecting his or her health in the doctor's history and physical.
- Provide information to patients about local programs to help older homeowners repair their homes. Some programs offer free repairs and others involve loans with no or low interest, only paid when the home is sold or the homeowner dies.

Case for Medical-Legal Partnership

Ingrid Swenson is an 82-year-old patient. She is very upset because her landlord sent her an eviction notice. This patient has mild cognitive impairment and some paranoia. The landlord claims she is disruptive because she complains about such things as "spies in the trees," "someone bugging my phone" and "ground glass slipped into my food." The MLP lawyer explains to the landlord that Mrs. Swenson has the right to a reasonable accommodation under federal law, just like a policy against pets must accommodate the needs of a blind tenant to use an assist animal. The landlord claims that because Mrs. Swenson's daughter lives in town, this should excuse the landlord from making any accommodation.

Questions for Discussion

1. How might the MLP team work together to help Mrs. Swenson stay in her home?
2. What treatments might help Mrs. Swenson and make it more likely that she can stay in her home?
3. Under what laws might she be protected from eviction?
4. Should the law provide an "out" for landlords, if the older tenant has adult children living nearby, as the landlord argues?

Long-Term Care

Medical Overview

Following a crisis of some type or as chronic disability progresses, patients may face challenges in securing the services needed to remain at home. The well-being (financial and otherwise) of patients and their families may be at risk if short- or long-term placement in a nursing facility is needed. Beyond the financial issues, patients face a variety of potential problems related to the transitions involved.

Choices for sites of short-term rehabilitation or long-term residential care can be limited by many factors: bed availability, quality and reputation, geographic needs, as well as preferences related to religion, language, culture and the like. Patients are often expected to accept a new set of primary care providers; the matter of continuity of medical care is often not prioritized.

Elements of the clinical database may be degraded during the transition: loss of details of the medical/surgical history as the data are compressed into a brief transfer summary, subtle issues regarding medications, details of advance directives and end-of-life preferences, and important portions of the social history. Demented patients without involved family are at particularly high risk. In these cases, little attention may be given to an inventory of community contacts, assets, legal issues and historical preferences based on personal experience. For reasons of cost, the facility may provide the patient with minimal social service and no legal support. Among other problems, the patient may also have trouble finding the assistance needed to return to the community when it is appropriate.

Coverage Issues and Patients' Rights

A legal advocate can be very useful for older people when coverage for long-term services is threatened or denied. The most common scenarios occur when a person needs to enter a nursing facility or needs home healthcare. All state and federal healthcare programs involve complex and changing laws, so whenever an older person is denied coverage or a healthcare benefit is cut off, legal assistance is key.

Medicare and private health insurance provide limited coverage for nursing home and home healthcare. Medicaid (not Medicare) is the nation's largest source of financing for long-term care, followed by out-of-pocket payments by those receiving care.[90] Although the number is growing, few families have private long-term care insurance.[91] Often this insurance is too costly or is denied because an applicant suffers from poor health.

Medicare and Home Care

Many people who want to stay at home when disabled have difficulty receiving ongoing services. Legal advocates are critical to ensuring that elders receive all the home care coverage they are entitled to under Medicare law. They have identified common errors that lead to denials of coverage. The nationally known Center for Medicare Advocacy counsels the following:

1. Medicare coverage should not be denied simply because the patient's condition is "chronic" or "stable."

2. Resist arbitrary caps on coverage. For example, do not accept provider assertions that aide services in excess of one visit per day are not covered, or that daily nursing visits can never be covered.

3. There is no legal limit to the duration of the Medicare home health benefit. Medicare coverage is available for necessary home care even if it is to extend over a long period of time.

4. The doctor is the patient's most important ally. If it appears that Medicare coverage will be denied, the doctor can demonstrate that the foregoing standards are met. Home care services should not be ended or reduced unless it has been ordered by the doctor.

5.   For the patient to appeal a Medicare denial, the home health agency must have filed a Medicare claim for the patient's care. The patient can request in writing that the home health agency file a Medicare claim even if the agency insists that Medicare will deny coverage.[92]

The healthcare providers play a critical role in supporting the patient's claim that he or she is in need of the services currently ordered. The treating physician should be the person who decides whether home health services are necessary and whether they should be reduced or terminated. The physician should not sign a discharge order if he or she continues to think the services are medically appropriate. The patient can also seek a second opinion from a different physician or home health agency.

Medicaid and Nursing Home Care

Many moderate-income elders stand to lose all or most of their savings when they need nursing home care. Like most Medicare recipients, they do not realize that Medicare covers very little nursing home care, and then only after a hospital stay of at least three days. Medicaid programs in all states must provide nursing home care coverage, but they limit what a person can own to qualify. A person who enters a nursing home often has to pay private rates out of pocket until the resource limits for Medicaid coverage are met.

Protecting Assets under Medicaid

Advocates familiar with Medicaid laws can advise a person, within the limits of the law, about how to keep some property. This property is for the person's use when they get out of the nursing home, or for the use of their spouse, children or grandchildren. Giving away property results in disqualification in most cases (42 U.S.C. 1396p(c)). Hiding property is illegal. These laws and regulations can be quite detailed and confusing. (Note that the protection of income is addressed separately, in the section that follows this discussion of Medicaid's rules about property.)

In most states, a single person can have only $2,000 in total savings, although the limit is higher in some states.[93] (The property rules also use the terms "resources" and "assets.") Some types of property do not count, such as a home, household goods, a vehicle, and some other types of property. If the patient has more savings or property than Medicaid rules allow, she will be ineligible until she has spent down those extra assets. Most patients would rather see their family benefit from their savings than have to privately pay the high cost of the nursing home. See Strategies for Spending Down for ways to help moderate-income elders access Medicaid coverage.

Strategies for Spending Down

- Pay for something that Medicaid does not count, such as a car or a newer vehicle
- Prepay funeral costs or a burial plot
- Pay off bills
- Make repairs or improvements to the home
- Buy appliances or make the house more energy-efficient or handicapped-accessible

- Transfer assets to a special needs or supplemental needs trust, which is a trust created for the sole benefit of a disabled person under the age of 65. This may be a child or other relative, or even a friend. If the terms of the trust comply with federal rules, the funds in the trust will not be considered to belong to the beneficiary in determining his or her own Medicaid eligibility (42 U.S.C. § 1396p (c)(2)(B)(iv)). One of the federal rules requires that after the disabled individual dies, the state must be reimbursed for any Medicaid funds spent on his or her behalf (42 U.S.C. § 1396p(b)).

Despite having these options, spending or transferring the extra assets is not always the best course to follow. With extra savings, the patient can privately pay for a nursing home stay. In some cases, nursing facilities tend to give priority to applicants who will be privately paying for care, so in some cases, it may be in the patient's interest to use those savings to open the door to a better facility.

There are property protections for a married Medicaid applicant's spouse if the spouse still lives in the community. The community spouse resource allowance (CSRA) can sometimes be increased with the help of a legal advocate. States vary in how they calculate the CSRA; some are much less generous than others. The federal government sets a minimum and a maximum on how much in savings (or other extra assets) the community spouse can keep. In 2010, the minimum was $21,912 and the maximum was $109,560. Only a few states allow the community spouse to keep this higher figure, so the $109,560 figure serves as the minimum and the maximum in those states.[94]

Protecting Spousal Income

Besides getting legal help to protect property or savings, a patient may be concerned about providing income for a spouse still living in the community. Medicaid rules generally provide that a person's income must be applied to help pay the nursing home, but certain deductions apply. Perhaps most important of these is the protection for the community spouse who is entitled to a minimum monthly maintenance needs allowance (MMMNA).[95] Excess housing costs and other expenses, with the help of an advocate, can be presented to Medicaid to increase the MMMNA. Particular problems emerge for older women who often have very low Social Security incomes. If the husband enters a nursing home, the wife may be left with very little income. MLPs can advocate for these women to improve their financial position and overall quality of life.

Residents' Rights in Nursing Facilities

By federal law, all nursing facilities certified by either Medicare or Medicaid are required to follow detailed procedures for the care of their residents. Residents get the protection of these laws regardless of how their bills are paid. The federal Nursing Home Reform Law, which is incorporated into the Medicare and Medicaid regulations, requires that every nursing home resident be given whatever services are necessary to function at the highest level possible. The law gives residents a number of specific rights, including these (42 U.S.C. § 1396r(b)(4)):

- To be free of unnecessary physical or chemical restraints, except when authorized by a physician in writing for a specified and limited period of time

- To participate in care planning meetings

- To receive a written description of legal rights including an explanation of state laws and the facility's policies and procedures regarding advance directives

- Privacy in all aspects of care
- To share a room with a spouse, gather with other residents without staff present and meet state and local nursing home ombudspersons or any other agency representatives
- To leave the nursing home and belong to any church or social group
- To manage their own financial affairs freely
- To get up and go to bed when they choose, decide what to wear and decide how to spend their time
- To self-administer medication
- To bring personal possessions to the nursing home
- To be treated with respect
- To not be moved to a different room or nursing home, a hospital, back home or anywhere else without advance notice, an opportunity for appeal and a demonstration of why such a move is in the best interest of the resident or is necessary for the health of other nursing home residents
- To be free of interference or reprisal in exercising his or her rights.

Best Practices and Advocacy Strategies for Medical-Legal Partnership

Here are ways that MLPs can assist patients and their families with issues involving long-term care:

- When home healthcare would benefit the older patient, document this and encourage Medicare patients to insist that their claim be filed by the home health agency with Medicare.
- Educate patients and their families about what property and income they can keep if a loved one enters a nursing facility. Often families attempt to provide care that is beyond their ability and might endanger the older person, out of fear that they will lose income or property under the rules on healthcare coverage.
- Educate patients and families about residents' rights when the patient enters a long-term care facility; prepare written materials that are easy to understand.
- Provide training to the healthcare staff and to the patient community about the rights of long-term care residents.
- Caution older patients not to give away property without getting legal advice, because this may be unnecessary and, if done improperly, may disqualify the patient from becoming eligible for coverage.

From Practice to Policy

Nursing home patients sometimes need hospitalization for a few days. In many states, these patients risk losing their place at the nursing home while in the hospital. Medicaid allows states to set the number of "bed hold" days the program will cover. Some states don't cover any bed hold days. Having to move from one nursing home, to the hospital, and then to another nursing home is very hard on sick, elderly patients. Transfer trauma, which can result from these moves, is a recognized and sometimes life-threatening condition. Some states have addressed this problem by requiring that nursing home facilities hold a bed for a certain number of days for patients covered by Medicaid. For example, Massachusetts requires that the facility hold the bed for 10 days (130 CMR 456.425). In Maine, after state funding was cut for bed holding for patients on Medicaid, advocates proposed legislation to restore the funding.[96]

Case for Medical-Legal Partnership

A 79-year-old patient, Jim Jackson, enters a nursing home. The facility admissions personnel tell his wife, Thelma, that she has to pay out of pocket when his Medicare coverage ends. However, facilities that are Medicaid certified cannot force a person to pay privately. Other than their modest home, they have a 10-year-old car, some debts for repairs on the car and a few medical bills that Medicare didn't cover. Their property taxes are coming due soon. The MLP team evaluates the couple's situation to see whether any of their savings ($33,000 total) can be used for Mrs. Jackson's benefit.

Questions for Discussion

1. What is the lowest amount of the couple's savings that federal law allows Mrs. Jackson to keep?

2. What ways might she use any extra savings to help her age in place? Should she deed the house over to their children? Why or why not?

3. What options might she have?

Elder Abuse and Neglect

Elder mistreatment may be physical, psychological or financial; it may involve active abuse or passive neglect in any of these domains. It may be perpetrated in a domestic setting, most commonly by family members but occasionally by formal caregivers or other providers of goods and services. It also occurs in institutional settings like nursing homes, most commonly by staff but occasionally at the hands of other residents.

Physical Abuse or Neglect

Physical mistreatment or abuse involves acts of violence that may result in pain or injury. Examples include pushing, striking, slapping, or pinching; force-feeding; incorrect positioning; and improper use of physical restraints or medications.[97] Sexual abuse can involve sexual coercion or assault or simply exposure without consent or when the older patient is incapable of giving consent. A physician has cause to suspect these types of abuse when the elderly patient presents with unexplained injuries, when the explanation is not consistent with the medical findings or when contradictory explanations are given by the patient and the caregiver.[98]

Physical neglect is characterized by a failure of the caregiver to provide the goods or services necessary for optimal functioning or to avoid harm. This may include withholding of care including adequate meals or hydration, physical therapy, or hygiene; failure to provide physical aids such as eyeglasses, hearing aids, or dentures; and failure to provide safety precautions. Physical neglect may be suspected in the presence of dehydration, malnutrition, pressure ulcers, poor personal hygiene, or lack of compliance with medical regimens.[99]

Psychological Abuse or Neglect

Psychological abuse or neglect involves conduct that causes mental anguish in an older person. Psychological neglect includes the failure to provide reasonable social stimulation. This may involve leaving the older person alone for long periods of time, ignoring the older person and failing to provide companionship or information. The possibility of psychological abuse or neglect should be investigated if the older person seems extremely withdrawn, depressed, or agitated; shows signs of infantile behavior; or expresses ambivalent feelings toward caregivers or family members.

Financial Abuse

Financial or material mistreatment abuse involves misuse of the elderly person's income or resources for the financial or personal gain of a caretaker or adviser. It may involve stealing money or possessions or coercing the older person to sign contracts, purchase goods or make changes in a will.[100] Financial neglect is failure to use available funds and resources necessary to sustain or restore the health and well-being of the older adult. Financial abuse or neglect should be considered if the patient is suffering from substandard care in the home despite adequate financial resources, if the patient seems confused about or unaware of his or her financial situation, or has suddenly transferred assets to a family member.[101]

Healthcare providers are in a critical position to witness, diagnose, and report elder abuse or neglect. In some cases, good medical diagnosis and treatment can improve the functional status of the patient, reduce dependency, simplify the details of patient care, and lessen vulnerability to mistreatment. In more grievous situations, legal protection of the patients and prosecution of the offenders is more appropriate.

The Medical Approach to Elder Abuse

Family members, adult children or spouses are implicated in 90 percent of the cases of elder abuse.[102] Psychiatric disorders and substance abuse often contribute to family problems.[103] In these cases, arranging effective treatment for those affected may be important to resolve problems. Frequently abusive scenarios involve some type of bidirectional dependency or co-dependency that may make the situation difficult to resolve. For example, an adult child may depend on a parent for housing and income for basic needs; the parent may need the child to provide personal care, instrumental help with tasks like bills and shopping, and psychological comfort. In some cases, exploring other ways to satisfy these needs may greatly decrease the severity of the problems. If patient safety can be ensured along with continued access to care, a focus on the entire family as the unit of care may be most acceptable to the elderly parent or spouse.[104]

Scenarios involving neglect sometimes reflect an imbalance between the abilities and personal needs of caregivers and the needs of the identified patient. Imbalances may emerge in several ways: the patient is more disabled and needs more personal care than the family has skills or resources to provide, or caregivers have relapsing substance abuse, psychiatric problems, financial troubles or other stressors that render them unable to meet the needs of the patient. Thoughtful geriatric care can improve these situations in many ways: timely rehabilitative approaches to the patient, care to avoid unnecessarily complex and expensive medication regimens, and ongoing attention to details of management that affect the patient's cognition, continence and mobility.[105]

Self-neglect is also a common form of abuse or neglect.[106] It is often the basis for a social services agency to start a guardianship or conservatorship case, based on reports of neighbors, relatives, or professionals who are concerned about the older person. Definitions of capacity are changing in the area of self-neglect for patients living at home. In the home setting, patients must perform the routine tasks necessary to manage medical conditions over time; alternatively they need to be capable of directing others to perform certain tasks. Assessing autonomy in this setting must be expanded to include both decisional and executive dimensions. Executive autonomy includes the ability to implement and adapt plans.[107]

Almost all states have laws that mandate the reporting of suspected elder abuse to local state agencies.[108] Physicians are often reluctant to report elder abuse by family members for fear of disrupting the doctor-patient relationship and limiting their own abilities to help the patient in the future. Ideally the referral can be portrayed as an effort to get additional services and support for the household, not as a merely judgmental and punitive action.

The Legal Approach to Elder Abuse

State laws, not federal laws, are the primary legal tools in the area of elder abuse. The primary role of the federal government is as a resource center, particularly the Administration on Aging's National Center on Elder Abuse. In 2010, Congress passed the Elder Justice Act, which would increase the federal role in preventing elder abuse; however, funding has not yet been appropriated.[109]

Laws Protecting Victims

All states have laws addressing elder abuse, neglect and self-neglect. Typically, state law definitions include physical abuse, neglect or deprivation of care that results in physical harm or pain and/or mental suffering. Many states include financial exploitation as well. (Also see Chapter 11 for discussion of child abuse and neglect and interpersonal violence.)

Some of the relevant laws are criminal laws, including domestic violence laws; others are civil in nature resulting in lawsuits. Many law enforcement agencies are reluctant to step into family situations or prosecute a case where the victim has impaired memory. There is a growing trend to treat elder abuse as a criminal offense with enhanced penalties and sentences. A special classification for the elderly or disabled victim may be included in a broad range of criminal statutes, including those that proscribe assault and battery, sexual assault, and property crimes such as theft and fraud.[110] Some laws apply to paid professionals or businesses that target the vulnerable older person. Offenders range from the door-to-door salesperson to the investment adviser, from the home health aide to the religious organization.

Statutes may create special penalties for those who defraud elderly consumers including double or treble damages. In some states, minimum sentencing ranges may be set for criminals convicted of committing crimes against the elderly. Sentencing schemes may be enhanced when the victim is elderly, for example, the victim's status as elderly may be an aggravating factor to be considered in imposing the sentence. There may be a separate penalty scheme for entities and workers who abuse the elderly in institutional settings. In some states, nursing homes and other institutional caregivers and their workers are subject to penalties, including loss of license, censure and fines.[111]

An older person who has been abused or exploited can generally sue the perpetrator. The possible claims include breach of fiduciary duty, which alleges that the defendant abused a position of trust for his or her advantage, conversion (taking of property) or fraud. Some states' elder abuse statutes provide for civil redress of abuse and allow for compensatory and punitive damages, costs and attorney's fees.[112]

Best Practices and Advocacy Strategies for Medical-Legal Partnership

In Texas, the Baylor College of Medicine has trained healthcare providers and caregivers to spot mild cognitive impairment and its effect on older patients' financial affairs. They developed a *Clinician's Pocket Guide on Elder Investment Fraud*, which outlines red flags for investment fraud, tips for discussing financial capacity with older patients and resources for reporting suspected abuse.[113] This type of resource is particularly useful for MLPs that serve elders.

From Practice to Policy

Some states and cities have particularly strong laws to protect older adults. Having laws on the books, however, does not always mean the public is aware of them or that the laws are enforced. Effective policy in this area often requires outreach, education and securing a commitment on the part of law enforcement to prosecute abuse and neglect. California has developed strong linkages between the community and law enforcement to identify, report and address elder abuse.[114] Because healthcare providers may be the first to spot elder abuse, MLPs are particularly well positioned to work with community partners to develop strategies to identify and respond to elder abuse and neglect.

Case for Medical-Legal Partnership

A patient, Gertrude Johnson, age 82, comes for her regular checkup and seems very subdued. She whispers to the nurse to ask if her son "Big Jim"—who has been asked to wait in the lobby—can hear her from where he's sitting. When asked why, she says he has a very hot temper and will be very angry with what she is saying. The problem is that Gertrude doesn't want her son to stay at her house anymore. He yells at her and threatens her. But she needs someone to help her. When asked about the bruises on her arms, she is evasive and claims she bumped into a door.

Questions for Discussion

1. If her doctor is concerned that Gertrude might be the victim of abuse, what steps should he or she take, and what referrals or recommendations might be offered to Gertrude?

2. What role might the MLP lawyer play?

Caring for the Caregiver

Most personal or custodial care is provided free by families. Typical caregivers are adult children who do not live with the parent and have their own families and employment concerns. Approximately 66 percent of family caregivers are women.[115] See Figure 14.6 for more statistics.

Over three-quarters of adults living in the community and in need of long-term care depend on family and friends (i.e., informal caregivers) as their only source of help; 14 percent receive a combination of informal and formal care (i.e., paid help); only 8 percent used formal care or paid help only.[116] Even among the most severely disabled older persons living in the community, about two-thirds rely solely on family members and other informal help, often resulting in great strain for the family caregivers.[117] Given the prevalence of informal caregiving for older community-dwelling patients, it is important for MLPs to do what they can to provide support for them.

Figure 14.6 Community Long-Term Caregivers

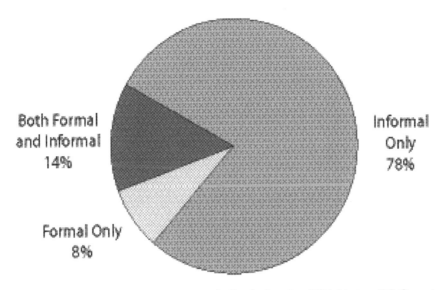

Source: Lee Thompson, "Long-term Care: Support for Family Caregivers," (Washington, DC: Georgetown University Long-Term Care Project Issue Brief, March 2004). Graph reprinted with permission. *Data Source:* Health Policy Institute, Georgetown University, analysis of data from the 1994 and 1995 National Health Interview Surveys on Disability, Phase II. *Note:* Based on people age 18 or over who, because of disability or health condition, receive help from another person with activities of daily living or instrumental activities of daily living.

Laws and Resources for Caregivers

Stressed caregivers are often unaware of their options for help. They might be eligible to apply for unpaid leave from their jobs under the federal Family and Medical Leave Act (FMLA). That law applies when the employee needs to care for a parent or spouse with a serious health condition. The law provides for leave up to 12 weeks (29 U.S.C. § 2612). (See Chapters 7, 12, and 13 for additional discussion of FMLA.) A few states, such as California, have enacted laws that provide for leave for caregivers.[118] Finally, another resource for caregivers may be found in their employer's human resources department. Companies feel the effect of the caregiving duties that employees carry out for parents and loved ones. They sometimes contract with agencies that advise their workers about services for older people. With an aging population, and considering the detrimental health impact that caregiving can have on families, MLPs have an important role to play in advocating for passage of family medical leave laws on a state and national level.

The Impact of Caregiving on Families Is Also a Health Concern

- Older caregivers are at a 63 percent higher mortality risk.

- 20 percent of employed female caregivers over 50 years old report symptoms of depression, compared to 8 percent of their noncaregiving peers.

- Depressive symptoms are an important indicator of general well-being and mental health among older adults. People who report many depressive symptoms often experience higher rates of physical illness, greater functional disability, and higher healthcare resource utilization.

- 40 to 70 percent of family caregivers have clinically significant symptoms of depression, with approximately a quarter to half of these caregivers meeting the diagnostic criteria for major depression.

- More than 1 in 10 (11 percent) of family caregivers report that caregiving has caused their physical health to deteriorate.

Sources: R. Schulz, Scott R. Beach, "Caregiving as a Risk Factor for Mortality: The Caregiver Health Effects Study," *Journal of the America Medical Association*, 282, no. 23 (1999): 2215; Leslie Gray, *Caregiving and Depression: A Growing Mental Health Concern*, a *Policy Brief* (San Francisco: National Center on Caregiving, 2003).

Best Practices and Advocacy Strategies for Medical-Legal Partnership

The American Medical Association refers to caregivers as "hidden patients." The organization encourages physicians to collaborate with social workers and other professionals to help caregivers with the goal of benefiting both the older patient and the caregiver. One tool suggested by the AMA is a brief questionnaire for caregivers to help them assess their stress and to give them options for help.[119]

From Practice to Policy

Here are three policies that MLPs may advocate for to relieve some of the burden being placed on caregivers and provide better care for older patients:

- Advocate for state paid family leave policies, such as provided under California law.[120]

- Educate the community about the Community Living Assistance Services and Supports Act (CLASS Act), which will allow employees to pay into a federal program that would later pay them a daily benefit for care. These funds can be used to pay family, friends or private caregivers.[121]

- Support legislation improving the working conditions and quality of direct care workers. High turnover, lack of training, and low wages for paid workers who provide care for the elderly have been cited as one cause of poor care. Advocates for direct care workers propose federal legislation to address these concerns. The Direct Care Workforce Empowerment Act is an example of legislation targeted at addressing this problem.[122]

Case for Medical-Legal Partnership

A 78-year-old patient, Bob Baxter, had a stroke several years ago and needs extensive help to remain at home. His wife, Susan, who is younger, still works full-time and is able to pay for a health aide during the day. Her nights, however, are very difficult because Bob needs help with eating, bathing, and walking and does not sleep well at night. She takes medication for depression but seems to be exhausted and upset. Without her care, Mr. Baxter would need nursing home care.

Questions for Discussion

1. What steps could the MLP team take to support Mrs. Baxter?
2. What resources could you refer Mr. and Mrs. Baxter to for assistance?

Conclusion

The unique and often complex health and healthcare concerns of older people require an interdisciplinary approach. Very often legal assistance is needed to address the medical concerns of the elderly. But just as important, preventive legal assistance can make a significant difference in preserving an older person's autonomy and quality of life. Working together, MLPs can provide more comprehensive and preventive care for elderly patients as well as for their families.

---

1. S. E. Levkoff, P. D. Cleary, T. Wetle, R. W. Besdine, "Illness Behavior in the Elderly." *Journal of the American Geriatric Society*, 36, no. 7 (1988) 622–29.

2. M. Sandel, M. Hansen, R. Kahn, et al., "Medical-Legal Partnerships: Transforming Primary Care by Addressing the Legal Needs of Vulnerable Patients," *Health Affairs*, 29, no. 9 (September 2010): 1697–705.

3. The attorney's duty of loyalty to a client can be modified if that client gives informed consent to allow someone else—with conflicting interests—to also be a client. ABA Model Rule of Professional Conduct 1.7 (b).

4. J. E. Soulders and G. A. Rooke, "Perioperative Care for Geriatric Patients," *Annals of Long Term Care*, 13, no. 6 (2005): 1524–9.

5. R. A. Smith, V. Cokkinides, and O.W. Brawley, Cancer Screening in the United States, 2008. Cancer Journal for Clinicians, 58 (2008): 161–79.

6. P. A. Singer, D. K. Martin, M. Kelner, "Quality End-of-life Care: Patients' Perspectives," *Journal of the American Medical Association*, 281, no. 2 (1999): 163–68.

7. Patients should be encouraged to take advantage of hospitals' assistance programs to complete advance directives. All hospitals, home health agencies and hospices that get federal funds must provide free help in executing these documents, in accordance with the Patient Self-Determination Act, 42 U.S.C. 1395 cc (a).

8. National Alliance for Caregiving in collaboration with AARP, Caregiving in the United States (Bethesda, MD: National Alliance for Caregiving, November 2009).

9. R. Pear, "Obama Returns to End-of-Life Plan That Caused Stir," *New York Times*, December 25, 2010.

10. R. Pear, "US Alters Rule on Paying for End of Life Planning," *New York Times*, January 4, 2011.

11. Y. Zhang, et al., "The Impact of Medicare Part D on Medical Adherence in Older Adults Enrolled in Medicare Advantage Products," *Medical Care*, 48, no. 5 (2010): 409–17.

12. D. E. Everitt, J. Avorn, "Drug Prescribing for the Elderly," *Archives of Internal Medicine*, 146, no. 12 (1986): 2393–96; See also Zhang et al., "The Impact of Medicare Part D," note 4.

13. Family Caregiver Alliance, "What Is Long-Term Care?," http://www.caregiver.org/caregiver/jsp/content_node.jsp?nodeid=440 (accessed February 11, 2011).

14. Over 96 percent of those age 65 and older were covered by Medicare in 2001. Employee Benefit Research Institute, *Facts from EBRI: Health Insurance and the Elderly* (Washington, DC: Employee Benefit Research Institute, August 2003); Henry J. Kaiser Family Foundation, *Medicare Fact Sheet: Medicare at a Glance* (Menlo Park: Kaiser Family Foundation, September 2010).

15. U.S. Department of Health and Human Services, *Medicare Benefits: What Is Medicare?* (Washington, DC: Department of Health and Human Services, 2011), www.medicare.gov/navigation/medicare-basics/medicare-benefits/medicare-benefits-overview.aspx (accessed February 11, 2011).

16. Ibid.

17. U.S. Department of Health and Human Services, Centers for Medicare and Medicaid Services, *Medicare Part B Premium Costs in 2010*, (Washington, DC: Department of Health and Human Services, 2009), http://www.medicare.gov/Publications/Pubs/pdf/11444.pdf (accessed February 11, 2011).

18. Medicare Payment Advisory Commission, "Medicare Advantage Program Payment System: Payment Basics" (Washington, DC: Medicare Payment Advisory Commission, October 2010).

19. Ibid., 1.

20. Center for Medicare Advocacy, "Medicare Part D Prescription Drug Coverage," http://www.medicareadvocacy.org/InfoByTopic/PartDandPrescDrugs/PartDMain.htm#LIS (accessed February 11, 2011).

21. U.S. Department of Health and Human Services, *Medicare Coverage of Skilled Nursing Facility Care* (Washington, DC: Department of Health and Human Services, September 2007), 14, http://www.medicare.gov/publications/pubs/pdf/10153.pdf (accessed on February 11, 2011).

22. Family Caregiver Alliance, "What Is Long-Term Care?"

23. A. Salganicoff, J. Cubanski, U. Ranji, T. Neuman, "Health Coverage and Expenses: Impact on Older Women's Economic Well-Being," *Journal of Women, Politics and Policy*, 30 (2009): 242.

24. U.S. Department of Health and Human Services, Centers for Medicare & Medicaid Services, *Medicare & You* (Washington, DC: Department of Health and Human Services, September 2010), 29.

25. National Academy of Social Insurance Study Panel on Medicare/Medicaid Dual Eligibles, Elizabeth Cusick, Ken Nibali, "Current Processes for Enrolling Medicare/Medicaid Dual Eligibles in Medicare Savings Programs and Efforts to Increase Enrollment" (July 2005), http://www.nasi.org/usr_doc/Current_Process.doc (accessed February 11, 2011).

26. Both Medicare and Medicaid are health insurance programs established in 1965 through amendments to the Social Security Act. Medicare is in Title XVIII ("Health Insurance for the Aged and Disabled"); codified in 42 U.S.C. 1395–1395ccc. The regulations are at 42 CFR Vol. 2, Chap. IV: 400–26, 482–93, 498. Medicaid is in Title XIX ("Grants to States for Medical Assistance Programs"), 42 U.S.C. 1396–1396(v), regulations are in 42 CFR, Vol. 2, Chap. IV: parts 402, 430–36, 440–42, 447, 455–56, 482–83, 485, 491, 493.

27. Henry J. Kaiser Family Commission, "Dual Eligibles: Medicaid's Role for Low-Income Medicare Beneficiaries" (February 2009), http://www.kff.org/medicaid/upload/4091_06.pdf (accessed February 11, 2011).

28. Ibid., note 13.

29. Patient Protection and Affordable Care Act of 2010 (PPACA), P.L. 111-148 (March 23, 2010), § 2602.

30. Center for Medicare Advocacy, "Advancing Fair Access to Medicare and Health Care" (July 22, 2010), http://www.medicareadvocacy.org/InfoByTopic/Reform/10_07.22.CHCO.htm (accessed February 11, 2011).

31. R. Ungaro, A. D. Federman, "Restrictiveness of Eligibility Determination and Medicaid Enrollment by Low-income Seniors," *Journal of Aging & Social Policy*, 21, no. 4 (Oct. 2009): 338–51.

32. Ibid., note 13.

33. Each state has a Senior Health Insurance Information Program (SHIIP), which can offer assistance in determining eligibility for Medicaid and other health insurance programs. The website www.benefitscheckup.org also offers a free assessment of eligibility based on information provided by the senior.

34. J. Leland, "Cuts in Home Care Put Elderly and Disabled at Risk," *New York Times*, July 10, 2010.

35. S. K. Inouye, "The Dilemma of Delirium: Clinical and Research Controversies Regarding Diagnosis and Evaluation of Delirium in Hospitalized Patients," *American Journal of Medicine*, 97, no. 3 (1994): 278–88.

36. P. S. Appelbaum, "Assessment of Patients' Competence to Consent to Treatment," *New England Journal of Medicine*, 357, no. 18 (2007): 1834–40.

37. Massachusetts General Law Chapter 201D §3 states, "No person who is an operator, administrator or employee of a facility may be appointed as health care agent by an adult, who, at the time of executing the health care proxy is a patient or resident of such facility ... unless said operator, administrator or employee is related to the principal by blood, marriage or adoption." N.Y. Public Health Law Article 29-C §2981 (3)(a) similarly denotes, "An operator, administrator or employee of a hospital may not be appointed as a health care agent by any person who, at the time of the appointment, is a patient or resident of ..." Article 29-C §2981 (3)(b) goes on to say, "but the restriction in paragraph (a) shall not apply to an employee of the hospital who is related to the principal by blood." In addition, Connecticut General Law Chapter 368w §19a-576 (d) says, "An operator, administrator, or employee of a hospital, residential care home, rest home with nursing supervision, or chronic and convalescent nursing home may not be appointed as a health care agent by any person who, at the time of the appointment, is a patient or a resident of ... This restriction shall not apply if such operator, administrator or employee is related to the principal by blood, marriage or adoption."

38. G. P. Eleazer, et al., "The Relationship Between Ethnicity and Advance Directives in a Frail Older Population," *Journal of American Geriatrics Society*, 44, no. 8 (1996): 938–43.

39. Lower Cape Fear Hospice and Life Care Center, *Begin the Conversation* (Wilmington, NC: Lower Cape Fear Hospice, 2011), http://www.begintheconversation.org (accessed January 7, 2011).

40. American Bar Association, Section of Real Property, Trust and Real Estate Law, "Estate Planning: Living Wills, Health Care Proxies and Advance Directives," http://www.americanbar.org/groups/real_property_trust_estate/resources/estate_planning/living_wills_health_care_proxies_advance_health_care_directives.html (accessed February 11, 2011).

41. Ibid.

42. Only 18 to 30 percent of Americans have completed an advance directive. See A. Wilkinson, N. Wenger, L. Shugarman, RAND Corporation, *Literature Review on Advance Directives* (Washington, DC: U. S. Department of Health and Human Services, Office of Disability, Aging and Long-Term Care Policy, June 2007).

43. See New York's Family Health Care Decisions Act as an example; See also Family Decisions Coalition website, which details surrogate decision making statutes in several states: http://www.familydecisions.org/otherstates.html.

44. For example, controversial cases such as *Cruzan v. Director, Mo. Dept. of Health*, 497 U.S. 261 (1990) and *Schiavo ex rel. Schindler v. Schiavo*, 404 F.3d 1270 (2005) have addressed this issue.

45. Center for Ethics in Healthcare, Oregon Health and Science University, *Physicians' Orders on Life-Sustaining Treatment Paradigm, Information for Patients and Families: Frequently Asked Questions* (Oregon: Oregon Health & Science University, 2008), http://www.ohsu.edu/polst/patients-families/faqs.htm (accessed February 7, 2011).

46. American Bar Association Commission on Law and Aging for the National Hospice and Palliative Care Organization, *The Legal Guide for the Seriously Ill: Seven Key Steps to Get Your Affairs in Order* (Alexandria, VA: National Hospice and Palliative Care Organization, 2009).

47. N.C. Senate Bill 145 of the 2003–2004 session.

48. D. A. Evans, H. H. Funkenstein, M. S. Albert, et al., "Prevalence of Alzheimer's Disease in a Community Population of Older Persons. Higher than Previously Reported," *Journal of the American Medical Association*, 262, no. 18 (1989): 2551–56.

49. D. B. Reuben, K. A. Herr, J. T. Pacala, B. G. Pollock, J. F. Potter, T. P. Semla, "Geriatrics at Your Fingertips, 12th ed.," in *Dementia* (New York: American Geriatrics Society, 2010), 57–62.

50. D. S. Geldmacher, "Differential Diagnosis of Dementia Syndromes," *Clinics in Geriatric Medicine*, 20, no. 1 (2004): 27–43.

51. G. J. McAvay, P. H. Van Ness, S. T. Bogardus Jr., et al., "Older Adults Discharged from the Hospital with Delirium: 1-Year Outcomes," *Journal of the American Geriatric Society*, 54, no. 8 (2006): 1245–50.

52. D. B. Reuben, et al., "Geriatrics at Your Fingertips," 54–56.

53. S. Borson, J. M. Scanlan, P. Chen, M. Ganguli, "The Mini-Cog as a Screen for Dementia: Validation in a Population Based Sample," *Journal of the American Geriatric Society*, 51, no. 10 (2003): 1451–54M.

54. E. Pfeiffer, "A Short Portable Mental Status Questionnaire for the Assessment of Organic Brain Deficit in Elderly Patients," *Journal of the American Geriatric Society*, 23 (1975): 433–41.

55. S. Folstein and P. R. McHugh, "Mini-Mental State: A Practical Method for Grading the Cognitive State of Patients for the Clinician," *Journal of Psychiatric Research*, 12, no. 3 (1975): 189–98.

56. For example, Section 9.60 of New York State Mental Health Law sets forth criteria judges must use in determining whether to require someone to undergo involuntary outpatient mental health treatment. Forty-four other states have similar laws (http://www.nysenate.gov/press-release/kendra-s-law-passes-senate). Massachusetts General Law Chapter 201 § 14(c) states, "No temporary guardian so appointed shall have the authority to consent to treatment with antipsychotic medication, provided that the court shall authorize such treatment when it (i) specifically finds using the substituted judgment standard that the person, if competent, would consent to such treatment and (ii) specifically approves and authorizes an antipsychotic medication treatment plan by its order or decree."

57. B. D. Lebowitz, J. L. Pearson, L. S. Schneider, et al., "Diagnosis and Treatment of Depression in Late Life: Consensus Statement Update," *Journal of the American Medical Association,* 278, no. 14 (1997): 1186–90.

58. B. A. Garner, ed., *Black's Law Dictionary*, 9th ed. (Eagan, Minnesota: West Group, 2009); "Springing power of attorney. A power of attorney that becomes effective only when needed, at some future date or upon some future occurrence, usu. upon the principal's incapacity."

59. S. K. Summer, ABA Senior Lawyers Division, *Guardianship and Conservatorship: A Handbook for Lawyers*, (Chicago, IL: American Bar Association, 1996).

60. Massachusetts General Law Chapter 201D § 17 states that several categories of people involved in the patient's situation "may commence a special proceeding in a court of competent jurisdiction, with respect to any dispute arising under this chapter, including, but not limited to, a proceeding to (a) determine the validity of the health care proxy."

61. National Committee to Preserve Social Security and Medicare, "Senior Income Statistics" (March 2010), http://www.ncpssm.org/ss_senior_income/ (accessed February 11, 2011).

62. Social Security Administration, *Physician's/Medical Officer's Statement of Patient's Capability to Manage Benefits, Form SSA-787* (Baltimore: Social Security Administration, May 2010).

63. Security Administration. "FAQs for Representative Payees" (modified December 2010), http://www.ssa.gov/payee/faqrep.htm (accessed February 11, 2011).

64. 42 U.S.C. § 1396b(f)(4)(C); 42 CFR 435.725(c)(1)(i).

65. For examples, see Massachusetts Uniform Probate Code § 5-101 (9); New Hampshire Revised Statutes Annotated § 464-A:2 XI; Connecticut General Laws Chapter 802h § 45a-644 (c) & (d)

66. American Bar Association, Commission on Law and Aging, *State Law Charts and Updates: Adult Guardianship State Legislative Charts: Limited Guardianship of the Person* (Chicago: American Bar Association, 2008).

67. National Academy of Elder Law Attorneys, *Wingspan: The Second National Guardianship Conference, Recommendations* (Vienna: National Academy of Elder Law Attorneys, 2001): 4; Section II.

68. Massachusetts Uniform Probate Code § 5-303 (a); Pennsylvania Consolidated Statute Title 20 § 5511 (a); Utah Code § 75-5-303 (1).

69. J. N. Alschuler, et al., *The Guardian ad Litem Handbook* (Madison, WI: State Bar of Wisconsin, 2000).

70. Pennsylvania Consolidated Statute Title 20 § 5511 (f); Massachusetts Uniform Probate Code § 5-409.

71. New York Public Health Law Article 29CC § 2994-D 4 (i); California Probate Code § 4714; Tennessee Code Annotated § 68-11-1706(c)(4)(A).

72. This form is available at http://www.pcpfc.com/webforms/MedCert-GuardMI-MR.pdf (accessed February 11, 2011).

73. J. Reischel, "Guardianship Reform in Massachusetts Proving Unpopular," *Massachusetts Lawyers Weekly*, March 22, 2010.

74. U.S. Census Bureau, "POV01: Age and Sex of All People, Family Members and Unrelated Individuals Iterated by Income-to-Poverty Ratio and Race: 2009," http://www.census.gov/hhes/www/cpstables/032010/pov/new01_100_01.htm (accessed February 11, 2011).

75. U.S. Census Bureau, "POV46: Poverty Status by State: 2009," http://www.census.gov/hhes/www/cpstables/032010/pov/new46_100125_14.htm (accessed February 11, 2011).

76. D. I. Smith, R.E. Spraggins, *Gender, 2000: Census 2000 Brief* (Washington, DC: U.S. Department of Commerce, Economics and Statistics Administration, 2001); Olivia S. Mitchell, Phillip B. Levine, John W. Phillips, *The Impact of Pay Inequality, Occupational Segregation, and Lifetime Work Experience on the Retirement Income of Women and Minorities* (Washington, DC: American Association of Retired Persons Public Policy Institute, September 1999).

77. E. O'Brien, K. Bin Wu and D. Baer, *Older Americans in Poverty: A Snapshot* (Washington, DC: AARP Public Policy Institute, April 2010), 12.

78. Ibid.

79. D. C. John, *Disparities for Women and Minorities in Retirement Saving* (Washington, DC: The Brookings Institution, Sept. 2010).

80. P. Purcell, *Income and Poverty Among Older Americans in 2008,* (Washington, DC: Congressional Research Service, 2009).

81. 26 U.S.C. 6305 ("Garnishment for Child Support"); Internal Revenue Code, 26 U.S.C. 6331 and 6334, which allows for collection of federal taxes.

82. Fair Debt Collection Practices Act, 15 U.S.C. §§ 1692c–f.

83. U.S. Department of Housing and Urban Development, U.S. Department of the Treasury, *Making Home Affordable: MHA Overview Presentation for Counselors,* https://www.hmpadmin.com/portal/resources/docs/counselor/presentations/mhacounselorpresenglish.pdf (accessed February 11, 2011).

84. U.S. Department of Housing and Urban Development, U.S. Department of the Treasury, "Making Home Affordable: FAQ," http://makinghomeaffordable.gov/borrower-faqs.html (accessed February 11, 2011).

85. See, for example, Arizona's law regulating debt collection at 20 A.A.C. 4.

86. See, for example, Annotated Code of Maryland § 15-601.1.

87. Fair Housing Act, 42 U.S.C. § 3601-3619; 24 C.F.R. § 100.204.

88. Bazelon Center for Mental Health, Advocacy Training and Technical Assistance Center of the National Association of Protection and Advocacy Systems, "Fair Housing Information Sheet # 5," http://www.bazelon.org/LinkClick.aspx?fileticket=ftg2oguJbkQ%3d&tabid=245 (accessed February 11, 2011).

89. Bazelon Center for Mental Health, Advocacy Training and Technical Assistance Center of the National Association of Protection and Advocacy Systems, "Fair Housing Information Sheet # 4: Using Reasonable Accommodations to Prevent Eviction" (Washington, DC: Bazelon Center for Mental Health, December 2003).

90. Health Policy Institute, Georgetown University, *Fact Sheet:Who Pays for Long-Term Care?* (Washington, DC: Georgetown University Long-Term Care Financing Project, July 2004).

91. Health Policy Institute, Georgetown University, *Fact Sheet: Private Long-Term Care Insurance* (Washington, DC: Georgetown University Long-Term Care Financing Project, May 2003).

92. Center for Medicare Advocacy, "Home Health Care," http://www.medicareadvocacy.org/InfoByTopic/HomeHealth/HomeHealthMain.htm (accessed February 11, 2011).

93. 130 C.M.R. § 520.003; See also, The Elder Care Team, "What Is Spending Down for Medicaid?," http://www.eldercareteam.com/public/539.cfm (accessed February 11, 2011).

94. 42 U.S.C. § 1396r-5; U.S. Department of Health and Human Services, *2010 SSI and Spousal Impoverishment Standards,* available at https://www.cms.gov/MedicaidEligibility/downloads/1998-2010SSIFBR122909.pdf (Last accessed February 11, 2011).

95. U.S. Department of Health and Human Services, *2010 SSI and Spousal Impoverishment.*

96. HP 0483, LD 700, (1), 124th Maine St. Leg., "Act to Restore Funding for Bed-hold Days at Private Non-medical Institutions."

97. M. S. Lachs, K. Pillemer, "Elder Abuse," *The Lancet*, 364, no. 9441 (2004): 1263–72.

98. Ibid.

99. Ibid.

100. John A. Hartford Foundation Institute for Geriatric Nursing, Eileen Chichin, et al., "Staff Development Partners Edition, Instructor Guide," *Module 16: Caregiving and Mistreatment of Older Adults*, quoted by Evidence to Practice, Benedictine Health System, "Topics developed by the John A. Hartford Foundation Institute for Geriatric Nursing: Caregiving/Elder Mistreatment," http://www.evidence2practice.org/topics/Hartford/data/guides/Module16CaregivingandMistreatmentofOlderAdults.doc (accessed February 11, 2011).

101. Ibid.

102. Institute on Aging, "Elder Abuse Prevention," http://www.ioaging.org/aging/elder_abuse_sf.html (accessed February 11, 2011).

103. Arizona Attorney General's Website, "Elder Abuse Information and Training Guide," http://www.azag.gov/seniors/elder_abuse_guide.html#9 (accessed February 11, 2011).

104. "Diagnostic and Treatment Guidelines on Elder Abuse and Neglect," *Archives of Family Medicine*, 2 (1993): 371–88.

105. Ibid.

106. M. J. Gorbien, A. R. Eisenstein, "Elder Abuse and Neglect: An Overview," *Clinics in Geriatric Medicine*, 21 (2005): 279–92.

107. A. D. Naik, C. R. Teal, V. N. Pavlik, C. B. Dyer, L. B. McCullough, "Conceptual Challenges and Practical Approaches to Screening Capacity for Self-Care and Protection in Vulnerable Older Adults," *Journal of the American Geriatric Society*, 56, no. S2 (2008): 266–70.

108. Forty-seven states have mandatory reporting requirements. Gerald J. Jogerst, et al., "Domestic Elder Abuse and the Law," *American Journal of Public Health*, 93, no. 12 (2003): 2131–36.

109. L. A. Stiegel, "Elder Justice Act Becomes Law, But Victory Is Only Partial," *Bifocal*, 31, no. 4 (March–April 2010).

110. State of Arizona Attorney General's Office, "Elder Abuse: Potential Legal Remedies" http://www.azag.gov/seniors/elderabuse.pdf (accessed February 11, 2011) Adapted from Wisconsin Coalition for Domestic Violence, National Program Development, Training and Technical Assistance, "Elder Abuse in Later Life" (Madison, WI: Wisconsin Coalition for Domestic Violence 2003).

111. ConsumerAffairs.com, "California Fines Nursing Home Chain $1 Million: Pleasant Care Hit with More than 160 Citations" *Consumer Affairs* (March 8, 2006), http://www.consumeraffairs.com/news04/2006/03/ca_pleasant_care.html (accessed February 11, 2011).

112. "Elder Abuse and Neglect Basics: Elder Abuse Laws," National Center for State Courts, Center for Elders and the Courts, http://www.eldersandcourts.org/abuse/laws.html (accessed February 11, 2011).

113. The Pocket Guide is available at http://www.investorprotection.org/downloads/pdf/learn/research/EIFFE_Clinicians_Pocket_Guide.pdf (accessed February 11, 2011).

114. State of California, Department of Justice, Bureau of Medi-Cal Fraud and Elder Abuse, "A Citizen's Guide to Reporting and Preventing Elder Abuse," (Sacramento, CA: State of California Department of Justice, 2002).

115. National Family Caregivers Association, Caregiving Statistics, http://www.nfcacares.org/who_are_family_caregivers/care_giving_statstics.cfm (accessed February 11, 2011).

116. Family Caregiver Alliance. "What Is Long-Term Care?," http://www.caregiver.org/caregiver/jsp/content_node.jsp?nodeid=440 (accessed February 11, 2011).

117. Ibid.

118. National Partnership for Women & Families, *Building Better Workplaces for Family Caregivers*, (Washington, DC: National Partnership for Women & Families, 2010).

119. The AMA's Caregiver Self-Assessment may be found at http://www.ama-assn.org/ama1/pub/upload/mm/433/caregiver_english.pdf (accessed February 11, 2011).

120. California Work and Family Coalition, "Paid Family Leave: Learn More," http://www.paid-familyleave.org (accessed February 11, 2011).

121. Leading Age, "Community Living Assistance Services and Support (CLASS) Act Summary," http://www.aahsa.org/classact.aspx (accessed February 11, 2011).

122. Direct Care Alliance, "The Direct Care Workforce Empowerment Act" (New York, NY: Direct Care Alliance, 2010), www.directcarealliance.org (accessed February 18, 2011).

Chapter 15

Adolescent Health and Legal Rights

Abigail English, JD
Debra Braun-Courville, MD
Patricia Flanagan, MD
Angela Diaz, MD, MPH
MaryKate Geary, BA

Adolescence is a time of normative developmental transition: from childhood to adulthood, from dependence to independence, from the world of school to the world of work. This time of life is dynamic and evolving. Adolescents experience simultaneous physical changes, psychosocial changes, psychosexual changes and cognitive changes. Adolescence is also a critical time for moral and social development. Recent studies of brain development show radical changes during this period, perhaps helping explain some of the risk-taking behaviors associated with adolescence. The health and health risks for adolescents reflect the dramatic changes during this period of life.

Society views adolescence with ambivalence. This ambivalence is particularly evident in the law, where adolescents are sometimes treated as competent adults, able to make their own decisions, and at other times treated as children in need of protection:

> With respect to age, individuals are categorized into two groups: children and adults ... Persons below the line (children) are incapable of action and require support and protection. Persons above the line (adults) have full capacity.... There is no separate legal status of adolescence.... The line is not necessarily drawn at age 18 for all purposes, however. In many states, a child can drive at 16, be sentenced to adult prison for certain offenses at 14, but be legally incapable of possessing alcohol until age 21.[1]

Protecting the parent-child relationship while also providing young adults with some level of independence and responsibility makes legal line-drawing difficult. Many laws, including those governing consent and confidentiality in the healthcare setting, reproductive rights of minors and access to services and the legal system, reflect this tension. The inconsistency may leave healthcare providers confused and unsure about how they should balance the need to develop trust with an adolescent patient while including parents in decision making. Particularly vulnerable teens, such as those who are homeless, LGBTQ (lesbian, gay, bisexual, transgender and questioning), pregnant or in state custody present challenges that make delivery of effective care even more challenging.

Although this chapter cannot begin to address all of the health concerns or legal issues that affect adolescents, it provides an overview of some of the ways in which health and law converge—or conflict—during adolescence and in which medical and legal partners can work together most effectively to address the needs of adolescent patients and clients. (Readers interested in the medical-legal concerns of adolescents may also wish to review Chapters 9 and 11, which provide greater detail about how those subjects affect adolescent health and legal rights.)

This chapter begins with an overview of adolescent health and the legal concerns in the healthcare context. It then provides a summary of some of the particular health concerns that arise during adolescence and the legal context surrounding those concerns. Finally, it discusses some particularly vulnerable subgroups of teens—homeless youth, youth in foster care and juvenile detention, pregnant and parenting teens, and LGBTQ youth—and addresses some of the health challenges and legal barriers these youth face. Throughout the chapter are examples of ways medical-legal partners can help youth overcome barriers that may impede their health and access the services they need to transition into a healthy and productive adulthood.

From Childhood to Adulthood: An Overview of Adolescent Health Issues

The Demographics of Adolescents in the United States

The adolescent and young adult population in the United States is increasing in number and diversity. Between 1990 and 2006 the population of 10–24-year-olds increased from 40 million to 63 million.[2] As shown in Figure 15.1, the racial and ethnic composition of

Figure 15.1 Racial and Ethnic Diversity of U.S. Youth Ages 10–24, 2006

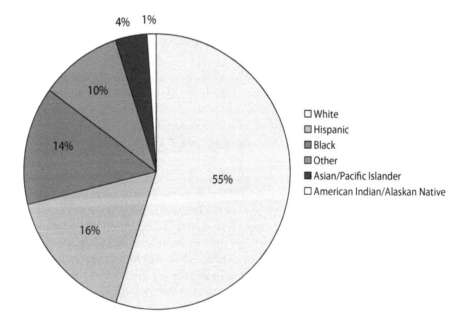

Notes: The adolescent and young adult population will continue to become more diverse in the next decade: by 2020, it is projected that it will include 6.3 percent Asians/Pacific Islanders, 14.1 percent blacks, and 22.2 percent Hispanics. More than 1 in 10 (10.6 percent) adolescents and young adults (ages 15–24) was foreign-born in 2006. The overall number of adolescents and young adults is expected to increase from 63.3 million in 2006 to 64.1 million in 2020.
Source: National Adolescent Health Information Center, 2008 Fact Sheet on Demographics: Adolescents and Young Adults, http://nahic.ucsf.edu//downloads/Demographics08.pdf.

U.S. youth in 2006 is changing as well. In 2006, one in ten 15–24-year-olds was an immigrant or foreign-born.[3] Many adolescents live in poverty. In 2009, 19.2 percent of children and adolescents between the ages of 5 and 17 and 20.7 percent of young adults between the ages of 18 and 24 were living below 100 percent of the federal poverty level.[4]

The racial and ethnic diversity and high percentage of poverty among the adolescent and young adult population, combined with the fact that adolescence is often a tumultuous time of life, presents many challenges for healthcare providers. To treat the adolescent patient effectively and sensitively, healthcare providers often must understand and navigate complex issues. These include adolescent development, sexuality, family relationships and stability, and social and cultural context.

Adolescent Health and Development

Practitioners often consider adolescence a healthy age demographic. According to the National Health Interview Survey, the percent of adolescents 12–17 years of age with fair or poor health is only 2.3 percent. Five percent of adolescents 12–17 years of age missed 11 or more days of school in the past 12 months because of illness or injury.[5] Morbidity among adolescents is modest, with very low rates of hospitalization and the majority of healthcare usage being outpatient (office visits or emergency rooms).[6]

Although adolescents are generally healthier than other age groups, the adolescent period is nevertheless affected by serious health concerns. Health risk behaviors among adolescents constitute the major reasons for mortality and morbidity. According to the Centers for Disease Control and Prevention (CDC), the leading causes of mortality and morbidity among youth in the United States are related to six categories of priority health risk behaviors. These are: (1) behaviors that contribute to unintentional injury and violence, (2) tobacco use, (3) alcohol and other drug use, (4) sexual behaviors that contribute to unintended pregnancies and sexually transmitted infections including HIV, (5) unhealthy dietary behaviors, and (6) physical inactivity.[7] As Figure 15.2 shows, the leading causes of death for adolescents are unintentional injury (primarily car accidents), homicide and suicide.

Health behaviors that begin in adolescence lay a foundation for lifelong health habits, behaviors and risks. Exposure to violence, alcohol consumption, substance abuse and sexual behaviors such as condom use and partner selection, can all strongly influence adult health behaviors, habits and status.

The CDC Youth Risk Behavior Survey

The CDC surveys in-school youth on a biannual basis, asking about behaviors and conditions experienced by teens. The Youth Risk Behavior Survey (YRBS) is a self-reported survey of a national sample of U.S. youth in grades 9–12. Results from the 2009 YRBS indicate that many students report engaging in behaviors that increase their risk for the leading causes of death among people aged 10–24 in the United States.

- Nearly 10 percent rarely or never wore seatbelts.

- 17 percent had carried a weapon.

- 19 percent had smoked tobacco in the past 30 days.

Figure 15.2 Five Leading Causes of Deaths among Persons Ages 10–24 Years (United States, 2005)

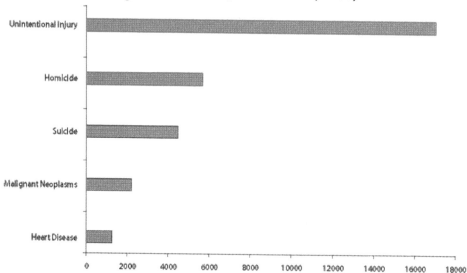

Source: Centers for Disease Control and Prevention, National Center for Injury Prevention and Control, Division of Violence Prevention, http://www.cdc.gov/violenceprevention/youthviolence/stats_at-a_glance/lcd_10-24.html.

- 28 percent reported having had at least a two-week period of persistent sadness and hopelessness in the past year, and 6.3 percent had attempted suicide.

- 28 percent report that in the month preceding the survey they rode in a car driven by someone who had been drinking alcohol.

- 31 percent had been in a physical fight.

- 34 percent were currently sexually active, and 38 percent of those reported not using a condom during their most recent sexual encounter.

- 42 percent had consumed alcohol, and 20.8 percent had smoked marijuana.

- 77 percent had not consumed five or more fruits or vegetables/day in the week preceding the survey.

- Over 80 percent were not physically active every day, and 12 percent were obese.[a]

When considering these behavioral risks to health, it is important to recognize that adolescent risk behaviors do not occur in isolation but often co-occur in the same individual. Over half of U.S. high school students reported that they engaged in two or more behaviors that carried significant health risks, and 15 percent were engaged in at least five such behaviors. Males and older students are the most likely to engage in multiple risk-taking behaviors.[b]

Source: [a] D. K. Eaton, et al., "Youth Risk Behavior Surveillance—United States, 2009," *Morbidity and Mortality Weekly Report*, 59, no. 5 (2010): 2, http://www.cdc.gov/mmwr/pdf/ss/ss5905.pdf; [b] H. B. Fox, et al., "Significant Multiple Risk Behaviors among U.S. High School Students, Fact Sheet No. 8," *The National Alliance to Advance Adolescent Health* (March 2010): 4, http://thenationalalliance.org/mar10/ factsheet8.pdf.

Adolescent Health: Risk and Opportunity

Because the profile of adolescent mortality and morbidity is so heavily influenced by behavior and decision making, it is important to understand adolescent health from a developmental perspective. The dynamic nature of physical, cognitive and social changes that are the hallmark of adolescence drive many of the health risks that young adults face. Between the ages of 10 and 18, physical changes are enormous. Height, weight, strength and hemoglobin all increase dramatically, often over very short time intervals. The myriad of changes occur with the emergence of secondary sex characteristics — breasts, hips, redistribution of fat and hair, deepening of voices, the onset of menstruation and the ability to procreate.

Just as dramatic as the physical changes are changes in psychosocial, psychosexual and cognitive realms. The processes of self-discovery, erotic exploration, experimentation, limit testing and risk taking are a necessary and healthy part of adolescence. At the same time, these changes can lead to increases in impulsivity, aggression, moodiness and introspection. They may also drive the underlying causes of adolescent mortality and morbidity. Cognitive development — including the ability to think abstractly, see alternative solutions to a problem, take another's perspective and link cause and effect — progresses throughout the adolescent years. At the same time, the inability to function wholly in the realm of adult abstract reasoning may lead to some poor decision making and putting youth in harm's way, resulting in unplanned pregnancies, car accidents and violence.

The Adolescent Brain

Recent advances have allowed study of the maturation of brain and thought processing in exciting and enlightening ways. Adolescents may take more risks, at least partly because they have an immature prefrontal cortex. The frontal cortex is the area of the brain responsible for executive functions, assessing multiple factors, and judgment of risk and benefit, cause and effect. Recent research into neurodevelopment reveals that the prefrontal cortex is late to develop and perhaps reaches its maturity in the early twenties.[8]

The brain early in adolescence differs from the late adolescent or adult brain in anatomy, biochemistry and physiology. In early puberty, the brain grows many neural connections. Over the course of adolescence and young adulthood, the number of these connections diminish.[9] "Scientists believe this process reflects greater organization of the brain as it prunes redundant connections, and increases in myelin, which enhance transmission of brain messages."[10] Figure 15.3 demonstrates this maturation process.

Development brings risks but also opportunities for good health among adolescents and young adults. As people progress through this epoch of their lives, they gain mastery of their world, insight and decision-making abilities, generosity and the perspective of others, and healthy connections and relationships. These developmental forces are strong

Figure 15.3. Changes in the Adolescent Brain

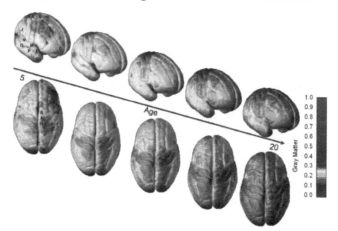

Source: N. Gogtay, et al., "Dynamic Mapping of Human Cortical Development during Childhood through Early Adulthood," *Proceedings of the National Academy of Sciences*, 101, no. 21 (May 25, 2004): 8174–79. Copyright 2004, National Academy of Sciences, U.S.A.

and, when appropriately nurtured, can have great impact on adolescents' health and their health behaviors. Recognizing the strengths and emerging abilities of adolescents, building on the new awareness and reasoning, and encouraging teens and young adults to make healthy decisions will improve their health during adolescence and into adulthood.

Chronic Health Conditions among Adolescents

In the United States, 16.8 percent of youth (12–17 years) have a chronic health condition. A chronic health condition for an adolescent is defined as a problem that has lasted or is anticipated to last greater than one year and has at least one of the following: (1) use of or need for prescription medicine on a regular basis; (2) use of or need for more medical care, mental health services or educational services than others of the same age; (3) an ongoing emotional, developmental or behavioral problem that requires treatment or counseling; (4) a limitation in ability to do things most children of the same age can do; and/or (5) the use of or need for special therapy (such as physical, occupational and/or speech therapy).[11]

However, the lack of illness or medical diagnoses among youth is not the same as good health or wellness. A recent report from the Lewin Group stated that 70 percent of female and 62 percent of male recruits failed to qualify for military service. More than half of the disqualifications were because of obesity (30 percent of both males and females); the other most common conditions included drug abuse, mental illness and asthma.[12] Parents and youth may not necessarily perceive obesity as a health concern because most of the excess morbidity and mortality related to obesity does not manifest until later in life. Nonetheless, the military views obesity as a major health issue related to lack of fitness for service among young adults. It also may reflect sociodemographic influences on an all-volunteer military and thus reflect health disparities of low-income populations. (For further discussion of obesity, see Chapter 17.)

Youth with special healthcare needs face particularly complex issues in transitioning from pediatric systems of care to adult systems. The Society for Adolescent Health and Medicine formalized a position paper on this topic nearly 20 years ago, and it is still an area of active research and progress.[13] It is often not a seamless process as adolescents are learning how to navigate the healthcare system as young adults and beginning to assume more autonomy and leadership for directing their medical care. A variety of patient- and provider-specific factors have been identified: lack of patient preparation, scarcity of appropriately trained providers and centers, inadequate insurance coverage, physician/ parent/patient attitudes and cognitive impairment.[14] Nevertheless, healthcare providers and legal professionals can help adolescents with this transition by providing supportive services, helping them access health insurance and connecting them to adult care providers.

Adolescents and the Social Determinants of Health

Perhaps because so much of adolescent health is driven by behavior rather than genetic or biological risk, the primacy of the social determinants of health in adolescents' lives is significant. An adolescent's health is closely related to the quality of his or her school, the safety of his or her neighborhood, the emotional and financial stability of his or her family and the opportunities for successful paths to adulthood. For example, genetic predisposition or biological risk does not drive rates of death from a gunshot wound among minority youth in urban areas, car accidents on Native American reservations or childbearing among young teens in poor rural communities. Moreover, these events are not randomly distributed across the adolescent young adult population of the United States.

Poverty and Race

Economically stressed adolescent populations carry an increased burden of illness. In 2008, the majority of youth in the United States reported they were in excellent (56 percent) or very good health (21 percent).[15] However, health status was clearly related to socioeconomic status. For example, the study showed that as the level of maternal education increased, the percent of children with excellent health increased. Children in poor families were five times more likely to suffer from poor health (5 percent) compared with children whose families were not poor (1 percent).[16] School days lost due to illness or injury also show nonrandom patterns. Children in single-parent households are twice as likely to report having missed more than 11 days of school in the past year due to illness or injury (7 percent vs. 4 percent).[17]

Rates of particular illness are also higher for lower-income and minority adolescents. For example, asthma rates for poor and minority youth are higher than for higher-income white youth. Though 16 percent of all U.S. teens age 12–17 years have ever been diagnosed with asthma, 21 percent of non-Hispanic black children have ever been diagnosed; 18 percent of poor children compared with 13 percent of higher income children have had asthma.[18] Similarly, attention deficit/hyperactivity disorder (ADHD) is another common cause of morbidity among U.S. youth that shows disparities based on income. The condition is twice as prevalent among youth in low-income families compared to high-income families with rates of 12 percent compared with 6 percent.[19] (For discussion of ADHD in relation to education, see Chapter 9.)

Access to Healthcare

Adolescents are uninsured and underinsured at higher rates than other groups in the population; young adults aged 18 to 24 are uninsured at the very highest rates.[20] Although increasingly adolescents are covered through public insurance programs such as Medicaid and the Children's Health Insurance Program (CHIP), many remain uninsured.[21] As discussed later in the chapter, the potential for very significant changes in insurance coverage for young adults has arrived with the enactment of healthcare reform legislation in 2010. Medical-legal partnerships (MLPs) play an important role in ensuring that eligible youth are enrolled in insurance programs, thus improving access to preventive care and helping reduce health risk behaviors.

Clinical Implications for Healthcare Providers Serving Adolescents

Healthcare providers who serve adolescents face unique challenges. They must balance gaining the adolescent's trust while getting important information about — and addressing — health risk behaviors. The cornerstone of adolescent medicine is confidentiality. Adolescents are more willing to disclose sensitive information when they trust the clinician.[22] (Confidentiality is discussed in detail later in this chapter.) Healthcare providers should take time to listen to their adolescent patients, be culturally sensitive and be nonjudgmental.[23] (For discussion of culturally sensitive care and nonjudgmental listening, see Chapter 5.) Questioning and interviewing a young adult also requires an understanding and appreciation of adolescent development. For example, younger adolescents tend to be very concrete thinkers, focused on the "here and now." In contrast, older adolescents may be more able to think about long-term planning. Finally, providers should take a full psychosocial history from adolescents to identify health and social concerns. Table 15.1 provides an example — the HEADSSS Screening.

Questions for Discussion

1. What are the particular challenges involved in healthcare for adolescents?
2. What are the greatest health risks faced by adolescents?
3. How does adolescent development affect the provider-patient relationship?
4. How do social determinants play a role in adolescent health? What does this mean for practice?

Legal Rights of Adolescents in the Healthcare System

Adolescence, by definition, is an important developmental stage of life, as well as a time of transition from childhood to adulthood. As already discussed, it is also a time of multiple physical, cognitive and emotional changes. Consequently, there is often societal ambivalence about how much freedom and responsibility to bestow on adolescents, particularly with regard to important decision making. Lawmakers must determine where to draw the line between treating adolescents more like adults who have the legal right to act independently or more like children whose parent or guardian maintain legal responsibility. Laws governing the rights of adolescents in the healthcare context strongly influence their access to care. Concerns about confidentiality or required parental consent may create barriers to adolescents seeking care.

Financial issues, such high costs and lack of a source of payment for care, may also impede the ability to provide timely care to adolescents. Therefore, a basic understanding of state and federal laws affecting the rights of adolescents and young adults in the healthcare setting is critical for healthcare providers. MLP lawyers are an important resource for educating both healthcare providers and young people about legal rights involved in

Table 15.1 The Psychosocial History Using HEADSS Screening Questions

Home
  • Where do you live?
  • How long have you lived there?
  • Who lives at home with you?
  • Do you feel safe at home?
  • Do you feel safe in your neighborhood

Education
  • Where do you go to school?
  • Have you changed schools recently?
  • What do you like or not like about school?
  • Do you feel safe at school?
  • What are your grades like?
  • What do you want to do after finishing school?

Activities/Employment
  • What do you do for fun?
  • Do you have a best friend?
  • Do you have a job?
  • Do you exercise?
  • Do you feel comfortable with your eating habits?

Drugs
  • Do any of your friends smoke or drink?
  • Do you know anyone who smokes or drinks?
  • Have you ever tried?
  • Have you ever ridden in a car driven by someone (including yourself) who was "high" or had been using alcohol or drugs?

Suicidality
  • Have you ever been so sad you thought about hurting yourself
  • Have you ever tried?
  • Do you feel sad now?
  • Have you ever cut yourself intentionally?

Sex
  • Have you ever dated anyone?
  • Boys, girls, or both?
  • Have you ever kissed anyone?
  • Have you ever had sex?
  • Has anyone ever touched you in a way you did not want to be touched or forced to do something you did not want to do sexually?
  • Have you ever had a sexually transmitted infection?
  • Are you sexually active now? Did you use a condom with your last sexual encounter?
  • Have you ever been pregnant?

Source: Rachel Katzenellenbogen, "HEADSS: The "Review of Systems" for Adolescents," *Virtual Mentor,* 7 (2005).

accessing care. In partnership with healthcare providers, they can also advocate on behalf of youth to address barriers to care.

This section discusses in general terms the legal requirements and protections that facilitate access to healthcare for adolescents. Specifically, it explains the state laws that determine whether adolescents who are legally minors (under age 18) can consent for their own healthcare, the federal and state laws that protect confidentiality for adolescents who are minors or young adults and the laws that help ensure that healthcare is financially accessible to adolescents.

Consent and Confidentiality

Parental Consent

Parental consent is usually required for a minor's healthcare, although exceptions to this requirement allow other adults, courts or minors themselves to consent.[24] Alternatives to parental consent may include consent by legal guardians, or by other adult relatives, caretakers, custodians and occasionally foster parents; courts may often give consent and may authorize others such as social workers or probation officers to do so for young people in state custody.[25] Prior consent is not required in emergencies because it is implied.[26] The requirement of parental consent is based in common law (court cases) and in many states is not found in specific statutes, although the alternatives and exceptions are usually spelled out in statutes. In addition to the exceptions previously mentioned, every state has some laws that expressly allow minors to give their own consent for healthcare either because they have attained a particular status or because they are seeking a particular type of care.[27]

Minor Consent

The minor consent laws based on status most frequently authorize minors to consent if they are emancipated; living apart from their parents, including runaways or homeless youth; serving in the armed forces; married; parents of a child; high school graduates; at least a certain age, such as 15 or 16; or "mature minors," who meet certain criteria for capacity to consent.[28]

The minor consent laws based on type of care most frequently include contraceptive services; pregnancy-related care; diagnosis and treatment of sexually transmitted diseases (often referred to in the statutes as venereal disease), HIV or AIDS and reportable or contagious diseases; counseling and treatment for drug or alcohol problems; mental health treatment, particularly outpatient care; and examination and treatment related to sexual assault.[29]

Not all states have statutes covering every status or all of these services. Some of the laws contain age limits, which most frequently fall between 12 and 15 years, or other specific limiting criteria.[30] Montana is a state with relatively comprehensive statutory provisions related to minor consent and confidentiality. Other states may have similar laws, or laws that are more comprehensive or more limited. It is essential for healthcare professionals to be familiar with the specific laws in their own state.

Example of State Law Provisions Related to Minor Consent and Confidentiality: Montana

The age of majority (the age at which the law considers a person an adult) is 18 in Montana. However, Montana law authorizes minors to consent for healthcare in several situations. For example, emancipated minors (those who are living apart from their parents and providing self-support by any means), married minors, minor parents and high school graduates are generally allowed to consent for their own healthcare. Pregnant minors are allowed to consent for pregnancy-related care, including contraception and prenatal and maternity care. Although Montana does not have an explicit statute that authorizes minors to consent for family planning services or contraceptive care, minors can do so in sites receiving federal Title X funds (explained later in this chapter) or when the services are paid for by Medicaid. Minors also are allowed to consent for care for sexually transmitted diseases (STDs) and reportable diseases, including HIV and AIDS; treatment for drug or alcohol abuse; and outpatient mental health services.

A law requiring notice to a parent before a minor can obtain an abortion was declared unconstitutional under the Montana constitution and is not being enforced, so minors may consent for their own abortions without parent or court involvement. Montana relieves parents of financial responsibility for care in most situations when a minor has given consent unless the parents agree to pay; the minors who have given consent are financially responsible, unless they are unable to pay and receive services in a public institution. Healthcare professionals who provide outpatient mental health services are relieved of liability unless they are negligent.

Information about the care for which minors have given consent may be disclosed to parents in specified circumstances affecting the health of the minor or family members, such as child abuse, imminent danger, crime victimization or life-threatening suicidal or harmful behavior. Information about the care of emancipated minors may not be disclosed. Information also may not be disclosed without the consent of the minor if the minor is found not to be pregnant, not have an STD or not be suffering from drug abuse. Minors who have consented to care have exclusive control over their medical records under the state's Uniform Healthcare Information Act. Healthcare professionals are not required to accept the consent of a minor for healthcare. Minors age 15 or older may enter into contracts for health and life insurance.[a]

Source: [a] A. English, et al., *State Minor Consent Laws, A Summary*, 3rd ed. (Chapel Hill, NC: Center for Adolescent Health & the Law, 2010).

Emancipated Minors and "Mature Minors"

Traditionally, minors who were married, serving in the military, or living apart from their parents with parental consent or acquiescence were considered by the courts to be "emancipated" from the custody and control of their parents.[31] More recently, a number of states have enacted specific statutes allowing minors who meet similar criteria to seek a court order of emancipation.[32] Some of these statutes mention consent for healthcare as a consequence of emancipation; others do not.[33] However, a strong argument can be made that minors who meet traditional criteria for emancipation should be able to consent for their own healthcare even without a law to that effect.

Based on the mature minor doctrine,[34] which was created by the courts, even in the absence of a specific statute, "mature minors" may have the legal capacity to give consent for their own care.[35] A mature minor is an older adolescent (typically at least age 15) who is capable of giving, and has given, informed consent. Other important features of allowing mature minors to consent for medical services: the care is not high-risk, it is for the minor's benefit and it is within the mainstream of established medical opinion.[36] The basic criteria for determining whether a patient is capable of giving an informed consent are that the patient must be able to understand the risks and benefits of any proposed treatment or procedure and its alternatives and must be able to make a voluntary choice among the alternatives.[37] Unless there is a court decision in a state specifically rejecting the mature minor doctrine, mature minors should be allowed to give their own consent for low-risk care even in the absence of an explicit statute.

Confidentiality of Healthcare Information

Numerous studies have shown that without assurances of privacy, adolescents sometimes avoid seeking care entirely, refuse specific services, alter their choice of provider or withhold significant information from healthcare professionals.[38] Subsequently this has the potential for deleterious effects on adolescent health. In recognition of this, state and federal laws provide significant confidentiality protections for adolescents (both minors and young adults), and healthcare professional organizations have adopted policies to promote the delivery of confidential care to adolescents.[39]

Even confidential information may be disclosed with the permission of the patient or another appropriate person. Often, when minors can legally consent to their own care, they also have the right to control disclosure of confidential information about that care. However, there are a number of circumstances in which disclosure over the objection of the minor might be required, even if the minor had consented to the care. For example, if a specific law requires disclosure to parents, if a legal obligation to report suspected physical or sexual abuse applies, or if the minor poses a severe danger to him or herself or to others.[40]

Even when a minor does not have the legal right to control disclosure, and the release of confidential information must be authorized by a parent or legal guardian, it is still advisable (from an ethical perspective) for the healthcare professional to seek the agreement of the minor to disclose confidential information or, at minimum, advise the minor at the outset of treatment of any limits to confidentiality.[41] Fortunately, issues of confidentiality and disclosure can often be resolved through discussion and informal agreement among a healthcare professional, the adolescent patient and the parents without reference to legal requirements.

Confidentiality Laws

The confidentiality obligation has numerous sources in law and policy. They include the federal and state constitutions, federal statutes and regulations related to funding programs, state statutes and regulations (such as medical confidentiality and medical records laws, physician-patient and psychotherapist-patient privilege statutes, professional licensing laws, and funding program requirements), court decisions and professional ethical standards. Extensive federal medical privacy regulations, known as the HIPAA Privacy Rule, affect the care of adolescents and adults and are of critical importance.

Confidentiality in State Minor Consent Laws

Some state minor consent laws specify that the information may not be disclosed without the permission of the minor patient, but others allow physicians to disclose information to a minor's parent, even over the objection of the minor. Such laws usually contain criteria for when this may be done, such as if it is necessary to protect the health of the minor.[42] Conversely, some of the minor consent laws require that parents be involved or informed, but contain exceptions if, in the judgment of the treating professional, it would not be in the minor's interest or would cause harm to the minor.[43]

Federal Laws Protecting Confidentiality

Federal laws that provide confidentiality protection for healthcare services received by adolescent minors based on their own consent include the Title X Family Planning Program (42 U.S.C. §§ 300 et seq.; 42 C.F.R. Part 59), the federal drug and alcohol confidentiality regulations (42 U.S.C. § 290dd-2; 42 C.F.R. Part 2), Medicaid (42 U.S.C. §§ 1396d(a)(4)(C), (a)(7)), and the HIPAA Privacy Rule (42 U.S.C. §§ 1320d et seq.; 45 C.F.R. Parts 160 and 164). The Title X Family Planning Program contains very strong confidentiality protections and allows minors in every state to receive confidential family planning services in Title X-funded sites without parental consent, regardless of whether their state has an explicit law authorizing minors to give their own consent for contraception or family planning services.[44] The HIPAA Privacy Rule also contains important confidentiality protections for minors.

HIPAA Privacy Rule

When minors are authorized to consent for their own healthcare and do so, the HIPAA Privacy Rule treats them as "individuals" who are able to exercise rights over their own protected health information.[45] Also, when parents have acceded to a confidentiality agreement between a minor and a healthcare professional, the minor is considered an "individual" under the Rule.[46] Documenting the parent's assent to confidentiality is important to avoid problems in the future.

Generally, the HIPAA Privacy Rule gives parents access to the health information of their unemancipated minor children, including adolescents. However, on the issue of when parents may have access to protected health information for minors who are considered "individuals" under the Rule and who have consented to their own care, it defers to "state and other applicable law."[47]

Disclosure of Adolescent Health Information

- If state or other law explicitly *requires* information to be disclosed to a parent, the HIPAA Privacy Rule allows a healthcare provider to comply with that law and disclose the information.

- If state or other law explicitly *permits but does not require* information to be disclosed to a parent, the regulations allow a healthcare provider to exercise discretion on whether to disclose.

- If state or other law *prohibits* the disclosure of information to a parent without the consent of the minor, the regulations do not allow a healthcare provider to disclose it without the minor's consent.

- If state or other law *is silent or unclear* on the question, an entity covered by the rule has discretion to determine whether to grant access to a parent to the protected health information, as long as the determination is made by a healthcare professional exercising professional judgment.[a]

Source: [a] A. English, Carol A. Ford, "The HIPAA Privacy Rule and Adolescents: Legal Questions and Clinical Challenges," *Perspectives on Sexual and Reproductive Health*, 36 (2004): 80–86.

Mandatory Disclosure

Some laws require disclosure of healthcare information that is otherwise protected as confidential. Particularly significant among such requirements are mandatory child abuse reporting laws that exist in every state and require healthcare professionals to make reports to child welfare and/or law enforcement authorities when they know or suspect a child has been the victim of physical or sexual abuse or neglect.[48] Significant confusion for healthcare professionals has resulted from the inclusion in some state laws and by some law enforcement officers of voluntary sexual activity of minors within the scope of mandatory reporting of child abuse.[49] The laws and their interpretation and application vary widely among the states, and healthcare professionals should learn about local requirements.

Other important situations in which healthcare professionals may be required to disclose adolescents' confidential health information include those in which an adolescent presents a serious risk of doing harm to self or others,[50] an adolescent is seeking an abortion and state law requires parental consent or notification or a judicial bypass proceeding,[51] (discussed below) or, in a small number of states, parental consent or notification is required for minors to receive contraception or family planning services paid for by state funds.[52]

Disclosure via Billing and Insurance Claims

Finally, the entire process of billing and submitting health insurance claims for confidential services is a major concern and may breach adolescent confidentiality rights. An Explanation of Benefits (EOB) is sent home by many commercial health plans to the primary insured or the primary beneficiary, listing services rendered by the provider and reimbursed by the health plan. Parents may receive these EOB documents, which reveal confidential information about the type of health services obtained by their child. Additionally, co-payments automatically generated with certain billing codes for office visits and medications can be a barrier for adolescents receiving care. This is a significant issue both for adolescents who are legally minors and for young adults who remain on their family's health insurance policy.[53]

Financial Access

In the effort to ensure that adolescents have access to comprehensive healthcare, laws that pertain to consent, confidentiality, research and payment are inextricably intertwined. Financial obstacles can seriously impede access to essential services. The issue is particularly critical for adolescents from low-income families or those, such as homeless youth or former foster youth, who have no family support, and even more critical when a young person needs confidential care.[54]

Financial Access and Confidentiality

Legal provisions that allow adolescents to give consent for care and protect their confidentiality do not ensure access. Financing the care is also an essential element of confidentiality. Some of the state minor consent laws specify that if a minor is authorized to consent to care, the minor (rather than the parent) is responsible for payment.[55] In reality however, few (if any) adolescents are able to pay for healthcare out of pocket, unless there is a sliding fee scale with very minimal payments required. Although many adolescents have private health insurance coverage, they can rarely use that coverage without information reaching the policyholder or primary insured, who is usually a parent.[56] The potential is greater for them to receive confidential care through Medicaid, but policies and practices in this regard are varied and uneven among the states.[57]

There are some federal and state healthcare funding programs that enable minors to obtain confidential reproductive care at little or no cost to them. Most notable is the federal Family Planning Program, funded under Title X of the Public Health Services Act (42 U.S.C. §§ 300 et seq.; 42 C.F.R. Part 59). As significant a role as these programs play, they do not ensure access to comprehensive health services for teens. The financing available through insurance is thus all the more important.

Financial Access and Insurance

The Patient Protection and Affordable Care Act of 2010 or the Affordable Care Act (ACA)[58] contains many provisions that, when fully implemented, will increase access to comprehensive healthcare for adolescents. Many important provisions pertain to expansion of private insurance, Medicaid and CHIP for adolescents; others promote preventive care or target benefits to vulnerable youth. The key provisions of the ACA are extensive, and a detailed discussion is beyond the scope of this chapter.[59] They are summarized in abbreviated form in Affordable Care Act: Key Provisions for Adolescents in an implementation timeline.

Affordable Care Act: Key Provisions for Adolescents

The requirements of the ACA are phased in over several years, beginning in 2010 and extending until 2014 and beyond. Several key provisions that are important for adolescents and young adults were scheduled for immediate implementation in 2010. Others are spread over the implementation period. The general timeline for implementation of some requirements with particular significance for adolescents and young adults is set forth here:

2010

- In private insurance:
  - Provide dependent coverage for adult children up to age 26
  - Prohibit preexisting condition exclusions for children
  - Require coverage of certain preventive services without cost-sharing (co-pays)
- In Medicaid:
  - Create a state option to cover childless adults (many of whom are young adults) through a Medicaid state plan amendment
  - Create a state option to expand coverage for family planning through a Medicaid state plan amendment

2011

- Establish new programs to support school-based health centers

2012

- Expand collection and reporting of data on race, ethnicity, sex, primary language, disability status and underserved rural populations

2014

- In private health insurance:

- ○ Create state health insurance exchanges for individuals and small businesses to purchase coverage, with a minimum essential benefits package, premium subsidies for low-income individuals and families and other protections such as elimination of preexisting condition exclusions

- In Medicaid:

  - ○ Expand Medicaid to all non-Medicare-eligible individuals under age 65 with incomes no greater than 133 percent federal poverty level with enhanced federal subsidies to states for new eligibles

  - ○ Continue Medicaid coverage to age 26 for youth aging out of foster care

  - ○ Conduct outreach to, and enroll in Medicaid and CHIP, several vulnerable and underserved populations, including unaccompanied homeless youth, children with special healthcare needs, pregnant women, racial and ethnic minorities, rural populations and individuals with HIV/AIDS.

Source: A. English, "The Patient Protection and Affordable Care Act of 2010: How Does It Help Adolescents and Young Adults," Center for Adolescent Health & the Law and National Adolescent Health Information and Innovation Center, http://www.cahl.org/web/index.php/the-patient-protection-and-affordable-care-act-ppaca-of-2010-how-does-it-help-adolescents-and-young-adults (accessed December 14, 2010).

Best Practices and Advocacy Strategies for Medical-Legal Partnership

Because studies show that adolescent access to healthcare is strongly influenced by confidentiality protections, practitioners need to be very sensitive to privacy concerns. As discussed earlier, the law provides confidentiality protections for adolescents in certain circumstances, but they are rarely (if ever) absolute. This may create confusion for providers. MLP healthcare providers and lawyers should work together to ensure that adolescent confidentiality is maintained whenever possible. MLP lawyers can train healthcare providers about their state's law and help them understand the nuances of when information may or must be kept confidential and when they have discretion.

In assessing confidentiality protections, three key questions must be answered. What *may* be disclosed based on professional judgment? What *must* be disclosed? What *may not* be disclosed? In answering these questions the following considerations are relevant:

- What information *is* confidential (because it is considered private and is protected against disclosure)?

- What information *is not* confidential (because such information is not protected)?

- What *exceptions* are there in the confidentiality requirements?

- What information can be released *with consent?*

- What other mechanisms allow for *discretionary* disclosure without consent?

- What *mandates* exist for reporting or disclosing confidential information?[60]

From Practice to Policy

As discussed, state laws and policies vary significantly with regard to consent and confidentiality for adolescents in the healthcare setting. In addition to ensuring that state protections are enforced on behalf of individual adolescents, MLP partners can work together to advocate for laws and policies that protect adolescent rights in their states. Following are suggestions for MLP systemic advocacy:

- Advocate for institutional (hospital, clinic, health plan) policies that allow minors to receive confidential care based on their own consent and that accept the mature minor doctrine, and the constitutional right of privacy (in the case of contraceptives), as a basis for doing so.

- Educate institutional (hospital, clinic, health plan) personnel about minor consent and confidentiality laws and ways to honor confidentiality for adolescents while encouraging appropriate parental involvement.

- Oppose efforts in state legislatures to restrict or repeal minor consent and confidentiality statutes.

- In states without an explicit statute authorizing minors to consent for contraception, educate institutional (hospital, clinic) personnel about referral of minors to Title X sites for confidential family planning services.

- Negotiate with health plans in the area about adopting procedures to protect confidentiality so that minors can use their health insurance (e.g., for contraception, STD screening and treatment) without sacrificing confidentiality.

- Advocate with the state legislature, department of insurance and Medicaid/CHIP agency to implement the provisions of the ACA that would be especially beneficial for adolescents.

Case for Medical-Legal Partnership

Susan is 16 years old and comes to the adolescent clinic for a camp physical accompanied by her mother. She tells the physician that for the past year she has been having vaginal intercourse with her boyfriend, who is the same age as Susan. They have used condoms intermittently, and Susan reports using no other form of contraception. She denies that she is sexually abused and prefers that her mother not know she is having sex. The physician does not identify any other physical or psychosocial issues.

Questions for Discussion

1. What healthcare services does Susan need?

2. Can Susan give her own consent for any of these services?

3. How would a clinician negotiate private time with Susan? What should be said about confidentiality to Susan? To her mother?

4. Is the HIPAA Privacy Rule relevant to Susan's situation? If so, how?

5. What issues, if any, might limit the confidentiality of Susan's care?

6. What are the options for making sure Susan can get confidential contraceptive services?

7. How can Susan's care be paid for?

Special Health and Legal Concerns of Adolescents

Mental Health

Many mental illnesses begin in childhood or adolescence. Studies suggest that symptoms of nearly half of lifetime diagnosable mental health problems begin by age 14, and three quarters of lifetime diagnosable problems begin by age 24.[61] In 2008, the National Health and Nutritional Examination Survey found that 13 percent of children ages 8–15 had at least one mental illness, a rate comparable to childhood diseases such as asthma.[62] Yet mental disorders often go undiagnosed and untreated for years.[63] In fact, more than 20 in every 100 teens have a serious mental health concern, yet only 4 of them will get the care they need.[64]

Depression and anxiety are among the most widespread mental health issues, affecting an estimated 54 million adults in the United States each year.[65] Twenty-six percent of U.S. adolescents reported feeling sad or hopeless for more than two weeks in the past year on the most recent 2009 Youth Risk Behavior Survey (YRBS).[66] Depression can adversely affect the development and well-being of adolescents because it has a wide range of impact: on school functioning, peer and family relationships, medical health and somatization, general motivation and activities of daily living. It is a risk factor for a number of other negative health behaviors that can adversely affect an adolescent's health, including high-risk sexual activity, poor school performance, involvement with the juvenile justice system, substance use and abuse and violence.

Adolescents and Suicide

Suicide is the most feared complication of adolescent depression.

- According to the CDC, suicide is the third leading cause of death among adolescent and young adults.[a]

- Depression and suicidal ideation are known risk factors for successful suicide completion.

- According to the 2009 YRBS, 13.8 percent of adolescents have seriously contemplated suicide in the past 12 months.[b] Almost half of these high school students had attempted suicide one or more times in the past year.

- Among those youth who reported a suicide attempt in the past year, more than 67 percent also reported symptoms of depression.

- Suicide rates are highest among Native Americans and whites.[c]

- Pill ingestion is the most common method of attempted suicide, but firearm use is the leading cause of suicide death.[d]

Source: [a] "Web-Based Injury Statistics Query and Reporting System (WISQARS)," National Center for Injury Prevention and Control, Centers for Disease Control and Prevention, http://www.cdc.gov/ncipc/wisqars (accessed November 15, 2010); [b] "Youth Risk Behavior Surveillance—United States, 2009," *Morbidity and Mortality Weekly Report* 59, no. 5 (2010); [c] "Suicide," National Center for Injury Prevention and Control, Centers for Disease Control and Prevention (2010), http://www.cdc.gov/violence prevention/pdf/Suicide_DataSheet-a.pdf (accessed January 12, 2011); [d] Ibid.

Unidentified mental health conditions such as anxiety and depression, particularly in children with a chronic condition, are a significant force that drives utilization of health resources.[67] Because symptoms of mental illness are so likely to manifest during adolescence and young adulthood, early identification and treatment during these years is critical to prevent significant morbidity and mortality.

Substance Abuse

Alcohol Use among Adolescents

Alcohol use and binge drinking among U.S. youth is a major public health problem. In fact, alcohol is used by more young people in the United States than tobacco or illicit drugs.[68] As of 1988, all states prohibit the purchase and consumption of alcohol by youth under the age of 21 years. Consequently, underage drinking is defined as consuming alcohol prior to the minimum legal drinking age of 21 years. Even though it is illegal, it is estimated that 75 percent of adolescents will drink alcohol before the age of 18.[69] According to the most recent data from the YRBS, alcohol use among high school students remained steady from 1991 to 1999 and then decreased from 50 percent in 1999 to 42 percent in 2009. However, alcohol use and misuse is still a significant problem. In 2009, 24 percent of high school students reported episodic heavy or binge drinking.[70]

The risks of adolescent alcohol use and abuse are well known. The leading cause of death among young adults is motor vehicle accidents, often the result of driving under the influence.[71] Zero-tolerance laws in all states make it illegal for youth under age 21 to drive with any measurable amount of alcohol in their system (i.e., with a blood alcohol concentration ≥ 0.02 g/dL).[72] However in 2009, 10 percent of high school students reported driving a car or other vehicle during the past 30 days when they had been drinking alcohol.[73] In addition, 28 percent of students reported riding in a car or other vehicle during the past 30 days driven by someone else who had been drinking alcohol.[74]

Among youth, alcohol and other substance usage has been linked to negative health outcomes such as unintentional injuries, physical fights, poor contraceptive usage, STDs, academic and occupational problems, and illegal behavior.[75] Long-term alcohol misuse is associated with liver disease, cancer, cardiovascular disease, neurological damage and psychiatric problems such as depression, anxiety and antisocial personality disorder. The immaturity of the developing adolescent brain may make it more vulnerable to the toxic effects of alcohol and other drugs.[76] Multiple studies have shown that drinking at early ages can enhance the development of alcohol-related problems and addiction.[77]

Illicit Drug Use among Adolescents

Marijuana is the most commonly used illicit drug among youth in the United States.[78] Other drugs include cocaine, inhalants, ecstasy, amphetamines, heroin and hallucinogens. Fortunately, the rates of abuse of these other drugs have decreased or at least remained stable in the past 10 years. Although illicit drug use has declined among youth, rates of nonmedical use of prescription and over-the-counter (OTC) medications remain high.[79] Prescription medications most commonly abused by youth include pain relievers, tranquilizers, stimulants and depressants. In 2009, 20 percent of U.S. high school students had ever taken a prescription drug, such as Oxycontin, Percocet, Vicodin, Adderall, Ritalin or Xanax, without a doctor's prescription.[80] Teens also misuse OTC cough and cold medications, containing the cough suppressant dextromethorphan, to get high.[81]

Misuse of prescription and OTC medications can cause serious health effects, addiction and death. For example, abuse of stimulants such as Adderall and Ritalin can result in an irregular heartbeat, elevated body temperatures, cardiovascular failure or seizure activity.[82] If dextromethorphan is taken in very large quantities, it can impair motor function, produce numbness and nausea/vomiting, and increase heart rate and blood pressure.[83] Severe respiratory depression and a resulting lack of oxygen to the brain has also been found to be a serious adverse effect, especially if combined with other OTC decongestants.[84]

Inhalants and OTC medications are often seen as gateway drugs that can lead to more hazardous abuse of prescription or illegal drugs. Given the potential adverse effects and health implications of these substances if used and misused, it is prudent for adolescent healthcare providers to screen for use and abuse at every healthcare visit. Providing adolescents with risk reduction and health education messages about the adverse effects of these substances may lead to decreased use and ultimate avoidance. Brief three- to five-minute interventions and motivational interviewing techniques can be helpful in the harm-reduction model of adolescent healthcare. Brief interventions are counseling strategies that primary care physicians can deliver during office visits to help patients change health risk behaviors and increase compliance with therapy. Often the goals of these interventions are to reduce or minimize risky behaviors but not necessarily completely resolve them. This technique is used with adolescents often in the form of education, counseling and anticipatory guidance.[85]

Legal Issues for Adolescents with Mental Health and Substance Abuse Problems

Adolescents suffering from mental health issues and/or struggling with substance abuse issues may face trouble accessing treatment because of their minor status. They also may have legal issues resulting from their mental health or substance abuse problem, such as involvement with the juvenile justice system. These concerns are discussed in the following sections.

State Minor Consent Laws for Mental Health and Substance Abuse Treatment

Just as minor consent laws generally vary by state, state laws also differ regarding consent requirements that affect access to mental health services and substance abuse counseling and treatment for adolescents who are minors. Some states allow adolescents to consent for treatment but encourage parental involvement. For example under California law, a minor, aged 12 or older, "may consent to mental health treatment or counseling on an outpatient basis, or residential shelter services, if both of the following requirements are satisfied: (1) the minor, in the opinion of the attending professional person, is mature enough to participate intelligently in the outpatient services or residential shelter services; and (2) the minor (A) would present a danger of serious physical or mental harm to self or to others without the mental health treatment or counseling or residential shelter services, or (B) is the alleged victim of incest or child abuse."[86] The mental health treatment "shall include involvement of the minor's parent or guardian unless, in the opinion of the professional person ... the involvement would be inappropriate."[87] More than half of states allow minors to consent for outpatient mental health services; and almost every state allows minors to consent for counseling or treatment related to alcohol or drug use.[88]

Healthcare providers should become familiar with the laws in their state. MLP lawyers should work with healthcare providers to ensure that misunderstanding about consent for services does not create a barrier to care and treatment for adolescent patients.

Mental Health and Substance Abuse Problems and the Juvenile Justice System

Almost two million adolescents less than 18 years of age are involved in the juvenile justice system each year.[89] Although arrest rates for violent crimes have decreased in recent years, overall arrests have increased.[90] Adolescent males predominate in the juvenile justice system; however, female delinquency is a rising problem and rates have increased substantially in the past 10 years.[91] Ethnic minorities are over-represented in juvenile detention facilities, with blacks and Hispanics involved at five times the rate of non-Hispanic whites.[92]

The role of mental health and substance abuse problems in the juvenile justice system appears to be twofold. First, mental health and substance abuse problems are strongly correlated with involvement in the juvenile justice system. These problems may lead adolescents to engage in illegal behavior that brings them to the attention of law enforcement or illegal drug use itself leads to arrest. According to the Federal Bureau of Investigation, 109,444 juveniles (under the age of 18) were arrested by state and local law enforcement for drug abuse violations during 2007.[93] Mental health issues are also strongly correlated to juvenile justice system involvement. One study found that 60–80 percent of adolescents in detention facilities have a serious psychiatric illness, and many have more than one disorder.[94]

Second, youth in the juvenile justice system may have limited access to appropriate healthcare and substance abuse treatment while incarcerated. On exiting the system, they may also have a difficult time accessing services, making intervention difficult. For example, a long-standing provision of the Medicaid program has precluded Medicaid coverage for youth confined in juvenile justice facilities. Thus, to ensure continuity of healthcare, recently incarcerated youth may require assistance from advocates to connect them with insurance providers after incarceration. This provision was not altered by the 2010 healthcare reform law. However, by expanding Medicaid significantly and providing subsidies for the purchase of private health insurance, the ACA increases opportunities for young people leaving juvenile justice custody to qualify for Medicaid or secure private coverage, thereby increasing their options for accessing healthcare including mental health and substance abuse treatment.[95] MLPs can work with youth to ensure they receive coverage.

MLPs working with youth, including those who are or may become involved with the juvenile justice system, can intervene early to help prevent the long-term health and social consequences of mental health and substance abuse. On identifying youth with mental health or substance abuse problems, healthcare providers can involve MLP partners to assess the broader social issues and potential legal remedies available to the youth and his or her family. Additionally, MLP partners can assess the needs of adolescents who have been involved with the juvenile justice system to ensure that they access health insurance and other services for which they may be eligible.

Best Practices and Advocacy Strategies for Medical-Legal Partnership

Healthcare providers who identify adolescents with mental health and substance use issues may face difficulty engaging the patient in treatment. This may be the result of patient, family, legal or logistical issues. Unfortunately, undiagnosed and untreated illnesses can have a broad range of impact on adolescent psychosocial functioning and long-term health. MLPs can work together to ensure adequacy and efficacy of treatment options by:

- Recognizing that in most states adolescents can consent to their own care for substance use disorders in the outpatient setting, without parental consent.

- Advocate for minor adolescents who desire mental health counseling but are unable to involve their parents in the process, to seek and receive these services.

- Ensure that adolescents with mental health concerns locate and secure health insurance to meet their counseling and treatment needs.

- Adolescents with mental illness may be involved in the legal system, and providing them access to a legal health lawyer may improve health and long-term social outcomes.

Sexuality and Reproductive Rights

Adolescent Sexual Health

Adolescence is a time when many youth become sexually active, putting them at risk of STDs and unintended pregnancy. At age 15, 13 percent of youth report ever having had sex; by their senior year in high school, nearly 65 percent report having had sex.[96] A sexually active adolescent girl who does not use contraception has a 90 percent chance of becoming pregnant within a year.[97] The particular health and legal issues facing pregnant and parenting teens are discussed later in the chapter.

Adolescent sexual health also has a great impact on utilization of healthcare resources. Of the 18.9 million new cases of STDs reported each year, 9.1 million (48 percent) occur among 15–24-year-olds.[98] This is despite the fact that this age group represents only about one quarter of the sexually active population.[99] For a variety of reasons such as multiple partners, short-term relationships, and engaging more often in unprotected sex, sexually active young people are more susceptible to acquiring STDs and HIV than are older adults.[100] Fully one in four sexually active youth contracts an STD each year.[101] Additionally, according to the CDC in 2006, an estimated 5,259 young people aged 13–24 in the 33 states reporting to them were diagnosed with HIV/AIDS, representing about 14 percent of the persons diagnosed that year.[102]

The implications of these data are that large numbers of adolescents require access to age-appropriate, confidential, and affordable services for STDs and HIV. That presents challenges for both the private and public healthcare delivery systems, as well as for prevention efforts in the public health arena.

In addition to STDs, one of the leading causes of healthcare use among adolescents is pregnancy. (Pregnant and parenting teens are discussed in more detail later in the chapter.) U.S. teen pregnancy, birth and abortion rates are considerably higher than most other developed countries.[103] Ten percent of all U.S. births are to teens.[104] The majority of teen pregnancies are unintended.[105] Seven percent of adolescent mothers receive late or no prenatal care. Infants born to teens are more likely to have low birth weight than births to older mothers.[106]

As discussed earlier, a vital aspect of adolescent healthcare is confidentiality, particularly for such sensitive topics as sexuality, STDs and reproductive health. If adolescents are worried about confidentiality, they will be less likely to communicate with healthcare providers about sensitive topics, which may affect information shared about essential health issues for this population. Furthermore, if privacy is a concern, adolescents may not be willing to receive services that should be standard, such as pelvic examinations and STD testing and treatment. Another concern among advocates is that adolescents will not seek help if they do not trust the adult providing the care.[107] The main goal in treating adolescents is to deliver high-quality, age-appropriate care, while encouraging communication between adolescents and their parents or other trusted caregivers without betraying the trust between adolescent and provider.[108]

Federal and State Consent and Confidentiality Laws for Adolescent Reproductive Healthcare

Adolescents' rights regarding consent and confidentiality in the area of sexual and reproductive healthcare vary from state to state and sometimes one federal jurisdiction to another. Although minors are entitled to constitutional protections, reproductive rights for adolescents are not as broad as the protections afforded to adults.[109] According to the U.S. Supreme Court, these rights are limited because of "the peculiar vulnerability of children; their inability to make critical decisions in an informed, mature manner; and the importance of the parental role in child rearing."[110] The statutes enacted by state legislatures and the decisions of state and federal courts reveal a tension between the rights of minors and the rights of parents. Optimally, legislators and courts attempt to strike a fair and appropriate balance between affording adolescents constitutionally guaranteed reproductive rights while also maintaining parental rights; sometimes the balance leans more heavily in one direction.

Contraception

There are several different bases on which minors may be able to consent for contraceptive or family planning services. These include state statutes explicitly authorizing minors to consent for contraception; state laws authorizing certain categories of minors to consent for medical care generally; the statutory and regulatory requirements of the federal Title X Family Planning Program and Medicaid; and the privacy provisions of the U.S. Constitution and some state constitutions.

Approximately half of states and the District of Columbia have an explicit statute that authorizes minors generally to consent for contraception or family planning services. In many other states, minors are able to consent for contraceptive services either because there is a statute authorizing a limited group of minors to do so or because they fall into a category of minors who are authorized to consent to healthcare generally (e.g., currently or previously pregnant, married, a parent, over a certain age or a high school graduate).[111] A few states currently have no clear state policy on minors' right to consent for contraceptive services.[112]

In every state, however, minors may give their own consent and receive confidential family planning services that are funded by the federal Title X Family Planning Program or Medicaid. Title X regulations provide particularly strong confidentiality protections.[113] Also in every state, minors should be able to give their own consent for contraception based on the constitutional right of privacy, unless there is an explicit statute requiring parental consent that has passed constitutional muster.

STDs

All 50 states and the District of Columbia allow minors to provide consent for health services for STDs.[114] About one fourth of states require that minors be a certain age (generally 12–14 years old) before they are allowed to consent for their own care for sexual healthcare.[115] No state requires parental consent for STD care or that providers notify parents that an adolescent minor child has received STD services, save for limited or unusual circumstances, such as suspicion of sexual abuse.[116] However, 18 states allow (but do not require) a physician to inform a minor's parents that he or she is seeking or receiving STD services when the doctor deems it in best interests of the minor's health to do so.[117]

Abortion

The one notable exception to the expansion of minors' right to consent to their own healthcare is abortion.[118] The laws related to abortion change frequently, so it is essential for lawyers and healthcare professionals to obtain up-to-date information about their state's laws relating to abortion. At the time of this writing, minors may obtain an abortion without notifying a parent or guardian in the following states: Connecticut, Hawaii, New Hampshire, New York, Oregon, Vermont, Washington, and Washington, D.C. On the other hand, a large majority of states have laws that require parental involvement (either consent of notification) of at least one parent in their daughter's decision making.[119] All of the states that require parental participation have an alternative process for minors who cannot or choose not to involve their parents in their abortion decision.

In the 1979 landmark case *Bellotti v. Baird*, the Supreme Court analyzed Massachusetts's attempted reconciliation of a woman's constitutional right to choose to terminate her pregnancy, in consultation with her physician, and "the special interest of the State in encouraging an unmarried pregnant minor to seek the advice of her parents in making the important decision whether or not to bear a child"(443 U.S. at 639). Ultimately, the Court decided that a state may require parental consent for an abortion, as long as the state also offers an alternative option, often referred to as "judicial bypass," which allows a court to authorize an abortion for a minor without parental consent or notification when the court is satisfied that "she is mature and well enough informed to make intelligently the abortion decision on her own" (443 U.S. at 647). Even if the adolescent is unable to prove to the court that she is mature enough to make the decision on her own, the court may authorize an abortion when it determines that doing so is in the best interest of the minor (443 U.S. at 647–48).

Parental Consent and Judicial Bypass: Rhode Island and New York

Rhode Island's law provides a good example of a parental consent law that provides for judicial bypass. In Rhode Island, if a teenager under the age of 18 who has not been emancipated and is unmarried decides to have an abortion, she must have the consent of at least one of her parents (R.I. GEN. LAWS 1956 § 23-4.7-6 (2010)). Under the Rhode Island statute, the parent of the pregnant teenager shall only consider what is in his or her child's best interest. Also, if the parents have both died or are otherwise unavailable to the physician, a legal guardian may provide consent.

If parental consent is refused or not sought, the pregnant teenager may petition the Family Court to authorize the physician to perform the abortion. The Family Court judge must determine that the minor is mature and capable of making an informed decision or that the minor is not mature but the abortion is in her best interest. During a confidential hearing, the pregnant teenager may participate, and a guardian ad litem will be appointed to represent the pregnant teenager's best interests to the judge.

By contrast, New York does not require parental involvement in a minor's decision to have an abortion. This means that a New York teenager may "consent to (or refuse) an abortion, as long as she understands the risks and benefits of the procedure and its alternatives."[a] One point worth noting is that New York law applies to a teenager seeking treatment in New York, even if the teenager is only there for a short time.

Source: [a] J. Feierman, et al., "Teenagers, Healthcare & the Law: A Guide to the Law on Minors' Rights in New York State," (2002): 32–33, http://www.nyclu.org/files/publications/nyclu_pub_teenagers_health care_law_english.pdf (accessed December 1, 2010).

An additional obstacle worth noting for low-income adolescents seeking an abortion is the Hyde Amendment. The amendment is a legislative rider that was attached to annual appropriations bills. Since it was initially introduced in 1977, Congress has continued to pass it. The Hyde Amendment bans the use of federal Medicaid funds from being used to finance an abortion with very limited exceptions. As of 2008, 32 states banned the use of Medicaid funds for abortion, except in cases of rape, incest or life endangerment. Some states provide state funding for abortion for low-income women. Studies suggest that for some low-income women and adolescents, the inability to pay out of pocket for an abortion can cause a considerable burden, delaying or precluding it.[120]

Questions for Discussion

1. What is the role of healthcare providers in addressing issues of substance abuse and sexual activity by adolescents? What is the most effective way to address these issues with patients?

2. What access issues are there for adolescent girls seeking an abortion? What, in your view, is the appropriate balance between adolescent consent and parental consent?

Violence
Adolescents and Violent Crime

Adolescents and young adults are the most likely age demographic to be both perpetrators of violence and victims of violence. Overall, trends in violence over the past two decades are encouraging. Nonfatal crime rates have decreased dramatically for young people between the ages of 12 and 24.[121] Homicide rates for youth 10–24 years old also declined from 1990 to 2005.[122] Despite these declines, homicide is the second leading cause of death for all youth and is the leading cause of death among African American male youth (see Figure 15.4).[123] In general, adolescents are less likely than any other age group to report crimes against them. Data from the U.S. Department of Justice suggests that people ages 12 to 19 report only 36 percent of crimes against them, as compared to 54 percent in older age groups.[124] Environmental factors, such as poverty, family conflict and living in a community with high rates of crime and violence, all present risks for teens becoming perpetrators and victims of violence.

Healthcare providers who identify youth who live in communities with particularly high rates of violent crime should provide anticipatory guidance to these adolescents and their families. Depending on the circumstances, healthcare practitioners may also refer adolescents who have been personally affected or have witnessed violent activities to

Figure 15.4 Rates of Homicide Per 100,000 among Males Ages 15–19 by Race and Hispanic Origin, 2007

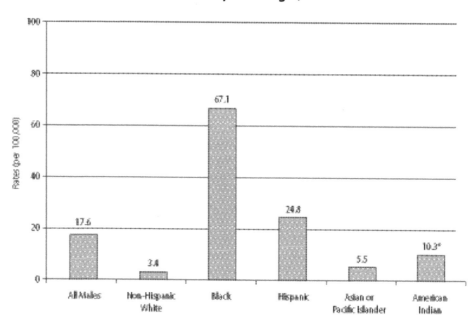

Source: Child Trends Databank, calculations using data from the Centers for Disease Control and Prevention Web-based Injury Statistics Query and Reporting System (WISQARS), http://www.cdc.gov/injury/wisqars/index.html.
Note: * Indicates rate is based on fewer than 20 cases

mental health professionals for counseling services. Adolescents and young adults who have been victims of crime may also need legal advice regarding their rights as victims. MLPs can be instrumental in this process.

Gang Youth

- It is estimated that there are 750,000 gang members in the United States, a major portion of whom are adolescents and young adults.[a]

- Approximately 80 percent of gang members are of African American or Hispanic background, and the majority are males.[b]

- Adolescents involved in gangs come from disadvantaged backgrounds to start with, often living in poor neighborhoods with preexisting family involvement in gangs, limited access to community resources, and lower socioeconomic status.[c]

- Health risk behaviors are prevalent among adolescents involved in gangs as they have higher rates of participation in criminal activities, violence, drug and alcohol use, and high-risk sexual behaviors.[d]

- The risk of death is augmented with this population, as youth gang members are about 60 times more likely to be killed than the general population.[e]

- Young adult gang members may be particularly vulnerable in terms of health disparities, as they may lack a medical home. Gang youths' primary source of medical care is often the emergency room.[f]

- Adolescents involved in gangs may not seek needed medical care for fear of legal or law enforcement involvement at the time of injury.

Source: [a] A. Egley and C. E. O'Donnell, *Highlights of the 2006 National Youth Gang Survey* (Washington, D.C.: Office of Juvenile Justice and Delinquency Prevention, 2008); [b] Ibid.; [c] V. Dupéré, et al., "Affiliation to Youth Gangs during Adolescence: The Interaction between Childhood Psychopathic Tendencies and Neighborhood Disadvantage," *Journal of Abnormal Child Psychology,* 35, no. 6 (2007): 1035–45; [d] M. H. Swahn, et al., "Alcohol and Drug Use among Gang Members: Experiences of Adolescents Who Attend School," *Journal of School Health,* 80, no. 7 (2010): 353–60. Ronald A. Brooks, et al., "Condom Attitudes, Perceived Vulnerability, and Sexual Risk Behaviors of Young Latino Male Urban Street Gang Members: Implications for HIV Prevention," *AIDS Education and Prevention,* 21 (2009): 80–87; [e] J. C. Howell, "Youth Gangs: An Overview," Office of Juvenile Justice and Delinquency Prevention (1998), 10; [f] B. Sanders, et al., "Gang Youth as a Vulnerable Population for Nursing Intervention," *Public Health Nursing,* 26, no. 4 (2009): 346–52.

Because many youths who are vulnerable to violence, particularly those involved in gangs, may not access primary care, identifying them for intervention is difficult. Connecting an MLP to an emergency department may help identify these youth and provide support when possible.

Intimate Partner Violence

As discussed in Chapter 11, intimate partner violence (IPV) is a significant social and public health problem. IPV among young people is a particularly serious public health concern, not only because of its high prevalence and profound health consequences but also because it occurs at a life stage when romantic relationships are beginning and patterns of interaction are learned that can carry through into adult relationships.[125] At three times the national average, females between the ages of 16 and 24 are the most vulnerable age group for IPV.[126]

Studies suggest that violence usually starts in younger couples, where verbal and physical aggression is often considered part of the "normal" pattern of interpersonal relationships.[127] Unfortunately, dating violence may start with teasing and name calling, which can then escalate into more serious violent behaviors like physical assault and rape. As teenagers find themselves exploring their sexuality through dating relationships, they may engage in extreme gender stereotyping.[128] Inherent in stereotypical role playing, young males may assume a dominant role, including feeling they have the right to "control" or "possess" their female partners, exhibiting masculinity through physical aggressiveness, and avoiding being attentive and supportive toward their girlfriends to "fit in" with their peer group.[129] Young females, in contrast, may believe that they are responsible, or that the jealousy, possessiveness, or physical abuse is "romantic," that this type of behavior is normal, or that help is unavailable.[130]

Some warning signs that a teenager may be experiencing dating violence include "physical signs of injury, truancy, dropping out of school, failing grades, indecision, changes in mood or personality, use of drugs/alcohol, pregnancy, emotional outburst, and isolation."[131]

Knowledge Gap: Association of IPV to Adverse Adolescent Health Outcomes

Victims of adolescent dating violence are at increased risk for a number of adverse health outcomes.

- A large study in 2005 showed that more than a third of adolescent girls tested positive for STDs or HIV, and more than half of girls actually diagnosed with an STD reported experiencing dating violence.[a]

- Fear of violence may prevent women from seeking help, testing or treatment for STDs and HIV.

- High school females reporting violence from dating partners are approximately three times more likely than their nonabused peers to have ever been pregnant.[b]

- Adolescent girls who have been sexually and physically hurt by dating partners are up to five times more likely to attempt suicide or have suicidal ideation than those who reported no abuse.[c]

- Female adolescents who report being sexually or physically abused are more than twice as likely to report smoking, drinking and using illegal drugs compared to nonabused teens.[d]

- Disordered eating is also prevalent among victims: 32 percent of teen victims report binging and purging, compared to 12 percent of nonabused teens.[e]

- Adolescent women who are battered are also less likely to attend school and less likely to receive good grades if they are in school.[f]

Source: [a] M. R. Decker, Jay G. Silverman, Anita Raj, "Dating Violence and Sexually Transmitted Disease/HIV Testing and Diagnosis among Adolescent Females," *Pediatrics,* 116, no. 2 (2005): e272–76; [b] J. G. Silverman, et al., "Dating Violence against Adolescent Girls and Associated Substance Use, Unhealthy Weight Control, Sexual Risk Behavior, Pregnancy, and Suicidality," *Journal of the American Medical Association,* 286 (2001): 572–79; [c] "Physical Dating Violence among High School Students— United States, 2003," *Morbidity and Mortality Weekly Report,* 55, no. 19 (2006): 532–35; [d] Silverman et al., "Dating Violence against Adolescent Girls"; [e] Ibid.; [f] Ibid.

Studies show that most teen victims refrain from telling anyone, especially their parents, about the violence experienced in dating relationships.[132] Teens are reluctant to report dating violence and may remain in abusive relationships for many reasons: fear of the perpetrator, self-blame, minimization of the crime, loyalty or love for the perpetrator, social or religious stigma, or lack of understanding.[133] Even after disclosure, victims of dating violence may face a number of obstacles if they seek assistance. Adolescent dating victims are often not adequately supported by the same services that provide help to adult domestic violence victims. For example, very few domestic violence shelters accept teens as the primary victim for protection. Teen victims also confront barriers to protection in the legal system, as discussed in the following section.

State Domestic Violence Laws and Teen Dating Violence
Confidentiality and Teen Dating Violence

As is true for reproductive health, confidentiality is an important factor for teens experiencing IPV. Healthcare providers struggle with maintaining the adolescent's trust while at the same time trying to keep the victim safe and free from harm. Helping teens access services and support to keep them safe means revealing the problem to other adults; but revealing information about the teen's safety concerns may undermine the youth's trust for the provider. This is complicated by some states' mandatory reporting laws in which certain professionals such as teachers, counselors and healthcare providers may be obligated to report the abuse to the authorities if the teen is less than 18 years of age.[134] (For more discussion of mandatory reporting of child abuse, see Chapter 11.)

Civil Protection Orders

One legal barrier faced by adolescent victims of dating violence that is not faced by adult victims is whether they are able to apply for a civil protection order against an abusive partner. Most state civil protection order statutes have two important components: definitions of what constitutes abuse and definitions of what constitutes family or household members.[135] Depending on how narrowly the statute defines household "family or household member," a teen victim may or may not be able to apply for a protective order. If the statute requires cohabitation, a teen victim of dating violence will be excluded. On the other hand, some state statutes may be interpreted more broadly to include dating relationships. For example, the Massachusetts statute defines "family or household member" as people who "are or have been in substantive dating or engagement relationship, which shall be adjudged by district, probate, or Boston municipal courts consideration of the following factors: (1) the length of time of the relationship; (2) the type of relationship; (3) the frequency of interaction between the parties; and (4) if the relationship has been terminated by either person, the length of time elapsed since termination of the relationship."[136]

Eleven other states' statutory definitions are written broadly enough to incorporate teen dating relationships.[137] In most states, however, adolescents will have trouble taking advantage of the protection of civil protection statutes because they require cohabitation or specifically limit protection to adults.[138] Occasionally a court has interpreted the state statute broadly enough to apply to adolescents. For example, in New Jersey, the court construed the domestic violence statute broadly because the legislature failed to precisely define household member.[139] Therefore, the court found that the parties were "de facto 'household members'" and that courts could make a case-by-case determination to ensure that it was "more than a casual dating relationship."[140]

An additional barrier for adolescents seeking civil protection orders is parental consent. A majority of states allow minors to obtain civil protection orders against dating partners, with some restrictions based on the age of the minor. However, most require that a parent or guardian file the petition for a protection order on behalf of the teen. This makes it even less likely that teens will choose this as an option for addressing violence. In states where adolescents may file without a parent, such as California and New York, the teen must appear in court.[141] This, too, may serve as a barrier for an adolescent unwilling to expose the violence publicly.

MLP is a particularly beneficial approach to teen dating violence. As discussed in Chapter 11, screening for IPV by healthcare providers is critically important for identifying it and providing an opportunity for safety planning with the victim. On-site legal assistance is important because opportunities to meet with victims may be limited by abusers who control their access to care. Because teen dating violence presents particular legal issues for adolescent victims as discussed, a collaborative medical-legal approach to safety planning and enforcement of legal rights is most likely to achieve results for victims.

Case for Medical-Legal Partnership

When asked about violence in her relationships, Michaela, a 16-year-old, discloses to her pediatrician that her boyfriend has hit her a few times. She explains that he only does it when he is mad that she is spending too much time with her girlfriends and not with him. She says he really loves her and that is why he gets mad. She forgives him for hitting her.

Questions for Discussion

1. How should the pediatrician respond to Michaela's disclosure? Should she/can she reveal this information to other professionals to help Michaela avoid the violence?

2. If Michaela acknowledges that the violence is unacceptable, how might an MLP lawyer help?

3. What are the barriers to protecting Michaela from dating violence given that she is an adolescent?

Vulnerable Populations of Youth

Homeless Youth

Homeless youth are perhaps the most vulnerable subgroup of teens. Their limited access to healthcare coupled with serious health concerns can make this population one of the most difficult to treat.[142] Mental health and physical conditions may be exacerbated by multiple barriers, including "limited financial resources and social disconnectedness ... and their status as minors and lack of an adult caregiver."[143] Serious health problems of homeless youth should be a societal concern because "they threaten the health of the individual adolescents affected; they threaten the public health; and they place young people at long-term risk for poor health, chronic homelessness, and inability to fully integrate into mainstream society through education, employment, and other means."[144]

Homeless youth are often dichotomized into the absolute and relative homeless. The absolute homeless have no identified housing and actually live on the street, often outside, in abandoned or unsafe buildings or the shelter system. Relatively homeless youth have insecure housing options, often renting rooms or space from others on a temporary basis, or "crashing" with friends or family. Regardless of the terminology, homeless youth face enormous struggles because of a precarious living situation. Estimates of homeless youth are problematic and likely underreported. Homeless Youth: Who Are They? provides some demographic information on homeless youth.

Homeless Youth: Who Are They?

• It is estimated that there are more than 1.6 million homeless adolescents and runaway youth in the United States.[a]

• Adolescent males and females are equally represented in the homeless population, with females being younger ages than males.[b]

- Homeless youth are comprised of a diverse population with 42 percent black, 38 percent white, 20 percent Hispanic, 4 percent Native American, and 2 percent Asian.[c]

- Youth who have run away from foster care placements or "aged out" without satisfactory transitional plans are overrepresented in homeless youth.[d]

- The most commonly cited reasons homeless youth report leaving home are:

  ○ Escaping disruptive family conditions, including neglect, physical, emotional or sexual abuse. In one study, almost half of homeless youth had been physically abused and 17 percent were sexually abused.[e]

  ○ Being thrown out by their family members. This may be particularly true for LGBTQ youth who may have been evicted from their family and home because of their sexual orientation.[f]

Source: [a] "Homeless Youth," National Coalition for the Homeless (August 2007), http://www.nationalhomeless.org/publications/facts/youth.pdf; [b] Katharine Kelly, Tullio Caputo, "Health and Street/Homeless Youth," *Journal of Health Psychology,* 12, no. 5 (2007): 726–36; [c] "Homeless Youth," National Coalition for the Homeless (2008), http://www.nationalhomeless.org/factsheets/youth.html (accessed November 9, 2010); [d] D. S. Bass, *Helping Vulnerable Youths: Runaway and Homeless Adolescents in the United States* (Washington, DC: NASW Press, 1992); [e] "Homeless Youth," National Coalition for the Homeless; [f] A. C. Molino, "Characteristics of Help-Seeking Street Youth and Non-Street Youth," paper developed for the National Symposium on Homeless Research, Washington, DC, March 1–2, 2007.

The Impact of Homelessness on Health and Well-Being

Homeless youth may experience a number of health issues that result from limited access to sanitary facilities for showering, sleeping and eating. They are at increased risk for respiratory infections (including tuberculosis) and skin infections such as scabies and lice. Inadequate monetary resources may lead to hunger and malnutrition, which can aggravate underlying medical conditions. A Canadian study in 2005 found that 74 percent of homeless youth indicated that they had one or more health problems.[145] These problems may be exacerbated by lack of medical attention and limited resources for pharmacologic intervention. Homeless youth are also at increased risk of mental health disorders and are affected by depression, suicidal ideation or behaviors, post-traumatic stress disorder, or conduct disorder at three times the rate of the general adolescent population.[146]

Homeless youth are at greater risk of victimization, as they report engagement in high-risk sexual behaviors, substance use and illegal activities such as dealing drugs, stealing or survival sex.[147] Homeless adolescents are at increased risk of STDs, particularly HIV, as engagement in prostitution and the sex trade may be their source of income. Pregnancy rates are exceedingly high as well, a consequence of inadequate contraceptive options.[148] Homeless adolescents are also more likely to be victimized through physical assault, rape trauma, violence or robbery.

Homeless adolescents report a variety of school problems, including learning disabilities, illiteracy, poor academic achievement and study skills.[149] Adolescents may be marginalized in the education system as a result of homelessness. Legal guardianship requirements, residency requirements, improper records and lack of transportation complicate access to education. This academic underachievement perpetuates the cycle by limiting their job options and subsequent ability to earn a living wage, and afford reasonable housing.

Legal Issues and Supports for Homeless Youth

Healthcare

Most homeless youth lack health insurance. Although many homeless youth may be unaware of it, most meet the income eligibility criteria for Medicaid and the Children's Health Insurance Program (CHIP).[150] Homeless youth may not be able to fill out the complex enrollment forms, may be unable or hesitant to provide identification or contact information, and may believe themselves to be ineligible, which led to 43 percent of homeless youth being uninsured in 1992.[151] Until recently, Medicaid and CHIP eligibility generally ended at age 19.[152] But at least three provisions of the ACA, the 2010 healthcare reform law, should be helpful in expanding health insurance coverage for homeless youth. First, in 2014 states will be required to extend Medicaid eligibility to everyone up to 133 percent of the federal poverty level who is not eligible for Medicare. Second, states will also be required to conduct outreach to and enroll in Medicaid eligible individuals who are members of specific vulnerable groups, including unaccompanied homeless youth. Third, states will be required to extend Medicaid coverage to all youth aging out of foster care up to age 26.[153]

Even if homeless youths are able to overcome the financial barriers, they may find themselves barred from healthcare because of issues with consent and confidentiality.[154] Unaccompanied youth, depending on their age, may not be able to consent to certain care.[155] "Slightly less than half of states have enacted statutes that enable minors who are living apart from their parents to consent for their own healthcare," two thirds of these states expressly authorize homeless youth consent, and the remaining third allows consent based on "age, unavailability of a parent, or sufficient intelligence to comprehend the risks and benefits of the care."[156]

To aid homeless youth, MLP lawyers should educate healthcare providers who serve homeless youth about their state rules for unaccompanied minors. In states where there are no provisions that enable homeless youth to consent for care, MLP lawyers and healthcare providers can work together to advocate for legislative change.

The Right to Education

In addition to healthcare barriers, homeless youth also face obstacles in education, housing, immigration, access to legal services and employment.[157] Homeless youth are often "denied access to 'good' schools because of school instability, previous poor school performance, discipline concerns, poverty or displacement."[158] Healthcare providers and MLP lawyers working with homeless youth can provide important support to youth seeking to remain in school. Under the McKinney-Vento Homeless Assistance Act (42 U.S.C. § 11431 (2002)), homeless children may not be denied access to a school based on failure to provide a permanent address. (See Chapter 9 for a detailed discussion of the Act.) Unfortunately, many school officials are not aware of their legal obligations under the Act and often turn away homeless students. MLP lawyers can be critical advocates for homeless youth to ensure that their rights are not violated and that they have access to an education.

Youth in the Foster Care System

The Special Healthcare Needs of Foster Care Youth

Adolescents enter the foster care system when their parents or legal guardians are no longer able to appropriately and safely care for them. Unfortunately, once these youths reach foster care, they may have already been subjected to a range of adverse experiences. Almost all adolescents are placed involuntarily into foster care by court order for reasons of parental abuse or neglect, abandonment or because they are "persons in need of supervision" or juvenile delinquents.[159] Children and adolescents can be voluntarily placed in foster care, although this is much less frequent than involuntary placement.

In 2009, more than 400,000 children and adolescents were in the foster care system.[160] Forty percent of these children were adolescents between the ages of 12 and 20, with an equal distribution of males and females. Racial and ethnic minority adolescents are disproportionately affected.[161] Foster care is meant to be a temporary placement, with the ultimate goal of reuniting with family members. However, this may not always be the case and foster care can turn into a long-term situation especially for adolescents. (See Chapter 11 for additional discussion of the child welfare and foster care systems.)

The American Academy of Pediatrics classifies foster care youth as children with special healthcare needs because of the high prevalence of chronic medical, developmental, emotional and behavioral problems that often occur at the time of or prior to placement.[162] Children entering foster care are often in poor health and have at least one chronic medical problem; one fourth of these children have three or more medical conditions. These medical problems run the gamut from problems related to prematurity, prenatal drug exposure, dental issues, hearing and vision impairment, elevated lead levels, infections, increased pregnancy rates, developmental disabilities, lack of prior healthcare, underimmunization, and educational, behavioral and mental health problems.[163]

Adolescents in foster care are also a vulnerable population because they are more likely to have experienced abuse and neglect, family and community instability, family dysfunction, poverty, poor medical and mental health, developmental delays and educational difficulties.[164] The increased rates of abuse and maltreatment in this population can lead to a host of emotional and behavioral problems. Depression is common, as nearly one-third of older adolescents in foster care have an affective disorder.[165] Trauma victimization is another major component of adolescents in the foster care system, as 25 percent of adolescents in one study had evidence of post-traumatic stress disorder.[166]

Adolescents in foster care often do not receive timely or appropriate medical care because of erratic home situations and multiple placements. They may not have a true medical home, and information about their current health status and past medical history may be difficult to obtain.[167] This fractures continuity of care for the healthcare provider and the adolescent patient. The American Academy of Pediatrics has created a resource manual for pediatric care providers that outlines the health concerns of children in the foster care system and provides guidelines for evaluating their physical, developmental, mental health and educational needs.[168]

Academic achievement may also be affected; children in foster care often struggle academically and may be behind expected grade level in school performance. By the time adolescents age out of foster care, 37 percent have not finished high school, and 50 percent are unemployed.[169]

Legal Interventions for Youth In and Transitioning Out of Foster Care

Healthcare providers who are sensitive to the particular vulnerabilities of foster care youth can help screen for potential barriers and problems that may be addressed through legal intervention. Many of the difficulties experienced by youth in foster care occur when they "age out" of the system and no longer have regular contact with the social service system or a foster family for support. MLPs may be particularly well poised to identify youth who are transitioning from foster care to independence and offer supportive advocacy on their behalf.

Healthcare

Foster care youth are eligible for Medicaid while under state custody (in foster care). However, MLP partners should screen these youth to ensure that they maintain their coverage when aging out of foster care. The ACA requires states to extend Medicaid coverage for youth aging out of foster care up to age 26.

Education

Because youth in foster care are more likely to suffer from disabilities, they often require special education services. Some studies suggest that children in foster care are three times more likely to have disabilities requiring special services than other school-age children.[170] As discussed in Chapter 9, the federal Individuals with Disabilities Education Act provides certain rights to special education services for eligible children. These rights are enforced primarily though procedural protections afforded to parents. Because foster parents are not legal parents for the purpose of representing a child's right to services, foster care youth may be left without an appropriate advocate. Though most state laws provide that it is the obligation of the state to ensure a child's right to an appropriate education while in foster care, this does not always occur.

If a healthcare provider identifies an adolescent who is not receiving appropriate special education services, an MLP lawyer may challenge the state child protective services agency to meet its obligation to ensure the child receives appropriate services or request that the state appoint an educational surrogate to step in.

Housing

"A housing crisis exists for youth aging out of foster care."[171] When children age out of foster care, on or about their eighteenth birthday, many begin living independently. Congress has enacted multiple laws to help the transition from foster care to independent living, most notably with the John H. Chafee Foster Care Independence Program (Chafee Act; 42 U.S.C.A. §677 (2010)). Congress began by federally funding the Independent Living Program to assist 16-year-olds and older adolescents with the transition. Eventually the age was decreased to 14 years old, and the funding was increased.[172]

Yet youth aging out of foster care still experience significant instability. Between 12 and 36 percent of youth aging out of foster care experience at least one night of homelessness.[173] Lack of education or poor achievement in education leads to unemployment or "employment that does not pay a living wage,"[174] thus exacerbating the housing problems.

To be effective, housing for youth aging out of foster care needs to be more than just a roof.[175] It needs to provide the youth with "sufficient security, safety, and a sense of home to anchor them," thus allowing them to take advantage of the various support systems they will need as they embark on independent living.[176] Programs funded under the Chafee Act are designed to address not just housing but the skills necessary to successfully transition to self-sufficiency, such as "assist in getting a high school diploma, career exploration, vocational training, substance abuse prevention, and preventive health activities (smoking avoidance, nutritional education, pregnancy prevention)" (42 U.S.C.A. §677 (2010)).

States are seeking alternatives to the housing problem. Connecticut has the Community Housing Assistance Program, a subsidized housing program that places youth in supervised or semi-supervised apartments throughout the community.[177] MLPs can work with child welfare agencies to ensure that youth aging out of foster care access appropriate services and housing.

Questions for Discussion

1. What are the similarities between homeless youth and youth in or leaving foster care? What are the particular health vulnerabilities that they share?

2. How might MLPs create better systems to improve access to healthcare and legal services for these youth?

Pregnant and Parenting Teens

Teen Pregnancy Rates

Approximately 750,000 adolescents 15–19 years of age become pregnant annually.[178] Teenagers aged 18–19 are three times as likely to give birth as those aged 15–17. The majority of teen pregnancies are unplanned (82 percent), accounting for more than one-fifth of all unintended pregnancies each year.[179] About 27 percent of unintended pregnancies among adolescents 15–19 years of age end in induced abortion.[180]

Fortunately, the teen pregnancy rate for girls ages 15–19 decreased 41 percent between 1990 and 2005.[181] However, after 14 years of decline in all 50 states and in all ethnic groups, the teen pregnancy rate increased slightly (3 percent) in 2006.[182] Birth rates vary considerably by race and ethnicity: black and Hispanic women have the highest rates of teen pregnancy.[183]

The consequences of unintended pregnancy for adolescents include unplanned births, reduced educational attainment, fewer employment opportunities, increased likelihood of welfare receipt and poorer health and developmental outcomes for their children.[184] Even though the adolescent female may be of childbearing age and potential, there are medical risks and complications to having a child at a young age. The medical risks for pregnant teens are well known: hypertension and pre-eclampsia, poor maternal weight gain, anemia and preterm birth.[185] The psychosocial concerns are also apparent. Pregnant and parenting teens have higher rates of depression, low self-esteem, school disruption, poverty, family separation or isolation and intimate partner violence. Multiple births further increase the risk of poor outcomes for young women and infants.[186]

Adolescent fathers are less well understood. However, much like adolescent mothers, teen fathers are at increased risk for poor educational and vocational outcome, with lower income levels and educational achievement. Studies also indicate that adolescent fathers have more emotional difficulties and are at greater risk for legal concerns and incarceration than adolescents who are not parents.[187]

Most adolescent mothers are not mentally, emotionally or financially prepared for the challenges of parenthood. Compared with their peers who delay childbearing, adolescent mothers are less likely to finish high school or have steady employment and are more likely to receive public assistance and experience marital strife. Furthermore, adolescent mothers are much less likely than older mothers to receive timely and appropriate prenatal care and are more likely to smoke during pregnancy.[188]

The infants and children of adolescent parents are also at risk for poor outcomes. Studies have repeatedly shown that children born to teenage mothers are at greater risk for low birth weight (almost twice the rate of nonteen mothers), higher rates of school failure, behavioral concerns, higher rates of developmental delay, early initiation of sexual activity and increased rates of substance use.[189]

In addition to physical and psychological concerns, a variety of barriers to medical care exist for adolescent parents. Adolescents often have difficulties accessing physicians due to time and financial constraints. Adolescent parents may feel judged or dismissed by the provider, especially if a grandparent or other adult accompanies them to the visit. Positive outcomes can be achieved by identifying a medical home for the parent and child, improving parenting practices, delaying or avoiding a second pregnancy, helping adolescent parents complete their education and educating them about normal child development.

Legal Issues for Pregnant and Parenting Teens
Healthcare Access

Generally, a teen who is covered by Medicaid before her pregnancy will continue to be covered by Medicaid throughout her pregnancy and after the birth.[190] State laws and policies vary considerably regarding eligibility for Medicaid. All 50 states and the District of Columbia provide Medicaid coverage for pregnant women, however, the income eligibility ranges from 133 percent of the federal poverty level (FPL) to 300 percent of the FPL.[191] Forty states and Washington, D.C. cover pregnant women with income at or above 185 percent of the FPL.[192] Washington, D.C., and 43 states do not require an asset test when determining eligibility.[193] Fourteen states have decided to adopt the Unborn Child Option, which allows them to provide CHIP benefits to pregnant women.[194]

Educational Rights

Research shows that women who complete their education have improved medical, social and psychological outcomes. They have significantly improved vocational and income outcomes as well. In 2009, median incomes for women with a high school education were $20,861 compared to $13,943 for those with less than a high school education.[195] Teen pregnancy is the leading cause of high school drop-out among girls.[196] Only half of teen mothers have a high school diploma, compared with 89 percent of nonparenting teens.[197]

Under Title IX, the federal law protecting educational equity for girls and women, a pregnant or parenting teen may not be denied access to education in a public school. Title IX states that "no person in the United States shall, on the basis of sex, be excluded from participation in, be denied the benefits of, or be subjected to discrimination under any education program or activity receiving Federal financial assistance, except [in certain delineated sections]" (20 U.S.C.A. § 1681 (1979)). Following the broad language and vague standards, the Department of Health, Education, and Welfare "enacted regulations to clarify the rights and responsibilities of schools and students, including pregnant students."[198]

The regulations have three main objectives: (1) access, (2) choice and (3) quality.[199] By requiring access, the regulations forbid expulsion of pregnant students.[200] Second, the student is allowed to choose between remaining at the school she attended before she got pregnant and an alternative school, if one is available.[201] The key here is that the decision regarding which school to attend belongs exclusively to the student.[202] The alternative schools for pregnant students must be comparable to the mainstream schools.[203] Last, the quality of the education needs to be the same to ensure the student's right to education.[204]

Despite protections under Title IX, school and administrative staff are often unaware of the educational rights of pregnant and parenting teens, or they do not provide the resources required to ensure that pregnant and parenting teens can continue with their education as required by law. A pregnant student may be reluctant to take action to enforce her rights because she views her pregnancy as temporary, she does not know her rights, or she wishes to choose the path of least resistance.[205] Table 15.2 outlines recommendations for strengthening enforcement of Title IX on behalf of pregnant and parenting teens.

Table 15.2 Recommendations for Strengthening Enforcement of Title IX

Report drop-out rates	"Recipients must isolate information about pregnant students, including dropout rates and reasons for dropping out. The information must be reported regularly, but no less than every three years, to the Secretary. Recipients must use the form issued by the Secretary to collect the required information."
Report academic requirements	"Recipients must also report to the Secretary on a regular basis, but no less than every three years, any difference in graduation or promotion requirements (such as permissible number of missed days, academic requirements, or physical education options and alternatives) between pregnant and non-pregnant students."
Report about alternative schools	"Recipients who offer alternative schools to pregnant students must also report to the Secretary on a regular basis, but no less than every three years, how many pregnant students attend those alternative schools in a given year and how many students, who are known to the Recipient to be pregnant, remain in the school they attended before becoming pregnant."
Swift action regarding complaints	"Upon receiving a complaint regarding pregnancy discrimination, the responsible Department official, or his or her designee, shall commence an emergency proceeding to determine whether the complaint has merit. The proceeding shall culminate in a preliminary injunction or temporary restraining order, where appropriate, to ensure that relief can be achieved as quickly as possible."
How educators must leave the choice to attend alternate school to the student	"A recipient may not, in any way, interfere with a student's decision to attend an alternative school. Interference includes, but is not limited to, encouragement to attend an alternative program by suggesting it would be superior to her current education, suggestion that her mainstream school might not be able to meet her needs during pregnancy, and telling her how many other students attend alternative programs (unless specifically asked)."
Procedural changes for regulators to publish changes for school administrators	"The responsible Department official, or his or her designee, should issue specific guidelines for distribution to all recipient schools with instruction about how to discuss with pregnant students their academic options during pregnancy. School districts that operate alternative schools should be specifically guided in how to avoid coercing pregnant students to attend those programs. The guidelines must be updated as necessary to apprise recipients of any changes in the law that would affect how they approach these discussions."
School's obligation to provide a comparable education that a nonpregnant student receives	"A recipient that operates an alternative school or program for pregnant students must adhere to the academic and programmatic requirements in the school district's mainstream schools. While alternative schools may accommodate the particular physical and emotional needs presented during pregnancy, they may not vary from the educational quality or programmatic options available to students in mainstream schools."

Source: Excerpted from K. Fershee, "Hollow Promises for Pregnant Students: How the Regulations Governing Title IX Fail to Prevent Pregnancy Discrimination in School," *Indiana Law Review* 43 (2009): 115.

Access to Income Supports

When Congress passed welfare reform legislation in 1996, much attention was directed toward teen parents. In its introductory findings for the Personal Responsibility and Work Opportunity Reconciliation Act, Congress cited studies showing the poor outcomes of teen parents and their children. It also pointed to the higher costs of public assistance for teen parents:

> Young women 17 and under who give birth outside of marriage are more likely to go on public assistance and to spend more years on welfare once enrolled. These combined effects of "younger and longer" increase total AFDC costs per household by 25 percent to 30 percent for 17-year-olds.[206]

In response to these concerns, the law included two important provisions directed at teen parents. As a condition of receiving cash assistance, teen mothers (1) must attend school or a training program, and (2) must live with a parent or other responsible adult (42 U.S.C. § 608(a)(4)-(5)).

Eligibility for the SNAP program (food stamps) is generally determined based on the household. Therefore, in some states, pregnant and parenting adolescents and young adults are not allowed to apply separately for SNAP if they are living with their parents. In Massachusetts, for example, a parent under the age of 22 living with her parents may be eligible for cash assistance but may not apply separately for SNAP.

> Jane Doe is 20 years old. She and her baby live with her mother Margaret and Jane's twin brothers, who are 12. Jane receives TAFDC [Transitional Assistance to Families with Dependent Children] for herself and her baby, and buys food and fixes meals separately from the rest of her family. Because Jane is under age 22, she cannot get food stamps/SNAP separately for herself and the baby. Jane, her baby and her brothers and her mother have to qualify for benefits as one household, or not at all.[207]

By asking questions about the social determinants of health, a healthcare provider can identify teen parents who are struggling financially or who are unlawfully being excluded from school. Referral to an MLP lawyer can help address these problems before they affect health or future opportunity for the teen parent.

Case for Medical-Legal Partnership

Jenna is 16 years old and pregnant. At a visit with her pediatrician, she says that last week her high school guidance counselor told her that it might be best for her to pursue her GED (an exam-based credential in lieu of a high school diploma) because getting to school on time once her baby is born is probably going to be very difficult.

Questions for Discussion

1. How should the pediatrician counsel Jenna? What questions should he or she ask her?

2. Should the pediatrician seek help from the MLP lawyer? What potential legal issues might be involved here?

3. What type of advocacy could the MLP team undertake on Jenna's behalf if she wishes to continue high school?

LGBTQ Youth

In addition to the same challenges faced by their heterosexual peers, lesbian, gay, bisexual, transgendered and questioning (LGBTQ) adolescents face additional health, safety and educational concerns. These concerns include "a much greater chance than straight youth of being abused and victimized, of abusing substances, of prostituting themselves, of attempting suicide, and of being homeless."[208]

Health and Mental Health Risks for LGBTQ Youth

Estimates suggest that 1 in 10 individuals struggle with sexual orientation issues and up to 8 percent of high school students identify as gay, lesbian or bisexual.[209] These may be underestimates, as adolescents may fear stigmatization and therefore delay coming out until later in adulthood. Sexual identity is not equivalent to behavior; many adolescents experiment with same-gender sexual relationships as a part of normal healthy development. Healthcare providers need to be aware of the complexities and fluid nature of sexual identity and behavior among adolescents and treat them accordingly.

LGBTQ adolescents engage in the same health risk behaviors as heterosexual adolescents but may be at greater risk. Men who have sex with men are at increased risk for contracting HIV and syphilis, which are infections on the rise. It is worth repeating that sexual identity does not always equate with behavior. As such, healthcare providers should screen for HIV and STDs based on an adolescents' sexual behavior, not whether he or she identifies as gay, lesbian or bisexual.

It has been postulated that suicide may the leading cause of death among gay males, even though it is third among adolescents overall.[210] Substance abuse appears to be higher among LGBTQ youth. It is an area of active research, and one study found that LGBTQ youth were 5 times more likely to use cocaine, 10 times more likely to use crack, and 10 times more likely to use IV drugs compared with their heterosexual peers.[211] LGBTQ youth are also subject to increased victimization, from bullying at school, to random acts of violence, to rejection from peers and family members.[212]

Harassment and Mental Health

In addition to the typical stressors of adolescents such as peer pressure and identity formation, many LGBTQ youth contend with regular harassment and victimization from peers in their schools. LGBTQ youth report feeling unsafe in school and unsupported by school administrators and teachers who fail to intervene or take harassment seriously. Recent highly publicized suicides by LGBTQ youth have raised the public's consciousness about the connections between harassment and mental health concerns. In addition to contributing to mental health problems, harassment may prevent LBGTQ youth from receiving the education to which they are entitled.

LGBTQ Students: Harassment and Bullying

The 2009 GLSEN National School Climate Survey findings suggest that LGBTQ youth experience frequent harassment and victimization at school leading to higher rates of depression and risk for suicide.

- 84.6 percent of LGBTQ students reported being verbally harassed, 40.1 percent reported being physically harassed and 18.8 percent reported being physically assaulted at school in the past year because of their sexual orientation.

- 63.7 percent of LGBTQ students reported being verbally harassed, 27.2 percent reported being physically harassed and 12.5 percent reported being physically assaulted at school in the past year because of their gender expression.

- 72.4 percent heard homophobic remarks, such as "faggot" or "dyke," frequently or often at school.

- Nearly two-thirds (61.1 percent) of students reported that they felt unsafe in school because of their sexual orientation, and more than a third (39.9 percent) felt unsafe because of their gender expression.

- 29.1 percent of LGBTQ students missed a class at least once, and 30.0 percent missed at least one day of school in the past month because of safety concerns, compared to only 8.0 percent and 6.7 percent, respectively, of a national sample of secondary school students.

- The reported grade point average of students who were more frequently harassed because of their sexual orientation or gender expression was almost half a grade lower than for those who were less often harassed (2.7 vs. 3.1).

- Increased levels of victimization were related to increased levels of depression and anxiety and decreased levels of self-esteem.

- Being out in school had positive and negative repercussions for LGBTQ students—outness was related to higher levels of victimization, but also higher levels of psychological well-being.

Source: J.G. Kosciw, E.A. Greytak, E.M. Diaz, and M. J. Bartkiewicz, *The 2009 National School Climate Survey: The Experiences of Lesbian, Gay, Bisexual and Transgender Youth in Our Nation's Schools* (New York: GLSEN, 2010), http://www.glsen.org/cgi-bin/iowa/all/library/record/2624.html.

LGBTQ Youth in the Child Welfare System

Because of family conflict over their sexual orientation, many LGBTQ adolescents end up in the child welfare system. These adolescents face disapproval and rejection from their parents, and if removed from "abusive or neglectful parents and placed with unsupportive foster parents, [they] may face hostility and rejection, compounding their plight."[213] The adolescents who end up in group homes or state facilities "encounter violence from both their peers and staff."[214]

Child welfare agencies may fail to ensure that the private foster home is a nurturing, healthy environment and the foster parents are not forcing the youth to attend "reparative" therapy or attend religious services "designed to convince them to renounce their sexuality or gender identity." Some child welfare organizations have created specialized foster care group homes geared toward LGBTQ youth, with sensitized workers and LGBTQ-friendly policies that honor the gender identification of the young person.[215]

Due to these pressures, a disproportionate number of LGBTQ adolescents end up homeless. Once homeless, LGBTQ adolescents face additional discrimination because fewer beds are specifically allocated to LGBTQ individuals. For example, in the "historically unwelcoming and hostile to LGBTQ individuals" New York City public shelter system, only 26 of the beds are allocated for LGBTQ individuals and there are nearly 7,000 homeless LGBTQ youth.[216]

Clinical Implications

Medical professionals who care for LGBTQ adolescents should be aware of the particular health risks of this population, and screen and treat them accordingly. This may require vigilance because of the increased risk of STDs, alcohol and substance use, depression/suicidality and victimization. The American Academy of Pediatrics produced a policy for adolescent healthcare providers that states:

> The goal of the providers is not to identify all gay and lesbian youths, but to create comfortable environments in which they may seek help and support for appropriate medical care while reserving the right to disclose their sexual identity when ready. Pediatricians who are not comfortable in this regard should be responsible for seeing that such help is made available to the adolescent from another source.[217]

Adolescent healthcare providers should be careful to ask about sexual behaviors, but allow adolescents to discuss their sexual identity when they are ready. Disclosure of sexual orientation to a healthcare provider, friends or family members may be challenging for these youth because they may fear stigmatization. Listening and providing supportive counseling is particularly important with this population. Because LGBTQ youth often have difficult relationships with family members because of their sexual orientation, healthcare providers should be aware of family dynamics and encourage active family involvement (or other social support networks) when possible. Finally, healthcare providers can help identify when LGBTQ youth are experiencing bullying or harassment and work with the MLP team to advocate on their behalf to ensure safety at school.

Legal Supports for LGBTQ Youth

Rights in School

LGBTQ youth have the right to a respectful, safe education in public schools.[218] This includes the right to be free from verbal, sexual or physical harassment by students or faculty, based on sexual orientation or expression of gender identity.[219] State laws vary, but many provide specific protections for students based on sexual orientation. In Vermont, for example, "schools are considered places of public accommodation and therefore they may not discriminate on the basis of sexual orientation or gender identity in their accommodations, advantages, facilities or privileges."[220] Furthermore, the Vermont Equal Educational Opportunity Act provides that the state must provide "substantially equal access" to education for all Vermont students, including LGBTQ students.[221] These laws prohibit express and implied discrimination or harassment. Although a school may not expressly prohibit an LGBTQ student from participating in an extracurricular activity, such as the basketball team, the school may also not imply participation would not be welcome through conduct.[222] Under the federal Equal Access Amendment, LGBTQ students have the right to start gay/straight alliances and have this club treated the same as all other clubs at school.[223]

MLP Assistance with School Harassment

When an adolescent patient indicates to a healthcare provider that he or she is being harassed at school, a referral to the MLP lawyer should be made. The MLP lawyer may serve as an advocate with the school on behalf of the student or advise him or her how to advocate. Key points in advocacy include:

- Reviewing the student handbook to identify the school's harassment policy.

- Identifying the appropriate person responsible for complaints under the policy.

- Documenting incidents and all reporting to the school in writing.

- Follow-up with the principal or superintendent, if the first point of contact does not address the harassment.

Source: GLAD, "Students and Schools," http://www.glad.org/rights/c/students-schools/.

Rights in Child Welfare System

Just as some states have passed specific laws protecting LGBTQ youth from discrimination and harassment in school, some states have laws protecting them in foster care as well. For example, in California, LGBTQ youth in foster care are protected by the Foster Care Non-Discrimination Act, which makes it unlawful for various child welfare agencies, including county departments, group home facilities and foster family agencies, to discriminate based on actual or perceived sex, sexual orientation or gender identity.[224]

State courts have also held that child protection agencies must accommodate youth based on gender identity. For example, in *Doe v. Bell*, the Supreme Court of New York held that New York City Administration for Children's Services had to make reasonable accommodations for a 17-year-old youth, who was born biologically male but identified as female.[225] The plaintiff was placed in an all-male foster care facility, was uncomfortable dressing as a male, and ran away from placements where she was forced to dress in male attire.[226] The court held that a reasonable accommodation would be to allow Ms. Doe to wear female attire while in the Atlantic Transitional Facility.[227]

Some youth correctional facilities have also created policies protecting LGBTQ youth from discrimination. For example, Hawaii's Youth Correctional Facility adopted a policy of Non-Discriminatory Developmentally Sound Treatment of LGBT Adolescents.[228] Of note, LGBTQ youth may not be placed in isolation as a means of protection from discrimination or harassment. Classification and housing must be based on an individualized decision, and staff are trained and must "affirmatively demonstrate" their commitment to providing a safe environment. Youth are given verbal and written warnings that name calling and other harassment is "hurtful and not accepted" at the Hawaii Youth Correctional Facility.[229]

MLP lawyers should inform healthcare providers and their patients about any legal protections against discrimination and harassment under state law. Like the school setting, if a youth is being harassed or discriminated against in foster care, a group home or a correctional facility, he or she should seek assistance from a trusted adult or advocate, follow the proper procedure for reporting, and keep a written record.[230] MLPs that work with LGBTQ youth should ensure that their rights are enforced in these settings and take appropriate legal action when they are not. Because not all states have specific protections for LGBTQ youth, MLPs can also advocate for legislation supporting the rights of LGBTQ youth in schools and out-of-home placements.

Best Practices and Advocacy Strategies for Medical-Legal Partnership

The Rhode Island Medical-Legal Partnership for Children at Hasbro Children's Hospital works closely with the Teens and Tots Clinic (which provides primary care to teen mothers and their babies). Through this collaboration, concerns were raised about the lack of enforcement of teen mothers' educational rights under local policies and Title IX. Medical students from Brown University and law students from Roger Williams University worked together to study the problems, advocate for teen parents, and create "know your rights" information for teen parents. Through a community health clerkship, a medical student documented the issues through interviews with teen parents, school officials, community agency representatives and healthcare providers in a report, *Educational Concerns of the Teen Mother in Providence, RI: The Law, School Policies and Real Experiences.*[231] Law students created a brochure to be used in the clinic explaining educational rights of teen parents.

From Practice to Policy

MLPs that serve particularly vulnerable adolescents, such as homeless youth or those in the child welfare system, can play an important role in advocating for policies that improve access to healthcare. Some examples of policy advocacy follow.

- Advocate to ensure that the state implements the Medicaid expansion option to cover youth aging out of foster care up to age 21 that is part of the FCIA immediately, pending implementation of the ACA requirement to cover youth aging out of foster care up to age 26.

- Work with the state child welfare agency to adopt "automated" procedures to ensure that as youth leave or age out of foster care, they are evaluated for Medicaid or CHIP eligibility and enrolled if they are eligible.

- Help Medicaid and CHIP agencies to evaluate and revise (if necessary) their application and enrollment procedures to make it possible for otherwise eligible former foster youth and homeless youth to enroll in Medicaid or CHIP.

- Work with other local partners to conduct direct outreach to former foster youth and homeless youth to encourage them to enroll in Medicaid or CHIP if eligible.

- Ensure that the state implements the provisions of the ACA that extend Medicaid eligibility to all individuals up to 133 percent FPL who are not eligible for Medicare.

- Develop a partnership with administrators of safety net health programs to evaluate their potential to serve former foster youth and homeless youth, and if necessary, revise their programs to meet the needs of these young people more effectively.

Case for Medical-Legal Partnership

Dr. Jackson, a healthcare provider for adolescents, always asks his patients a series of questions about their sexuality and sexual activity. During a screening, Justin, a 15-year-old patient, states that he is heterosexual but acknowledges that he has engaged in the past in some sexual activity with other males. He then complains that despite the fact that is heterosexual, he has endured significant harassment from some of his peers at school because they believe he is gay. He says that the harassment is so bad that he sometimes stays home from school and tells his parents he is sick.

Questions for Discussion

1. How should Dr. Jackson discuss sexuality and sexual orientation with Justin? What types of health concerns should he be concerned about for Justin?

2. Should Dr. Jackson refer Justin to the MLP lawyer for help in addressing the harassment at school?

3. If Justin is willing to talk to the MLP lawyer, what challenges might there be in advocating on Justin's behalf with the school given that he states that he is not gay?

Conclusion

Adolescent patients present distinct challenges for healthcare providers and the healthcare system. However, understanding adolescent development as a time of both risk and opportunity is important to providing sensitive and effective healthcare to this population. Inquiring about and addressing the social factors surrounding an adolescent's health is crucial to effective care. MLP lawyers can be key allies in helping healthcare providers understand the unique legal provisions governing consent and confidentiality for adolescents in the healthcare context, as well as legal protections for particularly vulnerable adolescents in a variety of contexts. Working together, healthcare providers and lawyers can be important advocates for adolescents as they navigate a range of issues during this critical time, including relationships with parents, schools and peers.

1. L. Cunningham, "A Question of Capacity: Towards a Comprehensive and Consistent Vision of Children and Their Status under Law," *U.C. Davis Journal of Juvenile Law & Policy* 10 (2006): 285–86.

2. "2008 Fact Sheet on Demographics: Adolescents & Young Adults," National Adolescent Health Information Center, http://nahic.ucsf.edu/downloads/Demographics08.pdf (accessed January 11, 2011).

3. Ibid.

4. "POVO1: Age and Sex of All People, Family Members, and Unrelated Individuals Iterated by Income-to-Poverty Ratio and Race, 2009," Current Population Survey, 2010 Annual Social and Economic Supplement, U.S. Census Bureau, http://www.census.gov/hhes/www/cpstables/032010/pov/new 01_100_01.htm (accessed January 15, 2011).

5. T. Paul Mulye, et al., "Trends in Adolescent and Young Adult Health in the United States," *Journal of Adolescent Health*, 45 (2009): 8–24.

6. Ibid.

7. D. K. Eaton, et al., "Youth Risk Behavior Surveillance—United States, 2009," *Morbidity and Mortality Weekly Report*, 59, no. 5 (2010): 2, http://www.cdc.gov/mmwr/pdf/ss/ss5905.pdf.

8. D. Weinberger, B. Elvevag, J. Giedd, "The Adolescent Brain: A Work in Progress," National Campaign to Prevent Teen Pregnancy, June 2005.

9. Ibid.

10. "The Adolescent Brain," Society for Neuroscience, January 2007, http://www.sfn.org/index.aspx?pagename=brainBriefings_Adolescent_brain.

11. U.S. Department of Health and Human Services, Health Resources and Services Administration, Maternal and Child Health Bureau, The National Survey of Children with Special Healthcare Needs Chartbook 2005–2006 (Rockville, MD: U.S. Department of Health and Human Services, 2008).

12. Lewin Group, "Qualified Military Available: New Estimates of the Eligible Youth Population," Lewin Group, Human Resources Research Organization, April 2005, in Bruce P. Frohnen, et al., "Concern for Our Teens: Opinion Leaders Speak Out on Adolescent Health," National Alliance to Advance Adolescent Health Report No. 4 (July 2010).

13. R. W. Blum, et al., "Transition from Child-Centered to Adult-Healthcare Systems for Adolescents with Chronic Conditions," *Journal of Adolescent Health*, 14 (1993): 570–76.

14. Ibid.

15. Mulye et al., "Trends in Adolescent and Young Adult Health in the United States."

16. Ibid.

17. B. Bloom, et al., "Summary Health Statistics for U.S. Children: National Health Interview Survey, 2008—Detailed Tables 5, 9," National Center for Health Statistics, *Vital Health Stat,* 10, no. 244 (2009): 17, 26.

18. Ibid.

19. Ibid.

20. S. H. Adams, et al., "Health Insurance Across Vulnerable Ages: Patterns and Disparities From Adolescence to the Early 30s," *Pediatrics,* 119 (2007): e1033–39.

21. Ibid.

22. C. A. Miller, et al., "Chlamydial Screening in Urgent Care Visits: Adolescent-Reported Acceptability Associated With Adolescent Perception of Clinician Communication," *Archives of Pediatric Adolescent Medicine,* 161, no. 8 (2007): 777–82.

23. L. S. Neinstein, ed., *Adolescent Healthcare: A Practical Guide,* 4th ed. (Philadelphia: Lippincott Williams & Wilkins, 2002).

24. A. Roddey Holder, *Legal Issues in Pediatrics and Adolescent Medicine,* 2nd ed. (New Haven, CT: Yale University Press, 1985).

25. Ibid.

26. Ibid.; A. English, et al., *State Minor Consent Laws, A Summary,* 3rd ed. (Chapel Hill, NC: Center for Adolescent Health & the Law, 2010).

27. Holder, *Legal Issues in Pediatrics and Adolescent Medicine.*

28. English et al., *State Minor Consent Laws.*

29. Ibid.

30. Ibid.

31. Adams et al., "Health Insurance Across Vulnerable Ages."

32. Holder, *Legal Issues in Pediatrics and Adolescent Medicine.* English, et al., *State Minor Consent Laws.* "Emancipation in the United States: Fact Sheet," Juvenile Law Center, http://jlc.org.c25. sitepreviewer.com/index.php/factsheets/emancipationus.

33. Holder, *Legal Issues in Pediatrics and Adolescent Medicine.*

34. Ibid.

35. Ibid; English et al., *State Minor Consent Laws.* Gary S. Sigman, Carolyn O'Connor, "Exploration for Physicians of the Mature Minor Doctrine," *Journal of Pediatrics,* 119 (1991): 520–25.

36. Holder, *Legal Issues in Pediatrics and Adolescent Medicine;* English et al., *State Minor Consent Laws.*

37. Holder, *Legal Issues in Pediatrics and Adolescent Medicine.*

38. C. A. Ford, Abigail English, Gary S. Sigman, "Confidential Healthcare for Adolescents: A Position Paper of the Society for Adolescent Medicine," *Journal of Adolescent Health,* 35 (2004): 160–67; Carol A. Ford, Abigail English, "Limiting Confidentiality of Adolescent Health Services: What Are the Risks?" *Journal of the American Medical Association,* 288, no.6 (2002): 252–53.

39. A. English, "Understanding Legal Aspects of Care," in *Adolescent Healthcare: A Practical Guide,* 5th ed., ed. Lawrence S. Neinstein et al. (Philadelphia: Lippincott Williams & Wilkins, 2008), 124–32; M. C. Morreale, et al., "Policy Compendium on Confidential Health Services for Adolescents," Center for Adolescent Health and the Law (2005), http://www.cahl.org/web/index.php/policy-compendium-2005.

40. Ford et al., "Confidential Healthcare for Adolescents."

41. Ibid.

42. Holder, *Legal Issues in Pediatrics and Adolescent Medicine.*

43. Ibid.

44. Ibid; Rachel Benson Gold, "Title X: Three Decades of Accomplishment," *Guttmacher Report on Public Policy,* 4 (2001): 5–8, http://www.guttmacher.org/pubs/tgr/04/1/gr040105.pdf.

45. A. English and C. A. Ford, "The HIPAA Privacy Rule and Adolescents: Legal Questions and Clinical Challenges," *Perspectives on Sexual and Reproductive Health*, 36 (2004): 80–86; Catherine Weiss, "Protecting Minor's Health Information under the Federal Medical Privacy Regulations," ed. Jennifer Dalven (ACLU Reproductive Freedom Project, 2003), http://www.aclu.org/FilesPDFs/med_privacy_guide.pdf.

46. English and Ford, "The HIPAA Privacy Rule and Adolescents"; Weiss, "Protecting Minor's Health Information."

47. Ibid.

48. "Protecting Adolescents: Ensuring Access to Care and Reporting Sexual Activity and Abuse: Position Paper of the American Academy of Family Physicians, American Academy of Pediatrics, American College of Obstetricians and Gynecologists, Society for Adolescent Medicine," *Journal of Adolescent Health*, 35 (2004): 420–23.

49. Ibid.

50. Morreale et al., "Policy Compendium on Confidential Health Services for Adolescents."

51. Amanda Dennis et al., "The Impact of Laws Requiring Parental Involvement in Minors' Abortions: A Literature Review," Guttmacher Institute (2009), http://www.guttmacher.org/pubs/ParentalInvolvementLaws.pdf.

52. C. D. Brindis, A. English, "Measuring Public Costs Associated with Loss of Confidentiality for Adolescents Seeking Confidential Reproductive Healthcare: How High the Costs? How Heavy the Burden?" *Archives of Pediatric and Adolescent Medicine*, 158 (2004): 1182–84.

53. Rachel Benson Gold, "Unintended Consequences: How Insurance Processes Inadvertently Abrogate Patient Confidentiality," *Guttmacher Policy Review* 12, no. 4 (2009): 12–16.

54. C. D. Brindis, M. Morreale, A. English, "The Unique Healthcare Needs of Adolescents," *Future of Children*, 13 (2003): 117–35; M. Halley, A. English, "Healthcare for Homeless Youth," Center for Adolescent Health and the Law (2008): 1, http://www.cahl.org/PDFs/HealthCareForHomeless Youth.pdfCh 15 tyler RTF.rtf; A. English, A. J. Stinnett, E. Dunn-Georgiou, "Healthcare for Adolescents and Young Adults Leaving Foster Care: Policy Options for Improving Access," Center for Adolescent Health and the Law (2006), http://www.cahl.org/PDFs/FCIssueBrief.pdf.

55. English et al., *State Minor Consent Laws*.

56. Gold, "Unintended Consequences."

57. Ibid.

58. Patient Protection and Affordable Care Act (PPACA, P.L. 111-148, March 23, 2010), as amended by the Healthcare and Education Reconciliation Act (Recon. Act, P.L. 111-152, March 30, 2010).

59. A. English, "The Patient Protection and Affordable Care Act of 2010: How Does It Help Adolescents and Young Adults?" Center for Adolescent Health & the Law and National Adolescent Health Information and Innovation Center, http://www.cahl.org/web/index.php/the-patient-protec-tion-and-affordable-care-act-ppaca-of-2010-how-does-it-help-adolescents-and-young-adults (accessed December 14, 2010).

60. English, "Understanding Legal Aspects of Care," 124–32.

61. R. C. Kessler, et al., "Lifetime Prevalence and Age of Onset Distributions of DSM-IV Disorders in the National Comorbidity Survey Replication (NCSR)," *Archives of General Psychiatry*, 62, no. 6 (2005): 593–602.

62. L. A. Pratt, Debra J. Brody, "Depression in the United States Household Population, 2005–2006," NCHS Data Brief 7 (September 2008).

63. National Institute of Mental Health, http://www.nimh.nih.gov/index.shtml (accessed November 12, 2010).

64. A. Chandra, C. S. Minkovitz, "Stigma Starts Early: Gender Differences in Teen Willingness to Use Mental Health Services," *Journal of Adolescent Health*, 38 (2006): 754.

65. "U.S. Census Bureau Population Estimates by Demographic Characteristics Table 2: Annual Estimates of the Population by Selected Age Groups and Sex for the United States: April 1, 2000 to July 1, 2004," Population Division, U.S. Census Bureau (released June 9, 2005), http://www.census.gov/popest/national/asrh.

66. "Youth Risk Behavior Surveillance—United States, 2009," *Morbidity and Morality Weekly Report,* 59, no. 5 (2010).

67. P. Bernal, "Hidden Morbidity in Pediatric Primary Care," *Pediatric Annuals,* 32, no. 6 (2003): 413–18.

68. National Institute on Drug Abuse, http://www.nida.nih.gov/nidamed/ (accessed November 19, 2010).

69. Lloyd D. Johnston, et al., "Monitoring the Future National Results on Adolescent Drug Use: Overview of Key Findings, 2008," National Institute on Drug Abuse, publication no. 09-7401 (2009), http://www.nida.nih.gov/PDF/overview2008.pdf.

70. "Youth Risk Behavior Surveillance" (2010).

71. "Web-Based Injury Statistics Query and Reporting System (WISQARS)."

72. "Sentencing and Dispositions of Youth DUI and Other Alcohol Offenses: A Guide for Judges and Prosecutors," National Highway Safety and Transportation Administration, http://www.nhtsa.gov/people/injury/alcohol/youthdui/section3.html (accessed November 19, 2010).

73. "Youth Risk Behavior Surveillance."

74. Ibid.

75. National Institute on Drug Abuse.

76. K. C. Winters, A. T. McLellan, "Immature Brain Structure May Place Teenagers at Greater Risk for Substance Abuse," Special Report Commissioned by the Treatment Research Institute (November 2004), http://www.tresearch.org/resources/specials/2004Nov_AdolescentBrain.pdf (accessed January 12, 2011).

77. National Institute on Drug Abuse.

78. Ibid.

79. Ibid.

80. "Youth Risk Behavior Surveillance."

81. National Institute on Drug Abuse.

82. "NIDA Info Facts—Stimulant ADHD Medications: Methylphenidate and Amphetamines, June 2009," National Institute on Drug Abuse, http://www.nida.nih.gov/pdf/infofacts/ADHD09.pdf (accessed January 12, 2011).

83. Ibid.

84. Ibid.

85. W. R. Miller, S. Rollnick, *Motivational Interviewing: Preparing People for Change,* 2nd ed. (New York: Guilford Press, 2002); Jim McCambridge, John Strang, "The Efficacy of Single-Session Motivational Interviewing in Reducing Drug Consumption and Perceptions of Drug-Related Risk and Harm among Young People: Results from a Multi-site Cluster Randomized Trial," *Addiction,* 99 (2004): 39–52.

86. Cal. Family Code § 6924(b) (West 2010).

87. Cal. Family Code § 6924(d) (West 2010).

88. English, et al., *State Minor Consent Laws.*

89. M. Golzari, S. J. Hunt, A. Anoshiravani, "The Health Status of Youth in Juvenile Detention Facilities," *Journal of Adolescent Health,* 38 (2006): 776–82.

90. Ibid.

91. Ibid.

92. Ibid.

93. "Juvenile and Drug: Facts and Figures," Office of National Drug Policy, http://www.whitehousedrugpolicy.gov/drugfact/juveniles/juvenile_drugs_ff.html (accessed December 1, 2010).

94. Golzari et al., "The Health Status of Youth in Juvenile Detention Facilities."

95. English, "The Patient Protection and Affordable Care Act of 2010."

96. S. Harlap, K. Kost, J. Darroch Forrest, "Preventing Pregnancy, Protecting Health: A New Look at Birth Control Choices in the United States," Guttmacher Institute (New York: AGI, 1991), in "Facts on American Teens' Sexual and Reproductive Health," Guttmacher Institute, (January 2010).

97. Ibid.

98. H. Weinstock, S. Berman, W. Cates Jr., "Sexually Transmitted Diseases among American Youth: Incidence and Prevalence Estimates, 2000," *Perspectives on Sexual and Reproductive Health*, 36, no. 1 (2004): 6–10. "Facts on American Teens' Sexual and Reproductive Health."

99. "Facts on American Teens' Sexual and Reproductive Health."

100. Andrea P. MacKay, Catherine Duran, "Adolescent Health in the United States, 2007," National Center for Health Statistics, http://www.cdc.gov/nchs/data/misc/adolescent2007.pdf.

101. "Sex and America's Teenagers," Guttmacher Institute (New York: AGI, 1994), in "U.S. Teen Sexual Activity," Kaiser Family Foundation (January 2005).

102. "HIV/AIDS Surveillance Report, 2006," Centers for Disease Control and Prevention, 18, no. 11 (2008), http://www.cdc.gov/hiv/topics/surveillance/resources/reports/2006report/pdf/2006SurveillanceReport.pdf.

103. A. Feijoo, "Adolescent Sexual Health in Europe and the U.S. — Why the Difference?" updated Sue Alford and Deb Hauser, 3rd edition, Advocates for Youth, 2008.

104. J. A. Martin, et al., "Births: Final Data for 2002," *National Vital Statistics Reports*, 52, no. 10 (2003), cited in "Facts on American Teens' Sexual and Reproductive Health," Guttmacher Institute, January 2010.

105. Ibid.

106. Ibid.

107. A. Maradiegue, "Minor's Rights versus Parental Rights: Review of Legal Issues in Adolescent Healthcare," *Journal of Midwifery and Women's Health*, 48, no. 3 (2003): 170–77.

108. Ford et al., "Confidential Healthcare for Adolescents."

109. See *Bellotti v. Baird*, 443 U.S. 622, 633–34 (1979).

110. *Bellotti*, 443 U.S. at 634. The right to access an abortion is different than requiring a minor to reach the age of majority to marry. Ibid., 642. Where a minor's right to marry will only be delayed, access to an abortion will be denied if not timely. See ibid.

111. "State Policies in Brief: An Overview of Minor's Consent Laws," Guttmacher Institute (last modified November 1, 2010), http://www.guttmacher.org/statecenter/spibs/spib_OMCL.pdf.

112. Ibid.

113. "Teenagers' Access to Confidential Reproductive Health Services," *Guttmacher Report on Public Policy*, 8, no. 4 (November 2005).

114. Guttmacher Institute, "Overview of Minor's Consent Laws."

115. Ibid.

116. Ibid.

117. Ibid.

118. "State Policies in Brief." English et al., *State Minor Consent Laws*.

119. "State Policies in Brief: Parental Involvement in Minors' Abortions," Guttmacher Institute (last modified November 1, 2010), http://www.guttmacher.org/statecenter/spibs/spib_PIMA.pdf.

120. "State Policies in Brief: State Funding for Abortion Under Medicaid," Guttmacher Institute http://www.guttmacher.org/statecenter/spibs/spib_SFAM.pdf (accessed January 15, 2011).

121. M. R. Rand, "Criminal Victimization, 2008 from the National Crime Victimization Survey, September 2009" last accessed January 11, 2011, http://bjs.ojp.usdoj.gov/content/pub/pdf/cv08.pdf.

122. Ibid.

123. "Key Facts at a Glance," Bureau of Justice Statistics, last accessed January 11, 2011, http://bjs.ojp.usdoj.gov/content/glance/homage.cfm; "Web-based Injury Statistics Query and Reporting System (WISQARS) [Online]," (National Center for Injury Prevention and Control, Centers for Disease Control and Prevention (producer), 2007) last modified June 14, 2010, www.cdc.gov/injury.

124. "Criminal Victimization in the United States 2001: Statistical Tables," Bureau of Justice Statistics, (Washington, DC: U.S. Department of Justice, 2003).

125. Sarah F. Lewis, William Fremouw, "Dating Violence: A Critical Review of the Literature," *Clinical Psychology Review*, 21, no.1 (2001): 105–27.

126. "Teen Dating Violence Facts," National Teen Dating Violence Prevention Initiative, American Bar Association (2006), 1, http"//www.clotheslineproject.org/teendatingviolencefacts.pdf.

127. Lewis and Fremouw, "Dating Violence," 105–27.

128. Ibid.

129. "Dating Violence," Alabama Coalition against Domestic Violence, http://www.acadv.org/dating.html (accessed January 23, 2011).

130. Ibid.

131. Ibid.

132. E. Joyce, "Teen Dating Violence: Facing the Epidemic," National Center for Victims of Crime (2003–2004), 2, http://www.ncvc.org/ncvc/AGP.Net/Components/documentViewer/Download.aspxnz?DocumentID=38039 (accessed January 23, 2011).

133. Ibid.

134. Ibid.

135. K. E. Suarez, comment, "Teenage Dating Violence: The Need for Expanded Awareness and Legislation," *California Law Review*, 82 (1994): 435.

136. MASS. GEN. LAWS 209A §1(e)(1), defining "Family or Household members" entitled to protection, cited in Suarez, "Teenage Dating Violence," 441.

137. Suarez, "Teenage Dating Violence," 439. "These statutes do not specifically include dating adolescents in their definitions of domestic violence. Rather, these statutes are significant because they do not necessarily exclude teen daters explicitly or effectively from their scope of coverage." Ibid., 439–40.

138. Suarez, "Teenage Dating Violence," 435.

139. Ibid. See *Desiato v. Abbott*, 617 A.2d 678 (N.J. Super. Ct. Ch. Div. 1992).

140. Suarez, "Teenage Dating Violence," 448. The case in *Desiato* involved adults, but the broad construction may be extended to adolescents. Ibid.

141. C. Green, L. Murray Mohlhenrich, "Dating Violence: Can Teens Access Protection Orders?" National Center for Victims of Crime (2005), 1–11.

142. M. Halley, A. English, "Healthcare for Homeless Youth," Center for Adolescent Health and the Law (2008), 1, http://www.cahl.org/PDFs/HealthCareForHomelessYouth.pdf.

143. Ibid.

144. A. English, "Youth Leaving Foster Care and Homeless Youth: Ensuring Access to Healthcare," *Temple Law Review*, 79 (2006): 440.

145. M. Goldberg, et al., *On Our Streets and in Our Shelters: Results of the 2005 Greater Vancouver Homeless Count* (Vancouver, BC: Social Planning and Research Council of BC, 2005), http://vancouver.ca/commsvcs/housing/pdf/homelesscount05.pdf (accessed January 23, 2011).

146. "Homeless Youth," National Coalition for the Homeless.

147. P. A. Toro, A. Dworsky, P. J. Fowler, "Homeless Youth in the United States: Recent Research Findings and Intervention Approaches," paper developed for the National Symposium on Homeless Research, Washington, DC, March 1–2, 2007, http://aspe.hhs.gov/hsp/homelessness/symposium 07/toro/.

148. "Program Assistance Letter: Understanding the Healthcare Needs of Homeless Youth," U.S. Department of Health and Human Services, Health Resources and Services Administration, http://bphc.hrsa.gov/policy/pal0110.htm.

149. N. Higgitt, et al., "Voices from the Margins: Experiences of Street-Involved Youth in Winnipeg" (2003), http://ius.uwinnipeg.ca/pdf/Street-kidsReportfinalSeptember903.pdf.

150. Halley and English, "Healthcare for Homeless Youth," 1.

151. Ibid. More recent data are not available, but it is likely that a significant portion of homeless youth remain uninsured.

152. Ibid. 1.

153. Abigail English, "The Patient Protection and Affordable Care Act (PPACA) of 2010: How Does it Help Adolescents and Young Adults?" Center for Adolescent Health and the Law (August 2010), http://www.cahl.org/web/wp-content/uploads/2010/08/CAHL-UCSF-HCR-Issue-Brief-Aug2010_Final_Aug31.pdf.

154. Halley and English, "Healthcare for Homeless Youth," 1.

155. Ibid.

156. Ibid., 5.

157. See A. Horton-Newell, K. Meyer, C. Trupin, eds., *Runaway and Homeless Youth and the Law: Model State Statutes* (American Bar Association Commission on Homelessness and Poverty and the National Network for Youth 2009).

158. Ibid., 1.

159. "Child Maltreatment 2005," U.S. Department of Health and Human Services, Administration for Children, Youth and Families, http://www.acf.hhs.gov/programs/cb/pubs/cm05/cm05.pdf (accessed January 23, 2011).

160. "Statistics and Research," U.S. Department of Health and Human Services, Administration for Children and Families, www.acf.hhs.gov/programs/cb/stats_research/index.htm (accessed January 23, 2011).

161. Ibid.

162. H. Ringeisen, et al., "Special Healthcare Needs among Children in the Child Welfare System," *Pediatrics,* 122, no. 1 (2008): e232.

163. Ibid.

164. L. K. Leslie, et al., "Health-Risk Behaviors in Young Adolescents in the Child Welfare System," *Journal of Adolescent Health,* 47, no. 1 (2010): 26–34.

165. M. E. Courtney, et al., "Foster Youth Transitions to Adulthood," study done at University of Wisconsin-Madison, Institute for Research on Poverty (1998).

166. P. J. Pecora, et al., "Improving Family Foster Care: Findings from the Northwest Foster Care Alumni Study," Casey Family Programs, Seattle, WA (2005).

167. AAP Committee on Early Childhood, Adoption, and Dependent Care, "Healthcare of Young Children in Foster Care," *Pediatrics,* 109, no. 3 (2002): 536–41.

168. AAP District II Task Force on Healthcare for Children in Foster Care, District II Committee on Early Childhood, Adoption, and Dependent Care, *Fostering Health: Healthcare for Children in Foster Care—A Resource Manual* (American Academy of Pediatrics, 2001).

169. Courtney et al., "Foster Youth Transitions To Adulthood."

170. A. J. Baer, et al., "Early Intervention and Special Education Advocacy: Challenges in Representing Children, Parents, and the Department of Education," *Practicing Law Institute: Criminal and Urban Problems,* 195 (2003): 110.

171. T. Naccaroto, et al., "The Foster Youth Housing Crisis: Literature, Legislation, and Looking Ahead," *St. John's Journal of Legal Commentary,* 23 (2008): 429.

172. Ibid., 430.

173. Ibid., 430–31.

174. Ibid., 433.

175. E. S. Pitchal, "Thickening the Safety Net: Key Elements to Successful Independent Living Programs for Young Adults Aging Out of Foster Care," *St. John's Journal of Legal Commentary,* 23 (2008): 472.

176. Ibid.

177. Ibid., 459.

178. "Facts on American Teens' Sexual and Reproductive Health," Guttmacher Institute (January 2011), http://www.guttmacher.org/pubs/FB-ATSRH.html.

179. Ibid.

180. Ibid.

181. Ibid.

182. Ibid.

183. Ibid.

184. J. D. Klein, "Adolescent Pregnancy: Current Trends and Issues," *Pediatrics,* 116, no. 1 (2005): 281–86.

185. Ibid.

186. Ibid.

187. D. Hollman, E. Alderman, "Fatherhood in Adolescence," *Pediatrics in Review,* 29, no. 10 (2008): 364–66.

188. "Health, United States, 2009, with Special Feature on Medical Technology: Table 10 Mothers Who Smoked Cigarettes during Pregnancy, by Selected Characteristics: United States, Selected Years 1990–2000 and Selected States, 2005–2006," National Center for Health Statistics, Hyattsville, MD (2010): 162.

189. Klein, "Adolescent Pregnancy," 281–86.

190. Elisabeth Ryden Benjamin, et al., "The Rights of Pregnant & Parenting Teens: A Guide to the Law in New York State," (2006), 29, http://www.nyclu.org/files/publications/nyclu_pub_rights_par-enting_teens.pdf (accessed December 1, 2010).

191. M. Heberlein, et al., "Holding Steady, Looking Ahead: Annual Findings of a 50-State Survey of Eligibility Rules, Enrollment and Renewal Procedures, and Cost Sharing Practices in Medicaid and CHIP, 2010–2011, Kaiser Commission on Medicaid and the Uninsured (2010–2011), 44–45, http://ccf.georgetown.edu/index/cms-filesystem-action?file=ccf publications/about medicaid/holding steady, looking ahead.pdf (accessed January 23, 2011).

192. Ibid.

193. Ibid. States requiring an asset test include Arkansas, Idaho, Iowa, Montana, South Carolina, South Dakota and Utah. Pregnant women whose income exceeds the percentage of the federal poverty level may still be eligible for some coverage. For example, in Hawaii, "pregnant women whose income exceeds 185% of the FPL can enroll in Quest-ACE by paying premiums. Coverage goes up to 200% of the FPL, but provides limited benefits." In 2014, Medicaid coverage will be expanded to adults at 133 percent of the FPL, which will increase the number of pregnant women covered.

194. These states include Arkansas, California, Illinois, Louisiana, Massachusetts, Michigan, Minnesota, Oklahoma, Oregon, Rhode Island, Tennessee, Texas, Washington and Wisconsin. Heberlein, et al., "Holding Steady, Looking Ahead," 12.

195. "California Postsecondary Education, Relationship between Education and Income," http://www.cpec.ca.gov/SecondPages/Index.asp?Query=Relationship between Education and Income#middle_column (accessed January 23, 2011).

196. "Why It Matters: Teen Pregnancy and Education," National Campaign to Prevent Teen and Unplanned Pregnancy (March 2010), http://www.thenationalcampaign.org/why-it-matters/pdf/education.pdf.

197. Ibid.

198. K. Fershee, "Hollow Promises for Pregnant Students: How the Regulations Governing Title IX Fail to Prevent Pregnancy Discrimination in School," *Indiana Law Review,* 43 (2009): 79.

199. Ibid., 84.

200. Ibid.

201. Ibid.

202. Ibid.

203. Ibid.

204. Ibid.

205. Ibid., 94.

206. 101 P.L. 104-193 (Congressional Findings).

207. "SNAP/Food Stamps," MassLegalHelp, http://www.masslegalhelp.org/income-benefits/food-stamps (accessed January 11, 2011).

208. N. Harris, M. R. Dyson, "Safe Rules or Gays' Schools? The Dilemma of Sexual Orientation Segregation in Public Education," *University of Pennsylvania Journal of Constitutional Law*, 7 (2004): 187.

209. R. J. Bidwell, "The Gay and Lesbian Teen: A Case of Denied Adolescence," *Journal of Pediatric Healthcare*, 2 (1988): 3–8.

210. Robert Garofalo, Emily Katz, "Healthcare Issues of Gay and Lesbian Youth," *Current Opinion in Pediatrics*, 13 (2001): 298–302.

211. R. Garofalo, et al., "The Association between Health Risk Behaviors and Sexual Orientation Among a School-Based Sample of Adolescents," *Pediatrics*, 101, no. 5 (1998): 895–902.

212. Garofalo and Katz, "Healthcare Issues of Gay and Lesbian Youth," 298–302.

213. S. E. Valentine, "Traditional Advocacy for Nontraditional Youth: Rethinking Best Interest for the Queer Child," *Michigan State Law Review*, 2008 (2008): 1059.

214. Ibid.

215. B. Fedders, "Coming Out for Kids: Recognizing, Respecting, and Representing LGBTQ Youth," *Nevada Law Journal*, 6 (2006): 795.

216. Ibid., 789.

217. Committee on Adolescence, "Homosexuality and Adolescence," *Pediatrics*, 92 (1993): 632.

218. "Students & Schools—At-a-Glance," GLAD, http://www.glad.org/rights/c/students-schools/ (accessed January 11, 2011).

219. Ibid.

220. 9 V.S.A. §4502 (2009); see also "Students' Rights in Vermont," GLAD, http://www.glad.org/rights/vermont/c/students-rights-in-vermont/(accessed January 11, 2011).

221. 16 V.S.A. §1 (1997); see also "Students' Rights in Vermont."

222. "Students' Rights in Vermont."

223. 20 U.S.C. §4071 (1984); see also http://www.glad.org/rights/c/students-schools/.

224. Cal. Welfare & Inst. Code §16001.9; Flor Bermudez, "Legal Rights of LGBTQ Youth in Out-of-Home Care," Lambda Legal, http://www.juvjustice.org/media/resources/public/resource_161.pdf (accessed January 11, 2011).

225. *Doe v. Bell*, 754 N.Y.S.2d 846 (N.Y. Sup. Ct. 2003); see also Bermudez, "Legal Rights of LGBTQ Youth in Out-of-Home Care," note 22.

226. *Doe v. Bell*, 754 N.Y.S.2d 846, 848 (N.Y. Sup. Ct. 2003).

227. Ibid., 853.

228. "Rights of Lesbian, Gay, Bisexual, Transgender, and Questioning Youth Involved in the Juvenile Justice System—Hawaii Correctional Facility, Policy Number 1.43.04," Lambda Legal, 21, http://www.juvjustice.org/media/resources/public/resource_161.pdf (accessed January 11, 2011).

229. Ibid.

230. "Know Your Rights: LGBTQ Youth and Youth Living with HIV in Foster Care and Juvenile Justice Systems," Lambda Legal, http://data.lambdalegal.org/publications/downloads/fs_know-your-rights-lgbtq-and-hiv-youth-in-foster-care.pdf.

231. C. J. Voelker, "Educational Concerns of the Teen Mother in Providence, RI: The Law, School Policies and Real Experiences," unpublished paper for Community Health Clerkship, Medical-Legal Partnership, Rhode Island Legal Services (2006).

Part V

Using Medical-Legal Partnership to Improve Population Health

Chapter 16

Medical-Legal Partnership: Strategies for Policy Change

Megan Sandel, MD, MPH
David Keller, MD
Ellen Lawton, JD
Leanne Ta, BA
Kevin Kappel, BS

The dynamics of policy change at the institutional, local, state, and federal levels are explored in some detail throughout this book. Indeed, virtually all chapters extol the opportunity for powerful policy change on behalf of vulnerable populations brought about by legal and health professionals working together in medical-legal partnership.

This chapter builds on the policy frames introduced in Chapter 1 and discusses strategies that will be covered in more depth in Chapters 17 and 19 to describe a sampling of approaches used by medical-legal partnerships (MLPs) which drive policy change at multiple levels. After reviewing the basic landscape of policy activity and stakeholders, brief examples from the national MLP network are presented to demonstrate how MLPs are uniquely situated to improve the health and well-being of vulnerable populations by shaping policies at every level—from local healthcare institutions to major federal government programs such as Supplemental Security Income and the Supplemental Nutrition Assessment Program.

Defining Policy

Many advocates prioritize policy change activities in order to achieve maximum impact for underserved communities and populations. But what does "policy" actually mean?

Public Policy: A Working Definition

In any society, government entities enact laws, make policies, and allocate resources. This is true at all levels. Generally, public policy can be defined as a system of laws, regulatory measures, courses of action and funding priorities concerning a given topic promulgated by a government entity or its representative.

Source: D.G. Kilpatrick, *Definitions of Public Policy and the Law*, Medical University of South Carolina. National Violence Against Women Prevention Research Center (2000). Available at: http://www.musc.edu/vawprevention/policy/definition.shtml.

What constitutes "public policy" can vary among states, counties and towns, but the policy process always involves efforts by competing interest groups to influence policy-makers—also known as advocacy, which is defined as "the act or process of advocating or supporting a cause or proposal."[1]

In the broadest sense, healthcare and legal institutions also have the capacity and opportunity to implement laws and regulations enacted by federal, state and local entities, as well as to allocate resources. Institutions such as hospitals and insurance carriers routinely interpret laws, regulations and policies, making the term "policymaking" relevant at multiple levels, from institutions to local, state and federal governments. Table 16.1 details MLP-initiated policy changes at all levels that improve health.

Table 16.1 Levels of Advocacy, Advocacy Intervention, and Policy Impact

Level of Advocacy	Advocacy Need	Advocacy Intervention	Policy Change
Institutional	Healthcare providers unsure how to document patient's disability to trigger eligibility for benefits and services	Electronic health records as screening tool for disability and a training series for healthcare team	Improved access to disability benefits and services adopted as clinical priority and quality indicator
Local	Housing codes insufficient to protect children from lead poisoning	Joint testimony by physician-lawyer team before city council details health risks and recommends policy actions to protect child health	Recommendations adopted by local city council and housing codes revised to strengthen protections and expand enforcement
State	Low-income chronically and terminally ill patients forced to repeatedly secure physician letters documenting health status to avoid utility shut-off	Regulatory comments jointly developed by physician-lawyer team recommends (1) expansion of qualified healthcare providers who can document need and (2) reduction of required documentation	Department of Public Utilities adopts regulations citing physician input as persuasive
Federal	Adults with disabilities mistakenly denied disability protections due to out-of-date disability standards	Physician-lawyer team publishes journal series on disability standards and submits regulatory comments recommending revisions to medical disability and functional limitation definitions	Federal disability agency revises disability standards to reflect current medical standards

In MLP terms, policy impact is both a core component and an outcome of the model. Policy change activities in the MLP context encompass both *internal* or *institutional* changes (such as improved medical home or improved clinical workforce skills) as well as *external* or *public* policy changes (such as improved policies, laws and regulations).

Key Strategies for Policy Change

The phrase "patients to policy" is used to describe a policy trajectory, whereby the MLP provides direct assistance to vulnerable, individual patients and families in the healthcare setting, identifying ineffective policies that have unintended health consequences. MLPs can then design and advocate for policy solutions to avoid negative health impacts, thus enabling the MLP intervention to improve the lives of many more vulnerable people.

When thinking about policy change, key questions to consider include:

- *Why* is this change important and worthwhile?
- *Who* are the stakeholders, decision makers, allies and opponents?
- *What* are the appropriate and most effective tactics and strategies to employ?
- *When* will individuals or groups be poised to act?
- *Where* are the opportunities to influence policy change?

The fundamental question in any policy change effort is "why." For advocates, the answer must be clear, since the policy process requires significant commitment of time, energy and other resources. For policymakers, it must be clear why the policy change is important to their constituents. Whether elected or appointed, in legislatures or administrative agencies, policymakers are accountable to their constituents; policy change, therefore, requires that advocates and policymakers both articulate the benefits of policy change. Using the above-referenced case example, answers to the question of "Why is this policy change important and worthwhile?" are different for each stakeholder group— patient, healthcare provider, hospital, and government insurer.

A worthwhile cause or strong motivating factor—such as an immigrant child's health, or the proper allocation of scarce healthcare resources—not only raises awareness and interest in policy change, but also can help to secure the level of support that is needed to push a policy change effort forward. The question of "why" thus has a broad impact on who is involved and their levels of engagement. This in turn affects other fundamental aspects of policy change, including media, political opportunities and timeline.

Who Makes Policy Change?

Individual and population health is affected by policies that are made at many levels of government, from community-based programs to major initiatives emanating from the Executive Office of the President of the United States. Healthcare policy in the United States is developed and implemented through serial communication between and amongst federal, state and local governments, together with a wide range of national, state and local organizations with varying and sometimes overlapping missions. (Chapter 17 contains a detailed discussion of the federal, state and local entities that may relate to obesity prevention initiatives.)

Table 16.2 Policy Stakeholders

Executive branch of government	The executive branch shapes the public policy agenda, but also initiates a budget and oversees the implementation of state and federal laws through regulations, policies and resource allocations.
Legislative branch of government	Legislators enact bills, approve and revise budgets, and appropriate funds. They influence policy by passing or rejecting legislation, resulting in creation or elimination of public programs or policies.
Judicial branch of government	Judges and juries at the local, state and federal level interpret laws created by legislative branch and resolve cases or controversies arising from policies or regulations implemented by the executive branch.
General Public	Public opinion polls are closely monitored by policymakers and widely used in the policy field to develop a policy agenda; both elected officials and other government entities communicate directly with constituents to gauge public opinion on specific topics.
Interest Groups and Lobbyists	Lobbyists are hired by individuals, corporations or organizations for their expertise in navigating political landscapes to represent the interests of those entities, their employees and the constituencies they serve.
	Interest groups—such as the American Bar Association or the American Medical Association—can wield enormous influence in the policy sphere due to their ability to mobilize their members and affiliated organizations to press for policy change.

Source: B. S. Jansson, *Becoming an Effective Policy Advocate: From Policy Practice to Social Justice, Fifth Edition* (California: Thomson Brooks Cole, 2008).

Policy Stakeholders in the MLP Context

In addition to the above-referenced groups, MLPs deploy their policy change strategies within the institutions where they practice, to "transform and improve institutions." Given the breadth of potential stakeholders in local communities—from hospitals to law firms, public health departments and academic institutions—it is helpful to highlight key allies for MLP policy initiatives.

Professional and Industry Associations

Professional and industry associations can be a critical force in efforts to effect policy change, largely because they epitomize two of the golden rules of advocacy—strength in numbers and recognized expertise in their focus area.

From the point of view of those trying to effect change, especially smaller and more isolated organizations, leveraging the support and/or position of a large respected association provides significant firepower with which to make an argument. First, the legitimacy afforded to many industry organizations can serve to validate the argument. Second, the fact that these organizations are inherently oriented toward consensus building among a larger group of stakeholders often mitigates positions that are perceived as extreme and that could isolate certain groups. These groups must find common ground in their positions as they seek to satisfy the demands across the spectrum of their membership— the air of compromise, especially in a contentious political climate, can help to improve the perception and opinion of a particular viewpoint. From the point of view of policymakers and those able to implement reform, these organizations provide a convenient way to adopt a consensus opinion without actually navigating to that consensus themselves.

Third, the resources, both financial and human (in terms of grassroots), available to spread the message can provide an effective microphone to an organization and its mission.

All of these factors become even more important for smaller, highly-specialized organizations like MLPs, which have not been active in the policy arena for very long. Gaining the support of industry associations can provide a much larger platform for entry onto the policy stage. However, engaging these groups can be complicated. In order to secure the support of outside organizations, it is important to promote *their* agenda and to keep their priorities and interests in mind.

Government Relations Offices of Law Firms and Hospitals

The government relations offices of pro bono law firms and hospitals provide a good opportunity for organizations like MLPs to leverage relationships with partners that have mutual interests for advocacy efforts. These offices often have close relationships to policymakers and can weigh in on the MLP's behalf.

These entities can be particularly useful for MLPs because (1) they have access to audiences that other partner organizations may not have, or have a certain standing or credibility within the institution that is useful, and (2) they can present the MLP's position to these audiences with a perspective they would appreciate.

It is important to properly leverage these relationships and engage key stakeholders at the appropriate time in the appropriate manner. The first step in that process is helping them to understand the MLP mission and activities, while highlighting mutual interests and the ways in which it is in *their* interest to become involved.

Institutions

Institutions, including hospitals, health centers, law offices and universities have unique policies and regulations that govern the way that services and resources are managed and delivered. In healthcare, institutional policies affect not only patients, but also the clinical staff in terms of workflow, actions and priorities.

MLP attorneys and healthcare providers, in caring for patient-clients in a healthcare setting, have a front row view of how institutional policies, laws and regulations affect individuals and families. In many instances, MLP staff can identify institutional policies that produce barriers to health for their patient-clients, and—with input from both medical and legal members of the team—can successfully campaign to change those *internal* and *external* policies.

Basic Strategies for Effective Policy Change

It is a common perception that successful policy change can only arise from a change in the law. But *legislative and political activity* is just one strategy, alongside *administrative advocacy*, *organizing* and *media outreach*. Each brings unique challenges and advantages, and these strategies are most effective when used together.

Legislative and Political Activity

Legislative activity refers to any action calculated to influence the status of impending bills before a legislative body. It encompasses both *policy* activity, e.g., analyzing potential bills, the strategy behind a particular bill and possible policy alternatives. *Advocacy* activities involve developing a comprehensive campaign to engage policymakers. See Figure 16.1. Advocacy activities naturally synchronize with media and organizing activities which attempt to mold public opinion and stimulate legislative action by supporting or opposing specific legislative issues or philosophical attitudes.

Figure 16.1 Connecting Policy and Advocacy

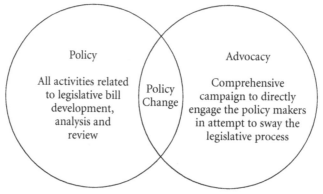

Policy and advocacy activities can include:

- Formulating policy positions on specific bills;

- Preparing and presenting testimony before legislative committees;

- Initiating telephone calls, sending faxes or writing e-mails or letters to concerned stakeholders to urge a particular action on specific or categorical legislation;

- Sponsoring or holding meetings, furnishing speakers or preparing and distributing pamphlets and other literature to stimulate reaction to legislation; and

- Circulating petitions, contacting legislators or participating in other efforts to impact legislative issues.

Within legislative activity, the boundaries between lobbying and educating can be difficult to define. These distinctions are important, however, since many attorneys, healthcare providers and others must conform to institutional and state rules regarding lobbying activities. In some states, there are strict laws concerning policy activities by persons not registered as lobbyists, and there are guidelines in many institutions and professions regarding how to participate in the legislative or political process. While LSC-funded agencies' lobbying activities are restricted, there are many legal aid agencies that do not receive federal funds and are therefore not restricted in their advocacy activities.

Permissible Legislative Activities for LSC-Funded Agencies

Employees of LSC-funded legal aid agencies acting in a professional capacity may:

- track legislative developments at the local, state and federal levels and inform others about the content and status of new or proposed statutes

- publish materials that report on the content or status of pending or proposed legislation

- discuss legislative developments in task force meetings and other settings

- advise clients and others about the content and effects of legislation
- advise clients and others about their right to participate in legislative proceedings or communicate with elected officials

Employees of LSC-funded legal aid agencies acting in a professional capacity may not:

- Engage in direct lobbying—that is, attempting to influence pending or proposed legislation
- Engage in grassroots lobbying, defined as "any written or oral communication in any form which 'contains a direct suggestion to the public to contact public officials in support of or in opposition to pending or proposed legislation, regulations, executive decisions' or ballot measures."

Source: A.W. Houseman, "Short Primer on Policy Advocacy," Center for Law and Social Policy (2007). Available at: http://www.nhlp.org/files/06%20Short%20Primer%20on%20Policy%20Advocacy%20Sept%202007.pdf.

MLP attorneys and healthcare providers seeking to understand legal restrictions on lobbying or policy activity frequently turn to government relations or government affairs offices in their stakeholder network. Many institutions, including hospitals, universities and law firms, have offices dedicated to serving as liaisons between the institution, government and community groups. They often have well-established relationships with local and national policymakers, and can help to ensure that policy efforts fall within institutional guidelines and are aligned with the broader mission of their partner institution.

In general, *political activity* refers to any action intended to influence the nomination, election or appointment of any person to public office. Similar to legislative activities, political activities are governed in part by restrictions for certain entities—for example, the tax status of the organization under the U.S. Internal Revenue Code.

Just as some legal and healthcare organizations have strict rules against lobbying, a tax-exempt organization under section 501(c)3 of the Code is prohibited from directly or indirectly engaging in certain political activity.[2] See Appendix 16.1. Political activities—including raising funds for legislators and candidates, making contributions to candidates' campaigns, distributing pamphlets or other materials regarding a specific candidate, or supporting a candidate at a sign-waving event or other rally—are all completely permissible activities for any private citizen.

Administrative Advocacy

Policies are developed at all levels of government, from the Executive Branch at the federal level, to federal or state agencies, to local governments or municipalities. Even institutions such as hospitals, medical or law schools have administrative mechanisms to create or change policy. One critical advocacy arena is commenting during a rulemaking process. For example, the Department of Health and Human Services (DHHS) and Centers for Medicare and Medicaid Services regularly issue regulations pursuant to legislation. During rule making, DHHS must respond to testimony or comments submitted by the general public or relevant stakeholders who can explain the unintended consequences of the policy and recommend remedies to avoid them. Policymakers can also reach out to certain professional groups to hold stakeholder meetings and submit comments and recommendations, creating separate advocacy opportunities. In this way, administrative and regulatory advocacy can be as impactful as other policy strategies.

Organizing for Policy Change

The multidimensional nature of seeking policy change in a complex, political climate demands that the groups and individuals seeking change *organize* in the most cohesive manner possible, aligning their message and coordinating their activities. "Grassroots" (bottom up) and "Grasstops" (top down) is a strategy that leverages the voices of many people across a community spectrum valued by policymakers: (1) their direct constituencies that they serve and who, in many cases, elect them (grassroots), and (2) leaders and "validators" with expertise and well-known gravitas in a particular field, such as health or economics (grasstops).

Essential components of a successful grassroots/grasstops campaign include:

- Ensuring diversity of voices but with a common, consistent message
- Aligning incentives for all potential partners to participate in the policy effort
- Providing effective social media strategies and the ability to mobilize a network rapidly

Successful organizing for policy change dovetails with the interests of multiple industry and professional associations and produces the political or community consensus described earlier that can accelerate policy change.

Telling the Story: Advocacy through Media Outreach

Whether journalists are the "watchdogs" of government, the "gatekeepers" of information or the "agenda-setters" for policymakers, it is clear that the media hold tremendous power to alter our society, values and behaviors. Mass media influence what we know, what we care about and the political decisions that are made each day, from our town halls to the steps of Congress.

The broad power of mass media is commonly demonstrated in the public health arena. In recent history, the media have been a prevailing force in shaping health policy and advancing public health goals. Since the late 1960s, anti-tobacco campaigns have been facilitated largely through print messaging and television and radio ads.[3] Mass communication has been a primary source of information about HIV/AIDS and other sexually transmitted infections.[4] The media not only enable the dissemination of important health information and ideas, they are also effective tools in advancing behaviors that promote health and well-being. A 1987 study estimated that more than 9,600 smokers in Erie County, New York, stopped smoking for at least one week as a result of exposure to a newspaper-based mediated smoking cessation program.[5] Numerous studies confirm that media campaigns are effective in preventing alcohol-impaired driving.[6]

It is also important to consider the pervasive influence of social networking sites in promoting advocacy and shaping policy change. Popular websites, including Facebook, Myspace, Twitter and thousands of blogs provide an open forum to discuss healthcare policies and change. These sites generate instant and widespread publicity for public health issues, inciting support or opposition. Not only are these resources an important source of information for many people, they also shape public opinion, which ultimately can affect social and political processes.

On a systemic level, the strategic use of mass media has brought about numerous opportunities to influence laws, policies and regulations related to individual and population health. Effective storytelling around medical issues — often focused on a single, dramatized example — has prompted both local and broad-scale policy actions in the U.S.

Policy experts have sought to analyze the use of powerful anecdotes alongside, or instead of, scientific research. Table 16.3 captures some of the strengths and limitations of each approach.

Table 16.3 Understanding Anecdotes and Evidence in Policy Advocacy

	Definition	Justification	Purpose
Anecdotes	Stories told to illustrate a problem or the failure of a policy, such as "I saw someone buy a steak with food stamps" or "welfare queen" stories	To justify starting or stopping programs by providing an easily understood story with obvious conclusions and underlying normative or moral principles	Good for staking out a position on an issue or motivating people to believe a certain way; less useful as part of serious analysis because they do not delve deeply into how programs work
Evidence from scientific study	Conclusions reached through scientific study of a problem or of the outcomes of a policy	To justify starting or stopping programs by providing the most scientifically sound information that policymakers can use to make decisions	Much stronger than anecdotes in understanding how and why things work the way they do; however, results of scientific studies are seldom straightforward and are always accompanied by unanswered questions. Many policymakers lack the technical expertise to fully understand the degree of uncertainty inherent in scientific analysis.

Source: T. Birkland, *An Introduction to the Policy Process: Theories, Concepts, and Models of Public Policy Making.* New York: M.E. Sharpe, Inc., 2005.

One memorable example is the case of Deamonte Driver. In February 2007, *The Washington Post* published a feature article on the 12-year-old Maryland boy who "died of a toothache." Without insurance and access to a dentist, Deamonte Driver lost his life to a case of untreated tooth decay that resulted in a fatal brain infection—something a routine, $80 tooth extraction might have prevented. The powerful story put a human face on the vast number of uninsured people in the U.S. and called attention to the life-and-death implications of a broken healthcare system. The shocking account generated enormous public outcry and dozens of follow-up articles in media outlets around the country. By 2008, a number of bills had been introduced to increase access to dental care, develop the dentistry workforce, increase the Federal Medical Assistance Percentage and prevent and manage early childhood caries.[7]

Deamonte Driver's story illustrates a key function of mass media which gives it a powerful and far-reaching influence in the policy realm—that is, the creation of images that remain in the minds of general audiences and policymakers alike. As seen in many news articles about complex public health issues, a single incident that affects an individual or family can serve as an example for millions of Americans facing similar situations. Deamonte Driver's story offered a convenient example for advocates to cite while making their case. It carried a high level of emotional appeal, and succinctly demonstrated the gravity of a particular healthcare problem and the urgent need for reform.

In recent years, public health organizations, associations and other industry stakeholders have succeeded in utilizing media to forward a diverse set of goals. The American Academy of Pediatrics, for instance, has effectively utilized the news media to bring a number of child-related issues to the legislative forefront, as detailed in a *Pediatric Annals* article.[8] These issues include state and national requirements for child auto restraints, product safety regulations on children's toys, safety caps on medications, bicycle helmet laws, restrictions on gun use and pediatric emergency care guidelines.

Consumers rely heavily on various forms of media to distill, process and analyze complex health information. Policymakers keep a close eye on the topics that media bring to light. Given the power of mass media to influence knowledge and decision-making, medical-legal partnerships and other public health programs can employ the media as an effective tool for advancing health-promoting goals. An excellent example of creating visibility in the media for health-related issues is through a letter to the editor in a local newspaper, responding to a media story.

Truly Smart Electricity Meters Should Aid the Elderly

The July 31 editorial "Gridlock," which called for a new regulatory doctrine for advanced metering or "smart meters," missed an important point: A truly smart approach protects access to electricity for our most vulnerable neighbors. Smart metering saves money when utilities can remotely disconnect service and avoid visits to houses. But this can be a missed opportunity to intervene in a crisis, as illustrated by the profile of the older couple in the July 19 Metro article "From good deed to dire straits." Despite their physician's request for a delay, this medically frail couple fell through the cracks during a heat wave, and Pepco temporarily disconnected their service for nonpayment.

Smart meters encourage conservation by enabling higher charges for peak usage, but for seniors on fixed budgets, this just motivates them to turn off the air-conditioning when they need it most. Low-income seniors use less energy than average and tend to have older appliances — they have little to conserve in response to higher prices.

Smart meters may be the prescription for our ailing energy grid, but they will be good medicine only if they also protect our most vulnerable people. Smart metering is smart only when peak pricing is optional and remote disconnections are prohibited for such customers.

Note: The writers are working on a health-impact assessment of advanced metering, supported by a grant from the Health Impact Project, a collaboration of the Robert Wood Johnson Foundation and the Pew Charitable Trusts.
Source: L. Snyder and M. Sandel, "Truly Smart Electric Meters Should Aid the Elderly," *The Washington Post*, Letter to the Editor (August 10, 2010).

Communicating about health through mass media can be a complicated and difficult task. More often than not, public health issues are multi-layered and controversial. In many instances, poor media communications about such topics generate confusion for the general public — and occasionally, ineffective communication can induce an outbreak of fear or outrage among the public. Effective communication requires a keen understanding of messages, audiences and potential reactions. As Liana Winett and Lawrence Wallack write in the *Journal of Health Communication*, "[U]sing the mass media to improve public health can be like navigating a vast network of roads without any street signs—if you are not sure *where* you are going and *why*, chances are you will not reach your destination."[9]

Without proper attention to messages and audiences, mass media can be counterproductive to public health goals. While media can be used to effect positive change for different populations, it can also lead to unexpected or unwanted consequences. In 1994, the *Boston Globe* ran an article on Clarabel Ventura, a crack-addicted mother who brutally abused her four-year-old son. Several days later, the newspaper ran a longer article focusing on the Ventura family—Eulalia Ventura (Clarabel's mother) and her 17 children, most of whom were unemployed and sustained by welfare programs, including AFDC, Food Stamps, WIC benefits and rent subsidies. Also featured were Eulalia's 74 grandchildren, many of whom were "beginning to apply for welfare themselves." The article perpetuated a stereotypical image of the idle, irresponsible welfare recipient. Within days of the article's appearance in the *Globe*, the Massachusetts Senate approved a floor amendment to terminate AFDC benefits after two years.[10]

Deamonte Driver and Clarabel Ventura's stories together make a compelling argument for the tremendous power of the media to influence healthcare policy decisions. In both cases, the media steered public dialogue toward a particular issue and created powerful images that served as examples for broader public health topics. These are just a few examples that demonstrate the crucial ways in which mass media guide popular opinion, influence public health priorities and shape local and national policy debates. Mass and social media, therefore, are important and powerful tools for any public health advocate.

Questions for Discussion

1. What are the benefits of collaborating with industry associations, government affairs offices and other key players in public policy change initiatives?

2. What are the benefits and drawbacks of each of the multiple strategies for policy change?

3. How can MLPs utilize mass media and social networking sites to promote positive information dissemination and support meaningful policy change?

MLPs: Powerful Drivers of Policy Change

When joined together on behalf of, and in concert with, vulnerable individuals and communities, healthcare providers and attorneys bring special skills and talents to policy work that result in exponentially more effective advocacy.

As detailed in Chapter 3, "advocacy" is perhaps more traditionally associated with attorneys than with healthcare providers. Attorneys are obvious advocates for the underserved—they are trained to challenge systems and to make arguments on behalf of clients who are not being adequately or appropriately served by existing policies, laws and regulations. But while many healthcare providers view themselves as advocates for their individual patients, they struggle to understand, and participate in, the policy domain—even where it is tightly connected to their clinical or professional goals as a physician.

Dr. David Rothman describes this issue in the New England Journal of Medicine:

> [Medical] professionalism today has to be invented, not restored. This proposition is even more true of the current effort to make civic and social obligations central to medical professionalism. Over the past century, physicians have been extraordinarily reluctant to enter the public arena. A few exceptions aside, most physicians have not taken part in national politics (even when healthcare reform was debated), let alone in state or local politics (e.g., serving on school boards).[11]

Earlier chapters, especially Chapters 2 and 3, describe some of the basis for this difference in civic attitudes, priorities and skill sets between attorneys and healthcare professionals. In the realm of policy change, how can MLP overcome—indeed, take advantage of—these differences to make policy change more effective?

Healthcare Providers as Policy Advocates

While all medical schools train future physicians in physiology and immunology, training in healthcare policy and advocacy skills is far from standard. Even schools that do teach healthcare policy "tend to describe the mechanics of our system, not the process of changing systems."[12]

Among medical sub-specialties, Pediatrics and Family Medicine have done the most to make community involvement and systemic advocacy part of their professional culture. Pediatrics as a specialty "split off" from the rest of medicine in the 1920s over federal support for the practice of preventive medicine for children, when a few pediatricians declared their support for the Children's Bureau's program to bring preventive pediatrics to rural and poor children throughout the country.[13] Since 1995, pediatric training programs have been required to have curricula "that prepare residents for the role of advocate for the health of children within the community"[14]

Family practitioners have, since the inception of Family Medicine as a specialty in the 1960s, taken an active role in the communities in which they practice. Their training programs are required to include a structured curriculum in community medicine, including "experience in developing programs to address community health priorities."[15] Like pediatricians, once in practice, the demands of providing care limit the ability of most physicians to build on those experiences.

There has been progress among other sub-specialties, including a recent statement by the American Board of Internal Medicine, the American College of Physicians, and the European Federation of Internal Medicine calling for medical professionalism to incorporate the principles of social justice and patient welfare in their work, and for physicians to be "activists in reforming health care systems on behalf of the patient community."[16]

Many pediatric leaders have also urged their colleagues to recognize the importance of physician activism in their work, calling it the "fourth dimension of medicine" after patient care, research and teaching.

> In addition to the lack of medical school training around civic engagement, there may be other explanations for why physicians and other healthcare providers are reluctant to enter the political sphere. In some ways, policy work is at odds with

a healthcare culture that emphasizes collaboration, respect for authority and rigid hierarchies. In most hospitals, for example, a wide institutional hierarchy exists, and providers know their places on the institutional ladder. Physicians in various specialties, nurses, and social workers learn to work together to address patient needs — a significant strength in coalescing broad policy change. But the instinct to challenge authority and change existing systems is not necessarily valued within the culture of medicine, which places a strong emphasis on teamwork and efficiency. In addition, though collaboration is emphasized, many silos still exist within hospitals and care systems, and the now common conundrum of fragmented healthcare is in fact evidence of a profound lack of collaboration across healthcare institutions and systems. New payment systems and healthcare reform hold promise to close some of the silos and gaps, but the sub-specialization of modern medical care continues to perpetuate discontinuity of care.[17]

While policy work can be viewed as relying on an American system of government that is largely adversarial,[18] healthcare providers tend to problem-solve using a paradigm that is grounded in the individual patient. Based on a deep knowledge of anatomy and physiology, physicians listen to the patient's problem, diagnose the cause and prescribe a regime of treatment that will alleviate or cure the problem.

Recognizing and addressing policy issues requires a different approach. First, physicians must be able to shift their focus away from the individual patient, and learn to recognize patterns of problems that indicate systemic need — a strategy that draws on public health. For instance, one child with asthma may be just that — a single case of asthma. But multiple children from a housing development with asthma may suggest that the origin of the problem is the conditions in the housing units. While embarking on policy work can be difficult, complex and time consuming for healthcare providers who have been trained to provide care for individual patients, in the era of healthcare reform, physicians will be expected to have a population health management approach to their care, and will be incentivized to find ways to keep patients healthy and out of the hospital.

Lawyers as Policy Advocates

Unlike healthcare providers, attorneys are natural policy advocates. While many attorneys are regularly called upon to make their case before decision makers such as judges and juries, legal training in general helps attorneys build an arsenal of advocacy skills regardless of the practice setting. All lawyers are trained to understand the legislative process and analyze how regulations and policies can affect their clients' lives.

More broadly, attorneys are trained to think critically about the ways in which laws enhance or harm our lives and to challenge an ineffective system. Attorneys count lawsuits among their arsenal of legal tools. Indeed, as described in Chapter 17, class action lawsuits have been the impetus for many of the biggest changes in healthcare laws in recent decades, from public safety regulations to tobacco advertising laws.

But despite this expertise, much of the legal profession — especially the legal aid community — does not have an accurate picture of either the health or the healthcare landscape for their clients or community. The broad, data-driven and eminently multidisciplinary view of the healthcare community, coupled with the ethic of prevention and upstream intervention that is inculcated in primary care medicine, are perspectives that have yet to take root in the legal profession, particularly among legal services providers.

What Healthcare and Legal Providers Can Learn from Each Other

Healthcare providers who engage in MLP are more likely to understand the interaction between social and legal systems and patient health. By working closely with an attorney, physicians, nurses and other members of the healthcare team can gain insight into the laws, policies and regulations that affect patient health and well-being. They can discover the legal remedies that can be taken to amend and improve an ineffective policy.

Attorneys who engage in MLP are able to reframe their work in terms of patient health and well-being, and can better understand the connections between policies and health outcomes. In addition, healthcare providers are able to substantiate claims with medical evidence. With appropriate coaching, a physician's science-based perspective can be used in preparing oral and written testimony for local, state and national hearings, comments on state and federal regulations affecting the health of patients, and even informing the writing of legislation to realign the rules regarding health. See Appendix 16.2 for examples of physician testimony on specific policies and regulations impacting low-income patients. In addition, healthcare providers tend to have a better understanding of the key interest groups within the world of healthcare, which can be beneficial to attorneys embarking on a health or public health policy effort.

Detecting Policy Change Opportunities

In addition to gaining insight and skills from each other, MLP teams—through frequent communication and casework—can recognize patterns of need, and the institutional or external policies that exacerbate these needs.

For example, one MLP received a series of referrals from different healthcare practices regarding children with cerebral palsy who were being denied physical therapy services under Medicaid, services that had historically been approved. The attorney noticed the cluster, contacted the local Medicaid office and found that new staff members were interpreting state regulations more restrictively than prior staff. A single conversation with the agency leadership was sufficient to reverse this change in policy. Because the healthcare providers knew that MLP attorneys could assist in reversing the denials, and the attorneys understood the medical context in which the denials were made, the MLP team was able to secure physical therapy services for children who needed them.

This example involved policy change on a small, local scale—that is, the local Medicaid office. Sometimes effective advocacy involves working at a higher level. Take the following example:

A family was concerned with the way in which a local school system was handling their daughter's mental illness. The medications for her bipolar disorder were being adjusted, so that the symptoms were intermittently causing "meltdowns," which appeared to school staff to be psychiatric emergencies. The school's policy at that time was to contact local police in such cases, as they were empowered to "commit" individuals to involuntary psychiatric treatment. While this was not consistent with the standards established by the State Department of Education, it was common practice by local school committees throughout the state. The family voiced their concerns to their daughter's doctor, who referred them to the MLP.

In the end, MLP attorneys worked with the Education Department to develop a new protocol for the management of psychiatric emergencies, and also joined a statewide initiative to reform children's mental healthcare throughout the state. This included the development of mobile emergency mental health teams to do onsite evaluations of child psychiatric emergencies. The policy change benefitted numerous children and families throughout the local school district. By improving policies at a district level, the MLP staff was able to maximize the impact and effectiveness of their work.

It is important to note that in both of the examples cited above, it is unlikely that the healthcare partners would have engaged in effective systemic advocacy without the perspective of the MLP. Without the medical component and support from healthcare providers, attorneys would also have been less effective in achieving these goals. MLPs are thus excellent vehicles to help physicians and other healthcare providers as well as attorneys gain the skills and expertise needed to become effective advocates.

Influencing Policy Change: Examples from the MLP Network

Internal or Institutional Change

MLP attorneys and healthcare providers have worked together to improve numerous policies within health and legal institutions that affect patient health. Several examples, some of which are discussed in other chapters of the book, are highlighted here.

> The **Cleveland Community Advocacy Program in Cleveland, Ohio** developed and disseminated dozens of Karody Special Education Calculators, an innovative tool that helps parents and providers understand special education processes and deadlines so that children are evaluated in a timely manner.

> **MLP | Boston in Massachusetts** developed templates for healthcare providers to use to advocate for vulnerable patients needing utilities shut-off protections in cold winter and hot summer months. The templates were integrated in the electronic medical record, and a department-wide policy regarding utility shut-off protection requests was implemented throughout the hospital.

> The **Children's Health Advocacy Project (CHAP) in St. Louis, Missouri** helped develop a new asthma clinic with their federally qualified health center partner, Grace Hill Neighborhood Health Center. Patients who live in the neighborhood of Grace Hill and who have visited the emergency room within the past month are contacted and scheduled to meet with a team of professionals. This team consists of a primary care physician, a lawyer and a child psychologist who all work together to address the barriers affecting these patients' optimal treatment of asthma.

> The **Cincinnati Child Health-Law Partnership in Cincinnati, Ohio** assisted families whose gas or electric service has been or will be terminated for nonpayment to keep their utility service on for up to 90 days each year if the service is medically necessary. For families to receive this service, they must provide the utility company with a certification of medical necessity from a medical provider. The MLP partner, the Pediatric Primary Care Clinic at the Cincinnati Children's Hospital Medical Center, receives many requests for medical certifications for utility service each month. In 2010, Duke Energy instituted a new Percent of Income Payment Plan (PIPP Plus) that gives families the opportunity to have their debt to the utility company forgiven. A Legal Aid attorney developed an information sheet and worked with the clinic to provide information on PIPP Plus and other home energy assistance programs which families might be eligible for and to assist patient families requesting a medical

certification. Legal Aid also facilitated training for partner clinics and other hospital social workers on public utility programs and consumer rights.

The **Medical-Legal Partnership | Boston in Boston, Massachusetts** developed a toolkit for healthcare providers working with immigrants: Communicable Disease Waivers for Immigrant Patients: A Toolkit for Providers (January 2010) (accessible at http://www.mlpboston.org/resources/for-health-care-providers/train ings-and-toolkits). MLP | Boston armed Boston Medical Center's Infectious Disease group (and other invested clinicians) with a guide to successfully complete the paperwork associated with certifying medical eligibility for patients with diseases like tuberculosis who are otherwise eligible green card applicants.

The **Lancaster Medical-Legal Partnership for Families in Lancaster, Pennsylvania** participated in an anti-asthma initiative launched by Lancaster General Hospital. The Lancaster MLP attorney collaborated with the AmeriCorps volunteer and physician who staff the initiative to discuss strategies for abating residential mold. They began developing a protocol for situations when the anti-asthma team identified a mold issue or potential mold issue, including informational letters on mold reduction strategies to go out to both the patient's parents and landlords of these residences, and they identified factors for recognizing when legal intervention might be appropriate. To improve external systems, the Lancaster MLP attorney was invited by the healthcare partner's medical director, who is also a chair of the City of Lancaster's Board of Health, to contribute to and assist in revisions to the City's Lead Paint Ordinance. The MLP attorney drafted detailed comments, suggested revisions and collaborated with city officials on the re-writing of the law. The revised ordinance was adopted by the city council on July 13, 2010, and contains greatly expanded protections for tenants.

The **Tucson Family Advocacy Program in Tucson, Arizona** partnered with law students from the University of Arizona College of Law and healthcare providers from a federally qualified health center to conduct advance directive clinics at low-income housing facilities. Medical residents from the University of Arizona Department of Family and Community Medicine discussed the importance of creating medical powers of attorney and living wills from a healthcare provider perspective. Legal staff and pro bono legal volunteers then supervised law students as they helped elderly and disabled residents at low-income housing complexes complete these advance directive forms. The residents were able to obtain the information and documentation necessary to make informed decisions and plan for end of life care.

The **Health Law Partnership (HeLP) in Atlanta, Georgia** created the Law and Medicine elective for fourth year medical students to spend one month with the MLP team and clinic interacting with lawyers, physicians, law students, faculty and clients, and collaborating with MLP staff. This elective allows students to address clients' legal matters and engage in interdisciplinary education and co-operation with the goal of improving preparedness for practice in the professions of law and medicine.

External Systems Change

MLPs have leveraged health and legal expertise to improve local and state laws and regulations that impact the health of vulnerable populations. Highlighted here are "practice to policy" examples, some of which are also discussed in other chapters in the book.

The **Cleveland Community Advocacy Program in Ohio** collaborated with the local police department to advocate for U Visas, a form of relief for immigrants who are victims of criminal activity and are suffering from physical or mental abuse. A resolution in support of U Visas was unanimously passed by the Cleveland City Council in 2010.

The **Peninsula Family Advocacy Program in San Mateo, California,** organized a regional MLP policy initiative to investigate the housing code inspection practices in the San Francisco Bay Area. Medical students researched the link between inadequate housing and poor health and medical partners documented the health connection. A policy brief was written and disseminated in September 2009 with policy recommendations to improve access to healthy housing.

The **Health Law Partnership (HeLP) in Atlanta, Georgia,** addressed a state-wide problem regarding access to home health agency services for Medicaid-eligible disabled children ready for discharge from the hospital. The physician and lawyer MLP teams advocated changing the rule and revising the policy with the state Medicaid agency, and corrective legislation was drafted with input from the MLP team. They also researched and developed a position paper and drafted proposed legislation and supporting educational materials to address a Medicaid administrative appeals problem. The legislation has been introduced in the 2011 session of the Georgia General Assembly.

The **MLP at Legal Aid of Western Missouri in Kansas City, Missouri,** advocated for a new policy to provide Orders of Protection in both English and petitioners' native languages, if other than English. The Missouri court system adopted the new policy in 2010.

Physician leaders from the **Syracuse MLP in New York** submitted testimony to inform the allocation of resources around civil legal services as part of a New York Access to Justice hearing.

Physicians and attorneys from **MLP | Boston in Massachusetts** participated in statewide Department of Public Utilities (DPU) hearings on utility shut-off protection. MLP documented the negative health impact of utility shut-off and proposed specific strategies to streamline the system, citing the clinical experiences of healthcare providers. The DPU subsequently revised its regulations, extending shut-off protection to vulnerable households, relaxing illness recertification requirements and allowing nurse practitioners and physician assistants to sign illness certification letters.

The MLP team from the **Children's Law Center/Health Access Project at Children's National Medical Center (CLC HAP) in Washington, DC** testified before the DC Council Committee on Housing and Workforce Development in support of the Tenant Access to Justice Reform Act of 2009. This bill gives tenants access to court, allowing them to sue when they are forced to live in unsafe and unhealthy housing conditions. The medical director's testimony educated the council and community about how many housing code violations negatively impact children's health.

Questions for Discussion

1. In what ways can physicians and lawyers promote effective policy change, both individually and in collaboration with one another?

2. Consider the policies, laws and regulations influencing the health of low-income patients or clients in your community. What are some ways in which these policies

could be changed or improved? What role could a healthcare provider-lawyer team play in advocating for these changes?

Conclusion

By bringing together the unique skills and expertise of lawyers and healthcare providers, MLPs can be influential drivers of policy change. To be effective policy advocates, MLP partners must be knowledgeable about the players and stakeholders involved in policymaking, the benefits and drawbacks of policy change strategies and approaches, and the opportunities to effect change at the institutional, local, state and national levels. Working on behalf of and in partnership with vulnerable individuals and communities, MLPs can identify and remove systemic barriers to health.

1. Miriam-Webster Definition of "advocacy," available at: http://www.merriam-webster.com/dictionary/advocacy.

2. Disability Insurance Benefits Payments, 26 U.S.C. §501(c)3 (2011), available at: http://www.irs.gov/charities/charitable/article/0,,id=181565,00.html.

3. National Library of Medicine, *Visual Culture and Health Posters*, available at: http://profiles.nlm.nih.gov/VC/Views/Exhibit/narrative/antismoking.html.

4. R.J. McDermott and T.L. Albrecht, *Mass Media*, eNotes.com (2011), available at: http://www.enotes.com/public-health-encyclopedia/mass-media.

5. K.M. Cummings, R. Sciandra, and S. Markello, "Impact of a Newspaper Mediated Quit Smoking Program," *American Journal of Public Health* 77, no. 11 (1987): 1452–53.

6. Centers for Disease Control and Prevention, *Mass Media Campaigns are Effective in Preventing Alcohol-Impaired Driving*, available at: http://www.cdc.gov/MotorVehicleSafety/Impaired_Driving/massmedia.html; R.W. Elder, R.A. Shults, D.A. Sleet, J.L. Nichols, R.S. Thompson, W. Rajab (Task Force on Community Preventive Services), "Effectiveness of Mass Media Campaigns for Reducing Drinking and Driving and Alcohol-Involved Crashes: A Systematic Review," *American Journal of Preventive Medicine* 27, no. 1 (2004): 57–65.

7. Academy of General Dentistry, *National Legislation* (2011), available at: http://www.agd.org/issuesadvocacy/advocacynews/nationallegislative/Default.asp?PubID=1&IssID=681&ArtID=3130.

8. S. P. Shelov, "The Use of Media to Impact on Legislation," *Pediatric Annals* 24, no. 8 (1995): 419–20, 422–5.

9. L.B. Winett and L. Wallack, "Advancing Public Health Goals through the Mass Media," *Journal of Health Communication* 1 (1996): 173–196.

10. L.A. Williams, "Race, Rat Bites, and Unfit Mothers: How Media Discourse Informs Welfare Legislation Debate," 22 Fordham Urban Law Journal (1994–1995): 1159–96.

11. D.J. Rothman, "Medical Professionalism—Focusing on the Real Issues," *New England Journal of Medicine* 342 (2000): 1284–86.

12. S.S. Cha, J.S. Ross, P. Lurie, G. Sacajiu, "Description of a Research-Based Health Activism Curriculum for Medical Students," *Journal of General Internal Medicine* 21, no. 12 (2006): 1325–28.

13. J. P. Baker, "Women and the Invention of Well Child Care," *Pediatrics* 94 (1993): 537–41.

14. Accreditation Council for Graduate Medical Education, ACGME Program Requirements for Graduate Medical Education in Pediatrics, available at: http://www.acgme.org/acWebsite/downloads/RRC_progReq/320_pediatrics_07012007.pdf.

15. Ibid., 30.

16. Medical Professionalism Project, "Medical Professionalism in the New Millennium: A Physician Charter," *Annals of Internal Medicine* 136 (2002): 243–46.

17. M. Baker, "Medical School Class of 2007: Changing the World, One Graduate at a Time," Center for International Security and Cooperation 2007, available at: http://cisac.stanford.edu/news/activism_is_medicines_vital_fourth_dimension_cisac_scholar_tells_graduates_20070629/.

18. R.A. Kagan, "Adversarial Legalism and American Government," *Journal of Policy Analysis and Management* 10 (1991): 369–406.

Chapter 17

Public Health Crisis: Medical-Legal Approaches to Obesity Prevention

Manel Kappagoda, JD, MPH
Samantha Graff, JD
Shale Wong, MD, MSPH

Skyrocketing obesity rates in the United States over the past three decades have prompted calls to action from diverse sectors of society, including policy makers, school administrators, healthcare professionals, military recruiters and individual citizens. Currently, two-thirds of adults[1] and one-third of children[2] are overweight or obese. A solution to this crisis undoubtedly demands that people take personal responsibility for their habits. But given the powerful influence that social and environmental factors have over the choices available to us, a critical component of the solution must involve not only individual education and health management but also population-based policy interventions targeted at the places we live, travel, shop, study, work and play.[3]

To make a physically active lifestyle possible, for example, our neighborhoods must provide opportunities for active living, such as safe walking and biking paths and parks and recreation centers. If we hope to prepare meals that include more fresh fruits and vegetables and less preserved or packaged foods, we need access to affordable, healthy food in local markets, restaurants and schools. Low-income people and communities often lack these amenities and consequently suffer poorer health and higher levels of obesity. To turn this around, we must create environments in which healthier choices become easier to make.

This chapter begins by laying out the data on the American obesity epidemic. Then it explains social norm change as an approach to obesity prevention policy. It outlines the legal and governmental systems in which policy change takes place. Finally, it explores different local policy strategies and ways medical-legal partnerships can work to lower obesity rates by promoting policy changes in communities and schools.

Obesity: Individual and Public Health Impacts

Both children and adults in the United States have shown dramatic increases in weight over the past several decades. As of 2008, 33.8 percent of adults[4] and 16.9 percent of children ages 2–19[5] in the United States were considered obese. Collectively, we have changed how we live our lives, causing us to become a so-called obesogenic society. The health consequences of obesity are increasing along with the weight gain: nearly $150 billion are spent per year to treat obesity-related illness and disease.[6]

Defining Obesity

Our best objective measure of body fatness is described by Body Mass Index (BMI). Although BMI is not a perfect measure of obesity, it is a calculation of body habitus determined by height and weight for age and gender. When an individual has a BMI above the 85th percentile, it identifies overweight; above the 95th percentile signifies obesity, and both indicate risk for health complications related to weight.

The tendency toward weight gain has been described as a simple energy imbalance. When an individual consumes more calories than he or she expends, the excess becomes added weight. Although this is a simple concept, the reality of making lifestyle changes to even the balance is truly complex and generally requires modification to both sides of the equation to achieve better health.

Obesity is best defined as a chronic condition. Many factors that cause an individual to be overweight as an adult begin in childhood and are more difficult to reverse in adulthood. Children who are overweight or obese are more likely to be obese as adults. Research has shown that obese six- to eight-year-olds were approximately 10 times more likely to become obese adults than children with BMIs in a normal range.[7] Food choices and dietary patterns, exercise habits, work hours and other lifestyle measures are well established among adults, making behavior change a challenge. Individuals make conscious choices every day that become habits of eating and activity and eventually become unconscious patterns. Regardless of the health impact of these daily choices, engrained behaviors are very hard to change.

Epidemiology and Prevalence of Obesity

According to the most recent surveillance data from 2007–2008, 32 percent of children and adolescents aged 2–19 years had a BMI at or above the 85th percentile for age.[8] Those children are at higher risk for diabetes , heart disease, asthma, cancers, high blood pressure and sleep disorders than their peers who are not overweight. Possibly the most prevalent concern related to being overweight is social stigmatization and bullying that may result in long-term psychological concerns, such as stress, depression, anxiety and low self-esteem. These mental health issues are shown to directly relate to poor school performance and decreased productivity.[9] The stigma creates a vicious circle: children who suffer from being overweight are less able to participate in physical activities and integrate into social circles, thus they are even more likely to have increases in weight and decreases in social supports.

The 2007–2008 surveillance data reveal that 33.8 percent of adults were obese.[10] In 2009, only Colorado and the District of Columbia had obesity rates lower than 20 percent.[11] Figure 17.1 shows the obesity rates for adults by state for 2009. Obesity in adults is a major risk factor for cardiovascular disease, type 2 diabetes, and certain types of cancer. Obese adults suffer greater number of days away from work related to health complications, shorter life span and higher healthcare costs compared to individuals of normal weight.

Although obesity is a condition that crosses all sectors, it disproportionately affects people of lower socioeconomic and education levels. Ethnic minorities are also more likely to be affected by obesity: compared to whites, blacks and Hispanics have 51 percent and 21 percent higher prevalence rates of obesity, respectively.[12] Figure 17.1 shows adult obesity trends and Figure 17.2 displays adult obesity rates by race.

Across the board, rates of obesity in young people have tripled over the past 30 years. The highest prevalence is seen among African American adolescent girls age 12–19 and

Figure 17.1 Percent of Obese (BMI ≥ 30) in U.S. Adults, 2009

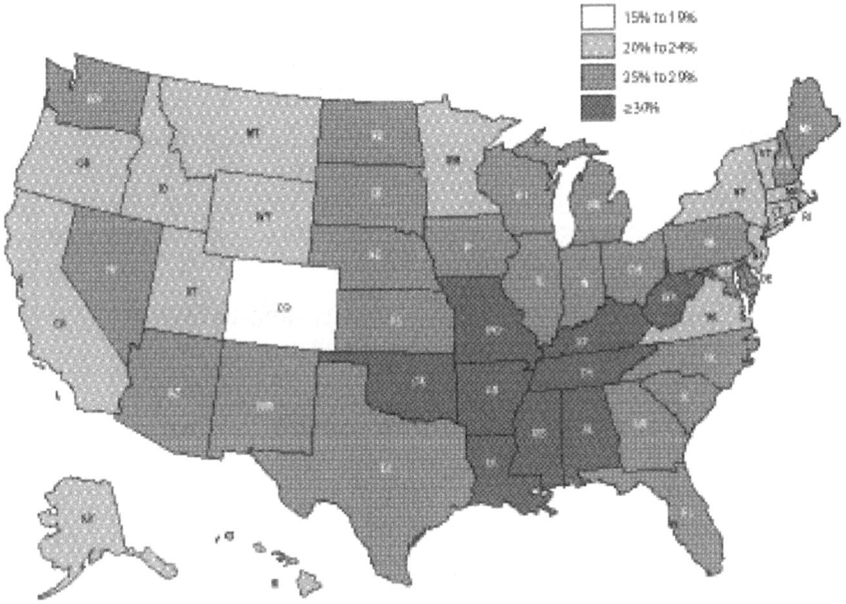

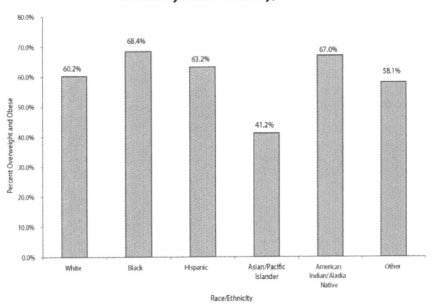

Source: Centers for Disease Control and Prevention, "U.S. Obesity Trends by State, 1985–2009," Overweight and Obesity (2010). The data shown in these maps were collected through the CDC's Behavioral Risk Factor Surveillance System (BRFSS).

Figure 17.2. Overweight and Obesity Rates for Adults by Race/Ethnicity, 2009

Source: Henry J. Kaiser Family Foundation, *Kaiser State Health Facts*, statehealthfacts.org. Data source: Centers for Disease Control and Prevention, Behavioral Risk Factor Surveillance System Survey Data, 2009, unpublished data.

Hispanic boys age 6–19.[13] Native American children in all age ranges have higher rates of obesity[14] than children of white, black, or Hispanic origins. Although prevalence of obesity among non-Hispanic white children is lower than among minority children, white children represent the largest absolute number of overweight and obese children in the United States. (See Figure 17.3 for prevalence of obesity among children by race and gender.

The origins of childhood obesity may date to the earliest moments of life. Emerging evidence suggests that a predisposition to weight gain or subsequent childhood obesity may have origins even before birth: maternal weight gain has been implicated as a risk factor for later obesity in an infant or child.[15] Furthermore, breastfeeding has been shown in several studies to be associated with decreased obesity later in life.[16]

Figure 17.3 Prevalence of Obesity among Children Ages 2–19 in the United States

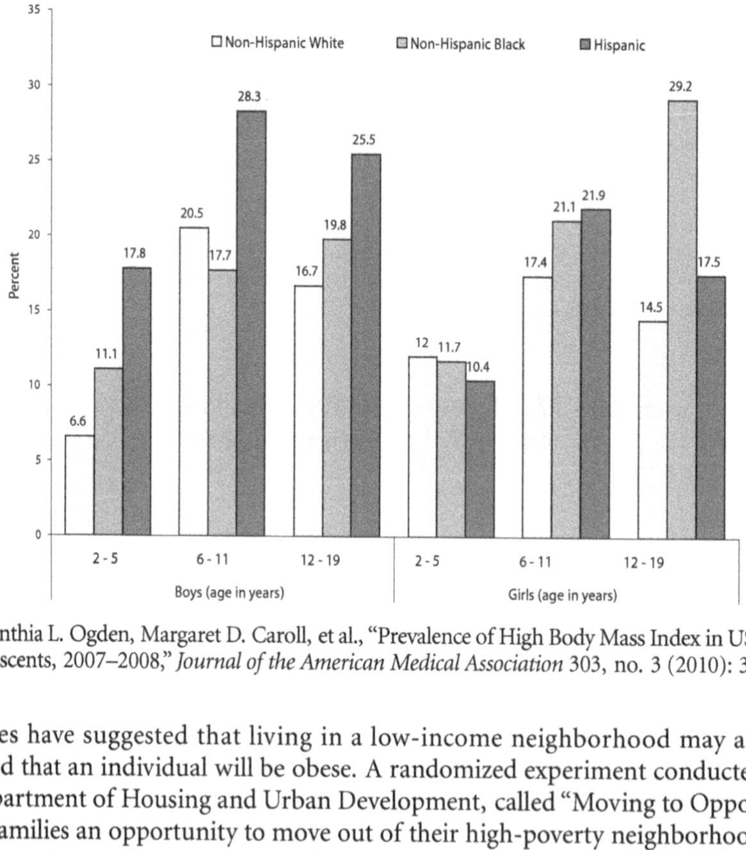

Legend: □ Non-Hispanic White ▨ Non-Hispanic Black ■ Hispanic

Boys (age in years):
- 2-5: 6.6, 11.1, 17.8
- 6-11: 20.5, 17.7, 28.3
- 12-19: 16.7, 19.8, 25.5

Girls (age in years):
- 2-5: 12, 11.7, 10.4
- 6-11: 17.4, 21.1, 21.9
- 12-19: 14.5, 29.2, 17.5

Source: Cynthia L. Ogden, Margaret D. Caroll, et al., "Prevalence of High Body Mass Index in US Children and Adolescents, 2007–2008," *Journal of the American Medical Association* 303, no. 3 (2010): 342–49.

Studies have suggested that living in a low-income neighborhood may affect the likelihood that an individual will be obese. A randomized experiment conducted by the U.S. Department of Housing and Urban Development, called "Moving to Opportunity," offered families an opportunity to move out of their high-poverty neighborhoods using housing vouchers in low-poverty neighborhoods. A control group remained in public or other assisted housing in high-poverty neighborhoods. The Robert Wood Johnson Foundation funded a study to consider the health outcomes of those who moved. The study found that obesity was reduced 11 percent among adults who were offered vouchers and had the opportunity to move to a low-poverty neighborhood.[17] One explanation for differences in obesity rates among low-income individuals is diet. As Figure 17.4 shows, low-income Americans are less likely to have good diets than middle- and upper-income Americans. As discussed in greater detail later, residents of low-income neighborhoods often live in "food deserts" where they do not have access to grocery stores that carry healthy foods.

Figure 17.4 Lower-Income Americans Are Less Likely to Have Good Diets

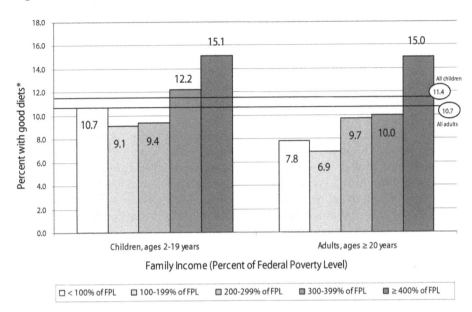

Note: * The mean healthy eating index (HEI) score measures intake of 10 key diet components (grains, vegetables, fruits, milk, meat, total fat, saturated fat, sodium, cholesterol, and variety), each ranging from 0–10 with higher scores indicating healthier eating. A good diet is defined as a having an HEI score above 80.
Source: Robert Wood Johnson Foundation Commission to Build a Healthier America, "Improving the Health of All Americans through Better Nutrition." *Data source*: Analyses conducted for the Robert Wood Johnson Foundation Commission to Build a Healthier America by the Center on Social Disparities in Health at the University of California, San Francisco, using data from the National Health and Nutrition Examination Survey, 1999–2002.

Putting a Human Face on the Problem:
The Individual Patient and Family in Context

Jamal Smith leaves his doctor's office on a Thursday afternoon. This is his first appointment since surviving a mild heart attack two weeks earlier. Although his salary as a data entry clerk will not permit him to move his family out of their crime-ridden neighborhood, Jamal is luckier than most because his employer provides private insurance that covers preventive cardiac care. His doctor told him he has a 20 percent chance of having another heart attack within 10 years if he does not change his lifestyle. At 5 feet, 8 inches tall and 250 pounds, he is obese and he knows that he has to lose weight. According to his doctor, if he exercises for 30 minutes a day five days a week, modifies his diet, lowers his blood pressure close to 120/80 mm Hg, and loses 60 pounds, he could significantly reduce his risk of another heart attack. Jamal is 45 years old, and he has two children ages 7 and 9. He is determined to make the necessary changes so he can watch his children grow up and set a good example for them.

Jamal lives about two miles from his doctor's office, but he drove to his appointment today as is his habit. On the way home, he passes three billboards proclaiming the happiness and convenience of fast food. He turns on the radio in his car. The first thing he hears is an advertisement for an ice-cold 44-ounce super-big soda for $0.89. He stops at his local corner store to pick up something for dinner. As there is no grocery store in his work-ing-class neighborhood, he picks up three fried chicken frozen dinners for his family and then, remembering the doctor's advice, grabs a can of tomato soup for himself. What he does not realize is that the can of soup he picks up has almost his entire Recommended Dietary Allowance (RDA) of sugar and salt. Like most typical consumers, he does not read nor understand nutrition labels—much less how to calculate the RDA of salt for people with high blood pressure from the RDA for healthy adults listed on the can. At the check-out counter he sees row upon row of candy bars and potato chips. With the conversation with his doctor fresh in his mind, he asks the cashier if they have any fruit. The cashier apologizes, saying that fruit goes bad quickly so they don't stock it.

By the time he gets home, his wife, Sarah, is already there. It's Thursday night and both parents are exhausted. As they warm up dinner, the children play "Flip the Mix" on the M&M website. Sarah feeds the children and then sets them up to do their homework while she and Jamal sit down to eat. Once the family has finished dinner and homework, they all settle down for the evening to watch *American Idol.* Jamal mentions to Sarah that the doctor told him to get more exercise. He would like to start walking around their neighborhood in the evenings. Sarah reminds him of the recent crime and shares her nervousness about him being on the streets in the evenings.

There is no doubt that Jamal and his doctor have the best of intentions. But there are many factors working against Jamal's desire to lose weight and prevent another heart attack. He is bombarded by advertisements in his community for unhealthy food in portion sizes that lead to rapid weight gain. Like most of us, he has become dependent on car-based transportation and cannot imagine using a form of active transportation like walking or biking to get to work or appointments. Moreover, his neighborhood does not have easy access to a grocery store that stocks fresh fruits and vegetables—an area considered to be a food desert. Instead, he has to rely on a corner store that stocks unhealthy products like soda and highly processed foods. The issue is acute in low-income neighborhoods, which often suffer disproportionate impacts from disinvestment and land use planning that do not support healthy living. Furthermore, he does not feel safe walking around his neighborhood, which makes it difficult for him and his family to engage in regular, inexpensive physical activity.

Like many Americans, Jamal faces an uphill battle in his desire to offset the negative impacts of his sedentary job and sedentary leisure activities. A 2009 Nielsen study found that the average American watched five hours of television a day.[18] In addition to the inactivity he experiences while watching TV, Jamal is barraged with advertisements for junk food, fast food, soda and beer—not only in between programming but also covertly via paid product placements in the background or even storylines of the shows themselves. Research suggests that repeated exposure to food advertising can affect eating behaviors without conscious awareness of the impetus.[19] The media environment also impedes Jamal's aspirations to set a good example for his children. The food industry spent $1.6 billion in 2006 alone marketing predominantly high-calorie, low-nutrient food to children.[20] About a third of those dollars were invested in child-directed television, where viewers see more than seven advertisements per hour for mainly unhealthy food products.[21] Another $186 million went to in-school marketing in 2006,[22] a savvy investment considering students are a captive audience. Food companies also target children with sophisticated interactive digital marketing techniques—from immersive "advergaming" websites to viral marketing on Facebook and Twitter, to electronic rewards for children who disclose their mobile phone numbers.[23]

Although physicians can encourage their patients to make better individual choices, a true improvement in population health requires tackling the social norms that have led to a 34 percent rate of obesity prevalence among American adults. This chapter looks at obesity prevention policy from this perspective and considers policy changes that can be made in our communities to make healthy choices easier for families.

What Kinds of Social Norms Currently Drive Obesity Rates?

There are many elements that influence the daily choices an individual makes about food and physical activity. At the core of the obesity epidemic in the United States is the fact that for many people, energy in does not equal energy out. That is, Americans consume far more calories than they expend. Table 17.1 provides a list of major factors that contribute to this behavior.

Table 17.1 Factors That Contribute to Obesity

Too Many Calories Consumed	Too Little Physical Activity
• Ubiquity of high-calorie, low-nutrient food options • Pervasiveness of junk food and fast food marketing • Relative affordability of highly processed food • Limited access to fresh fruits and vegetables, especially in low-income neighborhoods • Growth of portion sizes • Lack of knowledge about good nutrition	• Limited opportunities for physical activity in daily routines • Paucity of recreational venues, especially in low-income neighborhoods • Car-centric culture and land use planning • Multiple hours of screen time per day • Fear for personal safety

These factors and others have led to the current obesity crisis. Law and policy have played a part in creating these norms, and law and policy can change them.

Questions for Discussion

1. What factors do you think have lead to rising obesity rates?
2. Which factors do you think contribute most to obesity rates? Why?
3. What is the role of social determinants in obesity rates?

Social Norm Change and Public Health Policy

In the United States, the most effective efforts to address major public health concerns such as obesity have taken a comprehensive approach recognizing the many causative factors that shape our health.

The Spectrum of Prevention

The Spectrum of Prevention—developed in 1983 by Larry Cohen of the Prevention Institute in Oakland, California—provides healthcare practitioners with the elements of an effective prevention campaign and can be applied to almost any public health problem from injury to obesity prevention.[24] See Figure 17.5.

Figure 17.5 The Spectrum of Prevention

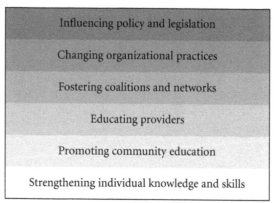

Source: Larry Cohen, Susan Swift, "The Spectrum of Prevention: Developing a Comprehensive Approach to Injury Prevention," *Injury Prevention,* 5 (1999): 203–7.

The bottom three levels of the spectrum reflect that individuals bear responsibility for their actions. These levels emphasize the importance of health education, with the idea that people who know what is in their best interests behave accordingly. Starting from the bottom, the spectrum calls for building the knowledge and skills of individuals — something healthcare providers do when they give information to patients. The second level focuses on educating groups, often through public health-related media campaigns. The third level is closely tied to the first, presuming that providers who have a good understanding of prevention offer better information to their patients.

The remaining three levels proffer that medical interventions and educational endeavors alone will not shift individual behaviors enough to solve a public health problem. Learning about the dangers of drunk driving, how to quit smoking, or how to eat a balanced diet might be enough to motivate some people to make different choices. But to change the daily norms of a critical mass of the population requires societal interventions. How can interventions be achieved society-wide? Interventions can be achieved through the efforts of strong coalitions and networks of stakeholders, through institutions modeling healthy living by adopting organizational practices, and through the passage and implementation of new policies and laws.

Medical-legal partnerships (MLPs) have enormous power to influence the upper three levels of the spectrum. They are perfectly situated to foster coalitions and networks of healthcare professionals, lawyers and community members who have a stake in improving public health. As for changing organizational practices, MLPs have the collective stature and knowledge to pursue reforms — such as healthy food procurement policies, public transit incentives and on-site farmers markets — by hospitals, law schools and other affiliated institutions. Finally, the medical, legal and community-based expertise comprised by MLPs put them in a unique position to propose and advocate for evidence-based public health-oriented policies and laws.

The Importance of Policy and Law to Social Norm Change Campaigns

Used well, the Spectrum of Prevention can lead to what some public health advocates call "social norm change." A *social norm* is defined as shared expectations of culturally appropriate and desirable behavior.[25] The goal of a social norm change movement is to influence behavior indirectly by creating a social environment and legal climate in which harmful conduct becomes less desirable, acceptable and attainable, and healthier conduct becomes the norm.[26] This approach to policy development creates system-level changes in a range of settings including households, schools, entertainment venues, corporations and government agencies. The changes are institutionalized informally through cultural expectations and peer pressure and formally through legislation and law enforcement. Many movements have shaped the society we live in today—from civil rights to seatbelt use to recycling—and almost all can be described as taking a social norm change approach.

This chapter focuses on the top level of the spectrum: Influencing policy and legislation. The bottom levels may feel like a more natural fit for healthcare professionals in their day to day work. However, the top level calls for their involvement, too. Policy and law shape the context for how people live their lives and make decisions—often providing the choices and setting the defaults. In addition, physicians have a history of gaining meaningful results through participation in policy and legislation efforts that promote public health. Working with legal partners, they can be enormously powerful advocates for policy change.

Another important advantage of the top level is that it results in enforceable mandates, including laws enacted by legislators, regulations implemented by executive agencies and binding contracts arising through voluntary negotiations or litigation settlements. Enforceable mandates have an advantage over customs and informal rules because when push comes to shove, the government can compel compliance. Legislation is only as strong and effective as its enforcement provisions. Sometimes the most powerful policy intervention is simply adding enforcement language to existing law so there are serious consequences for noncompliance.

Social Norm Change Campaigns

Current obesity prevention policy draws on lessons learned from more established prevention campaigns, such as tobacco control and drunk driving prevention.

Tobacco Control in California

The California Tobacco Control Program (CTCP) paved the way for a national and then international social norm change campaign that has had an enormous public health impact.[27]

In November 1988, California voters approved Proposition 99, the Tobacco Tax and Health Protection Act. This landmark legislation imposed a cigarette tax of 25 cents per pack, established the CTCP in the state health department, and earmarked 20 percent of the new revenues for state and local programs aimed at reducing tobacco use.[28] From its inception, the CTCP recognized that success would require investing at every level of the Spectrum of Prevention.[29] Table 17.2 shows the CTCP activities at each level.

Table 17.2 Sample CTCP Activities at Each Level of the Spectrum of Prevention

Influencing Policy & Legislation	Funding local health departments and community-based organizations to advocate for new tobacco control laws such smoke-free restaurants and increased tobacco taxes.
Changing Organizational Practices	Filling gaps in the law by, for example, encouraging rodeos to decline tobacco sponsorship or encouraging hospitals to implement smoke-free campuses.
Fostering Coalitions and Networks	Administering and coordinating the tobacco control efforts of 61 local health departments, approximately 40 community-based organizations, hundreds of public health workers, thousands of volunteers and several statewide technical support organizations.
Educating Providers	Teaching providers how to talk to patients about giving up tobacco and why referrals for cessation help patients reduce their risk of complications and improve their health.
Promoting Community Education	Running school-based tobacco prevention education programs and producing a much emulated media campaign aimed at reducing secondhand smoke exposure, countering protobacco influences and motivating Californians to quit.
Strengthening Individual Knowledge and Skills	Maintaining a statewide quit line with services available in six languages.

The CTCP's comprehensive approach is particularly notable for its emphasis on influencing policy and legislation. The CTCP has unabashedly empowered advocates and public health professionals to pursue cutting-edge laws at the state and local levels. In the wake of Proposition 99, California passed tobacco control laws, aimed at limiting secondhand smoke exposure (Cal. Lab. Code §6404.5), sales to youth (Cal. Pen. Code §308(a); Cal. Bus. & Prof. Code §22950 et seq.), and tobacco marketing (Cal. Bus. & Prof. Code §22961 et seq.). Moreover, localities throughout California have enacted tobacco control laws that plug loopholes or cover more ground than the state laws. For example, state laws prohibit smoking in most enclosed workplaces, in and around playgrounds, and within 20 feet of state buildings. Some municipalities have gone farther by enacting laws restricting smoking in outdoor service and dining areas (Santa Monica Munic. Code §4.44.020, 2004), multi-unit residences (Belmont Munic. Code Chap. 20.5,2007), and beaches (Carmel-by the-Sea Munic. Code §8.36.020,2008).

These tobacco control laws have been a key factor in the campaign to denormalize smoking and other tobacco use in California. The state achieved a 35 percent reduction in adult smoking rates between 1988 and 2007: from 22.7 percent to 13.8 percent.[30] It now has the second lowest rate of adult and youth smoking in the nation,[31] behind Utah (9.8 percent in 2006),[32] where the low rates likely reflect the religious prohibition on smoking followed by many Mormons. Statewide incidence of lung cancer in California has been declining at four times the national rate; assuming this trend continues, California may be the first state in which lung cancer is no longer the leading cancer cause of death.[33] The California tobacco control movement has saved not only numerous lives but also a significant amount of public funds. From 1999 to 2004, the CTCP saved the population $86 billion in healthcare expenditures—a 50-fold return on the $1.8 billion spent on the program during the same period.[34]

Note that an important backdrop to the CTCP's success is the 2008 Master Settlement Agreement (MSA) between the major tobacco companies and the attorneys general (AGs) of 46 states. The MSA is a binding contract that ended a lawsuit in which the AGs sought to recover tobacco-related healthcare costs shouldered by state governments. Under the agreement, the tobacco companies are required to make annual payments to each state in perpetuity, amounting to an estimated $206 billion.[35] The tobacco companies also agreed to finance a $1.5 billion antismoking campaign, open previously secret industry documents and abide marketing restrictions including a ban on the use of cartoons in tobacco advertisements, the elimination of most outdoor tobacco advertisements and limitations on certain sampling and sponsorship practices.

DUI Prevention

A social norm change approach has also been used to address the problem of driving while under the influence of alcohol. The leader in this field is the national advocacy organization, Mothers Against Drunk Driving (MADD).[36] Candy Lightner founded MADD in 1980 after her daughter, Cari, was killed by a repeat drunk driving offender. Cindy Lamb—whose daughter, Laura, became the nation's youngest quadriplegic at the hands of a drunk driver—joined Lightner's campaign shortly thereafter.[37] As the foremost organization working to change society's norms around drunk driving, MADD works on the multiple levels identified by the Spectrum of Prevention. In terms of influencing policy and legislation, they have won major victories at the federal, state and local levels, which include the formation of a National Commission on Drunk Driving, more stringent blood alcohol limits in state laws and aggressive state and local law enforcement measures such as checkpoints.[38] In fact, since its inception, MADD, in partnership with policy makers and government agencies, has pushed successfully for the enactment of more than 1,000 new laws.[39]

MADD bolsters its policy change strategy by working to change the social environment as well as the legal environment, a tactic essential to a social norm change approach and one that requires grassroots support. MADD is particularly adept at fostering coalitions and networks. In an article written for the 25th anniversary of the founding MADD, former president Mickey Sadoff explained, "[In the 1980s], MADD was sprouting up in communities all over the country. It wasn't top-down growth. It was a bunch of small fires that started a wildfire."[40] These grassroots activists have enabled MADD to be a leader in encouraging communities to adopt informal practices to change behavior. "The idea of the designated driver, which has now become inculcated into the social life of the nation, was created by this movement. The idea of a designated driver is reinforced in the advertising campaigns of beer distributors. On holidays, many public transportation agencies and private taxi associations now provide free or subsidized transportation as a socially sanctioned and convenient substitute for driving while drunk."[41]

Legislative efforts and grassroots campaigns have been bolstered by sophisticated media strategies that have served to educate providers, law enforcement and the community at large. Through advertising and other communications techniques, MADD has been extremely effective in changing public perception so that phrases like "designated driver" are now part of the national lexicon[42] and drunk driving "accidents" have become "crashes caused by criminal negligence."[43] MADD has also sponsored many high-profile national campaigns, such as "You Drink, You Drive, You Lose" and "Over the Limit, Under Arrest."

Litigation as a Tool for Public Health Change

The Master Settlement Agreement (MSA) is a powerful example of how strategic litigation can help propel a social norm change campaign. As described earlier, the MSA was negotiated by the major tobacco companies and a group of state attorneys general to settle a lawsuit regarding tobacco-related healthcare costs. The MSA resulted in huge financial gains for states, uncovered previously secret industry documents and produced some results that would be hard to achieve through legislation — such as the marketing restrictions, which could have raised First Amendment problems.

There is yet to be a lawsuit in the obesity prevention arena that has anywhere near the impact of the tobacco MSA. The state AGs and at least one progressive city attorney have gained some traction threatening and bringing lawsuits focused on unsubstantiated food labeling. In the 1980s, a group of about 10 state AGs known as the "food cops" challenged many food companies regarding false and misleading claims, including alleged misuse of the phrases "real cheese," "lean meal," "hypoallergenic" and "energy releasing."[a] These cases were important forces behind the passage of the federal Nutrition Labeling and Education Act of 1990, which regulates health claims and requires the Nutrition Facts Panel on packaged foods.[b] More recently, the Connecticut AG announced in late 2009 that he and several other AGs were investigating the Smart Choices Program, an industry-sponsored voluntary rating system that allowed a Smart Choices logo to appear on packaging for food products that met certain nutrition standards.[c] The program was widely ridiculed when it became clear that Froot Loops, Frosted Flakes and Cracker Jack qualified for the Smart Choices logo. After the Connecticut AG's announcement, the U.S. Food and Drug Administration (FDA) declared it was also going to investigate, and the program was suspended.[d] Also in late 2009, the San Francisco City Attorney and the Oregon AG issued letters to Kellogg demanding substantiation of the "Now helps support your child's immunity" banner splayed across the front of Cocoa Krispies boxes.[e] Kellogg quickly agreed to stop making immunity claims on its products.

Thus far, private lawsuits relating to the negative health effects of obesogenic foods have been unsuccessful. For example, in 2003, children and their parents filed a lawsuit against McDonald's alleging that as a result of consuming McDonald's food, they became overweight and developed diabetes, coronary heart disease, high blood pressure and elevated cholesterol.[f] The plaintiffs stated that McDonald's failed to adequately disclose the ingredients and/or health effects of ingesting certain food items containing high levels of cholesterol, fat, salt and sugar. McDonald's described these foods as nutritious, and through marketing enticed customers, including children, to purchase "value meals" without disclosing the detrimental effects of eating these foods.[g] Plaintiffs also alleged that McDonald's negligently sold foods high in cholesterol, fat, salt and sugar, even though studies show that such foods can lead to obesity and other detrimental health problems, and that McDonald's failed to warn consumers of the ingredients, and quantity and quality of fat, cholesterol, sugar and salt in their products.[h] The complaint was dismissed with the court finding that the plaintiffs failed to allege that the products were "dangerous in any way other than that which was open and obvious to a reasonable consumer."[i]

Notes: [a] National Policy and Legal Analysis Network to Prevent Childhood Obesity, Public Health Law Center, *State AG Enforcement of Food Marketing Laws: A Brief History* (St. Paul, MN: Public Health Law Center, 2010), http://www.nplanonline.org/childhood-obesity/products/State-AGs, 1–2; [b] Ibid., 2; [c] Ibid.; [d] Ibid.; [e] Ibid., 3; [f] *Pelman v. McDonald's Corp.*, 237 F. Supp. 2d 512, 519 (S.D.N.Y. 2003); Caleb E. Mason, "Doctrinal Considerations for Fast-Food Obesity Suits," *Tort Trial & Insurance Practice Law Journal*, 40 (2004): 76; [g] *Pelman*, 237 F. Supp. 2d at 520. These causes of action were based on violations of the New York Consumer Protection Act, New York Gen. Bus. Laws §§ 349 and 350, and New York City Administrative Codes, Ch. 5, 20-700 et seq.; [h] *Pelman*, 237 F. Supp. 2d at 520; [i] Ibid., 541; As of 2010, the case was still actively being litigated. The case was brought to the Second Circuit, remanded, and the docket indicates that the parties have been engaged in procedural disputes. *Pelman v. McDonald's Corp.*, 452 F. Supp. 2d 320 (S.D.N.Y. 2006); Joan R. Rothenberg, "In Search of the Silver Bullet: Regulatory Models to Address Childhood Obesity," *Food & Drug Law Journal*, 65 (2010): 204–5.

Questions for Discussion

1. How is public policy advocacy focused on obesity similar to or different from previous efforts focused on tobacco and drunk driving? What strategies used in these campaigns might be successful in obesity prevention campaigns?

2. Based on past campaigns, draft a list of strategies that might be appropriate to affect social norm change aimed at obesity prevention and reduction.

Role of Healthcare Professionals in Public Health Policy Development

Healthcare providers have valuable insights into the barriers that prevent their patients from engaging in healthy behaviors and often feel passionately committed to improving their patients' health outcomes. Frequently, however, they do not know how to marry policy work with their clinical practice. Medical educators in medical schools, residency programs and professional societies are beginning to address this deficit in training and provide more instruction around advocacy, policy development and public engagement.[44] Healthcare providers and lawyers can work together to ensure that health impacts are considered when policy is formulated. (See Chapter 1 for a discussion of Health Impact Assessments.)

Case Study: Mobilizing Healthcare Professionals as Policy Leaders in the Fight against Childhood Obesity

The National Initiative for Children's Healthcare Quality (NICHQ) engages healthcare professionals in the development of obesity prevention policy through its project called Mobilizing Healthcare Professionals as Community Leaders in the Fight Against Childhood Obesity.[a] Through this work, NICHQ has demonstrated that healthcare providers can be particularly effective advocates for strong nutrition and physical activity policies.[b] Community members view healthcare providers as a trusted source of information related to obesity prevention. A survey of parents revealed that they are more likely to have communicated with healthcare providers about obesity prevention than with school officials, grocery store or restaurant owners or other government officials.[c]

Although pockets of the healthcare sector have been activated, many areas have lacked the focus and prioritization to take on the epidemic, and the voice of the primary care provider has been virtually silent. NICHQ provides healthcare professionals with the trainings and tools to advocate for policy change at the local, state and federal levels.[d]

The Texas Pediatrics Society (TPS), based in Austin, is one of the grantees funded under the NICHQ initiative. TPS saw a great need to combat obesity in Texas. In 2004–2005, 42 percent of Texas fourth graders were overweight or obese, as were 39 percent of eighth graders and 36 percent of eleventh graders. Similarly, in 2007, a fifth of low-income children age two to five years enrolled in the Texas Women Infants and Children Supplemental Nutrition Program were overweight or obese. Overweight and obesity rates were highest among Hispanics and American Indian/Pacific Islanders.[e] Since receiving funding in 2009, TPS has held a number of advocacy trainings that focus on providing healthcare professionals with the tools to engage in local and state legislative advocacy on childhood obesity issues.[f]

Dell Children's Medical Center pediatrician Kimberly Avila Edwards is one of the physicians leading the TPS NICHQ project. She believes it is critical that healthcare professionals engage in policy change and her leadership in this area is based on her experience as a practicing pediatrician. "From the tremendous costs — both healthcare and societal — of obesity and the myriad associated diseases like hypertension and heart failure, to the faces of the 10-year-old boy hospitalized with type 2 diabetes, or the 9-year-old girl with adult diseases needing referral to a pediatric cardiologist.... I've seen the harm this disease causes." She added that the NICHQ initiative speaks to healthcare professionals' understanding that although the diagnosis and treatment of obesity is a much-needed service, the solutions to childhood obesity epidemic must also include the community at large.[g]

Notes: [a] This case study is derived from National Initiative for Children's Healthcare Quality, "Be Our Voice," http://www.nichq.org/advocacy/about/index.html. The Mobilizing Healthcare Professionals project has been developed by NICHQ, in cooperation with the American Academy of Pediatrics, the California Medical Association Foundation and the Robert Wood Johnson Center to Prevent Childhood Obesity with the goal of reversing the childhood obesity epidemic trend across the nation by training, supporting and providing technical assistance to healthcare professionals who wish to become advocates for change within their communities. It is funded through a grant awarded to NICHQ from the Robert Wood Johnson Foundation; [b] M. A. T. Flynn, et al., "Reducing Obesity and Related Chronic Disease Risk in Children and Youth: A Synthesis of Evidence with 'Best Practice' Recommendations," *Obesity Reviews,* 7 (Suppl. 1) (2006): 7–66; Helen M. DuPlessis, et al., "The Pediatrician's Role in Community Pediatrics," *Pediatrics,* 115, no. 4 (2005): 1092–94; F. Krebs, et al., "Prevention of Pediatric Overweight and Obesity," *Pediatrics,* 112, no. 2 (2003): 424–30; [c] Field Research Corporation, *Healthy Eating, Active Communities Neighborhood Survey: Findings at Baseline* (San Francisco: Field Research Corporation, prepared for the California Endowment, 2006); [d] National Initiative for Children's Healthcare Quality, "Advocacy Resources to Fight against Childhood Obesity," http://www.nichq.org/advocacy/obesity_resources/index.html. NICHQ Advocacy Toolbox available at http://www.nichq.org/advocacy/advocacy%20documents/Advocacy%20Toolbox.pdf; NICHQ Advocacy Resource Guide available at http://www.nichq.org/advocacy/advocacy%20documents/Advocacy%20Resource%20Guide.pdf; The American Academy of Pediatrics *Policy Opportunities Tool* available at http://www.aap.org/obesity/ matrix_1.html; [e] Texas Medical Association, "Physician, Health Care Professional Seminars Target Childhood Obesity in the Community," Texas Medical Association, May 29, 2010, http://www.texmed. org/Template.aspx?id=8497 (accessed June 24, 2010); [f] Dr. Kimberly Avila-Edwards, conversation with authors, June 14, 2010; [g] Ibid.

Case for Medical-Legal Partnership

When lawyers and healthcare professionals intervene to resolve a patient's health or legal problems, they are working at the bottom level of the spectrum; however, these interactions can be valuable drivers for larger policy change efforts. Consider this case.

Miguel Lopez is a nurse practitioner caring for Chun-Yan Fong, a patient with diabetes. At a recent visit, Miguel notices that his patient's blood sugar has risen alarmingly. When he asks Chun-Yan if her diet has changed, she says she lost her SNAP benefits (Supplementation Nutrition Assistance Program, formerly known as food stamps) because a fraud investigator mistakenly determined that her son lives with her and contributes to the household income. She says that in fact, her son only spends weekends at her apartment. For the past two months she has had to buy the food she can afford, which turns out to be more highly processed, less healthy food.

Questions for Discussion

1. What can Miguel do to help the patient improve her diet in the short term?

In addition to helping Chun-Yan strategize about improving her diet in the short term, Miguel brings in Jeanne Mason, a lawyer and colleague in a local MLP program. Jeanne starts preparing to file an appeal on behalf of Chun-Yan before the state agency that administers the SNAP program.

2. What can Miguel contribute to the appeal?

Jeanne soon discovers that the state agency had sent Chun-Yan a notice of denial of benefits and that she had already missed the appeal deadline. Chun-Yan is a Cantonese speaker with limited English proficiency (LEP), and she explains that the notice was written in English and she didn't understand it. Jeanne files a request that the agency hear the appeal despite the missed deadline because the notice should have been written in Cantonese pursuant to federal guidelines that some types of government documents be translated for each LEP language group that constitutes a certain percentage of the applicable population. The agency denies the request.

Meanwhile, Miguel tells Jeanne that he has begun to notice a pattern of LEP patients who have had their benefits terminated.

3. What can the MLP do to find out more about this pattern?

Miguel and Jeanne come to the conclusion that the state agency administering SNAP is violating federal guidelines by failing to translate essential documents into three languages spoken by a significant percentage of the local population.

4. What steps might the MLP take—ranging from negotiation to litigation—to encourage the state agency to comply with the federal guidelines?

The Federal Context for Obesity Prevention Policy

Although much obesity prevention policy develops at the local and state level, activity at the federal level has a significant impact on the policy environment in which public health advocates work. Advocates working on obesity prevention have been energized by First Lady Michelle Obama's Let's Move! campaign and President Barack Obama's

Interagency Task Force on Childhood Obesity. Additionally, there are major pieces of federal legislation that influence state and local obesity prevention policies.

Constitutional Authority

Our federal government technically has a limited dominion over public health policy because its three branches may exercise only the specific powers vested in them by the U.S. Constitution (Articles I–III). But these enumerated powers—including Congress's ability to enact laws "necessary and proper" to execute said enumerated powers, and its authority over international and interstate commerce—have been interpreted expansively, giving the federal government leeway to pass legislation on a broad swath of issues affecting the obesity epidemic. Federal law is the supreme law of the land, so it prevails over contrary state and local laws (Article IV, § 2).

There are, however, constitutional boundaries that the federal government (or any lower level of government) cannot cross. The Bill of Rights and the Fourteenth Amendment contain some of the most important constraints on the government's reach. Many of these constitutional provisions—including those pertaining to free speech, due process, equal protection and property ownership—mandate that a balance must be struck between the government's interest in advancing its vision of the general welfare and the interest of individual citizens in freedom and self-determination.

Federal Legislation and Initiatives

The following federal policies that govern child nutrition, transportation, farm policy, food financing and elementary and secondary education are of particular importance to obesity prevention policy.

Child Nutrition Act

The Child Nutrition and WIC Reauthorization Act (P.L. 108-265)[45] authorizes all of the federal school meal and child nutrition programs, which serve more than 30 million children each day. Because so many students take in more than half of their calories at school, these programs have a substantial impact on the health of children across the country. Every five years Congress reviews these programs through the reauthorization process.[46] It has six main components:

The National School Lunch Program: All children can participate in the program, but low-income children qualify for free or reduced-price meals. In 2009, the program served 28.9 million lunches daily.[47]

The School Breakfast Program: Children who qualify for free or reduced-price school lunch also quality for the School Breakfast Program. In 2009, the program served 10.2 million meals daily.[48]

The Child and Adult Care Food Program: The program reimburses child care centers, Head Start Programs, family child care homes, homeless shelters and after-school programs for snacks and meals served to children. Generally, children under the age of 12 (as well as certain disabled adults) can participate, but homeless shelters and after-school programs can serve children 18 and under. In 2009, the program served 1.9 billion snacks.[49]

The Summer Food Service Program: Children (18 and under) who depend on school lunch and breakfast during the school year have access to free meals and snacks during the summer when school is out. It provides reimbursements to schools, local government agencies, and private nonprofit organizations that serve free meals and snacks to children at sites located in low-income areas or that serve primarily low-income children. In 2009, the program provided 133.1 million total meals and snacks.[50]

The After School Snack and Meal Program: Children who participate in after-school programs can receive snacks through this program. It provides federal funds to private nonprofit and public organizations (including schools) so they can serve nutritious snacks and, in eight states, meals as part of after school programs.

The Special Supplemental Nutrition Program for Women, Infants, and Children (WIC): This program provides food, nutrition education and access to healthcare to low-income pregnant women, new mothers, infants and children up to age five. In 2009, there were 9.1 million participants each month.[51]

A major focus of public health advocates in recent years has been increasing the school lunch reimbursement amount, strengthening nutritional standards for all foods available during the school day, including "competitive foods" (i.e., foods and beverages available for purchase on campus that are not part of the school breakfast and lunch programs), and providing training for schools on how to serve healthier meals.

Robert Wood Johnson Foundation Commission to Build a Healthier America Recommendations on Nutrition Policy

Feed children only healthy foods in schools.

- Federal funds should be used exclusively for healthy meals.
- Schools should eliminate the sale of "junk food," including food sold outside of school cafeterias through vending machines, school stores and fundraising.
- Federal school breakfast and lunch funds should be linked to demonstrated improvements in children's school diets.

Fund and design WIC and SNAP programs to meet the needs of hungry families for nutritious food.

- These federal programs must have adequate funding to serve all American families in need.
- Federal programs should facilitate and support good nutritional choices.[a]

Note: [a] "Improving the Health of All Americans through Better Nutrition," Robert Wood Johnson Foundation Commission to Build a Healthier America, http://www.commissiononhealth.org.

The Transportation Bill

The Safe, Accountable, Flexible, Efficient Transportation Equity Act: A Legacy for Users (SAFETEA-LU) is the 2005 federal law that governs transportation funding. It provides guaranteed funding for highways, highway safety and public transportation. Funding is distributed to state transportation departments that in turn determine state transportation policy and programs.[52] The transportation bill is reauthorized approximately every six years.

Obesity prevention advocates are active in policy discussions related to SAFETEA-LU and SAFETEA-LU's reauthorization for a number of reasons. The bill provides funding that can be used for active transportation policies, programs and infrastructure development. These include creating Complete Streets policies ensuring that roadways are designed with all users in mind, including bicyclists, public transit and pedestrians of all ages and abilities. They also include implementing Safe Routes to School programs and traffic-calming measures (these are discussed in detail later in the chapter). All of these strategies increase physical activity opportunities, which may in turn impact obesity rates. However, both the language of the bill and state implementation decisions overwhelmingly focus on automobiles rather than walking, bicycling or public transportation. Some obesity prevention advocates oppose components of SAFETEA-LU that increase reliance on automobiles and promote suburban sprawl. These advocates strive to have the bill provide more equitable support for active transportation, seeking, for example, to get a larger share of safety funding dedicated to pedestrian and bicycling safety.

The Farm Bill

The Farm Bill governs federal farm and food policy, covering a wide range of programs and policies and is renewed approximately every five years. The Food, Conservation, and Energy Act of 2008 (P.L. 110-246) is the most recent version. It contains 15 titles encompassing commodity price and income supports, farm credit, trade, agricultural conservation, research, rural development, energy and foreign and domestic food programs such as food stamps and other nutrition programs, among other programs.[53] The Congressional Budget Office estimates the total cost of the 2008 bill at $284 billion between 2008 and 2012.[54]

Federal agriculture policy strongly influences what crops are grown, where they are grown, how they are grown and how much they cost through programs that provide subsidy payments and risk management support to farmers, incentivize conservation practices and fund research programs that explore new farming techniques. It also influences what people eat and where they buy their food through the numerous food assistance programs and agriculture marketing services. Almost 70 percent of Farm Bill spending is on nutrition programs,[55] making it of critical importance to the U.S. food policy generally and obesity prevention policy specifically.

The Healthy Food Financing Initiative

The Healthy Food Financing Initiative (HFFI) was introduced in the Obama administration's budget for fiscal year 2011 to bring grocery stores and other healthy food retailers to underserved urban and rural communities across the nation. The Departments of Treasury, Agriculture and Health and Human Services will issue competitive grants and new market tax credits making investments to increase availability and promote consumption of healthy food.

HFFI expands the availability of nutritious food through the establishment of healthy food retail outlets, including developing and equipping grocery stores, small retailers, corner stores and farmers markets to help revitalize neighborhoods that currently lack these options. The 2008 Farm Bill defined a food desert as "an area in the United States with limited access to affordable and nutritious food, particularly such an area composed of predominantly lower-income neighborhoods and communities." Residents of these communities are typically served by fast-food restaurants and convenience stores that offer little or no fresh food. A study by the USDA found that nearly 23 million Americans, including 6.5 million children, live in low-income neighborhoods where the nearest supermarket is more than one mile from their homes.[56] HFFI investments are intended to improve public health, create jobs, help revitalize distressed communities and open up new markets for farmers to sell their products.

The Elementary and Secondary Education Act

Education is primarily a state and local responsibility in the United States. States and communities, as well as public and private organizations of all kinds, establish schools and colleges, develop curricula and determine requirements for enrollment and graduation. The single largest source of federal support for K–12 education is the Elementary and Secondary Education Act (P.L. 89-10). As mandated in the Act, the funds are authorized for professional development, instructional materials, resources to support educational programs and parental involvement promotion. The Act was originally authorized through 1970, however the government has reauthorized it every five years since its enactment.[57] The law currently includes the Carol M. White Physical Education Program, which provides grants to local school districts and community-based organizations to initiate, expand or enhance physical education programs, including after-school programs, for students in kindergarten through 12th grade.[58] In the upcoming reauthorization, the Department of Education has requested that the legislation set aside funds under the Successful, Safe, and Healthy Students program to carry out strategies designed to improve school safety and promote students' physical and mental health and well-being, nutrition education, healthy eating and physical fitness.[59]

Key Federal Agencies

A wide array of federal agencies have jurisdiction over development, implementation and regulation of policy influencing obesity, ranging from healthcare practices to nutritional standards in schools to safety in parks, and even communication and marketing practices. Traditionally, the Departments of Health and Human Services (DHHS) and Agriculture (USDA) have been most recognized in this domain.

The DHHS is the principal agency for protecting the health of all Americans and providing essential human services, especially for vulnerable and underserved populations. The department's programs are administered by eight agencies in the U.S. Public Health Service and three human services agencies, and include more than 300 programs. Grant programs such as the Communities Putting Prevention to Work are just one example of funding specifically for obesity prevention programs at a community level.

The USDA manages food, agriculture and natural resources to support integrated delivery systems. Their responsibilities include improving nutrition and health by providing food assistance and nutrition education and promotion. Examples of well-known USDA programs include school lunch and breakfast programs; SNAP, which provides food subsidy to low-income families; and education through dissemination of dietary guidelines.

In response to the 2010 presidential memorandum designating an interagency task force to address the issue and seek solutions for childhood obesity prevention, 12 federal agencies and 5 executive offices participated actively. Working together to share ideas and cross the boundaries of their individual agencies, they shared expertise to develop recommendations for federal action, as well as steps to guide the private sector, state and local leaders, and parents to improve the health of children and reduce childhood obesity. These recommendations were compiled in a report entitled *Solving the Problem of Childhood Obesity within a Generation*.[60] Listed in the Table 17.3 are examples of contributing agencies and some of the recommendations found in the childhood obesity task force report.

Table 17.3 Federal Agencies Policy Recommendations for Reducing Childhood Obesity

Agency Policy	Recommendations for Reducing Childhood Obesity
Agriculture	Update federal nutritional standards for school meals; increase resources for school meals; connect school meal programs to local growers and farm-to-schools programs; disseminate information about 2010 dietary guidelines
Education	Encourage school wellness policies with strong physical activity components
Health and Human Services	Ensure that healthcare providers, hospitals and insurers encourage prenatal care, provide information about breastfeeding, and support programs in hospitals and workplaces for breastfeeding
Housing and Urban Development	Encourage communities to consider the impact of built environments on physical activity and health; increase the number of safe and accessible parks and playgrounds in low-income communities
Interior	Support outdoor recreational venues, including National Parks and public lands
Justice	Promote healthy behaviors in juvenile correction facilities
Transportation	Enhance safe routes to schools programs; encourage active transportation throughout communities
Environmental Protection Agency	Assist school districts in establishing guidelines to promote physical activity and walking to school
Federal Communications and Trade Commissions	Work with industry to develop standards for marketing to children, including nutritional guidelines and what constitutes marketing to children

State and Local Context

Although the federal framework greatly influences obesity prevention policy, a great deal of innovative public health policy change happens at the state and local levels.

Police Power and Preemption

States possess the police power, that is, the inherent authority to act in the interest of the health, safety and welfare of the public. States retained the police power as part of the constitutional compact,[61] and states and their subdivisions historically have had primary responsibility for protecting and advancing public health.[62] Every state delegates at least some police power authority to local governments, but the extent of local police power authority varies widely.[63] Because regulating public health is a quintessential police power function,[64] states (and localities with the delegated police power) have the presumptive authority to pass public health laws as long as the laws do not overstep constitutional limits. If challenged in court, basic police power regulations are generally subject to rational basis review, a legal standard that is very deferential to the government.

In addition to the constraints contained in the Bill of Rights (and analogous state provisions), another important restriction on the police power is a concept known as preemption. All public health advocates should understand preemption: the invalidation of the law of one jurisdiction by the law of a higher jurisdiction. Federal law is the supreme law of the land (U.S. Constitution, Article VI, §2). So when a state law conflicts with a federal law, the federal law wins. Federal and state laws trump conflicting local laws in the same way. The ability of a state or locality to enact a public health law thus depends in part on whether a higher level of government has already legislated on the topic, and if so, whether that law forbids the enactment of the lower jurisdiction's law.

Preemption is both a legal and political concept. Typically, public health policy evolves at the local or state level to ensure it is responsive to community needs. Industries generally prefer for policy change to happen at the federal level, so they can target their lobbying resources at one level of government and end up with one uniform set of rules to follow. Preemption has been used to undermine local public health law campaigns — most famously by the tobacco industry.[65] As one former tobacco lobbyist explained:

> We could never win at the local level. The reason is, all the health advocates, the ones that unfortunately I used to call "health Nazis," they're all local activists who run the little political organizations. They may live next door to the mayor, or the city councilman may be his or her brother-in-law, and they say, "Who's this big-time lobbyist coming here to tell us what to do?" When they've got their friends and neighbors out there in the audience who want this bill, we get killed. So the Tobacco Institute and tobacco companies' first priority has always been to preempt the field, preferably to put it all on the federal level, but if they can't do that, at least on the state level, because the health advocates can't compete with me on a state level. They never could.[66]

Preemption is by no means unique to tobacco control. In 2006, New York City passed a menu labeling ordinance requiring certain chain restaurants to post calorie counts on their menu boards. Numerous cities and states around the country followed New York's lead. Although the laws varied somewhat, they shared the goal of giving consumers important nutritional information about restaurant food. In 2010, Congress enacted a law requiring all chain restaurants with 20 or more locations to provide specified nutritional information to customers (21 U.S.C. § 343(q)(5)(H)). The federal law created controversy in the public health community. On one hand, it was widely considered to be very strong in comparison to the existing local and state laws. On the other hand, it quashed burgeoning local and state legislative action on menu labeling and precluded localities and states from experimenting with different approaches to nutrition disclosure requirements of the type covered by the federal law.

Attempts to preempt state and local regulatory authority are a concern for all policy makers and public health advocates who want to preserve opportunities for policy innovation and control at the state and local levels.[67]

State and Local Government Agencies

The term "policy maker" is often construed as synonymous with "elected official." It goes without saying that governors and legislatures at the state level — and mayors, county boards and city councils at the local level — enact laws that shape the context of the obesity prevention movement. Less conspicuous is the important policy and programmatic roles played by state and local administrative agencies.

Government agencies wield influence by engaging in a wide range of activities. They craft and implement regulations that flesh out the laws on the books. They are educating public school administrators, training citizens and organizations on issues of public concern and running public service announcements to raise awareness about solutions to social problems. Agencies generate and compile huge amounts of data and conduct research to inform policy. They are grant makers who support activities considered to be in the public interest. Agencies are an important participant in the economic marketplace, and they can use their contracting and purchasing power to encourage socially responsible business practices.

Listed in Table 17.4 are major state and local government agencies that have purview over topics relating to obesity prevention, as well as examples of agency functions that relate in some way to obesity prevention. (This list is *not* comprehensive and may not accurately reflect a particular state or locality's political structure.) It is important to note that several of the agencies identified here do not have a public health mission but do have the authority to affect public health.

Table 17.4 State and Local Government Agencies and Obesity Prevention

Agency	Examples of Nexus to Obesity Prevention
Agriculture	Oversees production of fruits and vegetables. Licenses farmers markets.
Board of Health	Fosters public participation in shaping the health system. Analyzes and recommends obesity prevention-related policies.
Economic Development and Redevelopment	Improves community infrastructure for physical activity. Promotes safe neighborhoods. Attracts retail (and can be used to promote healthy food access).
Education	Administers school nutrition programs. Provides physical education. Educates students about healthy living.
Environmental Conservation	Promotes clean air and thus increased active transportation. Supports urban greening.
Land Use Planning (local level only)	Uses zoning and general plans to regulate what is built where.
Parks and Recreation	Provides access to recreational venues.
Public Health	Pursues a mission of chronic disease—including obesity—prevention.
Transportation	Sets transportation policy and funds transportation projects, including active transportation.

These government actors work best when guided by strong community voices at the state and local level. The input of professional advocates, parents concerned about their children's school environment and citizens who want to improve their quality of life is critical in shaping a public health-oriented social norm change movement that actually responds to community concerns about obesity. MLPs have the potential to wield significant influence in the halls of government because they can provide policy makers with compelling individual stories, evidence-based proposals and interdisciplinary expertise.

The Important Role of Government Lawyers in Health Policy Development

Government lawyers at all levels play a central role in public health policy development. Municipal attorneys and county counsel are frequently on the front lines—advising localities on the legality of policies, drafting ordinances and defending local laws from legal challenges. For example, New York City municipal attorneys worked with a local board of health to draft the menu labeling law in

2006. They then represented the city (and ultimately prevailed) in a series of legal challenges brought by the New York State Restaurant Association.

State attorneys general are the primary enforcers of state consumer protection laws and thus are well positioned to address problematic food and beverage marketing practices. As already described, AGs have made an impact by threatening and bringing lawsuits focused on false and misleading food labeling.

At the federal level, government lawyers work in multiple ways to draft, enforce and defend laws related to public health policy. For instance, FDA lawyers filed an amicus brief in the New York City menu labeling case arguing that a specific federal law, the Nutrition Labeling and Education Act, did not prevent NYC from passing its 2006 menu labeling ordinance. In 2010, the federal government passed a federal menu labeling law, and FDA attorneys are charged with developing regulations that interpret this federal law.

Local Policy Strategies to Address Childhood Obesity

Altering our obesogenic environment is an enormous challenge, requiring interventions on many fronts—from changing the way unhealthy products are depicted in the media to passing local laws that limit access to the products in the first place. Advocates for policy change are thinking in terms of a systemic web of policies that, taken together, change social norms to create healthy environments for infants, children and adults.

Given the legal expertise of MLPs, this section focuses on interventions that result in enforceable mandates, such as local ordinances enacted by city councils, regulations implemented by government agencies, and binding contracts. It does not focus on interventions that rely on voluntary agreements or the development of new programs. The section begins by highlighting community-level policy strategies and then turns to what might be done in schools.

Policy Strategies for Neighborhoods

Many communities, particularly those with the highest rates of obesity, find that they are dealing with multiple problems when they evaluate their environment. They are saturated with unhealthy food outlets in the form of fast-food restaurants and corner stores, and they do not have access to grocery stores. Typically, in these same communities residents have limited physical activity options. Recreational facilities are in poor condition or nonexistent and safety concerns prevent many people from walking and bicycling in their neighborhoods. This section describes some policy strategies that promote access to healthy food, restrict access to unhealthy food and encourage physical activity in our communities.

Increasing Access to Healthy Food and Reducing Access to Unhealthy Food in Communities

As residents of many moderate and low-income neighborhoods know, highly processed, nonnutritious foods are more readily available for purchase than fresh fruits and vegetables. To reform food deserts, public health advocates support a range of policies aimed at improving access to fresh foods while reducing the surfeit of unhealthy foods. It is important to recognize that different policy approaches may be more appropriate for the unique needs of different communities and that combining diverse policy efforts strengthens the likelihood of improving a local food environment.

The federal Healthy Food Financing Initiative presents an opportunity for local leaders to bring grocers and farmers markets to underserved communities. A ban on trans-fats in restaurant food is an example of a policy aimed at diminishing the prevalence of unhealthy food,[68] and a menu labeling law (which was recently enacted at the federal level but allows local laws covering smaller chains and solo restaurants) is intended to inform consumers and thus deter demand for highly caloric food.[69] Communities can also consider adjusting food and beverage prices to influence consumer behavior by levying taxes on processed foods or sugar-sweetened beverages (soda taxes).[70] In the tobacco control context, tobacco taxes have been the most influential policy connected to lower smoking rates.[71]

The remainder of this subsection focuses on land use and zoning laws, which comprise a relatively new and promising approach to promoting obesity prevention policy. "Of all the implementary tools available to city planners, zoning is by far the most frequently utilized, and the most likely to have an immediately discernable impact on the lives of the citizens in the community."[72] This is because zoning, which is adopted by ordinance and carries the weight of local law, defines how residential, commercial, industrial, agricultural, open space and other uses are distributed geographically within a community.[73] "The basic concept of zoning is simple. The governing body divides the community into districts, or zones, and adopts land use regulations that vary by district but that are uniform within each district."[74] For instance, heavy manufacturing plants might be permitted in an industrial but not a residential zone. A typical zoning ordinance describes numerous zone classifications, which can go beyond specifying land use to include regulating design character, development intensity or other standards.[75]

From the early twentieth century onward, zoning has been recognized as an important tool to protect public health. A community's zoning laws control the amount of light, air, pollution and noise to which residents are exposed. The exercise of zoning laws falls squarely within the police power authority of states and communities. Zoning laws can be used to ban restaurants that serve unhealthy foods (fast-food outlets), to regulate or place a quota on the number of fast-food outlets in a community, to regulate the distance of fast-food outlets from other land uses, and to regulate the density of fast-food restaurants.[76]

Note that zoning out harmful businesses tends to be a longer term strategy because new zoning laws generally include exceptions for existing businesses to avoid "takings" problems. The U.S. Constitution (Fifth Amendment) and most state constitutions contain a takings clause limiting the power of state and local governments to take private property for public use without just compensation. A taking can be a literal seizure or permanent physical occupation of land, or it can be a regulation depriving an owner of essentially all economically viable use of his or her property.[77] State takings law often is more protective of private property than federal takings law. Most states mandate that new zoning laws grandfather in existing businesses (at least until they are abandoned or significantly altered) or give businesses a reasonable "amortization" period in which to phase out.

Prohibiting or limiting the sale of certain types of food addresses only half the problem. To improve a community's food environment, it is necessary to ensure access to fresh and healthy food. Zoning law plays an important role here as well and can be used to support the establishment of farmers' markets, community gardens and full-service supermarkets.[78] If a type of use of land is not defined and permitted in a zoning code, it is considered illegal (even if the use does not appear at all in the code). A zoning law that establishes farmers markets as an *allowed use* in the areas the community selects eliminates the need for a permit and increases the land available for markets. It can also help protect existing markets in the allowed use area.[79]

Until recently, zoning regulations in the city of Fresno, California, prevented farmers markets from being established because they were not a legally defined use in the city's zoning code. The lack of supportive land use policy for farmers markets here was particularly ironic: although Fresno County is one of the most productive agriculture areas in the world, its farmers could not sell directly to residents in their own community. Community members worked with the city's planning department to change the zoning code so that residents can now benefit from the fresh, local food that farmers markets bring (Fresno Munic. Code § 12-105(F)(4.5), 2009).

Case Study: South Los Angeles

In many communities, the lack of a supermarket or grocery store serves as the biggest barrier to fresh food access. Bringing a grocery store into an underserved neighborhood not only makes fresh produce and other healthy food more accessible, it can provide living-wage jobs, raise the value of surrounding property and anchor and attract additional businesses to the neighborhood. But grocery store attraction can be a long-term and difficult effort requiring leadership and teamwork by city agencies and aided by a strong understanding of local zoning requirements and business incentive programs.[a]

One community—South Los Angeles—used zoning law to make a strong statement about fast food in 2008 when policy makers decided to place a year-long moratorium on new fast-food restaurants in an effort to encourage other types of food retail to move into the area.[b] Of the more than 900 restaurants in the area, over 45 percent are fast-food establishments.[c] Although this policy certainly brought much-needed attention to the fact that 30 percent of adults are obese in one of Los Angeles's poorest neighborhoods (compared to much lower rates in wealthier neighborhoods), it did not address the issue of changing the existing food environment. In response to community concerns about the lack of healthy food, a city council member convened a team made up of city council department members and nonprofit organizations to develop a coordinated strategy to bring grocery stores to the neighborhood. The interdepartmental team included staff from the mayor's office and the city's redevelopment agency. The team produced outreach materials to promote the neighborhood, compiled incentive lists, provided community support, met with retailers and helped coordinate and shepherd the entire effort. Based on these efforts, three new supermarkets were scheduled to open in 2010.[d] This is a good example of using both zoning law and community economic development tools to create change in the local food environment.

Notes: [a] Planning for Healthy Places, *Getting to Grocery: Tools for Attracting Healthy Food Retail to Underserved Neighborhoods* (Oakland, CA: Public Health Law and Policy, 2009), http://www.phlpnet.org/healthy-planning/products/getting-to-grocery; [b] Kim Severson, "Los Angeles Stages a Fast Food Intervention," *New York Times*, August 13, 2008, http://www.nytimes.com/2008/08/13/dining/13calo.html?_r=1&pagewanted=2; [c] Ibid.; [d] Scott Gold, "Central Avenue Is Dreaming Again," *Los Angeles Times*, September 25, 2009, http://articles.latimes.com/2009/sep/25/local/me-southla-centralave25/2.

Decreasing Junk Food Advertising

Like Jamal Smith and his family, most people are bombarded with advertising for obesogenic food and beverages in their homes and communities. Thinking in terms of social norm change, can local governments exert influence to reduce junk food advertising?

Localities face two major constraints on their ability to enact advertising restrictions. First, federal law vastly limits state and local jurisdiction over television, cable television, radio, the Internet and other digital media. For example, federal law would preempt (i.e., invalidate) a local law that banned fast food advertisements during children's programming. Second, the First Amendment protects not only individual free speech but also corporate advertising (commercial speech). The First Amendment generally looks unkindly on laws restricting advertising based on its content—in other words, laws restricting advertising only on a specific topic like tobacco, beer, or prescription drugs. Such laws are subject to the rigorous *Central Hudson* test, named for the case that first enunciated this standard of review.[80] The *Central Hudson* test is very protective of business's right to share—and adult consumers' right to receive—truthful, nonmisleading commercial information. For example, under the *Central Hudson* test, a court likely would strike down a local law banning soda billboards within 1,000 feet of schools.

The *Central Hudson* Test

The *Central Hudson* test asks four questions:

1. Is the commercial speech protected by the First Amendment? Commercial messages are protected by the First Amendment as long as they inform the public about a lawful activity in a manner that is not false, deceptive or inherently misleading.[a] If the government has banned certain activity—such as selling marijuana—the government can also ban the marketing of that activity. Some scholars have argued that it is deceptive and misleading to advertise to children under a certain age.[b] Unless a court accepts that argument, however (and none has yet), it is likely to find that most junk food advertisements are protected because they accurately inform the public about a lawful activity.

2. Does the government have a substantial interest to protect by restricting the commercial speech? Courts generally recognize that the government has a substantial interest in passing laws that promote the public's health, safety and welfare.[c] In the context of preventing underage tobacco use, the Supreme Court found that the government's interest in protecting children's health "is substantial, and even compelling."[d]

3. Does the commercial speech restriction directly advance the government's stated interest? The third prong is harder to meet. The government cannot rely on mere "speculation and conjecture" that the restriction on speech will alleviate the articulated harms.[e] Instead, the government must provide at least some empirical data to justify the speech restriction.[f] In a Supreme Court case involving efforts to restrict cigarette advertising to youth, the government cleared this hurdle by providing several studies illustrating that advertising plays "a significant and important contributory role in a young person's decision to use cigarettes or smokeless tobacco products."[g] In another case, the Supreme Court struck down a state prohibition on advertising liquor prices because the government

failed to provide evidence beyond commonsense conclusions that the prohibition would serve the state's interest in promoting temperance.[h]

4. Is the regulation no more extensive than necessary to further the state's interest? The fourth prong is often the hardest to meet. The government must conduct a careful and thorough analysis of the impact the regulation would have on speech and explain why alternative non-speech-related regulations would be insufficient to advance the purported interest.[i] In addition, the regulation cannot be overly broad in its sweep; it must have as little impact as possible on businesses' right to communicate their speech to adults and adults' corresponding right to receive that information.[j] This last prong doomed one state regulation banning outdoor advertising of tobacco products within 1,000 feet of a school or playground.[k] The Supreme Court concluded that the government did not "carefully calculate the costs and benefits associated with the burden on speech imposed" because, among other reasons, in some urban areas the geographic reach of the 1,000-foot rule resulted in a nearly complete ban on communicating truthful information about tobacco products to adults.[l]

Notes: [a] *Central Hudson Gas & Elec. Co. v. Pub. Svce. Comm'n of New York*, 447 U.S. 557 (1980), 567; [b] Jennifer L. Pomeranz, "Television Food Marketing to Children Revisited: The Federal Trade Commission Has the Constitutional and Statutory Authority to Regulate," *Journal of Law, Medicine & Ethics*, 38, no. 1 (2010): 101–5; Jennifer Harris and Samantha Graff, "Ethics of Targeting Food Marketing to Young People and the First Amendment: Psychological and Legal Perspectives," publication pending, on file with authors; [c] *See*, e.g., *Rubin v. Coors Brewing Co.*, 514 U.S. 476, 485 (1995); [d] *Lorillard Tobacco Co. v. Reilly*, 533 U.S. 525, 563 (2001); [e] Ibid., 561 (quoting *Edenfield v. Fane*, 507 U.S. 761, 770 [1993]) (internal quotations omitted); [f] Ibid., 555; [g] Ibid., 558; [h] *Liquormart, Inc. v. Rhode Island*, 517 U.S. 484, 505 (1996); [i] *Thompson v. Western States Medical Center*, 535 U.S. 357, 373 (2002); [j] *Lorillard*, 533 U.S. at 561–67; [k] Ibid., 528; [l] Ibid.

All is not lost, however, for local governments wishing to reduce exposure to junk food. As for billboards, it is one thing to regulate commercial billboards based on their content and another thing entirely to outlaw all commercial billboards, regardless of their content. A local law would likely withstand First Amendment scrutiny if it banned all commercial billboards (except those located on the site of the advertised establishment), as long as the ban is based on non-speech-related considerations like traffic safety or esthetics.[81] A blanket prohibition on billboards is an indirect way to minimize junk food advertising in the community. But what if a locality wants to take an overt regulatory stand?

From a First Amendment perspective, it is much easier for government to impose restrictions on products than on speech about the products. So instead of focusing only on advertising, a locality might consider expanding its purview to the overall food environment — pursuing the trans-fat bans, soda taxes and zoning laws already discussed.

Another policy idea some communities are exploring is requiring food retailers to provide healthy check-out lanes devoid of soda, chips, candy and cookies. This would allow parents to head off the inevitable wrangle that results when their children ask for the high-calorie, low-nutrient food that is strategically located where every shopper must go.[82] Even childless shoppers might appreciate the chance to avoid impulse buys, determined primarily by the proximity of food rather than hunger or a conscious decision to buy or to eat.[83]

A strategy that received a lot of press was spearheaded by Santa Clara County, California. In April 2010, the county passed a first-of-its-kind ordinance that sets basic nutritional standards for restaurant meals that come with a toy. Meals and snacks away from home account for one third of the calories consumed by children each day,[84] and 93 percent of children's meals at chain restaurants fail to meet basic nutritional standards.[85] At the same time, the restaurant industry distributed more than 1.2 billion toys in one year — the vast majority if which were used to sell high-calorie, high-fat, high-sodium meals to children.[86] Most of the major fast-food restaurants already have combo options that meet Santa Clara's standards, so the effect of the ordinance is to encourage such restaurants to promote the healthier meal as the default choice.

Case for Medical-Legal Partnership

ABC Food Company decides to develop new potato chips called Spicy Jalapeño Snappers. To generate consumer interest, the company decides to give out coupons for the product and price them lower than other chips. The company pays grocery stores a fee to place the product on a shelf at the checkout aisle, making it more likely that consumers will buy a bag on impulse as they are paying for their groceries. Finally, the company creates an advertising campaign around these chips that involves a funny jalapeño cartoon character who finds the spicy chips irresistible, even though they make his tongue burn.

Questions for Discussion

1. You are working with a group of parents who want to make it harder for their children to get access to junk food in their town. Of the policy options listed in this section, which one would you encourage the parents to start working on first to address marketing campaigns like the Spicy Jalapeño Snappers campaign? What factors do you consider?

2. Medical: What medical or epidemiological information would be helpful to support the state or local law that the parents' group decides to work on?

3. Legal: What legal issues will you need to research thoroughly before moving forward with your policy campaign?

Increasing Physical Activity Opportunities in Communities

Regular physical activity is part of a healthy lifestyle and plays a critical role in mitigating obesity. Public health advocates are pursuing a range of strategies aimed at increasing exercise opportunities at work and school and on the way to and from work and school. Advocates should take a broad view of physical activity by looking at transportation policy, recreational opportunities, and school and child care policies related to physical education and physical activity. If this is an area that advocates want to focus on, it is critical to make connections with transportation and planning agencies.

A 2008 study that looked at national surveys of travel behavior and health indicators in Europe, North America and Australia found that walking and bicycling are far more common in European countries than in the United States, Australia and Canada and that active transportation is inversely related to obesity in these countries.[87] Although transportation policy is heavily influenced by both federal and state law, there are local policy strategies that local advocates can champion to create healthier communities.

One such policy strategy is called Complete Streets, which are streets designed and operated to enable safe access for all users.[88] Complete Streets policies ensure that streets and roads work for drivers, transit users, pedestrians and bicyclists, as well as for older people, children and people with disabilities. Creating Complete Streets means transportation agencies must change their orientation toward building primarily for cars. Complete Streets can be achieved through a variety of policies: ordinances and resolutions, rewriting design manuals, inclusion in comprehensive plans, internal memos from directors of transportation agencies and executive orders from elected officials, like mayors or governors.

Safe Routes to Schools (SRTS) is a policy approach closely related to Complete Streets. SRTS focuses on children's active transportation to and from school. Research demonstrates that children who walk or bike to school have higher daily levels of physical activity and better cardiovascular fitness than those who do not actively commute to school.[89] Advocates who wish to work on this issue can consider working with their school district to pass a district policy that promotes and supports SRTS programs.[90] The Case Study: Saratoga Springs Safe Routes to School Policy details an example of a successful SRTS program.

In addition to engaging in active transportation, it is important that people have access to open space and facilities where they can play and exercise. Many communities, particularly low-income ones, lack these amenities. Schools often have a variety of recreational facilities—gymnasiums, playgrounds, fields, courts, tracks—that could provide exercise opportunities not only to students but also to adults, after hours. Most states currently have laws that encourage or even require schools to open their facilities to the community for recreation or other civic uses. Nonetheless, school officials may be reluctant to do so, cautious about the expense of maintenance, power and security in times of increasingly tight budgets.

A *joint use agreement* is a formal agreement between two separate government entities—often a school district and a city or county—setting forth the terms and conditions for the shared use of public property. In San Francisco, for instance, the city and school district used a joint use agreement to open school playgrounds to the community on weekends. In Seattle, the city and school district implemented a more complex joint use agreement to centralize the scheduling of all school and city recreation facilities, making them more accessible and easier to reserve. In some communities, schools and cities have partnered to build new recreational facilities for schools and neighborhoods. Subject to overriding state and local laws, the agreements can allocate to local government some or all of the responsibility for costs, security, supervision, maintenance, repairs and potential liability. Advocates can get involved by urging school officials (including school board members) and city or county officials to pursue a joint use agreement that would make school facilities more widely accessible to community members.[91]

Case Study: Saratoga Springs Safe Routes to School Policy

On May 15, 2009, Saratoga Springs, New York, resident Janette Kaddo-Marino and her 12-year-old son, Adam, biked to school as part of a bike-to-work celebration. After they arrived, mother and son were approached first by school security and then school administrators, who informed Ms. Kaddo-Marino that students are not permitted to walk or ride their bikes to school per school board policy. The bike was impounded by school staff and Ms. Kaddo-Marino was told she would have to return with a car to pick the bike up.[a] She was outraged by this incident and started to push to get the policy changed. She turned to the Safe Routes to Schools National Partnership (SRTSNP), a national organization that works to get policies in place at the state and local level that encourage active transportation.[b] Former Speaker of the House Newt Gingrich joined the debate, coauthoring a letter with a director at the Center for Health Transformation that urged board members to revise the policy.[c]

As Ms. Kaddo-Marino and SRTSNP pushed for a policy supporting walking and biking in Saratoga Springs, the school board raised liability concerns as one reason they did not want to put such SRTS policy in place. At that point, Ms. Kaddo-Marino and SRTSNP reached out to the lawyers at Public Health Law and Policy (PHLP) in Oakland, California, to find out if a policy like this that put requirements around a SRTS policy could actually increase schools' liability. The PHLP team was able to explain that schools are generally not liable to students for injuries that occur when students are not in the physical custody or control of the district. Thus, the school would have very little risk of liability if it simply failed to interject itself into students' non-bus transportation to and from school. Armed with this information and strong support from groups like SRTSNP and local transportation advocates, Ms. Kadino-Marino went back to her school board and convinced them to change their policy.[d]

Notes: [a] Andrew J. Bernstein, "Student's Bike Ride Earns Punishment," *Saratogian*, May 23, 2009, http://www.saratogian.com/articles/2009/05/23/news/doc4a176696ca884152592474.txt; [b] Safe Routes to School National Partnership, "Home," www.saferoutespartnership.org; [c] Newt Gingrich, Laura Linn, Letter to Saratoga Springs Board of Education, http://www.healthtransformation.net/galleries/default-file/Saratoga%20Springs%20Board%20of%20Education%2010%205%2009%20_2_.pdf; [d] Saratoga Springs Board of Education, "Meeting Minutes" (Saratoga Springs, New York, October 13, 2009), http://www.saratogaschools.org/boardofeducation/boeminutes/09-10minutes/boeminutes-10-13-09.pdf.

Questions for Discussion

1. What role might an MLP play in helping establish the importance of passing an SRTS policy in a community?

2. What is the value of having a policy in place that permits children to walk and bike to school?

Policy Strategies for Schools

Like communities, schools are on the front lines of the obesity epidemic. Fifty-five million children are enrolled in primary and secondary school.[92] Along with the home environment, schools are largely responsible for shaping children's diet and exercise habits. Unfortunately, schools deal with same problems in their food and physical activity environments that our communities face: the nutritional value of food served in schools is often poor and opportunities for physical activity are limited. In 2007–2008, 62 percent of public elementary school students were able to purchase unhealthy foods or beverages such as soda, candy, cookies and french fries, through vending machines, à la carte lines, and school stores. Meals served through the National School Lunch Program often included higher-fat items such as pizza, french fries, and 2 percent or whole milk.[93] Only one-in-five third-grade public school students were offered daily physical education in 2007–2008, and only 18 percent were offered at least 150 minutes of weekly physical education, as recommended by the National Association for Sport and Physical Education.[94] As with the community policy interventions, public health advocates are exploring many strategies to address these issues; however, this section focuses on strategies that rely on legally enforceable tools for implementation: school district policies with enforcement provisions and binding contracts.

School nutrition is shaped by the Child Nutrition Act. Physical education, part of school curricula, is included in the Elementary and Secondary Education Act. In 2004, Congress passed a law (P.L. 108-265) requiring school districts that participate in federal school nutrition programs to establish a local school wellness policy. Schools have a strong tradition of local control, so the legislation places the responsibility of developing a wellness policy at the local level. The wellness policy must:

- Set goals for nutrition education, physical activity and other school-based activities to promote student wellness

- Establish nutrition guidelines for all foods available on school grounds during the day, with the intention of promoting student health and reducing childhood obesity

- Ensure that nutrition guidelines for reimbursable school meals are not less restrictive than federal guidelines

- Establish a plan for measuring the implementation of the wellness policy, with one or more people in the district charged with ensuring compliance (this requirement paves the way for community members to help enforce the policy)

- Involve parents, students, representatives of the school food authority, the school board, school administrators and the public in developing the school wellness policy

Ninety-nine percent of all students in the United States were enrolled in a school district with a wellness policy as of the beginning of school year 2008–2009.[95] A national study, published in 2009, found that a lack of enforcement has proven to be a major weakness of many local wellness policies.[96] Local wellness policies therefore make an excellent policy target for MLPs wishing to work on improving the school environment as they provide a mechanism for addressing both physical activity and nutrition in schools at the local level.

Increasing Access to Healthy Food and Reducing Access to Unhealthy Food in Schools

The USDA recommends that school districts adopt wellness policies that set comprehensive nutrition guidelines for food sold on school campuses. To this end, the school district should:

- Set guidelines for foods and beverages in à la carte sales in the food service program on school campuses. (À la carte foods are food items that are sold separately from school lunches — generally snack foods.)

- Set guidelines for foods and beverages sold in vending machines, snack bars, school stores, and concession stands on school campuses.

- Set guidelines for foods and beverages sold as part of school-sponsored fundraising activities.

- Set guidelines for refreshments served at parties, celebrations and meetings during the school day.

- Make decisions on these guidelines based on nutrition goals, not on profit making.[97]

MLPs can review school district policies, ensure they cover the areas listed, and recommend strengthening policy language if the nutrition standards in the wellness policy are not strong enough. Additionally MLPs can help ensure that strong policies are actually enforced by reviewing the policies and filing complaints at the school level and then the district level if policies are not being followed.[98]

In addition to working on wellness policies, advocates can implement strategies for improving so-called competitive foods, that is, food sold in à la carte lines, vending machines and school stores. Known as competitive foods because they compete with lunches served under the USDA's National School Lunch Program, these foods are often of poor nutritional value and are available to children during most of the school day. The USDA currently requires state agencies and schools to establish rules or regulations to prohibit the sale of these products in the food service areas during the lunch period (7 C.F.R. §210.11, 1994). The regulations permit state agencies and schools to enact further controls over these foods and beverages. At least 27 states have laws regulating the sale of competitive foods at schools.[99] Several states specifically regulate which beverages may be sold in schools. Connecticut, for example, only permits the sale of milk, nondairy milk, 100 percent fruit and vegetable juice (with no added sugars), and water (with no added sugars or caffeine) in schools and restricts portion sizes (other than water) to 12 ounces or less (C.G.S. §10-221q, 2006). Advocates can influence the nutritional content of these foods by strengthening language about competitive foods in wellness policies and pushing school boards to purchase healthy foods and beverages through their vending contracts.

Healthy Beverage Vending Contracts

Beverage vending agreements provide a special opportunity for public health advocates and school districts. Vendors who handle beverage contracts represent a single beverage company, selling and advertising only that company's brands; in contrast, vendors who service food machines tend to stock and sell products from multiple companies. Because a beverage vendor represents only one company, the vendor can offer financial benefits that come with exclusive contracts, in which a school district agrees to purchase only that vendor's products. These benefits might include sponsorship fees, cash advances and more lucrative deals. More important for children's health, that vendor might also have significant flexibility to change its product mix to improve the nutritional quality of beverages sold on district property. As a first step, MLPs can encourage local school boards to pass healthy beverage vending policies at the district level.[a]

Note: [a] National Policy and Legal Analysis Network to Prevent Childhood Obesity, *Developing a Healthy Beverage Vending Agreement* (Oakland, CA: Public Health Law and Policy, 2009), http://www.nplanonline.org/nplan/products/developing-healthy-beverage-vending-agreement.

Decreasing Junk Food Advertising in Schools

The constant onslaught of junk food advertising follows children even when they enter the sheltered realm of the school environment. The food industry reaches children at school in myriad ways, from providing branded "educational" materials, to splashing logos on school facilities, to sponsoring fundraising campaigns, to rewarding students with gift certificates for fast food, to giving schools rebates for including obesogenic brands in children's lunches.

Even though commercial speech receives significant protection in most circumstances, the First Amendment should not stand in the way of carefully crafted advertising restrictions on public school property—either through vending contracts or wellness policies.

In contract negotiations, a school district can request that a vendor agree to any type of advertising prohibition envisioned by the district. Assuming the vendor would otherwise have a First Amendment right to advertise in schools, it may waive that right through a contract as long as the waiver is voluntary and the party has full awareness of the legal consequences.[100] If a vendor signs a contract agreeing to an advertising prohibition, the provision is likely to be valid given that competitive food and beverage vendors tend to be large companies with sophisticated legal and business savvy.[101]

As for restricting junk food advertising through wellness policies, because a public school is a "nonpublic forum," special First Amendment rules apply.[102] A "public forum" is a place that, like a public park or city square, has for many years been made available to a wide variety of speakers. The First Amendment makes it very difficult for the government to restrict speech in public forums.[103] Because public schools have a fundamental mission to educate students, courts have ruled repeatedly that K–12 schools are nonpublic forums. As such, a school district may limit advertising as long as any restriction is both *reasonable* and *viewpoint neutral*.[104] A policy is *reasonable* if it is consistent with the district's legitimate interest in preserving the property for its dedicated use.[105] A policy is *viewpoint neutral* if it restricts all speech on a given subject.[106] A school district advertising policy has a strong chance of meeting these standards if it (1) bans all advertising on campus; (2) bans all food and beverage advertising on campus; or (3) bans the advertising on campus for those food and beverage products that are not allowed to be sold on campus.

Case for Medical-Legal Partnership

Ever since Jamal Smith suffered a mild heart attack, he and his family have been trying to make changes to their diet and exercise routines. Both Jamal and Sarah, his wife, have asked administrators at their children's school to improve the food available on the school grounds. Also, they have been spending more time at a local swimming pool run by the local Parks and Recreation Department. The parents have noticed that at both the school and the pool, the vending machines sell only junk food. Often when their two children finish their swimming lessons, they are hungry and it is hard to convince them to eat the healthy snack Sarah has packed for them when they can see the vending machines full of chips and candy bars. It's made even worse because the vending machines have big advertisements on the front panels with tempting pictures of unhealthy food.

Sarah decides that she wants to improve the quality of the food sold in vending machines on school grounds and at the Park and Recreation Center, not just for her children but for all the children in the community. She mentions her frustration to her pediatrician, who enlists the help of an MLP lawyer. What steps can Sarah take to make this change? How could a medical-legal partnership help her?

Questions for Discussion

1. What solutions might you recommend to Sarah?
2. Is your chosen solution a policy or a program? If it is a program, try to broaden it to a policy.
3. What's the rational basis (i.e., the public health reason) for the policy?

4. At which level of government should the policy be enacted?

5. Which government agencies will Sarah need to work with to make this policy change?

6. Can you identify any legal issues which might be triggered by the policy approach?

7. What kind of responses, both positive and negative, would you anticipate the policy will provoke?

Increasing Physical Activity Opportunities in Schools

Although increasing physical education and physical activity in schools is a critical element of combating childhood obesity, it also has other benefits. Research has shown that engaging in regular physical activity may improve student performance.[107] In many states, schools receive failing grades for their physical activity and physical education programs. For example, in 2007 Florida's physical activity policy required each district board to allow 150 minutes of physical activity per week for students in grades K–5 but did not define the term "physical activity." According to the *Miami Herald*, the state legislature discovered that some schools were counting the time it took to walk across campus between classes to meet the requirement.[108] In 2008, in response to parent outrage, Florida passed SB 610, which provides for "at least 30 consecutive minutes" of physical activity to be provided for students K–6.

When considering physical activity standards in schools, it is important to note that there are no federal standards. All states maintain policies on physical activity, but local districts have the discretion to interpret and apply policy and determine the manner of implementation. As with public health, there is a strong tradition of local control in the education arena. The power to change policy resides with the local school district administration, local school boards, individual schools and parent/teacher associations. Public health advocates can ensure that local schools interpret state legislation on physical activity in a manner that maximizes the benefits to student health. Local wellness policies should set clear guidelines for physical activity requirements, and MLPs can ensure this is the case. Lawyers can review the laws governing physical activity and physical education in schools and make sure the law is being followed. Healthcare providers can testify before school boards and legislatures about the importance of physical activity.

Case Study: Changing Physical Education Policy in Los Angeles Public Schools

Like many school districts around the country, the Los Angeles Unified School District (LAUSD) was not enforcing the physical education requirements laid out in state law.[a] In 2009, the City Project[b] and United Teachers of Los Angeles, parents and school officials initiated a strategic campaign to enforce physical education in Los Angeles's public schools. LAUSD serves a diverse and vulnerable student population: 91 percent are children of color, 74 percent are low-income and 26 percent suffer from obesity. Recreational facilities at LAUSD schools are extremely limited; schools with higher numbers of non-Hispanic white children have significantly greater access to playing fields and play spaces.[c] The ratio of students to teachers in middle school physical education classes average 93:1.[d]

According to the City Project, their campaign to improve physical education policy had four major elements designed to enforce physical education requirements and improve the health and quality of life for LAUSD students. First, the teachers' union organized a public organizing campaign to support physical education. Second, the City Project filed administrative complaints on behalf of parents, youth groups and health advocates under civil rights and education laws to require the school district to enforce physical education requirements. Third, in response to the campaign and complaints, the Board of Education unanimously adopted a resolution to enforce physical education laws. Fourth, the teachers, the City Project and the LAUSD superintendent developed an implementation plan to enforce the physical education laws and resolution and resolve the complaints.[e]

City Project Executive Director Robert Garcia notes that when developing their campaign, coalition members relied on social science research to document the disparities in physical education and health based on race, ethnicity and income.[f] The campaign also benefited from being able to use the threat of litigation as a negotiating tool. "Social scientists and attorneys need to collaborate to connect the dots between physical education, human health, racial and ethnic disparities, and civil rights and education laws. Foundations should fund analyses of evidence by legal practitioners, including social science research and disparities in physical education and health based on race, ethnicity, and income. Abstract policy reports and tool kits are not enough. Foundations should fund not only policy and legal advocacy outside the courts, but also litigation in the courts. Access to justice through the courts can be a profoundly democratic means of engaging, educating, and empowering people of color and low-income people to achieve concrete improvements in their lives."[g] This interdisciplinary approach to policy change includes many elements of the Spectrum of Prevention and serves as an excellent model for other communities.

Notes: [a] Robert Garcia, Chad Fenwick, "Social Science, Equal Justice, and Public Health Policy: Lessons from Los Angeles," *Journal of Public Health Policy*, 30 (2009): S27; [b] The City Project, "Mission," http://www.cityprojectca.org/about/index.html; [c] Garcia and Fenwick, "Social Science," S29; [d] Ibid., S27; [e] Ibid., S28–32; [f] Ibid., S30; [g] Ibid.

Increasing Physical Activity Opportunities in Child Care Settings

Obesity rates among American infants, toddlers and young children have risen along with rates among school-age children. Over the past four decades, obesity rates among preschool children ages two to five have nearly tripled, from 5 to 14 percent.[109] A new national study also shows that over 18 percent of 4-year-olds are obese.[110]

At the same time, the number of young children receiving care in child care settings has increased. At least 60 percent of infants and children up to age five currently spend an average of 29 hours each week in some form of child care setting.[111] Child care arrangements in the United States include care at home by relatives or a babysitter, by family child care providers (nonrelative child care providers who care for two or more children in the provider's home) and by child care centers (including nursery schools, preschools and Head Start programs). Yet few states have addressed regulating physical activity for young children supervised in child care settings.

Although child care is regulated at the state level, the federal government provides three major programs that subsidize child care. Head Start operates child care programs for low-income preschool-age children. However, Head Start's regulations do not address the amount, frequency or type of physical activity for preschool children, nor do they address or limit television or other screen time.[112] The two other major federal child care programs are the Child Care and Development Block Grants, which subsidize child care costs for low-income families, and the Child and Adult Care Food Program, a federal program that subsidizes meals and snacks for children and adults receiving day care. Neither program provides physical activity standards.[113]

Each state sets and enforces its own child care licensing regulations. Most states require both child care providers and child care facilities to meet specific standards to obtain and maintain a license to operate. Advocates working at the local level can consider working with local officials to develop standards for child care settings and then pushing for a city or county resolution urging local child care providers to adopt them, requiring that standards are included as conditions for subsidies or other grant funding by local governments or private funders, or asking that child care providers voluntarily adopt them.[114]

Practice to Policy

MLP's origins lie in providing individual patients and clients with integrated medical and legal care to address the social determinants of health. However, as described, both lawyers and healthcare providers can play a very powerful role as agents for policy change. Individual cases develop a practitioner's sense of broader concerns or trends in a community. It is often a recurrent problem seen as a pattern across many patients that triggers the need for policy action rather than individual attention. MLP develops both perspective and relationships that can facilitate the steps to influencing policy.

With respect to obesity prevention, healthcare providers have observed the trends for decades. They have tackled problems independently and are well versed in the statistics and the reality of this epidemic. The many examples included here illustrate the variety of areas where policy change could have a significant impact. Armed with this knowledge and perspective, MLPs are poised to help inform and affect policy in this area as well as develop coalitions. MLPs should consider bringing together new groups that may identify with different movements and can rally around the same policies, such as environmental organizations, civil rights organizations and sustainable agriculture organizations. Below are some of ways that MLPs may influence obesity prevention policy.

- Work with medical and legal societies and associations to publicly support an obesity prevention effort. Sponsor healthy activities like runs or walks that provide opportunity to highlight community development and physical activity policy.

- Help establish a local food policy council. The CDC provides resources online to develop community-based food policy councils.

- Track local health legislation, or ask law and medical students to follow the legislation as part of a MLP, health policy or advocacy class. Most communities maintain their legislative calendars online. If relevant policies come up for hearing, testify on behalf of the legislation at the hearing. Students can be persuasive speakers and can inform and impact the session.

- Consider a class project in which students present an obesity prevention policy to local council members or the mayor.[115]

- Participate in school leadership meetings with state boards of education, districts, PTAs or food services management. Each of these organizations has the opportunity to work with policy makers to influence the quality and standards for physical activity and food in schools.

- Develop relationships with your local health department and align with state and local government agencies to support infrastructure and system changes. Many government and health department staff feel a strong commitment toward social justice and want to partner with informed and credible community allies.

- Consider getting involved in the public commissions that govern much of the relevant policy development: for example, the local school board, the local board of health, citizen commissions dealing with children's health issues or chronic disease (usually run by city or county health departments), the local planning board and the local redevelopment commission.

- Don't have time to commit to a public commission? If you are aware of the passage of relevant local policies in your community, consider attending the city or county council hearing on the issue and testifying on behalf of the inclusion of strong health language.

Conclusion

Approximately a third of adults and 17 percent of children and adolescents are obese in the United States. It is a public health problem on an epic scale. As such, it demands a solution that works at all levels, from individual to societal. To address obesity for the long term, we need to rethink how we structure our communities and we have to address major infrastructure problems present in our food delivery systems, public transportation systems and school systems. To institutionalize these kinds of changes, public health advocates must work in the policy arena. Lawyers and healthcare providers can advocate for individuals and families that need access to healthy nutritious and affordable food, safe physical activities and recreational opportunities. They can also play an important role in a policy approach to address obesity rates by participating in policy development and actively engaging in the legislative process with policy makers.

Note

The authors appreciate the following people for contributing their expertise to the draft chapter: Kimberly Avila Edwards, Charlotte Dickson, Christine Fry, Nora Howley, Hillary Noll Kalay, Hannah Laurison, Rachelle Mirkin, Claudia Polsky, Melissa Rodgers and Sara Zimmerman.

---

1. Katherine M. Flegal, Margaret D. Caroll, Cythnia L. Ogden, et al., "Prevalence and Trends of Obesity Among US Adults, 1999–2008," Journal of the American Medical Association, 303, no. 3 (2010): 234–41.

2. Cynthia Ogden, Margaret Caroll, Lester R. Curtin, et al., "Prevalence of High Body Mass Index in US Children and Adolescents, 2007–2008," Journal of the American Medical Association 303, no. 3 (2010): 342–49.

3. Robert Wood Johnson Foundation, Commission to Build a Healthier America, "Issue Brief 7: Message Translation" (2009).

4. Flegal, et al., "Prevalence and Trends of Obesity."

5. Ogden, et al., "Prevalence of High Body Mass."

6. Eric A. Finkelstein, Ian C. Fiebelkorn, and Guijing Wang, "National Medical Spending Attributable to Overweight and Obesity: How Much, and Who's Paying?" Health Affairs, W3 (2003): 219–26.

7. David S. Freedman, Laura Kettle Khan, Mary K. Serdula, et al., "The Relation of Childhood BMI to Adult Adiposity: The Bogalusa Heart Study," *Pediatrics*, 115, no. 1 (2005): 22–27.

8. Ogden et al., "Prevalence of High Body Mass."

9. William Dietz, "Health Consequences of Obesity in Youth: Childhood Predictors of Adult Disease," Pediatrics, 101 (1998): 518–25. M. B. Swartz, R. Puhl, "Childhood Obesity: A Societal Problem to Solve," Obesity Reviews, 4, no. 1 (2003): 57–71.

10. Flegal, et al., "Prevalence and Trends of Obesity."

11. Centers for Disease Control and Prevention, "U.S. Obesity Trends by State, 1985–2009," Overweight and Obesity (2010). Data source: CDC's Behavioral Risk Factor Surveillance System (BRFSS).

12. L. Pan, D. A. Galuska, B. Sherry, et al., "Difference in Prevalence in Obesity among Black, White, and Hispanic Adults, United States, 2006–2008," *Morbidity and Mortality Weekly Report*, 58, no. 27 (2009): 740–44.

13. National Center for Health Statistics, *Health, United States, 2002*, with *Chartbook on Trends in the Health of Americans* (Hyattsville, MD, 2010); www.cdc.gov/nchs/hus.htm.

14. Yvonne Jackson, "Height, Weight, and Body Mass Index of American Indian Schoolchildren, 1990–1991," *Journal of the American Dietetic Association*, 93, no. 10 (1993): 1136–40.

15. Institute of Medicine, *Weight Gain during Pregnancy: Reexamining the Guidelines*, ed. Kathleen M. Rasmussen and Ann L. Yaktine (Washington, DC: National Academic Press, 2009).

16. Christopher G. Owen, Richard M. Martin, Peter H. Whincup, et al., "Effect of Infant Feeding on the Risk of Obesity across the Life Course: A Quantitative Review of the Published Evidence," *Pediatrics*, 115 (2005): 1367–77; S. Arenz, R. Ruckert, B. Koletzko, et al., "Breast-Feeding and Childhood Obesity: A Systematic Review," *International Journal of Obesity and Related Metabolic Disorders*, 28 (2004): 1247–56.

17. National Bureau of Economic Research, *Moving to Opportunity: Interim Impacts Evaluation*, Prepared for U.S. Department of Housing and Urban Development, Office of Policy Development and Research (2003).

18. *Nielsenwire*, "Americans Watching More TV Than Ever; Web and Mobile Video Up too," May 20, 2009, http://blog.nielsen.com/nielsenwire/online_mobile/americans-watching-more-tv-than-ever.

19. Jennifer L. Harris, Kelly D. Brownell, John A. Bargh, "The Food Marketing Defense Model: Integrating Psychological Research to Protect Youth and Inform Public Policy," *Social Issues and Policy Review*, 3, no. 1 (2009): 211–71.

20. Federal Trade Commission, "Marketing Food to Children and Adolescents: A Review of Industry Expenditures, Activities and Self-Regulation," report to Congress, July 2008, http://www.ftc.gov/os/2008/07/P064504foodmktingreport.pdf.

21. Carmen Stitt and Dale Kunkel, "Food Advertising during Children's Television Programming on Broadcast and Cable Channels," *Health Communication*, 23, no. 6 (2008): 578–82.

22. FTC, "Marketing Food to Children and Adolescents," 23.

23. Kathryn Montgomery and Jeff Chester, "Interactive Food and Beverage Marketing: Targeting Adolescents in the Digital Age," *Journal of Adolescent Health*, 45 (2009): S18–29.

24. Larry Cohen and Susan Swift, "The Spectrum of Prevention: Developing a Comprehensive Approach to Injury Prevention," *Injury Prevention*, 5 (1999): 203–7.

25. Gordon Marshall, ed., *A Dictionary of Sociology* (Oxford: Oxford Express, 1998), http://www.encyclopedia.com/doc/1O88-norm.html; Xueying Zhang, David Cowling, and Hao Tang, "The Impact of Social Norm Change Strategies on Smokers' Quitting Behaviours," *Tobacco Control*, 19 (suppl. 1) (2010), http://tobaccocontrol.bmj.com/content/19/Suppl_1/i51.full.pdf.

26. California Department of Health Services, Tobacco Control Section, *A Model for Change: The California Experience in Tobacco Control* (Sacramento: Department of Health Services, October 1998), 3–4, http://www.cdph.ca.gov/programs/tobacco/Documents/CTCPmodelforchange1998.pdf.

27. California Department of Public Health, California Tobacco Control Program, *California Tobacco Control Update 2009: 20 Years of Tobacco Control in California* (Sacramento, California: California Department of Public Health, 2009), http://www.cdph.ca.gov/programs/ tobacco/Documents/CTCPUpdate2009.pdf; Samantha Graff and Jacob Ackerman, "A Special Role for Lawyers in a Social

Norm Change Movement: From Tobacco Control to Childhood Obesity Prevention," *Preventing Chronic Disease,* 6, no. 3 (2009): 1–7.

28. Cal. Rev. & Tax. Code §§ 30122(a)(1), 30123(a), 30124(b)(1); Cal. Health and Safety Code §§ 104350–104480, 104500–1045450, 130100–130155.

29. California Department of Public Health, *California Tobacco Control Update 2009.*

30. Ibid.

31. U.S. Department of Health and Human Services, Centers for Disease Control and Prevention, *Sustaining State Programs for Tobacco Control: Data Highlights 2006* (Atlanta: U.S. Department of Health and Human Services, 2006), http://www.cdc.gov/tobacco/data_statistics/state_data/data_highlights/2006/pdfs/dataHighlights06rev.pdf.

32. Ibid.; Indiana Tobacco Prevention and Cessation, "Adult Smoking Rates by State," http://www.tobaccofreedelawarecounty.org/documents/Smokingratesbystate2006.pdf.

33. U.S. Department of Health and Human Services, Centers for Disease Control and Prevention, *Best Practices for Comprehensive Tobacco Control Programs — 2007* (Atlanta: U.S. Department of Health and Human Services, 2007), http://www.cdc.gov/tobacco/tobacco_control_programs/stateand community/best_practices.

34. James M. Lightwood, Alexis Dinno, Stanton A. Glantz, "Effect of the California Tobacco Control Program on Personal Health Care Expenditures," *PLoS Medicine,* 5, no. 8 (2008): e178.

35. California Office of the Attorney General, "Master Settlement Agreement," http://ag.ca.gov/tobacco/msa.php.

36. Edward Lawlor and Ann Dude, "Mobilizing, Framing, and Leading: Three Policy Thought Experiments for Covering America," in *Covering America: Real Remedies for the Uninsured, Vol. 2,* ed. Jack Meyer and Elliot Wicks (Washington, DC: Economics and Social Research Institute, 2002), 97–109.

37. Mothers Against Drunk Driving, "History," http://www.madd.org/About-us/About-us/History.aspx (accessed June 23, 2010).

38. Mothers Against Drunk Driving, "History," http://www.madd.org/about-us/history/madd-milestones.pdf (accessed June 29, 2011).

39. Nady El-Guebaly, "Don't Drink and Drive: The Successful Message of Mothers Against Drunk Driving (MADD)," *World Psychiatry,* 4, no.1 (2005): 35–36.

40. Laurie Davies, "25 Years of Saving Lives," *Driven* (Fall 2005): 11.

41. Lawlor and Dude, "Mobilizing, Framing, and Leading."

42. Davies, "25 Years of Saving Lives."

43. El-Guebaly, "Don't Drink and Drive."

44. Mark Earnest, Shale Wong, Steven Federico, "Physician Advocacy: What Is It and How Do We Do It?" *Academic Medicine,* 85, no. 1 (2010): 63–67.

45. Food Research and Action Center, *FRAC 101: Child Nutrition and WIC Reauthorization Act* (Washington, DC: Food Research and Action Center), http://www.frac.org/pdf/frac101_child_wic_actprimer.pdf.

46. Ibid. The reauthorization amends two existing statutes: the Richard B. Russell National School Lunch Act and the Child Nutrition Act of 1966. The Richard B. Russell National School Lunch Act, signed by Harry Truman in 1946, created the National School Lunch Program "as a measure of national security, to safeguard the health and well-being of the Nation's children." Twenty years later, Lyndon B. Johnson signed the Child Nutrition Act of 1966 into law, which established the School Breakfast Program. Not long after, programs such as the Child and Adult Care Food Program (CACFP), the Summer Food Service Program (SFSP), and other child nutrition programs were added to the National School Lunch Act.

47. Economic Research Service, "Food and Nutrition Assistance Programs: Charts," U.S. Department of Agriculture, http://www.ers.usda.gov/Briefing/FoodNutritionAssistance/gallery/FANR/programs.htm.

48. Ibid.

49. Ibid.

50. Ibid.

51. Ibid.

52. Federal Highway Administration, *Safe, Accountable, Flexible, Efficient Transportation Equity Act: A Legacy for Users* (Washington, DC: Federal Highway Administration, 2005), http://www.fhwa.dot.gov/safetealu/summary.htm.

53. Renee Johnson, *What Is the "Farm Bill"?* (Washington, DC: Congressional Research Service, 2008), http://www.nationalaglawcenter.org/assets/crs/RS22131.pdf.

54. Ibid.

55. Edwin Young, Victor Oliveira, and Roger Claasen, "2008 Farm Act: Where Will the Money Go?," *Amber Waves* (November 2008), http://www.ers.usda.gov/AmberWaves/November08/Data Feature/.

56. Economic Research Service, "Access to Affordable and Nutritious Food: Measuring and Understanding Food Deserts and Their Consequences," U.S. Department of Agriculture, June 2009.

57. K12 Academics, "Elementary and Secondary Education Act (ESEA)," http://www.k12academics.com/us-education-legislation/elementary-secondary-education-act-esea.

58. U.S. Department of Education, "Carol M. White Physical Education Program," http://www2.ed.gov/programs/whitephysed/index.html.

59. U.S. Department of Education, *A Blueprint for Reform: The Reauthorization of the Elementary and Secondary Education Act* (Washington, DC: U.S. Department of Education, 2010), http://www2.ed.gov/policy/elsec/leg/blueprint/blueprint.pdf, 33.

60. Available at http://www.letsmove.gov/pdf/TaskForce_on_Childhood_Obesity_May2010_FullReport.pdf.

61. Lawrence O. Gostin, *Public Health Law: Power, Duty, Restraint* (Berkeley: University of California Press, 2000), 47.

62. Ibid.

63. Paul Diller and Samantha Graff, "Regulating Food Retail for Obesity Prevention: How Far Can Cities Go?," *Journal of Law, Medicine & Ethics*, 39, s1 (2011): 89–93.

64. *Patrick v. Riley*, 209 Cal. 350, 354 (1930).

65. Michael Siegel, et al., "Preemption in Tobacco Control, Review of an Emerging Public Health Problem," *Journal of the American Medical Association*, 278, no. 10 (1997): 858; Robin Hobart, *Preemption: Taking the Local Out of Tobacco Control* (American Medical Association, 2003).

66. Andrew A. Skolnick, "Cancer Converts Tobacco Lobbyist: Victor L. Crawford Goes on the Record," *Journal of the American Medical Association*, 274, no. 3 (1995): 200–1.

67. See, e.g., National Conference of State Legislatures, *Preemption Monitor*, 6, no. 1 (2010), http://www.ncsl.org/default.aspx?tabid=20109 (noting that pressure for congressional and White House support for "federal usurpation of state authority" "continues to mount"); National Association of Attorneys General, *Interim Briefing Paper Presented for President-Elect Obama Transition Team* (Washington, DC: National Association of Attorneys General, 2009) (listing federal preemption of state laws as a top issue of concern).

68. See, e.g., Philadelphia Heath Code § 6-307, http://www.amlegal.com/library/pa/philadelphia.shtml.

69. See 21 U.S.C. § 343(q)(5)(H).

70. Kelly D. Brownell, et al., "The Public Health and Economic Benefits of Taxing Sugar-Sweetened Beverages," *New England Journal of Medicine*, 361, no. 16 (2009): 1599–605; National Policy and Legal Analysis Network to Prevent Childhood Obesity, *Model Sugar-Sweetened Beverage Tax Legislation* (Oakland, CA: Public Health Law and Policy, 2010), www.nplan.org.

71. Tobacco Free Kids, *Raising Cigarette Taxes Reduces Smoking, Especially among Kids (And the Cigarette Companies Know It)* (Washington, DC: Tobacco Free Kids), http://www.tobaccofreekids.org/research/factsheets/pdf/0146.pdf.

72. Charles M. Harr, "In Accordance with a Comprehensive Plan," *Harvard Law Review*, 68, no. 7 (1955): 1154.

73. Sean Walsh, Terry Roberts and Shauna Pellman, *California Planning Guide: An Introduction to Planning in California* (Sacramento, CA: Governor's Office of Planning and Research, 2005), 5–6.

74. Eric Damian Kelly, *Zoning and Land Use Controls* (Albany, NY: Matthew Bender, 2010), § 1.03(2)(a).

75. Walsh et al., *California Planning Guide*, 5.

76. Julie Mair et al., *The Use of Zoning to Restrict Fast Food Outlets: A Potential Strategy to Combat Obesity* (National Center for Environmental Health, Centers for Disease Control and Prevention, 2005).

77. Lynn Blais and Gerald Torres, "Regulatory Takings and Land-use Initiatives to Combat Childhood Obesity," report submitted to the National Policy and Legal Analysis Network to Prevent Childhood Obesity (May 19, 2008), available at http://www.nplanonline.org/nplan/products/takings_survey. Courts will occasionally find a taking occurred when an owner was not deprived of all economically viable use of his property but when two of these three factors are unusually severe: (1) the economic impact of the regulation, (2) the degree of interference with reasonable investment-backed expectations, and (3) the character of the governmental action.

78. Marice Ashe, et al., "Local Venues for Change: Legal Strategies for Healthy Environments," Journal of Law, Medicine & Ethics, 35 (2007): 141–42.

79. National Policy and Legal Analysis Network to Prevent Childhood Obesity, *Establishing Land Use Protections for Farmers' Market* (Oakland, CA: Public Health Law and Policy, 2009), http://www.nplanonline.org/nplan/products/establishing-land-use-protections-farmers-markets.

80. *Central Hudson Gas & Elec. Co. v. Pub. Svce. Comm'n of New York*, 447 U.S. 557 (1980).

81. *Metromedia, Inc. v. City of San Diego*, 453 U.S. 490, 507 (1981).

82. Anne Sutherland and Beth Thompson, *Kidfluence: The Marketers' Guide to Understanding and Reaching Generation Y — Kids, Tweens and Teens* (New York: McGraw-Hill, 2003).

83. Brian Wansink, *Mindless Eating: Why We Eat More Than We Think* (New York: Bantam Books, 2006).

84. Biing-Hwan Lin, Joanne Guthrie, Elizabeth Frazano, "Nutrient Contribution of Food Away From Home," in *America's Eating Habits: Changes and Consequences*, ed. Elizabeth Frazano (Washington, DC: U.S. Department of Agriculture, 1999), 217.

85. Margo Wootan, Ameena Batada, Elizabeth Marchlewicz, *Kids' Meals: Obesity on the Menu* (Washington, DC: Center for Science in the Public Interest, 2008), http://cspinet.org/new/pdf/kidsmeals-report.pdf, 8.

86. FTC, "Marketing Food to Children and Adolescents," 19.

87. David R. Bassett Jr., et al., "Walking, Cycling, and Obesity Rates in Europe, North America, and Australia," *Journal of Physical Activity and Health*, 5, no. 6 (2008): 795–814.

88. National Complete Streets Coalition, "Complete Streets FAQ," http://www.completestreets.org/complete-streets-fundamentals/complete-streets-faq/.

89. Kristen K. Davison, Jessica L. Werder, Catherine T. Lawson, "Children's Active Commuting to School: Current Knowledge and Future Directions," *Preventing Chronic Disease*, 5, no. 3 (2008): 1–11.

90. National Policy and Legal Analysis Network to Prevent Childhood Obesity, *Resources on Safe Routes to School Programs* (Oakland, CA: Public Health Law and Policy, 2010), http://www.nplanonline.org/childhood-obesity/products/SRTS-resources.

91. For information on joint use resources, see National Policy and Legal Analysis Network to Prevent Childhood Obesity, http://www.phlpnet.org/childhood-obesity/products/nplan-joint-use-agreements.

92. National Center for Education Statistics, "Projections of Education Statistics to 2018," http://nces.ed.gov/programs/projections/projections2018/sec1a.asp.

93. Lindsey Turner, Frank Chaloupka, Jamie Chriqui, et al., *Executive Summary: School Policies and Practices to Improve Health and Prevent Obesity: National Elementary School Survey Results: School Years 2006–07 and 2007–08* (Chicago: Bridging the Gap Program, Health Policy Center, Institute for Health Research and Policy, University of Illinois at Chicago, 2010), http://www.bridgingthegapresearch.org/client_files/pdfs/Publications/BTG_ExecSumm2_FINAL.pdf, 5.

94. Ibid., 6.

95. Jamie Chriqui, et al., *School District Wellness Policies: Evaluating Progress and Potential for Improving Children's Health Three Years after the Federal Mandate* (Chicago: Bridging the Gap, Health Policy Center, Institute for Health Research and Policy, University of Illinois at Chicago, 2010).

96. Robert Wood Johnson Foundation, *Local Wellness Policies: Assessing School District Strategies for Improving Children's Health. School Years 2006–2007 and 2007–2008* (Chicago: Bridging the Gap, Health Policy Center, Institute for Health Research and Policy, University of Illinois at Chicago, 2009), http://www.bridgingthegapresearch.org/_asset/hxbby9/WP_2009_monograph.pdf.

97. U.S. Department of Agriculture, "Local Wellness Policy," http://www.fns.usda.gov/tn/healthy/wellnesspolicygoals_guidelines.html.

98. National Policy and Legal Analysis Network to Prevent Childhood Obesity, *How to Enforce a Wellness Policy: A Guide for Parents and Community Advocates* (Oakland, CA: Public Health Law and Policy, 2009), http://www.nplanonline.org/nplan/products/how-to-enforce-wellness-policy.

99. Trust for America's Health, *F as in Fat: How Obesity Policies Are Failing America* (Washington, DC: Trust for America's Health, 2009), http://healthyamericans.org/reports/obesity2009/Obesity2009Report.pdf, 5.

100. *Overmyer Co., Inc. v. Frick Co.*, 405 U.S. 174, 187 (1972) (discussing requirements for waiver); *Fuentes v. Shevin*, 407 U.S. 67, 95 (1972) (discussing requirements for waiver).

101. Samantha K. Graff, "First Amendment Implications of Restricting Food and Beverage Marketing in Schools," *Annals of the American Academy of Political and Social Science,* 615 (2008): 158–77.

102. For more information about how these tests apply to schools, see ibid.

103. National Policy and Legal Analysis Network to Prevent Childhood Obesity, *Restricting Food and Beverage Advertising in Schools* (Oakland, CA: Public Health Law & Policy, 2009), http://www.nplanonline.org/nplan/products/restricting-food-and-beverage-advertising-schools.

104. *Educ. Ass'n v. Perry Local Educators' Ass'n,* 460 U.S. 37, 46 (1983).

105. Ibid., 50–51.

106. Ibid., 49.

107. Joseph E. Donnelly, et al., "Physical Activity Across the Curriculum (PAAC): A Randomized Controlled Trial to Promote Physical Activity and Diminish Overweight and Obesity in Elementary School Children," *Preventive Medicine,* 49 (2009): 336–41.

108. Hannah Sampson, "Florida Schools Struggle to Get Kids Active," *Miami Herald,* October 6, 2008, http://www.districtadministration.com/newssummary.aspx?news=yes&postid=51011.

109. Healthy Eating Research, *Promoting Good Nutrition and Physical Activity in Child-Care Settings* (Minneapolis: Healthy Eating Research, University of Minnesota, School of Public Health, 2007: 1–9), http://www.healthyeatingresearch.org/images/stories/her_research_briefs/her%20child%20care%20setting%20research%20brief.pdf, 1.

110. Sarah E. Anderson, Robert C. Whitaker, "Prevalence of Obesity among US Preschool Children in Different Racial and Ethnic Groups," *Archives of Pediatrics and Adolescent Medicine,* 163, no. 4 (2009): 344–48.

111. Healthy Eating Research, *Promoting Good Nutrition,* 1.

112. See 42 U.S.C. §9801 (Head Start Act); 45 C.F.R. §§1301–1311 (Head Start Program Performance Standards and other regulations).

113. See 45 C.F.R. §§98.1 et seq., 99.1 et seq. (Child Care and Development Block Grants); 42 U.S.C. §1766 (National School Lunch Act); 7 C.F.R. §226 (Child and Adult Care Food Program).

114. National Policy and Legal Analysis Network to Prevent Childhood Obesity, *Model Physical Activity Standards for Child-Care Providers (For Infant through Preschool-Age Children)* (Oakland, CA: Public Health Law and Policy, 2010), http://www.nplanonline.org/nplan/products/model-child-care-physical-activity-standards.

115. For examples of the kinds of policies that students may want to consider, with model legislative language and supporting legal research, go to www.phlpnet.org.

Chapter 18

Evaluating Medical-Legal Partnership: Approaches and Challenges

Rebecca Lawrence, MPH, MSW
Chong-Min Fu, BA
Megan Sandel, MD, MPH
Edward De Vos, EdD

As the medical-legal partnership (MLP) movement has grown over the past decade, one of the key issues for institutionalizing the model is how to evaluate its effectiveness and benefits. How does it change the practice of healthcare providers and lawyers? Does it improve health outcomes for individual patients and their families? Do systemic changes benefit the public health of particular populations? Although there is no shortage of literature about how to conduct social and behavioral research and program evaluation, studying the impact of an intervention such as MLP is quite complex. What is unique to the MLP model is the fusion of the medical and legal disciplines, among others. These disciplines have distinct approaches to research and evaluation and have traditionally asked different questions about impact. For example, lawyers tend to focus on the outcome of a legal case, whereas healthcare providers tend to focus on improved health in an individual patient or patient population.

This chapter presents the unique challenges and opportunities involved in evaluating MLP as an intervention. It is not intended as a comprehensive review of existing methodologies to study MLP. Rather, it presents an overview of some of the studies of MLP to date and how researchers may think about planning and implementing evaluation of the MLP model. Based on experience thus far, we outline some of the lessons learned, including many of the challenges, as well as potential solutions involved in studying MLP. Specifically, we detail challenges involved with designing a study based on the MLP program model, the types of data that can be used, identifying and recruiting study subjects from the populations that MLP typically serves, and its interdisciplinary nature. To frame our discussion of evaluation studies, we include discussion of basic research concepts to help readers understand the many ways in which MLP may be studied. This introductory information about research methods, although not exhaustive, serves as foundational background for students and practitioners interested in MLP research and evaluation.

An Overview of MLP Research and Evaluation

Domains of Impact

As the MLP network continues to expand across the country, demonstrating the efficacy of MLPs has never been more vital. The impact of MLP is generally measured in four key domains: patient health and well-being, medical homes and institutions, clinical workforce skills and provision of legal services. See Figure 18.1 for sample outcomes and impacts within each of these domains. Impact and outcomes can be demonstrated on multiple levels: the patient, the provider, the institution and the healthcare and legal systems. This chapter focuses on the evaluation of legal assistance in the healthcare setting or the provision of direct service, but MLPs are also studying the effect of trainings on provider knowledge, attitudes, and behaviors and the cost-effectiveness of MLP programs, as well as other aspects.

Figure 18.1 Domains of MLP Research and Evaluation

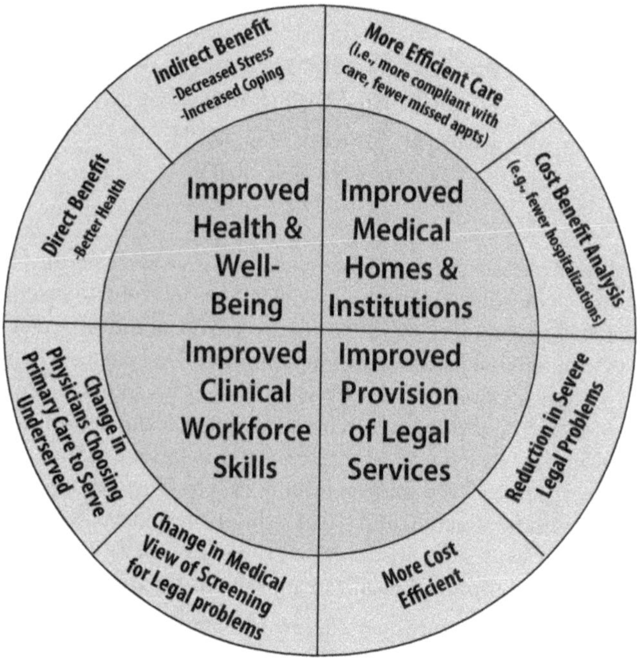

This chapter provides an overview of the components involved in a well-designed and implemented research or evaluation project. We review each component, beginning with who conducts research (the research team); what questions to answer in the research or evaluation project (formulating a hypothesis); how the question(s) will be answered (study design); and which patients will be studied (sampling). We discuss what outcomes should be tracked (defining and measuring MLP outcomes) and how to specifically define the MLP intervention that will change those outcomes. Though many MLP evaluations focus on the impact of direct service on certain outcomes, it is also important to focus on other ways that MLP can change health or legal institutions and practice as well as impact policy. Once outcomes are defined, deciding on methods of tracking or collecting the outcomes (determining data collection) are important as well. Last, we discuss the important considerations in MLP evaluation (conduct of research), including recruitment, ethical issues and engagement of vulnerable individuals and families in research studies.

Research vs. Evaluation

There are no universally recognized definitions for the terms *research* and *evaluation*; however, some important distinctions do exist. *Research*, according to the U.S. Department of Health and Human Services, is "a systematic investigation, including research development, testing and evaluation, designed to develop or contribute to generalizable knowledge."[1] An *evaluation* project or study is generally an assessment of an existing program based on some defined criteria. The field of evaluation differentiates between "formative" and "summative" evaluation. *Formative evaluation* assesses the delivery of a program, the quality of its implementation and organizational context, personnel, inputs and so on.[2] *Summative evaluation* examines the intended and unintended effects or outcomes of a program and sometimes attempts to demonstrate causality between program activities and outcomes.[3] Evaluation uses many of the same methodologies as research to form conclusions.

The Research Team

The first step in research is to establish the research team. Though it may seem easy to collect data about a particular program, it is best to have dedicated staff time and defined roles to effectively evaluate a program. It is important to realize that there are special expertise and skills that may be beyond those of the general MLP staff.

Table 18.1 outlines suggested members of the research team and their roles and responsibilities. Note that not all studies have a staff person for each position; sometimes, one individual will cover multiple responsibilities. Although members of the legal staff are not included in the box, the legal team is an integral part of the research process. As discussed later in the chapter, legal staff guide the research team through the MLP intervention, potentially identifying eligible patients for the study and helping to collect data.

Table 18.1 Roles and Responsibilities of the Research Team

Title	Roles and Responsibilities
Principal Investigator (PI)	Oversees all research related to the study; typically a PhD or MD; will be identified in the protocol as the principal investigator
Project Coordinator or Manager	Coordinates the day-to-day aspects of the study; supervises any research assistants or students; keeps the study on schedule; manages the protocol and application process
Data Manager	Maintains databases; checks data quality; leads data entry efforts
Statistician	Analyzes data during this later stage of the study
Research Assistant(s)	May recruit participants; may conduct surveys and interviews of participants; otherwise assists research team with study-related tasks

The research team should begin by identifying the problem to be studied and then reviewing the current literature in the field. Once these formative steps have been completed, the research team will need to engage in the following steps in the research process: (1) formulate research hypotheses, (2) choose a study design, (3) determine a method for identifying and sampling potential research participants, (4) create a plan for data collection, (5) devise a recruitment strategy, and (6) work through ethical considerations and obtain approval from the Institutional Review Board (IRB) of all appropriate institutions. In developing the research process, the research team also needs to consider the flexibility of the MLP model (discussed later in the chapter in "Challenges in Defining the MLP Intervention") and the families being served (see "Vulnerable Families and Research"). The following sections include discussion of the basic concepts of each of these steps, as well as the challenges each step presents to researchers designing studies of MLP.

Formulating Hypotheses

A *hypothesis* is a testable prediction about the relationship between one or more factors and the problem being studied.[4] In other words, a hypothesis is a possible explanation for a certain phenomenon. In program evaluation, a hypothesis is derived from the suspected outcome of program activities. Hypotheses help focus the study and help the research team identify the most pertinent variables for data collection. If the hypothesis is identified first, only variables that help test the hypothesis should be collected. This will save valuable time and resources. In an MLP context, hypotheses could explain or prove the improvement of health outcomes for patients, the change in attitudes and behaviors of healthcare providers, or the change in the provision of legal services to MLP patients (See "Example Hypotheses" from a study completed by MLP | Boston).

Example Hypotheses

1. Compared with the prevailing standard of care, exposure to MLP results in a decrease in parents' perceived stress and increased empowerment, self-efficacy, and more trust and better communication with physicians, which leads to improved health for the patient.

2. Compared with the prevailing standard of care, exposure to MLP results in fewer pediatric Emergency Department visits and fewer missed appointments, which leads to improved health for the patient.

3. Compared with the prevailing standard of care, exposure to MLP results in improved parental reports of child's overall health status, as well as fewer days of school and/or work missed due to health-related issues, which leads to improved health for the patient.

Formulating hypotheses to test for improved health in MLP patient-clients can present a major challenge. Measuring changes in health can be difficult, especially in pediatric populations where there are many variables affecting child health dependent on multiple types of legal issues. For ease of measurement, data collection, and analysis, hypotheses may need to be reductionist. In other words, researchers may need to focus on one health problem, such as asthma, or one social factor, such as housing conditions, instead of attempting to study multiple health outcomes and legal needs.

Study Design

The research team determines what study design will be used to address their research questions. Multiple study designs exist and could be used to evaluate MLP (see Appendix 18.1). Study designs include descriptive, cohort, case-control and randomized controlled trial studies. Each study design lends itself to certain research questions, hypotheses and settings. Evaluation teams should carefully consider what study design is feasible in their specific MLP.

An additional consideration in study design is the timing of the measurements. Ideally one would have a pretest, post-test design, where measures were taken prior to and then after program intervention, allowing for measuring changes over time. Baseline (preintervention) data is sometimes gathered through a *needs assessment,* which collects information about the population the program serves (e.g., sociodemographics, problems/issues faced, levels of knowledge, attitudes and behaviors) and existing resources. Gathering a baseline is important so that there is something against which change over time can be measured. Sometimes this is not feasible, and the only option is a post-test design. To improve the quality of data analysis, one could use a *control group* to compare differences. A control or comparison group is nearly identical to the group receiving the intervention and may allow the research team to verify that changes they observe are in fact due to the intervention and not other factors.

Qualitative vs. Quantitative Studies

Qualitative study design is a methodology generally used to *create* hypotheses by trying to identify new areas of research for further investigation. It is also particularly useful for gathering information about values, opinions, behaviors and beliefs of a group. *Quantitative* studies are designed to *answer* hypotheses with fixed variables, outcomes and previously developed questions and instruments (see Appendix 18.2 for a more thorough comparison of the two approaches). Depending on the research hypotheses, qualitative or quantitative methodology or a combination of both can be very useful. The rest of this chapter focuses on quantitative approaches to MLP program evaluation because many MLPs are seeking to test and answer hypotheses about the MLP model. See "Example of Qualitative MLP Research and Evaluation" for a summary of one qualitative study.

Example of Qualitative MLP Research and Evaluation

Study Title: Qualitative Legal Needs Study

Objectives: Researchers from Cornell University conducted a study in order to: (1) determine the extent of met and unmet need for legal and non-medical assistance in the population of families that seek services in Boston Medical Center's pediatric clinics; (2) identify and examine barriers to receiving legal and other non-medical services that are likely to affect child well-being and health; (3) determine the extent to which MLP | Boston is effective at identifying and helping the families with these kinds of problems; and (4) identify potential ways MLP | Boston can be more effective at providing services to families with children.

Methods: From February 2007 to January 2008, 72 qualitative interviews were conducted in English and Spanish with patient-families at six Boston Medical Center affiliated community health centers (three with MLP | Boston services and three comparison sites without).

Findings: Data from interviews demonstrates that: (1) MLP | Boston patient-families were more likely to acknowledge they had a problem when speaking with their doctors compared to patients at the comparison sites; (2) overall, MLP | Boston patient-families were more skilled advocates and felt more empowered to access the services they needed; (3) patient-families who received legal assistance from MLP | Boston felt they had better results than they would have had without that assistance.

Source: Diana Hernandez, "Qualitative Legal Needs Study Executive Summary," National Center for Medical-Legal Partnership, Cornell University (February 2008).

Challenges in MLP Study Design

The design of a program evaluation is dependent on the structural and organizational makeup of the program. Differences in partnership components (i.e., whether the local MLP program consists of an academic teaching hospital, a community health center, legal services program, pro bono attorneys/firms and/or some combination of these elements), the legal issue areas addressed and the resources available (both within the program as well as through the surrounding community) all influence the program model. These differences also influence the processes by which services are delivered, the outcomes or impacts the program have and the domains the program evaluation should consider measuring.

Patients seen at healthcare institutions affiliated with MLPs can be compared to patients from non-MLP healthcare institutions. However, such a design essentially requires the use of the hospital or community health center as the unit of analysis. This may be problematic due to the variability in the number of sites available; the demographic, systems, and resource differences across sites; and administrative and logistical concerns, given the addition of multiple IRBs to review and approve the research protocol. However, future evaluation studies with more time and funding may consider a large-scale randomized controlled trial with random assignment at the level of the individual program or program site.

Sampling

Next the research team must devise a plan for identifying study participants or the "sample" of people that will be included in the study. *Sampling* is the process of choosing a certain number of study participants from a defined population.[5] In some cases, all people from the intervention population can be included.[6] However, most studies include a large population; therefore, sampling of a subgroup is necessary.

First, the study team must identify the study population or the group of people the team is interested in examining.[7] For example, the study population of an MLP study could be identified as all patient-clients or patient-clients from a specific patient population, healthcare institution, or specialty clinic. Next, the team chooses a sampling method and a sample size (see Appendix 18.3 for descriptions of various sampling methods). In certain instances, a research team will make calculations to determine the needed sample size to make precise measurements or demonstrate significant differences between groups.[8]

Challenges in Identifying the Population/Study Sample

Each evaluation must first identify the study subjects. For example, an MLP program may use a model where the healthcare providers generally identify families with legal needs and refer them to a partnering legal services program. It may seem simplest to include every patient referred to the program in a study sample. However, it may be difficult to approach every patient referred. This approach also limits evaluation of the impact of the MLP program because many patients are helped through phone consultation or by trained healthcare providers who help with legal needs but do not refer the patient for a legal intake with a lawyer. Another important point: If a study design involves the use of a comparison group, then that group ideally should look demographically similar to the population receiving MLP services. This is done to assess what changes are attributable to the program intervention (MLP) versus the normal changes the population might experience over time that are not attributable to the intervention. Generally, the neediest patients are referred to MLP; therefore, it may be hard to find a similarly needy referent group.

Theoretically (and ideally), eligible families could be randomly assigned to treatment or control conditions (for example, "treatment" might receive MLP services and the "control" would receive the general standard of care). Where MLP is meant to be the *standard of care*, it would be extremely difficult (if not impossible) to use a randomized control trial and withhold treatment from eligible patients. Even in sites where MLP is oversubscribed or where the partnership cannot meet the demands of the patient populations, randomizing patients would be ethically complex. One solution may be to use a randomized model that allows patients to receive MLP intervention "now" versus "later." This method would allow researchers to track the difference between the "now" versus "later" groups but not withhold intervention from a needy participant permanently. However, this solution may also be ethically problematic if a patient who is in urgent need of legal assistance that may benefit his or her health cannot access services because of the study limitations.

Questions for Discussion

1. What are the relative advantages and disadvantages of qualitative and quantitative studies?

2. Formulate a hypothesis about MLP that could be tested through a research study.

3. What are some of the particular challenges involved in designing a study of MLP?

Defining and Measuring MLP Outcomes

Due to the interdisciplinary nature of MLP, each involved profession (legal, medical, social work, public health, etc.) brings with it different philosophies, theories, methods, and even terminology. See Chapter 4 for further discussion of these differences. How each profession measures success and failure varies greatly. To successfully evaluate an MLP, the evaluation team must identify and choose multiple outcome measures that will appeal to the various perspectives while keeping in mind the main goals of the evaluation itself (i.e., to provide evidence for potential funders, to convince a community to adopt the program, or to convince providers to participate, etc.). The target audience influences the choice of outcomes the evaluation should measure.

Choosing Variables

Variables are discrete pieces of information to be collected that will help the research team test their hypotheses. Variables can be *independent* or *dependent*. Typically, dependent variables represent an observed phenomenon, event or outcome of interest, whereas independent variables are explanatory or predictive. Variables are characteristics or attributes of a person, thing, or phenomenon that are measurable and can take on different values.[9] Examples of variables collected in MLP evaluations include age of patient, health status, number of doctor and ER visits, presence of legal needs and access to and use of government benefits and services.

The National Center for Medical Legal Partnership (NCMLP) and MLP | Boston developed a comprehensive list of metrics (including individual variables and concepts) that measure outcomes of interest (see Table 18.2).

Example of MLP Research and Evaluation

Study Title: Pilot Study of Medical-Legal Partnership to Address Social and Legal Needs of Patients

Hypothesis: Integration of legal services into pediatric settings will increase families' awareness of and access to legal and social services, decrease barriers to healthcare for children, and improve parent-reported child health.

Methods: 36-month prospective cohort study of the impact of clinic- and hospital-based legal services. The study sample was recruited from families who received services from the Family Advocacy Program (MLP). Assessments were performed at baseline (at the initial legal intake) and six months after the closing of the legal case.

Findings: Comparison of follow-up with baseline demonstrated significantly increased proportions of families who used food and income supports and significantly decreased proportions of families avoiding healthcare due to lack of health insurance or concerns about cost. Two-thirds of respondents reported improved child health and well-being.

Limitations: Small sample size, loss to follow-up, lack of long-term follow-up, and all outcomes data were collected directly from families.

Source: Dana Weintraub, Melissa A. Rodgers, Luba Botcheva, Anna Loeb, Rachael Knight, Karina Ortega, Brooke Heymach, Megan Sandel, and Lynne Huffman, "Pilot Study of Medical-Legal Partnership to Address Social and Legal Needs of Patients," *Journal of Health Care for the Poor and Underserved* 21 (2010): 157–68.

Challenges in Defining the MLP Intervention

One factor that has likely contributed to successful expansion of the MLP model across the country is its flexibility in adapting to local contexts. Yet that very flexibility in adaptation may present a challenge to evaluation. Even within a single setting, the types of services offered by the program span a broad continuum of activities, consistent with the program leadership's commitment to the practice of preventive law.

Level of MLP Involvement

MLP is designed to provide many different interventions. As noted, the NCMLP is committed to the practice of preventive law. Consistent with that framework, a program will be more "successful" the farther upstream it is able to intervene. Intervention may take a number of different forms and exists on a continuum. At the most indirect level,

Table 18.2 MLP Target Metrics

PROGRAM PERFORMANCE	
Advocacy capacity-building in healthcare partners	• Number of healthcare workers trained • Self-reported changes in knowledge, attitudes, and behaviors (currently documented via IRB-approved needs assessment studies) • Number of patients screened for unmet legal needs by providers; percentage of healthcare affiliates total patient population screened; percentage of healthcare affiliate provider panel engaged in screening • Number of provider-focused advocacy tools designed and deployed • Rate of provider utilization of MLP-designed advocacy tools (such as utility shut-off protection form letters, housing conditions advocacy letter templates), especially those integrated into the electronic medical record • Number of distinct providers making use of advocacy tools, including triage calls • Number of instances where MLP-supported (either through an advocacy tool or a triage call) provider advocacy was successful on behalf of a patient (will require new record-keeping on the clinical side)
Legal assistance outputs (aggregated by subject matter)	• Percentage of legal matters favorably resolved • Percentage of legal matters with a neutral output • Percentage of legal matters unfavorably resolved
Legal assistance outcomes (examples)	• Monetary value of SNAP benefits secured for patient-clients • Number of housing units whose unhealthy conditions were eliminated, etc.
SOCIAL & ECONOMIC IMPACT	
Improved health outcomes	• Number of health problems eliminated (or severity thereof reduced) • Improved patient problem-solving, self-efficacy, self-mastery • Reduction in patient stress and/or anxiety • Number of health-promoting laws, policies, regulations, or practices successfully implemented with MLP support; number of low-income people affected • Number of health-harming laws, policies, regulations, or practices successfully averted with MLP support; number of low-income people affected
Improved efficiency of healthcare delivery	• Reduced patient no-show rates • Improved treatment adherence among patients
Institutional return on investment	• Reduction in rate of individual hospital readmission • Timely discharge of inpatients (reduction in number of "stuck" patients) • Revenue generation (increased patient volume) due to increased efficiency of patient medical appointments • Improved reimbursement of healthcare services
ORGANIZATIONAL HEALTH	
Program capacity built	• Number of healthcare affiliates served • Number of new staff hires made • Number of new healthcare affiliates • Number of pro bono partnerships leveraged • Number of pro bono volunteers handling cases and projects • Number of law school partnerships leveraged • Number of legal services organization partnerships leveraged • Number of student volunteers leveraged
Improved efficiency of healthcare delivery	• Number of healthcare affiliates making direct investment in services • Budget v. actuals

Note: This table is based on MLP | Boston's Program Performance Metrics (2011).

the healthcare provider may consult with the MLP lawyer to ask for guidance regarding the patient's or family's legal issue(s). In this instance, a family may not be aware of the MLP's involvement; the healthcare provider's consult with the MLP lawyer serves to help him or her determine what steps may be in order regarding the patient's legal problems. At the next level, an MLP paralegal or lawyer may determine that a more hands-on approach is needed. In this case, the family may be scheduled to meet with MLP staff for an intake interview for assessment of legal needs. Moving further down the continuum toward more direct intervention, the legal team determines the next steps. Depending on the nature of the needs and the MLP's resources to address those needs, the staff may offer legal advice and counsel, referral to a pro bono attorney, or direct representation by the MLP program in court or at an administrative agency.

At the onset of an evaluation effort, distinguishing the level of MLP involvement to be evaluated is critical to studying the nature, results, and patient satisfaction with that involvement. Although all people who receive any direct service from MLP staff are considered "treatment" or "intervention" study subjects, not all of them receive the same level of service. Even people who receive a full legal intake vary in the level of service needed and provided. Level of service can be controlled for by limiting the study sample at the beginning of the study or through analysis at the end of the study. Sometimes level of service is also called the "dose" of the intervention. Limiting the study sample is done through inclusion/exclusion criteria. For example, the research team decides only to enroll subjects who have a defined level of service, such as those who receive a full legal intake or those who had a letter written on their behalf by a provider. The research team may also choose to limit the study by the type of legal issues patient-clients have, so the data collected on the subjects are more comparable. Alternatively, the level of service, or dose, can be defined after recruitment and data collection have occurred. However, if this is done, the study team needs to use a large enough sample size so that enough people fall into each level-of-service group for meaningful data analysis.

Working with Multiple Providers and Settings within a Single Site

Some MLPs work in many divisions or departments of a hospital or community health center (CHC) or in multiple healthcare institutions. Each division and department as well as CHC has its own priorities, administrative procedures, patient populations and perspectives on MLP and its services. Not only does this adaptation affect the answers to "what is the program?", it also affects recruitment and the availability of secondary data (see the section "Determining Data Collection" for a definition of secondary data). For example, patients who obtain their or their children's primary care at a community health center will not necessarily be part of the hospital's medical records for most routine care. Gaining access to the medical records within multiple CHCs for a study entails a lengthy process involving multiple IRBs and reconciling potential differences across oversight bodies. The different community sites also affect the availability of secondary legal data. Although some MLPs have developed a centralized client tracking database, a similarly centralized record of medical data may not exist across healthcare institutions. Inconsistency of secondary data, whether from the medical record or the legal case file, makes analysis and interpretation difficult.

One response to this difficulty is strong leadership from MLP medical provider partners, both practicing physicians and healthcare organization administrators. Medical provider partners who are invested in the research can work with the records department to build in case tracking within medical documentation. This can alleviate the need to track all data proactively. This is best done at the beginning of the research process, as the team defines its hypotheses and the outcomes to be measured.

Primary Care vs. Specialties

The wide appeal of MLP speaks to both the logic of the model in general, and its adaptability to a variety of settings. MLPs have expanded to various patient populations with different disease prevalence and severity. Although demonstrating health-related outcome benefits would appear to be the holy grail of this medically based legal model, the diversity of clinical settings and the diversity of patient populations make it extremely difficult to select a specific health outcome to measure. For an asthma clinic or for the treatment of asthma patients in a primary care setting, medical outcomes may be quite clear; reliable, valid, and appropriate biomarkers are readily available. Even thorough parental report, health-related behaviors, subsequent clinical involvement, and patient or patient-family health adjustments may be measured. But for primary care more generally, with both a range of potential conditions and a population of relatively healthy and resilient patients, the range of measures and the low prevalence of reoccurrence make the use of biomarkers to evaluate program effectiveness very problematic.

For primary care populations, more general measures of health and health-related adjustments may be suitable. If priority is to be given to showing change on specific biological outcomes, we recommend that specialty clinics and/or a disease/condition-specific target population be used. Again, it is important that the research team work with the medical provider partners to determine which outcomes are most relevant in the healthcare setting. The medical team in the various subspecialties should determine the health and well-being outcomes to be studied and which of those outcomes may be affected by legal intervention, whether through direct service or system changes in the healthcare institution.

Evaluating More than Direct Service

MLPs affect more than legal assistance to patient-clients, and therefore evaluations may measure broader outcomes than individual case resolution. The preventive law model of MLP also underscores the importance of internal and external systemic advocacy. Internal systemic advocacy creates change within a healthcare or legal institution. External systemic advocacy creates change within communities or local, state, and federal agencies. Coupled with the varying levels of legal assistance, it can be a challenge to determine which aspects of the MLP model are being evaluated and what constitutes good outcomes. Some examples of the outcomes that could be tracked are knowledge, attitudes, and behavior of healthcare providers before and after legal trainings, or systems such as the number of times a utility letter to prevent a utility shutoff is generated. These types of data measures are system-wide outcomes that do not involve individual legal service.

Determining Data Collection

Data collection techniques allow us to systematically collect information about the subjects we are studying. Techniques include collecting available information (i.e., from an existing client database or electronic medical record), observation, interviews, written questionnaires or surveys and focus group discussions.[10] Data collection can also be categorized as primary or secondary data. *Primary* data is data collected directly by the research team through methods such as direct observation, surveys or interviews. *Secondary* data is collected by someone other than the research team (by a hospital, legal aid office or organization such as the U.S. Census, the National Health Survey, or organizational records). Both kinds of data collection may be used in a study.

Challenges Collecting Data

Primary Data

Primary data for MLP evaluations are most often gathered with a survey administered to individuals. The survey consists of questions that obtain the data for the defined variables that measure the outcomes to be studied. When the outcome of interest is more complex than a yes-or-no question, it might require a composite of variables to accurately identify and measure the outcome. Some research teams may decide to develop new questions; others may opt to use already validated sets of questions from existing studies. These composites of questions that measure a concept are generally referred to as data "instruments." Consider the concept of stress, for example. It is inadequate to simply ask a person whether he or she is experiencing stress in a given moment. Perhaps that person always feels stress. Additionally, how people define stress may vary from person to person. To uniformly and consistently measure a person's level of stress, a researcher must clearly identify and define terms and concepts.

Fortunately, many behavioral and psychosocial concepts already have existing instruments composed of multiple questions/variables that have been tested repeatedly and have established *measurement validity*, which is the degree to which a variable actually captures what it strives to measure.[11] Table 18.3 provides a list of validated instruments that are frequently used and might be helpful for program/intervention evaluation. Finally, the Institute of Medicine (IOM) recently recommended that the HHS develop and implement a standardized set of health outcome indicators, as well as indicators of community health.[12] This set of indicators will be another invaluable measurement tool for researchers studying MLP.

The particular challenge with using established instruments has to do with their validity. Often, initial validity measures are based on a limited group of people, whose sociodemographic background might be very different from the population an MLP serves. Instruments also might not be valid in languages other than English. They may be too general or too specific, or they may not measure the right time frame. For example, there are those that measure a person's level of stress in the moment (or at the time of the survey), those that measure the level of stress of a person in the past month, and then those that measure a person's overall disposition and whether they are just "stressed" in general.

Secondary Data

Secondary data have already been collected and must be extracted for research purposes. Although this sounds ideal, use of secondary data presents its own challenges because these data were potentially collected for a different purpose, to answer different research questions than those of the current study, or for nonresearch purposes.

Collecting *secondary legal data* presents several challenges to the research team. The collection of secondary legal data is contingent on each MLP's database and/or record-

Table 18.3 Examples of Instruments Used in Evaluation of MLPs

Instrument	Outcome Measured	Authors
Perceived Stress Scale (PSS)	Stress	Sheldon Cohen, Tom Kamarck, Robin Mermelstein, "A Global Measure of Perceived Stress," *Journal of Health and Social Behavior*, 24, no. 4 (1983): 385–96.
Mastery Scale	Self-efficacy	Leonard I. Pearlin, Carmi Schooler, "The Structure of Coping," *Journal of Health and Social Behavior*, 19, no. 1 (1978): 2–21.
Consumer Assessment of Healthcare Providers and Systems (CAHPS)	Physician communication with patient and guardian	
Measure Yourself Concerns and Wellbeing (MYCaW)	Concerns in life	Charlotte Paterson, Kate Thomas, Andrew Manasse, et al., "Measure Yourself Concerns and Wellbeing (MYCaW): An Individualized Questionnaire for Evaluating Outcome in Cancer Support Care that Includes Complementary Therapies," *Complementary Therapies in Medicine*, 15, no. 1 (2007): 38–45. Elizabeth F. Juniper, "Can Quality of Life Be Quantified?," *Clinical & Experimental Allergy Reviews* 2, no. 2 (2002): 57–60.
Family Empowerment Scale (FES)	Family empowerment for families with children with disabilities	Paul E. Koren, Neal DeChillo, Barbara J. Friesen, "Measuring Empowerment in Families Whose Children Have Emotional Disabilities: A Brief Questionnaire," *Rehabilitation Psychology*, 37, no. 4 (1992): 305–21.
SF-12	Quality of life	John E. Ware Jr., Mark Kosinski, Susan D. Keller, "A 12-Item Short Form Health Survey: Construction of Scales and Preliminary Tests of Validity and Reliability," *Medical Care*, 34, no. 3 (1996): 220–33.

keeping system and their capacity to track legal outcomes. Each MLP has a unique system for entering data, storing data and recording outcomes for patient-clients. Many MLPs are based in legal aid offices that typically have a case management tracking system. That system may not be designed for research. Therefore, research staff should gain an in-depth understanding of how an MLP database is structured and what their systems and procedures are before designing and conducting an evaluation study.

There are several challenges to collecting secondary legal data from an MLP client database. For instance, the availability of complete and detailed legal data is contingent on the time dedicated to data entry and on minimal human error in data entry. Legal staff must enter data in addition to their other duties, which can include research into legal issues on behalf of patient-clients, advocacy work, training activities, and relationship building with legal and healthcare partners. Data entry poses an extra burden on an already burdened staff.

Additionally, the quality of each MLP's record of legal outcomes for patient-clients creates unique challenges. Legal teams may experience many difficulties following up with patient-clients for these outcomes. For instance, a patient-client might be referred by their healthcare provider for assistance with their application for SNAP (food stamps) benefits. The MLP legal team will help the patient-client with his or her application. After this point, the legal team may never know whether the patient-client's application was denied or approved and, if approved, the amount of benefits received. Variability across MLPs exists with regard to systematic follow-up and communication with healthcare providers or patient-clients about these outcomes. Without these outcomes, improvements in legal outcomes are difficult to prove in a research study.

MLP clients, however, rarely have only one legal need. Based on prior work with similar patient populations, it is reasonable to assume that most families referred to MLP for service will have multiple issues.[13] Intake screening asks directly about the range of issues (i.e., housing, public benefits, immigration, etc.) a family confronts. Typically, these include the legal matter or issue for which the family became an MLP client. However, as we examine the impact of MLP on the family and not necessarily on the matter in isolation from the constellation of issues that the family confronts, the other problem areas may show no or limited change.

The timing of the study can also limit an MLP's ability to collect data related to the outcomes achieved for patient-clients. Many legal matters that MLP lawyers address may take a long time to resolve. Matters involving educational rights or a family law issue, for example, may take a year or more of advocacy work to reach a resolution. This means that for many study participants, their presenting legal issue may not be resolved at the time of data extraction, and no outcomes are available for collection from the client database. The research team should keep this in mind as they determine the study period of an evaluation or research study.

Last, the research staff must acquire permission from each MLP to access the legal database. The medical and legal professions have distinct ethical standards and practices (see section on "Ethical Considerations in Research" for further discussion). Any research study must respect and operate under both sets of standards. To gain access to patient-client legal records, a question explicitly asking for permission to do so can be included in the consent form. Any future evaluation efforts need to work with the MLP early in the research process to gain access to patient-client legal records in a way that meets the ethical standards of both the medical and legal professions. Consideration should also be given to developing a standard release form for MLP patient-clients to sign to permit sharing of their legal record for purposes of research, evaluation, and program management and the conditions under which such access and use may be granted. It may be possible to analyze legal case records by aggregation of outcomes to ensure anonymity and protect confidentiality. If researchers aggregate results to ensure anonymity, it is crucial to decide which outcomes will be extracted from the case records ahead of time and only extract those outcomes. Also, it is important to have sufficient numbers of records extracted so legal outcomes cannot be tied back to specific patients.

The availability of *secondary medical data* depends on each MLP's relationship with and integration into a hospital, health center, or clinic. These data were designed to track medical course of disease or healthcare utilization, but were not necessarily designed for MLP research purposes and therefore may be complicated to access. Confidentiality and HIPAA concerns associated with this data are discussed in the "Ethical Considerations in Research" section.

Other considerations associated with using medical data include the following issues.

- When the MLP is comprised of multiple hospitals and health centers, the research team may need to work with different electronic medical record (EMR) systems and platforms. Each system may have a different format and therefore slightly different data. For example, race and ethnicity categories might be different; this will require some cleaning and reformatting of the data.

- The nature of the relationships between outcomes (medical and legal) should guide which time intervals are the most appropriate for data collection. For example, in the case where a child who has asthma lives in a home with mold and an MLP is helping the family enforce their right to require the landlord to remove it, medical improvement for the child will not necessarily take place as soon as the mold is removed and may require follow up on medical outcomes three months after MLP intervention.

- Sites must also consider the timing of data extraction required by the IRB. Because delays may be an inevitable part of the recruitment process (described in more detail shortly), the intervals approved for data extraction should be sufficiently broad to permit data to be collected for the relevant intervals. Also note that data may be abstracted for different intervals, depending on the relationship(s) to be examined.

Example of MLP Research and Evaluation

Study Title: Development of a Brief Questionnaire to Identify Families in Need of Legal Advocacy to Improve Child Health

Hypothesis: The medical-legal advocacy screening questionnaire (MASQ) will screen families for referral more effectively than the clinical interview alone.

Methods: A convenience sample of parents seen at healthcare partner practices of Family Advocates of Central Massachusetts (FACM) was recruited to complete the MASQ before a routine visit. Physicians independently and blindly assessed the families' need for referral. Both sensitivity and specificity of the questionnaire and provider assessment were calculated.

Findings: The MASQ would likely identify more patients who would accept referral than provider assessment alone.

Limitations: The study sample was limited to one MLP. Because child and family demographics are incomplete, the performance of MASQ could not be assessed in different subpopulations. There is no gold standard tool for assessing the presence of legal issues, so the MASQ performance could not be compared.

Source: David Keller, Nathan Jones, Judith A. Savageau, and Suzanne B. Cashman, "Development of a Brief Questionnaire to Identify Families in Need of Legal Advocacy to Improve Child Health," *Ambulatory Pediatrics* 8, no. 4 (2008): 266–9.

Questions for Discussion

1. What are some of the challenges of defining and evaluating MLP as an intervention? How can researchers address these challenges?

2. Discuss the difference between primary and secondary data sources, and give an example of each. Describe one limitation of each type of data source.

The Conduct of Research and Evaluation

Recruitment

Depending on the study design, the research team needs to take a number of steps to recruit potential participants. The basic steps include identifying potential participants in the population, assessing their eligibility and enrolling participants by obtaining informed consent. Eligibility should be assessed on inclusion and exclusion criteria. *Inclusion criteria* are characteristics a participant must have to be eligible, whereas *exclusion criteria* are characteristics that do not allow a person to participate in the study. For example, participants that do not speak a certain language may be excluded if the questionnaire cannot be translated into that language. For certain study designs, comparison or control groups must also be identified and enrolled to assess differences in outcomes. For transparency of the recruitment process and to record the enrollment and retention of study subjects, it is recommended that numbers are reported in a flow-chart (see Appendix 18.4 for an example of a recruitment flow-chart).

The Identification Process

Study recruitment, accrual and retention are important issues, and achieving the necessary number of consenting study subjects to participate to adequately measure outcomes can be challenging. Many obstacles exist due to characteristics of the study population, institutional culture or structure, logistics (time, travel, etc.) and interest or trust. Some of the obstacles to recruitment can be addressed in study design, but many can be addressed in the recruitment process itself.

One major challenge to recruitment is that families may interact with the MLP to varying degrees. Therefore, research teams must understand an MLP's referral and advocacy process before identifying a point of contact between the study and eligible cases. Research teams should also use program and legal staff in the evaluation's recruitment strategy. However, using the legal team as the study's first contact with potential participants may be problematic. For example, if legal staff members are asked to talk with patients about the study immediately following regular legal service provision, this may pose an added burden to the work they do. This kind of change in procedure may be in opposition to their standard of practice. Additionally, because it is usually not a part of the legal staff's regular workflow, they may sometimes forget to ask a client to participate. One way to address this specific issue is to conduct weekly reviews of the database with legal staff to identify potential cases that were missed and potential process challenges.

Furthermore, when patients come to see their healthcare provider, they have limited time to engage with the provider to address all of their questions and problems. A healthcare provider may not be inclined to give permission for the research team to speak with a patient because of time constraints. Although the provider may grant permission to contact the patient, he or she may not always have contact information readily at hand. Study staff could follow-up with providers to obtain contact information, but some providers may not be responsive, and these patients may be lost to recruitment. If study staff is granted access to the electronic medical record, they can relieve some burden on the provider by offering to look up the patient's contact information if the provider can only give a minimal amount of information (e.g., the medical record number, the name, and/or date of birth).

If the research team decides to conduct a research study involving controls (or comparison subjects), the team will also need to devise troubleshooting procedures for recruiting controls. In theory, controls never have any MLP contact, either directly or indirectly through their healthcare providers. The process of their recruitment will be very different from the recruitment of MLP participants. Potential control subjects could be identified through the medical record system and by matching to the MLP case type (subject) based on the participating MLP patient-client's gender, race, language, date of visit to the healthcare provider and/or type of visit. However, the greater the number of criteria used to match, the fewer the number of potential comparisons are likely to be identified. It is important to consider the number of characteristics one can realistically afford to compare and how that might affect recruitment. If possible, testing the matching criteria with hypothetical cases (using both common and rare combinations) will reveal how restrictive the criteria are before recruitment begins, allowing one to adjust accordingly.

The characteristics of the patient population of the healthcare institution will also affect the ease with which the study team can identify control subjects. For instance, language can be a limiting factor in identifying controls. If a healthcare institution does not serve enough speakers of a certain language, the recruitment of controls who also speak this language will be quite difficult. Study teams may want to limit study recruitment to certain language populations. Furthermore, a disconnect may exist between the patient's identified race and/or ethnicity and that recorded in the patient's medical or legal record. These discrepancies can also create challenges to identifying and recruiting well-matched control subjects.

One of the best solutions to recruitment is to think about integrating research staff into the MLP team. This can allow research assistants to work on multiple research questions and evaluations at a time, recruit patients either during one-on-one interaction with legal staff, or quickly contact a patient or provider after an interaction to recruit a patient. Also, integrating research staff into the MLP team allows healthcare and legal staff to feel more comfortable referring patient-clients to a known staff member for research purposes.

The Outreach Process

Making contact with low-income patient-clients who have unstable financial and housing situations for study recruitment can be a challenging endeavor in many respects (see a more detailed discussion in "Research Involving Vulnerable Individuals and Families"). Low-income patient-clients may be difficult to contact because their phone service may be disconnected or because they work irregular hours. Some particularly vulnerable participants, such as domestic violence victims, may live in shelters, which may present confidentiality concerns. Study staff may need to adjust recruitment hours to fit the lives of potential study subjects. One solution can be to have dedicated times to call families at night or during weekends to ensure contact can be made. Another solution is to provide phone cards as incentives to improve access to participants with cell phones.

The Consent Process

Once potential participants have stated that they are willing to hear more about the study, staff must then engage in a lengthy consent process with patients. If the research team recruits participants in person, they can provide a copy of the consent form to the prospective participant and can review it with them, highlighting the most important aspects of the study and their rights as participants. Similarly, in a face-to-face interaction, the staff member may be in a better position to identify areas that could require further clarification and answer any questions that may arise. If consent is gained by phone, the IRB requires that the entire form be read to eligible subjects aloud. The required language of the consent form is often technical and may be intimidating, even in studies involving no more than minimal risk. This process is time-consuming and some prospective participants may decide it is not worth listening to and hang up. Because this process is required by the IRB, there is not a good solution to this problem. However, to minimize the challenges associated obtaining consent, research staff should be well trained to interact with potential participants, interpret the form using common language and address concerns voiced and identified through body language or over the phone.

Some MLPs use research staff members who are dedicated to obtaining consent from research, alleviating the burden on legal staff to do this. This can ensure consistency of information, culturally competent interactions and better likelihood of people agreeing to participate.

Ethical Considerations in Research

When conducting research, there are numerous other issues and challenges that an evaluation team may experience as a result of researchers' responsibilities to protect human subjects. Some of these are outlined here.

Institutional Review Board (IRB)

Research is a regulated industry, and since the notorious instances of the Nuremberg Trials for Nazi prison experimentation during World War II, the Tuskegee syphilis study, effects of irradiated milk on children at the Fernald School, and others, government and international agencies have set about to protect human subjects from research risks. The regulations governing the protection of human subjects are promulgated by the U.S. Department of Health and Human Services (Title 45 CFR Part 46). Institutions that engage in human subjects research must have a duly executed *federal-wide assurance (FWA)* that indicates their commitment to comply with the federally articulated requirements for constituting and supporting a review team; conduct training and ensure the ongoing qualifications of all key personnel; review, oversee, and report on all covered research; and document and maintain records for all substantive and administrative procedures.[14]

Prior to conducting research that involves human subjects in any context, research teams must develop a study protocol and obtain approval from an IRB (or Human Subject Committee, as they are sometimes called). A protocol includes an in-depth description of the study, including the hypotheses, the procedures, forms, surveys, team composition and more. Once developed, the protocol is reviewed by the board. This process varies in length depending on the risk involved to the human subjects and depending on the IRB. Generally it takes anywhere from two to six weeks from submission for the IRB to approve the study protocol. Researchers should plan ahead and allot enough time for the process because no study activities may begin until the protocol is approved.

Not all MLP sites, such as community health centers and legal services agencies, will have a formal IRB to review research. These sites may contract with private companies that review research protocols to protect research subjects.

When an IRB Is Required: Evaluation vs. Quality Improvement

The requirement for IRB review varies depending on intent to disseminate findings, risks to subjects, confidentiality considerations, and whether the service is new. If research or evaluation is conducted with the goal of disseminating knowledge outside of the institution, then it is subject to IRB approval. It becomes more complicated however, with a formative evaluation that can also be considered quality improvement. If the intent is to gather information for improvement of service delivery and findings are kept in house, then IRB review is generally unnecessary. When in doubt, it is best to consult with the IRB.

Working in Interdisciplinary Teams

IRB review and approval is just one of the many legal and ethical issues that affect the evaluation of MLP. There are practice standards and regulatory frameworks within which clinical service provision takes place. In many ways, interdisciplinary research is no less challenging than interdisciplinary practice.

The first step in the Centers for Disease Control and Prevention's (CDC's) widely disseminated program evaluation framework is to identify and engage stakeholders.[15] Rossi et al. define stakeholders as "individuals, groups or organizations that have a significant interest in how well a program functions."[16] Not all the professionals who are invested in a program will have the same perspective or expectations about the program. They may not agree on what constitutes appropriate goals and objectives, and even when they do, they may not agree on the approach(es) that should be used to achieve them.

Clearly articulated means and ends are critical to developing program models and, in turn, for creating approaches to evaluate them and for research design and measurement. Yet even where such agreement can be found, the research and evaluation must take into account the professional ethics and statutory requirements of key stakeholders. MLPs have numerous stakeholders, but chief among these groups are lawyers and healthcare providers. Because these professions have such strict professional rules governing confidentiality of patient and client information, bridging the gap between these professions for purposes of research can prove challenging.

Confidentiality

The practices of medicine and law both adhere to strict confidentiality standards. For U.S. lawyers, the American Bar Association's Center for Professional Responsibility has enumerated model rules of professional conduct. Rule 1.6, "Confidentiality of Information," specifies the lawyer's obligation not to reveal information related to representation of a client without the client's informed consent except under six circumstances, none of which pertain to research.[17] Within medicine, ethical professional principles governing patient confidentiality have been codified and mandated in the Health Insurance Portability and Accountability Act (HIPAA) of 1996 (P.L. 104-191). The Privacy Rule in the Code of Federal Regulations further regulates the use and disclosure of Protected Health Information.[18] See Chapter 6 for a detailed discussion of the rules of confidentiality for lawyers and healthcare providers.

Informed consent for release of personally identifiable medical and legal information should be part of the research protocol, and the language used must be suitable to both professional groups' standards. The IRB process generally ensures that HIPAA regulations are followed and meet the ethical standards of the medical community. The legal services community has yet to determine a standard for protecting confidentiality when clients participate in research. Some MLP programs have created separate consent forms for the release of legal information specific to a research project. Although this is clearly an issue to address, it has not been resolved and requires careful consideration.

Incentives for Research Subjects

Understandably, IRBs need to be sure that eligible individuals are not coerced into participation through the recruitment process. Because many MLP evaluations will likely recruit from economically disadvantaged populations, the IRB needs to make a subjective judgment as to what level of incentive would be coercive insofar as it would be extremely difficult for a potential subject with financial needs to turn down a cash incentive. This determination is also influenced by considering the amount that would constitute fair remuneration and/or a stipend for the time involved, potential burden, and any additional costs incurred by the individual who participates in the study as well as the cost implications for the project budget.

Research Involving Vulnerable Individuals and Families

MLPs seek to address the unmet legal needs of the most vulnerable populations. The realities of vulnerable families' lives create unique challenges for researching and evaluating an MLP. The very issues that MLPs address (e.g., food and/or energy insecurity, housing conditions, immigration status) can themselves become barriers to recruitment and retention.

Consent without Legal Authority

During recruitment, the research team may encounter children in the care of individuals who do not have legal authority over the child. For instance, a grandmother who does not have legal custody of the child but is in effect the child's caretaker, may not be recruited into the study because she is not authorized to consent for the child to be a subject of research. On the other hand, foster parents have the power to make medical decisions on behalf of a foster child; therefore, these parents could be considered eligible for recruitment into the study. Future research should find ways to include children in nontraditional families in research studies. This issue is not unique to MLP; review of the research literature may reveal some applicable recruitment strategies to address this concern.

Language Diversity

The diversity of languages spoken by MLP clients can also present challenges for the case recruitment. Researchers should examine the specific program's case makeup for language diversity. If a substantial portion of the patient-client population speaks languages other than English and Spanish, the research team may consider expanding recruitment to other languages. However, researchers would also have to consider the additional cost of hiring and maintaining staff who speak those additional languages and the implications for instrument translation/back-translation as well as administration.

Immigration Status

In the current political and legal climate in which undocumented immigrants fear being deported if their status is revealed to authorities, immigrants may be particularly wary of participating in any study, regardless of whether their status issue is explicitly raised. All future consent forms should include information about confidentiality, and confidentiality can be reemphasized with individuals who express concerns about their immigration status. Immigrants with status concerns will probably be more comfortable participating in anonymous studies where they can be assured that the risk of identification is minimal. Although the risk may be minimal in a confidential study, however, identifiable information may be collected creating some risk. In this case, it is important to clearly explain to the prospective participant who will have access to the data and specifically what it will be used for (which is required in the consent process) and accept that the person may choose not to participate.

Housing

The instability of a family's housing can also affect recruitment and retention. MLP families and controls may be living in transitional housing or shelters, may be "doubling up" with other families or may be on waiting lists for public/low-income housing. All of these situations make the execution of an MLP evaluation more difficult. Families may not receive initial study information due to an incorrect address or because they have moved. The chances of missing a family can be minimized if recruitment takes place at the health or legal services center. In general, when initial contact is made in person, there are increased chances of enrollment and more solid data collection.

Families' housing situations can also affect retention. If a family does not have a stable address, they may not receive consent forms, study information and/or study incentives to which they are entitled. Families may be lost from the study because staff cannot reach them. Future studies will have to develop creative solutions to ensure that patients receive study materials through the mail and to reduce loss to follow-up due to housing instability.

Phones

Numerous barriers may be encountered by study staff related to participants' cellular phones, which will likely be the preferred method of communication for the majority of study participants. Because many families change phone providers and numbers frequently, phone numbers in legal and medical records may be out of date. Phones may also be temporarily out of service for some families who purchase pay-as-you-go cellular minutes and wait until the beginning of each month to add minutes to their accounts. Even if a mobile phone has available minutes, researchers often encounter full voicemail boxes or find that the participant screens calls and does not answer. Future studies may recommend free voicemail services to study participants. This would provide a way for staff to maintain contact with participants.

Questions for Discussion

1. What challenges do researchers face in recruiting subjects for MLP research studies? In what ways does integrating researchers into MLP staff help to overcome these challenges?

2. What are some of the unique challenges in research involving vulnerable individuals and populations? Can you think of ways to overcome these challenges that are not mentioned in the chapter?

3. How might studies of the impact of MLP be important to institutional and policy change?

Conclusion

Continued research is critical for MLPs to measure the impact they have on patients and their families, public health, and the healthcare and legal systems. This requires medical and legal service providers to work closely with other professionals engaged in evaluation research to answer a wide array of questions regarding how MLPs may impact health and well-being, clinical workforce responses to the social determinants of health and legal services as part of medical homes.

Though challenges exist in measuring the impact of all levels of MLP intervention, from direct legal service to public policy change, it will be crucial to find new evaluation methods to define this impact if fuller implementation of MLP is to happen. Expanding collaboration among researchers and MLP teams will provide the level of evidence needed to identify the benefits of MLP. Many MLP sites across the country are currently engaged in research and evaluation projects. Although each varies in its structure, the demographics of the population it serves, and the resources available for research, these studies will contribute greatly to the knowledge base and literature on MLP effectiveness.

Note

Rebecca Lawrence and Chong-Min Fu contributed to all writing, conception and execution of this chapter. Megan Sandel oversaw development and revision of the chapter with Rebecca Lawrence and Chong-Min Fu. Ed DeVos helped develop the categories of research at the inception of the chapter and contributed to early drafts.

---

1. U.S. Department of Health and Human Services, Title 45, CFR Part 46. Protection of Human Subjects, http://www.hhs.gov/ohrp/humansubjects/guidance/45cfr46.htm.

2. William M. Trochim, *The Research Methods Knowledge Base*, 2nd ed. (version current as of October 20, 2006), http://www.socialresearchmethods.net/kb/.

3. Ibid.

4. Corlien M.Varkevisser, Ann Templeton Brownlee, Indra Pathmanathan, eds., *Designing and Conducting Health Systems Research Projects, Volume 1: Proposal Development and Fieldwork* (Amsterdam: KIT, 2004): 86.

5. Ibid., 198.

6. Ibid.

7. Ibid.

8. Ibid., 208.

9. Ibid., 100.

10. Ibid., 144–53.

11. John M. Last, ed., *A Dictionary of Epidemiology* (Oxford: Oxford University Press, 1995), 171.

12. Institute of Medicine, "For the Public's Health: The Role of Measurement in Action and Accountability" (Washington, DC: National Academy of Sciences, 2010).

13. Mark Hansen, "Between a Rock and a Hard Place: The Prevalence and Severity of Unmet Legal Needs in a Pediatric Emergency Department Setting," Medical Legal Partnership for Children, Boston Medical Center (April 2008), http://www.medical-legalpartnership.org/sites/default/files/page/Between%20a%20Rock%20and%20A%20Hard%20Place(2).pdf.

14. U.S. Department of Health and Human Services, "Federal Wide Assurance," http://www.hhs.gov/ohrp/assurances/assurances/filasurt.html

15. U.S. Department of Health and Humans Services, Centers for Disease Control and Prevention, "Framework for Program Evaluation in Public Health," *Morbidity and Mortality Weekly Report (MMWR)* 48 (1999).

16. P. H. Rossi, M. W. Lipsey, H. E. Freeman, *Evaluation: A Systematic Approach* (Thousand Oaks, CA: Sage, 2004).

17. American Bar Association, Model Rule 1.6, http://www.abanet.org/cpr/mrpc/rule_1_6.html.

18. 45 CFR Part 160 (and Subparts A and E of Part 164).

Chapter 19

Looking Ahead: Opportunities for Medical-Legal Partnership in the Era of Healthcare Reform

Joshua Greenberg, JD
Joel Teitelbaum, JD, LLM

Given the central role that healthcare—and the enormous cost often associated with it—plays in the lives of just about everyone, healthcare policy and reform top many public opinion polls asking about Americans' greatest concerns.[1] In 2009, governments, businesses, and individuals collectively spent $2.5 trillion on healthcare, an amount equal to just over 17 percent of the country's gross domestic product[2] and a number that far exceeds the expenditures of every other country. As of the beginning of 2010, more than 50 million Americans were uninsured, with many more millions underinsured.[3] The World Health Organization ranks the United States as 72nd among member states in terms of overall level of health.[4]

Out of these and other sobering facts sprung the Patient Protection and Affordable Care Act (the Affordable Care Act, or ACA).[5] Over time, this hugely complex federal law could effectively reorder most aspects of the U.S. healthcare system and, if fully implemented, could stabilize the health insurance system and make insurance newly available and affordable to millions of Americans. Furthermore, although the law's reforms of health insurance and the markets through which it is sold have garnered much of the public's and political establishment's initial attention, the ACA also reforms healthcare quality, the healthcare workforce, health financing, health information systems and other key elements of the healthcare system.

Long before passage of the ACA, some states and healthcare organizations had been experimenting with reform efforts. These include a range of activities focused on, for example, expanding coverage, containing costs, developing more integrated care models such as patient-centered medical homes and more effectively managing chronic disease. As implementation of the ACA moves forward, states will be at the forefront of innovative systems design. Given the scope of the ACA and the fundamental reordering of the health system it aims to engineer, the environment for innovative delivery models, such as medical-legal partnership (MLP), is ripe.

The purpose of this chapter is to provide an overview of healthcare reform trends, including an overview of the ACA and state and local efforts, and to explore the potential role that MLP may play in reform initiatives as well as the opportunities for MLP brought about by these changes.

Key Reforms in the Affordable Care Act

The key to the many reforms envisioned in the ACA is a fundamental reordering of the relationships that lie at the heart of the healthcare system. Individuals, providers, insurers, employers, governments and others will be forced to alter normative behaviors in response to the legal and policy changes brought about by the law. Generally speaking, these behavioral changes will result from four major changes in the ACA, plus several other less fundamental shifts.[6]

1. The first major change is a requirement, known as the "individual mandate," that individuals maintain "minimum essential health coverage"[7] or face specified financial penalties. The individual mandate is perhaps the most important provision in the ACA because it creates a large risk pool of premium-paying individuals that operates as the quid pro quo to insurers forced to accept many other insurance market reforms present in the ACA. For individuals with incomes between 100 and 400 percent of the federal poverty level—that is, those likely unable to purchase the type of minimum coverage mandated by the ACA—and who do not qualify for Medicaid or have access to employer-sponsored health benefits, subsidies are made available.[8]

2. The second fundamental change key to health system reordering are reforms that prohibit or curtail existing health insurer and health plan practices (with exceptions for what are known in the ACA as "grandfathered" health plans[9]). Included among the many examples of these reforms are prohibiting the use of preexisting condition exclusions and discriminatory enrollment practices based on an individual's health status; guaranteeing the availability of health insurance and the renewability of an individual's existing insurance; requiring coverage of certain preventive screening and immunization services recommended by the federal government; and guaranteeing coverage for dependent children (married or otherwise) who are under age 26.[10]

3. The third key change is the creation of state health insurance "exchanges," the purpose of which are to establish stronger and more regulated markets for the purchase of individual and small group health plan products.[11]

4. The final major reform is expanded eligibility for coverage under the Medicaid program for all U.S. citizens and legal immigrants with incomes below 133 percent of the federal poverty level.[12]

Beyond these very visible changes, the ACA also includes dozens of other reforms and new programs; there is virtually no aspect of the healthcare system that goes untouched. Medicare, CHIP, healthcare quality, public health practice, health disparities, community health centers, healthcare fraud and abuse, comparative effectiveness research, the health workforce, health information technology, long-term care and more all receive attention by the ACA.[13] See Appendix 19.1 for an overview of some of the ACA's key provisions and Chapter 2 for a detailed discussion of some of the expansions under the ACA that will benefit low-income populations.

Nonetheless, there remain some individuals who will not benefit from the new law. Undocumented immigrants and individuals who are ineligible for subsidies under the new law will continue to have difficulty accessing affordable coverage. Even the newly eligible may encounter access problems as the ACA does not dramatically expand the number of healthcare providers, particularly those who accept Medicaid. Of course, it also remains to be seen whether legal challenges brought by states and individuals will lead to the repeal of some of the provisions underpinning these reforms.[14]

Anticipated Health Reform Trends: Federal and State Changes

Although there is no question that the ACA will make significant changes to healthcare policy and practice, the complexity of the law and the extended timeline for implementation mean that changes in policy and practice will unfold over many years. In the meantime, states continue their own experiments in reforming the delivery system, with an increased impetus to do so given the federal changes and the potential to capture federal investments in their reform efforts. Additionally, the healthcare marketplace has already been consolidating in many places with the development of comprehensive, integrated delivery systems and provider organizations alongside changes in the financial and clinical relationships between payers and providers. Finally, there are fundamental changes occurring within healthcare organizations themselves, resulting from enhanced access to information technology and a growing awareness of systemic approaches to managing care.

Given these factors, we can reasonably anticipate dramatic changes in at least four areas of healthcare over the next several years. These are described here.

Patterns of Insurance Coverage

Patterns of insurance coverage will fundamentally change in the coming years. The ACA aims to cover an additional 32 million people in the United States.[15] It provides financing and subsidies to individuals and businesses to purchase coverage in the private market and creates a hierarchy of exchange-eligible plans that can be purchased with these subsidies. The establishment of health insurance exchanges throughout the country will make access to information about available health coverage and prices more transparent, and will theoretically reduce market barriers to care. In many cases, these changes will depend on effective state-based implementation efforts. Under the new law, states have a great deal of flexibility to evaluate their coverage gaps and to design more comprehensive systems to fill those gaps. As discussed shortly, expansions in coverage will occur on several fronts. Figure 19.1 provides additional detail about coverage expansions under the ACA.

Private Insurance

The ACA makes significant alterations in private insurance regulation at the federal level. The phased elimination of preexisting condition exclusions and annual and lifetime limits as well as the opportunity for young adults to maintain coverage through their parents' health plans will create new private coverage opportunities for previously "uninsurable" individuals and families. These coverage protections will be directly beneficial to some of the populations described in this book. Specifically, the elimination of preexisting conditions exclusions and coverage caps should benefit patients with cancer and HIV, as well as other chronic diseases. Extended coverage for young adults should significantly reduce the percentage of uninsured 18–26-year-olds (see Chapter 15).

Medicaid

At the same time, almost half of the newly insured will be covered through a dramatic expansion of the Medicaid program. (See Chapter 2 for discussion of Medicaid expansions under the ACA.) This approach will create both opportunities and challenges for state Medicaid officials to find, enroll, and provide care to a previously uninsured population

Figure 19.1 Coverage under Health Reform, 2014

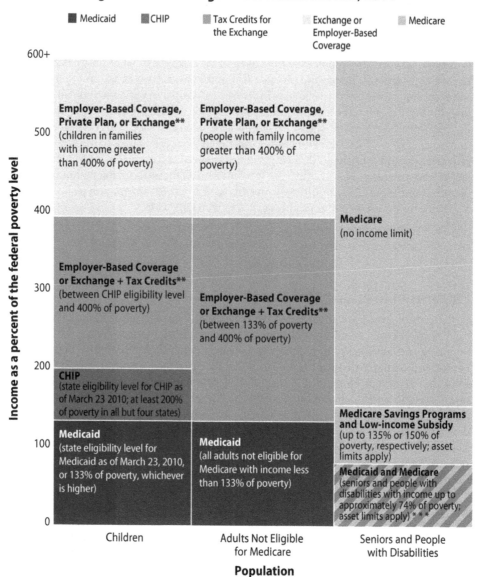

Notes: * This table does not reflect Medicaid eligibility for long-term services and supports such as nursing home, other institutional, or home- and community-based care, which will continue to vary by state. Health reform includes several programs that give states incentives to expand Medicaid home- and community-based services. Additionally, it establishes a new, voluntary long-term services insurance program that will be available to everyone.

** Employer-Based Coverage, Private Plan, or Exchange: People with employer-based coverage or individual private coverage can keep that coverage if they want. However, if the costs of participating in the employer's coverage are too high (or if the employer's plan pays less than 60 percent of the cost of covered benefits), people can instead purchase coverage through the exchange. If their incomes are below 400 percent of poverty and they buy coverage through the exchange, they may also be eligible for subsidies in the form of tax credits. (See Families USA, *A Summary of the Health Reform Law*, for details.)

*** During the two-year period when people with disabilities receiving SSDI are ineligible for Medicare coverage, they are eligible for Medicaid if their income is less than 133 percent of poverty.
Source: Families USA, *A Summary of the Health Reform Law* (April 2011).

that by definition is low-income and may generally experience other social and environmental barriers to care. MLPs have a key role in identifying newly eligible individuals and ensuring that they are enrolled.

There have been (and continue to be) numerous Medicaid expansion demonstration projects at the state level through waivers granted by the secretary of Health and Human Services.[16] These will inform effective outreach strategies combined with the new Medicaid expansion, the elimination of barriers to enrollment and retention and workable approaches to care management for vulnerable populations. Other lessons learned about challenges to maintaining coverage resulting from state fiscal crises,[17] the extreme vulnerability of safety net providers and the difficulties experienced by more traditional payers in managing care for low-income populations[18] will inform the expansion of Medicaid under the ACA and strategies for sustaining coverage for vulnerable populations.

New Models of Care

New models of care are likely to develop as a result of reform efforts. The ACA is replete with demonstration projects and care delivery pilots. Many of these proposals draw on existing work at the state and local levels. Included in the law is funding for the development of accountable care organizations (ACOs), patient-centered medical homes, chronic disease management programs and public health/wellness initiatives. In almost every case, the impetus of the law is for increased collaboration among providers, reorganization of the delivery system to have a more "patient-centered" focus and an enhanced emphasis on keeping patients healthy rather than treating them when they are sick. Even if the federal law were to be scaled back as a result of current repeal efforts, the business model for healthcare is increasingly moving in these new directions.

Integrated Patient-Centered Preventive Care Models

In recent years, a number of models of care have been introduced that focus on a more integrated, patient-centered approach to prevention, quality enhancement and cost savings. Two of the models that are particularly relevant to MLPs are highlighted here. The ACA provides support for expanding these models.

Patient-Centered Medical Home

The American Academy of Family Physicians (AAFP), American Academy of Pediatrics (AAP), American College of Physicians (ACP) and the American Osteopathic Association (AOA) developed "Joint Principles of the Patient-Centered Medical Home" in 2007. They describe the Patient-Centered Medical Home (PC-MH) as "an approach to providing comprehensive primary care for children, youth and adults." They explain the key principles as follows:

Personal physician: each patient has an ongoing relationship with a personal physician trained to provide first contact and continuous and comprehensive care.

Physician-directed medical practice: the personal physician leads a team of individuals at the practice level who collectively take responsibility for the ongoing care of patients.

Whole person orientation: the personal physician is responsible for providing for all the patient's health care needs or taking responsibility for appropriately arranging care with other qualified professionals. This includes care for all stages of life, acute care, chronic care, preventive services, and end-of-life care.

Care is coordinated and/or integrated across all elements of the complex health care system (e.g., subspecialty care, hospitals, home health agencies, nursing homes) and the patient's community (e.g., family, public, and private community based services). Care is facilitated by registries, information technology, health information exchange, and other means to ensure that patients get the indicated care when and where they need and want it in a culturally and linguistically appropriate manner.

Quality and safety are hallmarks of the medical home

- Practices advocate for their patients to support the attainment of optimal, patient-centered outcomes that are defined by a care planning process driven by a compassionate, robust partnership between physicians, patients, and the patient's family.

- Evidence-based medicine and clinical decision-support tools guide decision making.

- Physicians in the practice accept accountability for continuous quality improvement through voluntary engagement in performance measurement and improvement.

- Patients actively participate in decision making, and feedback is sought to ensure patients' expectations are being met.

- Information technology is used appropriately to support optimal patient care, performance measurement, patient education, and enhanced communication.

- Practices go through a voluntary recognition process by an appropriate nongovernmental entity to demonstrate that they have the capabilities to provide patient-centered services consistent with the medical home model.

- Patients and families participate in quality improvement activities at the practice level.

Enhanced access to care is available through systems such as open scheduling, expanded hours, and new options for communication between patients, their personal physicians, and practice staff.

Payment appropriately recognizes the added value provided to patients who have a patient-centered medical home.[a]

Chronic Disease Management Programs

The Congressional Budget Office provides the following definition of disease management programs: "Disease management programs vary widely in the specific techniques and tools that they use, but they share several common components that are designed to address those shortcomings. One component is to educate patients about their disease and how they can better manage it. The goal is to encourage patients to use medication properly, to understand and monitor their symptoms more effectively, and possibly to change their behavior. A second component is to actively monitor patients' clinical symptoms and treatment plans, following evidence-based guidelines. A third component is to coordinate care for the disease among all providers, including physicians, hospitals, laboratories, and pharmacies. A disease management program can provide feedback on individual patients and support to physicians about patients' status between office visits as well as up-to-date information on best practices for particular patients."[b]

Sources: [a] American Academy of Family Physicians (AAFP), American Academy of Pediatrics (AAP), American College of Physicians (ACP), American Osteopathic Association (AOA), "Joint Principles of the Patient-Centered Medical Home," March 2007, http://www.acponline.org/advocacy/where_we_stand/medical_home/approve_jp.pdf; [b] "An Analysis of the Literature on Disease Management Programs," Congressional Budget Office (October 13, 2004), http://www.cbo.gov/ftpdocs/59xx/doc5909/10-13-DiseaseMngmnt.pdf.

Changes in Financing

Changes in financing are a necessary complement to care-delivery reforms. There is a strong and growing belief among policy makers that the current system, which rewards providers for the number of services delivered rather than for the results of their care, incentivizes inefficient and uncoordinated care delivery. There have been numerous experiments around the country with "pay-for-performance" programs in both private and public markets designed to promote improved health outcomes, patient safety and the quality of care delivered. Because many of the proposed models depend on enhanced care coordination, we anticipate additional financial resources being made available to primary care practitioners and their "extenders" (such as nurse practitioners and physician assistants), especially in the context of medical home evolution.

We can also expect movement toward "bundled" or "global" payment systems. In a bundled payment, a healthcare system or multigroup practice contracts for a lump-sum payment for a specified (time-limited) episode of care for a specific disease or intervention; Geisinger Health System's contract for coronary artery bypass surgery is an often cited example.[19] Under the global payment framework, providers contract on a capitated basis for health services delivered to a specific patient.[20] Blue Cross Blue Shield of Massachusetts, for example, implemented "Alternative Quality Contract" agreements with providers to encourage a patient-centered global payment model.[21] More data are needed to determine if this type of agreement will lead to cost savings and quality improvement. Both arrangements often include incentives for high-quality performance and have provisions for "shared savings" between providers and payers if costs are kept below budgeted amounts. Several states have extensive planning processes in place designed to move in the direction of these payment frameworks.

Cost Pressures

Cost pressures on the overall healthcare system are likely to continue. Although the causes of healthcare costs are the subject of debate (higher cost technology, increased utilization, price inflation and more are all blamed), the result is an increasing share of the gross domestic product, state budgets, employer operating expenses and family income being devoted to health expenditures.[22] In some jurisdictions, this has led to a call for a return to rate setting. Furthermore, in almost every jurisdiction, as a result of the 2007–2009 recession, there have been severe rate cuts in Medicaid programs,[23] increased cost-sharing required of consumers and declining rates of private coverage.

There has also been a trend toward more extensive inquiry into relative costs and prices. The availability and aggregation of extensive information on healthcare costs allows significant comparative insight and public reporting. A number of states have proposed "all-payer claims databases" that allow for more extensive modeling of health costs across providers and delivery systems by payers, providers, and policy makers. Massachusetts is a good example of a state undertaking this type of effort.[24] Indeed, some argue that enhanced transparency will in and of itself facilitate cost containment by providers.

In response, providers will be required to develop more efficient systems, to reduce unnecessary utilization and to better understand and serve their patients. The most successful providers will adopt technologies and delivery models that allow lower cost innovations to replace more expensive ones. One way MLPs have sought to promote the importance of preventive legal services in the healthcare setting (and their potential cost savings) is to seek federal Medicaid reimbursement for those services. MLPs are poised to participate in and influence a range of healthcare reform efforts that focus on coordinating and integrating care, preventive approaches (particularly for vulnerable populations) and cost-saving and efficiency measures.

Medical-Legal Partnership Capacities and Opportunities

Many of the core components of MLPs—their emphasis on prevention, internal and external systems change, and the development of an integrated, collaborative healthcare model—are also key goals and strategies in healthcare reform efforts. Therefore, MLPs are uniquely situated to not only fit into healthcare reform efforts as they continue to unfold but also help shape those efforts in the years to come. MLPs' combination of medical expertise and legal insight provide an important perspective to reform efforts: at the most basic level, MLPs have insight into how individual patients experience their health, their healthcare, and the changes brought about by healthcare reform efforts. They are positioned to help interpret those experiences to policy makers and providers as they work to identify gaps, cost drivers, and inefficiencies in the system.

Because of their focus on addressing the social determinants of health, MLPs are also at the forefront of reform efforts aimed at reducing health disparities. Indeed, working to reduce "social disparities that greatly influence short-, intermediate- and long-term-health will require direct, concerted research, policy and programs that seek to alter significantly the negative influence of social determinants on diverse communities. The ACA's provisions for Community Transformation Grants and other related initiatives offer opportunities to test or bring to scale innovative community-based strategies that coordinate social and health services to fit individual and family circumstances."[25]

Thus, in addition to MLPs playing a key role in expanding and shaping healthcare reform efforts, there may also be new opportunities under the ACA and other government and foundation funding streams to expand the MLP model. As reformers think more creatively about healthcare delivery models in the wake of the ACA's structural and philosophical reordering of the health system, MLPs may have new opportunities to become more established and integrated parts of the healthcare system.

There are at least three core capacities of MLPs that are particularly relevant to a reformed healthcare system as envisioned by the ACA and other reform efforts. These are explored next.

Innovations in the Delivery Model: Integrated and Preventive Care

The collaborative and interdisciplinary nature of MLPs inherently promotes efforts to innovate through provider and patient education and by leveraging resources within the healthcare system. Under healthcare reform efforts, the emphasis on more efficient and integrated care models will be well served by the lessons learned by and about MLPs. MLPs have established a set of tools ideally suited to identifying patients with problems, explaining and enforcing legal protections, and resolving issues before those problems become acute. This preventive focus overlays neatly onto healthcare reform efforts, particularly under the ACA, focusing on developing preventive healthcare models that result in cost savings. MLP interventions in asthma care, described in Chapter 8, provide a good example. There is an increasing body of literature suggesting that community-based environmental interventions, combined with strong healthcare management and medication adherence, can dramatically reduce inpatient and emergency room utilization and costs.[26]

Additionally, new healthcare delivery models under the ACA emphasize disease management, focusing on interdisciplinary, integrated approaches. The ACA's support for expansion of the patient-centered medical home model builds on the prevention-focused holistic approach to health that is the hallmark of MLPs. There is also a particular opportunity to work with chronically ill patients as part of integrated clinical teams. Opportunities through these new models are likely to be specific to the clinical setting and at least partially dependent on the care delivery and financing arrangements the clinical setting employs. MLPs can help providers identify areas where they may have strong financial or performance incentives to better integrate care and think about ways that legal advocacy on behalf of vulnerable patient populations may improve care delivery performance. In addition to the many populations they currently serve—such as pediatric, geriatric, and patients with HIV or cancer—MLPs are well positioned to explore opportunities to expand service to chronically ill populations, including stroke patients, cardiac patients, diabetic patients, patients with mental health concerns, patients with neuromuscular disorders, and technology-dependent patients. An effective early stage approach to integrating MLP into these programs may be for MLP partners to sit in on healthcare team meetings on a consultative basis and learn more about legal and systems barriers faced by these patient populations.

Finally, MLP practitioners tend to be innovators and strong systems thinkers. They are skilled at interdisciplinary communication and finding ways to address bureaucratic hurdles that often stand in the way of patient-focused care. Effective programs designed according to healthcare reform goals will need to address how patients move through care delivery systems, how to efficiently transfer information among and between healthcare providers, and how to communicate optimally with consumers. These issues will be fundamental to the success of many of the health reform efforts to come. MLPs' proven success in providing a new standard of care through innovative interdisciplinary collaboration will be a strong example in these efforts.

Improved Individual Patient-Client Identification and Service

The expanded insurance coverage resulting from the ACA and other reforms will bring opportunities for MLP teams to expand and improve outreach. MLPs are well situated to develop patient education materials and help clinical and administrative staff identify target patients. One area of emphasis may be on patients who have previously been denied coverage, such as those who did not qualify for Medicaid prior to the ACA, but who are now eligible under the new law. MLPs know from experience that these patients tend to assume they are not eligible for programs despite either changes in their own circumstances or program rules. In addition to conducting outreach to these patient populations, MLPs should explore opportunities to interface with the financial counselors or enrollment staff located in the clinical setting for follow-up on denied applications.

For example, the MLP model got its start in Boston as a result (in part) of the Supreme Court decision in *Sullivan v. Zebley* (493 U.S. 521 (1990)), which expanded children's eligibility for Supplemental Security Income benefits. In the aftermath of the decision, the pediatric clinics at Boston City Hospital provided a tremendous opportunity to identify patients improperly denied benefits and to partner with local and national legal advocacy groups to enforce legal rights. Similarly, under the ACA, many of the private insurance protections—such as the elimination of annual and lifetime caps—present opportunities to find and assist particularly vulnerable patients who may have defaulted to Medicaid coverage but who now have access to private insurance. Given the creation of health insurance exchanges that will serve low- to moderate-income patients as well as new private coverage protections under the ACA, MLP practitioners will need to learn more about private insurance coverage and regulation to identify and enforce patient access to coverage. They will play a critical advocacy role for patients seeking private employer-based coverage, vouchers and subsidies, and information and evaluation of health insurance exchange options.

Identifying and Shaping Needed Systems Reforms

MLPs are ideally situated to identify how changes in the rules governing healthcare coverage impact patients. The combined MLP strategies of effective preventive screening, in-depth training, and case consultation and representation allow for on-the-ground assessment and triaging of individuals and families experiencing changes in their coverage status and seeking to take advantage of new regulatory protections. MLPs can identify trends in patient access and drive discussions about regulatory changes that address barriers. There are a number of important ways MLPs may influence the shape of healthcare reform efforts. Some of these are highlighted here.

First, MLPs should pay close attention to the development of pay-for-performance standards within private and public coverage programs, as well as payment policies that may impact care delivery. For example, payers are increasingly refusing to pay for inappropriate readmissions to hospitals, some of which may well result from external social or environmental factors. MLPs need to document not only the benefits of legal advocacy to patient health but also the potential cost savings rendered by addressing social and environmental determinants of health and healthcare usage. This information will help them educate and communicate with policy makers and providers about the value of preventive legal intervention.

Second, the evolving state and federal systems for quality assessment and performance (and current or eventual public reporting) will also influence clinical focus within healthcare organizations. MLPs should explore both local and national quality standards relevant to their work and incorporate quality measurement into their system design that are in sync with the healthcare organizations with which they work. This will be particularly important in the medical home model, in which MLP services should play a larger role in the future.

Third, there are enormous opportunities for MLPs to structure the healthcare reform "rules of the game" at the national and state levels. Who is covered, for what type of services, and who will get paid for those services will be fundamental issues as healthcare reform efforts continue to take shape. MLPs are well-positioned to translate on-the-ground clinical experience into regulatory insight. MLPs should use the expertise of partnering healthcare providers and lawyers to help policy makers charged with drafting regulations. The Department of Health and Human Services is tasked with over 1,000 regulatory processes under the ACA. Because much of the healthcare reform law will be carried out by states, there are similar opportunities to influence state-based interventions. For example, MLPs may be able to influence the selection of pay for performance or quality improvement projects, wellness initiatives, and the range of covered services.

One final opportunity for influencing policy development for vulnerable populations served by MLPs concerns accountable care organizations. Many health systems have begun to explore the development of accountable care organizations that theoretically offer improved integration of care delivery and allow for better patient care management, while holding the organization responsible for costs. However, there are going to be fundamental concerns raised about who controls these systems and how vulnerable patients are treated within them. The work involved may be very similar to past MLP advocacy around the regulation of Medicaid managed care plans (e.g., who should they cover, what should they pay, what patient protections are required, how should their performance be assessed?). There is likely to be similar work around the development of local insurance exchanges. MLPs have terrific opportunities to collaborate with clinicians in developing policy recommendations based on experience addressing the particular concerns of vulnerable populations.

There should be a natural flow of information from the system design opportunities discussed above into the policy-making sphere. *The Practice to Policy* examples throughout this book highlight how experience from individual MLP cases can help inform policy change. Choosing the system reform efforts that are likely to have the greatest impact in addressing health disparities should be the priority for MLPs in the future.

Questions for Discussion

1. What roles can MLP healthcare providers and lawyers play in ensuring that healthcare reform laws and initiatives address the needs of vulnerable populations?

2. What lessons from MLP service delivery might be helpful to those engaged in healthcare reform efforts?

3. In what sense, is MLP "healthcare reform"?

Conclusion

The country is entering a phase of healthcare reform that is nearly unprecedented, in which improved care integration and cost containment will become major thematic drivers. MLP partners should develop an understanding of the business imperatives driving system transformation and think about opportunities to add value to care delivery from both clinical and financial perspectives. They should extend their knowledge of private insurance regulation and clinical quality standards. They should also stay true to their missions and adapt and refine proven approaches. Continuing to pay special attention to the needs of vulnerable populations (children, elders, patients with significant chronic conditions) should provide a strong starting point for collaboration and intervention. The historic MLP emphasis on preventive legal care is well positioned given these imperatives. Maintaining or enhancing the back-and-forth flow between individual advocacy, systems reform and policy interventions will be crucial to the success of these efforts.

---

1. See *The Gallup Poll: Public Opinion 2007* (Oxford: Rowan and Littlefield, 2009), 60–62; "Problems and Priorities," PollingReport.com, http://www.pollingreport.com/prioriti.htm.

2. See J. Norman, "National Health Expenditures Now Grab 17.3 Percent of GDP, Study Projects," *Washington Health Policy Week in Review* (Feb. 4, 2010), http://www.commonwealthfund.org/Content/News letters/Washington-Health-Policy-in-Review/2010/Feb/February-8-2010/National-Health-Expenditures-Now-Grab-173-Percent-of-GDP-Study-Projects.aspx.

3. See J. B. Fox, C. L. Richards, early release of "Vital Signs: Health Insurance Coverage and Health Care Utilization — United States, 2006–2009 and January–March 2010," Centers for Disease Control and Prevention (Nov. 9, 2010), http://www.cdc.gov/mmwr/preview/mmwrhtml/mm59e1109a1.htm.

4. See "Annex Table 1. Health System Attainment and Performance in all Member States, Ranked by Eight Measures, Estimates for 1997," *World Health Report 2000* (Geneva: World Health Organization, 2000), 152–54. The United States is ranked 37th in terms of "overall health system performance" but only 72nd with respect to overall health. WHO hasn't completed another study rating the health and health systems of countries since 2000.

5. P.L. 111-148 (111th Cong., 2d sess.).

6. For a more detailed discussion of these changes, see S. Rosenbaum, "Realigning the Social Order: The Patient Protection and Affordable Care Act and the U.S. Health Insurance System," *Suffolk Journal of Health and Biomedical Law* (Winter 2011). For more specific descriptions of these changes and their implementation, go to www.healthreformgps.org.

7. Internal Revenue Code (IRC) § 5000A, as added by ACA § 1501.

8. IRC § 36B, as added by ACA § 1401.

9. ACA § 1251. Regulations issued in 2010 by the Obama administration establish a series of tests for determining whether a health plan can claim "grandfathered" status. See "Update: Health Reform and Grandfathered Plans," Health Reform GPS, http://www.healthreformgps.org/resources/health-in-surance-reforms-and-%e2%80%9cgrandfathered-plans%e2%80%9d/.

10. See "Immediate Private Health Insurance Reforms," Health Reform GPS, http://healthreformgps.org/resources/immediate-private-health-insurance-reforms/.

11. ACA § 1311; see also "Update: Health Insurance Exchanges," Health Reform GPS, http://healthreform gps.org/ resources/health-insurance-exchanges/.

12. 42 U.S.C. § 1396a(a)(10), as amended by ACA § 2001; see also "Medicaid Eligibility Changes," Health Reform GPS, http://healthreformgps.org/resources/medicaid-eligibility-changes/.

13. See generally, Rosenbaum, "Realigning the Social Order."

14. "State Legislation and Actions Challenging Certain Health Reforms, 2010–11," National Conference of State Legislatures (January 11, 2011), http://www.ncsl.org/?tabid=18906.

15. The Congressional Budget Office (CBO) estimates that by 2019, the number of nonelderly uninsured individuals would be reduced by 32 million. Put another way, by 2019 the percentage of nonelderly individuals with health insurance would increase to 94 percent. "Letter to Speaker Nancy Pelosi, March 20, 2010," Congressional Budget Office, p. 9, http://www.cbo.gov/ftpdocs/113xx/doc11379/AmendReconProp.pdf.

16. The Social Security Act authorizes the secretary of Health and Human Services to grant waivers to states for demonstration projects to provide greater flexibility in administering their Medicaid programs. These include: Section 1115 Research & Demonstration Projects that "test policy innovations

likely to further the objectives of the Medicaid program"; Section 1915(b) Managed Care/Freedom of Choice Waivers "to implement managed care delivery systems, or otherwise limit individuals' choice of provider under Medicaid"; Section 1915(c) Home and Community-Based Services Waivers that "waive Medicaid provisions in order to allow long-term care services to be delivered in community settings. This program is the Medicaid alternative to providing comprehensive long-term services in institutional settings." See "Medicaid State Waiver Program Demonstration Projects," General Information, U.S. Department of Health and Human Services, Centers for Medicare and Medicaid Services, https://www.cms.gov/MedicaidStWaivProgDemoPGI/01_Overview.asp.

17. For discussion of Medicaid and CHIP enrollment during the recession, see M. Heberlein, et al., "Holding Steady, Looking Ahead: Annual Findings of a 50 State Survey of Eligibility Rules, Enrollment and Renewal Procedures, and Cost Sharing Practices in Medicaid and Chip, 2010–2011," Henry J. Kaiser Family Foundation (January 2011), http://www.kff.org/medicaid/upload/8130ES.pdf.

18. For discussion of the challenges involved in Medicaid managed care, see "Medicaid and Managed Care: Key Data, Trends, and Issues," Kaiser Commission on Medicaid and the Uninsured, Henry J. Kaiser Family Foundation (February 2010), http://www.kff.org/medicaid/upload/8046.pdf.

19. See, for example, T. H. Lee, "Pay for Performance, Version 2.0?" *New England Journal of Medicine,* 357, no. 6 (August 9, 2007): 531–33, http://www.geisinger.org/provencare/nejm_pc.pdf.

20. A. Robinow, "The Potential of Global Payment: Insights from the Field," Commonwealth Fund (February 18, 2010), http://www.commonwealthfund.org/Content/Publications/Fund-Reports/2010/Feb/The-Potential-of-Global-Payment-Insights-from-the-Field.aspx.

21. M. E. Chernew, et al., "Private-Payer Innovation in Massachusetts: The 'Alternative Quality Contract,'" *Health Affairs,* 30, no. 1 (January 2011): 51–61.

22. See, for example, "Examination of Health Care Cost Trends and Cost Drivers Pursuant to G.L. c. 118G, §6(b)," Office of Massachusetts Attorney General Martha Coakley (March 16, 2010).

23. K. Sack, "For Governors, Medicaid Looks Ripe for Slashing," *New York Times,* January 28, 2011.

24. "All-Payer Claims Database: Overview of Efforts in Massachusetts," Division of Healthcare Finance and Policy, Massachusetts Office of Health and Human Service, http://www.mass.gov/Eeohhs2/docs/dhcfp/p/apcd/apcd_overview.pdf.

25. D. P. Andrulis, N. J. Siddiqui, J. P. Purtle, L. Duchon, "Patient Protection and Affordable Care Act of 2010: Advancing Health Equity for Racially and Ethnically Diverse Populations," Joint Center for Political and Economic Studies (July 2010): 14–15.

26. See D. R. Williams, et al., "Moving Upstream: How Interventions That Address the Social Determinants of Health Can Improve Health and Reduce Disparities," *Journal of Public Health Management and Practice,* Supplement (November 2008): S8–17.

Glossary of Terms

This section provides basic definitions of terms and concepts used in this book in the areas of poverty and health, public health, medicine, health and the healthcare system, law and the legal system, and medical/healthcare partnership.

Poverty and Health

Food Desert: Areas that lack access to affordable fruits, vegetables, whole grains, low-fat milk, and other foods which make up a healthy diet.[1]

Health Disparities: Differences in the incidence, prevalence, mortality, burden of diseases and other adverse health conditions or outcomes that exist among specific population groups in the United States; can affect population groups based on gender, age, ethnicity, socioeconomic status, geography, sexual orientation, disability or special health care needs and can occur among groups who have persistently experienced historical trauma, social disadvantage or discrimination, and systematically experience worse health or greater health risks than more advantaged social groups.[2]

"Heat or Eat": Federal research shows that while both rich and poor families increase their expenditures on home fuel during the winter, poor families offset this cost through decreasing food purchases, with an average 10 percent decrease in caloric intake.[3]

Low-income: Individuals and families are defined as low-income if their income is less than twice the federal poverty threshold.[4]

Socioeconomic Status (SES): Description of a person's societal status using factors or measurements such as income levels, relationship to the national poverty line, educational achievement, neighborhood of residence or home ownership.[5]

Social Determinants of Health: Conditions in which people are born, grow, live, work and age, including the healthcare system; circumstances shaped by the distribution of money, power and resources at global, national and local levels, which are themselves influenced by policy choices.[6]

Vulnerable Populations: Includes any group of people whose healthcare needs exceed the average or who are "at greater risk (than the average person) for poor health status and healthcare access."[7]

Public Health

Biostatistics: Involves the theory and application of statistical science to analyze public health problems and to further biomedical research.[8]

Centers for Disease Control (CDC): Part of the U.S. Department of Health & Human Services, the CDC is dedicated to protecting health and promoting quality of life through the prevention and control of disease, injury and disability; its mission: collaborating to create the expertise, information, and tools that people and communities need to protect their health through health promotion, prevention of disease, injury and disability, and preparedness for new health threats.[9]

Downstream Intervention: Has an explicit health purpose, a narrower range of benefits and tends to be targeted at those already suffering from increased health risk.[10]

Environmental Health: Addresses all physical, chemical and biological factors external to a person, and all related factors impacting behaviors; encompasses the assessment and control of those environmental factors that can potentially affect health; targets disease prevention and the creation of health-supportive environments. This definition excludes behavior not related to environment, behavior related to the social/cultural environment and genetics.[11]

Epidemiology: Study of the distribution and determinants of health-related states in specified populations, and the application of this study to control health problems.[12]

Population: Total number of individuals occupying an area or making up a whole, or a body of persons or individuals having a quality or characteristic in common.[13]

Primary, Secondary, Tertiary Prevention: *Primary prevention* is the prevention of a disease before it occurs; *secondary prevention* is the prevention of recurrences or exacerbations of a disease that already has been diagnosed; and *tertiary prevention* is the reduction in the amount of disability caused by a disease to achieve the highest level of function.[14]

Qualitative: *Qualitative analysis* ascertains the nature of the attributes, behavior or opinions of the entity being measured. *Qualitative data* is information that is difficult to measure, count, or express in numerical terms. *Qualitative research* involves detailed, verbal descriptions of characteristics, cases, and settings and typically uses observation, interviewing and document review to collect data.[15]

Quantitative: *Quantitative data* is information that can be expressed in numerical terms, counted, or compared on a scale. *Quantitative analysis* ascertains the magnitude, amount, or size, e.g., of the attributes, behavior, or opinions of the entity being measured. *Quantitative research* examines phenomena through the numerical representation of observations and statistical analysis.[16]

Social Epidemiology: Systematic and comprehensive study of health, well-being, social conditions or problems, and diseases and their determinants, using epidemiology and social science methods to develop interventions, programs, policies, and institutions that may reduce the extent, adverse impact or incidence of a health or social problem and promote health.[17]

Upstream Intervention: Concept of anticipating adverse effects of situations and events that, if unchecked, could lead to potentially harmful health consequences, in order that relevant early intervention can be initiated to break the causal chain.[18]

Medicine

Acute: Characterized by sharpness or severity, e.g., acute pain or an acute infection; having a sudden onset, sharp rise, and short course, e.g., an acute disease or an acute inflammation.[19]

ADD/ADHD (Attention Deficit Disorder/Attention Deficit Hyperactivity Disorder): Conditions of the brain that affect a person's ability to pay attention. It is most common in school-age children and is a chronic disorder, meaning that it affects an individual throughout life. The symptoms are also pervasive, meaning they occur in multiple settings, rather than just one.[20]

Allergy and Immunology: Study of the sensitivity of the immune system in response to exposure to substances such as food, medications, insect stings and environmental factors; includes treatment of asthma and hay fever.[21]

Allopathic (also conventional): System of medical practice which treats disease by the use of remedies which produce effects different from those produced by the disease under treatment; medical doctors practice allopathic medicine. [22].

Anesthesiology: Study of the administration of medicine to aid in pain management and sedation, often during and after surgery or other medical procedures.[23]

Attending Physician: Doctor responsible for the patient's hospital treatment or who is charged with the patient's overall care and who is responsible for directing the treatment program.[24]

Cardiology: Study of the heart and its action and diseases.[25]

Case Manager: Person who assesses an individual situation and implements and monitors a care plan to meet the needs of a patient; also identifies and arranges services such as transportation, home care, meals and day care; can help determine eligibility for entitlement programs, plan for long-term care and intervene in crisis situations.[26]

Certified Nurse Assistant (CNA): Employed by hospitals, nursing homes, outpatient clinics, and private individuals to take care of patients' everyday needs, including personal care duties such as bathing, dressing and feeding patients, as well as brushing teeth and combing hair. CNAs help patients in and out of bed and assist them with walking as they travel to and from surgeries and treatments. In certain settings — for example, senior-care and other assisted-living facilities — certified nursing assistants are responsible for helping patients get daily exercise, as well as leading or participating in field trips or group activities.[27]

Chief Complaint: Primary symptom that a patient states as the reason for seeking medical care.[28]

Chronic: Marked by long duration, by frequent recurrence over a long time and often by slowly progressing seriousness; not acute.[29]

Chronic Diseases: Noncommunicable illnesses that are prolonged in duration, do not resolve spontaneously, and are rarely cured completely, e.g., heart disease, cancer, stroke, diabetes and arthritis.[30]

Clinical: Practice of medicine in which physicians assess patients (in person or virtually) or populations in order to diagnose, treat and prevent disease using their expert judgment; physicians who contribute to the care of patients by providing clinical decision support and information systems, laboratory, imaging or related studies.[31]

Curbside Consultation: Process in which a physician seeks information or advice about patient care from another physician who has a particular expertise without obtaining a formal consultation between the patient and the consultant physician at that time.[32]

Dermatology: Study of the diagnosis, structure, function, and diseases of skin, hair and nails.[33]

Early Intervention: Specialized health, educational and therapeutic services designed to meet the needs of infants and toddlers who have a developmental delay or disability, and their families.[34]

Emergency Medicine: Diagnosis and treatment of life-threatening medical situations.[35]

Failure to Thrive: Description applied to children whose current weight or rate of weight gain is significantly below that of other children of similar age and sex.[36]

Family Medicine: Medical specialty which provides continuing, comprehensive healthcare for the individual and family and that integrates the biological, clinical and behavioral sciences; encompasses all ages, both sexes, each organ system and every disease entity.[37]

Fellow: Physician in a graduate medical education program accredited by the ACGME who has completed the requirements for eligibility for first board certification in the specialty; "subspecialty residents" is also applied to such physicians.[38]

Geriatrics: Branch of healthcare concerning the comprehensive healthcare of the elderly.[39]

Graduate Medical Education (GME): Period of didactic and clinical education in a medical or specialty or subspecialty which follows the completion of a recognized undergraduate medical education and for which prepares physicians for the independent practice of medicine in that specialty or subspecialty, also referred to as residency education.[40]

Gynecology: Study of the physiology and disorders of the female reproductive tract and breasts.[41]

Histology: Microscopic study of animal and plant tissues and cells, and examination of how cells process various nutrients, interact with other cells and get rid of waste. The focus on cell function and how cells combine and form larger structures like organs makes histology similar to cellular biology.[42]

Homecare: Services (as nursing or personal care) provided to a homebound individual (as one who is convalescing, disabled or terminally ill).[43]

Hospice: Facility or program designed to provide a caring environment for meeting the physical and emotional needs of the terminally ill.[44]

Inpatient Care: Medical treatment that is provided in a hospital or other medical facility, and requires at least one overnight stay; inpatients are often in the hospital for surgical procedures, or for monitoring after accidents or serious medical events which compromised their health in some way.[45]

Intern: Historically, a designation for individuals in the first year of GME; no longer used by the ACGME.[46]

Internal Medicine: Study of the diagnosis and treatment of nonsurgical diseases.[47]

Long Term Care: Coordinated package of services that includes medical and non-medical care to people who have a chronic illness or disability; helps meet health or personal needs including activities of daily living like dressing, bathing and using the bathroom, and can be provided at home, in the community, in assisted living facilities or in nursing homes.[48]

Medical Assistant: Performs administrative and clinical tasks to keep the offices of physicians, podiatrists, chiropractors and other healthcare practitioners running smoothly; duties vary from office to office, depending on the location and size of the practice and the practitioner's specialty and include administrative and clinical duties. [49]

Medicine: Science relating to disease and its study, prevention, diagnosis and treatment in the pursuit of facilitating health.[50]

Morbidity: State of being ill or diseased; the occurrence of a disease or condition that alters health and quality of life.[51]

Mortality: Quality or state of being mortal; the number of deaths in a given time or place or the proportion of deaths to population.[52]

Neurology: Medical specialty focused on the diagnosis and treatment of diseases and disorders of the brain and nervous system.[53]

Nuclear Medicine: Study of the use of radionuclides for diagnostic and therapeutic purposes.[54]

Nurse: Person who cares for the sick or infirm, specifically a licensed healthcare professional who practices independently or is supervised by a physician, surgeon or dentist and who is skilled in promoting and maintaining health.[55]

Nurse Practitioner (NP) or Nurse Clinician: Registered nurse (RN) who through advanced training is qualified to assume some of the duties and responsibilities formerly assumed only by a physician.[56]

Nursing Home: Privately operated establishment where maintenance and personal or nursing care are provided for persons (as the aged or the chronically ill) who are unable to care for themselves properly.[57]

Obesity: Excess proportion of total body fat, generally when weight is 20 percent or more above normal; a most common measure of obesity is the body mass index (BMI). A person is considered overweight if his or her BMI is between 25 and 29.9; a person is considered obese if his or her BMI is over 30.[58]

Obstetrics: Healthcare specialty concerning the management of pregnancy, childbirth and post-partum care.[59]

Ophthalmology: Study of the diagnosis and treatment of eye diseases and conditions.[60]

Orthopedics: Study of the nature and correction of disorders of the bones, joints, ligaments or muscles.[61]

Osteopathic: System of therapy founded in the nineteenth century based on the concept that the body can formulate its own remedies against diseases when the body is in a normal structural relationship, has a normal environment and enjoys good nutrition. While osteopathy takes a "holistic" approach to medical care, it also embraces modern medical knowledge, including medication, surgery, radiation, and chemotherapy when warranted. Osteopathy is particularly concerned with maintaining correct relationships between bones, muscles and connective tissues. DOs practice osteopathic medicine.[62]

Otolaryngology: Study of the medical and surgical management and treatment of patients with diseases and disorders of the ear, nose, throat (ENT) and related structures of the head and neck.[63]

Outpatient Care: Any type of service offered that does not involve an overnight stay in a medical facility; typically a visit to a doctor's office is outpatient, but so is a surgery in a hospital where the patient returns home the same day.[64]

Palliative Care: Medical specialty focusing on improving the quality of life of people facing serious illness; treats people suffering from serious and chronic illnesses including cancer, cardiac disease like Congestive Heart Failure (CHF), Chronic Obstructive Pulmonary Disease (COPD), kidney failure, Alzheimer's, HIV/AIDS and Amyotrophic Lateral Sclerosis (ALS).[65]

Pathology: Study of the essential nature of diseases and especially of the structural and functional changes produced by them.[66]

Pathophysiology: Physiology of abnormal states; specifically, the functional changes that accompany a particular syndrome or disease.[67]

Pediatrics: Medical science concerning the care of children from birth to adolescence.[68]

Pharmacology: Comprehensive study of drugs and their effects upon living organisms.[69]

Physical Medicine and Rehabilitation: Medical specialty concerning the prevention, diagnosis, treatment, and management of disabling diseases, disorders and injuries typically of a musculoskeletal, cardiovascular, neuromuscular or neurological nature by physical means, including electromyography, electrotherapy, therapeutic exercise or pharmaceutical pain control.[70]

Physician's Assistant (PA): Healthcare provider certified to provide basic medical services (as the diagnosis and treatment of common ailments) usually under the supervision of a licensed physician.[71]

Psychiatry: Medical science concerning the diagnosis, treatment and prevention of mental illness.[72]

Psychology: Science concerning mental processes, both normal and pathological, and their effects upon behavior; introspective (self-examination) or objective (the study of others' minds).[73]

Pulmonology: Branch of medicine concerning the anatomy, physiology and pathology of the lungs.[74]

Radiology: Medical specialty concerning the application of radioactive substances to disease prevention, diagnosis and treatment.[75]

Residency: After four years of medical school, graduates engage in a period of advanced medical training and education consisting of supervised practice of a specialty in a hospital and its outpatient department and instruction from specialists on the hospital staff; program accredited to provide a structured educational experience designed to conform to the program requirements of a particular specialty.[76]

Resident: Medical school graduates participating in a residency; any physician in an accredited graduate medical education program, including interns and fellows.[77]

Resident, Chief: Typically, a position in the final year of the residency (e.g., surgery) or in the year after the residency is completed (e.g., internal medicine and pediatrics).[78]

Review of Systems (Symptoms): List of questions, arranged by organ system, designed to uncover dysfunction and disease; can be applied in several ways:
- As a screening tool asked of every patient that the clinician encounters;
- Asked only of patients who fall into particular risk categories; and
- To better define the likely causes of a presenting symptom.[79]

Rotation: Educational experience of planned activities in selected settings, over a specific time period, developed to meet goals and objectives of the program.

Social Worker: Skilled individual who provides any of various professional services, activities, or methods concretely concerned with the investigation, treatment, and material aid of the economically, physically, mentally or socially disadvantaged; assists people by helping them cope with and solve issues in their everyday lives, such as family and personal problems and dealing with relationships. Some social workers help clients who face a disability, life-threatening disease or social problem, such as inadequate housing, unemployment or substance abuse. They may conduct research, advocate for improved services or do policy work. May also be called licensed clinical social workers, if they hold the appropriate state mandated license.[80]

Specialty Services: Specialized healthcare provided by physicians whose training focused primarily in a specific field, such as neurology, cardiology, rheumatology, dermatology, oncology, orthopedics, ophthalmology and other specialized fields.[81]

Standard of Care: Formal diagnostic and treatment process a healthcare provider will follow for a patient with a certain set of symptoms or a specific illness which follows guidelines and protocols that experts would agree with as most appropriate; also called "best practice." In legal terms, a standard of care is used as the benchmark against a doctor's actual clinical and diagnostic work. A standard of care in one community will not necessarily be the same standard in another. Further, one doctor's standard can vary from another doctor's.[82]

Surgery: Use of manual or operative interventions in the treatment of pathological states.[83]

Urology: Study and treatment of disorders of the urinary tract in women and the urogenital system in men.[84]

Health and the Healthcare System

AAMC (Association of American Medical Colleges): Represents all 133 accredited U.S. and 17 accredited Canadian medical schools; approximately 400 major teaching hospitals and health systems, including 62 Department of Veterans Affairs medical centers; and nearly 90 academic and scientific societies. Through these institutions and organizations, the AAMC represents 125,000 faculty members, 75,000 medical students and 106,000 resident physicians.[85]

Accountable Care Organization (ACO): Organization of healthcare providers accountable for the care of Medicare beneficiaries enrolled in the traditional fee-for-service program for whom they provide the bulk of primary care services.[86]

ACGME (Accreditation Council for Graduate Medical Education): Private, nonprofit council that evaluates and accredits medical residency programs in the United States. Accreditation is accomplished through a peer review process and is based upon established standards and guidelines.[87]

Allied Health Professionals: Clinical healthcare professionals including, but not limited to, rehabilitation therapists, physician assistants and medical technicians; perform tasks which must otherwise be performed by physicians or other health professionals.[88]

AMA (American Medical Association): Promotes the art and science of medicine and the betterment of public health; its vision is for doctors to help patients by uniting physicians nationwide to work on the most important professional and public health issues.[89]

Capitated Care: Of, relating to, participating in, or being a healthcare system in which a medical provider is given a set fee per patient (as by an HMO) regardless of treatment required.[90]

Community Benefits: Programs or activities by healthcare entities that provide treatment and/or promote health and healing as a response to community needs and are not for marketing purposes. Since 1969, the IRS has required not-for-profit hospitals to meet a community benefit standard that assesses a hospital's eligibility for tax exemption by measuring whether they promote the health of a broad class of individuals in the community.[91]

Department Chair: Faculty member who serves as the academic leader and administrative head of a department of instruction, research or clinical service.[92]

Disproportionate Share Hospital (DSH): Hospital which disproportionately treats low-income and uninsured patients; federal, state and local governments provide subsidies to DSHs to provide the uninsured with access to affordable healthcare.[93]

Federally Qualified Health Center (FQHC): Public and private non-profit healthcare organizations that meet certain criteria under the Medicare and Medicaid Programs of the Social Security Act and receive funds under the Health Center Program. FQHCs are "safety net" providers such as community health centers, public housing centers, outpatient health programs funded by the Indian Health Service and programs serving migrants and the homeless; purpose is to enhance the provision of primary care services in underserved urban and rural communities.[94]

Healthcare Landscape For Vulnerable Patients:

Figure 1 Healthcare Landscape For Vulnerable Populations

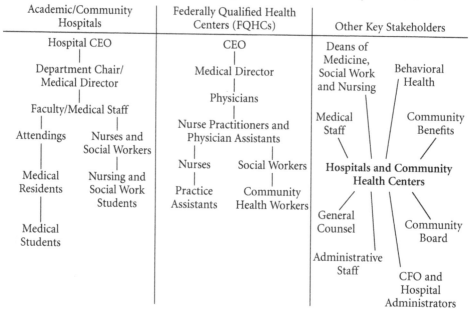

Hospital Administrator: Professional charged with the management of hospital activities and the application of hospital policies.[95]

Managed Care: Approach to healthcare intended to reduce unnecessary costs; providing incentives for cost-effective medical decisions, evaluating the need for specific services, controlling inpatient admissions and lengths of stay, etc.[96]

Medically Underserved: *Medically Underserved Areas (MUAs)* may be a whole county or a group of contiguous counties, a group of county or civil divisions or a group of urban census tracts in which residents have a shortage of personal health services. *Medically Underserved Populations (MUPs)* may include groups of persons who face economic, cultural or linguistic barriers to health care.[97]

NACHC (National Association of Community Health Centers): Provides research, training, advocacy and technical support for more than 1,000 community health centers throughout the United States.[98]

Nurse Manager: Nurse professionally qualified in administration and charged with the managerial responsibilities of a nursing unit.[99]

Patient-Centered Medical Home (PCMH): Healthcare setting which provides patients with comprehensive primary care and promotes partnerships between individual patients, their personal physicians, and, when suitable, the patient's family.[100]

Primary Care: Provided by physicians specifically trained for and skilled in comprehensive first contact and continuing care for persons with any undiagnosed sign, symptom or health concern (the "undifferentiated" patient) not limited by problem origin (biological, behavioral, or social), organ system or diagnosis.[101]

Quaternary Care: Advanced levels of medicine which are highly specialized and not widely used; experimental medicine, service-oriented surgeries and other less common approaches to treatment and diagnostics comprise the bulk of quaternary care.[102]

Secondary Care: Treatment by specialists to whom a patient has been referred by primary care providers.[103]

Tertiary Care: Treatment given in a healthcare center that includes highly trained specialists and often advanced technology.[104]

Law and the Legal System

ABA (American Bar Association): Largest professional membership organization in the world; provides law school accreditation, continuing legal education, information about the law, programs to assist lawyers and judges in their work and initiatives to improve the legal system for the public.[105]

ADA (Americans with Disabilities Act): Federal law which prohibits discrimination against people with disabilities in employment, public services and public accommodations.[106]

Administrative Law: Law governing the organization and operation of administrative agencies and the relations of administrative agencies with the legislature, the executive, the judiciary and the public.[107]

Administrative Law Judge: Official who presides at an administrative hearing and who has the power to administer oaths, take testimony, rule on questions of evidence, and make factual and legal determinations.[108]

Advanced Planning/End of Life Care: Describes the documents that specify the care a person wishes to have if he or she becomes unable to make medical decisions; generally includes a living will, a durable power of attorney for healthcare, "Do Not Resuscitate" orders and others.[109]

Advocacy: Attempting to influence public policy through education, lobbying or political pressure. Advocacy groups often attempt to educate the general public as well as public policy makers about the nature of problems, what legislation is needed to address problems and the funding required to provide services or conduct research.[110]

Attorney-Client Privilege: Client's right to refuse to disclose and to prevent any other person from disclosing confidential communications between the client and the attorney.[111]

Child Abuse/Neglect: Act or failure to act on the part of a parent or caretaker which results in death, serious physical or emotional harm, sexual abuse or exploitation of a child; or an act or failure to act which presents an imminent risk of serious harm.[112]

Civil Gideon: Constitutional guarantee to a lawyer in civil cases to match the guarantee in criminal cases announced by the Supreme Court in *Gideon v. Wainwright*, 372 U.S. 335 (1963).[113]

Civil Law: Resolution of legal claims by one individual or group against another.[114]

Civil Legal Process:[115]

Figure 2 How a Civil Case Is Processed

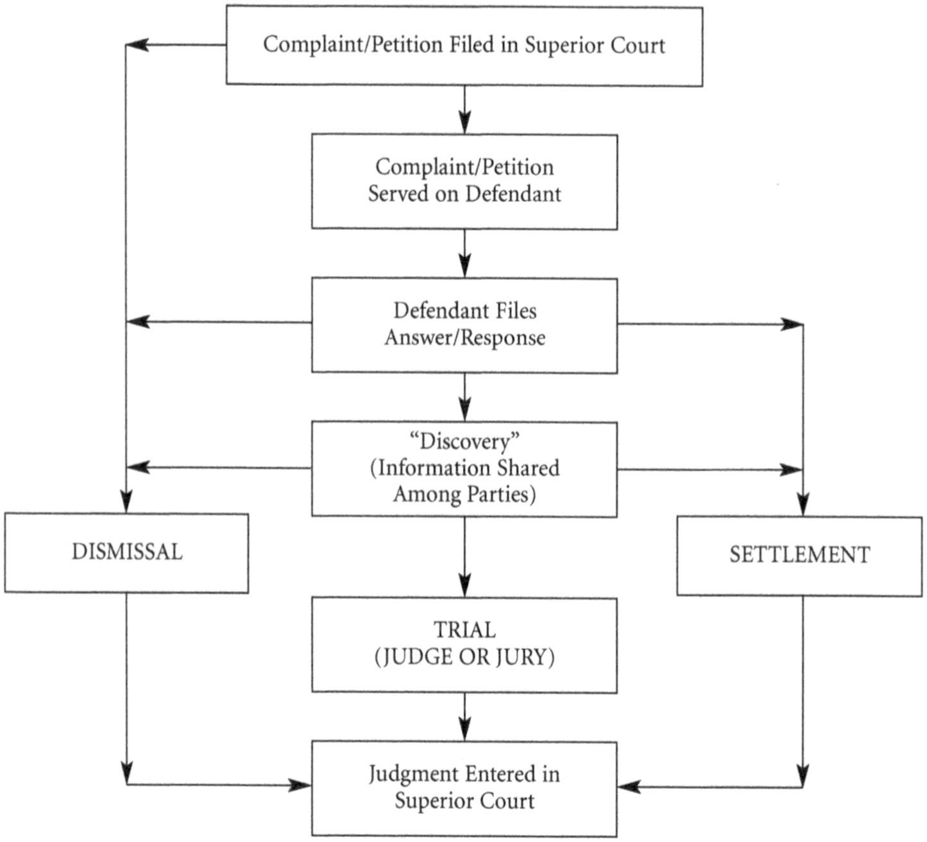

```
        ┌────────────────────────────────────────┐
   ┌────│   Complaint/Petition Filed in Superior Court   │
   │    └────────────────────────────────────────┘
   │                        │
   │                        ▼
   │         ┌──────────────────────────┐
   │         │    Complaint/Petition     │
   │         │    Served on Defendant    │
   │         └──────────────────────────┘
   │                        │
   │                        ▼
   │         ┌──────────────────────────┐
   │ ◄───────│      Defendant Files       │────────►
   │         │      Answer/Response       │
   │         └──────────────────────────┘
   │                        │
   │                        ▼
   │         ┌──────────────────────────┐
   │ ◄───────│        "Discovery"         │────────►
   │         │   (Information Shared      │
   │         │     Among Parties)         │
   │         └──────────────────────────┘
   │                        │
   ▼                        ▼                        ▼
┌──────────┐     ┌──────────────────────────┐     ┌──────────┐
│ DISMISSAL │     │          TRIAL            │     │SETTLEMENT│
│          │     │     (JUDGE OR JURY)        │     │          │
└──────────┘     └──────────────────────────┘     └──────────┘
   │                        │                        │
   │                        ▼                        │
   │         ┌──────────────────────────┐           │
   └────────►│    Judgment Entered in     │◄──────────┘
             │      Superior Court        │
             └──────────────────────────┘
```

Civil Procedure: Body of law governing the methods and practices used in civil litigation, usually rules enacted by the legislature or courts.[116]

Civil Protection Order: Court order prohibiting family violence; usually an order restricting a person from harassing, threatening, and sometimes merely contacting or approaching another specified person; also called Restraining Orders or Civil Restraining Orders.[117]

COBRA (Consolidated Omnibus Budget Reconciliation Act): Gives workers and their families who lose their health benefits the right to choose to continue group health benefits provided by their group health plan for limited periods of time under certain circumstances.[118]

Common Law: System of law derived from judges' decisions (which arise from the judicial branch of government), rather than statutes or constitutions (which are derived from the legislative branch of government).[119]

Constitution of the United States: Supreme law of the United States; framework for the organization of the federal government and for its relationship with the states, citizens, and all people within the United States. The Constitution creates the three branches of the national government: a legislature, the bicameral Congress; an executive branch led by the President; and a judicial branch headed by the Supreme Court. The Constitution specifies the powers and duties of each branch. The Constitution reserves all unenumerated powers to the respective states and the people, thereby establishing the federal system of government.[120] (See Figure 3.)

Contracts: Body of law dealing with agreements between two or more parties creating obligations that are enforceable or otherwise recognizable at law.[121]

Court Clerk: Court officer responsible for filing papers, the issuing process, and keeping records of court proceedings as generally specified by rule or statute.[122]

Criminal Law: Prosecution by the government of a person for an act that has been classified as a crime.[123]

Criminal Legal Process:[124] (See Figure 4.)

Defense Attorney: Lawyer who represents one or more defendants in a trial and asserts the defendant's or defendants' stated reason(s) why the plaintiff or prosecutor has no valid case.[125]

District Attorney: Attorney appointed or elected to represent the State in the prosecution of crimes within that District Attorney's jurisdiction.[126]

Elder Abuse/Neglect: Infliction of physical, emotional, or psychological harm on an older adult; also can take the form of financial exploitation or intentional or unintentional neglect of an older adult by the caregiver.[127]

EMTALA (Emergency Medical Treatment and Active Labor Act): Federal statute that ensures public access to emergency services regardless of ability to pay.[128]

Entitlement: Absolute right to a benefit, such as social security, granted immediately upon meeting a legal requirement.[129]

EPSDT (Early and Periodic Screening, Diagnosis, and Treatment): Medicaid's comprehensive and preventive child health program for individuals under the age of 21 which includes periodic screening, vision, dental and hearing services.[130]

Fair Housing Act: Federal law which prohibits discrimination in the sale, rental and financing of dwellings, and in other housing-related transactions, based on race, color, national origin, religion, sex, familial status and disability.[131]

Federalism: Principle of government that defines the relationship between the central government at the national level and its constituent units at the regional, state or local levels; power and authority is allocated between the national and local governmental units, such that each unit is delegated a sphere of power and authority only it can exercise, while other powers must be shared.[132]

FMLA (Family and Medical Leave Act): Federal law providing that qualifying employees may take unpaid, job-protected leave for certain family reasons, as when a family member is sick or when a child is born.[133]

Foster Care: Twenty-four-hour substitute care for children placed away from their parents or guardians and for whom a state agency has placement and care responsibility; includes, but is not limited to, placements in foster family homes, foster homes of relatives, group homes, emergency shelters, residential facilities, child care institutions and pre-adoptive homes.[134]

General Counsel: Senior lawyer of a corporation; most large companies have a team of in-house staff lawyers headed by a general counsel. This department, reporting to

Figure 3 The Government of the United States

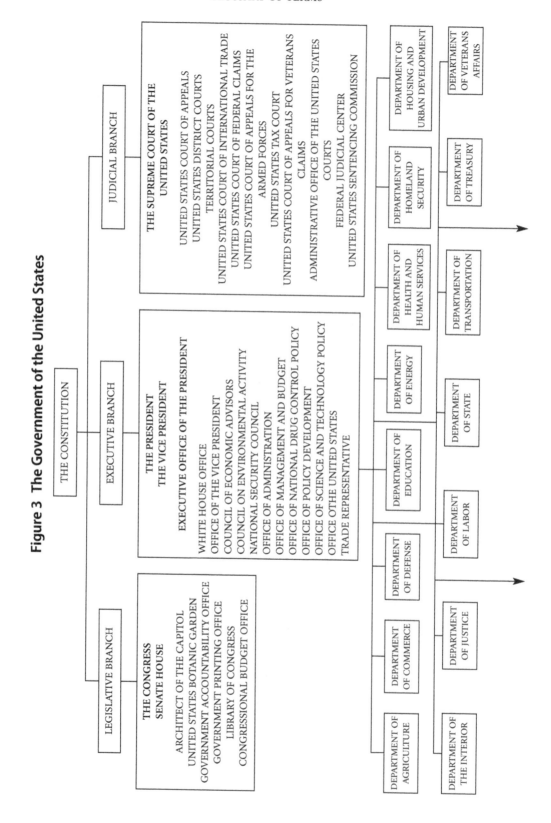

INDEPENDENT ESTABLISHMENTS AND GOVERNMENT CORPORATIONS

AFRICAN DEVELOPMENT FOUNDATION
BROADCASTING BOARD OF GOVERNORS
CENTRAL INTELLIGENCE AGENCY
COMMODITY FUTURES TRADING COMMISSION
CONSUMER PRODUCT SAFETY COMMISSION
CORPORATION FOR NATIONAL AND COMMUNITY SERVICE
DEFENSE NUCLEAR FACILITIES SAFETY BOARD
ENVIRONMENTAL PROTECTION AGENCY
EQUAL EMPLOYMENT OPPORTUNITY COMMISSION
EXPORT-IMPORT BANK OF THE UNITED STATES
FARM CREDIT ADMINISTRATION
FEDERAL COMMUNICATIONS COMMISSION
FEDERAL DEPOSIT INSURANCE CORPORATION
FEDERAL ELECTION COMMISSION
FEDERAL HOUSING FINANCE BOARD
FEDERAL LABOR RELATIONS AUTHORITY
FEDERAL MARITIME COMMISSION
FEDERAL MEDIATION AND CONCILIATION SERVICE
FEDERAL MINE SAFETY AND HEALTH REVIEW COMMISSION
FEDERAL RESERVE SYSTEM
FEDERAL RETIREMENT THRIFT INVESTMENT BOARD
FEDERAL TRADE COMMISSION
GENERAL SERVICES ADMINISTRATION
INTER-AMERICAN FOUNDATION
MERIT SYSTEMS PROTECTION BOARD
NATIONAL AERONAUTICS AND SPACE ADMINISTRATION
NATIONAL ARCHIVES AND RECORDS ADMINISTRATION
NATIONAL CAPITAL PLANNING COMMISSION

NATIONAL CREDIT UNION ADMINISTRATION
NATIONAL FOUNDATION ON THE ARTS AND THE HUMANITIES
NATIONAL LABOR RELATIONS BOARD
NATIONAL MEDIATION BOARD
NATIONAL RAILROAD PASSENGER CORPORATION (AMTRAK)
NATIONAL SCIENCE FOUNDATION
NATIONAL TRANSPORTATION SAFETY BOARD
NUCLEAR REGULATORY COMMISSION
OCCUPATIONAL SAFETY AND HEALTH REVIEW COMMISSION
OFFICE OF THE DIRECTOR OF NATIONAL INTELLIGENCE
OFFICE OF GOVERNMENT ETHICS
OFFICE OF PERSONNEL MANAGEMENT
OFFICE OF SPECIAL COUNSEL
OVERSEAS PRIVATE INVESTMENT CORPORATION
PEACE CORPS
PENSION BENEFIT GUARANTY CORPORATION
POSTAL REGULATORY COMMISSION
NATIONAL RAILROAD RETIREMENT BOARD
SECURITIES AND EXCHANGE COMMISSION
SELECTIVE SERVICE SYSTEM
SMALL BUSINESS ADMINISTRATION
SOCIAL SECURITY ADMINISTRATION
TENNESSEE VALLEY AUTHORITY
TRADE AND DEVELOPMENT AGENCY
UNITED STATES AGENCY FOR INTERNATIONAL DEVELOPMENT
UNITED STATES COMMISSION ON CIVIL RIGHTS
UNITED STATES INTERNATIONAL TRADE COMMISSION
UNITED STATES POSTAL SERVICE

Source: Office of the Federal Register and National Archives and Records Administration, "The Constitution of The United States," in *The United States Government Manual 2009/2010* (Washington, DC: US Government Printing Office, 2009), 21.

Figure 4 Example of How a Criminal Case Is Processed

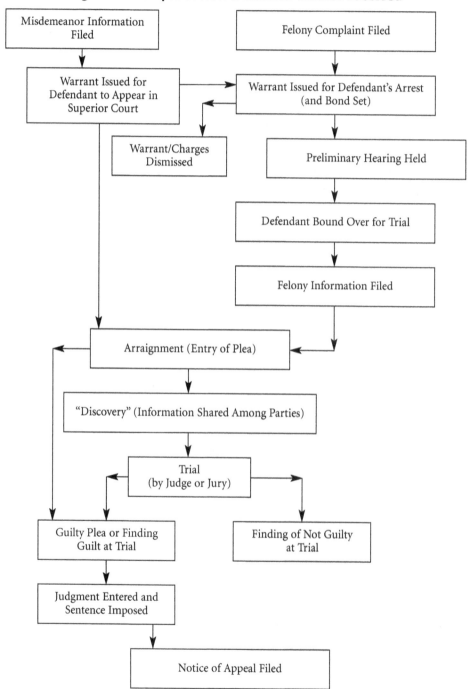

Source: California Supreme Court, www.scscount.org/general_info/courtsystem.shtml.

their board of directors, manages all legal services such as real property transactions, mergers and acquisitions, contracts and litigation although the latter is usually contracted-out to private law firms retained near the court where the claim has been filed.[135]

Guardianship: Legal process by which a probate court appoints one or more individuals to handle the personal and financial affairs of a minor or person of any age the court determines to be mentally incompetent.[136]

HIPAA (Health Insurance Portability and Accountability Act): Federal law which provides federal protections for personal health information held by covered entities and gives patients an array of rights with respect to that information; also permits the disclosure of personal health information needed for patient care and other important purposes.[137]

IDEA (Individuals with Disabilities Education Act): Federal legislation that governs the public education of children with physical or mental disabilities and attempts to ensure that these children receive a free public education that meets their unique needs.[138]

IEP (Individualized Education Program): Specially designed written plan of educational instruction for a child with disabilities.[139]

Income Supports: Supplemental income targeting low-income individuals and families which may include social security benefits, welfare benefits, food stamps and other forms of assistance.[140]

Informed Consent: Agreement, approval or permission given voluntarily by a competent person.[141]

Interpersonal, Domestic or Family Violence: *Interpersonal violence* includes violence between family members and intimate partners and violence between acquaintances and strangers that is not intended to further the aims of any formally defined group or cause. *Domestic violence* refers to situations where one partner uses a variety of tactics, whether mental or physical, to control another person in an intimate relationship. *Family violence* is a situation in which one family member causes physical or emotional harm to another family member.[142]

IOLTA (Interest on Lawyer's Trust Accounts): Legal aid funding source derived from pooling of interest from lawyer trust accounts.[143]

Judge: Public official appointed or elected to hear and decide legal matters in court.[144]

Lawful Permanent Resident: Any person not a citizen of the United States who is residing in the U.S. under legally recognized and lawfully recorded permanent residence as an immigrant; also known as "Permanent Resident Alien," "Resident Alien Permit Holder" and "Green Card Holder".[145]

Legal Aid/Legal Services: Free or inexpensive services of an attorney provided to individuals who are not otherwise able to afford an attorney.[146]

Legal Needs: Specific situations that raise legal issues, whether or not handled by a lawyer or taken to the justice system.[147]

LGBTQ: Initialism used since the 1990s as a self-designation by what was formerly known as the "gay community"; refers collectively to persons who are lesbian, gay, bisexual, transgender and to those who are queer or questioning their sexual identity.[148]

LSC (Legal Services Corporation): Nonprofit federal corporation that provides legal assistance in civil cases to those who cannot afford it through grants to legal aid and other organizations and by contracting with individuals, firms, corporations and organizations that provide legal services.[149]

Mandatory Reporting: Certain professionals designated by state law are required to report suspected child abuse and neglect; states may also have mandated reporting for vulnerable populations such as the elderly.[150]

McKinney-Vento (McKinney-Vento Homeless Assistance Act): Federal legislation which provides a range of services to homeless people including emergency shelter, transitional housing, job training, primary healthcare and education.[151]

Medicaid: Cooperative federal-state program that pays for medical expenses for those who cannot afford private medical services.[152]

Medicare: Federal program established under the Social Security Act that provides health insurance for the elderly and the disabled.[153]

Naturalization: Process by which U.S. citizenship is granted to a foreign citizen or national after he or she fulfills the requirements established by Congress in the Immigration and Nationality Act (INA). In most cases, an applicant for naturalization must be a permanent resident (green card holder) before filing.[154]

Paralegal: Person who assists a lawyer in duties related to the practice of law but who is not a licensed attorney.[155]

Preventive Law: Practice of law that seeks to minimize a client's risk of litigation or secure more certainty with regard to the client's legal rights and duties.[156]

Pro Bono: Involving uncompensated legal services performed, especially for the public good.[157]

Probate: Legal proceeding defined by state law in which the court determines the validity of a decedent's will and the correctness with which the provisions of the will are carried out.[158]

Professional Responsibility: Attorney's obligation to comply with rules of professional conduct, such as ethical considerations in the Model Code of Professional Responsibility.[159]

Property: Body of law dealing with the right to possess, use and enjoy a determinate thing (e.g., a tract of land or a chattel).[160]

Prosecutor: Legal officer who represents the government in criminal proceedings.[161]

Public Charge: In immigration law, an individual who is likely to become primarily dependent on the government for subsistence, as demonstrated by either the receipt of public cash assistance for income maintenance or institutionalization for long-term care at government expense.[162]

Public Defender: Attorney employed by the state or federal or state courts to provide legal defense to defendants who are unable to afford counsel.[163]

Public Policy: System of laws, regulatory measures, courses of action and funding priorities concerning a given topic promulgated by a governmental entity or its representatives; individuals and groups often attempt to shape public policy through education, advocacy or mobilization of interest groups.[164]

Reasonable Accommodation: Action taken to adapt or adjust for a disabled person, done in a way that does not impose an undue hardship on the party taking the action.[165]

Regulations/Regulatory: Rule or order having legal force and issued by an administrative agency.[166]

SNAP (Supplemental Nutrition Assistance Program): Federal program that helps people with low incomes and resources buy the food they need for good health; formerly food stamps.[167]

SSDI (Social Security Disability Insurance): Federal program funded by Social Security tax revenues designed to help disabled individuals who are "insured," meaning those who have worked long enough and paid Social Security taxes.[168]

SSI (Supplemental Security Income): Social welfare or needs-based government program providing monthly income to the aged, blind or disabled.[169]

Statute: Law established by an act of the legislature.[170]

TANF (Temporary Assistance for Needy Families): Combined state and federal program that provides limited financial assistance to families in need.[171]

Torts: Branch of law dealing with civil wrongs, other than breach of contract, for which a remedy may be obtained, usually in the form of damages; a breach of duty that the law imposes on persons who stand in a particular relation to one another.[172]

U.S. Attorney: Serves as the nation's principal litigators under the direction of the Attorney General; appointed by and serves at the discretion of the President with advice and consent of the U.S. Senate; has three statutory responsibilities: to prosecute criminal cases brought by the federal government, to prosecute and defend civil cases in which the U.S. is a party and to collect debts owed the federal government which are administratively uncollectible.[173]

VAWA (Violence Against Women Act of 1994): Federal law which seeks to improve criminal justice and community-based responses to domestic violence, dating violence, sexual assault and stalking in the United States.[174]

WIC (Women, Infants and Children Nutrition Program): Federally-funded health and nutrition program for women, infants and children that helps families by providing checks for buying healthy supplemental foods from WIC-authorized vendors, nutrition education and helps with finding healthcare and other community services. Participants must meet income guidelines and be pregnant women, new mothers, infants or children under age five.[175]

Medical-Legal Partnership (MLP)

Feedback Loop: Formal mechanism through which MLP teams share information about legal and health screening, triage, interventions and outcomes. MLP teams must devise appropriate, ethical strategies to share confidential information across the legal and health disciplines.

Healthcare Champion: Physician, nurse, social worker, case manager or other healthcare provider who serves as a leader and strategist as part of the MLP team. She or he works directly with the legal team to (1) develop and strengthen relationships with healthcare institutions, departments, clinics and providers and relevant graduate schools; (2) develop and strengthen relationships with legal institutions, departments, law schools, lawyers and paralegals; (3) provide insight into healthcare infrastructure that may affect MLP activities; (4) facilitates MLP presence and access in all clinical areas; (5) jointly develops and implements healthcare provider training and tools; (6) supports development of pro bono partnerships and initiatives; and (7) mentors other healthcare team members, medical residents and students engaged in MLP-related activities. See http://www.medical-legalpartnership.org/resources/library/1198.

Institutional Transformation: Core component of the MLP model; MLPs transform health and legal institutions by providing evidence-based recommendations to conduct quality improvement projects that can help make internal systems more efficient and effective to better serve patients and families.

Legal Champion: Lawyer who serves as a legal leader and strategist as part of the MLP team; he or she works directly with the healthcare team to (1) develop and strengthen relationships with healthcare institutions, departments, clinics and providers and relevant graduate schools; (2) develop and strengthen relationships with legal institutions, departments, law schools, lawyers and paralegals; (3) provide insight into healthcare infrastructure that may affect MLP activities; (4) facilitates MLP presence and access in all clinical areas; (5) jointly develops and implements healthcare provider training and tools; (6) supports development of pro bono partnerships and initiatives; and (7) mentor other healthcare team members, medical residents and students engaged in MLP-related activities.

Practice Transformation: Core component of the MLP model; MLPs transform health and legal practices in multiple ways, including training frontline healthcare providers to screen for and triage patients with potential legal needs and facilitating joint data tracking and the documentation of legal information within patient medical records.

Referral System: MLPs connect with clients via the healthcare setting in a team-oriented, integrated referral system, which facilitates critical, efficient, shared triage and problem-solving among health and legal teams who care for patients with complex multidisciplinary needs; enables lawyers to reach clients earlier, to focus on preventive action and to avoid the escalation of legal problems.

Note

The editors thank the following people for their contributions to the glossary: From the National Center for Medical-Legal Partnership: Brandy Gonzales; from Medical-Legal Partnership Boston: Leah Rappaport, Amy VanHeuverzwyn, Alingon Mitra, Venchele Saint Dic, Jessica Moyer, Rebecca Diamond, Michelle Wu and Jeffrey Lewis.

---

1. "Food Deserts," Centers for Disease Control and Prevention, available at: http://www.cdc.gov/Features/FoodDeserts/.

2. "Health Disparities," National Association of Chronic Disease Directors, available at: www.chronicdisease.org.

3. "Heat or Eat Dilemma," WK Kellogg Foundation, accessed February 22, 2011, available at: www.wkkf.org.

4. National Center for Children in Poverty, available at: www.nccp.org.

5. Center for Disease Control and Prevention, *2003–2008 HIV Prevention Community Planning Guidance*, available at: http://www.cdc.gov/hiv/topics/cba/resources/guidelines/hiv-cp/appendixD.htm.

6. "Social Determinants of Health," World Health Organization, accessed February 22, 2011, available at: www.who.int/en/.

7. C. Ferguson, "Barriers to Serving the Vulnerable: Thoughts of a Former Public Official," *Health Affairs*, 26 (2007): 1358–1365.

8. "Department of Biostatistics," Harvard School of Public Health, accessed February 22, 2011, available at: http://www.hsph.harvard.edu.

9. "Center for Disease Control and Prevention," Centers for Disease Control and Prevention, accessed February 22, 2011, available at: www.cdc.gov.

10. D. P. Ross, "Policy Approaches to Address the Impact of Poverty on Health," *Canadian Institute for Health Information*, June 2003.

11. "Environmental Health," World Health Organization, accessed February 22, 2011, available at: http://www.who.int/topics/environmental_health/en.

12. "Epidemiology," Center for Disease Control and Prevention, accessed February 22, 2011, available at: www.cdc.gov.

13. Merriam-Webster Online, s.v. "population," accessed February 22, 2011, available at: http://www.merriam-webster.com/dictionary/population.

14. "Overview of Prevention," Mental Health: A Report of the Surgeon General, accessed February 22, 2011, available at: www.surgeongeneral.gov.

15. "Glossary," Bureau Of Justice Assistance Center for Program Evaluation and Performance Measurement, available at: http://www.ojp.usdoj.gov/BJA/evaluation/glossary/index.htm.

16. Ibid.

17. J. Cwikel, *Social Epidemiology: Strategies for Public Health Activism* (New York: Columbia University Press, 2006).

18. Medical Health Encyclopedia Online, s.v. "Upstream Intervention" accessed February 22, 2011, available at: http://www.jrank.org/health/pages/38312/upstream-intervention.html.

19. Mirriam Webster Dictionary Online, s.v. "acute" accessed February 22, 2011, available at: http://www.merriam-webster.com.

20. " Attention Deficit Hyperactivity Disorder," National Institute of Mental Health, accessed February 22, 2011, available at: http://www.nimh.nih.gov.

21. "Physician Specialties," Medicare.gov, accessed February 22, 2011, available at: http://www.medicare.gov/find-a-doctor/staticpages/learn/physician-specialties.aspx.

22. Medicine Net, s.v. "allopathic," accessed February 22, 2011, available at: http://www.medterms.com.

23. "Physician Specialties," Medicare.gov, accessed February 22, 2011, available at: http://www.medicare.gov/find-a-doctor/staticpages/learn/physician-specialties.aspx

24. "Glossary," Presbyterian Healthcare Services, accessed February 22, 2011, available at: http://www.phs.org/PHS/healthplans/content/glossary/index.htm.

25. MedlinePlus Online, s.v. "cardiology," accessed February 22, 2011, U.S. National Library of Medicine and National Institute of Health, available at: http://www.nlm.nih.gov.medlineplus/mplus dictionary.html.

26. "Community Care Options," Family Caregiver Alliance: National Center on Caregiving, accessed February 22, 2011, available at: http://www.caregiver.org/.

27. "Duties," Certified Nursing Assistant, accessed February 22, 2011, available at: http://www.certifiednursingassistant.org.

28. MediLexicon Medical Dictionary Online, s.v. "chief complaint," accessed February 22, 2011, available at: http://www.medilexicon.com.

29. MedlinePlus Online, s.v. "chronic," accessed February 22, 2011, U.S. National Library of Medicine and National Institute of Health, available at: http://www.nlm.nih.gov.medlineplus/mplusdictionary.html.

30. "Chronic Disease Prevention and Health Promotion," Centers for Disease Control and Prevention, accessed February 22, 2011, available at: http://www.cdc.gov.

31. "Glossary of Definitions," ACGME, accessed February 22, 2011, available at: http://www.acgme.org.

32. C.M. Perley, "Physician Use of the Curbside Consultation to Address Information Needs: Report on a Collective Case Study," *Journal of the Medical Library Association* 94 (2006):137B44.

33. "Specialties, Credentials, and Glossary," Medicare.gov, accessed February 22, 2011, available at: www.medicare.gov.

34. "Overview of Early Intervention," NICHCY, accessed February 22, 2011, available at: http://www.nichcy.org.

35. "Physician Specialties," Medicare.gov, accessed February 22, 2011, available at: http://www.medicare.gov/find-a-doctor/staticpages/learn/physician-specialties.aspx.

36. MedlinePlus Online, s.v. "failure to thrive," accessed February 22, 2011, U.S. National Library of Medicine and National Institute of Health, available at: http://www.nlm.nih.gov.medlineplus/mplus dictionary.html.

37. "Definition of Family Medicine," American Academy of Family Physicians, accessed February 22, 2011, available at: http://www.aafp.org.

38. "Glossary of Definitions," ACGME, accessed February 22, 2011, available at: http://www.acgme.org.

39. D. Venes, *Taber's Cyclopedic Medical Dictionary, 20th ed.* (Philadelphia: F.A. Davis Company, 2005).

40. "Glossary of Definitions," ACGME, accessed February 22, 2011, available at: http://www.acgme.org.

41. D. Venes, *Taber's Cyclopedic Medical Dictionary.*

42. "What is Histology?," Degree Directory, available at: http://degreedirectory.org/articles/What_ is_Histology.html.

43. MedlinePlus Online, s.v. "homecare," accessed February 22, 2011, U.S. National Library of Medicine and National Institute of Health, available at: http://www.nlm.nih.gov.medlineplus/mplusdictionary.html.

44. MedlinePlus Online, s.v. "hospice," accessed February 22, 2011, U.S. National Library of Medicine and National Institute of Health, available at: http://www.nlm.nih.gov.medlineplus/mplusdictionary.html.

45. A. Santiago, "Inpatient care," About.com, available at: http://healthcareers.about.com/od/h/g/ inpatient.htm.

46. Glossary of Definitions" ACGME, accessed February 22, 2011, available at: http://www.acgme.org.

47. "Terms We Use About Quality," Legacy Health, available at: http://www.legacyhealth.org/body. cfm?id=751.

48. "Long-Term Care," Medicare.gov, available at: http://www.medicare.gov/longtermcare/static/ home.asp.

49. "Medical Assistants," Bureau of Labor Statistics, *Occupational Outlook Handbook 2010–11 Edition,* available at: http://www.bls.gov/oco/ocos164.htm.

50. D. Venes, *Taber's Cyclopedic Medical Dictionary.*

51. Agency for Toxic Substances and Disease Registry, "Glossary of Terms," Centers for Disease Control and Prevention, available at: http://www.atsdr.cdc.gov/glossary.html#G-M-.

52. MedlinePlus Online, s.v. "mortality," accessed February 22, 2011, U.S. National Library of Medicine and National Institute of Health, available at: http://www.nlm.nih.gov.medlineplus/mplusdictionary.html.

53. A. Santiago, "Neurology B What is Neurology," About.com, available at: http://healthcareers. about.com/od/n/f/Neurology.htm.

54. "Glossary," *ACHRE Report,* The Office of Health, Safety and Security, available at: http://www.hss.energy.gov/HealthSafety/ohre/roadmap/achre/glossary.html.

55. MedlinePlus Online, s.v. "nurse," accessed February 22, 2011, U.S. National Library of Medicine and National Institute of Health, available at: http://www.nlm.nih.gov.medlineplus/mplusdictionary.html.

56. MedlinePlus Online, s.v. "nurse practitioner," accessed February 22, 2011, U.S. National Library of Medicine and National Institute of Health, available at: http://www.nlm.nih.gov.medlineplus/ mplusdictionary.html.

57. MedlinePlus Online, s.v. "nursing home," accessed February 22, 2011, U.S. National Library of Medicine and National Institute of Health, available at: http://www.nlm.nih.gov.medlineplus/mplus dictionary.html.

58. "Obesity," WebMD, available at: http://www.webmd.com/diet/guide/what-is-obesity.

59. D. Venes, *Taber's Cyclopedic Medical Dictionary.*

60. MSN Encarta, s.v. "opthalmology," accessed February 22, 2011, available at: http://encarta.msn. com/dictionary_1861635169/ophthalmology.html.

61. MSN Encarta, s.v. "orthopedics," accessed February 22. 2011, available at: http://encarta.msn. com/dictionary_/orthopedics.html.

62. Medical Dictionary, s.v. "osteopathy," accessed February 22, 2011, MedicineNet, available at: http://www.medterms.com/script/main/art.asp?articlekey=4684.

63. "What is an Otolaryngologist?," American Academy of Otolaryngology, available at: http://www.entnet.org/HealthInformation/otolaryngologist.cfm.

64. Tricia Ellis-Christensen, Edited by O. Wallace, "What is the Difference between Inpatient and Outpatient?," WiseGeek, Last modified: January 5, 2011, available at: http://www.wisegeek.com/what-is-the-difference-between-inpatient-and-outpatient.htm.

65. "What is Palliative Care," GetPalliativeCare.org, available at: http://www.getpalliativecare.org/whatis.

66. MedlinePlus Online, s.v. "pathology," accessed February 22, 2011, U.S. National Library of Medicine and National Institute of Health, available at: http://www.nlm.nih.gov.medlineplus/mplusdictionary.html.

67. MedlinePlus Online, s.v. "pathophysiology," accessed February 22, 2011, U.S. National Library of Medicine and National Institute of Health, available at: http://www.nlm.nih.gov.medlineplus/mplusdictionary.html.

68. D. Venes, *Taber's Cyclopedic Medical Dictionary.*

69. Ibid.

70. Merriam-Webster Dictionary, s.v. "physical medicine and rehabilitation," available at: http://www.merriam-webster.com/medical/physical%20medicine%20and%20rehabilitation.

71. MedlinePlus Online, s.v. "pathophysiology," accessed February 22, 2011, U.S. National Library of Medicine and National Institute of Health, available at: http://www.nlm.nih.gov.medlineplus/mplusdictionary.html.

72. D. Venes, *Taber's Cyclopedic Medical Dictionary.*

73. Ibid.

74. MedlinePlus Online, s.v. "pulmonology," accessed February 22, 2011, U.S. National Library of Medicine and National Institute of Health, available at: http://www.nlm.nih.gov.medlineplus/mplus dictionary.html.

75. D. Venes, *Taber's Cyclopedic Medical Dictionary.*

76. Glossary of Definitions" ACGME, accessed February 22, 2011, available at: http://www.acgme.org.

77. Merriam-Webster Dictionary, s.v. "residency," available at: http://www.merriam-webster.com/medical/residency; Glossary of Definitions" ACGME, accessed February 22, 2011, http://www.acgme.org.

78. "Glossary of Definitions," ACGME, accessed February 22, 2011, available at: http://www.acgme.org.

79. "A Practical Guide to Clinical Medicine," University of California, San Diego, available at: http://meded.ucsd.edu/clinicalmed/ros.htm.

80. MedlinePlus Online, s.v. "social worker," accessed February 22, 2011, U.S. National Library of Medicine and National Institute of Health, available at: http://www.nlm.nih.gov.medlineplus/mplusdictionary.html.; *Social Workers*," Bureau of Labor Statistics, *Occupational Outlook Handbook 2010–11 Edition*, available at: http://www.bls.gov/oco/ocos060.htm#nature.

81. "Tertiary Care Definition," Johns Hopkins Medicine, available at: http://www.hopkinsmedicine.org/patient_care/pay_bill/insurance_footnotes.html.

82. Trisha Torrey, "Standard of Care," available at: http://patients.about.com/od/glossary/g/standardofcare.htm.

83. D. Venes, *Taber's Cyclopedic Medical Dictionary.*

84. MSN Encarta, s.v. "urology," available at: http://encarta.msn.com/dictionary_/urologic.html.

85. AAMC, "About the AAMC," available at: https://www.aamc.org/about/.

86. Centers for Medicare and Medicaid Services, "Medicare 'Accountable Care Organizations,'" available at: https://www.cms.gov/OfficeofLegislation/Downloads/AccountableCareOrganization.pdf.

87. Accreditation Council for Graduate Medical Education, available at: http://www.acgme.org/ac Website/home/home.asp.

88. MeSH NLM Controlled Vocabulary, s.v. "allied health occupation," available at: http://www.ncbi.nlm.nih.gov/mesh/68016390; MeSH NLM Controlled Vocabulary, s.v. "allied health personnel," http://www.ncbi.nlm.nih.gov/mesh/68000488.

89. "Our Mission," American Medical Association, available at: http://www.ama-assn.org/ama/pub/about-ama/our-mission.shtml.

90. MedlinePlus Online, s.v. "capitated," accessed February 22, 2011, U.S. National Library of Medicine and National Institute of Health, available at: http://www.nlm.nih.gov.medlineplus/mplus dictionary.html.

91. S. Rosenbaum and R. Margulies, "New Requirements for Tax-Exempt Charitable Hospitals," Health Reform GPS, December 20, 2010, available at: http://www.healthreformgps.org/resources/new-requirements-for-tax-exempt-charitable-hospitals.

92. Office of Academic Personnel, "The Importance of Being a Department Chair," University of California Irvine, available at: http://www.ap.uci.edu/Workshops/ChairRetreat_2008/Binder/Importance%20of%20Being%20Dept%20Chair.pdf.

93. K. Fonkych and G. Melnick, "Disproportionate Share Hospital Subsidies for Treating the Uninsured," *Medical Care* 48, no. 9 (2010): 809–14.

94. Health Resources and Services Administration, "The Health Center Program: What is a Health Center," available at: http://bphc.hrsa.gov/about/; Centers for Medicare and Medicaid Services, "Fact Sheet: Federally Qualified Health Center," available at: http://www.cms.gov/MLNProducts/downloads/fqhcfactsheet.pdf.

95. MeSH NLM Controlled Vocabulary, s.v. "hospital administrator," available at: http://www.ncbi.nlm.nih.gov/mesh?term=hospital%20administrator.

96. MeSH NLM Controlled Vocabulary, s.v. "managed care," available at: http://www.ncbi.nlm.nih.gov/mesh?term=managed%20care.

97. Health Resources and Services Administration, "Shortage Designation: HPSAs, MUAs & MUPs," available at: http://bhpr.hrsa.gov/shortage/.

98. National Association of Community Health Centers, "About NACHC," available at: http://www.nachc.org/about-nachc.cfm.

99. MeSH NLM Controlled Vocabulary, s.v. "nurse manager," available at: http://www.ncbi.nlm.nih.gov/mesh?term=nurse%20manager.

100. AAFP, AAP, ACP, and AOA, "Joint Principles of the Patient-Centered Medical Home," available at: http://www.acponline.org/advocacy/where_we_stand/medical_home/approve_jp.pdf.

101. American Academy of Family Physicians, "Primary Care," available at: http://www.aafp.org/online/en/home/policy/policies/p/primarycare.html.

102. Medical Dictionary, s.v. "tertiary care," available at: http://medical-dictionary.thefreedictionary.com/tertiary+care.

103. Medical Dictionary, s.v. "secondary care," available at: http://medical-dictionary.thefree dictionary.com/secondary+care.

104. Medical Dictionary, s.v. "tertiary care," available at: http://medical-dictionary.thefree dictionary.com/tertiary+care.

105. American Bar Association, available at: http://www.americanbar.org/aba.html.

106. *Black's Law Dictionary* 92 (8th ed. 2004).

107. *Black's Law Dictionary* 48 (8th ed. 2004).

108. Ibid.

109. American Academy of Family Physicians, "Ethics and Advance Planning for End-of-Life Care," available at: http://www.aafp.org/online/en/home/policy/policies/e/ethicsadvplan.html.

110. Dean G. Kilpatrick, "Definitions of Public Policy and the Law," Medical University of South Carolina, available at: http://www.musc.edu/vawprevention/policy/definition.shtml.

111. *Black's Law Dictionary* 1235 (8th ed. 2004).

112. Child Abuse Prevention Act, 42 U.S.C. 5106g sec. 111 (definitions).

113. B. H. Barton, "Against Civil Gideon (and for Pro Se Court Reform)," 62 Fla. L. Rev. 1227, 1227 (2010).

114. "Civil Procedure: An Overview," Cornell University Law School, Legal Information Institute, available at: http://topics.law.cornell.edu/wex/civil_procedure.

115. Superior Court of California, County of Santa Clara. "Overview of the State Court System," available at: http://www.scselfservice.org/home/overview.htm#2.

116. *Black's Law Dictionary* 104 (3rd pocket ed. 2006).

117. *Black's Law Dictionary* (9th edition, 2009).

118. United States Department of Labor, "Continuation of Health Coverage—COBRA," available at: http://www.dol.gov/dol/topic/health-plans/cobra.htm.

119. "Common Law," E.B. Williams Library Tutorials, available at: http://www.ll.georgetown.edu/tutorials/definitions/common_law.html.

120. Wikipedia, s.v. "United States Constitution," available at: http://en.wikipedia.org/wiki/United_States_Constitution.

121. *Black's Law Dictionary* 143 (3rd pocket ed. 2006).

122. *Black's Law Dictionary* 107–108 (3rd pocket ed. 2006).

123. Cornell University Law School, Legal Information Institute, "Criminal Law," available at: http://topics.law.cornell.edu/wex/criminal_law.

124. Superior Court of California, County of Santa Clara. "Overview of the State Court System." available at: http://www.scselfservice.org/home/overview.htm#2.

125. *Black's Law Dictionary* 190–191 (3rd pocket ed. 2006).

126. Madison County District Attorney's Office, 23rd Judicial Circuit, Huntsville, AL, available at: http://www.districtattorney.org/; New York County District Attorney's Office, http://manhattanda.org/.

127. American Psychological Association, "Elder Abuse and Neglect: In Search of Solutions," available at: http://www.apa.org/pi/aging/resources/guides/elder-abuse.aspx.

128. United States Department of Health and Human Services, *EMTALA Overview* (2010), available at: http://www.cms.gov/EMTALA/ (last accessed 2/22/11).

129. *Black's Law Dictionary* 573 (8th ed. 2004).

130. United States Department for Health and Human Services, *Medicaid Early and Periodic Screening and Diagnostic Treatment Overview* (2005), available at: https://www.cms.gov/MedicaidEarlyPeriodicScrn/ (last accessed 2/22/11).

131. United States Department of Housing and Urban Development, *Fair Housing Laws and Presidential Executive Orders* (2009), available at:http://www.hud.gov/offices/fheo/FHLaws/ (last accessed 2/22/11).

132. The Free Dictionary by Farlex, s.v. "federalism," available at: http://legal-dictionary.thefreedictionary.com/Federalism.

133. *Black's Law Dictionary* 638 (8th ed. 2004).

134. Department of Homeland Security, "Federal Definition of Foster Care and Related Terms," available at: http://www.dhs.state.mn.us/main/groups/county_access/documents/pub/dhs_id_027331.pdf.

135. Duhaime.org, s.v. "general counsel," available at: http://www.duhaime.org/LegalDictionary/G/GeneralCounsel.aspx.

136. MIT Workplace Center, *The Family Caregiver Handbook*, available at: http://web.mit.edu/workplacecenter/hndbk/sec7.html#P.

137. United States Department of Health and Human Services, *Understanding Health Information Privacy*, available at: http://www.hhs.gov/ocr/privacy/hipaa/understanding/index.html (last accessed 2/22/11).

138. *Black's Law Dictionary* 789 (8th ed. 2004).

139. Ibid.

140. United States Department of Labor, "Income Supports," Office of Disability Employment Policy, available at: http://www.dol.gov/odep/categories/employment_supports/income.htm.

141. *Black's Law Dictionary* 323 (8th ed. 2004).

142. World Health Organization, "The Economic Dimensions of Interpersonal Violence," Violence and Injury Prevention and Disability, available at: http://www.who.int/violence_injury_prevention/publications/violence/economic_dimensions/en/; New York State Office for the Prevention of Domestic Violence, "What is Domestic Violence?," available at: http://www.opdv.state.ny.us/whatisdv/about_dv/index.html.

143. Available at: IOLTA, www.iolta.org.

144. *Black's Law Dictionary* 386–87 (3rd pocket ed. 2006).

145. USCIS Website Glossary, available at: http://www.uscis.gov/portal/site/uscis/menuitem.5af9bb95919 f35e66f614176543f6d1a/?vgnextoid=070695c4f635f010VgnVCM1000000ecd190aRCRD&vgnextchannel=b328 194d3e88d010VgnVCM10000048f3d6a1RCRD.

146. Webster's New World Law Dictionary, s.v. "legal aid," available at: http://law.yourdictionary.com/legal-aid.

147. American Bar Association, *Legal Needs and Civil Justice: A Survey of Americans* (1994), available   at http://www.americanbar.org/content/dam/aba/migrated/legalservices/downloads/sclaid/legal needstudy.authcheckdam.pdf (last accessed 2/22/11).

148. Wikipedia, s.v. "LGBT," available at: http://en.wikipedia.org/wiki/LGBT.

149. *Black's Law Dictionary* 915 (8th ed. 2004).

150. New York State Office of Children and Family Services, "Child Abuse Prevention," available at: http://www.ocfs.state.ny.us/main/prevention/faqs_mandatedreporter.asp#mandated; California Welfare and Institutions Code Section 15630–15632, http://www.leginfo.ca.gov/cgi-bin/display-code?
section=wic&group=15001-16000&file=15630-15632.

151. United States Department of Housing and Urban Development, *McKinney-Vento Act*, (2007), available at: http://www.hud.gov/offices/cpd/homeless/lawsandregs/mckv.cfm (last accessed 2/22/11).

152. *Black's Law Dictionary* 1003 (8th ed. 2004).

153. Ibid.

154. USCIS Website glossary, available at: http://www.uscis.gov/portal/site/uscis/menuitem.eb 1d4c2a3e5b9ac89243c6a7543f6d1a/?vgnextoid=d84d6811264a3210VgnVCM100000b92ca60aRCRD&vg nextchannel=d84d6811264a3210VgnVCM100000b92ca60aRCRD.

155. *Black's Law Dictionary* 520 (3rd pocket ed. 2006).

156. *Black's Law Dictionary* 1226 (8th ed. 2004).

157. *Black's Law Dictionary* 1241 (8th ed. 2004).

158. MIT Workplace Center, *The Family Caregiver Handbook*.

159. *Black's Law Dictionary* 254 (3rd pocket ed. 2006).

160. *Black's Law Dictionary* 573 (3rd pocket ed. 2006).

161. *Black's Law Dictionary* 576 (3rd pocket ed. 2006).

162. USCIS Website Glossary, available at: http://www.uscis.gov/portal/site/uscis/menuitem.eb1 d4c2a3e5b9ac89243c6a7543f6d1a/?vgnextoid=829b0a5659083210VgnVCM100000082ca60aRCRD&vg nextchannel=829b0a5659083210VgnVCM100000082ca60aRCRD.

163. Law Server, s.v. "federal public defender," available at: http://www.lawserver.com/law/legal-dictionary/federal-public-defender-definition.

164. D. G. Kilpatrick, "Definitions of Public Policy and the Law," available at: http://www.musc.edu/vawprevention/policy/definition.shtml/

165. *Black's Law Dictionary* 1293 (8th ed. 2004).

166. *Black's Law Dictionary* 1311 (8th ed. 2004).

167. United States Department of Agriculture, *Supplemental Nutrition Assistance Program* (2010), available at: http://www.fns.usda.gov/snap/faqs.htm.

168. Social Security Administration, *Benefits for People with Disabilities* (2011), available at: http://www.ssa.gov/disability/.

169. *Black's Law Dictionary* 1480 (8th ed. 2004).

170. 'Lectric Law Library's Lexicon, s.v. "statute," available at: http://www.lectlaw.com/def2/s071.htm.

171. *Black's Law Dictionary* 1504 (8th ed. 2004).

172. *Black's Law Dictionary* 724 (3rd pocket ed. 2006).

173. United States Department of Justice, "United States Attorneys," available at: http://www.justice.gov/usao/.

174. National Domestic Violence Hotline, "Violence Against Women Act (VAWA)," available at: http://www.thehotline.org/get-educated/violence-against-women-act-vawa/.

175. California WIC, "Women, Infants and Children Program," available at: http://www.cdph.ca.gov/programs/wicworks/Pages/default.aspx.

Appendices

Appendix A

Example of a Medical Record

Chief Complaint: Routine Health Care Maintenance and Asthma

History of Present Illness:
Bobby is a 4 y.o. who has a history of necrotizing pneumonia and 6 other hospitalizations for asthma. He has been most recently hospitalized in July for asthma. He is followed by a pulmonary specialist who has referred him to Breathe Easy for his multiple environmental allergens. They are working with ISD and their landlord to have the mice exterminated. Mom is faithfully giving Bobby Flovent twice a day, however, she is using an old Flovent container and is not sure of the dosage. She has not started the Singulair and Loratadine at this time because she wanted to talk about this with me first.

His language development has improved in Head Start. He speaks in full sentences in Cape Verdian and English.

Mom has missed multiple days of work for Bobby's various admissions and has lost her job. She has recently found another job, however, it is part-time and she is struggling with her bills. She is in a market value apartment.

Bobby is a healthy eater and she tries to have him avoid juice and never gives him soda. However, his mom admits his grandmother does give him juice often.

Past Medical History:
Necrotizing Pneumonia
Anemia
Food and Environmental Allergies
Asthma

Medications:
ALBUTEROL SULFATE 0.083 % NEB SOL (ALBUTEROL SULFATE) Use one vial every 4–6 hours prn asthma
AEROCHAMBER PLUS-MEDIUM MASK MISC (RESPIRATORY THERAPY SUPPLIES) use w/ inhalers as directed. disp 2 for home & school
PROAIR HFA 108 (90 BASE) MCG/ACT AERS (ALBUTEROL SULFATE) 2 puffs up to q 4 hours prn asthma. disp 2 for home & school
SINGULAIR 4 MG CHEW (MONTELUKAST SODIUM) 1 tablet once daily at bedtime to control asthma.
CLARITIN 5 MG/5ML SYRP (LORATADINE) 5 ml by mouth once daily to control allergy. generic OK
FLOVENT AERO 110 MCG/ACT (FLUTICASONE PROPIONATE (INHAL)) Two puffs twice a day to control asthma. use chamber. rinse mouth after use

Allergies:
• NUTS
• PET DANDER, DOG CAT
• MICE, MOLD
• DUST MITES

Social History: Mom from Cape Verde, lives alone with Bobby. Biological father not involved, however, good friend has acted like Bobby's father since Bobby's birth.

Developmental Milestones/Activities

Developmental Age (months): 48

PEDS done today? Yes

PEDS Interpretation: negative

Asthma Visit

Levels of Asthma Control:
Daytime Symptoms: <= 2/week
Limitations of Activities: None
Night (with awakenings): Some
Need for reliever/rescue treatment: <= 2/week
Exacerbations: One or more/year

Medication Use:
ACTUAL frequency of controller use: 2 times/day
Are symptoms reduced by controller? A lot
Reliever use when NOT acutely ill: less than weekly

Asthma impact during last 12 months:
ER visits: 2
Acute Non-ER visits: 0
Hospitalizations: 4

Review of Symptoms

Gen: No fevers, fatigue
ENT: Mild congestion
Resp: 1–2 nighttime wheezing per week
GI: No constipation
GU: No polyuria

Vital Signs
Height / Weight
Ht: 44.2 in. 112.2 cm.
Wt: 49.50 lbs. 22.5 kg.
BMI: 17.88
BMI Percentile: 95th
BSA: 0.83

Vitals
P: 102
Blood Pressures
#1: 96 / 54 **HR:** 102

Oxygen Testing
O2 resting 100%

Physical Exam
Gen: well developed, well nourished, no acute distress
Skin: no rashes
H-Ear: no external deformities, canals clear, TM's pearly gray
Neck: neck nodes not palpable

CV: RRR, no murmurs, no gallops, peripheral pulses intact, <2 sec cap refill
Resp: clear to auscultation, no respiratory distress, no accessory muscle use
GI/Abd: soft, nondistended, nontender, no guarding, normal BS, no hepatosplenomegaly, no hernias
MGU: penis normal, testes descended bilaterally

Impression and Plan

AP: Bobby is a 4 y.o. with a significant history of asthma and necrotizing pneumonia.
1. Asthma: reinforced that mom should start the Claritin and Singulair. Mom will also check her Flovent bottle at home and ensure it is 110 mcg. He will follow up with the pulmonologist in September. I will call the mother after the appointment to ensure she understands the plan.
-Reviewed Asthma Action Plan with her today as well.
2. Language/Development: right on target! Head Start in September.
3. Trouble with bills, patient referred to family help desk. Will go and see them tomorrow. Mom given permission to e-mail or have me paged if she needs any letters.
4. BMI: 95%
-Encouraged to limit juice intake, will continue to follow.
5. RHCM: 4 y.o. vaccines given and caught up on PCV-13.

Lilly Frank, MD

Appendix B

Example of a Legal Intake

Name: Joceline Rocha Fortes
Referring Provider: Dr. Lilly Frank
MLP at Intake: Paul Sanchez
Issues: Income Supports, Housing, Education, Legal/Immigration Status, Personal Stability
Steps Taken: Conflict check and income eligibility check complete—passed both.

Summary

Legal permanent resident mom (originally from Cape Verde) with 1 U.S. citizen son (4 years old) is seeking assistance with housing, income supports, and education issues.

Income Supports

Mom applied for food stamps soon after losing her prior job. She was told that she does not qualify, but she could not understand why. Her new part-time work gives her $200/week (before taxes), and she would like to apply again for food stamps as well as any other benefits available to her. She has been skipping meals to pay rent and is concerned the food she can afford is not giving son proper nutrition. On occasion—approximately twice a month, though not consistently—mom's boyfriend will give them $50 to purchase groceries.

Housing

Mom lives in 1 BR apartment. She has contacted landlord multiple times about mice infestation and mold in housing. Exterminators were sent once, but mice have returned. Landlord has been unresponsive since and failed to address mold at all. Son suffers from asthma, which is being exacerbated by these conditions. Mom says that his physician is willing to write a letter stating this. She is particularly concerned about the mice droppings she finds near the kitchen.

Mom applied for public housing 4 months ago, but she says that she has not received any sort of response from the PHA [Providence Housing Authority] yet. She believes (but is not sure) her housing application made mention of her son's asthma.

Education

Mom is concerned about what will happen to son after Head Start since she does not know if his next school will be able to continue to teach according to his needs. Son is starting to speak full sentences in English and Cape Verdian, but he has developmental delays. She is looking for a school that will give him a proper assessment and possibly an IEP [individualized education program].

Legal/Immigration Status

Mom would like to get citizenship. She has taken the naturalization exam once, but was not able to pass. She was hoping to be referred to an organization that could help her prepare to take it again.

Personal Stability

Mom has birth certificate of son. Since biological father is no longer involved, however, mom would like to remove his name from the birth certificate. Instead, she would like add the name of her boyfriend, who acts like a father to her son.

Appendix 1.1

Health Impact Assessment

The following is excerpted from the Pew Charitable Trusts and the Robert Wood Johnson Foundation, *Health Impact Assessment Project: Advancing Smarter Policies for Healthier Communities, Policy Brief* (December 2010).

Bringing Public Health Data to Decision Making

Preventable health problems, including many cases of heart disease, diabetes, asthma, and injuries, are taking a huge toll on American families. For the first time in U.S. history, data suggest that today's children may live shorter lives than their parents. These problems also threaten our nation's economic vitality. Heart disease and diabetes alone now account for more than 700,000 deaths in the United States annually and cost the nation over $650 billion in medical expenses, disability, missed work and financial losses associated with premature death. These costs are rising every year. To improve Americans' health, the root causes of these illnesses must be addressed. By factoring health consequences into the process when drafting new laws and regulations, building a major roadway, planning for a city's growth or developing a school curriculum, policy makers can capitalize on hidden opportunities to improve health, save on health-related costs, and use limited resources more wisely. Health Impact Assessment (HIA) is a practical, evidence-driven tool to accomplish these goals. Many nations, large lending banks, and major industries such as oil, gas, and mining are adopting HIA to improve health, control costs, and build trust with communities.

HIA in Decision Making: A Flexible Approach

HIA brings together scientific data, health expertise, and public input to identify the potential health effects of a new proposal and to help craft policy recommendations that minimize risks and capitalize on opportunities to improve health. HIA gives federal, tribal, state, and local leaders the information they need to make better decisions today to prevent health problems in their communities tomorrow.

The basic HIA process can be readily adapted to fit the scope, resources, and timeline of a given decision. In a recent survey by the Health Impact Project, HIA practitioners reported that most HIAs take from six weeks to a year to complete and cost $10,000 to $200,000—a fraction of the time and resources that often go into environmental studies and permitting procedures. HIA also shows promise as a way to help policy makers who are facing difficult budgetary decisions. For example, the New Hampshire Center for Public Policy Studies is conducting an HIA to shed light on the health implications of proposed budget changes for 2011 in order to help legislators make the difficult choices necessary to balance the state budget.

713

Steps of HIA

1. SCREENING
↓ Determine whether an HIA is needed and likely to be useful.
2. SCOPING
↓ In consultation with stakeholders, develop a plan for the HIA, including the identification of potential health risks and benefits.
3. ASSESSMENT
↓ Describe the baseline health of affected communities and assess the potential impacts of the decision.
4. RECOMMENDATIONS
↓ Develop practical solutions that can be implemented within the political, economic or technical limitations of the project or policy being assessed.
5. REPORTING
↓ Disseminate the findings to decision makers, affected communities and other stakeholders.
6. MONITORING AND EVALUATION
Monitor the changes in health or health risk factors and evaluate the efficacy of measure that are implemented and the HIA process as a whole.
The HIA process encourages public input at each step.

Benefits and Best Uses of HIA

- *HIA can build community support and reduce opposition to a proposed project.* By ensuring that decisions are made with full attention to community concerns, HIA helps reduce conflicts that can delay projects. For example, an Alaska Native community considered litigation over plans to allow oil and gas lease sales in their traditional hunting areas. Instead, the Bureau of Land Management (BLM) worked with the local government to complete an HIA, which resulted in new protections that addressed community concerns while still allowing development to go forward. Owing in part to the success of this HIA, an environmental impact statement associated with the lease sales was never challenged in court. Since then, the BLM has begun using HIA more commonly in similar planning and permitting decisions.

- *HIA facilitates collaboration across sectors.* HIA provides a structured, pragmatic way for those in public health to collaborate with officials in other agencies and sectors, ensuring that these officials have the health data they need to make better decisions.

- *HIA is not always necessary.* If health is already a focus of a proposed policy or project, or if the potential health effects are too hypothetical, HIA may not offer any new information to decision makers. To avoid unnecessary time and expense, an effective approach to screening can determine whether HIA will add value.

Opportunities for HIA

Momentum is building in the HIA field as more and more cities, states, tribal, and federal agencies seek better ways to factor health into their decisions. The Health Impact Project and the Centers for Disease Control and Prevention (CDC) have identified nearly 120 HIAs that have been completed or are in progress in 24 states. Local planning departments, state environmental regulators, and federal agencies carrying out environmental impact statements are beginning to request health impact assessments as well. As initiatives progress at all levels of government, many opportunities exist to incorporate HIA and build healthier policies. Examples include:

- Government officials at all levels should use HIA for important new decisions outside the health sector—including, for example, transportation, housing and urban planning, educational programming, agricultural policy, and energy and natural resource projects—to minimize unnecessary risks and unanticipated costs and to help create healthier communities.

- Executive branch agencies involved in major infrastructure projects, such as Housing and Urban Development and the Department of Transportation, should consider ways to use HIA as a means to integrate health considerations in current and future initiatives.

- The newly established, cabinet-level and multi-agency National Prevention, Health Promotion, and Public Health Council should recommend that any federal agency that is making decisions with potentially significant health effects should use HIA.

- In spring 2011, the National Academy of Sciences plans to release a report on HIA, which is intended to provide guidance to federal, tribal, state, and local agency officials and others. Once this report becomes available, agencies should consult it to determine where there are opportunities to apply HIA in decisions that have a potential for significant health effects.

Examples of HIA Topics

Transportation and Land Use	Family and Employment	Energy and Natural Resources	Other
City planning, housing development and urban renewal Transportation corridor planning, highway projects and light rail systems	Paid sick leave policies Minimum wage ordinance After-school programs School siting decisions	Planning and permitting oil, gas and mining projects Carbon cap-and-trade regulations Permitting and siting new power plants	State budget decisions Food and agriculture policy

Note: See www.healthimpactproject.org for project descriptions and key findings.

Learn More about HIA at:

Health Impact Project: www.healthimpactproject.org

CDC Healthy Places: www.cdc.gov/healthyplaces/hia.htm

HIA Clearinghouse Learning and Information Center: www.ph.ucla.edu/hs/hiaclic

Human Impact Partners: www.humanimpact.org

World Health Organization HIA: www.who.int/hia/en

Appendix 3.1

National Center for Medical-Legal Partnership 2009 Site Survey Results, Executive Summary

Direct Legal Assistance for Vulnerable Individuals and Families

Medical-legal partnership teams at 137 hospitals and health centers:

- Provided direct legal assistance to nearly **13,000 individuals and families**
- Provided nearly **3,000 consultations** to healthcare partners about a particular individual or family's legal problem

Training the Next Generation of Healthcare and Legal Providers

- MLP teams trained nearly **8,000 front-line healthcare providers** to recognize the connection between unmet legal needs and health.
- MLP curriculum is incorporated in **52 residency programs** across the U.S. in pediatrics, family medicine, oncology, adolescent medicine, geriatrics and internal medicine.
- **25 medical schools** are affiliated with MLPs, 24% of which offer an MLP rotation, MLP elective and/or MLP course.
- **29 law schools** are affiliated with MLPs. 80% of which offer an MLP clinic or MLP externship.

About the 2009 MLP Partnership Site Survey

In January 2010, the MLP Network was comprised of 76 medical-legal partnership programs serving 180 hospitals and health centers in the United States and Canada with an additional 12-15 MLPs in active development.

Fifty-five programs (72% of the Network) serving 137 hospitals and health centers completed the annual MLP Network Partnership Site Survey.

This data reflects a portion of MLP work across the U.S.

Financial Return

For Patient-Clients

Thirty-three MLPs track the cash benefits they recover on behalf of patient-clients. In 2009, those programs **recovered over $5 million for vulnerable individuals and families.** Those benefits include:

- Over $1.3 million in Social Security Income
- Over $750,000 in Social Security Disability Income
- $65,000 in Food Stamp benefits
- Over $2.8 million in other public benefits

For Healthcare Institutions

Ten MLP programs track the amount of money they recover for healthcare institutions through insurance appeals. In 2009. those programs **recovered over $800,000 for hospitals and health centers** in Medicaid appeals.

From Patients-to-Policy: MLP and Systemic Advocacy

Medical-legal partnerships engaged in dozens of initiatives on behalf of patient-families to change institutional and regulatory systems, including:

Health and Law Partnership in Atlanta, GA addressed a state-wide problem regarding access to home health agency services for Medicaid-eligible disabled children ready for discharge from the hospital. The physician and lawyer MLP teams advocated changing the rule and revising the policy with the state Medicaid agency, and corrective legislation was drafted with input from the MLP team.

Peninsula Family Advocacy Program in San Mateo, CA organized a regional MLP policy initiative to investigate the housing code inspection practices in the San Francisco Bay Area. Medical students researched the link between inadequate housing and poor health and medical partners documented the health connection. A policy brief was written and disseminated in September 2009 with policy recommendations to improve access to healthy housing.

Investment in Medical-Legal Partnership in 2009

Cash Funding

Breakdown of Cash Funding (Total Cash Funding=$8,092,500; n=53)

Medical-legal partnerships received over $8 million combined in cash funding

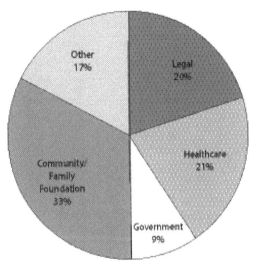

Legal Funding

Legal services (including LSC), state and local bar foundations, law firms, and law schools dedicated over **$1.65 million** in funds to medical-legal partnerships.

IOLTA funds accounted for **$400,000** of the legal funding for partnerships.

Law schools contributed **$530,500** while law firms provided **$414,500.**

Healthcare Funding

Hospitals, health centers, health foundations, healthcare conversion foundations, pharmaceutical companies and medical schools contributed over **$1.67 million** to medical-legal partnerships.

Health conversion foundations accounted for **$645,000** of healthcare funding while other health foundations dedicated **$330,000.**

Other Sources

The largest single contributor to medical-legal partnerships was community and family foundations at over **$2.68 million**.

Local, state and non-LSC federal government funding totaled over **$705,000.**

Pro Bono and In-Kind Funding

Medical-legal partnerships rely heavily on the contributions of *pro bono* partners. In 2009, *pro bono* partners provided nearly **$13 million** in in-kind services.

Medical-legal partnerships received over **$1.2 million** in other in-kind from partner legal and healthcare institutions in office space, equipment and staff time.

Appendix 3.2

American Medical Association and American Bar Association Resolutions on Medical-Legal Partnership

AMERICAN MEDICAL ASSOCIATION

Resident and Fellow Section
33rd Interim Business Meeting
November 5–7, 2009

Resolution 3:
Medical-Legal Partnerships to Improve Health and Well-Being

RESOLVED, That our American Medical Association encourage physicians, allied health professionals, hospitals, and community-based health centers to develop medical-legal partnerships to help identify and resolve diverse legal issues that affect patients' health and well-being (Directive to Take Action); and be it further RESOLVED, That our AMA work with key stakeholder organizations such as the American Academy of Pediatrics, the American Bar Association, the Legal Services Corporation and the federation to (a) educate physicians on the impact of unmet legal needs on the health of patients, (b) provide physicians with information on screening for such unmet legal needs in their patients, and (c) provide physicians, hospitals and health-centers with information on establishing a Medical-Legal Partnership. (Directive to Take Action).

AMERICAN BAR ASSOCIATION

Health Law Section
Report to the House of Delegates
Recommendation
August 2007

RESOLVED, That the American Bar Association encourages lawyers, law firms, legal services agencies, law schools and bar associations to develop medical-legal partnerships with hospitals, community-based health care providers, and social service organizations to help identify and resolve diverse legal issues that affect patients' health and well-being

REPORT

Introduction

Human health is affected not only by biology and behavior, but also by broader socio-economic factors present in the communities and environments in which people live. Health outcomes of persons diagnosed with chronic or acute illness are not dependent solely on pathology and medical treatment, but also on social and emotional support, economic stability, and physical safety, which play significant roles in whether and how well a patient can access and adhere to medicinal and psychological therapies.

Ensuring human health therefore is not exclusively the responsibility of the medical community. Lawyers, for example, assist patients with managing issues related to and often affecting their health, such as insurance coverage and advance planning. Since the early days of the AIDS epidemic, lawyers have assisted people living with HIV/AIDS in preventing or remedying discrimination and breaches of confidentiality, which is critical to encouraging HIV testing which, in turn, is a key to HIV prevention.

When lawyers, doctors, social workers, and others work together to address these concerns, patients are better served and their illnesses are better managed. Indeed, collaborations between legal, medical, and other professionals have proven effective in combating selective socio-economic impediments to health, relieving the anxiety that often accompanies a chronic health condition and improving quality of life for vulnerable populations such as the elderly, children, people living with chronic diseases, and low-income individuals and families.

The purpose of this recommendation is to encourage closer and more frequent collaboration between these professional communities in a truly holistic approach to health and well-being. Specifically, it seeks to promote "medical-legal partnerships," in which lawyers work with health care providers to identify and resolve legal issues affecting patients' health and well-being, including, for example:

- Substandard housing conditions, such as mold in an asthmatic patient's apartment that the patient's landlord refuses to remove;
- Eligibility for health insurance coverage, whether through private or government programs like Medicaid or SCHIP;
- Eligibility for employment benefits, like Family and Medical Leave Act (FMLA), to allow a family member to care for sick loved one;
- Eligibility for income supports, such as Temporary Aid to Needy Families (TANF), SSI benefits, or food stamps;
- Domestic violence, to provide for the physical safety of women and children;
- Family law, to arrange for guardianships, custody, and child support to stabilize a patient's living situation;
- Advance planning, to ensure continuity in health care decision-making; and
- Special education, to secure appropriate education for chronically sick or disabled children.

Typically, a low-income patient who is referred by a health care provider to a lawyer has multiple unmet legal needs that involve socio-economic problems that legal assistance can help to resolve. When these and other legal issues arise during an acute or chronic illness, they can compound the difficulty of resolving patients' medical problems. By working directly with health care providers, lawyers can often intervene to address the social, economic, and environmental determinants of patients' health, thereby improving their overall health and well-being.

Current ABA Policy

Current ABA policies recognize a connection between medicine and law and encourage legal professionals and bar associations to coordinate with health care providers in assisting patients. For example:

- The policy on public health law (04A102) "[u]rges American Bar Association members and lawyers throughout the United States to improve their knowledge of public health law in order to better serve their clients and public who will be affected by new public health threats such as bioterrorism and infectious disease outbreaks." The policy further encourages bar associations to provide pro bono assistance to local health authorities and to ensure "that public health measures are protective of civil and constitutional rights." It also recognizes the importance of involving legal professionals in designing public health protections that are effective and respectful of individual autonomy.

- The policy on long-term care for HIV/AIDS (8/95) supports "action to create legal mechanisms that allow people with HIV, AIDS or other debilitating, chronic, fatal illness to better plan for long-term care for themselves and their families, including standby guardianships, advance medical directives, and viatical settlements." The policy also recommends legislative and educational efforts to protect and assist patients with chronic diseases.

- The policy on breast cancer (00A112) urges legal professionals to "partner with the public health community and bar associations to improve access to legal services for breast cancer patients."

This recommendation builds upon prior policies by promoting development of long-term medical-legal partnerships to address a broad spectrum of health and legal issues that impact patient wellbeing and, by so doing, mitigate or even prevent that impact, thus promoting patient health and, in the process, preserving scarce legal and health care resources.

Medical-Legal Partnerships in Action

The medical-legal partnership model in a hospital setting was developed and established in 1993 by doctors serving low-income patients at Boston Medical Center. The model since has been adapted at more than 60 sites nationwide, many of which have expanded to include partnerships with legal services agencies and law schools. The partnerships improve patient outcomes by addressing—and, where possible, preventing—legal and socio-economic problems that can compromise treatment, seeking to ensure that basic needs of patients, such as food, housing, safety and stability, and education, are met. As appropriate, participating lawyers, doctors, and social workers also engage in systemic policy advocacy to help resolve or avoid these deficiencies in the first instance.

A number of professional organizations have recognized the importance of addressing these socioeconomic determinants of health in addition to providing medical care. The Accreditation Council for Graduate Medical Education, for example, includes among its accreditation requirements "advocating for quality patient care and assisting patients in dealing with system complexities."

The American Academy of Pediatrics residency review requirement includes addressing the multicultural dimensions of health care, community experience, and increasing "emphasis on the importance of the psychosocial, legal, economic, ethical, and cultural aspects of care." Medical-legal partnerships put these directives into concrete action.

Law schools provide a good opportunity to promote these partnerships among health care providers and the legal profession. Required by the ABA's accreditation standards to offer substantial opportunities for real-life practice experiences and for pro bono service, many law schools already offer clinical programs addressing legal issues of the elderly, children, people living with chronic diseases, and low-income individuals and families. By partnering with health care providers and thereby offering a holistic approach to clients' problems, law schools can increase the effectiveness of their clinical programs as well as foster a spirit of interdisciplinary cooperation among the professions. Similarly, legal services organizations can extend the reach of their programs and the effectiveness of client representation by creating these partnerships with health care providers in their communities.

Summary

Just as the medical profession advocates preventive health care, so too by entering into these partnerships with health care providers, the legal profession can advance a "preventive law" strategy for addressing clients' social and economic problems and thereby improve clients' health and well-being, especially those from low-income and other under-served communities.

Appendix 4.1

Medical Education Competencies

Institute of Medicine Core Competencies

Provide patient-centered care

Identify, respect, and care about patients' differences, values, preferences, and expressed needs; relieve pain and suffering; coordinate continuous care; listen to, clearly inform, communicate with, and educate patients; share decision making and management; and continuously advocate disease prevention, wellness, and promotion of healthy lifestyles, including a focus on population health.

Work in interdisciplinary teams

Cooperate, collaborate, communicate, and integrate care in teams to ensure that care is continuous and reliable.

Employ evidence-based practice

Integrate best research with clinical expertise and patient values for optimum care, and participate in learning and research activities to the extent feasible.

Apply quality improvement

Identify errors and hazards in care; understand and implement basic safety design principles, such as standardization and simplification; continually understand and measure quality of care in terms of structure, process, and outcomes in relation to patient and community needs; and design and test interventions to change processes and systems of care, with the objective of improving quality.

Utilize informatics

Communicate, manage knowledge, mitigate error, and support decision making using information technology.

Source: Institute of Medicine, *Health Professions Education: A Bridge to Quality* (2003).

Accreditation Council for Graduate Medical Education (ACGME) General Competencies

Minimum Program Requirements Language
Approved by the ACGME, September 28, 1999

The residency program must require its residents to obtain competencies in the 6 areas below to the level expected of a new practitioner. Toward this end, programs must define the specific knowledge, skills, and attitudes required and provide educational experiences as needed in order for their residents to demonstrate:

a. **Patient Care** that is compassionate, appropriate, and effective for the treatment of health problems and the promotion of health

b. **Medical Knowledge** about established and evolving biomedical, clinical, and cognate (e.g. epidemiological and social-behavioral) sciences and the application of this knowledge to patient care

c. **Practice-Based Learning and Improvement** that involves investigation and evaluation of their own patient care, appraisal and assimilation of scientific evidence, and improvements in patient care

d. **Interpersonal and Communication Skills** that result in effective information exchange and teaming with patients, their families, and other health professionals

e. **Professionalism,** as manifested through a commitment to carrying out professional responsibilities, adherence to ethical principles, and sensitivity to a diverse patient population

f. **Systems-Based Practice,** as manifested by actions that demonstrate an awareness of and responsiveness to the larger context and system of health care and the ability to effectively call on system resources to provide care that is of optimal value

Source: ACGME Outcome Project (September 28, 1999), http://www.acgme.org/outcome/comp/compmin.asp.

Appendix 4.2

Preparation for the Practice of Law

There are not equivalent professional "competencies" required by the American Bar Association (the accrediting body for legal education) to the ACGME general competencies required for medical education (see Appendix 4.1). However, recent reports have addressed the need to incorporate particular skills and competencies into legal education to better prepare lawyers for contemporary legal practice. The following is excerpted from the summary of an influential report by the Carnegie Foundation for the Advancement of Teaching, *Educating Lawyers: Preparation for the Profession of Law.*

Law school provides the beginning, not the full development, of students' professional competence and identity. At present, what most students get as a beginning is insufficient. Students need a dynamic curriculum that moves them back and forth between understanding and enactment, experience and analysis. Law schools face an increasingly urgent need to bridge the gap between analytical and practical knowledge, and a demand for more robust professional integrity. Appeals and demands for change, from both within academic law and without, pose a new challenge to legal education. At the same time, they open to legal education a historic opportunity to advance both legal knowledge—theoretical and practical—and the capacities of the profession.

Legal education needs to be responsive to both the needs of our time and recent knowledge about how learning takes place; it needs to combine the elements of legal professionalism—conceptual knowledge, skill and moral discernment—into the capacity for judgment guided by a sense of professional responsibility. Legal education should seek to unite the two sides of legal knowledge: formal knowledge and experience of practice.

In particular, legal education should use more effectively the second two years of law school and more fully complement the teaching and learning of legal doctrine with the teaching and learning of practice. Legal education should also give more focused attention to the actual and potential effects of the law school experience on the formation of future legal professionals.

Recommendations

1. Offer an Integrated Curriculum

To build on their strengths and address their shortcomings, law schools should offer an integrated, three-part curriculum:

(1) the teaching of legal doctrine and analysis, which provides the basis for professional growth;

(2) introduction to the several facets of practice included under the rubric of lawyering, leading to acting with responsibility for clients; and

(3) exploration and assumption of the identity, values, and dispositions consonant with the fundamental purposes of the legal profession. Integrating the three parts of legal education would better prepare students for the varied demands of professional legal work.

In order to produce such integrative results in students' learning, however, the faculty who teach in the several areas of the legal curriculum must first communicate with and learn from each other.

2. Join "Lawyering," Professionalism, and Legal Analysis from the Start

The existing common core of legal education needs to be expanded to provide students substantial experience with practice as well as opportunities to wrestle with the issues of professionalism. Further, and building on the work already underway in several law schools, the teaching of legal analysis, while remaining central, should not stand alone as it does in so many schools. The teaching of legal doctrine needs to be fully integrated into the curriculum. It should extend beyond case-dialogue courses to become part of learning to "think like a lawyer" in practice settings.

Nor should doctrinal instruction be the exclusive content of the beginner's curriculum. Rather, learning legal doctrine should be seen as prior to practice chiefly in the sense that it provides the essential background assumptions and habits of thought that students need as they find their way into the functions and identity of legal professionals.

3. Make Better Use of the Second and Third Years of Law School

After the JD reports that graduates mostly see their experiences with law-related summer employment after the first and second years of law school as having the greatest influence on their selection of career paths. Law schools could give new emphasis to the third year by designing it as a kind of "capstone" opportunity for students to develop specialized knowledge, engage in advanced clinical training, and work with faculty and peers in serious, comprehensive reflection on their educational experience and their strategies for career and future professional growth.

4. Support Faculty to Work Across the Curriculum

Both doctrinal and practical courses are likely to be most effective if faculty who teach them have some significant experience with the other, complementary area. Since all law faculty have experienced the case dialogue classroom from their own education, doctrinal faculty will probably make the more significant pedagogical discoveries as they observe or participate in the teaching of lawyering courses and clinics, and we predict that they will take these discoveries back into doctrinal teaching. Faculty development programs that consciously aim to increase the faculty's mutual understanding of each other's work are likely to improve students' efforts to make integrated sense of their developing legal competence. However it is organized, it is the sustained dialogue among faculty with different strengths and interests united around common educational purpose that is likely to matter most.

5. Design the Program So That Students — and Faculty —
Weave Together Disparate Kinds of Knowledge and Skill

Although the ways of teaching appropriate to develop professional identity and purpose range from classroom didactics to reflective practice in clinical situations, the key challenge in supporting students' ethical-social development is to keep each of these emphases in active communication with each other.

The demands of an integrative approach require both attention to how fully ethical-social issues pervade the doctrinal and lawyering curricula and the provision of educational experiences directly concerned with the values and situation of the law and the legal profession. As the example of medical education suggests, these concerns "come alive" most effectively when the ideas are introduced in relation to students' experience of taking on the responsibilities incumbent upon the profession's various roles. And, in teaching for legal analysis and lawyering skills, the most powerful effects on student learning are likely to be felt when faculty with different strengths work in a complementary relationship.

6. Recognize a Common Purpose

Amid the useful varieties of mission and emphasis among American law schools, the formation of competent and committed professionals deserves and needs to be the common, unifying purpose. A focus on the formation of professionals would give renewed prominence to the ideals and commitments that have historically defined the legal profession in America.

7. Work Together, Within and Across Institutions

Legal education is complex, with its different emphases of legal analysis, training for practice and development of professional identity. The integration we advocate will depend upon rather than override the development of students' expertise within each of the different emphases. But integration can flourish only if law schools can consciously organize their emphases through ongoing mutual discussion and learning.

Source: William M. Sullivan, et al., *Educating Lawyers: Preparation for the Profession of Law* (Carnegie Foundation for the Advancement of Teaching, 2007), 8–10.

Appendix 5.1

Culturally and Linguistically Appropriate Services (CLAS) Standards

Standard	Description	Category	Status
1	Healthcare organizations should ensure that patients/consumers receive from all staff members effective, understandable, and respectful care that is provided in a manner compatible with their cultural health beliefs and practices and preferred language.	Culturally Competent Care	Recommendation
2	Healthcare organizations should implement strategies to recruit, retain, and promote at all levels of the organization a diverse staff and leadership that are representative of the demographic characteristics of the service area.	Culturally Competent Care	Recommendation
3	Healthcare organizations should ensure that staff at all levels and across all disciplines receive ongoing education and training in culturally and linguistically appropriate service delivery.	Culturally Competent Care	Recommendation
4	Healthcare organizations must offer and provide language assistance services, including bilingual staff and interpreter services, at no cost to each patient/consumer with limited English proficiency at all points of contact, in a timely manner during all hours of operation.	Access to Language Services	Mandate
5	Healthcare organizations must provide to patients/consumers in their preferred language both verbal offers and written notices informing them of their rights to receive language assistance services.	Access to Language Services	Mandate
6	Healthcare organizations must ensure the competence of language assistance provided to limited English proficient patients/consumers by interpreters and bilingual staff. Family and friends should not be used to provide interpretation services (except on request by the patient/consumer).	Access to Language Services	Mandate
7	Healthcare organizations must make available easily understood patient-related materials and post signage in the languages of the commonly encountered groups and/or groups represented in the service area.	Access to Language Services	Mandate
8	Healthcare organizations should develop, implement, and promote a written strategic plan that outlines clear goals, policies, operational plans, and management accountability/oversight mechanisms to provide culturally and linguistically appropriate services.	Organizational Support	Recommendation

9	Healthcare organizations should conduct initial and ongoing organizational self-assessments of CLAS-related activities and are encouraged to integrate cultural and linguistic competence-related measures into their internal audits, performance improvement programs, patient satisfaction assessments, and outcomes-based evaluations.	Organizational Support	Recommendation
10	Healthcare organizations should ensure that data on the individual patient's/consumer's race, ethnicity, and spoken and written language are collected in health records, integrated into the organization's management information systems, and periodically updated.	Organizational Support	Recommendation
11	Healthcare organizations should maintain a current demographic, cultural, and epidemiological profile of the community as well as a needs assessment to accurately plan for and implement services that respond to the cultural and linguistic characteristics of the service area.	Organizational Support	Recommendation
12	Healthcare organizations should develop participatory, collaborative partnerships with communities and use a variety of formal and informal mechanisms to facilitate community and patient/consumer involvement in designing and implementing CLAS-related activities.	Organizational Support	Recommendation
13	Healthcare organizations should ensure that conflict and grievance resolution processes are culturally and linguistically sensitive and capable of identifying, preventing, and resolving cross-cultural conflicts or complaints by patients/consumers.	Culturally Competent Care	Recommendation
14	Healthcare organizations are encouraged to regularly make available to the public information about their progress and successful innovations in implementing the CLAS standards and to provide public notice in their communities about the availability of this information.	Culturally Competent Care	Suggestion

Source: U.S. Department of Health and Human Services, Office of Minority Health, "National Standards on Culturally and Linguistically Appropriate Services (CLAS)," http://minorityhealth.hhs.gov/templates/browse.aspx?lvl=2&lvlID=15.

Appendix 9.1

Disability Categories for School-Age Children under the IDEA

Disability Category	Legal Definition
Autism	A developmental disability significantly affecting verbal and nonverbal communication and social interaction, generally evident before age three, and which adversely affects a child's educational performance. (34 C.F.R. §300.8(c)(1)(i))
Deafness	A hearing impairment that is so severe that the child is impaired in processing linguistic information through hearing, with or without amplification, which adversely affects a child's educational performance. (34 C.F.R. §300.8(c)(3))
Emotional disturbance	A condition exhibiting one or more of the following characteristics over a long period of time and to a marked degree that adversely affects a child's educational performance. (A) An inability to learn that cannot be explained by intellectual, sensory, or health factors. (B) An inability to build or maintain satisfactory interpersonal relationships with peers and teachers. (C) Inappropriate types of behavior or feelings under normal circumstances. (D) A general pervasive mood of unhappiness or depression. (E) A tendency to develop physical symptoms or fears associated with personal or school problems. (34 C.F.R. §300.8(c)(4)(i))
Hearing impairment	An impairment in hearing, whether permanent or fluctuating, that adversely affects a child's educational performance but that is not included under the definition of deafness … (34 C.F.R. §300.8(c)(5))
Intellectual disability (formerly mental retardation)[a]	Significantly subaverage general intellectual functioning, existing concurrently with deficits in adaptive behavior and manifested during the developmental period, which adversely affects a child's educational performance. (34 C.F.R. §300.8(c)(6))
Multiple disabilities	Concomitant impairments (such as mental retardation-blindness or mental retardation-orthopedic impairment), the combination of which causes such severe educational needs that they cannot be accommodated in special education programs solely for one of the impairments. (34 C.F.R. §300.8(c)(7))
Orthopedic impairment	A severe orthopedic impairment that adversely affects a child's educational performance. The term includes impairments caused by a congenital anomaly, impairments caused by disease (e.g., poliomyelitis, bone tuberculosis), and impairments from other causes (e.g., cerebral palsy, amputations, and fractures or burns that cause contractures). (34 C.F.R. §300.8(c)(8))
Other health impairment	Having limited strength, vitality, or alertness, including a heightened alertness to environmental stimuli, that results in limited alertness with respect to the educational environment, that (i) is due to chronic or acute health problems such as asthma, attention deficit disorder or attention deficit hyperactivity disorder, diabetes, epilepsy, a heart condition, hemophilia, lead poisoning, leukemia, nephritis, rheumatic fever, sickle cell anemia, and Tourette syndrome; and (ii) adversely affects a child's educational performance. (34 C.F.R. §300.8(c)(9))

Specific learning disability	A disorder in one or more of the basic psychological processes involved in understanding or in using language, spoken or written, that may manifest itself in the imperfect ability to listen, think, speak, read, write, spell, or to do mathematical calculations, including conditions such as perceptual disabilities, brain injury, minimal brain dysfunction, dyslexia, and developmental aphasia. (34 C.F.R. § 300.8(c)(10))
Speech or language impairment	A communication disorder, such as stuttering, impaired articulation, a language impairment, or a voice impairment, that adversely affects a child's educational performance. (34 C.F.R. § 300.8(c)(11))
Traumatic brain injury	An acquired injury to the brain caused by an external physical force, resulting in total or partial functional disability or psychosocial impairment, or both, that adversely affects a child's educational performance. Traumatic brain injury applies to open or closed head injuries resulting in impairments in one or more areas, such as cognition; language; memory; attention; reasoning; abstract thinking; judgment; problem solving; sensory, perceptual, and motor abilities; psychosocial behavior; physical functions; information processing; and speech. Traumatic brain injury does not apply to brain injuries that are congenital or degenerative, or to brain injuries induced by birth trauma. (34 C.F.R. § 300.8(c)(12))
Visual impairment, including blindness	An impairment in vision that, even with correction, adversely affects a child's educational performance. The term includes both partial sight and blindness. (34 C.F.R. § 300.8(c)(13))

Source: [a] The original version of IDEA 2004 defines this category as "mental retardation." On October 5, 2010, President Barack Obama signed Public Law 111-256, which requires removing the term "mental retardation" from federal law and replacing it with "intellectual disability." See http://frwebgate.access.gpo.gov/cgi-bin/getdoc.cgi?dbname=111_cong_public_laws&docid=f:publ256.111.pdf (accessed December 13, 2010).

Appendix 10.1

Overview of Immigrant Eligibility for Federal Programs

Program	Qualified Immigrants Who Entered the U.S. before 8/22/1996	Qualified Immigrants Who Entered the U.S. on or after 8/22/1996	Not Qualified Immigrants
Supplemental Nutrition Assistance Program (SNAP)	Eligible only if: • Are under age 18[a] • Were granted asylum or refugee status or withholding of deportation/removal, Cuban/Haitian entrant, or Amerasian immigrant • Have been in "qualified" immigrant status for 5 years[b] • Are receiving disability-related assistance[c] • Lawful permanent resident (LPR) with credit for 40 quarters of work • Were 65 years or older and were lawfully residing in the U.S. on Aug. 22, 1996[b] • Veteran, active-duty military; spouse, unremarried surviving spouse, or child[b] • Member of Hmong or Laotian tribe during the Vietnam era, when the tribe militarily assisted the U.S.; spouse, surviving spouse, or child of tribe member[b] • Certain American Indians born abroad	Eligible only if: • Are under age 18[a] • Were granted asylum or refugee status or withholding of deportation/removal, Cuban/Haitian entrant, Amerasian, or Iraqi or Afghan special immigrant status • Have been in "qualified" immigrant status for 5 years[b] • Are receiving disability-related assistance[b, c] • LPR with credit for 40 quarters of work • Veteran, active-duty military; spouse, unremarried surviving spouse, or child[b] • Member of Hmong or Laotian tribe during the Vietnam era, when the tribe militarily assisted the U.S.; spouse, surviving spouse, or child of tribe member[b] • Certain American Indians born abroad	Eligible only if: • Member of Hmong or Laotian tribe during the Vietnam era, when the tribe militarily assisted the U.S.; spouse, surviving spouse or child or tribe member, *who is lawfully present in the U.S.* • Certain American Indians born abroad • Victims of trafficking and their derivative beneficiaries
Temporary Assistance for Needy Families (TANF)	Eligible[b]	Eligible only if: • Were granted asylum or refugee status or withholding of deportation/removal, Cuban/Haitian entrant, Amerasian, or Iraqi or Afghan special immigrant status[d]	Eligible only if: • Victims of trafficking and their derivative beneficiaries

		• Veteran, active-duty military; spouse, unremarried surviving spouse, or child[b] • Have been in "qualified" immigrant status for 5 years or more[b]	
Full-scope Medicaid	Eligible[e]	Eligible only if: • Were granted asylum or refugee status or withholding of deportation/removal, Cuban/Haitian entrant, Amerasian, or Iraqi or Afghan special immigrant status[f] • Veteran, active-duty military; spouse, unremarried surviving spouse, or child[b] • Receiving federal foster care • Have been in "qualified" immigrant status for 5 years or more[b] • Children under 21 (state option)[g] • Pregnant women (state option)[g]	Eligible only if: • Were receiving SSI on Aug. 22, 1996 (in states that link Medicaid to SSI eligibility) • Certain American Indians born abroad • Victims of trafficking and their derivative beneficiaries • Lawfully residing children under 21 (state option)[g] • Lawfully residing pregnant women (state option)[g]

[a] Children are not subject to sponsor deeming in the SNAP program.

[b] Eligibility may be affected by deeming: a sponsor's income/resources may be added to the immigrant's in determining eligibility. Exemptions from deeming may apply.

[c] Disability-related benefits include SSI, Social Security disability, state disability or retirement pension, railroad retirement disability, veteran's disability, disability-based Medicaid, and disability-related General Assistance if the disability determination uses criteria as stringent as those used by federal SSI.

[d] In Indiana, Mississippi, Ohio, South Carolina, and Texas, TANF is available only to immigrants who entered the United States on or after August 22, 1996, who are: (1) LPRs credited with 40 quarters of work; (2) veterans, active-duty military (and their spouse, unremarried surviving spouse, or child); or (3) refugees, asylees, persons granted withholding of deportation/removal, Cuban/Haitian entrants, and Amerasian immigrants during the five years after obtaining this status. Indiana provides TANF to "refugees" listed in (3) regardless of the date they obtained that status. Mississippi does not address eligibility for Cuban/Haitian entrants or Amerasian immigrants. National Immigrant Law Center, *Guide to Immigrant Eligibility for Federal Programs.*

[e] In Wyoming, only LPRs with 40 quarters of work credit, abused immigrants, parolees, veterans, active duty military (and their spouse, unremarried surviving spouse, or child), refugees, asylees, persons granted withholding of deportation/removal, Cuban/Haitian entrants, and Amerasian immigrants who entered the U.S. prior to Aug. 22, 1996, are eligible for full-scope Medicaid.

[f] In Alabama, Mississippi, North Dakota, Ohio, Texas, Virginia, and Wyoming, full-scope Medicaid is available only to immigrants who entered the United States on or after August 22, 1996, who are: (1) LPRs credited with 40 quarters of work; (2) veterans, active-duty military (and their spouse, un-remarried surviving spouse, or child); or (3) refugees, asylees, persons granted withholding of deportation/removal, Cuban/Haitian entrants, and Amerasian immigrants during the seven years after obtaining this status. Wyoming provides full-scope Medicaid to "qualified" abused immigrants and persons paroled into the U.S., regardless of their date of entry. In Texas, Amerasian immigrants are eligible only during the five years after obtaining this status; Mississippi and North Dakota do not address eligibility for Cuban/Haitian entrants or Amerasian immigrants. Virginia provides Medicaid

to lawfully residing children and Texas provides Medicaid to "qualified" immigrant children, regardless of their date of entry into the United States.

ᵍ For a list of states providing medical assistance to additional categories of immigrants, either with state funds or under the option to provide federal Medicaid and CHIP to lawfully residing children and pregnant women, regardless of their date of entry into the United States, and to provide prenatal care, regardless of the mother's status, under the CHIP program's "fetus" option, see the table "Medical Assistance Programs for Immigrants in Various States," http://www.nilc.org/pubs/guideupdates/med-services-for-imms-in-states-2010-07-28.pdf.

Source: National Immigration Law Center, *Guide to Immigrant Eligibility for Federal Programs*, 4th ed. (2002), 17–20; updated version, http://www.nilc.org/pubs/Guide_update.htm.

Appendix 16.1

Tax Law Restrictions on Legislative and Political Activities of Exempt Organizations

	501(c)(3)	501(c)(4)
Receive tax-deductible charitable contributions	YES	NO
Receive contributions or fees deductible as a business expense	YES	YES
Substantially related income exempt from federal income tax	YES	YES
Investment income exempt from federal income tax	LTD*	YES
Engage in legislative advocacy	LTD	YES
Engage in candidate election advocacy	NO	LTD

* Limited

Source: Common Tax Law Restrictions on Activities of Exempt Organizations, IRS.gov, last modified June 29, 2010, available at: http://www.irs.gov/charities/article/0,,id=170946,00.html.

Appendix 16.2

Example of Physician Testimony on Specific Policies and Regulations Impacting Low-Income Patients

Good Afternoon, Mr. Chairman and other Distinguished Members of the Committee. Thank you for the invitation to speak today.

As a pediatrician, I am not among the usual suspects to testify in support of HR 2895, the National Affordable Housing Trust Fund Bill of 2007. I am here today to share with you new research that recognizes housing as the foundation to excellent child health. I hope to convince you that often the best medical intervention for children is to get them an affordable home and that it is within your power to keep kids healthy through housing.

As many of you know, there are millions of families on waiting lists for affordable housing. In Boston it is not unusual for waiting lists to actually be closed and not accept applications because tens of thousands of families have already applied. Even families in homeless shelters with the highest priority often wait a year and half or more to get a home they can afford. For many families, as they wait on these lists, this means making terrible trade-offs between rent and food, or settling on a home with severe housing problems such as pest infestations or mold because it simply is all they can afford.

We know from the Children's Sentinel Nutrition Assessment Program (it is commonly known as C-SNAP) that food insecure children who are eligible but don't receive housing subsidies are twice as likely as those who do receive housing subsidies to have stunted growth by World Health Organization criteria (Meyers et al. Archives of Pediatrics 2005). This is important since one aspect of the bill targets the majority of National Affordable Housing Trust Fund, some 75% for extremely low-income families, defined at 30% of area median income. This means the children most at risk for stunting, those who are food insecure, could be protected by from stunting, simply by getting an affordable home. As you know, stunting not only limits children's physical growth in the short term but also stunts their life long potential because we know that if your body is not growing, your brain is not growing as well.

Because many families have very few limited choices of homes they can afford, and have to make trade-offs, they often live in substandard conditions, such as infestations with cockroaches. We know these can threaten their children's health. For instance, asthmatic children who are allergic to cockroaches and then exposed to cockroaches in their home are three more times likely to be hospitalized for asthma (Rosenstreich NEJM 1997). What can be surprising to people is that though 30% of urban children have cockroach allergies, 20% of suburban children also are allergic and exposed, suggesting these substandard conditions can go beyond the stereotypical inner city (Matsui JACI 2003). Further, new data suggest that exposure to cockroaches in early life may cause immune system changes that can lead to the development of wheezing and asthma. (Finn et al. JACI 2000) Young children living in other substandard exposures, such as older

741

homes with leaded paint, are well known to affect development and by recent estimates, can lead to billions of dollars in education and other costs (Landrigan EHP 2002).

Lastly, families having difficulty affording rent may double up with other families, resulting in crowding or moving frequently from one place to another. We know children who stay in the same home, and do not move frequently, have better child development outcomes and do better in school. (Zima AJPH 1994)

Another aspect of the bill that I support is the local flexibility offered by the bill. From my experience working in Boston with the Boston Public Health Commission, local Community Development Corporations and some state funded housing developments, the ability for state and local governments to match the best local solutions to their greatest housing needs makes the most sense. In some instances, rental-housing needs are the most pressing or in other localities, homeownership can be targeted as the best outcome. Research has consistently shown home ownership makes housing more stable and is better for overall health. In pediatrics, the best therapies are often tailored ones, and this bill clearly accommodates local needs.

I urge you to support HR 2895 the National Affordable Housing Trust Fund Bill of 2007 because it can ensure that our most vulnerable population, our children, have a safe, decent, affordable home. I leave you with the idea that **a safe, decent, affordable homes is like a vaccine. It literally prevents disease.** A safe home can prevent mental health and developmental problems; a decent home may prevent asthma or lead poisoning and an affordable home can prevent stunted growth and unnecessary hospitalizations. This bill's goal is 1.5 million affordable homes over the next 10 years, and that can mean more than 1.5 million healthier children as a result.

I would like to end with a story that drives home why I think housing can be a medical intervention to make kids better and can keep kids healthy. In my pediatric practice, I take care of a child, Whitney, who I first met when she was only 9 months old. Her family was homeless because they could not afford an apartment of their own. At that time she was already falling off the growth chart, and over the next three months she gained less than a pound, and I needed to hospitalize her because she was becoming dangerously malnourished. She ended up needing to be transferred to a rehabilitation hospital because she had an underlying swallowing problem and stayed for over a month, which you can imagine the cost of that to her insurance. At the rehabilitation hospital, she slowly began to gain weight but as soon as she went back to the shelter she began to lose weight again. After advocating with the help of lawyers from our Medical Legal Partnership at Boston Medical Center, Whitney and her family were finally offered an affordable home in a local public housing development. Once in her new apartment, Whitney began to gain weight, her developmental delays improved, and she was able to thrive. I recently saw her at her physical a few months ago, and at 4 years old, she is starting to learn to read. I tried my best to treat Whitney, with all my medical expertise, including very expensive medical care during hospitalizations, but the best medical intervention, the one that eventually made her well, was a safe, decent, affordable home. It is actually Whitney's birthday today, July 19, and I can think of nothing better to help her and kids like her to stay healthy than to pass HR 2895 the National Affordable Housing Trust Bill of 2007.

Thank you.

Literature Cited

P.W. Finn, et al., "Children at Risk for Asthma: Home Allergen Levels, Lymphocyte Proliferation, and Wheeze." *Journal of Allergy & Clinical Immunology,* 105 no. 5 (May 2000): 933–42.

P.J. Landrigan, et al., "Environmental Pollutants and Disease in American Children: Estimates of Morbidity, Mortality, and Costs for Lead Poisoning, Asthma, Cancer, and Developmental Disabilities." *Environmental Health Perspectives,* 110, no. 7 (July 2002): 721–8.

E.C. Matsui, et al., "Cockroach allergen exposure and sensitization in suburban middle-class children with asthma." *Journal of Allergy & Clinical Immunology,* 112 no. 1 (July 2003): 87–92.

A. Meyers, et al., "Subsidized Housing and Children's Nutritional Status: Data from a Multisite Surveillance Study." *Archives of Pediatrics and Adolescent Medicine* 159 (2005): 551–556.

D. Rosenstreich, et al., "The Role of Cockroach Allergy and Exposure to Cockroach Allergen in Causing Morbidity among Inner-City Children with Asthma," *New England Journal of Medicine,* 336, no. 19 (May 1997): 1356–63.

B.T. Zima, et al., 1994. "Emotional and Behavioral Problems and Severe Academic Delays among Sheltered Homeless Children in Los Angeles County," *American Journal of Public Health,* 84, no. 2 (1994): 260–264.

Appendix 18.1

Study Design

Study Type	Description
Descriptive	Nonintervention study, involving the description of a situation, event, case or phenomenon.
Cohort (prospective, time series)	Nonintervention study, where subjects exposed to the intervention (or the program) are compared to nonexposed individuals over time in terms of how often an outcome occurs.
Case-control	Nonintervention study, generally retrospective, where one group who has had the intervention is compared to another group who has not.
Cross-sectional comparative	Nonintervention study, in which researchers describe and compare groups to determine what variables may contribute to certain outcomes (design is susceptible to confounding or intervening variables).
Before-after (pre-experiment)	Intervention study, using no randomization or control group. One group is examined before and after the intervention. Differences are observed in the outcomes.
Nonrandomized (quasi-experiment)	Intervention study, typically using randomization or control group, but not both. For example, one group receives the intervention and the other, the control group, does not. Both groups are observed before and after the intervention.
Randomized controlled trial (true experiment)	Intervention study, where study population is randomized (have an equal chance of being in either group) into at least two groups, the intervention group and the control group. Both groups are observed before and after the intervention, which only the intervention group receives.

Adapted from Corlien M. Varkevisser, Ann Templeton Brownlee, Indra Pathmanathan, eds., *Designing and Conducting Health Systems Research Projects, Volume 1: Proposal Development and Fieldwork* (Amsterdam: KIT, 2004).

Appendix 18.2

Comparison of Quantitative and Qualitative Research Approaches

	Quantitative	Qualitative
General framework	• Seek to confirm hypotheses about phenomena • Instruments use more rigid style of eliciting and categorizing responses to questions • Use highly structured methods such as questionnaires, surveys and structured observation	• Seek to explore phenomena • Instruments use more flexible, iterative style of eliciting and categorizing responses to questions • Use semi-structured methods such as in-depth interviews, focus groups and participant observation
Analytical objectives	• To quantify variation • To predict causal relationships • To describe characteristics of a population	• To describe variation • To describe and explain relationships • To describe individual experiences • To describe group norms
Question format	• Closed-ended	• Open-ended
Data format	• Numerical (obtained by assigning numerical values to responses)	• Textual (obtained from audiotapes, videotapes, and field notes)
Flexibility in study design	• Study design is stable from beginning to end • Participant responses do not influence or determine how and which questions researchers ask next • Study design is subject to statistical assumptions and conditions	• Some aspects of the study are flexible (for example, the addition, exclusion, or wording of particular interview questions) • Participant responses affect how and which questions researchers ask next • Study design is iterative, that is, data collection and research questions are adjusted according to what is learned

Source: Family Health International, *Qualitative Research Methods: A Data Collector's Field Guide, Module 1* (Research Triangle Park, NC, 2005).

Appendix 18.3

Sampling Methods

Method	Description
Qualitative studies	
Quota	Used when a researcher wants insight into all variations of a certain phenomenon and samples a fixed number per group/variation
Typical case	Cases that are typical of a group/variation in which the researcher is interested are studied; does not produce results that can be generalized to the whole group
Snowball or chain	Researchers start with one or two key informants, who then recommend other key informants
Quantitative studies	
Simple random	A full list of all possible participants or units (sampling frame) is made; sample size is determined; the required number is selected from the list using a lottery method or random numbers
Systematic	Sampling frame is determined; participants are chosen at regular intervals (e.g., every fifth or tenth person)
Stratified	Sampling frame is determined; participants are then divided into groups according to certain characteristics (e.g., participants of different race/ethnicities); a set number of participants are selected randomly or systematically from within these groups

Adapted from Corlien M.Varkevisser, Ann Templeton Brownlee, Indra Pathmanathan, eds., *Designing and Conducting Health Systems Research Projects, Volume 1: Proposal Development and Fieldwork* (Amsterdam: KIT, 2004).

Appendix 18.4

Recruitment Flow Chart

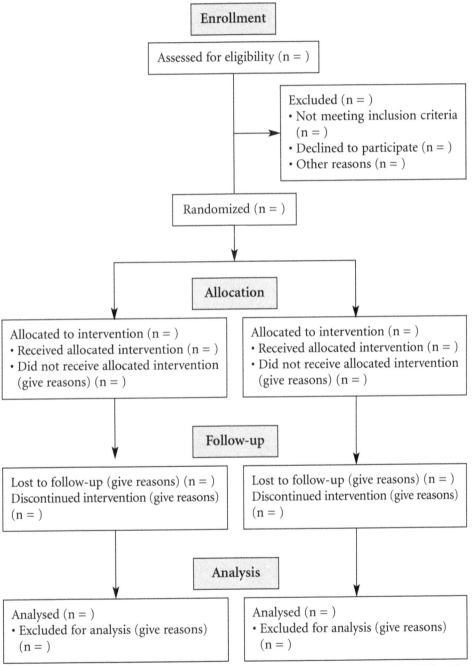

Source: Kenneth F. Schulz, Douglas G. Altman, David Moher, "Statement: Updated Guidelines for Reporting Parallel Group Randomized Trials," *BMJ* 340 (2010): 698–702.

Appendix 19.1

Overview of Key Reforms in the Patient Protection and Affordable Care Act

Health Insurance	
Market reforms	• Requires all plans to permit enrollees to elect coverage for children up to age 26. • Establishes temporary high-risk pools for individuals with preexisting conditions that have been uninsured for at least six months and cannot find affordable coverage. • Prohibits all plans from establishing lifetime limits on policies and restricts annual limits for essential benefits. • Prohibits the use of preexisting condition exclusions for children's coverage. • Prohibits new plans from discriminating based on health status, medical condition, claims experience, and other health-related factors. • Requires health coverage of preventive services with no out-of-pocket costs to patients. • Directs the secretary of HHS to define a package of "essential benefits" that all plans must cover to be offered through the exchange and eligible to tax subsidy. • Ensures mental health and addiction parity. • Establishes four insurance coverage tiers based on the actuarial value of the plan or policy.
Exchanges	• Establishes health insurance exchanges thorough which small businesses and individuals purchasing coverage on their own can select from a broad array of health insurance plans. • Permits the sale of national and multistate plans under certain conditions.
Individual mandate	• Beginning in 2014, requires U.S. citizens and legal residents to have health insurance or pay a tax; individuals may receive an exemption if the health insurance exchange certifies that premiums exceed a certain percentage of individual or family income. • Provides tax credits to individuals and families with incomes between 133% and 400% of the federal poverty level to help cover the cost of health insurance premiums. • Provides cost-sharing assistance for low-income individuals and limits out-of-pocket costs for covered services.
Employer responsibilities and incentives	• Provides temporary reinsurance to employers to help lower the cost of providing coverage to certain high-cost retirees between the ages of 55 and 64 who are not yet eligible for Medicare. • Requires employers with 50 or more employees that do not offer health insurance to pay an assessment for each employee who relies on tax credits to buy insurance through a state exchange. • Requires employers with 200 or more employees that offer insurance coverage to auto-enroll their employees in their employer-sponsored plans while permitting employees to opt out.

	• Provides tax credits to small businesses to make it more affordable to offer insurance to employees and their families.
Insurer accountability and patient protections	• Imposes minimum medical loss ratios for plans and requires a rebate of excess premiums. • Strengthens the appeals process for persons who have been denied coverage. • Ensures better information for patients and consumers about their health insurance coverage. • Ensures that key reforms apply regardless of whether individuals are covered through state regulated insurance products or self-insured employer plans regulated under the Employee Retirement Income Security Act (ERISA).
Medicare	
	• Phases in coverage of prescription drugs under the Medicare part D "donut hole." • Expands coverage of preventive services and eliminates copayments and deductibles for these services. • Provides coverage for tests, treatments for individuals exposed to environmental health hazards.
Medicaid and Children's Health Insurance Program (CHIP)	
Medicaid	• Requires states to provide Medicaid coverage to individuals and families with incomes up to 133% of the federal poverty level (FPL), with additional federal assistance to states to help defray costs. • Permits states to provide coverage for low-income populations with incomes between 133% and 200% of FPL as an alternative to enrollment in the health insurance exchange. • Permits states to provide family planning services to certain low-income women not otherwise eligible for Medicaid. • New coverage of primary and preventive services and improved provider payments for primary healthcare.
CHIP	• Authorizes CHIP through FY 2015, and increases federal payments to states for the cost of the program.
Healthcare Quality and Value	
	• Authorizes the secretary of HHS to implement delivery system reforms and pilot programs to test alternative delivery and payment systems in Medicare. • Establishes two new research bodies to recommend new approaches: the Center for Medicare and Medicaid Innovation, and the Patient-Centered Outcomes Research Institute. • Establishes the Cures Acceleration Network to speed access to promising treatments.
Healthcare Fraud and Abuse	
	• Expands Medicare, Medicaid, and CHIP program integrity activities. • Improves antifraud and abuse safeguards in the area of physician-owned services, physician referrals, prescription drug marketing, ownership disclosure, and nursing home safety and quality.
Public Health, Healthcare Infrastructure, and Health Disparities	
Promoting public health and wellness	• Establishes a council to develop prevention, wellness, and health promotion goals and to develop a national prevention strategy. • Establishes sustained funding for public health and prevention programs. • Promotes access to school-based health centers and preventive dental services. • Requires national nutrition labeling information be available in restaurants.

	• Provides for improved public reporting on diabetes, improvements in vital statistics collection, and surveillance for congenital heart disease. • Provides grant funds to develop small business workplace wellness programs.
Access and healthcare workforce	• Invests in workforce development through new federal programs and state grants to provide scholarships and loan repayment assistance, and other innovations. • Revises medical residency training programs to emphasize primary care. • Creates teaching health centers. • Authorizes investments in diversity training for healthcare providers and provides workforce diversity grants to promote minorities entering the field of healthcare. • Strengthens the Indian Health Service.
Reducing health disparities	• Improves data collection and reporting on race, ethnicity, sex, primary language, and disability status and directs the secretary of HHS to analyze data and report trends. • Restructures and elevates the HHS Office of Minority Health.
Tax Changes	
	• Provides tax credits to small businesses to help lower the cost of providing health insurance coverage to their employees. • Beginning in 2017, insurers will pay an excise tax on health insurance plans that exceed a threshold amount. • Limits the amount that can be set aside by individuals in tax-preferred accounts, known as cafeteria plans, and by increased penalties for early withdrawals or withdrawals for nonhealth purposes from Health Savings Accounts or Medical Savings Accounts. • Increases Medicare payroll taxes for high-income individuals.
Long-Term Care	
	• Establishes the Community Living Assistance Services and Support (CLASS) Act, a voluntary long-term care insurance program. • Establishes new Medicaid long-term care options to promote community-based care while protecting spouses from impoverishment.

Source: Adapted from "Summary of New Health Law," The Henry J. Kaiser Family Foundation, June 18, 2010.

Further Reading

American Bar Association Child Law Practice, Practicing Preventive Law, A Day in the Life of a Medical-Legal Partnership Attorney, Pilnik, 2008.

American Bar Association Journal, Wellness Program: Medical-Legal Partnerships Pinpoint the Legal Causes of Patient Ills, McMillion, April 2010.

Academic Medicine, Physician Advocacy: What Is It and How Do We Do It?, Earnest, Wong, Federico, Jan. 2010.

Ambulatory Pediatrics, Development of a Brief Questionnaire to Identify Families in Need of Legal Advocacy to Improve Child Health, Keller, Jones, Savageau, Cashman, Jul–Aug. 2008.

American Journal of Public Health, Editor's Choice, It Takes Lawyers to Deliver Health Care, Northridge, Mar. 2005.

American Journal of Public Health, Material Hardship and the Physical Health of School-Aged Children in Low-Income Households, Yoo, Slack, Holl, May 2009.

Archives of Disease in Childhood, From Principle to Practice: Moving From Human Rights to Legal Rights to Ensure Child Health, Zuckerman, Lawton, Morton, Jan. 2007.

Archives of Internal Medicine, So Much To Do, So Little Time: Care for the Socially Disadvantaged and the 15-Minute Visit, Fiscella, Epstein, Sept. 2008.

Archives of Pediatrics and Adolescent Medicine, Advocacy is Not a Specialty, Bergman, Sept. 2005.

Archives of Pediatrics and Adolescent Medicine, Estimating the Risk of Food Stamp Use and Impoverishment During Childhood, Rank, Hirschl, Nov. 2009.

Archives of Pediatrics and Adolescent Medicine, Medical-Legal Partnerships: Linking Housing, Health and Law to Improve Family Well-Being, Hernandez, Sandel, Lawton, Zuckerman, 2007.

Archives of Pediatrics and Adolescent Medicine, Subsidized Housing and Children's Nutritional Status, Meyers, Cutts, Frank, Levenson, Skalicky, Heeren, Cook, Berkowitz, Black, Casey, Zaldivar, June 2005.

Boston University Public Interest Law Journal, The Lawyer Is In: Why Some Doctors Are Prescribing Legal Remedies For Their Patients, And How the Legal Profession Can Support This Effort, Tames, Tremblay, Wagner, Lawton, Smith, Spring/Summer 2003.

The Child Health Impact Assessment Working Group, Affordable Housing and Child Health: A Child Health Impact Assessment of the Massachusetts Rental Voucher Program, Smith, et. al., June 2005.

Clearinghouse Review Journal of Poverty Law and Policy, Center for Children's Advocacy: Providing Holistic Legal Services to Children in Their Communities, Stone, Cote, Ghio, DeGraffenreidt, Sicklick, Nordstrom, July/Aug. 2005.

Clearinghouse Review Journal of Poverty Law and Policy, Lawyers and Doctors Partner for Healthy Housing, Cherayil, Oliveira, Sandel, Tohn, May/June 2005.

Clinical Law Review, Professional Ethics in Interdisciplinary Collaboratives: Zeal, Paternalism, and Mandated Reporting, Anderson, Barenberg, Tremblay, Spring 2007.

Clinical Pediatrics, Screening for Basic Social Needs at a Medical Home for Low-Income Children, Garg, Butz, Dworkin, Lewis, Serwint, 2008 (online)/2009.

Contemporary Pediatrics, How Substandard Housing Affects Children's Health, Sandel, Zotter, Oct. 2000.

Contemporary Pediatrics, Immigration 101 for the Pediatric Practice, Sandel, Morton, April 2005.

Geiger Gibson/RCHN Community Health Foundation Research Collaborative, Medical-Legal Partnerships: Addressing the Unmet Legal Needs of Health Center Patients, Shin, Byrne, Jones, Teitelbaum, Repasch, Rosenbaum, May 2010.

Georgetown Journal on Poverty Law & Policy, Public Health Services: A New Vision, Schulman, Lawton, Tremblay, Retkin, Sandel, Fall 2008.

Harvard Business Review, Turning Doctors Into Leaders: Medicine is in for a Radical Change as the Old Guard Gives Way to Performance-Driven Teams, Lee, April 2010.

Health Affairs, Medical-Legal Partnerships: Transforming Primary Care by Addressing the Legal Needs of Vulnerable Populations, Sandel, Hansen, Kahn, Lawton, Paul, Parker, Morton, Zuckerman, Sept. 2010.

Health Capital and Social Development, Disparities in Health, Disparities in Law: The Global Potential of Individual Advocacy, Lawton, Riseberg, Bogin-Farber, Knight, Cohen, Smith, 2008.

Health Lawyer, Lawyers and Doctors Working Together—A Formidable Team, Retkin, Brandfield, Lawton, Zuckerman, DeFrancesco, Oct. 2007.

Health Lawyer, Medical-Legal Partnerships: A Key Strategy For Mitigating the Negative Health Impacts of the Recession, Retkin, Brandfield, Hoppin, Oct. 2009.

Health Promotion Practice, Process and Impact Evaluation of a Legal Assistance and Health Care Community Partnership, Teufel, Brown, Thorne, Goffinet, Clemons, 2009.

Journal of Allied Health, What Attracts Students to Interprofessional Education and Other Health Care Reform Initiatives?, Hoffman, Rosenfield, Nasmith, Fall 2009.

Journal of Clinical Oncology, The Attorney as the Newest Member of the Cancer Treatment Team, Fleishman, Retkin, Brandfield, Braun, Mar. 2007.

Journal of Developmental & Behavioral Pediatrics, Poverty Grown Up: How Childhood Socioeconomic Status Impacts Adult Health, Conroy, Sandel, Zuckerman, Feb./Mar. 2010.

Journal of General Internal Medicine, Medical-Legal Partnership: Collaborating with Lawyers to Identify and Address Health Disparities, Cohen, Fullerton, Retkin, Weintraub, Tames, Brandfield, Sandel, 2010.

Journal of Graduate Medical Education, Medical-Legal Partnerships: Addressing Competency Needs Through Lawyers, Paul, Fullerton, Cohen, Lawton, Ryan, Sandel, Dec. 2009.

Journal of Health and Social Behavior, Racial/Ethnic Differences in Asthma Prevalence: The Role of Housing and Neighborhood Environments, Rosenbaum, June 2008.

Journal of Health Care Law & Policy, Allies Not Adversaries: Teaching Collaboration to the Next Generation of Doctors and Lawyers to Address Social Inequality, Tobin Tyler, Sept. 2008.

Journal of Health Care Law & Policy, Multidisciplinary Representation of Patients: The Potential for Ethical Issues and Professional Duty Conflicts in the Medical-Legal Partnership Model, Boumil, Freitas, D., Freitas, C., 2010.

Journal of Health Care for Poor and Underserved, Pilot Study of Medical-Legal Partnership to Address Social and Legal Needs of Patients, Weintraub, Rogers, Botcheva, Loeb, Knight, Ortega, Heymach, Sandel, Huffman, May 2010.

Journal of Higher Education Outreach and Engagement, Partners in Outreach and Advocacy: Interdisciplinary Opportunities in University-Based Legal Clinics, Pearson, Johnston-Walsh, 2006.

Journal of Law, Medicine & Ethics, How Bioethics Can Enrich Medical-Legal Collaborations, Campbell, Sicklick, Galowitz, Retkin, Fleishman, Winter 2010.

Journal of Law, Medicine & Ethics, Health Benefits of Legal Services for Criminalized Populations: The Case of People Who Use Drugs, Sex Workers and Sexual and Gender Minorities, Csete, Cohen, Winter 2010.

Journal of Palliative Medicine, A Medical-Legal Partnership as a Component of a Palliative Care Model, Rodabaugh, Hammond, Myszka, Sandel, 2010.

Journal of Public Health Management Practices, Moving Upstream: How Interventions That Address the Social Determinants of Health Can Improve Health and Reduce Disparities, Williams, Costa, Odunlami, Mohammed, 2008.

The Lancet, Medical-Legal Partnerships: Transforming Health Care, Zuckerman, Sandel, Lawton, Morton, Nov. 2008.

Management Information Exchange, The Family Advocacy Program: A Medical-Legal Collaborative to Promote Child Health and Development, Lawton, Summer 2003.

Management Information Exchange, Medical-Legal Partnerships: From Surgery to Prevention?, Lawton, Spring 2007.

New England Journal of Medicine, American Medical Education 100 Years after the Flexner Report, Cooke, Irby, Sullivan, Ludmerer, Sept. 2006.

New England Journal of Medicine, Closing the Gap: How Lawyers Help Doctors Address Health Disparities, Zuckerman, Sandel, Lawton, 2010.

New England Journal of Medicine, Payment Reform for Safety-Net Institutions — Improving Quality and Outcomes, Wang, Conroy, Zuckerman, Nov. 2009.

New England Journal of Medicine, Medicaid and National Health Care Reform, Sara Rosenbaum, Nov. 2009.

New York University Review of Law and Social Change, The Asthma Crisis in Low-Income Communities of Color: Using the Law as a Tool for Promoting Public Health, Das, 2007.

Pediatric Annals, The Effects of Housing Intervention on Child Health, Sandel, Phelan, Wright, Hynes, Lanphear, July 2004.

Pediatric Clinics of North America, Double Jeopardy: The Impact of Poverty on Early Child Development, Parker, Greer, Zuckerman, 1988.

Pediatrics, Families' Health-Related Social Problems and Missed Referral Opportunities, Fleegler, Lieu, Wise, Muret-Wagstaff, 2007.

Pediatrics, Revisiting the Social History for Child Health, Kenyon, Sandel, Silverstein, Shakir, Zuckerman, 2007.

Pediatrics, Social Determinants: Taking the Social Context of Asthma Seriously, Williams, Sternthal, Wright, 2009.

Pediatrics, Why Pediatricians Need Lawyers to Keep Children Healthy, Zuckerman, Sandel, Smith, Lawton, 2004.

Philadelphia Social Innovations Journal, Medical-Legal Partnership | Philadelphia: Meeting Basic Needs and Reducing Health Disparities by Integrating Legal Services into the Healthcare Setting, Lawton, Beck-Coon, Fung, Spring 2010.

Preventive Law and Problem Solving, Advancing the Integrated Practice of Preventive Law and Preventive Medicine, Morton, Barton, Maypole, 2009.

Social Work Today, Beacon of Hope for Immigrants: The Medical-Legal Partnership, Yacobucci, Sprecher, July/Aug. 2009.

Tennessee Law Review, The Law School Clinic as a Partner in Medical-Legal Partnership, Wettach, 2008.

Index

social environment/conditions
   children and, 6
   of clients, 141
   definition of social environment, 141
   and health, 4–5, 19–21, 81–82
   healthcare providers and, 77–78
   legal intervention and, 91–92
   of patients, 141
   and stress, 12–13, 141
   See also socioeconomic status (SES)
social epidemiology, 5, 27
social norms
   change in, 609–17
   defined, 609
   and DUI, 611–12
   and obesity, 606, 607
Social Security
   and elders, 497
   elders and, 502–3, 511
   Medicare and, 44
   protection of income, 503
Social Security Act, 206, 217, 369–70, 676n16
Social Security Administration (SSA), 205
Social Security Appeals Council, 208, 210
Social Security Disability Insurance (SSDI)
   about, 194, 205, 206
   appeals of denials, 421
   for cancer survivors, 417–18
   eligibility for, 206–10
   and HIV/AIDS, 458, 460
   work incentives, 210
social workers
   attributes of, 79*table*
   collaboration with lawyers, 180–82
   and confidentiality, 181
   and mandatory reporting, 180–82
   in MLP, 119–20
   stress and, 430
   training of, 114
Society for Adolescent Health and Medicine, 532–33
socioeconomic status (SES)
   and adolescent health, 533
   area-based differences in, 8–10
   and cancer, 397
   and child maltreatment, 362
   and health, 6–7, 533
   and IPV, 362

   and obesity, 602, 604–5
   racial differences and, 7
   and stress, 13
   See also income; social environment/conditions
Socratic method, 130
Solving the Problem of Childhood Obesity within a Generation, 619–20
Southern Poverty Law Center, 292
special education, 279, 282–86, 288–91, 303–5, 560
   Karody Special Education Calculator, 75, 289
Special Immigrant Juvenile Status (SIJS), 337
Special Supplemental Nutrition Program for Women, Infants, and Children (WIC), 215–16, 617
Spectrum of Prevention, 607–8, 609, 610, 611
SSDI. *See* Social Security Disability Insurance (SSDI)
SSI. *See* Supplemental Security Income (SSI)
Stanford University, Medical-Legal Issues in Children's Health, 110
STaT: Screen for Lifetime Intimate Partner Violence, 351
state governments
   and child care, 636
   and family planning, 48
   and food in schools, 632
   and free public education, 311n1
   HIPAA and, 167
   and housing for adolescents, 560–61
   and legal aid, 57–58, 59
   and Medicaid, 39, 41
   and obesity, 620–23
   and physical activity, 634
   as "police power," 620
   and preemption, 621
   public health policy, 620–23
state law(s)
   debtor protection under, 504–5
   federal law vs., 504–5, 620–21
   and HIV confidentiality, 447, 448
   and HIV discrimination, 451–52
   and HIV testing, 446
   housing code enforcement, 237–38
   and housing discrimination, 462